P9-CAN-680

Gun Digest

28th Anniversary

1974 Deluxe Edition

EDITED BY JOHN T. AMBER

DIGEST BOOKS, INC. NORTHFIELD, ILL.

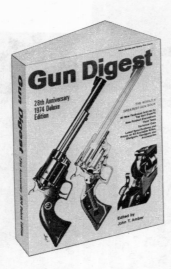

Our full-color covers this year, inside and out, are dominated by a trio of excellent handguns. The outside front shows the latest Ruger Super Blackhawk in its newly engineered, ultra safe form. The inset at lower right reveals clearly the interdependence of the hammer-transfer bar-trigger system, a notable achievement in fail-safe handgun design.

On our outside back cover there is Ruger's latest development, the Mini-14 autoloading carbine/rifle, surprisingly well put together for a quasi-military firearm, plus the Ruger Security Six revolver in softly gleaming stainless steel.

The inside front cover pictures the unique and interesting—if provocative—Colt Sauer bolt action sporting rifle, recently introduced. The inside of the back cover depicts the deservedly popular Colt Python revolver, a handsome and rugged sixgun.

Jim Triggs, master artist in this demanding work, created the Superb Ruger drawings.

GUN DIGEST STAFF

EDITOR
John T. Amber

ASSOCIATE EDITORS
Harold A. Murtz
Joseph J. Schroeder, Jr.

ASSISTANT EDITOR
Lilo Anderson

CONTRIBUTING EDITORS
Bob Hagel
W. Labisky
John Lachuk
Maj. Geo. C. Nonte, Jr.
W. L. Rickell
Larry Sterett
A. M. Wynne, Jr.

EUROPEAN EDITORS
Raymond Caranta
Derek Partridge

ASSOCIATE PUBLISHER
Sheldon L. Factor

MEMBER OF THE
NATIONAL
SHOOTING
SPORTS
FOUNDATION
INC.

Copyright MCMLXXIII by Digest Books, Inc., 540 Frontage Rd., Northfield, Illinois 60093. No part of this publication may be reproduced, stored in a retrieval system, or transmitted, in any form or by any means, electronic, mechanical, photocopying, recording, or otherwise, without the prior written permission of the publisher.

The views and opinions of the authors expressed herein are not necessarily those of the editor or publisher, and no responsibility for such views will be assumed.

Manuscripts, contributions and inquiries, including first class return postage, should be sent to the Gun Digest Editorial Offices, 540 Frontage Rd., Northfield, Ill. 60093. All material received will receive reasonable care, but we will not be responsible for its safe return. Material accepted is subject to our requirements for editing and revisions. Author payment covers all rights and title to the accepted material, including photos, drawings and other illustrations. Payment is made at our current rates.

Printed in the U.S.A.

ISBN-0-695-80395-6

Library of Congress Catalog #44-32588

IN THE BLACK

Remington Buys Norma

On May 17 Remington Arms Co. announced the tentative purchase of Norma Projektilfabrik, ammunition makers in Sweden, for a price between one and two million dollars.

Harvey A. Donaldson
1884-1972

A life-long shooter and ballistics experimenter, Donaldson died in Fultonville, N. Y. on November 6, 1972. Well known for his development of the 219 Wasp Ace, he was responsible in good degree for the initiation and growth of modern bench shooting. A founder and past president of the Pine Tree Bench Rest Club of Fulton County, Donaldson was the first president of the Eastern Bench Rest Shooters Assn. formed at Johnstown, N.Y. in 1947. That organization, four years later, became the N.B.R.S.A.

Harvey Donaldson's retentive mind held a vast reservoir of shooting lore much of which he imparted to many others through his numerous articles and letters. A great rifleman has gone.

Questions and Answers

Demands on the editors are such that not all letters can be answered, though we try. A stamped, address-to-oneself, envelope must be included. However, before writing to us for the location of suppliers, please see our Directory of the Arms pages—you'll probably save a stamp.

Weatherby Award

The 17th Weatherby Big Game Trophy went to James R. Mellon, II, a young man who has literally devoted his life to hunting. Many, if not most, of his thousands of birds and animals have been given to the Carnegie Museum in Pittsburgh. Some 50 of his trophies are in the Rowland Ward record book, with another large number awaiting official measurement and approval.

Wm. Caldwell
1935-1972

Bill Caldwell, ballistician for Speer Bullets, writer and shooter, died in a car accident on November 3, 1972. Others of his family were killed and injured.

Bill had brought fresh thinking to the ballistics field, as a reading of his "Pressures and the Revolver" in our 27th edition quickly reveals. His writings, marked by original insight and unfettered approaches to problems, presaged a most promising career. His work had appeared in *The Handloader, The Rifle, Gun World* and other publications. A sad and tragic loss.

John I. Moore
1897-1972

Old friend and veteran bench-rester-hunter, John I. Moore, died on April 4, 1972. He sparkplugged the building of the fine benchrest range at San Angelo, Texas. I had the pleasure of presenting to John the first awarding of the Gun Digest Trophy in 1960 for his winning of the Heavy Varmint Rifle Championship. That event was part of the first running of the National Varmint and Sporter Rifle Championship matches.

Townsend Whelen Award

The winner of this year's award—our 8th presentation honoring the late Colonel Townsend Whelen, who devoted his whole life to rifles and marksmanship—goes to Dr. Kam Nasser for his deeply researched and detailed study of a great rifle, "The Model 70 Winchester 1936-1963." We think riflemen everywhere—as well as owners and collectors of the Model 70—will enjoy and profit from this interesting and informative account.

This annual $500 award is given to the author who, in the opinion of our judges, made the best contribution to the literature of firearms, as published in this edition. The criteria are originality, clarity, readability and lasting value.

Our sincere congratulations to Dr. Nasser—and our thanks.

NBRSA Gun Digest Trophy

The National Bench Rest Shooters Assn. Varmint and Sporter Rifle championship matches were held June 6-9, 1972, on the John Zink Range near Tulsa, Okla.

I. F. (Jack) Williams of Casa Grande, Ariz., posted a .3334 MOA to take the Heavy Varmint Rifle grand aggregate and the GUN DIGEST trophy. He used a unisleeved Shilen action, Hart-barreled in 222½ caliber.

Gun Digest IBS Trophy

Carl Lynn (left) president of International Benchrest Shooters, presents the GUN DIGEST Trophy to Myles Hollister of Whitehall, N.Y., winner of the International Championship with the Heavy Varmint Rifle at Fassett, Penna. on July 27-30, 1972. He shot a .3151 MOA aggregate. He used a Clyde Hart sleeved action, a C.R. & P.J. Hart 222 barrel and a Hart stock. His scope was a Redfield 3200 in 24x.

CONTENTS

THE MODEL 70

H.I.H. Prince Abdorreza Pahlavi of Iran with No. 2 world's record Urial ram, collected in Northeast Iran. His rifle—a custom pre-64 Model 70 in 7mm Rem. Mag., made by Len Brownell of Sheridan, Wyoming.

WINCHESTER

1936-1963
a history of its halcyon years

by KAM NASSER

To THE AVERAGE hunter the Model 70 Winchester rifle may have no special meaning. To a man who knows guns and is a hunter, the Model 70 means a truly fine bolt action rifle. To a man who collects pre-64 70s there is no production rifle around today which can match the workmanship and appearance of the Model 70 made before 1964.

I am from Iran, a great land for hunting. Before I left there, in early 1956, I had taken part in many hunting trips and I'd always listened with a keen interest to those people who knew something about rifles. My first chance of looking over various rifles came during hunting trips I made, as a youngster, with some members of my family. Since one had to be 18 to own a rifle in Iran, my rifle shooting experience was limited to those times when I was allowed to handle someone else's rifle. During the course of some of those trips I began to understand better the arguments of my elders about the operation of Winchester 70 rifles compared to others. Even so, it was not until I graduated from college in this country, and had owned several rifles, that I could really appreciate the differences between the old 70s and other rifles. At that

point I got rid of several off-brand rifles and bought, in 1962, my first Model 70, a 30-06 featherweight. Since then, whenever I've had the opportunity and the money, I've invested in pre-64 Model 70s—and "investment" is the operative word!

Prices for old Model 70s have climbed steadily since 1964. Those who didn't consider this trend a few years back are today well aware of current market values. They also know that, along with several other discontinued Winchester firearms, the cash value and trading worth of their 70s are high—and getting higher! They've also learned that if one buys right that the chance of losing money on them is quite nil. The story of the Model 70 may very well follow in the footsteps of the Model 21 Winchester shotguns which, when produced, were sold for as little as $100 or less. Note that today, even though 21s are still being made, prices start at around $1,200 and go up. The old 21s have increased in value accordingly, if not more so.

The era of the old 70 goes back to 1925, with the introduction of the Winchester 54. Model 54 rifles, unfortunately, weren't very good looking and had several undesira-

ble aspects—an awkward wing-type safety, a disliked trigger system and a non-detachable floorplate, among other things. While the quality of the 54 improved considerably toward the end, Winchester discontinued it in 1935, offering in its place a new rifle—and a new action—the better-designed Model 70.

The 70s made before WW II look very much like the last of them except for the safety, which swung behind the bolt sleeve to the left, and a difference in the tang. This safety was OK with open sights but cumbersome and hard to manipulate with a scope mounted. By the way, pre-WW II 70s did not generally have the bridge tapped for scope sight screw holes. The top of the bridge was recessed, too, the recessed area showing a wavy-line matting.

As early as 1937 both Pachmayr and Tilden offered their own versions of Model 70 safeties, as did Griffin & Howe, no doubt to eliminate the awkwardness of the existing one when a scope was mounted. There is a strong possibility that Winchester adopted the plan of the Pachmayr and Tilden safeties, for one looking very like the Tilden was incorporated in their

Left, a pre-war Model 70 action; middle, a transition type compared to a later production rifle at right. Note the safeties, bolt appearance, contour of the back of the actions, as well as the shapes of the breech bolt sleeves.

post-war models. At the same time the appearance of the bolt handle was changed to allow proper clearance for the scope rings.

First Model 70s

The first announcement of the Model 70 rifles came toward the end of the year 1936. The indications were that the rifle was going to be produced in 250-3000, 220 Swift, 300 H&H, 257 Roberts, 270, 30-06, and 7x57mm calibers. From this period on the Model 70 went through interesting changes, with 3 distinct periods covering its life span: (1) the pre-war period, from 1937 to World War II, (2) the post-war period ending with the late forties—also known as the transition period, and finally the last chapter, (3) the early 1950s through 1963.

Model 70s were not only produced in standard and feather-weight grades, but in supergrades, target models, carbines and even a few sniper rifles. Supergrades resemble the standard and feather-weight 70s in every way but the stock—they have much more generous and better checkering, a capped pistol grip, a cheekpiece and a black fore-end tip. A sling strap with quick detachable swivels was also included, and the word "supergrade" was stamped on the floorplate. Usually the actions were smoother. Perhaps one reason the supergrades were not overly popular was that many potential buyers felt that the differences between them and the standard models were not great enough to warrant the extra cost.

Supergrades were not produced in all calibers. The chart below shows which calibers were produced in supergrades, in both featherweight and standard models.

The Winchester National Match rifle or the standard weight target rifle met most requirements of the big bore shooters. The N.M. rifle appeared in 30-06 caliber only, with a 24-inch floating-type barrel, a marksman stock with full pistol grip, and a weight of 9½ pounds. These came equipped with a Lyman No. 77 front sight on a forged ramp and the Lyman No. 48 receiver sight, plus target-scope bases. Another version of this rifle was also produced, known as the heavyweight target model, at 10½ pounds, without forged ramp. A still heavier style was also marketed, this one called the Bull Gun, its weight almost 13¼ pounds with a 28-inch barrel in 30-06 and 300 H&H calibers. A few sniper rifles in 30-06 caliber were also made, but their fate and details are not clearly known. The story goes that a few pre-war 70 actions were fitted with Model 54 30-06 barrels for this purpose.

A Model 70 rifle was also developed for long-range small game shooting, called the varmint rifle. It weighed 9¾ pounds. The receiver was not only tapped for most scope mounts and a receiver sight, but the barrel was also tapped for front sight bases. Target-type scope blocks were provided in much the same way as for the target models. A feature of one Model 70 varmint rifle was a checkered Monte Carlo stock. Others came with a plain, uncheckered marksman stock, these with wide, beavertail fore-ends. Over the years the target and varmint models appeared in 22 Hornet, 220 Swift, 243, 250-3000, 270, 30-06, 300 H&H and 35 Rem., almost in all instances with a 24-inch medium-weight barrel. Varmint rifles were made in 220 Swift and 243 with 26" heavyweight barrels and, in later years, with stainless steel barrels exclusively.

With the announcement of the Model 70s in 1936 it was clear that the rifle was going to be produced

Calibers	Supergrade Standards and Barrel Lengths	Supergrade Featherweights and Barrel Lengths
22 Hornet	24"	
220 Swift	26"	
243	24"	22"
250-3000	24"	
257 Roberts	24"	
270	24"	22"
7x57mm	24"	
300 Savage	24"	
308		22"
30-06	24"	22"
300 H&H	26"	
35 Remington	24"	
375 H&H	25"	
458	25"	

not only in the standard 24-inch barrel lengths but also with 20-inch barrels, then known as carbines. For some years carbines were offered in 22 Hornet, 250-3000, 270, 7x57mm, 300 Savage, 30-06, and 35 Remington. These carbines bring premium prices today, for they're unusual pieces in any collection. While the idea of a 20-inch barrel was certainly well ahead of its time, they did not sell well, and the ax fell in 1951.

Pre-War Quality

Pre-war 70s are outstanding examples of firearms craftsmanship. Their blueing is excellent, the checkering very fine, and the quality of the stock is much superior to those of a later date. The wood appears to be of a denser and darker walnut, and in some instances these stocks were very handsomely figured. Pre-war 70s also had a much smoother action, no doubt because of the time and trouble taken then in making each rifle.

There were at least two different barrel diameters available, as evidenced in the 375 Holland and Holland caliber; one reason was that the 375 was produced in a 24-inch barrel during the first year (serial numbers under 10,000), while those made later had a 25-inch barrel. In the 1960s a third variation appeared. In these the contour of the barrel was changed slightly, creating a more distinct drop a few inches away from the action. By the way, the early pre-war 375 H&H Magnums had the barrel boss-sight base of the standard 70s, but later-made barrels did not.

It is my belief that more special-order factory rifles were produced during the pre-war period than in any other period in the life history of Model 70 rifles. Fig.2 shows a couple of special-order supergrades made during 1943; a 30-06 and a 375 H&H, both having 22-inch barrels. The first 22-inch barrel production rifle, however, the featherweight 308, was not marketed until 1952. The 375 H&H was never cataloged with a 22-inch barrel.

The production of pre-war Model 70s stopped somewhere in the 63,-000 serial number range. Those 70s serially numbered from about 63,-000 to approximately 100,000 are considered "transition" models. In the transition period the safety was the leaf type and the shape of the receiver tang was still of the double radius type. It was just after this period that the cataloging of

many of the more important calibers—7x57mm, 35 Remington, 250-3000—as far as collectors are concerned, came to an end. However, it was possible to buy these or other calibers as late as the 1950s, but only on special order. Also, according to Winchester, in the past one could convert from one caliber to another, if feasible, such as changing a 270 to 7x57mm. This practice was discontinued after 1964 in order to make barrels and other parts on hand last for years to come. No, no matter how desirable you think it, you can't alter your 270 or 30-06 to a 7x57mm today! Not by New Haven, anyway.

The approximate serial numbers are quite important when it comes to knowing the pre-64 Model 70s. It is important to note that Model 70s after the war were serially indicated from 63,000 to 700,000; anything introduced after the 700,-000 serial number is classed as or called the "new Winchester Model 70," certainly a name given by the collectors to differentiate the old ones from the new.

Pre-64 70s were made in 20 different calibers, from the small "Mighty Mouse" 22 Hornet to the "Booming Bertha" 458 Winchester Magnum. The entire list of calibers follows:

Calibers	Introduced	Discontinued	Standard Barrel Lengths	F'weight Barrel Lengths	Carbine Barrel Lengths	Target & Varmint Barrel Lengths **	Supergrade Barrel Lengths ***
22 Hornet	1937	1958	24"		20"	24"	24"
220 Swift	1937	1963	26"			26"	26"
243 Win.	1955	1963	24"	22"		26"	22" 24"
250-3000 Savage	1937	1949	24"		20"	24"	24"
257 Roberts	1937	1959	24"		20"	24"	24"
264 Win. Mag.	1959	1963	26"	22"			
270 Win.	1937	1963	24"	22"	20"	24"	22" 24"
7x57mm	1937	1949	24"		20"	24"	24"
7.65x53mm	1937	1937	24"				
300 Savage*	not cataloged	not cataloged	not cataloged	not cataloged	not cataloged	not cataloged	not cataloged
308 Win.	1952	1963	24"	22"			22"## 24"
30-06 Springfield	1937	1963	24"	22"	20"	24" 26" 28"	22" 24"
300 H&H Mag.	1937	1963	26"			26" 28"	26"
300 Win. Mag.	1963	1963	24"				
338 Win. Mag.	1959	1963	25"				
35 Rem.	1944	1947	24"		20"	24"	24"
358 Win.	1955	1958		22"			
9x57mm	1937	1937	24"				
375 H&H Mag.	1937	1963	24"# 25"				25"
458 Win. Mag.	1956	1963					25"

*Factory records do not indicate that the 300 caliber was cataloged; however, research of the literature shows that a good many were produced, not only in standard 24" barrel rifles but also in 20" models.

**Authorities from the factory prefer to combine the varmint and target models in this category. The differences, though, are indicated in the text of this article.

***Supergrades were not produced in 20" barrels.

#During the first year of production, 375 H&H Magnums were produced in 24" barrels, thereafter in 25" barrels.

##Standard 24" barrels in 308 calibers were available on special order.

Two special-order pre-war Supergrade M70s, both with 22-inch barrels, made at the factory for Mr. John Moran of Indianapolis, Ind.

Only 243, 264, 270 and 30-06 were produced in both feather-weight and standard models. The 358 was introduced only in featherweight style and the 308 could be bought as a standard model on special order. Most calibers were produced in standard and super-grade form, but the 458 Winchester Magnum was the only one offered in supergrade alone. See our Model Chart for comments on the 300 Savage.

It is safe to say that the transition period ended with the beginning of the early 1950s. Many collectors considered that it was just after the transition period, and through the middle of the 1950s, that the Model 70 was at its peak. The Model 70 went through many small and major changes even after the transition period. The low-comb standard stocks of this period had a fatter and rounder fore-end. On rifles just after the transition period, the pistol cap area drops off about 3/16-inch to 1/4-inch, about the same as during the transition period. One of the common characteristics of

these rifles, and of those prior to this period, was the integral front sight ramp, ground off along the sides and blued; I have seen many Model 70s, serial numbered in the 300,000 range, with this characteristic. After this period, however, or perhaps toward the latter half of the 1950s, the sight ramps were sweated on and then blued.

Model 70s of this post-transition period were also fairly heavy, one reason being the steel buttplate and floorplate and, in most cases, the solid bolt handles. The checkering was full and very good looking. Up to about 1953-54 one could find the year of a rifle's manufacture stamped into the bottom of the barrel, just in front of the action. However, this does not necessarily mean that the entire rifle was produced at that particular date, since the component parts could have been put together, following a request for a particular caliber, at a later date. For example, my pre-64 Model 70 in 7x57mm is of early 1950 production, but the barrel is stamped 1942. Also, Winches-

ter barrels were not so-stamped for a time in the 1950s, and it is quite possible to see some without *any* marks under the barrel.

Featherweight 70s

In 1952 Winchester came out with a barrel innovation, the Model 70 featherweight in 308 caliber, which was subsequently produced in 5 other calibers—243, 264, 270, 30-06 and 358. Since many shooters thought the standard Model 70 was a bit too heavy, the featherweight was a welcome addition to the Winchester line. The major change was basically the 22-inch barrel, but Winchester also did away with that boss on the barrel which marks the standard grade rifle, and thereby eliminated as well the stud screw of the fore-end. The new shorter rifle came with an aluminum floorplate and trigger guard. All of these factors contributed to the lightness of the new feather-weight model, at 6½ pounds, and with an over-all length of 42½ inches.

This was the period during which

the high-comb stocks became popular. With the onset of these Monte Carlo, or high-comb stocks, Winchester eventually switched over from the Winchester 22G sporting rear sight, generally associated with low-comb stocks, to the Lyman No. 6 folding-leaf sight.

Of the 6 featherweight calibers produced the most sought after are the 243, 270 and 30-06, as far as the shooting public is concerned. The Model 70 featherweight could certainly be considered—at least by many—as one of the handsomest rifles ever factory-made in this country.

In the late 1950s an effort was made to lighten both featherweight and standard rifles even further. The steel buttplate was changed to aluminum on all models, as was the bolt handle ball, drilled to make it slightly lighter.

By the time the rifles were discontinued in 1963 many interesting changes had occurred. Because of the cost of production, and because other manufacturers had simplified their manufacturing techniques, increasing their sales by so doing, Winchester could not afford to continue with the old expensive methods. In this era no doubt everything was tried to save the life of the old 70 rifles. The checkering on both fore-end and pistol grip was reduced considerably, the steel or aluminum buttplates were replaced by plastic. On the Magnum calibers the factory solid-rubber recoil pads were changed to the see-through type. Less time was spent on staining and finishing the stocks, since some appear to be much lighter-toned, less well done than the stocks of previous years. Wood to metal fit fell off as well. The bolt sleeve, which originally had a straight vertical cut on the safety side, was left round. It is interesting that this period coincides with the boom in the Winchester short belted magnums, such as the 458, 338, 300 and 264. One can find "458" stamped under the action of 264, 300 and 338 rifles, perhaps denoting that the particular action could have been just as easily used in a 458.

In spite of its efforts, Winchester could not keep production costs down, and a complete change became inevitable. By 1964 the old Model 70 rifle had become a thing of the past in the annals of firearm history.

A few Model 70 calibers, such as the 264 and 220 Swift, were furnished with stainless steel barrels as well as in chrome-moly steel. The finish on these stainless steel barrels (standard or heavyweight) is obviously different, for they were first sandblasted, then blued, giving them a sort of Parkerized appearance rather than the highly polished finish of standard barrels.

All Model 70 actions, at least in profile and at first glance, look alike. The 300 and 375 Holland and Holland long-case calibers differed from the others in that the top rear edge of the receiver ring and the front of the bridge were cut away to accept these lengthy magnums. Other than this, without a close look, one can't tell the difference between the action of a 22 Hornet and that of a 30-06, a 257, et al. In such small-case calibers as the 243, 257, 308, etc., as opposed to the 270 or 30-06, the bolt carried a little metal piece on the left-hand side of the bolt body, generally known as the bolt stop

Cartridges for which the old Model 70 Winchester was chambered. Top row (from left) 22 Hornet, 220 Swift, 243, 250-3000, 257 Roberts, 264 Win. Mag., 270, 7mm, 300 Savage, 300

extension. The smaller-caliber magazines were fitted with partitions to decrease their inside length.

Many Model 70 parts are interchangeable from rifle to rifle because of the size or similarity of some calibers. For instance, the 308 magazine is the same as that for the 257; the 270 is the same as that of the 7x57mm and 30-06. Many small parts are the same for virtually all calibers, being usable from one rifle to another.

The Collector's Problems

Since pre-64 Model 70 actions are in great demand today by custom gunmakers, the collector is faced with a problem. Since many hundreds of these pre-64 70s were robbed of their original Winchester barrels to make room for a custom barrel, many of the old 70 barrels are floating around on the market. Some, of course, have been already

H&H Bottom (from left) 300 Win. Mag. 30-06, 308, 7.65mm, 338 Win. Mag., 35 Rem., 358, 9mm, 375 H&H, 458 Win. Mag.

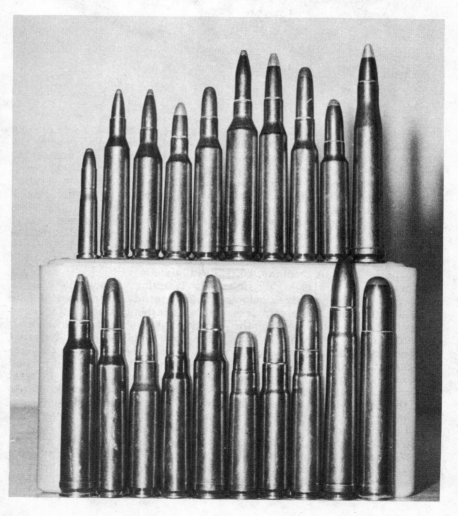

Outstanding examples of pre-64 Model 70 featherweights. From top: 30-06 with B&L 2½ to 8 scope, 270 with 4x Weaver in Buehler mounts, and a 243 with a B&L 2½-5x scope.

fitted to other Model 70 actions, resulting in "new" 70 rifles. Yet, as far as appearance is concerned, they all look the same. It is disturbing, to say the least, to come across a Model 70 with a barrel and caliber that is not appropriate for the action. For example, I've seen a 300 Winchester Magnum with a serial number in the 200,000 range, but that caliber wasn't produced until 1963. A genuine 300 Winchester Magnum is highly unlikely to be serial numbered below 400,000. Examining the proofmarks is another way of detecting the originality of the barrel and action. In almost all cases the proofmarks are perfectly aligned; that is, the proofmark on the barrel and that on the action are in straight line, with the exception of a brief period. During the very end of the pre-64 production years (about 1962-63), this exact alignment on 300 Winchester Magnums did not hold true. As a matter of fact, I own one of these and have seen several others showing this variation.

By the same token many old Model 70 stocks have flooded the market; it would be a mistake to use a latter-production stock, say of the 1960s, with its narrow checkering, on an early production model. All featherweight and standard stocks can be interchanged (except when the tangs differ), but in the instance just cited the inappropriate type of checkering would be a dead giveaway.

It is quite possible to alter a standard grade 70 to make it look like a carbine. One could cut 4 inches off the muzzle and sweat the front sight back on, but that won't work because the carbines were discontinued in 1951, and their front sights were integral with the barrel, not sweated on. As with other fields of collecting, real expertise doesn't come overnight; one must have looked at several hundred Model 70s before the authentic rifle can be told from the phony. Well, the situation isn't all that critical yet, but such fakers could be the collector's hangup in

the future—especially the novice collector!

One of the most unusual 70s I've seen was a 300 H&H Magnum converted to appear like a 300 Winchester Magnum. The idea behind this particular trickiness goes back to the 1950s, when the 300 H&H Magnum was the only 300 Magnum around, and at times the rifles were simply stamped "300 Magnum." If the breech end of the barrel is cut off a bit and the barrel rechambered to the 300 Winchester Magnum, the barrel would be shorter, all right, but it would look quite genuine. Nevertheless, the serial number would give it away. Here's another—restocking a standard grade 70 in 30-06 with a National Match stock would make it look like a target model, but the informed collector knows that the National Match barrel did not permit a hood or sight cover to be placed on the front sight ramp. Also the action of a National Match rifle had a clip slot cut into the bridge, whereas regular pre-64

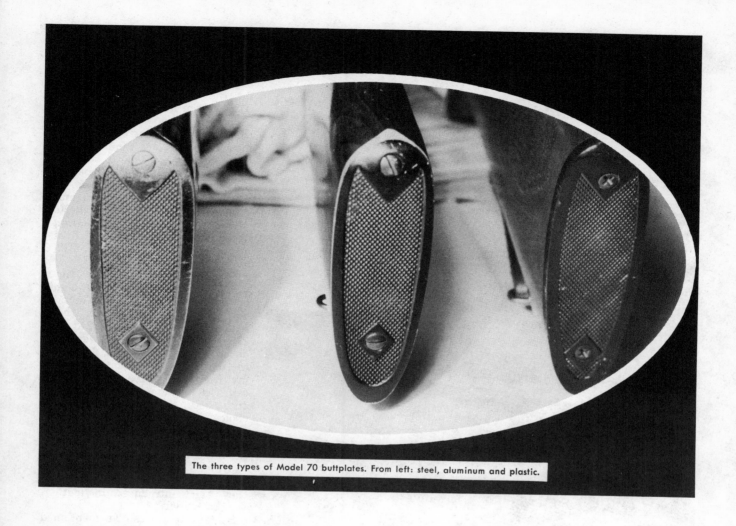

The three types of Model 70 buttplates. From left: steel, aluminum and plastic.

Model 70 standard rifles in 30-06 calibers did not except for the quite early ones.

Model 70 Prices—Then and Now

Let me now discuss and analyze prices of the most sought after Model 70s—what they cost when introduced and what they're worth today.

In 1936, when the Model 70 was first announced, the retail price was $61.25 for the standard rifle. That, incidentally, was only a few dollars over the retail price of the Model 54. In the 26 years of Model 70 production, cataloged prices more than doubled. In 1963 the list price was $139 for featherweights and standard grades, and about $15 more for the magnums, target or varmint models. An exception was the 458 Magnum, which retailed at $310. Since the discontinuation of the old Model 70 prices have sky-rocketed. Those who began collecting pre-64 Model 70s only a few years or so ago are finding out that they're not only becoming extremely hard to come by, but that their

prices are also getting too rich for the average man's pocketbook. So it is important to look at today's market prices honestly and realistically and, I hope, without any bias. There are books available today which set certain prices on these rifles, but I contend that most of these "Purple Book" values are misleading, unreasonable and unrealistic. The collector should not necessarily be misled by gunshop prices, either. Obviously these stores have to make a little profit on a rifle to meet their operating costs, and they can also afford to hang on to their merchandise for a lot longer time. Moreover, they must allow for trades.

Collector's values for pre-64 Model 70s are based on the following factors, not necessarily in this order:

1. Rarity of the caliber.
2. Type, i.e., standard, super-grade, carbine.
3. Special factory versions.
4. Originality and condition.

Generally, of the many Model 70

collectors to whom I've spoken or know, few tend to place more value on their rifles than the average going prices. On the contrary, some have got fantastic prices for theirs. So it may be pointed out that the old rule of thumb, "They are worth as much as you can get for them," still stands.

For a start, please note that any pre-64 Model 70 action in excellent condition is worth at least $100 because of their high demand by custom rifle builders.

The slow sellers of the past, such as standard grade rifles in 35 Remington, 250-3000, 300 Savage and 7x57mm calibers (which in most instances were produced for a short period of time and then discontinued) have become essential to any Model 70 collection worth the name. These calibers, in the original box or in mint condition, bring from $350 to $400. Those two rarest calibers (7.65mm and 9x57mm) that every one talks about but few have seen, would bring the very top prices; I've never seen either.

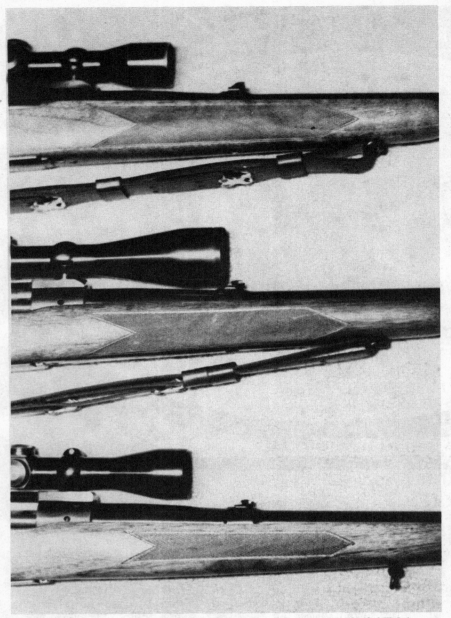

The checkering of Model 70s shown chronologically. From the top: a late 1940 257 Roberts, a 22 Hornet of the middle 1950s, and a 300 Winchester Magnum of the 1960s.

Even though some Model 70s—22 Hornet, 220 Swift, 257 Roberts—were continuously produced over the years, this does not make them any less valuable; as a matter of fact these 3 calibers, along with the 358, are the next biggest stumbling block in front of the collectors (the toughest calibers to find, for most collectors, are the 35 Remington, 7x57mm, 250-3000 and 300 Savage). Even though as many of these were produced as were the 270 and the 30-06, they are much more desirable for the collector, hence the values. The price range depends on the condition, of course, and is in the neighborhood of $200 to $225.

I've been asked many times which I prefer—the featherweights or the standard grades. There is not much choice between them, really, for only 6 calibers (243, 264, 270, 308, 30-06 and 358) were produced as featherweights. I like all the featherweights, though some of my friends disagree with me. I'd call it a matter of personal preference because I don't think the choice has anything to do with collecting values. There is no doubt in my mind, though, that some of the other calibers—the 257 Roberts, 7x57mm, 250-3000, 22 Hornet—would have done quite well had they been introduced in featherweight models.

So far the prices I've mentioned relate only to the standard grade Model 70s. However, within that same group the transition models and the pre-war Model 70s command special attention. In excellent or better condition these would bring slightly more money over the later issues. The supergrades, undoubtedly the cream of the crop, are the top pieces for the collector. Thumbing through the first issue (1944) of the GUN DIGEST, the supergrades were shown at the unbelievable price, today, of $107.85, compared to standard models selling at $78.45. Today, on the average, supergrades would bring roughly $100-$125 more than a standard model.

Model 70 National Match prices are right up there with those supergrades in the medium price range, such as the 220 Swift and 22 Hornet. The 70 Bull Gun perhaps, is in the same category. The 20-inch barreled Model 70 carbines, in such rare calibers as 250-3000, 7x57mm or 35 Remington, would no doubt top the field in terms of collector interest and value; since not many were made in the rarer

On the other hand, such very common calibers as the 243, 270, 30-06 and 308 are not very hard to find. Of these, the 243 and the 270 seem to be very good sellers, and in excellent to better shape bring $150 to $175. Even so, they are becoming scarcer. The magnum calibers are increasingly hard to find; among them the 300 and 338 Winchester Magnums and the 375 H&H Magnums are quite sought after by collectors and shooters; prices asked are around $200 to $250. Of these three calibers, since the 300 Winchester Magnum was produced only in 1963, it can be expected to climb considerably over

the rest of the magnum calibers in the near future. The slowest seller among the magnum calibers, besides the 264, seems to be the 300 H&H, which was pushed right out of the market by the appearance of the 300 Winchester Magnum. The market value of these last two is somewhere between $175 and $200, again if in excellent or better shape. The 264 Magnum, made with 22- and 26-inch barrels, sells best, in my experience, with the longer barrel.

Between the rare and the common calibers, a wide range of good to outstanding calibers exist which are not necessarily easy to obtain.

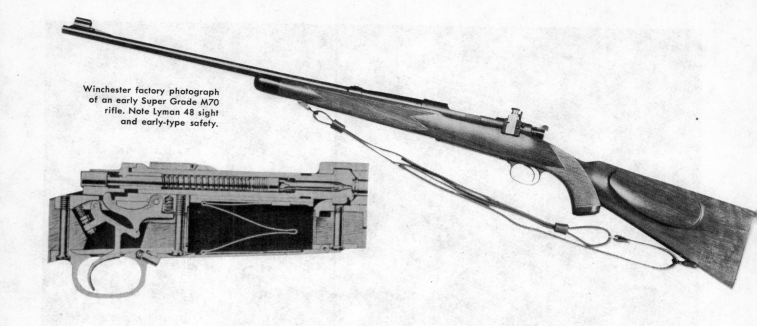

Winchester factory photograph of an early Super Grade M70 rifle. Note Lyman 48 sight and early-type safety.

calibers, any one of them would enhance the collection.

To some collectors any variation in Model 70 rifles is important, such as those of the post-war period without sight slot and front sight ramp, or a rifle of pre-war and transition vintage. Because the transition period covered only a few years, generally any rifle of this period is more in demand; naturally the supergrade of the same period is even more desirable and interesting, since logically there could not have been too many of them made during that period. Moreover, some of these Model 70s were factory engraved and gold inlaid on special order. An example of such workmanship is found in the 23rd issue of the GUN Digest, page 139. Here, obviously, we are talking about a four-figure price tag.

All prices mentioned, by the way, are relative—the condition of the rifles is highly important. Chances are most of them won't be in the original box, or mint or even in excellent condition. Accordingly, the price may take a sharp dip. I've seen a good many rifles in the rare calibers with their barrels chopped off two inches or so, rechambered, the bolt altered, with disastrous results. Naturally, if an individual has collected 18 of the 20 known calibers, the asking price for the whole collection would be higher, in spite of the condition of some of the rifles.

As far as I can tell, from information received in recent years,

pre-64 Model 70 collectors are specializing. Some stick to the supergrade models, some prefer the pre-war and transition periods, while others collect post-transition Model 70s with serial numbers in the 100,000 to 300,000 range. Some—perhaps after a good profit—are collecting everything in sight! Me? I'd like to have one example of each model and period.

Many people ask "Why a pre-64 Model 70?" The answer is very simple. If one is familiar with good workmanship and quality and is, as well, a collector who puts high value on any good firearm, he knows he can't go wrong by collect-

Two pre-1964 Model 70s—at left a 30-06, at right a 375 H&H Magnum, both standard grades. Note receiver ring and bridge cuts in the magnum.

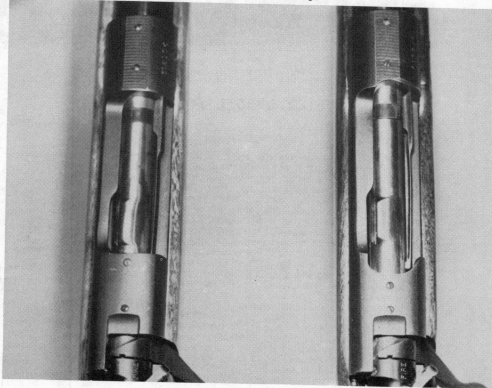

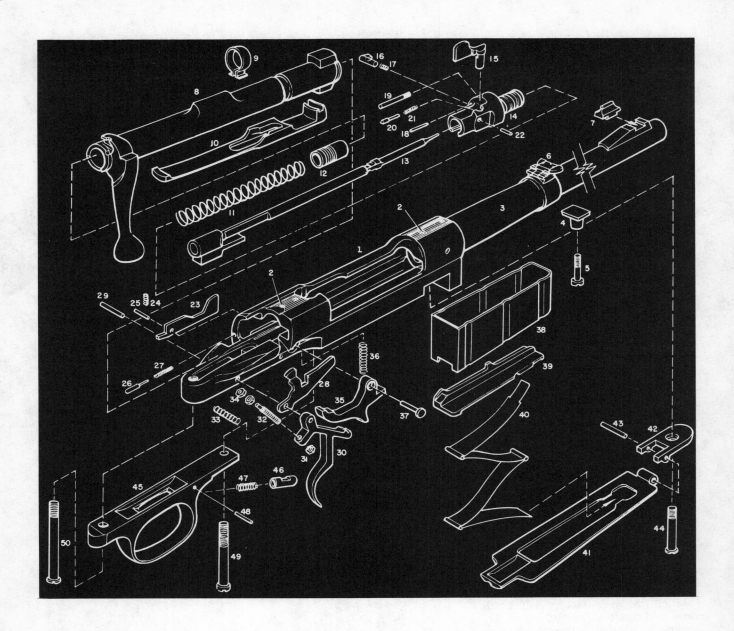

WINCHESTER MODEL 70

Disassembly—Depress bolt stop (28) and draw bolt to rear out of receiver. Remove barrel and receiver from stock by unscrewing fore-end stud screw (5), magazine cover hinge plate screw (44), and front and rear guard bow screws (49,50). Remove magazine cover assembly complete with spring (40) and follower (39). Lift receiver and barrel group out of buttstock. Guard bow (45) may be removed from buttstock. Ejector (23), bolt stop (28), trigger (30), sear (35) and their springs may all be removed from receiver by driving out their retaining pins. Bolt stop plunger (26) and spring (27) are removed from hole at rear of receiver after removing bolt stop. Extractor (10) may be turned slightly on bolt and is easily disengaged from lips of extractor ring (9). With bolt cocked, move safety lock (15) to its intermediate position between "safe" and "fire." Depress breech bolt sleeve lock (16) and unscrew breech bolt sleeve and firing pin assembly from breech bolt. Move safety lock to "fire" position. Pull firing pin sleeve (12) to rear slightly. Turn sleeve ¼-turn in either direction, disengaging sleeve from firing pin (13). Withdraw sleeve and spring (11) from firing pin, taking care not to let the compressed spring escape forcibly. Breech bolt sleeve (14) is removed from firing pin by unscrewing firing pin stop screw (19). Reassemble in reverse order.

Parts List
1. Receiver
2. Receiver Plug Screws
3. Barrel
4. Fore-end Stud
5. Fore-end Stud Screw
6. Rear Sight
7. Front Sight
8. Breech Bolt
9. Extractor Ring
10. Extractor
11. Firing Pin Spring
12. Firing Pin Sleeve
13. Firing Pin
14. Breech Bolt Sleeve
15. Safety Lock
16. Breech Bolt Sleeve Lock
17. Breech Bolt Sleeve Lock Spring
18. Breech Bolt Sleeve Lock Pin
19. Firing Pin Stop Screw
20. Safety Lock Plunger
21. Safety Lock Plunger Spring
22. Safety Lock Stop Pin
23. Ejector
24. Ejector Spring
25. Ejector Pin
26. Bolt Stop Plunger

27. Bolt Stop Plunger Spring
28. Bolt Stop
29. Trigger Pin
30. Trigger
31. Trigger Stop Screw Nut
32. Trigger Stop Screw
33. Trigger Spring
34. Trigger Spring Adj. Nuts (2)
35. Sear
36. Sear Spring
37. Sear Pin
38. Magazine
39. Magazine Follower
40. Magazine Spring
41. Magazine Cover
42. Magazine Cover Hinge Plate
43. Magazine Cover Hinge Pin
44. Magazine Cover Hinge Plate Screw
45. Guard Bow
46. Magazine Cover Catch
47. Magazine Cover Catch Spring
48. Magazine Cover Catch Pin
49. Front Guard Bow Screw
50. Rear Guard Bow Screw
Buttstock, buttplate and sling swivels are not shown in the exploded drawing.

A Model 70 National Match rifle, made about 1952.

ing these old Model 70 rifles. There is, of course, more to Model 70 mania than this simple explanation. In these rifles one finds the wide-head, reliable, Mauser-type extractor, noted for its smooth operation. Many parts of the action were forged and machined; the checkering was done by hand; the excellent 3-position safety, inoperative unless the firing pin is cocked; the ease with which the entire action can be taken apart and reassembled.

What the future holds for the old Model 70 design is anybody's guess. There are some who feel that Winchester will ultimately capitalize on the consumer demand and start reproducing the old Model 70 rifle on a limited basis, in much the same way the Winchester Model 12 shotgun is offered. This would, for a time at least, shake up the collectors. However, if and when they are reproduced the prices are

certainly not going to be any cheaper than those current for new Winchester Model 70s and chances are they'd go at top prices. Others contend that Winchester, by so doing, would downgrade their new 70s, thereby pulling the (sales) rug from underneath them.

At present there seems to be a pressing factor for Model 70 collectors. Parts easily available a few years ago are becoming depleted to a point where some of the rare calibers cannot be rebarreled to restore their original condition. Eventually, of course, all parts will be exhausted, as is the current situation facing the

owners of Winchester Models 75, 72, 43, etc. Some far off day pre-64 Model 70s will find their way into showcases or museums, along with such cherished firearms of the past as the Sharps, the early Colt, the Lefever, the Parker and many others.

While I don't mean to damn with faint praise, it is quite correct that the "new" Model 70 Winchesters are as good as any rifle made today anywhere—strong, reliable, accurate and well made—but neither they, nor any other rifle, can match the superb quality and craftsmanship of the pre-64 Model 70, the rifleman's rifle. ●

H.I.H. Prince Abdorreza with two record-class Red sheep, collected in northern Iran. The rifle—a custom pre-64 Model 70 in 7x57mm, made by Al Biesen of Portland, Oregon.

Some Special Seventies

A late Model 70 Winchester action forms the basis for this sporter built by Al Biesen, the barrel by Wm. Hobaugh in 7mm Remington Magnum caliber. The California American walnut has a rich, warm color and a swirling figure in the butt section, with fiddleback grain prominent in the fore-end section. Biesen fitted his trapped and checkered steel buttplate, a matching grip cap, checkered the bolt knob and the bolt release button, then installed the floorplate release in the thinned and re-contoured trigger guard. The bolt and raceways are engine turned. Excellent checkering covers most of the fore-end and pistol grip, with a diamond-shaped panel of finer checkering set into the underneath fore-end pattern.

This early Model 70 Winchester rifle, serial number 3338 and in caliber 30-06, was bought in 1937. The stock seen on it now was made by Hal Hartley of Lenoir, North Carolina, the wood a very tightly figured piece of fiddleback hard maple. The safety is a Tilden, the scope base just visible on the left side of the receiver is an early Echo. The Lyman 48 peep sight base, also on the left side, is filled with a dummy slide.

This is another factory-made "extralusso" Super Grade Model 70 Winchester. The wood is a superb piece of fancy American walnut, but its figure is obscured now by too many applications of oil over the years. The floorplate-guard, the trapped grip cap and the buttplate are well engraved. The scope is a Noske in Adolph Niedner's sliding-dovetail side mount, and that's a Lyman 48 receiver sight attached to the receiver.

This old Winchester Company photograph, dug out of our files, represents the 500,000th Model 70 Winchester, I believe. The wood is a special piece of ultra-fancy walnut, the checkering is in an unusual pattern, and the barrel and receiver are fully engraved, with gold inlaid lines and figures. The safety lever shows that it is an early Model 70, and I suppose this might be called a Super Grade.

This factory photograph shows a Super Grade Model 70 Winchester, probably made about 1952. Note change in cheekpiece form from earlier Super Grades, and the low Monte Carlo comb.

The AFRICAN BATTERY

a modern approach

by STEVE MILLER

THE AMERICAN SPORTSMAN planning his first trip to the Dark Continent usually spends hours studying ballistic charts and selecting kingsize cartridges, and then more hours going from sporting goods store to gun dealer, trying to find a suitable set of rifles chambered for these, when perhaps guns adequate for most African hunting already rest in his own gun cabinet. Years of propaganda have convinced us that African game is more tenacious of life than our own, with almost super-strength, and that our old favorite calibers, long in use here, will bounce off their tough hides.

This is pure hogwash. Most African game is no harder to kill than animals of comparable size on our continent. The average male lion will weigh between 350 and 500 pounds, is soft skinned and much easier to kill than a good-sized grizzly bear. That the lion is more

Time was, not too many years ago, when calibers for the big safari were predominantly British—the 470 or 465, the 416, 375 or 300 H&H. Not so today, even if you don't agree with all of the author's recommendations.

aggressive, I will admit, but the idea that he merely shrugs off 30-cal. bullets is ridiculous. The famous Blaney Percival, longtime African game warden, did much of his hunting with a 6.5x54 Mannlicher and even went on elephant control with this junior-size 264. All of us have read the exploits of W.D.M. Bell, the famous ivory hunter, who killed over 1000 elephants, most of these with the 7mm Mauser but a few with the 303 British and 318 Rigby. None of these rifles will approach the power of the old 30-06—which is standard deer medicine in the States! The larger African antelope, such as eland, average slightly bigger than an Alaskan moose, but are no harder to kill. The remainder of African antelope, which run from white-tailed deer to elk size, can be handled by any caliber rifle that will handle our game here in the States. This, of course, is not to say that your favorite 30-30 will do for buffalo, rhino or elephant, but don't overlook your favorite deerslayer when planning your African hunt.

On a trip to the Congo in 1964, I took my old Husqvarna 30-06 equipped with a Redfield 2-7 variable power scope. My ammunition was the Remington factory load with 220-gr. Core-Lokt bullets and 50 handloads assembled with Hornady's excellent, but alas, now discontinued, 220-gr. solids. As I was primarily on a business trip, I was unable to take other rifles with me. During the three weeks that I managed to get in the bush, I killed five lions, twelve bush cows—the Congo's answer to the Cape Buffalo—and numerous antelope. The one leopard I got was killed with buckshot, and was quite possibly the first leopard slain with the then new Western Mark V load. The lions were killed with the soft point loads. All were one-shot kills except for a lioness which required two shots to stop a charge.

Before you start thinking of me as a game violator, let me explain. Since the Belgians left the Congo a few years ago, game regulations have been nonexistent. Almost no hunters have been in the Congo for several years, because of the political trouble, and game has multiplied to dangerous proportions. Natives who now openly own guns kill a great many antelope, but avoid the dangerous game, and man-eating lions have become common. At least two of the lions I killed were confirmed man-eaters,

and one was actually feeding on a native when shot. The bush cows, which are slightly smaller than Cape buffalo, are noted for their bad tempers and travel in herds up to 50 or so, which can make hunting them a dangerous proposition. Those I shot, incidentally, were all killed with the solid bullets, and penetration was superb. After Hornady discontinued his 308-cal. solids, I switched to the 250-gr. Barnes solid, but have not yet used them on game.

African game, excluding rhino and elephant, ranges in weight from about 100 lbs. to maybe a ton. The dangerous species of cats run from about 150 lbs. for leopard to 500 for the lion. The leopard, which is quite easy to kill if hit properly, is probably the world's nastiest animal to track when wounded. The best medicine in this situation is a double barreled shotgun stuffed with buckshot.

Let's examine the average American hunter's rifles and consider them for African use.

243 Winchester and 6mm Remington

While both the 243 and 6mm are popular in America, they are a bit on the light side for African game. Using long 100- and 105-gr. handloads, preferably of the Nosler type, they could be used successfully for the lighter plains game. Thompson's gazelle, impala and the like are no harder to kill than a small white-tailed buck and easier than large mule deer. Heavily constructed bullets at about 3000 fps would prove good medicine for plains game and the flat trajectory of these cartridges would prove a valuable asset.

250-3000 and 257 Roberts

Of these two, the 257 would be the writer's choice, as heavy handloads using 117-125-gr. bullets far surpass anything possible in the 250-3000. The 100-gr. Nosler, however, easily handloaded to 2900-plus fps in a bolt action 250-3000, would be a good leopard medicine and be capable of handling plains game up to 500 lbs.

264 Winchester and Various 6.5mm Rifles

The 6.5x54mm Mannlicher-Schoenauer has killed every species in Africa—possibly every one in the world—but for most hunters it can be considered on the light side for dangerous game, with the possible exception of leopard. It will handle any plains game easily, the long

156-gr. bullets offering deep penetration because of their exceptional sectional density.

The 264 Winchester Magnum would easily handle any of the plains game in Africa, and with a strong, well-constructed bullet I would not hesitate to take on a lion providing I was backed up by a heavier gun—and of course any of us who hunt in Africa will be out with a white hunter who is carrying a heavy-caliber double or magazine rifle. Non-dangerous game as heavy as the eland should prove no problem for the rifleman armed with a 264.

270 Winchester

The 270 is a favorite of American hunters and long has been recognized as one of the better cartridges for this continent. It is also very popular in Rhodesia and South Africa, and no American hunter now alive will ever see as much African game as has been piled up by this caliber.

Handloads using heavy bullets such as the 150-gr. Nosler or the 170-gr. Barnes or Speer, or Canadian Industry Ltd.'s 160-gr. factory load, should make it a perfectly adequate lion rifle, and its flat trajectory will make easy meat out of any plains game. In a recent letter, Jack O'Connor, who deserves most of the credit for the 270's popularity, told me he killed most of his game in Africa, except elephant, with a 270. Jack has killed several grizzly bears with this cartridge and he agrees that a lion is no more difficult to kill than a grizzly of comparable size. The important thing is to use bullets that hold together. Good factory ammo, of course, can be bought almost anywhere—another point in the 270's favor.

The 7mms

The 7x57mm Mauser, or 275 Rigby as it is known in Africa, is a standard medium or light caliber there. Many settlers and almost all white hunters have a 7mm in their battery, and that is good enough recommendation for me. As to the 7mm Remington Magnum, that is just frosting on the cake. Anything the 270 will do, the 7mm Remington will equal or surpass, with the added advantage of having an excellent, heavily constructed 175-gr. bullet available in a factory load. Any of the plains game, as well as lion, should prove no problem for this caliber. This also is true to a lesser extent of the 280 Remington and 284 Winchester.

American calibers adequate for some African game. Left to right: 257 Roberts, 117-gr. Core Lokt; 270 Winchester, 150-gr.; 7x57mm Mauser, 175-gr. SP; 30-06 180-gr. Core Lokt; 338 Win. Mag., 300-gr. Western Power Point; 35 Rem., 200-gr. SP; 360 Nitro Express (also known as the 9.3x57R), 285-gr. SP; 444 Marlin, 240-gr. SP. The leopard was killed with one shot from a 30-06, the 165-gr. Hornady SP bullet handloaded with 53 grains of 4320, at approximately 2850 fps.

308 Winchester

The 308, in reality a junior 30-06, will handle all African game except possibly buffalo, rhino and elephant. Using the factory load with 200-gr. bullet at about 2450 fps you should be able to handle any plains game plus lion and leopard. If this weight bullet was available in a solid, I wouldn't hesitate to take on buffalo or rhino with it, but as penetration is unsure using soft-noses I'd stop at lion with these.

Kudu, okapi, eland or the desert dwellers such as gemsbok are easy meat for an accurate, scope-sighted 308.

30-06 Springfield

Since about the end of World War I, when Springfield rifles became generally available for sporterization, thousands of hunters have used the 30-06 for everything from crows to elephants. While on the light side for ele-

phant, the 30-06 is one of the most versatile cartridges available. Factory loads have bullets for 110 to 220 grain, and handloaders can choose from the 90-gr. jacketed types, while with cast bullets he can just about name his own poison.

For most of my stateside hunting I have used the almost-perfect 165-gr. Hornady spire point which can be pushed to about the same velocity as the 150-gr. factory load

300 Weatherby and 300 Winchester Magnums

Everything stated about the 30-06 also stands true for the big 30s. The 300 Weatherby got its reputation where it counts, on the game fields of the world. Internationally known hunters Elgin Gates and Herb Klein have used the 300 Weatherby on almost every possible game animal. I consider the various 300 Magnums on the light side for steady use on elephants, as in control shooting, but with appropriate solid bullets I wouldn't hesitate to take on all the average sportsman can get licenses for. For leopard hunting you are frankly over-gunned with a big 30, but it will lay them down like lighting and a dead leopard is a safe leopard.

338 Winchester Magnum

This comparatively new offering by Winchester is what I would consider the lightest practical rifle for the Big Three—rhino, buffalo and elephant—although some of those already mentioned would do in a pinch. Supplying ballistics only slightly below that of its big brother, the 375 Magnum, the 338 offers less recoil and better sectional density with bullets of similar or equal weights. The 300-gr. Winchester Power Point should penetrate deeper than the 300-gr. 375, and the 250-gr. Silvertip is almost a twin of the 375's 270-gr. load.

With handloads using Hornady's strong 250-gr. solid in front of 57 grains of IMR 4064 for a velocity of some 2450 fps, I am going to take on an elephant or two in the next few months. I doubt that I'll have anything to worry about. John Taylor, who wrote that bible of hunting, *African Rifles and Cartridges* (Harrisburg, Pa., 1948), stated that the 350 Rigby and 333 Jeffery were ideal for most hunting on the Dark Continent, and ballistically the 338 Winchester has both beat. Taylor also stated that 4000 fp of muzzle energy was more than enough for the largest African game and the 338 scores on that point too.

358 Winchester, 350 Remington Magnum and 35 Whelen

These three 35s, which have excelled for heavy American game, and the similar 348 Winchester, which is becoming obsolete, will all suffice for African game up to lions. Using a well-constructed 250-gr. bullet at about 2400 fs might even be sufficient for buffalo in a

Your own "deer" rifles may prove effective on African game, given the chance. In my gunrack, left to right: 1. Custom Mauser in 257 Imp. Roberts, the Weaver K-10 scope with Rangefinder reticle. 2. My favorite Husqvarna 30-06 sporter has a Redfield 2-7x variable with post reticle. 3. Winchester 70, caliber 338 Win. Mag., carries a Bushnell 2½x scope with Command-Post reticle and auxiliary Williams receiver sight. 4. Custom Remington 722 in 358 Winchester, the scope a Redfield 2½ with post reticle, auxiliary Williams open sight and custom muzzle brake-ramp sight combination.

I consider the 338 Magnum adequate for all African game, including elephant, buffalo and rhino, with solid bullets. Hornady and Colorado Custom (Barnes) supply 338 solids—Hornady's 250-gr. and Barnes' 300-gr.

and will supply over 3000 fp of energy. It's a mystery to me why the factories don't load this weight, as it combines the trajectory of the 150-gr. with the penetration of the 180-gr. bullet.

While the 165-gr. handload or 180-gr. factory bullet would have been sufficient for most of my African hunting, I used the 220-gr. bullet exclusively. I wanted this weight for the bigger stuff and my gun groups the lighter bullets some 12" away from its zero at 200 yards, which would have necessitated re-sighting.

The old 30-cal. Hornady 220-gr. solid had almost unbelievable penetration. I shot one buffalo through the shoulder and he fell as though pole-axed. The bullet passed completely through him, breaking both shoulders on the way. Another bull was shot centrally in the chest from the front and I couldn't reach the bullet with a 38" piece of bamboo shoved into the hole. I tested the load on a bull elephant just killed by a companion, and on a side brain shot the bullet completely penetrated the head. Soft points give less penetration, of course, but on the smaller antelope you should be sure no other beast is standing in line with the one you shoot at, as the 220-gr. soft point will sometimes pass through as many as three impala. Indeed, the 150-gr. bullet would prove more suitable on this sort of game.

Steve Miller at the bench with a Custom 358 Winchester on a Remington 722 action. Using factory 250-gr. Silvertip ammunition this caliber is adequate for 90% of African game; with handloads using the 300-gr. Barnes solid, it would do for Cape buffalo. I recommend that solids be used on buffalo from any caliber gun.

pinch. While I prefer solids for buff hunting, many hunters swear by soft points, and the Winchester-Western Silvertip and Remington Core-Lokt are heavily enough constructed to stand up to almost any job. My only objection to the 350 Remington—a purely personal one —is the rifle supplied for it. Just thinking about the recoil of this powerful load in a 6½-lb. carbine scares me to death. Now that the 350 is offered in the Remington M700, it should be a best seller. You, of course, might handle it with no trouble in the Model 660.

375 H&H Magnum

The 375 Magnum is primarily an African caliber to begin with, but I am including it here because many Americans have one in their battery for Alaskan use. If I had to use one gun for hunting everything in the world from grizzlies to elephants, the 375 Magnum would probably be my choice.

John Taylor calls the 375 the best all-round load for African use and tells of many cases where charging elephants and buffalo

were smacked down for keeps with the 300-gr. solid. Because the caliber has been around a long time, 375 Magnum cartridges are available wherever men hunt, from Fairbanks, Alaska, to Dar es Salaam, and this can be important. If you run low on cartridges out in the blue, you are in deep trouble.

The combination of high velocity,

excellent sectional density and deep penetration of its solid bullets has made the 375 one of the most versatile guns available. While it admittedly doesn't have the muzzle energy of the 458 Magnum, it will handle most anything that the larger cartridge will and with considerable less recoil. For the professional elephant hunter, who might

"Making up his mind." If you're that close to a buff, you're too close. This photo was taken in Rhodesia from much farther away, using a 300mm lens.

An extremely large bull elephant, for the Congo, he's carrying at least 150 pounds of ivory (75 to the side). He is in perfect position for a heart or lung shot. Most hunters shoot too low on the side heart shot, and should aim at a point at least in the center of the elephant. Using solids the best shot would be directly through the shoulder blade, which would break the elephant down, and penetrate deep into his lungs. He wouldn't move out of his tracks.

have to face an enraged elephant alone in the wilds, I would definitely suggest a 458 or even better, one of the English double rifles such as the 470 or the 475 No. 2. But for the American who will be hunting with a whole company, I frankly wonder if it is necessary.

Sights for African Use

Experienced hunters know they can dependably hit only what they can clearly see. Usually you see best with a good scope. The best scopes in the world, I believe, are now being made in the U.S., and they seem to be the preferred sights of Americans. Even the conservative British are slowly coming around, and more and more professional white hunters are carrying glassware on their medium-bore guns.

A low powered scope with a good, stand-out reticle, mounted on a low, quick-detachable mount can often make the difference between a hit and a miss. The vast majority of African game, with the exception of the desert dwellers, is shot at while standing at less than 200 yards. The hunter usually has plenty of time to make his shot. Most of us, after reading stories of African hunting, imagine that every day we will be faced with dangerous, charging game, but this is not so. The average hunter could make half a dozen safaris and never see a charging animal. Indeed, the only animal that is inclined to charge is the rhino, which, in its stupidity, will sometimes blunder into a hunting party. As he is comparatively easy to turn, I don't consider him as potentially dangerous as a lion, leopard or buffalo, which will charge to the death—but not usually without considerable provocation. On different African hunts I have used the Bushnell 2¾x scope with Command Post, the Redfield 2-7 variable with post reticle, and a Weaver K4, also with post. I prefer the Redfield variable, but only because the high power settings enable me to forego carrying binoculars. Whatever the scope you choose, its reticle should stand out

Elephants crossing a Congo river. Elephants such as these, that spend most of their lives in the thick forests, are considerably smaller and carry smaller tusks than their East African cousins. Using a smallbore rifle with solids, they are easy meat for a side brain shot or a high heart or low lung shot. However, with smallbore rifles, a heart or lung shot should never be attempted when the elephant is headed your way, as he will be able to travel from 200 yards to ¼-mile before expiring. If he's facing away from you, though, he will invariably follow his trunk on receiving such a shot.

This rhino was killed in the Congo with a 30-06 Springfield sporter, using Kynoch factory solids.

conspicuously in poor light. A *heavy* crosshair, post or 6-minute Lee Dot would probably be equally good.

Any scoped gun for African use should have auxiliary iron sights. I prefer an open rear sight, but a good receiver model should prove almost as fast and perhaps a little more accurate. The scope normally will be used for 99% of the hunting, and even a charging lion is easier to stop with one than with open sights, unless within a few yards of you. If a variable power model is used, it should be set at the lowest magnification, to obtain the widest field and brightest illumination.

The important thing pertaining to iron sights is the choice of the front bead. For some reason gun manufacturers furnish an almost invisible bead. This might prove the most accurate on the 100-yd.

for hunting. I prefer a brass or gold sight like the Redfield Sourdough, but any bead smaller than ³/₃₂″ is too small to suit me and I would prefer ⅛″ or even a ¼″ shotgun bead for fast snapshooting. Sight in the iron sights at 150 yards and even if the scope is smashed, the trip will be saved.

Shotguns for Africa

Most African countries ban the importation of repeating shotguns, so we are limited to the double barrel types. I have found a 12-ga. Browning Superposed suitable for all use, from birds to leopards. Because shotgun ammo is readily available in only 12 gauge, any other shotgun bore could prove a headache, but if you want to take that 20-ga. Model 21, go ahead. Just make sure you take plenty of ammo with you. Bird hunting in Africa is second best to nowhere in

the world. If you are taking a 12-ga. gun, buy your shells when you get there.

For too long the American hunter has allowed himself to be told that he is the neophyte, and the British sportsman with the long handle before or after his name is the real hunter, and the only authority on big game hunting. This isn't true. Before most Americans plan an African trip, they have usually hunted this continent thoroughly and are experienced enough to know what hunting is all about, while the average well-to-do Britisher (not the African settler) frequently hunts because it is expected of him and is "the thing to do." This doesn't make him an expert. So go if you can, and take your old favorite rifle that has delivered the goods here in the U.S. It'll do the same in Africa, if you give it a chance. ●

THEY MADE THE

When single shot breechloaders were kings of
Axel Peterson, George Schoyen and A. O.

Harry M. Pope rifling.

A typical A. O. Zischang barreled rifle, with false muzzle built on the Sharps Borchardt dropping block action. The outside of the action has been modified and streamlined.

THERE WAS great jubilation among riflemen in Denver on January 16, 1904. D. W. King, Jr., president of the Colorado Rifle Club, had that day established a new world's record score of 917, shooting on the Standard American Target offhand at 200 yards. This surpassed Harry M. Pope's long-standing record score of 908. All but one of Dean King's 100 shots were in the black bull's-eye. Especially jubilant was George Schoyen, maker of the barrel on King's single shot rifle which had shot this remarkable score.

It was not unusual for records to be held by Colorado riflemen around the turn of the century. C. W. Rowland and C. C. Ford held world records in addition to that made by D. W. King, Jr.

The man behind the gun was, of course, the determining factor in producing high scores, but the finest rifleman in the world could not punch holes in the center of a target unless he had a highly efficient rifle. To supply such rifles, Denver was fortunate in having two of the nation's best—George Schoyen and Axel Peterson.

George Schoyen

George Schoyen, a native of Norway, migrated to the United States soon after the War between the States. Following a short period of residence in Chicago, he headed west, obtaining employment in Denver with the popular gunmaker Carlos Gove.

From 1873 to 1885 Schoyen worked diligently at the Gove shop,

helping to establish a fine name for the shop and firmly establishing his own reputation as a skilled craftsman. In 1885 Carlos Gove retired from business and Schoyen decided to hang out his own shingle. Not quite ready to go it alone, though, he took one D. W. Butt as a partner. This association did not last long, and in 1887 Schoyen teamed up with F. A. Burgen.

The Schoyen-Burgen partnership did quite well for about 10 years, but in 1897 the partnership was dissolved. From 1897 to 1904, working alone, Schoyen's fame as a fine gunmaker continued to grow, and he was swamped with work. At this time, making one of the best decisions of his life, he teamed up with Axel W. Peterson. Thus began a great partnership at 1415 (and later 1417) Lawrence Street in Denver.

Like Schoyen, Axel Peterson was proficient in all fields of gunmaking. While Schoyen's skill as a barrelmaker had perhaps gained more acclaim than his other abilities, Peterson's skill as a stockmaker added to his fame as gunmaker, inventor and maker of telescopes. Schoyen and Peterson, it was soon evident, made an excellent team.

It is significant, perhaps, that the following appears on the cover of a small folder prepared for the partnership: "Schoyen & Peterson, gunmakers ... manufacturers of Schoyen Rifle Barrels, Peterson's Patent Elevating Cross-Hair Telescopes, etc."

In addition to data on barrels

BEST BARRELS

the range, custom rifles barreled by Harry Pope,
Zischang were favored by the top marksmen.

by JAMES E. SERVEN

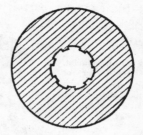

George Schoyen rifling.

and telescopes, a new powder measure, described as a "New Loader," was illustrated with the notation that Schoyen & Peterson were the patentees and manufacturers.

New *muzzle-loading* barrels with a loading outfit were priced at $25. The outfit consisted of a barrel, false muzzle, bullet starter, a special bullet mould which cast from the point, a lubricating pump and ramrod. New *breech-loading* barrels were only $12.

The ad said that Schoyen barrels were fully guaranteed "for accuracy, quality, and workmanship." Barrels of 32 caliber and larger were guaranteed to make a 2½-inch group at 200 yards from machine rest. Schoyen considered 30-inch barrels best, but would furnish them two inches longer at the same price. For calibers under 32 Schoyen recommended 28-inch barrels.

The partners considered it sufficient to mention only their No. 4 barrel, which weighed about 7½ to 8 pounds. Such barrel weights resulted in rifles of some 12 to 14 pounds and more. Heavier barrels could be furnished at $1 a pound extra.

Schoyen's rifling was different than that of rival Harry M. Pope in several ways, especially in the number of grooves and his ideas on the width of lands and grooves.

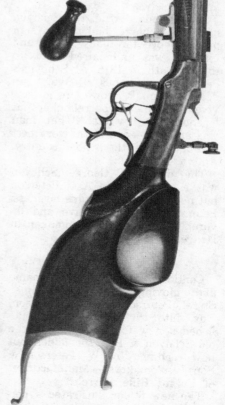

A Schoyen Ballard, made with 3 barrels—32-40, 38-55 and 22 Long Rifle. False muzzle and other tools were furnished with the 32-40 barrels.

George Schoyen, great custom barrelmaker of Denver. His superb workmanship spoke for itself through the world records established with his barrels and rifles.

Schoyen barrels usually had 7 grooves, one turn in 16¼ inches. Bore diameter of a 32-40 rifle was .314", groove depth of the rifling was .005". Grooves ran .115" wide, the land width ordinarily .05".

Rifle stocks came in for their share of attention, too—"We also make a specialty of rifle stocks of our own design that are made to fit the person and allowing the shooter to stand and hold in a perfectly natural position." These stocks were priced up to $25, equalling the cost of a barrel with loading outfit.

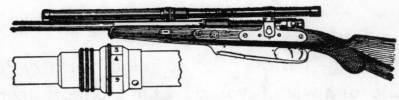

PETERSON'S PAT, ELEVATING CROSSHAIR TELESCOPES
Made to Order a Specialty

VIEW OF METHOD FOR ELEVATING CROSS-HAIRS   ⅞ TUBE, 16 TO 20 IN. LONG

Axel W. Peterson, a quiet, gentle man with a touch of gunmaking genius. He was partial to the Ballard action for his single shot match rifles.

The Schoyen & Peterson folder was quite brief, concluding with "The records that have been made with our special target rifles speak for themselves."

It was indeed true; the Schoyen name on a barrel had been a sign of excellence for many years, and his skill was unimpaired right up to his death in 1916. At Schoyen's death, the famous Denver gun dealer John P. Lower (who survived the master barrelmaker but a short time) wrote: "That man was an artist—one of the very best gunmakers in the whole country. And a fine man, too."

The death of George Schoyen was a sad shock to Axel Peterson but not a fatal blow to his business. Peterson had been active and favorably known as a gunmaker in Denver since 1886.

Axel Peterson

Continuing under his own name and moving to 1429 Larimer Street, Peterson soon took his son, Roy, into the business. He published a new folder, similar to the old Schoyen & Peterson folder, but now reading: "A. W. Peterson & Son—Riflemakers—Manufacturers of Target Rifle Barrels."

The new folder illustrated a perfect machine-rest score of 10 shots at 200 yards, shot by the great Colorado marksman C. W. Rowland with a 32-40 Peterson barrel.

Smaller calibers seemed to have the greater emphasis now, and the folder stated: "We specialize in low pressure barrels and recommend 22 caliber barrels, not over 28 inches long, and make only the highest grade barrels—No seconds."

The Peterson No. 3 barrels weighed 6 to 7 pounds, and cost $25 if made round. Octagon or half-octagon barrels were $5 extra. Some emphasis was placed on "Gunsmithing in all its branches," and advice was given that a stock of rifles, shotguns and revolvers, both new and used, was kept on hand.

A great increase was seen in the

Schoyen & Peterson

GUNMAKERS

Manufacturers of

Schoyen Rifle Barrels
Peterson's Patent Elevating Cross-Hair Telescopes, etc.....

1417 LAWRENCE STREET
DENVER, COLORADO

A New Loader
SCHOYEN & PETERSON,
Patentee's and Manufacturers.

The Latest and Best Loader on the Market. The Easiest and Best Working Machine Made. Price..............$5.00

Can't Make a Mistake in Loading.

maximum cost of gun stocks, which went from $6-$25 in the old folder to $10-$75 in the A. W. Peterson & Son folder. As in one of the several Schoyen & Peterson folders, this Peterson folder illustrates two Ballard rifles with what are indicated to be his No. 1 and No. 2 shapes of stocks. The No. 2 is what is sometimes called a "perch-belly" shape, with deep under curve and long-prong metal buttplate. Both the No. 1 and No. 2 have high, full cheekpieces. The rifles illustrated are equipped with a long telescope sight, a palm rest, double-set triggers and fancy finger lever.

One day I asked Axel Peterson where he had obtained the beautifully grained wood I had observed in many of his stocks. "A feller from here used to go vunce a year to New York," he replied in his

Scandinavian accent. "He vas a good vun to know vood. He knew vot ve vant, and he picked out only the best planks."

Axel Peterson, like Schoyen, had migrated to America from the old country at an early age, arriving in Denver in 1879. His life was spent mostly at the lathe and rifling machine. One of the things that attracted me to this gentle, talented man was his hands. He was slow and deliberate in all his motions, never "grabbing" anything. His hands just seemed to move gracefully and close smoothly on anything he held in them—that sure, skilled touch that distinguishes a craftsman.

The Denver climate was apparently favorable, for both Schoyen and Peterson lived well beyond their three score and ten years.

But after they had gone off to that great range beyond, the golden era of barrelmaking in Denver came to an end.

It is perhaps worthy of note that Ballard actions appear to have been the favorites of Schoyen and Peterson, even though Ballard rifle production by Marlin had ceased before the turn of the century.

The Ballard system was first manufactured by Ball & Williams in 1861. Manufacturing rights were acquired by John M. Marlin in 1875, but by 1890 the manufacture of repeating rifles had led Marlin to ease off on the single shots. Marlin did claim that in the 1870s and 1880s more matches had been won with Ballard rifles than any other. James Grant, the author of three excellent books on single shot rifles, describes the Ballard as "the

This shows the "working section" of the Axel Peterson gunshop in Denver, where for many years top quality custom gun work was performed.

Established 1886

ᐁᐃᐁ

A. W. PETERSON & SON

RIFLE-MAKERS

ᐁᐃᐁ

MANUFACTURERS OF

Target Rifle Barrels

1429 Larimer Street

DENVER, : : : COLORADO

ing at New York City, he soon found employment (despite his unfamiliarity with the language and American customs) at the Sharps Rifle Co. of Bridgeport, Conn. Here he became acquainted with the Sharps Model 1878, better known as the Borchardt. This may have influenced him to use this action extensively for many fine rifles he built in later years.

Zischang's stay in Bridgeport was relatively short. From the Sharps factory he went to work for Nichols & Lefever in Syracuse, New York.* By 1879 he had enough

gunsmith. Colonel Tewes, Captain Gindel and Dr. W. G. Hudson were others of an extensive clientele that kept the Zischang shop filled with more rifle orders than the master riflemaker could easily produce.

William O. Zischang, a son, wrote me some years ago that he remembered Dr. Hudson quite well. He met him first at a Schuetzenfest near Brooklyn, New York, at about the time Dr. Hudson had first taken up the then ever-popular 200-yard offhand shooting. Dr. Hudson was at the time negotiating with A. O. Zischang for a new

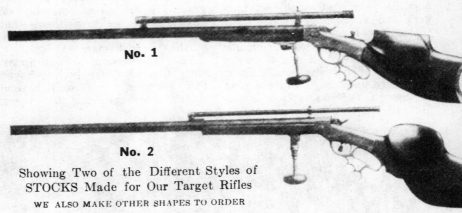

No. 1

No. 2

Showing Two of the Different Styles of
STOCKS Made for Our Target Rifles

WE ALSO MAKE OTHER SHAPES TO ORDER

most famous and beloved of all the single shots."

Dr. Maynard's patent rifles, contemporary with the Ballard, were made by the Massachusetts Arms Co. of Chicopee Falls. They enjoyed some popularity among the single shot target shooters, especially the Model of 1882. However, these rifles were never favored by the custom barrelmakers, and they, like the Marlin-Ballard, began to fade from the picture by the 1890s. The company's assets were eventually acquired by the J. Stevens Arms & Tool Co.

Let us turn, now, to custom gunmakers of the East where the Stevens, Maynard, Ballard, Sharps, Winchester and other single shot rifles were in use on ranges like Walnut Hill in Massachusetts.

A. O. Zischang

A contemporary of Schoyen and Peterson, and a man with somewhat similar background, was A. O. Zischang. The Zischangs, generation after generation, had been gunsmiths in Saxony, Germany. In 1876 A. O. Zischang, then 30 years old, migrated to America. Land-

command of the English language that he could open his own gunshop, performing all kinds of gunsmithing, but making a specialty of building fine target rifles.

Zischang's shop in Syracuse began to gain considerable attention, and before long his target rifles appeared in the hands of some of the nation's leading marksmen. It is quite probable that his German background may have helped in making his guns popular with members of the powerful National Schuetzenbund of the U.S.A., with headquarters at the German Artillery Hall in Charleston, South Carolina. This organization boasted of over 1000 members with affiliated clubs nationwide.

Among Zischang's friends was Dr. Franklin W. Mann, author of *The Bullets Flight*, a well-known textbook on ballistics. Zischang and Harry Pope both assisted Dr. Mann in his experiments, as did A. O. Niedner, himself a fine marksman and

barrel. Later, when Dr. Hudson was getting a United States team in readiness for matches in England, he sought Zischang barrels for its members, but the Syracuse gunmaker was unable to accept the order because of the short time specified for delivery.

Dr. W. G. Hudson was one of the truly great rifle shots our nation has produced. In the early 1900s he held many records. He was a member of the victorious American Palma team at Rockcliffe, Canada, in 1907, and made the highest individual score at the first International Smallbore Matches in 1909.*

In 1905 Dr. Hudson's health had been such that a period of relaxation in the invigorating mile-high climate of Denver was prescribed. There he met many who shared his great interest in match shooting, and he became a popular figure at meetings in the Schoyen & Peter-

---

*Nichols & Lefever were in business together for only some four years (1878-1882). Chiefly makers of shotguns, the firm did make also a few heavy-barreled percussion target rifles as well, one of which is in the editor's collection.

---

*Dr. Hudson wrote a book in 1903 called *Modern Rifle Shooting from the American Standpoint*. This well done volume, dealt mainly with the caliber 30-40 Krag rifle (the official U.S. rifle at the time) and military shooting. The "little blue book" of Dr. Hudson's was, for some years, the bible of those shooting the service rifle.

son shop and on the range of the Colorado Rifle Club.

Writing to Tom East, a fellow member of the Colorado Rifle Club, C. W. Rowland, had this to say of Dr. Hudson:

"I have formed the opinion that he is a quiet, pleasant, very intelligent and agreeable man, and a wizard in all that pertains to explosives and fine work with firearms. As an offhand shot he is a wonder in holding, pulling, and judgment of weather.

"He shoots a Zischang 38 caliber breech-loading barrel in a Remington Schuetzen* action (Hepburn pat.)The barrel is throated or freed to allow an easy seating of bullet in the breech."

Mr. Rowland added that he considered Dr. Hudson's rifle one of the finest and most advantageous Schuetzen style of rifles possible to use with the current knowledge of ballistics. He gave these reasons: The windage needed was 40% less with a 38-caliber 308-gr. bullet than the 32 caliber with a 200-gr. bullet; the increased size of the hole cut in the target gave a 14% advantage on the German ring target; a

---

*Rowland's reference here to a "breech-loading" barrel is done so to distinguish it from the barrel with false muzzle, which permitted the seating of the bullet through the muzzle. Either could be used as breech-loaders, of course. The Remington Schuetzen action was housed in the Hepburn receiver, but internal design differed considerably from the standard Hepburn. Dr. Hudson had designed a bullet—soon called the "Hudson bullet"—which had a base band of greater diameter than normal, in addition to having other bands dropping, by steps, to a bore-riding diameter. These were made normally by Ideal in 32-40 and 38-55 sizes, and in 33-40 caliber on special order.

From left: Deluxe Sharps Borchardt with panelled receiver; Bullard single shot; Low-wall Winchester; Ballard; last two are No. 52 Stevens "Schuetzen Jr" rifles, both in the 44½ action. Author's collection.

A. O. Zischang, the aristocratic-looking and highly skilled craftsman from Syracuse, was one of the nation's leading custom barrel- and gunmakers, specializing in fine target rifles.

decrease in recoil with the powder used; the quickness and "get out of" barrel qualities of the bullet.

When preferred by men of this stature it can be seen that Zischang barrels were considered among the very best that could be obtained anywhere.

A. O. Zischang turned his shop at 451 Salina Street in Syracuse over to his son William in 1919, but he couldn't stay away from his workbench. He managed to do some work in the shop until his death on May 21, 1925. He would have been 80 years old on his next birthday.

Zischang was a fine penman, writing in firm Spencerian style. In appearance, he looked more like a professor than a man who labored at a lathe or rifling bench. If doctorates were awarded in his profession, he would certainly have received one *cum laude!*

Harry M. Pope

The only American-born member of the great foursome of barrelmakers covered in this account was Harry M. Pope. Born in 1861 at

Walpole, New Hampshire, he was of studious bent and took special courses at the Massachusetts Institute of Technology, emerging with a degree in engineering in the class of 1881. He became involved in several manufacturing ventures (including the making of bicycles) but, once he had made his first rifle in 1887, he decided this was the field in which he wanted to devote his efforts. He called himself "a rifle crank."

Pope's great interest in marksmanship (as a shooter) and his technical engineering knowledge gave him an ideal background for a career as one of the nation's all-time great barrelmakers.

Early in his career Pope became interested in the Schalck system of rifling, and he became convinced that this technique possessed advantages (especially for offhand shooting) that placed it far in advance of any other method then employed.

George Schalck who had migrated to Pottsville, Pennsylvania, from Germany in 1854, pursued the gunmaking trade until his death in

This old photograph, found in the files of the Jersey City, (N.J.) Journal, is thought to have been made at a schuetzen match held in the Greenville section of Jersey City some 60-70 years ago. Pencilled on the back, but barely legible, are these names, among others impossible to read: Harry Pope, Fred Ross, G. Schlicht, Zettler, Mike Dorrler, Louis Buss, Hubalek, Owen Smith and Begeros (?). Harry Pope is in the middle row, 7th from the right. If a reader can identify any of the rest, we'll be pleased to have the information.

1893. An ardent marksman as well as a highly skilled gunmaker, Schalck did much experimental rifling.* At the urging of a scientific rifleman named William Hayes he developed a rifling style that made a deep impression on Harry Pope.

Pope found that barrels he made on Schalck's rifling and loading systems gave such a marked improvement in accuracy that he was besieged by his friends, and then by outsiders, to make barrels for them. This eventually led to the establishment of Pope's shop at 59 Ashley Street in Hartford, Connecticut.

Pope had refined and improved on the Schalck rifling designs. The major differences were in the shape or form of the rifling, and that Pope's rifling was *cut* to correct shape, while Schalck's had been leaded or lapped. Schalck rifling had 8 flat grooves and 8 narrow lands, with sharp corners where the lands and grooves joined.

Harry Pope's rifling also has 8 grooves, but they are formed with a radius about three times the radius of the bore, and the corners are rounded out, so fouling is easier removed, and the barrel kept cleaner in use. The grooves are cut just deep enough to clear the bore diameter, in the middle, and give a depth at the corners of about

*Schalck began making rifles in the percussion cap period, his specialty being offhand rifles in the Schuetzen style—stocks with high combs and face-fitting cheek pieces, long-prong buttplates, and false-muzzled barrels—an idea which had been patented in 1840 by A. Clark.

Offhand shooting positions, when they "stood up on their hind legs and shot like a man!"

Harry M. Pope, the old master, would do a job right or not at all, telling customers who were in a hurry to "take it when it is done or take it somewhere else."

.004-inch. The lands are very narrow (about ⅕th to ⅙th the width of the grooves).

Pope moulds produce a tapered bullet, with a base large enough to fill the grooves completely; the body decreases until the forepart is the same diameter as the bore. Such a bullet is gas tight, loads easily and, on upsetting or expanding, instead of the body of the bullet being cut by sharp lands perhaps more or less unevenly, it is held in place by the nearly flat center of the broad grooves and swells into the grooves evenly and perfectly central, with resulting fine accuracy—always assuming *good* bullets!

The greatest accuracy, Pope always claimed, was had by loading the bullet from the muzzle, using a false muzzle and bullet starter. He believed that loading in this way tended to assure a clean bore for the bullet's passage down the barrel, prevented fins of lead on the base of the bullet, which inevitably appeared when inserted from the breech, and that loading in this manner was less tiring for the shooter, an important factor in a long match. Unlike some of the prominent shooters, Pope did not favor the 38 or larger calibers, claiming they were harder on the nerves in a long match.

Pope's barrels were cut with a gain twist (unless specially ordered otherwise) and so bored and rifled as to have a slight but gradual taper from breech to muzzle. He considered a round 30-inch barrel of about 7¾ pounds best for 200 yard offhand shooting, "where you stood up on your hind legs and shot

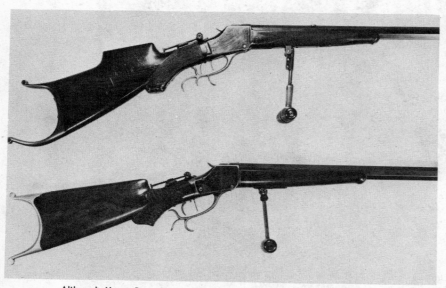

Although Harry Pope barrels were fitted to Ballard, Stevens and other single shot actions, the Winchester high wall was quite frequently selected for his custom jobs. Note differences in levers, stock treatment and dimension. Harry Pope did virtually no stock work.

SOME PROMINENT AMERICAN RIFLEMEN.

A photograph that appeared in the December Christmas issue of *Shooting and Fishing* for 1896. Assembled here are some of the finest schuetzen shooters of their day—or any day. From left to right, top row—F. C. Ross, NY; Wm. Hayes, NJ; Capt. Mat Gindele, OH; Adolph Strecker, CA; F. J. Rabbeth, MA. 2nd row —Gus Zimmerman, NY; G .H. Wentworth, NH; J. E. Kelley, MA; O. M. Jewell, MA; A. J. Van Deusen, MN. 3rd row—A. H. Pape, CA; Andrew McBean, MO; H. M. Pope, CT; J. Busfield, MA; Dr. E. R. Chadbourne, NY. 4th row—N. S. Brockway, VT; D. L. F. Chase, MA; H. V. Perry, NY; Salem Wilder, MA; R. C. Rice, OH. 5th row—Lt. F. C. Wave, GA; Maj. C. W. Hinman, MA; Sgt. T. J. Dolan, NY; Sgt. John Corrie, NY; C. S. Richmond, GA.

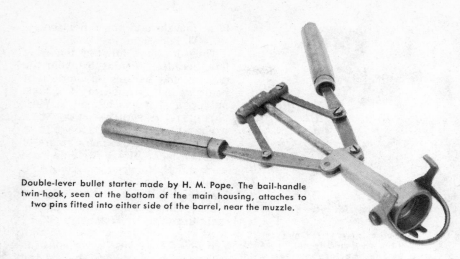

Double-lever bullet starter made by H. M. Pope. The bail-handle twin-hook, seen at the bottom of the main housing, attaches to two pins fitted into either side of the barrel, near the muzzle.

like a man," and preferred the 28, 32 or 33 calibers. Groups of 2½ to 3 inches on a 200-yard target, machine rest, were guaranteed, under favorable weather conditions.

A catalog titled "Pope Rifle Barrels" published March 1, 1899, at the Hartford address included (in addition to the special bullet moulds, *in which the lead is poured in from the nose end rather than the base*), false muzzles and starters Pope's lubricating pumps, double loading flasks, wind gauge rear sights and machine rests. The "double" flasks had two reservoirs, one for a priming charge of smokeless powder, the other and larger container for the main black powder charge.

As the fame of Harry Pope and his quality barrels grew, he was constantly flooded with more work than he was able to turn out—but he would not sacrifice quality for haste. Finally a solution appeared to present itself. In 1901 Pope was bought out by the J. Stevens Arms & Tool Co. of Chicopee Falls, Mass., which had just brought out their great line of "Ideal" target rifles, these on the No. 44 action.

Under date of April 1, 1901,

Harry Pope mailed this notice to friends and patrons: "My business having increased beyond my capacity, and being anxious to fill my orders more promptly, I have sold all my tools and special machinery to the J. Stevens Arms & Tool Co. The business will be conducted by them, but I am to remain in full charge of all the work on the high class rifles and tools on which I have been working in the past, and no such work will leave the factory without my personal inspection and approval."

Soon afterward, the Stevens No. 51 catalog announced the acquisition of Pope's tools and services on April 1, 1901. It also pointed out that Pope then held the 50-shot 200 yard record (467x500) and the 100-shot record at the same distance (908x1000), both records made in 1903.

And so it was from 1901 to the end of 1905, when Harry Pope terminated his association with the Stevens company. In that period it is estimated that about 1200 "Stevens-Pope" barreled rifles were turned out. These had been made under Pope's close supervision, but the factory continued the sale of Pope-Stevens rifles for some years after Pope had left.

Soon after Pope had joined the company they published a "Catalog of Stevens-Pope Specialties." This interesting little booklet describes and prices the various Pope-type accessories from moulds to re- and de-cappers and illustrates the Ideal rifle models available with Pope barrels, false muzzle or not. The better guns are priced at an average of $80. In addition, record targets are illustrated which had been made by Pope barrels, and data provided regarding barrel design and manufacture.

Possessed with an independent and restless nature Harry Pope, at 45 years of age, decided to try his fortunes in the West. He had not been contented at Stevens. He chose San Francisco as his new location, opening his shop there on April 17, 1906. He could not have chosen a worse time and place, for early the next morning San Francisco's tragic earthquake and fire struck. In a few terror-filled hours San Francisco became the scene of devastating destruction. Practically everything Harry Pope owned was destroyed.

The following two years were lean ones for Harry Pope. He worked for awhile in the John Sidle telescope shop and at odd

Machine rest made by H. M. Pope, this specimen Serial No. 1. The central unit attaches to a vertical bench-face via the 4 mounting holes seen. Elevation is had by rotating the bottom T-handle. Lateral adjustment is of the opposed-screw type, again using the T-handles seen. The other elements are barrel holders, the one at top for an iron sighted barrel, the other two for scoped-barrel use.

jobs.* Then in April, 1908, he got together enough capital to start his own shop at 18 Morris Street, Jersey City, New Jersey. In May he sent this letter to some of his old friends and customers:

"I beg to announce that I have resumed the making of Pope Barrels, etc., at address above, where I shall be pleased to hear from you and to execute any orders that you may be able to give me.

"Mine is the original and only genuine 'Pope Barrel' that holds most of the off-hand records, and future work will be even better than the past standard of excellence.

"I have no circulars or catalogs at present, but will be pleased to correspond with you in regard to any work you would like to have done.

"As I have lost my address book, together with everything else, in the San Francisco fire, I am without the names of most of my old friends and customers, I will thank you, if you write to me, to give me the names and addresses of such riflemen as occur to you."

It was not long before orders were again crowding in on the great barrelmaker at his small, cluttered Jersey City shop.

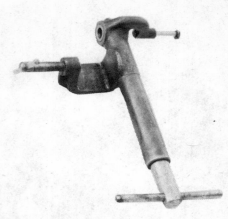

Bullet lubricator made by H. M. Pope. Tapered or multi-diameter bullets, as cast by Pope moulds (and others) could not be greased in conventional push-type tools. The lubricating die in the tool pictured was machined to match a given bullet, and such dies were interchangeable. The T-handled piston drove the lube into the bullet's grooves.

false muzzle. In addition to his name, generally shown on the top and underneath the barrel as "H. M. POPE," he often dated his barrels in his New Jersey period, at least. For instance, I have one

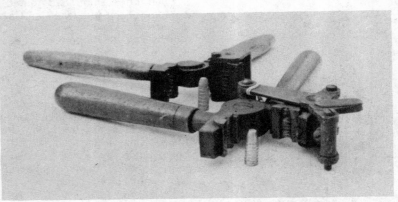

A pair of point-cutoff moulds made by H. M. Pope. In the foreground is his scarce automatic sprue-cutter type, the mould cavities interchangeable. The other is the more common double-cutoff type.

A significant feature of Pope barrels is the marking. He usually numbered his barrels on the underside and, for those guns with a false muzzle, he put the same number on the bottom face of the

dated "5/19/10," which tells me that the rifle, a deluxe hi-wall Winchester, was barreled at Jersey City in 1910.

On these false-muzzle barrels, at least, he also stamped the underside of the barrel with numerals indicating the rate of twist and the gain factor. On a Stevens Model 52, the action the 44 type, and the rifle made before Pope joined Stevens, this twist marking appears as "21/1.4/1," in two lines. The Stevens serial number of this 32-40 rifle—which has a matching-numbered

false muzzle and the other tools—is 7503. Pope's number is 235.

Thus it went for the following four decades. Wishing to avoid the troublesome backlog of work that had plagued him at Hartford, Pope put up a sign which read in part: "NO DELIVERY PROMISED. TAKE YOUR WORK WHEN DONE OR TAKE IT ELSEWHERE." Tired from many years of exacting labor, Harry Melville Pope went quietly to sleep on October 11, 1950. At 89 he had outlived most of his barrelmaking contemporaries.

Yes, Harry Pope was temperamental and a bit crotchety, but he was a genius and a man of high principle. He was never one to compromise on quality—he did the job right or he didn't do it at all. This was, indeed, the common trait of the four great riflemakers discussed on these pages. None left substantial riches, but all established reputations money could not buy; they will always be remembered as the best in their profession in a golden era of rifle shooting. That is why, today, rifles bearing their barrel signatures are actively sought as choice and valuable specimens of the gunmaker's art.

It is not intended to give the impression that these four great barrelmakers have been the only masters in their field. There have been others in this select group down the years, right up to such men of the present as Clyde Hart—and others—who carry forward the tradition of striving for the highest degree of excellence human hands and minds can devise. •

Bibliography

Jas J. Grant, *Single Shot Rifle*. New York, 1947.

——————, *More Single Shot Rifles*, New York, 1959.

——————, *Boys' Single Shot Rifles*, New York, 1967.

N. H. Roberts and K. L. Waters, *The Breech-Loading Single Shot Match Rifle*, Princeton, N.J., 1967.

F. W. Mann, *The Bullet's Flight from Powder to Target*, New York, 1909 and Huntington, W. Va., 1942 *et seq.*

Ray M. Smith, *The Story of Pope's Barrels*, Harrisburg, Pa., 1964.

*Some years ago I bought a Pope machine rest, the type allowing the use of a telescope sight held separately from the rifle. On removing the heavy coat of aluminum paint which covered it, I found "JOHN W. SIDLE, PHILADA, PENNA." stamped into one face, and the several components parts marked with the numeral "1". Pope suggested the use of Sidle scopes with these machine rests, and it may be that he gave Sidle the first one made.

Drawn after a faded old photograph, here is the 3-year-old Houston Stiff, standing a bit lopsided to offset the weight of the holstered Colt 45 auto.

Model 1918A6 Gun Nut — a case history

For almost fifty years the author knew and owned, bought, sold, traded and lost, fixed and ruined, was shot at and killed with, longed for and loved guns. Here are his nostalgic notes on the past, his cogent comments on the present, and words of warning for the darkling future.

by HOUSTON STIFF
(Col. USMC, ret'd)

THAT I GREW up in Texas with guns is scarcely a mark of distinction. Almost anybody of my vintage who grew up in Texas grew up perforce with guns. In those days, guns were as much a part of the average Texas household as a kitchen stove.

But my father was a gun buff, and whatever gene or chromosome it was that caused that affliction in him came through to me full strength. A yellowing snapshot taken when I was three shows me listing hard to port to balance the weight of my father's Government Model 45 Colt strapped on my right hip. (This, incidentally, was the same pistol with which my father later shot himself in the leg while practicing quick draw.)

The big Colt was strictly a prop for the photo—I wouldn't want you to think I was allowed to play with guns at the age of three. I must have been

6 or 7 before I got my own real gun, a topbreak "Saturday Night Special" with no firing pin, and not until my 10th birthday did I get my first shooting gun—a little Remington rolling block 22 which I could shoot only under my father's supervision. I had hoped for a repeater, and thus first experienced the perennial dissatisfaction with guns on hand that is the gun nut's lot in life.

That 22 was the first of more guns to pass through my hands than I care to think about, much less try to count. There has never been a day since that I haven't owned at least one firearm and at times the total was closer to 20. For almost half a century I have known, owned, bought, sold, traded, shot, cleaned, lost, fixed, ruined, played with, looked at, killed with, been shot at and hit with, longed for, and loved—yes, *loved*—guns. If that doesn't qualify me as a gun nut, I don't know what it takes.

As I've said, I got the bug from my father, a character in more ways than one. For one thing, I didn't call him Father or Dad or Papa—I called him "Colonel" and so did everybody else in the family, including my mother. The highest military rank he'd ever held was lieutenant, in the National Guard in 1918—"Colonel" was a nickname given him when he was a small boy. I never called him anything else when he was alive, and I might as well call him that here.

Colonel was a secret dandy. His street clothes were conservative enough but what I think of as his costumes were something else. He had riding breeches from Abercrombie & Fitch and the boots that went with them were made somewhere in the East. His western boots usually had white stars inset around the tops, and were made to his last by Old Man White of Ft. Worth. He had gold-plated spurs and silver hatbands, and fancy saddles turned out by Tom Kinney of Nobby Harness.

Father's Favorites

His favorite pistol was a Colt Government Model, silver-plated and engraved: it had carved ivory grips with a ruby-eyed Texas Longhorn on one grip and I forget what on the other. Most of his handguns had stag grips and the rest walnut—he couldn't stand pearl or hard-rubber.

He regarded rifles and shotguns as working tools, and his were usually standard off-the-shelf models. Occasionally he would bring home an unusual item—I remember a nickel-plated Winchester, a Model 92 carbine with about a 12-inch barrel; I think he got it from a Texas Ranger. For a

while he had a Thompson submachine gun: an older man he'd befriended had once owned gold mines in Mexico and the Thompson had been used by his guards. One day in his hotel the old man pulled the gun out from under a bed—it was in a fitted leather case—and gave it to Colonel. Colonel, of course, was in hog heaven and so was I; other kids' fathers had rifles and shotguns and the like, but a Tommy Gun?

A few months later, however, Colonel got drunk on bathtub gin and fell to brooding about ancient wrongs

The author, age about 10 years. All set for a backyard safari and already wearing military habiliment—Sam Browne belt, pegtop breeches and high boots.

done him by the Law in his home town, some 40 miles away. Revenge seemed the only answer and he began loading 50-round drums in preparation for a midnight massacre. Fortunately for all, the gin put him out before he was ready to leave, and next morning my mother took a stand. The Thompson had to go. Colonel sold it to the local police, and I wouldn't be surprised if they have it still.

Another time he came home with a Spencer saddle-ring carbine plus several *pounds*—not rounds—of ammunition and a pouch of extra tube magazines. He used to shoot it at tree stumps and old barns, and we would marvel at the size of the holes. He called it his "bear" gun but it was really never anything but a toy.

My own collection was growing; there was a beautiful cap-and-ball boy's rifle with Kentucky lines, and an 1851 Navy Colt 36. I got my first Single Action Army about this time, a

black powder model with one-piece walnut grips and no finish. It was a "play" gun, however: the firing pin was filed down. My shooting arms now included a Model 39 Marlin (my repeater, at last), a Lefever 410 shotgun, and an Iver Johnson 22 revolver. A little later I was to get my first "high powered" rifle, actually a Model 92 carbine in 25-20 caliber: this one came secondhand with a pitted bore but Colonel sent it off to Winchester for a new barrel.

When I was about 12, I was given a gun I wish I could forget. Colonel, then on the fringes of the oil business, had a number of rich friends; one of them had a large room full of guns, old and new. We visited this man often, though not often enough to suit me. He wasn't known for his generosity with guns, dollars or anything else, but he must have had a soft spot for wistful small boys because he finally gave me a Single Action Colt that looked brand new. Colonel said it had never been fired and was worth at least $30. Obviously too good for a play gun, it would be kept for me until I was older.

Ungrateful brat that I was, I never really warmed up to that particular Model P. For one thing, the barrel was too long—5½ inches. To me, 4¾ inches was the *only* length for a Peacemaker. For another, it had hard-rubber grips and it was in a sissy caliber—22. That's right, it was a 22 rimfire Model P Colt and, according to Parsons, one of only 107 made!

What happened to it? Ah, that's a painful story. A year or so after my benefactor had missed a West Texas bridge while doing 90 in his Packard, and while Colonel was away in Mexico, I smuggled that rare revolver out to a small gunshop and traded it for a well-worn Police Positive Special, which I proceeded to ruin by hacksawing its barrel down to a ragged 2 inches. You see, I was watching gangster movies by then and just had to have a Detective Special. I kept the trade and its consequences secret from Colonel as long as I could, but he eventually found it out, and thereby hangs (pardon the pun) another painful tale.

A Trader's Pigeon

This example of my prowess as a gun trader is, unfortunately, reasonably typical. I can't blame it on youth and inexperience because I didn't improve much with age. As a trader I never came out on top in a trade: as a buyer I never got a bargain, as a seller I never got my price. The other guy always had me at a disadvantage—*he* could take the deal or leave it, or so I was conditioned to believe. I remained an ideal target for gun dealers and traders everywhere, and they found me, all right.

It's heresy to say it, I know, but in a way I should be grateful to the Gun Control Act of 1968. After I moved away from Texas, I seldom stayed in one place long enough to cultivate a favorite gun dealer and so was shielded from direct temptation. But the advertisements found me wherever I was, and when the buying fever struck my letter and remittance to Klein's Sporting Goods or Stoeger or Hunter's Lodge, or whatever, would soon be in the mail. For me, then, and no doubt for other impulse buyers, GCA '68 has meant a kind of forced savings program. Sure, there are still ways to order by mail but it isn't so easy any more and I'm getting old and lazy.

In my case, too, it's just as well. A few years back I got swept up in the Luger craze. I acquired two via *Shotgun News,* neither rare in any respect but price, even though I had never liked Lugers and still don't. Then came the rush for prewar Peacemakers: I paid $150 for one, also by mail, that came with an old cold-blue job and a broken half-cock notch.

Guns sometimes took me by surprise. In 1954 I was in Vienna, on leave from my post as Assistant Naval Attache in Moscow. One day, out for a stroll, I spotted a gun store and went in. Most of the guns displayed were shotguns, but there was one Mannlicher-Schoenauer carbine, a rifle I'd always had a secret yen for. This one was in some European caliber, but the clerk—a woman who spoke English—told me they could be had in American calibers as well. For some reason the 257 Roberts cartridge appealed to me at the time, obsolescent though it was. I mentioned this caliber to the woman and she said it would have to be a special order. Feeling safe enough, I told her I would like to have one but was leaving in two days. What I didn't know, of course, was that Mannlichers are made in Steyr, just a few miles away. So—you guessed it—I boarded the plane to my next stop clutching a Mannlicher-Schoenauer carbine in 257 Roberts caliber. (I've often wondered what the Russians thought when I returned to Moscow with that gun. As I had a diplomatic passport, they didn't search my baggage, but they knew about it, all right.)

My carbine from Vienna never saw the game fields. For a while in Moscow there was talk of a wolf hunt, something the Russians occasionally organized for foreign diplomats, but nothing came of it. The Mannlicher came back to the States with me, miraculously surviving the beating the trunk it was in took from the longshoremen. I was going to get a scope for it but never did. In the 10 years I had it, I fired it less than 20 times, just plinking.

Firearms in the Service

It has been the same story with many—too many, I guess—of the guns I have owned. How many times have *you* been asked, "What good is a gun if you don't use it?" A stupid question, of course, but not always easy to answer. I have in fact used guns quite a bit but they were usually Uncle Sam's guns, not mine. During 24 years in the Marine Corps, including two wars and a peek at a third, guns were a part of my official as well as my private life. During World War II and the Korean conflict, I was variously armed with and sometimes used M1911A1 pistols, a Reising submachine gun, hand grenades, M1 and M2 carbines, a 38 S&W and a Detective Special of my own, and an M1 rifle or two in the tight spots. On Saipan I picked up a Thompson SMG and carried it for a couple of days before it got too heavy. I didn't carry but used machine guns, mortars, artillery, tanks, flamethrowers, attack aircraft, cruisers, destroyers, rockets, recoilless rifles—almost everything available to an infantry officer trying to do his job. In my case, then, I suppose you could say guns are either tools or toys, and not interchangeable. You wouldn't be entirely accurate, but I will admit I hate to see a pretty gun get scratched up in the field.

For example, when in 1961 I received orders to Korea for the second time, the officer I was to relieve of a staff billet in the top headquarters there wrote and said my toughest challenge would be to find ways to pass the time. He suggested hunting—wild game was coming back, he said, from wherever it had gone during the fighting. This made sense, and I decided I'd go for deer—said to be plentiful—and maybe the tigers that were alleged to exist. So what rifle to take? I had at least two that were suitable, a 30-06 Super Grade Model 70 and a 270 F.N. Mauser. Both had Weaver K4 scopes. But both were like new, and I couldn't bring myself to take them to a God-forsaken spot like Korea. One of my recent impulse purchases had been an "El Tigre" 44-40 carbine, a well-made Spanish copy of the M92 Winchester. Mine was in sound if battered condition—good bore and tight action, just the thing for rough work. I had it converted to 44 Magnum and the barrel cut to 16 inches. With a Williams Fool-Proof rear and a ramp front sight installed, and the whole thing blue-chromed, the *Tigre* was almost too pretty for Korea but I took it anyway.

Did I get a deer or a tiger with it? Well, no—but that's another story, too long and sad for these pages. However, I did tote it over a fair number of Korean hills, hills that had become remarkably steeper in the 10 years since I first climbed them. The carbine was much admired by other hunters, and one of them talked me out of it—for what it cost me—before my tour was up.

When I retired from the Corps in 1964, the guns I owned at the time unexpectedly became a problem. I wanted to see some parts of the world I had missed and, having no fixed base, my idea was to take off and keep going until I had enough. Perhaps I would even settle in another country. Guns don't travel well (for me, anyway) unless carried by hand, and in any case are unwelcome or prohibited in many parts of the world. When I asked a couple of movers about storage facilities for guns, I got only blank stares. There were no gun-oriented friends nearby, so I finally decided to sell my guns. I didn't have time to advertise so I hauled them down to my friendly neighborhood dealer. At the last moment I held back two S&Ws, a Model 1926 44 Special and an as-new M39 with a serial number below 1500.

Selling my guns hurt, but none was rare or custom-made and I consoled myself with the knowledge that they could be replaced when and if I found a compatible place to live. But it hasn't turned out that way.

As it turned out, my travels lasted for most of 4 years and took me in directions I hadn't planned on. Twice, for instance, the Marine Corps put me on active duty for brief trips to Vietnam: when I retired in '64 I would have bet any amount that neither I nor any large number of Marines would ever see Vietnam, which makes me as good a prophet as I am a trader. But I did get to some of the spots I'd wanted to see, and in general enjoyed kicking around on my own, even in Vietnam.

Now I find myself back where I started, in southern California. I'm as settled as I'll ever be, I suppose, but I haven't replaced those guns I sold. It isn't just the money, either, although the prices would average at least 20% more now. And it isn't availability—I might have to wait a few months for a Combat Magnum, for example, but I could get one.

The Urge Lessens

One reason is a sneaking doubt in my mind as to the general quality of the current gun crop, even in the name brands. This stems not only from personal observation but from some surprisingly frank comments on the subject by one or two of the better known gun writers. (There must be something to it, else why the demand for pre-'64 Model 70s?)

But the main reason is, I think (knock wood), that I have somehow developed an immunity to buying fever. I find I can read about all the glamorous new guns without automatically wanting to own them. But if I *have* stopped buying guns, I'm pretty sure I'll never stop reading about them.

To one who grew up on Bannerman catalogs, Stoeger's Bible and *The American Rifleman,* the postwar boom in gun publications was like manna from Heaven. As one new gun magazine after another appeared on the newsstands, my only concern was that I might miss one. It seemed too good to last, but last it did and I have been from the beginning as faithful a reader as gun magazines are likely to have. I guess my appetite is insatiable.

But when you read about guns as much as I do and for as many years, you are bound to find yourself wading through some very familiar stuff: old gun writers, it seems, neither die nor fade away; they just keep grinding out the same old words. You must learn to accept verbosity: gun writers are usually paid by the word, and for them to write "bullet" instead of "250-grain copper plated .429″ Keith-type slug" would be fiscal folly. Finally, you must be prepared to read a lot of just plain bunk.

Now bunk is nothing new in gun periodicals but of late there seems to be more of it. Perhaps it has something to do with all those pages that have to be filled. Also certain subjects appear to attract bunk as a light attracts moths. Take "knock-down" power—I can't prove it, of course, but I would bet that more drivel has been written on this firearms topic than any other.

In the face of scientific facts to the contrary, gun writers are forever touting the "knock-down" ability of this or that cartridge.* Whether they are big bore men or super-high velocity advocates, they can tell stories about the big elk or big grizzly or large animal of some sort that was knocked off its feet when hit solidly by a favorite combination of brass, powder and projectile. I will grant these writers a

*See "Knock Down Nothing," by Warren Page (GUN DIGEST, 16th ed.) which debunked the concept of bullet knock down power. Ed.

certain amount of literary license, but some of them expect us to take them literally. Well, it so happens that a bullet—any *bullet*—is not a good instrument to use if literally knocking an animal down is what you're after. A missile less than a half-inch in diameter, weighing an ounce or less, and moving at three times the speed of sound, is not designed to knock things down—it is designed to penetrate, to make a hole, to destroy tissue and break bones, and to cause shock (in the medical sense); when it does these things to a living target, that target is quite likely to *fall* down sooner or later. But is it knocked to the ground by the initial impact? Not likely.

The same is true when men are the targets involved. My first visit to Vietnam coincided with some of the early fighting around Khe Sanh, a spot later much in the news when the Marines were surrounded there. The Marine colonel in command at Khe Sanh was an old buddy of mine, and I spent several days with him. The Marines had only recently been issued the M16 rifle, and they were having their problems with it. M16s, they said, jammed too often. There was a minor scandal in the press about defective design, etc., but the real source of trouble turned out to be mostly bum dope about care and cleaning. However, there was also discontent with the "knock-down" power of the new rifle. Advance word had it that just one of the hot .223-inch bullets would tear a man's arm off or, if it hit him in the foot, would break his leg. But on the hills west of Khe Sanh, it wasn't happening that way. North Vietnamese were being killed and wounded by M16s often enough, but no arms were being blown off and a hit in the foot resulted in little more than a pronounced limp. On the other hand, I was told, the enemy was using a special sniper rifle that could *really* knock a man down. Curious about this mystery marvel, I investigated and found it to be a scope-sighted 7.62 Moisin, a Russian design dating from the turn of the century and firing a cartridge ballistically inferior to the 30-06. Having personally observed more than a few men take hits from 30-06 bullets at close range and still stay on their feet, I was forced to conclude that Marines were being knocked down as much by vivid imagination as by ballistic effectiveness. Who knows, maybe the same thing happens to all those big elk and grizzlies.

The 45 Auto

Jeff Cooper's discovery of the Government Model Colt 45 led to a

general re-opening of the old "Revolver vs. Automatic" argument, which in turn has resulted in considerable printed bunk. Most of the well-known gun writers have jumped on this theme, and some it seems would rather switch than fight. One of the big-name experts recently announced with no warning that he shoots "only automatics," meaning, presumably, only semi-automatic pistols. Coming from one who was instrumental in having the Colt New Service—"Old Ugly"—in *38 Special* caliber, this has got to be a quantum jump in handgun preferences.

Pity the poor police! First they get dragged over the coals for clinging to the pipsqueak 38 when they could have 41 Magnums; now they're castigated for carrying revolvers when they should have automatics. Oh, well, maybe the police don't read gun magazines.

Given the number of men who have been armed with it (and its close copies) in various military services and various wars, the Government Model Colt is very likely the best known pistol of all time. For 60 years it was both praised and damned by those exposed to it, and the brickbats were as numerous as the bouquets. Then, not long ago, it suddenly emerged as the best all-round combat handgun in the world, with few voices raised against it. Because of something called combat pistol shooting—or "High Noon" on the pistol range—the 45 Auto has finally found its niche.

Even though I first strapped on a 45 Auto at the age of three, I won't count that as the beginning of my own experience with this pistol. My father was a pre-Cooper fan of the Government Model and owned several but I never shared his enthusiasm. I had one of my own for a spell, more or less by accident, and so was quite familiar with the weapon when I became a Marine and had to carry it on occasion and fire it for record at regular intervals. I could make Sharpshooter with it, and that was about all. The 45 Auto just wasn't my gun but I respected it for what it was: an efficient military sidearm, reliable, rugged, easy to clean and repair, accurate and powerful enough for its intended purpose, that is close-range self defense. These features are just as valid today as they were in 1911, which probably accounts for the fact that the Model 1911A1 Colt, despite its weight and bulk and lack of such modern refinements as a double-action capability, is still our standard military sidearm. Army Ordnance has made some spectacular blunders in its time, but hanging on to the M1911A1 is not one of them.

As for the niche the 45 Auto has found for itself in combat pistol shooting, however, it seems to me there is less to this than meets the eye. Jeff Cooper writes well and is outstanding among gun experts if for no other reason than that he doesn't wear a cowboy hat. But when he says, of combat pistol shooting, "We are now able to pose simulated combat problems for the pistol which cannot be handled as well with rifle, shotgun or submachine gun," I have to reply, "So what?" I could pose simulated combat problems in which a knife, a blackjack, or a garrote would be the best weapon to use, but that doesn't mean I would voluntarily go into actual combat armed only with one of the three. Cooper may be thinking of those Viet Cong tunnels—the "tunnel rats" who search them out can't manage any firearm bigger than a pistol — but that is a very special combat situation. No, I have to think we readers are being promoted a bit here: no doubt Cooper and his cohorts are deadly with their pistols but if I ever team up with them in a *non-simulated* combat problem, I hope they bring along their rifles, shotguns and submachine guns as well.

Quick Draw

"Quick draw" is a somewhat related subject that has accounted for at least its share of baloney in print, and not all of it in gun magazines. The old Hopalong Cassidy series—the books, not the TV shows—made me a quick draw addict at an early age, and I spent hours trying to outdraw myself in the mirror. My father was tolerant of this—surprisingly, I think, in view of that 45 caliber scar he carried from his own experiments in the field—but often quoted an old Texas Ranger to the effect that "If a man thinks he's going to have to use his gun he's a damned fool to carry it anyplace but in his hand." My own combat experience convinced me the old Ranger was right; quick draw has no military application that I know of, and I doubt that its application to police work is significant. Furthermore, just to be contrary, I contend that it was never much of a factor in the heyday of Western gunfighters.

With the phony glamor stripped away, those old gunfighters were, by and large, killers. It didn't matter which side of the law they were on—some in fact switched sides more than once—they were killers and therefore picked their shots and their victims. Fair play was a standard they couldn't afford. The face-to-face confrontation

with hands poised over gun butts and bystanders scurrying for cover was invented by script writers from Brooklyn, and has practically no basis in historical fact. Western gunmen didn't need to draw quickly because they knew *when* they were going to draw and the other poor devil didn't.

Which brings me to my final beef with gun writers—a complaint not about the nonsense they include but about some critical factors they often ignore. Generally, in their articles the emphasis is on hardware—scopes, stocks, actions, slings, barrel lengths, sights, calibers, brass, powder, bullets, etc. The reader is presumed to know how to shoot—all he needs is

Colonel Stiff (right) presenting a Team Trophy two days after President Kennedy's death.

the right equipment.

But the fundamental purpose for which firearms were developed and for which they are designed today is— whether we like to admit it or not— to kill something or somebody. And when a firearm is put to this ultimate use, elements other than barrel length and stock design come into play. Luck is one such element, and the character of the man behind the gun is another. This is scarcely an original thought, I realize—gun writers are surely aware of the human element but they seem to shy away from it, perhaps because it is hard to put into words. They may also feel that if a reader hasn't got what it takes to be a good hunter no amount of printed advice will make him one, and I would agree with this. Yet the constant reader of gun periodicals is likely to be lulled into the belief that all he needs is the right gun for the job.

The Right Gun

The right gun for the job! I think

back to a day in 1963 when I was commanding The Weapons Training Battalion, Marine Corps Recruit Depot, San Diego. As the name implies, the Battalion conducted all marksmanship training for West Coast recruits as well as annual re-qualification training for regular personnel. We also had the Depot Rifle and Pistol Team. On this particular day, the Team was hosting a match with several other military teams, and in addition we had the regular weekly record firing for recruits and requalifiers. It was Friday, November 22d, and the Commanding General was on hand, as he often was on Record Day.

The General and I watched the recruits shoot for a while, then moved over to see how things were going in the team match. As we approached the 1000-yard line where firing was in progress, a sergeant intercepted us, crying, "General, General! The President has just been shot!" We went over to the parked car where the sergeant had been listening to the radio, and heard the shocking news. (One of my first reactions was to hope that no ex-Marine had done the shooting: by the following Monday we were combing old files for information concerning Lee Harvey Oswald, ex-PFC, USMC, who had fired for record on our ranges six years and eleven months earlier.)

At the end of the day, President Kennedy was dead and so was a Dallas policeman named Tippit. Lee Harvey Oswald was in custody with less than 48 hours left to live. As the story unfolded on television and radio and in the papers, I shared the national sense of incredulity.

We learned (eventually) that at least three shots had been fired, at least two of which were hits. The range was fairly short, 60-90 yards, but the gun/target angle was downhill and the target was moving at a speed of 11 miles per hour. A difficult shot? Not for the Marines on my rifle team, perhaps, but tricky at best for less distinguished marksmen. A fellow Marine later told the Warren Commission it was an "easy" shot. I submit that there can be no such thing as an easy shot when the target is the President of the United States.

We saw photographs of the assassin's weapon. First reports called it a "German Mauser" but we gun nuts recognized it for what it was—a Mannlicher-Carcano designed in 1891 and disdained by gun experts ever since. Its cheap Japanese scope and flimsy side-mount made it scarcely more credible as a gun that had changed the course of history.

The right gun for the job? Here was a battered old rifle of mediocre design and obsolete caliber. It had already seen hard service when it was shipped from Italy. There is no conclusive evidence that Oswald *ever* sighted in his rifle, and it is certain that he did not after the rifle had made a round trip between Dallas and New Orleans in the back of a station wagon and thereafter kicked around for two months in a garage wrapped in a blanket. It was a gun/sight/caliber combination no gun expert would have recommended, and the circumstances surrounding its use on November 22d were heavily weighted against success. Yet the President was dead. Luck and the character of the man behind the gun: a warped kid with a junk rifle shook the world.

A Loyal Fan Still

My piddling complaints notwithstanding, I am a loyal fan of gun writers. Not only do they write what I want to read, but they inform me, instruct me, and entertain me, and I am grateful.

It is easy to overlook the fact that gun writers, as a body, are as strong a force for the proper use of guns as we have. If their counsels were strictly heeded, there would be no misuse of firearms and consequently little basis for gun control laws. Unfortunately those who misuse guns are rarely gun buffs and therefore cannot be expected to read, much less heed, sound advice on the use of guns.

So we *do* have misuse of firearms in this country, and it seems obvious this is the root problem vis-a-vis the continuing threat of anti-gun legislation. Misuse by criminals hurts us most but hunting accidents, suicides, and accidental shootings are no help.

There is little hope the problem can ever be eliminated, human nature being what it is—no more hope than there is that people will stop misusing automobiles, speedboats, alcohol or drugs or almost anything else you can think of. Kids are killing themselves with hair spray, for God's sake! The anti-gun extremists may claim there is no such thing as legitimate use of guns by private citizens but *misuse* is their bread-and-butter and they will probably continue to have it.

It becomes a matter, then, of which side, pro-gun or anti-gun, can muster the most votes. Clearly neither side constitutes a majority—far from it. This means that the issues will be resolved by voters who are neither gun lovers (although they may be gun owners) nor gun haters. This, I believe, is cause for optimism. I believe that the majority, given the facts, will usually vote against willful destruction of traditional liberties.

New Gun Laws Needless

The right to keep and bear arms is not only a constitutionally guaranteed liberty but a traditional one. To say our forefathers shot their way from coast to coast would be a cynical exaggeration but it is a fact that firearms in the hands of private citizens were an essential ingredient in the development of this nation from Plymouth Rock onward—and I doubt that any significant number of Americans considers this a shameful aspect of our history.

But if there is cause for optimism there is surely no room for complacency. Nor is it enough for us gun nuts to run around quoting the Second Amendment to each other—the majority can be misled so we must make sure they have the facts.

It seems to me that a basic weakness of the anti-gun proponents is their fanaticism—their arguments tend to go well beyond the boundaries of logic, reason and fact, thus becoming vulnerable to dispassionate and factual counter-attack. Consider, for example, the continuing push for Federal gun registration. The basic argument for gun registration is that it would keep guns out of the hands of the wrong people—criminals, minors, mental defectives, et al—and would make it easier for police to trace guns used in crimes. The factual counter-attack? Simply that no *new law is required to attain these two objectives*.

In the matter of the "wrong" people obtaining guns—we're talking about obtaining guns *legally*, remember— the 20,000-odd pertinent state and Federal laws now on the books already provide more controls than can be effectively enforced on who can le-

gally obtain a gun. Also, of course, there are laws against stealing guns, which is the way criminals prefer to obtain them. So, unless there is a category of "wrong" people we don't know about yet, no new law is needed here.

Tracing guns used in crimes? Considering the many state and Federal laws requiring records for tax purposes (as well as police purposes), and considering GCA '68 with its voluminous requirements for records, licenses, identification, etc., etc., the question is—just how much more help can the police use?

In 1962 Oswald's rifle was traced to him in a matter of hours although he ordered it under a false name. In 1964 the late ex-Senator Dodd traced handguns sold by certain dealers to "children, crooks, dope addicts, assorted imbeciles (etc.)" by using the dealers' own records. For years, collectors have been able to trace guns through factory and dealer records to such notables as Bat Masterson and George Patton, not to mention obscure cavalry lieutenants and minor-league outlaws. Stolen guns? Under *any* system guns can only be traced to the last honest person who had possession. In other words, tracing firearms has never been all that difficult, and with GCA '68 it should be a snap for even the most Keystone-like police force. Again, no new law is needed.

Arguments for most measures in the typical gun control package are equally vulnerable to facts, and the facts must be placed before the uncommitted majority and Congress. They must be made to appreciate the fact that any further proposals for restrictions on legal gun owners can only be regarded as attempts to destroy a traditional liberty which, at its worst, is one of the least of the *internal* threats confronting the nation; at its best it's a very real deterrent to *external* threats as well as to homegrown crime. Between the two extremes, of course, it is a source of recreation and pleasure and, to be sure, profit for many millions of Americans.

As I said, I am optimistic. I believe that the gun nut is still very much a respected part of the American scene. When he raises his voice he is heard —as a number of ex-members of Congress can testify. Much of our heritage has been frittered away or watered down but our traditional ties with guns are, I believe, as strong as ever. In this country we have gun nuts, anti-gun nuts, and the rest of the American people, with the rest being the majority—and in that majority I have faith.

As an old model gun nut, how else could I feel? ●

MOST SHOOTERS, especially clay busters and live pigeon shooters, are familiar with the standard method of assessing choke, but I'll recapitulate briefly for tyros. Choke is the degree of constriction between the diameter of the barrel, just beyond the chambers and forcing cones, and the diameter at the muzzle. The resultant patterns produced are graded in terms of the percentage of pellets from the original shot charge, which find their way into a 30-inch circle on a sheet of paper 40 yards away. Full choke has 70%, Improved Modified 65%, Modified 60%, Improved Cylinder 50% and Cylinder 40%.

It is often said, erroneously, that Cylinder indicates a complete lack of constriction. English barrel-chokers found that a barrel totally devoid of choke produces uncontrolled and widely varying patterns. Therefore, almost surreptitiously, they put .003" to .005" constriction into the guns of customers who specified true cylinder.

For new scattergunners, the simplest analogy to describe the practical effect of choke is to liken it to the attachment on the end of a garden hose. When fully open, it allows the water to spray out in a wide circle over a short distance. The more it is tightened down, or constricted, the smaller the circle becomes—but the farther it travels. Being a little more precise—choke allows us to present the target with about the same size "circle" filled with about the same amount of shot at different distances.

However, there's a great deal more to choke than the simplified explanation above gives. So much, in fact, that it is fair to say that no one knows all the factors which can affect choke, and which produce good and bad patterns from seemingly identical sets of dimensions and loads, in different sets of barrels. This may seem surprising in view of the highly advanced techniques and testing apparatus

Uptight about choking? You want more pellets in the magic circle? Here's how it's done, even to 98 percent patterns—in some guns. In spite of some minor qualms, the author surrendered his pet Perazzi to Doc Cordaro for a major operation.

CHOKES CHOKES CHOKES

by DEREK PARTRIDGE

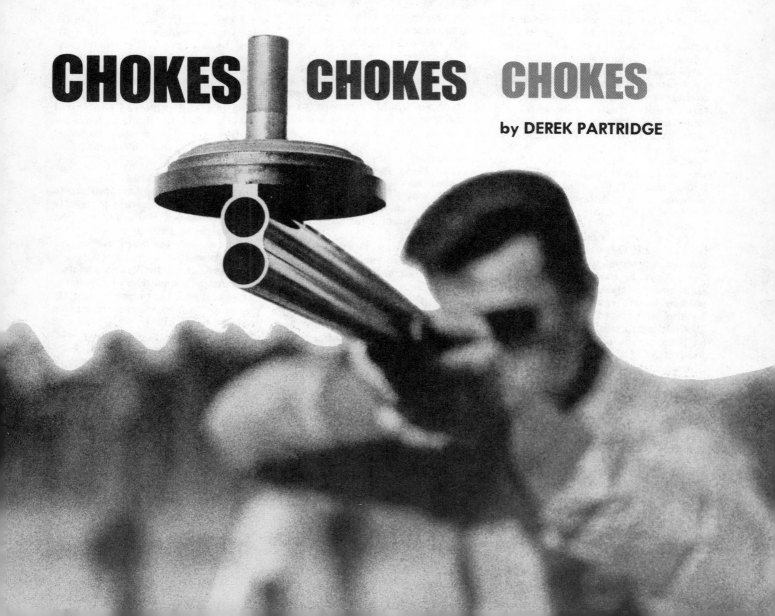

available to the world's leading gun-makers—and especially to those in America. A number of today's expert American gunsmiths have devised various methods of improving the performance of standard factory barrels. This is really not too difficult, for the cost of hand-finishing a mass-produced gun barrel would be so prohibitive as to price the gun out of its market. Francis Sell, a noted firearms consultant, has recently completed a survey of various aspects of choking and he concludes, as do most leading authorities, that one prime essential is smoothly polished bores. It could therefore be concluded that an improvement over the factory barrel could be made merely by hand-polishing (lapping is the professional term) the interior of the barrel.

Some gunsmiths have taken the improvements a lot further than that. Names which spring to mind are Herb Orre, Al Ljutic, Bill Atkinson (rifled shotgun barrels) and Doc Cordaro. The strange thing, which I believe all have in common, is that each discovered his particular method by accident! The accident was generally caused by a broken reamer leaving an unwanted configuration inside the bores which, for one reason or another, they happened to test fire and found, to their amazement, that "super" patterns resulted. I also recall, with fond amusement, another friend and amateur "expert," Franz Rotthinger. He is a well-known trapshooter on the west coast and a capable mechanic, who bought my F.N. (Browning) after I had "married" my beloved Perazzi. We shot a lot of International Trap together and between each round, Franz could *always* be seen, peering down the barrels of either the F.N. or his Krieghoff. Out would come a hand reamer, a few deft turns—to improve the pattern or move it up or down, right or left—then off he'd go to the pattern board, reappearing in time for the next round. We used to kid about it unmercifully, but his search for perfection in patterning obviously paid off, for it won him the State Championship of Upper Austria with 98/100—and in International Trap that's a darn good score. I am not a handloader, nor am I a ballistician, because I don't want red and green dots dancing before my eyes when I'm out on the firing line: "Maybe I should have dropped 18 instead of 17 grains? Ouch! I must have dropped 22 grains in that one! My God! The wife forgot to put the primer—shot—wad in this one, etc.!" To shoot successfully, there must be only one thought in mind while on the line: The next target, and killing it. But I do have my own

approach to the question of choke. What's this 60%, 70% at *40 yards* nonsense? How many people shoot at 40 yards? Why not the maximum possible number of pellets, *evenly distributed* in a 30-inch circle at the *average range* each of us shoots?

The Cordaro System

Dr. Sal Cordaro told me he could achieve this. To my amazement, I found myself believing in him to the point where I was prepared to put my Perazzi on the operating table and allow the doctor to carry out the delicate, high precision surgery required. The fact that the worthy doctor had been an experimental tool maker and was also Italian—my gun's nationality—seemed to provide the assurances I needed. Doc Cordaro felt as I did, that there's no point having pellets outside the killing circle; they don't do anyone much good except a consistently inaccurate shot. His aim was to contain as many as possible inside the 30-inch circle—expanded to about 35 inches for ranges over 40 yards (the margin of error increases with distance)—and to concentrate utterly on achieving their absolutely even distribution. I was interested only in the final, pragmatic result on my targets, but I was prepared to go through all the ballistic theory involved, so I could eventually go out on the line with complete practical and theoretical confidence in the performance of my gun—a definite psychological factor in aiding good shooting. Many years ago, I had realized that shooting top scores consistently started from having such confidence in my equipment that I would *never* blame a lost target on it, but only *myself*.

Factors affecting the creation of an optimum pattern include total trueness or roundness of barrel interior; length, taper and diameter of forcing cones and chokes; powder charge and resultant muzzle velocity; size of shot, relative to choke constriction, and whether it's lead, hard lead or nickel plated. Other aspects to be considered are the type of target—clays, live pigeon, game birds, length of shot column and, when necessary, effect of wind.

From many years of trapshooting, observing trapshooters, examining their guns and firing thousands of rounds in exhaustive testing procedures on pattern sheets, Doc Cordaro made the following claims: by altering the dimensions of the above factors to tolerances of precision never before attempted (through his experience in experimental tool making), he could customize the pattern of any gun for

the 16-yard man, the 27-yard handicap shooter, the doubles, live pigeon or International Trap competitor. Moreover, he would do this by working only from dimensions he had worked out over 5 years of testing to perfect his method, which is known as Cordo choking. He's so sure of their infallible accuracy that he tells clients after working on their guns: "I haven't test-patterned it—but please feel free to do so, you'll find it's what you asked for." A very remarkable claim—especially when you consider that his technique, like those of the other choke-improvers, was stumbled on by accident:

A previous accident had left a stepped ridge in the end of a barrel. He hadn't noticed it, but when he patterned the gun he got almost double the percentage he had been aiming for—in the region of 90%. On discovering the ridge, he ran a series of tests which showed him that the wad was being momentarily stopped by the ridge, avoiding any possibility of its breaking up the shot column and ruining the pattern. Shortly afterwards, also as a result of an error caused by a broken reamer, Al Ljutic came out with a barrel having a spiral in the end, to spin the wad away from the shot column. Then the protective shot-cup wad and the sleeve came out and rendered the spiral choke obsolete for shells so loaded—for they would spin both protector and shot and so cause too much pellet dispersion.

First Steps

Stage one was for Doc Cordaro to watch me shoot, ascertain at exactly what distances I consistently broke targets and to pattern my gun with various loads to see how it performed. The reason I was even prepared to consider altering the Perazzi was this: The gun, patterned to give 72% lower barrel and 80% top barrel, absolutely pulverized International targets—a second barrel kill being equally as dramatic as the first—or more so, considering the greater distance. So I thought the pellet density might be too concentrated in one area and that the evenness of distribution could therefore be improved—along with putting the maximum number of pellets in the circle at the distances *I* was shooting.

Briefly, the differences between International Trap and American Trap are: I.T. travel 77-87 yards—and sometimes around 100 yards, (A.T. 48-52), at a speed of nearly 100 mph (A.T. about 55 mph), through an arc of 90 degrees (A.T. 44 degrees) and through height variations be-

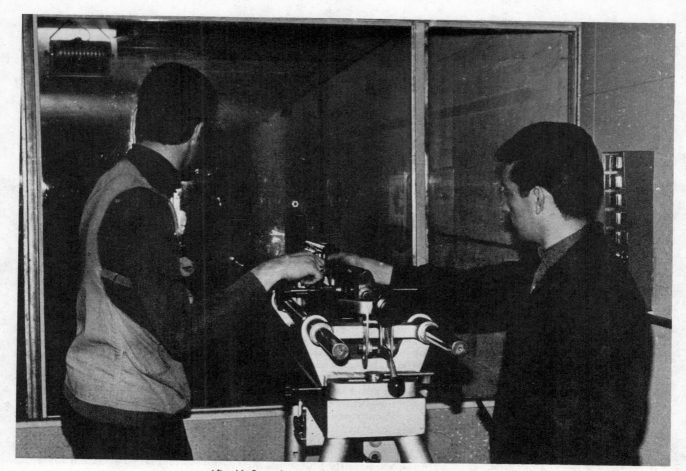

After his Perazzi over-under received the Cordo Choke treatment, Partridge returned to Brescia for the ultimate tests. The machine rest shown here confirmed the improvements.

tween 3 and 13 feet off the ground at a point 11 yards from the trap (A.T. have a constant height of about 9 feet at that distance). The average experienced American trapshooter breaks his target at around 35 yards and takes from 0.9-second to 1.10. At International you're allowed two shots; the first shot averages 36 to 38 yards and the second between 41 and 45. Average time for a straight-away shot is 0.6-second and, for an acute angle, 0.7- to 0.8.

At our test site, we had a Winchester-Western Continental trap, which gave us all the vertical and horizontal variations and angles, but because we didn't have any of the harder International targets, it was only throwing American targets 70 yards, just short of the International minimum. Doc Cordaro set out wooden stakes at 5-yard intervals, then watched to see just where I broke targets. First barrel kills were consistently broken at 31 yards. Then, by deliberately missing first-barrel shots, we were able to determine that 35-38 yards was my breaking distance for second-barrel shots. We debated whether to add a few yards to the

distances he would work to in his choking, to allow for the slighter greater distance of true International targets. We decided on a very few yards, as we felt that my reaction time would speed up in relation to the faster ejection of the International targets. (Subsequent tests in Europe on International targets established the distances as 34 yards and 38-40 yards). Out of curiosity he had me shoot 16-yard American targets and found that I consistently broke them just under 10 yards from the trap—a distance of 25 yards from the gun, or 10 yards nearer than the average trapshooter. To further test the effect of my then choke, he had me shoot the 70-yard modified International targets from the 27-yard line—the gun still pulverized targets and, when there were any left, also pulverized tiny chips with the second barrel!

We moved to the pattern board and fired patterns at 30, 35, 40, 45 and 50 yards with Remington, Federal and Winchester International Trap loads in 3¼/1¼/7½s and 8s and also tried some 3¾ dram shells. We used nickel-plated, lead and Federal's hardened lead shot. In keeping with what Doc

Cordaro had expected, from previous years of testing, Remington loads showed the least variance with the Federals a very close second.

The 7½s gave slightly higher percentages than the 8s, but so slight that the 8s still delivered more pellets in the circle. The hotter 3¾ loads definitely blew the pattern more open —to my mind, too open. (The blown-pattern effect of a high velocity shell will decrease in proportion to the increase in choking). However, the most striking feature of the patterning procedure was that my gun consistently threw elliptical patterns, crowding the upper right portion of the sheets with pellets and leaving the lower left markedly bare. Could that be the reason for my more than normal amount of "unaccountable" misses on low, acute left angle targets? Doc Cordaro said this was quite typical of any barrel and denoted that the barrels—from chambers, through forcing cones and bore to chokes— were out of true. This setup can give a very misleading patterning report. The pellets will be on the sheet, hence will give a good percentage figure but, when you divide the pattern sheet

98% patterns? Yes, Dr. S. V. Cordaro, who does the bore surgery entailed in his Cordo Choke treatment, says the density pictured here hits nearly 100%.

into clock-face segments, the bad effect of elliptical distribution is immediately obvious.

Dr. Cordaro Operates

Doc Cordaro now knew what my gun did, where I shot and what his experience told him I needed as optimum patterns for my first and second barrels. His intention was to put more pellets in the lower barrel pattern for 35-yard shooting, just a few more in the top one for 40 yards, and to improve the even distribution and density of both. It was a tear-jerking moment when I handed Doc Cordaro the Perazzi, put a hand on his shoulder, looked him squarely in the eye and said: "Look after her, old boy, she's the only woman I've ever been faithful to." Doc, being an emotional Italian, was visibly moved, whereas I, being British, kept a traditionally stiff upper lip, squeezed his shoulder, and strode away into the gathering gloom without another glance back.

Knowing that I would probably crack up under the strain of a long wait, he treated my Perazzi as an emergency case and burned the midnight oil in the operating shed. Next morning we met again at Bob Gegerson's Mid Hudson Winchester Club. Doc's Italian features had taken on a decidedly oriental appearance—suitably inscrutable, they gave me no indication as to the outcome of his barrel-doctoring. I squinted nervously down the barrels. I could see the fine polishing marks where he had trued up the bores (later polished out to a mirror finish) and relieved the forcing cones (too sharply angled a forcing cone can produce increased recoil). The chokes had also been relieved

and there were signs of some more top secret activity at the muzzles! As I prepared to shoot, it was Doc Cordaro's turn to assume the role of nervous father, pacing up and down in anticipation of the performance of what had become his baby, too.

I missed the first target out—a simple straight-away—Doc staggered and fell . . . then I turned round, grinned sheepishly and explained that I had forgotten that I had started to use a release trigger only the week before and in the excitement of firing the now Cordo-choked gun, had completely overlooked this! Doc was revived by a still-smoking hull being passed under his nose and sat up in time to see targets breaking with a confidence-inspiring consistency. The difference being that now, instead of smoking most targets, with the occasional chip (from the fringe of the pattern) and the even more occasional miss, they just disintegrated into tiny, evenly-sized pieces. This showed that the pellets had been evenly distributed throughout the killing circle and that, instead of having a dense central (or off-center elliptical) killing area and a sparsely filled outer ring, now the whole circle was equally lethal to any target venturing into it!

As an experiment to test the second barrel's efficacy—without resorting to deliberately missing targets, which can have a slightly detrimental effect on timing—I used some skeet 2¾/1⅛/9s in the first barrel, erroneously presuming that they would merely dust the targets, instead of breaking them. Not only did they break them perfectly first barrel but, as a further experiment, we found that 9s even broke them out to 35 or 40 yards from

the second barrel. We concluded that 9s could be effectively used for 16-yard trap and the first shot of doubles, except in high wind conditions, which will be referred to later. After conditioning myself to miss the first barrel shots, just before reaching the target, I broke 22/25 with the second shots, and so proved the equally even-breaking capacity of the upper barrel. I had been afraid he might take too much out of this barrel and so destroy its legendary capacity to smash second barrel shots and bits remaining from first barrel kills. I had to forget about the latter, because the way the Cordo-choked first barrel now broke targets, there was rarely anything left to shoot at. I then tried different combinations of shells with Doc Cordaro noting the results in his notebook as before; disintegrated; broken into so many pieces; chipped; dusted; missed.

We moved to the pattern board for final confirmation of what I was already fully satisfied with. Immediately noticeable from every shot, regardless of the shell, was the even distribution of pellets throughout the clock-face segments of each pattern sheet. Yesterday Doc had brought a new pattern board he had built. At the end of the previous patterning the top and right wooden frame sides were spattered with pellets, whereas the left and bottom struts were virtually unmarked. Today we reversed the frame and found, as expected, that each of the four struts had a completely even covering of fringe pellets. The frame was built to hold sheets approximately 36 inches square. Doc pronounced himself satisfied, but he told me he could "Cordo" the barrels a fraction more if I found I wanted it. He suggested, though, that I try it first on true International targets in top competition. The actual comparative pattern percentages were to be left until my forthcoming trip to the Perazzi factory, when I would pattern the barrels under the same conditions as when the original percentages were calculated.

Best Score Ever

A few days later, I left for the Interservice International Trap Championships at Fort Benning, Ga. On the first day, I ran my first-ever 25 straight, first barrel only—a rare occurrence in International Trap—and turned it into a 50 straight. On the last day I missed the 14th target in the first round and then ran a heart-pounding 75 straight to finish with 99/100. There were two lucky chips, and two to three second-barrel shots per round which, along with the rest of the first barrels, were all completely disintegrated. It was my best-ever score. (As a comparative note of the relative value of scores between American Trap and International: at the 1968 Grand American, 44 shooters tied with 200/200; in the whole history of International Trap, 200/200 has been fired only 5 times, one of which was in America).

On my return, I discussed some points about shot size with Doc Cordaro. We had already learned that a light load of skeet 9s would break targets out at 35-40 yards, but Doc had said they weren't to be used in a strong wind. His experiments had shown that strong winds could affect the smaller pellets to the extent that hardly a pellet would be found on the pattern sheet at 40 yards. He had found that the same thing applied even to 8s, in similar conditions, when 7½s would still produce good patterns.

It is quite obvious that the more pellets we can put into our patterns the less chance there can be of a clay slipping through a hole. The four square inches of target area the clay presents to a trapshooter is horrifyingly small — especially when you think about it in those terms! The smaller pellets must have sufficient energy to break the clay. In the case of the International target, which is deliberately made harder (and slightly smaller), to withstand the shock of being thrown at twice the speed of the American target, this must definitely be considered.

Shot Sizes

To successfully use the smaller sizes of shot, you may have to open your chokes slightly, for the smaller the pellet the more it deforms in tightly constricted chokes. This opening of the chokes to accomodate continuous use of smaller pellets will not result in a reduction in percentage, but rather an increase and an attendant improvement in distribution. A number of live pigeon shooters successfully use 9s — except perhaps during the winter months, when the birds are in their heavier plumage. Some years ago there was an interesting "duel" between the Jenkins brothers and Bob Allen at live pigeons. While Bob Allen ordered double extra full chokes and used 7½s, the Jenkins brothers conversely opened up their chokes and used 9s — consistently beating Allen. But a pigeon is not a clay, and the final word on that I'll leave to Winchester-Western pro Al Mosier, who reckoned that one-and-a-half times as many 8s as 7½s were

needed to achieve the same breaking effect.

The best combination in my experience, which Doc's technical knowledge backed up, is 3¼/1¼/8s first barrel and 3¼/1¼/7½s in the second. Both should be nickel plated or be specially hardened lead. Nickel plating helps by protecting against pellet deformation — a good pattern's worst enemy and one which is not *entirely* eliminated by the plastic shot collar. If you want to open up your first barrel pattern, without touching the chokes, use lead shot, without a shot collar. Although some International shooters prefer 3¾ dram loads, particularly in Europe, careful patterning tests should be made to learn whether such a load shows good patterning — especially at ranges over 38-40 yards.

Shortly before I left for Italy Doc and I shot more patterns, demonstrating to some interested shooters the results of his work. Although percentages and distribution were good, the centers now seemed a little thin, giving "doughnut" patterns. Searching for a reason, we recalled noticing the Power Piston wad was sailing prominently down range almost to the 40-yard-distant pattern board. It was a cold, clear day and the atmosphere was very thin — offering little resistance to the passage of the wad. We then checked the fall of the wad each time. They fell to within one to 1½ yards from the pattern sheet, so there was the cause of the doughnut patterns. A brief adjournment to Doc's workshop, then more shooting. Now the wads fell some 15 yards from the sheets, which once again showed patterns of uniform density, no worrying hole in the center. Doc had performed some further mechanical alchemy in the barrels, retarding the wad just enough to prevent it disrupting the pattern.

I tried to prise some more information from Doc about the high-precision surgery he had performed on my Perazzi, but he figured he had worked too long to perfect his technique to make a free hand-out of it — a reasonable enough feeling! He would only allow that he had "altered" the dimensions referred to earlier, and the mirror finish spoke for itself. Another way of achieving this finish is by chrome-plating the barrels, but this does have the disadvantage of making any subsequent choke alterations extremely difficult. A more recent idea is the use of Teflon lining. Teflon, developed for space use, now adorns many household cooking pans. Its extremely low coefficient of friction makes it ideal for reducing pellet de-

formation to an absolute minimum. Naturally, Doc Cordaro is working on a practical application!

Last Tests in Brescia

Now came the final test, which was only for the sake of ballistic record, as the practical results had already more than satisfied me. I shot a series of patterns in the test tunnel at the Perazzi factory in Brescia, Italy. The original percentages, shot in my presence, had been 72% and 80% at 38 yards — European standard test distance is 35 meters. Now the figures were 83% and 85%, with distinctly improved distribution and a slightly larger number of pellets in the top half of the circle where you "look at" and therefore normally shoot the clay. At 34 yards, my first barrel shooting distance, the figure was 85%. So I had what must be considered perfection for an International shooter — identical patterns at the two distances I was shooting. It's the same target, so there's no point in having different patterns! Doc had achieved what he set out to do: put more pellets in the first barrel pattern (11% more), just a few more in the top one (5% more); equalize the distribution of both and customize them identically for my two shooting distances. The barrel gauge showed that he had opened the lower barrel only 0.001-inch and the top the same; I also noticed that, in the perfect, still conditions of the tunnel, the bottom barrel also gave identical percentages with 8s and 7½s. This would seem to bear out Doc's theory that wind can affect the smaller 8s, as all our outdoor tests had consistently shown the 7½s to give better percentages. His barrel polishing and other mystery ballistic engineering had definitely reduced pellet deformation of the smaller 8s to give them parity with 7½s under *windless* conditions

Sal Cordaro has now become more interested in technicalities and ballistics than in his own shooting — to the point where he is in the process of designing and building a Cordo gun. It will probably be the first gun which will enable the trapshooter to sit back while the gun does the job for him! In the meantime, if your gun is tightly constricted, over-choked for your type of shooting or throwing elliptical patterns, let Doc Cordaro perform his "opening and evening" operation. At $50 per barrel, it's a small investment which could net you a handsome return — with a gun customized to your type and style of shooting. His address is 28 Seven Bridges Rd., Chappaqua, New York 10514. ●

Forty Years with the Little 7mm

"I think," says the author, "I've seen more game killed with fewer shots from this modest little cartridge than any other." Here's the why and how, all of which may well explain the current spate of interest in the little seven millimeter.

by JACK O'CONNOR

Eleanor O'Connor with a 53-inch greater kudu shot with the 7x57 in Mozambique in 1962. Her professional hunter is Harry Manners.

For almost 40 years I've been having an off-and-on romance with a sweet little cartridge known as the 7x57, the 7mm Mauser, and the 7mm Spanish Mauser. There is nothing spectacular about the 7x57. It does not have a big case. Even when the charge is tightly compressed it is possible to get only about 53 grains of 4350 or 4831 powders into the Western 7x57 case, which is roomier than Remington's. This modest little cartridge does not have a belt. It isn't a magnum. It doesn't bellow like a 105mm howitzer and scramble the brains of the firer. It doesn't shoot through three elk, one moose, two grizzlies and a forest ranger and then mow down a grove of jack pines on the far side. The hole in the barrel is so little that even a small, thin, underprivileged mouse would have difficulty in entering, and the cartridge itself isn't as long as a maiden's arm.

Yet I think I have seen more game killed with fewer shots from this modest little cartridge than with any other. The explanation for its deadly efficiency does not lie in blinding velocity, in big bullets, in a frightening number of foot pounds of energy. It lies in the light recoil, coupled with

the excellent hunting accuracy of so many 7x57s. Those who use it are not afraid of it and, as a consequence, they tend to shoot it well—and to place their shots well. In case no one has told you, the most important factor in killing power is putting that bullet in the right spot.

The 7x57 is so-called because the bullet has the number of millimeters which add up to a diameter of .284" and the barrels a bore diameter of .276". The bullets have a slightly greater diameter than those of the 270 WCF, which measure .277". The 7x57 case holds about 10 grains less powder, as you can stuff 62-63 grains of 4831 into a Western 270 case. The cartridge gets the "57" tacked onto its name because the case is 57mm long. The head size is the same as that of the 30-06 and the 270. It is simply the 8x57J Mauser case necked down to 7mm.

As I write this, late in 1972, the cartridge is 80 years old. Developed in 1892 at the Mauser Werke in Germany, it was adopted the next year by Spain as a military cartridge. We Americans first got acquainted with it in 1898 when, in Cuba, the Spanish used it to shoot small, neat holes in a considerable number of

gringos in such ructions as the American charge up San Juan hill. The American army came out of the war with a profound admiration for the 7x57 and for the Model 1893 Mausers the cartridge was used in. American ordnance developed the 1903 Springfield rifle, which is a modified Mauser, and the 30-03 and 30-06 cartridges, which are enlarged 7x57s.

Early History

Until recent years, the 7x57 was enormously popular as a military cartridge. It was adopted by Mexico, Brazil, Colombia, Chile, Honduras, Uruguay, and Serbia, as well as by Spain. It became popular as a sporting cartridge in England, on the Continent, and in Africa. W.D.M. Bell, the famous elephant hunter and excellent writer *(Bell of Africa, Tales of an Elephant Hunter, Karamojo Safari)*, used it with the full metal-jacketed 172-gr. military bullets (solids) to bump off over 1,000 elephants. Most of these were big, tough bulls with good ivory. Bell never bothered much with cows.

Americans became acquainted with the 7x57 as a big game cartridge after the Spanish-American War, as many American soldiers brought rifles back

This 42-inch sable antelope was a one-shot kill with the 7x57 in Angola.

with them and used them on deer, elk, moose, and bear. For a long time the only American factory cartridge available was one loaded with a 175-gr. soft point bullet at a muzzle velocity of 2,300 foot seconds. Later the velocity was stepped up to 2,490 fps. I do not know, but I suspect that this velocity was taken in a 30-inch barrel as, until recently anyway, it was the practice to take velocities in the barrel length for which the cartridge was developed. In the case of the 7mm, the early military rifles had 30-inch barrels.

The long 175-gr. bullets gave satisfactory penetration because of good sectional density, made a satisfactory wound channel because the bullets had plenty of lead and expanded easily. All in all, with that bullet, the 7mm was a good 175-225 yard cartridge for about any sort of game. Trajectory with the heavy bullet was about like that of the 30-06 with the 220-gr. bullet. Recoil was less. If you were smart enough to sight in to put the bullet 3 inches high at 100 yards, there was no necessity to hold high even at 200 — and I'm sure I don't need to tell my gentle readers that more game is killed at under 200 yards than over.

Along in the middle 1920s, the Western Cartridge Company shot the old 7mm full of testosterone and vitamins Z, P, and X, by bringing out a load that gave a 139-gr. open point bullet an alleged velocity of 3,000 fps. If that velocity were the McCoy (and I doubt that like hell) it was achieved in a 30-inch barrel. Remington likewise introduced a load with a 139-gr. bullet but said it was stepping along at 2,900. Prior to World War II, Winchester loaded a 150-gr. bullet at 2,750, a velocity probably taken in a 24-inch barrel. Currently Norma loads a 110-gr. bullet at 3,068, a 150 at 2,756, and a 175 at 2,490.

7x57 Actions

The 1893 and 1895 Mauser actions are on the soft side, cock on the closing motion of the bolt, and do not have the auxiliary locking lug at the root of the bolt handle. Pressures, consequently, should be kept down to around 45,000 pounds per square inch. Some of the actions made in Spain are particularly soft. Beginning around 1908, the Mauser Werke at Oberndorf, Germany, began turning out 7x57 sporters in various styles on a slightly shortened Model 98 type action. I have heard this action called the Model 1908 and also the Model

1912. It is, I believe, ⅜-inch shorter than the standard Model 98. Actions of similar, if not identical, lengths were used by Mexico, Czechoslovakia, and Yugoslavia. Just before and after World War I hock shops in the Southwest and Southern California always had for sale 7mm Mauser carbines that had probably come across the line with fugitive Mexican soldiers. These could be bought for a song and were widely used for hunting deer and desert sheep in the Southwest.

In Germany, the Mauser Werke and various custom gunsmiths built 7x57s. In England, Rigby made them on Mauser actions, calling the cartridge the 275 Rigby. In the United States, Remington turned out 7x57 rifles on the Rider Rolling Block actions for various foreign governments, and also chambered Lee sporting rifles for the cartridge.

During the 1920s and 1930s, Griffin & Howe made many handsome sporters on Mauser and Springfield actions for the cartridge. The first caliber that W.A. Sukalle, the famous Arizona gunsmith and barrelmaker, tooled up for was the 7mm.

Remington chambered the Model 30 bolt action for the cartridge, and Winchester produced 7x57s in the

Mrs. O'Connor's 7x57 Mauser, metalsmithing by Burgess, stock by Russ Leonard. Shown here with Buehler mount and Weaver K4, but it now carries a Leupold 3x.

Models 54 and 70. But what had been a mild boom for this fine little cartridge petered out. Both Winchester and Remington dropped the load with the 139-gr. bullet. They also discontinued the caliber in their line of bolt action rifles about the time WW II began.

However, in the past 20 years or so in the United States, thousands of 7x57 military rifles have been sold, turned into sporters in one way or another, and used for hunting. The cartridge has always had its admirers and hundreds of expensive custom sporters have been built for it. In 1972 Ruger made a few thousand 7x57 rifles in the Model 77 (as well as a near number of 257 Roberts rifles) and all were spoken for before they could be produced. The cartridge is a long way from being dead yet. Besides the regular load with the 175-gr. bullet, Federal Cartridge now loads a 139-gr. bullet; Dominion, one of the same weight. Velocities are in the neighborhood of 2,800 fps. Pressures are O.K. for the older Mausers. With both of these loads pressure is kept down to around 45,000 psi, I am sure, because most of them will be used in older rifles of the Model 93 type. The cartridge makes new converts every day. People like it because of its light recoil, its good killing power, and its good accuracy—not that you can't get bum 7mm barrels!

My First Little Seven

I got my first 7x57 rifle in 1934. I saw it at Bill Sukalle's shop in Tucson. Bill had put a 7x57 barrel on a remodeled action from a World War I German Model 98 Mauser sniper's rifle. It had been magnificently stocked in handsome French walnut by Adolph G. Minar of Fountain, Colorado, one of the finest classic stockers that ever lived. The stock had a German trap buttplate and a trap grip cap. It had as iron sights a Lyman 1-A peep on the cocking piece and a ramp front sight with gold bead. With iron sights, the rifle weighed slightly less than 7 pounds. However, it was equipped with a big German Gerard scope on claw mounts, which outfit added about two pounds. The scope was good optically, but because of the soft mount, it would not hold a constant point of impact. I traded the scope off. However, the rifle with iron sights was an astounding bargain at $75. That's right—$75! I took off the Lyman 1-A and had a 4x Noske scope put on with the Noske mount. The outfit then weighed less than 8 pounds.

I shot my first desert ram with that rifle, one of the best Rocky Mountain mule deer I have ever knocked off, and various other game—all with the Western factory 139-gr. open point bullet load. With one exception, everything I shot at with a 7x57 was a one-shot kill. That was a desert mule deer which I shot in one ham as he ran directly away and on which I used two cartridges. Then about 1952, I caught up. Hunting on Idaho's Snake River with another 7x57, I picked out a nice fat doe and took a crack at her. Down the hill she rolled—and also a forkhorn buck that had been standing behind her.

Sadly enough, I traded off that lovely little Sukalle-Minar 7x57, along about 1940, for an equally handsome 2-R Lovell on a Sharps-Borchardt action. Like the 7x57, it had been barreled by Sukalle and stocked by Minar. The O'Connors felt civilization crowding in on them, moved away from Tucson to Lewiston,

The 7x57 is loaded all over the world. Here is some of the good RWS (German) ammo.

Idaho in 1948. Not long after I had Tom Burgess, a crack metal man (who was then in Spokane, but who's now located in Kalispell, Montana), remodel a Czech VZ33 action and fit a 22-inch 7x57 barrel. The late Russ Leonard made the stock. Before long, my wife latched onto it. I had the stock shortened and a recoil pad installed. This 7x57 has been her favorite rifle ever since. I have no idea how many North American animals she has collected with it, but I believe I can name the species—mule deer, Rocky Mountain goat, black bear, caribou, elk, Stone sheep, Dall sheep, Corsican mouflon in Texas, and pronghorn antelope. She has also used it on the mountain sheep called *urial* in Iran and has collected most of the African antelope—including such large ones as eland, greater kudu, roan, and sable—with it on safaris in Tanzania, Mozambique, Angola, Botswana, South West Africa and Rhodesia. When she went after tiger in India, and elephant and lion in Zambia, she felt she needed a very powerful rifle, so she acquired a 30-06.

In Mozambique, our professional

hunter was the famous Harry Manners. He looked askance at her little rifle, told her she was undergunned. Before the trip was over, he was calling her One-Shot Eleanor, because—with the exception of a greater kudu, a handsome antelope about the size of a spike bull elk—everything she shot at was taken with one bullet. This kudu jumped into the air as she fired, and I called it a heart shot. My wife hit it again as it ran and yet again when it stopped. It fell at the third shot, but it had one bullet through the heart. From its actions, I am convinced it was the first one.

In the summer of 1972 my wife, our son Bradford (who is the outdoor editor of *The Seattle Times*) and I decided to make modest safaris in South West Africa and Rhodesia. Bradford took a Ruger Model 77 in 30-06 and a restocked Winchester Model 70 in 375 H&H. My wife and I did all of our shooting with two 7x57 rifles—her Mauser and my Model 70 Winchester.

Last Model 70 in 7x57

About that Model 70 in 7x57 there is a tale. It was the last 7x57 ever turned out at the Winchester factory. When I felt myself coming down with another 7x57 in 1955, I asked friends at Winchester if they could put a Model 70 in that caliber together for me. I was told this was possible as they still had exactly one (1) 7x57 barrel left. When the rifle came I sent it to Al Biesen, the Spokane, Washington, gunsmith and stockmaker. He turned down the barrel, shortened it to 22-inches, put a release button for the hinged floorplate in the trigger guard, checkered the bolt knob, made a stock of good French walnut, mounted a Weaver K4 scope on a two-piece Redfield mount. Complete with scope, this rifle weighs 7¾ pounds and will keep good bullets into less than an inch. Partly because of the light recoil, I shoot this rifle quite well. I would be hard put to imagine a much better mountain rifle. For the record, the serial number of this little dream is 361582. Prince Abdorreza Pahlavi of Iran has the next to the last Model 70 in 7x57 turned out at Winchester. He has used it extensively in Asia, Africa, Europe and North America. Likewise put together on special order, its number is 222222!

When my wife and I arrived in South West Africa in the summer of 1972, the professional hunters there told us we were undergunned—an opinion I had heard before. There, and in Rhodesia, we shot greater kudu, sable (in size midway between mule deer and elk), mountain zebra, gemsbok, and various other antelope.

Most of the animals were anchored with the first shot.

I used the 140-gr. Nosler bullet in front of 45 grains of 4320. Velocity in my Model 70 with 22-inch barrel is 2,825. This is the velocity I get in the same rifle with the Dominion 139-gr. bullet load. The Federal load, with the 139-gr. bullet, produces somewhat less velocity.

For years my wife has used various 160-gr. bullets pushed by 52 grains of 4831. Velocity in the 22-inch barrel of her rifle is 2,660. As far as I can tell, this load shoots just as flat as the 180-gr. bullet in the 30-06 and kills just as well.

In South West Africa the only animal she did not kill with one shot was an enormous kudu bull with 60-inch horns. The bull was about 300 yards away and moving. She shot twice, paunched it, broke a hip. He went about 100 yards and fell. A good bull sable she shot in Rhodesia was quartering away. The 160-gr. Nosler bullet angled through and came to rest under the hide behind the right shoulder. It ran about 150 yards. Only one lung had been hit.

Tough African Antelope

I have heard many a fanciful tale about the incredible toughness of African antelope. After much prayer and meditation and ten African safaris I cannot for the life of me see that African game is any tougher than North American game. I have used as "light" rifles on safari the following calibers: 300 Weatherby, 30-06, 270, 7mm Remington Magnum, 338 Winchester Magnum and the 7x57. I have also used on heavier animals a 416 Rigby, a 450/400 Jeffery double rifle, a 450 Watts (the predecessor of the 458 Winchester) and various 375 magnums.

As far as I can tell the little 7x57 kills African antelope from the largest to the smallest just as well as any of the cartridges I have used. I have, for instance, shot greater kudu with a 300 Weatherby, a 30-06, a 375, a 7mm Remington Magnum, a 270 and a 7x57. All kill well if the bullet is well placed, but the hunter who paunches his animal or breaks a leg is generally in trouble with any of them.

Just before writing this I read a piece by a writer who dotes on the magnums more than I do. He uses the 7x57 as a dreadful example of the non-magnum. He says that "200 yards is close to the practical killing limit of the 7x57." He adds that this is because the energy has then fallen off to about 1,400 ft. pounds.

Well, I've got news for the lad. Two hundred yards is not only the practi-

Winchester chambered the Model 54 and the Model 70 for the 7x57. A Super Grade pre-'64 Model 70 like this early one in 7x57 would bring a nice sum from a collector.

cal killing range of the 7x57, but also the practical killing range of the 30-06, the 7mm Magnum, the 300 Weatherby Magnum, and what have you. The reason for this is that very few hunters can lay the bullets into

Jack O'Connor and friend with a 38½" gemsbok, the kill made in Southwest Africa in 1972, Jack's rifle a 7x57.

This 32½-inch Mozambique waterbuck rolled over with one shot from the 7x57.

the vital area of a game animal at any greater distance, even under the most favorable conditions. In fact, I'd bet a sugar cookie that most hunters could kill stuff farther away with the 7x57 than they could with the 7mm Magnum. It would not kick them so hard. They wouldn't be afraid of it, and they would shoot it better. I have some more news: game is *not* killed by foot pounds of energy. In fact, the energy has little to do with killing power. Animals are killed by putting in the right place a bullet that penetrates deep enough and opens up adequately.

Some of the most spectacular kills I have ever seen have been made with the 7x57. A very large mule deer, standing on a frosty hillside at about 8,000 feet above sea level in northern Arizona, was hit behind the shoulder and went over like a paper deer in a puff of wind. He was literally killed in his tracks. A greater kudu bull in South West Africa was hit through the upper leg bone and heart at about 150 yards. He fell as if he had been electrocuted. A Hartmann mountain zebra, that may have weighed 700 on the hoof, went down as if poleaxed when hit through the shoulder blade at about 275-300 yards. A sable in Rhodesia was hit too far back when trotting at about 250. It ran about 50 yards and stopped. I held slightly high (6-9 inches probably) and squeezed one off. The bull sable hit the deck.

I haven't made any very long shots with the 7x57, but I try to avoid long shots with any rifle. Most game is killed at 200 yards or less, but many of these kills get stretched out when they are processed through a typewriter.

I have never used a 7x57 to kill a bear of any sort—black, blue, brown, or grizzly. However, I saw the Storm & Strife knock off a nice black with one shot. I have never shot an elk with the 7x57, but I have seen her lay two good bulls low, each with one 7mm bullet, not to mention zebra, greater kudu, sable, roan, eland, four different kinds of sheep, and what-not.

Many very fine hunters have sworn by the 7x57. I have mentioned W.D.M. Bell. That hunter of man-eating tigers, the late Capt. Jim Corbett, used a 7x57 (which he called a 275 Rigby) and a 450/400 Jeffery on these 400-500 pound cats. Prince Abdorreza Pahlavi has shot all sorts of Asiatic sheep and goats, all species of North American sheep, and most African antelope, with the Little Seven. One of the greatest sheep hunters who ever lived, the late Charlie Ren, used to shoot antelope and desert sheep with the 7x57 and the 300 Savage. He considered the 30-06 and the 270 too noisy, too violent, and too destructive of meat. If a dude had ever shown up with a magnum I think old Charlie would have busted a gasket.

Shooting the 7x57

The 7x57 is a sweet little number to shoot. Recoil is about one-third less than that of the 270, about half that of the 7mm Remington Magnum. This is going to be a hard one for a lot of people to swallow: I have shot about the same amount of game with the 7x57 and the 7mm Magnum, and if, with the same shot placement, the magnum kills any better than the 7x57, I have been unable to see it.

The handloader will rejoice to learn that the 7x57 owner has his pick among a great variety of .284'' bullets. Speer alone makes bullets weighing 115, 130, 145, 160 and 175 grains. Nosler has three weights—140, 160 and 175. Hornady can supply bullets in weights of 120, 139, 154 and 175 grains. The last can be had in either round nose or spire point styles. Anyone with a yen to shoot an elephant can usually scrounge up some old 175-gr. military "solids."

Such lighter weight bullets as the 120-gr. Hornady and the 130-gr. Speer, which can be pushed along at velocities ranging from 2,900 to above 3,000, should be excellent for antelope and open country deer. I have shot around 35-40 head of game ranging in size from Thompson gazelles (30 pounds) to greater kudu (600 pounds) and mountain zebra (700 pounds) with 140-145 grain bullets. No complaint. My wife has always stuck with one bullet weight—160 grains. In her rifle this bullet leaves the muzzle at 2,660. She sights in for 200. The bullet drops 9 inches at 300. At 400, it would probably drop about two feet, but she doesn't believe in shooting at things that far away. She says doing so is silly. I'm inclined to agree with her.

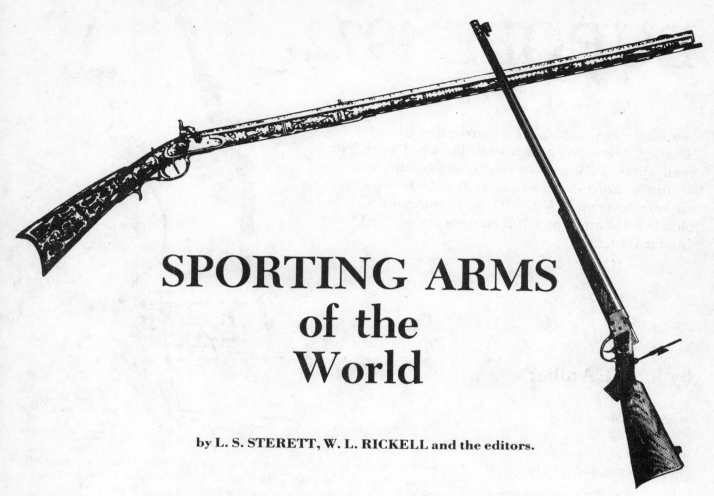

SPORTING ARMS of the World

by L. S. STERETT, W. L. RICKELL and the editors.

Though there is little letup in the introduction of new and different
modern sporting firearms, there's a strong harkening to the past, too.
More and more firms are showing single shot rifles—breechloaders
and caplocks—and the revival of various older cartridges grows
apace. Here you'll find almost all that's new in arms, ammunition and
accessories, imported and homegrown, in full detail and short.

NOSTALGIA SEEMS to have set in among manufacturers and consumers alike. The merry-go-round is moving too fast, and the idea of a time when it went slower seems to have considerable appeal. As an example, the trend a few years back was toward autoloading shotguns and rifles, but more recently the pendulum has been swinging toward muzzleloaders, single shot rifles, and replicas or modifications of old designs. The autoloaders are not dead — far from it — and they probably never will be, but more and more firms are climbing on the bandwagon with single shot rifles — breechloaders and muzzleloaders.

During the past year Harrington & Richardson brought out 4 single shot rifles — two front loaders and two centerfires. Browning has reintroduced the 1887 High-Wall single shot rifle, Jim Riedl has an excellent new SS rifle, Clerke is trying, Ruger's No. 3 carbine is available and they can't keep up with the orders for his No. 1. Thompson/Center has one in the works, besides a new 6-lb. caplock halfstock rifle, the Seneca, and North Star has a darn good muzzleloader. Mowrey has several, Navy Arms has Remington rolling block replicas and Martini target models, a host of imported muzzleloaders and a couple of new Hawken-style versions. Remington introduced a modern version of the old and long-gone Model 32 over-under shotgun, though greatly improved (wish they would reintroduce the M1816 muzzleloader). Lyman now has the Plains Rifle ready, and their own Zouave, Marlin brought out their 1895 for the 45-70 cartridge, and the M1861 Enfield Musketoon is back in production. Doubtless there are many other single shot rifles, muzzleloaders and replicas on the way.

Even some of the older cartridges, such as the 220 Swift, 250 Savage, 257 Roberts, 7x57 Mauser and the 45-70, are rapidly regaining popularity as new rifles are being chambered for them. As the man said: "Time, oh time, turn back in thy flight. Make me a boy again, just for tonight." Maybe it is pure nostalgia, but from here it looks like good times are ahead in the sporting arms field for whatever reason. LSS.

EUROPE 1972

We had an enjoyable and instructive trip to
Sweden, Germany and Switzerland last year. You'll
read about FFV and its numerous operations,
a hunt in northern Sweden that didn't come off, and
visits to Norma, RWS, SIG and Hämmerli—
plus the shooting of a full custom made Carl
Gustaf rifle.

by John T. Amber

FFV plants in Sweden.
See code below.

● HEAD OFFICE
● FACTORIES, MAINTENANCE WORKSHOPS
◐ SURPLUS SALES
○ LAUNDRIES

Sweden and the FFV

As my faithful readers (both of 'em)
will remember, my notes in this space
in our 27th edition about the FFV
Sports, Inc., (nee Husqvarna) operation in Eskilstuna, Sweden, were
relatively brief. I reported on what
seemed interesting—Gyttorp, Norma,
Saab, et al—at some length, but because my solo trip to Sweden in 1971
was no more than a curtain raiser
for the visit I made in 1972 (with
other members of the clan), I kept my
1971 notes on the short side as far
as FFV was concerned. The big year
was to be 1972—several of us would
make the trip and, unlike 1971,
we'd take part in a big älg (moose to
you) hunt in northern Sweden.

Three of us—Jim Carmichel, arms
and ammo editor of *Outdoor Life,*
and Bob Zwirz, eastern editor of
Gun World—and your agent left New
York for Stockholm on August 27.
Capt. Eric Claesson—an old, old
friend and export manager for FFV—
met us at the airport and whisked us
quickly to Eskilstuna, site of the FFV
plant and general offices. It was a
brilliant day, temperatures in the
70s, and in minutes after leaving
Stockholm airport we were surrounded by tall pine forests, deep
and dark on either side of our road.

The weather, in fact, was to continue
bright and sunny for the rest of the
Swedish visit.

Our brief stay in Eskilstuna included a trip through the FFV-Carl
Gustafs factory—which I told you
about last year—and an all-day session at John Alderin's remarkable
operation, a few miles outside Eskilstuna. Alderin owns and manages a
large distributorship handling sporting goods in great variety. To help his
customers' salespeople, Alderin built
his business on a large acreage in
the countryside. Here he erected
facilities for rifle and shotgun shooting of various types, plus similar
areas devoted to other sports. Included is a fully mechanized running
moose target—about which more
later. Alderin's idea was to bring
salespeople to his place for several-
day familiarization courses and training with the products they'd be selling
—handle them, take 'em apart and use
them, learn how they functioned, et
cetera. This excellent idea had worked well—the sales people became
more knowledgeable, learned to
discuss and describe products intelli-
gently and adequately—and they'd
enjoyed the visit to a charming rural
setting, spending much of their time
outdoors.

Why did we need to put in a full

day, nearly, at Alderins's attractive
place? A good question! That running
moose target I've mentioned—at 80
meters from the firing point, the cardboard moose travels about 15-18
miles an hour in both directions. To
obtain the required Swedish hunting
licenses we had to hit that moose four
out of 5 tries in the critical heart-
lung area (about a 10-inch rough circle) in each of three efforts! That is,
12 out of 15 shots had to hit home or
no license. Don't laugh—that vital
area isn't as easy to connect with as it
may sound. At least it wasn't for us,
which is why it took a few hours and
a fair expenditure of ammo before we
all made it—including Will Moore,
FFV's representative in the U.S.,
George Thornton, a researcher hired
by FFV, and his wife—though Mrs.
Thornton didn't shoot.

The Hunt That Never Was

Early on the morning of September
22nd we headed north for the moose
camp—us and our gear in two cars, a
Volvo and a Saab, what else? During
the preceding four days we'd visited
the Carl Gustafs factory, the FFV
main offices and the Hugelsta shooting range. We also spent an interesting several hours at the Norma
factory in Amotfors, plus another ed-
ucational and pleasurable trip to a

knifemaking plant, Knivfabrik.

All hands carried a new FFV 30-06 rifle, scope mounted—except me. During my 1971 trip to Sweden I'd ordered a custom-built FFV rifle (FFV actions and barrels are improved versions of the old and excellent Husqvarna) in 7mm Remington Magnum caliber, the stock to my order and dimensions. This is the rifle I carried, and which is shown here.

(The wood is a handsome piece of highly figured walnut, and it's equally well and extensively checkered. Rather than having caps on the butt and the grip, both are checkered. The stock is very straight, as can be seen, the line from comb nose to heel running without change in dimension—this line is a good ¼-inch higher than the bottom of the bolt sleeve, hence the long handhole and the comb nose far enough back to miss the retracted bolt. Because of the high heel position, the butt is extra deep to maintain the correct line from the toe to the guard and through it. I readily agree that the farther back location of the comb nose makes the buttstock area as a whole look a bit odd, but it fits! I can cheek the comb hard and I'm looking through the scope dead center. I don't have to raise my head any.)

Here are some dimensions—the pull length is 13¾", the drop at comb nose and heel, from the scope centerline, is 1⅝"; the butt is 5¾" deep and amply broad. The 24" barrel tapers to 0.585" at the muzzle.

Late that same afternoon we reached the hunting lodge run by Lars Wahlberg, a few miles from the town of Messlingen, almost 3 degrees from above the Arctic Circle. Lying in an area of low hills, stands of pine and hardwoods broken frequently by lush meadows, the lodge consisted of several squared/log chalet-type cabins, each with 3 or 4 rooms. All interior walls are pine paneled, with electric lights, controlled heating and hot water in all of them. All meals were laid on in a well done hilltop restaurant, belonging to the lodge, some 50 yards away. One of the chalets served as a post office and small shop, where toiletries, canned goods, candies and the like were on sale.

Our meals, of course, were essays in the Swedish cuisine—meaning cheeses and herrings in wide variety and fish, but there were other things in abundance as well. The food was excellently prepared, fresh and ample —we couldn't have eaten better in Stockholm's best restaurant, really.

Above—Amber tries a shot offhand at the running moose target. He soon sat down.

From the expression on Bob Zwirz's face, I don't think he believes a thing Carmichel is telling him. That's George Thornton looking on.

Bottom—A crossroads in northern Sweden, not far from the Arctic Circle, and a short distance from Messlingen. Carmichel and I couldn't decide whether to go upstairs or down.

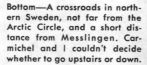

Above—the hunting lodge dining room. From left—Rolf Nordstrom, Will Moore, Bob Zwirz, Eric Claesson (skoaling someone), Jim Carmichel and George Thornton. Roughing it, huh?

Left—Rolf Nordstrom in typical Swedish hunting clothes. The dog is Lars Wahlberg's elk hound.

Left, below—there's a lot of water in northern Sweden. We made several of these short ferry trips. Good looking country, isn't it? Moose country!

Right, below—this is the 2-headed moose used as a qualifying target at our hunting camp in northern Sweden. I'm pointing to the heart-lung area that must be hit to qualify—shots striking elsewhere don't count.

Bottom—I think Jim Carmichel, pointing to the sighting-in target, is trying to tell our German co-hunter why he didn't hit into the X-ring.

I've described these primitive accommodations at some length, but I've got a reason, as you'll see.

After dinner the first night a council of war was held—all of us, some 10 people, including two Germans who'd be hunting with us, assembled in a big lounge below the restaurant. Our host, aided by Eric Claesson, briefed us on Swedish hunting customs, where to hit a moose most effectively, and told us about the area we'd be hunting in and the strategy that would find moose.

I don't know just what to call the kind of hunting we were taking part in. It wasn't a drive hunt, for there were no beaters used, and it certainly wasn't still hunting. Anyway, here's what we did. The sun gets up quite early in those latitudes, so we were roused out at 3.30 A.M., took in a

hurried breakfast (Carmichel learned to love cornflakes and sour milk), and piled into the cars for a fast, short ride to the hunting areas. Then, after walking for some 30 minutes or so, all of us, with one exception, were stationed on a long line —each man some few hundred yards (sorry, meters) from his fellow hunters on either side. In the meantime Lars, along with Rolf Nordholm (Eric Claesson's aid) had gone into the bush, taking with him the one man of our crowd not on stand. Lars had with him also a fine elk hound— well, everybody said he was a damned good dog. The plan was this—when the dog picked up a trail the small party, including our fellow hunter, would tear out, hot on the trail of the moose (or mooses). Our boy might— he hoped—get a shot or, we hoped, the animal (s) would come busting up to and/or through our line.

That, as I say, was the drill. Sad to say, it never happened—during three days of such hunting, in which we worked different country each day, man's best friend didn't pick up a single scent! I'm not low-rating that pooch, either, for after the first day I'd have been more surprised if he'd found a fresh moose track or spoor—I saw almost no tracks at all, the few I did see very old, faint traces.

In a word, we were skunked—nobody got nothin'! O, one of the fellows, I forgot who, saw a moose a hell of a ways off, or thought he did. If he did, he was the only one, and that's what hurt the most—I'd have been pretty well satisfied just to catch sight of the big critters.

But it was truly an enjoyable outing—the weather was ideal, the skies blue and the sun bright, the temperatures in the 60s and 70s. It is beautiful country, too—the terrain soft and a bit spongy, something very like the northern Scottish moorlands, the water level not far from the surface. I was glad to be a part of it all, no

No, he's not in the wild — this European bear roams about in a natural-habitat zoo in Stockholm.

matter the lack of luck. I'm long since past the time when I'd have felt frustrated and annoyed that I'd downed no game. All of us foregathered for our midday meals in some wind-sheltered glen, a good fire going, to say nothing of the usual lies and hunting tales—but that's redundant, isn't it.

We'd get back to the lodge in the early darkness, ready for a few belts, a good dinner and the sack, in that order. Half-past three would be coming round all too soon.

Our farewell to Lars Wahlberg and his beautiful lodge was a reluctant one, despite our hunt that never was, but I'm not sure it would have been so pleasant a parting if the place, the warm and friendly people, the great food hadn't been there. If only we could have spent a few more days...

Shooting the FFV/Carl Gustaf Custom Rifle

Because of rough winter weather I found few chances to fire the deluxe 7mm Remington Magnum that FFV Carl Gustaf had delivered to me during my visit to Sweden in 1972. As I've explained, we found no moose, so the rifle remained unshot when I got it home—aside from a proof round or two and my shooting to sight it in, some 3 rounds.

Setting at my 100-yard bench, early in March, I put 5 Remington 150-gr. soft points (code Y115) down range after having pushed a patch through the barrel to remove any junk it might hold. That first string shot badly—strung out vertically to 5 inches plus. Lateral dispersion was good, though, just over an inch. Those 5 did include the first shot, the bore still slightly oily and, of course, cold. I expected I might find a problem with fore-end tip pressure—or lack of it—and I checked the 3-9x Redfield scope to see if it was slipping in the rings. It wasn't.

Five Norma cartridges were shot next, these also 150-gr. weight, the bullets their semi-pointed soft point boat-tails—lot number 503124. These 5 did a lot better, going into a good round group 1.6" on centers, so my fears about the scope and the fore-end were now stilled—at least for the

moment.

Then two 5-shot groups were shot with the Remington 150's again, but though the group sizes were a bit better, the vertical component was still there—one group went 3.2", the other 2.9", these also showing slender horizontals of an inch and .92" respectively. This FFV rifle doesn't like the Remington load for some reason.

After a cleaning of the barrel, the remaining 15 Norma loads (as above) were fired in 5-shot bunches, with each performance getting slightly better. The last 5 were 1.2", the other two averaging 1.45". Quite good, I feel, for what is a rather light rifle (8¼ pounds), including the scope—and with factory ammo. Too, this session saw only 35 rounds total down

John Amber's custom FFV rifle in 7mm Remington Magnum, photographed in a Swedish glade while he waited, and waited, and waited, for a moose.

the barrel, not enough really to settle and smooth the bore.

A while later I shot some handloads, one of which is an old favorite in this caliber, a load that's done well for me on big game, here and in Africa. This old load uses 69.0 or Norma 205 and the 160-gr. Nosler bullet, seated for a total length of 3.20″. This is a full-power, near-max load, intended for game, not top accuracy, yet in this FFV rifle two groups of 5 went into a hair over 1.2″ on average. Another handload, this one with Sierra 160-gr. spitzer boat-tails and 67/4831 — a load that has given good accuracy in my Al Biesen rifle and in a Remington 700 — did only about like the Norma factory loads, or about 1.4″ for two 5-round groups. This load should do better than that, and I think altering the charge a little, up or down, should improve performance. I got a clue to that, too, for I didn't load that much 4831 right off — I started with 66.0, for 2 shots only, which showed no pressure signs, but they had printed quite close to each other.

Checkering on the custom FFV rifle is extensive, running without a break over the top of pistol grip, fully around fore-end. Bottom of pistol grip and butt are also checkered. The deep handhole and rearward location of the comb nose were necessitated by the very short drop at comb and heel.

This is a good-performing rifle as of now, and I'm sure it will do an inch or less soon. The deep butt spreads recoil nicely, and the action is beautifully smooth. The bolt moves in and out almost effortlessly, seating and extracting all of the cartridges fired with ease. Lifting the bolt handle to pull the fired cases out felt almost as though the chamber were empty — and that chamber is exceptionally well polished.

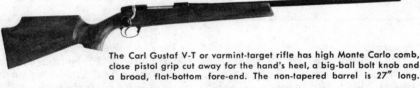

The Carl Gustaf V-T or varmint-target rifle has high Monte Carlo comb, close pistol grip cut away for the hand's heel, a big-ball bolt knob and a broad, flat-bottom fore-end. The non-tapered barrel is 27″ long.

FFV-Carl Gustaf 1973

For openers I don't think I can do better than to tell you what Eric Claesson (President of FFV Sports, Inc.) had to say in his introduction to the 1973 Carl Gustaf catalog. Here's old friend Eric:

"At FFV Sports we have combined our fine steel, our advanced technology and a 350-year tradition of arms making to bring you one of the world's truly great sporting rifles — the Carl Gustaf.

"Although our factory is totally new and equipped with the latest in precision machinery, the same pride, skill and attention to detail which went into each matchlock, flintlock and percussion rifle for the last three and one-half centuries is embodied in the current Carl Gustaf line.

"For 1973 we have added many new items which we are confident will warrant the interest of the discerning hunter and competitive shooter — a new centerfire target rifle; a new 22 match rifle; a true mirror image left-hand action and many cartridge chamberings, a few of which are not available in any other production rifle — among them the 35 Whelen Improved, a cartridge long acknowl-edged for its fine performance."

The new target rifle mentioned is the Model CG-T in 6.5x55, 308 and 30-06 calibers, with a new stock, very much in the American tradition of match stocks, designed and made by Paul J. Wright, well-known competition marksman, handloader-wild-catter and tireless experimenter. Every stock bears his name. The special order CG-T lists at $349.50, with stainless steel barrels available at extra cost. The CG-T has a *big* bolt knob, as does the V-T rifle, to be described below.

Another new target rifle, this one in 22 rimfire and called the CG-22T (to be available late in 1973), has a high comb and tight, close pistol grip associated with European match rifles. Lock time is very fast — 1.8 milliseconds — and firing pin fall is only 0.09-inch. The barrel is 19.2″ (26.8″ with a balance tube), and the trigger can be adjusted for a really light letoff — 1.1 to 1.7 lbs. Cost, $259.50.

The third Carl Gustaf varmint-type rifle, the V-T, will probably appeal to more shooters than either of the above rifles. The V-T is offered in all popular varmint calibers, from the 17 Remington through 222, 22-250, 243 and 6mm, to 6.5x55 and 25-06, though the 17 and the 6mm are special-order calibers only. The stock has a high Monte Carlo comb, a normally close pistol grip, and a broad, flat-bottomed fore-end. The stock dimensions are great enough to permit thinning it down here and there easily, but if that won't do, FFV can supply a truly rough-outside stock (fully inletted) to carve on. The straight-tube barrel is 27″ long (no iron sights fitted), the trigger can be set to as little as 18 ounces, and that big-ball bolt handle knob makes for fast, sure repeat shots. This V-T rifle let the Swedish Shooting Team take two World Records at Phoenix (Arizona) in 1970. Price of the V-T is $309.50.

The Carl Gustaf sporting rifles (Grades II and III, in regular and magnum calibers) remain about as

One of the barrel operations in the Carl Gustaf rifle factory at Eskilstuna, Sweden.

Left—the Carl Gustaf "Swede", a classic rifle with a well handled schnabel fore-end treatment, the barreled action the Grade III type. Right—the Grade II Carl Gustaf rifle in standard-caliber form. The Grade II Magnum differs only in caliber and in having a recoil pad fitted.

they were, but a number of small refinements can be readily seen—stocks are more in keeping with current American taste, checkering covers more ground, and wood quality generally has been up graded. The good aspects of all CG sporters remain unaltered—externally adjustable trigger pull, short (80°) bolt lift, silent safety that locks sear and bolt, a recessed bolt face that enshrouds the cartridge head a full 360°, and a guard-released hinged floorplate. Operation of the Carl Gustaf bolt is incredibly smooth, loaded or not; of course the well-polished chambers assist in this slick operation.

Now, in addition to offering virtually all standard calibers (from 22-250 to 30-06) the Grade II can be had chambered for the .250 Savage, 257 Roberts, 7x57mm, 280 Remington, 358 Winchester and 35 Whelen Improved—a truly wide range.

All of the Magnum chamberings are offered in the Grade II Magnum, including 458 Winchester, and recoil pads are standard on these Magnums.

Grade II rifles are $259.95, the Grade II Magnum $10 more.

Grade III rifles (standard calibers $309.50, Magnums $10 extra) are of deluxe quality—specially selected French walnut, given a high gloss

finish; special hand-cut checkering patterns; a jeweled bolt, an engraved floorplate and quick-detachable swivels.

The Carl Gustaf Grade V is new for 1973. This special-order rifle goes well beyond the deluxe Grade III— only the finest, fanciest-grain French walnut is used, a rare commodity

Triggers are being adjusted by this workman in the new FFV-Carl Gustaf sporting arms plant at Eskilstuna, Sweden.

today, and it is checkered in special patterns, generously covering the fore-end and pistol grip. The receiver,

guard and floorplate are hand-engraved in scroll designs. Price of the Grade V is $544.95, in Magnum calibers $559.95.

All of these sporting rifles (Grades II, III and V, both in standard and magnum calibers) are available with full mirror-image, left-hand actions at about $15 extra—a pretty low price differential, and one I don't think southpaws will grumble over.

The lowest cost CG rifle is the Swede, formerly called the Continental. This is a relatively simple, unadorned rifle distinguished by its schnabel fore-end, classic straight comb stock (a Monte Carlo stock is also offered) and, in my eyes, its overall gracefulness. The regular stock version comes with iron sights fore and aft; the Monte Carlo style has none. Either may be ordered with Grade II or III barreled actions ($229.95 and $264.95), and there is a wide choice of calibers, including the 257, 7x57mm and 35 Whelen Improved, the latter two new for 1973. Magnum calibers are not offered in the Swede, nor are left-hand rifles.

Barreled actions are supplied in all types except the CG-22T, prices from $162 to $419.95. Actions alone (4 types or styles) cost $109.95 to $143, the Grade V engraved action not included.

This is a Norma gunsmith testfiring a rebarreled military target rifle in Norma's 100 meter basement range. The scope seen is an auxiliary one for test purposes, not normally mounted on the rifle. Note the full sized sighting bull on the closed circuit TV screen; the screen has been pulled around to show what it looks like for this picture. The bull seen is projected on the 100 meter target and, as each shot is fired, the TV screen shows the point of impact clearly. The special spring-loaded rest absorbs all recoil; none is taken up by the shooter, thus uniformity is insured. The board on the wall behind the shooter folds down for prone position shooting.

These racks hold the several hundred rifles and barrels used in pressure testing and chronographing RWS cartridges at the Fürth factory. Handguns and shotguns are stored nearby.

Below is the long line of firing test ranges—to 500 meters—at the Dynamit Nobel (RWS) ammunition factory near Nuremberg, West Germany.

Visit to RWS

Jim Carmichel and I didn't return home after leaving Sweden. After visiting the fleshpots of Copenhagen for a day or so—including a night excursion to the famed Tivoli Gardens which proved to be pretty much all things to all people—we flew to Munich and the 20th Olympic Games. Not that we actually saw any events in the flesh—we arrived only a couple of days before the end of the Games, and we soon learned that final-event tickets were being scalped at upwards of $100 each. We gave that a pass, and settled for watching the results on a big color TV over the back bar of the hotel's cocktail lounge.

We enjoyed our brief stay in Munich—we walked several times over the pedestrian mall, always filled with crowds of people, and we went through the Hunting Museum thoroughly. An interesting collection, including a pre-historic red stag that had antlers some seven feet wide!

RWS—Europe's largest ammunition makers probably, now that DWM has gone—were our hosts at Munich, where they had a busy reception center for Olympic contestants. A charming and competent young man of their's, Franz Wolfgarten, took us in charge there and on our trip to Nuremberg and the vast RWS factory. Most ammo factories are pretty much the same, to a good degree, but we saw some interesting and different things in the RWS plant—primer manufacture, for one thing, is quite differently done compared to U.S. practices. Because of a chronic labor shortage throughout Germany, RWS employs a considerable number of foreign-born help, and among this group are many women. Jim Carmichel and I saw the entire RWS plant, but by the time we reached the test-firing and chronographing section, they were closed—inside we could see long racks filled with rifles and shotguns, a collection that's been accumulating for many years, probably since the 1870's or earlier. There must have been a thousand pieces, easily. It was frustrating!
                                                    J.T.A.

SIG and Hammerli

Our next stop was at Rhinefalls, the site in Switzerland where the Swiss Industries Gesellschaft has its factory. We made the trip from Nuremberg, via Schaffhausen, by rail, and a pleasant journey it was. We passed through lovely forested country. Rhinefalls is named for the great and broad waterfall there, the roar of the great water mass audible throughout the area. It was here that Raymond Caranta, our European editor, joined us.

At the SIG plant we saw the various models being made, much of the work

Mr. Hediger (right) general manager at Hämmerli's Lenzburg plant, explains details of the new Model 150 free pistol to Raymond Caranta, European editor for the GUN DIGEST.

on them by hand, and we saw, too, the many steps in the manufacture of their assault rifle, the Sigamt.

It was easily seen why SIG firearms, including the assault rifle, are rather expensive—close tolerances and precise workmanship were evident in all models, the military types as well. Admittedly it is a bit hard to understand why such meticulous attention should be spent on an assault rifle, but that is the SIG approach.

We also saw the two new auto pistols (not yet on the market) SIG is readying—the Models 210 and 230. However, we were asked not to reveal any of their features at this time! The three of us were allowed to shoot these new pistols—as we did the assault rifle—and accuracy of all was impressive. Car-

John Amber examines a long rackful of Hämmerli match rifles.

knew a great deal indeed about the firearms being produced everywhere else.

From Rhinefalls we went to Lenzburg and the Hämmerli factory, now owned by SIG. Target arms only are made by Hämmerli, both rifles and handguns, and I think we saw them all, including the yet-to-be-marketed models 120 and 150, both single shot match pistols in 22 Long Rifle caliber. (A 150 Hämmerli pistol was sent to me a while back. You'll find a report on it in this issue.) The handwork that goes into any of these Hämmerli handguns must almost be seen to be believed. Again, and as everyone knows, these Swiss pistols are quite expensive, but at today's prices for labor, there's a good

degree of justification for the high costs.

We also saw the manufacture of the Hämmerli "free" rifles—on which as much or more care is lavished during their building—and then we got to see the Hämmerli collection, housed in a top-floor room and seldom visited. Just about every type and variant they've ever made is stored there, all in about new condition—a collector's dream!

Raymond Caranta drove Jim and I to Zurich, where we spent a couple of days despite weather that had become a bit chilly and overcast. It was at this time that the dollar suffered its first devaluations so, apart from a few small things we didn't buy a damned thing.   J.T.A.

michel put 10 shots from the assault rifle into about an inch at the 100 meter range—and at a fairly rapid rate.

The gentleman who conducted us through the busy SIG plant was Mr. Willy Schad, and a more knowledgeable firearms man I've yet to meet. Not only was he thoroughly familiar with every machine and hand operation going on in his factory, he also

Raymond Caranta (left) and John Amber watch one of the final assembly stages of the Hammerli match auto pistol.

That's Jim Carmichel hiding behind a big Hammerli free rifle. Mr. Hediger is coaching.

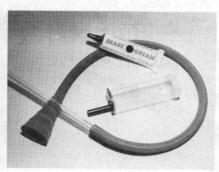

Some handy items for the black powder shooter from Caution Tool Co. Beare grease for cap-and-ball revolver; a transparent powder flask with either or both of two different-size nozzles, and a flushing-rod/hose for cleaning that muzzleloader with boiling water. All 3 items were tested, and they perform as they're supposed to.

Dem-Bart

Bill McGuire (see "Super Smoothbores" in this edition) demonstrated two Dem-Bart products at the N.S.G.A. show, and both merit mention and recommendation.

One, Continental Style Stock & Checker Oil, is simple to apply initially on new stocks, even easier for subsequent coats. The result is a low-sheen, waterproof, London-type oil finish that I find highly attractive. It also fills the pores and may be renewed at any time. The other is a Stock Filler & Sealer (no silicas or pigments) that works with two coats on most woods, and which can be applied and finished in an hour or less.

Supplied in 2-oz. bottles, either is $2.00 postpaid.   J.T.A.

BROWNING 1973

Lots of new things from Browning in 1973—the Liege over-under, a gas-operated auto shotgun, a single shot rifle, new ammo, even bicycles! Here they all are, except the new smoothbore auto, so far unseen.

This firm is going great guns—but far from exclusively! Not only has the name been changed from Browning Arms Company to just plain Browning, but the past few years have seen an expanded line of merchandise for all sports. The 1973 additions for the hunter include three new guns, plus a host of other goodies. The B-SS is now available in 20 gauge with 26- or 28-inch barrels having 3-inch chambers, a weight of 7 pounds, and a price tag of $239.50. A new 12-gauge over-under in Field and Magnum models is ready at $429.50. With a single selective mechanical trigger, the new Liége (pronounced Lee-age) can be obtained with 26½-or 28 inch barrels in the Field version and there's a 28- or 30-inch barreled Magnum.

Browning also has a new line of shotgun shells in 12, 16, 20 and 410. A new feature is a Power Rating (from 35 to 60) shown on the front of each box except on buckshot and slug loads. This rating, based on a calculation using the velocity and weight of the shot charge, can be translated into effective range via a chart on the back of every box. This enables the hunter to compare or rate one load against another for maximum effectiveness. The shells are packed 25 per box, except for the slug and buckshot loads, which come in handy 5-round packs.

In mid-1972, Browning introduced a line of rimfire cartridges in 22 Short and Long Rifle sizes. Labeled "Nail-Drivers," they carry a headstamp "B," and come packed 50 Shorts per box, while the 22 LRs come 100 in plastic slide-top boxes. The latter serve as handy loading blocks, and each also has a 3-inch rule on top to measure group size. All bullets are copper coated with a dry wax lubricant.

Browning's centerfire metallic line now includes a 180-gr. 30-06 round nose, two 25-06 rounds with 87- and 120-gr. soft points, a 9mm Parabellum with 100-gr. JHP, a 357 Magnum with 110-gr. SJHP, a 32 S&W Long with 98-gr. lead load, and the 44 Remington Magnum with a 240-gr. SJHP bullet.

Slated for introduction about the time this appears in print, or shortly thereafter, is a new gas-operated automatic shotgun. This is quite a switch from the recoil-operated autoloaders Browning has sold for so long, and it should be welcomed with open arms.

Other new items include 1-inch ring mounts for the 22 rifles, a fitted luggage style case for the B-SS shotguns, a bore cleaner and metal conditioner called "Liquid Gunsmith," and a host of new items in the outdoor clothing line, plus new sleeping bags, tents, packsacks and archery equipment, including three new bows. Bicycles, too,

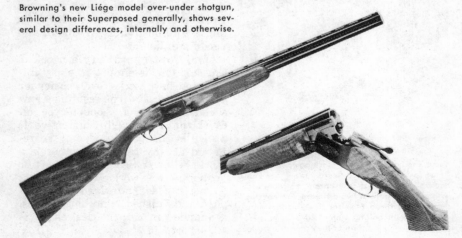

Browning's new Liége model over-under shotgun, similar to their Superposed generally, shows several design differences, internally and otherwise.

Belgian made in three grades, all 10-speed types. John M. would be proud of the way things are going.   LSS.

Browning's Big News

Browning's long-rumored new over-under shotgun, the Liège, and their gas-operated autoloading smoothbore are realities now, and both will be seen in the local gunracks about mid-summer '73, if not earlier. But more on these later, for the surprising word from Browning's Ted Collins, just received this 10 of January, is that a *single shot rifle* is ready, too, for 1973!

No picture here yet, much less a sample rifle, but it will have a dropping block action with a visible hammer, so it may well be a copy of John M. Browning's first rifle, the one he patented in 1878 and later sold to Winchester. That 1879 Model single shot, as Winchester termed it for years, became very widely known and loved as the high wall Winchester —with a low wall version, usually for the less potent calibers, appearing some years later. Me, I'm on tenterhooks; I can hardly wait to see, handle and shoot the new Browning S.S. I can't decide which caliber to get.

Four calibers will be offered initially—22-250, 6mm Remington, 25-06 and 30-06—all barrels 26" long, but differing in style, type and weight. There'll be heavy and medium weight round sporter barrels, these resulting in rifles weighing about 7¾ or 8 pounds, and a full octagon barrel in medium weight at about 7½ lbs.

Browning says high-grade steel is to be used, that barrels are tapped for scope bases, and that the trigger is adjustable—to what degree I don't know. Price of the Browning S.S. rifle, which comes without sights, is going to be about $240.

Add Browning

More details on the Browning single shot rifle have just arrived, also the picture you see here, which shows the stock treatment—shallow-curved pistol grip, schnabel tipped fore-end, checkered fore and aft, etc. In profile, at least, the receiver appears identical with the old Winchester High Wall, and I'd guess that Browning has also used the long tangs of the original, judging from the length of the hand hole and that long pistol grip. The lever top is a bit different, and the trigger seems to have an unusual form.

No metallic sights are fitted, but the rifle is supplied with the scope bases and rings pictured. According to the news release sent by Browning, "Extraction and ejection" are automatic, which may or may not indicate a kicking ejector.

I'm showing a photograph of the Liège superposed—which I haven't seen yet, either, which also goes for their gas-operated auto and another new Browning development, a 20-gauge companion to the Browning B-SS 12 bore side-by-side. From the picture I can't see that it differs materially from Browning's long-standard Superposed. The price, incidentally, is about $430, which I must say surprises me—I'd thought it would be in the $300-$350 area, if a new market were to be uncovered. At $430 it is priced exactly the same as the Browning standard grade O-U brought in 1972. Well, we'll just have to wait until the gun itself is available for inspection and discovery, which will be around the first of February at the National Sporting Goods Assn. meeting in Houston, Texas.

For now, then, the specs received from Browning on the 12-gauge Liège show it to be normal in barrel length, chokes and weights—30″ and 28″ magnums, with the usual 3″ chambers, 28″ and 26½″ standard 2¾″ chambers, and weights from 7⅞ to 7¼ pounds; the trigger is of mechanical type, the safety is manual.

The 20-gauge B-SS has 3″ chambers (the B-SS 12 does not), and two barrel lengths are listed—28″, Mod. or Full; 26″, Mod. and F. or Imp. Cyl. and Modified. The weight given for the shorter barreled gun is 6⅞ pounds, 7 for the 28″ type. I'd thought—and rather hoped—that this new side-by-side 20 would be lighter, but I suppose those shooting 3″ magnum 20 loads need a gun of fair heft.

I received no dope at all on Browning's gas-operated auto, and it isn't scheduled, I gather, for display at the NSGA show. However, its advent is firmly committed, with its announcement set for mid-1973. Still, maybe we can unearth something before press time, and if so... J.T.A.

New Browning "Power Rated" Shotshells

Browning has added shotgun shells to their ammunition line. Centerfire rifle and handgun ammunition was introduced early in 1971. Rimfire 22 Nail-Drivers in the summer of 1972, and now—Browning offers shotshells in all popular gauges.

These new shotshells feature a fast "Power Rating Index" (PRI) that lets you instantly rate one load against another.

A 35 to 60 Power Rating is clearly stamped on every shell and every box except on buckshot and slug loads. The PRI is based on a calculation using the velocity and weight of the shot charge.

Browning's new single shot rifle, a handsome addition to the line.

Depending on the choke of a shotgun and the shot size selected, the Browning PRI can be translated into effective range. The higher PRI shells are used for the longer shots and tougher game. Lower ratings are for smaller game, shooting over dogs or close-in hunting.

Different PRIs can be combined for maximum effectiveness, say, a 40 Power for the first shot followed by a 45 and 50 Power for the second and third shots.

A chart on the back of every box shows the Power Rating of all Browning shotshells. Dram equivalency,

Browning's Power Rated shotshells, a new concept in performance evaluation.

weight of shot charge, and shot size are stamped on the lid of every box for detailed identification. However, the PRI goes a step further—it reduces drams equivalent and weight of shot charge to a simple common denominator. A common denominator loaded with benefit for every hunter.

Browning's Variety Big

Time was, and not awfully long ago, when "Browning" meant firearms, and firearms only. Not today. Though Browning has more guns than ever, it also covers much of the outdoor world—and what it doesn't offer this year you'll probably find a Browning label on a year or so

hence.

Bicycles? Yes, three grades of 10-speed bikes show the Browning marque for 1973 (priced from $114.50 to $240.50) and they're also made in Belgium. These were seen at the Houston N.S.G.A. meeting, in styles for men and women, and excellent quality was the keynote throughout. The Model V, at the top of the line, weighs only 26 pounds.

Now, in addition to the products added to the Browning camp in recent years—scopes, mounts, ammo (see details on their cartridges elsewhere in this section), foot wear, fishing tackle, knives, archery gear, boats, golf carts, vaulting poles, and gun cases—you'll find hunting clothes, sleeping bags, pack frames, binoculars, tents, trap and skeet shell carriers and, quite recently introduced, Browning Liquid Gunsmith. This last, sold in spray cans, is equally useful before and after shooting. It prevents powder and primer fouling build-up, cures the same condition after shooting. It also inhibits rust and has good lubricating qualities. In addition to their big catalog, Browning has detailed brochures on these several sidelines, all for the mere asking. J.T.A.

Browning's B-SS shotgun, now offered in 20 gauge.

COLT SAUER

The new bolt action rifle introduced by Colt is most unusual, even unique in several areas. Here's how it works, plus a shooting report.

Colt Sauer Rifle

Colt's first seminar for gun writers was held in a beautiful part of the country—Cimarron, New Mexico was the scene for this initial gathering, a small town lying in the high hills of the northeastern part of that "Land of Enchantment."

Cimarron is in good mule deer territory, which is why Colt brought a gaggle of writers and company men that far off instead of having the session at Hartford or somewhere closer to home base. Not only would Colt introduce a new bolt action big game rifle to us; there'd be enough of the Colt Sauers on hand to let each of us grab one and go ahunting.

First, though, we put in a morning going over the new rifle, getting the full story on it via a slide show in color that was expertly done.

The Colt Sauer is a well-turned-out rifle, and a handsome one in the modern fashion—wood and metal, finished to a high gloss, are closely and smoothly joined at all points, including the edges of the fore-end inletting. The barrel is nominally free-floated except for a 2-point bearing about two inches abaft the fore-end tip, but in the rifle I have the left rear side of the fore-end, for about two inches, bears against the barrel. That area of contact showed up in the bench shooting I did after getting home, which I'll come to later on.

If you're familiar with the less-gaudy grade Weatherby rifles, you have a good idea of how the new Colt Sauer looks—flattish fore-end bottom and sides, Monte Carlo cheekpiece-comb, a slanted fore-end tip and grip cap (of rosewood) set off by white-line spacers, as is the ventilated rubber recoil pad. The multi-point checkering, hand cut and well executed, covers a goodly area of the fore-end sides and pistol grip. The stock is American walnut, most of them showing a nice amount of figure, though by the luck of the draw—

we pulled numbers from a hat at Cimmarron—Neal Knox and I got somewhat plainer grades.

It's the action and the barrel-action joining that makes the Colt Sauer highly unusual and, I think, genuinely unique in some aspects. First, here's a turnbolt rifle—which owes virtually nothing to Oberndorf am Neckar—with a bolt that doesn't turn! Lifting the bolt handle—which takes only about 55 degrees to open—and removing it reveals a uniform and big diameter bolt from front to rear, no lugs readily visible. But they are there, *at the rear,* three of them spaced equally around the circumference of the bolt body. Here's how they work—the lugs pivot at their front ends, being cammed into open (locking) or closed position as the bolt handle is lowered or raised. This is a fully positive locking-up, note, so there need be no fear that the lugs may retract into their bolt recesses accidentally—each lug locks firmly into a mating recess inside the bridge. This locking action is caused by studs or projections, at the rear of the firing pin, forcibly moving the locking lugs outward as the firing pin or striker rotates. Concealed cam tracks, engaging a short stud at each lug's rear, retract the locking lugs as the bolt handle is lifted.

Barrel Lock-Up

This is essentially a simple system, but it must be costly to produce, as must be, also, the method of fitting the barrel to the receiver ring. The Colt Sauer receiver ring becomes a heavy, square mass underneath, and it is divided by a vertical cut that extends upward to the barrel threads. After the barrel is threaded home, opposing Allen screws of big size, passing through the squared ring extension, are control-torqued to factory specs. Into the center of this cut or slot goes a threaded bolt or pin, which acts to equalize the mating thread pressures all around the barrel. This same pin serves as an action bolt; its external threads are engaged by a screw-slotted cap passing through the front of the plate that surrounds the magazine recess. The back face of this split ring acts as a recoil lug. The stock also beds at the sides of the square section and on the long flats at the rear of the action.

The Colt Sauer rifle has no box magazine, cartridge follower or floor-plate as these are usually understood. Instead, quick detachable 3-shot magazines are used, their base lying flush with the bottom of the fore-end. A spring-loaded release lever permits their instant release. Cartridges lie in a single column, not staggered, thus the top round is carried higher than usual, offering a nearly straight-line feed into the chamber. Cartridges, I found, are stripped out of the magazine very smoothly and surely. Twin vertical grooves in the magazine walls prevent the cartridges from slamming forward as the rifle recoils—pointed soft points will remain pointed.

Headspacing of barrels is adjusted in an unusual way, too. The breech face of the barrel abuts against a steel washer made of shim stock, the individual laminations some 0.002" thick. One or more of these is removed to control headspace on initial assembly. After proof firing, head-

Above—This is the 1973 Colt Sauer centerfire bolt action rifle in standard form. Below is the 1973 Colt Sauer Grand African model, caliber 458 Winchester.

space is checked and, if necessary, re-adjusted. At first glance this would seem to be a time-consuming technique, hence costlier than the standard method of running a finish reamer in, but perhaps Sauer has found a way.

New Trigger System

The Colt Sauer trigger system is new and quite different. Its outstanding feature is a roller that acts as a sear, the idea being to reduce friction and hence gradual wear, as occurs with the usual sliding sear-firing pin system. On pulling the trigger—which is adjustable for preliminary take-up or slack, weight of pull and over-travel—a toggle linkage, which holds the roller against the firing pin, gives way, letting the firing pin move forward to strike the primer as the roller

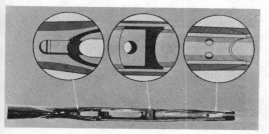

Colt Sauer bedding. The receiver bottom rests squarely on two points—around the top tang screw and on the flat behind the recoil lug opening. The barrel is free-floated all the way forward except for two integral wood pads, these positioned 45° from the barrel centerline.

sear drops downward. An ingenious system, but one not without a fault—to break the toggle joint, the sear body must be pushed upward a little, so in practice a 3½-pound pull is said to be about the lightest obtainable.

My sample Colt Sauer had a trigger pull of 5¼ pounds when I got it. Weight of pull can be altered, without removing the stock, by means of a spring-loaded rod bearing against the back of the trigger, near its top. A small pin or paper clip, inserted into one of 4 holes in this rod and turned counterclockwise, decreases pull weight, say the instructions. It didn't work that way—turning the pin counterclockwise made the pull heavier, and I reached 6½ pounds after some 3 full turns or so. Turning the pin the other way, or clockwise, I got a 3-lb. pull—or I did according to my pull gauge.

The adjustment screw for take-up is reached through a hole in the front-top of the trigger, but because it is a slotted-head screw it is impossible to turn unless the guard is removed or the short side of an Allen wrench is ground to make a blade form. An

Allen screw at this point would be an improvement.

Two more design aspects of the Colt Sauer are different and unexpected. At the root of the bolt handle, on top and readily accessible, is a small (about ³⁄₁₆″) plunger pin. With the top tang safety pushed to "on," which locks bolt and sear system, thumb pressure on this plunger permits raising the bolt handle to eject a chambered round in perfect safety, or the magazine load, for that matter.

Chamber Telltale

The second of these innovations is a "loaded chamber" indicator, a short headed-pin inserted into the left side of the receiver ring, about at 10 o'clock. The bolt face is recessed in the modern fashion; the ejector is the plunger-pin type, the extractor a short and narrow (³⁄₁₆″ wide by ¹⁷⁄₃₂″ long) pivoting piece which cuts into the bolt face wall the same ³⁄₁₆″. However, to make room for the loaded-chamber indicator pin, there's another ³⁄₁₆″ U-shaped segment cut in the wall of the recess. With a cartridge in the chamber, the spring-loaded indicator pin is raised slightly from its otherwise flush position, and can be readily felt, no need to even glance down. A convenience and a safety factor as well, but if a case burst on firing gas could escape easily via the bolt-face cut and the hole for the indicator pin. The pin itself, in this remote contingency, would not be blown out, I think. It has a rim or flange at its inside end.

The bolt has 3 gas-escape ports, holes of about ⅛″, sited at 3 o'clock along the bolt body. There is no gas port in the receiver ring. The bolt sleeve is capped to contain or divert escaping gases. An extension of the sear body projects rearward, its top painted red, to show that the bolt is cocked.

The Colt Sauer isn't that long an action, but it looks bigger and longer because of its design. The left wall of the receiver rises solidly to well beyond the centerline of the action—which should make for good stiffness. From the front of the receiver ring to the rear of the bridge proper is 6¾ inches (compared to 7 inches for a Model 70 Winchester), but the receiver actually continues rearward to give a length of 8 ⁵⁄₁₆ inches; adding the tang-safety section makes overall length 10 inches. The M70 is 9⅜ inches long, top tang included. The Colt Sauer bolt is 7 ⁵⁄₁₆ inches long, its diameter with my mike .744″.

Bolt takedown is easily done. After removing the bolt, a short pivoting lever, lying in the bolt body an inch ahead of the bolt handle, is depressed

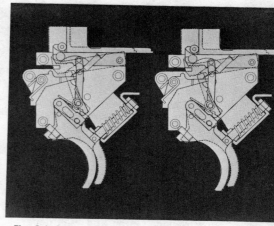

The Colt Sauer trigger system. A roller-bearing sear eliminates friction compared with the usual sliding surfaces arrangement.

and the bolt handle turned down. This action cams the locking lugs outward (as it does with the bolt in the rifle) and the cocking sleeve-firing pin, etc., may be pulled out to the rear. Re-insertion is equally fast and foolproof—the bolt cannot be assembled incorrectly.

My Colt Sauer weighs an even 9 pounds with the 3-9x Redfield Wide Field scope, but without ammo in the magazine. It is a 30-06, as were all the others used on the Cimarron outing. Other calibers available are 25-06, 270, 7mm Remington Magnum and 300 Winchester Magnum, all with 24-inch barrels. There's also the Grand African, caliber 458, with a 26-inch heavier barrel. This one weighs 10½ pounds, and is stocked in African bubinga wood, whatever that is. The barrel carries an ivory bead on a hooded ramp, the rear sight a sliding adjustable type. The Grand African is priced at $425.

* * * * * *

The Colt Sauer bolt. Arrow A shows bolt handle release button, used to unload safety-locked bolt. B indicates locking lugs, shown here in locked position. Arrow C is lever used to take bolt apart, D points to extractor hook. The 3-gas-escape holes lie at 3 o'clock when the bolt is closed.

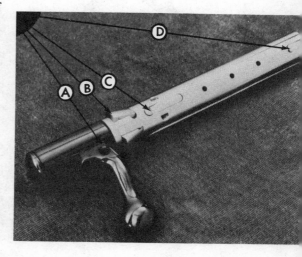

Back to the hunting. After our morning briefing, sighting-in was in order. My rifle printed about 1½ inches high at 100 yards, after a few scope clicks, using the 180-gr. Peters Core-Lokt ammo supplied by Colt. That would put me on aim at some 175 yards, I thought.

Early the next morning we all rolled out—some of us to hunt on horseback, others from various FWD vehicles. Old friend Pete Barrett (gun editor for *TRUE*) and I went off together, our guide Gene Bales of the New Mexico Game and Fish department. All the hunting would be on the big acreage of the UU-Bar ranch, where plenty of mule deer and wild turkey, plus some elk, are generally found. We'd all be hunting deer; our licenses didn't cover elk.

The first day Pete and I had a bit of climbing in great weather, but no shots. We saw several deer, way too far off or too high up in the timber. The next day was more of the same, but we knew the country a little better now, so Pete and I made a long haul on the contours of the slope, one of us high up, the other (me) below. We'd driven the Jeep higher, too, which helped—Gene stayed with the vehicle for a while, ready to signal us if a deer was seen, but it was Pete's good hunting on his own that paid off. He put down a nice buck some couple of hundred yards off. I didn't get lucky, so that was that, for the next day we'd all be heading for home. But in view of the hunting lasting only a couple of days, the

High above the lower UU-Bar Ranch country near Cimarron, N.M. The rifle is the new Colt Sauer.

group's success was excellent, some 70%, I believe, having scored. Pete and I are going back to New Mexico this fall, though—Bales told us he'd seen several antelope in a certain location with horns better than 16 inches, including a couple he swore went 18 inches!

All of the Colt Sauer rifles had performed well during the brief hunting, though admittedly no big number of shots was fired. I find the hills steeper these days, so I'd have felt better with a lighter rifle, but none of the young guys were

bothered, not audibly at least. Certainly the Colt Sauer operates beautifully smoothly—the non-rotating, well-fitted bolt accounts for much of that slick, Krag-like motion.

Accuracy from the bench, later on, was quite good. The same Peters 180-gr. loads went into an average 1½ inches for 5 shots, but some W-W 180-gr. soft points touched about 2 inches. As I'd suspected, that left-side barrel and fore-end contact put my groups several inches to the right of where they ought to have been; I'd collimated the crosshairs of the Redfield 3-9x to dead on zero before firing. I went left some dozen turret divisions to put me on the target, but group sizes remained about the same. My best group was shot with 48/4895/165 Speers, 5 into an inch even, slow fire. Not a top load, of course, but pleasant to shoot and usually quite accurate. If I shot at all fast I got angled groups—upward and to the right. The 24-inch barrel is pretty light, only .550″ at the muzzle, and it seems to heat pretty fast.

All in all, a well-made, good performing and—if the Now styling is your bag—a good looking rifle. I'm afraid I find it also a little over-engineered, but that's progress, I suppose. At $394.95 ($399.95 for Magnums) it isn't cheap, but the quality workmanship and materials in the Colt Sauer run high, especially these days, so the new rifle is good value.   J.T.A.

Earmuff Hearing Protectors

Most shooters of my generation are deaf to one degree or other—even ear plugs weren't around at the time of the Spanish-American War! Maybe

the shooters of today and tomorrow will show more sense, and wear a set of the now-numerous brands of hearing safeguards offered.

David Clark Co. (360 Franklin St., Worcester, MA 01604) has several such devices, all efficient protectors of their type and all with replaceable ear seals. Clark's Straightaway Universal Hearing Protectors cost from $6.75 for the E-305-S, an overhead type, to $12 for the 10As model, said to be the "most effective" of its kind. There are also 3 intermediate versions ($6.75 and $7.50), one of which, the E-310-S, can be worn with headband over, behind or underneath the earmuffs.

The Silencio earmuff can also be used in any desired position—the lightweight thermoplastic ear cups rotate 360 degrees, and each may be adjusted for best comfort in any direction separately as well. The Silencio protects the hearing in the critical 1000-4000 cycle range, and its component parts are easily dis-

assembled for washing and sterilizing. At $6.95 a set, these are a good investment in hearing loss protection. The makers are Safety Direct, Box 8907, Reno, NV 89507.   J.T.A.

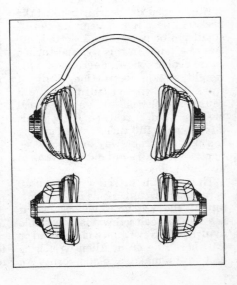

This is the David Clark Straightaway hearing guard, wearable in most any position.

REMINGTON 1973

It looks much like the old and long dead Model 32, but there are many important design changes in the new Remington 3200.

Remington Seminar 1973

Well, the 11th Remington annual gathering of writers and editors having to do with firearms—and related stuff—actually took place in November 1972, but it was '73 products we were introduced to, with one exception I'll get to later.

The big news from Ilion this time around is big news indeed—the long-rumored, long-awaited, Model 3200 over-under shotgun—a much-delayed lineal descendant of the famous Model 32 was shown to the assembled hands in all of its glory. That's not entirely hyperbole either, for Remington didn't do things by halves at this latest Seminar.

We saw and handled—maybe fondled's a better word—five (5) versions of the 3200, each more handsome and alluring than the last, and more expensive, too! Like $1050 for the top of the new series, the 1 of 1000 grade, a trap gun that is going to be produced in exactly that quantity, no more.

Word about this relatively limited production figure got noised abroad mighty quickly, it seems, for as early as late January virtually all of the Model 3200s in the 1 of 1000 grade had been spoken for or reserved. Many of these orders were by individuals, too, though jobbers got their requests in, of course. Is, then, $1000-plus a lot of dough for a shotgun or are enough of us at such an affluent stage that a grand is no longer big money?

As I've said, the new 3200 derives in good degree from the long-defunct Remington 32—that gun was made from 1932 to 1942, the total number delivered not very many, really. Today the old 32, a highly innovative design itself, is much sought for, by Skeet shooters particularly, and they bring a premium price, one well over their cost some 30 years ago.

Make no mistake, though—the new over-under by Remington is *not* the old 32. Sure, they're superficially alike, for much of what was good in the 32 is retained in the 3200—the distinctive separation of barrels and the sliding top lock over the breech. Side by side the two over-unders (see our illustrations) look quite similar, but a close look reveals several important changes, improvements that make the 3200 a truly new design.

Model 3200 Features

The open air space between the barrels (increased over the 32 design) offers advantages over barrels joined conventionally. Rising heat waves (mirage) are more quickly dissipated and the barrels cool faster between shots because the air circulates fully around them. Expansion and elongation of one barrel can't affect the other, which can happen in ordinary over-unders and thus change the point of impact for both tubes. This freedom of barrel movement in the 3200, without any penalty, is achieved through Remington's unique system of banding the barrels together at the muzzle. This dove-tail spacer design allows the barrel(s) some fore-and-aft movement and, because it is adjustable, it allows the factory to pre-set the spacer element for the optimum point of impact, whether the gun be a field, Skeet or trap Model.

Not least, by no means, the non-joined barrels mean less steel out front, making for a better-balanced gun, with more weight between the hands. The 3200 barrels appear more tapered, too, for the muzzle-wall thickness seemed less compared to a 32 examined. That, if true, would aid further in bringing balance rearward.

Neither the old 32 nor the 3200 have underlugs for locking (bolting), thus both have low-profile frames. However, the 3200 has massive divided lugs on each side of the lower barrel, these looking into frame buttresses for high strength and rigidity. A semi-circular cut in the front of each side lug bears against short and integral frame pins, these acting as pivots when the gun is opened or closed. There is, of course, no full-width hinge pin as such. These locking lugs, located just below the centerline of the bottom barrel, direct recoil nearly straight back to the shoulder, lessening the upward thrust of the comb against the shooter's cheek. There's less muzzle jump, too, and faster recovery for the second shot.

The triggers on the 3200 are not, I'm glad to see, of the inertial type. Their action is mechanical, meaning that the second barrel fires even if the first barrel was empty or held a dud cartridge. Practice firing has been taken care of, too—a new design feature prevents the hammer striking the firing pin when the chamber(s) is empty—a good idea indeed, no snap-caps needed.

At the Remington Seminar—John Linde (left) head of the design-team that produced the Model 3200 over-under. Center, Sam Alvis, now-retired research chief, and his successor, Wayne Leek.

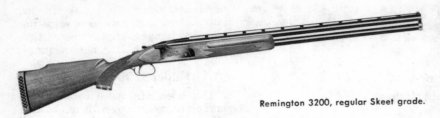

Remington 3200, regular Skeet grade.

Barrels at left are on the new Remington 3200 over-under, those at right on a 32. There's more airspace between barrels and an airier ventilated rib on the 3200, plus a different muzzle lockup as well. one that's adjustable for varying point of impact and that allows barrel elongation when the barrel(s) heat up.

The safety on the 3200 is wholly new. Lying atop the upper tang is a short lever which, when positioned straight ahead, is on "safe". Pushed left, it leaves the bottom barrel ready to fire; moved right, the top barrel fires. Removing this lever, which is readily done, locks the device in place for one barrel or the other, leaving the gun ready to fire at all times. This system will appeal to claybird shooters, for the gun cannot, then, be inadvertently made "safe" and a target thereby lost, perhaps.

Lock time of the Remington 3200 is remarkably fast—1.4 to 1.8 mille seconds, which Remington engineers believe to be faster than that of any other available shotgun. According to Remington, the shot leaves the muzzles of a 3200 before the shell crimp opens in most shotguns. This ultra-fast lock time could take some getting used to; it might alter lead practices!

Genuine American walnut is used on the 3200, the finish Remington's tough RK-W treatment. The 20-line checkering—applied by a so-far secret Remington technique—is surprisingly good. Every raised diamond is perfect, and covering is generous, especially so on the fore-end. Checkered brown plastic forms the buttplate and grip cap, blending in nicely with the warm-toned walnut. Wood-to-metal jointing is excellent, though the wood stands slightly above the frame flats and tangs. That's not ideal or perfect, of course, but better than having the stock widths undersize.

Remington's Gamble

This is as good a time as any to comment on the whys and wherefores of the 3200's emergence at this time, a period of high costs generally, and certainly high costs for hand labor and craftsmanship. Remington was determined that the new 3200 would have to exhibit—or exceed—the quality and craftmanship of olden days; that it would have to be priced competitively with the best over-unders available, and that it would have to be a better gun than the old 32.

I think Remington has succeeded

admirably, and I'm not alone. Everyone at the Seminar, with no exceptions I could note, was highly enthusiastic over the 3200, introduced there by the head of its design department, John P. Linde. I've rarely seen such acclaim for a new firearm, and such a vocal one.

Modern machine design—automated yet precision machine tools for fast, high quality production of steel and wood components—is responsible in good part for the existence of the Remington 3200, the only quality over-under made entirely in the United States. There is, to be sure, hand work and hand fitting in the 3200, but it's not the almost wholly handmade shotgun the 32 was.

My 3200, standing in a corner over there, is their Skeet grade, one of 5 variants offered. I think it's a handsome over-under—it shows a trim, graceful profile, its balance—at the hinge—putting the main mass between the hands, and it comes up very well. It isn't quite as long in the pull length as my conformation demands—no standard shotgun is—

A couple of the cock pheasants shot at Shagbark Game Farm with the Remington 3200 over-under Skeet grade.

Center right—Lower gun is old Remington 32. Note 3-position safety-barrel selector on tang of Remington 3200.

There are considerable differences in fore-end latches between the old 32 (right) and the new 3200, both visible and hidden.

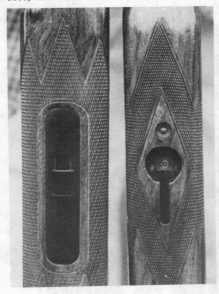

and it is a bit heavy at 8¼ pounds as a field gun.

But it handled and shot well the other day at Shagbark Game Farms (near Hebron, Illinois) where several of us had some good pheasant shooting. I was using target-load 8s on those close-rising birds, and only twice did I shoot the top barrel—unavoidably! I'd hoped to report on pattern performance, but there's been too little time.

Models and Grades

Here's a rundown on the various Remington 3200 models, their specs and prices, as of March 1973:

The new gun will be made initially in 12-gauge only, and in trap, Skeet and field versions, each with appropriate barrel lengths and choke combinations.

Trap and Skeet models have full, beavertail fore-ends; field models have a slimmer, less bulky type. Trap models have regular or Monte Carlo stocks, both with recoil pads. Field and Skeet models have the "rosewood-toned," checkered buttplates and grip caps I've mentioned.

There is, in addition, the 3200 "Special" trapgun, made with selected choice American walnut and carrying distinctive cut checkering.

The big Special, as noted above—and to commemorate Remington's return to over-under shotgun production, is their One of 1,000 trap grade. Remington will produce, in 1973 only, exactly 1000 of these guns, each marked *One of 1,000* in gold on the side of the frame. These will have consecutive serial numbers, from 1 to 1,000, also appearing in gold.

Stocks and fore-ends on these One of 1000 guns will be best quality, highly figured American walnut, the cut checkering extremely attractive. The frame, trigger guard and fore-end latch will be floriate engraved in a style and quality usually found on guns costing thousands of dollars. A gold-inlay grip cap sets off the stock. In keeping with their high quality, each One of 1000 comes in a special carrying case.

All 3200 guns have 2¾" chambers, auto ejectors, wide selective single trigger and vent-rib barrels, a top-tang safe combined with barrel selector lever. The frame is one-piece steel, with shield-covered, locking breech. Ivory front and middle beads are put on target models; there's a metal front bead only on field grades. Average weight of trap guns, 8¼ lbs., Skeet and field types (26" barrels) 7¾ lbs.

Barrel length, chokes available and prices follow:

Barrel Lengths, Chokes, Stock Dimensions and Prices

Field	26", 1C & M	1½" x 2⅛" x 14"	$ 450
	28", M & F		
	30", M & F		
Skeet	26", Sk & Sk	1½" x 2⅛" x 14"	470
	28", Sk & Sk		
Trap	30", IM & M	1½" x 1¾" x 14⅜"	490
	30", F & F	1½" x 2" x 14⅜" (MC)	540
			1050

Remington's Model 541S

This is the non-new 22 rimfire rifle shown at Remington's late-1972 Seminar—which was also unveiled at the 1971 Seminar, for the first time. For some reason unknown to me (maybe they were too busy with the 3200?), the 541S failed to appear in 1972.

The 541S is a handsome bolt action rifle, light and trim at 5¼ pounds. A pretty happy compromise was reached in its general dimensions, too—pull length is 13⅜", distance from trigger to fore-end tip is 16½"; the 24" tapered barrel is not a featherweight,

either; the muzzle mikes 0.620". It can be seen from these figures that the 541S is well suited to shooters in their teens and to adults also.

Pistol grip and fore-end carry a good bit of Remington's new cut checkering—the diamonds raised and excellently done. The wood on our sample is real walnut, of good density and nicely figured. Buttplate, grip cap and fore-end tip are dark brown plastic, joined to the wood with the omnipresent white spacers. There's no cheekpiece, I'm glad to report, but the comb-nose fluting isn't as well designed or executed as it might be—they're too broad and they angle downward too much. The wood carries Remington's RK-W glossy finish, durable and scratch resistant.

All metal parts are softly blued—not shiny—and there's some foliate engraving on the receiver top and the guard. Metallic sights are not supplied, but the barrel is tapped at the muzzle and about 18" rearward for such sights. The receiver top is grooved for tip-off scope mounts, and tapped fore-and-aft as well for use of conventional scope bases. Swivels or swivel studs are not fitted to the 541—which will please some, but doesn't me. The plastic-shell 5-shot clip magazine—which functions well if a little hard to remove—drops below the bottom stock line about ⁵⁄₁₆-inch, as does the clip release device, to a lesser extent. These protruding

pieces spoil the lines, for me, of what is otherwise a handsomely profiled rifle.

The trigger pull in our test 541S was too heavy to suit me at nearly 5 pounds, but it didn't take long to get it down to just over 2 pounds—the 541S trigger system lets pull weight be altered, but Remington frowns on tinkering with the trigger-engagement or trigger-stop screws. Striker fall on this 541S, at least, is very good indeed—just about dead, no vibration or clatter.

A light 6-8 mph wind, out of the northwest, was working over my 50 yard range, with some gusting, but I don't think the performance of the 541S suffered much. With a 6x Weaver scope aboard, and using Remington Kleanbore 22 Long Rifles mainly, several 5-shot groups of an inch or so were made—the biggest went into 1.3 inches, and two groups were barely under 0.85 inch. A few rounds of old Western Match ammo failed to do well, for some reason—age, maybe. Two groups of 5 averaged 1.4 inches.

A very well done rifle, this Reming-

Remington's Mike Walker here holds the 1973 left-hand version of the Model 700 rifle.

The Remington 1100 special gun made for Ducks Unlimited.

ton 541S, though I'd like to see sling swivels supplied and an out-of-sight magazine and release lever. It's pleasant to handle and shoot, and I like the excellent trigger.

Remington's Southpaw 700

A left-hand version of the Model 700 Remington bolt action rifle—a rifle that's prime choice of so many shooters—was seen at the 11th Seminar and later introduced officially at Houston early in 1973. These lefty 700s are full mirror-image versions of the right-hand rifles—bolt handle, safety and ejection are all to the left.

The Remington 700 is too well known to need elaboration here and now, but for 1973 the left-hand 700s will be available in BDL grade only.

Special Remington 1100 Auto Shotgun For Ducks Unlimited

This special and limited edition of Remington's highly popular 1100 shotgun commemorates the completion of Ducks Unlimited's 1,100th wildlife habitat project.

The DU Special 1100 will be made in 12 gauge with a 30-inch full choke, ventilated rib barrel. Centered in the gilded scrollwork on the left side of the receiver is a colorful Ducks Unlimited medallion in red, white, blue and gold. In addition, these DU commemoratives will be serialized using a selected block of numbers with a DU prefix, also in gold.

Included in the price of the DU Special 1100 is a monetary contribution to Ducks Unlimited. Individual owners, as a result, will have not only a handsome, limited edition shotgun, but visible evidence of their DU support wherever the gun is displayed or used.

By issuing this commemorative gun, Remington recognizes the valuable work done by Ducks Unlimited for the past 36 years in restoring, maintaining and creating new water foul habitat in North America.

Oakley & Merkley

The Oakley & Merkley booth at the NRA 1972 meeting attracted all the custom gun buffs, including the custom gunmakers, of course. At left, Clayton N. Nelson of Enid, OK and Dale Goens of Cedar Crest, NM, neither needing much introduction.

Esopus Gun Works

A new name to most shooters, this New York state firm has only one sporting arm at present, the TB-1. A 2-shot percussion, muzzle-loading rifle in 45 caliber, weighing 8½ pounds with 28-inch barrels, the TB-1 is an over-under rifle with rotating barrels, and only two moving parts in the lockwork. The buttstock is American black walnut with solid brass buttplate, trigger guard, and patchbox with steel lid. A two-piece walnut fore-end is used, giving the rifle a better appearance and a more positive grasping surface for the supporting hand. Each of the barrels carries a V-notch open sight and a brass blade front sight. With two ramrods, the TB-1 is $139.50.

The second arm is a totally new concept in percussion muzzle-loading rifles. Using a one-piece, pistol grip walnut stock with beavertail fore-end, the Pacer is modern in every detail. The 26-inch tapered round 45-caliber barrel carries a ramp front sight and a Williams adjustable rear sight. The breech mechanism has a side-mounted straight line striker, or hammer, and an automatic safety that goes "on" when the mechanism is cocked. Priced at $99.95, the Pacer weighs about 6 pounds, and comes complete with an aluminum alloy ramrod.

RUGER 1973

New from Southport is a great Single Six revolver, designed for utmost safety, and a military-police styled autoloading rifle, the Mini-14. The Single Six report is in our Handgun Review section, but here's a Testfire Report on the Ruger No. 3 Carbine, and detailed data on the Mini-14.

Sturm, Ruger

Originally a handgun manufacturer, Ruger entered the long arm field with the introduction of his 44 Magnum Carbine, followed by a similar rimfire, the No. 1 single shot rifle, and the M77 line of bolt action rifles. A No. 3 single shot rifle, chambered for the 45-70 cartridge, was introduced last year, but deliveries did not get under way until early 1973. The over-under shotgun, still in development, may have its first showing at the 1973 NRA meeting in Washington, but it probably won't be on sale before the 1974 hunting season...if then. New designs take a long time from drawing board to delivery.

The No. 3 carbine will be available in 22 Hornet and 30-40 Krag by the time this appears in print, and the M77 rifle will be offered in 220 Swift caliber, though perhaps in a limited run. The M77 was also made in 1972 in 7x57 and 257 Roberts, these calibers also in short runs, some 3000 rifles of each. All, we were told, sold very quickly.

Three variations of the excellent double action Security-Six handgun have been introduced, including a stainless steel version that goes for $135, plus greatly improved lockwork on the Single-Six single action models, but the biggest news is the Mini-14. This last gem is a semi-automatic carbine chambered for the 223 (5.56mm) cartridge. Looking much like the military 7.62mm M14 rifle, but scaled down for the smaller cartridge, the Mini-14 is based on the M14 and M1 Garand designs, yet it's not a direct copy of either. Gas-operated, with a rotating bolt, its barrel is 18.5 inches. Over-all length is 37-25 inches, weight about 6⅝ pounds. Stock and handguard are of good American walnut. A detachable box magazine of 5, 20 or 30 rounds capacity will be available. The rear sight is fully adjustable, the front has a sporting style bead. $200 is the announced price, but delivery probably won't begin before late 1973, if production goes well. In any event, law enforcement agencies and varmint hunters alike should be waiting eagerly for the Mini-14. LSS.

No. 3 Ruger Carbine
A Testfire Report

The Ruger No. 3 carbine, though advertised for almost two years, only became available in early 1973. A rather timely introduction however, since the 45-70 cartridge it chambers was introduced in 1873.

The action is the same reliable and rugged one used on the No. 1 rifle, but the underlever looks like those on the old Stevens single shots. An internal hammer is mounted on the underlever; when the carbine is cocked a tip on the hammer projects through that part of the lever acting as the trigger guard: in this position the hammer tip serves as a cocking indicator. The handy sliding tang safety of the No. 1 is also on the No. 3.

The American walnut stock and fore-end resemble those on the Ruger 44 carbine, as do the barrel band and buttplate. However, the No. 3 grip is straight, whereas the 44 carbine has a pistol grip. The wood finish is excellent, but there is no checkering.

Metal finish and the wood-to-metal fit are very good, though the buttplate is about ⅛-inch smaller all around than the stock. The receiver top has *RUGER NO. 3* stamped thereon; the caliber stamp is on the left side of the barrel, ahead of the receiver.

The 22-inch barrel results in a handy over-all 39⅝ inches. Weight is 6⅝ pounds, fine if you have to lug it many miles.

Unlike the No. 1 rifle the carbine is not tapped for scopes. It is intended to be used only with open sights; a folding rear sight, adjustable for windage and elevation, is dovetailed into the barrel, and the muzzle band holds a .07" gold bead. The 45-70 cartridge collected a lot of game in the past century, most of it taken with open sights. After a session at the bench with the No. 3 this writer will agree that the new Ruger carbine should collect its share of game in the future, too.

All shooting, done from the bench,

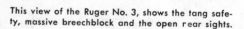

This view of the Ruger No. 3, shows the tang safety, massive breechblock and the open rear sights.

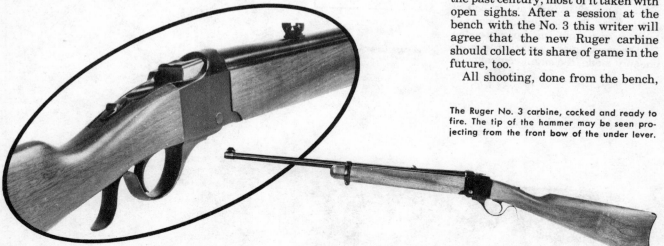

The Ruger No. 3 carbine, cocked and ready to fire. The tip of the hammer may be seen projecting from the front bow of the under lever.

consisted of 3-shot groups with a cooling interval between groups. Remington and Winchester factory loads, with 405-gr. jacketed soft points were shot, plus some old UMC 500-gr. RN lead bullet cartridges. Surprisingly, the old ammo did as well as the new stuff—the UMC and Winchester loads shot into 2-⅞" on centers. Twenty groups averaged just over 3-¼"—highly acceptable for big game hunting, and what hunter uses the 45-70 for varmints?

The UMC loads were probably made about 50 years back. When one of these old timers was touched off, you could hear the primer ignite, followed shortly thereafter by a *Brrroom* and a cloud of smoke. Once in awhile one of the old cartridges failed to fire, which is a good way to find out if you're flinching!

Recoil with the No. 3 isn't heavy, even with the 500-gr. load, but the gun does raise off the rest a bit with the shot. Ejection is very positive: The snap-action mechanism threw the cases straight back.

At $165 the No. 3 represents good value. As for handloading, the No. 3 will handle all loads listed as safe in the various loading manuals. Dies are readily available, and Ohaus, Lee and others offer 45-cal. moulds. Soon, too, the No. 3 will be chambered for the 22 Hornet and 30-40 Krag cartridges, good news indeed.   L.S.S.

Ruger Mini-14 Production Carbine

I shot an early prototype of the Ruger Mini-14 several years ago during a visit to the New Hampshire factory—during which brief session the carbine functioned without a sign of trouble. Some half-dozen of us fired a total of 300-plus rounds, slow fire and rapid, and in rapid fire it was easy to keep 5 shots within a 6-inch bull at 100 yards.

About 10 days ago I received a production specimen of the Mini-14. Only minor changes appear to have been made in comparison with the one I shot, but it was readily apparent that the sample carbine here had been materially improved in various ways—the fit of wood to metal is excellent, as is the sliding fit and friction-free operation of moving parts. The wood and metal, too, are smoothly finished and well polished.

This is not the type of construction one usually sees on what is, after all, an essentially military or police-use firearm. On the contrary, many of today's guns, including those intended for the sporting arms market, exhibit cheaply made, too-small components,

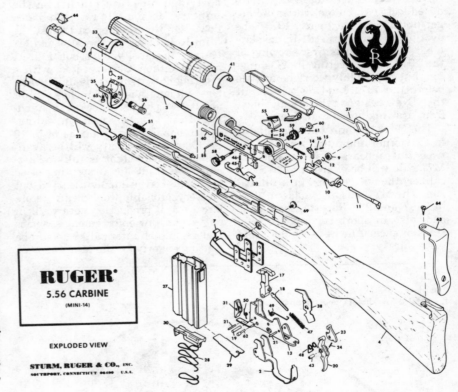

RUGER
5.56 CARBINE
(MINI-14)

EXPLODED VIEW

STURM, RUGER & CO., INC.
SOUTHPORT, CONNECTICUT 06490   U.S.A.

often of substitute materials, parts readily damaged or broken after relatively short use. That's not the Ruger way – the Mini-14 is made up of comparatively few parts, ruggedly made. The breech and firing mechanisms are held to minimum size and weight by the use of hardened chrome-moly steels. The one-piece American walnut stock is strengthened at stress areas by steel reinforcements.

The Mini-14 is indeed a quality firearm, its materials, assembly and appearance harking back to the days of the Krag and the early Springfields. Ruger has achieved these surprising results – in these labor-costly times – by the use of specialized, innovative engineering and manufacturing techniques, a total-design cum construction system that lets the Mini 14 be priced at a *lower* figure than its most crudely made opposite numbers!

The safety blocks hammer and sear, and the breechblock can be opened with the safety on – the latter lies in the front of the trigger guard, moving fore and aft, and can be moved to fire position without taking the trigger finger from the guard.

The trigger is of double-stage type, military style, and on the sample here the letoff pull is a crisp 4 pounds by my scale. The firing pin is retracted mechanically on the first motion of the bolt in unlocking. The rifle can be fired only when the bolt is fully locked.

Production during 1973 will not be big, and sales, as of now, are limited to police and federal agencies. Suggested list price is $200, which makes the Mini-14 excellent value.　J.T.A.

Ruger 223 (5.56) Mini-14 Carbine

Technical Data

Weight (mag. empty)	6.4 lbs. (2.9kg.)
Length	37.25" (94.6cm)
Length, std. barrel	18.5" (47cm)
Rifling—6 grooves, right twist, one turn in	12" (30.5cm)
Sighting radius (100 yd. setting)	22.10" (56.1cm)
Sight gradations (adj. for windage and elev.)	One MOA
Stock	Steel-reinforced American walnut
Mechanism	Gas-operated—fixed piston
Feed (5 or 20 round)	Staggered box magazine
Trigger pull	4.5 lbs. (2kg.)
Caliber: 223 (5.56mm)	Standard U.S. Military ball or commercial cartridges
Chamber pressure (max. ave.)	51,500 psi (3504at.)
Maximum range (approx.)	3000 yds. (2740m)
Muzzle velocity	3300 fps (1005m./sec.)
Muzzle energy	1330 ft. lbs. (183.9kg./m)

Austrian Gunworks

No, the Hiptmayers – Klaus and Heide – don't work in Austria, though they were both born there in the 1940s and apprenticed there as well, spending the required 4 years in gunsmithing and engraving. This young husband-and-wife team – she engraves, gold inlays, et cetera, while Klaus does custom stocking, metal smithing and restoration of antique arms – now live in Canada, their address Box 136, Eastman, Quebec.

I've got room for only two photographs of their work, unfortunately, but in them you'll see the style of their excellent efforts – note the unusually bold scroll and leaf designs surrounding the animal figures, the wealth of well-drawn detail in the differing backgrounds.

The two moose fighting are very well delineated, I think, and if the bears are not as well portrayed as they might be, remember that North American fauna aren't as familiar to the Hiptmayers as red deer, boars and chamois are, and that the work shown is an early effort of theirs.

Good engraving photography, too, by Marcel Coté, of Waterloo, Quebec.　J.T.A.

Revival of the Swift

The Ruger round-top Model 77 here has the new bolt handle.

Maybe. Jim Carmichel and I, late in 1972, were visiting Bill Ruger at his New Hampshire place and, wouldn't you know it, we got to yakking about rifles in particular and firearms in general. Ruger, as you may have heard, intends to chamber his No. 3 Carbine single shot for calibers other than the 45-70—among those given serious thought were the 30-40 Krag, the 30-30, the 22 Hornet and the 220 Swift.

"Why don't you," Jim and I asked, "put the 220 Swift into the Model 77 line-up as well?" At that time Ruger had sold out a run of several thousand M77s in 7x57 and 257 Roberts, calibers which had been put through production as a special run and, perhaps, on a one-time basis only. These 5000-odd rifles (both calibers) had not been advertised, given no fanfare of publicity, yet they'd moved off the dealers' shelves inside of 40-50 days! Our feeling was that the 220 Swift—not chambered for by any U.S. maker for several years—would easily sell as well as the 7x57 and the 257, particularly if the news of its availability was made public and if it were to be listed in Ruger's retail and trade catalogs. I said that 5000 rifles in 220S caliber could be sold handily, in my opinion, well within a year of its introduction. I still feel that way, and I'd not be surprised a damn bit if 220S sales went well beyond 5000 rifles.

Bill Ruger evidently expects to sell at least 1000 rifles in 220 Swift! He's told us that many will be made early in 1973, using the regular (shorter) action, I believe. The two rifles we have are on the Long M77 action.

At this point in our talk Jim and I suggested that Bill Ruger send each of us a Model 77 rifle fitted with a 26″ medium heavy varmint barrel, caliber 22, and unchambered, but with a 14″ twist rate. Ruger's plant had no 220S chamber reamers on hand, but the rifles would be sent to Bill Atkinson (Atkinson Gun Co., P.O. Box 512, Prescott, Arizona 86301), famed riflesmith and barrelmaker in the former partnership of A&M Rifles, also at Prescott, and also Carmichel's home base now. Atkinson would do the chambering, no more—no tuning of the bedding, etc. The rifles could be factory standard otherwise.

Jim and I would then put these rifles through the mill, fire them with factory ammo and handloads, then report to our readers—as I'm now doing.

Jim and I are hopeful that our reports will stimulate renewed interest in the much-maligned Swift, and justify my belief that this great cartridge can rise from the ashes. It's long been a favorite of mine, as many of you know. I never had any trouble with the Swift, either, except in the early days of my ownership of one, about 1938. I failed to clean my rifles adequately then, as so many others didn't, either, and consistent grouping suffered.

That first 70 Winchester Swift was a standard sporter. Some dozen years ago I bought one with a heavy barrel, another with a Marksman stock, paying an exhorbitant $60 because "it was shot out," the owner said. This one was brought back to life with copious amount of J-B compound, and half-inch groups became common. More recently I fell for a Super Grade 70 in 220S caliber, and the gamble paid off—it also does a half-inch with good handloads under good conditions.

So, you could say, I like the 220 Swift. I do indeed, and I hope Ruger permanently adds it to his line or lines, M77 and Single Shot. It's truly a remarkably fine cartridge—given an equally fine barrel—and it deserves better than it has received.

My Ruger Swift rifle arrived here at Creedmoor Farm early in January. Because the barrel is not tapped for target scope blocks, I used the regular Ruger rings to mount a Leupold 10x on the integral receiver bases. I pushed a patch through the barrel and sat down at the bench.

I was in for a surprise, a couple of them, in fact, and at first a pleasant one—the very *first* 5 shots, using Remington 48-gr. SP factory cartridges (lot No. R19S, and rather old), printed a respectable ¾-inch, a nice rounded cluster, too. There hadn't been any fouling shots, though I'd thought the first 2 or 3 would be just that, and the group formed right around the first shot. Then the accuracy fell off badly—the second 5 made 1½ inches, the third 5 went almost 2 inches! I've no idea why unless the first string was a fluke or the bore had fouled rather badly, or the bedding was acting up. There's also a fourth possibility, which I'll get to in a moment.

Range conditions were OK, too, if a mite chilly—30°-32°, fairly bright overcast skies, a light wind from the southwest at 3-6 MPH, gusting now and then to 8-10.

(I'm responsible, of course, for whatever results you'll read here, but I've still got that floating, translucent mass inside my right eyeball, the aftermath of the eye hemorrhage I experienced a few years back. I usually have to wait and wait to get a clear or semi-clear sight picture, and sometimes I don't! I'm quite sure a good young shooter could halve my results, or nearly so.)

The erratic grouping mentioned earlier may, possibly, spring from the chambering job. The leade or throat seems rather short, for all of the Remington loads required extra effort to get the bolt closed, this strain occurring just before final bolt closure. After this had happened a couple of times I seated a couple of cartridges, then extracted them. Marks of the 6 loads were clearly engraved on the bullets, the top of each mark about 1/16-inch above the bullet's base. Bullet seating in handloads will be adjusted to avoid this condition, of course. Don't go 'way.

On January 25 the weather was good—bright, about 40°, and little wind—but I was too busy otherwise to shoot the handloads I'd made—ten rounds each of Sierra 53-gr. HPs, Remington 53-gr. dittos, Nosler's new 52-gr. semi-boattail 52s, and Hornady's 53-gr. HPs, all with 38.0 grains of 4064 and Norma primers. Norma cases were used also, all checked for length and uniformity. Because of the short throating condition mentioned earlier, I had to seat all of these bullets to give a total cartridge length of 2.666 inches,

This is the Ruger 77 which will be chambered for the 220 Swift—it has the shorter action and integral dovetail scope-base recesses, as well as the new bolt handle.

whereas Lyman gives 2.680 inches as a maximum.

The next day, Friday, was ideal—bright overcast, about 45° and no wind—and I quickly learned that the Ruger 220 Swift could perform well, despite my misgivings, and a mediocre trigger pull.

Gratifyingly, all 4 bullets shot nicely, but it was the new Noslers that surprised me. The Remingtons, shot first, made 9/16″ and 11/16″, though 4 of the last 5 went into 1/2″. The Hornadys gave me a round 3/8″ for the first group, but the next string measured 9/16″. Next up were the Noslers, and the first 5 gave the tightest of the day—5/16″. The second 5 Noslers did almost as well, or 3/8″. The Sierra 53s went 1/2″ and 7/16″, but these 10 were the last to be fired of the second 20—I'd cleaned the barrel after 22 rounds, having put two factory-load foulers down range at the start.

I was wishing for the Canjar set trigger today, the type I'd recently put on the Ruger 77 in 7×57mm, which has a crisp, no-movement let-off when set of 3 ounces. The trigger on this Ruger 220 Swift has a bit of creep and a heavy release, about 5 pounds, and I had a tough time holding center with that much pull weight.

Those first-trial handloads, by the way, were simple, unsophisticated—no outside neck turning, no selection for weight-case capacity and no bullet-case spinning tests.

Neither was the rifle tuned at all—Carmichel told me he'd had double grouping with his mate to mine, and he had opened up the barrel channel to cure that, which it did. He then got groups similar in spread to those I shot, but some of them smaller, I believe. My shooting of this new Swift has been "as is," out of the box.

Jim also found that this long-action 77 wouldn't feed from the locker, nor will mine. Jim said he had widened the rails a little and beveled them also at their under edges, which licked his feeding problem, but I've had no time for that chore. The production 220 S rifles, to be made on the shorter 77 action, should feed satisfactorily.

In sum, then, here are two new 220 Swift rifles, both shooting quite well, as so many Swifts do. The barrels are standard Douglas, nothing special about them—1-14 twist, 6 grooves, .2243 groove diameter. Mine weighs 8⅞ pounds without scope or rings. The production Ruger rifles in 220 Swift will, I believe, also have 26-inch medium-heavy barrels. I hope so, for most varminters and accuracy fans want barrels of about this length and weight, not shorter or lighter.

I'm looking forward to shooting the Ruger production 220 Swift and, if only 1000 are going to be made, they'll soon be collectors' items.

Ruger Relents

Just as we were about to close this story, word came from Ruger (on February 22, 1973) that a limited issue (exact number not available) Model 77 rifles will be offered in 220 Swift caliber, these on the standard or shorter action, the one with integral scope bases. The barrel will be special—a heavy 26″ length, tapped for target scope blocks. Price, $176.50 retail, and your dealer ought to have them as you read this.   J.T.A.

Richard Hodgson

Some time back I bought a double rifle, an over-under made by Anton Sodia of Ferlach in Austria, the caliber 375 H&H Magnum.

The top rib held iron sights, but no provision for a scope. Hodgson agreed to see what he could do about making a mount.

The result, pictured here, shows a superb piece of metalsmithing. Two transverse cuts, made in the rib, were fitted with dovetail bases. Each carries two integral lugs, preventing forward movement of the rings during recoil, and also serving to maintain zero when the scope is re-mounted after removal.

Except for the locking elements, these rings are solid steel, radiussed fore and aft to flow smoothly into the scope tube metal. The short levers lock the rings rigidly to the bases. When rotated into locked position, the joint between the movable section and the solid part can barely be seen. I've opened the rear ring to show you where the joint lies!

The rear lever is left-hand threaded so that both levers lie toward each other when locked. The bases are recessed front to rear so that the iron sights are usable when the scope is removed.

In all, a remarkably fine job, and I can't see how its simplicity or elegance could be improved on.   J.T.A.

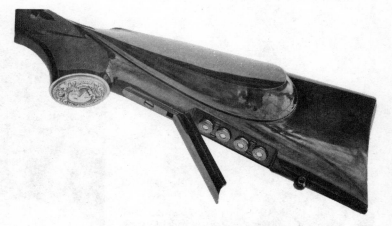

Norman Schiffman

The custom rifle seen here—made by Schiffman—carries the 4-round spare cartridge trap he makes and installs. I've always considered these emergency reservoirs an excellent idea, and they're available in the white at $24.50. For a full length view of this rifle see our Custom Guns pages.   J.T.A.

ARMI FAMARS

Most western world gunners view outside hammer
shotguns as archaic as button shoes. They'd change that
opinion after seeing these Italian beauties!

Armi Famars — Brescia

Most of the world's gun users, certainly most shotgunners in the western hemisphere, look upon smoothbore doubles with open, visible hammers as relics of the 19th century, as archaic as high button shoes, nickel movies and simple courtesy. They'd be right, too, on all counts, for outside-hammer shotguns—those of high quality and twin tubes, at least—haven't been made in several decades. True? Well, not quite, and that's where Armi Famars comes in.

This highly reputed firm's shotguns have won several awards at sporting arms exhibits in Florence, Turin and Brussels, the Belgian prize a gold medal and diploma for quality, precision construction and elegance. Over a dozen different types are made—double guns mostly, side-by-side or over-under, full sidelocks or boxlocks and—will you believe it, external hammer doubles costing as much as $1800! That's the dollar-devalued price in 1973 for a sidelock/hammer horizontal double, the Model 270 Castore E. A.—as our illustrations show, a handsome shotgun with its classical English-style buttstock and slender fore-end. All of the breech area metal is engraved with fine scroll work except the lock-

plates—hammers, both tangs and top lever, safety, guard, etc. A gold crown is laid into the top lever, and a gold shield—a coat of arms—is set into the fore-end.

Ordinarily, the customer ordering the 270 Castore—or any other better grade Armi Famars double—asks for extra engraving, which the firm offers in profusion. I wish I could

The three hammer styles used on Armi Famars double guns. That at lower left, the breast flat faced, may be substituted for the rounded cock on the Castore model. I like the top one for its bold sculpturing and top treatment.

reproduce some of the color pages in their catalog, these showing samples of their gold inlaying that are strikingly original and beautifully done. Nor is this gold work as florid as it so often is—it's artistry of the highest order and in good taste. Writing in *Armieri*, Dr. Franco Vaccari called his article "When Engraving Becomes True Art," and compared favorably Armi Famars chiseling in steel and gold with the works of Cellini.

Make no mistake, though—this Castore double is no turn-of-the-century hammer gun. Modern steels are used throughout, the action being made of nickel-chrome moly steel. Auto ejectors are standard, and the hammers go to full cock on opening the gun, though they may be lowered or cocked manually as well. The tang carries a normal sliding safety, and the front trigger is hinged. This 28-inch barreled 12 bore, beautifully finished, weighs about 7½ pounds. It is furnished with a best leather trunk-style case, as are most better-grade Armi Famars guns.

King George V used hammer shotguns exclusively until his death in 1936. A greatly skilful game shot, his shooting obviously wasn't impaired by using outside hammers. They might, perhaps, have even

This view of the Armi Famars Model Castore shows the rounded body of the hammers and the flowing lines of the fences around the firing pins.

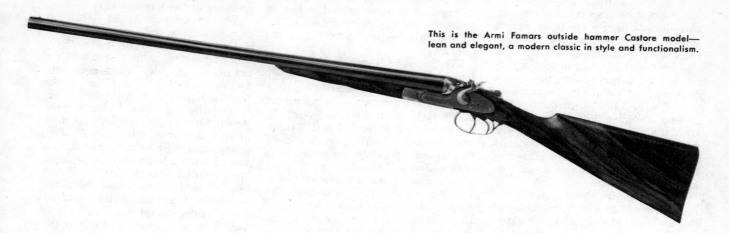

This is the Armi Famars outside hammer Castore model—lean and elegant, a modern classic in style and functionalism.

helped! I imagine he'd have been pleased to shoot an Armi Famars Castore.

The firm makes a couple of other outside hammer doubles as well, both attractive sidelocks, but less embellished than the Castore—these are the Polluce at some $500, and the Nettuno E.S. at $400. These also have auto ejectors and are self-cocking.

I don't have space for describing the hammerless sidelock double called the Venere Extralusso (extra de luxe hunter), but it is the top of the Armi Famars line except for a like gun built entirely to the customer's order. Built on the H&H sidelock form, it is also English in stocking and general styling, fine scroll engraving, etc. Treble locking, it has auto ejectors and hinged front trigger, inlaid gold crown and shield like the Castore. Made in 12 gauge only, it weighs about 7 pounds with 28-inch barrels and costs today, in Italy, about $1350.

The Venere Golden Star (similar to the Venere E.L. above) is Armi Famars top quality shotgun. The price today is about $2500 *without engraving!* The client (he's no longer a "customer") selects the decoration he wants, perhaps even designs it, given the ability. This super double can be made with extra sets of barrels —20, 28 and 410, for example—and has been so made for several U.S. Skeet shooters.

If space allows you'll see two more photos of Armi Famars work in our Art of the Engraver pages, right and left side lockplates showing Diana, the goddess of hunting, at the bath. Superb work, and different.

Armi Famars has a 1973 catalog ready, and in it you'll see their newest engraving patterns, these celebrating our Revolutionary War and depicting various battle scenes from that conflict. Send $1 for surface mail delivery, $2 if you want it airmailed, to them at Via Cinelli 33, 25083 Gardone Val Trompia, Italy.
J.T.A.

Black Duck Game Calls

These word-of-mouth game calls are made in good variety and qualities, ranging from several duck and goose callers through others for doves, crows, quail, turkey, pheasant, deer and elk, among others. Excellent calls they are, too, with fine tone and sound. I had the pleasure of listening to their creator, Ed Mehok, run through a group of them on a TV show recently, and the effects were impressive. Ed not only makes 'em good, he uses them good. He also had a birch bark moose call—the old fashioned kind—which he'll make up if asked for.

If you want calling instruction, Ed has 45 RPM records as well—separate ones for ducks, geese and crows, each $2. His calls cost from $2.95 up. Write Black Duck at 1737 Davis Ave., Whiting, IN 46394 for the 1973 brochure.
J.T.A.

North Star Arms

This fairly new firm has one of the best looking muzzle-loading rifles I've examined. Tabbed the "Plainsman," it is a typical (45- or 50-caliber) half-stock caplock at $144.50 without a cap box, or $149.50 with one. The octagonal barrel measures 32 inches, and the bolster-type breech plug has a cleanout screw. The stock is American cherry, with a beautiful stained oil finish. Buttplate, trigger guard, cap box and other stock fittings are polished brass, the fore-end tip white metal. The lock uses V-type main and sear springs, as did the original rifles, and the trigger is a plain single, non-set type. The rear sight is a standard open field style, adjustable for elevation via a stepped elevator, and for windage by tapping. The front sight is a plain brass blade.
LSS.

This is the Venere Extralusso, a 12 gauge double gun in the traditional classic pattern. Fine-cut scrollwork covers all metal except the barrel.

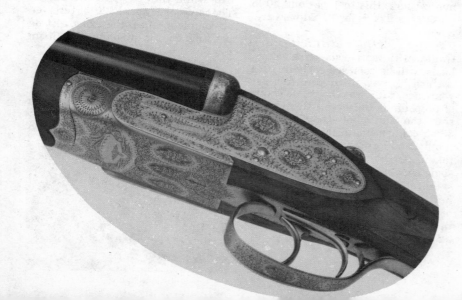

Garcia

Newest Rossi import is a plain side-side double barrel shotgun with a simple boxlock action and a raised matted rib. Rossi shotguns with outside hammers have been on the U.S. market for several years, but the new double—12, 20 and 410—is hammerless. The 12 has 28-inch barrels, the 20 and 410 have 26-inch barrels, all with the usual chokes. Double triggers and a plain pistol grip stock with a beavertail fore-end are standard, but the under $125 price doesn't allow a lot of frills.

The Saddle Ring Carbine mentioned in our 27th edition isn't available yet, but the Sako Model 72 has appeared. It's plain, with a tangent rear sight on the barrel, but the quality is of the same excellence expected from Sako.

Another new Garcia product is a line of blow-molded polyethylene decoys. Each one is hand-painted, the paint flat so it won't shine or glisten, even when wet. Currently available are mallard, black duck, pintail, blue bill, green and blue wing teal, and crow models.   LSS.

Garcia/Sako Model 72

This rifle, based on the Sako L61R action, is minus the usual Sako refinements. The top of the receiver dovetails are smooth, without matting, as is the bolt sleeve. The bolt handle is straight, instead of being slightly swept back. The rifle tested, caliber 375 H&H Magnum, weighed 7⅞ lbs. Add another pound for a scope and mounts and it's about right for the caliber, particularly if it has to be carried for any great distance. The trigger pull was a crisp 4½ lbs., without creep.

The straight taper barrel, 24½" long, held a hooded front blade on an unmatted ramp. A tangent-type rear sight is mounted on the barrel ahead of the receiver in the usual position. Though it is marked 1, 2 and 3, there are 8 elevation positions via a sliding fingerpiece. Windage adjustment is obtained by loosening two small screws and sliding the notch right or left. These removable sights are adequate, but I prefer a receiver peep—the regular Sako peep will fit the dovetail—or better yet a scope.

The plain French walnut stock lacks a fore-end tip or grip cap, but there's a recoil pad, and swivel studs are fitted. Hand checkering on the pistol grip and fore-end is 18 lines-per-inch. The checkering was not always full, but there were few run outs. The cheekpiece and Monte Carlo comb—fluted on both sides—are standard. Wood-to-metal fit is good. A metal crossbolt behind the recoil lug bespeaks the caliber; there isn't one on the smaller bores. The barrel is free-floating except for some pressure at the fore-end tip.

After examination the M72 was topped with a 4x scope in Weaver mounts and taken to the range—though paper punching with a 375 is not exactly my idea of fun, even with a 9-lb. rifle. The M72 lifted off the front sandbag with every shot, but every bullet went into the black of the 6-inch bull at 100 yards, and most groups (3-shot) were under 2". One group, using Browning ammunition loaded with 270-gr. soft point semi-spitzer bullets, measured ¹⁹⁄₃₂". Firing over forty 375 cartridges from the bench in one session isn't exactly pleasurable, but the recoil isn't really bad. This particular M72 can really put them where it counts.

At $198 in the 4 magnum calibers or $188 for the 8 standard calibers (222 through 30-06) the M72 has all the features of the standard Sako rifles—adjustable trigger, sliding safety, hinged floorplate, forged cold-hammered barrel, recessed bolt face, etc., but it's without the extra frills of the standard and de luxe models. In the 375 chambering you save almost $50, which will buy 4 boxes of ammo, with change!   L.S.S.

The M72 now offered has standard checkering—not skip-line, and no white spacers (small cheer). The test rifle had a rubber recoil pad, as do all the magnum calibers.

High Standard

Having sold for years only solid, non-detachable barreled shotguns, the new H-S pump action shotguns will have full interchangeability of barrels in the 12 gauge models. Now the owner of the basic gun can change to a slug barrel with rifle sights for deer hunting, or to an adjustable-choke model, or to a longer, full-choke barrel with ventilated rib for use at trap. The stock finish has been improved and the steel receiver now has classic scroll engraving to set off the high-polish blue job. To top it off, the original buyer of a new High Standard shotgun—pump or autoloader—is given a lifetime guarantee. The autoloaders, newly slicked up like the pumps, don't have interchangeable barrels...yet. H-S is also expanding their revolver line with a new 357 Magnum, the Mark II and Mark III Sentinels, and some additional improvements show in the rimfire handguns, including the autos.   L.S.S.

New DuPont 4759 Ready 4831 Introduced!

DuPont announces the return of SR4759 after a survey showed a big demand existed. Four-lb. and 12-lb. kegs are available. DuPont will also introduce (?) IMR4831, a surplus powder Hodgdon's been selling for many years, this in 1-, 8- and 20-lb. containers. Loads for 10 calibers are ready.

A revised *DuPont Handloaders Guide*, with emphasis on shotshell loads, will be released early in 1974.

Until it was discontinued a few years ago, 4759 was the prime choice of propellants by those riflemen who shot the oldtimers—the 32-40 and 38-55 caliber single shots, to name a couple, and no other powder has quite taken its place. However, there's some hope now—but no firm promise—that 4759 will be made again, perhaps only a single run. Whether it is or not depends on how much interest in and demand for 4759 exists. It's as simple as that.

R. S. Lampert

Lampert has a well-equipped metalsmithing shop, and one of his specialties is working over '98 Mauser actions. He can fit Model 70 style bolt handles and safeties ($20, either job) and he will heat treat receivers at $10 while they're being worked on. The same job is about $20 for receivers or complete rifles, the exact cost depending on the amount of refitting required.

The '98 action pictured, worked over as described and also shortened, has a hinged floorplate also made by Lampert. He's a careful, precision-quality craftsman, capable of the most critical work.   J.T.A.

Harrington & Richardson

In mid-'72, H&R introduced the Blue Streak varmint rifle in 222 caliber, along with Blue Streak cartridges for it. The Model 322 rifle is based on the Sako L461 action, but with the receiver dovetails left off and tapped for conventional scope mounts. At $159.50 the M322 has a 24-inch barrel and a plain walnut stock with cheekpiece, Monte Carlo, hand checkering, and swivel studs. The ammunition, also by Sako, is headstamped H&R. The 50-gr. soft point bullet leaves the muzzle at 3220 fps. Blue Streak cartridges, 20 per box, are $4.10, packed with a plastic divider usable as a loading block.

Many of our arms makers have hopped on the "commemorative" rifle bandwagon. H&R is out with the 268 Custer Memorial Collection of 45-70 Springfield trapdoor rifles, 243 of them in the Enlisted Model and 25 Officer's Model grades. Each rifle honors one of the men who died at the Little Big Horn on June 26, 1876. Each rifle is heavily engraved with soldier's date of birth and location, company, date of assignment to the 7th Cavalry, rank, and date and location of death. Each of the 268 rifles comes in a velvet-lined American walnut case with piano hinges and furniture finish, along with two leather-bound books—a biography of the 7th Cavalry by Hammer, and *The Reno Court of Inquiry* by Utley. The tab is $2000 for the Enlisted Model and $3000 for the Officer's Model. 5000 of a third model, called the Little Big Horn, are offered at $200. This one has no engraving, inlays or fancy wood, but it does have a tang-mounted rear sight, and it, too, comes with a book—*In the Valley of the Little Big Horn.*   LSS.

H & R Blue Streak

H&R sent me a new rifle in September of 1972, this 222 called the Blue Streak. They also sent a batch of Blue Streak cartridges. Rifle and ammo are made in Finland, the action a Sako without the usual scope base dovetails.

The Blue Streak has clean and simple lines which I like—nothing elaborate. The walnut stock has a cheekpiece and Monte Carlo comb, but neither is exaggerated.

My first shooting test of the new H&R Blue Streak 222 rifle came on Wednesday, September 27. A bright sky prevailed (though my targets after 2:30 PM or so are in shade), and it was almost windless. The temperature was 60°.

Unable at the time to find a scope base to match the holes in the receiver (this Sako L-461 action has a rounded bridge and receiver top, not the Sako tapered dovetails), I'd mounted a 20x Lyman by putting bases on the barrel and the receiver ring, the distance between bases only 4⅝ inches on centers, which left a fair amount of scope tube overhanging the action.

The new rifle weighs 6½ lbs., including the target scope bases. No iron sights are fitted, front or rear, on the 24-inch round and tapered barrel.

The trigger pull, clean and without creep, is a consistent 3½ lbs. Oddly, though, it seems heavier than that to me, and I'm going to reduce the pull weight to about 2 lbs. or so before the next firing session.

The trigger/striker fall is not as "dead" as I'd like it—there's an element of vibration and clatter after the letoff—but then few triggers have that desirable attribute.

After cleaning the bore of factory lube and putting three foulers/sighters through the barrel, the first 5 for record at 100 yards, from the bench, went into a big spread—2.85 inches for the 5, with 4 shots in just over 2″. Not very good, but that's only the beginning and I'm confident that ultimate groups will tighten up considerably. It often takes a hundred shots or so to condition a barrel, work in the recoil lugs and bedding generally, and in the process to try other brands of ammo, handloads, etc.

The ammo used was also new, H&R's Blue Streak 50-gr. soft points, made in Finland, too, and rated (per the box) at 3200 fps at the muzzle, with an indicated 39,800 psi chamber pressure. The carton gives other ballistic data, by the way—velocity at 100 and 200 yards, plus trajectory and drop figures out to 200 yards.

The pressure figure just cited sounds rather low comparatively, and it is belied a bit by the performance of the cartridge. DuPont shows pressures as high as 46,000 psi in their Loading Guide, but perhaps Finnish pressure testing procedures differ from ours. Certainly the psi in these Blue Streak rounds isn't maximum—cases fall from the chamber, though a very slight cratering of the primers is seen—a meaningless item in itself, of course.

In mounting the 20x Lyman I resorted to bore sighting (couldn't use the Alley collimator with such scopes), and I fired the first sighter at 20 yards to be sure I was on. My target for this purpose is a sheet of ½-inch plywood mounted on those handy Bonanza folding legs. That first shot was a surprise—the bullet must have expanded fully almost on contact, for the hole in the paper, and through the plywood, went over ½-inch! These Finnish bullets must be of the thin-jacket, quick-expansion type, for the second shot at 100 yards must have hit a weed stem or the like, for the bullet never reached the target.

More later after I've checked the bedding, lessened the trigger pull, and perhaps the trial of some up pressure at the fore-end tip. As delivered the barrel is fully free floating all the way to the front of the receiver ring.

The H&R Sako has two guard screws, one front and rear. The factory must have set the forward one up with an impact tool, for I had to resort to the drill press and a short screwdriver blade to loosen it.

Once I'd got the barrel and action out of the wood I found thin steel shims had been used at three places in the inletting. One lay at the bottom of the recoil-lug recess, another was placed in the cutout for the rear of the guard. Two others were forward, lying in the front of the guard recess. These guard-shims—about an inch long over-all—are holed to let the guard screws pass through them.

Because I next wanted to shoot the Blue Streak 222 with some fore-end pressure, I removed one of the forward guard shims and also the recoil lug shim. After snugging up the guard

The H&R Blue Streak rifle, Model 322, chambered for the 222 Remington ctg.

screws I found that the fore-end tip (for some 2″-2½″) bears against the barrel with light pressure; at a guess, not over 2-3 lbs., and quite possibly less. The rest of the barrel floats as before, including the section forward of the receiver ring.

On Sunday, October 1, 1972, the 222 H&R Blue Streak was shot again. The temperature was 66°—the sky clear and bright, with a very light west wind. The first 5 shots with B.S. ammo again, went into 3.4″! Then Norma 50-gr. SPs went into a better 1¼″, but the next 5 Normas went into a lateral 2½″ (though only ½″ vertically) for some reason; wind gusts, maybe, but I doubt it. The last 4 Normas, all that were left, went into 2½″, but with these last 4 I used a heavy card shim between fore-end tip and barrel to see what heavier up pressure might do.

The combination of fore-end pressure with two shims removed from the Sako not having worked, I put all shims back except one at the forward guard screw, and removed all fore-end pressure; I'd used card stock there.

The groups that followed showed some small improvement, as can be seen: the last of the Blue Streak ammo, 12 rounds only, averaged 1.78″ for two groups of 5, two being used for foulers. Next, Remington 50-gr. Powr-Lokt loads were shot, after a thorough cleaning, and these gave the best promise of all—four 5-shot groups 1.35″, but had it not been for fliers in all but one string, the average would have been 1.11″. Smallest string went .87″, largest 1.82″ because of a wide flier.

Now that I've got Weaver bases to fit the H&R rifle, I removed the 20x Lyman Super Targetspot, and mounted a 3x-9x Weaver scope. I've been thinking that the weight of the long 20x Lyman on the floating barrel might have accounted for some of the vertical grouping I've had; we'll see.

Only 20 cases were handloaded—10 with 52-gr. Sierra BRHP bullets, the others with Nosler's new 52-gr. Solid Base HPs. The powder was the same for all 20—24/Ball C, Remington 7½ primers.

With almost no wind, I sat down to shoot. After wasting a couple of fouling rounds, I got a hell of a surprise! Whatever had been wrong before was now fixed—and I can't think of anything but that 20x Lyman scope as the cause. With the Weaver at 9x, the first 4 Sierras went ⁹⁄₁₆″, the first 4 Noslers doing ½″! The remaining 5 of each averaged ⅝, the Noslers again shooting slightly tighter.   J.T.A.

Sterett's Blue Streak

My Blue Streak, fitted with a Weaver V8 scope, was taken to the range with Blue Streak, Browning, Federal, Speer/DWM and Winchester ammunition.

The weather during two sessions was anything but good. The overcast sky made the targets at 100 yards look like those seen at dusk on a normal day. Three-shot groups were bench-fired, with time out between groups to let the barrel cool.

Trigger pull was a nice 2-¾ pounds. The smallest group, with Speer/DWM 50-gr. PSP ammo, went ¹³⁄₃₂″. Browning cartridges did almost as well (one ⅜″ group) and the H&R Blue Streak 50-gr. loads (made in Finland) shot from ⁷⁄₁₆″ to ½″. No group, whatever the ammunition, went over 2″. The Federal stuff averaged just over one-inch.   L.S.S.

H&R Springfield Stalker

This muzzleloader combines modern materials and design with some features of the pre-Civil War Springfield rifle. Available in 45 or 58 caliber, the Stalker has an American walnut stock almost identical to that found on the M1873 Springfield Carbine, except for the fore-end tip.

Our 45-caliber Stalker weighed 7⅜ lbs.; the 58-caliber version goes slightly less. Trigger pull measured 7½ lbs., and the big hammer falls with authority. Thumbing the hammer back results in 3 rather loud clicks, which could scare game. The trigger hangs loosely, even with the hammer cocked, as there is no tension on it. This may bother some shooters, but one can get used to it.

The bar action lock has the old-fashioned V-type springs like the muzzle-loading Springfields. The breech-plug is the bolster-type with a slotted-head cleanout screw.

Appearance of the Stalker is military all the way, from the massive hammer and trigger guard to the fore-end band and stock profile. Except for the sights it could pass for a military rifle of the late 1850's with the forestock cut back for sporting use.

The crowned barrel is 26¾″ long

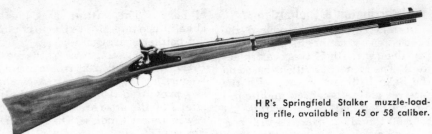

HR's Springfield Stalker muzzle-loading rifle, available in 45 or 58 caliber.

to the bottom: over-all length is 43⅜″. Point of balance is just to the rear of the open rear sight; and the rifle comes up well in the offhand position.

Sights are a Williams Dovetail Open Sight, adjustable for windage and elevation, and an .085″ blade, adequate for the rifle.

All metal parts are finished to a highly polished blue-black. U.S. is stamped on the buttplate tang, U.S. Springfield and a spread eagle appear on the lockplate, ahead of the hammer. Springfield Stalker and 45 Cal. are stamped on the left side of the barrel. Wood-to-metal fit is very good.

Priced at $150 the Stalker comes with a wood-handled, telescoping brass ramrod, a spare nipple and nipple wrench. The unique ramrod's main section is boresize (for the 45 caliber). After the ball is started, the tip section of the rod can be turned counterclockwise to permit a smaller section to be pulled out and turned to lock rigidly for seating the ball the rest of the way. The removable tip accepts a standard cleaning jag.

The T-handle nipple wrench, it was found, needs to be offset to clear the hammer. A few taps with a brass hammer turned that trick.

I shot the Stalker from the bench, firing 3-shot groups. H&R recommends 50 grains of FFg powder with a .009″ patch and a .445″ ball, as a start, but these ingredients were not available. Other components were tried. The first load consisted of 53.2 grains of Curtiss & Harvey's Fg powder, slightly smaller than Du Pont FFg and approaching FFFg. Using a Thompson/Center .018″ linen patch lubed with Hoppe's No. 9 Plus and a .434″ ball, this load produced one group of almost 3″, but most groups went just over 3″ at 100 yards. Remington No. 11 caps were used exclusively.

Switching to 52.4 grains of Du Pont FFg and the same patch/ball combination opened the group size. A different patch—.032″ polyester—was tried without improvement. The first load, of course, is more than satisfactory for use on deer-size game.   L.S.S.

Marlin Firearms

Nostalgia, as we've noted, seems to be the name of the game. Marlin boasts of having kept one shoulder arm in continuous manufacture longer than any other firm. The arm? Their lever action M39A rimfire rifle, which began as the M1891. In keeping with the "return to the past" the 39A is now available with a 24-inch octagon barrel at $125. At the same price the 39M may be had with a 20-inch octagon barrel and a straight-grip stock. In the larger calibers, the 336 is offered with a 22-inch octagon barrel in 30-30 Winchester caliber, with straight-grip stock, for $135. A special commemorative Zane Grey Century model with pistol grip stock, brass buttplate and fore-end cap, and special portrait medallion, goes for $150. The Marlin 1894—44 Magnum caliber and 20-inch octagon barrel, straight-grip stock and old-style squared bolt—lists at $135.

Several special barrels have been added to Marlin's shotgun line. The excellent 120 Magnum is now obtainable with a 40-inch barrel. (Yes, 40 inches!) Chambered for 3-inch shells, the 40 MXR Magnum barrel comes only with a full choke, and without a ventilated rib. The Goose Gun has apparently sold so well with a 36-inch barrel that Marlin decided to go even further. (Now, if you can't hit 'em with the shot charge, just reach out and rap 'em with the muzzle.) A 26-inch slug barrel, with rifle sights and a rear base tapped for scope mounting, is a welcome addition. The 120 can be bought with these barrels or the barrels may be ordered separately for $50 each.

A special 120 Trapgun, at $229.95, is going to find some friends. With a walnut Monte Carlo stock and full fore-end, this trapgun has hand-cut checkering and standard trap dimensions. The 30-inch barrel, with a ventilated rib, may be had in full or modified choke.

The bolt action Goose Gun with 36-inch barrel has been around for a number of years, but a companion—

the 55S—has been introduced with a 24-inch barrel having rifle sights for slug use. The barrel is drilled and tapped for scope mounting. Complete with recoil pad, carrying strap and swivels, the 55S weighs about 7 pounds, and lists at $73.95, or $94.95 complete with 1.5x scope mounted and ready to go.   LSS.

1895 Marlin 45-70
A Testfire Report

The last repeating rifle made in 45-70 caliber was, I believe, the 1886 Winchester, very much a collector's item today. But now, and for those of us who prefer a scoped 45-70 rifle, Marlin has the answer in the new Model 1895.

The new 1895 (not to be confused with the old 1895) uses the basic Marlin 336 lever action, modified to accept the larger cartridge. Feeding and ejection in the test gun were flawless as long as cartridges were kept under 2.550″ long. (The tubular half-magazine holds 4 rounds.) The stamped steel gate in the loading port was a little sharp-edged, making it rather tough on the thumb, but this is a minor point, and with gloves on it isn't a problem. Fired cases are forcibly ejected to the right, out of the line of sight.

The 22″ tapered barrel, rifled with 8 grooves, has a set of conventional open sights. The receiver top is tapped for scope mounts, and the hammer spur carries an offset thumb piece for ease in cocking. For the test shooting I used a Redfield 1-4x scope with post reticle in the Marlin No. 10 mount, which combination worked very well.

Stock and fore-end are of American walnut—a Marlin tradition. The fore-end has a blued steel cap, and the squared-off finger lever fits right up against the straight grip. The hard rubber buttplate is without a white spacer! Since this recoil is rather mild (the 1895 weighs 8 1/16 lbs.) no recoil pad is needed, and the wide, rounded comb makes the 1895 comfortable to shoot.

All metal parts are a polished blue, except the receiver top—the latter is sand-blasted to prevent glare. Finish on wood and metal is good, as is wood-to-metal fit. Trigger pull was 5½ pounds, not overly heavy for a hunting rifle.

Three-shot groups were bench fired, range 100 yards. The Redfield scope was set at 4x, and the barrel was allowed to cool slightly between groups. All cartridges were fed through the magazine, as they would be in the field.

The smallest group, 1-3/32″ on centers, was made with W-W 405-gr. cartridges. Even some old UMC loads shot well—one group went under 2″. With handloads and other bullet weights the 1895 might even get under that magic single minute of angle!

Priced at $185 the Marlin 1895 is, at the moment anyway, the only lever action repeater chambered in 45-70 caliber. In fact it's the *only* repeater that is, though a bolt action 45-70 rifle may appear soon. If the upswing in popularity of this century-old cartridge continues, others will be climbing on the bandwagon. No matter, it will be tough to beat the 1895 at $185 for functioning, accuracy and value.   L.S.S.

Interarms '73

That's the title of their new catalog, a small format (about 5½″ x 7½″) booklet of 24 pages that is handsomely done in full color. Place of honor in the new catalog is given to the Churchill "One of One Thousand" bolt action (commercial Mauser 1898) sporting rifle—it appears on the cover and on page 3. As the name implies, only 1000 of these will be made,

and a special descriptive catalog on this handmade rifle is now ready. The price? $1000, what else? The rest of the catalog is taken up with Interarms' other products—Walther pistols and rifles, the Mark X bolt action sporters, Star Gauge shotguns, Mauser auto pistols, including the Luger, Mauser scopes and actions, Brenneke rifled shotgun slugs, the Arsenal line of military rifles, Sako

cartridges and the excellent Virginian, a single action revolver in traditional form that's made by Hämmerli of Switzerland, no less. This version of the old single action Army has a special base-pin system that prevents the gun being fired accidentally. In 375 Magnum and 45 Long Colt only, the Virginian is $159. The new Interarms '73 catalog is free.   J.T.A.

Marubeni America

This Japanese firm markets the Miida over-under shotgun, 12 gauge only. Five grades are available, priced $381.50 to $1194.50. The action is a standard boxlock design, the price differences due to the type of receiver finish, amount of engraving, and the grade of stock wood. Select French walnut is used, and the checkering is 20 lines-per-inch, but extra fancy woods raise the cost. All grades have ventilated-rib barrels, selective ejectors, single selective triggers similar to the Browning design, and receiver engraving proportional to grade. The top of the line—the Trap Grandee—has fully engraved dummy sideplates. Barrel lengths and chokes in good variety, and the trap models carry Pachmayr recoil pads. To top it off, the original owner receives a lifetime warranty against defective parts and workmanship.   LSS.

Marubeni

Because of a mail mixup, one of the Miida Model 2300 Skeet guns reached us too late for a field test, I'm sorry to say. Doubly so in this instance, for the 2300 is a real beauty—the well-checkered stock and fore-end, of good French walnut, show a nice bit of figure plus some fiddleback grain. Stock dimensions, though nominally standard, bring my eye well above the ventilated rib, so I'm sure the bulk of the pattern will print over the point of aim. The fore-end appears trim and slender in profile, but flares out below the finger ledges to form a highly adequate beautiful effect. This broader section tapers to a larger dimension at the rear, too, thus tending to lock the hand into place. The comb-nose fluting is very well handled; so many times these days it isn't. Wood-to-metal jointing is first class.

All metal save the barrels shows a soft satin-chrome finish and a tasteful amount of foliate-scroll engraving. The gold-plated and checkered single trigger is of the inertial type. Some of the world's best shotguns have the same system, though I prefer the mechanical design.

The underlug boxlock action is 2⅝" deep. Selective ejectors are standard in the 2300, and the top tang safety-barrel selector is non-automatic. This sample Miida Skeet gun has 27-inch barrels, the total gun weight 7¼ pounds. The balance point, just behind the hinge pin, puts the gun's weight mostly between the hands.

Altogether, the 2300 is an attractive double, well-designed and well-executed, and I'm sorry there's no shooting of it to report.   J.T.A.

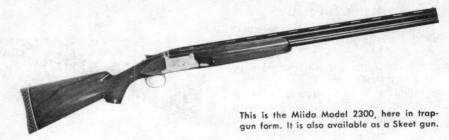

This is the Miida Model 2300, here in trap-gun form. It is also available as a Skeet gun.

Lyman Gun Sight

The new Lyman Plains Rifle is a handsome 45-cal. halfstock caplock, traditionally styled with brass patchbox, guard and buttplate. Double set triggers are fitted, and fully adjustable sights are standard on the black powder muzzleloader. Factory proof-tested for insured safety, the new rifle is $175. An accessory kit—mould, nipple wrench, ball starter, etc., is $20.50, less if bought with the rifle.

The other new Lyman long gun is a replica Zouave rifle, caliber 58, with the customary brass furniture and color case-hardened lock. $145 or, with a kit of accessories, it's $160.

Lyman's mate to their 1860 Remington replica 6-shooter caplock (44 or 36 caliber) is an 1851 Colt Navy copy, cal. 36, highly attractive in its gleaming blue and brass finish. $95 buys one, $109.95 for gun and kit.

Lyman's new 100 SL shotshell press is styled like their Easy to some degree, but it's an improved design that includes an Auto Primer Feed (with optional Primer Reservoir), floating wad guides and crimp starters, plus powder and shot measures that can be emptied quickly. Made only in 12 and 20 gauge, and without convertibility to roll crimping, cost is $79.50. Conversion kits are available.

The Easy shotshell loader remains in the line, versatile as ever, starting now at $49.50 in fold-crimp form, or at $58.50 in roll-crimp/slug style.

Lyman's new 3x-9x Variable scope, its body a hard-anodized alloy for light yet rugged toughness (14 oz.), shows a smooth, clean design. Half-inch click adjustments are standard, as is a regular crosswire or a reduced-center crosswire reticle. Parallax adjustment is not a feature.   J.T.A.

Savage Arms

The Model 333 over-under has a new wide vent rib and other custom features; ejectors replace the extractors, plus an increase in price to $273.50. The stock has been completely redesigned on the Model 110-C, CL, D, and DL bolt action centerfire rifles, by adding a cheekpiece and checkering. The Fox B side-side shotgun is now available in 12 and 20 gauges with a 24-inch barrel; this should be handy for use on quail and rabbits in thick brush where a long barrel sometimes gets hung up. The fore-end on the Model 170 pump action rifle no longer has the rattle that bothered some hunters.   LSS.

> The product prices mentioned in these review pages were correct at presstime, but may be higher when you read this.

Universal Firearms

This Florida firm hasn't changed much of their carbine, scope or shotgun lines, but Universal has become the sole importer and distributor of Soviet-made sporting arms. Included are rimfire rifles, single barrel and double barrel side-side and over-under shotguns, target rifles and pistols. The complete line includes 44 models, most of them never before available to U.S. shooters. At least two other importers have tried to distribute Soviet arms in the U.S. in the past decade, but apparently without much success. Maybe Universal will do better. Prices are not completely set yet, but they should be competitive.

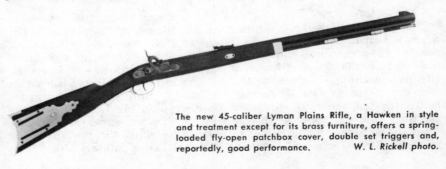

The new 45-caliber Lyman Plains Rifle, a Hawken in style and treatment except for its brass furniture, offers a spring-loaded fly-open patchbox cover, double set triggers and, reportedly, good performance.   W. L. Rickell photo.

South African Rifles by Musgrave

One of the exhibits at the NSGA-Houston meeting—and a very big display it was—surprised the hell out of me! Can you imagine a firm making bolt action rifles in South America bringing them in various grades to the U.S. and selling them here? That's what it was, and I suppose it does make sense—after all, the U.S. is far and away the biggest market in the world for sporting firearms. Too, the Musgrave people have established an agency here (J. J. Sherban, 2655 Harrison Ave., Canton, OH 44706), which will warehouse the rifles and make fast deliveries.

Musgrave is not a new firm except here. They've been making rifles in South Africa for some years, including a target type that won every match—national and local—in South Africa in 1972. Musgrave, then, knows something about making rifles, whether match type or sporter, and because many rifles sold in South Africa are put to a rigorous test on dangerous game, such rifles must be reliable, accurate and durable.

I examined the Musgrave line carefully, and I think I can say that they meet those requirements easily. The action, while deriving from a '98 Mauser basically—and there's nothing at all wrong with that—is distinctively a Musgrave design. The forged receiver, carefully machined from a steel billet, holds a bolt made the same way. It has 3 locking lugs forward, making for a shorter bolt lift, and the wide hook extractor of the original Mauser. It's my opinion that nobody has improved on that form yet, especially if a ticklish situation develops. Gas-escape ports are provided.

Bolt handles on the sporters sweep gracefully rearward; the bolt on the Model RSA target rifle, caliber 308, drops down straight. The single-stage trigger, well back in the generously sized guard, is 3-way adjustable. The rifles I tried had crisp, clean letoffs. The cocking-piece safety permits low scope mounting, and is a highly positive type.

All Musgrave barrels are hammer forged and rifled, the F.N. steel of 145,000 psi tensile strength. The bores are hand polished to a mirror finish, too. The Premier models have 25.5″ barrels, the Valiant 24″. None have metallic sights, but the receiver is tapped for standard scope bases.

The premium priced Premier ($244.95) has a restrained Monte Carlo cheekpiece walnut stock, multipoint checkering, and contrasting wood fore-end tip and grip cap. The

Here are the three regular Musgrave rifles and one other. From the top—The Valiant, then a custom grade rifle, the metal nicely engraved and gold inlaid. Third down, the Premier version and, last, the RSA target rifle in standard stocking and medium-heavy 26.4″ barrel. Other stocks can be had for the RSA. As shown, the cost is almost $300.

Valiant has a straightline stock, without Monte Carlo or cheekpiece, hence it is usable by the lefthander, and skip-line checkering. It is also minus grip cap or fore-end tip, otherwise it is like the Premier.

Both grades carry swivel studs, integral magazines with hinged floorplates (button-in-the-guard release). The literature says that the Valiant has a fixed-leaf rear open sight and a hooded ramp front sight, but the photos don't show them, and I can't recall seeing them at Houston. Each Musgrave rifle is zero- and accuracy-tested at the factory, and the test target accompanies the rifle. What degree of accuracy is not mentioned in their handsome color catalog.

As you might expect, I like the Valiant model for its simple and classical lines and good proportions, not to speak of its $180 price. I'd prefer the regular checkering, but that's a minor point. I think it is as good looking a production rifle as we're offered today, and I'm looking forward to a trial of one. Unfortunately, the expected sample hasn't shown up yet, but if it does . . . . .

J.T.A.

The product prices mentioned in these review pages were correct at presstime, but may be higher when you read this.

Cole's Acku-Rests

Color and brilliance has reached the rifle rest field. No longer need bench shooters put up with drab canvas or buckskin bags. Cole's new line uses a scuff-resistant, sturdy vinyl, this material ranging from grained to smooth finishes and in color from browns and tans ($8.55 for two bags) to Cole's Zodiac colors—gleaming and sparkling blue, red, green, gold and silver; these last are $11.55 per set (an in-between grade is $9.95). The most colorful is called the Heritage Set, these using all 5 Zodiac colors, the whole a red, white and blue confection. These $11.95 bags carry the motto, "Protect our Heritage," stamped in gold, and your name can be stamped in this fashion for $1.95 extra.

Send for Cole's color brochure on this new line. Full details and all measurements are given.

J.T.A.

Winchester Seminar 1972

It was enjoyable, as it always is, to meet old friends and make new ones at Winchester's 15th gathering of the clan, this time at Nilo Farm and Alton, Illinois. As usual, too, we all got in some good shooting—wildfowl, upland birds, and clays—and for once the weather was nice, crisp but not frigid, and a fair bit of blue sky.

Regrettably—from your standpoint and mine—Winchester's one truly new firearm, shown to all hands, can't be talked about in any detail, not until 1974, for God's sake. It is a single barrel repeating shotgun, I'll say that much (without getting sent to Coventry, I hope), and it was generally agreed by the gun writers present that it was an impressive piece, very well put together, and with excellent handling qualities. All steel, too, I believe, and only ultra modern machining technology has made the intricately tooled action possible. Incredibly small dimensional tolerances are now achieved via these tape-fed and programmed automatic tools. This does away with, to a good degree, much of the costly hand labor that would otherwise be called for in a smoothbore of this quality and precise dimensions.

That's as much as I can say. Perhaps someone else won't observe the solemn ukase from W-W, and you'll learn more about it elsewhere!

The only new firearm from Winchester that can be described is another shotgun, this the new Model 37A, a single barrel, top snap, break-open style with an auto ejector, gold-plated trigger, new stock/fore-end design and an "engraved" receiver. At its modest price, the 37A can hardly be hand engraved, of course.

The full size 37A will be made in all gauges except 10, and with barrels from 26 to 36 inches, all bored full. (See our catalog pages for details.)

The Youth's 37A, offered only as a 20 or 410, both with 26-inch barrels choked improved-modified and full respectively, carries a shorter but full size buttstock and a recoil pad. Fore-ends on both versions are of walnut-stained hardwood, attractively fluted for good control, and checkered, as are the pistol grips on their sides.

To paraphrase the Great Emancipator, the inevitable and ubiquitous white spacers found on the 37A's grip and buttplate are just the thing for those who like this kind of embellishment, if that's the right word.

All 37As are $46.95 except the Youth's model and the 36-inch barreled 12; these last two are $47.95, which is only 25c an inch over the 32-inch guns. A bargain if I ever heard one.

The third item on Winchester's bob-tailed agenda this year will, I think, please handloaders. Certainly the advent of an extensive new propellant powder line-up pleases this long-time assembler of shooting components, and here's what the W-W powder plot for 1973 looks like:

SHOTGUNS **452AA**—a normal 12 gauge powder. **473AA**—a normal 20 gauge powder. **540**—a powder for high velocity and magnum loads. **571**—a powder for extra heavy duty magnum loads, for 3-inch cases particularly. **RIFLES** **760**—for normal rifle use, but not for magnum. **748**—a number for benchrest, 222 and such like usage. **680**—a fast-burning powder for such cartridges as the 22 Hornet, 218 Bee, *et al.* **HANDGUNS** **630**—a powder for high velocity loads and M1 Carbine loads. **230** and **296**—both for magnum and 410 loads.

Full information on the above Winchester-Western powders should be available by early summer, most probably by the time you read this. Full load data also ought to be offered at or around the same time.

Texas Ranger M94

To celebrate the 150th anniversary of the famous Texas Rangers, Winchester will honor this outstanding group of Texans by issuing a limited edition (5000) Texas Ranger Commemorative Model 94 rifles.

Sanctioned by the Texas Ranger Commemorative Commission, these rifles will be available only in the State of Texas. The first 150 units, bearing serial numbers one through 150, will be special-editions sold only through the Texas Ranger Assn. The rest, 4,850 models, will be available at regular Texas retail outlets.

The Texas Rangers carbine has a 20-inch barrel equipped with a post front sight and semi-buckhorn rear sight, plus the traditional barrel band. The tang carries the inscription "Winchester Model 1894." The stock and fore-end are of semi-fancy walnut, and the buttstock features the classic square comb and curved metal buttplate. A facsimile of the famous "Texas Ranger Star" is imbedded in the buttstock. The caliber is 30-30 only, the magazine holds 6 cartridges. The gun weighs about 7 pounds and will be available in Texas after April 1, 1973. Price, including a saddle ring, is $134.95.

> **The product prices mentioned in these review pages were correct at presstime, but may be higher when you read this.**

The 150 special-edition models, which will be sold through the Texas Ranger Assn., have hand-checkered, full fancy walnut stocks and 16-inch barrels with full buckhorn type rear sights. The special-edition version weighs some 6 pounds and holds 5 rounds—4 in the magazine and one in the chamber. They're sold in a special presentation case, with the Texas Ranger Commemorative Star mounted inside the case, not on the gun. At a mere $1000 each they'll probably all be sold before you read this!

J.T.A.

Top—Winchester 1973 single barrel Model 37A in standard form. Below it, the same gun in the Youth's Model made only in 20 and 410 gauge.

The new Winchester Texas Ranger carbine.

Bill Ballard

Ballard started out, some years ago, making cases for long-gone rifles—Sharps, Remingtons, Ballards, et al, cases in 40, 44 and 45 calibers. From that beginning he went to old style tools for reloading and bullet-making—mould, swages, capping-decapping tools, bullet seaters, tall tang sights and so on.

His moulds cast a plain cylindrical bullet, without lube grooves, and these can be adjusted for light or heavy bullets. Such bullets are intended for paper patching. As with most cast bullets, these come from the mould less exactly dimensioned and formed than they ought to be. These moulds are $22.50, extra cavity units $12.50.

The Ballard swage set brings the cast bullets to a smooth, uniform diameter, hollow based for easier patching—and a swaged bullet shoots better. $20.00 for the swage complete, $15.00 for extra die sets.

His re- and decapper is much like the old Pope style, but Ballard makes the tool with detachable heads so that various calibers can be served. About $20-$25 depending on over-all length.

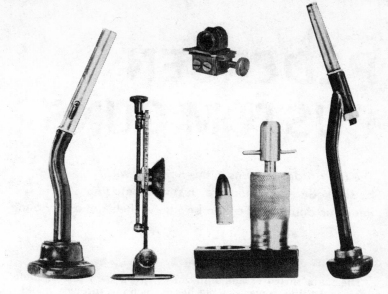

Some of Bill Ballard's handmade tools for oldtimers. From left—breech bullet seater; long range tang sight; one-piece swage, with patched bullet swaged in it; Remington Creedmoor style windgauge front sight; and another form of breech bullet seater.

Ballard's breech seaters (for seating bullets into the throat, ahead of the case mouth), come in two styles at $17.50, and his straightline bullet seaters are made for various old calibers, these $10. His tang rear sights are in Remington and Sharps Creedmoor rifle styles and heights usually, but he can furnish others. About $35-$45 for the tang types, between $27.50 and $35 for the spirit-level fronts.

Ask for Ballard's new folder—it's got full details and good hints on loading, swaging, etc.   J.T.A.

Case-Gard

MTM's Case-Gard 50, great ammo boxes for metallic cartridges (rifle and handgun, 5 heights available at $1.25-$1.95 each), have been described at some length in these pages—as have their well designed and functional loading trays, standard and 5-in-1 powder funnels—so you'll hear now about MTM's new items for the shooter.

MTM's big item for 1973—in import and physically—is the Case-Gard 100, a truly new product and one that's meant, this time, for the shotgunner. I said it's big, but that's relative—it's a compact 7" deep by 9" high by 11" long, big next to the Case-Gard 50s. Take a look at the picture we're showing—two of those 50-round trays go into the case, one atop the other, and they're available with 12, 16 or 20 gauge trays. Because the top tray rests on a shelf, the space below can be used for various other things if desired—a thermos bottle, a small lunch, loose empties, you name it. Obviously, the separate trays can be used at the loading bench, too. All components are made of a tough, high-impact ABS plastic, precision moulded to last a lifetime unless abused. The broad double handles make the Case-Gard 100 easy to tote, and you can forget about rust or water seepage, no matter how wet the day in the duck blind. Black, brown or gray, they're $7.95 complete (case and 2 trays), but dead-grass green will be offered, too. Extra trays are $1.45 each.

MTM (Dayton, Ohio 45414) has a new item for the rifleman hunter this year, too. Case-Gard 20 holds 20 rifle cartridges in separate wells, protecting them against damage of any kind and making them readily accessible. Case-Gard 20 slides onto a belt or slips into a pocket—though it would have to be a roomy pocket for the bigger sizes. Made of the same tough ABS plastic, the covers lock into place over a flange, making the Case-Gard 20 water- and dustproof to a good degree. Case-Gard 20s are $1 each in Small (17 Rem., 222), Medium (22-250 to 308) and Large, for 270 to 458.   J.T.A.

Case-Gard 20 is made in 3 rifle cartridge sizes, goes on belt or in pocket, has dust- and waterproof snap-locking cover.

New Case-Gard 100 case holds 100 shotshells in piggyback trays. Light, sturdy and virtually waterproof.

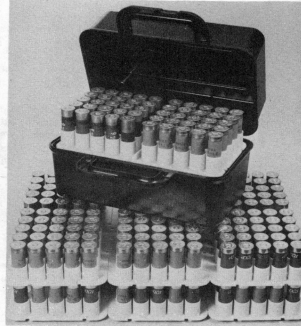

PEDERSEN CUSTOM GUNS

The top grade shotguns in this new line will
be stocked to your measure. Just walk into your
Pedersen dealer and ask to be fitted—he's got a "try gun."

The main thrust of this ambitious effort is, I think, something not heretofore attempted. The Pedersen project is, in a few words, a plan to offer quality shotguns of a certain grade—the top of the line—with stocks made to the buyer's dimension. Such individualized stocks are nothing new, of course, and some few armsmakers, in the past and even now, to a much limited extent, have furnished stocks to the customer's specification, the metal too, but invariably at quite high cost, at prices well over and in addition to the price of the basic firearm. The cost of this kind of work today is considerably greater than it was only a few years ago. For example, a custom made rifle at the present time, made by one of several top-flight craftsmen, can easily start at a thousand dollars—using your barreled action and your wood! With any embellishment—engraving, special metalsmithing and checkering—the total outlay can reach $3000 and more.

Pedersen's idea is to offer a made-to-measure stock and yet keep the price relatively low by standardizing on the rest of the gun. To this end a crew of experts has been recruited, seasoned craftsmen all, who will handle the custom stocks, the assembly of the gun when finished, men who will make sure that the customer gets what he's ordered, that he'll be well satisfied with the gun. To make this plan work Pedersen must, I think, get enough volume of orders to keep its men busy

week on week. A handful of orders coming through would raise the unit custom-work costs too much.

To help obtain the needed orders, and to insure that the customer is properly fitted for his or her custom stock, Pedersen has another "first" to its credit—all authorized dealers will be furnished with a costly and sophisticated "try gun". This has never been attempted before on anything like such a scale. In the heyday of London gunmaking every first class maker owned a try gun, some of them more than one, and each usually made in the various shops. There probably aren't more than a dozen or so in the entire U.S., and hardly more than that number of men capable of using the try gun adequately. Gun-fitting with the try gun isn't nearly as simple a task as it may sound. The practitioner has to really know guns and shotgunning (fitting a rifle stock is relatively easy), he has to study the customer, his configuration, stance and habits if the bespoke stock is going to fit him as well as a standard-dimension stock—or as good!

To make this delicate and painstaking job a bit easier for its dealers, many of whom have never seen a try gun, Pedersen has issued a comprehensive and detailed manual, *The Lore of Custom Gun Fitting,* for study and application by its dealers. It's a well-written booklet, too, and it should be a big help to those unfamiliar with a try gun.

Pedersen Models

The new Pedersen line is extensive, some 4 over-under shotgun grades, each offered in field, Skeet and trap form; 3 side-by-side double guns, all nominally field types, though conceivably target dimensioned stocks and barrels could be ordered (in the M2000, Grade I), and a bolt action, high-powered rifle in 3 grades. Only the top grade in the shotguns is available with a custom-fitted stock.

The over-under leader is the Model 1000, Grade I, a deluxe double with fancy American walnut stock, hand checkered, an engraved and gold-filled frame, a rosewood grip cap, gold-plated trigger and fore-end release, etc. A high gloss finish appears on wood and metal. The boxlock action has an unusual locking system (aided by side buttresses) for these days, though a similar design was used by Dan Lefever in the 1880s. This consists of twin steel bolts, projecting from the standing breech, that mate with holes in the monobloc barrel breech. A strong system, and one that lets a low-profile frame result.

The barrels are air-gauge inspected to insure uniform dimensions and circularity (a practice usually carried out only on bench-rest barrels), firing pins are spring-loaded and the mainsprings are of coil type for long life and trouble-free service. This M1000 Grade I, made in 12 and 20 gauge, is $970 in field, Skeet or trap style, the stock made to order.

The M1000 Grade II is like the top Pedersen except it does not have custom stock option, and there's a little less engraving and gold filling, etc. 12 or 20, $650. The M1000 Grade III, like the others above in basic respects, cost $500, 12 or 20.

The M1500, 12 gauge only, is a cut below the M1000 series, but has a European walnut stock, vent rib and selective ejectors, sells for $400.

Single trigger, selective ejectors, ventilated rib barrels and English style (solid) rubber recoil pads are found on all M1000 grades. Skeet and trap guns in the M1000 and M1500 grades are slightly higher priced ex-

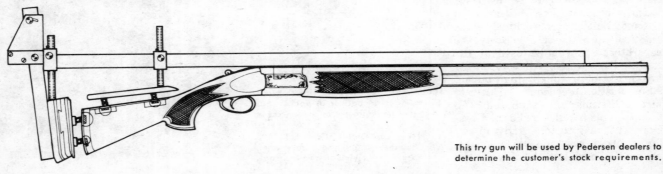

This try gun will be used by Pedersen dealers to determine the customer's stock requirements.

These are three of the Pedersen Custom guns. From the top—the $970 Series 1000 Grade I, a de luxe over-under that is stocked to the buyer's dimensions, and is fully engraved, etc. Center is the Series 2500 side-by-side double, below it the Series 3000 bolt action rifle, here in fully engraved presentation quality, retail price $650. See text for details.

cept for Grade I; they're also $970.

The Pedersen 2000 and 2500 Series, lateral doubles, have boxlock actions, are double underlug locked, and come with single trigger and selective ejectors. They do not have ventilated ribs. The wood is again select U.S. walnut, hand checkered, the fore-end a semi-beavertail type.

In this Series the Grade I offers the stock built to the owners dimensions, has an engraved frame, premium grade wood and so on. Cost is $970.

The Grade II, with less engraving, etc., is $650; the M2500 Grade III, like the foregoing grades in all respects except engraving, has European walnut, sells for $275.

All Pedersen double guns are furnished without added charge in a handsome luggage or trunk style case, built on a hardwood frame and with plush lined compartments. Three locking latches are standard. A pair of snap caps is also supplied at no extra cost.

Pedersen Rifles

The basic Pedersen rifle is their Model 3000 Grade III, a bolt action centerfire in 4 calibers—270, 30-06, 7mm Remington Magnum and 338 Winchester Magnum. This smooth looking action has 4-in-line locking lugs, a streamlined bolt sleeve, a checkered bolt handle knob and a hinged floorplate, 3-shot magazine. The trigger is adjustable and sling swivels are standard. The barrel carries an open rear sight and a hooded ramp front.

The Grade III stock has a flared pistol grip and a high, rollover comb-cheekpiece as standard. A low-comb, iron-sight stock is optional. Grip and fore-end are checkered. Price. $375.

The Grade II rifle is identical to the Grade III in all major aspects, but carries some engraving and ornamentation, cost $450. The Grade I, top of the Pedersen rifle line, shows extensive hand engraving, including the whole bolt handle and well forward on the barrel. The stock is of best grade American walnut. This rifle, identical to the Grades II and III otherwise, sells for $650.

All Pedersen rifles come with a plastic-coated steel cleaning rod, no extra cost, and several grades of slings are available at various prices.

I saw all of these Pedersen guns during the NSGA meeting and examined some of them closely. With no exceptions noted, all styles at whatever price seemed nicely put together—good fitting up, attractive wood quality and general appearance. I'd prefer finishes less shiny, but that's a minority view, I know. My pick of the shotguns was the Grade II side-by-side, a light, well balanced gun and not over elaborate.   J.T.A.

Mossberg's Lever Action Rifle

The Deer Slayer—Model 472—is the name of Mossberg's new lever-action rifle. A 7-shot full-length magazine carbine, its 20-inch round barrel carries open sights. The walnut pistol grip stock and fore-end are not checkered, I'm glad to see, rather than bearing today's impressed diamonds. The new carbine has three excellent features, two of them with safety aspects—1) Integral lever and trigger—the trigger travels with the operating lever, thus prevents jamming the finger against the trigger, causing a misfire or a bent finger. 2) Disconnecting trigger—the gun cannot be fired until the action is closed and the trigger released, with finger pressure then being re-applied. 3) New hammer block safety—the rifle cannot be fired when the hammer-block lever is moved to a "Mark Safe" position, thus preventing accidental discharge when the rifle is being loaded or unloaded.

The new 30-30 has a semi-hard recoil pad and sling swivels; it can handle a scope easily because of its side ejection and heavy-duty solid steel receiver. Cost, just over $100, we hear.   J.T.A.

Bill Large Barrels

I don't know anyone offering a greater variety of muzzle-loading barrels—or anybody with the long experience—than Bill Large. He makes 'em all—from small pistol barrels to extra heavy bench types, and everything between; rifled or smoothbore, false-muzzle slug barrels, musket or sway-belly fowlers, right- or left-hand twists of almost any pitch desired. Moreover, he'll duplicate an old barrel *exactly*. His prices are quite reasonable, too.

In addition, for the benefit of any reading this who need the job done, Bill is a long-time specialist in rescraping and spot finishing of machine bedways or flatways, slides or any mating surfaces. Ask for his brochure if you need a barrel.   J.T.A.

Mossberg's Model 472, the Deer Slayer lever-action carbine.

Laporte Trap Machines

As I've said, I didn't get to see everything at Houston's N.S.G.A. meeting, and one of the exhibitors I almost missed was Laporte, makers in France of a truly great variety of machines for throwing claybirds. I'm glad I found them—their booth wasn't on a well-travelled aisle—for I wound up spending a good hour there.

I'll confess I hadn't realized the importance of Laporte in this field, yet some 80% of all competition trap layouts throughout the world use Laporte equipment (except in the U.S.) and the percentage is even higher when other brand names are considered, in that many of these companies manu-

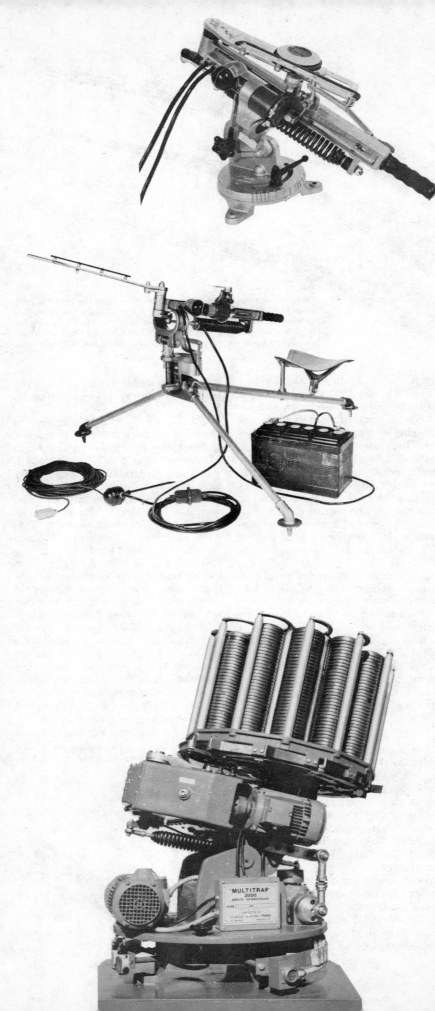

Above—the LaPorte Senior Trap 80, shown fitted with electrical release for use in single or 5-machine setups. Various electronic release consoles and microphone (voice) releases are available. Targets can be thrown between 45° and 130° horizontally, and from 10° to 42° vertically. • Right—the LaPorte Junior Trap 75, shown with remote electric release control and tripod mounted. The machine can also be mounted on a post or fixed to a base. Limited or unlimited cams allow lateral and vertical target variations internally. • Below—the versatile LaPorte Model 2000 trap, auto-angling to as much as 340° laterally, up to 60° vertically.

facture under license from Laporte. At this time Laporte machines—trap and skeet—are used in 32 countries for Olympics and International events as well as being in daily use at many clubs in those countries. Laporte traps were used in the Olympic Games at Rome and Tokyo in recent years.

Laporte makes some 15-16 different trap machines, these ranging from very low-cost hand traps to the most sophisticated devices I've seen or heard about, with a big selection of intermediate models at various price levels. In the popular-price range I was particularly impressed with their Models 75 Junior and 80 Senior—both showed excellent workmanship and the use of heavy duty, corrosion-resistant steels. Both, too, may be had with fail-safe 12-volt battery operation by remote control, and both are quite portable, too. The 75 Junior can be mounted on a tripod (supplied optionally) or on a post, etc., and a variety of control plates are offered to allow controlled alteration of flight angles, horizontal or vertical.

The Laporte Olympic 85 trap, though, is my choice for a backyard, casual setup because of its automatic, one-man usefulness—this machine has a clay target capacity between 35 and 80, is pneumatically cocked, and may be manually or electrically released. A voice-controlled (microphonic) release system is also available. Obviously, the lone shooter could use this Olympic 80 for hours—no helper needed—and he'd need to stop only infrequently to reload the magazine. I think this is a great idea.

But the most spectacular of the Laporte traps are their ultra-high capacity skeet and trap machines. I could hardly believe it, but their Skeetrap 1000 or Multitrap 2000 system have a magazine capacity of 1250 birds—that's right, 1250, enough for 100 rounds of skeet, for example, without reloading the machines! That is also some 6 hours of shooting for 6 people.

Both machines are, of course, fully automated. In fact, their most elaborate control box for straight trap offers 75 different angles, a system that is unpredictable and can't be "read."

The Multitrap 2000 is a particularly versatile machine. Because it is auto-angling to as much as 340 degrees horizontally and to 60 degrees vertically, plus variable speeds, the possibilities are almost endless. It can be positioned low or high, birds can be programmed to fly toward the shooter—simulating driven birds—and clay-birds can be thrown as fast as one per second and at *varying* speeds! As many as 14 birds can be thrown before the first one hits the ground and, easily managed by the operator, the second bird could be flying fast enough to overtake the first clay. No, I'm not making this up.　　　　J.T.A.

Because of the great versatility of this Multitrap 2000 model, Laporte showed me pictures and details of a new development that's now available from them. This is an 80-foot steel tower—the company calls it the Laporte Pylon—which accepts from one to 4 Multitrap 2000 machines. Each of these traps can be positioned anywhere on the tower—from just above ground level to 75 feet high—by pushing a button! The shooter has a big variety of shots—incomers, high or low, quartering left or right at various elevations and, by simply turning his back to the tower, all of these shots can be taken "going away." Because of the high rate of speed with which clays can be thrown—and only rarely at the same angle—flights of driven birds, flocks of ducks and geese, can be readily simulated.

Imagine this Laporte Pylon with two Multitrap 2000 mounted, each at a different level. In one hour those two traps can be put to flight 900 clay birds. That could be a lot of fun for some 6 or a dozen shooters, fanned out in a semi-circle around the tower.

Jean Laporte plans to erect one of these Pylons in the U.S., this year perhaps. When he does I very much want to see it in operation.

Well illustrated brochures on their traps can be had by writing Laporte S.A., B.P. 212, Pont de la Brague, Antibes, France, 06600.　　J.T.A.

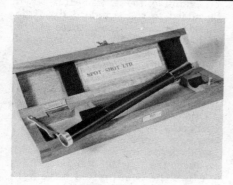

Spot-Shot

Drop this device into your 12, 16, or 20 gauge shotgun barrel—single or double, it won't work with pumps or autos because it is 10 inches long—close the gun and shoot. Instantly a circular spot of light appears on the wall or whatever, about the size of a cylinder-bore spread at any range, from a yard or two out to 40 yards. At longer ranges the light intensity falls off, of course, but paste-on reflective material is provided with the Spot-Shot, pieces of which can be temporarily mounted anywhere feasible.

What is seen on pulling the trigger is exactly where the point of aim was at that moment. This lets the shotter assess his gun mounting and the smoothness of his letoff. This can be, obviously, good practice, though at a stationary mark; a moving target would be ideal, naturally, but aside from clay birds propelled from a trap, that would be hard to achieve.

Our sample 12-gauge Spot-Shot weighs 6 ounces with its 3 Mallory Dura-Cell 1.5V batteries installed. Furnished in a fitted hardwood case (containing a small wrench and spare firing-pin impact unit of brass) the Spot-Shot sells for about $50. Custom made units can be furnished, and designs for use in magazine shotguns are being readied.

Abercrombie & Fitch (Madison at 45th St., New York, N.Y. 10017) are U.S. agents for the English-made Spot-Shot.　　　　J.T.A.

New S. S. Action

I don't know how many single shot actions have been offered in recent years, but it's a lot more than anyone would have expected, say, 25 years ago. Bill Ruger, of course, started the ball rolling with the Ruger No. 1 and, I suppose, the yen nowadays for the old and quaint has helped to bring the S. S. rifles back.

The action pictured is made and offered by the Falling Block Works (Box 22, Troy, MI 48084), cost $99. Called the Model H, it is a center-hammer under-lever, the breechblock dropping vertically. The receiver is an investment casting of chrome-moly steel. The hammer has a half-cock safety notch; the firing pin is in the breechblock. The extractor is of semi-ejector type. Trigger-hammer engagement is direct and adjustable. The action weighs about 2½ lbs., is 1⅜" thick. Stock attachment is via a through-bolt.

I haven't had this Model H action here for examination, but it appears attractive and well proportioned. I like the octagon top treatment. Judging only from the photo, the screws seem somewhat overlarge, and the short-length lever might lack grasping power in the event of a hard-to-move fired cartridge.　　J.T.A.

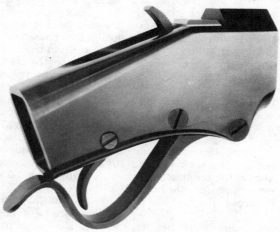

Rifles by James Riedl

I suppose it's an exaggeration to say that new single shot rifles seem to appear every week or so, but there's no denying their revival in fair numbers.

At this writing (January 1973, Riedl's Standard Rifle will be offered with a choice of 5 barrel weights, these with lengths proportional to their intended use—Light, Standard, Medium or Heavy Sporter, and the Magnum Sporter. As you can see from our picture, the rifle James Riedl (Box 308, San Juan Capistrano, CA. 92675) designed is an underlever, falling block type, stocked in classic, simple fashion—I'll describe the action in better detail a bit later on.

The single-shot rifle from Jim Riedl was delivered to me in mid-December, 1972. This new single shot, caliber 25-06, is not quite his production model, but it's close. The specimen here is, I believe, Riedl's last prototype and, as far as basic design and general appearance go, it's very close to what he'll market sometime in 1973.

Here is what the production rifle will offer: a truly unique action, operating via a rack-and-pinion system; the forward face of the breechblock carries the short rack, the end of the finger lever acting as the pinion. Action takedown is simple and fast, the trigger is adjustable for pull weight, and fired cases are extracted or ejected by varying manipulation of the finger lever.

The straight line firing pin is struck by a semi-concealed hammer; that is, the hammer is visible in the open top of the receiver, but may not be manually released or thumbed back after firing. Hammer cocking is automatic, but since no part of the hammer rises above the receiver opening, the hammer cannot be jarred off by a blow to it or the like.

The serrated safety lever lies *be-neath* the receiver, protected by the guard-lever, and is pushed off or on laterally. The safety locks the trigger and sear, and it may be reversed for left-handed shooters.

The action is made throughout of 4145 chrome-moly steel, but the hardened breech block is stainless steel; all springs are of coil type in stainless steel. As of this writing (January, 1973), five barrel weights and lengths are offered on Riedl Standard Rifles, these making up into rifles running from about 5¾ to 8½ lbs. and with 24″, 26″ or 27″ barrels. Standard calibers range from 17 Rem. ($15 extra) through all popular chamberings up to and including 375 H&H Magnum, but not all of these are available in all barrel types, of course.

Riedl's marketing approach is certainly different, for any Standard rifle, despite barrel weight (and length), will be sold at the same price, $199.50. I call that an attractive figure for a handmade rifle that's guaranteed against all parts failures.

The pistol gripped buttstock, held to the receiver by a ⅜-inch through-bolt, is quite straight, the shotgun-type butt deep. The classic lines are very attractive, I feel, and the 2-inch wide Varmint type fore-end nicely complements the buttstock. Deluxe wood is used, even on Riedl's standard-grade rifles, both fore-end and butt cut from the same blank for good matching of figure and color. Real buffalo horn buttplates are standard, and the fore-end screw will have a like horn inlay around it.

Metallic sights are not furnished except on 45-70 rifles; this caliber carries a front ramp and open rear sights. A raised quarter rib, designed to accept Weaver rings, abuts the receiver ring, and is a standard fitting.

Changes and Options

The scope base may be had, optionally, in steel or alloy, and a fore-end

Larry Sterett about to touch one off in the single shot rifle made by James Riedl.

hanger will probably be used at no extra cost. Riedl had thought to attach the fore-end by means of the usual simple screw. A single set trigger may be available, too. Other calibers will be added to the standard list if demand warrants. Among these will be, probably, 220 Swift, 257 Roberts, 458 Magnum and several others.

The Riedl single shot will be offered with a wide range of custom options, too many to list here, but special woods, stocks and finishes, barrels of all types and styles, including full or half-octagon, are just a few of many extra-cost options. Riedl has a free leaflet describing all of these, as well as brochures on the standard rifles.

I like the Riedl rifle I have here very much. I think it's a handsome piece, and it has functioned unfailingly for me so far. As my shooting results show, I'd say it has performed well, even for me! I think its capable of a lot better results, too, in the hands of a younger, clearer-eyed marksman. I'm not the sharpshooter I used to be, if I ever was!

Photo shows clearly the rack-and-pinion system used in Jim Riedl's single shot rifle. The component parts shown are not yet fully polished.

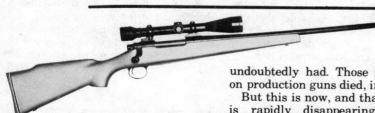

The Riedl rifle full length. The fore-end on this specimen is broad yet graceful in profile. The pistol grip curves well on this quite straight stock. The prototype scope mount, too high, will be lowered for production rifles.

There is, however, one thing on the new Riedl rifle I didn't like. That's the current over-high scope base, which lets even a big-objective scope clear the barrel top by ½-inch or so. Bringing this scope base down would help the shooter in another way, of course. As it is, the good high comb line of the stock is negated; one has to raise his head too far. I've suggested the base height be reduced, which Mr. Riedl says will be done. I'd like to see the rifle available with target-type scope blocks attached to the barrel, the current quarter-rib base left off. I'd like to mount one of the short-tube target scopes such as the Lyman or Unertl.

Shooting the Riedl

The weather turned good on December 28 — high, bright overcast, virtually no wind and the atmosphere crisp and clear. Temperature was about 40° F.

The new single shot rifle, now carrying a Weaver V9 scope in Weaver rings, was fitted to Riedl's quarter rib base; weight is an ounce under 8¾ lbs. The scope and rings make up for a pound of that weight.

During this enjoyable shooting session at my indoor bench (the muzzle peers out the westernmost garage window) I put 55 bullets through the Riedl 26″ medium weight barrel — the first lengthy shooting I'd done in several weeks. Trigger pull is a crisp 1½ lbs., which I like.

Twenty rounds were Remington's 87-gr. hollow points (their Index 2506), another 20 were Winchester's 90-gr. EXP (Expanding Point) cartridges (W25061), and 15 were hand-loads — 46.0/4064/87-gr. Sierra soft points/Norma primers, these in some GI brass I'd had around, primed and ready to load.

I'd used Dean Alley's Sweany-designed collimator to adjust the scope — having a touch of trouble seeing the collimator crosshairs because of the height of Riedl's quarter-rib base. The first couple of shots, however, were well on, printing about 4 inches high and some 2 inches to the right.

After expending a few of the W-W cartridges to condition the barrel and bring the point of impact closer to the point of aim, the first 5 of the 90-gr. bullets went into just under an inch. The next pair of groups, both of 5 shots, opened the groups a small amount, the 3 strings averaging about 1⅛ inches.

Then, after cleaning the barrel, I turned to the Remington ammo, wasting a couple of rounds again before making any groups for record. Three strings of 5 bettered the W-W ammo, but only slightly, and helped by the fact that one 87-gr. group went exactly .75-inch. The last remaining 3 of the R-P loads printed a hair under ⅝-inch. I'm not much of a believer in 3-shot groups validly establishing a rifle's norm, so this tighter run of 3 wasn't used in figuring the averages.

Both of these Remington and Winchester cartridge lots made the same point of impact at the 100-yard range, too, which is a nice trait in any rifle. I'm not sure, of course, but I'd guess that the coincidence of these two ammos springs from compensating barrel flip rather than from any inherent barrel stiffness. The Douglas-made barrel is the usual 1.20-inch at the receiver shoulder, and it's .665-inch at the muzzle — not a heavy barrel by any means.

The handload I'd put together was a first-trial effort, hence one on the mild side, as the results showed. The 87-gr. Sierras hit the paper some 3 inches above the group centers shot with the factory cartridges. Moreover, there was no decided improvement in group dimensions. One 5-shot cluster went into ¾-inch plus, but the average for the 3 groups, of 5 shots each, was just under 1⅛ inches, or about like the factory-ammo. — J.T.A.

Sterett's Riedl

The barrel channel of my Riedl rifle is thoroughly sealed. The barrel is glass-bedded ahead of the receiver for 7″ and free-floated the rest of the way. The fore-end is held to the barrel by one screw. The test rifle, caliber 300 Winchester magnum, had a glass-bedded recoil lug fitted ahead of the retaining screw.

Three-shot groups were fired at 100 yards from the bench, semi-slow fire. One session had winds gusting up to 25 m.p.h. — which wouldn't shrink group sizes. With the Weaver K-7 scope set at 7x the Riedl consistently shot between one and two inches with all three bullet weights. The smallest group measured 1¼″, made with Federal 180-gr. Hi-Shok loads. The 150-gr. Federal loads did almost as well; one group measured 1½″. With the proper handload the Riedl would no doubt shoot minute-of-angle groups or smaller. — L.S.S.

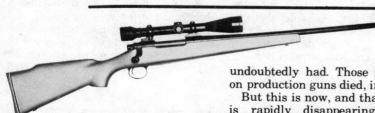

A Remington 700 barreled action in the Brown Precision fiberglass stock and fully finished.

Brown Precision Stocks

Time was when plastics in general were pretty much anathema to those with any feeling for natural materials. This attitude — amply justified in good part — was particularly prevalent among shooters. Who wanted plastic stocks, despite some advantages some undoubtedly had. Those few offered on production guns died, in the main.

But this is now, and that prejudice is rapidly disappearing — at least among target shooters, who will accept anything and any material if their scores and groups can be bettered thereby.

Brown's fiberglass rifle stocks, ultra light weight and impervious to warping and distortions due to weather-humidity changes, have been accepted, even welcomed by many bench-resters and hunters alike. In their first year of competition, 3 Brown stocks were among the "Top 20" at the Varmint Rifle Nationals.

Offered in blank at $55 (you do the final bedding, finishing, etc.) for Remington 700 and other actions, they're also available in finished form at $185. A third option, at $110, includes bedding your barreled action, ready to shoot, but no finishing or recoil pad.

Write for a price schedule and full details. — J.T.A.

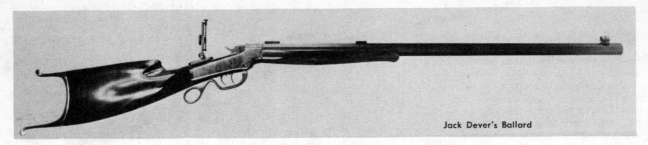

Jack Dever's Ballard

Jack B. Dever
Custom Gunsmith

The handsome Ballard single shot rifle shown here could well be mistaken for an original specimen in top condition. In actual fact, it's an old and loose Ballard Pacific action that Dever rescued and restored in traditional fashion. He fitted a Douglas barrel, all new pins and screws, and chambered the barrel for the seldom-seen 22-15-60 centerfire cartridge—a long, skinny little case that's oddly attractive. All metal was either rust blued or case-hardened in color, as appropriate.

Dever made the stock and foreend—using a nicely-figured piece of American walnut—to appear exactly like the original he found except for the buttplate and a buttstock without the semi-perchbelly profile and the high comb seen here. The Pacific Ballard came usually with a shallow-curved plate. He checkered the new wood to closely match the original's patterns. Dever's work seems to be first class.   J.T.A.

DS Antique Arms Co.

David F. Saunders, head of this company, had his replica Hawken rifles on view at the NSGA meeting —and very well done they are. With everything in and on them exact duplicates of the famous St. Louis-made caplock rifles, Saunders has re-created handsome and sturdy rifles in the old fashioned way.

Modern steels are used, of course, to make these Hawken copies eminently shootable—barrels are by Douglas in 45 to 54 caliber, locks have the tumbler fly, triggers are double set, double bar and adjustable, while the hook breech has a 5½" tang, as in the original. The buttplate, guard, toe plate, etc., are of steel, duplicating the original.

The wood used is hard maple, with fine figure, acid-etched and oil sealed in and out. As described, these "Hawkens" sell for $375, but variations can be made, too, as our illustration shows. Saunders puts his logo (a rams head with **D** and **S** on either side) on the breech and lockplate to let it be known that the rifles are of modern make.

Clerke's near replica of the High Wall Winchester single shot rifle, this Deluxe Grade about $245.

Saunders also does antique arms restoration, gunsmithing in this field in general, and fully guarantees his work "against everything but abuse," as he puts it.   J.T.A.

Clerke SS Rifles

Clerke has finally got his single shot rifles going—it's been a long wait! There are two models, the Standard (around $190) and the Deluxe at $245. Both are without sights or scope mounts but are tapped to accept the most popular styles. Redfield will, it's said, offer a one-piece mount later this year.

The Deluxe grade test model, in 45-70 caliber with a 26-inch round barrel, carried iron sights. The rifle pointed and handled well, much like a good brush gun. The lever opened easily but had to be forcefully returned to lock or latch into place. Extraction and ejection were smooth and positive. Accuracy at 50 and 100 yards was excellent, with 100-yard groups going 2½ inches with factory ammo—not too bad with open iron sights.

These rifles should appeal to classic buffs, since they carry the lines and feel of the old Winchesters, yet offer the dependability of coil springs. Clerke SS rifles will be available with fully adjustable trigger(s), round, full and half-octagon barrels, and in all popular calibers from 222 Rem. Mag. to 45-70.   W.L.R.

Redfield's
New Scope Mounts

If you're looking for a reliable way to mount a scope at low cost—and especially if you want ultra low weight—the new Redfield Frontier bases and rings really fill the bill. Precision machined of a tough alloy, each base has an integral locking lug that insures a rigid, immovable setup. The attractively-styled rings, designed to fit the scope tube perfectly, eliminate any problems of tube compression, optical distortion or seal breakage.

For the same reason, slippage of the scope in the rings won't happen, even under heavy recoil. Each ring has a thumb screw for easy mounting and removal, with no need to touch the scope screws. Only 3 ounces a set (4 units), Frontier mounts sell for $11.90, and they're ready now for all popular rifles.   J.T.A.

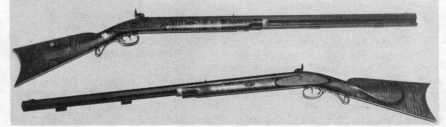

Two DS replica Hawkens, the lower one made for Lynton McKenzie, the New Orleans engraver.

Rangematic Mark V

This rangefinding instrument (made by Ranging, Inc., Rochester, N.Y. 14625) is not completely new—we reviewed an earlier form of it a while back—but the Mark V is a much-improved device, and at the same time more simple and easier to use. Essentially a split-image rangefinder, turning a calibrated dial while looking through the 6X scope element determines the range (50 yards to 2 miles) when the twin images blend together. It is as simple as that, really, and accuracy is guaranteed—99% at 100 yards, 98% at 200 yards, and so on to 95% at 500 yards. The standard scale furnished reads that way—in yards—but other scales are furnished that let the hunter know just how much he needs to hold over. These interchangeable scales are available for cartridges from the 22 Hornet to the 460 Weatherby, and just about every thing between—and there's a blank one for wildcats, too.

All Rangematics have been sturdy, near shockproof instruments—fiberglass reinforced outer case, welded steel interiors that are dustproof, insensitive to temperatures—that are guaranteed for 2 years. Roughly 10½″ x 2″ x 2½″ in its maximum dimensions (not including the detachable 6 x 18 scope, which is usable separately, of course) the Rangematic Mark V weighs 22 ounces complete. A well-padded vinyl case is furnished, which can be belt-hung and zipped open or shut in a moment.

As I've said, the Mark V works better and faster than the earlier models—the bright blue and yellow images make it easy to overlap them, and that in turn means more accurate range-finding. Admittedly, no ranging device is going to be used in many hunting situations, and none is really needed on shots to 200 yards or

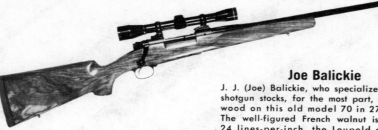

so, but there could well be occasions when it would help greatly to know whether that elk, say, was 350 yards off or 400. In any case the Mark V is reliable—you decide whether you can benefit from its use—and good value at $34.95.   J.T.A.

Fusil V

Here is a small stainless steel device, precisely made, that I wish I'd had some years ago when I was doing more caplock rifle shooting! Percussion caps were often a problem then—erratic performance, the right size not always available, bits flying about to sting the hands or face.

Fusil V replaces the percussion nipple or cone, allowing the use of large primers instead—just screw in the bottom element (¼-28 or 5/16-24, specials to order at $2 extra), drop in a primer, snap the top unit over the lower one and it's ready to fire. The flash hole is quite large, permitting a hot flame, yet there can be no blowback—an internal ball acts as a check valve.

The Fusil V has obvious advantages—the use of non-corrosive primers, avoidance of misfires in wet weather and strong and reliable ignition, so much so that even damp charges ought to fire.

Price, $9.95 from Anderson & Co., 1203 Brodway, Yakima, WA 98902—the same firm that makes the excellent Storm King and Storm Queen lens caps for scopes and other shooting items.

Joe Balickie

J. J. (Joe) Balickie, who specializes in certain shotgun stocks, for the most part, shaped the wood on this old model 70 in 270 caliber. The well-figured French walnut is checkered 24 lines-per-inch, the Leupold scope is in Conetrol mounts.

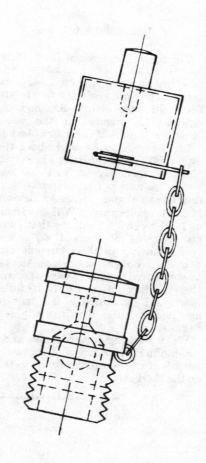

Howard V. Grant
Gun Engraver

New to the gun world, but an engraver for years on precious metals, Mr. Grant made the switch to hard steel very nicely indeed. I've seen some dozen examples of his work, and all of it was well executed and well designed. The 3-piece illustration of his work shown here—two grip caps and an exercise piece—readily reveal his expertise. The low-relief grip caps would grace and enhance any fine rifle, but Mr. Grant's talents extend to handguns and shotguns, of course.

Write to him at Box 396, Lac du Flambeau, Wisc. 54538 for full information.   J.T.A.

Engraving in steel by Howard V. Grant—the grip caps are executed in low relief, the backgrounds darkened for excellent light-and-shadow effects.

Champlin/Merkel

Champlin Firearms of Enid, Oklahoma—makers of handsome and practical sporting rifles to customers' tastes and dimensions, using the Champlin bolt action—are now exclusive U.S. agents for the world famous shotguns of Gebrüder Merkel.

Little needs to be said about the high quality and functional beauty of Merkels, certainly not to those who know the name. Their reputation is impregnable and, to assess modern Markels against pre-WW II specimen, as I did recently, I can say that I saw no lessening of the old skills and craftsmanship in their current production. I bought a sidelock Merkel over-under nearly 25 years ago, and the quality of some half-dozen Merkels I examined a few months ago hadn't suffered in the slightest degree.

We're showing some Merkels and a Champlin rifle nearby, and I'm rather surprised at the relatively low prices on the Merkels. J.T.A.

Left—the Merkel 203E, a sidelock O-U with H&H type hand-detachable lockplates. Double sears and double cross-bolts are standard on the 203E, but all else is optional—straight or p.g. stock (of de luxe walnut), twin or single triggers, fine scroll or hunting scene engraving, stocks to order, etc. With selective single trigger, in 12, 16 or 20 gauge, $1675. Merkel's 303E—their best quality—is like the 203E but has better wood, finish, engraving, etc., and lock-up includes double hook (Kersten) bolting. With all options, $2500.

Second, Merkel's best boxlock O-U, 12, 16 or 20 (3-inch chambers available), is the 201E, with a double Kersten-bolted action; double, single or SS triggers, straight-hand or p.g. stock to the customer's specification, cocking indicators and fine hunting scene engraving. At about 7¼ lbs. in 12 gauge (16s and 20s available also), the 201E with SS trigger is $1037.

Third, here is Merkel's 47S, a sidelock side-by-side double, made in 12, 16 or 20, with double-lock bolting and the usual Merkel options on barrel length, chokes, stock dimensions, triggers, etc. Lightweight at 6¼ to 6¾ lbs., the scroll-engraved 47S is $743 with single trigger.

Last, this custom Champlin 25-06 bolt rifle has an octagon barrel, the ramp front sight and sling-swivel stud integral. The handsome and classic French walnut stock is by Maurice Ottman, metal work—including checkered bolt knob and blind magazine—by Bill Rinie, both with Champlin Firearms.

New 1973 Williams Catalog

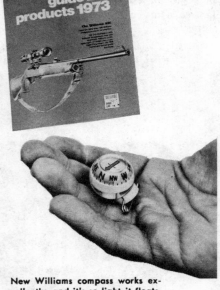

New Williams compass works excellently, and it's so light it floats.

Williams Gun Sight (7300 Lapeer Rd., Davison, Mich. 48423) has a new 36-page catalog that features the Williams 500 Custom Designed products for shooters, including their Twilight, Guide Line and Wide Guide scopes. Shown, among many other interesting items, are their new models of Sight-Thru mounts, Quick Convertible top mounts, Foolproof and 5D receiver sights, Guide receiver sights, trigger shoes and hammer extensions.

A convenient 4-page Accessory Chart lists all popular rifles and shows which Williams products will fit each —a handy reference for anyone and everyone interested in firearms. Free copies of the 1973 catalog are available for the asking.

Brand new is a small, spherical compass, the type meant to be pinned to a shirt or jacket. The 1⅛" diameter plastic globe holds a half-ball compass, a night-luminous arrow pointing to North. No matter how the sphere is tilted or rotated, the compass is always uppermost. Handy, useful indeed, and highly recommended. J.T.A.

Len Brownell's new grip cap, investment-cast in steel, shows a beautifully crisp and simple design. Their elegance, though, is hard to attain—they're not easily cast or polished.

Len Brownell's custom-made scope mount locks immovably on dovetail bases by turning two small levers. It can be quickly removed, yet it will go back to original point of impact perfectly.

Len Brownell's new investment-cast bolt handles, intended for gunsmith attachment to 98 Mauser bolts in the main. They're 98% finished, needing only light polishing after cleaning of the weld.

Len Brownell

One of the finest stockmakers of our time—and a topnotch metalsmith as well—Len Brownell spent several years working for Bill Ruger. Those handsome classic handles found on the Ruger Single Shot and Model 77 rifles are Brownell designs.

But Len also kept his eyes open during his stint at Ruger's New Hampshire plant. He saw how investment castings were made, and now he's put that knowledge to work.

Len has, as of now, three products he's designed—two for the gunsmith and one for the rifleman/hunter. Dissatisfied with the forged bolt handles that have been the only type available heretofore—their usual roughness, the time needed to bring them to finished state—Brownell offers a cast handle, one that's 98% finished. All it requires is welding to the bolt body, the cleaning up of the weld area and a minimum of bolt polishing before bluing.

It's a handsome handle, too—gracefully swept down and back, designed to clear a low-hung scope, and the perfectly-round knob is hollow for least weight. They're priced at $1.75, over the cost of a forged handle, but the labor saving more than makes up for the small difference, especially to the gunsmith who uses a fair number of them in the course of a year. They're fully guaranteed, of course.

Len's new 2-piece scope mount (separate bases and rings) is the result of long thought and great experience with existing mounts. It is beautifully clean—no protruding knobs to catch on this or that, just a small lever on each ring that locks the rings rigidly to a dovetail base. I'm going to quote from Len's letter: "This mount is rugged. It has large areas of support firmly locked together. Quick detachable, it will go back to the point of aim as good as a target scope—which is pretty damn good."

Bases for popular rifles, of course, plus blank bases for use on custom rifles, quarter-ribs and the like, are in the works. Prices are not yet determined, but Len's mounts are not meant to compete with other mounts.

Last, Len sent along a pistol-grip cap that is a masterpiece of simple good taste and elegance. I hope our photograph does justice to this little jewel, but it must be seen for real appreciation. These are $6, and they're available now.   J.T.A.

Gunk Neo-Met

The makers of Liquid Wrench—a popular product known to about everybody for its rust-busting ability—have a new Gunk-derived solvent that removes tar, grease, gum, wax, you name it, and it's safe to use on guns, typewriters, instruments, etc. Gunk Neo-Met is non-flammable, dries fast, and it contains no acetones, petroleum distillates or silicones. L.S.C. is another product made by the Radiator Specialty Co., Charlotte, NC 28201, which acts as an all-purpose lubricant, displaces moisture, and frees rusted parts. See your automotive supply dealer or hardware store first.   J.T.A.

George M. Fullmer

Fullmer is a metal working gunsmith—no bluing or stockwork, and he prefers to spend his time and labor on benchrest and varmint rifles. In conjunction with such work, Fullmer is also—perhaps primarily—a specialist in precision chambering. He uses only Red Elliott or Keith Francis reamers, pilots held to 0.0001", and he offers "absolute alignment of chamber and bore." At this time he's able to cut over 130 different chambers, these generally held to minimum standards, and he can, in most cases, furnish precision loading dies to match. 130 chambers—that must include a hell of a lot of wildcats, huh?   J.T.A.

Texas Platers Supply

If you'd like to give your guns—or other metal objects—a gold, silver or nickel finish, TPS has the materials and the techniques. Each kit contains detailed instructions and re-order information (the full information is offered by itself for a stamp), and there's enough plating materials in even the lowest-priced kit to plate three handguns. These kits cost as little as $5.40 for nickeling to $15 for their Gunsmith Special, which offers gold, silver and nickel plating. All kits carry a money-back guarantee, all are shipped prepaid. TPS is at 245 W. 5-Mile Parkway, Dallas, TX 75233.   J.T.A.

The Creedmoor Sharps

If all goes well we'll soon see the famed 45-3¼-inch Sharps straight taper rimmed case offered in good quantity—and at a reasonable price for what will be, most likely, a single production run.

These long-desired cases are not yet a reality, but it begins to look promising. Hundreds of people, perhaps thousands, have hoped that this historic cartridge case might one day become available, not that any big percentage of those same wishful thinkers own a big Sharps—or other rifle—so chambered. But that's the beauty of having the 45-3¼ returned, for from it can be made some 18 other much-sought-after cases, all with the same head-rim diameters. This covers such 45-caliber cases alone as the 2.4″, 2.6″, 2⅞″, to say nothing of the various 40-caliber cases that could be made from the same brass.

How has this project come about? A few months ago Bill Ruger told me that he would like to offer the Ruger No. 1 Single Shot rifle in this old and storied caliber if only the cases could be obtained. If they could, he added, he would deliver with each rifle so-chambered a number of the long cases—quantity not fully specified, but at least 25 or 50. Cost of the cases and how many would be manufactured would have a bearing, of course.

Of the several ammo makers I approached with this project, only Norma of Sweden evinced any interest. At that time I did not know that a prominent reloading tool maker had had the same idea, or that he had also approached Norma.

Now, via a letter from Norma's Nils Kvale, I've learned that the "other guy" is my old friend and hunting partner, Fred Huntington of RCBS. Fred had, I gathered, been in touch with Norma on much the same project I had.

For that reason Huntington may have sole distribution of these 45-3¼ cases if and when they're ready. In any event, their advent here seems reasonably assured, but prices remain unset at the moment.   J.T.A.

R.W.S.

Dynamit Nobel (105 Stone Hurst Ct., Northvale, NJ 07647) has several new loadings for 1973, most of these using their cone-shaped bullet, a fairly recent development that gives excellent game performance. See the sketch of it nearby.

The calibers using the cone-point are the 243 (95-gr.), the 6.5x57, rimless or rimmed, the 6.5x68 and 6.5x68R, these last four holding 127-gr. bullets. The cone point in 162-gr. weight is used in the 7x57, rimless or rimmed, and in the 7x64 and 7x65R.

A completely new cartridge for RWS is the 375 H&H, one with the cone bullet, the other version with a full-jacket projectile, both of 300 grains weight.

Beside these centerfire rifle cartridges, RWS also offers the R50, a match grade 22 Long Rifle rimfire, a 22 Short, the R25, a 7.65mm Luger (Parabellum) load, a new 45 ACP round with full metal-jacket 231-gr.

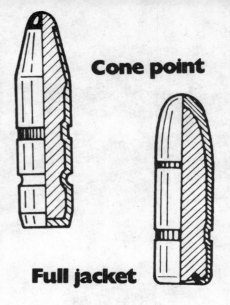

Cone point

Full jacket

bullet, and a 38 Spl. cartridge, also in FMJ form, the bullet weight 157 grains, muzzle velocity 870 foot seconds.

RWS makes first class ammunition, and I've used a lot of it over the years with good success.   J.T.A.

Chapman Screw Drivers

The makers of the highly useful screwdriver set pictured here are long-time toolmakers to industry, but the No. 8320 Kit now offered to gun fans is their first venture into the firearms world. Each kit holds 28 different driver bits—12 slotted-head, 10 Allen types, 2 Phillips head and four jeweler's blades. There's also a large handle, a rotating handle for the tiny bits, an extension and a ratchet having a torque strength of 200 inch pounds. All of the blades are made of chrome-nickel-moly steel, and the slotted bits are parallel sided, not tapered, for a strong, non-slip bite. Everything is contained in a handsome red-vinyl

covered steel case (4½″×7½″), and all elements nest in their separate compartments.

All of the regular bits may be used in the extension or not, and may be driven by the ratchet alone, or by the larger handle, with or without the extension. Each also has a "spinner top" for fast finger tightening.

A $20 bill buys the entire lot, as described—just ask Chapman Mfg. Co., Route 17, Durham, CT 06422, for No. 8320. Extra bits, including Bristol ¼″ square drive and other Allen and Phillips heads, the latter in metric sizes too, are available.

An excellent outfit, one designed to keep your screwdrivers handy and ready for instant use. We recommend it highly.   J.T.A.

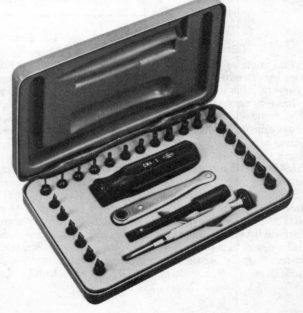

Chapman No. 8320 screwdriver kit.

Goens Custom Rifles

Shown here are three excellent examples of Dale Goen's high craftsmanship, each clearly exhibiting his mastery of flowing line and graceful, coordinated contour.

Top is a Model 70 Winchester, caliber 280, made for Paul DeMeis. The wood is curly, burl maple, checkered fore and aft in a ribboned fleur-de-lis pattern.

Next below is a lightweight 7×57, made for Richard Harris, also on a pre-64 M70 action. The wood is American crotch walnut, the checkering done to a pattern Goens has named for Jack O'Connor.

Bottom is a full-stocked rifle, made for Lou Ostendorp, an old hunting partner. This rifle is a mate to one made for me but completed earlier (see GUN DIGEST 25th/1971 ed., inside back cover). It has the same engraved silver fittings—and a like Böhler octagon barrel with raised rib. The wood is a handsome piece of French walnut, the action an FN Mauser. J.T.A.

Ingram Carbine Conversion for Thompson-Center Contenders

Until recently the T/C Contender pistol has been limited to factory pistol barrels only, in lengths of 8½″ and 10″. Now David L. Ingram (P.O. Box 4263, Long Beach, CA 90804) offers a carbine conversion kit in several variations for this popular single shot pistol.

This kit consists of a buttstock, fore-end and rifle barrels, 16½″, 18″ or 20″ long, ready for attachment to the Contender action. Retail, $114.50, includes the T/C pistol. There are two barrel contours—standard taper and straight bull type. Right- or left-hand stocks at no extra cost, and there are three fore-end styles: standard, beavertail and full length Mannlicher. The latter is available only with the standard 20″ barrel. Over 35 chamberings, wildcats and standard, are available.

There are de luxe and super de luxe models also, with prices at $179.50 on up.

Here are the legal aspects of these units: they are perfectly legal as long as the buttstock is used in conjunction with a rifle barrel over 16″ and a shotgun barrel over 18″. W.L.R.

Top—Ingram conversion T/C Contender with beavertail fore-end and bull barrel.

Middle—Ingram conversion with standard 20″ barrel and full length stock.

Bottom—Ingram T/C Contender conversion with standard barrel and fore-end.

F&H Machining

F&H makes 3 types of front rifle rests and 2 basic styles of rear rests, all intended for use by bench rest competition shooters in the main, but eminently usable by anyone wanting high-precision equipment.

Front rests are offered in standard, ball-bearing or Delrin ball-slide forms. All of these have angle-locks on the elevation screws, hardened-tip rest screws (for use on concrete benches) that are reversible to rubber-tipped style, and one-inch elevation screws. The best quality alloy is used in the base castings, and workmanship is excellent.

The standard rest (38.95) serves well for bench shooting, particularly in the Varmint and Sporter classes, or for informal rest shooting, of course. The ball-bearing and Delrin-ball-rail rests are for use in unlimited class shooting, their cost as much as $89.95, but these are made also as top units, attachable to the regular F&H rest, and sell for less.

The F&H rear rest systems, also meant for unlimited class competition, are priced to about 75.00, and various accessories are available to enhance performance.

F-H standard rest with bag clamps.

F-H rest with precision bearing top.

F&H also offer a very good rack-and-pinion type loading (arbor style) press, weight 8½ lbs., capacity under the ¾" rack of 5½". The pinion shaft is bronze bushed for long life, and the 3-point base makes for steady positioning even on rough or uneven surfaces. Cost, $47.50. F&H's Bill Hill will gladly send full information for a stamped envelope.   J.T.A.

M. H. Canjar Co.

The reliable and easily fitted (usually!) Canjar triggers have brightened the outlook for many riflemen for a long time, so no elaborate review of them is needed here. For the benefit of the new boys, they're made in regular and set types, and for many models of rifles.

However, Canjar has three new triggers that I know about — and by this time (mid-March 1973) he may have one for the De-Haas-Miller single shot rifle-action. Two triggers are now ready for Ruger rifles — the Models 77 and Single Shot, and another for the 88 Remington. Samples of each of these were sent to me last November.

I was particulary pleased to get the Ruger 77 set trigger, for I'd also obtained not long before a 77 in 7x57mm caliber — which needed a better trigger. It didn't take long to install it — some metal had to be removed from the guard top and trigger opening in the guard widened a bit. The trigger itself performed beautifully, with no adjustment of it needed — I got 2½ pounds unset, a few ounces set. Both letoffs are crisp and clean, and I'm delighted with it.

I haven't fitted the Canjar trigger for the Remington 788 yet, but it took more time to fit the new trigger

(also a set type) to the Ruger Single Shot — and a bit more time to get the trigger adjusted. The rather tricky innards of the Ruger SS account for a good part of this, of course — it's not as simple as most bolt actions are. Anyway, I managed to get just under 3 pounds unset, and again a very light release when set.

Excellent triggers, these two, and I'm sure the set trigger for the 788 will be equally satisfactory.   J.T.A.

Canjar Tang Safety Trigger

M. H. Canjar, well known for the good triggers he's long made, has just introduced a top tang safety that may be ordered as part of his triggers. Made in two types — one meant to be welded to the action, the other not — the new system is made for '98, FN, Mark X and Santa Barbara Mausers, for Springfields, Winchester 70s and the 3 sizes of Sako actions. The linkage between tang safety button and trigger — on both types — was designed to be as small as practicable; only a minimum of wood need be removed in the grip section. Full details and prices on request.   J.T.A.

Charles Clement's Leathercraft

For the past 8 years Clements has been making fine holsters, fitted gun cases, antique reproductions and restorations, binding and case fitting books, sheathing fine knives and doing presentation carved and tooled work. He'll also attempt industrial prototypes in innovative techniques.

Having trained for nearly 20 years to produce the quality of design ornamentation and construction reflected in his articles, he doesn't compete with saddleries, harness shops and department store leathercrafters. Clements' style is in the English tradition of fine construction, the motifs derived from western carving, bookbinders modeling and a background in fine art.

Clements sent us several color shots of his work, which I regret we can't show. He works by appointment only, and he'll be glad to answer any questions posed.   J.T.A.

Kropatschek Rifles and Carbines

Century Arms has brought a limited number of these early breech-loading military arms into the U.S. Made first around 1878 or so, these tubular-magazine firearms were built at the famous Steyr factory in Austria for the Portuguese government. Because they were made before 1898 they're freely deliverable to individual buyers in the U.S. Two models are available, the 1886 and the 1886-91, either in rifle or carbine. The 86-91 version differs only in having a handguard, but contemporary data shows a shorter barreled M1886-91.

These are bolt action arms, the bolt sticking straight out on the rifles, bent down on the carbines. There's a cut off lever for single-shot firing, and a thumb safety that blocks the firing pin. The caliber of the Portuguese Kropatscheks is 8mm, commonly called the 8x60R, and loaded with a 247-gr. jacketed bullet of .326" diameter. Muzzle velocity was about 1700 foot seconds. This cartridge is similar

Top—the Kropatschek bolt action M1868 rifle; below, the carbine form. Both are chambered for the 8x60R Kropatschek cartridge.

to the earlier 8x60R Guedes, but they're not interchangeable. The rifle magazine holds 8 cartridges, the carbine 6. Century Arms tells us quantities of 8x60R cartridges will be available by the time you read this.

One of the carbines had been promised for a shooting trial, but it didn't arrive in time, regrettably. However, we've examined both rifles and carbines recently, and the evidence of old fashioned fine workmanship and assembly was readily evident.

These are not, however, *new* arms—they've seen a degree of service, but they'd classify as about N.R.A. Good to Very Good generally. As usual with such lots, some specimens will be better than others, but at their relatively low price, they're a good buy.

The Kropatschek rifles are priced at $29.50 (either model), the scarcer carbines selling for $34.50, these prices FOB St. Albans, Vt., headquarters for Century Arms, and orders can be sent directly to the company.

Keith Stegall

The 270 rifle pictured here was made for Mr. Chad Neilson on a near new 1898 Mauser action. Handsomely stocked with an exceptionally nice piece of French walnut—note good fiddleback quality—the 24 lines-per-inch checkering shows a multi-point and inset panel combination. The checkered steel buttplate is one of Al Biesen's; the classic steel grip cap is the new one made by Len Brownell.   J.T.A.

Frazier's Custom Guns

Jay Frazier seems to be an up-and-coming young fellow as a custom stocker in the classic tradition—shown here is a Ruger single shot rifle he recently completed for a left-handed shooter. Good lines and good checkering—24 lines per inch—distinguish the black walnut stock of this attractive 22-250 rifle.

Our Custom Guns section shows another well done rifle by Frazier,

this one a 1909 Argentine Mauser in 6mm Remington caliber. The action was much altered and the bolt knob checkered in three panels. The American walnut stock—checkered

24-line—shows a very handsome crotch-feather pattern. Frazier says he welcomes and answers all inquiries—address him at Hayden, Colo. 81639.   J.T.A.

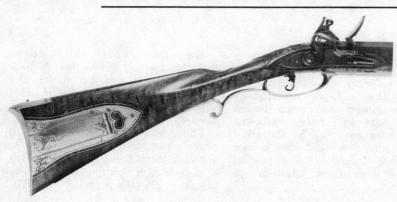

John Bivins

The buttstock area seen here is found on a beautifully done light rifle made for a youngster. Weighing only 6½ pounds, this handsome Pennsylvania rifle has a 36-inch Paris barrel, the caliber 40. The grace and simple elegance of Bivins' work is hardly to be surpassed, his mastery of flowing line and form beyond reproach.   J.T.A.

Smith Wildcats

Bob Smith (Smitty's Gun Shop) is the creator of the six wildcats pictured here, all developed some time ago. We show these cartridges because they're moderate-performance loads, each carefully designed for excellent case-capacity ratio to caliber and bullet weights. None of them are intended to burn barns or destroy tanks, but all are effective in their several areas of performance.

For full load data and other information see P.O. Ackley's 2-volume work, *Handbook for Shooters and Reloaders,* or write to Bob Smith. Ackley, you'll note on reading his comments, finds the Smith wildcats useful.

From left—the "Smith 25," his 277 and 7mm Magnums, the "Thirty Smith" and his 350 and 450 Magnums.

NHF Day Involves Millions

With reports still coming in, National Hunting and Fishing Day headquarters in Riverside, Conn., reports that direct word has been received on 1,875 Open Houses so far, with total known attendance exceeding 2½ million persons.

Since it is nearly impossible to gain reports on every NHF Day activity held, the NHF Day organizers estimate that more realistic figures indicate that some 2,500 special NHF Day observances were held, involving between 3 and 4 million persons.

Virtually all clubs which held activities on Sept. 23 report they are already planning for NHF Day, 1973, to be held on September 22.

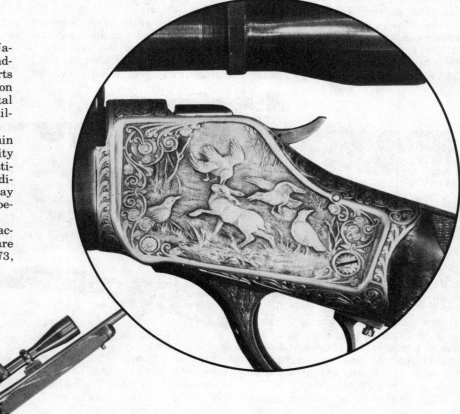

Hal Hartley

Two views of a de luxe rifle done by Hartley recently, except for the engraving—that is Albin Obiltschnig's (Ferlach) superb work, even though he is 80 years old! Hartley, who owns several guns engraved by the great Austrian engraver—and who has seen many more—considers this as good as any he's seen from Obiltschnig's hand.

The action is a high wall Winchester, the barrel a Douglas 26-inch heavy sporter chambered for the Remington 6mm, but with a rim. Hal uses 7x57R cases, altering them as needed.

The wood is hard maple, with sharply-contrasting fiddleback grain showing throughout its length. With a K-6 Weaver scope aboard, the weight is 8¾-plus pounds.   J.T.A.

Hyper Single Rifle Test

Sam Lair sent me the rifle pictured here at a time when I couldn't do any shooting—too cold, too rainy, too busy—but today the sun shone, if briefly, so I fired a few handloads—but fewer than I intended, as you'll see.

This Hyper Single, in 225 Winchester caliber, is stocked and sighted as a varminter—high and dished comb-cheekpiece, a 12x Redfield scope, and it has Lair's fluted barrel. The fluting is well done, too, the net result a stiff barrel for better accuracy, yet one that lets the complete rifle, with scope, go only 8½ lbs.

Shooting it from my 100-yard bench was both frustrating and rewarding! The light was good, but a 6-8 mph wind, gusting to 10 or better, was blowing from the southwest. A test of the trigger showed a crisp letoff of about a pound, the internal hammer fall satisfyingly dead. The crosshairs were steady on the target—no paral-

Lair's S.S. action is the basis for this 22-250 varmint rifle with fluted barrel.

lax.

I'd loaded 22 rounds, all with 32.0/4064/CCI primers, and with 7 Nosler 52-gr. Solid Base match grade (unpolished for a special test); 5 of Nosler's 52-gr. regular SB bullets; 5 each of Sierra 53s and Remington Match 52s, all hollow point.

In trying to waste the first two shots (Nosler 52s) I ran into trouble—the first load failed to fire! The primer had been too lightly struck, it was easy to see. Either headspace is a touch loose or firing pin protrusion is short, and I suspect the latter is the case. I continued shooting and, despite another misfire, four bullets went

into a tight 7/16″ laterally, but with near-zero vertical dispersion.

I then shot the 5 Remington bullet loads, again getting another misfire, with about the same results. 3 bullet holes were touching horizontally (for ½″), with no elevation differences. The 4th shot went a half-inch away, my fault, I'm sure.

The few cases actually fired—8 total, plus the 3 misfires, showed the same shallow firing pin indent. In view of what was probably not ideal ignition conditions, and the gusting wind, those tight groups indicate that this Hyper Single wants to perform. I'll try again when it's fixed.   J.T.A.

Camillus Knives

Camillus has been making knives—of all kinds, but in the main pocket knives of folding type—for a great many years. Since 1876, in fact, which means that this New York State manufacturer has been in the blade business for almost a century.

Camillus knives, however, were for a long time distributed and sold through hardware jobbers. That's changed now, though, and the sporting goods field is being covered and catered to as rapidly as conditions permit.

Make no mistake—Camillus knives, though factory made, are fabricated of excellent quality high-carbon steel, tough and durable, and their edges hand-honed for extra sharpness. However, several folding knives are

now offered in stainless steel (for anglers, seamen, et al), and there is also a line of new sheath knives offered, these last in addition to several earlier hunting knives. The new sheath blades have real stag handles, vary in length from 3½″ to 7″, and in price from $12.50 to $16.50.

A short while ago, the Boy Scouts of America elected Camillus as the maker of their official knife (no illustration), and the company has now embarked on a program to make a very wide range of the famous "Swiss Army" knives, so-called. These last have been big sellers for years, particularly those with a number of blades, can openers, screwdrivers, scissors, you name it. Some of these "Swiss Armys" are hardly more than over-sized curiosities, of

course, with their multiple blades and fittings (like up to 25!) but others can be quite handy. I've been carrying one for years—an Elinox, made of stainless steel, and with two blades, a screwdriver, a combined can-bottle opener and a corkscrew. What with most U.S. wine bottles holding a plastic stopper or cap these days, I've little use for the corkscrew here, but it's handy in Europe.   J.T.A.

Herman Waldron—Metalsmith

Waldron offers a variety of excellent custom items for Mauser and other actions—his latest work includes making octagonal-sided bolt handles, scope bases, trigger bow bottoms, etc. He produces precise, carefully done jobs, as the trigger bow pictured here attests. He alters bolts and checkers bolt knobs, makes side-swing floorplate release levers, and streamlines, by fluting, Redfield scope bases. Waldron's address is Box 475, Pomeroy, WA 99347—ask for his price list.   J.T.A.

Mauser Models 71 and 71/84 Rifles

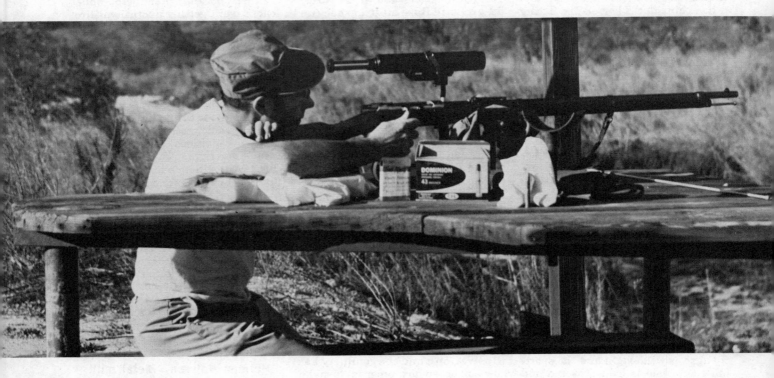

A detailed and valuable study of Peter Paul Mauser's first successful action systems, plus full data on the 11mm Mauser cartridge and a modern load table.

by FRANK C. BARNES

MAUSER MODELS 71 and 71/84 military rifles chambered for the 11mm Mauser cartridge have been sold in the United States by military surplus dealers at various times since around the turn of the century. There was another influx of these rifles about 10 years ago, many of them brand new. It is the more recent introduction that has stimulated renewed interest in the rifles and the cartridge they shoot. The 11mm Mauser cartridge has never been widely used in the U.S. and information, particularly loading data, is quite scarce. The author has received sufficient mail on the subject over the past five or six years to warrant a fairly comprehensive coverage. As a matter of fact, the Mauser Models 71 and 71/84 rifles are among the best and most accurate of the old black-powder military rifles. There is no reason why they should not be used, and perhaps the information provided here will encourage more owners to take them off the wall and out into the field.

The Mauser Model 1871 and the later M71/84 bolt-action rifles were

Checking out the Mauser 71/84 rifle and 11mm ammunition. The rifle will shoot as well as any modern hunting rifle but effective range is limited by the high trajectory of the bullet.

designed by Peter Paul Mauser, well known to gun enthusiasts as one of the world's foremost firearms designers. The Model 71 was the first truly successful bolt-action rifle firing centerfire, self-contained ammunition. As such, it represents an important milestone in small arms development, one that influenced military thinking and tactics through World War II, a span of almost 75 years.

The Model 71 Mauser

The Model 71 is a single-shot, breech-loading, bolt-action rifle with a split-bridge receiver and a two-piece bolt having a removable head. Over-all length is 52.75 inches and barrel length is 33.5 inches (a shorter carbine version with a 20-inch barrel was also manufactured). The rifling has four grooves, right-hand twist, one turn in 21.7 inches.

Nominal bore diameter is supposed to be 0.433-inch, with groove diameter 0.448- to 0.450-inch. However, there is a wide variation in the bore and groove diameters actually found in these rifles, and some barrels will measure from 0.452- to 0.455-inch groove diameter. This fact undoubtedly accounts for the poor results reported by some shooters when handloading with the usually recommended 11mm bullets. It is important to measure the bore diameter of 11mm Mauser rifles before ordering bullet molds or sizing dies in order to end up with the correct size for your particular rifle. Both the M71 and M71/84 rifles were manufactured at various commercial plants and arsenals, which may account for the differences in bore dimensions. This will be covered in greater detail later.

The M71 is operated by raising the bolt handle and drawing the bolt to the rear. A cartridge is inserted in the chamber and the bolt pushed forward and down until the action is closed and locked. The action is self-cocking and is ready to fire as soon as the bolt is locked. There is a manual safety at the rear of the cocking piece; when the lever is to the left, the gun is ready to fire; if pushed up and all the way to the right, it is on SAFE. The bolt can be removed by loosening the bolt stop screw on the right side of the bolt (on top when the bolt handle is lifted), raising the stop and, with the trigger held back, withdrawing the bolt. The barrel can then be cleaned from the breech end.

Accurate production records are not available, but the number of M71 rifles made must have been close to a million. In addition to Germany, many were sold in the Balkans, China, and to some South American countries.

The Model 71/84

The M71/84 Mauser rifle has the same basic action as the M71, but has been altered to incorporate a tubular magazine system, converting it to a 10-shot repeater. The magazine extends forward under the barrel and is covered by the fore-end. At first glance the uninitiated might not be able to differentiate the M71 from the M71/84. One feature that immediately marks the repeating version is the magazine-cutoff lever on the left side of the receiver. On opening the bolt, the cartridge lifter will confirm the model.

The M71/84 weighs a shade more than 10 pounds, is 51 inches long, and has a 31.5-inch barrel. (There was also a carbine version of this model). The rifling is the same as that of the M71—four grooves, right-hand twist, one turn in 21.7 inches. Nominal bore diameter is given as 0.433-inch, with a groove diameter of 0.442-inch. Again, however, as with the M71, there is considerable variation to be found. The author's M71/84, marked as having been manufactured at Spandau Arsenal in 1887, has a groove diameter of 0.445-inch, and other rifles may vary from 0.444- up to 0.447-inch.

The operation of the M71/84 is the same as operation of the single-shot M71 except for the magazine system. The magazine is charged by first raising the bolt and drawing it to the rear. With the bolt open and the cartridge lifter in the down position, ammunition is pushed forward (bullet first) into the magazine. The magazine holds 8 rounds, but a ninth can be placed on the lifter after the magazine is full. The tenth round is chambered by hand as the bolt is closed, and at that point the safety should be put in the ON or SAFE position. In practice, it is safer and easier to simply load the magazine and use the rifle as an 8-shot repeater.

With its magazine-cutoff lever in the rear position, the M71/84's magazine system is active, and the rifle will function as a repeater. With the cut-off lever in the forward position, the magazine is disconnected and cartridges will not feed to the action. The magazine is held in reserve and the rifle is singly loaded until such time as the repeating feature is desired. This is of value mostly for military use. The cutoff lever can only be pushed forward (ON position) when the cartridge lifter is up (bolt open). To remove the bolt, the cutoff lever must be properly positioned, which is more or less straight up. It may be necessary to feel for the clear position in order to withdraw the bolt. As with the M71, the trigger must be held back when removing the bolt.

Modifications of the M71/84 were adopted by Serbia and Turkey in 10.15mm and 9.5mm, respectively. Rifles firing the original 11mm cartridge were bought by China and some South American countries. Many of the more recent imports originated in Ecuador.

M71 and M71/84 rifles were manufactured at the Amberg, Danzig, Erfurt and Spandau arsenals as well as at the Mauser works in Oberndorf. Steyr in Austria also manufactured large numbers of 11mm Mauser rifles.

The material and workmanship that went into these 11mm Mauser military rifles was the very best of the day. The action is considered quite strong for a black powder rifle. I understand that some of the single shots were rebarreled and

Table I.
11mm Mauser Cartridge Data

Bullet diameter	
Military	0.440
CIL	0.445
Correct for handloading	0.446
Case neck dia.	0.465
Case shoulder dia.	0.510
Case base dia.	0.516
Case rim dia.	0.586
Case length	2.37
Loaded length	3.00 (max.)
Rim thickness	0.095
Primer size	0.254 (6.5mm)
Shoulder angle	9° 28′
Case capacity, grs. H_2O, average	70
Case capacity, grs. Fg black powder	
Military	74
CIL	77

All dimensions in inches

chambered for the 7x57mm and 8x57mm Mauser cartridges. However, neither the M71 nor the M71/84 action can be considered suitable for building a sporting rifle in any modern caliber. They were not designed or intended for high-pressure cartridges as were the later, more advanced Mauser actions such as the Model 1893 and Model 1898. Also, any alterations made in these older rifles will destroy their value as collection pieces. I strongly recommend they be used as is, and in the original caliber.

Historical Background

To properly evaluate the 11mm Mauser rifles and appreciate their place in history, it will be helpful to know something of contemporary military weapons and the tenor of the times. The period of the late 1860s and early 70s was an era of transition when the world military powers, large or small, were changing from the muzzleloader to the breechloader and from rimfire to centerfire ammunition. All this happened in a comparatively short space of time and the shift to the breech-loading rifle was hardly completed when there was another scramble to rearm with repeating rifles. This was not because the repeating rifle followed as the logical outgrowth of the single shot because the repeater had already been battle tested in the American Civil War. However, ammunition development got ahead of gun design and there weren't any repeating actions available to handle the long centerfire military cartridges of the day.

Many authorities have praised the M71 Mauser as a very advanced piece of ordnance for the date of introduction. Actually, when compared with other single-shot rifles of the period it wasn't all that spectacular. The Remington rolling-block, Peabody-Martini and Sharps single-shot actions, to name a few, were as fast and reliable as the M71. The true significance of the M71 was in the fact that it could be quickly and easily converted to a repeater, and it served as the prototype for later improvements that culminated in the best turnbolt rifle action developed by any designer. The Mauser system is still the basis of practically all modern bolt-action sporting rifles. Many have changed it, but none have succeeded in truly improving it.

In the matter of advanced armaments, the United States was (at least for a few years) ahead of the rest of the world in the transition period to the breechloader. Breech-loading single-shot and repeating rifles and metallic cartridges were used in quantity during the Civil War (1861 to 1865). In 1866, the U. S. Army officially adopted the single-shot "trapdoor" Springfield rifle in 50-70 caliber. The British followed suit a year later with their Snider conversion to the 577 cartridge. The Russians probably had a more advanced single-shot rifle when they chose the American-designed Berdan rifle in 10.75mm (0.42") caliber during 1868. In 1970, the Egyptians adopted the Remington rolling-block in 11mm (0.43" Egyptian Remington) and the following year the Spanish adopted the same rifle in a slightly different 11mm caliber (0.43" Spanish-Remington). The Remington rolling-block is considered to have been one of the best single-shot actions ever developed. It made the transition into the smokeless-powder era and was a dead-end design insofar as any possible conversion to the repeating principle is concerned.

Obviously, the Germans were not really the front runners in the matter of good single-shot rifles. However, in 1884, when the basic M71 action was converted to a repeater, they made a big jump in arming their troops with a good repeating rifle several years ahead of everyone else. All the other powers were eventually forced to adopt a completely new system in order to rearm with repeaters, and this took time. When smokeless-powder, high-pressure cartridges appeared, the same basic Mauser bolt action was improved to handle these. As the result, Germany was able to use the same general military rifle action for almost 75 years. The time and money this saved must have been considerable.

The man responsible for this was Peter Paul Mauser (1838-1914). Paul Mauser, as he is more generally known, was born in Oberndorf, Wurttemberg, Germany, the youngest of 13 children. Almost all the male members of the family were involved in the gun business. The father was a master gunsmith at the local governmental arsenal, and it was predictable that young Paul would follow the same general path. In fact, when 14, he hired on at the same plant where his father worked, remaining there for about 7 years. His work on small arms development began in the early 1860s, culminating in his greatest success, the design and development of the Mauser turn-bolt system. The design grew out of what was an original effort to improve on the action of the Dreyse needle gun.

In 1867, Paul Mauser entered into an agreement with the American Samuel Norris, the European representative of the Remington Arms Company. In consequence of this relationship, the first Mauser patent was taken out in the United States (June, 1868). Norris tried to interest Remington in the Mauser system, but they were heavily committed to the rolling-block single-shot and could see no commercial advantage in what at the time was just another single-shot rifle no better than their own.

After two frustrating years of trying to market the new Mauser rifle, Norris withdrew from the venture. Shortly thereafter, Prussia

The Mauser Model 71/84 bolt action repeating rifle. Some of the dealers who sold these rifles turned the bolt handle down, as shown. The standard issue rifle has a straight bolt handle.

completed a series of evaluation tests, adopted the rifle, and in 1871 placed a substantial order for the Mausers. Deliveries began in 1872. This was the beginning of the Mauser arms empire that endured through World War II.

The 11mm Mauser Cartridge

Paul Mauser claimed that he personally designed all of his own cartridges, and in this field he demonstrated as much genius as he did in gun designing. The Mauser cartridges, military or sporting, were all excellent, although some achieved greater popularity than others. The 7x57mm, for example, is probably one of the most widely known and used of the Mauser cartridges. It originated as a military round, but at present is loaded only for sporting purposes.

1873 U.S. 45-70 military round used a 405-gr. bullet at 1350 fps and 1640 foot pounds. The 11mm case is 0.27-inch longer than the 45-70 case and has about 20% greater volume. This may not sound right, but it is true. Anyone who has loaded the 45-70 with black powder knows that the case won't hold 70 grains of powder unless the bullet is seated so far out that the completed round won't work through a repeating action. With the 405-gr. bullet properly seated, the case only holds 55 to 60 grains of Fg black powder.

At one time, the 11mm Mauser was loaded in the U.S., but was discontinued during the 1920s. It is listed in the 1891 Winchester and 1905 UMC catalogs and appears in the 1918-19 Remington catalog. Contrary to some published state-

Table II. 11mm Mauser Ballistics

Bullet/grs.	V/fps				E/fp			
	Muzzle	100	200	300	Muzzle	100	200	300
[1]385	1360	1150	1030	940	1580	1130	910	750
[2]386	1425	1260	—	—	1740	1360	—	—

[1]With this CIL smokeless powder load and the rifle sighted in for 100 yards, point of impact will be 2″ high at 75 yards; 3.5″ low at 125 yards.
[2]Kynoch 77-gr. black powder load.

The 11mm Mauser, the first to be introduced, cannot, however, be considered a highly original design. It is so similar to the preceding 42 Berdan, 43 Egyptian, and 43 Spanish that it is obvious these exerted considerable influence on the designer's efforts. The 11mm Mauser must be viewed as a good but conventional military cartridge within the state of the art at that particular period of history. Even Paul Mauser knew it was subject to improvement, for in 1878 he introduced the 10.15mm Serbian Mauser, and in 1887 the 9.5mm Turkish cartridge, both improved military rounds based on a caliber reduction of the original 11mm Mauser case.

The 11mm Mauser is a rimmed, slightly bottlenecked cartridge with a case length of 2.37 inches (Table I). The original military loading had a 386-gr. lead bullet backed by 70 to 77 grains of black powder. The actual powder charge was determined by the presence or absence of a felt or wax over-powder wad. The muzzle velocity is given as 1425 feet per second (fps) and the muzzle energy as 1752 foot pounds (Table II).

As a matter of comparison, the

ments, the Remington rolling-block was not chambered for the 11mm Mauser, although it was furnished in the similar 43 Egyptian and 43 Spanish calibers. As a matter of fact, there does not appear to have been any American commercial rifle chambered for the 11mm Mauser. All references in cartridge catalogs show the round as being made for the Mauser 71 and 71/84 rifles only.

However, the 11mm Mauser was regularly loaded by European and British ammunition manufacturers up to World War II. At the present time, Canadian Industries, Limited (CIL), is the only company loading the 11mm. Theirs is a Boxer-primed case with smokeless powder (23 grains of an unidentified perforated-disc type) behind a 385-gr. lead bullet. Muzzle velocity and energy are given as 1360 fps and 1580 foot-pounds, respectively.

Stocks of old black powder military cartridges, with either paper patched or lubricated bullets, have been sold by surplus dealers. Some of this shoots quite well, giving good practical hunting accuracy, even though more than 80 years old. Military cases and other British or European loaded ammuni-

Three very similar cartridges. The 10.75mm Russian (top) and the 11mm Spanish (middle) cartridges predate the 11mm Mauser. The 11mm Spanish is often confused with the 11mm Mauser (bottom) but, as the photograph shows, there is a difference in form and bullet diameter.

tion have the Berdan-type primer of 6.5mm (0.254″) size. Alcan 645B primers made for all-brass Berdan shotshells work fine in loading these cases.

The 11mm Mauser was used by German colonial units and native troops in Africa as late as WW I. The rifles, fairly well-distributed, were used for hunting in some areas. John Taylor* rates the 11mm as "generally useless" and not worth serious discussion as an African big-game caliber. Presumably, it would have been OK as a "meat" cartridge for shooting the lighter, non-dangerous animals.

The author has used the 11mm Mauser and the M71/84 rifle for deer and elk hunting and witnessed its use on an even wider variety of game. At ranges up to 150 yards, it appears to have good stopping and killing power, and it certainly makes a fine brush or woods cartridge for any of the deer found in this country. In the hands of a good hunter, I'd rate the 11mm Mauser as adequate for any North American big game under normal hunting conditions. If a wider variety of bullets, particularly gas-check and jacketed types, were available it could be upgraded substantially. A 385-gr. jacketed bullet could be hand loaded to 1600 or even 1800 fps without straining the 71 or 71/84 action. This would flatten the trajectory and bring the muzzle energy up to 2200 or nearly 2800 foot-pounds (depending on velocity), creating a very respectable big-game cartridge under any circumstances.

One frequently asked question is: How does the 11mm Mauser compare with the 45-70 for sporting purposes? In the original black powder loading, there is not a great deal of difference in effective range, accuracy, or killing power. However, I do believe the 45-70 with its heavier 400- to 500-gr. bullets has a superior short-range knockdown capability on heavy game. Field observations lead to the opinion that the modern factory-loaded 45-70 with the 405-gr. soft point bullet enjoys this same advantage over the 11mm CIL lead bullet load of 385 grains.

In the matter of handloading improvements, the 45-70 enjoys a considerable advantage because of the large variety of 458 bullets available, both cast and jacketed. In a strong action, the 45-70 can be loaded to truly formidalbe per-

*African Rifles and Cartridges, Harrisburg, Pa., 1948

formance. If one of the bullet manufacturers would bring out a good jacketed bullet for the 11mm, the gap could be narrowed.

Handloading the 11mm Mauser

Developing smokeless powder loads for obsolete black powder cartridges and rifles presents many problems, and the results are not always fully satisfactory. Certain tradeoffs or compromises are an integral part of the game. Maximum velocity and top accuracy are seldom compatible, so if either is the ultimate goal, then one must accept some sort of reduction of

Table III.
11mm Mauser Loading Data

Powder/grs.	MV/fps	Remarks
347-gr. (Lyman 446110) cast bullet sized to 0.446″		
4064/44	1260	accurate
47	1400	
3031/40	1250	
42	1370	
4198/30	1275	very accurate
32	1380	accurate
35	1510	max.
N200/30	1370	good accuracy
32	1460	
4227/29	1350	
31	1470	max.
2400/26	1340	
387-gr. (Lyman 439186) cast bullet unsized, 0.444″		
3031/41	1270	
4198/30	1205	accurate
32	1335	
4895/42	1350	
*Black Fg/70	1435	

*Duplex load—6 grs. Red Dot beneath FG charge.

the other. The best over-all performance is usually obtained at or near the original black powder ballistics. In fact, it is not unusual for the original propellant to prove significantly more accurate than any smokeless loading that we can come up with. Also, these old rifles tend to be highly individualistic in the way they digest smokeless powder loads and therefore the combination that shoots best in one rifle might not perform quite as well in another. If accuracy is the name of the game, then some adjustment of the loading data is inevitable. My advice is to use the loading data presented here as a general guide. Start about two grains below the lightest charge given and work up in increments of a half-grain

until the point of greatest accuracy is reached. The top loads given are about the maximum that is consistent with acceptable accuracy. However, bullet hardness and the lubricant used will have a bearing on this.

The 11mm Mauser is an easy cartridge to load, and there are no special problems. Loading dies are available from Lyman, RCBS and most other diemakers. Good Boxer-primed cases are made by CIL for their 11mm ammunition, the latter available from many sporting goods stores, or on order. Surplus black powder military ammunition is also a source of reloadable cases, although the Berdan primers are a little bothersome. Cases fired with black powder should be soaked in a detergent solution and scrubbed clean inside as soon as possible after use; otherwise, the powder fouling will corrode the cases, making them unsuitable for further loading. In a humid climate, this will happen within a few days. It is not necessary to do this when the cases are fired with smokeless powder.

The foremost loading problem, and certainly the point of greatest confusion concerning the 11mm Mauser, is the correct bullet diameter. Several factors have conspired to confuse the question. For one thing, and as previously pointed out, there is considerable variation in the groove diameter of different 11mm Mauser rifles. Secondly, most information on bullet diameter comes from measuring bullets, and this has led to some erroneous conslusions. Few modern shooters are aware of the practice during black powder days of using undersized bullets. Projectiles were made from very soft, nearly pure lead, so they would upset or swage to a proper fit under the gun's gas pressure. In practice, this worked OK and gave perfectly acceptable military or hunting accuracy. However, later experiments proved that better accuracy was possible with bullets of groove or nearly groove diameter, and that is what match shooters came to use. Also, an undersized bullet cast from a hard alloy will give very poor accuracy, and modern handloaders are accustomed to using hard alloys. One other factor is the confusion between the 11mm Mauser cartridge and the 11mm Spanish round. Many individuals think they're the same, but this is not true. Both case dimensions and bullet diameter are different.

The author measured the bullets from a variety of 11mm Mauser black powder cartridges and found them to vary from 0.4397" to a maximum of 0.4425". The average diameter was 0.4405". The 1904 DWM catalog gives the bullet diameter of the 11mm Mauser as 11.2mm, which is 0.4409 inch. CIL 11mm ammunition has a bullet diameter of 0.445". Cast bullets sized 0.439" to 0.440" give terrible accuracy in 11mm Mauser rifles, although they might work all right if cast with a soft alloy. The bullet diameter that works best in most M71/84 rifles and many of the M71s is 0.446". Lyman loading- and bullet-sizing dies are made to this specification; some others are not.

used with good results, but one soundly cursed by others is the Lyman No. 439186 (387 grains). This bullet is intended for the 43 Spanish-Remington cartridge and, if sized to the recommended 0.439", doesn't work at all well in 11mm Mauser rifles. The secret for success is to use these bullets unsized just as they drop from the mould (0.444" diameter). They can be run through the Lyman 0.446" sizing and lubricating die if light pressure is used on the lubricating screw; otherwise the lubricant will flow out around the base and nose of the bullet. This bullet should also be cast from a fairly soft alloy, not harder than about 1 part tin to 20 parts lead. Type metal or similar

ter round ball mould available (about 135-137 grains), and these can be used to load up light, short-range plinking or small-game loads. Seat the ball flush with the case mouth and cover it with a blob of bullet lubricant; 15 grains of 2400 gives about 1250 fps and good practical accuracy. When using a round ball, a lubricated felt wad and a heavy cardboard wad under the ball will often improve accuracy. Sometimes it goes the other way, though, so try it and see how it works in your rifle.

Two other cast bullets tried in the 11mm Mauser were Lyman's No. 446109 (365 grains) and No. 446187 (470 grains). Neither worked at all well, giving poor

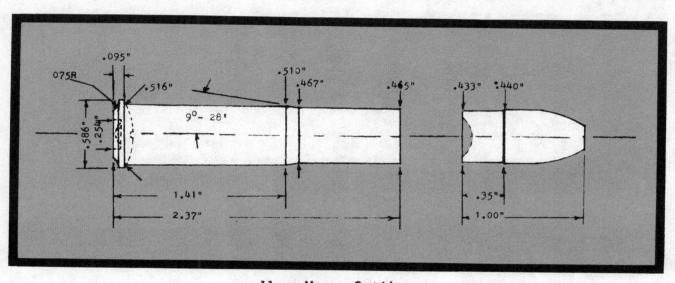

11mm Mauser Cartridge
Diameter of military bullets averages .440". These are not recommended for handloading. Use .446" bullets instead.

Many of the M71 single-shot rifles require a bullet of even larger diameter than this for best accuracy. There is, however, a limit to the diameter that can be used, because the chamber dimensions are normal for the 11mm Mauser cartridge. If the bullet is too large, it will over-expand the cartridge neck when seated, and the round won't chamber. The solution appears to be in using the largest diameter bullet that will chamber and a relatively soft alloy. (Not harder than approximately 1 part tin to 30 parts lead.)

Unfortunately, none of the bullets available were designed for the 11mm Mauser. They are all intended for some other round, but can be used successfully because weight and diameter are about right.

One bullet the author has long

hard alloys do not give good results with this bullet. When cast as indicated here, it shoots well with moderate smokeless loads and gives excellent accuracy with black powder loads.

Probably the best all-round bullet available for the 11mm Mauser is Lyman's No. 446110 (347 grains), even though it is intended for the old 44-77 and 44-90 cartridges. This bullet should be sized to 0.446" and it may be cast from type metal or other hard alloys. It will give better accuracy with heavier smokeless-powder loads than will No. 439186. It is also available in a hollow-point configuration that weighs some 315 grains. Only the solid type was used for these tests. An Alox-base lubricant was used on all bullets.

There is a Lyman 0.445"-diame-

accuracy at any velocity.

There are two more bullets that might work in the 11mm Mauser, but time and circumstances did not allow including them in this test series—Lyman's Nos. 441267 and 446188.

Selecting the best smokeless propellant for loading obsolete black powder cartridges requires close attention to the performance limitations imposed by available components and the firearm involved. In loading the 11mm Mauser, only plain-base cast-lead bullets are currently available. This immediately restricts the performance level to about that of the original black powder loading. Muzzle velocities of around 1400 to 1500 fps appear to be about the maximum consistent with acceptable accuracy. The author found that as velocity in-

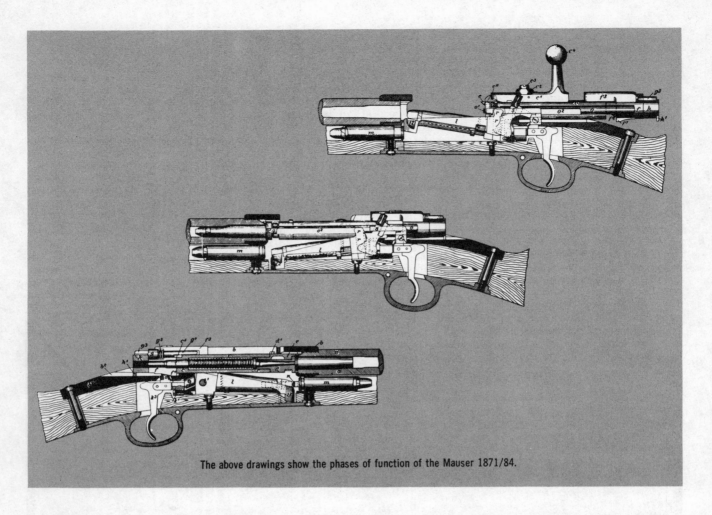

The above drawings show the phases of function of the Mauser 1871/84.

creased accuracy decreased. The smallest groups were always with the lighter powder charges.

Duplicating black powder ballistics means using relatively light to moderate loads of smokeless powder, thus such medium- to medium-fast burning powders as 4198, Reloder 7 and 4227 give the most satisfactory results. However, the slower-burning 3031 and Reloder 11 also shot well in the 11mm.

One problem when loading light-to-moderate charges of smokeless powder in large-capacity cases is that the powder does not bulk well. One of the best powders for bridging this gap was the now obsolete DuPont SR 4759. Unfortunately, dealer stocks of this are now practically exhausted, so there was no point in working up data, even though the author does have a small supply. One solution to the bulk problem is the use of an inert filler material. Some shooters use dry cornmeal, oiled sawdust or Cream of Wheat to fill the space between the base of the bullet and the powder charge. My own experience with these has always been poor, and I think there is an

element of danger in using them to compress charges of fast-burning powders such as Bullseye, Unique, or 2400.

Probably the best solution to the bulking problem is one suggested by Col. E. H. Harrison in his excellent articles on accuracy and performance with cast bullets (*The American Rifleman*, February and March 1969 issues). This involves using small quantities of Kapok or Dacron fiber as a filler. Small tufts are pushed down on top of the powder charge prior to seating the bullet. Tufts of Kapok weighing approximately 1.5 grains or 2-gr. Dacron tufts work well in the 11mm and will keep the lighter powder charges uniformly positioned against the primer from shot to shot. This may also provide a measure of protection to the bullet base against the hot powder gas. Both materials gave improved accuracy. The amount of shooting did not indicate any clearcut superiority of one over the other, but the Dacron was easiest to work with.

Kapok and Dacron fiber can be purchased at most large dry goods stores or through the big mail-order houses. It comes in various

sizes, and a one-pound bag is about the smallest that can be bought. A pound, cost around $1.00, will last a very long time.

Loading data for the 11mm Mauser is listed in Table III. The three most accurate loads tested were as follows: (1) 347-gr. Lyman 446110 bullet with 30 grains of 4198; (2) the same bullet with 29 grains of Reloder 7; (3) 387-gr. 439186 bullet with duplex loading—6 grains of Red Dot and 70 grains of Fg black powder.

The information presented here should provide owners of 11mm Mauser rifles with a better understanding of their rifles as well as the basic information for loading good target or hunting ammunition. Either the 347-grain or 387-grain bullets at initial velocities of 1300 to 1500 fps are quite adequate for most big-game hunting at ranges up to 150 yards. The M71 and M71/84 Mauser rifles are excellent black-powder rifles, and those willing to invest a little time in working up handloads will be rewarded by many hours of pleasant shooting recreation. ●

WHEN SHOOTING GOES METRIC

Come the day, what will metrication mean to the average shooter? Will such favorite cartridges as the 30-30, the 270 and the 30-06 be made obsolete? Not because we go metric, certainly. The author supplies metric-English conversion tables covering values and ballistics.

by HAROLD O. DAVIDSON

Yep, she's a perfect 91-61-91 — centimeters, that is.

IN YEARS PAST few American shooters had reason to be concerned with the metric system of measurement. Competition shooters in the international events, collectors of European firearms and cartridges, and a very few others would complete the list. Of course, the rest of us have some familiarity with metric terms to the extent of knowing that 6 millimeter caliber is .243″, and 7mm is .284″, and maybe that 50 meters is about 10% more than 50 yards. Mostly, however, the shooting measurements we deal with are in the old English units of grains of bullet weight, grains or "dram equivalents" of powder, feet per second muzzle velocity, inches of mid-range trajectory, and yards of range. Now, in England, the familiar old English units are on the way out. The English measurement system has been declared obsolete. Britain is going metric.

The decision was made in 1965 and "metrication" is well underway. The easier changes, such as the conversion from "fifths" and gallons to liters, were made first. However, such more complicated changes as those from English to metric thread standards are also involved in their program, which is to be completed by 1975. The English are slow to give up their traditional ways, but they've concluded that conversion to the metric system is important to keep them in competition for world markets. (Japan converted between the end of WW II and 1960).

Trends of the Times

What's happening in Great Britain and in other countries all over the world is cause for wonder 1) whether the U.S. may soon start on a nationwide metrication program, and if that happens 2) will shooting go metric? Supposing that it does, 3) what exactly will that mean for the average shooter? 4) Will such favorite cartridges as the 30-30 become obsolete?

Based on our research into the subject, the answers in brief are:

1) Probably, 2) Almost certainly, 3) Very little, and 4) Not likely. With this thumb-nail summary, let's take up the questions one at a time.

In predicting that the beginning of a U.S. metrication program is probably close at hand we have several facts to go on. We know, for example, that a key factor in Britain's decision to go metric without waiting for the U.S. was a shift in the attitude of English businessmen from a majority opposed to a majority in favor. That happened rather quickly in the early 1960s and their program began about two years later.

The strongest opposition to past proposals for conversion to metric measurement in this country has also come from business, because of concern over tool and drawing change problems and other costs of conversion. However, more and more businesses are finding that the costs of *not* changing are even higher in the long run. Thus there has been a shift in the attitude of American businessmen to the extent that a majority now favor metrication, according to a survey completed in 1971. Even among small businesses with less than 20 employees the survey found most in favor of some kind of metrication program.

It's pretty clear that one of the factors involved in this change of attitude is the world-wide trend. All of our export markets in North and South America, Europe, Asia, Australia and most of Africa are metric countries. All of our competitors vying for these markets are also metric. In fact, the only nations other than the United States that have not yet started on conversion programs are: Barbados, Burma, Gambia, Ghana, Jamaica, Liberia, Musat & Oman, Nauru, Sierra Leone, Southern Yemen, Tonga, and Trinidad.

Another factor was the trend toward increased knowledge and use of the metric system in the United States itself. The U.S. Army and Air Force, for example, have been using metric map coordinates for some years (specifically, the "UTM" or Universal Transverse Mercator grid system). Also, in 1957 the Army established a regulation that all weaponry and associated equipment would be based on the metric system. About half of all labelling on canned goods gives net weight in grams as well as in English units. Skis are now produced exclusively according to the metric size standards. The prescription drug industry converted to the metric system over a decade ago and the optical industry also uses metric measurement and standards. Metric wrenches are available in many hardware and auto supply stores, and every foreign car mechanic is familiar with them. Some of the cars assembled in the United States now have engines built to metric standards. A bare 10 years ago most grade school mathematics books made no reference to metric system, whereas it is now covered in every grade school arithmetic book. Amateur radio operators tune to metric wave lengths (e.g., "5-meter band" etc.) and photography is about 50% converted to the metric system.

These and other factors were undoubtedly taken into account when the Nixon Administration came out in favor of metrication in 1971, and the Senate voted approval in 1972. They must also have been considered when the American Management Association set up conferences for business men to help them plan conversion in their own companies. Altogether they add up to the conclusion that the United States will soon begin a program of conversion to the metric system. When that happens it's a virtual certainty that shooting will go metric along with everything else. But...

There'll Always Be a 30-30

That's too strong a prediction really, since any cartridge could become obsolete if shooters lost interest in it. The point here is that conversion to the metric system will not make any cartridge obsolete. The

Table 1

Common Conversion Factors for Metric and English measurement.

Metric to English		English to Metric	
1 meter	= 3.281 ft.	1 foot	= 0.3048 m
	= 1.0936 yds.	1 yard	= 0.9194 m
1 cm	= .394 ins.	1 inch	= 2.54 cm
1 mm	= .0394 ins.	1 inch	= 25.4 mm
1 kg	= 2.20 lbs.	1 pound	= 0.454 kg
1 g	= .0353 ozs.	1 ounce	= 28.3 g
	= 15.43 grs.	1 grain	= 0.0648 g
1 kg/cm²	= 14.22 lb/in²	1 lb/in²	= 0.0703 kg/cm²
1 m/sec	= 3.281 ft/sec	1 ft/sec	= 0.3048 m/sec
1 mkg	= 7.23 ft/lb	1 ft. lb.	= 0.1383 mkg
1 liter	= 1.06 quarts	1 quart	= 0.9463 liters
1 cc	= 0.016 fl. oz.	1 fl. oz.	= 59.1 cubic cm.

Table 2

Equivalent Metric and English Designations for Rifle Cartridges.

Note: Data in this table are intended for general information only, and are not sufficient for determining interchangeability of English and metric cartridges. It should be also be appreciated that inconsistencies exist in both systems. Thus, the 8mm metric designation is applied to both .318″ and .323″ groove diameters although the cartridges are not interchangeable. The reverse situation also exists; the English designate the 7mm caliber as 275, while in Canada it's 280, and in the U.S. both 280 and 284 designations have been applied to the same caliber.

English, inch	Metric, mm
.177	4.5
.20	5
.22	5.5/5.6
.243/.244	6/6.2
.25/.256/.257	###
.264	6.5
.270	###
.275/.280/.284	7
.30/.308	7.62
.310	7.65
.32	8
.338	###
.35/.358	9
###	9.3
.375	9.5
###	10.75
.458	11.5

indicates calibers not normally available today in the system under which the symbol appears.

30-30, for example, has had a fair amount of popularity among sportsmen in metric countries, who sometimes refer to it in metric terms as the 7.62×51R. (The first number is the bore diameter in millimeters, the number after the "×" is the case length in millimeters, and the "R" designates a rimmed case). The adoption of metric designations is about the only change the casual rifle shooter is apt to notice, and it's likely that both English and metric designations will be used on cartridge boxes for some time after conversion takes place.

Actually, the changeover to metric units in ordinary affairs will be quite easy. This conclusion is based on the experience of people in countries where conversions have been made, and on the experience of American military personnel and their families in NATO countries where they have learned to buy milk by the liter, meat by the "kilo" (kilogram = 1000 grams = 2.2 pounds), and to keep within kmh (kilometers per hour) speed limits driving American cars with mph speedometers.

Without really trying, hunters will start to think of range in meters instead of yards, and to size up their bucks in kilograms instead of pounds. The truth is that while conversion to metric measurement will involve a good deal of work and expense for some businesses, it won't be nearly as difficult for the average citizen as some people have said. A number of frequently used conversion factors are given in Table 1. Table 2 gives English and metric caliber equivalents, already familiar to many shooters.

Few Changes For Shotgunners

There'll be no basic changes in shotgun gauges, chambers, or chokes since these are all internationally standardized at the present time. European gunmakers have, for some years, chambered their shotguns to the metric equivalents of U.S. and English chambers, as shown below:

English/U.S.	Metric
2⁹⁄₁₆"*	65mm*
2³⁄₄"	70mm
3"	76mm

*obsolete

Metric shot size designations are simpler than ours, being the diameter of the shot in millimeters. A common set of European shot sizes is based on increments of half a millimeter, as shown below in comparison to the U.S. standard sizes and their metric equivalents:

U.S. Shot Sizes	Metric
No. 9	*2.0mm
7½	2.41
—	*2.5
6	2.79
5	*3.0
4	3.30
—	*3.5
2	3.78
—	*4.0

*Indicates sizes now standard in Europe. Note that No. 5 and 9 sizes correspond exactly to current metric sizes.

Conversion to the metric system would not necessarily mean a change to European shot sizes, though some form of international standardization would probably come about in time. Suppliers would welcome a reduction from 6 sizes to 5. Some pheasant and grouse hunters might find the 2.5mm shot size a useful compromise between 6s and 7½s; others might prefer to keep the existing sizes. At this point it's pure speculation what shot standards might eventually prevail.

Changes for Handloaders

Handloaders will have two choices when metrication takes place: continue using their old scales until they wear out, or replace them right off with metric scales or metric scale beams. In the first case, new loads given in grams can be converted to English measure at 15.43 grains to the gram. In the second case, loaders can convert their old loads stated in grains by the factor 64.8 milligrams = 1 grain (6.48 mg = ¹⁄₁₀-grain).

Metric Ballistics

The conversion of muzzle velocity from feet per second to meters per second is a simple multiplication: mps = .305 (.3048) × fps. Breech pressures are converted from pounds per square inch to kilograms per square centimeter when multiplied by 14.22.

The conversion of remaining velocity, drop, and mid-range trajectory data is complicated by the fact that metric ballistic tables will be constructed on metric increments of range (50 or 100 meters) instead of English (yards). Thus it is necessary to use special conversion factors that take account of the change in distance at which the measurement is made as well as the change in measurement units. The author has calculated those factors which are needed to convert velocity and trajectory data from metric to English tables, and vice versa.

Precise conversion of ballistic tables is rather complicated since the conversion factor is dependent on both muzzle velocity and ballistic coefficient. In general practice it's not worthwhile trying to calculate precise conversions since actual ballistic performance may deviate by 5% or more from theoretically correct values because of round-to-round variations in muzzle velocity, changes in bullet drag under different atmospheric conditions, and several other factors. This being so, the author concluded that approximation errors averaging around 2% or less could be tolerated in a conversion factor table with essentially no effect on the practical accuracy of the results. By using close approximations instead of mathematically exact factors it was possible to condense a complex set of tables down to the relatively simple results seen in Tables 3 and 4.

In order to use these conversion tables one must know the ballistic coefficient within the limits set forth in the tables. If the value of the ballistic coefficient is not known, the following guidelines may be used:

1) Tables 3 and 4. If 100-yard velocity is 80% or more of muzzle velocity, use conversion factors for ballistic coefficients (C) greater than .20 in Tables 3 and 4. If less than 80% of MV, use conversion factors in Table 3 for C figures between .10 and .20.

2) Table 4. For 100-yard velocity between 75 and 80% of MV use conversion factors for C figures between .15 and .20. If 100-yard velocity is below 75% of MV, assume a C figure of .10 to .15.

Energy Conversions

The metric unit of energy in ballistics is the meter kilogram (mkg), which is equal to 7.23 foot pounds. Conversely, 1 foot pound equals .1383 mkg. Energy may also be determined from the basic formula wv^2/K. For results in foot-pounds, "w" is bullet weight in grains, "v" is velocity in feet per second, and K is the number 451,000. For results in meter kilograms, "w" is bullet weight in grams, "v" is in meters per second, and K is the number 19,630. That's all there is to it.

When Will It Happen?

The beginning date for conversion can't be given at this time. One thing is sure, however. Conversion cannot take place overnight, but will be accomplished gradually over a decade or so. Thus, there will be ample warning for the relatively minor accomodations that we'll have to make as individual shooters and citizens. ●

Table 3
Remaining Velocity Conversion Factors

	Range (yards or meters)						
Conversion	0	100	200	300	400	500	600
Ballistic Coefficient greater than .20							
ft/sec @ 'x' yds. to m/sec @ 'x' mtrs.	.305	.302	.299	.295	.292	.290	.286
m/sec @ 'x' mtrs. to ft/ sec @ 'x' yds.	3.28	3.31	3.34	3.39	3.43	3.45	3.50
Ballistic Coefficient less than .20							
ft/sec @ 'x' yds. to m/sec @ 'x' mtrs.	.305	.298	.292	.290	.289	.288	.287
m/sec @ 'x' mtrs. to ft/ sec @ 'x' yds.	3.28	3.36	3.43	3.45	3.46	3.47	3.48

Table 4
Drop and Mid-Range Conversion Factors

	Range (yards or meters)					
Conversion	100	200	300	400	500	600
Ballistic Coefficient greater than .20						
inches @ 'x' yards to cm @ 'x' meters	3.05	3.08	3.11	3.14	3.16	3.18
cm @ 'x' meters to inches @ 'x' yards	.328	.325	.322	.318	.316	.314
Ballistic Coefficient between .15 and .20						
inches @ 'x' yards to cm @ 'x' meters	3.08	3.14	3.19	3.21	3.24	3.28
cm @ 'x' meters to inches @ 'x' yards	.325	.318	.314	.312	.309	.305
Ballistic Coefficient between .10 and .15						
inches @ 'x' yards to cm @ 'x' meters	3.10	3.19	3.30	3.31	3.32	3.33
cm @ 'x' meters to inches @ 'x' yards	.322	.313	.303	.302	.301	.300

Confusion of Words

"The English language is a confusing tongue at best. When it comes to the words used to describe the various birds, fish and animals of the world, however, the confusion turns to dismay," according to Ted McCawley, manager of public relations for Remington Arms Company, Inc. "Even the same species are sometimes called by different names under various conditions.

"For example, a group of geese on the water is called a plump. When airborne, however, these same birds become a skein. Put them on the ground and they are called a gaggle.

"Ducks are just as much of a problem. It's proper to call a number of them a flock—sometimes. On the water they are called a paddling except for teal which come in a spring, coil, knob or bunch except on Thursdays when they are a—but where was I? Oh, yes—in flight you see a team of ducks except for widgeons, and it's proper to call a group of them a bunch, flight or company.

"Sometimes the collective nouns are very descriptive—a clamor of rooks, a murder of crows, a mutation of thrushes or a murmuration of starlings.

"Mammals have their descriptive terms, too. Several camels are known as a rag. A group of mules is a barren, while a number of sheep are called a hurtle or flock.

"The business goes on and on. In the fish world, perch come in packs, smelt in quantities and herring in shoals.

"Some years ago a story appeared in the Richmond(Va.) *Times-Dispatch* which sums up this mumbo-jumbo pretty well. Here it is:

"'A flock of ships is called a fleet; a fleet of sheep is called a flock; a flock of girls is called a bevy; a bevy of wolves is called a pack; a pack of thieves is called a gang; a gang of angels is called a host; a host of porpoise is called a shoal; a shoal of fish is called a school; a school of buffalo is called a herd; a herd of seals is called a pod; a pod of whales is called a game; a game of lions is called a pride; a pride of children is called a troop; a troop of partridges is called a covey; a covey of beauties is called a galaxy; a galaxy of ruffians is called a horde; a horde of rubbish is called a heap; a heap of oxen is called a drove; a drove of blackguards is called a mob; a mob of worshipers is called a congregation; a congregation of theater-goers is called an audience; an audience of peacocks is called a muster; a muster of doves is called a flight; a flight of larks is called an exaltation and if they are starlings, it's murmuration; a murmuration of bees is called a swarm; a swarm of foxes is called a skulk; a skulk of pigs is called a stye; a stye of dogs is called a kennel; a kennel of cats is often called a nuisance.'"

You Call Them— they won't call you!

Calling geese in by word of mouth, so to speak, is a hard-earned art, but the kind of calls you can buy are mighty effective, too—if you'll practice!

by ART REID

ALTHOUGH I had long fancied myself a pretty fair caller of Canada geese, I was completely fascinated by the exhibition of calling taking place in the goose hunting pit next to mine. It was one of those days when only an occasional honker ventured over the cornfield decoys, even though there were birds in the air constantly. When the rare goose did cross the boundary line of the Crab Orchard National Wildlife Refuge, it was promptly drawn to my competitor's shooting pit, over 200 yards away. Not only did I look on with admiration, but I was envious, too. The caller over there sounded more like a goose than the real McCoy did.

I'd met Charlie Sullivan briefly only that morning, when Jack Bowman, owner of the daily fee shooting club, introduced him as a goose caller and professional guide. Frankly, he looked anything but. Six feet five and gangly, with a shock of hair too long to be establishment and too short to be

called hippie, and sporting rusty-colored bib overalls, Sullivan looked like a scarecrow in search of a field to protect. A grimy green, wide-brimmed corduroy hat slouched on his head, apparently held in place only by his ears. He appeared to be about 30 years old.

It wasn't until after I had stood by helplessly that day, watching Sullivan call in all those wayward geese, that I learned he was Illinois State Champion goose caller, with a string of victories dating back to 1967. Incredibly, he does it the hard way—by mouth.

Calling Canada geese with what's commonly known as a "horn" or mechanical call, is one thing, but doing it successfully with the vocal cords is a horse of a different hue. One prerequisite for voice calling is the ability to yodel or control the voice in a similar manner. It's not easy. Youngsters seem able to produce the various tones more easily than adults,

but some young callers lose this ability as their voices change. Constant practice throughout this trying period is the only way to retain it.

Sullivan has remained so dedicated to the challenge of fooling this most majestic and wary of waterfowl species that his effectiveness has actually improved over the years. He quickly admits, also, that his accumulating store of goose lore helps him know what to say and when to say it to the wise old monarch of the migration routes.

Goose Lore

"Some days," he said, "you can call too much, and others you can't call them enough. You just have to begin each day by feeling them out to see what they'll respond to, then work with that pattern of calling and forget about anything else."

Emphasizing that his basic opening tones are a series of sounds like these —har-uuuk, har-uuuk, har-uuuk, with a definite emphasis on the final syllable, and about 5 in a single series—Sullivan then did a strange thing while demonstrating his method. He cupped his right hand behind his right ear and cocked his head as if listening intently. "Oh, that," he explained, "that's to hear myself so I can give the right pitch."

"Volume!" he suddenly blurted. "Volume is the key to calling success. If you haven't got enough noise so the geese can hear you on a windy day, forget it. Have you ever noticed how shrill and strong the voice of a honker really is? You can hear them for a mile or more at times, and the caller has to be just as noisy to attract their attention."

Sullivan compares his method to having the birds attached to a long cord. "When I start calling geese and feel they are paying attention," he explained, "all I do from that point on is keep them interested with just enough short and fast calls to keep them from aborting. It's like I had strings tied to their legs—all I do is gently pull 'em down. Once they've cupped their wings and dropped their landing gear, I generally stop calling right then. That timing is critical." Sullivan's eyes flashed the significance of his statement. "You can keep a firm hold on the string or lose it right there. More often than not you'll keep it by not calling another note."

Interestingly, despite the large number of excellent mechanical calls available, voice callers prefer their own natural efforts. It's also true that men with such talents are few and far between. Thus it falls to the lot of most goose hunters and would-be callers to snap up those handy devices which substitute admirably for yodel control. Even the stoutest of voices becomes cracked and raw from overwork during the hunting season, and even the Sullivans must relieve their throats by using a wooden horn on occasion.

There's no question that a mechanical call can bring a fair number of honkers into range on any given day. Learning to call geese isn't that hard. I feel strongly that the tones and volume necessary to successful goose hunting are not half so intricate or demanding as duck calling is.

Learning to Call

The easy way to start is to buy one of the well-known brands of calls. Back that purchase with another, equally important—an instructional recording of the calling sequences and tones. Diligent practice will take care of the rest.

Charlie Sullivan was no different.

Although for years his home during each hunting season has been those damp holes in the ground surrounded by corn stubble, he wasn't born a champion goose caller. Says the elder Sullivan, "He used to drive me nuts with all that goose noise around the house. Why, he'd practice all year long, then intensify his efforts to build up his voice as goose season approached. It got so that I looked forward to hunting season more than he did, just to get him out of the house for two months," he laughed.

A goose call recording will tell you that a planned series of calls will be most productive under most circumstances. Professionals such as Kenny Martin (who grew up with the wintering Mississippi flyway geese at Horseshoe Lake near Cairo, Illinois) confirm this. Though he moved to Lamont, Illinois, a few years ago, Martin still returns to Horseshoe Lake and the Canadas each season, and he's known internationally as the manufacturer of the famed Kenny Martin calls.

I first met Martin during the 1967 season at Horseshoe. The way he could blow one of his horns was not surprising, yet I was amazed at the energy he poured into his efforts. I quickly learned that at times calling is a real chore, requiring great lung power, to sustain the required sounds and to produce the necessary volume. Rivulets of sweat popped out on Martin's forehead as he became completely engrossed in his work. At the same time, the series of tones was simplicity itself, as he explained it to me.

The inner organs of all mechanical goose calls are basically the same, no matter who stamps a brand on them. They consist of two pieces of wood, or plastic blocks which, when placed together snugly in the barrel of the call, hold the most important ingredient of the whole shebang—the reed that makes the noise. The reeds found in most goose calls today are made of plastic, carefully adjusted so they will actually flap back and forth freely when air pressure from the mouth is forced down to them.

The sounds emitted by a call depends on the type and position of the reed. All goose calls come pre-tuned,

Charlie Sullivan, State champion voice caller, limbers up his "chords."

ready to be put into action. However, after extensive use, plastic reeds often become cracked or broken. It's important to replace a reed with one of the size, shape and material of the original. Spare reeds can be had usually from your friendly sporting goods dealer or from the call maker. Plastic shirt collar stays won't work — I've tried 'em.

Goose calls also have a tendency to dry out when they're not in use for long periods. Before each hunting season the call should be taken from mothballs and checked. Blow in it a couple of times and listen to the sound. If it seems ok, fine. Many won't be in such good shape, however. They will need tuning up.

This requires simply removing the lower portion of the call, the part that holds the plastic reed. By carefully moving the reed up or down a fraction of an inch or so, and rechecking each time it's moved with a few blows into the mouthpiece, the desirable quality will be restored. This adjustment procedure can be used any time the call seems out of whack.

Today's goose hunter is indeed fortunate that so many horns are available to him. They can be found just about anywhere in the nation where goose hunting is pursued. Here in the Midwest it's accepted that Martin and Olt shuck out fine calling devices. Black Duck Game Calls of Whiting, Indiana, and the Mallardtone Company of Moline, Illinois, have never found it necessary to tip their hats to superior products, either. These calls are all good. They all do exactly what they are designed to do, if they are manipulated efficiently by the man who owns one.

Most Effective Sound

The most effective sound is created by slapping the tongue against the roof of the mouth, following a forceful emission of air from the lungs. This sound is made by bringing air up from the lungs and pushing it into the call as if you were trying to blow a gnat off your chin. Instead, say the word *hut* directly into the call. Try it. Bring air from the lungs and blurt out the word *hut*. Now push up the word slowly. Say *huuuuuu-ut* and slap your tongue sharply against the roof of your mouth at the very end.

That, in a nutshell, is the basic sound made by Canada geese and one which can easily be duplicated with a mechanical call, by anyone. Moreover, modern calls are made to give these noises with minimum effort. The only taxing of lungs and breath control comes when these sounds are made in rapid succession, as is often required

Julio, half-Labrador, half-Boxer, climbs from the pit to retrieve a downed goose.

An 8-pound Canada is no problem for a good retriever.

Sullivan watches more geese approaching as Julio gives up prize.

when calling geese into gun range. Practice takes care of that.

But getting a spooky Canada goose to answer an artificial note and fooling him into range, as Sullivan pointed out, is quite another story. Attract the attention of flying honkers by giving them a single series at most. Many professionals contend that one welcoming call is generally enough. A crisp *huuuu-ut,* followed by silence, is all that's necessary until the geese answer back. When they do, offer the birds another single call. If they continue to answer each call, and show signs of boring in closer, increase the rapidity of calls into a series to retain their attention.

To Call or Not

But herein lies a controversy that promises to go unsettled as long as there are goose hunters: to give or not to give what many people feel is the feeding call. This sound is made by shortening the *huuu-uts* to a staccato series of *hut-hut-hut-huts,* made just about as fast as it's possible to do all that tongue slapping.

Grounded Canada geese do make this sound, most often when other geese are hovering overhead or passing close by. The feeding geese apparently become excited at the prospect of visitors dropping in, and they make this guttural, murmuring sound.

Sullivan seldom uses it, saying, "I don't think it's necessary as long as I can keep them climbing down that string." Martin occasionally goes right from the welcoming series into the feeding chuckle. I've heard him do it.

"Yes, I use the feeding murmur," Jim Olt said, "but it doesn't always work. I'd say it depends on a number of things, including the age and experience of the geese. Young birds are more easily fooled by a feeding call. Experience includes how long they've been around these refuge areas and their consciousness of hunters in blinds and pits outside. Wise honkers soon become pit-shy, I think, and they won't be fooled with the feeding call."

Other Geese, Other Habits

Jim Olt and Al Sonderman, also of the Olt Company, brought up a good point. Geese in different parts of the country react differently to calling. While birds are en route, they often expect to stop and feed with others on the ground, and the feeding call is often effective on these birds. Around the refuge areas, however, where Canadas spend months wintering, there is generally ample food inside refuge boundaries. They are not all

that anxious to dive into a hunting field to eat or to respond to an artificial call for lunch.

Jim Walker, another hunting companion, who often uses the feeding call with success, adds that some Canada geese can't be called into range, period. On this everyone agrees.

Landing geese among the blocks near a pit or blind is the exception rather than the rule. Too many times it's necessary to make a judgment as to whether birds are in range of the gun's and the hunter's capabilities. Most geese seen in the air will never be fooled into approaching within effective range of the most powerful scattergun the federal migratory waterfowl hunting laws permit—the 10-gauge magnum. There are days when the best one can hope for is to

A pair of calls by Black Duck—one for ducks, the other a goose call.

lure birds into what is called effective pass shooting range.

It goes without saying that if one man can entice geese within range, two callers can often be twice as effective. The trick is to let the calls be completely uncoordinated, making it sound as though a number of live geese with different vocal tones were voicing their opinions. This technique often brings birds into range when the single caller goes ignored.

High Canada geese are 50-yard geese. Few are killed cleanly past that yardage, the 3-inch magnum 12s used by most professional guides notwithstanding. Almost all honkers bagged have fallen from the 25- to 40-yard range. If a hunter knows his onions and can call birds in that show an inclination to work over decoys, geese can be taken closer to the 30-yard marker.

Unlike most other goose hunters I know, Walker insists that all hunters

with him place their shotguns *outside* the pit, on the ground within easy reach. I can't disagree with the effectiveness of the safety measure, but at the same time I feel that the practice is bound to flare spooky geese.

Spooky and Suspicious

Cautious birds shy away from the slightest indication that all is not well with that hole in the ground. Honkers have keen eyesight. They are especially wary of any visible movement from below. They also have the advantage their high position offers while reconnoitering out-of-the-ordinary conditions. Even while responding to a call, Canadas constantly search the ground suspiciously, their heads swiveling from side to side on extended necks. The glint of a shiny gun barrel, the gleam of polished wood—the whole setup is out of the norm and quite visible to the discerning eye of a goose.

Gauges and Loads

Which gauges and loads are best for Canadas is never at issue with veteran hunters of the Southern Illinois area. Almost to a man they prefer the 12-gauge 3-inch magnum, most bored full and with 30-inch barrels. Averaging about 7-8 pounds, a Canada is plastered with thick layers of feathers that must be penetrated by the shot pellets. This can be too much of a chore for some 2¾-inch loads, especially from long yardages.

Some will argue that ballistically there are short 12-gauge loads more than capable of performing admirably on Canadas to 50 yards or so. I don't dispute this. However, 3-inch magnums pouring out a cupful of No. 2s will do the job one helluva lot more efficiently.

Unpredictable Geese

There are also times when flaming orange flags waved aloft over a goose pit wouldn't prevent these unpredictable waterfowl from literally fogging into a set of decoys. Once they've made up their collective mind to invade a field, for reasons known only to another Canada, a battery of howitzers fired at 5-second intervals wouldn't drive 'em away. On rare occasions I've seen gaggles of Canadas swarm into cornfields loaded with pits and hunters who had never put a mechanical call to their lips. Everyone got his limit.

In November of 1969 I was visiting Art Hanseman, an old friend then operating a hunting club south of the Crab Orchard Refuge boundaries near Marion, Illinois. Geese that day had been especially active. Most hunters had bagged their limits during the

Experienced hunter and novice alike thrill to Canada geese brought in by calling.

early morning flights. Since some pits were not filled, Hanseman and I elected to try for our birds.

As we crossed the few hundred yards to the cornfield shooting site, honkers began streaming in from three directions. Moreover, they were landing among the decoys at our destination ahead. These, of course, spooked at our approach. Uncasing the guns as we reached the pit, we dropped down and loaded. Almost immediately 5 geese bored straight in. We waited until they were within 25 to 30 yards before we broke above ground level. All 5 of them flared up and to the left. Hanseman took the two on the far left side while I concentrated on the final pair. Four fat honkers thumped audibly to the ground. We'd been in the pit less than 5 minutes, and had not placed a call to our mouths.

By the same token, many geese that "look good" from a distance don't have to be induced by calling. These are the ones with a predetermined course of "working," such as the 5 birds that dropped in on Hanseman and me that morning. Working honkers are exactly what the name implies: they are willing to work into a set of decoys.

In contrast to those cooperative working geese are the "flyers" or "unworkables." Some Canadas appear to be out exercising just for the hell of it. The pros quickly size them up for what they are — high flyers — and don't even attempt to call them. These birds can be identified by their reluctance to waver off course or relinquish an inch of altitude no matter how appealing the caller might sound to his own ears. The very most the unworkables offer in return is a rasping *arrunk,* if they respond at all. The intricate workings of a honker's mind can be exceedingly trying at times.

That is, perhaps, the very reason why so many men become captivated by the challenge of hunting Canada geese. Canadas refuse to be summarily filed into a category of known moods and attitudes from day to day. They can be and often are confusing at best, annoying at the least. About the time you feel you are finally becoming acquainted with what makes them tick, they'll reveal another quirk and fake you clear out of the ball park.

As Jim Walker is prone to say, "The only thing predictable about a honker is his baffling ability to be totally unpredictable."

End of a perfect goose hunt; a limit of two honkers each.

Custom Guns

Paul Jaeger

A 98 Mauser action, stocked in the simple and elegant style typical of Jaeger. The wood is French walnut.

Bob Johnson

A 98 Mauser with 338 Winchester barrel by Apex, built for Jack O'Connor. The handsome stock, in classical form, is of high contrast English fiddleback walnut.

Frazier's Custom Guns

1909 Mauser action, much altered, Douglas Premium barrel in 6mm Rem., Timney trigger, 3-panel checkered bolt knob. Classic stock in fancy feather-crotch black walnut, checkered 24 lpi in multi-point design.

Earl Milliron

A pre-64 Model 70 stocked in the graceful, severely simple style seen in all of Milliron's work.

Bob Smith

A conversion, including bolt alteration, of a military 98 Mauser to a handy carbine, caliber 7x57mm.

Hal Hartley

This Ruger No. 1 single shot, richly engraved by Albin Obiltschnig, was stocked in tight-grain fiddleback maple, the checkering a ribboned fleur de lis design.

Consult our Directory pages for the location of firms or individuals mentioned.

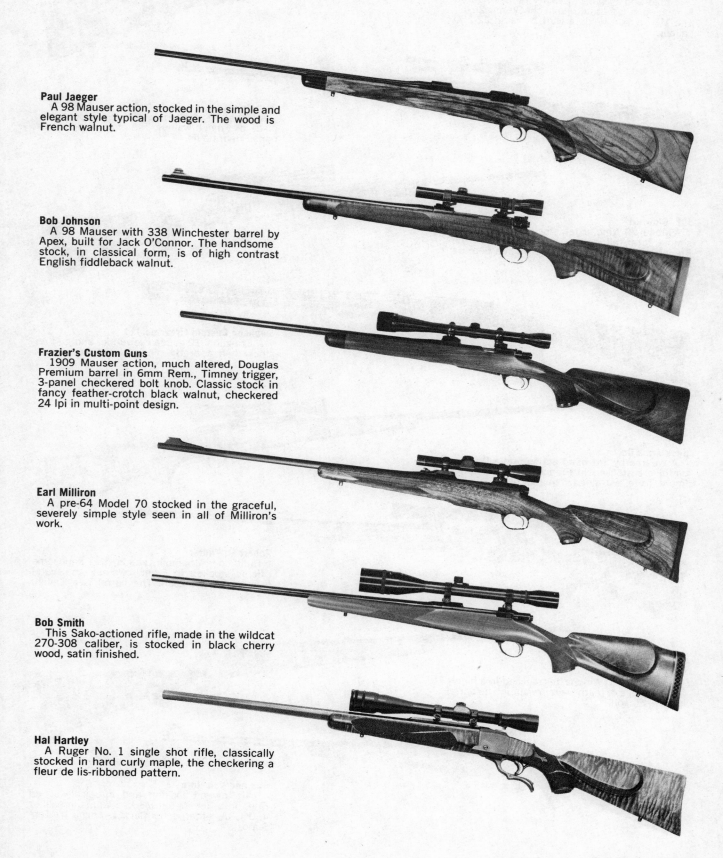

Paul Jaeger
A 98 Mauser action, stocked in the simple and elegant style typical of Jaeger. The wood is French walnut.

Bob Johnson
A 98 Mauser with 338 Winchester barrel by Apex, built for Jack O'Connor. The handsome stock, in classical form, is of high contrast English fiddleback walnut.

Frazier's Custom Guns
1909 Mauser action, much altered, Douglas Premium barrel in 6mm Rem., Timney trigger, 3-panel checkered bolt knob. Classic stock in fancy feather-crotch black walnut, checkered 24 lpi in multi-point design.

Earl Milliron
A pre-64 Model 70 stocked in the graceful, severely simple style seen in all of Milliron's work.

Bob Smith
This Sako-actioned rifle, made in the wildcat 270-308 caliber, is stocked in black cherry wood, satin finished.

Hal Hartley
A Ruger No. 1 single shot rifle, classically stocked in hard curly maple, the checkering a fleur de lis-ribboned pattern.

Clayton N. Nelson
Simple and elegant stocking in well-figured French walnut, the multi-point checkering 26 lpi. The M70 action holds a Hart barrel in 22-250 caliber.

Dale Goens
A Model 70 stocked in a brilliantly contrasty piece of French walnut. The checkering is ribboned fleur de lis.

J. K. Cloward
A Model 70 Winchester, stocked in classically simple form, all elements well handled. The French walnut stock is checkered in a fleur de lis-ribbon design.

Swanson Custom Firearms, Ltd.
A Krieghoff 12-gauge over-under shotgun restocked in a pretty piece of French walnut.

Kess Arms Co.
A Weatherby left hand action and a Douglas barrel are stocked in French walnut of fancy figure. Note restrained schnabel tip.

Robert M. Winter
Built on a Champlin action, this handsome rifle is stocked in French walnut, the metal fittings by Al Biesen. The barrel is a Shilen.

R. E. Anderson
A pre-64 M70 Winchester stocked in a highly figured piece of feather-grain walnut. The barrel is half-octagon.

Abe and Van Horn
This rugged looking and classically-styled rifle, on a Remington M30 action, is in caliber 460 G&A, ordered for **Guns & Ammo** by Tom Siatos.

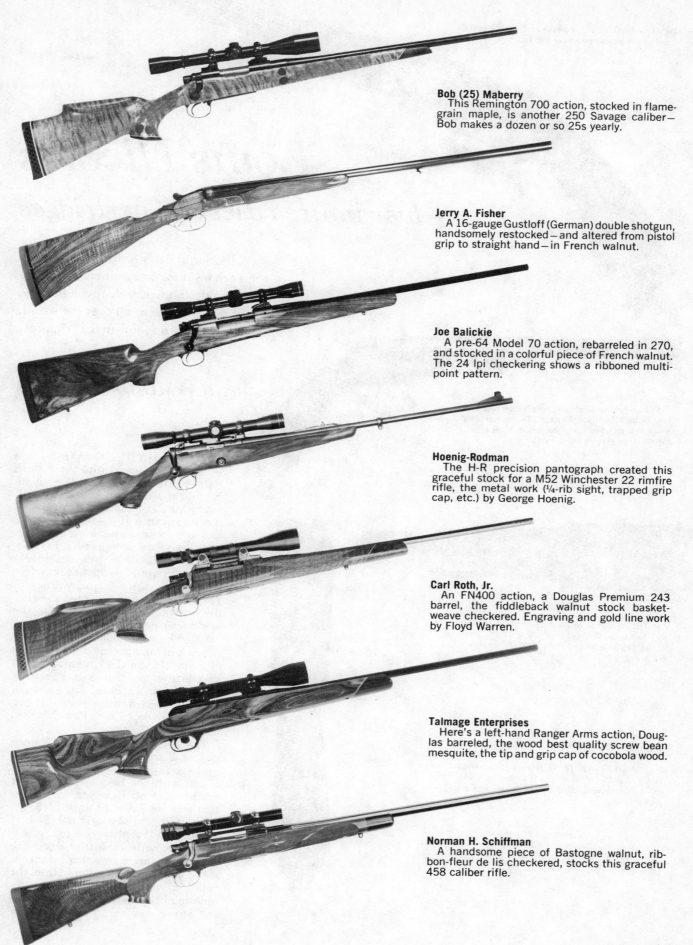

Bob (25) Maberry
This Remington 700 action, stocked in flame-grain maple, is another 250 Savage caliber—Bob makes a dozen or so 25s yearly.

Jerry A. Fisher
A 16-gauge Gustloff (German) double shotgun, handsomely restocked—and altered from pistol grip to straight hand—in French walnut.

Joe Balickie
A pre-64 Model 70 action, rebarreled in 270, and stocked in a colorful piece of French walnut. The 24 lpi checkering shows a ribboned multi-point pattern.

Hoenig-Rodman
The H-R precision pantograph created this graceful stock for a M52 Winchester 22 rimfire rifle, the metal work (¼-rib sight, trapped grip cap, etc.) by George Hoenig.

Carl Roth, Jr.
An FN400 action, a Douglas Premium 243 barrel, the fiddleback walnut stock basket-weave checkered. Engraving and gold line work by Floyd Warren.

Talmage Enterprises
Here's a left-hand Ranger Arms action, Douglas barreled, the wood best quality screw bean mesquite, the tip and grip cap of cocobola wood.

Norman H. Schiffman
A handsome piece of Bastogne walnut, ribbon-fleur de lis checkered, stocks this graceful 458 caliber rifle.

Fig. 1c—Right side perspective of the Flobert salon pistol described under fig. 1a.

Fig. 1a—Left side of a superb salon pistol in the Flobert family collection. The metal and wood are engraved and carved in high relief, the metal gold plated throughout.

Fig. 1b—This view of the Flobert pistol seen in fig. 1a shows the deep chiseling of the steel barrel. The inscription reads: FLOBERT inventeur Bte A PARIS.

Fig. 1d—Underside of the Flobert pistol shown in fig. 1a. The steel guard is elaborately chiseled, a grotesque mask carved in the forward part.

Louis Nicolas
—his rimfire rifles and cartridges

A short and lively history of the great French inventor and manufacturer. His cartridge design was truly revolutionary, and Flobert arms went all over the world. His name became a synonym for "rimfire!"

by RAYMOND CARANTA

WHEN A YOUNG man with a short beard stepped into the French Patent Office, on 21 July 1849, holding four sheets of paper carefully written by his own hand, nobody suspected the importance of the inventions he had to propose. As a matter of fact, in addition to the astonishingly simple breech mechanisms he'd designed—and which would be applied to indoor and gallery arms for more than 75 years, Flobert had invented the rimfire cartridge, still in wide use the world over nowadays.

When he was 14, Louis Flobert went to work as an apprentice in the shop of a one M. Sattler, gunmaker and sword-cutler at 22 Rue du Faubourg Saint Martin in Paris. On June 20, 1840, he married Louise Rosalie Rémy and had a son by her, Paul Nicolas, born in 1846.

The year after, according to French papers of the time, Flobert invented his famous system of guns and ammunition with the help of his younger brother Ernest. However, the invention was not patented until 1849.

According to the original Flobert patent, his invention covered "a new firing mechanism able to produce with great economy new guns," that is, shotguns, rifles and pistols, "from the smallest size to the largest, in combination with metal cartridges deriving their energy from the use of

Auguste Flobert –

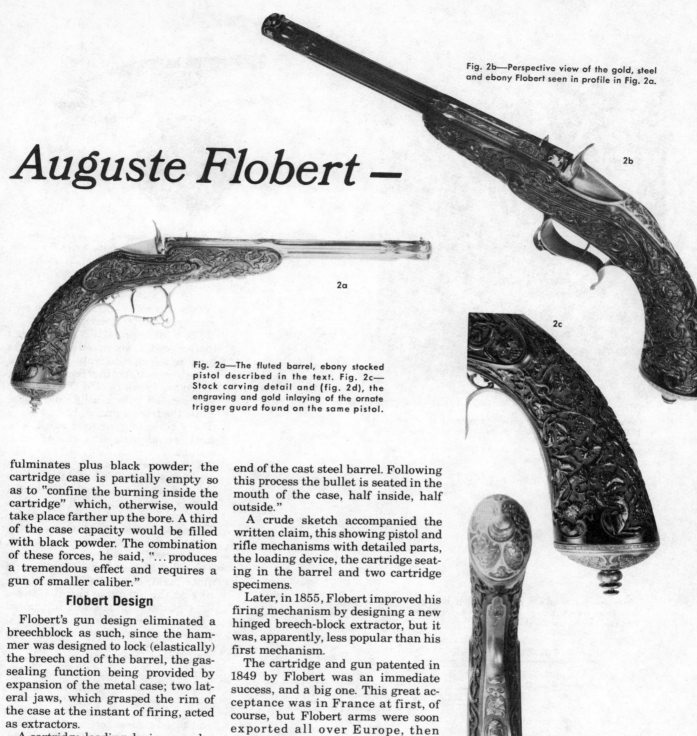

Fig. 2b—Perspective view of the gold, steel and ebony Flobert seen in profile in Fig. 2a.

Fig. 2a—The fluted barrel, ebony stocked pistol described in the text. Fig. 2c— Stock carving detail and (fig. 2d), the engraving and gold inlaying of the ornate trigger guard found on the same pistol.

fulminates plus black powder; the cartridge case is partially empty so as to "confine the burning inside the cartridge" which, otherwise, would take place farther up the bore. A third of the case capacity would be filled with black powder. The combination of these forces, he said, "...produces a tremendous effect and requires a gun of smaller caliber."

Flobert Design

Flobert's gun design eliminated a breechblock as such, since the hammer was designed to lock (elastically) the breech end of the barrel, the gas-sealing function being provided by expansion of the metal case; two lateral jaws, which grasped the rim of the case at the instant of firing, acted as extractors.

A cartridge-loading device was also patented, plus some particulars of the Flobert cartridge:

"The invention also covers a device for forming the cartridge cases. The original cylindrical blanks (cups) are sized down at the mouth one or more millimeters narrower than the bottom, the exact reduction depending on the caliber. The purpose of this sizing is to match the mouth diameter of the case to that of the bore. The barrel chambering is cut to match the case dimensions and to accept the cartridge rim, which seats against the breech

end of the cast steel barrel. Following this process the bullet is seated in the mouth of the case, half inside, half outside."

A crude sketch accompanied the written claim, this showing pistol and rifle mechanisms with detailed parts, the loading device, the cartridge seating in the barrel and two cartridge specimens.

Later, in 1855, Flobert improved his firing mechanism by designing a new hinged breech-block extractor, but it was, apparently, less popular than his first mechanism.

The cartridge and gun patented in 1849 by Flobert was an immediate success, and a big one. This great acceptance was in France at first, of course, but Flobert arms were soon exported all over Europe, then throughout the western world, including the United States. Flobert guns there were first handled by Schuyler, Hartley and Graham of New York City.

Flobert's Shop

In short order Flobert had earned enough money to open his own shop in Paris, at number 12, Boulevart (as it was then spelled) Saint Michel. There he produced some of the best specimens of Flobert pistols ever made. Three of them, still in the pri-

Louis Nicolas Flobert, inventor of the system Flobert in 1849, stands beside a display of arms made in his Paris shop.

A miniature Flobert pistol, stocked in ivory and with the inventor's name inlaid in gold atop the barrel. The coin is a French 5-franc piece.

These are the relatively crude drawings that helped Flobert gain his landmark French patent in 1849. Note cartridge tools (upper right) and chambering details at lower right.

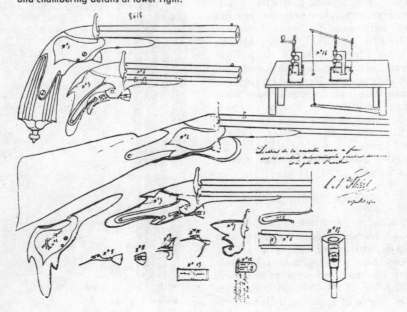

vate collection of the family, are well worthy of a brief description.

The most impressive is a large salon (parlor) pistol, engraved in elaborate high relief and entirely yellow-gold plated except for the flower petals, which are in white gold. The buttcap is decorated with a solid gold eagle, while the trigger guard shows a beautifully chiseled grotesque mask. The stock is made of superb quality French walnut.

The same collection includes a smaller pistol with a blued fluted barrel and an ebony stock. All metal parts are finely engraved and inlaid with gold vine-leaves and borders. The ebony stock is deeply carved, the intricate design showing vine-leaves, animals and masks.

A third Flobert pistol, smaller and quite plain, bears the Flobert signature on the top of the barrel. Besides its elegantly simple and functional lines and the excellence of its lock, this very nice pistol has a stock made of a single, solid piece of horn!

In addition to these masterpieces of gunmaking, Flobert made—either in his Paris shop or by French and Belgian subcontractors—huge quantities of popular-priced salon rifles and pistols. Most pistols were chambered for a 6mm rimfire cartridge, and the rifles were usually in 6mm or 9mm rimfire calibers. All of these guns were available with smoothbore or rifled barrels.

The smoothbore Floberts fired shotshells made of copper and heavy paper or metal cartridges carrying round balls. The rifled arms were chambered for metallic cartridges holding sharply-conical bullets. The 6mm version of this type of ammunition is popularly known in France as the *6 millimètres Bosquette*.

The 9mm conical-bullet load is no

A Flobert target rifle of top quality, its caliber 6mm rimfire. Note double set triggers and palm-rest guard. This illustration, which appeared about 1900, was supplied by Manufrance, the great French mail-order house with headquarters at St. Etienne.

MANUFACTURE FRANÇAISE D'ARMES ET CYCLES DE SAINT-ETIENNE (Loire)
MAISONS ... PARIS ... 12, Rue du Louvre, MARSEILLE, BORDEAUX, LILLE, TOULOUSE, NANTES, ROUEN, TOURS, etc.

CARABINE DE HAUTE PRÉCISION
POUR SOCIÉTES DE TIR

Cartouche calibre 6 m/m double culot, percussion annulaire. (Grandeur naturelle.)

This Flobert pistol, graceful of line and proportions, has a stock of solid horn. Such stock design allows the hand a high hold, an almost automatic sight alignment with the target as the wrist is dropped.

longer listed by French ammunition manufacturers. The 6mm and 9mm round ball cartridges or shotshells are still available in Europe, and so is the *Bosquette.*

Encouraged by his commercial successes, Flobert submitted his guns to the Emperor Napoleon III for possible adoption by the French government services. We know from contemporary reports and correspondence that Flobert was energetically supported by Gevelot, the famous ammunition maker.

The Flobert military guns or conversions of the muzzle-loading service rifles were inexpensive and easy to produce. A hinged breechblock, probably derived from his 1855 patent, was fitted to the rear end of barrels previously bored-through. The proposed cost of these Flobert rifles was 35 gold francs (seven U.S. dollars at that time) instead of the 65-70 francs for the regular Chassepot rifle. However, Flobert failed to interest the Emperor and his military guns never went beyond the prototype stage.

In 1873 Flobert lost his son, Paul Nicolas, who left a young child, Charles Nicolas, born that same year. This Charles Nicolas Flobert, curiously known as "Paul Flobert," later founded the *Cartoucherie Francaise* company, still a famous French ammunition maker and the importer, in France, of the Belgian F.N. Browning guns. He died in Paris in 1946.

Louis Nicolas Flobert died in Paris in 1894. He had not even received a medal from the French government for his inventions and technical achievements. However, his name, now known everywhere in the world, was a synonym for "rimfire" in Europe. France had hundreds of "Flobertist" shooting clubs and Flobert's name was listed in the famous La-

A brass-barreled Flobert pistol of target type. The excellently designed grip lets the hand ride high, giving a very low line of thrust and sight line.

rousse encyclopedia, the French equivalent of Webster's dictionary. Even today, Beretta automatic pistols chambered for 22 Shorts are marked on the slide *Tipo Flobert* and the crack of the 6mm Bosquette is a familiar one on European shooting ranges.

The family still operates the Flobert company, since moved to No. 3, Boulevard Saint-Michel, with Raymond Paul Louis Flobert, the son of

Charles Nicolas, in charge. The company, however, no longer makes rimfire guns; their efforts are devoted today to the import of sporting goods. However, with the current boom in replica firearms, renewed production of a rimfire Flobert may well be resumed one of these days by Bertrand Nicolas and Thierry Nicolas, direct descendants of the great Louis Nicolas Auguste Flobert. •

This short-barreled, gold-inlaid Flobert "derringer" was the personal property of the inventor, probably one that he carried. The rifled barrel, chambered for an unknown 3.7mm (0.145") rimfire cartridge, has not been shortened.

This graceful and handsome G&H rifle, caliber 30-06, was built on a Sauer Mauser 98 action, color case-hardened, the bolt handle not altered for scope mounting. A long-slide Lyman 48 micro rear sight was fitted (the base engraved to match other areas on the rifle) and a matted-ramp band front sight with hood. Contrary to what's often been said, the double set triggers on this rifle work excellently, set or unset. The checkering covers an ample area, running fully around the pistol grip and fore-end.

Details of the G&H seen in Fig. 1—engraved sight base, matted receiver ring and engine-turned bolt and raceways.

Long matted ramp front sight on the G&H Sauer Mauser is surrounded by engraving.

GRIFFIN & HOWE

GRIFFIN AND HOWE are custom gunsmiths. The company, founded some 50 years ago, soon became famous for building big game rifles of high quality. No similar company has gained or maintained as much prestige.

I think, looking back over the years and remembering what I have observed and what I have learned from others, that the story of Griffin and Howe is primarily the story of Seymour Griffin. As a young cabinet-maker who loved rifles but didn't have any, he read Theodore Roosevelt's *African Game Trails*. That was in 1910. Roosevelt had taken a sizable battery of rifles to Africa the year before. One was a slightly modified Springfield Armory rifle, Model of 1903, for the 30-06 cartridge. Roosevelt spoke well of the 30-06. Griffin had to have one stocked as a sporting rifle.

He got a Springfield and went hunting for a blank from which to make a stock. He told me that he found a fine piece of French walnut in the store of Von Lengerke and Detmold, a company later absorbed by Abercrombie & Fitch. He paid $5 for the blank as against the $100-$200 that such a blank would cost

today. When he had inletted and shaped the stock he spent many hours of hard work—mostly hand work—polishing the metal parts. Finally he found a man who could blue the barrel and action.

For 13 years after that, Griffin made stocks for Springfield rifles in the time he could spare from his regular job. He also made some valuable friends. The late Col.

Sunburst engraving of the steel grip cap on the G&H Sauer Mauser.

The late Lucian Cary wrote this article several years ago, but we were unable, for a variety of reasons, to print it until now. This material represents, we believe, the last unpublished story by Mr. Cary. Ed.

Townsend Whelen was one of these. In the spring of 1923 Col. Whelen, who was then in charge of Frankford Arsenal, wrote Griffin that the Arsenal had a particularly fine workman in metal. His name was James V. Howe. Col. Whelen got the two men together. Not long afterward Griffin and Howe formed a company. Griffin got enough backing to buy the necessary machine tools and supplies. The company began work on June 1, 1923.

Engraved steel buttplate of the G&H Sauer 98 has trapdoor.

In many ways the time was favorable. Capt. E. C. Crossman, then one of the most highly regarded gun writers, had published a good deal on the merits of the Springfield rifle and the 30-06 cartridge.* So had Col. Whelen. About 1910 Crossman had got a Los Angeles gunsmith, Louis Wundhammer, to make up four sporting Springfield rifles.† Stewart Edward White, famed writer on the outdoors, took one of these to Africa. He killed a great many lions on his several trips to Africa and came to prefer the Springfield to the Winchester Model 95 in 405 caliber. He decided that the Springfield was more accurate, pleasanter to shoot, and killed just as well. It was with the Springfield that White earned the reputation—for that day—of being the best shot who ever came to Africa. There probably weren't a dozen truly competent gunsmiths in the country in 1923. The commercial arms companies were not producing bolt action big game rifles. If you wanted a bolt action rifle, as the most knowledgeable big game hunters did, you chose a Springfield or imported something from Germany. Hunting scopes made in Germany were beginning to appear but there was no good mount for them.

There was, however, what promised to be a worthy rival to Griffin and Howe. This was the Hoffman

*Notably *The Book of the Springfield* (Marines, N.C., 1931), and *Military and Sporting Rifle Shooting* (Marines, N.C., 1932); the former was issued in an edition updated by Roy C. Dunlap in 1951. One of the first of these Wundhammer Springfield sporters appears on p. 55 *et seq.*, and it is described as well.
†Crossman calls his specimen of this group "the first sporter Springfield ever made. The two others for whom these sporters were made were named Rodgers and Colby. While Roosevelt's Springfield rifle was used by him a bit earlier than 1910, the T.R. rifle was not a full-fledged sporter, in the sense that a new stock was fitted to it.

As it happens, the Wundhammer sporter in this group of four that was made for White was added to Editor John Amber's collection some years ago. As Crossman points out *(op. cit.)* the fore-end is a somewhat spindly affair, a fault later to be well-corrected by Wundhammer. The buttstock dimensions of 13¾ x 1⅝ x 2½ show a drop at heel greater than Crossman later advocated, and the pistol grip is, perhaps, of greater radius than we prefer today. This rifle weighs 8 lbs. The original Armory barrel is used (this one dated Feb., 1910), and the rear sight base remains on the barrel though a Lyman peep receiver sight—not the later Lyman 48—is fitted also.

a history and a tribute

This famed firm, makers under the guiding hands of Seymour Griffin of the finest in firearms, flourished even in the dark days of the depression. The sportsman who owned a rifle custom made by G&H had the ultimate in craftsmanship, grace and shooting qualities.

by LUCIAN CARY

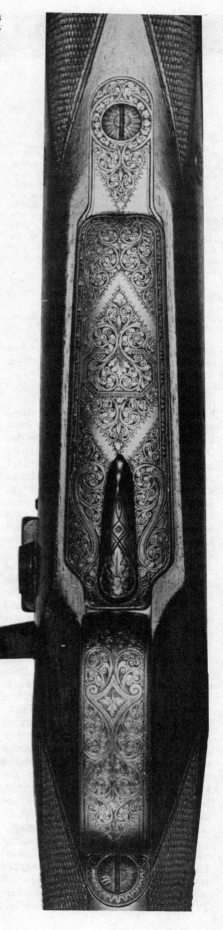

Guard and floorplate engraving on the G&H Sauer 98.

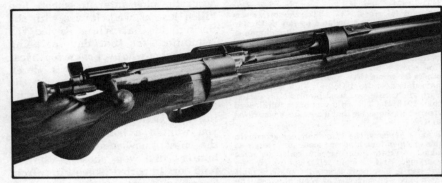

The G&H single shot rifle seen here, serial number 1413, is a Krag that was given unusual treatment. Both sideplate and magazine feed were removed, but enough of the feed mechanism were retained to eject the fired case and to offer a loading platform, semi-circular in section. The rounded wood inside appears as if moulded to the metal pieces. Caliber is 25 Niedner Magnum, a rimmed cartridge in the performance class of the 219 Zipper or 22 Savage Hi-Power. The medium-heavy barrel is 28 inches, rifle weight empty is 10 lbs.

Interior of the G&H Krag shown above.

Arms Co. of Cleveland. It was founded the same day as Griffin and Howe. After a few months Howe left Griffin in order to work for Hoffman. For nearly seven years Griffin held on by himself. He was able to find trained gunsmiths who came over here from Europe, chiefly Germany and Austria. One of these, the late George Hyde, was as accomplished a gunsmith as I ever knew. He left Griffin in order to found his own shop in Brooklyn, where he did some remarkable jobs. Griffin had the reputation of being a hard driver, but his men respected him. He drove himself harder than he drove any of them.

Griffin told me that in those first years he worked seven days a week except for one Sunday a month. He spent that Sunday in Harry Pope's Jersey City shop. Pope, then in his 60's, was well-known as the maker of the most accurate rifle barrels obtainable. For years Pope's specialty was making muzzle-loading barrels with false muzzles for such single-shot, breech-loading actions as the Winchester, Ballard and Sharps Borchardt, but he made 22-cal. target barrels that outshot anything the commercial arms companies could produce at that time. He also made some 30-cal. barrels, first for the Krag and then for the Springfield. It was widely held that Pope knew more about what makes rifles shoot than any other man in the country.

Pope told me that Griffin came over one Sunday with a barrel blank that a customer wanted turned down to three diameters, all within a thousandth of an inch. Pope thought this was nonsense, but

he did the job. On another Sunday Griffin arrived with a 30-cal. barrel that a customer wanted chambered for the 300 Magnum cartridge. Griffin had had some trouble with the chambering. Pope helped him complete the job—the first 300 Magnum rifle that Griffin and Howe turned out.

Early Days

Like most of us, Griffin had his foibles. Carl Estey, who once worked for Griffin and later was a salesman on Abercrombie's seventh floor (which contains more new guns than any other place I know of, here or abroad), told me of the time an emissary of the White House came in to order a rifle to be presented to some Eastern potentate. The rifle had to be made in one week. Griffin was out to lunch. When he came back he blew a gasket. Harry Truman was then president and Griffin, for whatever reason, or no reason, hated Truman. He said he would not make up a rifle for Harry Truman.

Estey waited until he thought Griffin had calmed down, then said: "After all, the President of the United States has chosen you above all others to build a rifle for presentation." Griffin yielded and turned the shop upside down in order to get the rifle out in the specified time.

Custom gunsmiths commonly try to fill their orders in rotation. I say "try." Being human, they do sometimes yield to a favorite customer. One of Griffin's customers—not a

favorite—once appeared with a bottle of whisky and the suggestion that he was in a hurry for his rifle. Griffin refused the whisky. Then turned to Estey and said: "I don't think you'll take it either, will you, Carl?"

I first met Seymour Griffin in 1928 or 1929. The shop was then on East 44th Street. You entered a room that was full of guns and accessories. This was a retail store. The much larger room behind the store contained the shop. You weren't free to go into the shop except by invitation. In the fall the store was rather a madhouse. Many men seem not to know that the time to order a new gun or have an old one repaired is quite a few months before the hunting season opens rather than the week before. I saw a man bring in a beat up pump shotgun that had a bad dent in the barrel. He was told that the job could be done in three weeks. He said: "I can't wait three weeks. I want to shoot ducks three days from now."

Griffin and Howe had some most unusual customers. One was a man who often ordered two or three rifles at a time. When asked what calibers he wanted his stock reply was: "Any I haven't got."

Finally he reported that he had gone hunting. Phil Johnstone, the then manager, asked him which of his Griffin and Howe rifles he had used. The man shook his head. He hadn't used any of his fine custom made rifles. He had used a factory 30-30 carbine. Johnstone asked what luck he'd had. The man answered that he had hit three tin cans in five shots.

Griffin and Howe finally ran out of calibers for this man, who then began to collect Purdey shotguns. Even second-hand these are likely to cost $3500-$4000 today!

Surprising Lady Customer

Another surprising customer was a little lady who looked as if she were crowding 70. Her chauffeur came in behind her carrying a rifle in a leather case. When he took the rifle out of the case it proved to be one made by Gibbs of Bristol on a magnum Mauser action for an elephant cartridge. Gibbs was one of the best English makers of rifles, maybe the best. The factory was bombed out by the Germans during World War II. When Griffin looked the rifle over he saw signs of use — dents and scratches on the stock and blueing was worn off toward the muzzle.

The little old lady said that she wanted a similar rifle as a present for her husband. Griffin was concerned. How many women know what kind of rifle would please a big game hunting husband?

"You see," the lady said, "my husband has always used a big double for buffalo and rhinoceros and elephant. But I had such luck with the Gibbs that he wants a rifle like mine when we go to Africa again."

Griffin was amazed. He couldn't picture the lady, who didn't weigh 110 pounds, swinging that Gibbs elephant rifle and taking its recoil.

The rather early G&H rifle shown here, made on a Springfield 1903 action, its serial number 827, has handling and balance qualities superior to any other rifle I've owned or used. Its stock dimensions are about normal (13⅝x1⅞x2⅝ inches) for iron sights, but it's the lean, slenderness of the pistol grip and fore-end, the in-the-hands balance that its tapering 23¼-inch barrel contributes to, that make this rifle come alive. Chambered for the 7x57 Mauser cartridge, the rifle weighs 7½ lbs. empty. The bolt has not been altered for scope use. Sights are a Lyman 48 micro rear and a matted-ramp front with hood.

The oil finished stock, now too dark, shows good figure. Grip cap and buttplate—the latter engraved and with trapdoor—are of steel. The fore-end tip is genuine buffalo horn, with not a check or crack in it. The checkering all but covers the fore-end, and runs from top edge to top edge. Checkering on the pistol grip goes across the top, though it doesn't join perfectly there.

"What about the stock dimensions?" Griffin asked.

"Make the stock the same as mine only an inch longer and not so much cast off. A man doesn't need as much cast off as I do."

After the lady left, Griffin picked up the telephone and called a customer who had hunted more than once in Africa and told him about the order. When he gave the lady's name the man said: "Oh, yes. She is as good a hunter as her husband. No white hunter shoots her game for her. If he tried to, he'd get fired on the spot. She has killed the Big Five without help from any other shooter."

By the Big Five the man meant elephant, rhinoceros, buffalo, lion and leopard.

A Gold Canary

Another customer who gave the place a surprise was the man who

The G&H 7x57mm Springfield, right and left side views. Note G&H's stock styling at this period—the raised ridge, rising out of the grip checkering, then falling away in a trajectory-like arc forward.

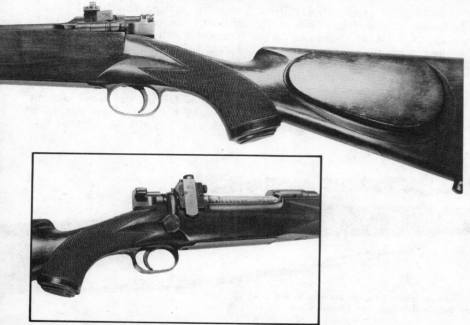

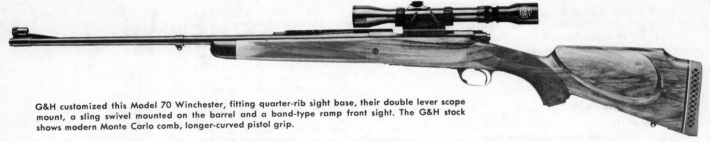

G&H customized this Model 70 Winchester, fitting quarter-rib sight base, their double lever scope mount, a sling swivel mounted on the barrel and a band-type ramp front sight. The G&H stock shows modern Monte Carlo comb, longer-curved pistol grip.

wanted a canary engraved on the top tang of a double barreled elephant rifle. This was so odd that Phil Johnstone asked him why.

"My pet canary just died," the man said. "I want a monument for him."

The job went to Joe Fugger, who studied art in Austria and has been with the company for many years. He's one of the best engravers of guns in the country. Maybe the best. I saw an engraving he did on the sidelocks of a double barrel Purdey elephant rifle. Three elephants were followed by an elephant calf, while beyond them a cheetah pursued an impala. The mountain in the background may have been Kilimanjaro. The animals were beautifully lifelike, the whole a magnificent composition. A coiled cobra in gold relief decorated the top lever. The engraving took 200 hours and cost the man who ordered it—back then—$1500 in addition to the cost of the rifle, which was more than $2000.

I asked Joe Fugger about the canary. He remembered it well. He said it was three-eighths of an inch high, a gold inlay. No doubt gold is the proper color for a canary.

Griffin and his crew designed a scope mount that is still highly regarded because the scope can be removed and replaced without changing the sighting of the rifle. This is rare in scope mounts. The Griffin and Howe mount is in two parts. The base, screwed and pinned to the receiver of the rifle, has a male dovetail along the top. The other part, in which the scope is held, has a female dovetail. After the two parts are slid

together, they are clamped by two levers that operate half-round rods. When the two levers are rotated back half a turn or so, the scope can be slid off.

Many of us remember that when Winchester first produced the 22 Hornet cartridge there was no rifle for it on the market. Griffin's answer was to adapt the Springfield rifle made in those days for the 22 long rifle cartridge to take the Hornet. Later a wildcat cartridge, much superior to the Hornet, came along. This was known as the 2R Lovell. It used the 25-20 single shot case necked down to take a 22 bullet. Griffin chambered rifles for the cartridge. The 25-20 single shot was obsolete and the cases were in short supply. Griffin got Winchester to make up some thousands of the cases. The rifle I had for the 2R, on a Sharps Borchardt single shot action, was, up to 200 yards, the most dependably accurate rifle I had ever shot. It averaged 1.70" for seven successive 10-shot groups at that distance. This was away back—some 35 years ago. We have much better bullets today, and the results are better. The 2R Lovell is now obsolete. Newer woodchuck cartridges have surpassed it.

Griffin also produced a 350-cal. cartridge at the suggestion of an American, Leslie Simpson, who hunted a great deal in Africa. It was the 375 H&H Magnum case necked down. If the slow burning powders we have now had been available in those days, the 350 might have been a considerable success. As it was, it reportedly gave a 250-gr.

bullet 2740 fs velocity and a 275-gr. bullet 2600 fs.

To Shoot or Not to Shoot...

In the early years Griffin and Howe were said to make big game rifles for Park Avenue nobs and other toffs, and that the owners, not being hunters, never shot their rifles but used them as conversation pieces. There was some truth in this allegation. Not much, but some.

Actually, Griffin and Howe have made rifles for many big game hunters. The late Grancel Fitz, who was the first man to kill all 25 of the legal varieties of big game on the North American continent, used a Griffin and Howe 30-06 for practically all of his hunting. The list of big game hunters who used Griffin and Howe rifles includes Ernest Hemingway, Russel Aitkin, Townsend Whelen, Edward Queeny, the Maharajah of Bikaner, Michael Lerner and Donald Hopkins. Col. Whelen told me, a few years before his death, that he believed Hopkins had more experience in big game hunting than any other living American. He has hunted in this country, in Alaska, Canada and on many long trips to Africa. The last I heard, Hopkins was in Africa hunting for a particular bull elephant said to have bigger tusks than any other. On one occasion when I visited the Griffin and Howe shop, Hopkins had six rifles in there to be restocked.

In 1930 Griffin and Howe became the subsidiary of Abercrombie & Fitch that it still is. Griffin con-

G&H built this Mauser 98-actioned rifle in 225 Winchester-caliber as a varmint rifle. Fore-end is heavier, more full, yet Monte Carlo comb is absent. Double set triggers were fitted, a good choice on a varmint rifle.

tinued in charge until his retirement a few years ago. Today the G&H shop is located at 589 Eighth Avenue. No retail business is done now, as it was on 44th street.

One of the problems of a custom gunsmith is the man who comes in early and stays around all day. One custom gunsmith I know put up a sign saying: "Conversation $5 an hour. Argument $10 an hour." Griffin and Howe's answer was to divorce the shop from the retail store. Whether you want a new recoil pad or a complete Griffin and Howe rifle you go to Abercrombie & Fitch at 45th Street and Madison Avenue, go up to the seventh floor and see John Realmuto, who is now the manager of Griffin and Howe. If you want a particularly fine piece of wood for a stock, John will arrange for you to look over the supply. The shop has some beautiful French walnut. Aber-

crombie & Fitch once put on exhibition an outstanding piece with the proviso that it was not for sale. However, a man came along and offered $200 for it. He got the piece. Such a blank weighs around eight pounds, so the man paid about $25 a pound for it. By the time the stock is finished it will weigh only a fraction of what it weighed in the blank, of course.

I am inclined to be cautious about using a fancy blank for a bolt action rifle where it is important that the grain run right in the grip and in the fore-end. The buttstock of a single shot rifle or a shotgun can be as fancy as you care to pay for, however.

In the 44th Street days Griffin and Howe had a strange machine that looked a little like a wide ladder. When I first saw it I didn't know what it was for. It was a machine for shaping and inletting rifle stocks. A stock maker did the final fitting.

Commercial stocks now are made by a much improved variety of the old Griffin and Howe machine. Even so, they need an amount of hand fitting that they seldom get. Most top stock makers prefer to start with the solid blank and do all the work with hand tools. This is sometimes called "block stocking".

Griffin and Howe discarded the old machine for shaping and inletting stocks when the company moved down to East 13th Street. All of their stocks now are made entirely by hand. This has greatly increased the price. Individual custom stockmakers today often charge $250 to over $500, plus the cost of the wood and the fittings. This may seem like a high price, but if a stock maker spends many hours in making a stock he is not getting rich. Stock making is the poorest paid part of a gunsmith's trade.

Griffin & Howe Check List

G&H rifles have long been collected by enthusiasts for the classic sporting rifle, and of course G&H made some few rifles in target grade or form also.

We are pleased to present here, through the courtesy of Abercrombie & Fitch, a check list of G&H serial numbers. We regret that the numbers for the 1923-1929 period inclusive are no longer available, but serial numbers started with 1 in 1923, and some 820 rifles were made through 1929. Thus an average of some 117 rifles were made each of those seven years. A rather high figure, it would seem in comparison with the near-60 average for the following ten years (1930-1939), but it must be remembered that the pre-depression period was one of prosperity and high *real* income, while the next ten years saw luxuries much less indulged in.

Please do do not write to Abercrombie & Fitch or to G&H for further information on a G&H rifle you may have. They will not reveal the names of the original purchasers under any circumstances, and neither do they have time to correspond on other aspects of G&H rifles.

Year	Serial Numbers		Year	Serial Numbers		Year	Serial Numbers	
1930	1001	- 1053	1947	1798	- 1828	1964	2505	- 2519
1931	1054	- 1109	1948	1829	- 1947	1965	2520	- 2534
1932	1110	- 1168	1949	1948	- 2007	1966	2535	- 2542
1933	1169	- 1228	1950	2008	- 2034			
1934	1229	- 1348	1951	2035	- 2066			
1935	1349	- 1462	1952	2067	- 2096	G&H is unable to		
1936	1463	- 1536	1953	2097	- 2126	supply exact figures		
1937	1537	- 1599	1954	2127	- 2156	for each year after		
1938	1600	- 1623	1955	2157	- 2186	1966, but the total		
1939	1624	- 1659	1956	2187	- 2216	number of rifles		
1940	1660	- 1678	1957	2217	- 2246	made for 1967-1972		
1941	1679	- 1707	1958	2247	- 2276	inclusive was about		
1942	1708	- 1737	1959	2277	- 2306	42, and the last rifle		
1943	none		1960	2307	- 2336	made (as of February		
1944	none		1961	2337	- 2426	1973) bears serial		
1945	1738	- 1767	1962	2427	- 2456	number 2584.		
1946	1768	- 1797	1963	2457	- 2504			

Stock Is Classic

Your typical Griffin and Howe stock is of a design I shall call classic. In recent years many stocks have been made, particularly on the West Coast, that I would call elaborate. They have deeply hooked pistol grips, oddly shaped fore-end tips, a variety of inlays made of plastic or contrasting wood, and finally the extreme Monte Carlo comb that is—sadly—on the way to becoming universal.

Now a rifle is a tool. As such it must be designed to suit its purpose, but there is no necessity for making it ugly. I have had two stocks made with the Monte Carlo combs. Then I discovered that this excrescence was entirely unnecessary. The same goes for a deeply hooked pistol grip. There never was any excuse for decorating a rifle stock with contrasting inlays. They merely distract the eye from something that should be seen as a whole.

The typical Griffin and Howe stock does not go in for nonsense. It is a clean, racy job, good to feel in shooting and good to look at. Griffin and Howe would undoubtedly make a stock with a restrained Monte Carlo comb for a man who wanted it, but I don't know what they would do if somebody came along who wanted a white diamond inlay the size of a postcard on one side of the stock and maybe a few more inlays scattered around.

The day of the Springfield is gone. The Director of Civilian Marksmanship no longer sells it. So also is the day when no other bolt action rifles for big game shooting were made in this country. Winchester, Remington

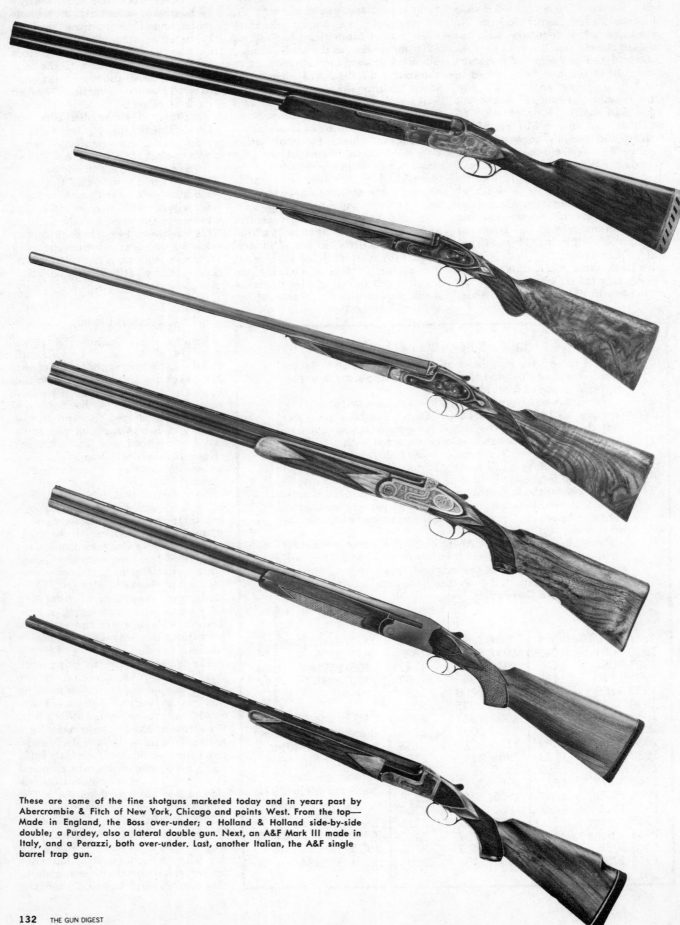

These are some of the fine shotguns marketed today and in years past by Abercrombie & Fitch of New York, Chicago and points West. From the top— Made in England, the Boss over-under; a Holland & Holland side-by-side double; a Purdey, also a lateral double gun. Next, an A&F Mark III made in Italy, and a Perazzi, both over-under. Last, another Italian, the A&F single barrel trap gun.

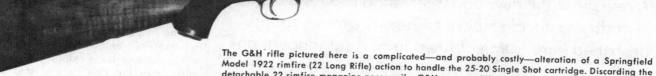

The G&H rifle pictured here is a complicated—and probably costly—alteration of a Springfield Model 1922 rimfire (22 Long Rifle) action to handle the 25-20 Single Shot cartridge. Discarding the detachable 22 rimfire magazine necessarily, G&H converted the action to conventional centerfire—1903 style floorplate, cartridge follower with W-spring, etc.

Fitted with a medium-heavy 26-inch barrel, making for a total weight of 9½ lbs. empty, this G&H rifle is arche-typical of their work in the Springfield period. The stock is classic—no Monte Carlo, not even a cheekpiece, and the multi-diamond checkering is ample indeed. The wood, probably American, is well figured in the butt section. The pistol grip cap and buttplate are of steel, a band-type ramp, matted, finishes off the muzzle, there's a genuine horn fore-end tip, and the bolt knob, flatted underneath, is fully checkered. Serial number of this well-made rifle is 1379.

The bolt body, follower and receiver raceways are engine turned.

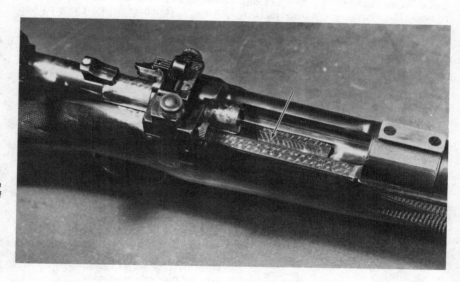

This action close-up shows the conversion from clip magazine to cartridge follower system of the G&H 25-20 S.S. rifle.

and Savage make them now, and so do H&R, Mossberg, et al. In addition, bolt action rifles are made in Finland, Sweden, Germany, Belgium, England and probably elsewhere. I had an excellent Springfield action and I toyed with the idea of having it made up into a sporting rifle. This requires a good deal of expensive work. I finally decided against the project for a reason that may seem odd to guncranks. The reason was that I didn't need it. I already had three excellent custom stocked big game rifles.

How Much Do They Cost?

Like the price of everything else, that of a Griffin and Howe rifle has gone up. The base price is $850. This does not include such things as a trap buttplate. That costs $25 extra. A Griffin and Howe scope mount fitted to the rifle costs $50 or more. A scope costs anywhere from about $40 to over $100. Engraving costs almost anything you care to pay. I saw some years ago a Winchester Model 70 that Griffin and Howe had restocked and engraved. The price was $1350. A similar job would cost much more today.

You can buy a good commercial bolt action big game rifle for from about $115 to $175. What does a man gain by paying Griffin and Howe several times as much? You might ask a man what he gains by paying $350 apiece for his suits when ready made suits are available at one-third that price or less. If he answered you truly he would probably be reduced to saying: "I just like them better." Griffin and Howe is not a large company. As of last January 1 it employed 12 men in the shop. For years the company has turned out from about 30 to 75 or more rifles a year. Because the company's production ceased during World War II when it went over to war work, its current serial number isn't much over 2600.

It is in the nature of things that a custom gun shop doing fine work cannot be big.

A custom gunsmith has done nice work for me over 15 years. I went to his shop at first because it was only an hour away by car from where I was living in northwestern Connecticut. I continued to go because his work was so good. He works alone. His charges are not much different from those of Griffin and Howe. He is critical. He knows the work of Griffin and Howe. He has had occasion to examine many examples of it.

I asked him when I was writing this what he thought of Griffin and Howe. He said: "If I needed some work that I couldn't do for myself I would go to Griffin and Howe."

I consider that statement, coming from the man who made it, a high tribute to Griffin and Howe. An accolade.

•

HANDLOADING

A review of the new and interesting products offered today's cartridge loader. There are many things described here, some of them important innovations.

by John T. Amber

B-Square

Dan Bechtel, owner-operator of B-Square—which makes a big variety of useful products for the gunsmith, gun nut and handloader—sent us a revised and improved couple of precision tools meant for the serious reloader/benchrester. As our picture shows, his Case Neck Gauge consists of a round steel block, the case going into the center of it over a hardened and ground spindle. Washers supplied permit necks to be measured at various points, those dropping over the spindle. Two spring-loaded pins, set into the perimeter and adjustable, push against the case being checked, holding it against the spindle. The dial indicator used, reading to 0.0005", goes through the perimeter also, between the two locating pins, impinging on the case to effect a reading.

Several cases were used to test the B-Square tool, and all readings were closely comparable to readings had from two other neck-wall thickness gauges—one the Brown Little Wiggler, the other a Starrett tubing micrometer. The spring-loaded pins exert a fair amount of pressure against the spindled case, so much so that at first it was hard to rotate the cases. A touch of oil on the tips and into the pin cavity helped considerably, but I think these pins would work easier and better if they were under less spring tension.

The B-Square Case Neck Gauge does a good job, though it's a bit slow to get going—the spring pins require readjustment when going from one caliber to another—and the $37.95 price includes a sturdy, dustproof case for the DI, two Allen wrenches and a set of washers.

Bechtel's other tool for handloaders is a combined case/cartridge spinner, using a dial indicator identical to that described above. (If both B-Square tools were ordered only the one D.I. would be required, the

saving $14.50). This B-Square spinner differs from most others in *not* having a means of locating the front and rear of the cartridge (or case) on lathe-type centers or spindles. This was done by design—in testing loaded rounds for bullet concentricity with the case axis, any inequalities in bullet noses resting in a circular opening can well indicate off-center bullet seating where little or none exists. This also holds true for case bases held in cupped arbors—case rims are rarely smooth edged or fully concentric.

As our illustration shows, the B-Square spinner consists of two steel rods, ground and polished, held slightly apart and parallel by two steel blocks. The D.I. rides vertically in the center of one block, and an adjustable steel pin serves to locate the case or cartridge as desired to let the D.I. plunger rest on case body, neck, bullet or whatever. The case alone lies between the larger rods—nothing touches the bullet being checked, and only the small diameter (.250") locating rod touches the case.

In use the case/cartridge is finger rolled on its twin-rod bed as the operator watches the D.I. Alternately the D.I. plunger can be lifted free of engagement and then lowered to a new position on the case/bullet circumference. Again a trace of lube on the case or bullet eases the job, lessens friction.

This B-Square spinner also worked well, in fact rather better than two other spinners—the Wilson and Brown tools, both of which let the case/cartridge rotate on one center or two. Belted cases, however, need a rebate or reduced-diameter section cut into the twin rest rods. This would let the belt—very often irregular dimensionally—lie free of the rods in rotation. B-Square will furnish such rods without extra cost.

Cost of the B-Square spinner, with D.I. to .0005", $34.95. Add $1 to each unit for shipping costs.

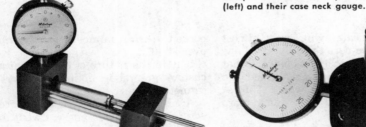

B-Square case-bullet spinner (left) and their case neck gauge.

New Speer Bullets

By my count Speer has 5 new rifle bullets this year, and one they've redesigned. Four of these are labeled *Mag-Tip*, the name indicating an interior ogive treatment that results in controlled expansion on game. The walls are "contoured" to a hexagon form and tapered, so that on impact the front section deforms readily until the thicker-walled rear section is reached. At that time expansion ends and better penetration results. These *Mag-Tip* bullets also have flat

noses, odd as that may seem at first glance for a bullet of high velocity potential. There's a reason advanced, though—at high speed, it was determined, pointed soft points shed their points through melting, to one degree or other. Because the amount of point loss varied, accuracy did too, so the answer seemed to be, "Why have any points?"

Velocity wouldn't be materially affected, but bullet uniformity would be improved, thus the *Mag-Tips*.

The Mag-Tip bullets are made in two 7mm weights, 160-gr. and 175-gr.,

and in .308" size another two—150-gr. and 180-gr. The 175-gr. 7mm *Mag-Tip* is the one Speer calls "redesigned."

Other new Speer bullets are: a 110-gr. HP Varminter in 30 caliber, a 9.3mm semi-pointed SP of 250 grains (when was the last previous 9.3mm bullet made in the U.S., if any?), and a 400-gr. .458" flat-nose bullet, strong jacketed for use in 458 Magnums and in those 45-70s of modern design that can stand higher pressures than the Springfield trapdoor and the Winchester 1886.

Electro-Loader

If you load lots of shotshells the Electro-Loader may be just what you need. This compact unit — 9x12 inches of bench space needed — weighs less than 25 pounds, and it's made for MEC's 600 Jr., 650 and Versamec 700 presses.

These kits are fully electric, they're easy to install, and operation is simple — a touch of the foot switch does all the work. Prices are $137.50 to $175 with a full year's guarantee. Write to Griffin Shooter's Specialties Co., 7801-A9 Hillmont, Houston, TX 77040.

CH-50 Digital Chronograph

This well-made instrument was introduced in 1972, I believe. Our test sample, delivered in mid-January, 1973, was carefully examined but was not put through its paces until warmer weather rolled around.

The CH-50 is a compact unit (8" x 3" x 6"), weighs 3.7 lbs. and offers a 4-digit readout via 7-segment incandescent lamps. Their visibility is excellent, even under bright ambient light. All circuits are fully transistorized for stability, maintenance of accuracy and long life. The pulse-counting system uses a one-MHz (one million cycle) quartz crystal. Usable with 110 VAC or dry batteries (6 D-size cells, Nicad or flashlight), it has a Nicad battery charger built in. Time-base accuracy is 0.01%, plus or minus one microsecond. 10-foot screen spacing is suggested, and the fully detailed manual-readout table is so computed. Other screen spacings can be used, of course. Velocities from 1000 to 10,000 fps can be measured using the 10-foot screen distance.

The all-metal case is ruggedly made, and has a carrying handle atop. Underneath is a sturdy folding stand to let the instrument be set to a convenient viewing angle. Screen holders and support feet (2 of each) are furnished (these designed for use

JASCO Reloader's Labels

How many times have you said to yourself: "*?!!× Now what the hell have I got in these loads?" Me, too, and I certainly knew better — just plain carelessness. There's little excuse, if any, for such neglect nowadays — ammo box labels, metallic or shotshell cartridges, are available in many shops — or by mail.

Jasco (Box 49751, Los Angeles, CA 90049) labels, self-adhesive and reusable, are $1.15 PP a pack (27 units for metallics or 40 for shotshell boxes). They'll help you keep track. Jasco shotshell caddys hold 50 cases, are a handy loading bench item, sell for $2.35 each PP.

with thin-wall conduit), as are 10-ft. and 20-ft. cables, Nicad batteries, silver-coated screens, etc.

Operation of the CH-50 is simple — insert the 2 screens, check the screen circuitry by means of 2 front-panel lamps, shoot and look up the velocity in the velocity tables. When power is "on," pressing the reset button reveals a reading of 8888 on the tubes, thus indicating that the unit is functioning correctly. If a screen fault exists (poor contact, a faulty screen, etc.), it is detected by either or both of 2 lamps on the cabinet face.

Our test CH-50 machine worked very well. There were no circuit or other instrument problems of any kind, and the large figures were easily read in bright sunlight — a polarizing filter provided assures excellent visibility. I did have some trouble hitting both screens — these are 2" x 4" and they're positioned in the stainless steel friction holders with the long side horizontal. That leaves only 2 inches available for bullet penetrations and a useful readout. I failed to hit the second screen a few times. The suggested system of mounting the screens could be altered to position them vertically, which would give almost 3 inches of screen availability in a vertical plane.

Rather than make that screen-orientation change, I tried something unorthodox. I placed the screens a

The product prices mentioned in these review pages were correct at presstime, but may be higher when you read this.

mere 2 feet apart and divided my velocity-table figures by 5. Hitting both screens dead center was easy, of course, but more to the point I didn't find any appreciable difference in velocity figures. I was careful to get the short screen separation exactly right, and since the CH-50 has a million-cycle crystal, it is inherently more accurate than are those chronographs with 100,000 MHz systems.

Thirty rounds of 22 LR Match ammo, tested on the 10-ft. screens, showed an average of 1087.5 fps from a 20" barreled rifle. That is well below the advertisied MV of 1120 for W-W's Mark III stuff, of course, but 1190 or so fps is what I generally get from the same rifle. (An old Winchester M52 with 28" barrel approaches 1120 more closely).

Another 30 cartridges, same load and rifle, fired through the 2-foot screens, showed a 1089.6 average, not enough difference to worry about. However, the high and low shots were a bit farther apart than before, though that could easily reverse itself if another 30 shots were to be fired. Anyway, as far as I'm concerned, the 2-foot separation worked well enough — we're never going to duplicate factory figures, except by accident. We don't use the *exact* same ammo, our barrels and conditions differ and so on.

I like the CH-50 chronograph and the way it performs. At $295 complete (nothing to add, 6 Nicads included) it isn't cheap, but it is indeed well designed and well executed. It can be bought without supports, screen holders, screens on Nicad batteries, for $268 — you may already have these items or some of them. Any screens of less than 500 ohms resistance can be used; CH-50 screens are $6.95 per 100.

Display Electronics, Box 1044, Littleton, CO 80120, are the makers of the CH-50 chronograph. They'll be glad to supply full details.

Left—Lee's Production Pot. Below—his Precision Melter (the lower-priced Bullet Caster is the same but lacks the heat control). Right, Lee's great new hollow-base mould.

Lee Engineering

Lee has lots of good stuff for the handloader this year, most notably items that represent fresh, new thinking. Witness their latest surprise in a mould, one for the Minie bullet with a hollow base. Those of you who have used hollow base—or hollow point— moulds know well how troublesome they can be. The new Lee mould (two weights in three calibers; 45, 50 and 58) has an automatic core pin that's as ingenious as it is simple and effective. Just fill the mould, hit the sprue cutter, open the mould upside down and the HB ball falls off right now! The core pin, attached to the mould, is automatically cammed out of the cavity as the handles are spread. Someone at Lyman (or SAECO or LEC, et al) is bound to say "Now why the hell didn't I think of that!"

I *know* they work well, too, for I've tried two—one in 45 caliber, the other a 50. Because Lee uses a light alloy for his mould blocks, even the first bullet cast is often useful, especially if Lee's instructions are carefully followed.

In each of the three calibers, Lee has made two bullet forms available —one a traditional Minie, the other a new and quite different style. Twelve very shallow lube grooves (.005" deep) are cut, this little depth permitting a much thinner than normal skirt, which in turn should make for better and faster expansion on firing. However, there's been no opportunity to shoot these novel Minies yet, but I'm anxious to try 'em.

They're $13.98 each.

Lee has numerous other bullet moulds for 1973—many rifle calibers now, in addition to his original moulds for handgun bullets—plus round ball moulds made in a new fashion. Using a technique called hobbing, the cavities are rough cut to within .005"-.010" of finished size. Then a tungsten-carbide ball, of desired caliber, is placed between the mould halves and squeezed in a 30-ton press. The result—a near-perfect cavity, much smoother and rounder than it could be made ordinarily. Lee's round ball moulds are made in 22 calibers, from .295" to .495", each with handles, at $8.98, I believe.

Lee rifle bullet moulds come in three calibers so far—270, 110- and 125-gr., and 9 in 30-caliber, weights from 113 grains to 200. All are gas check types, all are guaranteed to have a roundness within .001" or less, and each is $8.95, *with* handles. Three 45-70 moulds are also made (same $8.98 price), weights of 405, 450 and 500 grains. These are regular flat base types, though.

These new rifle bullet moulds show careful, thoughtful designing, too— adequate grease grooves, with band edges radiused for distortionless sizing; but minimal sizing is needed, usually, for diameters are kept groove-size or nearly so, and bullet fore parts are designed to be bore-riding.

I've left Lee's big-ticket products for the last because I wanted to be sure there'd be adequate space to describe them—and there is. Lee now offers for 1973 **three Electric Lead Melters**

—all of them relatively low power-consumption (wattage), yet all unusually fast in making solidified lead molten.

The Lee Production Pot holds 10 lbs., has a melting time of less than 20 minutes, and it's a bottom-pour type with infinite heat-control range. Because the heating element is separate from the lead pot (as is also the case with the other two Lee pots), only 500 watts are required during heat-up and much less than that to maintain temperature. Made with a mould guide and guaranteed 2 years, this unit is $29.98.

Lee's Precision Melter, a dip pot, holds 4 lbs., melts that quantity in less than 15 minutes via a 400-watt adjustable element, and sells for $19.98. The Lee Bullet Caster, also 4-lb. capacity, heats a bit more slowly. Its fixed heat element draws only 275 watts, its price $14.98.

I've used all three of these units recently, and all performed excellently. The rapidity with which they melt lead is surprising, but Lee's novel design explains it. The pot, of drawn steel, is surrounded by an aluminum jacket that reflects heat back to the pot. The tubular heating element (like those used on electric ranges) has a high efficiency factor and, because of the separation of pot from heater, there's virtually no on-off electrical fluctuation during heat-up. My only criticism applies to the big pot—clearance between its pouring spout and the base is too little to let some of my old hollow-base moulds clear. I'll have to build a riser block!

The Fergusons

These makers of top quality products for the bench rest shooter—or for any serious rifleman—have been written about before in these pages, but they continue to design and develop new items, interesting and unusual stuff that calls for commentary.

Their line now includes arbor-type presses (2 types); bullet and cartridge concentricity gauges, including a combined one, the Combo-Check; a primer seating tool, case-neck gauges, custom-made rear rifle rests, etc. The items pictured here—their Straight Line Sizing Die and S.L. Bullet Seating Die—differ markedly from those usually seen. As our caption explains, both use locating pins and mated holes for maximum concentricity, and the neck-sizing tool comes with precision bushings, interchangeable at any time (in case you change brass or neck-turn) and furnished in any desired sizes. All this for the moderate cost of $30 for the neck die, $20 for the seating die.

Really good stuff, all of these Ferguson pieces, and I wish I had space to show all of them.

Ferguson also builds "experimental" or return-to-battery type rifles and the various rests, front and rear, that support the iron monsters—which "shoot so well it's hard to talk about them without bragging," he says. I can believe it, easily.

Above—Top quality neck-sizing/decapping die set made by The Fergusons. Alignment holes and pins permit assembling the die only one way, the way it was made. Concentricity is also assured and, with care and good cases, cartridges can be assembled with less than 0.0005" runout. The small cylinder may be ordered to exact neck-sizing requirements, and is interchangeable in all Ferguson dies of this type. • Below—Precision made straight-line bullet seating die from The Fergusons. Locating pin and matching hole insure constantly uniform assembly and concentricity—the way the die was made. Bullet seating depth is amply adjustable. Die base (left) is anodized aluminum.

LEC-Lachmiller Engineering Co.

Jim Bell, a very long-time friend, is back at the controls of LEC—there'd been a change in ownership that didn't work out well. The recent takeover by Bell didn't give him enough time to get all his new products fully ready (several are on the way), but here's some news.

The low-leverage priming tool, short handled and cam operated, gives the user a highly sensitive feel—oversize or too-tight pockets can be easily detected. Complete for large or small primer (for use with your LEC, Lyman, Pacific or RCBS shell holders), it's $9.95. A Universal No. 206 Shell Holder is $2.50 extra.

The LEC Berdan decapping tool is back, usable with cases from the 11.7 rimmed to 6.5 M-S. This hardened tool is $13.95.

LEC has a line of new bullet moulds for 1973—for rifles, handguns and muzzleloaders (round balls and Minies), most in 2- or 3-cavity blocks at $12 and $15 without handles. Handles for either size—and these will fit Lyman and Ohaus moulds also—are $4.95, and they're extra long and sturdy for low heat transference and long service. Zinc plated, they won't rust. The extra-strong mould blocks are made by a new technique that assures perfect matching of the block halves, making for easier bullet release and better bullets, too. Sprue cutters, held flat by a pressure washer, won't work loose either because they're locked in place by Allen-head set screws. Square bases are a must for lead bullet accuracy.

Also new for LEC is an unusual melting pot of the bottom pour type. Designed to be used with a propane tank (a 14-oz. cylinder is said to be enough for 5000 bullets!), the pot's 11-lb. capacity can be melted in 10 minutes—that's fast. With no electricity needed, this LP pot can be used anywhere, and there's nothing to go wrong. $19.95, including a wooden V-block to support the LP torch. For those using a dip lead pot and multicavity moulds, LEC has a truly big-capacity dipper, cost $2.50. Write LEC for their new big catalog.

Sundtek Chronographs

Makers of the excellent Models 150 and 1500 chronographs reviewed in our 6th ed. Handloader's Digest (p. 56), Sundtek is at work on a couple of interesting projects. One is a one-foot separation optical detector of very high accuracy—at least to ±0.003", and normally even closer. This unit is designed for use with such 10 MHz chronographs as Sundtek's 150 and 1500 Models. The detector will be sold as a kit, the electronics package fully assembled and wired. The buyer makes the box. These kits will be about $200, perhaps less.

A new 4-digit chronograph, compatible with the optical detector mentioned, will be made also, accuracy on a par with other popular-priced, standard chronographs. This new unit, projected price about $200, will have a time readout only, requiring a set of conversion tables. Included at the price will be a paper/plastic screen package, thus the unit is ready to go as received—the optical kit is not a necessity.

TNT Bullet Swaging Dies

T. R. Thacker has made these efficient and well-liked dies since 1967, at least. These dies were described at length in HANDLOADER'S DIGEST IV, but briefly here is what they are and how they work.

Made for use in any sturdy 7/8-14 press (a tie-bar is indicated for the average C tool), the two-unit die is easily installed and adjusted. The main die is threaded into the top of the press, then the punch (which drives the core and jacket into the forming die) is placed in the shell holder of the ram. Next the jacket and lead core are dropped into the main body, then the point-forming die head is threaded onto the top of the die body. Now the press handle is moved down (or up) to form the bullet and, if the required initial adjustments have been made correctly (which is readily done), you've made a well-formed soft point bullet.

We won't pretend that TNT die sets will make prize-winning match bullets, or those comparable to top factory bullets, but the bullets we made (22s and 243s) gave excellent game and varmint accuracy. Many ½-inch to ¾-inch groups were made at 100 yards, some of these in a Remington 40× rifle in 6mm, the 22s in a 22-250 Remington 700 HB varminter. Not bad for a moderately priced die set.

Cores cut from lead wire can be used, of course, but Thacker sent us a twin-cavity core mould, adjustable for core length, which we found fully satisfactory—if adding to the labor! This unit has been succeeded, how-

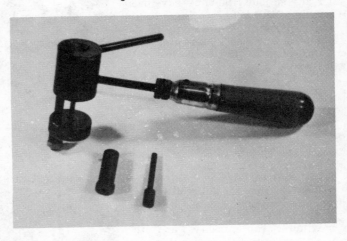

Thacker's TNT universal lead core mould ($28.50) offers interchangeable sleeve and punch sets, these $6.50 each in his 6 calibers, and available as well for casting cores into the jackets. See text for details.

ever, by a new TNT core mould that has unusual and valuable aspects. By means of various-caliber bushings the one solid mould body—it is *not* made in two halves—can be used for whatever caliber is required. More importantly, in our opinion, Thacker furnishes bushings which take the jackets themselves, so that the molten lead can be poured directly into the jackets. This technique assures two things that are of high importance in swaging good bullets—such cores will be in intimate contact with the jacket walls and bottom, which isn't always the case with hand-seated cores. Secondly, moving the mould's sprue cutter across the open end of the jacket leaves the hot core flush with the jacket mouth. That alone makes for greater uniformity of jacket-plus-core weight—and uni-

formity of all elements is the name of the game if accurate shooting is the goal. To further aid this jacket-core-weight-length sameness, either or both could be trimmed to arrive at the bullet weight desired.

A bonus of this system is the saving in time; pouring the lead directly into the jackets eliminates considerable handling of both units.

TNT die sets, offered in .224", .243", .257", .277", .284" and .308" (the latter two in spitzer point or round nose, the rest in pointed SP form only) sell for $67.50. His new universal core mould, complete for any one of the above calibers, is $28.50. Extra punch and sleeve sets are $6.50 each, cores or jackets, any listed caliber. All are fully adjustable for jacket-core length, with the core punch acting as core ejector also.

RCBS

Fred Huntington has a new Precisioneered reloader's scale for 1973, one that looks at first glance to be a conventional sliding-poise type. It isn't, though, for while the main poise slides, the fine adjustment is via a rotating drum.

One full turn of this small cylinder equals one grain; 1/10-turn gives a 1/10-gr. weight charge. A total of 10 grains is available by means of this rotating drum.

The main beam covers 500 grains, calibrated in 10-gr. increments. The beam notches are cut adequately deep to lessen chances of the poise shifting accidentally.

The beam is damped magnetically, a copper, non-conducting vane being brought quickly to rest through the resistance of an electrical field created by the fixed magnets. Accuracy and

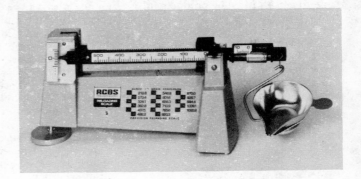

sensitivity are quite unaffected in the process. The pan is well shaped with a tapered pouring spout. The base is an alloy casting, with a leveling screw at the front end. A handy ounces-to-grains table is carried at the front.

The RCBS scale has the same approach-to-weight function used by

Ohaus. When using a powder trickler the operator is warned that his pre-set weight is about to be reached by early pointer movement. He thus avoids over-filling the pan. This is a well-designed, highly useful scale, amply sensitive and a real value at $22.95.

Texan Reloading Tools

Latest, biggest, best—and most costly—of the much-liked Texan tools is their M-IV at $279.95. It has been Texan's policy over the years to improve and update their equipment generally, yet to offer such system changes to owners of older Texan models. That's the case here—the M-IV is an outgrowth of their excellent M-II and M-IIA presses (both now out of production), but with conversion kits offered to make those earlier types into the M-IV, and at relatively small cost. More later on these.

The M-IV is a massive press, automated and self-indexing, that offers fast shell production and virtually foolproof operation. An empty case is inserted, a wad is placed in the wad guide, and the handle pulled down. Keep that routine up and, as the indexing action moves each case through the various stations, a completed shotshell is ejected for each pull of the spade grip. The new auto primer feed

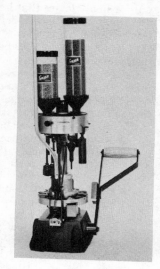

The Mk IV press.

operates only if a case is in position to be primed. The new wad guide, self-lowering, prevents deformed cases, and there's a new technique for adjusting and reading wad pressure.

A new shell-retention system maintains correct alignment of shell and die (with cases removable instantly from any station), and a new final crimp die produces the "Texan Tapered Crimp," resulting in a finished load easily usable in any shotgun. The M-IV is delivered fully adjusted and ready to go (12, 16, 20, 28 or 410), in 6-point or 8-point crimp (6-point only in 28 and 410), and a gauge conversion kit is offered at $39.95.

The M-II and M-IIA tools can be converted to the M-IV type piece-meal or completely—the new auto primer system is $39.95, the wad guide change costs $7.95, as does the wad pressure alteration. The complete changeover package is $49.95, a saving of $5.90 against the separate unit costs.

I examined the M-IV closely at the N.S.G.A. show, and watched as it produced some 25 shells. It worked without a bobble, and the completed shotshells showed a hard, tight crimp, the case firm and solid all over.

Chronograph Specialists

How would you like to have a reliable, crystal-controlled digital chronograph, battery operated and usable anywhere, for a fraction of what many others cost? You can—it's the CS-100, a small package (6" long by 2" by 2¾") that is fully transistorized, and costs only $27.50 plus $1 shipping charges. That's complete, too, ready to work—screen holders and screens (10), cables, velocity chart and instructions. An excellent value.

For $42.50 their CS-200—essentially like the CS-100—offers a double check on dud screens, internal or external power (6 volts) and can be

operated also on 110V via an adaptor at $27. The screen test function is a big convenience and a time/money saver. You know in advance that both screens are OK, that you won't fire and fail to get a reading.

CS offers two other chronographs, which we've covered before, one with a 9-lamp readout decimally, the other the lowest-cost *direct velocity* instrument available—no conversion table needed. The CS-400 is $84.50 complete (100 screens furnished); the MV readout CS-600 is $185, operable on 12V DC or on 110V AC via a $30 adaptor unit. Extra screens are $5 per 100, plus postage.

Continental Primer Pocket Cleaner

There are a dozen and one tools for cleaning primer pockets, most of them manually-operated gadgets, but Continental's device is the first motorized one to appear, I think. Sure, some brush types can be mounted in a drill, but this new one has its power built in. As our picture shows, a vertical spindle, operating at 3000 RPM and powered by a small 110-volt motor, takes a cleaning brush (one size for all pockets), of which 3 are furnished —two bristle and one wire. Brushes are installed and changed by turning a setscrew.

The plated housing, 4" wide by 3½" deep, has a mar-proof base. Cost complete is $12.95 plus 45c for postage and insurance; extra brushes are $2 the set of 3. The maker is CKKC, Box 40, Broomall, PA 19008.

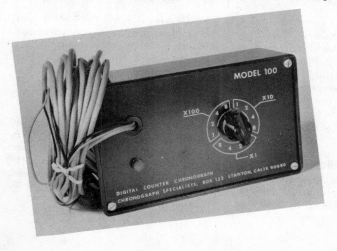

Telepacific Electronics Co.

I described the operation and functioning of this company's Model TPS-02 system in detail on page 267 of our 27th edition, but for those who've just come in, I'll tell briefly what it is.

The TPS-02 outfit consists of a chronograph instrument (the TPB-02) and a pair of photoeye screens, Model TS-E, which the makers call "Electroscreens." The TPB-02 chronograph has several important and highly useful aspects, one of them an exclusive, unique function.

First, the TPS-02 reads out in foot seconds—no requirement to consult conversion tables. Velocity is revealed by 4 groups of lamps on the face of the instrument box; quickly and accurately in true muzzle velocity!

Next, also on the front of the

housing, there's the "MV Corrector" unit, a small device that lets the user dial in a ballistic correction factor for the bullet being shot. It is this aid that lets muzzle velocity be read, not instrumental.

Lastly, the Electroscreens—these units, small (3"×5"×2") and compact, detect the bullets passage over them through ambient light (sky light or artificial) alone, no other light source, AC or whatever, being needed.

These features make the TPS-02 system completely portable. Everything operates on two 6-volt dry cells, these giving some 30 hours of operation life. All of this—foot-second readout, true MV operation anywhere—for a surprisingly low $265, plus shipping. Cooke is trying hard to hold this price, which was last year's figure also, but with times what they are... The utmost in convenient operation, too. Just push a button to clear the readout, and shoot.

At the time I wrote about the Telepacific electronic chronograph, in early 1972, I'd had no opportunity to shoot-test the Model TPS-02 system. I had worked with their Model TPB-01 —similar to the one discribed above, but without the photoeye screens or the MV Corrector—which I'd found accurate and reliable.

The TPS-02 system units arrived too late for comment in GD 27, but I've used the outfit for several hundred test shots to date (January, 1973), and entirely successfully. I did have a problem initially, but that was because of conditions prevailing here at

Creedmoor Farm. My outdoor chronograph-bench setup lies in a grove of oak trees. When the sun is shining through the leaves I get a dappled light condition in the area. These light fluctuations, going quickly from sunshine to shade, trigger the Electroscreens, giving false readings.

When this developed with the T.E.C. screens I knew right off what the trouble was, as I'd had the same experience with my older Potter photoeye screens. With the latter I'd rigged a makeshift shield above the screens, so I did that again and cured the trouble. Functioning now became faultless but, to test the TPS-02 further, I shot again on the next overcast day, without my top light shields, and once more the Electroscreens worked fully satisfactorily. Please note that this does *not* imply that the Electroscreens require dull or cloudy-day illuminations. They'll work just as well on brilliantly sunny days as long as the light descending on them is reasonably uniform or alters slowly. They're engineered to adapt themselves to virtually any light intensity—it's only rapid fluctuations in the usable light that could cause erratic readings. I don't want to cut those noble old oaks down, so I guess I'll have to make my light deflectors permanent!

An excellent tool, the TPS-02, and attractively priced for all it does and its convenience. I recommend it highly. Write to the company at 3335 W. Orange Ave., Anaheim, CA 92804, for full information.

New Federal Components

Several new reload components were introduced in late September, 1972, along with Federal's new plastic Champion II target shotshells. Reload data for these and other Federal components, in combination with the new shell, should be available at your local gunshop.

12C2 Champion II Wad. This is a slightly slimmer version of the regular Champion plastic wad. Although either can be used to reload the Champion II shell, the 12C2 wad is better for volume 3-dram loads when using some canister powders, and is needed for 18-gr. loads with some powders to stay within acceptable pressure limits.

12S1 Pushin'-Cushion Wad. This spring-action wad, now available, offers greater height flexibility than the Champion design, for use in a variety of hulls and for loads up to 1¼ ounces. The Pushin'-Cushion is ideal for use in the new Champion II plastic shell.

Federal's 12-ga. spring-action Pushin'-Cushion wad #12S1.

399 Shotshell Primer. This new primer has the same dimensions as the regular Federal 209, and both can be used to reload the Champion II plastic shell. However, for high power charges with some powders, the 399 is recommended. See the Federal reload data for full details.

Beginner's Handloading Guide

Want to get your feet wet in this interesting and satisfying hobby—and expand your shooting dollar as

well? Ask your sporting goods store or gunshop for a copy of *A Beginner's Guide to Handloading* or, if he can't supply it, write to the National Reloading Manufacturers Assn., Inc., Box 1697, Prescott, Ariz. 86301. This booklet shows the basic steps in reloading cartridges—for handgun, rifle or smoothbore.

100-Round Ammo Boxes

Varmint hunters, competition shooters, others who load in big numbers, will like the new big-capacity, sturdy plastic box that Reel Tool Co. (924 Grace St., Elgin, IL 60120) offers. Made to stack easily by means of moulded-in projectors, this large square case makes an excellent loading block or transport unit. A deep telescoping cover lets the box accomodate all popular standard rifle calibers and most magnums. Postpaid anywhere in the U.S. for $3 or $2.50 at the shop.

Nosler Bullets

New for 1973 is a line of "solid base" Nosler bullets in .224″ and .243″ diameters. Four styles are made in 22 caliber—a 50-gr. spitzer, a 52-gr. hollow point in two grades, standard and match, plus a 55-gr. spitzer. The two 6mm bullets weigh 70 or 85 grains; the former is a HP, the heavier one a spitzer.

These 6 new Noslers are all made under a new precision technique—*impact extrusion.* Most bullets start life as a more or less thick disk (depending on caliber), which then goes through a number of cup-and-draw steps. The unique new Nosler technology starts with a solid gilding-metal billet, which is then bumped and impact extruded for precise control of wall thickness—and this exactly controlled wall thickness, plus the heavy base section, are the main ingredients of this new bullet's success at the bench and in the game fields—the uniformly tapered jacket gives controlled expansion on impact; the lead core, swaged under heavy pressure, fully fills the jacket for uniform density and eliminates air pockets. It's the deeper and heavier base, however, that contributes greatly to performance and improved ballistic balance.

That heavy base makes for enhanced hitting power and penetration. As for better accuracy, read my account of the way the 52-gr. *standard* Nosler 22 bullet performed in my special Ruger M77 in 220 Swift caliber, elsewhere in this 28th edition.

Nosler partition bullets—used world wide by those who want the best production game bullet made—have also undergone a change in manufacturing recently, one that lets this great bullet perform even better than ever! The Partition bullet, too, has absolute concentricity and uniform wall thickness, assuring that center of mass and center of rotation conform for optimum accuracy. The solid intergral partition supports the expanded mushrooming of the thin-tapered forepart, and at the same time confines and retains the lead core behind the partition for deep penetration and high weight retention—about two-thirds of original bullet weight!

Truly fine performers, Nosler bullets—to paraphrase an old slogan, ask the man who's used them.

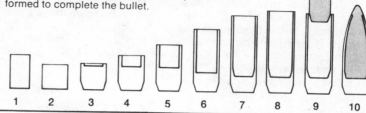

1. A measured slug is sheared from solid copper wire (a special gilding-metal alloy). **2.** Slug is "bumped" within a die to form a precisely-shaped billet. **3, 4, 5, 6.** Billet is impact extruded, in four successive dies, for accurate control of wall thicknesses. **7, 8.** Jacket is drawn, in two steps, to increase length and taper walls. **9.** Almost-finished jacket is trimmed to exact length and precision-fit lead core inserted. **10.** The lead core is swaged into position, and the ogive and tip are formed to complete the bullet.

News from Lyman

I had an interesting talk today (15 December, 1972) with Phil Chase—Phil is handling publicity and other matters for Lyman and Sierra, both members of the Leisure Group of companies.

Phil told me that quite a few new products will be introduced by Lyman sometime in 1973. Some of these products, perhaps all of them, will be shown at the NSGA show in Houston in the first week of February, but in any case here is such information as Phil was able to give me at the moment.

Notable will be Lyman's first variable scope, this one a 3×9, but I was unable to learn whether this will have an adjustable objective ring to offset parallax.

This next item will be great news for people who cast their own bullets, rifle or handgun. There is to be a new *Lyman Cast Bullet Handbook,* and I'm sure it's going to be a terrific seller in view of the heavy demand for their previous book on the same subject. That older book has been out of print for several years.

Lyman will also have a brand new shotshell press, but that's all I can say about it at the moment. I don't mean to imply that I know more, I don't, but I hope to have better information before long.

Champion II 12 Gauge Target Load

Federal's new 12 gauge Champion II target load was unveiled to competitive shooters at the 1972 National Skeet Shooting Tournament in Rochester, New York, and the 1972 Grand American Trap Shooting Tournament in Vandalia, Ohio.

The Champion II shotshell offers the performance of Federal's famous paper Champion target load, plus the long reload life of one-piece plastic construction.

The Champion II shell body is made by Federal's patented "draw-forming" process. In this method a punch forces a preformed slug of plastic through a die; the resulting shell has an integral base wad and greatly strengthened sidewalls. These features spell long reload life.

The mouth of the shell is chamfered to assist in crimping. The name and load data are marked on the shell by hot stamping with gold leaf. The marking is guaranteed to "stay on."

Performance ingredients of the Champion II shell include all those that have made the Champion paper load so successful:

Federal's original extra hard shot, the hardest made, which contributes to uniform patterns and more target-breaking power. The top performing Champion plastic

wad column with its shot cup, the totally enclosed air-cushion and center pillar for controlled collapse. Federal's extra-hot #209 primer for consistent ignition. During the National Skeet Tournament, the new shell was used in a long run of 734 straight. Its acceptance, along with other Federal loads, helped make Federal "number one" in sales at the tournament.

The Champion II shell will be offered in 2¾- and 3-dram equivalent loads in shot sizes 7½, 8, 8½, and 9. The price will be equivalent to other one-piece plastic target loads and slightly higher than the Federal paper Champion.

Winchester Ball Powders

By the time you read this, a new line of Ball powders—introduced at the 14th Seminar for Writers and Editors—should be available to handloaders throughout the U.S.

As many of you know, Ball propellant powders have several advantages not found in "log" or extruded-rod powders. Among these are:

Unexcelled chemical stability, making for very long life and uniform performance.

High grain density, which permits high loading density.

Longer barrel life through lower flame temperature (which reduces erosion), and less muzzle flash thereby.

More uniform charges from powder measures because of high flow qualities.

Ball powders give a high degree of accuracy for the reasons cited above, assuming a properly selected charge weight. If Ball powders have a fault, it's their tendency to foul the bore when charges are less than optimum. But that's something easily corrected or allowed for, even when working up loads.

A new Winchester data book will also be offered for use with their Ball powders. Over 300 shotshell loads will be listed, these covering a wide variety of components. Rifle and handgun data will be very extensive, for all practical applications of Ball powder will be covered.

Here's a short rundown on the new line:

452AA A completely new shotshell powder, one which replaces AA12S and 450LS. It is the same powder used in 12-gauge Double A factory

The 10 new Ball Powders, designed for reloading a wide range of shotshells and metallic cartridges, will be available in 8-oz. to 12-lb. containers.

loads. It has a wide range of usefulness in target and field loads and, of it, Winchester says, "It is...the ultimate in target load powder."

473AA Also brand new, this shotshell powder replaces AA20S and 500HS. It is the same factory propellant used in Western Double A 20-gauge factory loads. It has many uses in 12 to 20 gauge shells. Like 452AA, it offers exceptionally clean burning and uniform ballistics.

540 Formerly 540MS, this powder is a fine choice for heavy 12-gauge and 20-gauge loads, as it is also for 28-gauge shells.

571 Another new powder that's been specifically designed for use in the heaviest of 12- and 20-gauge loads, including 3-inch cases, of course.

296 A new 410 powder designed to produce the optimum in case volume considerations. It replaces AA665S. Its exceptional ballistics indicate it will prove quite useful in magnum pistol loads and such small-capacity rifle cartridges as the 30M1 carbine.

230 Formerly 230P, this is a very

fast, high-energy handgun powder designed for target and standard-velocity loads. It's been a proven and very popular powder with reloaders and many police departments.

630 A moderately slow but high-energy handgun powder (formerly 630P), well suited to such cartridges as the 45 ACP, 45 Colt and various magnum loads.

680 A very fast rifle powder (which replaces 680BR) designed specifically for such small cases as the 218 Bee and 22 Hornet. In fact, Winchester says, "It is the only powder we know of that can be safely handloaded to duplicate factory ballistics in these cartridges."

748 A centerfire rifle powder (previously 748BR) that has been highly popular with bench rest shooters in such cartridges as the 222. It has a very wide range of applications in a large number of calibers.

760 A broad-range rifle powder (formerly 760BR) that is a proven performer, 760 has been a popular choice in a very large range of calibers.

Avtron Chronographs

Avtron has a new instrument, so far unseen, not even a picture. The K973 offers visual readout in milliseconds, with velocities found by referring to the table furnished.

The K973 housing is rather unusual, but certainly sensible—it can best be described, perhaps, as a tackle box, one made of a heavy-duty, sturdy plastic. Lifting the handled lid reveals the chronograph, snugly bedded in the bottom.

Designed for use with Avtron's standard screens, the K973 operates from a self-contained 6-volt lantern battery, and sells for $169.

Wamadat Berdan Decapper

The sturdy, well-designed tool

shown here is made to remove Berdan primers hydraulically. The heavy steel container or reservoir (6″ high by 3″x3″ and about 7 pounds) holds the liquid, and the makers recommend a mixture of water and enough washing detergent to make a solution of some viscosity. Two decapping cylinders are included, one for cases of 9mm size and smaller, the other handling cases up to and including 303 British or those of like head size. There is also an optional larger cylinder offered, this one for such cases as the "577 Snider and other monsters," to quote the makers.

To operate the Wamadet, the container is filled with enough fluid to reach the holes in the top sides of the cylinders. The cylinder selected

is then inserted into a hollow round pillar, welded to the base inside the container, then a capped case is dropped into the cylinder, base down. Next, the close-fitting steel plunger or ram is placed in the cylinder, letting it ride down to a level with the rubber O-ring seals when decapping normal cases; with hard-crimped military cases, the makers suggest pushing the plunger some ¼-inch or so beyond the O-ring.

Then, with the container resting on a firm, solid base, the plunger is struck with a hammer, one weighing about 1½ pounds being suggested. Hydraulic pressure pushes the spent cap out, and a rate of several hundred an hour can be achieved, say the makers. After use, the fluid is decanted and all parts of the tool should be thoroughly oiled to prevent rust.

The advantages of hydraulic decapping by the Wamadet system result from the equalization of pressures — that's the same inside the case and out — no bulged cases, no expanded primer pockets or flash holes, no injured anvils.

Our test sample of the Wamadet, which included the big cylinder, worked excellently on standard or sporting caliber cases, though we did not attempt a fast rate of operation. This was done with a steel-headed hammer that weighed nearly 2 pounds, and our support for the container was one corner of a heavy work bench.

However, when quite old 577 cases were tried, these having a strong cir-

cumferential crimp, we had problems. The steel hammer and the container bounced, and the caps stayed put! After trying various solutions (no

pun intended) we placed the container on a biggish lead pad and used a 5-pound lead hammer. That technique did away with all bouncing, and it moved the fired caps out, too, though a second blow was sometimes needed. Once the old crimped caps are out, and the crimp removed, further decapping is easy.

All in all, an excellent tool, and a bargain, in our opinion, at $17 plus $3.50 postage. Included are the two standard cylinders, extra O-rings and detailed instructions. The big special cylinder is $7 plus 80c postage. So far the Wamadet is obtainable only from the makers, though they'd like to have an importer, of course. Write to Wamadet, Silver Springs, Goodleigh, Barnstaple, Devon, England. How's that for a full address?

C-H Tools

The new bullet swaging dies shown nearby are excellently made, and offer a great advantage over die sets for making handgun bullets. At last we can buy — at a nominal price — dies that work well with ¾ jackets, giving the user bullets that cannot lead the bore! These new C-H dies produce a bullet with the jacket rounding over the bullet's ogive, thus preventing any contact between the lead core or bullet nose with the bore of the barrel.

Made in standard ⅞-14 thread size, these dies can be used in any press capable of full length case sizing. Bullets can be varied in weight by simply adjusting the dies and/or through obtaining jackets of varied lengths.

Ejection of finished bullets or seated cases can be done by tapping the die tops, but the Ejector pictured is a time- and effort saver, believe me. I tried both techniques, and the heel of the thumb soon gets sore! At only $9.95, I suggest getting the Ejector unit.

The C-H Cannelure Tool shown is just about a must if your bullets are to be used effectively. Cannelures can be rolled into bullets or cases at any location desired, and once the tool is adjusted, thousands of bullets can be grooved. This sturdy tool, solid steel throughout, sells for $14.95.

Our sample C-H swaging tools worked easily in an old RCBS A2 press, making 38-caliber bullets of high uniformity in weight, length and dimensions. In addition to 38/357 dies, 41, 44 and 45 calibers are available, cost $24.95 in solid-point form. Die sets in hollow-point type are $27.45.

New C-H cannaluring tool handles cases or bullets, is fully adjustable for depth and location of cannelure.

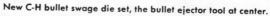

New C-H bullet swage die set, the bullet ejector tool at center.

THE GUN WRITER of today is in a highly competitive business. Not only must he be well informed on all aspects of firearms and cartridges — from the 22 rimfire to the most powerful cartridges the world has ever known — he must have some pretty sophisticated equipment with which to test his theories. Unless he wants to lay his head on the chopping block he doesn't assume that a certain load will give X velocity; he runs it on a good chronograph to make sure. Neither does he lob a bullet at a rock of unknown size at an unknown range on the mountain across the canyon; he shoots from a bench over bags stuffed with sand at a measured range.

If he wants to save time and get things done in the most efficient manner possible — and he will if he wants to eat regularly — he does his accuracy

as possible. That's all to the good, but there is one area that is often sadly neglected — illustration of the various components we use. The old adage that "one picture is worth a thousand words" never carried more weight than in gun writing.

The modern gunwriter just about has to be a reasonably good photographer, or he must know someone who is; the latter solution, though, is a poor substitute. In the first place, it is next to impossible to have someone come in and do the photography *when* you need it, and worse to try to box up the items you are currently working with and take them to the photographer. Second, the photographer usually has little interest in the project beyond the fee involved, and he frequently hasn't the faintest idea of what you want anyway.

The obvious solution is to get a

a studio and he won't want to pour a lot of dollars into equipment he will not use for anything else. I don't claim to have all of the answers to lighting and various other techniques, but I've learned a few things in many years of firearms photography and I'd like to pass them on.

Cameras

The first consideration is, of course, a suitable camera. I've used cameras of various sizes and designs, and I've concluded that for shooting cartridges and any other of the small items connected with firearms photography you don't need a large negative size. In fact, in many instances you are better off with something smaller. One reason always present, of course, is cost of camera, lens and film. More importantly, though, the larger the negative size the longer the lens it

FIREARMS FOTOGRAPHY

This instructive and well-illustrated article, directed particularly to those who write about guns and shooting matters, can benefit anyone wanting to produce first class pictures. Lighting, exposure, processing, tools and techniques are ably handled, clearly and simply explained.

Text and photography
by BOB HAGEL

testing and chronographing at the same time by the use of a photo-electric screen hookup. It is also mighty convenient to have the chronograph setup inside where he can control the temperature to within a couple of degrees, and shoot under nearly any weather condition at a 100-yard target outside the building.

If we are to know anything about what we are doing in relating pressures to velocity, we also have to use some reliable method of checking those pressures; everything from measuring case head expansion with a good micrometer caliper to compressing a copper crusher in a pressure barrel.

We experiment with dozens of powders, bullet weights, makes and designs; we use the finest barrels, custom stocks and scopes we can obtain to eliminate as many variables

camera and do your own shooting, then have your film and prints processed by someone else. This sounds reasonable but doesn't work worth a damn. You often find that you must use only part of a negative to make the point you want to put across. This means cropping, dodging or burning in of the finished print and, unless you stand over the guy making the print he doesn't know what you want or need. Obviously, you can't do that. The only sensible answer is to have your own equipment from camera to darkroom and enlarger, and herein lies the basis for this article.

Let's make one thing plain right now: if you're an accomplished photographer with a lot of sophisticated equipment and ideas, read no further. I'm writing to help the gunwriter make better use of the equipment he may have or can add to. He won't have

takes to cover it, and the longer the lens is the shallower the depth of field is (range of near and far sharp focus). It follows that the greater the depth of field the sharper everything in the photo will be; this is highly important (usually) in this type of illustration.

The 35mm camera is excellently suited to this kind of work, assuming good lenses, film and processing. Too, you can often employ the same camera used for your normal outdoor activities. However, not all 35mm cameras are eligible. You'll have to see exactly what you are doing at all times, with every detail exactly as the lens sees it, so the only answer is the SLR or Single Lens Reflex.

The SLR chosen should be able to accept various detachable lenses, which ability is a must for any kind of diversified photography.

We are concerned mostly with close-up photography, and there are several ways to approach it. There are extension tubes and bellows (which comes to the same thing), close-up supplementary lenses, the extender lens that increases the power (often 2x or 3x) of the normal lens, and the macro lens. Extension tubes, and bellows require considerable increase in illumination, and so does the extender. This not only means computing increased exposure times, but also requires going to a larger lens opening or f-stop, which cuts the depth of field. To overcome this shutter speed can be slowed down, but even with the camera mounted on a tripod and tripped by cable release, an unsharp image, due to slight movement caused by vibration, may result.

Supplementary lenses are made in various powers and require no change in exposure, but at higher powers depth of field is very shallow. Nor does the quality of such lenses do much for sharpness.

The Macro Lens

This brings us to the excellent macro lens. These are capable of focusing from very near the subject to infinity, and can be used for scenic and other outdoor photography in

Here is setup for photographing bullets or complete cartridges. This angled view shows method of draping background paper over box at rear of projector table, then down in arc under subject to dissipate shadows. Lamps are placed about 14"-16" above subject, and slightly to each side. They are aimed at the foreground in front of subject, which is placed about 8" back from front of table. This does not light subject directly, but "bounces" light on subject from white foreground. This gives even lighting that helps eliminate highlights caused when direct lighting is used. By using two lamps focused slightly to the sides of subject, bullets or cartridges, their edges are lighted to give even detail there as well as at the center. Paper used should be white with fairly high gloss surface for good light reflection, but do not use a highly reflective surface such as metal foil; these will create excessive highlights on subject, foreground and background.

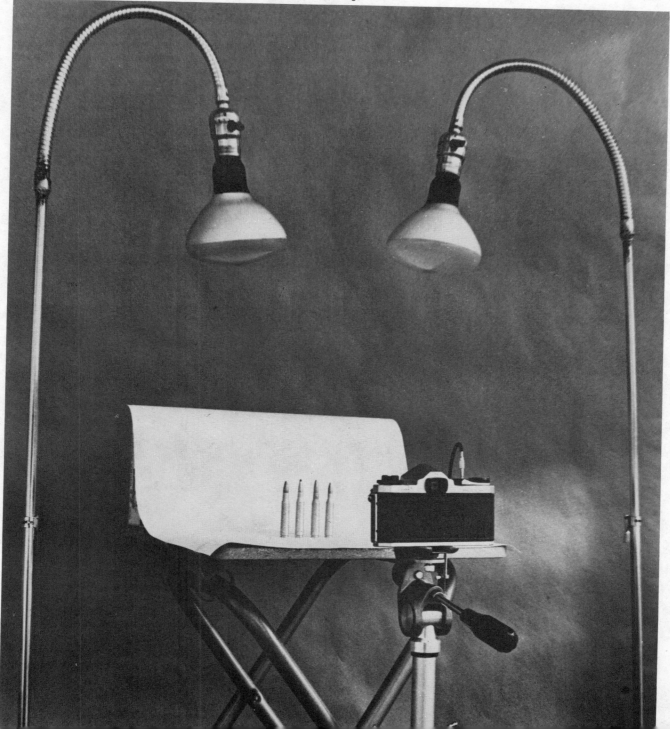

These partially sectioned cases were not treated prior to photographing so that the interior would be left black, which results from being fired, and which gives higher contrast to bullet base. They were, however, selected from an old lot of GI brass that had turned dark and dull. Such cases photograph quite well with lighting method used.

These cartridges, treated in Case-Brite cleaning solution, were photographed by using two lights aimed at foreground in front of and slightly to sides of cartridges. Note even lighting and fine detail. Cartridges at far left, third from left and far right, are new factory rounds, but the second cartridge from left is a reload which clearly shows where case has expanded to fill chamber just forward of web.

This is one of the most difficult types of bullet photography; the shooting of unfired, expanded and sectioned bullets with their many different shades and textures. These Alaskan bullets have a rear core of tungsten with a lead core forward. The only dodging done was a slight amount on un-fired bullets at left to compensate for darkness caused by polished surface.

This line-up of 30-caliber bullets includes about all shapes. This makes them highly difficult to photograph without excessive highlights but with good detail everywhere. Even though there are several brands represented here, with several different jacket alloys, the Case-Brite treatment brought them all to nearly the same shade, with resultant fine detail in all shapes, sizes and brands.

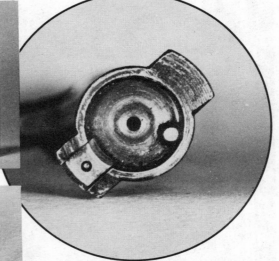

In photographing expanded bullets like these Bitterroot Bonded Cores, there is only one way to know where to position the light or lights: by looking through the lens of a single lens reflex camera. You'll want the lights at an angle that will give enough shadow detail for sharpness of critical irregularities.

This picture of the bolt face of a post '64 Model 70 Winchester shows what a good macro lens and correct lighting can do.

place of a normal lens as well as for close-up work. Some of these lenses will focus so close that a 1:1 ratio will be attained (actual size), but 1:2 (½ actual size) is plenty for this type of work. These macro lenses do require some compensation for exposure when racked out for very close work, but it is so minor as to make little difference when shooting in black and white.

Most macro lenses come in both pre-set and automatic diaphragm versions, so if your normal lens is automatic by all means use a macro automatic—you won't ruin film by forgetting to reset the f-stop after focusing wide open. Your auto-macro lens may cost nearly as much as your camera (around $150), but if you are serious it is worth it. If you're ordering a new camera, get the macro lens

single cartridge can be taken, but if you rely on a built-in metering system you will get a reading from the background as well. As we shall see later, such over-all readings are often misleading.

Now, as for lighting to be used in *any firearms photography,* forget about flash of any kind. With flash there is no way of knowing where the reflections and highlights will be, and you must be able to see these, just as the lens does, to be successful.

What is needed are at least three floods or spots. You won't use spots much but you should have a bulb or two around. Sealed beam, self-reflector types are preferable to those with separate reflectors. The sealed beams can be set closer to both camera and subject without interference with either. You can get by nicely with 500-

—usually under $10—would do nicely. However, such stands can only be rotated, left or right, and the lamp socket(s) swiveled for some degree of vertical positioning. The Smith-Victor Mini-Boom stand has an arm that allows overhead lighting, cost around $20. Larger, boom-arm stands, such as the Ascor Starliter and Coloration, run from around $50 to nearly $75. They are, however, too large for both the limited space usually available for firearms photography or storage.

Another economical possibility is the Smith-Victor socket-reflector set-up, which has spring clamps that may be attached to anything from a chair back to a pole stand. However, unless you also make up a stand with an overhead arm, overhead lighting is almost impossible.

If there are any light stands that are ideal for this kind of photography without modification I have never seen one. The lamp we require needs to be placed anywhere from a few inches above the floor to 5 feet or so above it, and from directly below the subject for low-angle lighting to directly above it for overhead lighting. To obtain such a light stand you will about have to make them up or have them made.

One of the small Smith-Victor stands, or a common music stand for folding sheet music, will work well; the shorter it telescopes the better. Buy a piece of stiff but flexible spiral tubing, such as used on desk lamps, with standard-thread ⅜" male fittings on the ends (these will fit standard light sockets); 18 inches is about right. One end will have to be soldered or brazed to the telescoping stem of the stand. Attach the lamp socket directly to the spiral tubing and let the cord run down through the tubing and stand. Be sure to use plenty of cord so that when the stand is extended you'll have an ample length left to position the stands correctly away from a heavy extension cord. You will need at least two of these stands, and should have three.

These cartridges are mixed as to size, shape, brand and age, yet with cleaning treatment before photographing and the type of lighting explained in the text, they all show good detail from rim to bullet point. Some dodging of the bullet end of cartridge was used here to reduce dark tones for better detail.

instead of the standard lens. My own macro lens, a Pentax Auto Takumar with a 1:2 ratio, is superbly sharp from extreme closeup to infinity, and it shows outstanding color rendition.

Lighting and Stands

Aside from camera and lens, the most critical thing in making good closeup shots is lighting, but before we get deeply into lights and placement, let's look at exposure metering systems. Today's trend is to built-in meters, of which the through-the-lens system (as found on the Pentax Spotmatic) is one of the most useful. I won't go into the merits and disadvantages of this system for general use, but while I use Pentax cameras I do not use a Spotmatic. For close-up work I much prefer a separate meter, one capable of reading a very small area. With these a reading from a

watt lights, but those from 750 to as much as 1500 watts are superior. In practice you won't need more than 750 watts at any time for photographing cartridges and other small objects, but the larger lights work better for photographing complete rifles. Their greater light output lets them be kept out of the field of view and cuts down on reflections. High powered quartz lamps would be ideal for gun photography, but they are very expensive.

Light stands are most important in firearms photography, stands that will put the lamps *exactly* where you want them. Unfortunately for our purposes, very few commercial light stands will serve. If all the lighting required in this work came from the front or sides, such standard light stands as those made by Smith-Victor

Tables and Backgrounds

You'll need some kind of table or stand for photographing such subjects as cartridges or bullets. A standard projector table—the kind used for a slide or movie projector—is of ideal height.

Next you'll need background material, something which will serve for a base as well as background. For nearly all cartridge, bullet or case photography, this background will be white. It will be placed on the table running from the forward edge and held down flat on the table for about

12", then bring it up in a gradual curve and drape it over something about 10" high. This gives an even curve in the background to dissipate shadows, especially where frontal lighting is used. On objects that present a flat side to the camera, such as sectioned bullets and cases, cast shadows can be completely eliminated by focusing a spotlight on the background, behind the subject. This does not work well with such round objects as bullets and cartridges. It does erase the shadows but it also causes the edges (the sides of bullets and cases) to be indistinct or softened because of the backlighting (halo) effect from reflected light coming from the background. Sharp lines on the sides of bullets and cartridges are more important than a fully shadowless plain background.

How to Light

The simplest way to photograph bullets or cartridges is to use two lights, each facing the subject from about 45°, left and right. However, such lighting creates reflection streaks that run the full length of the cartridge. These light-reflecting areas show no detail whatever, giving the viewer a general impression of a silhouette rather than a rounded, three-dimensional and detailed cartridge.

I have achieved the most even lighting obtainable by placing the lamps about 16" above the subject (for 500-watt lamps), one on either side, about 10"-14" apart, the distance depending on the *white foreground* just in front of the subject. The subject is placed about 8" back from the forward edge of the table. This lights the cartridges or bullets with reflected light (bounced, in photographic nomenclature) and not by direct lighting. This lighting is much more even than the usual 45° lighting mentioned, and there are fewer highlight areas. There will, of course, be some *direct* light on the subject that, if the lamps are correctly positioned, will add to the detail. By placing the lamps so that the beam is aimed at the sides of the subject, as well as forward, illuminates both sides and the front of the cartridge(s). You'll have to keep moving them around until as many reflections as possible are removed and the greatest detail obtained.

Even with this lighting system it is soon obvious that a new and shiny case or bullet still has a highly reflective surface, and that no matter how the lamps are aimed there are still many areas where detail has been killed by the highlights. Old cartridges, cases or bullets that have turned dark and dull produce much better prints. But it is at times necessary to use new cartridges mixed with the old, which not only places light-colored cartridges alongside dark ones, but bright and shiny surfaces beside old dull surfaces—an impossible situation to photograph for detail in all of them.

The solution lies in treatment of the cartridges, bullets or cases to produce nearly the same shade and surface as possible. If cases, complete cartridges, or bullets are treated in Case-Brite—a commercial case cleaner—this problem will be solved. Case-Brite not only cleans the cases and bullets, but it does so by a slight etching process which gives the surface a light-colored but dull finish that serves to break up the light and practically eliminates highlights.

While nearly all brands of cases will come out almost identical in color, there will be considerable variation in bullet shades because of the different alloys in jacket material. This treatment is also highly successful in treating sectioned bullets. It darkens the core to almost dead black, giving good contrast with the light jacket material. It should not be used on cases sectioned full length unless they are new cases; fired cases are better left untreated so they'll retain the black interior to contrast with the polished case wall to show case construction.

You may be tempted to try polarizing screens or filters to eliminate reflections on cartridges and other metal objects, but save your money unless you have other use for them. They are quite effective at angles up to 30 degrees on wood, but of no value on metallic surfaces.

Expanded Bullets

I cannot tell you how to arrange your lights for photographing fired, expanded bullets. Their irregular shape and the amount and form of expansion will dictate the position of the bullet in relation to the camera lens and, therefore, the positioning of the lights. Only a close study of the subject through the camera lens while moving the lights and/or subject will tell you when everything is right. The same thing is true when photographing gun parts, bolts, actions, boxes of bullets, powder canisters, loading tools, et al.

If you are forced to photograph untreated cartridges and bullets that are of different shades and reflective surfaces, it is better to place the dark subjects at one end of the lineup and

In photographing sectioned cases the lights are placed at sides of camera to show detail and give contrast between dark concave inside of case and new, bright cut of body. No background lighting is used because contrast of dark background and bright case wall is desirable.

the light ones at the other. Don't mix them if you can avoid it. Here's the reason: in printing the negative the timing for the enlargement will be different for light and dark, as well as for dull or highly reflective surfaces. If they are separated you can dodge or burn in the print to bring the various subjects to almost the same shade and detail, but if they are intermixed it will be impossible to do so.

It is almost impossible to light cartridges so that exactly the same amount of light falls on both the top or bullet end and on the base. Therefore, a little dodging of the print, usually at the upper part of the cartridge, will give much more uniform density and better detail to the whole.

Another point to remember—don't photograph any more cartridges or bullets at one time than absolutely necessary; the fewer items in a lineup the easier it is to light them correctly. Also, don't try to crowd too near the subject with the camera if it means filling the frame tightly with the subject items. Better to enlarge a little more because you will usually get better detail near the edges of the print. The finest lens made will not give detail quite as sharp and clear at the extreme edges as it does near the center, so don't overdo it. If this is carried to extremes there can be distortions of image size or dimensions at the extreme edges, particularly if a wide-angle lens is used.

Films and Processing

The next consideration is film and processing. There are many good films of different brands, but perhaps the best close-up roll film is Kodak Panatomic X — it's fine grained, gives sharp detail and good contrast. However, it is a slow film, one that often requires slow shutter speeds which, as indicated earlier, is not always conducive to sharp negatives. Neither is it ideally suited to outdoor work, and most of us often shoot part of a roll inside and part outside, and we often need added speed for action shots. True, you can goose Panatomic X up in processing for higher ASA indexes, but when you do that it increases graininess and puts it in the same class with such films as Plus X, which is already faster.

I have settled on Plus X for both firearms and all outdoor photography, wildlife included, as a happy medium. I use Microdol X fine-grain developer to partly compensate for its coarser grain. I use it full strength, but you can dilute it and increase developing time and/or solution temperature for even finer negative grain. In either case you will come up with a print that shows no grain whatever in the degree of enlargement you will need. You can enlarge at least 10-1 without graininess, assuming well-exposed negatives made with a good lens.

The enlarging paper used will definitely affect the sharpness and contrast of the finished print. For this work you need paper that gives black blacks and white whites! Bromide papers excel in this respect for all-round use. I use Kodak Kodabromide paper, glossy, of course, for glossy prints. Most prints from normal density negatives are made on #2, but for much cartridge work where high contrast is needed, #3 is ideal. For that under-exposed negative #4 will usually give a good print.

If you wish to use variable contrast paper with contrast filters, and have an enlarger set up for it, only one grade of paper need be kept on hand. This will save money and eliminate waste when the seldom-used numbers go bad by the age route.

You don't need an expensive enlarger. I used an old Federal for many years with good results. Some enlargers have better systems and advantages over others, of course. Lens quality is the main factor, but convenience of focusing and negative carrier arrangements are also strong considerations. I use a Simmon Omega B-22XL with lenses and carriers for both 35mm and 2¼x2¼ negatives, an excellent outfit. Beseler and many other enlargers are also excellent. I prefer glassless negative carriers for small negatives, but sandwiching the negative between glass does hold it flat for better over-all focus. But there is one piece of common glass between negative and paper that does nothing good for print sharpness.

Equipment Notes

As for other equipment, I use Pentax H3v cameras and a Seconic L-206 battery-operated (CdS) meter for reading the small spots of light so necessary in cartridge photography. The Spotron Pentaview Zoom Spot Meter is excellent for reading small areas of light, as is the Spotron Professional Spotmeter, but these are very expensive — $60 to $100, and too heavy and bulky for much outdoor use.

Aside from my Takumar automatic, macro lens, I have others of different make. I use Pentax cameras not only because they're among the top cameras in quality and rugged reliability, but because they are light and compact for use in the back country, where every ounce counts. I usually carry two of them, one loaded with black-and-white film, the other with color. There are several other brands of cameras that are of high quality and reliability if you don't mind a little extra weight and bulk; the Nikon F, the Beseler Topcon, to mention a couple. The Nikkor lenses furnished with the Nikon cameras, and also sold separately, are some of the finest made.

I am not trying to influence anyone as to the brand of equipment he should use. I merely mention the equipment I know is good, stuff that does all the work necessary in photographing firearms and related items from the smallest bullet up. If you know of other equipment, especially cameras, lenses and meters, that will do the same work as well, and you like it better for one reason or another, by all means try it. Just don't go gad-get happy or you'll have spent a lot of money on items you'll never use and can't get rid of.

As I've said, I don't know all the answers to lighting, equipment or processing, but they work well for me and I hope they'll be of some help to the gunwriter. ●

Photographic Terms

A.S.A.I. (American Standard Association) index. Speed of film given in direction sheet furnished with film for setting film speed index of light meter. Expressed in such index numbers as 64, 125, 160, etc.

F-stop: Diaphragm openings that regulate amount of light admitted through lens to film. The larger the number the smaller the opening; f:4 admitting more light (16 times as much) than F:16.

Extension tubes: Metal tubes of various lengths used between camera body and lens so that normal lens can be focused on objects very near camera. The longer the tube the closer the subject can be placed to the lens.

Extension bellows: Same principle as tubes but made like camera bellows to serve as extension between camera and lens. Both systems require more light (larger diaphragm openings) than with normal lens. The longer the tube setup the more light that is required to properly expose the film. A factor number furnished with the directions gives amount of light increase required for various lengths.

Supplementary lens: Lenses made to fit over normal lens by use of adapters that allow camera to be placed nearer subject and focus sharply. This in turn gives larger subject image on film. Increased exposure or larger lens openings not required.

Macro lens: A lens designed for extreme spread of focus by extending the front lens element much farther than normal from the rear element when focused for close work. Such lenses focus from a few inches to infinity.

Infinity: The longest distance at which the lens may be focused, marked ∞. The area between the last marking in feet or meters to as far as the eye can see. The area beyond which critical focus is not necessary with the lens used.

Depth of field: The area between the nearest and farthest points from the camera that will be in relatively sharp focus on the negative. The smaller the diaphragm opening (the larger the number) the greater the depth of field. F:22 will give much greater depth of field than an F-stop of 3.5. Remember that approximately 1/3 of the subject forward of the focusing point will be in sharp focus and 2/3 behind that point will be in focus, so always focus on a point about 1/3 of the way beyond the area where sharp focus is desired. Most lenses have depth of field scales that show distance of sharp focus for the F-stop used.

Dodging: Holding back the image from the enlarging lens to the enlarging paper for part of the enlargement time to avoid that area becoming too dark on the finished print. To do this a piece of paper of appropriate size and/or shape is held in a handle of thin wire between enlarger lens and easel so that its shadow blots out the image falling on the area desired to be lightened. It must be kept moving slightly so that the edge of the area dodged blends into the image on the finished print.

Burning-in: The opposite of dodging, when part of the image requires more light to darken it for more detail or evener shading. Light is held back from the remainder of the print for part of the enlarging time by use of the hands or a piece of paper with a correctly shaped hole for light to pass through.

brno SUPER

NEW BRNO SHOTGUN

Super Sidelock 12 Bore

Czechoslovakia's latest smoothbore double gets a critical and searching test — in the field and on targets — and stands up well.

Text and illustrations by
WALLACE LABISKY

OUR BLIND THAT day was a pit dug into a 6-foot-deep snowdrift, and 20 yards or so on the upwind side we had staked out a half-dozen oversize crow decoys. The first contingents of the main migration were still two day's flight to the south, so things were slow, with plenty of time for gun talk. But then a sudden, harsh *Caw-caw!* broke the quiet of the late win-

ter afternoon. Instantly we pressed ourselves tightly against the walls of the pit.

Even a true cylinder-bore would have more than gift-wrapped that black bandit when he finally spotted us and desperately tried to swap ends at hardly more than 15 yards range. The full-choke barrel with 1⅛ ozs. of 8s produced a genu-

inely disintegrating effect. For an instant the hit looked like a well-centered claybird. One wing cartwheeled into the pit, while a piece of the other was left dangling in a nearby plum thicket. As my crow-shooting amigo remarked, the bird was "badly dead."

This kill was one of half a hundred chalked up in recent weeks while using a scattergun

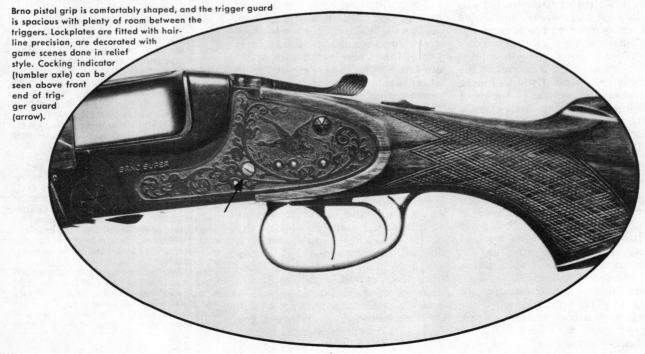

Brno pistol grip is comfortably shaped, and the trigger guard is spacious with plenty of room between the triggers. Lockplates are fitted with hairline precision, are decorated with game scenes done in relief style. Cocking indicator (tumbler axle) can be seen above front end of trigger guard (arrow).

which had its origin behind the Iron Curtain. I'm referring to the Brno Super 12/12 over-under, manufactured by the Brno Armament Works, Czechoslovakia, and brought to these shores by Continental Arms Corporation.

By way of brief review, the Brno plant has been in operation since 1918. Prior to World War II the emphasis was on military arms. Since then this Czech firm has widened its horizons by turning to the production of bolt-action rifles in big-game calibers, bolt-action and autoloading smallbore rifles, and shotguns.

If our test gun can be taken as a criterion, and surely it can, it becomes immediately evident that the Czech gunmakers have that certain touch for turning steel and wood into a highly presentable firearm. The sample over-under shows sound design along with good materials and workmanship, and it handles and shoots equally well.

Design Details

Basically, the Brno Super is a sidelock ejector gun with double triggers and quadruple bolting. Stocking is done in European walnut, neither ordinarily plain nor extra fancy, but with just enough contrasting figure to make it pleasingly attractive. The various metal components are of machined steel throughout, with a nicely blued finish on all exterior surfaces, ex-

cept for the gold-plated triggers. The Poldi steel barrels are topped with a solid sighting rib. Seen as distinctly European features are the sling swivels and the cheekpiece buttstock.

This Brno has a breech lock-up as unshakable as Fort Knox. There are Purdey-type double under-lugs integral with the under barrel, and these are engaged by a conventional flat bolt which moves fore and aft in the floor of the frame. Supplementing this is a Kersten-type lock featuring a round cross-bolt that mates with extensions on either side of the over barrel. The standing breech has a pair of slotways to accommodate the barrel extensions.

Multiple bolting such as this is sometimes found to be just so much window dressing, with one or more of the bolts failing to make contact. In this case, however, a smoke test revealed that the bolts were bearing solidly on all four surfaces. This, in itself, speaks quite highly for Brno craftsmanship.

Simplicity, ruggedness and careful fitting pretty well describe the Brno sidelocks, which are of the back-action type. Inner surfaces of the lockplates, as well as the bridles, carry a damascened finish. The tumblers are driven by husky coil springs, these centrally positioned just above the bridles, and with a power source such as this there seems little likelihood of misfires due to weak hammer fall.

The lockplates are held to the frame by a single transverse joining screw which makes removal for periodic cleaning and oiling a simple matter.

It's also worth noting that the Brno locks are fitted with an intercepting safety. This is in the form of a standby sear, and normally it is not engaged. But if the main sear is jarred out of its notch, the standby takes over by catching a projecting shoulder on the tumbler, thus blocking its fall and preventing accidental discharge.

The tumblers do not turn on their support axles. The axles themselves rotate and thus do double duty by serving as cocking indicators. The outer ends of the axles are left in the "white" and have a rib-like shoulder across their centers. So either visually or by feel, the shooter can tell whether the locks are cocked or fired.

Trigger Pulls

The trigger pulls on the test gun can be rated as excellent. Pull for the front trigger (under barrel) weighed 3½ pounds with a very small amount of travel preceding let-off. The rear trigger (over barrel) checked out at 4 pounds, the let-off being crisp.

The Brno trigger system, by the way, is unique in that the triggers can be rotated. If the shooter prefers a non-typical firing order of front/over and rear/under, he can have it. However, it is not an

Breech-end view of the Brno barrels show the damascened finish on the extractors and underlugs. Note extractor stop pins (arrow) on the underside of each barrel extension.

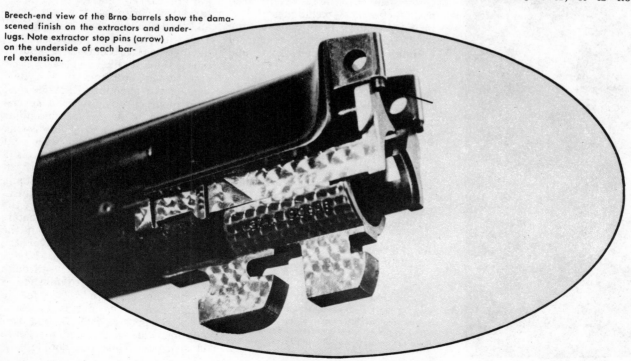

instantaneous thing. Switching the triggers does require removing the trigger guard and trigger plate from the frame—in most instances probably a job for a gunsmith, as few shooters will have a proper screwdriver to handle the narrow-slotted screws.

As most of you shotgun buffs well know, selective ejectors kick out the empty shells and lift the unfired rounds for manual removal. With the Brno Super primary extraction of unfired shells is 3/16", while full extractor travel on ejection is nearly 7/16". Stop pins are screwed to the bottom side of the barrel extensions to check extractor travel when the barrels are removed from the action.

The ejector system is one that

Floor of the Brno frame has "windows" to accommodate the lower part of the under-lugs. Without these openings, frame depth would have to be increased. Cocking levers are seen at the knuckle.

promises long, trouble-free service. The extractors are dovetailed to the sides of the under barrel and are powered by coil springs housed within the barrel breech. This eliminates the usually complicated hammer-and-sear arrangement in the fore-end and means there are fewer parts to get out of whack. The direct-contact coil springs take care of both primary extraction and ejection, while a camming action seats the extractors rather than having them drag down the action face as the gun is being closed.

As for the test gun, the mechanisms were timed to perfection and apparently the coil springs were carefully matched for strength. Invariably the empty hulls landed side by side after being tossed roughly 6 feet, though being a handloader I stopped most of them before they cleared the breech.

It is fairly common practice among European armsmakers these days to employ the monoblock method for joining together the two barrels at the breech. But the Brno factory has its own way of getting the hide off the proverbial cat. The forged barrels of the Super 12/12 are dovetailed together in the chamber area, are then soldered and further secured by a pair of screws.

As I've already mentioned, the barrels are crafted from Poldi steel and, according to the Brno catalog, so are all other parts of the gun. Quoting in part, in regard to Brno manufacturing techniques: ". . . heat treatment (in reference to the steel) meets all requirements of optimum strength, elasticity and wear resistance."

Chambers and Chokes

One would have to be a genuine nit-picker to find even small fault with the bore and chambers of the Super 12/12. Bright and smooth all the way. Too, the forcing cones are smoothly cut, running about 5/8" in length. Chokes are of the conical type, which is to say that the sections (each about 2¾" long) taper all the way, with no parallel at the muzzle end. Muzzle roundness is excellent for the test gun, this staying within .001" for both tubes.

My measurements taken at a point 5" from the muzzle disclose a bore diameter of .718" for both tubes. This is some .010" to .012" smaller than for most U.S.-made guns, but quite in line with European practices in general.

The Brno catalog says that the over barrel is choked "maximally" 1.1mm (about .043"), and the under barrel 0.9mm (about .035"). A constriction of .043" would be rather excessive. However, the test gun has actual measured constrictions of .025" (under barrel) and .030" (over). The barrel markings do not quite agree with this, showing the difference to be .008".

Pattern testing, of course, has the final say. At 40 yards the under tube printed modified-choke density with 8s, and full-choke density with both 6s and 4s.

The tighter topside barrel ran close to improved modified with 8s, and full choke with both 6s and 2s. (See pattern summary table for details.) Pellet distribution for all shot sizes and loads was typically full choke for both tubes—that is, nearly all patterns were characterized by dense centers.

Pattern Tests

The shooting for patterns was done from sand-bag rest, so this also gave the story on barrel alignment. The under barrel centered perfectly in the vertical plane when the two beads were "stacked" and the 2½" aiming marker was "floated." But the over barrel called for seeing less rib. To center, it was necessary to superimpose the two beads and hold about 5" low.

This difference in pattern centering between the barrels is a little more than I like to see, yet it created no problems in the field while crow shooting, Regardless of which barrel was fired, no special effort was made to see dissimilar amounts of rib, and if my swing was right the birds were hit squarely enough for clean kills.

The Brno Super is fitted with an automatic safety on the top tang, which means that the mechanism returns to "safe" each time the action is opened. Some shooters cuss the automatic safety, but the writer prefers this type over the manual — probably because I have grown accustomed to it through long use. When the thumbslide is pushed forward to "off safe," a bright orange-red dot is exposed.

Trigger spacing is a fraction over one inch, toe to toe, and the guard is spacious. Thus the double trig-

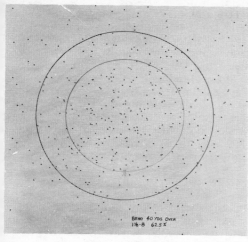

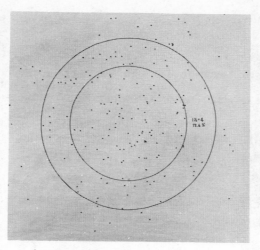

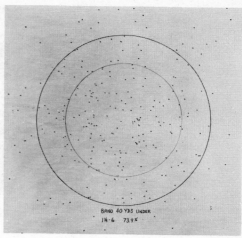

Brno over barrel averaged 63% with S&W field load of No. 8 shot. This 40-yard pattern went 62.5%, has dense center.

Average performance for the under barrel with 1½ oz. of Super-X 4s leveled out at 70.5%. This 72.6% pattern represents the norm in regard to pellet distribution.

Under barrel of the Super 12/12 handled Remington Express 6s for a 74% average at 40 yards, printing high center density. This pattern is typical, counts out to 73.9%.

gers can be handled while wearing gloves, providing they're fairly close fitting.

Long-armed shooters who like to position the left hand well forward will appreciate the Brno fore-end—it's a full 12″ long. Here we find a somewhat narrow and flat-sided design, with a depth of 2⅛″ and a width of 1⅝″ over the rear half. Both width and depth taper to smaller dimensions over the forward half. A push-type release is centrally located in the belly of the wood.

The bolt loop for engaging the fore-end catch is fastened to the barrel in an unusual way. The loop is an integral part of a steel band which completely encircles the under barrel. The more general practice is to attach the loop simply by soldering.

Checkering on the fore-end is confined to the sides and the covered area is adequate for a non-slip grip. This is cut checkering, running about 20 lines per inch in a modified skip-line style. Five lines are cut and one is skipped to produce something of a basket-weave pattern. The pistol grip is checkered in the same style.

It cannot be said that the checkering is flawlessly cut, as there are a few miscues here and there around the double-line borders. Nor are the diamonds sharply pointed up. But the work is quite good on the whole, certainly much more functional and more pleasing in appearance than checkering of the die-impressed type.

American shooters are likely to snicker at the idea of sling swivels on a shotgun, but I can call to mind a good many times when I've wished my gun had a carrying strap so as to free my hands for other tasks, such as lugging decoys, cameras and a lunch kit. The sling swivels on the Brno do not, to my thinking, detract from the gun's appearance; they are not in the way when shooting; and they do

40-YARD PATTERN TESTS

BRNO SUPER 12/12 OVER-UNDER
(AVERAGE OF 5 SHOTS)

Barrel	Load	Density 20″ Circle	Density 30″ Circle	Efficiency 30″ Circle	EDV 20″ Circle	EDV 30″ Circle
Under	S&W Field 3¼=1⅛=8 (441)	148	256	58.1%	39	50 (11.3%)
Over	Same as above	163	278	63.1%	32	37 (8.3%)
Under	Rem. Express Power Piston 3¾ - 1¼ - 6 (280)	128	207	74.1%	21	16 (5.8%)
Over	Same as above	121	202	72.1%	25	41 (14.6%)
Under	W-W Super-X Mk-5 4=1½=4 (212)	87	149	70.5%	14	14 (6.6%)
Over	W-W Super-X Mk-5 4=1½=2 (134)	56	97	72.6%	21	31 (23.1%)

EDV = Extreme variation in pellet hits between high and low patterns.

not add any weight to speak of. These will accommodate a ⅛″ strap. The front base is soldered to the under barrel at a point 1½″ ahead of the fore-end tip.

Dimensions and Weight

As for stock measurements, the 2¾″ drop at the heel is perhaps greater than many of us are accustomed to, but it can be easily adapted to by keeping one's head a bit more erect. On the other hand, the drop at the comb of 1⅝″ and a pull of 14 1/16″ from the front trigger are pretty much in line with our present-day stocking practices. The comb on the Brno, however, is noticeably thinner than those we find on most guns made here, so the nicely styled cheekpiece pays its way. It tends to keep the shooter's face away from the comb during recoil and this is quite effective in protecting the cheekbone from bruises.

The stock wears a modern, glossy-type finish which enhances the natural beauty of the wood. Unfortunately, the finish does not seem to be highly impervious to weather. On one of my crow-shooting forays, the right side of the stock was exposed to a moderate rain for about two hours as the gun stood in the corner of the blind. A few days later it was noticed that the finish on that side was slightly checked in places.

Weighing in at 7½ pounds empty, the Brno 12/12 is no featherweight. As was expected, recoil was quite mild when busting crows with the new Smith & Wesson field load (3¼/1⅛/8), and not at all disturbing when, on two different occasions, I switched to Federal Hi-Power loads with 1¼ ozs. No. 7½ shot for working over roost-bound flights that were passing overhead at considerable height. But patterning the gun with short magnums did produce considerable buttstock authority, though it must be remembered that shooting from a rest at a stationary target always accentuates apparent recoil, and the same loads when fired in the field at game never seem quite as rough.

The solid top rib on this Czech stack-barrel gun is of the level type, and the surface is engraved with finely cut longitudinal lines which do a very good job of suppressing glare. But as 12-ga. ribs usually go, this one is uncommonly narrow, measuring only .230″ across. I personally feel that a slightly wider rib, and possibly one of tapering design, might be employed to good advantage. On the other hand, the massive frame (measuring nearly 1¾″ across at the top of the standing breech) serves as an eye-catcher that seems to enhance fast, accurate pointing, so perhaps there would be little gained in increasing rib width.

Not only is the Brno frame wide, it is also deep, measuring 2¾″ in this latter dimension. This, along with the deep fore-end, contributes to an appearance that suggests handling qualities might not be up to par. But like the old saying goes, one should never judge a book by its cover. The Brno does handle and point in a very responsive way.

Weight distribution is such that the point of balance occurs roughly ¾″ ahead of the hinge pin. This is just about optimum — at least in the opinion of this shooter. With a balance point farther to the rear, a gun tends to become muzzle light. Such a gun will be a lightning-fast pointer, but the muzzles do not "steady down" nor do they swing with as smooth a carry-through as when the balance is more forward. This is not to say that the Brno is muzzle heavy, which it certainly isn't, but rather to point out that its weight distribution represents a good compromise.

Fit and Finish

On the matter of fit and finish, there is little room for complaint. All wood-to-metal and metal-to-met-

Cheekpiece on Brno gives gun Continental styling, but it also serves in a functional capacity. Grip cap and buttplate are of plastic, both with white-line spacers. Checkering is in skip-line style, runs about 20 lines per inch.

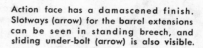

Action face has a damascened finish. Slotways (arrow) for the barrel extensions can be seen in standing breech, and sliding under-bolt (arrow) is also visible.

Brno locks have few parts, and hammers are driven by husky coil springs. Each lock has an intercepting safety to prevent accidental discharge due to jarring off. Bridles and inner surface of the lockplates have damascened finish.

al fitting is very well done, including those joints that are hidden behind the lockplates. As mentioned previously, the inner surface of each lockplate has a damascened finish, and the same is found on the action face, the ejectors and under-lugs.

This is nit-picking, pure and simple, but two places were found at the base of the top rib where the bluing did not take, and likewise around the base of the front sling swivel. In both instances, it is a matter of failing to clean away excess solder. Also, the outer perimeter of both muzzles is burred just a tiny bit, though the condition is not readily apparent. A minute or two with a fine-grit emery cloth would remedy this.

Any sidelock gun looks absolutely naked without some form of ornamentation on the lockplates, and the Brno people have taken care of this aspect with scroll work and game scenes in relief. The right-hand lockplate shows a duck in flight, the left plate a running hare. The work appears to be etched, and is similar in quality to that found on the Thompson/Center Contender pistol. A higher-priced model of the Brno Super is offered with hand-cut engraving.

Only one spot of trouble surfaced during my test shooting. The locks are not of the rebounding type and the firing pin for the over barrel would sometimes hang up in the indent of the fired primer. This made the action "sticky" on opening, often requiring that the bottom of the frame be struck smartly with the heel of my hand to "start" the barrels. The trouble occurred more frequently with some brands of ammo than with others. Corrective measures were not taken, but it appears that slightly rounding off the tip of the pin would take care of this matter.

All facets considered, this over-under may not be the greatest ever to come down the pike, but the gun certainly merits the stamp of approval for any shooter who likes a double-trigger stack-barrel with distinctly European styling. The under barrel could be given less choke, and if that were done the Brno Super 12/12 would become a much more versatile piece of ordnance, suitable for both upland work and waterfowling. ●

SPECIFICATIONS
Brno Super 12/12 Over-Under

Action Type: Superposed, hammerless, top-break, sidelock double with selective ejectors.
Breech Lock-up: Double under-lugs in conjunction with Kersten-type round cross-bolt.
Gauge & Chambers: 12; 2¾″.
Barrels & Chokes: 27½″; Poldi steel; .025″ (under) & .030″ (over).
Trigger: Double (front/under bbl. & rear/over bbl.), gold plated.
Safety: Thumb-slide on upper tang, automatic.
Sights: .110″ metal bead front; .045″ center bead on top rib.
Weight: 7½ pounds (empty).
Overall Length: 44¼″.
Buttstock & Fore-end: European walnut, cheekpiece; cut skip-line checkering; sling swivels; plastic capped pistol grip and plastic buttplate, both with white-line spacers.
Stock Dimensions (test gun): Length of pull from front trigger 14¹/₁₆″ (from rear trigger 13¹/₁₆″); drop at comb 1⅝″; drop at heel 2¾″; downpitch 2¼″; cast-off ³/₁₆″.
Price: $210
Mfr: Brno Armament Works, Brno, Czechoslovakia.
Importer: Continental Arms Corp., 697 Fifth Avenue, New York, NY 10022.
Remarks: Also available in 16 gauge.

KNIVES

Heinrich H. Frank
Knifemaker-Engraver

I received a most interesting letter in mid-March from Mr. Frank. In it he told me he'd moved to Montana in late 1972, where he's going to devote full time to knifemaking and engraving. He was previously associated with R. W. Loveless of Lawndale, California.

Frank's knives are entirely handmade. So far he has not found a stainless steel that meets his critical standards. He has his own heat-treating furnaces, and his superb engraving is completed before hardening of the blades. All of his hunting folding-knife styles have one (locking) blade only—he doesn't make many sheath-type knives. He uses gold and platinum on occasion, and he can make matched pairs if desired.

I believe the photograph reproduced here easily demonstrates Frank's great skills and artistry. These knives are graceful and elegant, yet fully useful, functional. His prices start at $125 for a 3-inch caper, not engraved, to $425 for his No. 4ENF (top of picture) or his 3ESF (second from bottom), a 3¼-inch bladed skinner. Sometime soon he will have a knife in the $100 area.   J.T.A.

Mr. Frank at work.

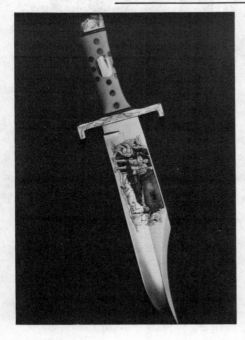

Dan Dennehy Knives

The bold and handsome Bowie knife seen here has an ivory handle inlaid with 22 pieces of turquoise and twin escutcheon plates. The etched scenes, by Shaw-Leibowitz, depict events in the turbulent life of Jim Bowie. The 7th ed. of Dennehy's catalog is now ready and well worth its $1 cost.   J.T.A.

Charles Dickey Knives

Excellent quality, these—first class design, construction and final assembly-finishing, all with a professional look, all handmade of high carbon or 440 C stainless steels. Dickey forges blades on special order, but he prefers the stock-removal technique. Tempering is done in an atmosphere-controlled furnace.

His tangs are rectangular in section, and his handle material (virtually anything you want to order) have squared holes to match. He then inserts a steel pin through the end cap —brass usually but nickel silver can be used—and into the tang. This is followed by a brass pin, also inserted and welded by metal upset. The result —a smooth exterior, without signs of attachment, yet the handle can never turn on the tang. Dickey's guards are hard silver soldered. Dickey also makes slab-handled knives by a special technique, equally rigid. All of his methods are gone into thoroughly in his new catalog. His prices start at about $48, delivery time now about 5-6 months.   J.T.A.

Baker HXD Knives

Fred Baker makes genuinely hot-forged knives, one of the few makers using the process nowadays. He claims that it is *only* through controlled forging that the steel grain or fibers can be oriented to the shape of the part. Because of this the grain is refined and made denser, he says, the steel then being in optimum condition for best response and strength from the subsequent heat treatment. Baker blades are thereby very hard, yet tough—they're made of alloy steels, but not stainless.

The Baker handle design, U.S. patented, uses nearly full tangs. The special-shape body consists of thick leather washers, guard and cap of brass or aluminum—the light metal is recommended for better balance.

Baker makes only one hunting knife, each handmade and differing only in length (5″, 6″ or 7″ blades). Deliveries are running about 9 months late on these $85 knives. A descriptive color leaflet costs $1, refundable if a knife is bought.   J.T.A.

Chas. Dickey knife

Scrimshaw by Barringer

I can't tell you who made the blades seen nearby, but C. Milton Barringer (217 2nd Isle North, Leisure Beach, Port Richey, FL 33568) did the well-executed full rigged ship carved into the walrus ivory of the big knife. Barringer, a modern practitioner of this ancient art form, exercises his skillful touch in many other directions, too—he offers scrimshaw on medallions, cufflinks, tie tacks, earrings, etc., and the motif need not be necessarily naval. This is excellent work. **J.T.A.**

Sparks Handmade Knives

The long and short of it seen here are paired favorites of Sparks, who also likes the angled guards the bigger knife shows—the angle can also be had cut in the other direction (which is the type I prefer) or conventionally straight across, of course. Sparks' new 24-page catalog—and nicely done—shows his extensive line, cost $1 postpaid. The larger knife pictured, a good one for bigger game jobs, has a 5″ blade and Sparks' "Power Grip" handle, costs $58. The small knife, with a 3″ blade good for caping, is $42. **J.T.A.**

W-K Knives

Walt Kneubuhler—at the sign of the anvil—is a maker of knives in the great mountain man tradition. With few exceptions, WK knives are named for mountain men and mountain places, names with a savor of the old West—Cache Valley, Wind River, Jed Smith, Grand Teton, Manuel Lisa and Broken Hand, among others. WK's knives, made in hunting, skinning and fighting types, are entirely handcrafted in his shop, and they're fully guaranteed. The knife illustrated is the Pierre Chouteau, named after a famed 18th century French trapper. Its 4¼-inch tapered blade is made from ³⁄₁₆- inch stock. The handles—wood, stag or Micarta—are miter joined to the guard, and all hardware is stainless steel. The cost, including a handmade sheath, is $80.

WK's new catalog for 1973 is now ready, cost $1. In it you'll see various extras offered as well—ivory handles, sheaths mounted in German silver, engraving of initials, etc., plus a showing of hunting bags—with or without powder horns, patch knives, and so on. **J.T.A.**

Above left, Barringer's scrimshaw work; Spark's workmanlike pair below.

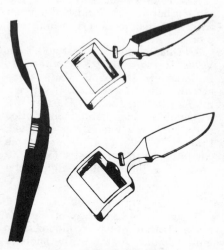

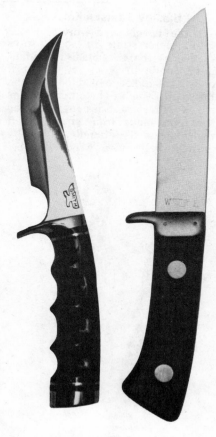

Collin Bros. Knives

The unusual and useful belt knife knives pictured here originated with the Collins brothers, though it has been pirated by some several other makers. As with all their knives, these different blades are made of 440C stainless steel, hardened to 58 Rockwell C and delivered with a razor sharp edge.

The knife at top is their 105 Survivor type, both edges flat ground, the blade 2⅞″ long. The lower one, called the Hunters Survivor, has the same length blade. It has a single edge and carries a built-in bottle opener. Both are furnished with a handsome 9-oz. cowhide belt (black or brown), which holds a sheath that conceals the blade. Cost, with belt, is $30. Extra belts are $8 each, even sizes to 50 inches.

Collins Bros. make a variety of knives, all of stainless steel—their one-piece, open-handle skinner-capers are a top favorite, made with trailing-or dropped-point. A like knife, but with a 4½″ hunting-style blade, rounds out this assortment. Each is $25, furnished with a sheath (patent applied for) that fits any belt up to 3″ wide, and can be worn normally, inverted or in the pocket with perfect safety. **J.T.A.**

John T. Smith Knives

The knife pictured is Smith's Model 1, a skinner type that he'll make with blades up to 5″ long, handles finger-grooved or not, and of wood, stag or Micarta ordinarily. Some 18 other styles are available, and handle materials can be almost anything you'd like. All of Smith's knives are handmade entirely, they're 100% guaranteed, and he invites full custom-order knives as well. His prices start at $40—the knife shown is $60, without finger grooves $55. Send 50c for his latest illustrated catalog. **J.T.A.**

J. T. Smith's Model 1 knife (left) and the Walt Kneubuhler Pierre Chouteau blade.

Rigid Knives

The three ruggedly handsome knives shown here, handcrafted by a company only three years old, have already gained national recognition.

These three Rigid Knives are, from left—the Ripper, a combination skinner-all purpose 4¼″ blade; at right is their Caribou, a professional type with a 5″ blade. The folding knife is the Apache, its blade 3¾″ long.

Individually made from sawn blanks of high carbon, rust resistant steel, these blades are carefully heat-treated to insure an even temper over-all, and each blade is tested for a hardness figure of 58-60 on the Rockwell C-scale. That degree of hardness makes for a blade that's tough without being brittle, and one that takes an edge easier. Rigid Knives, semi-hollow ground for faster re-honing, are delivered with a razor-sharp edge.

All Rigid sheath knives are full-tang type (the strongest possible form), have solid brass bolsters at hilt and butt, and the slab handles are made of Brazilian rosewood or black-grained Micarta. These handles, shaped to fit the hand, are finger grooved for better control. Because they're handmade, Rigid blade and handle lengths may depart slightly from listed lengths.

At this time Rigid offers 8 hunting style sheath knives, priced from $25 to $60, and two others of traditional form—a Bowie with an 11½″ blade at $125, and an Arkansas Toothpick for $70. Newest of Rigid knives is their Apache, a folding style with a 3¾″ blade. Made to the same quality standards as other Rigid knives, and of the same general form, the positive-locking blade and rocker of the Apache rotate on special oil-impregnated bearings for smoother action and longer life. The brass bolsters are fused and riveted to the 18-gauge stainless steel liners, which also accounts for the easy action of this folding knife. Cost of the Apache is $30.

All Rigid knives are furnished in black, solid leather belt sheaths which, while not exactly works of art, are fully adequate to protect the blade and the owner. The Apache comes in a belt pouch of the same heavy leather.

Rigid Knives carry a lifetime guarantee to the original buyer, assuming normal use, and if you'd like them to make a knife to your design—and by their quality methods —they'll be glad to do just that. Brochures and leaflets are free for the asking.   J.T.A.

Hartley-Bamsen Knives

These bevel-edged knives are, I think, interesting in more ways than one—the 4⅜″ blade is a laminate, made in Norway, the high carbon cutting edge held to 60 on the Rockwell C-scale. The outer sections are of softer iron, designed to keep the hard blade from snapping off under stress. The handle, of nicely-grained palisander wood, lies be-tween a nickel-silver guard and cap.

It's a comfortable feeling knife, and the leather sheath furnished is lined with stiff plastic as a retaining and protective unit.

All this for only $15, postpaid, from V. W. Hartley, 1602 S. Hunter Rd., Indianapolis, IN 46239. Blades alone are also offered, these $3. If you're a muzzle-loading shooter, Hartley has a "possibles" bag, handmade of oiled and tough cowhide, nylon stitched, that is 8″x8″, has an adjustable carrying strap, and sells for $8.50 postpaid. A bullet pouch, high on the inside back, is handy.   J.T.A.

Track Knives

Shown here are two of Track's blades, both of which are among their most popular. At top in the photo is the Montana Trapper, made with a serrated thumb rest and an extra finger groove for optimum control in skinning. The 4½ "dropped-point" blade allows careful ripping. About $55 with moose antler handles, $51 in walnut.

Chubby Hueske Knives

The knife pictured is a new model by Hueske, handmade like his various others. This Model 411 of his full tang Pro Hunter series, all of 3/16″ stock, can be had with a blade length of 4″ to 5″. The blades are specially ground for fleshing and skinning, and the handles are wood-grain Micarta slabs, which he recommends. About $60. Send 50¢ for his new catalog.   J.T.A.

The other cutter is the Flathead Skinner, a lightweight 4″ bladed knife that is usable on large and small game. With moose handles, about $52; walnut runs $47.33.

The Track catalog (50c postpaid) shows clearly some—but not all—of the knives in the line. Special purpose knives can be ordered, too, but all are entirely handmade of best steels and fully guaranteed.   J.T.A.

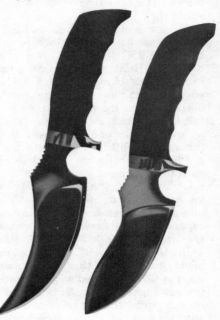

Flathead Skinner (l.) and Mountain Trapper.

Hartley-Bamsen (left) and Chubby Hueske knives.

H. O. McBurnette, Jr.

As our photograph shows, this young cutler makes attractively done knives, nor do the three samples pictured exhaust his blade patterns and handle treatment. All of his blades are fully handmade from GraphMo steel he orders in slab form or from 440-C stainless steel. He holds hardness to Rockwell C-scale figures in the mid-50's, heat-treating done in an electric oven. He hollow grinds all blade edges, and his knives are furnished with heavy saddle-leather sheaths, also handmade.

McBurnette uses two tang styles, for the most part—the knives in the photograph have his full-length round tangs, made ¾-inch wide at the guard for extra rigidity and to prevent the tangs turning. His flatter-handled knives are made with a ¾-tang,

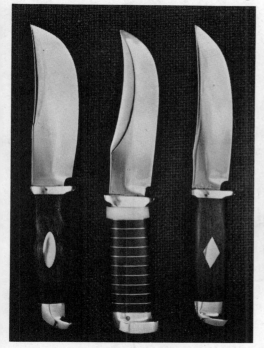

deeply notched to obtain a secure bond with the epoxy used to lock the tang to the handle. He can also supply a full slab or scale tang if desired—he'll make knives to the customer's design or ideas.

I received a sample knife from McBurnette, made with his ¾-tang, the 440-C Blade 5 inches long and brilliantly polished, and its hardness about 56 Rockwell C. The walnut handle, oil-finished to a soft sheen, is fitted with a solid brass guard and butt cap. This Model J knife shows graceful lines and good unity of blade and handle—it fits me well, and I'm going to enjoy using it.

McBurnette's prices start at about $50, and his knives are guaranteed for the life of the buyer unless abused. J.T.A.

Doc Johnston's Stuff

I don't think old friend Johnston can be doing much lawing these days—he's too busy making knives, blades alone, bolo ties (and knife handles) made from antler butts, these carved into 17th century style grotesque masks. Doc has a new brochure ready describing his creations, some of which are pictured here. Excellent quality, too, and moderately priced. The handmade knife (left) has a bleached stag handle of one piece, cost about $50. J.T.A.

Bourne Knives

The original of this "rifle knife" was made about 1835. The modern steel blade is 5¼" long, the hexagonal ebony handle trimmed with nickel-silver ferrule, but cap and thong ring. Inlays in the handle are of nickel-silver and mother of pearl. Cost, $75, from H. G. Bourne. J.T.A.

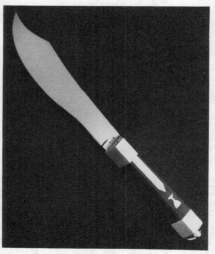

H. G. Bourne

Ralph Bone Knives

Two of Bone's latest designs are pictured here—the Bowie style has an engraved guard, the dropped handle is Sambar stag, and the blade top is serrated and grooved. The folding knife is engraved, carries Bone's initials, and has ivory plates. The Bone catalog, full of color, is 50¢. J.T.A.

Jimmy Lile Knives

Shown here are but two of Lile's many styles. The smaller knife is a folding type, the handle inlaid with select wood. The same knife can be had without the wood, the metal given a brushed finish. About $75. The same folding style can be made as a drop-point skinner, as a clipped-point or with two blades. The larger sheath knife is Lile's Big Seven—with wood handles about $60; stag is $10 extra. J.T.A.

Doc Johnston

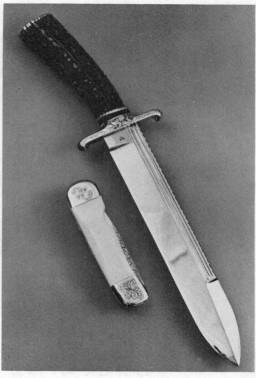

Ralph Bone

Jimmy Lile

During recent Arizona varmint hunt, Dale Miller sights his long barrel 44 Magnum at approaching varmint, author is drawing 41, and Dave Caldwell keeps on calling the critter into close pistol range.

THE MAGNUM REVOLVERS
which one for hunting?

The big 44 is still king of the hill among factory handguns, but the 41 is a strong contender. The 357? Well...Here's how they compare, with extensive data on performance, loads, recoil, suitability for hunting and much more.

by JOHN LACHUK

"I CAN LICK anybody in the house!" truculently declares the 44 Magnum. And you'd better believe it!

The lordly Forty-Four Magnum is still tops in killing power among factory-made hunting handguns, but he is not without contenders. The original one-hand Magnum, the 357, still has a potent right-cross and the young, ambitious 41 Magnum boasts a wicked uppercut. A welterweight, the 9mm has lately learned a few deadly tricks, and some light heavyweights, the 44 Special and 45 ACP, are

hard to count out. The 45 Long Colt, an old heavyweight who retired undefeated, is trying for a comeback.

So there you have the contenders in this ring of holster-handy hunting arms. Regardless of their relative merits, only the trio of Magnums shares the distinction of approaching, and sometimes overlapping, the killing power of many popular hunting rifle calibers. As with ring fans, handgun buffs all vociferously extol the virtues of their favorite caliber in song and verse, and each can put forth

valid claims for top claims in the brisk rivalry that flourishes among them.

The 357 Magnum probably has more staunch fans than all other high-intensity handgun calibers combined. If for no other reason, because it came first, and has had more time to win friends and influence people. It was introduced in 1935 by Colonel Douglas B. Wesson, of Smith & Wesson, based upon development work that he and Philip B. Sharpe carried out over a number of years. Many people forget that it was preceded by the 38-44, a revolver built on the same heavy N frame, originally designed for the 44 and 45. For it, Winchester loaded the Super Speed 38 Special, with a 158-gr. lead bullet traveling 1,115 fps.

The 357 Arrives

After years of experimenting with various bullet shapes, Sharpe and Wesson finally settled on a 158-gr. Keith-style lead slug, launched by 15 grains of Hercules 2400, burning at 45,000 psi, in a case stretched by 1/10-inch, at a phenomenal 1510 fps, from a revolver the likes of which we will never see again! The flawless workmanship and finish on the original 357 Magnum revolvers were the result of loving care by a battery of devoted craftsmen with life-long experience. All of these men, long since dead or retired, can never be replaced. Today, the manufacturers must depend upon precision machining for good fit, rather than deft strokes of a sharp file. The wonder is that they succeed so well.

Colonel Wesson's hunting feats with the new 357 were a wonder to all, as he bagged at least one of every species of dangerous big game found upon the North American Continent. For over two decades the 357 stood virtually alone in the role of hunting handgun, until the advent of the 44 Magnum in 1956.

The 357 is the smallest bore diameter to rate serious consideration for handgun-hunting big game and, in my opinion, that is stretching it a great deal. Only the most practiced, coolest marksman can be assured of certain kills with this smallest of centerfire magnums. Even hunting coyotes and bobcats, the long 38 plays third fiddle in a band headed by the 44 and 41 Magnums.

Accuracy with the 357 ranges from great to fantastic. My 6-inch barreled Colt Python, Buehler-mounted with a 10-inch eye relief Leupold M8-2x scope, produces one-hole bench rest groups consistently at 25 yards, with a wide variety of bullets and loads. A scope detracts from the normal handiness of a handgun, but increased aiming precision makes it worth the bother and burden to many holster-gun nimrods.

About the only practical holster that I've seen for such a scoped handgun is the "Trooper Hook" from Andy Anderson, the "Gunfighter" of North Hollywood, CA. The holster has a full flap to protect the gun, yet allows a reasonably fast draw. It swings freely on a GI-style brass claw hook, hung in reinforced holes that run the length of the leather belt. Ammo loops are confined to the sides, to avoid discomfort when riding in a vehicle.

The 357 can justly claim top honors for versatility. It chambers the entire range of factory-loaded 38 special ammo, from target wadcutters to 110-gr. Super Vels, and Speer's Shotshell snake ammo, plus every brand of commercial 357 cartridges.

My first hot handgun was a 357 Magnum. I was inordinately proud of the loud boomer, and felt with youthful smugness that it was unbeatable, until one day I suffered an emotional trauma from which I have never quite recovered. I went jackrabbit hunting in the Mojave desert with a couple of friends who were armed with 44 Special handguns and matching Model 92 Winchester lever action rifles.

All of us were shooting cast hollow-pointed bullets, loaded to near cylinder-bursting pressures. No doubt my bullets were traveling faster, but the results on those jacks showed my revolver was coming off a poor second in the killing power department. Later, when the inevitable plinking session developed, with tin cans stacked against a near hillside, I got another lesson in the benefits of increased bore size. My bullets drove through the cans and raised an impressive cloud of dust beyond, but when the 44s boomed, half the hillside erupted in geysers of flying dirt and rocks!

I straightaway sold my 357, complete with loading dies, bullet moulds, etc., and joined "The 44 Associates," a loosely-knit, nation-wide organization of men devoted to the 44 Special revolver cartridge, with Lawrence I. Newton, of Auburn, Mass., at its head. The society took on the fervor of a religious sect, with glassy-eyed disciples repeating the incantations of such high priests as Elmer Keith and Al Barr. The 44 Associates published a compilation of nearly 1,000 high intensity 44 Special loads, in an edition limited to 200. I still prize mine, number 103. Many of my friends and I loaded the 44 Special to the hilt without ever experiencing so much as a jugged chamber in the single action Frontier Colts we used.

Nearly a decade before introduction of the 44 Magnum, I developed a wildcat round that later proved to be a dead-ringer for the commercial product. I used 405 rifle cases, which had the same O.D. as 44 Specials, with heads trimmed to match, but cut off to the longest length possible without having bullets protrude from the cylinder of the custom-fitted Frontier Colt that I chambered with a custom

reamer. The cases chanced to be the same length as the real Magnum when it was later introduced. I had to neck-ream my bastard brass to accept the bullets, and suffered an actual loss in case capacity over the balloon-head 44 Special, because the 405 was thicker around the solid web. My optimum load of 22.5 grains of 2400 with the 244-gr. Thompson gas-check bullet came pretty close to current factory velocities.

Enter the 44 Magnum

Of course, Elmer Keith was the leader of the 44 Special revolution that led ultimately to the 44 Magnum. His book, *Sixgun Cartridges and Loads*, copyrighted in 1936 by Thomas G. Samworth, was my bible. About the only powders that were then capable of providing maximum velocities were Unique and 2400, but we attained some impressive results with them. Later I discovered the wonders H-240 and H-110, both an improvement over 2400. A book, *Sixguns by Keith*, is still widely available. It was copyrighted in 1955, before Elmer cajoled S&W and Remington into introducing the 44 and 41 Magnums, but it contains some timeless information of great interest to any real handgun buff!

When first introduced the S&W 44 Magnum was a pretty impressive "Big Iron," nearly a half-pound heavier than the 1950 Model S&W 44 Special Target Revolver. With counter-bored chambers, the cylinder was .18″ longer, and the barrel was full-diameter end-to-end, without the customary taper, topped by a broad rib and the finest set of field/target sights ever seen on any commercial revolver. The white-outlined rear sight was fully micrometer adjustable for elevation and windage, and the forward-slanting, ramp-mounted, Patridge style front sight held a red plastic rectangle that stood out boldly against backgrounds light or dark.

Even some revered gun experts of the day were rather overawed by the new gun. General J. S. Hatcher wrote in the March 1956 *American Rifleman* "...we found it advisable to wear gloves, as the recoil can only be described as severe." He went on to describe how the checkering shaved off bits of skin, and "...we suddenly experienced a sharp stinging sensation over the entire hand, as though hitting a fast ball with a cracked bat."

The irrepressible Colonel Charles Askins came back in the 1957 *Gun Digest,* "Word comes to me that some joes, probably with lace on their panties, are putting on gloves to shoot

Author's nickel-plated 41 Magnum fired top group of 10 shots at 50 yards from Ransom Rest, using 22.5 grains of H-110 and 220-gr. cast Saeco bullet. Lower group was fired by author from hand rest at 25 yards, using same load. Flyer in top group resulted from inadvertently chambering a Peters factory round.

Colt Trooper Mark III 357 with some groups fired by the author from hand rest at 25 yards. Lachuk holds that 5-shot groups are more realistic for hunting than 10-shot strings.

Two fine old time rounds that can be handloaded to high velocity with modern bullets for use in hunting handguns: the 44 Special and 45 Long Colt. These factory loadings, traveling at low velocities, have round-nosed bullets with little shocking power.

Sectioned cases reveal powder capacities of (from left) solid head 44 Special, author's 44 "magnum," and factory 44 Magnum. Note very thick case walls and web of 405 rifle case used by Lachuk to make his wildcat brass.

Author's favorite, a Colt Frontier 44 Special, has fired many rounds over the nearly 30-year span he's owned it!

Colt New Frontier 45 Long Colt with Buntline barrel makes a formidable hunting handgun, especially when handloaded with modern jacketed hollow points at high velocity.

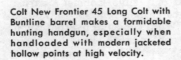

Magnum lineup in order of power, led by 44 Magnum, with lead 41 and jacketed soft point 41 next, 357 last, followed by the bullets used in each factory-loaded round.

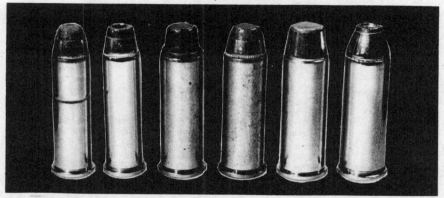

From left—Remington-loaded 357, Super Vel 357, Remington lead load for 41, and soft point jacketed Remington 41, Norma soft pointed 44, and Super Vel hollow pointed 44. Super Vels offer light bullets at high velocity, add increased shocking power.

Comparison of normal factory loadings and Super Vel ammo. From left —standard 9mm with round-nosed full jacketed 124-gr. followed by Super Vel 90-gr. JHP and 112-gr. JSP. Standard 45 ACP with full jacketed 230-gr. bullet, then a Super Vel 190-gr. JHP.

it. I shot the big 44 all one afternoon, and found the recoil nothing more than stimulating."

A year later, in the 1958 *Gun Digest*, Elmer Keith told of dropping a wounded mule deer on the run, with two hits out of six tries, at an estimated range of 600 yards. One bullet dusted the deer both sides, taking out ribs at entrance and exit. I've never known Elmer to stretch a long bow, and I'm sure it happened just the way he told it, but he still gets chided unmercifully for that one to this day.

It appears doubtful that any conventional handgun round will ever surpass the 44 Magnum for sheer brute power. Any significant escalation of either bullet weight or velocity would surely result in a pistol too heavy and bulky to be practical, or a level of recoil that even Charley Askins would find somewhat discomfiting! Mayhap the Gyrojet or some other exotic one-hand arm will one day accomplish more destruction at the target without unduly increasing the punishment to the shooter.

Introduction of the 44 Magnum was greeted by all hands with much fanfare and high-sounding ballyhoo. Heaven knows it was well deserved. But when the Johnny-come-lately 41 Magnum crept on stage, quietly from the wings in 1964, it was greeted by a collective yawn from the gun writers who normally wax eloquent at the drop of a firing pin. It was widely berated as too little and too late. Fact is, the 41 was a damn fine round that filled a specific need. While surely second to the 44 in ballistics, it also reduced recoil to a more tolerable level, while retaining a high level of energy delivered at the target. Had it preceded the 44 Magnum, the 41 would likely have been hailed as a major breakthrough. Coming as it did behind the 44, it probably never will emerge from the shadow of its bigger brother, although it offers near equal performance with a measurable reduction in recoil and racket.

The Compromise 41

Everyone has a tolerance level for recoil that can't be exceeded if he is to shoot well and enjoy it. The big 44 may be just too much for some. If those individuals can handle the 41, that is the gun for them. It far outclasses the 357 in killing power! Anyone who doesn't own a 357 or 44 Magnum should take a hard look at the 41 before investing in a hunting handgun.

All three major makers — Colt, Smith & Wesson, and Ruger — have put forth their finest efforts in making revolvers to handle the magnum trio. In the 357 Magnum, Colt offers their time-proved Python, with ejector rod shroud and broad ventilated rib running full length of a husky untapered barrel, topped by a serrated ramp Patridge front sight, backed by a micrometer adjustable rear. Workmanship is impeccable!

Time was, the Python was the top of the Colt line, but it has lately acquired some competition in the form of the new Colt Trooper Mark III. Colt built an entirely new plant just to fabricate this fine handgun. In outward appearance, the Trooper closely resembles the Python, whose frame it shares, but inside the works are completely new. The familiar V-mainspring of traditional Colt double action revolvers has given way to a modern coil, and a more positive internal safety has been added.

Rather than attempting to throw a block under the hammer to prevent firing pin contact, Colt put the shoe on the other foot. The hammer *has no contact* with the firing pin at any time. Instead, it depends upon a small flat plate, with an arm that attaches at the lower end to the trigger, and slides up and down a vertical slot behind the firing pin. Drawing the trigger rearward raises the plate, interposing it between the hammer and firing pin, delivering the impact from one to the other. With the trigger forward, the hammer rests directly upon the frame, with no possible way of impacting the firing pin. By way of test, I repeatedly released the single action sear, held the hammer back at that point for a moment, then let go with my thumb allowing the hammer and trigger to return to normal without interference. In every case, the trigger returned under spring pressure before the hammer could make contact, thus the plate was down, and unable to deliver the message to fire from hammer to firing pin. There's no way you can make this gun go off accidentally.

The forward bearing surface of the cylinder is at least 60% on the frame itself rather than bearing almost entirely upon the yoke, as do most other swingout cylinder revolvers. I would like to see the diameter of the barrel abaft the frame increased. This is a bad point of wear on most magnum revolvers. However, it appears that Colt reduced this diameter in order to increase the thickness of the frame surrounding the barrel—not a bad idea.

The trigger, in a complete reversal of recent practice, has been left completely smooth rather than grooved. It appears to facilitate double action shooting without any harmful effect in single action mode. The trigger is wide and deeply curved to fit the finger, with a generally very comfortable feel. An Allen screw, accessible from outside, offers backlash adjustment.

Anyone having even a passing acquaintance with Smith & Wesson Magnums doesn't have to be told that they're the finest handguns ever made, anytime, anywhere. They offer grooved wide triggers, broad-spur, deeply-serrated hammers, fine target sights on thick ribs, well-shaped stocks, and the highest degree of craftsmanship available in modern times. If you are pondering the purchase of a Smith 357, buy the heavy-frame Model 27. The lightweight Model 19, though a fine arm, is more for lawmen who *carry* much and *shoot* little.

Single action fans will be well served by the Ruger Blackhawks, with a look to excite any lover of things Western, and brute strength to match the look. Three generations of constant shooting couldn't wear out one of these guns! Excellent Patridge-style micro-adjustable sights, plus target-styled trigger and hammer are only a few of the assets found in the Rugers.

The original Colt Single Action is still available in either 357 Magnum

Lineup of 357 Magnum bullets. From left—Super Vel 137-gr., Remington 158-gr., Sierra 110-gr., 150-gr., 158-gr., and Speer 146-gr. and 160-gr.

Lineup of 44 Magnum bullets. From left—Speer 225-gr. and 240-gr., Super Vel 180-gr., Hornady 200-gr., 240-gr. and 265-gr., Sierra 180-gr. and 240-gr.

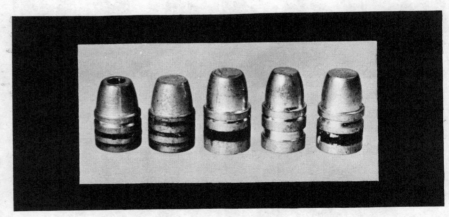

Much cheaper to shoot than jacketed bullets, lead bullets are entirely practical for hunting small game, as well as for practice. Left to right: 215-gr. Thompson/Ideal #431215, with and without hollow point; 250-gr. Saeco #290441 and Saeco 220-gr. #290441, and Elmer Keith's famous bullet, the Lyman #429421 250-gr. The Saeco #290441 turned in the best machine-rest groups fired by the author and Chuck Ransom.

or 45 Long Colt caliber. If this is your choice of hunting sidearm, take the New Frontier, with flat-topped frame and micro-adjustable target sights.

Picking a Magnum

Whatever revolver you buy, choose it with the longest barrel that's comfortable in your hands (hunters shoot two-handed). Numerous holsters are available that make them handy at the hip. A short-barreled magnum sacrifices velocity to compactness, bellers like a castrated bull, and rears up like a wild stallion.

Both the Colt Python and the Mark III come with 6-inch tubes. Take them! The Smith 357 Magnum comes with 6-inch or 8¾-inch barrels, the 41

ditto, the 44 with 6½-inch or 8⅜-inch tubes. The standard barrel lengths certainly provide effective hunting velocities, coupled with eye-appealing balance and reasonable compactness for carrying, but there is much to be said for the Buntline-style tubes. The long barrels appear clumsy, but in the hands of a practiced hunter they come to bear on-target with amazing swiftness, hold as steady as an anvil, and track running game like a radar beacon. The long sight radius reduces sighting error to a minimum. Velocity gain in all three magnum calibers ranges from 50 to 75 fps, depending on the ammo. Such slower-burning powders as 2400, H-110, and 630-P have more time to burn in the long tube, while such quick powders as Unique offer little advantage.

Rugers come 6½-inch in the 357 or 41 Magnums, 7½-inch in the 44, perhaps the best compromise between carrying ease and the optimum utilization of Magnum power. In the Colt SA, choose the 7½-inch option.

We don't plan to debate the pros and cons of revolvers versus autoloaders here. Suffice it to say that no autoloading pistol has the power to match the Big Three wheel guns, save for the moribund Automag, which was bulky and cumbersome, and lacked the versatility of the revolver, which can handle anything from primer-powered wax loads to thundering dynamite without a stutter.

Cost? The double action Magnums all run around $200, regardless of caliber. Would you believe that the original S&W 357 sold for just $60 about 30 years ago? The Ruger Blackhawks certainly rate as bargains, with the 357 and 41 selling at under $100, and the 44 Magnum Super Blackhawk retailing at $125 (as of this writing). The Colt New Frontier is costliest of all at $229.95. As might be expected, across-the-counter ammo costs more as the bore size increases — $8.55 per box of 50 for the 357, $10.60 for the 41, and $11 for the 44 Mags. Reloaders will find the cost contrast much less important to their choice.

Comparing the Magnum Triumvirate in terms of accuracy seems to be an exercise in futility. All of them, chambered into a Colt, Ruger, or Smith and Wesson, possess inherent accuracy far beyond the field marksmanship capabilities of even skilled handgunners.

Ransom Rest Tests

Chuck Ransom, inventor and manufacturer of the C'Arco Ransom Master Series Pistol Rest, loaned one of his excellent machines and his expertise in its use to help me compare the accuracy of several representative magnum handguns — a 357 Colt Trooper Mark III, a S&W 41 and 44. All were in new condition, the Colt Trooper being fired for the first time.

Chuck, a long-time pistol competitor, originally designed his rig just to find out if his own reloads were delivering acceptable target accuracy. At first he made his rest to hold only target pistols, but as demand grew among the big bore buffs, he provided adapters to handle most of the popular hunting handguns, including the magnums.

Chuck measures handgun accuracy in terms of 10 rounds at 50 yards.

Nothing less will satisfy him. I would have been perfectly happy with 5-round groups, but as it turned out, we were both satisfied. As often as not, the guns would shoot two separate 5-shot groups on the target. Chuck said that this was not at all uncommon, even with the most precise target handguns.

There is no doubt that a 5-round group shows considerably less dispersion than 10 shots will from the same gun and ammo. By the way of illustration, the first five 146-gr. Speer HPs from the Mark III, using 14.5/H-110, clustered impressively into 1¼ inches (center to center). The next 5 opened the group to 3½ inches. Super Vel 180-gr. 44 Magnum factory ammo grouped 5 into 1⅛ inches. The next three rounds made a tight cloverleaf ½-inch to the right. Number 9 shot landed in the original group for a respectable nine in 2⅛ inches. Then No. 10 blew it by wandering off at 4:00 o'clock to open the final group to 4¼ inches.

The 44 Magnum, loaded with 240-gr. Sierra Hollow Cavity slugs and 22.7/2400, put 4 shots into one ragged hole, ⅝-inch center to center. Then, while my hot breath fogged the Weatherby spotting scope, Chuck pushed down the lever that squeezed the trigger on the fifth shot — opening the group to 1¼ inches! The next 5 shotgunned around the original group, resulting in a 10-shot total of 3⅛ inches.

It was only coincidental that my favorite load printed the best group of the day. Chuck clamped my 6-inch S&W 41 Magnum into the rest and pumped out 10 rounds of Saeco 220-gr. cast bullets, ahead of 22.5/H-110, new brass, CCI Magnum primers. Seven shots cut each other for a 1⅛-inch group. Two, out at 11:00 o'clock, opened it to 1¼ inches. The tenth was out at 1:00 o'clock for a final 2⅛-inch group. However, I noticed that the flyer was not a clean-cut hole and brought it to Chuck's attention. We counted cartridges and discovered he'd absent-mindedly slipped a Peters factory round into the last loading.

Back in 1965, when Speer revised their ¾-jacketed bullets, Dave Andrews came up with some interesting information. He found that .410″ bullets were more accurate than .409″ size in the 41 Magnum. The revised Speer design with a heavy jacket, tapering to the mouth and flat on the bottom, was more accurate than the previous thin-jacketed, obtuse-ogive-based bullet. Hollow points were found to be slightly more accurate than soft points.

Most impressive groups to come to light thus far, resulted from marathon testing by Kent Lomont, who operates Lomont Precision Bullets, 4425 Fairfield Ave., Fort Wayne, Indiana. Kent has fired numerous 100-yard 5-shot groups that could be covered by an ordinary playing card, using scope-sighted magnum sixguns, across a sand bag rest; many of them measured from 2 to 4 inches, center-to-center. Kent and his father, who offer custom reloading as well as cast bullets in a wide variety of sizes and configurations, often fire as many as 5,000 rounds a week from their collection of 30 magnum handguns, mainly Rugers and Smiths. Kent fired over 220,000 full-loaded rounds through one S&W barrel, about 20% jacketed, the rest cast lead. "At the end of that time," he says, "it was still shooting 4-inch groups at 100 yards, even though the forcing cone was worn away to the edge of the barrel." Kent returned the revolver to the factory, and had the barrel set back one turn, and refaced at the rear. He is still shooting it. "The rifling is still perfect," he adds. Still the most accurate and saleable bullet in his inventory, says Kent, is the original Keith 250-gr. hardcast lead.

Comparative Recoil

One interesting sidelight that developed during accuracy testing with the Ransom Rest was the obvious contrasts in recoil exhibited by various guns and loads. The portion of the rest that supports the gun, via moulded rubber adapter plates clamped to the grip frame, rotates on a close-fitting shaft located below and to the rear of the pistol grip. A heavily spring-loaded "friction disc" holds the unit in battery. Considerable effort is required to rotate the gun muzzle upward manually. The muzzle rise of the 357 Magnum Colt Trooper Mark III with full-house hunting loads was just 9 degrees. The maximum rotation of 100 degrees resulted from firing the Hornady 265-gr. jacketed soft point ahead of 18.0 grains of 630-P in the S&W 44 Magnum. The theoretical difference measured in foot pounds of recoil between these two guns and loads was only about 2.4 to 1. However, the mechanical difference proved to be well over 10 times!

Changing to a load of 24 grains of H-110 behind a 240-gr. Norma bullet reduced the rotation to 87 degrees. Super-Vel ammo displayed the least recoil in the 44 Mag, rotating only 56 degrees while launching a 180-gr. jacketed hollow point at a listed 1830 fps.

Using the standard Remington/Peters factory loading, a 210-gr. soft point at 1500 fps, the 41 Magnum rotated 57 degrees. The 170-gr. Sierra hollow point loaded to about the same velocity turned the gun muzzle up to 48 degrees. This only demonstrates mechanically what the impact in my hand had told me years ago—all else being equal, lighter bullets kick less.

I find that the specter of recoil causes much trembling and trepidation among prospective big bore owners. However, this bugaboo can be conquered. You can reduce muzzle-flip by holding as high as possible on the stocks and using as tight a grip as possible, short of trembling. Stand nearly facing the target, to let the shoulder move back, absorbing some of the recoil energy.

It's a short step from this stance to the two-handed style developed by combat competition shooters in recent years. You can emulate these boys who shoot quick and deadly. Stand almost facing the target, left foot slightly forward. Start always from the leather, bringing the gun to eye level with the right hand, into the curled fingers of the waiting left. At the instant of contact, the left fingers wrap around those of the right, thumbs overlap. The elbows may be locked or slightly flexed. With the muscles of both forearms rigid, this gun mount is almost as steady as holding a rifle, and recoil is more readily overcome. The muzzle rises less and returns more quickly to the target. Good double action fire is possible and the left thumb can be used to cock the hammer for rapid single action fire, without disturbing the right-hand hold or shifting the gun.

Taming the Magnums

The shape and fit of the grips have a direct influence upon recoil effect. I find the issue grips on the Colt Python 357 distinctly uncomfortable to shoot. I'll take the 44 Mag Smith any day! The latter has stocks that are shaped better for my hand, and distribute the load better, over a larger area of contact. Best of all are custom-fitted grips, such as those available from Herrett's, Twin Falls, Idaho. In general, the more you shoot, the less recoil will bother you.

Various muzzle compensator devices have been offered over the years to reduce recoil but the most promising ever to appear is the "Mag-na-port," which consists of two inconspicuous slots cut into the top of the muzzle, one on each side of the front sight. The metal is removed neatly, without disturbing the finish on the

gun, by means of a space program spinoff electronic device that ionizes the metal away without leaving any burrs or machining marks. The gun can be shipped by any FFL licensed dealer to Mag-na-port Arms, Inc., 34341 Groesbeck, Frazer, Michigan, 48026.

More disturbing than recoil, especially on a covered target range is muzzle blast. Wear ear muffs during target practice to prevent a flinching habit that can come via the eardrums alone. In the field, the sound is dissipated by open space, and relatively few rounds are fired during a hunt.

Because the end requirement of a hunting handgun is to bag game, it can only be compared with its rivals in terms of killing power *first* and the ability to deliver that power to a vital spot in the game *second.*

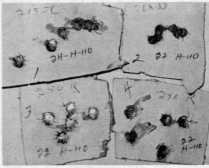

Four truly amazing 100-yard 5-shot groups from Kent Lomont's S&W 44 Magnum. No. 1—215-gr. gas check bullet, 24/H110, 2¾". No. 2—268-gr. JHP, 22/H110, 1". No. 3—250-gr. Keith lead, 22/H110, 1⅜". No. 4, same load as No. 3, 1⅝".

The primary aim of any hunter is not merely to kill game, but to drop it quickly and humanely. It is the hunter's responsibility to use the cartridge that will best assure humane kills, and to confine his shots to those within his certain kill range. For most handgunners, that is 100 yards or under for deer-sized game, and no more than 60 yards on the larger predators.

All three magnum handguns have demonstrated roughly equal ability to deliver the missile at the time and to the place required, but how do you find an objective measure of killing power? My own field experience shooting predators with handguns has shown that the 357 is sorely outclassed by the 41 and 44 Magnums. The latter two are so close in their effect on game that no measurable difference is apparent.

Magnums on Game

Most big game experience has been acquired with the 44 Magnum by such stalwarts as publisher Bob Petersen, who downed both an Alaskan brownie

and a polar bear, plus moose, deer, elk, and myriad smaller game. Lee Jurras, Super Vel empresario, took a 7½-inch Ruger Blackhawk to Africa, and using his own Super Vel 180-gr. jacketed soft point ammo, he bagged nearly a dozen species of African plains game, including a 350-lb. red lechwe, a fine tsessebe, and a tough old wart hog. The relatively light bullets provided ample penetration and excellent expansion in every case. In the course of a year, Lee will touch off as many as 100,000 rounds of big bore pistol ammo, and he has taken most of the big game animals on the North American continent with Super Vel ammo in Magnum handguns.

Lee says that "Velocity is 90% of bullet performance. The other 10% is bullet construction. Chamber pressures can be held down by trimming bullet weight, and limiting bearing surface, while maintaining the proper relationship between core hardness and jacket materials for a given pressure/velocity level." Lee's experience with lighter bullets in the 44 Magnum makes the 41 Magnum look good too, inasmuch as it can fire like bullet weights with superior ballistic coefficients at roughly equal velocities. The explosive expansion of modern jacketed bullets largely cancels out the slight edge in bullet diameter possessed by the 44.

Only when you get above deer-sized animals and begin hunting bear, moose or elk, does the 44, with its greater bullet weight, actually outclass the 41. The 220-gr. Speer soft point is about the heaviest practical bullet for the 41. The 44 can use bullets of 250 grains to advantage.

Trying to make valid ballistic comparisons of the magnum trio is highly speculative, but nonetheless interesting. A moving bullet has two attributes by virtue of its motion: *momentum*, which equals the bullet's mass times velocity, and *kinetic energy*, which equals half the bullet's mass times the square of its velocity. *Power*, as used here, is a measure of the work performed by the bullet's kinetic energy upon impact.

Ballistics for Magnums

Kinetic energy rises sharply with an increase in velocity, making light bullets look very good on a ballistics chart. However, a bullet must have sufficient mass and structural strength to penetrate into vital areas on big game, thus dictating a compromise. To kill quickly and humanely, a bullet must expend its kinetic energy in the vital organs of the animal,

In the 44 Magnum, Super Vel ammo exhibited the least recoil, rotating just 56 degrees.

A full-house 44 Magnum loading with the Norma 240-gr. soft point moved the muzzle 87 degrees.

A hefty hunting load behind a 265-gr. Hornady soft point displayed the most recoil, lifting the 44 Magnum muzzle 100 degrees.

not in superficial surface wounds or dust kicked up beyond the target. Animals of different size and toughness of sinew and bone, present differing resistance to bullets. That's why one type of bullet construction or one weight of bullet in a given caliber cannot be used to best advantage for hunting every type of game. In general, light, fast-expanding bullets at high velocity work best on small game, these offering little resistance, and heavy bullets of tougher construction are best for large animals that require deeper penetration in a more resistant mass.

Ballistics charts do not reflect a true measure of stopping power of any given cartridge/bullet/velocity combination. In his Textbook of Pistols & Revolvers, the late noted arms authority, General Julian S. Hatcher, detailed means of calculating the probable stopping effect of a given combination. The "Hatcher Scale" has been analyzed, adopted, adapted, quoted, and misquoted, but to my knowledge, no one has ever before noticed that Hatcher's math left something to be desired!

Hatcher's concepts were valid, being based upon extensive testing carried out by Colonel T. Thompson, Ordnance Department (inventor of the Thompson Sub-machine Gun), and Colonel Louis A. La Garde, for the U.S. Army, using cadavers and live cattle to analyze tissue disruption and effects upon the nervous system of various calibers and bullet shapes at differing velocities. Hatcher's comparisons have been largely upheld by actual field experience accrued through the years since his book was published in 1935. Hatcher's formula for calculating "Relative Stopping Power" results in figures

that *do not* represent feet or pounds, or any other meaningful unit of measure. They are nothing more than a comparison of one cartridge against another. Taken out of context, they have no meaning. Perhaps that's why no one ever spotted the flaw in his calculations.

Hatcher Factors

Hatcher injected a constant of his own, a "Factor for bullet shape and material," using an ordinary round-nosed lead bullet, such as that found in the factory-loaded 38 Special, as the starting point, equalling number 1000. Fully jacketed bullets such as the 45 ACP were rated as 900. Flat-nosed, sharp-shouldered Keith-types were rated at 1250. In my accompanying charts, I have added one more factor, 1500, to represent modern jacketed hollow point bullets with their explosive expansion

and resultant extensive tissue disruption. Hatcher didn't live to see these bullets. If he had, he would have left a factor. As it was, I was forced to extrapolate, based upon my own observations of the relative disruptive effects of Keith-style bullets compared to the new Super Vel type hollow pointed bullets, in such mediums as clay and wood, and in the field on various animals.

Beyond that, I simply followed Hatcher's original formulas (without the flaw) to arrive at "Stopping Power," based first upon energy, then upon momentum. After proposing the formula based upon energy in his early writings, Hatcher later changed to using momentum as the basis, to bring down what he came to believe were inordinately high ratings of small bullets at high velocity on the original scale. He wrote, on page 433, "The use of momentum instead of energy in the formula would give a

Chuck Ransom (left) supervises as author loads a S&W 41 Magnum mounted in the excellent pistol rest invented and marketed by Ransom. Machine rest testing of the various calibers indicated all shot better than an above-average marksman could hold in the field.

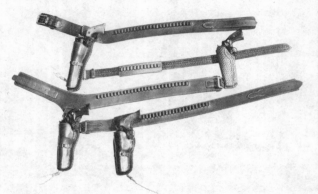

The sidearm is handy afield because it can be carried holstered, out of the way, yet always at hand when needed. Here are some of author's holster rigs, all holding 44 Magnums.

truer picture of the relative power of different bullets to put into motion the particles with which they come into contact. Moreover, it would give the factor of bullet weight more importance."

Hatcher's formulas, simply stated, were: Stopping power equals, *energy* times the frontal sectional area of the bullet in square inches, times the shape factor; and SP equals *momentum* times sectional area times the shape factor.

The chart printed herewith was calculated both ways. It can be seen that various cartridge/bullet/velocity combinations compare quite differently under the two systems. You can relate the *momentum* figures on my chart to those on page 435 of Hatcher's book, by multiplying his "Relative Stopping Power" figures by two. You will then have the correct figures according to his own formula. It appears that Hatcher arrived at his final figures by calculating backwards, using the erroneous formula, "If the energy and velocity of the bullet are known, the momentum is obtained by dividing the energy by the velocity," as noted in paragraph four, page 433, of his book. He could have arrived at the correct momentum by the back door, if he had divided the velocity into *two times* the kinetic energy. As it is, all of the "Relative Stopping Power" figures on the Hatcher Scale are actually half of what they should be.

Of course, Hatcher didn't have the benefit of an electronic computer, or a son such as my Mike, a physics major, to do all of the work!

The charts list several standard calibers along with the magnums to afford comparison. The contrasts are obvious. If you're really intent upon handgun hunting, get a Magnum! If you balk at the Magnum price tags, and an accurate 9mm or 45 ACP is on hand, you can make do with loaded ammo from Super Vel or appropriate reloads. Perhaps Lee Juras wasn't the first man to experiment with lightweight jacketed bullets in hand-

guns, but he was the first to make them commercially feasible. Jurras is handgunning's High Priest of High Velocity. He did for the holster-hunter what Roy Weatherby did for rifle nimrods. Jurras took handgun high velocity out of the garage and attic, and made it available across the dealer's counter, in the form of Super Vel cartridges.

Super Vel ammo loaded with rapid-expanding jacketed hollow point bullets has given the 9mm and 45 ACP marginal status as field guns. The 9mm Super Vel 90-gr. JHP at 1485 fps is adequate for coyotes and other predators out to about 50 yards, given *hits in vital zones only*. The 9mm won't bowl over a coyote with a bullet through the flanks like a 44 magnum will. The Super Vel 190-gr. JHP 45 ACP at 1060 fps stretches predator range to about 70 yards. Neither cartridge has any place in big game hunting.

Super Vel bullets are available to reloaders, along with similar offerings of Hornady, Sierra, and Speer, all of whom publish excellent loading manuals showing high velocity loadings for their jacketed bullets.

44 Special/45 Colt

If you're using a 44 Special or 45 Long Colt, you *must* reload to realize their potential as hunting sidearms.

Commercial loadings are useless in the field. The 44 Special barely accelerates to target velocity, with an accurate but ineffective bullet. The 45 Colt packs more foot pounds, but uses a bullet shaped as though it were deliberately designed to be as inefficient as possible, with rounded contour to slip through tissue without imparting appreciable energy in passage.

Half a century before the 44 Magnum saw labor pains, the 44 Special came from Russia with love. It was designed by a Russian technician, sent to Smith & Wesson by the Czar to supervise the making of 200,000 revolvers for his majesty. The original 246-gr. round-nose lead bullet remains unchanged to this day, although the original 26-gr. load of black powder, giving 780 fps, has given way to a smokeless powder load of about the same velocity.

Modern-day cases for the 44 Special are solid-head, and loading information in the manuals is based on those. I prefer the old balloon-head cases because they have about the same case capacity as the 44 Magnum. Admittedly, the thin-at-the-head cases fail sooner than the solid web variety, but if you retire them from heavy loads after about a half-dozen cycles, they will last indefinitely from then on if loaded light.

In 1948 Hercules Powder Company chronographed some loads for pioneer 44 Specialist Ray C. Thompson, using his 215-gr. gas-checked hollow point (Ideal mould 429215) ahead of 21 grains of 2400. Velocity was 1400 fps, pressure 25,000 psi. Ray killed deer and elk with his 44 Special before the Magnum was ever dreamed of!

Using the lighter 44 caliber jacketed bullets meant for the Magnum, the 44 Special can be made into a mean round, capable of taking

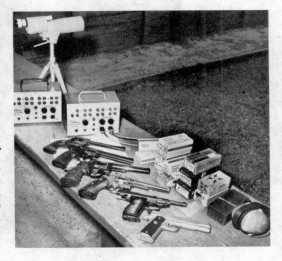

In testing for this article the author chronographed the Ruger 357 Blackhawk, the Colt 357 Python, the S&W 44 Magnum, the S&W 41 Magnum, the P-38, and a Colt Gold Cup 45 ACP, using a Telepacific chronograph, and factory ammo as well as reloads.

357 Magnum—Field Factor Chart
(All Bullets—Sectional Area = .100. Stopping Factor = 1500)

Bullet/grs.	MV/fps	Momentum	K.E.[1]	ST/Momentum[2]	ST/K. Energy[2]	Recoil/fp	Charge/grs.[3]
110 JHC Sierra	1550	.757	586.782	113.57	88.017	4.982	14.1 AL-7
125 JHC Sierra	1450	.805	583.535	120.73	87.350	5.415	12.7 AL-7
150 JHC Sierra	1300	.866	562.858	129.89	84.429	5.971	17.5 H-110
158 SP Sierra[4]	1200	.842	505.173	105.24	63.147	5.575	16.3 H-110
125 SP Speer[4]	1466	.814	596.484	101.72	74.560	5.536	20.0 H-110
110 HP Super V.	1550	.757	586.782	113.57	88.017	4.982	19.0 2400
125 HP Super V.	1450	.805	583.535	120.73	87.530	5.415	16.8 630-P
110 HP Hornady	1550	.757	586.782	113.57	88.017	4.982	18.7 630-P
125 HP Hornady	1400	.777	543.985	116.57	81.598	5.048	14.5 630-P
158 HP Hornady	1200	.842	505.173	126.29	75.776	5.575	14.8 2400
158 SP Rem.[4]	1425	.998	715.0	124.8	89.49	6.3	Fac.

[1]Kinetic energy. [2]Stopping power. [3]Powder weight, grains. [4]Stopping factor = 1250

41 Magnum—Field Factor Chart
(All Bullets—Sectional Area = .132. Stopping Factor = 1500)

Bullet/grs.	MV/fps	Momentum	K.E.[1]	ST/Momentum[2]	ST/K. Energy[2]	Recoil/fp	Charge/grs.[3]
170 HC Sierra	1550	1.170	906.845	231.68	179.555	10.161	23.3 630-P
210 HC Sierra	1400	1.305	913.894	258.50	189.951	11.936	21.7 630-P
210 HP Horn.	1400	1.305	913.894	258.50	180.951	11.936	19.5 630-P
210 SP Rem.[4]	1500	1.40	1050.0	231.0	173.50	12.70	Fac.

[1]Kinetic energy. [2]Stopping power. [3]Powder weight, grains. [4]Stopping factor = 1250

44 Special—Field Factor Chart
(All Bullets—Sectional Area = .144. Stopping Factor = 1500)

Bullet/grs.	MV/fps	Momentum	K.E.[1]	ST/Momentum[2]	ST/K. Energy[2]	Recoil/fp	Charge/grs.[3]
180 HC Sierra	1150	.919	528.554	198.552	114.168	7.310	22.3 H-110
240 HC Sierra	1100	1.172	644.789	253.226	139.274	11.192	16.3 2400
200 HP Horn.	1200	1.066	639.460	230.206	138.123	9.665	17.4 630-P
240 HP Horn.	1100	1.172	644.789	253.226	139.274	11.192	10.3 4756
180 HP Super V.	1150	.919	528.554	198.552	114.168	7.310	21.0 2400
225 HP Speer	1171	1.170	685.042	252.722	147.969	11.313	12.0 AL-7
240 SP Speer[4]	1104	1.177	649.487	211.789	116.908	11.273	13.0 N-1020

[1]Kinetic energy. [2]Stopping power. [3]Powder weight, grains. [4]Stopping factor = 1250

9mm Parabellum—Field Factor Chart
(All Bullets—Sectional Area = .099. Stopping Factor = 1500)

Bullet/grs.	MV/fps	Momentum	K.E.[1]	ST/Momentum[2]	ST/K. Energy[2]	Recoil/fp	Charge/grs.[3]
115 HP Horn.	1150	.587	337.687	87.21	50.146	3.183	4.5 230-P
125 HP Horn.	1050	.582	305.992	86.55	45.440	3.058	5.1 Unique
90 HP Super V.	1450	.580	420.145	86.06	62.392	3.371	7.8 Herco
90 HC Sierra	1450	.580	420.145	86.06	62.392	3.371	7½ Unique
115 HC Sierra	1350	.689	465.357	102.38	69.106	4.386	6.9 Herco

[1]Kinetic energy. [2]Stopping power. [3]Powder weight, grains.

44 Magnum—Field Factor Chart
(All Bullets—Sectional Area = .146. Stopping Factor = 1500)

Bullet/grs.	MV/fps	Momentum	K.E.[1]	ST/Momentum[2]	ST/K. Energy[2]	Recoil/fp	Charge/grs.[3]
180 HC Sierra	1650	1.319	1088.08	288.836	238.290	12.964	25.0 H-110
240 HC Sierra	1450	1.545	1120.387	338.434	245.365	16.550	22.7 2400
180 HP Super V.	1830	1.463	1338.429	320.345	293.116	15.947	Factory Loaded
180 SP Super V.[4]	1830	1.463	1338.429	266.955	244.263	15.947	Factory Loaded
200 HP Horn.	1400	1.243	870.376	272.303	190.612	11.197	23.5 2400
240 HP Horn.	1300	1.385	900.572	303.424	197.225	13.303	19.6 630-P
265 SP Horn.	1200	1.412	847.284	257.716	154.629	13.532	18.0 630-P
240 SP Rem.[4]	1470	1.565	1155.20	285.0	209.0	16.4	Fac.

[1]Kinetic energy. [2]Stopping power. [3]Powder weight, grains.

45 ACP—Field Factor Chart
(All Bullets—Sectional Area = .160. Stopping Factor = 1500)

Bullet/grs.	MV/fps	Momentum	K.E.[1]	ST/Momentum[2]	ST/K. Energy[2]	Recoil/fp	Charge/grs.[3]
185 HC Sierra	1100	.904	497.025	216.88	119.286	7.278	8.5 Unique
190 HP Super V.	1100	.928	510.458	222.74	122.510	7.621	10.0 Herco

[1]Kinetic energy. [2]Stopping power. [3]Powder weight, grains.

45 Long Colt—Field Factor Chart
(All Bullets—Sectional Area = .162. Stopping Factor = 1500)

Bullet/grs.	MV/fps	Momentum	K.E.[1]	ST/Momentum[2]	ST/K. Energy[2]	Recoil/fp	Charge/grs.[3]
185 HC Sierra	1200	.986	591.001	239.558	143.735	8.445	11.0 PB
190 HP Super V.	1200	1.012	607.487	246.032	147.619	8.843	12.5 Unique
185 HP Horn.	1200	.986	591.001	239.558	143.735	8.445	9.7 700-X
250 HP Horn.	1100	1.221	671.655	296.749	163.212	12.036	22.0 H-4227

[1]Kinetic energy. [2]Stopping power. [3]Powder weight, grains.

Ballistic Comparison Chart

	Bullet, dia.	Bullet, grs.	Bullet	Barrel, ins.	MV/fs.	ME, fp.	Load/grs.
9 mm	.355"	90	JHP	5	1450	420	7.8/Herco
357 Mag.	.359"	158	Lead	8⅜	1400	690	Fac.
41 Mag.	.410"	210	Lead	8⅜	1150	515	Fac.
41 Mag.	.410"	210	JSP	8⅜	1500	1049	Fac.
44 Spl.	.431"	200 Horn.	HP	6½	1200	639	17.4/630-P
44 Mag.	.430"	240	Lead	6½	1470	1150	Fac.
45 ACP	.4515"	190 Super V.	JHP	5	1100	510	10.0/Herco
45 LC	.452"	250	JHP	7½	1100	671	22.0/H-4227

most small to medium game animals. A long-barreled handgun, such as a Colt SA 7½-inch, makes the most of the velocity potential in this fine old round.

The 45 Long Colt boasts ample case capacity and bore size to qualify as a hunting handgun, when properly reloaded. However, the large case chambers into a thin-walled cylinder, always in danger of swelling with a too-heavy load. Experimenters have constructed single action 5-shot revolvers, thus placing the slot for the locking bolt between chambers rather than right over them, eliminating the weakest spot. Ruger could easily convert his Blackhawk into a "45 Magnum" by making it a 5-shooter. The Blackhawk frame is plenty strong enough for Magnum 45 loadings. Until that happy day, you can use your standard Blackhawk, Colt Peacemaker, or Colt New Service revolver, loaded with modern jacketed hollow point bullets traveling over 1000 fps, in complete safety.

Reloading the Magnums

Magnum shooters don't have to reload. A wide range of bullet weights and loads are available across the counter. The 357 Magnum can use the entire range of 38 Special ammo, from target wadcutters to Super Vel, plus Speer Shotshells, as well as 357 Super Vel 110-gr. JHP or JSP, and 137-gr. JSP. Conventional-weight jacketed ammo comes from Norma, Remington, and Winchester. The 41 Magnum is offered by Remington in a lead ball sub-load and jacketed hunting load. The 44 Magnum can use 44 Special ammo for target practice, in addition to Super Vel 180-gr. JHP or JSP, and Norma, Remington, Winchester full-weight, full-house loads.

However, reloading does offer some solid pluses. Besides saving many deflated dollars, reloading expands your horizon to include excellent bullets from Hornady, Sierra, and Speer, plus myriad moulds for cast bullets available from H&G, Lee, Lyman, Ohaus, and Saeco. Saeco's bullets are noted for superb accuracy, and their Keith-style shapes are field-feasible for predators big and small. The Saeco 45 Colt mould (290452) especially, presents maximum frontal area to provide a high degree of shock effect.

Space doesn't permit dwelling at length on reloading methods, except to say: use RCBS Precisioneered four-die sets, that neck-size tight without putting an unsightly shoulder near the case head, plus seating the bullet and crimping in separate dies. Use cast bullets sized at or near groove diameter with light loads for plinking and practice. They are cheaper and easier on the gun. In the field, use modern jacketed bullets of a weight commensurate with the size of the game being hunted. The loads listed are already maximum. *Don't improve* them by adding more powder!

With the help of my son Mike and Butch Miller, his boss at Advanced Kinetics, a Costa Mesa electronics firm, I chronographed the listed loads on my Telepacific Chronograph, and found that most clocked about as shown in the various reloading manuals. Some variations inevitably result from different components and guns.

Once settled upon caliber, your last decision will involve the finish on your hunting handgun. No one who heard them will ever forget the words of General George S. Patton in reply to a reporter's question about his "pearl-handled" revolvers. "These are ivory-handled," declared Patton. "Only a New Orleans pimp would carry pearl-handled pistols!" I used to feel about the same way about nickel-plated revolvers, until a friend sold me a used 44 Magnum with a nickeled finish. I discovered that the gun withstood neglect without rusting, and the bore was less given to metal fouling. The finish is shiny, and I would prefer a satin-nickel such as Colt now uses on their Commander. Another option is Teflon-S coating by Fluoro Tek Co., Inc., Anaheim, Cal. It is dark blue and free of bright shine, yet withstands immersion in sea water for a month without a sign of corrosion! Treated guns will operate in sub-zero temperatures without any lubrication. ●

Pistol and Revolver
BLUE DOT™
Handloading Data

Caliber	Bullet	Charge/grs.	MV	CUP*
357 Magnum	110 JHP	16.0	1968	39,300
	125 JSP	15.5	1815	38,700
	158 JHP	13.5	1568	37,000
	160 JSP	11.0	1380	37,000
41 Magnum	200 SJHP	14.6	1525	37,900
	210 SP	15.0	1530	37,900
	220 SJHP	14.3	1462	36,800
44 Magnum	225 SJHP	18.6	1575	37,700
	240 JSP	18.5	1523	36,600

*Copper units of pressure.

THE PAST TWO DECADES have probably witnessed more new commercially chambered cartridges introduced than in any other like period in the history of firearms. In a little over 20 years, starting in 1950 with the 222 Remington, at least 26 new cartridges have appeared, either made here or extensively sold in the U.S. Three of these, the 7x61 Sharpe & Hart, and the 308 and 358 Norma Magnums, though never loaded commercially or chambered for by a major U.S. company, have been imported or custom built in fair numbers. This, plus the general availability of Norma ammunition, makes them pretty popular with the American hunter.

Of these 26 cartridges, 15 have been in belted form. Add the 257, 270, 7mm, 300 and 375 Weatherby Magnums, plus that pair of oldtimers of British origin, the 300 and 375 H&H, and it's easy to see why loading the big cases is so popular. Also, of course, there are dozens of wildcats made from the basic 300-375 H&H case, as well as wildcats both up and down from the short belted cases that came along. Reloading magnum cases warrants special consideration, hence this article.

A few of these cartridges—the 224 Weatherby, the 6.5mm and 350 Remington Magnums—can't really be considered of magnum capacity because there are standard rimless cases that hold nearly as much; there are also other belted cases that have far more capacity than the last two. However, being belted, these cases have many of the same characteristics as the larger belted cases, and they create some of the same problems.

This brings up one of the most common and least-known problems in reloading belted cases. The situation it creates is often blamed on belted-case design, poor brass or sloppy full length sizing-die dimensions. Usually none of the trouble, though all but case-design can be. Some people feel that if it weren't for belted cases the trouble would never occur in the first place. That's a strong point, but we do have such cases, and there's nothing about them that understanding and knowledge can't cope with.

This problem consists of incipient or, infrequently, complete head separation or parting just forward of the web. The condition exists in many belted cases after the first firing of a factory or handload, but

is seldom recognized until it is almost complete. I have had a head separation so nearly complete—on firing a *factory* round—that a crack was visible almost completely around the case. If the chamber happens to be a little rough a complete separation and a stuck case body would be a result. This is not to say that the same thing can't happen with a rimless case, but here it is usually the fault of the chamber and not the case, assuming a new case. With the belted case it may be either or both.

Case and Chamber Fit

This all boils down to headspace. When using rimless cases that headspace on the shoulder (distance from bolt face to chamber shoulder), this distance has to be very close to a tight fit between cartridge and chamber or you may be in for trouble, either from excessive headspace and consequent head separation, or from a misfire. The latter is caused by the case driving forward under the impact of the firing pin on the primer, and the latter not detonating, or because the case is already forward by pressure of the spring-loaded ejectors found in most modern actions. Either can be disastrous under the right conditions.

With the belted case the headspacing is between the bolt face and the forward edge of the belt. Here is where the trouble originates. This need not be so if cases and chambers were dimensioned to also make near-contact at the shoulder, but this is where the fly dives into the soup. I am well aware that SAAMI (Sporting Arms & Ammunition Manufacturing Institute) has set up specifications that should take care of this situation if adhered to by both rifle and ammunition manufacturers. Regrettably, they are not.

Both the makers of rifles and cases, at times, lose sight of the

Loading

With few exceptions, big and small, differs —but those exceptions

by BOB HAGEL

trouble this condition can cause the reloader. It is, of course, rare for a full head-separation (or a partial one that shows up on the outside) to occur on the first firing, so they really don't have to worry much about factory-loaded ammo. But the case is often ringed inside to the point of reducing wall thickness at this point by more than half on the first firing as the body stretches forward to meet the shoulder.

There isn't one damn thing the reloader can do about this on the first firing, but he can do something to prevent it happening in future firing. One, he can neck size only with a neck-size die, which is usually not desirable for more than a couple of reloads when working at high pressures, or he can make certain that his die is not pushing the shoulder back or down in full length resizing. Normal full length resizing practice (the die base firmly against the shellholder) will not necessarily result in the correct shoulder-to-bolt-face distance. This situation occurs because the die-maker is hard pressed to know just how long his dies must be made, knowing as he does the variation found in belted chambers. About all he can do is make his dies to SAAMI specs, which have some tolerances, of course, and which in theory, at least, give the correct head-to shoulder dimension when the die base makes contact with

enough to prevent the case from being seated in the chamber without undue pressure. (Be sure that an over-long neck is not the cause of tight chambering.)

Adjusting the Sizing Die Correctly

The best way to set a belted-case die for correct headspace—or any other, for that matter—is to first thread it into the press only far enough to let the neck be resized part way down. Leave about 1/32"

between the resized portion of the neck and the shoulder. Now, if you try to chamber a cartridge so-sized, and it's one that has been fired at fairly high pressure, it may chamber hard (if it chambers easily use it that way until it does show resistance to chambering). If it chambers with some effort set the die down about ¼-turn in the press, then resize and try case again. The case will continue to chamber hard until the die is turned down enough to set the case shoulder back only enough to clear.

the Belted Magnums

the technique of handloading the belted magnums,
little from the methodology used with standard cases
are highly important. Hagel clears away the mists.

the shellholder. However, when your chamber is over-long in this dimension the result is that the shoulder of your fired case is pushed back in resizing if the die is set all the way down on the shellholder, and a head separation is inevitable if the case is loaded many times.

The answer would seem to lie in only partially resizing the case by adjusting the die to miss the shoulder far enough to make certain you did not set it back. This, however, will not work with big cases loaded to high pressures. When you resize in this fashion—almost full length—the expanded brass of the body is forced back to near-original outside diametral dimensions, thus fitting somewhat loosely into a standard-dimension chamber. But some of the brass is forced *forward* instead of inward, which pushes the shoulder forward

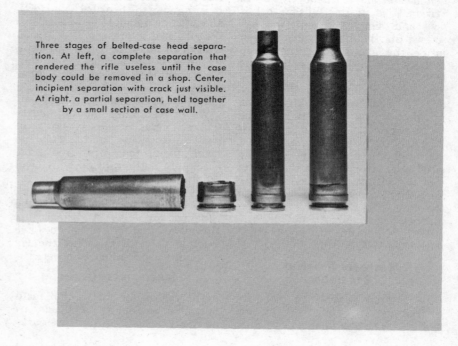

Three stages of belted-case head separation. At left, a complete separation that rendered the rifle useless until the case body could be removed in a shop. Center, incipient separation with crack just visible. At right, a partial separation, held together by a small section of case wall.

Belted cases are head-spaced on the belt (distance from forward edge of belt to bolt face), but chamber length, from bolt face to shoulder, is often longer than that dimension on new unfired cartridges. On firing this allows the case to stretch to fill the chamber, causing the start of head separation in such over-long cases. A close look at these specimens shows that the shoulders of both fired cases are pushed forward a great deal more than those of the original factory cartridge. Both cartridges were fired in new rifles, the rifles and ammo furnished at the same time for test and evaluation.

These two cartridges, the 7mm Weatherby Magnum (left) and the 7mm Remington Magnum, are almost identical in powder capacity, yet the Weatherby can be loaded with several more grains of the same powder with same bullet than can the Remington. This is due to the free-bore chambering of Weatherby rifles, not the cartridge, which acts in two ways: it reduces initial pressure by allowing friction-free bullet travel as speed builds up. It also allows seating bullets farther forward, which increases powder capacity of the case—if magazine length permits. The extra powder increases velocity but pressure levels remain the same.

At this stage, if you look closely you'll see lubricant on the case shoulder, just before the case shows a free fit in the chamber. I like to back the die up or out a small amount, after the case fits freely, so I can just feel contact when the bolt is fully closed. With such a die adjustment you now have the cartridge headspaced both on the belt and on the shoulder, *as it should be*, and there will be no further stretching of the body to cause a head separation—assuming you keep that die so-adjusted.

(A shortcut alternative to this somewhat tedious trial-and-error technique is to use the adjustable belted-case gauge made by L. E. Wilson. Use of the Wilson tool is fast and simple—loosen two setscrews that hold a movable section inside the gauge body, then drop a fired [not resized] case into the tool. Then, making sure that the case base is flush with the gauge base [or flush with the higher step in the stepped type], tighten the two setscrews. The gauge is now adjusted for *your* rifle. Next, adjust your full length sizing die until the sized case, dropped into the Wilson tool, lies with its head about halfway between the upper and lower steps of the gauge. The same tool checks overall case length as well, and clear instructions in its dual use are included with each Wilson gauge.   J.T.A)

Tests for Incipient Separation

It is often possible to place an unfired and fired round side by side and see, with the unaided eye, that the shoulder is pushed forward on the fired round (see photo). If this is so it is almost certain that the case has started the thin interior groove or ring, just forward of the web, that leads to a head separation. There are two methods of checking this incipient separation. One, section the case from end to end and take a look, but this takes time and is good only for that one ruined case. Two, bend a stiff wire or small rod so that a short 90° hook is formed at one end, then bring that end to a point with a stone or file. Slip it into the case as far as it will go, pressing the hook against the side of the case and start to withdraw it. By moving the hook back and forth about ¼" you should be able to feel the ring if it is present. It is a good plan to do this with belted cases you intend to resize and use, cases that have been fired, perhaps, in another rifle you know nothing about. It can prevent a head separation.

We've mentioned high pressures several times while speaking of head separations, but it should be made plain that pressures have absolutely nothing to do with head separations if headspace (cartridge shoulder-to-head length) is correct. I mention it only because of the resizing problems it brings up. However, high pressures do have a lot to do with reloading the big magnum cases, belted or otherwise.

Magnum Pressures

The reason for this is that factory ammo, as well as handloads, are normally loaded to high pressures.

While this is as it should be, it can give the unwary reloader certain problems that he would not encounter when loading at lower pressure levels. It has often been asked why a magnum cartridge should be loaded to high pressures. There are a number of good reasons, but paramount to all others is the reason you bought a mag-

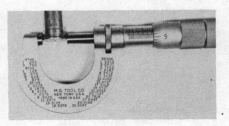

If the web section of a belted case is thin and does not completely cover the belt, the forward edge will start to expand before maximum pressure is reached. If expansion seems premature check rear edge to make sure the head is actually expanding. With mike set to cover belt (lower photo) reading is .532". The upper photo shows mike set on rear edge of belt, the reading now .531", or .001" less. Both photos of same case. Original belt diameter of unfired case was .530".

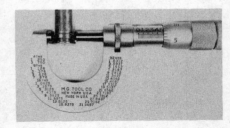

This photo shows a method of determining if a case has started the inside ring or circular depression than can lead to head separation. The bent wire's sharpened point is moved back and forth from the web for ¼" or so, the point pressed against the case wall. If the ring is there you should be able to feel it.

num in the first place. If you hadn't wanted extra power in that caliber you would have bought a standard cartridge instead—and you are not going to get that extra punch, velocity and flatness of trajectory unless you load it to its full potential, which means high pressure. This does not mean that you are necessarily working at higher pressures than with standard cartridges—the 270 Winchester has one of the highest factory-loaded pressure levels of any cartridge at 54,000-55,000 psi—but it does mean that to realize the potential of the big case you will be working constantly with this kind of pressure. The only real difference is that in the same calibers the big case burns more of slower-burning powders, with a little longer pressure peak, to obtain more velocity than the smaller case with the same bullet at similar pressures.

Another way of looking at it is that you are normally working with maximum pressures for the rifle and cartridge case you are using. "Maximum" here does not mean all that the rifle will stand without coming apart, but rather all that you can get out of it, with the case and bullet you're using, and still stay on the safe side if some variable should raise pressure a bit. Neither does it mean that the maximum safe pressure for the belted case you're using in that rifle is what is normally considered as maximum for another cartridge. Few magnum cartridges are held down in pressure because of old actions floating around that are

chambered for them, as with such other cartridges as the 7x57 Mauser and even the 30-06. But the kind of brass you use can make a lot of difference in the pressure it will stand and still remain usable and safe. Different makes of cases have different interior design, aspects that makes them differ in weight, wall thickness and web thickness. They are also made of brass that has different hardness in the head section where it counts, as well as different grain structure. These things are too complicated to go into here, but they have a decided bearing on how much pressure the case will stand without giving way. This in turn makes a load that is perfectly safe in one make of case prohibitive in another, and below maximum in still another.

As an example, I recently ran some tests with several rifles chambered for the 7mm Rem. Mag. cartridge. I found that with one brand of cases I could use 2 grains more of H-4831—with the same bullet and primer—than I could with another brand, yet both cases were of almost identical weight. The cases were checked to the same belt expansion, and the only differences that could be seen were in primer flatness and firing-pin indentation. Primers remained

equally tight in both cases. Velocity was 90 fps higher in the case handling the 2 extra grains of powder. While the one case brand continued to handle the charge round after round with no trouble whatever; the other make, while not giving way or blowing a primer, expanded the belt on the first firing by .002", and successive firings continued to expand it until the primer pocket loosened too much for use on the third to fourth firings.

Checking Head Expansion

In checking belted case head expansion with a micrometer caliper I prefer to use the belt instead of the rim. Many reloaders that go this far in pressure testing seem to prefer the rim system, but I don't for several reasons. The rim is nearly always rough, which makes it very difficult to get the same reading twice even on an indexed case, unless it is polished or turned. The rim is also often burred by the extractor in further use between shots. It also takes more pressure to give a significant reading on the rim than on the belt, therefore you have more warning of excessive pressures building up when measuring the belt. When you do get rim expan-

Different brands of cases have different interior head design and construction, the result webs of different thicknesses. Note that the center case has a thin web, one that does not support the belt forward while the other two cover it fully. As high pressures are reached the forward end of the belt on the center case may expand prematurely and give false readings if miked at that point.

sion you have to back off that much more, so why go up there in the first place? Don't worry about the belt so filling the chamber after a little expansion so that you can't tell what you're doing; there is enough clearance in most chambers to allow from .009″ to .014″ expansion, depending on the belt diameter of the original case! Also the primer will blow and the bolt freeze up long before this point is reached.

Some factory ammo or a good stiff home-brewed load will expand the belt .001″-.0015″ on the initial firing, but the same load fired in the same case will give no further expansion. You will be able to increase the load somewhat—the amount depends on the bore, bullet weight and powder used—before expansion again takes place. The second time the belt starts to expand enough for you to be sure of it, say .0002″-.0005″, back off at least a grain, in some cases two, for a maximum but safe load in that cartridge for that rifle.

In measuring the belt to detect a rise in pressure, certain case-wall dimensions may lead to a false impression of pressure. As mentioned earlier, some cases have thin webs, which come only part way up (inside) the belt, while others with thick webs fully cover the belt. If the case has this thin web the forward edge of the belt will expand before the rest of it does. If the belt seems to be ex-

panding with what would be considered mild loads, take a reading on the rear of the belt and compare the two. If the belt rear is still normal go on up until it shows expansion, then back off. Usually, however, the taper of the web into the case body will not allow the forward section to expand enough to cause any trouble. The photo illustrates how to take both measurements. Incidentally, the rim of the belted case is nearly always enough smaller than the belt so this is possible with a standard flat-surface mike. Checking for high pressures by visual inspection of primers is not too reliable unless you have checked primer appearance and the rifle against head expansion, so that you're familiar with the comparison. Some primer makes are softer than others, therefore show flatness and/or cratering at less pressure. Also, a small or sharp-pointed firing pin, a larger than normal firing-pin hole in the bolt face, or a weak spring, will cause cratering (extruding of primer metal into the firing-pin hole) or a pierced primer at lower pressure than normal. On the other hand, very hard primers may resist these things when pressures are extremely high.

Powder Selection

The powders to be used in the big belted cases are no different than powders used in cases of standard size, except that they are

Cartridge cases, sometimes, are not only sloppy dimensionally, they're occasionally imperfect. In upper photo a normal 7mm Remington Magnum case (left) is compared to one that lacked a belt. Fortunately the shoulder-to-head dimension was close enough so that headspace was nearly correct. In lower photo the 264 Winchester Magnum case at right is normal but other case has much heavier rim and wider extraction groove. It would not fit into the shellholder but chambered and fired with no trouble. Both of these odd cases were from factory-loaded ammunition.

nearly always slower in burning rate. Many such powders—4350, 4831, Norma 204 and 205—are also the most efficient in standard cases in calibers from 243 to 30, with the heavier bullet weights, as are such ball powders as Olin 760 and 780 BR and H-450. But these powders prove to be the best for even the lightest bullets in the same calibers in the big cases. In such cases as the over-bore 264 Winchester Magnum and wildcats of even larger capacity, powders of the very slowest burning rates deliver the highest velocity, and often the best accuracy. The slowest, 5010, is no

Not all of the big belted cases require the slowest-burning powders, even with the heaviest bullets. From left: the 164 Win. requires the very slowest available powders to deliver the highest velocity with 120/160-gr. bullets. The 300 Win., with 180/220-gr. bullets, does best with powders that are just a little faster. The 338 Win. will use the same powders as the 300 for 250-300-gr. bullets. But the big 458 Win. does much better with fairly fast powders behind its 500-gr. slug. Bullets from left, 140-gr. Speer, 200-gr. Nosler, 250-gr. Nosler, and 500-gr. Hornady.

longer available, I think, but H-570, a log type powder, and H-870 of ball type, are available and give outstanding performance both in velocity and accuracy with the heaviest bullets in large capacity cases of small caliber. If the case is large enough and the bullet heavy enough in relation to the bore, these are the powders to use. However, few cases have this kind of propellant capacity when bullet diameters pass 30 caliber. You simply can't squeeze enough powder into the case to build up maximum pressure. I tried H-870 in the 340 Weatherby case behind the 250-gr. Nosler bullet, but even with a charge of 98 grains, which was all that could be crammed in, despite bullet seating with extreme compression, pressure was mild and velocity was only 2729 from a 24" barrel. An 86-gr. charge of 4831 or 83 grains of Norma 205 gave 2925 with the same bullet. Both of these very slow powder numbers give higher velocity in the 264 Winchester, with all bullets from 120 grains up, than any other powder.

On average, magnum cartridges of up to 338-caliber will give the highest velocity, for all bullet weights, with 4831, 4350 and Norma 205. Many of these cartridges will deliver the highest velocity and the best accuracy, with most bullet weights, with Norma 205. One word of warning, though, where Norma 205 is concerned: *Don't* assume that you can use a certain amount of Norma 205, either above or below the charge you use of 4831 or 4350. You'll find that Norma 205 charges will vary by a few grains from the other two with the use of various case capacities, bullet diameters and bullet weights. However, regardless of the amount of N205 you're able to use in any case behind a given bullet weight, velocity will normally be slightly higher than with other powders.

One other advantage in using Norma 205, under certain conditions, is its high density. It is possible to use heavier charges without as much compression under long bullets. You often run out of room with 4831 even in big cases with today's deep-seated bullets in cartridges designed to work through short or standard actions. Here the dense Norma powder is at its best because you just can't seat a bullet over enough of the larger-grain powders, propellants that are slow enough to be effective with that bullet weight in that case.

Primers are not always a reliable indication of high pressures. To judge pressure by visual inspection of primers one must be familiar with the primer he is using and the rifle he's using it in. This photo shows that while the primer at right is pierced and quite flat, the one at left is only cratered. However, a close look at the two case heads show that the one at left carries the mark of the plunger-type ejector (over the numeral 2) where brass was forced into the hole in the bolt face. This indicates much higher pressure than the other case experienced. This situation can be caused by a soft primer, a weak firing-pin spring or a small firing pin in a large hole in the bolt.

This would seem to indicate that some of the ball powders would be the answer in the big cases with heavy bullets. However, with the exception of H-870, which is useful in only the very largest cases with the heaviest bullets, I've never been able to attain top velocity and pressure levels without running into erratic pressures. I don't like to use powders that become erratic when fired under maximum working pressures. It can get you a basket full of trouble when some slight variations take place. Conversely, if you hold pressures down to where uniform results are obtained with such ball powders, velocity will be less than you expect from the big case.

Compressed Loads

I receive many letters asking about the use of heavily-compressed loads. Many reloaders seem to think that if they compress a powder charge they are laying themselves open to all kinds of hazards, and that accuracy will suffer. This is far from true. There is, of course, a limit as to the amount any charge of powder should be compressed, and I don't like compressed charges of the faster powders in small cases, but compressed charges of slow powders are normally just as accurate as those not compressed—more accurate if there is too much air space otherwise. Also, the most uniform loads I've ever chronographed have been heavily compressed!

Which brings up another point in favor of high velocity loads that also develop high pressures. These loads are often the most accurate ones in the big cases. Many case-powder-bullet combinations give the best accuracy at the highest permissible pressures levels. Another thing to remember is this—many of the big cases that fire long, heavy bullets at high velocity may give only fair accuracy at 100 yards, but from 200 yards on out accuracy may be truly excellent. What happens is that the long bullet still has some yaw or wobble at 100 yards, not having settled into a true spin around its axis and the line of flight.

Last but not least: If you want to use and load a magnum cartridge don't buy a magnum rifle with a short barrel just because it will be light and handy. If you do you're defeating the purpose you bought the rifle for, at least in part. Here's why: First, you'll be using large doses of slow powders that have a long pressure peak, and these require a fairly long barrel to attain the best velocity. Second, a too-short barrel with a big cartridge will cause terrific muzzle blast. Third, muzzle jump, recoil and torque will be increased greatly. None of the big magnum cartridges are ideal with barrels of less than 24". If you feel you have to have a rifle with an 18-22" tube, better stick to a standard cartridge; you'll get almost as much out of it, and you'll find it a lot pleasanter to shoot. ●

The 257 Rides Again!

A shooting review of the Ruger Model 77 as chambered for the 257 Roberts. The bouquets outnumber the brickbats, the author finds, in assessing this limited-issue rifle.

by DON HUSER

AT ONE TIME or another I've owned a 25-3000, two 257s, a 25/06 and various other small bores, including two 243s, a 244 and a 6mm Remington, plus scads of centerfire 22s. These last included the 22 Hornet, the 22/250 and that old speed demon, the 220 Swift, but nothing holds my interest as does the old 257 Roberts. Some of you oldtimers may wonder why I don't call this the 257 Remington Roberts. Tis plumb simple—with all due respect to Remington, they haven't been very kind to the 257 in years past or now either, for that matter.

I don't and won't argue with the fact that when the 257 was first put on the market the powders then available wouldn't do justice to what the 257 is capable of today. 3031 was *the* powder in those days and, while this may be a fine powder for the 87-gr. bullets or those of lesser weight, it leaves a lot to be desired with 100-gr. and heavier bullets. For these weights 4320, 4350, 4831 and N-205 gives a much better pressure/velocity ratio. They make the 257 shine. When better powders did become available the 257 wasn't updated, as it should have been, to give higher velocity with safe pressures. Even today DuPont loading data is held to 45,000 psi in the

257. This is rather surprising in that the 257 was never offered on a weak action. Another fault is that all factory ammunition has deep-seated bullets, and all factory rifles have short throats. Deep seating of bullets intrudes on the powder capacity, which isn't any aid to increased velocity. When the 257 was introduced there wasn't any reason for such deep bullet seating, for factory rifles had actions long enough for shallower seating. In some rifles it's a simple matter to increase magazine length, but in others this is almost a major operation; lengthening the throat, however, is something most gunsmiths can easily do. It is a little odd that while Remington introduced the 257, they now have but one loading, the rather mild 117-gr. Winchester-Western, bless their hearts, have the 87-, 100- and 117-gr. weights available.

Wanted—Winchester 257

From what has been written so far you might assume that I'm in the pay of Winchester. Tain't so! I'm a working type gunbug like most of you and, at present, I own three Remingtons but nary a Winchester. However, if Winchester would like to do some-

thing about this, a Model 70 in 257, with a long throat and magazine, would be greatly appreciated.

While domestic production of the 257 died with the pre-'64 Model 70 and 722 Remingtons, a good second-hand 257 in either of these models can still be found. Be prepared to pay a slight premium, though, as the 257 is a popular cartridge among gunbugs.

The 257 was also chambered in Remington's slide action centerfire, but accuracy left a little something to be desired. If memory serves me correctly Browning-FN also offered the 257 in their bolt action rifles.

What really killed the 257 (and also the 250/3000, which has recently been re-introduced by Savage in their Model 99) was the introduction of the 243 Winchester and 244 Remington. These "new" 6mm cartridges were touted as being vastly superior to the 257 and 250/3000. That's correct, too, as there is no way you can compare an underloaded cartridge with one that is loaded to higher pressure levels and expect both to perform as equals. This is a loaded deck anyway you look at it. But reloading the 257 with proper powders, plus using a rifle with a longer throat and magazine, makes a different cartridge out of the 257 Roberts.

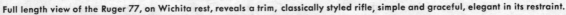
Full length view of the Ruger 77, on Wichita rest, reveals a trim, classically styled rifle, simple and graceful, elegant in its restraint.

New Ruger 7x57

Recently Ruger announced that they would have a short production run of their Model 77 bolt rifle in 7x57mm and, later on, would also run off a batch of 257s. When this bit of information filtered down to the boondocks of Missouri, no time was lost in placing an order for a 257. Delivery took a few months but the wait was worth it.

While I've owned several Ruger handguns, this was my first Ruger rifle. Up to this time the only Ruger rifles I had seen and handled were in dealer displays, so the first thing was to give the new Ruger 257 a good going over. The genuine walnut stock is rather plain grained, with little figure, but the grain was straight as a die, and I'll take a straight-grained stock any day of the week to one that has figured but crooked grain.

The stock has a dull oil finish, which I also prefer to these modern day high-gloss plastic finishes. At least the oil finish is easily re-finished when normal use brings about scratches and stains. The wood pores are well filled, which can't always be said for the plastic-finished stocks of most gunmakers. If you prefer a slicker finish there isn't any reason why a few coats of G-B Linspeed or Tru Oil can't quickly and easily do the job.

The stock is hand checkered at both fore-end and grip; nothing fancy, but generous and well done in borderless design, with no overruns. In recent months another gunmaker has run an ad showing the checkering of one of their higher priced rifles, but the checkering of the Ruger, in my opinion, shows higher workmanship.

The barrel is free floated except for an area about two inches at the tip of the fore-end, which has a two-point bearing surface. More of this later on. The metal parts have a nice polish and blue. Though not equal to the high polish of a SAKO, the cost between the two makes also happens to be a little different. The trigger guard and floorplate are alloy castings. I'd have preferred steel but these are available, at least according to the parts list. I understand these cannot be ordered on a rifle but must be ordered separately.

Studs are mounted for quick-detachable sling swivels. This is something that should be standard issue on all factory rifles. The amateur gunsmith can and frequently does ruin a good stock in trying to install sling swivels. The Ruger 77 comes with a solid rubber pad, red in color. Why

Close up of the good grip checkering on the 257 Ruger 77. Note new bolt knob and form, short extension of pistol grip and correct comb-nose fluting.

Ruger 77 rifle has top-tang safety, Mauser-type bolt release.

Bottom view of Ruger 77 shows trigger adjustment screw, quick release button for floorplate, new bolt knob.

are red pads so popular? Brown or walnut color would seem to be a better choice.

Weight of the rifle as it came from the box is 8 pounds 2 ounces, rather heavier than the 7 pounds listed for regular M77 Rugers. No doubt this weight difference is due to a rather heavy looking barrel, which in my book is a plus factor. I'm not a lover of lightweight rifles, even though my long, lanky frame is better suited to them. The receiver of this 257 (and of other recent M77 rifles) has a rounded contour, and is tapped for popular scope mounts. The receiver is *not* machined for the clamp-type Ruger mounts. My 257 came with open sights, front and rear, but it may be had without them. This latest receiver allows the owner to choose his mount not only as to make but also as to height. In ordering a scope mount ask for the Remington 700 long-action mount, which is the one for a proper fit. The bolt handle has been redesigned, too, which is to the good. The first M77 bolt handles were as crooked as a dog's hind laig.

The bright follower appears to be made of stainless steel, a material rapidly becoming popular for this use. The Ruger adjustable trigger can stand a lot of work. As it came from the box it would lift 5¾ pounds or more, but this happened to be the limit of my weights. By adjusting the screw in the trigger it was possible to get this down to just under 5 pounds. This was still too heavy for my liking so the gun was shipped off to a gunsmith in Montana who is a whiz on triggers and any other gunwork. Unfortunately, having as much business as he now wants he shall have to remain among the unknown. When the rifle came back the trigger was as it should have been in the first place, no creep or backlash and with a nice crisp letoff. It is useless to try and test loads in a rifle with a hard creepy pull, and I prefer my pulls to be around two pounds, both for target and field use. This might well be too light for many hunters, though, with 3 pounds or so better for field use.

Components were no problem, for already on hand were 40 new Western unprimed cases, a wide variety of bullets and powders along with a set of RCBS dies. Over the years, after using just about every make of loading dies and/or tools, I've standardized on RCBS as being top quality everytime, something I can't say about some other makes. About the only pieces of loading equipment I own not made by RCBS are an old, old Redding scale and a Forster case trimmer. Too, no one is so anxious to please as are the crew at RCBS.

Load Preparations

First chores were to run the 40 new cases through the full length size die to straighten the case mouths, then trim them .010″ shorter than maximum length and chamber. Next, 5 cases were loaded with different powders and bullets, the loads fairly stiff because I wanted to see what the

chamber looked like from these fired cases. None of the loads showed the least signs of pressure but they did show that the chamber was a trifle large—shaped somewhat like a goose egg would be closer to the truth! One trouble did develop—cases fired in my other 257 wouldn't chamber in the Ruger. These loads had been neck sized only after firing. A quick check with a No-Go headspace gauge showed that the Ruger chamber was on the minimum side. I'd much rather have had a chamber with a little looser

headspace instead of that out-of-round rear end, but you can't seem to have everything. On the other hand large chambers aren't unknown in factory chambered 257s, for there seems to be a lot of room between the minimum chamber and the maximum cartridge. Just another place where the 257 was shortchanged.

One other side effect of the tight headspace shows up in re-sizing. If too little case lube is used cases will be a very tight fit in the chamber. So for field use all cases are first run through the chamber to be on the safe side. This could be easily cured by sending three or more fired cases to RCBS and having a size die cut for this chamber.

But before any accuracy shooting could be done a scope had to be

mounted and the choice fell to the Leupold 3-9x with Duplex reticle. This new Leupold has an adjustable objective head so that parallax can be eliminated, a must for serious test work. Most fixed power scopes are factory adjusted for parallax at 125 to 150 yards, so shooting at ranges other than these can and will introduce sighting errors. This isn't really harmful as far as large game is concerned, but a no-no for test shooting and shooting at the smaller varmints. Leupold scopes are top notch, sharp as

Bullets used in testfiring the 257 Roberts.

a tack, with windage and elevation adjustments that are truly precise. Workmanship is of top quality throughout. Of 8 scopes now owned, four are Leupold. Just before I mounted this scope on the Ruger I had fired a 5-shot group with this same scope on a Remington 788 in 22/250, each shot made with a *different* power setting. The group measured .72″ and, considering that at 3x the aiming square was almost covered up by the reticle, I was impressed. This is one variable where there isn't any shift in impact when the power is changed. As this scope already carried Redfield Jr. rings in medium height, a Redfield Jr. base was used on the Ruger 257.

While I'm talking about scopes and mounts, one other thing should be

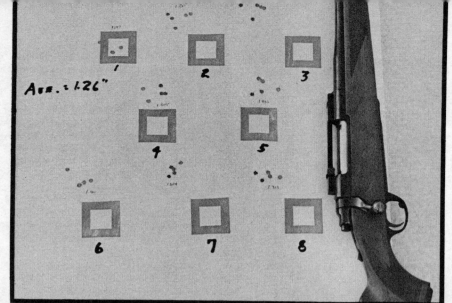

Average 100-yard accuracy of 8 groups, with four different loads, was 1.26".

mentioned—use the mount, where possible, to adjust the scope for lateral center. With very few exceptions, mostly in the photo reproduction field, optics are sharpest in the center, with a falling off of sharpness as you move away from the center of view. Also variable power scopes, because of their construction, have a much smaller range of adjustments. The Redfield Jr. windage adjustments were used to center the reticle, and it took only 2 minutes of elevation to center the group 1" high at 100 yards. This speaks highly of the machining of the receiver contour and the base mount. It isn't the least bit unusual to run out of adjustments in non-adjustable mounts, especially when these are teamed with a variable power scope with scanty internal adjustment. Adjustable mounts may cost a little more, but in the long run they can easily be worth the difference.

Accuracy Tests

First load used for accuracy tests was an old favorite—44.0 grains of 4064 and the Sierra 75-gr. hollow points, with Alcan large rifle primers as the sparkplugs. Only this one load was taken to the range for the first firing test, and these gave very good results. The first two shots, after sighting in, were rather wide but the next three were all touching. The rifle was allowed to cool and the next group of 5 shots measured slightly less than .72", which insn't at all bad for a varmint load.

As mentioned earlier the fore-end has a two-point bearing surface with the barrel. Before any firing was done the action was raised so that the barrel was free floating, for over the years I've had better accuracy with such barrels. On the other hand, I've never

liked or owned any whippy, lightweight barrels; on those I've shot a barrel bedding contact has been an accuracy help at times.

On the next trip to the range 87-, 90- and 100-gr. bullets were tried, and groups with all weights were on the order of 2". The action shims were removed but accuracy was no better. Finally the fore-end bearing points were removed with a fine rasp. Still no help. Then one to three shims were tried under the barrel but this wasn't any help either.

It was noticed during testing that the barrel fouled rather heavily. When the barrel was left overnight filled with Hoppe's the first clean patch through the barrel the next day showed only a grayish color; apparently the Hoppe's had cleaned out the fouling. Close examination of the bore at the muzzle showed numerous machine marks. It was found that by keeping the barrel as clean as possible accuracy was improved. Average with all loads was on the order of 1¼ to 1½ inches. While this is sufficient accuracy for large game, and such

larger varmints as coyotes and foxes, this is a little large for crows and groundhogs—providing the Fish & Wildlife Service allows us to shoot crows! No bullets heavier than 100 grains were used because of the short throat in the Ruger; while I have complained about this it really isn't all that bad, for the powder capacity of the 257 is such that weights of 100 grains and lighter are a better choice. For bullets of 100 grains or more the larger 25's, such as the 25/06, are much better suited.

My best loads are listed below:

The Ruger 257 isn't perfect, what with a trigger that needs to be redesigned or at least more attention paid to it before leaving the factory. Perhaps one of our trigger makers can be induced to make a replacement trigger if enough Ruger owners write.* The barrel smoothness and chambering could also be improved upon. But despite its faults, I like mine and Bill Ruger and his gang should be commended for having the guts to bring out a rifle chambered for two cartridges—the 257 and the 7x57—that have been considered moribund, if not dead, by our other gunmakers. Happily, his gamble paid off, too, for he's sold all that were made, some several thousands of them. ●

---

*Late in 1972 Canjar began making triggers for the Ruger 77 bolt action rifle (as well as for the Ruger Single Shots) in single set and standard types. I can attest that these are excellent trigger designs, having fitted one of the set styles to a 7x57 Ruger 77. JTA

Best 257 Loads

Bullet/grs.	Powder/grs.	MV/fps
Sierra 75 HP	4064/44	3485
Sierra 87	4320/44	3370
Hornady 87	H-380/47	3365
Sierra 90 BTHP	4350/47	3241
Sierra 100	4831/51	3157
Speer 100 HP	N-205/51	3228

Powders used in M77-257 test included N-205, H414, H335, 3031, 3895, 4350 and 4320.

This 22 Long Rifle automatic target pistol is among the most sophisticated produced in Europe in recent years. The new pistol is made in France by the Manufacture d'Armes des Pyrenees Francaises, in Hendaye, near the Spanish border, founded in 1923 by Mr. Joseph Uria.

Early production was devoted to police and pocket auto pistols, but the company soon began to design original sporting arms, first for the French market and then, when new models were fully developed, for export.

In 1937, Unique created the first French-made 22 LR selfloading rifle which, after several modifications, became the Model X-51. One of the most expensive guns of the world in its class, it is currently considered by some as the best selfloader on the international market.

In 1948 Unique made a 22 LR version of their Rr Police Model, this time the first French-made 22 LR auto pistol.

This design, improved over the years, evolved into the D line of popular plinkers once sold in the U.S. by Firearms International. Other models followed; among them a full line of excellent bolt action rifles made for target shooting and hunting.

UNIQUE D.E.S. '69

This modern 22 match pistol, made by the Manufacture d'Armes des Pyrenees in France, is performing excellently in competition. Our European editor tells about it.

by RAYMOND CARANTA

However, Unique management was not satisfied with their functional but cheap automatic pistols. Too, the pride of the skilled Basque craftsmen asked for more—they knew they could build top class target pistols and, in spite of strong international competition, they wanted to enter the game *pour l'honneur*.

The recent introduction of the "Standard Pistol" event by the "Union Internationale de Tir" (U.I.T. —International Shooting Union) gave them the opportunity they were looking for. This match, similar to the N.R.A. "Small Bore Pistol Shooting," calls for the shooting of 60 shots rapid fire in 5-shot strings at 25 meters, which demands sophisticated equipment.

The new Unique D.E.S. 69 perfectly meets these exacting requirements and those of the U.S. National Rifle Association Grouping Ability.

Grouping Ability

Built on a relatively small receiver, like most European auto target pistols, the D.E.S. 69 has a fixed barrel for maximum accuracy. One centimeter (.39") groups, center-to-center, are routine at 25 meters from a bench rest. The U.I.T. requirement is 1.96" (the 10-ring diameter of the target).

European shooters do much more gun cleaning than their American counterparts. Field stripping must, therefore, be extremely easy. To remove the slide of the Unique, just raise the slide catch, located on the receiver above the front end of the trigger guard, pull the slide to the rear as far as it will go and lift it.

The wrap-around stockplates, made of nice diamond-checkered French walnut, are quite fat, as they should be on a modern target pistol. There is ample wood for fitting the grip to the specific requirements of every shooter.

The wide thumb-rest is well located (a la Hammerli) and the swinging palm-rest is very clever.

The factory trigger position is excellent for average hands, but it can be easily adjusted for long or short hands by removing or adding material to the grip—as most seasoned shooters do.

weight, backlash, sear engagement and sear-spring strength over a wide range. With some practice, there is no trouble getting the clean 1 kilo (36-oz.) pull required by the international regulation.

Two barrel weights (260g=9 oz. and 350g=12 oz.) are available, but shooting with the plain barrel may be preferred by those who like a muzzle-light balance.

The sights are neat and low; the undercut square blade front is on a ramp. The micrometer rear sight, adjustable for windage and elevation, is mounted on a receiver extension, bringing the sight radius to 8.6" (220mm).

Beside carrying the rear sight, the receiver extension contains an original dry firing device—a telescopic pin is notched to retain the

hammer when it falls. This device has, therefore, no negative effect on the cleanness of the trigger pull. It permits home training and trigger adjustment with a maximum of safety.

The face of the chamber is protected against battering by a patented device that limits firing-pin travel. Dry firing need cause no worry. The D.E.S. 69, of course, has a thumb safety, an external hammer

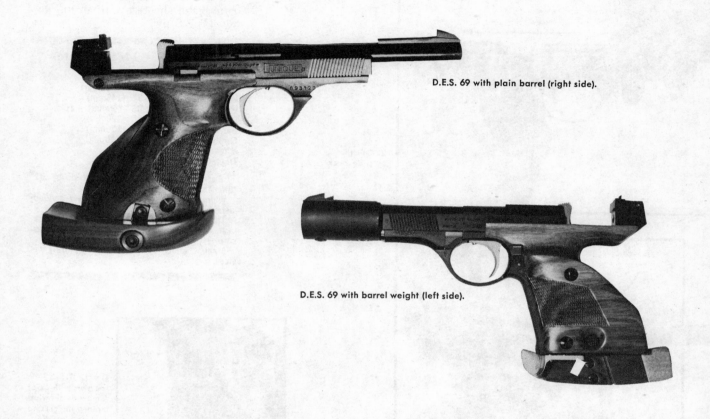

D.E.S. 69 with plain barrel (right side).

D.E.S. 69 with barrel weight (left side).

showing when the gun is cocked, and a slide hold-open device.

The D.E.S. 69 is truly a target pistol of international class. It is pleasant to shoot, the grip fits the hand well and, when the trigger pull is properly adjusted, rapid-fire accuracy depends only on the shooter's skill.

At Hendaye, Mr. Uria's pet gun is carefully followed by the whole Engineering Department: every problem reported by him is thoroughly investigated, with remedies immediately introduced. Production pistols are periodically withdrawn from the line and submitted to severe testing. Unique wants top accuracy and does what is needed to get it.

For instance, the technical staff recently selected 10 D.E.S. pistols at

random and fire-tested them from a bench at 25 meters, using several brands of European 22 LR ammo. The results (average *external* diameter of two 5-shot groups for each gun tested) follow:

Ammo Brand	Group Dia.
All Right (French)	0.56" (14.2mm)
Eley Tenex (British)	0.59" (15.0mm)
Eley Pistol (British)	0.71" (18.2mm)
Lapua Match (Finnish)	0.82" (20.8mm)
Eley Rifle Club (British)	0.97" (24.6mm)
R.W.S. Red Strip (German)	0.99" (25.2mm)

These results do not represent the quality of the cartridges used; rather, they show what brand is most suited to the bore of this particular model.

Another time, the Unique engineers took two standard, untuned production D.E.S. 69 pistols and

bench-tested them at 50 meters by firing 160 rounds (40 French All Right, 40 Eley Pistol, 40 Eley Rifle Club and 40 R.W.S. Red Strip) at the ISU international target.

All 160 rounds were in the 10 ring (1.96" dia.).

144 were contained in the inner ring (X-ring) (0.98" dia.) of the same target.

With such a high level of accuracy, the Unique pistol could hardly do otherwise than win some top competitions.

While used almost entirely so far by French shooters, the D.E.S. 69 has won the following honors in ISU "Standard Pistol" matches:

World Championship (Phoenix, Arizona 1970).

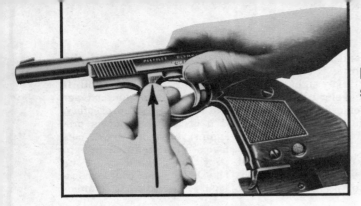

Field stripping:

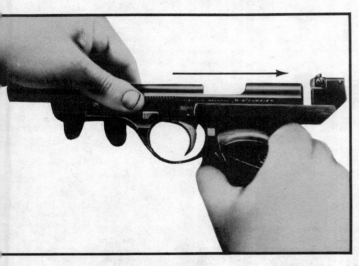

1. Raise the slide catch

2. Pull the slide back

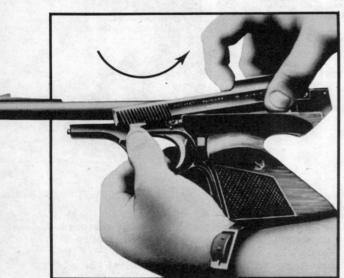

3. Lift the slide

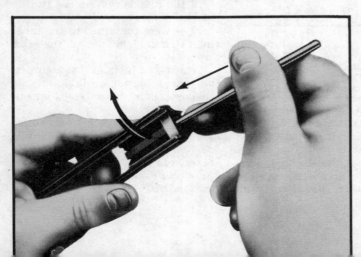

4. Firing-pin removal

Fourth individual with 574-600 by Trauch (France).

Fourth team with 2265/2400—average 566-600 (France).

The French record (2220-2400) was broken on this occasion.

French National Championships: Nancy, 1970—First; Gehres (567-600).

Tourcoing, 1971—First; Trauch.

France-Spain Match, Barcelona, 1971.

First-Vigneau (574-600)

Unique management won't rest on its laurels, that's sure. Target shooting in France is in full swing, and at the moment new and enthusiastic pistol shooters wait in line to buy a D.E.S. 69! ●

Unique D.E.S. 69 Match Pistol

Caliber	:	22 Long Rifle
Over-all	:	10.6″ (270mm)
Height	:	5.7″ (145mm)
Width	:	1.96″ (50mm) max.
Sight Radius	:	8.6″ (220mm)
Barrel	:	5.9″ (150mm)
Empty	:	36 oz. (1000g)
Magazine Cap.	:	10
Trigger Width	:	.47″ (12mm)

Micrometer rear sight adj. for W.&E. by .31″ (8mm) clicks at 25 meters (82′).

Walnut target grip with thumb-rest and adjustable palm-rest.

Trigger click-adj. for weight of pull, backlash, sear engagement and sear-spring pressure.

Manual safety. Hold-open and dry-firing devices.

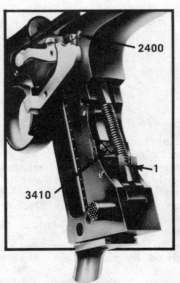

(Left) D.E.S. 69 receiver with grips removed, showing mainspring (1) and sear-spring adjustment screw (3410). No. 2400 is not identified.

Rear sight bridge with hammer cocked; dry-firing device holds hammer after trigger release.

The author's Bulgarian guide, a state forester.

Gunning in Eastern Europe

by SIDNEY Du BROFF

Hunting behind the Iron Curtain can be a rewarding experience. The plentiful game includes roe, red and fallow deer, wild sheep and boar, big brown bear, the auerhahn and black cocks, other species. But getting in and about needs foreknowledge—here are all the facts and figures needed.

THE MAN IN THE gun shop in Trieste, Italy, handed me the Beretta over-and-under. I threw it to my shoulder, then fondled it longingly. For a mere $92 it could be mine, but I already had a couple of perfectly good guns back home in Los Angeles. Still, I felt reluctant to return the Beretta to the man's waiting hands. It was either the gun or 57,000 lire.

There was only one thing to do. I laid down the fistfull of lire. But I didn't walk out of there clutching my gun; this was form-crazy, bureaucratic Europe. I had to give them my passport and fill out documents, one of which would be turned over to customs on my leaving Italy. It took almost a week before they said I could have my gun, but when at last I got it I was one happy guy. It was a 12-gauge over-under, bottom barrel modified choke, the top full, and a perfect fit. It was as if it had been waiting in that shop for me to come and claim it.

At the Italian-Yugoslav border I offered the form, which was ignored. I'd have been perfectly content to ignore it, too, but if I did that there'd be trouble when I wanted to return to Italy. I offered it again to the indifferent Italian customs man, who suddenly became fully animated when he realized that I was a foreigner in possession of a firearm. We were detained in the customs house. Trieste was contacted. None of this was really necessary; he had only to take the form and wave me on, but that would have been too easy, too efficient, too much as it should have been.

Entering Yugoslavia I anticipated trouble, but none came. On their form they wanted only to know the make, type and serial numbers of any guns in my possession; they didn't even bother to look at the gun. But later, in France, they not only looked, but took possession of my Beretta, apparently because it was new and did not come under the heading of personal property. Just by coincidence, of course, there was a clearing agent at hand who could arrange for customs to release the gun and ship it through to London in bond—for a fee that was astronomical. I wasn't going to London but to Paris, and told the clearing agent that I would do without his services, which, he let me know, would be virtually impossible. I trotted down to the American Embassy and told them my sad tale, where they were surprisingly sympathetic and helpful. Apparently deciding that I was no serious threat to the regime, and that I would not be taking the gun down to the Rue des Rosiers in Paris for a quick sale, it was, after several more hours in the customs house, returned to me.

England was easy, requiring, at the time, only that one buy an annual shotgun license at the post office, costing $1.40. Sadly, this has since been altered, with registration and a police-issued certificate required for smoothbores.

My work as a journalist kept me in Europe. Eager to get into the field and use my Beretta, I arranged some hunting. Despite the fact that the Beretta and I were made for each other, I couldn't connect! I had used a side-by-side double for many years and was an average shot, but I hadn't been able to make the adjustment rapidly. Eventually the Beretta and I became full partners.

England

In England guns are frequently made to measure, cost up to $8,000 for a pair of sidelock hand-made doubles that can take 18 to 36 months for delivery. The parts are not interchangeable, which means that they would have to be machined and hand-fitted should replacement become necessary. It is said to take about 600 man-hours to produce such a gun. But adequate guns, bought off the rack, can be had for about $500, second-hand over $250 and up. Guns are imported into Britain from virtually all the countries that make

them—Russia, Germany, Japan, Finland, Czechoslovakia, Italy, Hungary, the U.S.A., Spain. The cheaper Spanish guns cost about $100 in England, including some 36% purchase tax. A Beretta over-and-under like mine costs about $300, an American pump action about $150. Pumps and autos are not popular in England, and on some shoots would be forbidden altogether!

Ten-gauge guns can be used for waterfowl, and so can an 8-gauge, or a bigger gauge still, if you have one, and if you can find the shells to fit, or load them yourself. Cogswell & Harrison in London sells an 8-gauge shell, 3¼ inches long, two ounces of shot and 57 grains of powder, for about $13 for a box of 25. Thomas Bland has the makings for 4-gauge shells—4 inches long, 112 grains of powder, 3¼ ounces of shot. More typical would be the Eley ICI Grand Prix High Velocity cartridge, 12 gauge, 2½-inch, with 1⅛ ounces of shot and 32 grains of powder. A box of 25 costs about $2.50, including purchase tax.

In Europe game is sold on the market. In London a pheasant costs about $3; a hare, weighing about 7-8 pounds, about the same. Ducks are about $2.50, a woodcock —the European species is almost twice the size of the North American variety—about $2; deer steak— up to $2.64 a pound. Grouse, growing more scarce each year, sell for about $3 each.

The hunting season is a long one in England—pheasants from October 1st through February 1st, with no bag limits. The man who owns the land sets his own limit, since he knows approximately how many birds are on his land—he may have put them there as chicks at the beginning of the season, or released them the night before for the day's shoot—and he knows how many he wants to kill. He also decides if hen pheasants should be taken, and if so, how many.

Czechoslovakia

Czechoslovakia has some of the best pheasant shooting in Europe— probably in the entire world—with frequent bags of 1500 and 2000 birds. Recently, 12 gunners took 3000 pheasants. The Czech rearing program is a model for other countries. I arrived in Prague too early for the pheasant shooting, but the duck season was already under way.

I picked up a Czech-made 12 bore, sidelock double, the Model

DuBroff used his BRNO ZKK rifle, chambered for the 7x64mm, on this roe deer hunt. The scope is a Zeiss 4x.

The author (right) carries the 16x16x7x65R drilling he used in East Germany. District Forester Trensch, his gun a 16x7x65R also, but an over-under, holds Veronica's leash. The dog is a *Wachtelhund*, originally bred for quail, but nowadays these dogs trail wounded deer, bay only when the fallen animal is located. Quail haven't been hunted in Germany for a hundred years.

ZP, and another Brno 12 over-and-under, their Model ZH. In a sleek, torpedo-like Tatra sedan we drove onto the Bohemian plain, about 90 minutes from Prague, not far from the ancient town of Podebrady and settled into the comfortable lodge.

Next morning, and still quite dark, we met with the Chief Forester and five foresters from other districts, men who would also be shooting. Leaving the lodge we walked in silence for some distance, the air still and cold, then stepped onto what appeared to be a long, narrow wooden bridge. On the left there was a hand rail, on the right a fence of saplings, about 6 feet high, and every so often an indentation in the fence for a man to stand and shoot. The bridge, built across the marsh, was about 400 feet long, about four feet above the water.

We took our places. It was growing light now. Soon the birds started coming in. I missed two shots at an overhead mallard, but connected the next time on an incoming bird that somersaulted down into the water almost directly in front of me. Ducks came fast and thick from the front, from the back. Shots rang out from either side of me.

There were 4,000 ducks calling this marsh home. As it grew later the birds stopped moving, except for the occasional high flier. It was time to gather in the harvest. The foresters sent their dogs into the water after the dead birds. Three of the dogs were Czech griffons, the fourth a German short-haired pointer. They worked superbly, following the commands of their owners with precision. They were on display here, each man eager to show how well his dog could perform. They would call out to their dogs in the water below - *right*, or *left*, or *further on.* The dogs understood perfectly, found the ducks and came swimming back with them in their mouths.

One of the men sent his griffon after a downed mudhen lying in the reeds a short distance from the bridge. The dog ignored it. I thought he didn't see it, but it soon became apparent that's what he wanted everybody to think. Twice he practically stepped over it. When he couldn't play the game any longer, he picked it up, pretending that only now had he come upon it. The dogs didn't like the smell of mudhens; the other dogs had avoided it—he didn't see why he should be the one to pick it up.

After the shoot the birds were laid out. The Chief Forester had 5, I had 4, the others less. All game belongs to the State, and even the foresters are required to pay for it if they want it. Otherwise it is sold in the market. A duck costs about a dollar.

Our foresters, by the way, seemed partial to 20-gauge guns, feeling that it is the gun of the expert, and in all modesty, few will deny being experts. One of the foresters had a pre-war 20-gauge hand-made Belgian double, of which he was very proud.

In order for the Czech citizen to go hunting he must apply to the Hunting Association, and then put in a total of 66 hours of schooling at evening classes. Here he learns about hunting, using a gun, biology, "canineology," the care of wildlife, and all other subjects connected with hunting. After completion of class work, he becomes a member of the Association, and must work in the forests or field, part time, for a year, before he is allowed to carry a gun for the purpose of hunting. During this period he is taught to shoot, to look after the different types of guns, and to study them in detail. He then takes an examination, which is said to be difficult, consisting of both theory and practice. If he passes, he may then become a full member and buy a gun. The cost of membership is 120 crowns a year. The Zbrojovka will cost him about 1,700 crowns, the over-and-under, 1,900. An average salary is about 1500 to 2000 crowns a month —about $230-$307 today.

A break for lunch during a hare shoot in East Germany. Hot food and drink was brought out from the village.

Back at the lodge I wanted to try out the over-and-under, having used the ZP for the duck shooting. Obligingly, tin cans were thrown up for my benefit. In the past I have rarely been able to hit a thrown tin can, but now, after some initial missing, I scored every time, if not with the first barrel, then on the second. The Brno ZH over-and-under is not, to some eyes, an impressive looking gun, lacking the graceful lines of many over-and-unders, but it handled well, and I could hit what I was shooting at. Seven interchangeable barrel sets are offered for the ZH including one with a 7x57R caliber rifle on top, 12 bore below. All parts are interchangeable. The Orlov scope, specially made for use with the rifle/shotgun, comes in 2.5 and 4 power. In England the over-and-under costs about $230, and is said to be over-priced.

Bulgaria

The next time I got to use Czech firearms was in Bulgaria. I was handed one of the ZH over-and-under 12-bore Skeet guns, each barrel with its own built-in recoil-choke device, rather like the Cutts Compensator. It was in rather bad condition, suffering from neglect and abuse. I did not go out into the field with particularly high hopes. One can only shrug, and hope for the best. I did both.

The safety on the Brno ZH1 works through the top front of the trigger guard. I would touch my finger to it from time to time to remind myself, and repeat silently, "safety on the trigger guard."

The brush ahead of me exploded. I reacted by taking my hand from the safety on the trigger guard, searching for it on the stock, pushing with my thumb as hard as I could. Fortunately it was a hen pheasant that had jumped but, conditioned to use one kind of gun, I reacted intuitively and forgot current training. When a hare got up a few minutes later, I remembered where the safety was and got it with the second barrel at the edge of a thicket. A cock pheasant escaped my first barrel, but crumpled to the second, from a considerably greater distance. The second barrel accounted for another hare and another pheasant that had cleared the trees and looked like nothing would be able to stop it. Even in poor condition, with short barrels, just under 26 inches, that gun could nail them. I regarded it

with new respect.

Our game was collected and prepared for lunch, · served with tomatoes from a nearby collective farm, and helped down with local wine. Afterwards I dropped a pheasant with the first barrel, just to make sure that that barrel was really operative, and got another from a distance I never would have thought possible. It seemed like hardly more than a dot against the sky, but down it went, dead by the time it hit the ground. I was congratulated on my shooting, the success of which surprised me a

DuBroff's translator, Kaderka, stands on the long bridge/blind built over the wildfowl marshes in Czechoslovakia. His shotgun is the side-by-side Model ZP, a 12 bore made by Zbrojovka at Brno.

great deal more than it did anybody else.

This shooting was in Plovdiv, in south-central Bulgaria, in the direction of Greece. Now we turned the Volga, our Russian-made car, eastward toward the Turkish border. Here, in a place called Harmonley, we were after Chukar partridge, among the dry and rocky crags. I was handed a Merkel, a highly-regarded East German-made over-and-under that had once been a very fine gun, before it had been so shamefully abused. The safety was off completely. It was a dangerous gun and I didn't want to use it. Einchev, our guide-interpreter, an indoor addict who consumed three cokes and three cognacs at every meal, explained this to the forester, who took the Merkel and gave me his Russian-made double barrel Baikal, a 12-bore 7-lb. boxlock. I wasn't interested in merely *exchanging* guns, but in abandoning the safety-less Merkel altogether. If it were to be used, I would prefer to be carrying it rather than let somebody else do so; better it should go off in my hands than his. But he proved fairly safe, and I always made it a point to be well out of his way.

The Chukar were scarce, the going rough, the weather hot and dry. Then, when I fired the Baikal it refused to break open! With that one shot the hunt ended, which wasn't as bad as it sounds—our prospects had never looked very bright, anyway.

Next we made our way into the Balkan Mountains, to a beautiful lodge about 5,000 feet up. The mountains were a sea of autumn colors, rolling waves of mixed orange, red and brown. Here I was given a 7x64mm Brno bolt action rifle, the Model ZKK600, and a pair of 8x30 Zeiss binoculars. Missing from the rifle was a scope, which I sorely needed but never got. The morning air was chilly, though not yet really cold. We sat in a high seat built into the trees, about 20 feet from the ground, the European method of hunting deer. They come to you, and you shoot them. Through the glasses I saw a doe off in the distance. Does are shot, but no one particularly wants them, and the foresters usually wind up culling them from the herds at the end of the season.

A couple of times I spotted bucks through my glasses but they never came close enough to me for an effective shot with my open sights.

Leaving the Balkan Mountains we headed north toward the Rumanian border for wild boar in the flat forest and farmland district of Voden. Here I spent the night

The author's hunting companions in Czechoslovakia. From left, translator Kaderka, a Chief Forester and DuBroff. The retriever is a Czech griffon.

sitting in a tree, waiting for a boar to come and wallow in the pond just below me, and to help himself to the ears of corn that had been strewn about.

I was using another 7x64mm Brno bolt action rifle, this time with a 3x scope attached. This had been chosen for its light-gathering value to enable me to shoot in darkness. But it began to rain, and the boar had no need for a pond. The next afternoon, seated on a platform only a few feet above the ground, I heard something crashing about in the undergrowth. It could be a boar. I eased the safety off. A magnificent sika deer stepped into the clearing, unafraid, unconcerned, about 50 feet from me. He walked slowly toward me. But I had no permit to shoot a deer here, and all I could do was watch. He neither smelled me nor saw me. He came within 20 feet of where I sat, then stood for a long time. I felt as if I could reach out and touch him. Then slowly he walked on and disappeared back into the woods.

The roe deer permit was arranged, but only for a doe, which I got the next morning from a high seat, at about 90 yards. My deer turned a somersault and went down in its tracks, not moving

from where it had been hit. Roe deer, common to Europe, are small —about 40-50 pounds—living in areas of intense cultivation, as well as in remote mountain areas. The forester broke off a branch with some leaves attached, dipped it in the deer's blood, touched me with it symbolically, and gave me the branch with the bloodied leaves to wear in my hat. I rather missed the "Waidmannsheil!" one hears in Germany after a successful shot.

The guns of many countries are available in Bulgaria—Italian, Czech, Russian, English, Belgian, for the Bulgarians don't make any of their own sporting guns. Cartridges cost about 6¢ each, but most hunters do their own reloading. Ivan Sokolov, Chief of the Hunting Department, said, "It is a social occasion. They drink cognac while they fill their cartridges." The cost is about 4¢ each reloaded, but it isn't a question of saving money. The most ardent Bulgarian hunters never use factory-made ammunition; they reload according to the weather—less powder for dry weather, more for wet. Each man has his own idea of what he wants a cartridge to do, is often emotionally involved in his reloading.

Mr. Sokolov prefers quail and

partridge shooting. "Hunters with more imagination, the more intellectual, want to go after birds," he said.

I wasn't able to go hunting in Rumania because it was closed to foreigners. Their story is that a German shot a deer he wasn't meant to shoot, and this was so upsetting to the Rumanians that they closed hunting to outsiders, which sounds like an unlikely tale.

Visiting the headquarters of the Rumanian Hunting Association, I was a bit skeptical about their 5-legged mounted roe deer, and got down underneath to see if the fifth leg had been stitched or glued on.

Hunting Chief Duda said through the translator that individuals going after hare on their own reduced the number of hare because they were killing the females. Rumanian gunners must be exceptional if they're able to determine the sex of a running hare—or was I being put on again!

Hungary

I had never shot driven pheasants until I got to Hungary. It is the kind of shooting in which the European aristocracy engage, as well as just plain every-day rich people. I can't help feeling that there is something un-American about it. It's not hunting, but *shooting*. You try to hit what comes flying past, which isn't as easy as it sounds, but it can be a lot of fun when the birds come whizzing over faster than you can reload.

Dr. Studenka, whose title is legal rather than medical, was our guide-companion in Hungary. A one-time estate owner, he went to college in Scotland, where he studied agriculture, and he *knew* that the only proper way to shoot pheasants was to have them driven. We went to the Puszta, the great Hungarian Plain, near a town called Kecskemet, in the south, where the Hungarian apricot brandy is brewed. There, we were told, you can get drunk from the fumes just by walking down the street in the fall. But now it was December and we were relatively safe, though not from the already bottled stuff that was always being poured for our benefit.

An early snow covered all of Hungary and most of the roads were closed, except for those in the south. The Doctor had provided a 12-gauge Belgian sidelock, a handmade double with automatic ejectors that was 50 years old. It had

One of the Bulgarian foresters holds DuBroff's 12 gauge Merkel.

belonged to his father. It was well-used, but probably in as good shape as when it was new. He used a similar gun, in 16-gauge, about 40 years old. He kept both guns wrapped in strips of greased cloth. I told him that I had a Hungarian-made double, a 12-bore, which didn't impress him.

Our entourage moved out into the field, traveling in a Russian command car that maneuvered the rough, snow-covered roads with relative ease. Two sleighs were pulled along effortlessly by the sure-footed horses. The Doctor and I took up positions about 50 yards apart in an open field covered by deep snow. The beaters came through the woods toward us, calling, banging the ground with their sticks. Dr. Studenka dropped his coat to the ground, despite the falling snow, ready for action. It came. Slowly, almost casually, he raised his gun to his shoulder and fired, and just as casually, the bird dropped. As usual I missed my early shots, took a while getting used to the gun, and eventually connected. The drivers appeared. The drive was over. The dogs picked up the birds scattered in the field. They were collected and deposited in the sleigh. We climbed back into the command car and went on the next field. On such drives there are usually a number of shooters participating and, after each drive, they rotate positions until everyone has had a chance at a different location. Our beaters were finding it rough going in the deep snow, and we stopped early on their account.

The next day it was still snowing. The birds, bunching up because of the snow, were refusing to fly according to plan. This time we, my wife Nedra and I, rode out in a sleigh, the driver covering us with blankets. When we arrived at our destination, the blankets were removed and put back on the now stationary horses. I moved out into the field accompanied by the District Forester, who indicated that he would like my gun, which I handed over to him. Walking along, it became apparent that he wanted my gun in order to save me the effort of carrying it. This thoroughly embarrassed me, and as soon as possible I told the good Doctor, who conveyed my message to the forester, that I always carried my own gun.

My shooting was rather inconsistent with the Belgian gun, sometimes on, sometimes off. I once

nailed a cock coming in high and to the right with my first barrel, swung to the far left on a hen that was almost past me, and dropped her with the second. But there were plenty of empty shell cases scattered around me, serving as evidence of all the shots I'd had. Given a choice I like to do the looking, as well as the finding. There are few things as exciting as having a pheasant get up from almost under your feet—unless it's quail—startling you out of your wits as he beats his wings noisily to gain altitude.

The Hungarians have developed an outstanding game propagation program, and many record heads come from there. In the fall of 1971 their International Hunting and Fishing Exhibition was held in Budapest, where their trophies, and the trophies from nearly 50 countries were on display. About 2,000,000 people, no less, attended the 5-week event!

Dr. Studenka notwithstanding, my Hungarian 12-bore side-by-side is an outstanding gun. It has a walnut, oil-finished Monte Carlo stock, 28-inch barrels, and weighs about' 7¼ pounds. A boxlock type, it has automatic ejectors, but can be used as a non-ejector at will—a boon for reloaders—by removing the ejector mechanism in the fore-end—an instamatic operation. In Britain the gun sells for under $150. The over-and-under model costs about $170.

East Germany

On an assignment in East Germany I had the opportunity to meet and talk with Hans Schotte, Chief Forester of that country. As he was telling me about guns, game and game management in the German Democratic Republic—which they call themselves—I got the idea that I'd like to have a chance in the field myself. I asked Chief Schotte about the possibility of this. He never blinked an eye—just got on the telephone and made all the arrangements. I became the first American—the first Western civilian—to ever go hunting in East Germany.

Chief Schotte uses a 20-gauge double for hunting, and he breaks 85 out of 100 clays with that same 20! Starting at the bottom as a forestry worker, he had made his way to the top, having returned to school for a degree in Forestry Management. His 16-year-old son, who shoots with the Youth Champion Team, is learning to become a gunsmith. For his final examina-

DuBroff with pheasants bagged near Plovdiv, Bulgaria. He's holding the Czech-made ZH over-under 12 used on this trip.

tion he will have to make three drillings — 3-barrel rifle / shotgun combinations—within one year, by hand, without anyone's help.

Our hunt started off in the Spree District, an hour's drive from Dresden. Here I met Forester Trensch, who has the good fortune to be married to a woman who makes magnificent apple cake, besides being very pretty. The gun they had waiting for me was a drilling, a type I'd never hunted with before. It was a 16-gauge side-by-side double on top, with a 7x57rmm rifle barrel below. At the time it seemed somewhat strange, but out we went, after ducks. The safety is on the left side of the small of the stock, just above the triggers; this was something new to get used to, which I didn't quite manage by the time the ducks flew directly over me at 20 yards—and I never got in a shot. We then walked off a short distance, and I now saw what the drilling was for. I pushed now what I had pushed before, thinking it the safety, atop the stock where it is normally on a double-barrel gun. Up came the open rifle sights, which had until this moment been lying flat. Pushing that top button

also cut off the shotgun mechanism, activating the rifle mechanism, and allowing the front trigger to function with the rifle barrel. That wasn't all—I snapped the 4 Zeiss scope into the 4 slots atop the gun in an instant. The scope sits high, so I could use the gun either scope-sighted or open-sighted as I chose, merely by looking through one or the other.

We waited behind a convenient haystack and, before long, 5 roe deer emerged from the woods. The bucks had dropped their antlers, and the foresters were culling the herd now. Herr Trensch picked out the deer he wanted shot and gave me instructions. From that moment on I became a drilling fan. It isn't the most practical gun in the world for use in England, which I now call home, but I am in so much awe and admiration of the fine craftsmanship of this versatile gun that I feel compelled to own one. They're available in 12 or 16 gauge above, rifle calibers below in a wide variety of rimmed cartridges from 22 to 8x57mm. They are not usually available in England, but they can be bought in West Germany for about $400 and up. There are also over-and-under rifle/shotgun combinations, which is what Forester Trensch uses, made in the same gauges and calibers as the drilling. These are somewhat less expensive.

The next day we drove out from Dresden, past the Moritzburg Castle, once the summer residence of

King August III, the 17th century Saxon king who had 300 children, it's said. The castle is now a hunting museum. A half-hour later we were in Ebersbach, where I was to partake in a hare shoot. The District Forester welcomed me to the group, told everyone to exert caution, and announced that 120 hare were to be shot that day. I was equipped with a 12-gauge Merkel over-and-under, from one of the four gunmaking cooperatives in Suhl, East Germany. It was light and fast, with a raised rib, hunting scenes engraved on either side of the lock, and costs about $500 in England.

Three foresters blew a hunting tune on their round horns—the signal to begin the hunt. Most of the guns were side-by-side doubles, a few over-and-unders. There were 22 hunters and 31 drivers, local farmers who came along for the fun of it, and who would be presented with a hare each as a symbol of their participation in the hunt.

We were hunting in flat, open fields. The leader of the hunt would send one man off to the left, accompanied by a driver or two, then another man, with drivers, to the right, until we were all distributed, forming a giant circle about a half-mile in diameter. When we were spread out a man with a horn signalled that we were ready. We loaded our guns. The second horn sounded and we could proceed, hunters and drivers together,

Hungarian pheasant shoot in a snowstorm. The beaters and dog handlers are about to collect the downed birds.

"Hunting-Shooting" in East Germany, or what we term a quail walk. Asst. Chief Forester Richter is trying to sneak up on the next claybird.

moving toward the center. We could shoot at hare in front of us, or behind.

As the circle grew smaller the surrounded hare tried to break through. The guns barked continually. Usually the hunter stopped his hare on the first shot, occasionally the second; they were very good shots and connected more often than not. There was usually a fair amount of time to see your target and get a bead on it. My shooting wasn't particularly good, even though I had what is considered to be one of the finest guns in the world.

When we had advanced about three-quarters of the way toward the center of the circle, the horn sounded again. The hunters stopped. The drivers continued forward. Now we could shoot only in the direction from which we had come—behind us—to insure that we did not shoot toward the drivers.

A total of 115 hare were bagged. The top man got 10, and was crowned King of the Hunt. In his honor the horn blowers played "The Dead Hare." The second man got 8, and four others got 6 each. On some hunts, I was told, a kill of 400 hare is not unusual. I wound up with four—and used 26 shells to do it! "The King of the Hunt" is expected to buy drinks for everybody, as is the low man. The hunter receives half a mark for every hare, and 20% of his kill, the remainder being sold in shops that specialize in game. Each local Hunting Association is responsible for its own grounds, looking after the game during the winter, and destroying predators. Rifles and shotguns are not ordinarily privately owned, but are provided free of cost to members. It is possible, if

a member wishes, to buy his own gun.

In East Germany 120,000 roe deer are shot annually, 60% of the herd. 22,000 wild boar are killed; 400,000 hare, out of the million-odd population. The pheasant population is still relatively small, and the Czechs are providing assistance.

I wondered why I had performed rather poorly with such a fine gun as the Merkel, and fairly well with the Brno. I concluded that a heavier gun—like the Brno—is often more effective than a light one, as a result of changing the center of gravity. Certainly a light gun is a great advantage when carrying it around in the field all day, but will it be as effective?

In the spring we were back in the GDR. Chief Forester Schotte greeted my wife Nedra and me as old friends, and arranged a morning's clay pigeon shooting. He told us that during the past season 40,000 wild boar were bagged. The

quota had been 27,000, but the animals were in such abundance that the quota was upped another 13,000. About 200,000 head of big game had been taken by the 35,000 members of the Hunting Association—at no cost to themselves. After taking their percentage, GDR shooters had turned over 34 tons of game to be sold.

We drove out to the shooting grounds near Oranienburg, about 45 minutes from the center of Berlin, with Assistant Chief Forester Richter in his tough little Russian Moskowitch. Richter, a jovial and friendly man of about 40, told us that during the past season he had bagged two red deer, one fallow deer, 10 roe deer, 5 boar, 5 foxes, 20 ducks and 15 hare.

At the shooting ground, Mr. Runge, Secretary of the Oranienburg District Shooting Society, was waiting for us. Now he moved underground to operate the clay target traps. I started out with a 16-gauge Suhler side-by-side double, doing a lot of missing at first— always embarrassing in front of others, who assume that you've actually fired a gun before!

Richter used his 16-gauge drilling, his companion for all shooting, and managed to do some missing himself. I switched over to Runge's over-and-under, the kind of gun I'm used to, pretending my bad show was due to the unfamiliar gun. But I breathed a sigh of relief when the clays I was shooting at began breaking. Gunners in the GDR have to keep up a certain standard of shooting and pass shooting tests each year; if they are consistently bad shots they will be dropped from the organization—a precau-

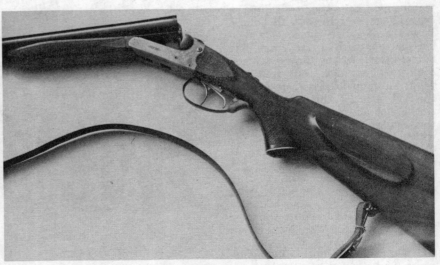

The Hungarian-made boxlock double 12 bore DuBroff bought. Note cheekpiece, sling and recoil absorber at rear of guard.

tion against wounded animals.

We were "walking up" the clays, called "hunting shooting" in the GDR. I'd never done it before, and Richter instructed me. I had to crouch, my right foot had to be sticking out to the right of the rest of me—but not too far—and I had to move slowly, as if stalking something. When Richter, standing behind me, saw whatever it was I'd been stalking, he hollered *"Hut!"* and Runge would send the clay hurtling into space. It was a lot to try to remember. But I wasn't the only one having trouble; crack Olympic shots, on their first encounter with "hunting shooting," didn't do as well as ordinary GDR Hunting Association members.

Richter then changed places with Runge, the latter using the side-by-side double that had been brought for me. He couldn't hit with it, and switched over to Richter's drilling, but with no greater success. He called out to Richter to tell him that his gun didn't shoot very well, and took back his over-and-under—the one I'd been using. Suddenly the double I'd gone back to got the range and started hitting. I couldn't figure out what I did right on the hits, or wrong on the misses, but the gun showed unmistakable signs of improvement; in fact, I did better with the side-by-side than with the over-and-under.

If this proves anything, it is only that it doesn't appear to matter very much what type of gun I use. Ignoring the misses, and counting the hits, Runge broke 18, I got 15.

I was told about an acoustic clay bird machine that had been developed in East Germany—a pneumatic device that catapults the clays through the atmosphere when it hears *"Hut!"* called out. The shooter has to act fast—or else the target is a hundred yards away.

Since that day in Trieste when I first bought the Beretta, I've been lucky enough to have fired a lot of shells in a lot of different places. I only hope that this is just the beginning. ●

European Hunting Data

Bulgaria

Initial Procedure

Tourist Entrance Visa $1 at border.

Arms, ammunition, cameras, binoculars, hunting equipment—freely imported.

$50 deposit required—minimum 20 days prior to commencement of hunt. Balkan Tourist Hunting Department, 1 Lenin Square, Sofia, Bulgaria.

License fees paid for hunting constitute only license required.

Costs

Red Deer—$300-$2,710 (13-to 26-lb. antlers). Plus $36 per day for lodging, food, guide, translator, car with driver. Wounded animal not recovered, $100.

Fallow Deer—$80-$480 (6-to 11-lb. antlers). Plus $21 for lodging, meals, services. Wounded animal, $30.

Roe Deer—$35-$255 (10 oz. to 18 oz. antlers). Plus $13 per day for lodging, services. Wounded animal, $25.

Wild Boar—$20-$200 (6-in. to 10-in tusks). Plus $12 per day for lodging and services. Wounded animal, $30.

Hare—$3 each, plus $9 per day for lodgings and services.

Partridge and Pheasant—$3 each, plus $12 per day for lodgings and services.

Quail—$2 each, plus $9 per day for lodgings and services.

No bag limit on hare, partridge, pheasant or quail.

A riding horse, where available—$4 per day.

Gun dog, when not provided—$3 per day.

Czechoslovakia

Initial Procedure

Visa required, available at border, through Czech Consuls, or accredited travel agency.

Sporting gun permit, issued by the Consul, or through accredited travel agencies, is required.

Hunting reservations to be confirmed 21 days before hunt begins. Cedok, Czechoslovak Travel Bureau, Prikopy 18, Prague 1, Czechoslovakia.

License—required of all foreign hunters. $15 for one month, $35 for one year, including third-party insurance.

Costs

Organizational hunting fees—$8-$50. Plus $8.40-$12.55 per day for lodging, food (regardless of species hunted).

Red Deer—$80-$620, determined by size of antlers. Wounded animal, $80.

Roe Deer—$15-$110, determined by size of antlers. Wounded animal, $15.

Fallow Deer—$50-$350. Wounded animal, $50.

Mouflon—$40-$350. Wounded animal, $90.

Chamois—$350. Wounded animal, $150.

Lynx—$200. Wounded animal, $100.

Wild Boar—$15-$250. Wounded animal, $70.

Bear—$1,200. Wounded animal, $600.

Capercaillie—$50. Wounded bird, $20.

Black Grouse—$35. Wounded bird, $10.

Pheasant and Hare shoots—Organized for 12 gunners. Cocks only —up to 200, $1.50 each; to 300, $2 each; over 1000, $4 each. $5 fine for each hen shot.

Up to 1000 shotgun shells and 20 rifle cartridges may be imported duty-free. Additional cartridges may be bought at about 9¢ each.

Shotguns may be hired at $5 per day, rifles at $7.

East Germany

At present East Germany does not generally make facilities available for foreign hunters.

Hungary
Initial Procedure

Visa obtainable at border, through authorized travel agencies, or Hungarian Consuls. Vouchers, bought through recognized travel agent, must first be presented. These cost $5 a day per person and are exchangeable in Hungary for lodgings and food.

Firearms import permits are obtainable through Hungarian Consuls. Ibusz, Felszabadulas Ter 5, Budapest V, Hungary, is chief travel agency.

License fees paid for hunting constitute only license required.

Costs

Red Deer—$100-$3,100, determined by size of antlers. A miss, $50.

Fallow Deer—$120-$1,300, determined by size of antlers. A miss, $40.

Roe Deer—$5-$1,375. A miss, $5. Mouflon—$150-$600. A miss, $40. Wild Boar—$50-$1,200. A miss, $20.

Cock Bustard—$200 (each). Three missed shots count as one killed bird.

Boar Drive—$15 per day per gun plus usual fee for each animal bagged.

Pheasant and Hare Drive—$125 per day (up to 10 guns), plus $1 per head of game up to 300. 1,000 or more, $3 per head.

Walking up: Pheasants, Partridge, Hare—$10 per day plus $1 each up to 30 head. $1.50 each, 50 or more.

Wounded animals not recovered —50% of kill price.

Room and board—$8-$10 per day.

Hungarian food—outstanding. The Game Restaurant in Budapest serves wild boar that will always be remembered with great pleasure.

Poland
Initial Procedure

Visa required, available through Polish Consuls on presentation showing of pre-paid vouchers representing total number of days of visit. Vouchers issued through approved travel agencies, redeemable in Poland for local currency. Visa application is then forwarded to Warsaw for approval.

Sporting firearms permits obtainable through Polish Consuls. Valid for 14 days. Should the visitor remain in Poland longer, he must report to nearest Militia headquarters in order to obtain a license for the possession of the firearm.

Travel agencies Orbis, 16 Bracka Street, Warsaw, and Sports-Tourist, 84-86 Marszalkowska St., Warsaw.

License fees paid for hunting constitute only license fee.

Costs

Red Deer—$300 and up, determined by size of antlers.

Fallow Deer—$100 and up.

Roe Deer—$50 and up. Does and fawns are less.

Wild Boar—$50 and up.

Pheasant, Partridge, Hare—$3 each.

To these costs must be added prices for lodgings and food, which varies.

Notes

Visas not granted to those whom the Polish Government feels may be unsympathetic or in any way unfriendly to it.

Those buying vouchers will have a portion of the fee withheld should the visa be denied.

Vouchers redeemed in Poland are at the rate of 23 zloties to the dollar, the official rate; the free market rate, 100 to the dollar.

Rumania
Initial Procedure

Hoping to re-open hunting to foreigners, the following data was made available. But nothing is quite firm yet.

Visa issued, no cost, at Consuls or border.

Sporting arms may be freely imported; make and serial number is written into the passport by Consul or frontier officials.

Ammunition may be imported or bought locally for 5¢-7¢ per cartridge.

Rifle calibers may not be smaller than 6.5mm.

License fees paid for hunting constitute only license required.

Costs

Red Deer—$300-$4,800. Wounded animal, $300.

Fallow Deer—$150-$850. Wounded animal, $100.

Roe Deer—$50-$300. Wounded animal, $50.

Chamois—$100-$350. Wounded animal, $70.

Wild Boar—$50-$150. Hunts for 6 persons minimum $30 each per day. Wounded animal, $70.

Bear—$1,000-$1,800. Wounded animal, $300.

Lynx—$200. Wolf—$50 (for the skin). 6 hunters minimum, $30 each per day.

Quail, Woodcock, Snipe—$10 per day per hunter, plus $1 for each game head.

Pheasants, Hare—minimum, $30 each hunter per day, plus $5 for each game head.

Lodgings, food, $18-$20 per day— which includes the price of a guide.

Yugoslavia
Initial Procedure

Visa required of U.S. citizens, obtainable at border or from Yugoslav Consuls; no cost. Vouchers not required. Arrangements for hunting can be made within Yugoslavia, but they should be made before visit.

Sporting arms may be freely imported, merely recording the serial number of each on entering the country.

Liability insurance necessary.

U.S. travel agents can make hunting arrangements.

Putnik Travel Agency, Dragoslava, Jovanozica 1, 11000 Belgrade.

Savez Lovackich Ogranizacija Jugoslavije, Alexse Nenadovica 23, Belgrade.

Kompas Travel Agency, Ljubljana (hunt organizer).

License fees paid for hunting constitute only license required.

Costs

Red Deer—$500 up, determined by size of antlers. Wounded animal not recovered, 50% of fee.

Wild Boar—$50 up, determined by size of tusk.

Kompas offers several all-inclusive hunts: Minimum of two hunters.

1 day. $59 each; meals, guide, beaters, porters, incl. Bag limit: 6 (1 hare, 5 pheasants/partridges).

Game costs, extra: Pheasant, $4.80; Partridge, $4; Hare, $7.20

2 days. $102. Bag limit, 12.

3 days. $149.50. Bag limit, 18.

Roe Deer—$83.50, one day, one buck all-inclusive.

No minimum number in party. Meat included at no additional cost. Fees include the use of dogs and game preparation.

Notes

Because of the 1972-1973 dollar devaluation, the prices quoted here may well be higher now. These should be checked with the various agencies mentioned.

Rocky Mountain Hunts –
You can make 'em or break 'em!

Jobson has the proper gear for *Osborni* caribou hunting. Binocs, 270 rifle, down jacket, cashmere sweater, cap with earlaps, ol' Seabiscuit with saddle bags full of necessities and goodies, pack horse with supplies.

Your outfitter may be tops, his guides and cook the best, his horses, trail and country perfect. But your personal gear, selected wisely or wrongly, can make the trip a delight or a disaster. Don't let it happen to you.

by JOHN JOBSON

A BIG GAME horseback-packtrain hunt in the Rockies is far more complicated and expensive than an ordinary 48-states weekend outing for whitetails—which may read to some, as belaboring the obvious. Yet I get stacks of mail from aspiring nimrods who confidently confide that they're past masters on Maine black bear, sheer murder on California blacktails, or absolutely deadly on Georgia swamp deer. So now, they continue, they've reached the plateau of big game a cut above the home-grown stuff, and will I please tell them where to go in the Yukon, the N.W.T., British Columbia, Alberta, Alaska, or wherever, as they have a powerful hankering to knock off a 44-inch ram, a 9-foot grizzly, and loads of moose, caribou, and Rocky Mountain goats. The only thing is, they aren't (heh heh) rich men, and consequently can't pay those outlandish prices that outfitters require. Since they are already expert hunters, they don't need guides. So will I please tell them how to have their $3000 hunt for $213.56? Sadly, practically all of these innocents are doomed to failure before they start. I know plenty of oldtimers in the city of Whitehorse, Yukon Territory, who have never shot a Dall sheep. Reason?

Glassing for rams and grizzlies. Note perfectly equipped saddle horses carrying chaps, saddle bags, and proper rifle scabbards.

They have no horses. It is the outfitters who've gone to the expense and enormous trouble of maintaining a horse string. The fact is, though, that many a good man who is not rich has taken a prime, top drawer, Rocky Mountain horseback hunt, with dependable pack horses carrying the supplies. Nor were these one of those questionable "quickie" in-and-out "hunts" for one species, but a wonderful outing lasting upwards of three weeks to two months—where a man luxuriates in pristine wilderness *for the hunt of a lifetime,* where he bags a full complement of the area's game species. All you've got to do is to *want* to go. Save the money (about what a good used car costs), get booked with a reliable outfitter, and get yourself into reasonable shape for mountain hunting.

'Ware the Pitfalls

There are a few pitfalls that can ruin an otherwise perfectly conceived pack trip, and among these, believe it or not, is choice of personal gear. Any of more-than-several items, chosen wrong, can handicap and even ruin a cherished trip. I'll touch on some that I've seen do just that, and I'll recommend the goodies which will work for you, not the stuff that won't. Oddly enough, a service piece such as this very often saves the day. A few outfitters are commendably conscientious in recommending a list for personal gear, others are not blessed with this perspicacity and laser-like insight. Others (particularly those of Indian descent) are most apt to advise you to fetch to roads-end what works best for *them.* One time a Yukon outfitter told me to wear tennis shoes, and bring blankets instead of a sleeping bag. Two pair of woolen socks would do me (for a 45-day pack trip!), he said; and one suit of long-handles.

Saddle Scabbards

When you seek out the noble ram and the truculent grizzly, the chances are you'll be using an expensive, scope-sighted, pet rifle. This should be carried aboard the saddle horse in a scabbard of saddle-skirting leather, and it does not hurt a bloody thing if it has been constructed to fit that particular rifle, and then *water* fit. Which is, you dampen the leather, place your rifle in thin sheet plastic, insert it, and let the whole works dry. Then it *fits.* Your scope will not get knocked out of alignment (or squeezed out, as frequently happens). If you are having a new scabbard made don't get the old-fashioned ones which reach away back to the button-shoe era—those which cover the entire rifle, with skirting or sole leather, back to the buttplate, and then have a cumbersome, heavy leather boot which fits over the open end. These are out with most of the cognoscenti. They're needlessly weighty and complicated. Once upon a time, back in the pre-1968 dear dead days, sportsmen used to ship their rifles in these rigs. No more. It is suicidal, if you dote upon your pet rifle, to unleash to the thieves rampant in the various shipping agencies any container showing that it's carrying a rifle. Nowadays, use a stout foam-lined container such as Saf-T-Case (one of the best), made of metal alloy and really hell for stout. I mark my own as containing "maps" and it has been all over the world. Use the leather scabbard only where it belongs, on horseback, and get one suitable for fast action yet fully protective against the elements and scratches. Have the saddle skirting (heavy leather) cover the rifle from muzzle to rear of the scope, and from there on, permanently attached (sewn to the main body of the scabbard) a snood-like cover of flexible, work-glove leather with full-length heavy duty zipper. When the sun benignly beams and you're riding in the open (or know you're approaching game) unzip the snood and fold it back on the scabbard, out of the way. If you go into bugbrush, timber, rocks—or the heavens clabber—zip securely and your rifle is adequately protected. Many firms and individuals have made the types I've described, but the first I ever saw were those made by the master of them all, Capt. Hardy. He told me he'd designed the heavy ones, with separate boot, for shipping

These are the packhorse panniers the author designed years ago. Sturdy and tough, Jobson told how to make this type of box (two are needed to balance the load) in the December 1971 issue of *Sports Afield.*

or for transporting a rifle on a pack horse. Those with the lighter weight, pliable snood-cover were for saddle horses. I'm with him. I'd be less than a conscientious reporter not to mention that, catching on here in the Mountain States, at least, is a rather remarkable scabbard-case of high-impact, light, rugged plastic which is "fur" lined and an all-round good deal. It has the separate boot (which, in leather, I've just advised you against) for use on a pack horse, in a pickup, or for shipping (the manufacturer says). I would not ship a rifle in one, for the reason that the contents surely would be no mystery to a felonious transport employee. With cover removed, it makes a dandy saddle scabbard for some, although my horse shied from it at first. Extremely interesting device, and sporting rifle enthusiasts could do worse than investigate it. Brochure from: Do-All Mfg., 3206 Plant Dr., Boise, Idaho 83703.

Other Leather Gear

Having other good leather products can add joy to a pack trip. You'll hear leather chaps called an "affectation," but in my experience this is bedside crockery, probably written by someone who'd never been on a big time pack trip. Relatively inexpensive, they are life savers (well, leg savers) in cruelly cold, blizzardy weather and, just as important, cushion and save the knees and shins from lacerations, which alone could handicap a trip's success. There are several varieties, but unless you are an agile youth, I'd shy from the form-fitting "stove pipe" design, which are more like Indian leggings. The sesame seed under the lower denture here is that unless you're a contortionist you can't shed them in a hurry when you pile off ole Seabiscuit on a steep hillside for a quick stalk. They are hot and induce sweat. Better are the rodeo "batwing" chaps, with three conchos and snaps for fast on-and-off.

You will find it pleasurable and mighty convenient to have your own saddle bags. Some outfitters furnish them, and some do not, but some of those supplied are poor things indeed. Safest to have your own for your lunch, camera, film, candy bar, spare ammo, maybe even a wee drap!

Pack Horse Panniers

During the 10-year stint I've been camping editor at *Sports Afield* my departmental pieces have brought me pleasing volumes of mail, some times postal canvas bags of it. But never have I received such a torrent, a raging maelstrom of enthusiastic respondence as when I have written,

Big Alaska/Yukon moose *(Alces gigas)* harvested by John Jobson—two shots, one not needed, with a 270 and Nosler 130-gr. bullets, WW brass and primer, 62 grains of 4831. Bull, quartering away, was hit in short ribs; one bullet came out of the chest, the other lodged under the chest skin. This bull stood 7' 8" at the withers, his antlers 68¾" wide ● You will note my outfitter packs a 44 Magnum handgun. Some experts tell you that never, under any circumstances, should you carry a large caliber handgun in big game country. Let's scotch this bit of balderdash—we were in the midst of some exceedingly truculent barren-ground grizzlies, who often sought us out and charged various members of our party. I was charged once and had to kill a small bear I didn't want. Grizzlies came into camp 7 different times, all different bear ● This outfitter couldn't carry his rifle with him all of the time, for he needed to use both hands to do his chores and jobs. Yet he required peace of mind and actual protection, so there are times when a big handgun is called for.

(several times now) on panniers (pack boxes) and how to make them. It's an exceedingly astute maneuver to acquire a pair of your own. Whether you buy or make them doesn't matter so much, but having them makes a world of difference. A pair of them, necessary for good balance, fits on a patient, usually willing pack horse. These contain all your goodies and necessaries with the exception of your bedroll, rifle, and scabbard. At home, your equipment can be stored in them and, when you're ready to take off, you can leave with no worries. Of various shapes, most possess the aesthetic conformation of apple crates. I prefer the horse-hugger design, shaped to fit the horse. These can be seen in my *Sports Afield* departmental piece for December 1971.

Sleeping Bags

For the Rockies, there is only one sleeping bag for fall hunts, and that's the heavyweight, insulated with 5-6 pounds of prime waterfowl down.

There is no shortcut to this that I've ever heard of. Those trying to cut corners on a quality bag end up the loser. One *must* have his rest on a big game hunt. You can still have fun and get around on tasteless food, leaky boots, and other hazards, if you must. But if you don't have sound sleep you're in trouble, in a hurry, and the trip is a write-off. Also carry a thick woolen blanket to fold several times under your kidney region, where the bag is coldest from compression of the down. On the rare warm night, sleep atop the bag with the blanket for a cover. Wrap the bag and blanket in a 10'x8' (or 10'x10') *canvas* tarp. The multi-layers will protect the bag in transit, and you can use it as a ground cloth. In emergency, you can make a shelter with it. Secure the tightly rolled "bedroll" with a couple of 3-inch wide web straps. The mattress can be either foam (if you're small and light) or air. I prefer air. It's necessary to include a patching kit.

Jobson holds a scabbard, of high-impact moulded plastic, that's becoming highly popular in the mountain West. About indestructable, it doubles as a carrying-shipping case or saddle scabbard. On the right, it's shown as it usually goes on saddle horses. Note integral strap loops. Left, the boot which fits over the open end of the scabbard, making one rugged, compact unit of protection for the finest rifles. The scabbard and part of the boot are lined with thick, protective man-made fiber "fur." It is not at all harmed by a horse rolling on it. Great in car trunk, boats, 4WD or wherever a compact, formfitting rifle case is required. Made by Do-All Mfg., and Kolpin of Berlin, WI 54923.

Jobson's outfitter (Bill Fraser) with rain suit and broad-brimmed hat. Jobson shot this caribou mainly for meat and the double-shovel he wore.

Personal Stuff

Personal gear should include binoculars for locating game—and the best you can buy. For the Rockies—10x40, 9x35, 8x30, or a 7x35 will do. These are for spotting game animals, hopefully before they see you (the primary rule of successful big game trophy acquiring). While you can locate game with binocs, to size up the horns-antlers you will save yourself many heartrending climbs and tedious hours if you fetch along a quality spotting scope of 20 to 30x. 22.5x is excellent.

Most everyone has his favorite camera, most of them in use today taking 35mm film, so I won't go into tiresome details about what *you* should buy or use. My favorite still camera for day-to-day use afield is the twin-lens Rolleiflex in 2¼x2¼-inch film size, but not by any means do I say this is the only camera. In truth, it's a bit on the bulky side, but I'm used to it. A good rule of thumb on the film supply (far from a source) is to calculate, generously, what you think you'll need, then double it. This usually works well for both amateur and professional photographers. Have a quality pocket knife, and a sheath knife with sharpening stone in the saddle bag or pack frame. Sun glasses, windproof lighter, wet strength tissue, Chap Stick, bandannas, and at least 100 rounds of ammunition (if you have only one rifle). My blood runs cold when writers advise burgeoning big game hunters to take only "40 rounds." This is wholly illogical. Put the case that your rifle gets bumped now and then, and must be carefully resighted? Or that you get temporarily misplaced from the others and have an overwhelming craving to let off a few salvos of three-shots-help-I'm-lost. Some guys like to cut loose at varmints, and/or shoot the heads of ptarmigan and other grouse, for the pot, when there is little likelihood of its spooking big game trophies. That eats up ammunition in a hurry. Me, I take 140 rounds for each rifle. The fact that generally I return with more than 100 has little to do with it. The ammunition is compact, relatively lightweight, and inexpensive compared to total trip costs. On most well-organized pack trips, you'll be in country where its possible to be weathered in, tent bound, occasionally. Anticipate by having a few paperback books. Playing cards are fine, as long as you do not gamble with the hired help. This has caused many a pack trip to go sour. Medicines, spare lens, and other wee impedimenta should be carried in little waterproof, protective

Many worthwhile leather items, such as chaps, saddle bags and rifle scabbards, can be made on cold winter nights, to while away the time and dream of next year's hunting. It's simple to do, and only a few tools, such as those shown here, are needed: leather (from leather supply house), needles of the harness-makers variety, wax thread and beeswax, sharp knife, chalk, leather cement, hole punches, rawhide mallet, ice pick (or awl), ruler pencil, and simple compass (to use as dividers). Here we're making saddle bags, hence the buckles.

Saddle bags are easy to make, so here we go. First step—make a paper pattern. If you can't locate a pattern easily, take the dimensions from saddle bags you admire. Use stiffer leather for the main body and thinner, softer leather for the gusset. It looks 700% harder than it actually is. Scabbards and chaps go just as easy, though chaps have to be fitted individually for best results. Use harness-makers double stitch. A shoemaker can show you how, or get a library book on leather-working, if you think you need it.

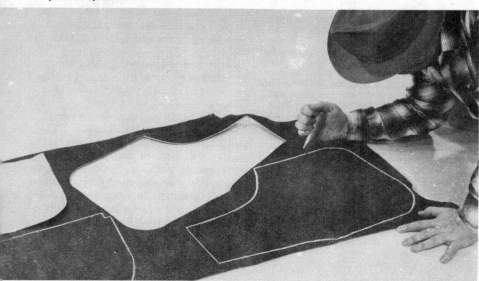

Tupperware containers (your wife can get them).

A good hat layout for the Rockies always includes a visored cap with ear muffs, a Navy woolen watch cap or the like, and a 10-gallon felt wide-brim. A roomy rain suit is called for, rather than a slicker. Slickers spook some horses, and they're so unwieldly as to be nearly impossible to walk or climb (stalk) in. An excellent rain suit is that offered by Action Sportswear, Box 1264, Wausau, Wis. 54401. You can experience an amazing spectrum of temperatures and general weather in the Rockies. Once in the Yukon, in early September, we had weather so bloody sizzling hot that life-long residents of Yuma, Arizona, would have been prostrated. That same day, climbing to the sheep pastures, we got into a howling snow storm with a vicious, cutting wind that would have frozen the *cojones* off Michaelangelo's stone statue of David.

Down Jackets

The number one, indispensable item of equipment to help cope with sub-arctic weather is a good quality down jacket. It is hard to get cold in one—I have ridden standing on the back of a stake bed truck in Wyoming in winter, wearing one, and wasn't chilled where the jacket protected me. They have an enormous temperature accommodation, and can be worn unzipped or partially zipped. An extremely versatile item of equipment. Next to the down bedroll, this is surely a must. Everyone has his own ideas about the things that follow, but after 14 major and many lesser pack trips,

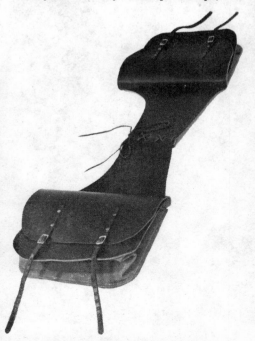

Jobson's Yukon Indian outfitter and guides know the necessity of binoculars (for locating game), and a spotting scope for judging the quality of the trophy. That's Johnnie Johns, world famous outfitter, at center.

are now made which break down in short length. In the olden days, it was nothing to see a 3½ or 4 foot aluminum tube atop a pack horse, carrying valuable Hardy-quality bamboo rods. The unconcerned horse would stroll under a tree, a branch would catch the tube, and copious tears the size of papaya seeds flowed like May wine. No, not from the horse.

Tips and Hints

A tip about clothing, in case you haven't experienced it — garments afield are much tighter and more constrictive about the crotch and armpits, etc., than in the store or at home. You get into many extreme positions on a trip that you never have reason to assume at home. You crawl, like a Comanche after a sodbuster. You bend, and turn — twist and stoop. Therefore experienced hands more often than not buy clothing roomier than they usually do. If you can, get "full cut" clothing. Loose clothing is, ounce for ounce, much warmer as it traps more insulating air. Multilayers of lightweight clothing are far, far warmer than an equal weight of a single layer. Again, air is trapped in the layers and folds. As you climb a mountain and blood circulates, a shirt can be shed. As you top out into a zephyr right off the Polar Cap, you add. Simple, but like many uncomplicated things — workable. Stockings should fit snug, for a fold in one can cause a peach of a blister or, worse, an injured (bruised) Achilles tendon. The latter, if one is striken with it, the first few days, will literally ruin the trip as this tendon, surprisingly subject to bruising afield, heals deplorably slow.

Boots, however, should be a size longer and *wider* than normal, as the feet swell that much under hard daily use, and you need a bit of extra room for two pair of wool socks. I put on one athletic, and one knee length. This thwarts the chill, but more important, acts as a bulwark against stone bruises.

Don't sell proper equipment short. You can save your nickels until you achieve that heady goal of being able to book the hunt, take time off, and *go*. Your outfitter may be the best, with top guides and a Cordon Bleu cook. His tents, horses, and country may be just perfect. But just one single item of personal gear, selected incorrectly, can and often does handicap a sportsman in degrees varying from being miserable to completely, totally ruining that long-dreamed-of, once-in-a-lifetime big game hunt in the Rockies. Don't let it happen to you.

I take the following clothing: two cotton flannel shirts, two woolen shirts (one light, one heavy), a *cashmere* (none other!) sweater, two suits of Duofold underwear (best quality), two undershorts, two stagged woolen lumberjack-type trousers, one pair of denim riders (Lee or Levis), a down vest, three pair of knee-length Norwegian heavy wool stockings and three pair of wool athletic socks.

Footwear

Boots: Number one, most used, are good oil-tanned mountain boots with 6-7 inch tops and Vibram lug soles. A pair of leather-rubber Bean pacs, some sort of insulated boot (these days, rubber-covered felt), and camp slippers. It is no problem anymore to pack an excellent fishing rod — several

I have tried all carrying-shipping cases I've ever heard of, but none compares with the two-rifle shipping case made by Saf-T-Case, Box 10592, Dallas, TX 75207. My case has ridden thousands of miles in the back of an African hunting car, over the Alaska Highway by commercial freight truck 8 times, has been over the Alaska Highway several times in my own rigs, has been shipped to Africa and return twice, to Hawaii, Fairbanks and Whitehorse; New York City and return several times. It's logged thousands of miles in 4WD and pickups throughout the West. The rifles remain in *perfect* shape through all this—no dust, no moisture. For me this is the only practical way to ship two rifles. The case does not scream "firearms" as do most cases, inviting thievery. I mark mine "maps" and, when going overseas, I remove the rifle bolts. Made of rugged alloy, with extra thick foam lining, two leather tie-down sets hold guns immovable. I saw this case thrown 30 feet from a ship to the dock below, as did four other people. No damage to the case or—more importantly—to the guns.

HANDGUNS
DOMESTIC AND FOREIGN

Comments and critiques on the new and soon to be seen pistols and revolvers.

BY GEORGE C. NONTE,
WALTER L. RICKELL AND THE EDITORS.

The Outstanding American Handgunner of the Year Award was officially unveiled in Indianapolis on Feb. 1, 1973. The noted sculptor (center) is Adolph G. Wolters. At right is Lee E. Jurras, co-sponsor of the award. John T. Amber, left, acted as master of ceremonies at the award dinner.

Outstanding American Handgunner First 1973 Award

The concept, planning and fulfillment of this praiseworthy effort to honor and recognize American handgunners was the joint effort of Lee E. Jurras and Ernie Wallein, chief officers of Super Vel Cartridge Corporation at Shelbyville, Indiana.

The award ceremonies and dinner, held in Shelbyville on 2 February, 1973, was a successful one indeed. The featured speaker was U.S. Senator Ted Stevens of Alaska, a strong opponent of restrictive firearms laws. Representative Wm. G. Bray of Indiana, likewise a friend of legitimate gun users, expressed his clear and unequivocal views on the subject as well. The compiler of these notes acted as master of ceremonies, a pleasant and rewarding job that he's to do again in 1974.

It is the hope of Jurras and Wallein that the Outstanding Handgunner Award will serve to acquaint the general public with handgunning as a sport, that handgunning is a legitimate activity, whether the individual's interest lies in target shooting, collecting, hunting or simple ownership.

While it is true that Super Vel initiated and sponsored this Award, other companies in the shooting sports participated to one degree or another. The sponsors hope that such participation will grow.

It could hardly have surprised anyone that Elmer Keith, Mr. Sixgun himself for these many years, became the first recipient of this new—and magnificent—trophy. Elmer Keith's numerous and varied contributions to the handgunning world need little explanation here—he's known the world over as a leading exponent, perhaps the leading figure, in his

tireless devotion to handguns and handgunning, whether for sport, competition or law enforcement. This dedication to the one-hand gun does not, of course, detract in any way from Elmer Keith's great ability with rifle or shotgun, yet to the world at large and to English readers in particular, Keith stands out like a shining light among handgunners. Small wonder, then, that Elmer Keith received the unanimous votes of the award committee, many of them top flight figures in the pistol and revolver field themselves.

The roster of judges for the 1973 award reads like a stellar cast of shooting stars—and no pun intended: George C. Nonte, chairman; Charles Askins, Pete Brown, Jim Carmichel, Jim Crossman, Dean Grennell, Steve Herrett, Neal Knox and Skeeter Skelton. Gun writers all, with one exception.

The 10 contenders for this first handgunner award had been chosen by ballots circulated nationally, the final choices selected from among scores of others voted for. The nine runners-up were and are, of course, prominent figures in the handgunning galaxy—Bill Blankenship, top competition shot for many years; Jeff Cooper of *Guns & Ammo*, writer and combat handgunning authority; Bill Ruger, famous handgun manufacturer; Lyman P. Davison, handgun advisor-expert and writer (and a friend of my youth); James Cirillo, police officer and a foe of most handgun controls; J. D. Jones, noted handgunner; Bob Milek, writer and consultant; Nate Silverleib, competition shooter and a battler against bad gun laws, and Hal Swiggett, writer and hunting handgunner.

These men were given memorial placques and a handgun, most of the

latter contributed by their manufacturers. The main trophy—a superb sculpture by Adolph G. Wolters of Indianapolis, a man famed for his work throughout the country—is the first of 10 only to be made from the Wolters original. There will be no more.

Plans are already being formed for the 1974 award ceremonies. If you would like to nominate someone you believe entitled to consideration, write to Super Vel.   J.T.A.

Elmer Keith, winner of the Outstanding American Handgunner Award for 1973. This was the first award of what will be an annual event, the sponsor Super Vel Cartridge Corporation.

HÄMMERLI

A Visit to Lenzburg

by JOHN T. AMBER

Hämmerli

This noted Swiss firm has long made some of the world's finest free pistols. After much development it has introduced a new Model 150 Free Pistol, caliber 22 Long Rifle.

Built on a Martini-type action, fitted with a slender 10.2-inch, free-floating barrel, it has a sight radius of 14.4 inches. Breech opening is accomplished through a thumb lever on the left side, and directly below it is a cocking lever for the finely adjustable single-set trigger. Both levers are pressed downward and are readily operable by the left hand. Trigger reach and angle may be adjusted to suit the individual. Stocks are typical free-pistol, wrap-around style with an adjustable palm shelf, accompanied by a long wood fore-end under the barrel, but separate substantially from it. Main purpose of the fore-end is to protect the barrel from impacts and to house the adjustable weights, which can vary total pistol weight between 42.3 and 49.4 ounces.

The striker firing mechanism (no hammer) has an extremely fast lock time of .0016-second and less than ¼-inch of travel. Accuracy of 10 consecutive shots into a 20mm (.80-inch) circle is guaranteed at 50 meters from a machine rest.　　　G.C.N.

Hämmerli's Model 120

As I've mentioned elsewhere in this edition, Jim Carmichel and I, as well as Raymond Caranta, spent a most interesting day at the Hämmerli factory in Lenzburg. We examined closely every model available then, including a couple I'm not permitted to describe, and particularly the new 22 rimfire pistols, the Models 120 and 150. The M150 Free Pistol won't, we were told, be ready for sale before late 1973, if that soon, but a sample of the M120 has just been received, packaged in a handsome red case or carton, foam-rubber lined, that no one will want to discard. Included with the pistol are a cleaning rod, brushes, two screwdrivers, a drift (all in a plastic pouch), a signed target, and an Instruction Manual in several languages. More on this manual later.

The M120 is a truly big pistol — it's almost 15 inches (375mm) long over-all, and its cataloged weight is 40 ounces (1250 grams). The sample pistol weighs 44 ounces. The tapered round barrel is 254mm long (10 inches), with a sight radius that's either 370mm or 250mm (optionally on the shooter's part), which is 14.13 or 9.84 inches. The rear sight has click adjustment screws, the click value for elevation and windage 15mm or about 0.6-inch — presumably at 50 meters, though that isn't stated. The front sight is a slightly undercut blade that's 0.140″ wide and deeply sloped toward the front, making for a sharp top edge. The rear sight is a flat steel plate (11x34mm wide), movable laterally for replacement by loosening two screws. The square notch in its top edge is only 0.11″ wide, but the long sight radius gives ample side light. The blade notch is not chamfered or undercut at its front.

The M120 is a bolt action, the cocking lever swinging laterally from its left-side pivot. The bolt face fully encloses the cartridge rim except for the narrow (about 0.10″) segment of the extractor. Cartridges must be seated manually, as there is no loading platform, but the loading port is amply large — it's 1.5 inches long, open at the top and extending well down the right side. Bolt locking is achieved through a steel arm, ½×½″ square in section, which is attached to the operating lever. As the lever closes, the locking bar or arm moves into position behind the breech-bolt. The rear of the locking bar bears against a broad-diameter plug, threaded into the rear of the receiver. This appears to be a strong and rigid system (Hämmerli has applied for a patent on it), and there is no shake or looseness of any degree when the bolt is closed, either in the cocked or fired mode.

The trigger system is highly unusual. The lower end of the trigger itself attaches to a round pin, the pin angling upward into the frame. The trigger may be adjusted to lie forward in the guard or back, and may be rotated as well to give an angled pull. The normal pull is a 2-stage, final letoff between 150 and 200 grams (53 to 70 ounces). A single stage pull can be adjusted for letoff running about 17 to 35 ounces. The trigger is otherwise adjustable for after travel and creep as well, though Hämmerli says this should be done by a qualified workman. Nevertheless, the Manual tells how to make all adjustments, if a bit obscurely!

The main frame (*not* including the steel receiver) is in two halves, made of aluminum. The one-piece walnut grip, strippled on both sides and made with a thumb rest for right-handed shooters, slides onto the frame from

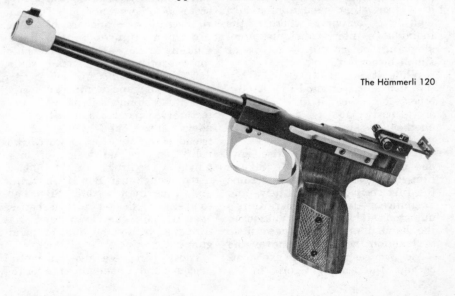

The Hämmerli 120

the rear.

Firing pin travel is only 7mm, lock time a fast 0.0018-second. Firing pin fall is quite dead, entirely without vibration.

An important design aspect of the 150 pistol is the extremely low position of the barrel in relation to the shooting hand. This allows, in turn, a very low line of sight, and at the same time decreases the amount of muzzle jump or flip on firing. Also, because of the nature and position of the low-slung fore-end, the center of gravity and the balance point of the pistol can be adjusted to suit the marksman's wishes.

Why the guard is so big I don't know. In part, maybe, to let the trigger be moved forward for those with long fingers. Perhaps, too, for some gloved marksman high on a frosty alp?

Fired from a machine rest, Hämmerli guarantees an accuracy at 50 meters of a high level – 10 shots within a 25mm circle – about an inch, compared to the 50mm 10-ring at that range. I don't have a machine rest, none that will take the M120 Hämmerli, at least, but from a 2-hand hold on sandbags, shooting at 20 yards indoors, groups of 10 shots – using RWS match 22 Long Rifles – averaged 0.88-inch for my old eyes, 30 rounds fired in all. Groups might have been smaller, I think, had the grip been a better fit. I found it too big, even for my size 9½ hands – I couldn't release the trigger confortably or uniformly. Hämmerli calls this the "standard" grip, but I can't locate anything in their literature offering smaller handles or a do-it-yourself rough grip. Nor is there any mention of a grip for southpaw shooters.

The Hämmerli 120 is an ingeniously designed, precision made match pistol, with a high potential, I believe, for top performances in competition. Despite its long length over-all and a 10-inch barrel, it has good balance, seeming to me neither muzzle light or heavy in offhand shooting. The retail price is $205, as of late 1972, so it's hardly inexpensive, but I imagine it will move well anyway, once match shooters can test its performance. Its even more sophisticated running mate, the Hämmerli Model 150 Free Pistol, may well be priced at near $400 when it appears – which won't be very soon.

I regret there wasn't time to give the Model 120 a lengthier workout – using other ammos, an altered grip or a makeshift one, and other shooters – but time ran out. We go to press with this 28th edition several weeks earlier this year!

Hämmerli 150

Hämmerli 230

The old Model 33

Astra

Astra Unceta, of Guernica in Spain, has been known since the turn of the century for good-quality handguns. The various so-called "Water-Pistol" Astra autoloaders have always exhibited very fine workmanship. Unlike the other major Spanish handgun makers, Astra has produced few true locked-breech autos, and its 1921-vintage M400/600 series is the only commercially successful *unlocked* design handling the powerful 9mm Parabellum and 9mm Bergman-Bayard cartridges. Its one locked-breech effort was the Mauser-like M900 series of 7.63mm military pistols and machine pistols.

After WWII Astra began producing solid-frame double-action revolvers, these copying the Smith & Wesson in appearance, and differing only slightly internally. This gun, called the Astra Cadix, has been imported and distributed for many years by Firearms International, a division of Garcia Corp.

The basic design, now updated and strengthened, is being offered as the "Astra 357," a very substantial 38.8-ounce, 6-shot 357 Magnum revolver. Our first sample, received in January, has proven to be a very sound and well-made piece. Offered in 3'', 4'', and 6'' heavy-ribbed barrels with full underlug, the 357 might be taken for a S&W Combat Magnum at a casual glance, but there are differences. The trigger guard is shallower forward, the crane and frame are radiused in profile, and the underlug angles upward. The hammer shape is also much

different (and less attractive) than the S&W.

Our sample gun (serial No. 152719) carries the 4-inch barrel and standard adjustable target-type rear sight, with quick-draw ramp front. Sights and rib top are neatly serrated to reduce glare. The serrated trigger face is narrow, only .280-inch wide, while the hammer spur is quite wide, .430-inch. The trigger looks fine, but the hammer is awkwardly shaped, though perfectly functional—both are finished

bright. Stocks copy the S&W magna style, but are thicker and not so comfortable.

Operation is strictly S&W: push forward the left-side cylinder latch, swing the cylinder out to the left, push extractor rod rearward to empty the chambers, and the rod locks up front in the familiar way. A spring-retracted, frame-mounted firing pin is used, and the hammer is retracted by a rebound slide when the trigger is released. A safety lever is fitted which rises to prevent the hammer from striking the firing pin unless the trigger is deliberately held fully

rearward. In short, the action has all the characteristics of the S&W, with the addition of a separate firing pin.

Our sample has a very smooth 10-pound DA pull, and a 4-pound SA pull with some creep and roughness. Functioning with several brands and loads of factory ammunition was faultless, and extraction load is moderate—not only with 38 Spl., but with the heaviest 357 loads. Cylinder lockup and alignment are excellent, and the barrel-cylinder gap measures only .005''-.006'', though about .001'' tighter on the left side than on the right.

As for accuracy, the Astra 357 did as well with 38 Spl. wadcutters and Super Vel 357, 110-gr. JHP loads as an old standby S&W M19 Combat Magnum I keep at hand for checking ammunition. I haven't shot it enough to pin down precise group-size averages with various loads, but put in the old-timer's vernacular "She shoots close, and she shoots where she looks." For a modern 357 Magnum revolver priced at about $100, that ain't bad at all. Astra's founders would be proud.
G.C.N.

Automag Corp.

Much has been made in the past of the Automag Corporation and the unusual autoloading pistol it made briefly. Apparently several hundreds of the guns were produced, perhaps as many as the 2500 claimed.

Then, though, the firm bankrupted, and its assets were sold. All finished parts, reported enough for several thousand guns, were all purchased by one party. We are told that eventually these parts will be assembled into complete caliber 44 Automag pistols which will be sold on the open market. Just when, how, and at what price this will occur, we don't know.

One bright spot for owners of Automag pistols is that factory-loaded ammunition is now available. Probably only this single lot, produced by the Remington Mexican plant, will

ever be offered—so those who need it had best get it now. Write to Pacific

International Import Co., 2416 16th St., Sacramento, CA 95818.   G.C.N.

New Bar-Sto Stainless Steel 25 Auto

Bar-Sto Precision (633 S. Victory Blvd., Burbank, CA 91502) makers of stainless steel 45 ACP, 38 Super, 9mm barrels and various parts for the old 1911 warhorse, now produces a small 25 auto pistol made entirely of 400-series stainless steel.

The little pistol looks, at first glance, like any other pocket pistol of this type but that's where it all ends. Close inspection shows superior workmanship, for this piece is completely machined from solid bar stock and finished in a semi-dull style. This 2⅛"-barreled gun weighs 11½ ounces, over-all it's 4" long by 2⅞" high, width less than ¾-inch. Basically like the baby Browning, it has a sear and firing pin of Stone's design. The sear, sealed in at the factory, can't be removed without destroying the frame. The safety, located at the rear, on the left side of the frame, operates easily with the left or right hand, and it's positive—Stone says that a live round can be safely carried in the chamber when the safety is on.

Accuracy is good. Six shots from the magazine of this high quality semi-auto stayed well within the black at 25 yards. The price is $125.00, a mite steep, but then what isn't? The workmanship, though, justifies the investment. W. L. Rickell.

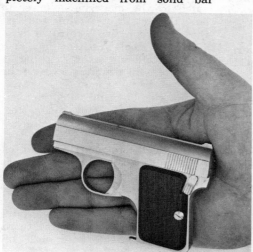

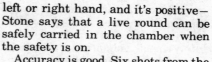

The new Bar-Sto stainless steel 25 auto pistol, the finish a non-glare matte.

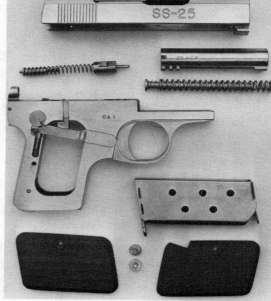

Bar-Sto's new stainless steel 25 auto pistol, here field stripped. The sear is permanently sealed in.

Alloy Frame Test

From time to time we receive queries from shooters concerned with the service life of aluminum-framed, big-bore autoloaders. Periodically there have been the usual latrine rumors and unsubstantiated reports of frame failures or abnormal wear after only 1000 rounds or less have been put through them.

Disbelieving such stories—since I'd never been able to dig out any details—I took a new S&W M39 and a new Walther P-38 and fired them 5500 rounds each as rapidly as possible. At the end of the test both guns were quite serviceable, still acceptably accurate, and displayed only modest wear on the frames, hardly any at all on the steel components. Also, you can add to this Skeeter Skelton's experience firing an identical amount of ammunition through a Colt Commander—which alloy-framed pistol remained serviceable, safe, and accurate after all that shooting of full-charge service ammunition. This would—or it ought to—seem to dispel once and for all the stories that aluminum frames don't hold up as well.

American Firearms announced a stainless steel 380 and 9mm Ultra autoloader last year, but as of this writing this gun is not yet available.

A similar situation exists with the **Budischowski** TP-70 stainless-steel, double-action, 25 ACP auto pistol; no samples of this gun have yet been made available. The big 20-shot 9mm Budischowski is also still absent from the marketplace.

P. R. Lichtman, 50 Sun St., Waltham, Mass. 02154, has announced "The world's smallest 380 auto," a diminutive gun hardly larger than many 25 autos. It measures 4.7" long, 3.3" high, and 0.75" thick, with a 5-shot magazine capacity. It is domestically made—and alleged to be available—but we have no more information than the description above, and haven't yet been able to obtain a sample for testing.

Two other guns announced sometime ago and mentioned in GD 27 have not yet materialized as production items. One is the **Plainfield Machine Co.** 380 auto, the other the unusual **Clerke** in 380 and 22 LR.

Armoloy

There is a new (new at least to guns) finish we've been checking out on handguns—though it is equally applicable to long guns. This the Armoloy process of chrome impregnation of the steel surface, forming a finish two microns thick by a solid molecular bond. This differs from the mechanical bond of electroplating, for the Armoloy finish actually becomes a part of the steel surface—it cannot crack, chip or peel. It has a hardness of about 72 on the Rockwell C-scale, and has a natural lubricity which greatly reduces friction. In addition, the finish is fully as resistant to corrosion as chrome plate.

At the present time, Armoloy is being applied only to handguns by Armoloy (206 E. Daggett St., Ft. Worth, Texas 76104), and only to external surfaces and internal parts. Bore interiors and very small springs are not yet being treated, though methods for them are being developed. In addition, Armoloy greatly improves the casting qualities of bullet moulds, and eliminates forever the need for oiling to prevent rust.

The completed Armoloy surface, which does not increase dimensions measurably, follows even the most minute surface inequalities. It does *not* build up in thick spots or fade out over sharp edges. In appearance it displays a very fine-grain matte surface and a semi-bright, slightly grayish color, much like finely sand-blasted bare steel. It will *not* hide surface imperfections, so an absolutely smooth polishing job must exist. Price for the average handgun runs $20-$35.   G.C.N.

Behlert

Interest continues to increase in autoloading pistols especially modified or customized for law enforcement use. The most recent example examined is a Browning High-Power extensively modified by Austin Behlert of Cranford, N.J.

Behlert first shortens the slide and barrel by one inch, then fits a special-threaded barrel bushing to improve accuracy, and also removes the front locking lug to make room for the bushing. A compound recoil spring with a full-length guide follows, along with a new screw/spring/plunger method of securing and detenting the slide stop. Refinishing and new sights — customers choice, but usually the S&W revolver target sight — completes the routine job. Behlert also offers a special enlarged, square-front, combat trigger guard, stippling of front and back straps, and special thin-profile stocks from Cloyce which reduce butt thickness by 3/16''. To go even further in weight and bulk reduction, Behlert will shorten the butt and magazine to suit. The sample

we've been shooting has the butt shortened over a half-inch, which makes the gun much more concealable. Numerous other mods are also available for the big Browning.

Behlert performs similar surgery on the Colt Government Model series, making them much more convenient to carry. Prices aren't cheap, for the average job goes around $250 — on *your* gun. Unlike most other combat conversion specialists, Behlert attempts to keep new guns on hand for conversion so customers won't always have to supply the basic gun. Retail price of the new gun is then added to the conversion cost. The sample we've been shooting performs quite well, being totally reliable and quite accurate, as well as very easy to carry and conceal.   G.C.N.

Budischowsky

The Budischowsky TP-70 double-action autoloader was an enigma until just recently. Though advertised for sale and announced last year, no sample guns could be obtained. However, we've recently learned the company's (Norton Armament Corp. 41471 Irwin, Mt. Clemens, Mich. 48043) problems are well into solution, and guns are now being produced. Friend Amber and I have examined samples which look quite good indeed.

This is a most pleasing little gun, quite the nicest 25 ACP auto ever to be made in this country, in this scribe's opinion. With a 2.60" barrel it measures 4.65" long, 3.31" high, 0.92" thick, has an exposed hammer, and a magazine capacity of 6 rounds. Weight is 12 ounces, empty. Thus it is approximately the same size as the Colt 25 Pocket Auto, but it has much more to offer.

First and foremost, it is of *double-action* type, complete with a Walther-style, slide-mounted manual safety; secondly, it possesses an external, manual slide stop which also is activated by the magazine follower to hold the action open after the last shot has been fired; third, it is of stainless steel construction and, fourth, it offers instant stripping by means of a dismounting lever on the right side of the frame.

Disassembly couldn't be simpler: engage safety; remove magazine; draw slide back about ¼"; turn dismount lever downward; move complete slide/barrel unit forward off frame; lift recoil spring and guide up and out rearward; same for barrel.

A very nice little gun, indeed — at about $100 it's a bit high for a pocket 25, but none of the lower-price guns can even approach its features. It will be available later in 22 LR caliber.   G.C.N.

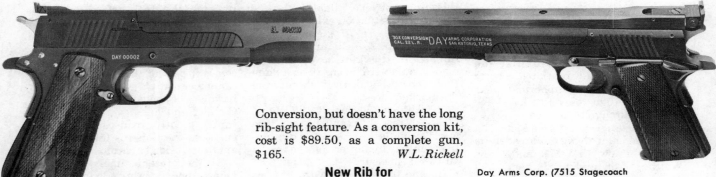

Conversion, but doesn't have the long rib-sight feature. As a conversion kit, cost is $89.50, as a complete gun, $165.   *W.L. Rickell*

New Rib for Combat Matches

Interest in police combat shooting continues to grow. The S&W K-38 and Model 19 revolvers with 6-inch barrels are easily the most popular handguns used, but they lack that necessary forward weight found in the Colt Python. To fill this need Day Arms Corp. (7515 Stagecoach Lane, San Antonio, TX 78227) developed a heavy rib for these S&W revolvers.

It attaches to the barrel rib by two 6-32 Allen capscrews, adding 3½ ounces to the important forward area. Two blades guard the front sight, keeping it away from the holster — blacking on the front sight so it won't rub off. The new rib doesn't interfere

Day Arms Corp.

The Day Arms 30x Conversion unit — a 22 Long Rifle caliber system designed for use on big Colt auto frames — was described in these pages some time back — and it's still available at $99.50, with full length sight rib and 10-shot magazine.

Now, however, Day Arms offers the whole package — a new alloy frame-receiver, your choice of trigger and mainspring housing (arched or flat) — all match conditioned, at $175.

The El Macho, another Day Arms development, is very like the 30x

Day Arms Corp. (7515 Stagecoach Lane, San Antonio, TX 78227), makers of the 30-X Conversion Unit for the 45 Auto, will soon offer a broad and heavy rib, with an adjustable rear target sight of their design. Prices unknown now, but the new sight-rib will be made for all popular target handguns.   *W. L. Rickell*

with any revolver functions.

Heretofore shooters have gone to great expense, having custom barrels turned from heavy blanks which limit the use of the gun, but this new Day Arms rib is $19.95. It can be attached by a competent pistolsmith in minutes and, once fitted, it serves as a useful addition to the officer's duty gun.   *W. L. Rickell*

Charter Arms Bulldog 44

During the past year or so there have been rumors aplenty about a new revolver from Charter Arms, gossip that could hardly be credited—who'd believe in a 20-ounce 44 Magnum? Who would want to shoot one?

The truth is out—and it's only a little less surprising than the back-door reports! The new Bulldog 44—chambered for the 44 Special cartridge—should be on the dealers' shelves about mid-year or a bit later, price $110.00.

Barrel length will be 3 inches, the cylinder will hold 5 rounds, and weight unloaded is a mere 19 ounces. The new revolver will, naturally, have all of the safety and other features found on the Charter Arms Undercover models, but numerous dimensional changes were made to handle the 44 Special cartridge—revised frame, new barrel and cylinder, of course, and there's a new hammer and trigger, both very broad.

Like the Undercover revolvers, the new Bulldog 44 has the Charter Arms hammer block or "transfer bar," a safety device which transmits the hammer blow to the firing pin only when the trigger is pulled fully back. The hammer *cannot* hit the firing pin

The new Charter Arms Bulldog 44 Special.

otherwise.

Short single- and double-action, plus an unbreakable beryllium firing pin, are additional features of the Bulldog 44.

Sights are fixed on this first-issue Bulldog 44, but a target-sight version will appear later, probably in 1974. Grips will be their Bulldog style, as standard, quite like the same style handles that are optional on the other Undercover handguns. J.T.A.

Charter Arms Bulldog Grips

A larger, checkered grip, made of hand-rubbed American walnut, is optional with all Charter Arms handguns; the Undercover 38 Special, Undercoverette 32 and the Pathfinder 22.

These "Bulldog" grips, available as original equipment or as replacements, are furnished with escutcheons, medallions and grip screw.

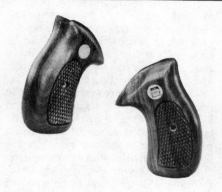

Plain, uncheckered grips of American walnut are furnished as standard on all Charter Arms handguns. The Bulldog grip meets the demand of those who prefer the size, heft and feel of a larger grip. In the case of the Undercover, in wide use as an off-duty handgun in the law enforcement field, the Bulldog grip does not detract from concealability.

Bulldog grips may be had through your local dealers or by writing to Charter Arms Corp., 265 Asylum St., Bridgeport, CT 06610. J.T.A.

Burris Sights and Mounts

A new firm has entered the metallic sights and scope mount field, and if their line looks somewhat familiar to you, you're right. Don J. Burris was, for some time, with Redfield Gun Sight Co., and his scope rings and bases, in particular, demonstrate that previous experience.

No matter, Burris scope mounts are well designed and well crafted, judging from the pair of samples here. The rings, nicely contoured and streamlined, are of special steel and made in three heights—low, medium

and high. The bases, both 1-piece and 2-piece, are also smoothly rounded—as are the base windage screws—for snag-free functioning. Extension front rings in two heights are offered, too, and virtually every popular rifle can be fitted with Burris bases—which are guaranteed to stand the recoil of any shoulder-held rifle. Burris, in fact, guarantees all of his products for the life of the original owner against defects in workmanship or materials!

Burris also makes a good range of open sights, front and rear, including

sweat-on and band-type ramp front sights. Both styles show smooth, graceful lines, and protective hoods are available for either form. Only receiver sights are not offered by Burris.

Our Burris one-piece base for a Remington 700 went on the rifle perfectly. Vertical alignment with the barrel was just right, according to the collimator, with a near-equal amount of clicks for elevation on either side of zero. Lateral line-up was also easily got by adjusting the base windage screw. J.T.A.

The other version of the Carl Gustaf/FFV gas-powered auto pistol, also in prototype form.

One of the two Carl Gustaf/FFV gas-operated autoloading pistols, here seen field stripped and gas nut loosened. Both versions are prototypes, with production pieces some two years away.

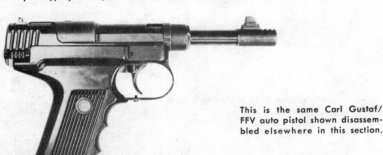

This is the same Carl Gustaf/FFV auto pistol shown disassembled elsewhere in this section.

Carl Gustaf/FFV

Early in 1972 we got a brief look at a pair of experimental autoloading pistols developed a number of years ago by the Carl Gustaf plant in Sweden for a military requirement. Since then a great deal of interest has developed in the basic design. As a result we recently had an opportunity to examine two guns closely and to give them a range workout. We were also advised that production is planned of two versions—the Model 1 in 45 ACP, 38 Super and 9mm P. (Luger), and the Model 2 in 357 and 44 Magnum. This sounds most interesting.

The design is gas-operated, something never yet accomplished successfully in a handgun. An annular gas piston, surrounding the fixed barrel, is driven rearward by expanding gases to accelerate the slide's motion backward. After a short "dwell" travel a cam groove in the roof of the slide first rotates the small cylindrical bolt to unlock, then carries the bolt rearward to extract, eject, and cock. Twin recoil springs are compressed by the slide movement. The slide is stopped by a removable breech plug set in vertical grooves in the receiver, then the recoil springs drive the slide forward to feed, chamber, and lock, leaving the gun ready to fire.

The barrel is screwed rigidly to the receiver. The bolt reciprocates and locks inside the receiver, the slide surrounding the receiver. The breech plug, which stops the slide, is removed downward, after depressing the exposed recoil spring guide head, to allow slide and bolt to be stripped rearward off the receiver.

The receiver is unique among autoloading handguns. It ends just below the bolt-way, just like the typical bolt-action rifle receiver. Only the trigger and a threaded grip stud protrude below it. The trigger guard is a separate unit screwed in place, and there is no grip frame. The entire grip/magazine seat is a plastic molding secured to the stud, carrying the magazine catch at its bottom rear edge.

The design incorporates a cocking indicator formed by the mainspring guide which protrudes from the rear of the receiver when the hammer is cocked. A typical manual safety rides on the left side of the receiver and a safety lug on the hammer prevents firing unless the slide is fully forward in battery. The fire control system is otherwise fairly conventional.

The guns are now rather squarish and esthetically they're not particularly appealing. This can and will be corrected in the production version, we're told, and mechanical improvements will also be made. Reportedly a program is under way to adapt this design particularly to the U.S. market.

We've shot two of the guns and found their performance quite acceptable. Grips are a bit boxy for small hands, and pointing could be improved (an easy change with the separate grip used). Functioning was fine with one gun, the other experienced occasional failures to lock because of its weaker (apparently well-used) recoil springs—an item easily replaced. Accuracy seemed equal to comparable guns. In final form, we'd expect the rigid barrel to produce better—or at least more consistent—accuracy than any of the mobile-barrel, recoil-operated designs we've lived with all these years.

We can't say when any Carl Gustaf pistols might be available here. Despite hints of 1 to 1½ years, we'd estimate *at least* a couple of years before production models could be available. All the same, we'll be looking forward to that day.   G.C.N.

A. R. Sales

Colt Mark IV/Series 70 auto pistols with alloy frames—total weight only 34 ounces—are offered by A. R. Sales in the standard 9mm, 38 Super and 45 ACP calibers. All of the Colt-made components are brand new, of course. Price, $125.00.

In addition, the same pistol, in 22 L. R. caliber (Colt's conversion unit is used) are $135.00.   W. L. Rickell

Bauer Firearms

The Bauer stainless steel 25 ACP auto described in detail in GD 27 has been coming off the production line in good quantity for quite some months now. Production guns in the field are generating excellent acceptance. The samples we've seen and used perform flawlessly, something that can't be said about a good many of both old and new 25 autos that are around these days.   G.C.N.

G&S Practicaps

Though it is less a problem than it once was, sustained "dry" firing for practice can easily be injurious to certain makes and models of revolvers and autoloading pistols, particularly older models—firing pins can break or become battered; firing-pin holes may enlarge or internal parts or surfaces suffer.

The use of Practicaps eliminates such potential problems. These "dummy" cartridges carry a special nylon pad in simulation of the live primer. These pads, spring-loaded to be compatible with the handgun they're intended for, cushion and absorb the firing pin blow—and Practicaps will, the makers imply, give good service virtually indefinitely, if not abused. The makers' warranty says that any Practicap that fails in normal service will be replaced without charge, except for postage or shipping costs.

Practicaps have a blacked steel case, the bullets red-colored. They

weigh roughly half as much as does a real cartridge.

Sample Practicaps were received in several calibers, 6 to a set. A Colt Mark III was loaded with the six 38/357 size, and the gun "fired" a hundred times, mostly fast double action. Only the slightest marking of the nylon pad appeared, and pad depth remained the same as before—our depth gauge gave the original reading. As of now, Practicaps are offered in 45 Long Colt, 44 Spl./44 Magnum, 41 Mag., 38 Spl./357 Magnum and 38 S&W. These cost $9.95 for 6 in 385 pl. The others are $11.95 for 6.

By the time you read this Practicaps in 380, 9mm Luger and 45 ACP calibers should be available. An all-plastic practice cartridge for 22 rimfire guns will be offered soon by G&S. These inexpensive dummy 22 rounds should be good for a thousand or so impacts. For full information, write to G&S Engineering Co., 11529 Tecumseh-Clinton Rd., Clinton, MI 49236.   J.T.A.

Griffin Gun Cases

No, the handsome case pictured here—as elegant as it is sturdy—is not made from well-seasoned oak—that's Formica's "sculptured" Spanish oak, a material highly resistant to scratching or stains. The piano-type hinge and dual latches are brass, and a "set-it-yourself" 3-digit combination lock will discourage prying fingers. The interior is equally attractive—the resilient material, which readily moulds itself to a handgun, is reversible, red or black, With the lid closed, the interior is sealed—a soft gasket, containing a corrosion inhibitor good for 2 years, does the trick. Griffin cases are made in 9 different sizes, from those for small derringers to a big 4-handgun attache type. The case pictured (No. 1173) measures 11½"x7½"x3" and sells

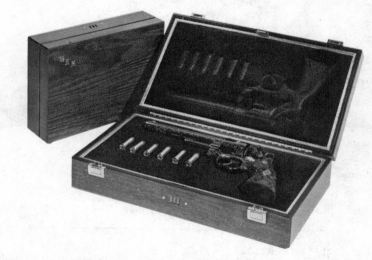

for $32.95. Three attractive "gold" initials of your choice are $1 extra.

Write Wamco, Box 280, Oquossoc, ME 04964 for free information.   J.T.A.

Hornady

In line with today's revival of older cartridges, Hornady is now making a bullet for the 33 Winchester—it weighs 200 grains and has a flat-point design, and retails for $10 per 100.

Hornady's new 45-70 bullet is a replacement for an earlier .458" diameter bullet intended for old 45-70 rifles. The new bullet has a longer and thicker jacket, giving it better performance when shot at the higher velocities and faster twists used in modern 45-70 rifles. Like its predecessor, the new bullet weighs 300 grains and has a hollow point design—and cost is still $7 per 100.

Other "old favorites" in the Hornady line include a 25-cal. 60-gr.

SP bullet, a 25-cal. round nose of 117 grains, a 32-cal. 170-gr. flat point and a 348-cal. flat point of 200 grains.

Another recent addition to the Hornady line is a 7mm bullet of 162 grains, a boat-tail HP in match quality—it should shoot very well.

The Hornady bullet selection now numbers 93 bullets, including 16 handgun types.   J.T.A.

New Hornady stronger jacket 45-70 bullet, weight 300 grains.

> **The product prices mentioned in these review pages were correct at presstime, but may be higher when you read this.**

Los Gatos Grips

This firm has been making handgun grips of various natural materials for some time—ivory, Cape buffalo horn, Sambar (India) stag—and some of their best liked are hand-carved on genuine ivory by J. M. Evans. However, such grips ran into money, the starting price $75, and it takes 3-6 months of waiting. Now Los Gatos offers exact duplicates of Evans' carved grips, in a wide range of motifs,

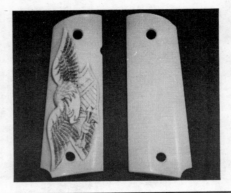

but in a synthetic material. Note, though, that these are *handmade,* yet the price in only $12.95 a pair, one side only carved. They're hand-fitted, too, we understand, and the carving appears sharp and crisply done. Their catalog is 25c.

Iv'e put a set of these, their No. 200 with buffalo skull carving, on a Ruger Super Black Hawk. The fit was 99% percect, just the slightest overlap at the bottom edges, almost too little to measure.　　　　　　　　　　J.T.A.

Right—High Standard's new Mk III revolver, caliber 357 Magnum, has target sights. The Mk II is identical except for having fixed sights.

Olympic High Standard

To help celebrate 1972's XX Olympic Games, High Standard offers—in limited numbers—the Supermatic Military 22 autoloader pictured here.

Engraved by Walter Kolouch, an Austrian now living in the U.S., the 5-ring Olympic symbol is inlaid in gold.

Serial numbered 1 to 1000 and cased, this deluxe High Standard pistol will sell for $550. In its standard form this is the only U.S.-made rimfire handgun to ever win an Olympic Gold Medal.　　J.T.A.

Ransom Master Rests

C'Arco (Box 2043, San Bernardino, CA 92406), makers of the excellent Ransom machine rests for accuracy testing of handguns, continues the same prices set last year—$112.50 for the complete outfit, including one set (2) of inserts for the 45 ACP (or similar) frame, unless ordered for some other handgun. Cost of insert pairs is the same, too, or $12.95, but the selection has been greatly expanded—you can pretty well name your choice, for among those now listed are the Hämmerli 208 and their free pistol, the Walther P-38 and OSP Rapid Fire pistols, the Ruger Security Six and many more.

Complete gun specifications for most of the guns described in this article may be found in our catalog pages. The addresses of the companies mentioned are listed in the Directory of the Arms Trade.

Ask C. R. Ransom for his latest brochure. It gives full information and it's free.　　　　　J.T.A.

This is the Ransom Master Rest, here holding a S&W Model 41.

Pachmayr Gun Works

Frank Pachmayr has spent the last couple of years working on a new system for accurizing the 45 Colt automatic pistol. Now the tooling for the several new component parts has been completed and, by about the time you read this—or maybe a bit later—the "Pachmayr Signature" accuracy treatment will be available on a first-come, first-served basis. In the beginning, at least, Frank won't be able to produce these jobs rapidly—much meticulous, critical work is required, of course, for this first class accuracy job to be delivered on a production line basis.

How does the Pachmayr Signature gun differ from some other and good accuracy treatments? Well known to targeteers using the Colt 45 auto—or like auto pistols—is the need for a firm, evenly-bearing fit between frame and slide, a fit that's without lateral looseness particularly. Well, it is in this region that Pachmayr's innovative design talents took over—below the frame, and just ahead of the guard, Pachmayr installs a specially-designed part called a Slide Guide. This relatively small device can be adjusted, at will, to increase or decrease the slide-frame clearance. In fact, as I did myself, the adjusting screw can be tightened until the slide cannot be retracted!

That aspect of the Pachmayr accuracy job—though it is, I think, the major element—is only part of the new treatment. First, of course, the slide edges and frame guides have to be made entirely smooth, without burrs or nicks, if the Slide Guide is to work effectively.

Another important component of the job is a new Barrel Bushing Housing-Retainer and its related Spherical Barrel Bushing. This combination, of course carefully fitted and adjusted, is also a special part. It is responsible for guiding the barrel back into battery uniformly and consistently every time—which it does very well.

Other parts that affect accuracy if they're not entirely right are also worked over—link, link pins, trigger, etc.—before Pachmayr returns the gun to you.

At the moment a firm price for the Pachmayr Signature job hasn't been set, but the basic work on your gun will cost about $250. Target sights, rebluing, etc., will be extra-cost options, of course.

The photo seen here doesn't show much, but it's all we have. The Slide Guide and the protruding Barrel Bushing can be seen, as can the new rubber grips Pachmayr makes for the Colt auto frame. These one-piece grips, wrapping around the handle, form an excellent means of handling the pistol. The checkering, perfectly done, has good grasping qualities, aided in good part by the semi-softness of the material. Each side of the grips has a steel plate moulded in for rigidity and strength.　　　J.T.A.

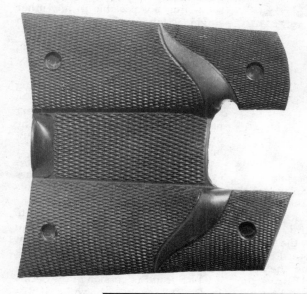

This 45 Auto has had the Pachmayr Signature accuracy treatment (see text) and on it are Pachmayr's new one-piece steel-reinforced rubber grips, also shown (inset) spread out.

Handgun Barrel Liners

A fair number of shops are prepared to do rifle barrel relining, but few have catered to handgunners. David R. Woodruff is one such—if you've got a bad barrel on that Luger, Mauser or some old revolver, write to Woodruff and get his brochure. Prices are quite moderate—from about $8.50 up, and he can furnish liners in most calibers, from 22 through 50 (yes, 50!)　　　J.T.A.

Pacific Bullet/Cartridge Chart

A handsome wall chart, picturing 95 actual-size, full color, rifle and pistol cartridges has been introduced by Pacific Tool Co. Useful to hang above reloading benches and attractive enough for the sportsman's den, it's the only available reference source of its kind.

The new chart displays and identifies 95 loaded cartridges from the 17/222 to the 458 Winchester Magnum. Printed on the dark-green background, alongside each cartridge, are bullet diameter, case length, primer size and shell-holder size. The chart also shows 91 full-size Hornady bullets, a Pacific reloading press with full nomenclature, and cut-away photos identifying the parts of Durachrome reloading dies.

35" wide by 25" high, the new wall chart is printed on heavy stock for easy hanging. Cost, individually rolled in a mailing tube, is $4 prepaid. Pacific, a division of Hornady, manufactures complete lines of tools, dies and accessories for both metallic and shotshell reloading. For information write Pacific Tool Co., P. O. Drawer 2048, Ordnance Plant Rd., Grand Island, Neb. 68801.

Spray Lube Misfires

Police personnel have been warned that use of many spray lubes can render primers inert, causing misfires, when the lube is applied freely to cartridges. This situation came to light when loaded revolvers were spray-lubed, then misfired some 3-4 months later—even with cartridges whose primers were "sealed." The moral—use spray lubes only after cartridges have been removed. J.T.A.

No-Sho SS Holster

As our illustration shows, the new No-Sho is a handgun holster made with a minimum of materials—16-

gauge stainless steel flat bars, covered with Corfam (a synthetic leather) to protect the guns. Made to exactly fit most any belt width, and quickly put on or detached via the twist-lock principle, the 2-oz. No-Sho allows a really fast draw. Less than 2 inches of vertical lift frees the handgun—even a 6-inch barreled sixshooter—faster than a 2-inch belly gun can be lifted from a conventional holster. It has so little bulk, say the makers, that No-Sho users have graduated from small guns to big ones with no loss of concealment. It is indeed a compact, narrow handgun holder.

The patented No-Sho is sold on a 10-day free trial or money back basis, cost $19.95, right- or left-handed, high rise or cross-draw. A safety strap can be had, price $2, but few use them, we're told.

We tried two No-Sho holsters—one for the Colt 45 ACP, the other for a Chief's Special. Admittedly this unusual-looking rig takes a little getting used to, but after some prac-

tice there's no question either gun could be moved from the No-Sho with high speed. The No-Sho doesn't wobble, either, the twist-lock angled fit on the belt seeing to that. No-Sho is at 10727 Glenfield Ct., Houston, TX 77035.   J.T.A.

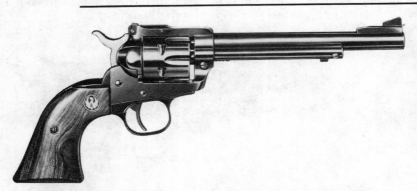

Sturm, Ruger

Bill Ruger's most significant new handgun this year doesn't *look* new at all. In fact, the new Single-Six looks exactly like the one we've known so long. The newness is all internal. The lockwork has been redesigned to meet all the safety limitations specified in GCA '68 and in the handgun control bill offered—but not passed—by Sen. Birch Bayh in the 92nd session of Congress. The general idea was to make the basic single-action design as mechanically safe as possible.

The main feature is a "transfer" bar, which must be between the hammer and the firing pin before the gun can be fired. This bar is linked to the trigger so that *only* when the trigger is deliberately held rearward does it move into position to allow the hammer to strike it and thus drive the firing pin forward. When the hammer is at rest, it bears on a solid surface of the frame and cannot reach the firing pin. This makes carrying all chambers loaded perfectly safe—something not possible in any other single action revolver. This system eliminates the usual intermediate hammer notches, so during cocking the old "clickety-click-clack" is missing.

In addition, opening the loading gate frees the cylinder to revolve, so there's no need of the old loading notch in the hammer. Too, when the loading gate is open, the gun cannot be fired, an added safety factor.

In our opinion this is the finest SA system yet devised, one that will pass all the safety tests put forward thus far.

Further, we have ample reason to believe that at the earliest practical date Ruger will use the same great system in the entire big-bore Black Hawk series.

The Speed-Six version of the Security-Six DA revolver shown on GD27's front cover isn't yet available, but we are informed it will be shortly after you read this.   G.C.N.

News From Speer

Lawman Ammunition is what the name implies—handgun cartridges in all popular calibers and types, including 9mm Luger and others in

modern high velocity loads. All of these new cartridges have been assembled by Speer with certain police handguns kept in mind, such as the short-barreled types used by plainclothesmen. A new police training film, in color, covers use of Speer's sub-velocity plastic case-bullet ammo. Called "Ready on the Right," it's available free to law enforcement groups.   J.T.A.

TDE

Late word from Ed Lomax of the TDE Corp. (11609 Vanowen St., No. Hollywood, CA 91605) is that Auto Mag pistols, 44 and 357, will be marketed, as will parts, for some intermediate time. Reason? TDE bought up Auto Mag, has permission from the courts to assemble, fabricate needed parts, and sell off the inventory—which was badly out of balance when TDE took over. Prices for either gun are $298.00. The 357/44AM conversion units are priced at $150.00.

Whether TDE will be allowed to resume full production of Auto Mags, once the inventory is disposed of, is unknown at present. TDE Corp., please note, is not responsible for or obligated to pay any Auto Mag Corp. bills or liabilities.   J.T.A.

New Safariland Holster

So-called "paddle" holsters have a bendable-steel, cushioned leather pad that the holster proper attaches to. The paddle slips *behind* the shooter's belt or waistband, held there by its curved fit and friction. A good rig that many like, but it has had problems— sweaty in hot weather and the leather pad stained the shirt or trousers.

Safariland's new version of the paddle style holster, called the Hip-Hugger, is offered on their Nos. 2, 18 and 29 regular holsters. The metal-lined pad, now covered with a rubbery substance, won't stain clothes and it is attached to the holster on a ratchet/swivel which can rotate 360 degrees. The holster is locked in any desired position by the screw which holds it to

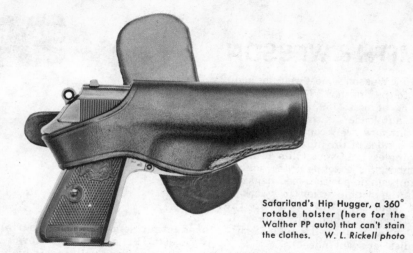

Safariland's Hip Hugger, a 360° rotable holster (here for the Walther PP auto) that can't stain the clothes.   W. L. Rickell photo

the pad. Thus the holster can be worn at a standard right-hand carry at various angles or in cross-draw fashion.

The holsters mentioned can be had with the rotating pad system for $4 over the regular price of the holster.   *W.L. Rickell*

Dan Wesson Pistol Pack

The new Wesson pistol kit should be attractive to many sixgun fans.

The cased set includes—beside the revolver of your choice—6", 4" and 2½" barrel assemblies, two finished grips and an inletted stock blank that can be whittled away to suit the owner's taste. The case, made from high-impact, luggage-quality plastic, is filled with a custom-cut foam-rubber interior. The case, designed for storage or travel, offers good insurance against damage in almost any circumstances. Prices range from $165 to $225, according to the revolver model selected.   J.T.A.

Dan Wesson

New for 1973 will be a line of 22 rimfire heavy frame revolvers, but that's only one of the new models coming from Wesson for '73. New long-action guns will be seen, as well as a selection of finishes and grip styles. Custom engraved models are also available. Price of the new 22 rimfire revolver has not been set, but it'll be around $100-plus. If we can snag one of these in time for a Test-fire Report, you'll read it elsewhere in this space or in this edition.

Dan Wesson revolvers are now offered in a matte nickel finish as well as in their highly polished blue. The new satin nickel plate, virtually glareless, looks a lot like stainless steel.

Dan Wesson's Models 14 and 15 have an improved barrel retaining nut, this nut now fully enclosed by the barrel shroud. This eliminates the exposed, serrated nut previously used, giving the gun smoother and more appealing lines.   J.T.A.

SMITH & WESSON

Smith & Wesson A most welcome addition to the Smith & Wesson handgun line is the new M59, a double-action 9mm autoloader. In this scribe's opinion this new S&W combines the best of two sides of the autoloader world. It mingles a 14-shot (plus 1 in the chamber, for a total of 15) double-column, single-position-feed magazine with the double-action lockwork of the excellent M39 S&W—in the highly popular 9mm Parabellum caliber—and in a total package that handles very well indeed.

The M59 is, really, only a modification of the highly successful S&W M39, the latter changed to handle a double-column magazine that's virtually identical to the one popularized by the single-action Browning Hi-Power pistol. Maximum parts interchangeability with the M39 has been achieved—the complete slide/barrel assembly being identical, as are many internal and lockwork parts. The enlarged magazine is accommodated by a new frame that's been widened, rearward of the trigger, to accept the thicker box. Accompanying this are very thin, checked black Nylon grips to hold over-all width within acceptable limits. To further reduce the circumference of the enlarged grip the backstrap has lost its characteristic M39 bulge and high-relief checkering, with generous relief cuts provided behind the trigger, a la Colt Gov't Model, to give easy trigger access to those with small hands or short fingers. The slide stop and magazine catch appear identical to those of the M39, but their stems are extended to reach through the widened frame. Internally, other changes have been made to accommodate the new magazine, particularly in a wider drawbar yoke through which the magazine must pass.

Functionally the M59 is identical to the M39. It uses the simple pivoted extractor of the M39-2, and the straight-feed ramp applied to all M39

New M59 S&W

production sometime after serial #150,000. This ramp design provides reliable feeding with all modern high-performance 9mm loadings, including the Super Vel 90-gr. JHP; most of these gave some feeding problems with the earlier M39 double-angle ramp.

Our experience thus far has been limited to two production M59s, numbered in the 170,000 range. Functioning has been flawless with every factory load we could drum up on short notice, and in handling the gun feels like a cross between the M39 and the Browning Hi-Power. The grip actually feels just a wee bit less bulky than that of the Browning, yet retains much of the excellent pointability of the M39. Fully loaded with 15 rounds the M59 weighs a mere 36 ounces—in good part because of its aluminum alloy frame—several ounces less than the only other pistol readily available of similar magazine capacity, the Browning H-P.

For those having a fondness for large-capacity magazines and double-action lockwork, the M59 is a most excellent choice. At the moment, it is the only choice with these attributes, though there are indications that other guns of similar characteristics may arrive on the scene in the not-too-distant future.

In the 1972 edition of this tome we reported on a new series of stainless steel revolvers from Smith & Wesson—the M64 (M10), M66 (M19), and M67 (M15). These are respectively

the Military and Police 38s, the Combat Magnums and the Combat Masterpieces. These guns were shown to the trade a year ago, but have only now become available (Dec. '72). We have just obtained production samples, and to date have examined and shot two each of the M66 and M67, and one of the M64. All have performed flawlessly, and none have exhibited those quality defects that we've noted in some previous S&W production pieces. Trigger pulls have been uniformly good—both SA and DA—accuracy has been excellent, while fit and finish are quite good. Thus far our only objection to these new stainless guns is the same one we make to virtually all bright-finished models—the front sights tend to become lost under bright light. This could be eliminated by using the old S&W separate insert of plain steel in blued finish. We'd like to see that.

Particularly good news is the fact that prices as originally announced have been reduced—the $175 previously asked for the M66 coming down to $157.

The only other current news from S&W concerns the discontinuance of the poorly received and executed 22 caliber M61 pocket auto and the hammerless Centennial model, which never quite achieved the market success originally anticipated. We do know of other developments under way at the S&W plant, but there's nothing we can talk about at this time.   G.C.N.

S&W Texas Rangers

Smith & Wesson, for 1973, will offer their first commemorative models. These will celebrate the 150th (Sesquicentennial) of the Texas Rangers. Here, briefly, are their descriptions.

All told, four Texas Ranger S&Ws will be offered. The big ticket Sesquicentennial TR20s ($1000) will be fully engraved revolvers in Class A grades, and will carry an oversized Seal of the Texas Ranger Commemorative Commission. The style of engraving may be selected by the buyer.

S&W Texas Ranger

Only 50 of these will be made, no more, and the price includes the handsome case and the Bowie knife illustrated.

Next in price, at $250, is a like Model 19 Combat Magnum, but which is not engraved; it does have the Seal on the sideplate, with 1823 and 1973 above and below, plus "TEXAS RANGERS" on the barrel; all are filled with 24K gold leaf. The Bowie knife and case are included.

A cased Model 19, as above but without the Bowie knife, is $215, while the Bowie alone in its case sells for $41. All of these S&W Bowie knives carry the Texas Ranger Seal set into the Pakka wood handle. The blades are of stainless steel, with "TEXAS RANGERS — 1823-1973" roll engraved.

The grades under $1000 will be serial numbered from TR1 to TR10,000.   J.T.A.

New 9mm Cartridge

Early in February the S&W Ammunition Co. announced an industry first — 9mm full jacketed semi-wadcutters. This new 9mm load is the fourth in that caliber made by S&W, and it should bring 9mm pistols into the target world.

Average accuracy figures with the new 115-gr. SWC cartridge ran to .616″ for 8 groups of 5 rounds at 25 yards; at 50 yards the figure was 2.188″.

Muzzle velocity is 1145 fps; velocity at 50 yards is 981 fps, at 100 yards it is 891 fps. Muzzle energy is 335 ft. lbs.; energy at 50 yards is 246 ft. lbs., and at 100 yards 198 ft. lbs. Mid-range trajectory is 1.0″ over 50 yards, 4.4″ over 100.

Good news indeed for 9mm fans, certainly, but the tariff is a touch steep. $8.30 for 50!   J.T.A.

COLT

The most widely publicized new firearms from Hartford as of this writing is the Colt-Sauer bolt-action rifle, an item beyond the purview of this section and covered elsewhere in this volume. Incidentally, this marks Colt's third attempt in barely a decade to break into the sporting long gun market. The first two were less than entirely successful.

Colt is considering the possibility that two-inch barreled revolvers might be prohibited in the near future — something we sincerely hope doesn't come to pass. Anyway, during a recent visit to the Hartford plant, we were shown some variations on the basic Detective Special to meet that problem. One is the existing 1972

D.S. with its heavy barrel extended to three inches, another a three-inch barreled version of the Diamond Back. We were told, too, that 3-inch barreled versions of all other Colt six-guns are likely to be offered if the legislative picture gets any bleaker.

These mid-length guns probably won't be available for some time. We think a 3-inch Detective Special would be quite popular.

Of much greater immediate interest is the introduction of a new Colt 380 Automatic. The old M1908 Colt Pocket Model 380, which went out of production at the end of WWII, has been much mourned in recent years, what with the increased performance and popularity of the 380 cartridge.

The new gun bears no real resemblance to the old. Instead, it is surprisingly familiar in both design and appearance. If you're a student of the Spanish Star (Bonifacio Echeverria, S.A.) pistols, you'll recognize the new Colt 380 as a modified Starfire of bygone years, the Spanish model DK. The since-modified gun is now being manufactured under the sign of the rampant colt, just as is the original Astra Cub, now built in this country as the Colt Junior.

The new Colt is an interesting design, with the locked breech and external appearance of the Colt/Browning 45 Government Model. After all, the entire Star auto series was developed from the C/B in the early 1920s.

It has an integral solid backstrap, with the mainspring seated in a well drilled therein. A pivoted trigger ac-

tuates an exposed sear bar on the right side of the frame, where a vertical disconnector rides in a dovetail. The exposed hammer is effectively blocked by a positive manual safety in the usual location. The barrel is locked to the slide by two ribs engaging grooves in the slide, and is raised and lowered by a pivoted link, just like the big Colt.

With a barrel length of 3⅛″, over-all length is 5½″ and height is 3.7″. Width over the stocks is 1.1″ and magazine capacity is 6 rounds. Empty weight (magazine in) is 20 ounces; fully loaded, 22¼ ounces.

The gun handles well and our sample produced 100% reliability with both ball and Super Vel 88-gr. JHP ammunition. Some other guns don't do so well with the latter, but Colts conducted an extensive test program to insure the gun would handle it, the most effective 380 round available. Accuracy is quite up to par, hand-size groups being easily obtained two-handed at 25 yards. Its locked-breech design will make it popular with handloaders who like to magnumize the little 380 cartridge.

All in all, quite a nice 380, quite suitable as a small — if not truly pocket-size — arm for fun or defense. General workmanship is excellent for its moderate price of $99.95.

Of course, there is the storied new Colt big-bore autoloader with all sorts of desirable features. We've seen prototypes, and so have some dealers, but its introduction is at least a year or so away. We like it, but we can't tell you anything about it yet.   G.C.N.

The new Colt 380 auto pistol is only 6″ long by 4⅛″ high, total weight 20 ounces. It fits the hand nicely. Price, $99.95. Photo by Walter L. Rickell.

The offhand position without sling is the real test of practical hunting rifle skill. A steady hold and precise trigger technique is demanded for good results. In wooded areas, more venison falls from this stance than any other. The gas-operated rifles' rapid recovery from recoil permits quick, well-placed second shots.

Checked out from the sitting position, the BAR handles well. Personal variations of the 4 basic rifle positions should be worked out to take full advantage of all field shooting conditions.

The BAR with Browning 2½-8x variable wide angle scope is representative of the fine autoloading sporting rifles available today. Simplicity and reliable operation characterize these increasingly popular arms.

Deliberate long-range shooting afield is aided by this mushroom shooting bag. Notice the one-point support of the rifle just under the receiver. Autoloaders and many bolt-action rifles group more consistently when they are supported under the receiver. Light 308 bullets—110-130 grains—can be loaded down to provide good accuracy and plenty of zap for varmints at realistic ranges.

Autoloading Rifles-- their care and feeding

by JAMES D. MASON

The autorifle has come
a long way in the past decade. They're fully reliable today,
strong and sturdy, the recoil softly sprung
and their accuracy level amply adequate. Here's
a discerning, organized report, full of facts and figures,
with valuable tips on management and handloading for the autos.

GROWING numbers of shooters in the past decade have elected to use selfloading centerfire rifles to bag big game. Largely taken for granted, these self-actuating sporting arms raise many questions among shooters. How accurate and reliable are they? What advantages do they have over other types of rifles? How do they work, and what are their peculiarities? All these questions and more have shown that the self-loading big game rifle is not well understood or appreciated, even by the many hunters who own them.

Historically, selfloading designs date back to the turn of the century. John Browning designed a rifle using a recoil mechanism similar to that of his Model 5 shotgun. Introduced as the Model 8 Remington in 1906, this rifle fired medium-power rimless cartridges in 25, 30, 32 and 35 Remington calibers. It was modernized in 1936 as the Model 81 Woodsmaster. Recoil design dictates the over-all mass distribution in operating parts and total weight of the firearm. Because of this, the Woodsmaster was rather heavy for the power of the cartridges it fired.

Winchester marketed the Models 05 and 07 autorifles, the latter in 351 and 401 calibers. These were blow-back-operated using a heavy inertial breechblock. The weight and rearward velocity of the breechblock during the operating cycle contributed to a rather sizeable felt recoil that was out of proportion to the power of the cartridges. Popularity of these early autoloaders was not outstanding, but it was good enough to maintain their production for over 40 years. The romance of the Frontier made lever action rifles the hunter's favorite during those years, but bolt action rifles, the military standard, saw increasing use by sportsmen, especially for full power cartridges. Interest in selfloading sporting arms only grew significantly after WW II.

Adoption by the military of semi-automatic rifles before WW II conditioned several million GIs to the use of this action type. Moreover, the M1 Carbine introduced the short-stroke-piston gas system, one which has made possible economical production of all current commercial full-power game rifles. It also allows the actuating mechanism to be contained within the rifle's fore-end with no exposure of unsightly operating parts.

How They Work

Located about halfway to the muzzle, the gas cylinder assembly is brazed to the bottom of the barrel. Hard chamber gasses, tapped off the bore, are conducted into the gas cylinder via the gas port, driving the piston backward a fraction of an inch. During this time, the piston pushes on a heavy inertia block, connected to the bolt assembly by operating rods. This heavy block delays breech opening time so that chamber pressures can drop to safe limits. The block is given enough impetus by the piston to assure reliable functioning.

All current selfloading sporting rifles have rotary bolts that lock into

Autoloading Rifles...

TESTFIRE GD REPORT

abutments located at the breech-end of the barrel. This arrangement makes a lightweight, strong, safe locking system. Bolts are supported in a carrier piece that provides for rotation of the bolt through a lost-motion cam. Force from the gas piston via operating rods moves the carrier to the rear, first camming the bolt to unlock, then retracting it rearward, subsequently effecting extraction and ejection. When the action stops its rearward motion, the compressed operating spring returns a new cartridge from the magazine, then locks the bolt for the next shot.

While there are design variations in the operating mechanisms among the four major domestic self-loading centerfire rifles, they all function according to the same general operating sequence and configuration outlined above. Remington produces their Model 742, Winchester the Model 100; Harrington and Richardson markets the Model 360 and, most recently, Browning has the BAR (not to be confused with the infantry support weapon of WW II.) Although classified as a domestic rifle because of the Browning company, the BAR is made in Belgium. Ruger has a 44 Magnum Carbine that's ideally suited for short-range woodslot hunting. However, because of its medium-power chambering, it is excluded from this discussion. Most remarks here about autorifle care and feeding apply to the Ruger Carbine.

Auto Ammo

Calibers suitable for autoloading sporters are limited but include some of the most popular and versatile hunting rounds available. The listing below covers all common high-power chamberings.

Rifle	M100	M360	M742	BAR
243 Winchester	X	X	X	X
6mm Remington			X	
270 Winchester				X
284 Winchester	X			
280 Remington			X	
308 Winchester	X	X	X	X
30-06			X	X
7mm Remington Mag.				X
300 Winchester Mag.				X
338 Winchester Mag.				X

The choice of calibers bears heavily on personal considerations. My own selection would be the 308 Winchester because it gives the broadest performance in a selfloading rifle with a 22-inch barrel. Except for the BAR Magnums, with 24-inch tubes, standard barrel length for all the rifles is 22 inches. The 742 and 100 have optional 18½/19-inch carbine offerings. In relatively short 22-inch barrels the 30-06 has no appreciable ballistic edge on the 308, and the same wide latitude in bullet choices and loads is available for the shorter case. The 6mm and 7mm bores offer flatter trajectories, but the short barrels again significantly

Dropped, damaged or lost magazines can plague the hunter, especially in cold climates where numbed fingers can fumble this important assembly. The BAR has its magazine attached to a floorplate that pivots down on a hinge pin. Loading is quick and convenient.

limit the potential ballistics of these lower-expansion-ratio cartridges. The slow-burning powders necessary for maximum velocities in 6mm and 7mm bores cause considerable muzzle blast from 22-inch barrels.

Bar 308 Chosen

To gather performance data, a BAR was acquired in 308 caliber. The gun came equipped with a Browning 2½x-8x wide angle scope sight. The action of the gun was exceptionally smooth. Craftsmanship was evident in small details and its finish. The scope and mounts, made for Browning by Redfield, embody all the quality features and performance one expects from the Denver-based firm. The wide-angle eyepiece, which increases the horizontal field of view considerably, has been used to good advantage in the field to find and track moving game.

Accuracy is always a consideration with any rifle but many shooters try to make too big a thing out of it. What is critical in a hunting rifle is its ability to deliver hits consistently and predictably from a cold barrel. For all practical purposes the ability to group within 3-4 inches at 100 yards is adequate for any hunting rifle. This is closer shooting than the average hunter will be able to hold at that distance, and it is all an excellent shot needs to bring home the venison. When ranges extend to where this 3-4 MOA (Minute of Angle) degree of accuracy is inadequate, the hunter had better choose another type of rifle rather than the selfloader.

Making selfloaders shoot better than 3-4 MOA is something else. Particular guns and loads will do better than this. Some BARs in magnum calibers can be made to print 3-shot groups, with tailored loads, just under 1 MOA. What is called for is some experimentation with various primers, powders and bullets to get a particular combination that suits the needs of the hunter. The cartridges chambered in today's selfloading arms are designed for high-intensity loading, and they're known to shoot well with maximum or near-maximum pressures. The shooter may find, though, that just dropping the maximum powder charge by one or two grains will show marked improvement in grouping without sacrificing much velocity or energy.

Levels of Accuracy

There is some debate as to which types of selfloader shoot more accurately. Test firings of several makes seems to show more variation in performance between individual rifles than between the basic designs. The early Remington 740 had some difficulties holding consistent groups when it was first introduced in the early 1950s. Shortly after introduction the fore-end mounting arrangement was altered to improve stabilizing tension on the barrel. The current 742 has corrected most of the early problems, for these latest Remington rifles are capable of delivering groups within acceptable norms. Optimum tension must be applied to the barrel mounting and the forestock screws, however.

Some people think the Winchester 100 and the H&R 360 shoot more accurately than do those with two-

Some of the great variety of 308 bullets available to the handloader. The BAR 12-inch twist handles all weights shown here. Left to right—110-gr. Speer, 130-gr. Speer HP, 150-gr. Speer Mag-Tip, 165-gr. Hornady Spire Point, 168-gr. Hornady HP Match, 180-gr. Speer SP Spitzer.

Loaded rounds carry the same l. to r. sequence of bullets above. Notice seating depth is adjusted to provide adequate length for efficient feeding in autoloaders. The 168-gr. Match load is the longest practicable LOA for feeding in 308 magazines.

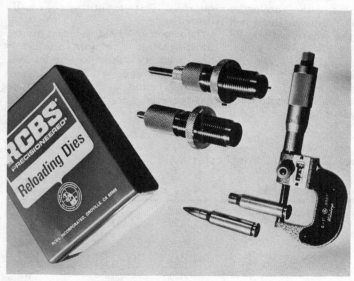

Many functional ills of autoloaders are solved by using small-base loading dies that reduce cases to factory minimum dimensions. Many feeding and extraction failures with reloads in self-loading rifles can be traced to insufficient sizing of once-fired brass.

piece stock, since the one-piece stock theoretically stabilizes the action better. However, the thin wood sidewalls at the receiver on these guns partially offset the advantage. Most 100s I have seen respond readily to glass bedding in the back of the recoil plate, just ahead of the magazine well on the bottom and sides of the receiver, under the gas-cylinder assembly, and in the barrel channel at the front of the fore-end. The principle here is to bring the stock, barrel and receiver group into a single, stable unit. The same principles apply to the H&R 360. I've seen two Model 100s respond to this treatment and deliver 1 MOA groups.

The BAR probably delivers the best out-of-the-box accuracy of the current crop of selfloaders. The substantial mounting gland for the barrel in the steel receiver provides a rigid base. The one-piece barrel assembly screws into the receiver so barrel reference is constant to the receiver. Working parts of the gas-actuating

Autoloading Rifles...

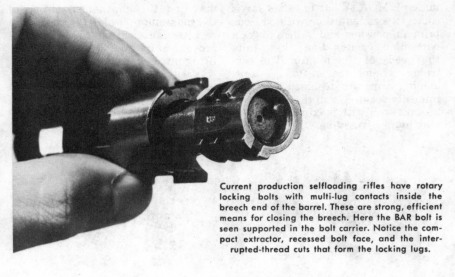

assembly are virtually free-floating on a single guide rod, eliminating or minimizing disturbances to the barrel. The forestock, attached at only one point to the gas cylinder, is free to articulate with barrel vibrations. Whether anything can be done to the BAR to *improve* accuracy is another thing. But the rifle shot exceptionally well in tests to be discussed below.

Testing Techniques

In testing autorifles for grouping capability, a sandbag rest should be used on the bench. Rest the rifle on the bottom of the receiver, preferably with the magazine removed. Resting the forestock on the sandbag will give erratic groups with vertical dispersions. The exceptions here would be a glass-bedded M 100 or H&R 360, but they too will give best results using the receiver support point. A rabbit-ear bag under the toe of the buttstock provides adequate control.

A new type of rifle rest called the "mushroom bag" was used for these tests, really two bags in one. A wedge-shaped upper section, which supports the rifle, is sewn to a round-base section to make an inverted-mushroom shape. When filled with white silica plasterer's sand, it makes an ideal, flexible rest for bench or field. To reduce weight the field bag can be filled with diatomaceous cat litter. The bags are available through Triple-K Mfg. Co., (568 Sixth Avenue, San Diego, CA. 92101), who offer a free catalog of their complete line of leather goods upon request.

Levels of Accuracy

Selfloading rifles offer many ad-

Current production selfloading rifles have rotary locking bolts with multi-lug contacts inside the breech end of the barrel. These are strong, efficient means for closing the breech. Here the BAR bolt is seen supported in the bolt carrier. Notice the compact extractor, recessed bolt face, and the interrupted-thread cuts that form the locking lugs.

Short-stroke pistons actuate modern self-loading high-power rifles. Here, the Browning piston is in its full rearward position as it thrusts against the action inertia block. Economy of Browning design uses the operating spring guide rod to support the block and limit rearward motion of the piston.

vantages to the shooter who'll exercise a bit of concentration and skill development. Unfortunately, too many hunters choose the autoloader for its *firepower*. Many of them feel that spraying the woods with rapid shots makes up for proper bullet placement. This does a great disservice to hunting as an honorable sporting activity. An overly aggressive tyro can turn a legitimate hunt into a shambles—who has not been

repelled at the sight of a dressed-out deer carcass, riddled with three or four bullet holes across the quarters. This sort of thing is totally inexcusable.

To shoot any rifle well the hunter must mount the gun uniformly and securely. Today's autoloaders, lightweight and well-balanced, handle and mount to perfection. These gas-operated guns reduce the effect of felt recoil, so as not to jostle the

Ballistic Performance Data—308 Winchester

Load	Powder/grs.	Bullet/grs.	Muzzle Velocity	Muzzle Energy	Variance	200 Yards* Velocity	200 Yards* Energy	100-yds. Groups/ins.
1	H335/42	180 Speer	2454	2407	31	2044	1670	3.750
2	H335/44	165 Horn	2615	2506	19	2155	1701	2.125
3	4895/42.5	168 Horn	2540	2406	10	2218	1835	1.820
4	H335/47	150 Speer	2844	2696	8	2206	1620	2.750
5	H335/50	130 Speer	3033	2655	28	2323	1557	3.900
6	H335/51	110 Horn	3184	2472	30	2389	1394	4.200
7	Factory†	180	2551	2601	12	2155	1856	3.375
8	Factory†	150	2735	2492	104	2282	1734	2.875
9	Factory†	125	2849	2254	24	2101	1226	2.000

Readings taken on an Avtron K233 chronograph with K101 photo screens spaced on 10 foot centers.
All loads fired from BAR with 22" bbl. Reloads used W-W cases with Winchester #120 primers.
Ambient temperature 55°. *Extrapolated data. †Browning factory loads.

shooter or seriously throw the gun off the aiming point. Shot-to-shot recovery is so rapid that *aimed* shots are easy after a little practice. Light recoil permits more practice, more shooting to zero the rifle, to calculate the proper leads, hold off and hold over for windage and range corrections. That second shot if needed calls for a deliberately placed one, not an irresponsible fusillade in the general direction of the quarry. And used properly, the self-loader is King at this second shot game!

Recoil effect is reduced by the re-

Major Self-Loading Rifles

	Barrel/ins.	Weight/lbs.	LOA/ins.	Price
BAR				
Standard	22	7⅜	43.5	229.50
Magnum	24	7½	45.3	248.50
H&R				
M360	22	7½	43.5	189.00
Remington 742				
Rifle	22	7½	42.0	179.95
Carbine	18.5	7¼	38.5	179.95
Winchester 100				
Rifle	22	7¼	42.5	174.95
Carbine	19	7	39.5	164.95

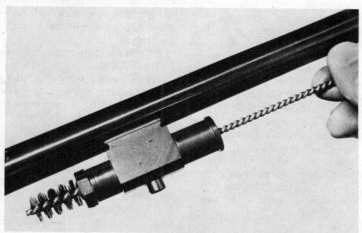

The gas cylinder of the BAR gets a cleaning with Hoppe's #9 on a nylon bristle brush. Periodic cleaning of gas-actuating parts reduces the likelihood of malfunctions due to the accumulation of powder residues.

action of the gas piston. When the rifle is fired, gas pressure forces the bullet forward and the rifle backward with equal force. Since the bullet is much lighter than the gun, it accelerates much faster. The weight of the gun is a factor in how much acceleration the rifle gets during recoil, and this velocity is a function of how hard it "kicks." In a gas-operated arm gas pressure, trapped from the bore, pushes the piston and the operating mechanism to the rear. At the same moment, equal and opposite *forward* force is applied to the cylinder housing, which drives the barrel, receiver, and stock forward. This forward motion counteracts some of the initial rearward recoil; the net effect is to soften the felt recoil. Because of this the shooter need not be so apprehensive of recoil effect as with bolt action rifles firing the same load.

Modern Autos Trouble Free

Modern selfloaders are relatively free from functional ills. Only a few precautionary maintenance steps

are needed to insure their flawless performance. Feeding problems occasionally plague individual autorifles. Check magazine lips for dents or malformation, cracks at the upper edges, or buckling of its sidewalls. Rough feed lips—burrs, sharp edges—should be stoned smooth; dirty magazines should be cleaned. A bad magazine is usually the culprit when feeding problems arise; replacing it usually eliminates stoppages due to this cause. Detachable magazines on most selfloaders are vulnerable to damage if dropped. The BAR secures the box to a hinged floorpiece so the magazine is held to the gun and cannot drop to the ground during loading; a decided advantage during the excitement of the hunt, especially during cold weather. Burrs or sharp edges on chamber openings invite hangups. These areas should be polished and eased slightly to reduce the possibility of stoppages.

Comparative Ballistics Typical Autorifle Loads*

Load **A** — 243 Winchester/87-gr. Load **D** — 7mm Reming. Mag/175-gr.
Load **B** — 270 Winchester/130-gr. Load **E** — 308 Winch./150-gr.
Load **C** — 284 Winchester/154-gr. Load **F** — 300 Winch. Mag/165-gr.

	Muzzle	100	200	300	400
Velocity/fps					
A	3100	2790	2490	2220	1970
B	3000	2750	2520	2290	2090
C	2800	2580	2380	2180	2000
D	2800	2590	2390	2200	2020
E	2800	2540	2300	2070	1860
F	3000	2740	2500	2280	2060
Energy/fp					
A	1852	1503	1198	952	749
B	2600	2183	1833	1513	1261
C	2681	2276	1937	1625	1367
D	3047	2606	2219	1880	1586
E	2612	2148	1761	1425	1152
F	3300	2751	2290	1904	1544
Bullet Path/ins.					
A	− 1.5	+ 1.05	- 0 -	− 7.63	− 25.85
B	− 1.5	+ .86	- 0 -	− 7.96	− 24.28
C	− 1.5	+ 1.18	- 0 -	− 8.93	− 27.68
D	− 1.5	+ 1.28	- 0 -	− 8.42	− 27.35
E	− 1.5	+ 1.37	- 0 -	− 9.49	− 30.59
F	− 1.5	+ .98	- 0 -	− 7.00	− 25.11

*Data taken from the Hornady Handbook. Based on nominal expected velocities from representative autoloading rifles.
Bullet Path—line of scope sight height, zero at 200 yards.

Autoloading Rifles...

Failure to eject can cause double feeding if the gun fails to cycle fully. This can be the fault of a light load and/or a dirty gas-cylinder assembly. A regular cleaning with Hoppe's #9 will keep the gas piston working freely. Do not over-oil any assemblies in the gun since the oil attracts and holds residues and dirt. Leaving a little Hoppe's in the cylinder helps keep movement free and residues soft. It is also a good idea to lightly stone all contact surfaces and edges of action parts that slide on one another. Added friction from rough surfaces and edge burrs, plus sluggish operation from over oiling, can cause cycling failures, especially in cold weather.

Too-heavy loads can batter operating parts. All current autorifles are very tolerant of overloads but they can cause early-opening symptoms Such hot loads let higher than normal gas pressures cycle the action faster. Meanwhile, chamber pressures are sustained for a longer interval at higher levels. So, when the breech unlocks, higher than normal residual pressures are encountered. Brass can be much more "sticky," especially if the chamber neck is covered with residues. Set back primers, gouged case rims, and stretched brass are symptomatic of early opening. Serious malfunctions can result in autorifles from using improperly loaded ammunition. Keep loads safe and sane; never exceed maximum load levels given in authoritative manuals. Do not use pet high-intensity loads in an autorifle just because they shoot well in bolt action guns.

Dirty chambers can cause case rims to be pulled off, especially with hot loads. Use a nylon bristle brush and nitro solvent to clean chambers; bending the wire handle 90° allows the brush to be inserted in the chamber and worked back and forth or rotated from outside the ejection port. Using the faster, cleaner-burning powders for reloads is recommended for autorifles. Some slow-burning powders leave unburned granules in chambers and bores that play hob with proper functioning. Using magnum primers can help, provided powder charges are adjusted downward 10% to 15% so as not to increase cham-

ber pressures unduly. Some lots of ball powders may leave excessive residues due to an accumulation of the calcium carbonate used during manufacturing to neutralize acids in the powder base. Such lots will require more frequent cleaning of bores, chambers and gas-cylinder assemblies for the most reliable functioning.

Reloads for Autos

Probably the most frequent source of trouble for autoloaders is reloaded ammunition. Fired cases get pretty rough treatment. Variations in pressure at opening time of the action have considerable influence on case distortions. Casehead expansions and headspace length may vary accordingly. Regular reloading dies do not ordinarily size cases to original factory minimum dimensions; this fact, coupled with variable spring-back characteristics in individual cartridge cases, can cause intermittent chambering and/or extraction problems when such reloaded rounds are fired. With a bolt action rifle a little "Armstrong" persuasion usually gets a snug case into the chamber, but with self-loaders, even the extra force won't let the action close completely.

For this reason RCBS makes small-base dies designed especially to solve many of the function ills of the self-loading rifle. Such sizing dies bring the casehead diameter back to factory minimum chamber specs, but leave the shoulder within field headspace dimensions for the particular rifle chamber. It is a good idea to tell RCBS the make of gun in use, since special dies are made for certain rifles. Or send RCBS several fired cases for custom dimensioning. For instance, ultra small sets take cases down to chamber minimums in *all* dimensions. Such RCBS dies, needed for BAR magnum reloading, solve most of the common feeding and extracting ills met when handloading for autorifles. Their use also extends case life, normally fairly short in self-loading rifles.

A series of loads was tried in the 308 BAR to determine rough performance characteristics. Then results were played back against references in *Speer's Manual #8*, the Lyman, Hornady, Sierra and Hodgdon manuals. Since hunting loads were being sought, velocity levels were studied to maximize muzzle energy levels without undue sacrifice of accuracy. Winchester 120 primers and H335 powder served well in all loads.

Another series of loads was assembled and chronographed with the Avtron K233 and their K101 photo-electric screens. A convenient arrangement, too, since photo screens don't require screen replacement after each shot.

Browning factory ammunition shot in the BAR gave quite interesting results. Shooters who've kept track of factory ammo in recent years know that the quality has come up considerably. Many factory brands produce excellent results, better sometimes than handloads. This certainly isn't true in all cases, but the 125-gr. Browning load showed much improved accuracy over the 130-gr. handload.

Backing off powder charges usually improves light-bullet performance— the most common theory being that heavy muzzle blast erratically affects light-bullet launching characteristics. Shooters who want to take varmints with their game rifles should roll back velocities about 200-250 fps from maximum and use a fairly bulky powder for good loading density. In the 308 this usually calls for 4895 or 3031. The 12" twist barrel of the BAR is capable of shooting the light 110- or 125/130-gr. bullets quite well!

Bullet Selection

Most hunters agree that the 180-gr. bullet weight is about maximum for most game suited to the 308 cartridge. 200-gr. bullets can be used but they must be seated well down into the case, sacrificing efficiency. My choice for an all-round game getter

Variances in Velocity
gas-operation vs. bolt action

Load	M70	BAR	Var. (fps)	%Δ
1	2551	2454	97	− 3.8
2	2674	2615	59	− 2.2
3	—	2540	—	—
4	2860	2844	16	− .6
5	3129	3033	96	− 3.1
6	3329	3184	145	− 4.4

Both test guns chambered for .308 Winchester, both with 22 inch barrels. Load designations keyed to master data table.

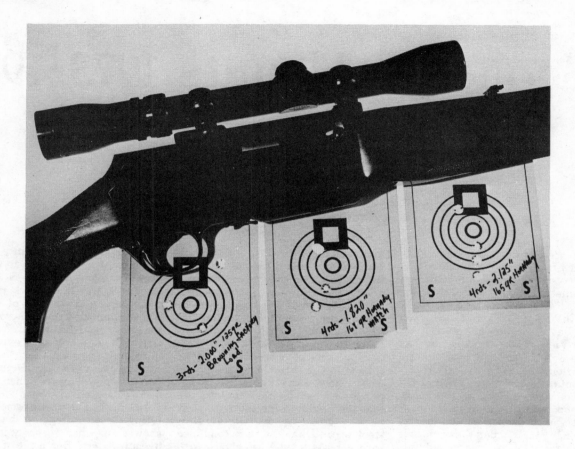

Autoloaders are no slouches when it comes to delivering hunting accuracy. Handloads and commercial ammunition will shoot well in these guns. The BAR is one of the most accurate out-of-the-box selfloaders. All modern autorifles can deliver acceptable hunting accuracy, 3-4 MOA or better, when proper attention is given to the rifle and ammunition.

is the 165-gr. weight. This weight combines a rather high ballistic coefficient, adequate velocity, and energy levels with accuracy from 308 bores. The 165s are hard to beat. Some regard it as the maximum efficient weight for the 308 case.

Hunters rarely think of using match bullets for game, but in the past two or three years the 168-gr. 308 match series have been judged "perfect" for long-range hunting. Their usual hollow point form assures adequate expansion even to 300-400 yards, and their quality maximizes accuracy in most any rifle. The load chosen here with the 168-gr. Hornady Match bullet has performed with distinction in target rifles, and it's no slouch in an autorifle, either. This load may very well be one answer for the man who wants a longer range game load in the 308 for plains or sheep country.

Another pleasant surprise was the performance of the new Speer Mag-Tip 150-gr. 308 bullet. This bullet weight, though, has always given ef-

ficient results with several powders in the 308 case. The Mag-Tip design grew out of the discovery that, at high magnum velocities, the regular softpoint spitzers lost their small lead tip shortly after ignition through acceleration forces and heat friction. If the tip gets burned off anyway, why put it on in the first place? So Speer started making a series of projectiles explicitly for use in magnum loadings.

Load No. 4, using this Mag-Tip bullet, came closest to matching the internal ballistics of a bolt-action rifle shooting the same load. Selfloading rifles use a small portion of the total energy to actuate their mechanism. Studies show a nominal energy loss between 1% and 3%. However, considerable ballistic variation can be found when the same loads are shot from two rifles of the same make and design.

The 150-gr. Mag-Tip load came quite close to external bolt action performance in this test series as well. Accuracy and velocity levels surely

nominate this as one of the prime candidates for all-round use in the 308. The stubbed-off Mag-Tip design eliminates the possibility of lead-tip deformation when the cartridge goes up the feed ramp. This factor alone would recommend the bullet for use in self-loading rifles.

* * * * *

While it is doubtful that a ¼-minute varmint shooter would ever find happiness with an autoloading rifle, there is no question that the state of the art for autos has developed to a high point in the past decade. Choose one of these arms for its simplicity of operation, learn to use its advantages, and the hunter will soon forgive its few shortcomings. For the technical buffs selfloading guns offer their own challenges in loading and small gunsmithing refinements. Bolt action riflemen need not look down on the autorifle as an inferior hunting tool. Used by savvy gunners, these "splattermatics" can hold their own in most any company.

●

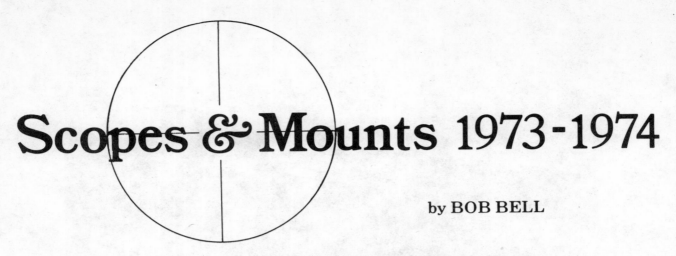

Scopes & Mounts 1973-1974

by BOB BELL

A comprehensive review of all that's new and interesting in scopes, mounts and related accessories.

W.R. Weaver Co. has made a lot of changes in their scope line for 1973. New scopes this year—or at least new versions of old favorites—are the K3-W, K4-W, K6-W, V4.5-W, V7-W and V9-W. The "W"—for those of you who haven't guessed—stands for Wider-View. These models have an eyepiece enlarged in the lateral dimension, which gives a greater horizontal field of view. Their listed fields of view, in feet, at 100 yards, are compared with the original round-eyepiece models in the table below. Obviously the Wider-View models have significant increases and this can be important, especially to the man hunting fast-moving game in brush or thick woods.

K3	K4	K6	V4.5	V7	V9
37	30	20	54-21	40-15	33-12
K3-W	K4-W	K6-W	V4.5-W	V7-W	V9-W
55	37½	25	70-26	53-20	41-16

The slightly larger eyepiece adds a whisper of weight to these Wide-View scopes—an ounce in the straight powers, ¾-ounce in the variables—but this seems a small price to pay for the increased field.

To be perfectly candid about this altered eyepiece/added field approach, I'm not personally convinced it's necessary. Maybe I'm old-fashioned, but I still feel a slight shock when I peer into a scope and don't see a round field of view, and I've been using a couple of wide-angle hunting models from another manufacturer for several years now. However, I don't use them exclusively, so maybe I haven't really overcome this feeling as the fellow who hunts with only one or two scopes might do. I hunt a lot with scopes, so I'm used to catching quick aim with them; perhaps I don't need the enlarged field as much as the 3-days-per-year hunter. There's no

doubt that a large field is an advantage over a smaller one, all other things—such as magnification, eye relief, and so on—being equal, so this general design of scope could well be just the thing for many hunters.

Those other things *are* equal in these Weavers, incidentally. Eye relief approaches 4 inches (and it doesn't change in the variables as the power is switched), and of course the power is whatever is specified. Reticles are like those offered for the regular K models—crosshair (actually an alloy steel wire), Dual-X (a CH combined with 4 posts, now a top choice with me), post and crosshair, rangefinder and at extra cost, a center dot.

There are other big changes in this year's Weavers. The K and V models are now completely steel (except for the lens surfaces, of course). They always had one-piece steel tubes, but in some models brass, aluminum or plastic was used for such things as lens cells and turret plates. None such material is used now. I feel sure this will please a lot of hunters, for in the minds of many steel connotes strength when compared to other metals. Whether this thinking is completely justified I can't say—obviously a thick piece of another metal would resist deformation better than a thin piece of steel—but the belief is there just the same.

Steel-tubed scopes normally weigh a bit more than equivalent sizes built with an aluminum alloy. Also, they rarely show a glamorous finish, tending toward a duller black. (The Classic models offered by Weaver for several years did have a high-gloss finish, but these have been dropped). At any rate, such characteristics are of minor importance on a hunting rifle, in my opinion. Certainly the matte, non-reflective surface won't "Flash" badly.

Of far greater importance is scope fogging. At a talk given to the Outdoor Writers Seminar at Nilo Farms late in 1972, William Steck, president and general manager of Weaver Scopes, indicated that this was one of the most vital factors in scope construction in the opinion of experienced hunters. He also said that Weaver had tested scopes of all manufacturers and found that all fogged when temperatures dropped to minus 20 degrees Fahrenheit. This is extremely interesting because fogging has rarely showed up when scopes were tested by gunwriters. But a bit of thought perhaps supplies the reason. Everyone I know who has conducted such tests has used a household deep freeze for his "cold box." Most of these maintain a temperature of about zero—well above the temperature mentioned by Mr. Steck . . .and the temperatures encountered at times by big game hunters.

We are talking here of interior fog, not exterior. The latter can be easily cleaned off, but fog inside the scope is a real problem when it occurs. It forms when the dewpoint (the temperature at which water vapor condenses) of the gas within the tube (air, nitrogen, or whatever) is equal to or higher than the temperature being experienced and there is moisture in the gas.

During manufacture, most of the better makers replace the air within their scopes with dry nitrogen. This lowers the dewpoint and makes fogging unlikely. However, on occasion this purging process leaves residual moisture behind. Moisture also enters some scopes because they are not perfectly sealed and changes in temperature cause the internal gas to expand and contract, pumping in and out through the leaks and bringing vapor inside. Then, too, there are also the kooks who enjoy taking things apart to see how they work, so they remove eyepieces, turret plates and anything else that can be detached without the use of a pipe wrench. All manufacturers advise against this—it normally voids the warranty—but some curious fellows persist in tinkering. All we can say is, don't do it.

According to Steck, a new process at Weaver assures that the gas within their current scopes will remain dry, and that their scopes won't leak. Each scope is tested following assembly.

Other testing carried out at Weaver deserves mention. One process has to do with ruggedness. Big game rifles generate noticeable recoil, and every time the gun is fired the scope is subjected to considerable shock. If anything in the unit—scope or mount—moves, your rifle is out of zero to some extent. It may not be enough to notice except on a bench, or it might be enough to make you miss a standing elk at 75 yards. This is something not many hunters realize. It's possible for a scope and mount to perform flawlessly for some years; then, as the continued pounding of recoil goes on, minor failures creep in. Eventually, the sighting unit simply becomes unsatisfactory. The fellow who fires only a few shots a year may never encounter this problem, but the man who does a lot of shooting could well find it significant. Any unit is going to fail eventually, no matter how good it is to begin with —as with any other manufactured item. The time will come when the Golden Gate Bridge will be unsafe to cross, despite the safety factors built in to begin with. The same principle applies to everything else, scopes included. This being the case, it's only sensible for the hunter to obtain the most rugged scope he can get; it's the cheapest approach in the long run.

Weaver tests their scopes for ruggedness this way: the scope is attached to a horizontal steel bar, which rides up and down between two vertical steel rails. The scope and bar are dropped from heights up to 4 feet. Impact is against a steel floor plate, simulating recoil. Weaver says that 4 feet of drop subjects the scope to about 5 times the recoil effect of a 458 Magnum, and that 2 foot drop gives about twice the effect. They feel that a good scope should take the 2-foot drop indefinitely, and Steck reports that samples of the new K and V models have been dropped 4 feet 50 times without ill effect.

Other makers of high-grade scopes do similar testing, of course, as we've mentioned in the past. All such com-

Weaver's "Qwik-Site" sighting system is adaptable to rifles or shotguns.

The Weaver V9-W Wider-View with enlarged eyepiece.

Streamlined 1″ Pivot Mount rings from Bushnell.

The Tasco 3-9x Omni-View with range finding reticle.

New SPI 3-9x utilizes new one-piece photo-etched reticle which reduces fogging.

panies do everything practicable to make sure they're marketing scopes that will give years of service under tough conditions.

Another change this year in Weavers is that the new K and V models have friction lock adjustments rather than the long-familiar clicks. It reportedly is easier to make a scope leak-proof if friction adjustments are used. Dial graduations equal ½-minutes for powers under 4x and V4.5, ¼-minutes for the K4 and above. (Maybe "inches" should be read here for "minutes.") The scopes for rimfire rifles—V22, D4 and D6—have 1″ graduations.

American Import Co. has made some changes in their line of L. M. Dickson "Signature" scopes. Four new fixed powers now carry this name, and these have the "hidden adjustment system" in which the windage and elevation dials are located beneath a protective ring just forward of the eyepiece, rather than amidships on the tube. A 2½x and a 4x have 32mm objectives (which gives an unusually large exit pupil, about 12½mm, in the lower power scope, making it easy to catch rapid aim., while another 4x and a 6x have 40mm objectives. Eye relief is 3 inches in all and all have a 4-post reticle (Duplex style).

Three variables are listed, a 1½-4x and two 3-9x s, one of the latter having a 33mm objective, the other a 42mm. Last year's 2½-7x has been discontinued. As with the straight powers, all are on 1-inch tubes and all have 4-post reticles.

Bausch & Lomb is resting on its laurels this year, with no new scopes or mounts, so this seems like a good time to give a quick rundown on the two lines they've been offering for some years now, for the benefit of new hunters.

In the mid-50s, B & L made quite a splash with a highly impressive 2½-8x variable power hunting scope. That particular scope is no longer made, but many are still seen on big game rifles in the field. A similar model, the Balvar 8A, is available in that power range, and the smaller Balvar 5, a 2½-5x, serves big game hunters well. The Balvar 8A has enough magnification at the top level to suit average varmint hunters, thus makes a good choice on a rifle chambered for a high-velocity load that will handle varmints and deer-size game. The 2½x Baltur A and 4x Balfor A round out B & L's Custom line. These models do not have internal adjustments, thus require an adjustable mount, such as the one- or two-piece models made by B & L to fit most any gun you'll come across.

A few years back, apparently in response to the American hunter's fondness for solid mounts and internally adjusted scopes, Bausch & Lomb marketed their Trophy line. The Baltur B is a 2½x, the Balfor B a 4x, the Balsix B a 6x, and the Balvar 8B a 2½-8x variable. Along with these came a solid bridge-type mount having no adjustments, also called the Trophy model. We've used several of these scopes and mounts over the years since they first appeared, and have nothing but praise for them. They're optically excellent, mechanically rugged, and they're good looking. Specs and prices are in the catalog section.

B&L offers many related items, of course—spotting scopes, binoculars, shooting glasses, etc. One little item which has proved practical and useful is their Accu-Pod rifle rest. This is a padded, vertically adjustable bipod which is held on the rifle by an elastic strap that goes around the fore-end and barrel. It weighs 5¼oz., sells for $5.95, and sure helps a lot when you're trying to hold the crosswires on a chuck a few hundred yards distant. It adjusts to 11 inches high, so it's usable primarily from the prone position.

Colt AR-15 Scope Mount

B-Square—makers of many products for the reloader-shooter, offers a new base for the Colt 223 rifle. The B-Square base accepts any type of Weaver rings, thus letting a vast range of scopes be used on the AR-15. The new base is furnished with a wrench for easy and fast attachment and removal. At $14.95, users of AR-15 rifles should welcome this base.

Buehler, Inc., entered the scope mount field just after World War II—almost three decades ago. At that time they made one style of mount base in a half-dozen models. Today there are four styles of Buehler bases in over 70 models in regular production, with special runs to fit quality rifles which don't happen to be so plentiful that they require a regular

Bausch & Lomb's Balfor A 4x on the Remington 700.

The B & L Balsix B 6x on a Remington 660.

Buehler 1-piece bridge mount.

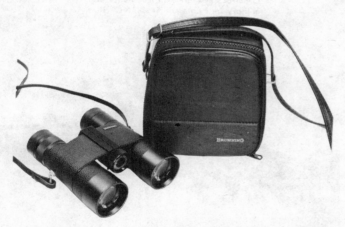

Browning's new 7x35 Sportsman's binoculars weigh only 18½ ounces.

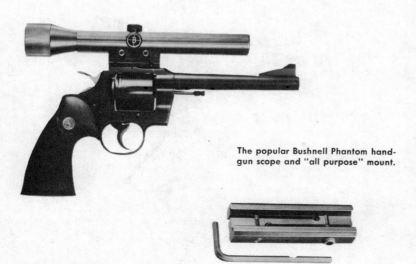

The popular Bushnell Phantom handgun scope and "all purpose" mount.

run...for instance, the Champlin, Steyr-Mannlicher, Omega and Brevex Magnum actions. They also make special bases to cover dovetailed receivers such as the Sako.

A note from Bob Ray, general manager at Orinda, Calif., plant, says Buehler bases are now made to fit the new lefthanded Remington M700 action (Code R 2-piece base will fit). He adds that the Mauser Mark X has been changed to standard FN drilling, so all four styles of bases will fit; the Code 3 2-piece base can be installed on the Mauser M3000 by reversing the front base, and Code C handgun bases for the Colt Python and Trooper Mark III are back in production, at regular prices. The millimeter-size rings have been taken out of regular production and become specials at added cost.

We might have said it before, but it bears repeating: Buehler scope mounts are excellent units; we've known of some that have been used since they first came on the market, and they're still doing their job.

Browning has nothing new in the scope line this year—they have a Wide Angle 5x and a pair of variables for centerfire rifles, along with a fine 4x for rimfires—but their Ted Collins says that a new optical item is a 7x35 roof prism binocular. Outer dimensions are about 5x5 inches, weight 18½ oz., field 446 ft. at 1000 yds. Price, $149.75.

Bushnell markets a veritable plethora of optical goods, as ol' Howard Cosell would say. Several lines of scopes, mounts, binoculars, bore sighters, what have you. Even a fish spotter for fish hunters, if that isn't a contradiction in terms. Not being a fisherman, I don't know about those things. (I once tried to peddle a story called "Fish is a Four-Letter Word," but I got no bites. Fishing-mag editors don't have much sense of humor, I guess.)

Anyway, Bushnell is another scope company which doesn't have much new this year. That's how it goes when you already pretty well blanket the hunting scope field. The Scopechief IV line, Bushnell's best, comes in 2¾x, 4x and 6x fixed powers and 1½-4x, 2½-8x and 3-9x variables. All are offered with Multi-X (combination CH and posts) and Command Post reticles, the latter being standard crosswires with a flip-up post for bad light conditions.

The less expensive Banner line has four fixed powers and four variables, all now featuring a neoprene eye guard on the rear end of the tube. Cross-wire or Multi-X reticle. (Complete specs in the catalog section.)

The Scopechief V "Lite-Site" models—4x, 1½-4x and 3-9x—have a lighted-dot aiming point for use under the worst seeing conditions. Battery powered, you switch it on or off as desired. I've used one in the 4x and it does make accurate aiming possible under conditions when it would be impossible with any other arrangement I know of.

The popular Phantom handgun scopes are still available in 1.3x and 2.5x, and "All Purpose" dual mount now is offered to fit the Phantom rail or two chrome molybdenum studs seated in 6-48 holes. $6.50.

Bushnell also offers impact resistant shooting glasses in green, yellow and gray lenses. I've used a pair of the yellow ones for a lot of claybird shooting on dark days, and they do markedly improve seeing ability and contrast, as well as give protection to the eyes. Twenty-some years ago I had a varmint rifle blow up when I fired a shot. I wasn't wearing glasses and got a number of tiny pieces of brass in my eyes…some of which still remain there. I've made it a habit ever since not to fire any kind of gun unless I'm wearing shooting glasses, and I strongly recommend that you do likewise. They're the cheapest insurance I know of. It was no fun when the doctor used a tiny steel pick to remove bits of brass from my eyeballs!

Conetrol Scope Mounts have not been around as long as some others, but plenty long enough to prove themselves. They're made for almost any rifle you might want to scope. Three lines—Huntur, Gunnur and Custum—are made, and each comes in either bridge or 2-piece style, with either solid or split rings in low, medium or high dimensions. Rings are available for 1″, 26mm, and 26.5mm tubes—something worth knowing if you're trying to fit a foreign glass on your pet rifle.

New this year are dovetail bases for the small BRNO rifles of both commercial and military persuasion. Bases will fit the ZKW-465 and ZKB-680 as well as the Krico and Steyr rifles with integral receiver dovetails. Bases require no drilling or tapping; they slide onto the dovetails and are secured by cross-clamping screws. They can be reversed if necessary to obtain optimum eye relief. Huntur bases are $9.95, Gunnur $12.95, and the Custum $14.95. Rings are extra.

Davis Optical scope with sliding objective lens for range focusing.

Conetrol's new dovetail mounts for both military and commercial BRNO rifles.

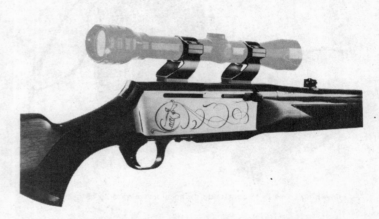

Kwik-Site See Through mounts are now available in Wider View models.

New Jason/Empire 20-60x zoom spotting scope.

Davis Optical Co. makes two comparatively inexpensive ($69.50 and $89.50) target scopes. They come in most powers from 10x to 30x and are unusual in that they focus for range by sliding the objective lens forward or back instead of screwing it in and out. Davis also makes power-boosting units for hunting scopes, adapting them for varmint use. These sell for $18, $25 and $29.50. These fit Weaver, Lyman Alaskans and some others.

J. B. Holden's Ironsighter, a mount which raises the scope high enough to use the iron sights by aiming through oval apertures in the rings, now is made to fit most rifles and the M350 fits many shotguns (they must be tapped). Scopes of the general size of a straight 4x or 2-7x variable will normally be handled by a low version of the Ironsighter, while large-objective models require the high unit. Mounts for the M70 Winchester in 300 H&H and 375 H&H are made on special order.

Hy-Score Products (S. E. Laszlo) sells hunting scopes ranging in price up to $98.50. Called the Red Dot Field & Stream, Gold Dot Seefar, Blue Dot Woodsman, and Green Dot Sierra models, they pretty much blanket the field, from inexpensive 22 rimfire designs on up to the big game variables. All regular powers are available, with crosshair, dual crosshair or post reticle.

Paul Jaeger's quick detachable side mount has been a favorite of many hunters for a lot of years now. Side mounts aren't seen as much now as they were a few decades back, but they have some advantages over top mounts. With these, a dovetailed steel base is fastened permanently to the side of the action. A set of scope rings is part of a unit that locks to the base by means of a lever-operated clamp. The scope and rings can be removed in a moment, leaving nothing to interfere with the use of the iron sights. No tool or coin is necessary to detach the scope or to reinstall it, which also takes but a second or two. If desired, the scope rings can be made high enough to use iron sights beneath them without removing the scope.

Jason/Empire

A new Jason spotting scope was announced for 1973, a 20x-60x zoom with a 60mm objective lens. All focusing and power control is at the ocular end for convenience and all lenses are fully coated for a brilliant image. A heavy-duty tripod (included at the $125 list price) adjusts between 15" and 18" when fully extended.

J.T.A.

Kuharsky Bros, Inc., who make the B&L-style mounts, have been turning out Trophy-design rings to fit Weaver-type bases, with good results. These use allen screws, which make it easy to get a secure fit without worrying about twisting the edges off the screwdriver slots, and have a high-polish finish which appeals to most gunners.

Kwik-Site See Thru mounts also raise the scope high enough to use the iron sights. These are a set of figure-8 rings, the upper holes holding the scope, the lower ones forming the tunnel that exposes the iron sights. New this year is a Wider-View model, which has a wider hole for fast open sight aiming. It's priced at $15.75, a dollar more than the original type.

Also new is the Kwik-Mount/94, for the M94 Winchester carbine. This one attaches to the side of the action, using existing factory holes and off-setting the scope for the top ejection. $19.95. For those who don't care about using iron sights, another added item is the Low-Profile Kwik-Mount which is basically the Kwik-Site without the tunnel . . . in other words, a set of mount rings which screws to the receiver bridge and ring. $14.75. These units are made for most popular rifles.

Leupold scopes are top-quality items. I've been using four of them – different models – for years now, and have had the opportunity to observe their performance on the rifles of friends in the field and of casual acquaintances when sighting-in, etc., so I believe I've had a reasonable amount of experience with them. And they've always done what was asked of them. Sometimes that was a lot, for in the natural course of hunting they've been subjected to all kinds of weather, rough handling, etc. I feel it's only fair to mention things that perform well – as I have in the past – and Leupolds have for me.

Of interest this year is the Adjustable Objective now offered on a number of the higher powered models. This permits precise focusing for any range from 25 yards to infinity, which eliminates all parallax and gives a somewhat better image. This feature is now available on the 7½x, 10x, 12x and 3-9x.

Five reticles are offered in Leupold's Golden Ring scopes: crosshair, CPC (a tapered crosshair), dot, Duplex (the combination CH and 4 posts introduced by Leupold in 1962 and now requested by some 80% of their buyers), and a variation of the Duplex in which the horizontal crosshairs are overlain by pointed posts that do not meet in the center, while a pointed post projecting up from the bottom touches the CH intersection. These three posts are somewhat heavier than in the regular Duplex, thus more conspicuous for fast shooting at short range. Personally, though, I'd prefer the Duplex.

Leupold has a new mount this year. Called the "STD" or Standard Mount, it is of the same basic design as the well-known Redfield Jr. That is, a base that bridges the action opening is screwed to the receiver ring and bridge, and a set of rings (1" diameter only) cradles the scope. The front ring has a projecting dovetail stud which fits into a recess in the base. It is disengaged by rotating 90° and lifting out. Opposing windage screws hold the rear ring and make rough zeroing easy. Rings come in three heights, measuring .650, .770 or .900 from the top of the base to the middle of the ring, so will handle scopes with any diameter objective. Rings and bases interchange with Redfield Jr. or Sr. components. Made for many popular rifles, including Remington's new lefthand models and M77 Ruger round receiver. Price of rings, $15.95, bases $9.95.

Lyman's biggest news this year is a variable power scope, which I'm glad to see. For some reason Lyman has for years resisted the obvious swing to variables in this country over the past decade. The Lyman variable is a 3-9x, which seems to be the one most scope makers start with in the switch-powers. A natural selection, as it provides usable magnifications for big game hunting at any range and for varmints at what might be called ordinary distances.

The Lyman 3-9x variable is built on a 1-inch anodized alloy tube, is 10½ inches long, weighs 14 ounces, has half-minute internal adjustments, an eye relief of 3¼" at top power, 3-¾" at 3x, and a field of 39-13 feet at 100 yards. Currently, a standard crosswire subtending 1½" at 3x, ½" at 9x, is available, plus a Center-range (4-post/CH) reticle. The fine center wires in this design subtend ¾" and ¼". Price, $109.95.

Marble Arms markets four good hunting scopes for centerfire rifles.

All are built on 1-inch tubes, machined from a solid bar of duralumin to decrease jointing and make weatherproofing easier. In fact, Marble's literature claims these scopes are waterproof, which is going out on a limb, seems to me, but maybe it's so.

Three of these scopes—the A2.5, A4 and VS3-9—have clear objective lenses of 32mm. This is plenty large for the straight powers and gives enough light for the variable's settings under anything like normal conditions. But for those who want more at high magnification, a second 3-9x variable has a 40mm objective. This gives an exit pupil of 4.4mm and a relative brightness of 19.3, compared with 3.5mm and 12.2 for the smaller unit. Since under bad light conditions the pupil of the human eye expands to about 5mm diameter, it's obvious that the larger lens can be an advantage on occasion. But when that light isn't needed, you still have to carry a bit more weight and put up with a bit more bulk if you choose the bigger model. So like anything else, you pay your money and take your choice.

Marble also supplies their dual sighting Game Getter mount, which lifts the scope a bit and provides a tunnel through which iron sights can be used.

Marlin Firearms Co. continues to offer their 1-¾-5x Zoom scope and straight 4x Model 425 for big game and two rimfire scopes. These are reasonably priced models that work well. The M750 is a 1½x having a 20mm objective in a 1″ tube, enlarged eyepiece and internal adjustments. It is designed for use on shotguns firing rifled slugs, particularly the Marlin M120 with slug barrel and their M55S. Eye relief is long, 9-15 inches, and field of view is about 25 feet. It is fitted with the optically centered 1-MR reticle—3 pointed posts and crosshair. $29.95

Nickel Supra scopes, imported by Continental Arms Corp., are high-grade scopes. Made in Germany, they come in an interesting variety of sizes, with a 1x for use on dangerous game or shotguns, two 4x and two 6x models, different size objectives offering different light transmitting properties and a choice of scope sizes, which can be satisfying to a hunter who wants a given power but doesn't like a scope so big that it gives an unbalanced look to his rifle, say. Supra variables also are made in 1-4x, 4-6x, 1½-6x, 2½-7x, 2½-9x and 3-10x. On these the entire ocular unit turns

Marlin's 1¾-5x Zoom scope fitted to their 444 Sporter.

Top—Nickel Supra 1-4x variable power; above—Nickel 4x fixed power scope.

The Lyman 3-9x Variable with 1″ tube.

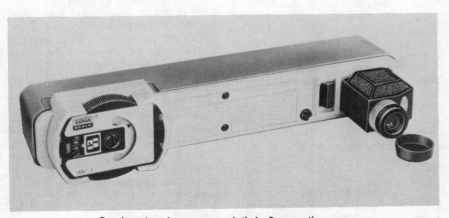

Ranging, Inc. has re-vamped their Rangematic range finder. Mark VI measures distances from 19 to 250 yards.

to raise or lower magnification, rather than a separate power selector ring. These have binocular type adjustment for focusing to the user's eyesight. Prices are high on these Supras—from $130 for the 1x to $250 for the 2½-9x, but as we said, those we've seen have been quality units.

Pachmayr Gun Works approached the scope/iron sight problem from a different direction, by developing their well-known Lo-Swing mount. This unit permits the scope to be flopped to the left when desired, offering a normal view of the iron sights. When the scope is used, it is in a very low position, so a comb height that serves well with the iron sights is suitable for the glass one.

With this mount, stop pins on the bottom of the mount loops center the scope above the rifle. Loops having longer stop pins are made for the installation of large-objective scopes. These hold the scope higher and a trifle to the left of center. The pins come extra long so they may be filed down until the proper clearance is obtained between the scope and the rifle barrel. These should never touch; you should have at least ¹⁄₁₆" clearance here.

The Lo-Swing mount is made for scopes having tubes of ¾, ⅞ or 1 inch, and 26mm. It will fit many popular rifle actions, including such military models as the M1 Garand, Krag, Springfield, and various SMLEs, and some shotguns, including the Browning Standard auto, Remington Models 1100 and 870, and Winchester's M12.

Ranging, Inc., makes the Wrist Scope, a monocular about the size of a pack of cigarettes, which is worn like a watch and so is readily available when you want to study some distant target but don't want to carry binoculars. It's a 6x prismatic design which focuses from 10 feet to infinity, weighs but 3½ oz. and has a field of about 40 feet at 100 yards. $17.50.

Ranging also markets a pair of range finders small and portable enough (10½x1½x1¼ inches, 22 oz.) for routine varmint hunting. Called the Rangematic Mark V and Mark VI, these units employ the split-image principle. Each uses a 6x18 scope for sighting. The outer case is of reinforced fiberglass, with welded steel inner construction. Each is claimed to be 99% accurate at 100 yards, scaling down to 90% at 1000 yards for the Mark V (I expect it would be shrewd to take several readings and average

them). The Mark VI is listed as measuring distances from 19 to 250 yards.

Interchangeable ballistic scales which tell how far to hold over for a Rangematic-determined range when zeroed at 200 yards are offered.

Price of Mark V is $34.95, Mark VI, $39.95. Leather holster and pouch, $7.95.

Realist, Inc., offers an interesting line of American-made scopes. They have conventional models in 2½, 4 and 6 power, a 1½-4½x with enlarged objective, which gives a very large field of 65 feet at bottom power, and a 3-9x. They also have four models called Auto Range scopes (4x, 6x, 1½-4½x and 3-9x) which we'll describe briefly for new readers; they were covered fully a few editions back. What makes these unique is a ring which is turned until a set of horizontal wires in the scope field brackets an 18" target area (this is assumed to be the average withers-to-brisket distance on various game animals). When this is done, a trajectory cam on the scope which makes contact with the rear top of the mount base tilts the scope up or down to compensate for bullet drop, so you can hold right where you want to hit. The cams are engineered to work with the bullet paths of different loads, and of course the scope must be zeroed in conventionally to begin with. In the variable powers, the unit is tied in with the power selector ring so that magnification increases for the longer range shots. We've tried three of these Auto/Range scopes on an accurate target rifle, firing at unknown ranges up to about 400 yards, and they work. This always assumes, of course, that the target or the given portion of it that you're using is close to 18 inches in depth; it also assumes you can hold the rifle on target reasonably well while you turn the adjusting ring. In all honesty we've got to admit these things are easier done on a bench rest than in the field. However, they often can be done under long range hunting conditions, and these Auto/Range units become particularly deadly then.

Redfield Gun Sight Co. has one of the largest scope lines in the country, and there's no doubt that it's one of the best. For many years Redfields have been known for the accuracy and consistency of their adjustments, high image quality and fine definition. Furthermore, this company long has been noted for its innovations. It was the first to produce a variable in which the reticle appeared smaller

at high magnification than at lower, it made the solidly mounted "3200" target scope, and a few years back it introduced the "Widefield" design.

This year, three new scopes are offered. They're conventional in looks, but interesting for Redfield in that two of them fall into the medium-price bracket. The other is a fairly high-priced rimfire scope. Considering this one first, called 4x Westerner, it's built on a 9" tube with enlarged ocular and objective, it is 9½" long and weighs 6¼ oz. Though ostensibly intended for 22s, Redfield says this little glass will take the recoil of magnum calibers, so with its 3½-inch eye relief and 25-foot field, it could well be chosen by a mountain hunter who wants to trim every possible ounce from his sheep-shooter. It has the highly useful 4-Plex reticle. Price, $29.95.

The other two new scopes are called FRontier models. One is 4x, the other 2-7x. Both are built on 1" tubes and both have 4-Plex reticles. The former costs $53.50, the latter $77.25. Storm Queen lens covers are offered for all three models at $3.45; for a half-buck more you can get Storm Kings for the FRontiers. Doubtless the new models are named to complement the FRontier scope rings and bases announced some time back but only now in full production. Machined from aluminum, these are light in weight (under 3 oz. complete) and sell for considerably less than the long-popular Redfield Jr. bridge mount.

Redfield has dropped the small 1-4x variable. I don't know why, but chances are it didn't sell well. This seems strange to me, as this size scope and this power range are a nearly perfect complement to most big game rifles. Rarely does anyone shooting at deer or larger animals need more power than 4x, yet there are many times when less power is desirable—and a larger field is a definite advantage. Too, a small, straight-objective scope looks more natural on a hunting rifle than a big one, is more convenient in the brush, etc. I guess too many hunters still want extra magnification, regardless of what it costs them.

It seems to me there is one place where Redfield should be adding power, but it's not in the big game line. There is a growing demand among bench and accuracy shooters for a short, light, high-magnification scope that mounts on the action only; that is, a scope which gives at least 20x but doesn't require the front block on the barrel or cantilevered out from the action. The 12x Redfield would seem to be a good starting point for such a unit. As is, this is a fine varmint scope, for it has an adjustment for eliminating parallax and the one we tested had accurate adjustments. However, 12x isn't enough power for the super-accurate rifles the short-range benchresters use. (Strangely, some 1000-yard bench shooters find this power adequate—or perhaps more usable would better describe their situation, as other problems are more bothersome at their distance than medium-low magnification.) At any rate, there seems to be a market here, despite the difficulties inherent in building an optically good scope of high power in such short length. I hope Redfield gives it a try.

Another new Redfield item this year is a tiny monocular. Of 8x with 20mm objective, it weighs only 2 oz., is an inch in diameter and about 3½ inches long. Field is 38 feet. Could be a darn useful item for a woods hunter, say, who doesn't want to be bothered with binoculars but occasionally needs a way to study something suspicious looking a few hundred yards out there. With case and lanyard, $38.95.

Elsewhere, we've mentioned that other makes of scopes are subjected to recoil simulation, etc. Redfield also has a gizmo that puts their glasses through this kind of treatment. To prevent internal fogging, current models are filled with dry nitrogen which reportedly has a dew-point of minus 80 degrees Fahrenheit. I don't have any way of testing a scope at that temperature, but that is an impressive figure.

Sanders Custom Gun Service continues to supply the Bisley scopes listed in earlier GD's. Those wanting German-made scopes will be interested to learn that Sanders also stocks the M.S.W.-Wetzlar line. Included are a 3x with 22mm objective at $60.50; a 4x30, $62.50; a 4x36, $64.50; and a 6x42 at $66.50. These are steel-tube models. The 4x36 and 6x42 are available on special order with light metal (aluminum alloy?) tubes. A 2-6x is offered at $98.50, and a 2-¾-8x at $107.50. Most of these imported scopes have 26mm tubes, while a few have attached rails. This can complicate mounting, but several American mount makers supply 26mm rings. (See catalog section.) Standard reticle is the European 3-post design; various others are available at $10 additional. Two-way adjustments are internal; elevation only, if preferred.

S&K Mfg. Co. makes Insta-Mounts for rifles ordinarily hard to latch a scope onto. They're adapted to various military rifles and can be installed without drilling or tapping. For instance, on the 1949 FN Auto satisfactory results could not be obtained by normal means because the bolt housing would not support a scope well enough to hold its zero. So S&K replaced the housing with a machined unit that became the mount base. A neat mounting job results, added weight only 2 ounces.

The Insta-Mount is also made for such rifles as the AR-15—it installs on the iron sight/carrying handle unit with no alteration to the rifle—the German M43 autoloader, the various Lee-Enfields, etc. On the M1917 Enfield it is installed between the "ears" of the GI rear sight.

W. H. Siebert's alteration of such medium-power varmint scopes as the Weaver Ks, Lymans and Leupolds to what might be called short bench rest scopes of 15 to 24 power was mentioned in these pages last year. Siebert now alters the Unertl BV-20 ($30)

and Lyman 20x LWBR ($25) scopes to 25x or 30x also. He recommends finer-than-standard reticles in all conversions and installs superfine crosshairs (for those with 20-20 vision), extra fine crosshairs, or ¼" or ⅛" center dot, if desired. $10, your choice.

New for the hotshot handgunners, particularly those out in the Northwest who like bench shooting with the Remington XP-100, is an alteration of the Redfield 12x which pushed it to 14x and, even more importantly for such shooters, gives it *one foot* of eye relief. I haven't seen this particular conversion, so don't know what, if anything, is sacrificed in the scope's other characteristics to obtain these. I'd expect a decrease in field. Even so, this won't bother a bench shooter, while the great increase in eye relief can make for much more comfortable handgun shooting.

Savage Arms has discontinued its scopes.

Scope Instrument also has discontinued its rifle scope line and will no longer supply scopes or related items.

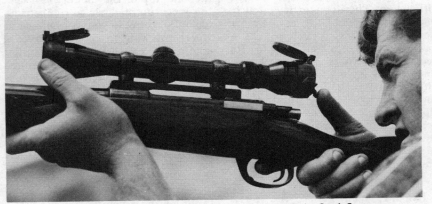

The excellent Supreme lens covers are now made by Butler Creek Corp.

Redfield's new scopes, from top: FRontier 2-7x, FRontier 4x, Westerner 4x, and 8x Monocular.

Southern Precision Inst. Co. now uses a one-piece duplex reticle, photo etched from a single sheet of stainless steel, in their big game line of scopes. This has no glass backing, according to Nat Halperin, which eliminates one area of possible fogging.

SPI's Optex Riflescopes are made in 4x and 3-7x on ⅞″ tubes for rimfires, with a 4x on ¾″ tube for 22s. The big game models are built on 1″ tubes in all normal magnifications from 2½x to 10x, and in 1½-5x, 2-7x and 3-9x variables. Centra-Set reticles include CH, post, tapered CH and duplex styles. Prices range from $26.50 to 49.50 for the big game models.

Supreme Scope Covers

Ed Vissing's Supreme Scope Cover Co. has been bought by Butler Creek Corp. of Box GG, Jackson Hole, Wyo., according to a note from J. F. Stone, general manager. The business has been moved to Wyoming. Current models of these lens covers have the release buttons molded into the ring mount to prevent any chance of loss. If anyone doesn't know how they work, these are cup-type covers which fit snugly over each end of the scope, shielding the lenses from rain and snow. To clear the scope for sighting, you just touch a release button with each thumb while raising the gun and the covers flip out of the way. $7.50 per set.

Swift Instruments Inc. has added two new scopes to its line, the 4x Gopher, for plinking rifles (15mm objective, 26½-foot field), which comes complete with tip-off mount, and a 4x for big game called the Buck model. This one is unusual, for it has no conventional turret to enclose the adjusting dials. Rather, a ring just forward of the eyepiece covers the adjustments, giving a long straight section of tube to accept the mount rings. This gives considerable leeway in ring spacing, if the longer enlarged section at the rear does not necessitate mounting the scope farther back than you like. Chances are this will bother no one except possibly those who really crawl a stock. The Buck has a Quadraplex reticle (CH and 4 posts), a 31½-foot field and 3″ eye relief.

Tasco has one of the most extensive scope lines going, with over two dozen models for centerfire rifles, a half-dozen or so for rimfires, a big target scope in 12, 16, 20 or 24 power, and—new this year—two 4x models and a 3-9x variable having European-style rails integral with the bottom of the tube for mounting. This rail fastens to a set of quick-detachable blocks which can be attached to the ribs of some combination guns, a firearm design long popular on the Continent and now gaining favor with quite a few Americans.

The 3-9x has a 32mm objective, as does one of the 4xs. The other has a 40mm lens. A German-style reticle—the long-familiar triple post which serves so well under bad light conditions—is available in all, or crosswires can be had in two of these. Adjustments are internal—quarter-minute clicks. The 3-9x is $79.95 with German reticle, $10 more for CH; the 4x40mm is $69.95, $3 more for CH. The 4x32mm is $59.95.

Tasco calls its TV-shaped eyepiece "Omni-View," and its available on a number of models. A half-dozen styles of reticle also are offered in various scopes. It gets too complicated to try to boil everything down to the space available here, but a full-color catalog explaining everything can be had from Tasco. See the Directory of the Arms Trade for address.

One new item should be mentioned here, the 25x Angleview Spotter. This spotting scope, as the name suggests, has an angled eyepiece for easy use from the prone position, a 60mm objective lens, quick-focusing knob, screw-on lens covers and extendible sunshade. The literature says it will resolve to 2 seconds of arc at 100 yards. $159.95. Extra eyepieces are available at 19.95 in 15x or 40x, $29.95 for the 60x.

Unertl Optical Co. has long been recognized as the producer of absolutely top-quality scopes. Their target scopes, in particular, are favorites of many experienced and knowledgeable riflemen. They weigh more than some, but where saving the last ounce is unimportant, they're often first choice. The company was founded in 1934 by John Unertl, a skilled rifleman as well as a great optical designer and producer of precision equipment. He was involved in this field from 1909 until his death in 1960. I remember talking with him at bench shoots many years ago, and he was always most helpful.

Unertl scopes are made for big game, varmints, target and benchrest shooting. They have no new models this year. A quote from their catalog probably explains this: "Changes that are made must be for the improvement of the product and not just for the sake of something new." Their catalog is worth obtaining, incidentally...not just for the scope listings and descriptions, but also for the definitive information on related subjects such as parallax, focusing, etc.

Universal Firearms Corp. now offers two 4x and two 3-9x models with Quadraplex reticle, the most noticeable differences in these scopes being the use of 32mm objectives on one of each power, 40mm lenses on the other. Universal also supplies a fairly low-priced line of scopes for centerfires. ($26.50 to 59.50.)

Williams Gun Sight Co. has not changed its scope line since last year, so has the Guide Line models in straight 4x and three multi-magnification models, a small 1½-4½x model of the type I prefer on a hard-use hunting gun, and 2-6x and 3-9x scopes with 38mm objectives, for ample light transmission. The Twilight models are made in 2½x20mm, 4x32, and 3-9x38. In addition, the 4x Wide Guide, which gives an unusually large lateral field, is still made.

S&K Insta-Mount on FN-1949 replaces original bolt housing, adds only 2 ounces.

Customizing Contrary Snubs

In spite of its numerous disadvantages and deficiencies, the smaller combat revolver has a place in the current scheme of things. Here are detailed data on how to have a smoother and better snub-nose.

by Jan A. Stevenson

THE SNUBNOSED revolver is a slender reed on which to prop one's hopes of longevity. Every design aspect of it contributes to ineffective ballistics, hopeless inaccuracy, and a piddling low volume of fire. The pipsqueaks are too light by far to hold steadily on target. The sight radius is so meager that gross errors in sight alingment go all but unnoticed by the shooter. The sights themselves, with rare exceptions, are far too tight and narrow. The snubs have little point or feel for instinctive shooting, and errors in trigger control are magnified manyfold over what they would be with a more substantial sidearm. Trigger reach is too short for all but debutantes, and the grips the factory fits are usually worthless. On discharge the shooter feels an uproar like King Kong unleashed, but the bullet leaves the sawed-off snout at a pace far short of the published ballistics figures, which are based on a 6" barrel. The short barrel means a short ejector rod, which means the empties have to be plucked out by hand, save for a couple of new designs. Whether fired deliberately or instinctively, it's one of the most inconsequential handguns in the book.

But despite its multitudinous disadvantages the much over-rated 38 snub does have its place. It fills a

Colt's 1972 Detective Special is a sturdy but small handful, weight just right at 23 ounces. Its improved grips are pretty good combat handles as found.

definite need, and in certain circumstances it is the only arm to choose.

For instance, the off-duty cop who must lug his equalizer to the movies, supermarket, beach and church, summer and winter, often finds anything larger than a snub a nuisance to hide. Likewise the undercover operative, the narcotics agent, or the vice squad officer can sometimes get away with a small 38 and have a far more effective firearm than any derringer or watch-fob automatic. The doctor, pharmacist, banker, jeweler, or shopkeeper who works in shirt sleeves, needs a gun that's concealable in a pants pocket holster — so the answer is obvious. Finally, he who insists on concealing his sidearm in a shoulder rig is restricted to the snub because the best of the half-breed harnesses will take nothing else.

Choice of Snubs

So if you really need a little shortnose hideout gun, what's there to choose from? Smith & Wesson has the largest offering: three models in steel frame at about 19 oz. and in airweight at about 14 oz. Their basic model is the Chief's Special. The Bodyguard is a Chief's with built up sidewalls shrouding the snag-prone hammer

Snubs, by nature, are the hardest handguns to shoot. The way the factories leave them, though, makes things harder than necessary. Author's battery includes (from left) Colt Agent, S&W Chief's Special (note chopped spur), and Charter Undercover. All have been customized to some extent. Charter wears factory optional Bulldog grips while other two get by with Ace shoes and Tyler adaptors.

spur. The Centennial model is slicker still, with the hammer completely concealed in the frame; it can be fired double action only and was designed for pocket use. Each of this trio is built on Smith's small "J" frame, is of the same size and heft, and takes 5 rounds. The Chief's is also available in all stainless steel at 19 oz., if you can find one!

Colt's snubs hold 6 rounds, and are consequently somewhat bulkier than the competition. The steel-framed Detective Special hefts 21 oz., and its aluminum alloy look-alike, the Cobra, goes 15 oz. Colt's Agent is simply a Cobra with shorter grip straps.

Colt's 1972 Detective Special, built on the Mark III system, is a big improvement over the older version of the DS. The new ejector rod, now .875-inch long, almost punches the empties out into the clear, but not quite. The ejector is now encased in a housing under the barrel, this adding a couple of ounces to total weight (now 23 oz.), shifting the balance forward, with improved handling and recovery from recoil.

The new grips are a major improvement, too. They're beefier, making for better control, with a second-finger filler built-in. They drop below the straps over a half-inch, another plus.

The Baughman-style ramp front sight, nicely cross-grooved for glare reduction, is ⅛-inch wide.

Otherwise the new Colt DS is much like its predecessor, and the latest model appears well put together—good finish, good quality control.

The knowledgeable customer usually selects a steel frame, and puts up with the extra weight involved. These guns are small enough to start with, and a few extra ounces are a big help in dampening their vicious recoil. Moreover, besides the extra strength of a steel frame, steel contact surfaces tend to work harden, and the more you fire the gun, the smoother it operates. Aluminum alloys have no such virtues, sometimes deteriorate after long usage.

In addition to such hoary names as Colt and Smith & Wesson, a relative newcomer to the field, the Charter Arms Corp. of Bridgeport, Connecticut, also offers an excellent 38 Special snub, their Undercover model. Externally resembling the Chief's Special, the Undercover weighs 16 oz., has a chrome-moly steel frame, high carbon or chrome-moly critical parts, and an aluminum alloy grip strap/trigger guard unit—clearly a nonstress part. I favor the Charter as perhaps the best compromise since

it's the lightest steel-frame 38 made, has the widest sights of the lot, and is offered with a fine pair of combat grips direct from the factory. But take a good look at the 1972 Colt DS as well.

Having now chosen one or the other, how do we go about wrenching the maximum potential accuracy and controllability from the perverse little gun?

This problem wants considerable thought, and then a good bit of work since, as they come from the factory, the little guns are rather barren of virtue and each of the limitations enumerated in the opening paragraphs must be overcome as far as possible.

Sights

Snubs come with non-adjustable milled sights, and in any altercation beyond off-the-muzzle range, your health and welfare are likely to depend on their quality. Ideally they're big, eye catching, and open enough to allow quick alignment even in dim light.

Smith & Wesson is the worst offender. Their front blade, nominally a slender 1/10", often mikes to a mere .073"-.075", and it's combined with a too-narrow rear notch. I've seriously considered having a competent pistol-smith knock the things off entirely and replace them with something usable. If going to this extreme, a 1/10"-1/8" gold or ivory bead in a wide "V" British Express-style rear leaf might prove an interesting combination.

The old Colt, with an .011" wide front post, has considerably more going for it. The rear notch is narrowish but can be opened by careful filing. You'll probably have to do this to sight the gun in anyway. The new Colt DS front sight mikes about the same, but the rear notch is a bit wider.

Charter's Undercover is by far the best of the three. Their front blade, nominally ⅛" (.125") actually measures a generous .139" and .141" on my guns. The rear notch is beautifully shadow-boxed into the frame and gives a dead-black picture. It too is a bit on the tight side, and stock removal is best done on the providentially fat front post.

Snubs are usually regulated at the plant to throw 158-gr. factory loads 2"-2½" high at about 15 yards, 6 o'clock hold. It's unlikely that your gun, from your hand, will put the load you want to use to the point of aim. If she shoots low, just file down the front sight a bit at a time till you're on target. If she shoots high, well, that's bad. You have to have a higher front sight. A good gunsmith may be able to lay a welding bead up there, or he may have to braze or dovetail on a complete new ramp and blade. If windage is adrift, the group can be brought to taw by carefully filing a bit of stock from the rear sight notch or from the front sight blade, on the side toward which you want the group to move. As we've noted, this operation has the additional advantage of opening the rear sight, giving more light on each side of the front sight blade—a distinct advantage for defense shooting.

Actions

A small revolver, if it is to deliver any sort of double action accuracy, needs a butter-smooth action. Many hours of careful handwork, which the factories simply can't afford to do, will be required. A few aristocratic gunners obviate this laborious action smoothing by having each moving part gold plated. This slicks the action right up, but us pore boys better do it the hard way.

Besides disassembly tools—screwdrivers, pin drifts, a brass headed hammer, etc., you'll need an India stone, a hard Arkansas stone, and several sheets of crocus cloth. Medium grade emery cloth may be substituted for the stones. A ⅛" power tool with an assortment of rubber abrasive heads is handy but not essential. Felt buffing wheels and Tripoli compound on the same tool will bring things to a mirror finish, but so will worn crocus cloth. A hand-held small parts vice is invaluable, and a pair of spring snips sees good use on a Smith & Wesson. All these items and a wealth of others are available from such good gunsmith's supply house as Brownell's (Main and 3rd, Montezuma, Iowa 50171) or Mittermeier's (3577 E. Tremont Ave., New York, New York 10465).

Colt's

Colt actions are the easiest to work with, and usually show the most marked improvement for your efforts. Tool marks are rampant (no pun intended), and the object is to make every contact surface absolutely smooth—to take off all the burrs and bumps and scratches and rough areas the factory left in. Go over everything lightly with the stones (India first, then Arkansas) or emery cloth, then finish up by polishing with the crocus cloth. Be careful to keep the stone and the cloth back-up (a file or a wooden block) absolutely flat on the work; *don't* change any angles or bevels. Keep corners square but not sharp. Bear in mind that you're removing burrs, not stock.

The rebound lever, which has the lower leg of the V-mainspring bearing on its back, is the heart of the regular Colt mechanism. On the right side of it (inside), about 3/5 of the way up at its widest point, is a triangular shelf (called the "cam" at the factory) which engages the cylinder stop or bolt. Stay clear of this cam like the plague. The cylinder stop itself is another verboten zone—don't touch it under any circumstances; likewise the two teeth on the top of the hand which engage the ratchet.

There's no point wasting labor on areas which aren't abrading. As for which parts *do* need work, the best approach is to dry snap the gun several dozen times, then take it apart and look for scrape marks. Probably that portion of the trigger adjacent to its axis pin will be grinding against the frame on one side and against the sideplate on the other. Forget the frame since you can't get at it, and polish instead both sides of the trigger and the inside of the sideplate.

The nose of the rebound lever has a long sliding contact with a shelf on the hand. Polish both of these surfaces, but take pains to keep them flat. The outside of the hand tends to grate against its recess in the sideplate, so here's another good place to work; the sideplate recess poses accessibility problems, though. For that matter, polish the entire hand—except for the ratchet engagement teeth—but be careful not to thin it appreciably lest it tip away from the ratchet during cylinder rotation.

The front face of the rebound lever, just ahead of the cam, engages the back of the hammer to rebound it to safety position. Polish both parts (the hammer and the lower angle on the front face of the lever; *not* the cam). Remove the safety bar and go over it very lightly to remove any really prominent burrs.

The back of the hammer, below the spur, is apt to rub on the frame or the sideplate or both; look for contact marks and polish if need be. The lower part of the hammer, below the axis pin, is quite rough, but generally doesn't touch anything, so don't worry about it.

The most important engagement in a Colt, from the point of view of the D.A. pull, is that between the top of the trigger and the lower inside of the hammer strut. Tool marks run across the trigger from side to side creating a gritty hop-hop-hop sequence as the hammer rocks back. Polish it smooth. Rounding off the top shelf of the trigger at the back helps double action, but plays hob elsewhere, drastically increasing the weight of the single action pull and causing the hammer to fall off early on D.A., thus inducing misfires and perhaps throwing the gun out of time. Best to leave it as flat as the factory did, and tolerate a bit of pressure buildup at the end of the D.A. pull. Again, *polish;* don't remove stock.

Likewise for the hammer strut. Drift its pin far enough to remove it from the hammer and polish both its underside and outside scrupulously. But don't change its length or profile; don't round it off at the bottom. Polishing the underside of the strut will make for a smooth double action and polishing its front face will contribute to a snappy trigger return.

Stay away from the single action sear surfaces on both trigger and hammer, and don't monkey with the mainspring. Colt hasn't made a too-stiff spring since the Great Depression, and weakening it will invariably cause misfires and a mushy trigger return.

The Colt, as we said, is a gratifying action to work on. Smoothing it up will not only take the grinds and jerks out of the pull, but will reduce its weight by two pounds or more. Ignition will be improved and trigger return will be speeded up. In short, the gun will feel like a pre-war Colt.

These instructions apply in no way

Colt's action, despite its seeming simplicity, is incredibly subtle and complex. Work with caution, never weaken springs in this gun.

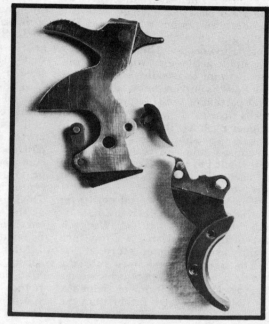

Sides and back of Colt hammer, bearing flats on each side of trigger, can stand polishing, but trigger-strut engagement is the prime governor of the D.A. pull. Don't drift hammer pin all the way out—just far enough to free the strut.

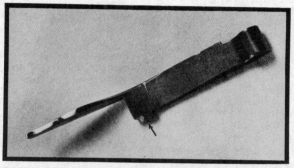

Rebound lever is the heart of the Colt mechanism. Underside of its extension, which bears on hand, needs polishing, but stay away from the cam (arrow) at all costs.

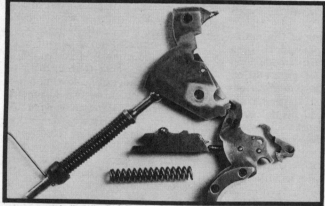

Smith & Wesson action is straightforward and efficient by design, wants only minimal smoothing. Note hammer-trigger engagement—this is where the hammer trips off on double action.

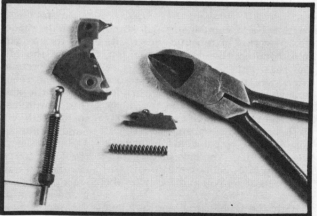

Smith's two massive coil springs can both stand pruning—generally up to two coils. Bob the rebound spring first. A dehorned hammer, like this one, has less mass than normal, needs an extra margin of mainspring behind it.

Double action sear surface on Smith hammer can stand a very light stoning—just enough to knock off the tall spots—but stay off the single action notch just a little above it.

to the new Mark III, which uses an entirely different mechanism and doesn't lend itself to this procedure.

Smith & Wesson

Smith & Wessons usually show very fine internal machining and come with creditably smooth actions. That's fortunate, since the trigger and hammer are case hardened to an average depth of 6 or 7 thousandths, and there's not a whole lot that can be done with them. The surface is almost glass hard, and while it's deep enough to take a bit of stoning, too vigorous an approach will break through into the softer core and the part is ruined. Just a light stoning to take off upstanding burrs (and there won't be many) is all these parts want or need.

I like to polish the rounded area at the upper back of the trigger where it contacts the hammer strut, but I'm willing to leave a bit of roughness lest I stone too deeply. This is just above the single action sear, with which you do *not* want to meddle. The strut on the S&W is only in contact during the first portion of the D.A. cycle. It soon rocks clear as a lower shoulder on the trigger picks up the hammer proper. I make a wishful pass with the fine Arkansas stone on both these locations, but I'm careful not to touch the adjacent single action sear notch on the hammer.

The hammer strut need not be removed, and indeed its working surface shouldn't be touched. Wedge it forward and polish its front face lightly to assist trigger return.

The hammer sometimes rubs the frame or sideplate, in which case it's best to polish the frame or sideplate, as the case may be, rather than the hammer. On my Chief's, the cylinder latch screw protruded through and interfered with the hammer. Check that.

Other S&W components can stand a bit of work. The rebound slide wants smoothing on all sides except on top, and the frame flat on which it rides can do with polishing. Again, no stock removal or you'll foul up clearance between the hammer and the safety bar. The ramp face on the lower body of the cylinder stop and the trigger nose can both be polished for a smooth trigger return. The side of the cylinder stop body sometimes galls the sideplate; if so, polish directly on the stop.

Both the trigger and the hammer ride between bosses on the frame and sideplate respectively; those on the sideplate may be profitably polished, but be careful to stay flat on the work.

And that's about it. Be cautious and tread lightly.

The Colt springs were off limits under pain of certain malfunction. Not so the Smith. The Smith & Wesson snub comes from the factory equipped with the lustiest springs in the business. There are two of them we're interested in, both coil type, and they are so placed as to do their job in the most direct and efficient fashion possible. The rebound spring, or trigger return spring, pushes the trigger forward with such gusto that two coils probably won't be missed. Lopping them off will help take some of the stiffness out of the trigger pull, and won't sap an iota of punch from the hammer. Removing more than two coils may result in a mushy trigger return—a clear liability in fast double action shooting. Bob the spring a half-coil at a time, trying it as you go. Prudence dictates having some spares on hand before we go grinding off springs.

The Smith hammer belts the primer a hearty smack. I've often found that cartridges which repeatedly misfired in other revolvers would dutifully discharge in the Chief's. This sort of reliability is comforting. It also contributes to the stiff trigger pull, and offers safe margin for improvement. First try polishing the outside of the mainspring swivel, a cup-shaped part which seats in the grip frame and is pierced through the center by the mainspring guide rod. Then, to ease things still further, have at the spring itself, a half-coil at a time; you can cut off two full coils with no great fear.

After any weakening of the mainspring, the revolver should be testfired double action with at least 50 rounds of each type of ammunition you expect to use. If any misfires occur, go back to a full-strength spring.

The Smith, it should be noted, is 75% impossible to reassemble without a special tool which, fortunately, is easily made. Take a screwdriver and file or grind about ⅛" off either side of the bit, leaving a sufficient nubbin protruding at the center to enter the rebound spring coil. Each side of the spring then will rest on the shoulders of the tool, and the spring and slide may now be shoved handily into place.

Here's the philosophy of it. With the Colt, grittiness, jerkiness, unevenness of pull was the problem. We smoothed the action for smoothness' own sake, and in order to help the spring put more energy where it was needed. The Smith was smooth enough, but too stiff. Smoothing its action merely gives a bit of safety margin for spring bobbing. For it's the compounded forces of the mainspring on top of the rebound spring that make the S&W stiff on double action.

Charter Arms

The Charter is a bit of a hybrid. The hammer is case hardened like an S&W, whereas the trigger and other action components are full hardened like a Colt, and can well stand working over. There's no sideplate on this gun, and polishing the inside faces of the frame with emery and crocus cloth over a file blade sometimes yields good results. Spring tension in those Charters I've seen is about right, and I don't recommend reducing them.

Grips

As vital as a smooth double action is for combat accuracy with the miniguns, the improvement brought about will hardly be as monumental as that which can be attained by simply screwing on a set of new grips. This point was painfully reemphasized the other day while I was testfiring a Charter Undercover. It carried the splinter-like standard factory grips and had almost no feel or sense of direction, and consequently squirmed about in the hand. Volley firing or accurate burst shooting was all but impossible, and establishing a good shooting grip from the leather was hopeless. On each shot my middle finger took a bruising blow from the trigger guard, and the right thumb was in danger of laceration by the cylinder latch. Trigger reach was so dismally short that my trigger finger kept ramming other assorted digits, and the muzzle flipped from side to side during trigger pull.

Merely screwing on a pair of well-designed combat grips—in this instance Jay Scott Gunfighters—made the miserable little beast a deadly accurate piece of equipment, and a pleasure to shoot, even with full charge loads. The grip was firm, solid, and substantial, and shifted not a whit in recoil. Recovery time was optimum, and follow up shots were rapped out in rapid succession with very pleasing accuracy.

Smith & Wesson grips are of the same configuration as the Charter's, and should be removed from the weapon and used for kindling fires.

Colt's earlier DS grips were designed upside down, being bulbous at the bottom where compactness is a virtue, and emaciated at the top where a healthy span for the encircling middle finger and the tender, recoil-absorbing web of the hand is needed. However, they are more substantial than the others, and since they ride on a larger-framed gun, they are usable if a grip adaptor and trigger shoe are added. Colt's rasp-like checkering should be sanded down flush along the backstrap for comfort's sake, and the tops of the diamonds

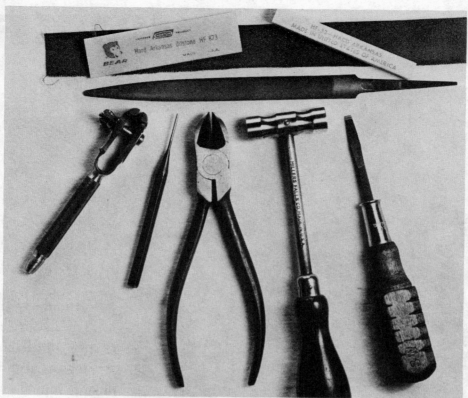

Basic tools for action smoothing include stones and crocus cloth (top) and (from left) small-parts vice, pin drift, spring snips, brass headed hammer, and screwdriver. File is used only to back up the cloth.

smoothed generally to avoid undue wear on clothing. As noted earlier, Colt's new DS grips are much better, being pretty good combat types as is.

One of the most crippling liabilities of an off-the-shelf snub is the rarely mentioned factor of insufficient trigger reach—the distance from the face of the backstrap to the curve of the trigger. For instance, the reach on a Chief's Special is a scant 2⅜", compared to 2¾" for the larger M&P. The tiny Charter, likewise at 2⅜'', is equally as sad a case as the Chief's. Fingers just don't ordinarily come short enough. I know one gunner whose trigger finger was amputated at the first joint, and the remaining stub fits the Charter reach just right. The Colt, being a larger-framed gun with a more sweeping trigger pull, is much better provided for—it has a full 2½" reach.

The problem can be attacked from both ends. Any of these weapons will benefit from the addition of a trigger shoe. The sharp serrations and edges of the shoe should be ground down smooth prior to installation.

The reasonable, and only really effective, way to lick the problem, though, is by the installation of a set of custom combat grips which increase trigger reach by putting lumber behind the backstrap.

Steve Herrett's popular "Shooting Star" grips unaccountably fail to cor-rect this problem. They're lovely to look on, but stop flush with the backstrap. His more recent "Shooting Ace" is almighty ugly, but puts the wood where you need it. Besides Herrett (in Twin Falls, Idaho 83301), Jay Scott Grips, of 81 Sherman Place, Garfield, N.J. 07026, or the Caray Sales Co. (Enforcer Brand Grips), 1394 15th Street, Palisades, N.J. 07650, also do things right. Charter Arms, with the introduction of their optional equipment "Bulldog" grips, became America's only gunmaker to offer decent combat stocks straight from the factory. They're good, too.

Custom grips usually add bulk by extending below the bottom of the grip straps and giving enough wood to seat the little finger. This makes for better handling, but is awkward if you carry the gun in a pocket. However, the excess timber can be whittled off flush with the straps for a conventional 2-finger grip. If your shooting style demands that the pinky be anchored, the extra bulk has to stay.

Other Alterations

Snubs in the hands of pseudo-savants are often seen with the front of the trigger guard chopped out. This alteration does give more elbow room in the crowded guard, but trigger guards were designed for fingers, not elbows. So, unless you have to shoot with gloved hands, venting the guard is a poor notion, and is inherently unsafe. If the gun is inadvertently dropped or instinctively used as a bludgeon (a remarkably poor application, by the way), a chopped guard can easily bend up to jam the trigger. The function of a trigger guard is to guard the trigger, and if it's not there, it can't do it. However, slimming the leading starboard edge of the obstruction to half of full width is not a bad idea on a steel-framed Smith or Colt.

One desirable alteration is grinding off the hammer spur. This claw-like appendage, constantly snaring itself on pockets, jacket linings, and shirt tails, is quite unnecessary on a gun primarily intended for double action use. Witness the justifiable popularity of Colt hammer shrouds and Smith's Bodyguard and Centennial models. A dehorned hammer can readily be cocked for single action shooting if the top edge is serrated, or even if it's not. Cock it part way with the trigger, roll the thumb over the top of the hammer, and finish the job just as if the spur were there.

• • • • • •

These modifications will make your snub—most contrary of handguns—accurate and easily handled, a gun to bank on in the worst circumstances. A customized snub, for its purposes, is the best possible choice, and the mark of a knowledgeable shooter. •

SHOTGUNNERS

by CHARLES F. WATERMAN

Particularly the good ones.
The better scattergunners,
craziest of all, are immune to
logical argument, ballistic
data or filmed evidence—they
just hit 'em! Here they are,
passing in review.

by

CHARLES F. WATERMAN

Red Monical of Montana uses a 3-inch 12-gauge magnum for high-flying mallards, but he wouldn't be helped with small shot in his full choke.

Even in those long ago days a custom Parker pigeon gun was expensive—I believe the price of this one had been around $3500, give or take a few hundred, but the well-heeled owner wasn't satisfied.

"I'm shooting over the blamed birds," he quavered as the week-end live pigeon program neared an end. "They made the damned stock too straight, and if I can't get down on 'em this trip is going to cost me money."

He stamped disconsolately about the grounds, clutching the offending weapon as if it smelled badly. Finally he saw a small tree with a fork about four feet up. He stuck the richly engraved barrels in the notch and leaned back hard. There was a cracking noise, the ventilated rib popped loose and the barrels bent a little. He shot better after that and when I saw him 20 years later the rib was still flapping like loose siding in a Kansas wind.

There aren't as many live pigeon shooters nowadays, but shotgunners are still artists if riflemen are scientists. After shooting pistols and rifles for years I took up shotgunning a bit late in life (possibly too late) and wrongly assumed a logical approach would make me a passable gunner in time.

Happening to know some scattergunning greats, I approached some of them for a good, sound foundation in shotgun shooting. It was a mistake— shotgun artists are not necessarily teachers. I should have interviewed someone just a few pages ahead of me in the shotgun book instead of the champions who had forgotten how they learned.

Never Watch the Bird!

The first—and most repeated—advice was to look at the bird, never at the gun. I tried that at an informal practice trap setup, missing the first

11 straight! A case of handloads later I realized the champions simply saw their barrels subconsciously, but with no recollection of them after the shot. As a beginner I learned I had blamed well better see the barrel and my hits picked up immediately when I did. Many sessions later I began to break occasional targets with no recollection of seeing the barrel or sights.

I also asked these wizards about the use and desireability of various gun models, but most of them knew less about that subject than I did.

Some experienced experts, as you may have heard, can see the shot charge in the air on nearly every shot. Some others can't, but it's a point of honor with them not to concede it. I have a secret method for checking out my coaches on this subject.

One friend told me I had shot low on four successive misses at clay birds.

"You'll have to get 'em up!" he insisted.

Are Strange People

In my routine check on the next try I shot an estimated eleven feet high. "Low again!" he snorted accusingly. To a rifleman used to the discussions of minute-of-angle groups and what it takes to get them, shotgunners' ballistics sound a bit sketchy. A deadly dove shot of my acquaintance insists on a heavy powder charge for long-range dove poking, explaining he doesn't need more shot in the trap gun he uses—just more powder.

"I don't have to lead so far with fast loads," he explains, "and you can hear 'em smack the dove quicker."

I checked into this—at the range he was shooting his "fast" loads gave

Shooting pintails over a Florida mangrove bay, these gunners are using improved-cylinder guns. Most shots are within 30 yards.

Until he saw this photograph this Hungarian-partridge shooter never suspected he bent both knees in game shooting.

him about 25 feet per second more velocity than his "slow" loads. That's hardly measurable in lead or shock but I am not going to tell that to a fellow who sometimes makes limit runs on doves—in the wind—and has a degree in engineering.

I am a little confused about the pros and cons of long and short shot strings. They tell me a long shot string helps a guy who shoots too far ahead but not the fellow who shoots a little behind. What's that again? I guess it depends on which end of the pattern he's aiming with.

I do believe now that after 40 years of preaching by gun writers it is gradually getting rumored about that overly long shotgun barrels don't make a gun shoot appreciably harder. Once, proud of my then-new knowledge I explained this to an old friend who has been pointing 30-inch repeater snouts for 40 years. He cross-questioned me until I began to resent it, but he then went

out and bought a double with 24-inch barrels. He always had hated those long guns.

This Gauge Business

Watch it, though, on the gauge business! Old shotgunners are convinced a 12 is more potent than a 16 bore, and a 16 more deadly than a 20. They'll stick to this even if the 12 carries one ounce of shot and the 20 is a magnum shooting a 3-inch Roman candle with an ounce and a quarter. The hole in the end is bigger, and that settles it.

A retired surgeon I know asked my advice about a new upland gun. He wanted a light, handy double, and he'd heard I fooled with shotguns and had written something elementary about them.

I explained that a 20 would be small, light to handle and, if a 3-incher, could handle the equivalent of 12-gauge express ammo. The doctor, a brilliant medical man, heard me out but he bought a 12. He said he'd decided a 20 just wasn't powerful enough so he shoots light field loads in his big 12. I went back and read the ballistic chart to him again.

"I know what you say is true," he apologized, "but a 20 just can't shoot as *hard* as a 12."

Keen eyesight has so long been associated with all kinds of shooting that even the experts get a little confused about it. Since it's pretty hard to prove any shotgun theory, the keen eye gets credit for the accomplishments of trained reflexes, nerve control and concentration.

A pheasant rooster getting up at your feet can look like a wet Rhode Island Red, but once he lines out and crosses at right angles he requires a fast swing.

Patterning

When one of the world's finest shotgunners credited his long runs at skeet to his acute perception of a target, I wondered a little, thinking of how the best pistol shots fire at a fuzzy target while focusing on their sights.

Feeling a little stupid but very scientific I wrapped layers of cheesecloth over my eyes until the world was in twilight, then had a go at some clay pigeons. The targets were vague, hurtling blobs and the gun barrel a shadow, but I hit about as many as without the blinders.

When it comes to chokes and patterns, however, shotgunning is really a never, never land.

The late Louis Montague, a fine trap and live pigeon shooter, made a profound statement about patterns. "Never," said Monty, "pattern your shotgun. It will ruin your whole life."

It is true that unhappily viewed pattern gaps may come back to haunt shotgunners after unexplained misses, but most of them have rather romantic notions about patterns. It is a source of wonderment that a man will buy a gun marked "improved cylinder" to give himself an open pattern on grouse and then brag about how close it shoots. He's delighted that it gives him modified patterns.

The plastic-sleeved loads of recent years have almost invariably improved patterns and, in many cases, tightened them considerably. It may be partly coincidence but in my limited testing the tightening shows up strongest on modified bores, these generally producing weak, full-choke patterns.

Many modified shooters had quick trouble with the new shells but couldn't recognize it. That caused, for a while, a strong demand for the old shells.

A few shooters, running out of other excuses, even blamed themselves, still refusing to believe the new shells made a difference.

"I have streaks when I can't hit anything" one bird shooter reported. "Then I'll hit a bird and tear it to shreds. When I do get on, I'm really on."

His old gun, of course, had simply tightened up with modern ammunition, but his patterning had been confined to the gratifying plastering of a tin bucket at unknown range when his fusil was new.

And the same crank who weighs individual bullets for his varminter may have startling views about shotgun shells and what goes into them.

Shooters, skimming through the literature on chokes and loads, seldom catch the possibilities of choke-load combinations. If they did, unhappy manufacturers might have to complicate their beautifully simplified ammunition lines.

New Loads

For example, a 20-gauge Skeet gun with 1⅛ ounces of 8s would be a potent killer on grouse, quail and woodcock. You'd have a big pattern and enough density for kills out toward the No. 8 range limit—the equivalent of a 12-gauge Skeet boring in a compact 20—but you can't buy a 1⅛/8s in factory 20s. No demand?

Within limits, of course, the rule is that the more open the bore the smaller the shot, and a Skeet pattern generally loss density before it loses penetration unless there's a lot of shot.

Stuff an open-bore 3-inch magnum 20 case with 1¼ ounces of shot, and you'd have a load that might cause a new appraisal of your local bobwhite

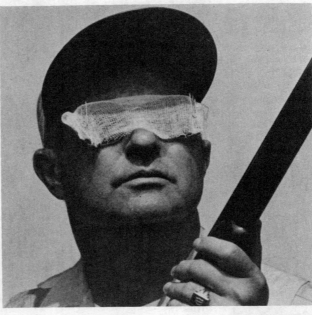

Several layers of cheesecloth clipped over his shooting glasses caused a partial eclipse for the author, but he broke clay targets just about as well as with clear vision.

population. Such a bomb isn't commercially loaded but I've built a few for patterning purposes. You still have all that destruction coming through a handy little 20-bore muzzle, In factory stuff, the nearest you can come to it is No. 7½ shot in the heavy load. A 12-gauge Skeet gun with 1½ ounces of No. 8s is another poor shot's dream.

Since every red-blooded shotgunner knows full choke guns are for ducks, even when they're banging over decoys at 25 yards, I am viewed sympathetically when I crawl hopefully into a blind with my improved cylinder 12.

Now that piece is loaded with 1½ ounces No. 6s in a short magnum case, so I have something akin to saturation fire out to 40 yards. That makes a fine combination for a sketchy pointer like me, who shouldn't shoot much farther than that anyway. Better shots are always explaining carefully to me that heavy loads are for long range guns but in my ballistic simplicity it has always seemed the reverse is true.

For example, a light field load of 6s would probably do just about as well as a heavy load in a full choke gun out as far as they'd penetrate satisfactorily. In my spray nozzle they would get

too thin, and No. 4s in an open bore don't have many worthwhile applications. Some hunters, however, would use fours in a 410 Skeet gun for waterfowl to give the little gun all the help they could!

On the other side of the blind there's a fellow who uses a full-choke 3-inch magnum 12 with No. 6s. He still has more pattern density than he needs, out there where the tired little 6s refuse to do more than sting an overweight mallard, but when he makes a center hit on a 25-yard decoying ringbill his prey disappears in a pink haze. Just try to explain these pedestrian facts to a veteran shotgunner and see what happens to your friendship. You might as well try to tell him how far to lead a bird.

Good shooters not only disagree as to proper methods of leading, they don't even use the same terms while they argue about swing through, sustained lead and snapshooting most of them use a combination of all three on game. One of the best Hungarian partridge gunners I know says that when he swings on a right-angle bird he takes dead aim with his front bead and then tells himself, "Now, push!" The true interpretation of these words is a bit vague but I take it he means to push out ahead before shooting. Anyway, he does something, because the birds fall!

Some of my trap and Skeet heroes were found to have feet of clay when they faced a modified "Crazy Quail" setup in which the birds flew in all directions, at varying speeds and at adjusted heights. Some of them had forgone live game shooting to preserve their target timing, and few broke more than 4 out of 10 on the Crazy Quail field the first time out. Although the Skeet or trap shot undoubtedly has excellent basic training he doesn't often score well on unpredictable game birds without *that* kind of practice.

Most true game artists, certainly, haven't the slightest idea of what they're doing when they hit or miss.

I diligently studied an English book on game shooting in which the author advocated following the bird with the muzzle while the gun is being mounted so that when cheek and stock meet the shot is just about ready for discharge.

That's Just Snapshooting!

"That's just snapshooting!" yelled my hotshot friend. He then went hunting and learned for the first time he'd been using that method himself for 20 years.

Assessments of various game birds is a favorite topic of shotgunners, the opinions being based largely on where or how the speaker hunts.

The ruffed grouse, recognized king of eastern shotgun game, gets the name of "fool hen" (actually another bird entirely) in Western U.S. and Canada. It is true that in these locations he will frequently sit in plain view on a limb while you throw rocks and sticks to start his flight. Report this to a New Englander and he will sulk or swear it isn't the same species. He will dribble tears all over his English double when you report how big game hunters pistol shoot friendly ruffs for the pot.

There's a sidelight of this western grouse business. After you finally haze him off the limb ready or not, he is a tough target, possibly even tougher than when he surprises you with a thunderous takeoff from the ground. Sometimes he dives almost straight down, and always he keeps much of the forest between you and him. After shooting off the limb old ruff is using for his takeoff, many a gunner has missed him with any other shells he happened to have in his gun.

With grouse behaving this way the tension can build to a deadly level. Ben Williams of Livingston, Montana, introduced me to the "throw a stick and shoot" method but one stick is seldom enough if the grouse is fairly high in the tree and I've watched Ben throw for 15 minutes straight while I stood by with my shooting confidence seeping away.

Once we saw a grouse go into a tree, where he remained invisible, so Ben climbed far up and probed about until he boosted the bird out. Unnerved, I missed with both barrels. Limb-clinging grouse may be undignified but I can't call them easy.

I have felt sorry for pheasant roosters who flapped off at my feet, but I have swung wildly at the same birds drilling downwind at 40 yards when flushed by other shooters. Most shotgunners take one side or the other about pheasants.

After being told by top gunners that Hungarian partridge were easy marks

Nearly all who have hunted the heavyweight sage grouse consider them an easy mark, but once you try pass-shooting them when someone else has put them up, you get a new respect for their speed.

I stepped into the midst of a solidly pointed covey, swatted down a double, and was inclined to believe it. Then I became involved with a big bunch in a small, steep-walled canyon, and fired a dozen times while the scattered covey sizzled back and forth overhead by twoes and threes. I picked up a pair of birds, apologized to my sulking Brittany, and slunk toward home.

All of these things lead to unresolved arguments.

Take woodcock, which are sometimes bagged during straight and level flight in the wide open spaces, and at other times are softly whistling ghosts in the brush.

Snipe Are Easy

As a relative newcomer to the ranks I was enraged by the statement that snipe are easy to hit. Having rolled up a score of 18 straight misses on snipe at about that time I investigated and learned my former friend had kicked his birds out of tall switchgrass whereas mine had twisted off from a distance of about 20 yards on a mud flat. This teaches both tolerance and humility, as well as the policy of hunting snipe downwind so they'll hop toward you before choosing a course.

Two years later I found some snipe

in tall grass myself and, even I, made two limit runs of 8 birds without a miss in three trips. Of this, I ain't a bit ashamed; I've been looking for a good place to get it in.

The physical form, the postures, used in shooting get pages of pictures in shotgun texts. Extreme poses and exaggerated crouches are universally ridiculed, but any trap or Skeet shoot will generally run up poses worth careful noting by cartoonists.

One high-scoring quail shooter straightened me out on shooting positions and emphasized a relaxed, moderate stance which I practiced diligently. I then made some photographs of him shooting quail in a tight corner and the relentless film showed that when actually at work he squats like a Japanese wrestler. He had no comment.

One book says a game shot should bend this front knee a little. Another says he should bend his back knee a little. Both say the other knee should stay straight. I know what I do when I shoot at a clay target but I don't know at all what I do when I'm game shooting. Can it be that I'm joining the club?

Range Savvy

Range judgment makes interesting conversation, but it isn't practiced much, really. Oh, some experienced duck shooters are inclined to experiment on slow days, and they'll make an occasional try at 100 yards. It's pretty easy to count your steps to a fallen target in upland gunning, but few do it, and when patterning a gun for the first time at a true 40 yards the average gunner is so surprised at how far that is he'll measure it twice.

The tendency is to shoot too far at geese and too close at quail, neither extreme proving satisfactory. Many quail are missed at 20 feet, and timing is a big factor there. I know a fellow who had a reputation as a real bobwhite thumper but couldn't hit doves until he turned his head away upon first sighting approaching birds. He'd wait until he thought the birds should be in range and then turn 'back and fire quickly. His score improved. Otherwise, he'd take too much time and miss.

Many a too-ready upland gunner has missed with both barrels at a quail rise, then watched the birds flapping away like pelicans—his gun already empty and the birds still in good range.

Now if these observations seem simple to you you're probably a mediocre shot, because most good scattergunners find them overly complex and will change the subject when you speak of pattern percentages, shot speed and shooting positions.

Ballistic baloney, they insist, is for riflemen and they don't know why they're good shots or why I'm a poor shot. Art is an ethereal thing. ●

Dream Gun or Zombie?

by H. V. STENT

The Winchester 30-30 has been done to death a thousand times—at least in print. Yet the old slab-sided companion of countless trails and campfires is alive and well—and flourishing everywhere.

SOMETIMES I wonder if Winchester's Model 94 30-30 is what the Haitians used to call a "zombie," a living corpse.

Lord knows it looks healthy enough, in this its 80th anniversary year, outselling practically every other sporting rifle, spawning special editions—the Buffalo Bill, Antique, Centennial, NRA and Teddy Roosevelt models—with an energy which would be remarkable at half its age.

Yet 35 years ago it was so nearly dead that a lot of us were just waiting for the black-bordered announcement from New Haven. Many gun writers, at least, claimed it was. They were bolt action enthusiasts all, of 30-06 or bigger caliber persuasion, and to them any lever gun was an obsolete has-been. The 94 was generally represented as too poopless to kill even deer effectively, too inaccurate to hit a deer farther than 125 or so yards away, too fast-shooting for anyone to use what little accuracy it had anyhow; weak, unreliable. Fit only for the boneyard, and darned near there.

When World War II stopped the manufacture of sporting rifles for the duration, bolt rifle advocates confidently predicted that the lever action would not be made again.

Back from its temporary tomb it bounced after war's end, however, and proceeded to sell like half-price hotcakes. Television came in, with Westerns easily the most popular of TV shows from the first, and rare is the Western that does not have a lever-action rifle prominently displayed—usually shooting 47 times without reloading. This has created—or helped create, certainly—such a popular demand for lever action guns that now we have lever action 22s made by more manufacturers than ever before, and high-powered lever actions pouring from Marlin, Savage and Winchester in a very healthy stream. Browning too!

Is this popularity all TV-inspired? Would the Model 94 and its cartridge be mouldering in their graves now, as the single-action Colt almost certainly would, had it not been for the living-room screen?

Today's leading gun writers and experts no longer condemn the lever action roundly in print as their predecessors did, but they're still almost unanimous in using bolt actions for their own hunting and target shooting. Are the old criticisms still valid, and the host of 94 and similar carbines carried into the hunting fields this fall really just ineffective ghosts riding along on a reputation built up in horse-and-buggy days, when no better rifles were to be had?

30-30 Resurgence

It would be foolish to deny that some of the two million or more Model 94s now used in North America were bought because of romantic dreams inspired by Chuck Connor, Dean Martin, or big John Wayne. How many it's hard to say.

But aren't toters of modern magnums often victims of hallucinations, too? Dreams that North American big game is dinosaur-tough, when actually every species of it has been killed with a 22 rimfire? Dreams of awful long ranges being practically compulsory now, when really most big game is still shot under 100 yards, almost all of it under 200; only the few who hunt the open plains or above timberline have much chance of getting long shots. Not to mention that being able to make a *sure* hit on big game at long range is also just a dream for most of us?

All trips aside, the killing power of the 30-30 is by now a well-established fact, as far as it goes.

The grin on this kid's face is understandable, for that's a nice buck, brought down with his 30-30 Model 94. He wouldn't have done any better with a belted magnum.

The author prefers a white bull for casual target shooting, floating the bead front sight into the circle. That's a 100-yd. 5 shot group—and not at all bad for metallic sights.

Some of the old thutty-thutties up north must have almost as long a record of moose slain as a Model 94 recently mentioned in *Outdoor Life* has achieved on elk. When the latter's owner, a Montana guide, bought it, 45 years ago, it had already killed scores of elk, and he and his sons have used it for elk ever since! I've known other woodsmen who found the 30-30 all they needed for these big critters, and several who were satisfied with the same gun for grizzly bear. Jim Osman, though not really a 30-30 man, killed four grizzlies with one, and thought them easier to kill than moose. Wasn't it the same humble weapon which recently dropped the world's record grizzly in northern British Columbia?

Makes you wonder, doesn't it, if it's just a matter of having confidence in your gun. Maybe if some of our magnum users switched to the 30-30 and believed in it, they'd be amazed at what it could do. When Bud Helmericks first went to Alaska he unwillingly used a 30-30 carbine because it was the only rifle available, and brought down a moose with it at 500 yards. Pretty good for a zombie!

How far is that? Well, a rather surprising distance. At actual—not imaginary—game ranges it is generally admitted to be an effective deer gun, combining oomph enough to kill with any reasonably-well-placed shot, reliably consistent performance, and a minimum of meat damage. It is said to have brought more venison to the table than all other calibers put together.

Nor is it limited to deer. Up in northern Canada, where men must be realistic because dreams can freeze solid in the grim winters and run into nightmares when they melt in the spring, the 30-30 is almost a standard arm for moose hunters. Some of them may use its speed of fire to drop their game by pumping it full of lead, but very few do that, for two reasons: one, ammunition is expensive and hard to come by, and two, the big black buggers are extremely prone to vanish in the bush before you've time for more than one or two shots.

A rifle in that stark country is not a dream gun but a tool on which men depend, sometimes for their lives. They would not depend on the 30-30 if it had not repeatedly proved itself adequate for the job.

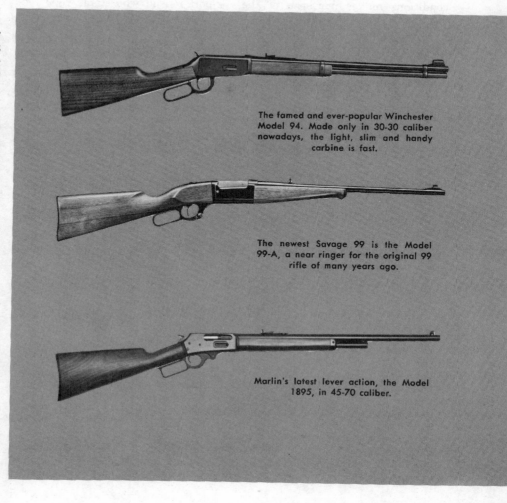

The famed and ever-popular Winchester Model 94. Made only in 30-30 caliber nowadays, the light, slim and handy carbine is fast.

The newest Savage 99 is the Model 99-A, a near ringer for the original 99 rifle of many years ago.

Marlin's latest lever action, the Model 1895, in 45-70 caliber.

Shooting at bigger game is most often like this, the shot made standing and hurriedly, not in other positions.

30-30 Accuracy

Its extensive use for 80 years by wilderness men under the toughest conditions makes nonsense of the old claim that the 94 action is unreliable—and it certainly isn't weak. Not only will the action handle handloads considerably hotter than the factory product, but when it gets too worn, that springy back-loaded action just lets the case expand enough to give sticky extraction, a clear warning to back off a little.

What about its accuracy? It was, after all, a very prominent old-time expert indeed who stated repeatedly that lever actions were not accurate enough to keep all their shots on a deer's body over 125 yards.

Tests on targets indicate that this was perhaps the most virulent of all the false propaganda that used to be spewed out about the 30-30. Although I'm no expert, I've made 1⅝-inch groups with a Model 94 and factory ammo, smaller ones with handloads, and I know others who have done better; all, incidentally, with iron sights. These were with the longer-barreled rifles, mine being a 24-inch Model 64. What little targeting I've done with the carbine has corroborated a claim I've seen made by others, that they won't do much better than 2½-inch groups at 100 yards. Still, that's good enough for big game well beyond the usual limit of 200 yards. There are indications that could be wrong, too.

Writing in the 1964 GUN DIGEST, Helbig and Cain found that loosening tight barrel bands and improving trigger pulls would improve accuracy considerably. More recently, in a popular gun magazine, the editor told of testing a new Model 70 and a new Model 94 carbine at about the same time. The 94 proved the more accurate of the two! The 30-30 cartridge itself seems very accurate; an ammunition company representative once told me that they got frequent 1-inch groups with it in testing, and in a heavy barreled special rifle it had grouped down to .55″.

It has accuracy enough, anyhow, power enough, reliability and strength to spare. Aside from romantic TV appeal, these provide solid background for the Model 94's popularity. Its greatest attraction, though, has yet to be mentioned— its wonderful handiness.

The Handy 1894

Shoot me at sunrise if you must for saying it, but the bolt action is not a handy hunting gun. True, it's got lots going for it in comparison with the lowly lever; greater accuracy, even if only by fractions of an inch; more strength, more rigidity, better suited to handloading, chambered for more powerful cartridges. Also—there's nothing like getting myself in wrong with both camps at once—the bolt rifle is better looking. I've always felt that the lever rifle, with its magazine as long as the barrel, looks as clumsy as a man trying to walk with both legs tied together.

But it sure is handy. Hunting, for most of us, means hiking for hours with a gun in your hand. You have only to pick up first one and then the other to see that the lever gun's slender steel breech fits more comfortably in the hand than the bolt gun's wider walnut waist; and every hour you carry either one accentuates the difference. Usually the bolt action weighs more

This grouse was shot with a lead-bulleted light handload during a deer hunt.

than the lever carbine, too. If the bolt rifle is scoped—and a bolt gun looks as naked without a scope as a 94 looks over-dressed with one—its comparative weight and awkwardness of hand cartage increase still more.

If you travel a-horse, the weight difference is unimportant, but the lever gun's flatness and lack of projecting knobs make it distinctly the better of the two to carry in—or snatch hurriedly out of—a saddle scabbard.

But we were afoot, gun in hand. Now swing each one up from the side to the shoulder. Notice how much easier and faster the short carbine comes up compared with most of the bolt rifles; especially if you try this in thick willow scrub or alder brush. Not only is the 94 carbine shorter in the barrel than most bolts, but its action is about two inches shorter as well.

Next step in comparison is to fire the two guns. You'll find the 94 noticeably pleasanter on shoulder and ears than the big bolt calibers usually recommended.

Finally, work the action for a second shot. Note that the bolt takes six motions, and you have to take your hand completely away from the trigger-guard; the lever takes just two, with your hand staying in the trigger-guard and its lever extension. Much handier, much faster.

Speed of fire does sometimes encourage careless shooting; many hunters frown on automatics for this reason. But it also makes quick accurate shooting possible, and a good lever man can toss a tin can in the air and hit it two or three times while it falls 20 feet. Such shooting will make sure of a running deer or moose if the first shot missed, but trying to hurry through the complicated six motions of operating a bolt fast in such circumstances is frustrating enough to make a saint swear.

A bolt action is a fine gun for leisurely shots in open country, but in the woods where most big game is sought, and where buck or bull can duck out of sight in seconds, it is a good feeling to be carrying a rifle that can be easily and swiftly pumped for a second shot.

Probably none of the above-mentioned comforts and conveniences will cut much ice with gun nuts who have already lost their hearts to some other action. Nevertheless, they're real and important to the great mass of hunters, men who handle a big game rifle for only a

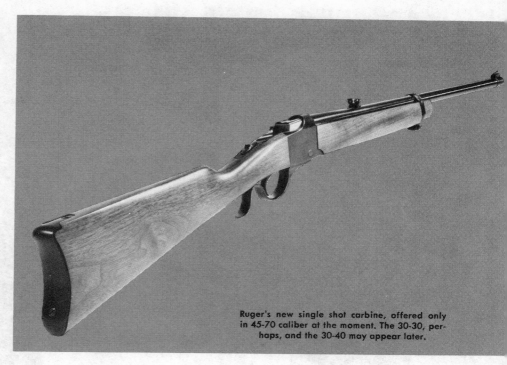

Ruger's new single shot carbine, offered only in 45-70 caliber at the moment. The 30-30, perhaps, and the 30-40 may appear later.

few days each year, men who don't give a hoot about superfine accuracy, handloading, or long-range knockdown power. For them the 30-30 carbine is probably the best all-round combination of desirable qualities that has ever been devised.

Only two of its rivals are even close. The M1 30 caliber carbine has lightness, convenience, rapid fire, mild recoil—that's why GIs so universally preferred it to the Garand or Springfield—but it hasn't

enough power for big game. The Remington 660 has the power, and is both light and short; but its kick and muzzle blast are far from gentle in its stronger calibers, and it retains the awkwardness for carrying or fast repeating that is a drawback to all bolts.

It will take something more convenient and competitive than these —or anything else so far produced —to make a ghost or a relic of the old 94. ●

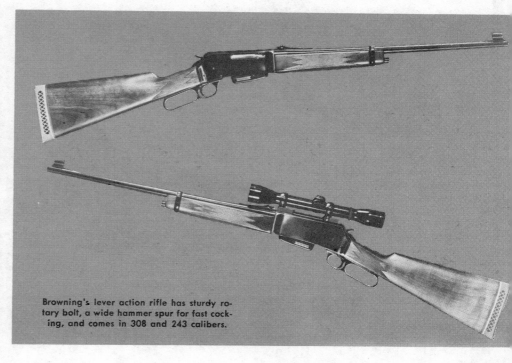

Browning's lever action rifle has sturdy rotary bolt, a wide hammer spur for fast cocking, and comes in 308 and 243 calibers.

Shaw-Leibowitz
(W. F. Moran Knife)

Miller Gun Works

Lynton McKenzie

Armi Famars

B. "Jim" Gwinnell

Jos. Bayer

Art of the

A display of engraving in
fine-line etching. The ad-
here will be found in our

Engraver

steel—as well as samples of dresses of the artists named Directory of the Arms Trade.

Shaw-Leibowitz
(W. F. Moran Knife)

Jos. Condon

Franz Marktl

Franz Marktl

Armi Famars

F. E. Hendricks

Neil Hartliep

John Warren

Max E. Bruehl

Max E. Bruehl

John Warren

Winston Churchill (A&F)

Lynton McKenzie

A. A. White

Winston Churchill (A&F)

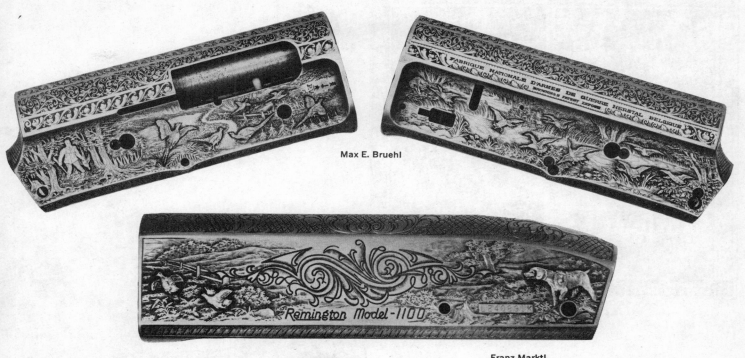

Max E. Bruehl

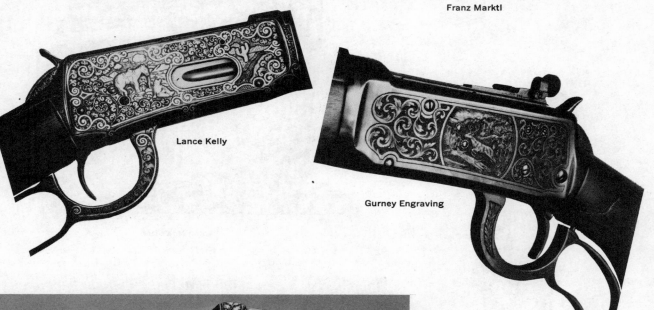

Franz Marktl

Lance Kelly

Gurney Engraving

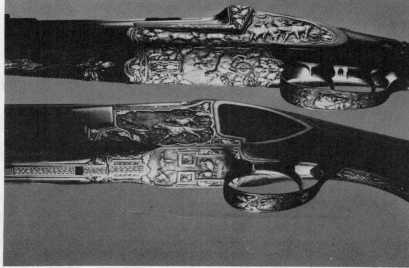

Al. Obiltschnig

R. J. Smith

F. E. Hendricks

Jos. Bayer

Lynton McKenzie

Al. Obiltschnig

HALLOWEEN GOBBLER

That was a wild turkey I had quartered in my crosswires...wasn't it? I thought so, but how could I be sure, when the first day of the hunting season fell on All Saints' Day, the day that witches and goblins haunt the deserted woods   ...Don Shiner

A WILD GOBBLER stood before me, framed in a small opening among beech and oak trees. The crosshairs of my scope centered on it and my trigger finger started to tighten. Normally I'd have touched off the explosive pill then and there, but this time I hesitated. Did I see a real wild gobbler—or was it a goblin, a spook, or maybe a mirage?

This was the opening day of Pennsylvania's turkey season. By sheer coincidence it was also—or would be at dusk—Halloween, eve of All Saints' Day, the time when goblins and ghosts supposedly galavant across the countryside. Could this gobbler in my gun scope be a goblin in turkey disguise?

An hour earlier, just after daybreak, I had slipped into these turkey woods. Climbing into a makeshift blind behind a wind-felled tree, I fiddled turkey talk at scattered intervals from my call box. Turkeys were here all right. There were scratch marks and feathers among the leaves. Besides, I'd counted a flock of fourteen birds, one day during the previous week, in the field at the base of this towering Appalachian ridge. Nevertheless, I hadn't rightly expected a turkey to appear in my sights so soon after the opening hour.

It stood rigidly, plumage glistening with a metallic sheen in the patch of filtered sunlight. As I studied the magnificent figure, the pounding in my chest caused the crosswires to wander all over the place. Suddenly, the bird

Selecting a wind-felled tree for a makeshift blind, I began making turkey talk on my cedar box.

spooked. It crouched low, neck stretched full length, ready, any instant, to leap into flight. It was now or never! My finger tightened on the trigger . . .

Every fourth or fifth year finds Pennsylvania moving its usual November gun season ahead a couple of days into October. This puts the opener on Saturday, giving most hunters a chance to get afield on their day off. Thus, the season's opening day falling on Halloween was no earth-shaking coincidence. That is, unless you believe that ghosts and goblins, and maybe wild gobblers, spook about on this day in lonely woods and near deserted farmhouses.

By some quirk of fate, my gun gear this day included, of all things, a fear-

some gorilla face mask, typical of those used with Halloween masquerade costumes. I'd had no intention of toting such a grotesque mask into these woods, and it came as a bit of a shock when I discovered it in my pocket. The mask had figured earlier in a school party of my older son's, during which he dressed the part of a "gorilla" warfare fighter, borrowing my gun coat to complete the Halloween getup. The mask got stashed in the game pocket at the program finale, and there I found it this morning, when I searched for my turkey caller. I tossed the spooky mask into some nearby leaves, to keep from accidentally leaning on and breaking it.

This turkey hunt centered at the base of a tall and extremely beautiful

I grabbed my rifle and got the scope on the big gobbler-like apparition that I saw in the clearing between the beech trees.

mountain in the Allegheny Plateau, one of the ridge-and-valley areas of Pennsylvania's Appalachian highlands. The general region called by this name has received some notoriety of late because of the federal war-on-poverty program. Perhaps it's therefore best, at the outset, to explain just what this territory is really like, and why there's no poverty here when it comes to turkey hunting.

Appalachia abounds with tall ridges and valleys which run as bold, sculptured lines from New York state south to Alabama. Driving westward across Pennsylvania, starting at the famed Blue Ridge mountains in the east, a series of formidable forest-clad mountain ridges or folds is crossed. Traversing the tall ridges and descending into the valleys is like passing from one world into another. Coal mining may be the chief activity in one, with culm banks and polluted streams the dominant features; the next might hold well-kept, modestly-prosperous dairy farms or miles of apple groves.

The high country is heavily covered with mixed hardwood and coniferous forests that stretch as far as the eye can see. Progressing across these rugged, tree-clad ridges, covering a span of perhaps a hundred miles, one finally encounters a bold, high escarpment, the Allegheny Front. This front, which begins the Allegheny Plateau, is so steep that roads and railroads ascend it with difficulty. It rises abruptly and majestically, with almost canyon-like slopes, to an elevation half a mile or more above the limestone valley. This ridge runs continuously, as do many of the others, from the Catskill Mountains in New York state, southward through Virginia, Tennessee and into Alabama. It is through this formidable country that Daniel Boone sought a pass, almost 200 years ago, to the blue grass prairie region.

The millions of acres in this Allegheny escarpment form some of the best turkey areas in the U.S. Pennsylvania is close to the top of the list in wild turkey population, and perhaps three-fourths of the commonwealth's turkeys live along the escarpment.

Heavy crops of mast from beech, cherry, white and red oaks provide nourishment to support unusually large flocks. Even before Pennsylvania undertook a wild turkey stocking program some 20 years ago, a fair number of birds inhabited this region. I bagged several, years back. The last two seasons I got none. It's wise to locate a particular flock's whereabouts before season and this year, fortunately, I did.

I stopped one early fall day at a small country store not far from Williamsport. As I paid the elderly lady for tobacco, I asked whether anyone had seen turkeys recently in the area.

"Yes," she replied. "A flock's been

The pounding in my chest made the cross-wires jump all over the place, but I managed to hold them on the butt of the wings long enough to squeeze off a single shot.

feeding almost every day in the fields on the old Boston farm."

It figured. A state park encompassing a tract of virgin pines and hemlocks lay next to the Boston place. With hunting forbidden in the park area, turkeys enjoyed a safe retreat, I thought.

However, the lady assured me birds were being seen in fields which lay about a quarter-mile north of the park. This threw a different light on the situation and I decided to drive there and investigate.

I drove five miles or so to reach the Boston farm. Parking the station wagon in a cutout beside the highway, I climbed the bank and used binoculars to scan the fields which reached upward to meet the steep, heavily wooded ridge. No turkeys were in sight. With sundown still several hours away, I crossed the fields and scouted the woods for signs. Once inside the trees, I found a tremendous crop of mast on the ground. Acorns were so numerous it felt as though I were walking on marbles.

Turkey Sign

Climbing to a shelf, the last bit of level ground before ascending the cliff-like escarpment, I found several fan-shaped scratch marks among leaves. Turkeys, like chickens, scratch along the humus floor to uncover goodies. Moving along the shelf, I spied a moulted wing feather among leaves. Soon I found more turkey feathers, and at one place handfuls were scattered in a small area. In my mind's eye I saw a wildcat, or possibly a big tiger owl, both of which are plentiful, floating in and cutting a turkey out of that flock.

Opening day was less than a week away when I again visited the Boston farm. Sure enough, I soon spied a flock feeding in the dead grass cover.

I studied them with my binoculars. Several ran around like chickens, as though chasing grasshoppers in the weeds. I laid plans then and there to be in those woods when the season opened.

Darkness still enveloped eastern Pennsylvania when I began the 30-mile drive from my home to the Allegheny Front on opening day. As I descended the last ridge, ten miles before reaching the escarpment, the upper part of the plateau was touched by golden sunlight, reflecting an eerie glow over the valley. Twenty minutes more brought me to the base of the Front. I turned northward, paralleling the ridge, passed the state park and finally reached the Boston farm.

The weather had been unseasonably warm. It was also tinder-box dry. State officials had threatened to ban hunting if rains did not soon materialize, and television commentators and newspapers pleaded with sportsmen to be careful about smoking and lighting matches in the dry woodlands. The lack of moisture made walking in the woods extremely noisy.

Packing lunch, binoculars, turkey call and other assorted gear in my pockets, I slung my rifle—a M70 Winchester 225 with Weaver V8 scope—over my shoulder and began the hike across the fields toward the ridge. Leaves crunched loudly underfoot.

I'd debated, as most turkey hunters do, whether I should tote a rifle or a shotgun into the woods this day. Many gunners prefer a 12-ga. shotgun loaded with #4 shot. Others favor something like a 222 or Hornet. Whichever is taken, the hunter almost invariably wishes he had the other. I've been thinking of buying a Savage M24 over-under in 22 rimfire magnum and 20 gauge, as it comes close to being the ideal turkey gun, but hadn't got to it. With the foliage dry and

As the rifle cracked, the bird collapsed. I raced down to see whether my prize was a gobbler—or a goblin!

noisy, shooting this day would be at long ranges, I figured, so I packed the rifle.

Daylight flooded the terrain as I climbed to the shelf and found an old wind-felled tree for a blind. From this vantage point I could see a long distance along the shelf, a corner of the field, and part way up the ridge.

I raked leaves away from the log so I could move a little without creating a lot of noise, and stuck up branches here and there to help conceal my presence. My watch showed fifteen minutes until the season's opening.

The excessive leaf noise underfoot would force me to remain in the blind most of the day. I planned to call every 10 to 15 minutes, hoping to coax the flock, or a lone bird, into range.

That's when, reaching into my pocket to produce the call, I found the gorilla mask. I chuckled. Here it was, Hallowen, eve of All Saints' Day when goblins and ghosts supposedly spook about the countryside. I could certainly dress for the occasion. With this mask I'd likely scare any wandering hunter clear out of the woods — or be thrown into the clink for being a nut loose with a rifle! I tossed the mask aside.

Waiting the last few minutes for the appointed hour to arrive, I rubbed some resin to the lips of the cedar box. Over the years I had experimented with no less than eight different turkey calls. These ranged from my grandfather's favorite, consisting of a deer's rib bone, through dry corn cob and slate stone, to a horseshoe metal disk folded over a rubber diaphragm. The latter is highly popular throughout the area. Of late I've settled on a model that resembles a narrow box, fitted with hinged handle that swings freely across the rocker-shaped side boards. Carried loosely in a pocket, this model talks turkey with every step the hunter takes, as the handle rubs across the thin side boards. Few hunters agree on the best call box, but many agree this model rates high.

I sounded the first group of notes at a few minutes past seven. These were slow, drawn-out p-e-r-t-s. They resembled hen talk, a hen which has suddenly uncovered a bonanza of beechnuts. I waited. There was no response. Only the incessant barking of a squirrel and cawing from far-off crows broke the silence.

Minutes lapsed into an hour. During this period I called three or four more times. Still nothing. A big-racked whitetail buck escorted two lady deer past me. A little later, I suddenly spied a bird with huge wingspread sailing scarcely six feet off the ground, banking between trees and bearing down hard in my direction. I jerked aside to keep from being hit. It passed so close that I felt the wake from its wings. I thought it was a tiger owl, but it turned out to be a broadwing hawk — undoubtedly the culprit which cut down that turkey whose feathers I'd found scattered among the leaves.

A Gobbler's Answer

Then about 8:30 I heard the electrifying call of an answering turkey. I'd barely finished making two light strokes across the call box, when the answer came, clear and sharp as a bell. I grew tense. Slowly I put aside the call and reached for my Winchester. The answering call had sounded awfully close.

Clutching the rifle tightly, I waited, afraid to breath, trying to discern the outline of a turkey among the trees and underbrush. My gaze suddenly shifted to that hideous gorilla Halloween mask. Why had I thrown it into such a conspicuous place? What if it should spook a gobbler just as he strolled into range? I fumed inwardly, but there was nothing to do now but let it be.

A movement among the trees, off to my left, jolted me. A big bird, black as a witch's cloak, now stood in an opening among the beech trees some 60 yards distant. It had appeared as quietly as a ghost. Was it gobbler or goblin?

Too shaky to try for a head shot, I decided to aim for the backbone to minimize meat damage. The crosswires in the scope moved onto the wing butts.

Just as I started to squeeze the trigger, a squirrel barked badly. The turkey whirled, ready to leap into the air. It was now or never. I touched off the shot. The crack echoed sharply against the steep escarpment, and the turkey pitched into the leaves, thrashed about for a moment, then lay still. In that instant, the air was filled with a thundering roar of beating wings. Ten or twelve turkeys took flight. I saw five or six sail through the trees, heading for the ridge top.

I raced toward my prize, but there was no need for haste. The gobbler lay motionless, partly buried in a pile of dry oak leaves, its beautiful bronze-black plumage glistening in the sunlight.

I took a minute to admire my Halloween gobbler, then slung it over my shoulder and set out for the station wagon. Suddenly I remembered that gorilla face mask which lay among the leaves beside the blind. I went back and got it, remarking to myself that maybe my gobbler had planned to join such other goblins on All Saints' Day.

Sure, I know perfectly well that there can be no connection between gobbler and goblins — at least I think I do — but this was All Saints' Eve, wasn't it? Who could be certain? ●

I hadn't planned on totin' a gorilla mask into the woods, but maybe it brought me luck somehow. After all, the season's opening had coincided with Halloween, the eve of All Saints' Day—and didn't I have my turkey?

If the front sight of your handgun zags when it should zig, try...

A SCOPE ON YOUR HANDGUN

by BOB STEINDLER

Testing scoped and unscoped handguns at 150-200 yards showed marked superiority of guns with glass.

I BELIEVE IT WAS the late Al Goerg who first scoped a handgun and then wrote about it. Since then, putting a scope on a sixgun or autoloader has become socially acceptable — but only to some extent. Most of those who scope handguns admit to being middle aged, since their eyesight ain't what it used to be. Dedicated hand gunners sort of sneer at the idea, feeling that putting a scope on a handgun is like using a shoulder bag when bench-shooting a 22-250. Nothing could be further from the truth!

I scoped my first handgun about 15 years ago. Since then I've shot varmints, edible small and big game with one, and I've shot at and hit flying clays. I've also shot various combat courses with scoped handguns during demonstrations for police departments. I do most of my long-range load testing with scoped handguns to eliminate the human-error factor from my testing.

If you're undecided about scoping a handgun, try this test. Set up a target at 25 or 50 yards. Grab your favorite handgun, and fire 10 imaginary rounds at the target. After the first few seconds of gripping the gun, you'll notice your front sight wobbling around on the target. As seconds turn into a minute, the wanderings of the front sight all over the target begin to bother you, and the harder you try to keep the sight on the target, the worse the situation seems to get.

Now try the same thing with a low-powered scope. If you can, borrow one of the scopes made especially for handguns. If you can't do that, use a Leupold 2x or any other low-powered scope. Take two stout rubber bands and fasten the scope to your handgun. Then repeat those 10 imaginary shots at the same target — see the difference? That, fellow shooter, is what handgun scoping is all about!

Early Types

The first special handgun scopes were 1x, that is, they did not magnify the target; they simply defined it better, making it easier to stay on target. Some shotgun sights can be

To scope or not to scope? These groups were shot at 100 yards, one with a scoped 256 Win. Contender, the other unscoped. Both guns were fired from a solid rest but hand held and trigger release was manual rather than electrically. T/C Puma scope shown was designed for T/C single shot Contenders.

used, too—I put an old Nydar sight on a Remington XP-100 and I topped one of the barrels for my Thompson/Center Contender with a Weaver Qwik-Point sight to my complete satisfaction—and to the consternation of every handgunner who sees those rigs.

Most currently made revolvers and many selfloaders can be scoped without much trouble. The XP-100 and Contender barrels can be scoped by anyone who owns a screwdriver, but most Colt, S&W, Charter Arms, Ruger guns, and the various imports may require a gunsmith to tap the mounting holes for the scope bases.

One problem manufacturers have faced in making scopes and suitable bases for handguns is recoil. Unlike rifle scopes and bases, the handgun scope is considerably scaled down. Bases, by necessity, are smaller, as are their mounting screws. Some automatics are hard to scope because of recoil and the relatively thin slide that makes secure anchoring of the base difficult.

One of the best handgun scopes was withdrawn from the market a few years ago since too many complaints were voiced by handgunners who had mounted the scope on a heavy-recoiling hand cannon. If you ever find a used German-made Nickel 1½x scope that isn't badly battered, grab it. The 357 Magnum is about the maximum caliber this scope should be used on,

and you will need special rings and bases. I still use my old Nickel a lot and, despite years of hard use and even some abuse, it works well.

Scoping a Magnum

If you must scope a magnum, be sure that scope and base are properly anchored. Six or 7 years ago Lee Jurras, J.D. Jones and I hunted in Montana's Bob Marshall wilderness. The primary purpose of the hunt was to test the performance of Super Vel ammo on game. I was using a scoped magnum revolver. Base and mount screws were locked into place with Loctite. Before heading west, I had fired 250 rounds of ammo through that scoped handgun—to check load performance, for practice and to dope out the trajectory of the load. We hunted high and we hunted low, but we saw nary hide nor hair of anything worth shooting. On the last day of the hunt, we decided to have an impromptu shooting fest. Picking a mark, I unlimbered my sixgun, grabbed it with both hands, sighted, and pulled the trigger—and all hell broke loose. While the gun was still in recoil, I sensed that something had zipped past my ear. When I recovered from the surprise, my scoped S&W was now an unscoped S&W. The screws holding the scope base on the top strap had sheared off. Although the scope, with the base still attached,

landed on a large boulder, the scope was undamaged.

Because of this recoil problem, the choice of available glassware that can be hung onto a handgun, particularly magnums, is relatively limited.

Weaver and Singlepoint

Among non-magnifying optical sights, the Weaver Qwik-Point is probably the most widely used at this time. Unfortunately this sight rides quite high above the bore, so it isn't the ideal choice. However, this slight drawback is completely offset because you can use the Weaver sight with one or both eyes—thus you need not force yourself to keep the non-shooting eye open if you are used to closing it. The rugged Qwik-Point is sighted in just like a scope. I had one on my Ruger 44 Magnum for a while, and later moved the sight to several other handguns without the slightest bit of trouble. Mounting, depending on the gun frame, may be a bit tricky; in that case turn the job over to an experienced gunsmith.

A somewhat similar sight is the British Singlepoint. Designed for use on shotguns, it can be fastened onto a sixgun or a selfloader without much trouble. The binocular system of the Singlepoint makes it mandatory that the shooter keep both eyes open—if he's to get full benefit from the sight when the illuminated dot is superimposed on the target. I've used this sight on several handguns, making temporary bases from aluminum bar milled to the contour of the slide or top strap.

Optical sights that feature some sort of illuminated dot have another advantage—they are superb for night hunting, such as calling varmints or running coons with hounds. Proved in jungle warfare, the British Singlepoint successfully withstood the constant pounding of the L7A2 Machine Gun allowing hits on targets out to 600 yards with considerable regularity. I mounted a Singlepoint on a Browning Hi-Power pistol with complete satisfaction, later moved the sight to a High Standard Supermatic Tournament autoloader. Such a handgun rig will make a second Joe Benner out of most any duffer at the range.

Several years ago Bushnell offered a special adapter for his old Phantom handgun scope. This allowed fast scope mounting on the 45 ACP—the left grip was removed and replaced by Bushnell's alloy grip-scope holder. This worked well, but the short grip-screws sometimes gave way through

Small Nickel scope (no longer made) did well on a 41 Magnum. Because recoil is hard on light mounts and screws, select these with care. This is a steel Buehler, now used on a 44 Magnum revolver.

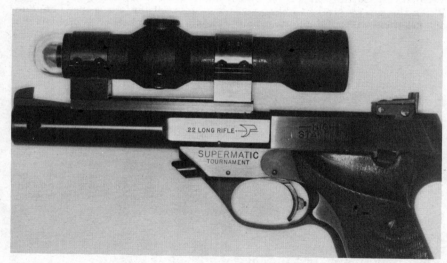

The now unavailable Westley Richards shotgun sight made a very acceptable aiming system for the Browning Medalist. Binocular vision was required for this sight.

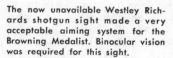

Not born for the job, the British Single-point shotgun sight worked out well on the High Standard Supermatic Tournament pistol. I have not tried this sight on a magnum handgun, but it does well with 9mm Luger and the 38 Spl.

recoil. Longer screws often helped. With this grip-base you need an old Bushnell Phantom scope, one without the integral rail meant for the later mounts. Installed, the scope is somewhat offset, but don't let that bug you. A few practice sessions will show you that even the loosest GI 45 can shoot better than most of us can hold.

Bushnells and Others

Bushnell's Phantom scopes have undergone quite a few changes in the past few years. The eyepiece is now adjustable so that the shooter can focus his handgun scope the way he does his rifle scope. Click stops have

The Hutson Handgunner scope is readily installed on any domestic revolver. Before permanently installing any scope on my handguns, I test the new sight on the S&W 41 Magnum—the Hutson Handgunner, shown here in older style—passed test easily.

This Leupold 2x has spent more time on various handguns than on a rifle. Ruggedly made, it has excellent optics and won't fog.

been added to the windage and elevation adjustments, and the cuts in the integral mounting rails have been deepened to improve scope anchoring. Beefed up to handle even the hottest 44 Magnum handloads, the scopes have been renamed the Magnum Phantom. As all-round scope, his 1.3x scope is a good choice, but for the long-range shooter and hunter, the 2.5x is easily worth the extra $10.

Bushnell has mounts for most Colt, S&W, and Ruger sixguns. I especially like the All Purpose mount, one which can be used on a great many handguns, including the Ruger semi-auto pistol.

Hutson Hangunner Scopes now have a 20% bigger eyepiece to admit more light, and are offered in 1x (no magnification) and a 1.7x. I find the latter great for hunting, shooting or plinking, and it costs only $4.50 more. I like the 1.7x better since it offers greater versatility. However, at extreme ranges, the extra magnification of the slightly larger 2.5x Phantom may be just what you need.

Hutson offers mounts for most domestic revolvers, plus a base for the T/C Contender and a blank base that can easily be adapted to many other wheelguns and autoloaders.

If you're shooting a Contender single shot pistol, you should try the T/C Puma scope. A cinch to install, this well-made scope can withstand the pounding of the 30 Carbine round without coming unglued. T/C mounts are also sturdy enough to withstand the heavy recoil of this cartridge in a handgun.

I'm currently whittling a couple of bases for a Weaver K1.5 scope that, I hope, will find a home on one of my black powder revolvers. This scope is 9¾" long, so it's only suitable for a large, long-barrelled gun; otherwise it would appear too top-heavy. Black powder guns have been scoped quite successfully, though this is frowned on by purists. Still, black powder guns are no different from other handguns —they tend to develop a wandering front sight, too.

The Leupold 2x is about the only

rifle scope short enough to be suitable for handgun mounting, in my experience. If you decide to go that route, you may have to fall back on special bases. I've used several Buehler pistol bases. These fit S&W sixguns, and there is no need to tap for them except when a magnum revolver or a semi-auto pistol is used. Buehler pistol bases are offered for most domestic handguns and, like his rifle bases, they're well made and will give long and satisfactory service.

Conetrol also has bases for the T/C Contender. I use a set of them with the Leupold 2x scope on a 22 Hornet barrel. That short-tubed Hornet is a fairly noisy proposition, so watch where you do your varmint hunting with that combination.

Recently I scoped another Contender barrel, using the B-Square scope base made for them, with a Redfield 4x scope. Although this scope is a bit large, my first 50-yard shooting tests to check handloads proved that this could become a potent varmint outfit.

If you decide to mount the scope yourself, remember to cinch all screws tight, using a drop of shellac, varnish or Loctite on all screws. When the screws are as tight as you can get them without damaging their

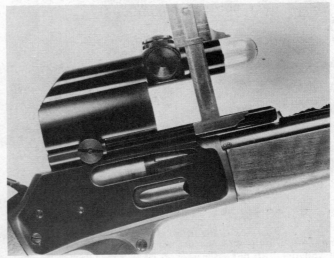

Installed on a rifle here, it's easy to see how high the Weaver Quik-Sight lies above the bore. This same device would make most handguns it was mounted on top-heavy, cumbersome.

slots, keep the screwdriver blade in the slot and give the screwdriver handle a solid wack with a plastic or leather mallet. Then tighten the screw a bit more.

Since bore sighting is not possible, except of course with the Contender, use an optical collimator, just as you would while pre-sighting a rifle. Then do your test shooting from a solid rest, preferably a set of sandbags, getting into the most comfortable position you can assume. Muscular strain on neck and arm muscles makes shooting a chore instead of a pleasure, and

it will also affect your shooting aversely.

A scoped handgun sitting on your closet shelf does little to give you more shooting fun afield. You will want a holster for that scoped handgun. Here are the names of some who can supply such holsters:

The late Al Goerg designed a special shoulder rig for scoped handguns. This holster, available from Goerg Enterprises (3009 S. Laurel, Port Angeles, WA 98362), can be made up for any gun-scope combination, and you'll have to go a long way to find a better rig.

The George Lawrence Co. (3065 W. 1st Ave., Portland, OR 97204) stocks holsters for scoped Contenders, and will make up custom holsters.

Seventrees (315 W. 39th St., New York, NY 10018) specializes in combat holsters, but they have made up custom holsters as have John Bianchi (100 Calle Cortez, Temecula, CA 92390) and Don Hume (Box 351, Miami, OK 74354), although the latter did it primarily to accomodate a friend. Since most of the holster makers are also active handgunners, and since they have the gun forms for making the basic holsters, producing a custom holster for a scoped handgun shouldn't be much of a problem for them.

You may want to have a custom holster made up for your gun-scope combo, but go slowly—another scope on the same gun—or vice versa—may not fit that custom rig. However, a good holster is a worthwhile investment.

Even if you're not a varmint or big game handgunner, you should try a scoped handgun. It will improve your shooting tremendously, for once you stop worrying about your sight picture, you can concentrate on improving your trigger squeeze. •

AIR RIFLES
—underlever or barrel cocking?

Both styles, inevitably, have their good points and bad, but our air arms expert offers a guiding light in general and specific choices as well.

by LADD FANTA

THERE ARE MANY commercially successful CO_2, pneumatic and spring powered pellet guns. Debate over the best propulsion system is pointless because multitudes of satisfied owners can attest to each type.

The prospective buyer settling on a sporting spring-air rifle often faces one more hurdle of decision: whether to get the underlever or barrel-cocking system.

Since the better grade barrel-cockers are close in price to the underlevers, one might wonder just how significant and useful the differences between them are.

First, it should be understood that none of the quality spring-powered pellet rifles "launch" their charge. Underlever, sidelever or barrel-cocking, only the barrel bore contacts the pellet as it is driven by suddenly compressed air generated at the moment of shooting.

Nearly all spring-air rifles made today for serious shooting are of the barrel-cocking type. These are also called "hinged-barrel" or "barrel-breakdown" systems. In these arms, forcing the barrel down on its pivot or hinge exposes the breech for loading, simultaneously cocking the mainspring. After inserting the pellet into the chamber, the barrel is snapped shut and locked by some form of spring-loaded detent. This system is the easiest to load, and pellet brands can be selected for an exact thumb-press fit, which in effect pre-sizes

Left—Made by Diana as the Model 50, this underlever solid-barrel air rifle is known here as the Winchester Model 450.

Right—The underlever BSF Model S54, shown in Match Grade, has micrometer rear sight.

the pellet for best performance. With little familiarization, a rapid rate of fire is attainable if the pellets are conveniently carried in a small pouch at the waist.

Modern underlever cocking systems, expensive to make, are considered by some as an elite class, bridging the gap between sporters and match grade air rifles. A pivoting lever under the barrel (hence the name) cocks the gun. The propulsion mechanics of U/L and barrel-breakdown rifles are the same. Loading, however, is quite different. Because of the solid frame and fixed barrel-cylinder (receiver) relationship, a small lever-operated "plug" or "tap" is provided at the breech for pellet insertion. The loading lever located on the side of the gun turns a small crossbolt 90° from the firing position (in line with the bore) to the loading position (tapered open end up) and vice versa. I

often are—*inherently* as accurate as U/L types, day-to-day maintenance of the B/C rifle's "Zero" or point-of-aim can suffer, as carefully observed shooting and the keeping of records will show. This shift in zero is brought about by a rear peep sight being receiver mounted while the front sight is on the barrel, thus any slight shift in receiver-barrel lock-up affects and alters zero. Such changes may go unnoticed by the casual plinker, but they're irksome to the serious marksman. Anyone who wishes to, or must use, a peep sight or scope, should give preference to a fixed-barrel system.

It is commonly believed that underlevers are more powerful than barrel cockers. This was true at one time, but not in recent years.

I don't like the popular penchant to put a scope on everything, but certainly there are those who cannot use the open sights that are

Whereas the U/L all-metal crossbolts may normally be considered a trouble-free, lifetime loading device, the B/C guns rely on a leather or rubber breech seal for positive power sealing. Needless to say, these may get cut, abraded, scorched (from diesel firing) or become leaky from other causes. Replacement, however, is relatively easy in most cases. On some of my experimental rifles I have fitted very enduring breech seals made of teflon and nylon.

Docile firing behavior and stable accuracy are key factors desirable in any air arm. Sometimes the spring gun has to be accurized with such helpful products as Loctite and silicone/MOS2 lubricants. New spring air rifles reach the buyer in various stages of lubrication need. For example, BSF and Weihrauch air rifles arrive the best prepared of any for "as is" immedi-

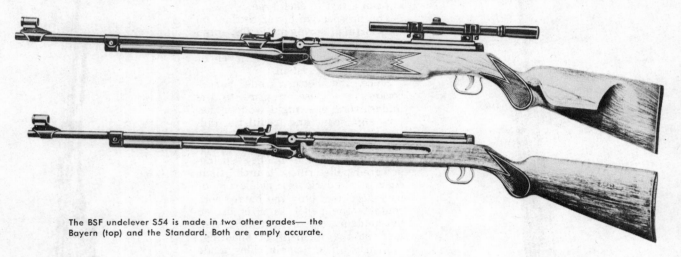

The BSF undelever S54 is made in two other grades— the Bayern (top) and the Standard. Both are amply accurate.

find 22-caliber rifles much easier to load than the 177s.

Regardless of shooters dexterity, the U/L load and shoot sequence requires more manipulation. Some U/L guns have the loading lever on the right, others on the left side. For many people, the heavier gun weight necessitates shifting both hands forward while loading, which adds work and time. Typical U/L gun weights are 7.5 to 8.75 pounds in contrast to barrel-cockers of 5.5/6.8 pounds. For long shooting sessions and all-round use, the lighter rifles are handier and more comfortable, but for more serious work, such as hunting and pest control, the greater weight of the U/L makes for steadier holding and lets that first, perhaps only, shot count.

While B/C rifles may be—and

standard on air rifles, people who require a peep sight or a scope. On the other hand, mediocre marksmanship often springs from lack of practice. Air rifles can be used so often, in so many places, that there is little excuse for poor proficiency. They are basically short-range arms, and adequate open sights *on the barrel* should serve well in most cases. The B/C rifle is then a stable, efficient and accurate shooting instrument.

The loading tap-crossbolt on all U/L air rifles rarely will need replacement, requiring only an occasional drop of oil under normal usage. It cannot be supplied as a separate component, for it is tapered and precisely reamed in position after being fitted to the rifle body to ensure correct alignment of the holes.

ate use. On the other hand, BSA Meteor and Webley air arms are frequently so dry as to make initial operation difficult. It should be realized that imported air arms can be up to 2 years or more old before reaching the consumer.

The Underlevers

BSA. Following WW II and their earlier models 1 and 2, Birmingham Small Arms produced the modern, streamlined BSA Airsporter (22 cal.) and the equivalent 177-cal. BSA Club U/L air rifles. These have a specially-designed compression chamber, a cocking lever completely housed in a standard length fore-end and with the loading lever automatically tripped open with the cocking stroke.

Exterior finish is much better on these guns than the less obvious interior detail. The fore-end, split

The BSA Meteor Super model is a barrel-cocking air rifle.

full length to accomodate the cocking lever, lacks solidity for firm bedding and has a hollow sound when the cocking lever is snapped into place or the gun discharged. Nonetheless, these rifles are handsome and powerful, their owners seldom willing to part with them. Both models are currently being redesigned and unavailable.

BSF. In Erlangen, West Germany, Bayerische Sportwaffen Fabrik makes their sturdy S54 U/L model with several stock options: a beech or walnut "Standard;" the "Bayern" and the heavier "Match." These are U.S.-available in 177 and 22 caliber, with identical hardware used on all models. Superior design of the cocking linkage allows non-split fore-ends at a cost of some muzzle heaviness.

BSF makes guns in the best old world traditions, solid and strong, with no use of cost-cutting plastics. Certified muzzle velocities are 669 fps in 177 and 551 in the 22s. In my tests, newly unwrapped S54s consistently have more penetration power than new BSA, Diana or Webley U/L guns. They also fire with minimum vibration (spring resonance) because S54 mainsprings are heavy-grease lubed.

Incongruously, out of the entire BSF air rifle line, only the S54 models have a rear sight with a

somewhat loose-fitting adjustable leaf. Typically, U/L air rifles have the cocking handle end spring-loaded so that it can be snapped back under the barrel after cocking. The S54 cocking handle has a spring-loaded tubular sleeve, which provides an excellent grip, but requires conscious pulling back each time to replace. This small nuisance does have some merit in that it keeps cocking linkage rattle free.

Although plastic-bag-and-paper wrapped, S54 air rifles are not factory boxed in individual cartons, thus small dents or impressions on the stocks are common. General S54 quality is always good, and while the rifle's rugged appearance may not please everybody, its great strength is a more important factor.

Diana. Dianawerk Mayer und Grammelspacher is the largest German air arm manufacturer, and their products are also marketed under other well-known labels. The Diana model 50 U/L, available in the U.S. only in 177 caliber, comes impeccably packaged.

The general finish—and one's first impression—of the Diana 50 is very good, but I find many minor detractions. For example, it has a split semi-Mannlicher length fore-end which hides the cocking under-

lever. While neat in appearance and securely held, stock removal requires a special spanner wrench, which is not supplied! Impressed pistol-grip checkering should have sufficed; the additional deep parallel grooves from trigger guard downward have grain-end roughness more annoying than useful. The straight, high-combed stock makes the factory sights difficult to use by a full-faced individual. It also forces those wearing prescription glasses into a degraded, off-center view through them.

The fact that the rear sight is partly made of plastic is enough to turn off many, but the material used is quite break-resistant and the sight is precise and click adjustable. Large or small U- and V-shaped notches may be selected, and the sight is exceptionally broad to help prevent canting. The sights are completely removable for an unhindered scope view.

Diana makes generous use of non-captive ball bearings in a smooth double-pull trigger, and to annularly grasp the piston shaft in cocked position instead of the usual large claw. This is good technology, making for low friction and less reliance on lubricants. It is said that "Knowledge comes from taking things apart, wisdom from put-

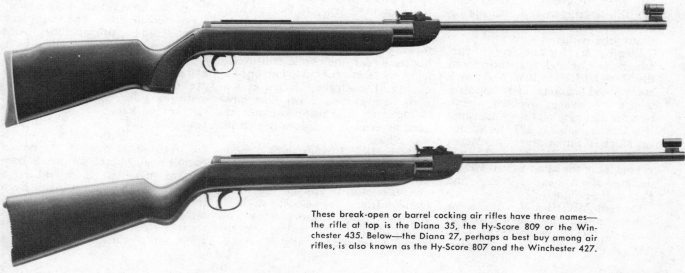

These break-open or barrel cocking air rifles have three names— the rifle at top is the Diana 35, the Hy-Score 809 or the Winchester 435. Below—the Diana 27, perhaps a best buy among air rifles, is also known as the Hy-Score 807 and the Winchester 427.

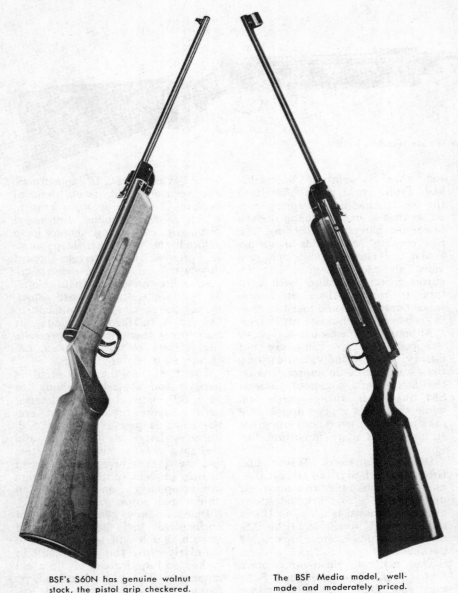

BSF's S60N has genuine walnut stock, the pistol grip checkered.

The BSF Media model, well-made and moderately priced.

ting them together." Reassembling the Diana trigger and mainspring units is one way to become mechanically wiser!

Webley. Webley and Scott of Birmingham, England, first introduced the Mark III U/·L in 1949. Now, with many modifications and improvements, it enjoys an excellent reputation for accuracy and workmanship. It is U.S.-available in 177 and 22, but the Mark III Supertarget Club Model (177 only) is not offered here. The target model, of the same proven MK III design, has a heavier barrel and Parker-Hale sights.

Current MK III U/L rifles show minor production shortcuts so much in evidence everywhere today. Among these is a simpler, stamped trigger guard, and gone is the contoured trigger. The loading lever, once so delicately curved, is now a robust piece of flat metal. Metal finish was previously of the highest order and, while still excellent, it lacks the old mirror-like quality. The stocks, always of superb hand-rubbed finish, are now ¼" shorter. The select walnut, as good as ever, is occasionally rich in nice fiddleback.

Mark III U/L rifles show a quality of construction unmatched by other manufacturers. The cocking lever/associated linkage, all machined from bar stock, is held together with screws instead of rivets or pins, and mainspring removal is easiest of any. Such ac-

comodating maintenance features are endearing to the owner, should they ever be needed.

One problem with some current MK III rifles, especially the 177s, is that the rear sight cannot be adjusted low enough.

The Barrel-Cockers

While U/L selection in the U.S. is currently limited to 3 makes, there are dozens of hinged-barrel sporting models available. Some in the serious adult $40 to $80 category are BSA Meteor; BSF Bavaria 55, Media and S60; Diana 27 and 35, and HW 50 and 35.

Like other daily-life commodities, the middle of the line is frequently the exceptional buy. BSA Meteor, BSF Media and Diana 27 are good examples of first-air rifle, moderate-priced values. The Diana 27, available here in 22 only, is a standout laden with important refinements borrowed from more expensive Diana guns. The BSF Media has slightly more power and a larger, adult-proportioned stock than the Diana 27, while the BSA Meteor, despite some distinctive features, power and accuracy potential, is handicapped by quality control in-differences like bore and paint finish, damaged breech seals and gratingly stiff operation.

A word of encouragement to the newcomer vacillating on his first choice: Statistical facts are that once the pneumo-bug gets you, you will not stop until you've tried several makes or models, so don't sweat the first choice too seriously. Nearly everyone is interested in power, but this should not be the sole criterion on which to base selection. The BSA S60, its 3″ shorter cousin the BSF Bavaria 55, and the HW35 are potent contenders. I've used a 22 BSF S60 to account for dozens of crows; as many as three in rapid succession.

For conditions requiring long term stand-by preparedness, such as pest control, spring rifles have a decided advantage over the CO_2 and pneumatic rifles. The spring gun can have a pellet chambered and mainspring uncocked, only requiring the cocking stroke for instant firing readiness.

Regardless of the air arm selected, remember that it is not a complete substitute for small bore firearm shooting. It is rather a natural *collateral* sport. Aside from training value, it provides all the recreational value of firearms sports at short ranges with a minimum of effort and at a fraction of the cost. ●

The BSA Model 1923 Rifle and 33 BSA Cartridge

Belted cartridges—long or short—are far from being new or even recent. The first patent appeared in 1893, the first commercial success in 1912—the justly famed 375 Holland & Holland Belted Magnum

by LARRY S. STERETT

The BSA 1923 Model Sporting Rifle, caliber 33 BSA.

MANY OF TODAY'S shooters seem to think the now-popular belted short magnum cartridges originated in the mid-1950's. It is true the 7×61 S&H was brought out in 1953, and that with the appearance of the 458 Winchester Magnum in 1956 the old ball really got to rolling. But new? We have mini-skirts today, but there were some just as short in the 1920s.

The longer belted magnums aren't new either. On August 15, 1893, one Thomas Bennett was granted a U.S. patent for a belted bottleneck cartridge case, and he in turn assigned it to the Winchester Repeating Arms Company. But the first belted cartridge of modern design appeared in England way back in 1905, when Holland & Holland introduced their Eley-manufactured 400/375 Nitro Express. This bottleneck cartridge, intended as competition for the 9.5mm Mannlicher-Schoenauer, had a rather long neck and used .371″ diameter bullets in a case 2.47″ long. The cartridge has been referred to as the 375 Holland-Schoenauer, and cases may be headstamped "Holland's Patent" or "Holland Pat. .400/375 Axite." (This cartridge was never too popular and in 1912 Holland & Holland introduced the 375 Belted Rimless Nitro Magnum [375 H&H] in a case 2.85″ long.) Next H&H brought out the 275 Belted Rimless Nitro Magnum to compete with the very popular 280 Ross Rimless. The 275 Magnum, with a case 2.50″ long, is modern even by today's standards.

Then in 1921 the Birmingham Small Arms Company introduced a series of belted cartridges for use in rifles built on the P14 Enfield action. First, and least popular, was the 40 BSA. It was a straight taper belted case—35 years before the 458 Winchester Magnum—2.80″ long, loaded with 69.0-grains of Cordite to push a 250-gr. bullet at 2850 fps. This particular cartridge failed to catch on and, although produced by Eley (and later Kynoch) the rifle and cartridges are seldom seen today.

The two other cartridges of the series— the 26 Rimless Nitro-Express (26 BSA) and the 33 Belted Rimless Nitro-Express (33 BSA)—proved more popular, remaining in production until WW II. Both cases were belted and their length* (2.39″ by actual measurement of the cartridges) qualifies them as the first short magnum cartridges, although the 300/375 and 275 H&H should share part of the honor. The 26 BSA was loaded with 53.0 grains of nitro-cellulose powder to push a 110-gr. bullet at 3100 fps, while the 33 BSA used 60.0 grains of nitrocellulose powder behind a 165-gr. bullet for 3000 fps.

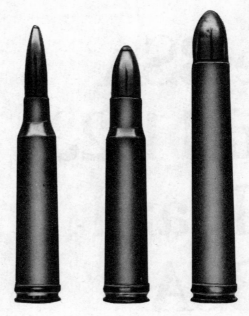

BSA Magnum cartridges. From left: 26 BSA, 33 BSA and 40 BSA.

BSA Magnum Cartridges Scarce

Rifles chambered for any of the BSA magnum cartridges are seldom seen in the U.S. Thus, when the opportunity was presented to shoot an original Model 1923 BSA rifle chambered for the 33 BSA cartridge, it was almost too good to be true. There was a catch. The BSA cartridges are not readily available and the few that might be found are Berdan primed. So, for over two years, the rifle went unshot. Loading dies were not available, nor was loading data. 33 BSA headsize is the same as the modern magnums—7mm Remington,

*Herein lies a slight mystery. The 26 BSA cartridge was manufactured by Eley Bros., and later Kynoch, for the Birmingham Small Arms Co. The 26 BSA and 33 BSA cartridges are listed in the various Kynoch (ICI) catalogs of the 1930s, through 1939. The listed and actual measured length of the 26 BSA case is 2.390″, yet the author owns a copy of a 1937 blueprint of Kynoch (ICI) origin for a 30 Super/26 BSA cartridge. The drawing shows a case length of 2.854″, an over-all length of 3.448″, and a listed bullet diameter of .265″. No actual cartridges fitting this description have been seen by the author; maybe none was ever manufactured. Interesting?

300 Winchester, et al—so any of these could be cut down and sized in various dies until they would fit the chamber. Fireforming and trimming would complete the process, but this would require more trimming than was desired. Then it was found that the 7×61 S&H Magnum case was just about the right length. A couple of cases were sized in various dies until they would just enter the 33 BSA chamber. They were then primed, charged with a Lee 039 dipperful of Bullseye (about 6 grains), and the remaining space filled with Cream-of-Wheat. After fire-forming the cases could hardly be told from the original Kynoch manufacture; they need no trimming, being a couple of thousandths under maximum case length for the 33 BSA of 2.40″.

A supply of cases found, the next step was to make a chamber cast, which in turn was rushed off to the Raton Gun Shop (Raton, N.M. 87740) for a sizing reamer. In due course the reamer arrived and it and two fire-formed cases were forwarded to RCBS. for a set of loading dies. (RCBS

can produce loading dies for almost any caliber if provided with 3 fire-formed cases. The 33 BSA was something else; they had no data on it, hence the need for the sizing reamer.) Special orders require some extra time, and during the interim the needed components were gathered.

The 33 BSA cartridge uses .338″ diameter bullets—the same as the 338 Winchester Magnum. However, only a 165-gr. bullet (soft point or full patch) was used in the Kynoch-loaded cartridges in order to achieve high velocity, and this weight of bullet is not produced in the U.S. The closest weights available were the 200-gr. Speer and Hornady bullets in this caliber; Bitterroot has an excellent 200-gr. hollow point bullet in this caliber also.

When the RCBS loading dies arrived, the depriming punch was removed from the sizing die, and lightly lubed 7x61 cases were sized until they would just enter the 33 BSA chamber. These were then loaded as mentioned previously and fire-formed. The excellent Norma brass blew out from

Headstamps of the three cartridges shown in fig. 2. The headstamps vary; note the 33 BSA is marked "33 Nitro" on this particular case.

Barrel markings on the BSA rifle. Note folding leaf sights.

7mm to 33 caliber perfectly without the loss of a single case.

The fire-formed cases were washed and dried, and reloading began in earnest. A check of the Powley Computer, plus loading data for some wildcats of the same approximate capacity, provided a start. Powder charges were started low and increased 0.5-gr. at a time until primers started to flatten. The 200-gr. Hornady spire point and Speer spitzer bullets were used exclusively. Once a load had been established, so far as case capacity or pressure was concerned, a quantity of each load was assembled for chronographing and accuracy tests.

Accuracy Tests

For the accuracy tests 3-shot groups were fired at 100 yards from the bench, using sandbag fore-end and butt rests. The BSA rifle is not tapped for scope sights so it was necessary to stick with the iron sights — regulated for that one load using the 165-gr. bullet. What would happen when only 200-gr. bullets were used?

Using the 200-yard sight the bullets just barely printed at the bottom of the target at 100 yards. Switching to the 400-yard sight the groups moved into the black and up to 12" high, depending on the particular load used. The largest group measured 2⅜" center-to-center, not bad for open sights. Most of the groups measured between one and two inches, the smallest 1-plus. (This particular load consisted of 65.5 grains of Hodgdon 380 O/S powder, with Federal 215 primers and 200-gr. Speer bullets.

Following the accuracy session considerable time was spent in chronographing the various loads using an Avtron T333 chronograph. None of the loads shown in the table were considered maximum in the rifle used; the primers were not flattened nearly as much as some currently loaded factory cartridges in other calibers. Alcan Max-Fire primers were used for all the loads, except the first and second — H-450 and 380 O/S — which used Federal 215 primers. The third, seventh, and eighth loads — H-4831, H-57 and H-570 — were compressed, and the powder shook down before attempting to seat the bullets. These latter loads gave fair accuracy, but not equal to that of the first two loads and the velocity obtained with H-4831 and H-570 was rather low. Surprisingly enough, the highest velocities were obtained from the loads that were most accurate. For this reason, if no other, all loads used for hunting will be either 65-5 grains of H-450 or 380 O/S. Both consistently group into less than 2" at 100 yards with the open sights, and about 3" high, which is just fine.

The fact that the 3000 fps of the original 33 BSA factory load was not obtained is of minor importance because that velocity was made with a 165-gr. bullet, while all of the loads shown in the table used 200-gr. bullets. A 200-gr. bullet moving at 2740 fps can collect a lot of game; it might even be possible to push it up to the so-called magic 3000 fps.

The 33 BSA cartridge will soon have been around for over 50 years. Like many of the other cartridges developed in the same period, it was ahead of its time. Today, with improved powders it is right at home; in fact it surpasses some of the ultra-short magnums, and it is usable in standard length actions.

The BSA rifle weighs 8½ pounds, its over-all length 47½". The 26½" barrel is stamped B.S.A. .33 1923 MODEL SPORTING RIFLE. The trigger is standard "issue" type, but with a pin installed to remove the double-stage pull. Letoff is a very clean 50 ounces.

The front sight is a .09" bead mounted on a ramp. A set of folding, shallow-V field sights are located on the barrel for 200- and 400-yard shooting. The "ears" on the military action were removed and a very neat pair of folding peep sights installed; these are 200- and 400-yard also, but can be adjusted for windage through the use of opposing cone-tip screws.

The safety lever has been slimmed and the dog-leg bolt handle has been straightened and given a butterknife shape. The

Loading Data
33 BSA Cartridge

Powder	Charge/grs.	Bullet*	I.V.†
H-450	65.5	Speer	2,725
H-380	6.5	Speer	2,740
H-4831	65.5	Hornady	2,392
N-203	48.5	Hornady	2,667
N-204	55.0	Speer	2,289
Herter 100	48.5	Speer	2,207
4320	57.5**	Speer	2,660
H-570	57.0	Speer	2,113

*All bullets 200-gr.
**Reduce this load 5% or more and work up.
†Instrumental velocity, taken at 10 feet.

The BSA 1923/33 receiver (above) and folding peep rear sights, regulated for 200 and 400 yards, at right.

Photo (bottom right). From left: 33 BSA factory load with 165-gr. full patch bullet; 7x61 Norma case after being sized in the 33 sizing die; 7x61 case fire-formed and loaded with a 200-gr. Speer bullet; 7mm Remington Magnum case expanded, trimmed, and loaded with a 275-gr. Speer bullet—this case has not been fire-formed yet.

trigger guard was not straightened, so the hump is till present; the magazine holds 5 cartridges, and has been altered for sporting cartridges, as has the feed ramp.

The stock has a slim fore-end, checkered 17 lines-to-the-inch all the way around. The capped grip is checkered the same. The black plastic buttplate carries the BSA trademark. The butt has an eye for a sling hook, with a similar eye located just ahead of the fore-end below the barrel. The grip, rather long and oval in cross-section, is comfortable. The comb is a bit thin, but no discomfort was noticed when firing the BSA rifle.

By current U.S. sporting rifle standards this Model 1923 would not exactly qualify as the "rifle of the year." It cocks on closing, it has no Monte Carlo or cheekpiece, it is not tapped for mounting a telescopic sight, it looks rather full in the mid-section, and it has a short fore-end and a long barrel. The metal finish is excellent—the stock shows some dents and nicks picked up in its near-50 years—as is the metal-to-wood fit; the weight and stock design are such that it is actually comfortable to shoot—at least 40 rounds per session—without benefit of a recoil pad. The sights are fast in use and the rifle handles better than many newer models. The cartridges I've developed can handle any North American game, so as it stands the 33 BSA 1923 rifle and cartridge make quite a combination.

Some 66 years ago, a 12-year old boy made his first hunt for deer, his rifle an old Winchester 38-40. Black bears were an unexpected bonus!

WHITETAILED DEER
WITH
BLACK POWDER

by Jack McPhee

LOOK AT the big deer walking through the orchard, whispered my mother. He was the largest we had ever seen and, with his horns in the velvet, his rack seemed to be as large as that of a moose. When he was gone, Mother said, "There's a deer you should try for this fall." At that moment I began making plans which included that big buck.

This was in the summer of 1907, when I was twelve. My mother and I were on a raspberry-picking expedition which lasted a week. We were camped in our summer cottage on a block of land, belonging to my father and his partner, that comprised several thousand acres at the head of Long Lake. Most of it was covered with a virgin forest of white ash, basswood, beech, birch, hemlock, hard and soft maple, hornbeam (or ironwood), elm and oak. Here and there a few balsam firs and butternut trees grew among the hardwoods. In the swales and swamps were black ash, white cedar, tamarack and spruce, with willows and alders growing along their edges. In the openings made by fires or logging there were raspberries in profusion, and these also grew all around the clearings made by the 6 old timers who had originally homesteaded

the land. There were hazel bushes and beech trees, too, their nuts a favorite food of the deer and black bear. A clearing in the woods, known as Fisher Field, grew a crop of volunteer buckwheat each year, and was a favorite feeding ground of deer and ruffed grouse. Our place, between Long Lake and Grand Lake, and connected with our Alpena (Michigan) home by poor roads, wasn't much bothered by town hunters.

Our cottage had been the home of the Hamilton brothers; they had homesteaded the land shortly after the end of the Civil War. Built of logs, it was two stories high, with a covered porch on all four sides. It was also surrounded by an apple orchard of at least 200 trees, an attractive feeding ground for deer, bear, coons, rabbits, squirrels and ruffed grouse, all of whom came to the orchard from the surrounding forest. To me it was a heavenly place and one that I never left willingly.

Earlier that day, while picking berries, we'd both seen very large deer tracks; now we felt we had seen the deer that made them. Many times, that summer and fall, my mother and I had talked about that deer: how to get him, how good his meat

would be, and just where his mounted head would hang in the house.

Deer season opened on November 10. I left home early that morning with permission to stay away from school for 5 days; that allowed me a whole week of hunting. My saddle horse, Pontiac, was loaded with my buffalo robe and a dried deer skin to put under it. Secured in my packsack was my food: whole-wheat bread, sausage, several dozen doughnuts and jerked venison. My cotton-drill leanto tent was wrapped around the bedding. Across the saddle bow, suspended from the horn in a strong leather sling, rode my Winchester 38-40 rifle. Pat, my dog, trotted along beside Pontiac and me. My mother said it was all right to take him along as a watch-dog, but not to use him to hunt deer.

The weather was cold, but I was dressed comfortably in woolen underwear, socks, shirt and cap. Since I had grown too large for my buckskin shirt, my mother had made me a hunting shirt of gray cotton twill. It pulled on over the head something like a parka, had 4 covered pockets and, when the cold wind blew, I belted it around my waist. This confined the warm air against my body and made it a most com-

BLACK POWDER DEER

fortable garment for cold weather. As always while in the woods I wore my buckskin moccasins, the most comfortable footwear I've ever found. In my packsack I carried a pair of rubbers to slip over the mocs in case of rain or wet snow.

Our caretaker, Harry Warner, lived alone in a good log cabin; he was a good hunter, trapper, maker of maple sugar and syrup, weaver of ash-splint baskets, and a man who understood boys. He always treated me as though I were a man, and when we were doing things together, it was his custom to ask me what I thought of some idea of his. I always agreed with his more-mature judgement, so we got along well.

I stopped for half an hour to visit with him, told him where I would camp and where I intended hunting. He, in turn, told me that when I got a deer to come to his cabin, and he would harness his horse and drag the deer out of the woods for me. He also gave me a piece of maple sugar that had been moulded in a milk pan and was about 14 inches in diameter by three inches thick. Beside that, he gave me a slab of bacon he had cured that fall. I felt that I was supplied with enough food to last me until spring.

My camp was pitched on the north shore of Long Lake, in a big clearing known as the LaFave Place. Once there had been a group of log buildings there, but they had been burned by careless campers. Pontiac was put out to graze on a long line; I made a supper of bread, bacon and maple sugar; Pat ate some scraps of old bread and meat which I had brought from home; then he and I turned in, I under the robe and he on top of it. The deer skin with the hair on it proved a great improvement in my bed, lots warmer than balsam boughs.

Bacon and bread for breakfast, then I mounted Pontiac and rode back toward Harry's, with Pat scouting through the brush. The sun was barely up, so twice he flushed partridges picking up gravel in the road and up into trees. I easily brought them to the ground with head shots. While passing our cottage, I dressed both birds and Pat ate the insides. I climbed up on the roof with my rifle and looked over the orchard in hope of seeing a deer feeding on frozen apples. I saw nothing except the beauty of the eastern sky as the sun was rising.

I gave the partridges to Harry, stabled Pontiac and gave him both corn and hay; that would keep him satisfied and comfortable for the day. Pat and I then walked down the road toward the Fisher Field. My mind was on the big deer but Pat, his belly full, seemed to be looking for a nice bed in the sun.

There were fresh deer tracks in the dusty road, but no real big ones. I found I was handicapped by hunting right into the sun; a deer had probably seen me and faded back into the brush. Several partridges flew noisily into the "popple" trees at the edge of the field, but I didn't want to shoot for fear of losing a chance at a deer. Hunting slowly through the field toward the south, I had a better chance of seeing deer before they spotted me, so I followed an old trail down toward the north shore of East Bay. This was slow work; one step, a good look around, then another step. Nothing was moving but a skunk, who paused to look me over, then moved on about his business. Pat knew all about skunks, and kept close to my heels.

At the lake shore there was a dry log in the sun, and I sat there, watching the shore on my side as well as that across the bay. The warm sun made me sleepy, so I put my cap on the sand and sat on it with my back against the log. Pat moved up beside me and both of us fell asleep.

A snarl from the dog woke me, and frightened me, too; he was standing beside me, his tail between his legs, with every hair on his back erect. My eyes followed his into the thick white cedars and my rifle was at my shoulder; no doubt my hair was standing on end, too, but I saw nothing nor heard a sound. Gradually the dog's hair subsided, his tail came out from between his legs and he wagged it in satisfaction. What ever had been in the cedars and had frightened him had moved away without noise. Both Pat and I were glad, and I didn't have the nerve to go into the woods to look for tracks. Probably it had been a bear that was glad to get out of our neighborhood, but at the time I felt as though it could have been anything from a man-eating African lion to a ghost.

We headed west along the beach, thoroughly awake now and on the alert. Pat startled a rabbit and I shot it after a run of 10 minutes or so. Finally we came to an opening in the woods where a portable saw mill had been set up to cut lumber for a large barn which had been erected near Harry's cabin. Along the east side of the clearing raspberry bushes were thick and I noticed that they had been freshly browsed. On seeing these signs, I had sense enough not to go any nearer and leave my tracks and scent; it might be a good place to watch for the deer that had been cropping those bushes. There was an old road from the mill site to Harry's place, so we hunted slowly along it without seeing anything except another partridge. Pat treed it and I shot it.

I had an early supper with Harry, then left about 3:30 P.M. to watch for deer at the mill site. Pat was tied up because I had learned not to have him along when there was any waiting to be done. Finding a smooth spot on a low pile of sawdust, about 30 yards from the berry bushes, I lay down facing them, with my rifle lying in front of me and held out of the sawdust by some old slabs.

Again I must have fallen asleep, for I was awakened by the sound of a deer cropping the bushes. I could see only his horns, and when he lowered his head for another bite, I slowly raised myself on my elbows with the rifle at my shoulder and my eye on the sights; it was a comfortable prone position. In a minute or two the deer took a step forward, raised his head for a higher bush, the sight settled on the white patch on his throat, the rifle cracked and the deer went down with a broken neck. A lucky shot, and I knew it.

Later, weighed on the barn scales, he went 130 lbs. There were 6 points on his small horns and he was very fat. I gutted him at once and, with tongue, heart, liver and kidneys in my packsack, I struck off for Harry's to haul him out with my horse.

Harry didn't seem surprised that I had a deer so quickly. He seemed to look on me as a good hunter, and that made me feel like a man. We had the deer back at the barn before it was very dark, and hung clear of the ground with a block and tackle. I felt good as I rode back to my camp on Pontiac with Pat trotting beside us. There was liver to eat with the bacon for my breakfast, and Pat was assured of high living on the rabbit and kidneys; Harry wanted only the heart and tongue.

No matter where I hunted the next day, I saw nothing except deer tracks and partridges. At last, growing impatient because no deer showed, I shot several of the grouse that Pat frightened into the trees. Pat grew lazy when filled with their innards, and I turned back to Harry's cabin. We visited until supper time, then after helping wash the dishes, I got Pontiac ready to ride back to my camp.

Harry drew my attention to the western sky, bright red from the setting sun. "The Indians say that when you see such a sunset at this time of year, you can expect a big wind and snow, a regular blizzard. Why don't you move down here, just in case it does snow and blow; or you could move into the cottage. There's lots of wood there, and you will be warm and comfortable. Your horse will be more comfortable in a warm barn than standing with his rear end to the storm. Think it over."

I did think it over on my way back to camp, but, as the weather seemed fine, I decided to move in the morning. Mindful of his promise of a big wind, I made my leanto double secure and packed everything except the bedding into sacks. I would move camp in the morning.

In the night I awoke to the flapping of my canvas shelter. The wind was howling from the north, but as yet there was no snow, even though it felt as cold as in January. Not having a watch, I didn't know exactly what time it was, but from the position of the Big Dipper, it seemed to be about 3:00 A.M.

Even with the best of pine kindling, and fine fire wood, I couldn't start a fire as the wind blew both flame and kindling away. Pontiac stood just as Harry had described him, his head hanging down and tail to the wind. That decided it; we would strike camp and move into the cottage.

Putting the saddle on the horse was not easy as the wind tried to snatch it away. I did make it at last, then loosened the leanto canvas and grabbed it as it was starting to blow away. The bedding had been rolled up before saddling Pontiac; next, I wrapped the canvas around the bundle and tied it on behind the saddle. Pat looked as miserable as the rest of us, but was glad to follow along.

At the cottage, I took the load off the

horse, placed it inside the door, then led the horse to the old log barn. Its door had been wired open, and as far as I could remember, we had never used it. Pontiac stopped and snorted when I tried to lead him inside. When I pulled on the reins, he backed up. On hearing him snort, Pat came on the run, stopped beside him snarling, then backed up, too. That was enough for me: there was something in there that both dog and horse feared. I led them down to Harry's place, where Pontiac entered the barn willingly and Pat did no growling to show that all was not well inside. As I came out of the barn, I saw a light in the cabin and Harry moving around, so I went in and told him how the animals had acted at the old Hamilton barn.

"By George," he exclaimed, "I'll bet there's a bear denned up in there! When it is daylight, we'll go up and find out. A bear that was feeding on apples in the orchard could easily have used that old place for his winter quarters. Just think how handy it must be for him. Some fat bear meat right now would come in handy, too."

It was daylight when the breakfast dishes had been washed, and we walked up the road to the old barn. Harry had his 45-70 and a lot of experience with bears; I, with my little 38-40, was content to watch what happened and see the fireworks, if any.

The inside of the barn was a wreck; it hadn't been used in the 10 years that we had owned it, and the hay-mow had rotted down and fallen into the center of the floor. On top of it was some old hay. A small opening showed between the barn wall and the old logs that had been the floor of the hay-mow. Harry's experienced eye noted a trail leading into this hole. He tried to get Pat to enter, but that worthy felt better out in the open. We got a small cedar rail off the old snake fence and with it, Harry felt around in the hole until his prodding was answered with a growl. There was a bear in there! My hair stood on end with the very thought and I wished myself safe at home.

But Harry had other ideas. "Take this rail, Johnny," he said, "go behind the barn, find a hole between the logs and poke around there. I'll wait out in front with my rifle."

I did as directed, found a space between the logs and thrust in the rail. I felt it bump something yielding and was rewarded by a savage growl.

"Good work, Johnny," encouraged Harry, "give him some more, and he'll come out where I can get a shot at him."

I poked some more, touched the bear again and heard him moving. Then Harry's rifle roared, and the bear bawled; another shot and the bawling stopped. With

my cocked rifle at the ready, I went carefully around the barn. The bear was dead, or at least, quiet. Harry watched him carefully for a few minutes, then said it was all right to take hold of him.

To me he seemed almost the size of a cow, but Harry said it wasn't a real large one, but he thought it would weigh about 250 lbs., and at that time of the year, would be fat and good eating. Pat stood off about 50 feet, and couldn't be coaxed nearer. He wasn't a bear dog, and didn't intend being one.

I went for Harry's light wagon and horse while he started gutting the bear. When I returned, the bear had been dragged behind the barn.

"That will be a good place to set a bear trap," he told me. "Probably another bear, or maybe more, will be coming to the orchard for apples, and the trap may take what ever comes this way."

We hauled the bear to his place, hung it up in the barn and skinned it. Probably Harry could read my thoughts as he promised me some bear steak for supper. He cut steaks and left them out in the cold, but covered with a clean cloth, remarking that with such cold weather, the steak would be well-chilled and good eating.

Remembering how frightened Pat had been at something in a clump of cedars on the lake shore the first day we had hunted

BLACK POWDER DEER

here, I told Harry about it. He understood that I had been frightened too badly to enter the brush and investigate, but now his opinion was that a bear may have been there; he suggested we go and find out. "Might as well have another bear," he remarked.

How the wind blew and how cold it was! Harry was too much of a woodsman to walk down wind, so we angled across the wind to the lake shore, then east across the wind. This time we left Pat tied in the barn with Pontiac. Harry decided he might frighten the bear by barking at the wrong time.

My heart speeded up as we came in sight of the grove of cedars, but with Harry along, his 45-70 across his arm, I felt braver than when Pat and I had been there alone. We walked softly among the trees. Harry whistled softly and pointed with his chin at a mound of moss and leaves heaped up at the butt of a windfall. A bear's den! I was thrilled, but cautious at the same time. Harry motioned me back out of the trees. There he whispered that our bear was in a hole made by the upturned roots of the tree, and the moss was material that it had gathered to close the door of its winter home. If I wished, I could stand a bit to one side, but where I could get a clear shot when the bear emerged, and Harry would do the prodding this time. Down in my heart I felt that I would rather he did the shooting, but I knew I couldn't back out of such a generous offer; I nodded my head in agreement and took my stand where directed.

The only pole long enough to prod the bear was a downed cedar about 8 or 9 feet long, and with a lot of limbs sticking out from its trunk. Harry took his stand opposite me and began breaking off the branches. Their snapping must have aroused the bear because he started out of his bed with a rush, not in my direction but toward Harry. He jabbed the pole at the bear, who, in turn, grabbed it between his jaws and gave it a jerk; Harry's arms were tangled in the remaining branches and he fell to his knees. The bear sprang out of the den, dropped the pole and ran. I was afraid to fire for fear of hitting Harry, still on his knees and grabbing for his rifle; the bear was gone and not a shot was fired.

I was heartily ashamed of my part in the act, but he said I had done the right thing and the bear deserved escaping for his bravery. It had been an exciting few minutes, and both of us felt that one bear was enough for one day. We went home, and you can bet there was a lot of talking done on the way back, and a lot more during the day. It started snowing on the way home, and I was glad to be inside out of the storm and close to the frying bear steaks. For me it had been a most exciting day.

The wind howled around the cabin that night and the snow flew past the windows. The cabin creaked and groaned with the force of the wind and it was a good night for a boy to sleep.

In the morning there were places where the snow had drifted and places where the ground was swept nearly clear of snow. The snow had ceased falling, the wind had died and the sun was shining. It was a good morning to try for deer. Neither of us knew when the wind had stopped blowing, but Harry suggested that I try the old orchard first, then hunt down toward the lake and, if the wind started ever so easily, for me to hunt quietly up into the wind. He reminded me that if I trailed a deer it would probably go up wind, and that from time to time I should circle across the wind and back into it with my rifle at my shoulder and ready to shoot, because a deer was in the habit of lying down early in the morning after feeding and always turned to the downwind side of the trail. There it lay where it could watch its back trail and, at the same time, keep its nose pointed into the wind. This was a good position to watch for a small boy following its trail; the next move was to let him pass up wind while the deer would sneak away in the opposite direction. He reminded me that with snow on the ground, I would be able to see the deer more easily than before; but the deer also could see me more easily too.

I found big deer tracks in the orchard where the buck had eaten some frozen apples lying under the trees. Following the tracks into the hardwoods, I saw where snow and leaves had been pawed aside under the beech trees. The trail went through the hardwoods toward the lake shore, turned left and went directly into the sun. Soon the trail turned northeast, and then I felt the breeze starting up. As Harry had said, the deer traveled into the wind. It avoided the drifts, walking where the going was best, its big hoofs sinking through the carpet of frozen leaves on the forest floor. I knew that, though a hunter walked quietly and carefully in snow, he made enough noise that a deer, with much better sense of hearing than a man, could hear easily. I felt that being down wind, now that the wind was blowing strongly again, I had a better chance of following without being heard, provided I walked softly in my moccasins.

To my inexperienced eyes the trail looked very fresh, and I didn't know if it was time to take a circle down across wind and then come back toward the trail, as Harry had advised. I felt I should do it, so with the rifle at my shoulder and thumb on the hammer, I turned toward the sun for 50 paces, then up and back into the wind toward where I thought the trail should be. Probably that was about the most exciting stalk I ever made. My heart pounded, my mouth felt dry and I strained my eyes to see the deer before it saw me. I took a step, looked carefully ahead and to both sides, then another step and the same careful inspection of the ground and woods ahead. With the sun at my back, everything ahead was well-lighted, but I saw nothing resembling a deer. Then I was back at the trail.

With a low sigh of relief, I relaxed, dropped the rifle into one hand, and took a few minutes of rest. Leaning against a big

My 38-40 rifle of those long-ago years was a Winchester Model 1892, with a 24-inch octagon barrel, an ivory bead front and a Marble peep rear sight. My old friend, Ed Wesson, the gunsmith, had found it for me, along with a complete outfit for casting bullets and loading the cartridges. The loading tool was an Ideal No. 4, with a bullet mould at the far end of the handles. There was a cap extractor, a dip measure for black powder, a shell resizing tool, a lead melting pot and pot holder—about like a stove lid with a hole in it, this accepted the melting pot, both being set on a cook stove to melt the bullet metal. There was also a bullet-sizing opening in the handles, but after we had sized bullets with it and fired them, Ed Wesson decided that such sized bullets added nothing to accuracy. Thereafter the bullets were lubricated as-cast and shot that way.

My entire outfit, aside from the powder, primers and cleaning rod, was bought used, the total cost only $13.00!

These tools were a mystery to me at first, but Ed Wesson soon taught me how to use them. He showed me how to weigh the lead and tin in proper proportions, 16 ounces of lead to one of tin. This was heated over the fire in our stove, fluxed with a piece of beeswax, stirred and skimmed. The cast bullets, weighing some 180 grains, had two grooves and a flat nose. Beeswax and tallow were then melted and mixed together. Into this warm lubricant each bullet was dipped nose down so that both grease grooves were filled. Then the bullet was set nose down on a sheet of paper until the grease had hardened and it was ready to load. I used FFg-size black Kentucky rifle powder, sold then in 6¼-lb. kegs at $1.65. My primers, Winchester No. 2s ($2.00 per thousand) were seated in the case with the tong tool; the primed case was then filled, using the dip measure, which was supposed to contain 40 grains of powder; the bullet was seated well down on the powder and the case mouth crimped into the upper grease groove. I don't think,

looking back, that my method of dipping powder gave me the supposed 40 grains each time, but the loaded cartridges shot well and I soon learned to use the rifle with some degree of skill. Our grocer gave me lead salvaged from chests of tea, and Ed Maynard, a plumber friend, gave me a piece of beer coil made of tin. This I cut up in small pieces with his tin snips, my lead and tin then weighed by Wesson on his scale. My mother enjoyed casting bullets and did it a lot better than I. After firing a few rounds I cleaned the barrel thoroughly because black powder fouled it quickly, I learned, and my lead bullets never shot well unless the barrel was clean. At first I used a pull-through cleaner on this job, but later I found a small jointed wooden shotgun rod which worked better. Also, when knocked down it could be easily packed in my hunting bag.

by Jack McPhee

Heading into the wind, which I knew had been blowing from the direction in which the road lay, I soon smelled smoke. Thinking that Harry's cabin was too far away for the smoke to have drifted over here, I was puzzled until I heard the sound of an axe. At first I felt lost, but I reasoned that a little more walking would bring me out on Fisher Field, so I kept on. About 100 more steps and I was in the brush at its edge. Across the field, I could see a column of smoke rising above the brush, which was blown in my direction by the strong wind. I also got occasional glimpses of red, probably the coat of some hunter.

Right then I didn't feel so important; it dawned on me that my deer had smelled the smoke when the fire had been started, and probably heard the noise of the axe, too, and had craftily turned back. It had been pure luck that I leaned against the tree when I did. Had I been moving, the deer would have seen me and run. I never would have seen him.

Walking back until I cut his trail, I turned and followed it back toward the field. It went only a few yards, then stopped; probably when the deer first scented the smoke. The tracks showed that it stood still, stamped a little, then started its sneak back which my bullet had ended. Well, I had the deer, but it was not by my expert stalking; merely beginner's luck.

I circled to the right until I came out on the road, cut the trail of a man wearing lumberman's rubbers; and followed it to the fire. The man was a middle-aged fellow, wearing a bright-red coat; the first of its kind I had ever seen. His rifle was a big one, a Winchester Model 1876, probably a 45-75. I had heard of a homesteader on Grand Lake with such a rifle, so I knew that this man was Wolf Manion.

"Any luck?" I greeted him.

"Naw," was his reply. "They ain't no deer left in the hull country. They used to be a good runway acrost the aidge of this field, an' I stood here fer nigh onto two hours 'thout seein' a hair."

"Wouldn't the fire keep the deer from crossing here?" I asked.

"Hell, no!" was his answer. "A deer ain't afeared of fire ner smoke. I've killed wagon loads of them a sittin' beside a fire, jist like this. But now that you've done all this talkin', the deer—if there is any—has got skeered of your voice an' lef' the country. An' I'm agoin', too." With that he turned back up the road and left his fire burning.

I extinguished the fire by kicking snow on it, then continued my walk. Harry made me a lunch, and after eating it, we hitched his horse to a home-made sleigh, locally known as a "jumper," and drove to the deer. It lay close to an old logging road with which Harry was familiar, so we had easy going on the way back.

The scale at the barn showed the buck's weight at 267 lbs., more than I had hoped. That weight puffed me up a lot, and I felt I just had to get home and tell about it. My father would come for the deer with the driving team and a light sleigh. The hunt had been a great success, and as I rode home on old Pontiac with Pat trotting beside us, I wouldn't have traded places with Daniel Boone. ●

beech tree trunk, my eyes roamed over the nearly-open forest ahead. After about 5 minutes of this, a movement caught my eye; it was a deer about 60 yards distant, head and tail down, sneaking slowly along in the same direction from where I'd come. I didn't dare make a quick movement, so I gradually got the rifle butt to my shoulder, raised the barrel slowly to horizontal, cocking the hammer softly as the barrel came up. By this time the deer had come about opposite me, some 40 yards away. He raised his head as I shifted the sights low on his right shoulder and squeezed the trigger. At the report he broke into a run with his tail still down, and I fired twice more. He kept on his run even though I felt that I couldn't have missed the first shot as everything seemed perfect when I fired. With a live round in the chamber, I walked through the black-powder smoke to his trail. There was cut hair and blood on the snow; then I heard the thrashing of his feet on the frozen ground, and then silence.

With the rifle at my shoulder, my heart pounding, I walked silently beside the trail for almost 100 paces. There was blood on the trees along the trail and on the snow. With all that blood I felt he was mine; then I saw him, lying on his side on the snow.

Oh, boy! what a deer! He was round and fat-looking, with thick heavy horns that, later, measured 20 inches in spread. His neck was swollen to about twice normal size—a big deer! My bullet had taken him through the upper part of the heart and stopped against the skin on the opposite side, well-flattened. I had thought such a wound would have thrown him in his tracks, but I had a lot to learn about bullet performance on game animals. My other 2 shots had missed.

After admiring him and handling his rack of horns, I got the jointed wooden rod out of my packsack and cleaned the rifle barrel of black-powder fouling, slipped a live round into the chamber, lowered the hammer to half-cock, then gutted the deer. I was doing just what Ed Wesson had taught me; he had explained that it took only a couple of shots with black powder to foul a barrel and make the rifle shoot wild.

I felt pretty satisfied with myself, even that I was darned good as a still hunter. It seemed that I had done everything exactly right, even to leaning against the tree and catching the deer on his way to watch his back trail. Feeling elated indeed, I set out to find the road and bring Harry after the deer with his horse.

U. S. Cartridge Revolvers 1856 to 1899 Brand Names and Makers

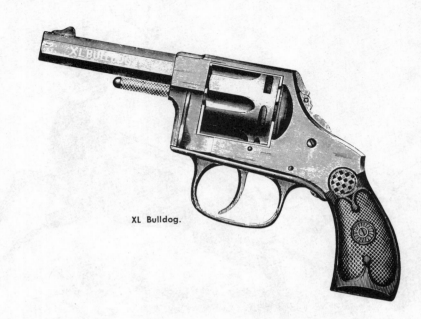

XL Bulldog.

The list that follows is an excerpt from *Collector's Handbook of U.S. Cartridge Revolvers*, by William B. Fors. The book, published in 1973, covers 600 brand names in the 40-year period, history sketches of 82 manufacturers, and over 200 patent listings. The hard cover book is available for $5 postpaid from the Barlow Book Co., P.O. Box 334, Northbrook, Illinois 60062.

ACME — (H.&A.), various calibers and markings, sold by Merwin, Hulbert Co.

ACME ARMS CO — (maker unknown), 22, 32 marked *Acme*, DA, cncld. hmr. Sold by J. Stevens Arms Co.

AETNA — (H.&R.), 22, 32 marked *1, 2,* or *2½* plus pat. date of May 23, 1876.

AJAX ARMY — (maker unknown), 44 marked *Ajax Army*, sold by E. C. Meacham Co, St. Louis, Mo.

ALASKA — (Hood FA), 22 marked *Alaska Cast Steel* plus pat. dates.

ALERT — (Hood FA or H.&A.), 22, marked *Alert 1874*.

ALEX — (H.&A.), 22, 32, 38, 41; marked as seller desired.

ALEXIA — (H.&A.), 22, markings vary by seller.

ALEXIS—(Hood FA), 22, marked *Alexis-Turner & Ross* plus pat. dates. Sold by Turner & Ross, Boston.

ALEXIS — (H.&A.), 22, markings vary with seller.

ALLEN — (H.&A.), 22, marked *Allen 22*.

ALLEN, ETHAN — (Ethan Allen Co), 22, 32, 41, all marked with company name.

ALLEN & WHEELOCK — (same), 22, 32, 38, 44, all marked with company name.

ALL RIGHT — (maker unknown), not the same as Wright Arms Co. model, name probably adopted to capitalize on Wright name popularity.

AMERICA—(B.&G.), 22, marked *America Patd April 23, 1878*.

AMERICAN ARMS — (same, Boston), 32, 38CF, 41, marked with company name, city and state plus pat. dates: Oct. 31, 1865 and June 19, 1866. Hmr. and h/less models.

AMERICAN BOY — (B.&G.), calibers, markings unknown. Sold by Townley Hardware Co., Kansas City, Mo.

AMERICAN BULLDOG — (I/J), 22, 32RF, 38CF, 38 S&W, 44. Large eagle on grip, sold by J. P. Lovell Arms Co. of Boston.

AMERICAN EAGLE — (H.&A.), various cals. and markings depending on seller.

AMERICAN GUN CO — (Crescent FA), no identification, sold through H.&D. Folsom Co.

AMERICAN STANDARD TOOL CO — (same, Newark, N.J.), 22, marked with company name. Made with original Manhattan FA tooling.

AMERICUS — (H.&A.), no identification.

AMERICAN DA — (H.&R.), 32, 38, marked *American*, variant model known as Safety Hammer DA.

ARISTOCRAT — (H.&A.), various cals., made for Supplee Biddle Hardware, Philadelphia, Pa. Usually with name marking only.

AUBREY — (Meriden FA), 32CF, 38CF, marked with name only. Made for parent company sale, Sears Roebuck Co.

AUTOMATIC — (H.&A.), 32CF, 38CF, marked *Automatic*, DA, concealed hammer (poss. also after 1899).

AUTOMATIC HAMMERLESS—(I.J.), 22, 32, 38CF, marked with owls-head and company name.

AUTOMATIC POLICE — (F.&W.), 32, 38 DA model carries company name.

AVENGER — (maker unknown), 32, marked *32 Avenger NY Pat Appld For*.

BABCOCK — (maker unknown), 32RF, marked *Babcock's Pat.*

BABY BULLDOG — (I.J. tent.), 22, 32, markings unknown, fld. trig., sold by J. P. Lovell Arms.

BANG-UP — (H.&A.), 22, markings vary by outlet adopting.

BABY RUSSIAN — (American Arms), 38

Table of Abbreviations

AE	automatic ejector	gd.	guard
A&W	Allen & Wheelock	H&A	Hopkins & Allen
bbl.	barrel	hgd.	hinged
B&G	Bliss & Goodyear	hmr.	hammer
bh.	birdshead (grip)	H&R	Harrington & Richardson
bs.	backstrap	I.J.	Iver Johnson
bt.	butt	met.	metallic
cncld.	concealed	mfg.	manufacturer
cal(s).	caliber	pt/pat	patent
CF	centerfire	OAS	Otis A. Smith
ctg.	cartridge	Rem	Remington Arms
cyl.	cylinder	RF	rimfire
DA	double action	SA	single action
FA	firearms	S/E	self ejector
F&W	Forehand & Wadsworth	SW/O	swing out (cyl.)
fld.	folding	SG	side gate (load)
frm.	frame	sp.	spur
		S&W	Smith & Wesson
		trg.	trigger
		tent.	tentative (ident.)

marked with *A A Co* in circle with two stars, copy of S&W Russian model.

BICYCLE — (H.&R.), 22, 32, DA; hinged frame marked *Bicycle* and date: Oct 8, 1895.

BIG BONANZA — (Bacon Arms), no further information.

BLACKFIELD — (maker unknown), sold by Hibbard-Spencer-Bartlett Co, Chicago.

BLOODHOUND — (H.&A.), 22, marked *Bloodhound*, other markings depending on seller.

BLUE JACKET — (H.&A.), 22, 32, marked *Blue Jacket* plus numbers 1, 1½ for 22; 2 for 32.

BLUE LEADER — No information.

BLUE WHISTLER — (H.&A.), 32RF, marked *Blue Whistler*, other markings depending on seller.

BONANZA — (Bacon Arms), 22, marked *Bonanza Cast Steel* plus patent dates.

BOSTON BULLDOG — (I.J.), 22, 32CF, variant of American Bulldog. Nickel finish only with bulldog insignia and I.J. name.

BOY'S CHOICE—(Hood FA), 22, marked *Boy's Choice - Pat. Apr. 6, 1875.*

BRIDGE GUN CO — (maker unknown), sold by Shapleigh Hardware, St. Louis, Mo.

BRIDGEPORT ARMS — (maker unknown), sold by Rohde-Spencer Co, Chicago.

BRITISH BULLDOG — (F.&W.), 22, 38, 44, marked *British Bulldog.*

BRITISH BULLDOG — (H.&A.), 22 only, probably marked with name only.

BRITISH BULLDOG — (I.J.), cal. unknown, DA model made only in 1881.

BROWNIE — (C. F. Mossberg), May not be on revolver model.

BRUTUS — (Hood FA), 22, marked *Brutus Cast Steel, Feb. 23, '75- Mar 14, '76.*

BUFFALO BILL — (maker unknown), 22, marked *Buffalo Bill*, Sold by Homer Fisher Co, New York.

BULLDOG — (F.&W.), various cals. marked *Bulldog*, plus pat. dates.

BULL DOZER — (Norwich Falls Pistol Co), 22, 38, marked *Bull Dozer Cala 38.* Sold by J. Bride & Co.

BULLSEYE — (maker unknown), 22, marked *Bullseye.*

CADET — (maker unknown), 22, sold by Maltby-Curtiss Co.

CAPT JACK — (H.&A.), 22, marked *Capt Jack- Pat Mar 28, 1871.* No other markings on author's specimen.

SAROLINA ARMS — (Crescent FA), sold by Smith-Wadsworth Co, Charlotte, N.C.

CARUSO— (Crescent FA), sold by Spencer-Bartlett Co, Chicago.

CENTENNIAL 1876 — (Deringer R.&P.), 22, 32RF, 38RF, marked *Centennial 1876.*

CENTRAL ARMS — (Crescent FA), sold by Shapleigh Hardware Co, St. Louis, Mo.

CHALLENGE — (B.&G.), 32, marked *Challenge Pat'd Apr. 23, 1878.*

CHALLENGE EJECTOR — (Meriden FA), various cal., sold by Sears Roebuck Co.

CHEROKEE ARMS—(Crescent FA), sold by C.M. McClung Co, Knoxville, Tenn.

CHICAGO—(Meriden FA), sold by Sears Roebuck & Co.

CHICAGO ARMS — (poss. Crescent FA), 38CF, marked *Chicago Arms Co*, DA hammerless, grip squeeze safety,

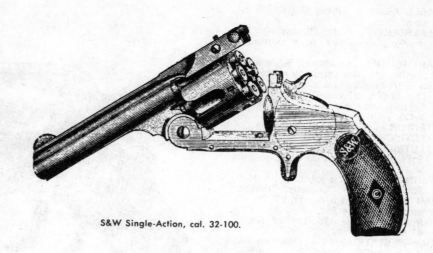

S&W Single-Action, cal. 32-100.

breaks to eject, sold by Fred Bifflar Co, Chicago.

CHICAGO LEDGER — (Ames Sword Co, Chicopee Falls, Mass.) No further information.

CHIEFTAIN — (B.&G.), 32, marked *Chieftain Pat'd April 23, 1878.*

CLIPPER — (maker unknown), 22 reported.

COLT — (Colt Pt.F.A.Co), Company markings and rampant colt insignia.

COLUMBIAN — (J.T. Smith, Rockfalls, Conn.), 22, 32S&W, 38S&W, marked *Columbian- Maltby Henley 1/24/1888- 10/28/1889.* Sold by Maltby Henley Co.

COLUMBIAN DA — (Crescent FA), 38CF marked *Columbian New York Arms Co.* Made for Garnett Carter Co, Chattanooga, Tenn.

COMET — Name reported on revolver, no further information.

COMMANDER — as previous listing.

THE COMMERCIAL — (Otis A. Smith), 32RF, made for Hibbard-Spencer-Bartlett of Chicago, may carry OAS grip insignia.

COMPEER — (Crescent FA), sold by Van-Camp Hardware Co, Indianapolis, Ind.

CONE, D.D. — (poss. Sharps & Hankins), 22, 32RF, marked *DD CONE, JP LOWER* or *WL GRANT.*

CONQUEROR — (Bacon Arms), 22, 32, 38, 41, marked *Conqueror- Pat Dec 10, 1878*, which may appear also on H.&A. models.

CONSTANT — Name reported on revolver.

CONTINENTAL — (same, Norwich, Conn.), 22, marked *Continental No. 1*; 32 marked *No. 2.*

COPELAND, F. — (same, Worcester, Mass.), 22, marked *F. Copeland.* Resembles Prescott models.

COWBOY — Name reported on revolver.

COWBOY RANGER — (maker unknown), sold by Rohde Spencer Co, Chicago.

CREEDMORE — (Chicago FA), 32, marked *Creedmore.*

CREEDMORE NO 1 — (H.&A.), 22, so marked.

CRESCENT — (Crescent FA), various cals. and markings requested by seller.

CRESCENT — (B.&G.), 32, marked *Crescent Pat Apr 23, 1878.*

CROWN — Name reported on revolver.

CROWN JEWEL — (B.&G.), 32, so marked.

CUMBERLAND ARMS — (Crescent FA), sold by Gray Dudley Hardware Co, Nashville, Tenn.

CZAR — (Hood FA), 22, marked *Czar- Cast Steel Pat Feb 23, '75-Mar 14, '76*, and TR on frame. Sold by Turner & Ross Co., Boston, Mass.

CRISPIN — (Smith Arms NYC), odd cartridge 32, marked *Smith Arms Co New York City Crispin's Pat Oct 3, 1865.*

DAISY — (Bacon Arms), 22, marked *Daisy Pat Dec 10, '78.*

DALY ARMS — (Maker unknown), 22, ring trigger, sold by Daly Arms Co, New York City.

DANIEL BOONE GUN CO — (maker unknown), sold by Belknap Hardware, Louisville, Ky.

DEADSHOT — (L.W. Pond), 22, marked *Deadshot*, half-circle insignia on grip.

DEFENDER — (I.J.), 22, 32, 38, marked *Defender.*

DEFENDER 89 — (I.J.), 22, 32, so marked.

DEFIANCE — (B.&G.), 22, marked *Defiance Pat'd Apr 23, 1878.*

DELPHIAN ARMS — (maker unknown), sold by Supplee Biddle Hardware, Philadelphia, Pa.

DERINGER-PHILA — (Deringer R.&P.), 22, 32, tip-up so-marked.

DESPATCH NO 1 — (H.&A.), 22, so-marked, some specimens spelled "Dispatch."

DIAMOND ARMS — (maker unknown), sold by Shapleigh Hardware, St. Louis, Mo.

DICTATOR — (H.&A.), 22, 32, marked with company name and patent date- *May 27, '79.* 32 marked *No. 2.*

DICKINSON — (E.L. Dickinson Co), 22, 32, marked *E L & J Dickinson, Springfield, Mass.*

DUPLEX — (Osgood Gun Works), oddity with two bbls, 22 & 32, marked *Duplex- Dec 7, 1880.*

DOUBLEHEADER — (H.&A.), Sold by Renwick, New York, a sales firm.

DREADNOUGHT — (H.&A. or B.&G.), 30RF, so-marked.

DUNLAP SPECIAL — (Davis Warner Arms), Sold by Dunlap Hardware, Macon, Georgia.

EAGLE — (I.J.), 22, 32, 38, 38CF, 41, so-marked.

EAGLE ARMS — (Plant Mfg.), 22, 32, so-marked.

EARLHOOD — (E.L. Dickinson), 32, marked *Earlhood* plus company name.

EARTHQUAKE—(as above), 32, marked *Earthquake* plus company name.

EASTERN ARMS — (Meriden FA), 32CF, DA, hnged fr. cncld. hmr., marked *Eastern Arms*. Sold by Sears Roebuck & Co.

ELECTOR — (H.&A.), no information.

ELECTRIC — (F.&W.), 32, so-marked.

ELECTRIC CITY — (maker unknown), Sold by Wyeth Hardware, St. Joseph, Mo.

ELGIN ARMS — (Crescent FA), Sold by Strauss-Schram Company, Chicago.

EMPIRE — (Rupertus Arms), 22, 38, 41, marked *Empire Pat. Nov. 21, '71-J. Rupertus, Phila.* 38 marked *No. 1,* 41 marked *No. 41.*

EMPIRE STATE ARMS — (Meriden FA), 32CF, 38CF, hng'd frm., self/ej., marked *Empire State Hammerless.* Sold by Sears Roebuck & Co.

EMPRESS — (J. Rupertus), 32, so-marked.

ENCORE — (I.J.), 32, so-marked, name also used by H.&A.

ENDERS — (Crescent FA), Sold by Simmons Hardware of St. Louis, Kentucky.

ENTERPRISE — (Enterprise Gun Wks.), 22, 32, 38, 41, marked 1 through 4 plus *Enterprise-Jas. Bown & Sons, Pittsburgh.*

ESSEX—(Crescent FA), Sold by Belknap Hardware Co, Louisville, Ky.

ETNA — Reported, no information.

EXPERT — (H.&A.), no information.

EXPRESS — (Bacon Mfg.), 22, marked *Express-Pat Dec 10, '78 Reissued May 10, '81.*

EUREKA — Reported, no information.

EXCELSIOR — (B.&G.), 32, marked *Excelsior Pat'd Apr 23, 1878.*

Improved British Bull-Dog (F&W).

FAULTLESS — (Crescent FA or H.&A.), Sold by Smyth Merchandise Co, Chicago.

FAVORITE — (I.J.), 22, 32, 38, 44, marked *No. 1* through *No. 4.*

FAVORITE NAVY—(I.J.), 44, so-marked, long bbl.

FEATHERLIGHT — Private brand sold by Sears Roebuck.

FEDERAL ARMS — (Meriden FA), 32, 38, DA, hng'd. fr., sold by Sears Roebuck.

FISHER — (maker unknown), sold by Fisher Co., Lynchburg, Va.

FOREHAND HAMMERLESS—(Forehand Arms), 32, 38, marked with company name.

FOREHAND & WADSWORTH — (same), 22, 30.32, 38.44, hmr. and h/less models in 32 and 38, marked with company name, city and state.

FRANK HARRISON ARMS — (maker unknown), sold by Sickles Preston Co, Davenport, Ia.

FRONTIER — (Norwich Falls Pistol Co), No information.

Some Tips to Remember for Ducks in December

The rush of air against feathers as a flock of ducks cup their wings over a set of decoys are among the most thrilling sounds and sights of the fall and winter hunting seasons. For those who have already started their annual waterfowling jaunts, or are about to, here are a few basic reminders from Remington.

Setting up the outer fringe of your decoys no more than 40 yards from the blind insures that decoying flocks will be in range and establishes an accurate distance reference for you.

On inland ponds and streams, 6 to 12 decoys are usually enough for dabbling ducks. Over larger, open bodies of water, however, rigs of two dozen or more tend to be more effective on diving species.

Avoid setting up a blind with the wind in your face. Since ducks invariably try to land upwind, your position should permit them to come in from left or right or toward your blind, but not directly over you, going away.

This means that ducks crossing your stool downwind are on an "inspection" pass, don't intend to drop in, and are moving at speeds that make them doubly hard to hit. If they don't spot any suspicious looking objects or movement, they'll come back into the wind on the next run.

To assure this, remember to camouflage or cover any items of equipment that are shiny or bright in color. Pick up any fired shells from the ground or water around the immediate area of the blind.

Ducks don't like to set down on a crowded landing strip, so be sure to leave an open space *inside* a large set of blocks.

Under today's bag limits and points systems, proper identification of species, even by sex, is important. Work on your ability to distinguish one type from another by their most prominent markings at a distance, as well as by individual silhouettes and flight characteristics. It's actually more important to be able to tell one duck from another at 40 yards before you shoot, than when you have them in hand.

Last of all, don't forget: your hunting license, your duck stamp, actual days of the legal season, a plug that limits your shotgun's shell capacity to three.

Remember, too, that good duck hunting doesn't depend solely on your skills in the blind. Support your local Ducks Unlimited chapter and attend its annual D.U. fund-raising dinner.

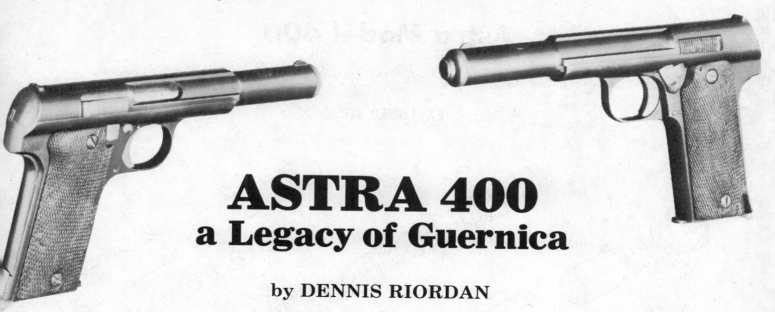

ASTRA 400
a Legacy of Guernica

by DENNIS RIORDAN

A thoroughly researched, definitive study
of this famous Spanish service pistol.
Included are three excellent drawings and other
illustrations, plus a parts legend, detailed
takedown instructions and a full bibliography.

THE ARMED FORCES of Spain adopted their first automatic pistol in 1913. Designed by the Spanish Count of Campo Giro and named in his honor, the gun was manufactured under contract by Esperanza y Unceta at Guernica. The Campo-Giro was a straight blowback pistol, chambered for the powerful 9mm Bergmann-Bayard, known in Spain as the 9mm Largo (long). Several modifications were incorporated into the gun during its life, but it was superseded in 1921 by a new pistol, designed and manufactured by Esperanza y Unceta. This pistol, to become commercially known as the Astra 400, was the largest and most powerful of a series of similar automatic pistols; the model 300 chambered in 32 and 380, the model 200 in 25 caliber and, eventually, the model 600 in 9mm Luger, developed for sale to the German military as the Model 1943.

Astra was the company's trade name, and most Model 400 pistols, both commercial and military, carry the Astra trademark on slide and magazine floorplate. The device consists of the word "Astra" superimposed over a starburst and enclosed within a circle. Esperanza y Unceta was to become Unceta y Compania, probably about 1925. The firm is still registered under that name.

The Astra 400 is a straight blowback pistol in caliber 9mm Largo.

It shares other characteristics of the Campo-Giro, such as a cylindrical slide moving within frame grooves and a barrel-mounted recoil spring. However, many Astra features apparently derived from Browning guns, particularly one F.N. Military Pistol of 1903. Like the F.N., the Astra has a grip safety operated by a flat spring. The hammer is located internally, the barrel secured to the frame by a series of lugs. The Astra's breech-block is an integral section of the slide forging, and a removable barrel bushing is fitted to the slide's forward end. Other features, such as the sliding sear located at the rear of the hammer, the clever grip-safety ratchet that locks the sear, the vertically-moving slide stop, and the desirable "L" shaped pins, may have been Astra developments.

The Model 1921 marked a great advance over the Campo-Giro. It is a stronger, safer pistol, far more rugged and reliable, infinitely simpler to strip and clean. The excellence of the design is indicated by its long military life, during which no modifications or improvements were found necessary. The Astra remained the standard Spanish military pistol until after World War II, when it was finally replaced by the Super Star from Echeverria of Eibar. The Star is

also in 9mm Largo, but has a fully locked breech and is externally similar to the 1911 Colt 45.

Straight blowback systems are rarely found in pistols chambered for ammunitions more powerful than the 9mm Browning Long. The Astra Models 400 and 600 are the only ones that have proved completely successful, both empirically and commercially. These pistols, totally unlocked at the moment of discharge, rely solely on the inertia of their heavy recoiling parts to prevent premature opening of the breech. To supply the necessary weight, Astra 400 slides are particularly massive forgings, yet while the pistols are heavy, they still run 3 ounces lighter than 1911 Colts.

The Astra's long, heavy slide is not entirely a liability, the weight and its distribution promotes steady holding and good muzzle control; the massiveness offers a great margin of safety; the length permits a long sighting radius.

Trigger Pull and Safeties

W.H.B. Smith has said that the Astra 400 won many European awards for accuracy. There are several good reasons why the pistol should produce good target scores. Beyond the weight and long sight-

Astra Model 400

EXPLODED VIEW

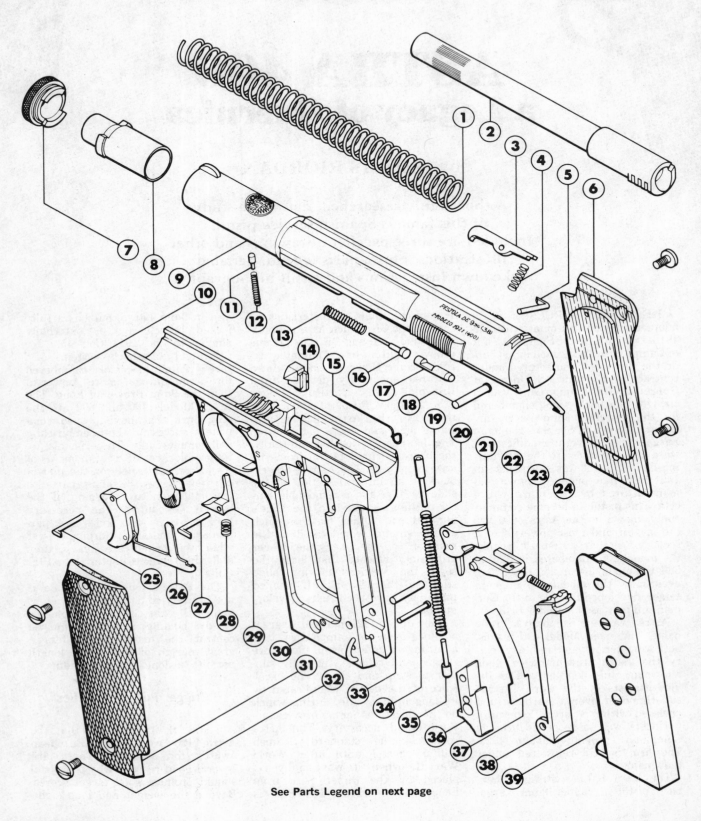

See Parts Legend on next page

Field Stripping

To field strip, remove magazine and clear chamber. Depress barrel bushing (8) flush with face of bushing lock (7), using lip of magazine floor plate. Turn bushing lock slightly so that it holds bushing depressed; grasp bushing lock firmly and rotate about ¼-turn until it unlocks from slide (9). Ease off bushing lock and bushing and remove recoil spring (1). Draw slide fully to the rear, then move slightly forward while engaging safety catch (10). Rotate barrel (2) counterclockwise to the limit of its movement, release safety and run slide and barrel forward off frame. Turn barrel lugs out of slide recess and pull barrel forward and out. In reassembly, locate barrel so that extractor notch faces downward while slide is mounted on the frame. Align lugs on barrel bushing and lock with slide channels when replacing these parts. Turn bushing lock until bushing snaps outward to retain it.

Disassembly

To strip slide, pry out extractor pin (24) with a small screwdriver inserted under its head. Remove extractor (3) and spring (4). Firing-pin extension (17), firing pin (16), and spring (13) are released by removal of their retainer pin (5). Notch in firing-pin extension must face toward extractor on replacement.

To strip frame, unscrew grip screws (32) and remove grips (6)(31). Push out magazine-safety pin (27) and lift out magazine safety (29) and spring (28). Insert magazine-safety pin in frame hole beneath rear end of trigger bar (26), pull trigger and lower hammer (21) with thumb. Push out hammer pin (18), releasing hammer, slidestop spring (15), and slide stop (14). Depress hammer plunger (19) with punch and remove magazine-safety pin. Push out magazine-catch stop (34) and grip-safety pin (33) to free magazine catch (36) and grip safety (38). Magazine-catch plunger (35), hammer spring (20), and hammer plunger can now be removed from bottom of frame. On replacement, the hammer plunger is identified by its concave head. With safety catch in disengaged position, push straight out of frame. Lift out safety detent (11) and spring (12). These parts must be depressed well into frame with a small punch while replacing safety. Pull downward and outward on trigger bar, while moving sear (22) and spring (23) forward into magazine well. Push out trigger pin (25). To remove and replace trigger and bar, pivot trigger forward, fully compressing the internally housed trigger-bar spring. Reassemble in reverse order.

ASTRA MODEL 1921 (400) Sectioned View

PARTS LEGEND

1. Recoil spring
2. Barrel
3. Extractor
4. Extractor spring
5. Firing-pin retainer pin
6. Right grip
7. Barrel-bushing lock
8. Barrel bushing
9. Slide
10. Safety catch
11. Safety detent
12. Safety spring
13. Firing-pin spring
14. Slide stop
15. Slide-stop spring
16. Firing pin
17. Firing-pin extension
18. Hammer pin
19. Hammer plunger
20. Hammer spring
21. Hammer and strut
22. Sear
23. Sear spring
24. Extractor pin
25. Trigger pin
26. Trigger and trigger bar
27. Magazine-safety pin
28. Magazine-safety spring
29. Magazine safety
30. Frame
31. Left grip
32. Grip screw (4)
33. Grip-safety pin
34. Magazine-catch stop
35. Magazine-catch plunger
36. Magazine catch
37. Grip-safety spring
38. Grip safety
39. Magazine

Cutaway shows relationship between internal parts. Pistol is pictured cocked and with chambered round, manual and magazine safeties disengaged, sear locked by grip safety. Parts are number-keyed to the parts legend.

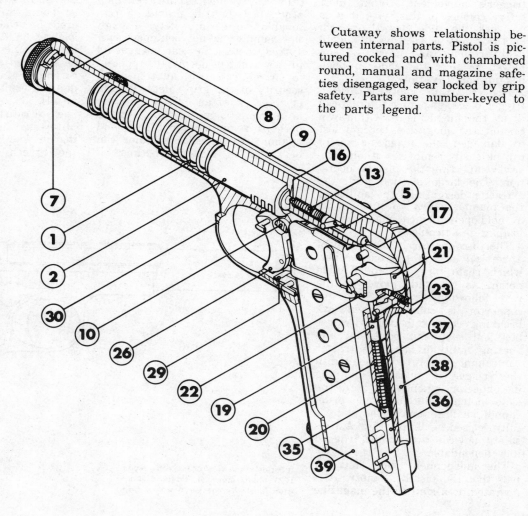

ing radius, the slide is well guided within grooves running the length of the Astra's frame. These grooves were fitted quite closely for a military pistol. Because the barrel is not required to move in firing, its lugs were made to engage their frame recesses tightly. For the same reason, the barrel bushing was given a close-tolerance fit to the barrel. Finally, the pivoted trigger operating a freely moving trigger bar, and the sliding sear engaging the rear of the hammer, combine to produce a smooth and unchanging trigger pull. Because the sliding sear is the vulnerable part of the trigger mechanism, it is important that the contacting surfaces between frame and sear be kept clean and smooth.

The grip safety is the primary safety device of the Astra 400. Its pivoting ratchet locks the sear and, resultantly, the hammer. Regardless of the condition of the manual safety, the sear is always locked until the pistol is actually held in the hand with the grip safety depressed by the palm.

The manual safety blocks the trigger's movement. Unlike most safety catches of this type, it does not lock the slide closed. An arm on the safety is used as an aid to field stripping, and it can be employed to lock the slide in open position at any time.

The magazine safety is also a trigger block, engaging automatically as the magazine is withdrawn. Should the magazine become lost or damaged, the magazine safety can be easily removed without otherwise affecting the pistol's operation. The large ejection port, the extractor design, and the ability of the manual safety to function as a hold-open device make single loading practicable.

The disconnector is comprised of a vertical arm of the trigger bar, which seats into a rounded slide notch. As the slide moves to the rear following discharge, the disconnector is cammed downward, breaking contact between trigger bar and sear and positively preventing multiple fire. The trigger bar cannot recapture the sear until the trigger is released and the disconnector again rises into the slide notch. Therefore the pistol cannot be fired unless the slide is fully closed. All of the Astra's safety devices are simple, rugged and dependable.

The independent slide stop signals that the pistol is empty. It is operated by a step on the magazine follower. The Astra's heavy gauge steel magazine is of seamless construction.

Field stripping the Model 400 is not difficult and it requires no tools. Such takedown results in 7 parts, none so small as to be easily lost. Complete disassembly presents no special problems and is facilitated by the slip fits given the pins, all of which can be pushed or pried out with little effort. All pins are mechanically retained within the assembled pistol.

Few Faults

Unfavorable characteristics are not particularly serious. The pistol is heavy and somewhat awkward to carry. The powerful recoil and hammer springs require a considerable effort to cycle the slide manually. The fixed sights cannot be knocked out of plumb and are virtually indestructable, but they do not allow of adjustment except by filing or brazing. There is no external indication of a chambered round. The manual safety is located a bit too far forward for thumb release in firing position. The Astra's safety devices are not foolproof, but they do provide a reasonable degree of safety. Though the hammer is not equipped with a safety notch, the sear engages its full-cock notch deeply, is unlikely to jar off, even without the added security of the grip safety. Whether the lack of an outside hammer is a point against the Astra is perhaps a matter for theory and opinion. An external hammer can be a mixed blessing, because it exposes a vital part of the firing mechanism to outside influences. The Astra's hammer cannot be struck a direct blow.

Probably the worst problem with this Astra is the difficulty of obtaining proper ammunition. The Model 400 has acquired a reputation for some reason, as having been designed to fire a variety of cartridges. This is a misconception; the pistol was designed and chambered for the 9mm Largo and no other. The use of substitute ammunitions has never been anything more than a matter of expediency.

Dimensions of the 9mm Steyr cartridge are so close to the Largo's that this ammunition has been used in the Astra pistol with great success. The rear of the case bulges slightly to conform to the Astra's chamber, but not to a serious degree. Unfortunately, Steyr ammunition is no less elusive than the Spanish Largo.

The 38 ACP round is nearly identical in length, but where the Largo and Steyr cartridges chamber on the case neck, the straight-sided Colt case simply wedges in the Astra's tapered chamber, driven home through the blow delivered by the heavy slide. When loading 38 ACP ammunition, it is therefore necessary that the slide be slammed closed to fully seat the cartridge. Manual extraction can be quite difficult in tightly chambered pistols. 38 ACP ammunition will operate satisfactorily in most Astra pistols, not at all in others, depending on whether the counterbore in the breech face is of sufficient

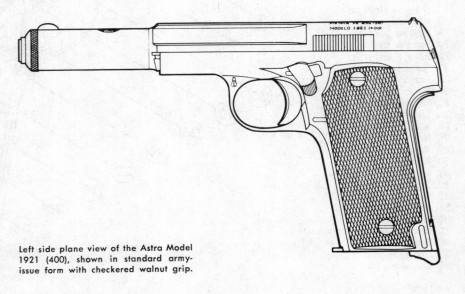

Left side plane view of the Astra Model 1921 (400), shown in standard army-issue form with checkered walnut grip.

diameter to accept the larger rim of the 38 case.

While the dimensions of the 38 Super case are the same as those of the 38 ACP, this round is too powerful for use in the Model 400. The 400 pistol does not use a recoil buffer, so 38 Supers cause excessive battering between slide and frame at the end of the recoil stroke.

The 9mm Luger cartridge can be dangerous. Much shorter than the Largo round, it must wedge at the rear of the chamber to operate properly. Some types of Luger ammunition, such as U.S. commercial and Canadian surplus, don't have a big enough base diameter to do this. As a result the extractor cannot snap over the case rim, but rather pushes the cartridge ahead of it, deep into the chamber. The Astra firing pin has a long reach and will usually fire a round so located, under a condition of grossly excessive headspace. Even with Luger ammunition that chambers adequately, the shorter cartridge has stacking difficulties in the magazine, with resultant jams.

If extensive shooting is wanted with the Astra 400, the 38 ACP is the logical choice. If necessary the counterbore can be opened up slightly to accommodate the larger rim.

Astra 400 Variants

Astra 400 pistols have evoked collector interest because of the variations reported. The standard Spanish model with moulded black composition or checkered walnut grips is by far the most common, though pistols displaying *Guardia Civil* markings are available in plenty. A mechanical variant has long been known, this version bearing a side-mounted magazine catch similar to that of the Astra 600. Astra pistols marked with German ordnance stamps, models with various commercial markings and special grips, and contract types carrying distinctive markings for individual Spanish services have all come to light in recent years. Additionally, copies of the Model 400 by other Spanish makers have been recognized, ranging in quality from poor to excellent.

But the big Astra is not essentially a gun for collectors; it has been brought into the country in numbers sufficient for distribution among shooters, and it is a gun well worthy of use. Fine quality steels, properly hardened, were used throughout its construction.

The quality of finish and fit is on a uniformly high level. The parts are rugged and strong, direct acting and simple. The action is very well enclosed against the entry of dust and sand. Above all, the gun

has rock solid dependability. It is weighty, but that weight means also strength and safety; homely, but absolutely the functional machine it was designed to be, a man's gun without compromise. ●

Astra Model 600 in 9mm (Luger). This model has a shorter barrel and redesigned magazine release located below the grip on the left side. Grips are of checkered walnut.

Bibliography

Study of Astra Model 400, Nos. 89188 and 103453, by Unceta y Compania S. A., Guernica, Spain.

Study of Astra Model 600, No. 37028, as above.

Dean A. Grennell, "Grand Olde Gun," *Gun World* magazine, September, 1968, p. 39. (F. N. Browning 1903)

E. J. Hoffschmidt, "Astra Models 400 and 600 Pistols," N.R.A. Firearms Assembly Handbook, vol. 2, p. 32.

Maj. Dick Keogh, "An Orphan Astra," *The Gun Report* magazine, August, 1970, p. 27. (Astra 400 copy)

Harold Murtz, "Astra Condor," *Guns* magazine, December, 1970, p. 42.

Maj. George C. Nonte, Jr., "Star's Modelo Super," *Gunfacts* magazine, July, 1969, p. 31.

Maj. George C. Nonte, Jr., "The Versatile Astra 400," *Gun World* magazine, September, 1969, p. 72.

Dale T. Shinn, "Campo-Giro—Spain's First Automatic Military Pistol," *The American Rifleman* magazine, November, 1969, p. 78.

Donald M. Simmons, Jr., "In Defense of a Tarnished Trio," *Guns* magazine, April, 1968, p. 24. (Astra 400)

Donald M. Simmons, Jr., "High-Power Blowback Pistols," *The American Rifleman* magazine, November, 1967, p. 61.

W. H. B. Smith, *Book of Pistols and Revolvers,* 6th ed. Harrisburg, 1965, "Astra 400," p. 370; "Browning 1903," p. 326.

W. H. B. Smith and Joseph E. Smith, *Small Arms of the World,* 7th ed., Harrisburg, 1964, "Spanish Pistols,"p. 543.

Capt. Robert D. Whittington, III, "Astra Pistols in the German Army," *Guns* magazine, November, 1968, p. 41.

J. B. Wood, "Viva Astra," *Gun World* magazine, February, 1966, p. 26. (Astra 400)

J. B. Wood, "The Adaptable Astra," *Shooting Times* magazine, September, 1968, p. 39. (Astra 400)

J. B. Wood, "The Count of Campo-Giro," *Guns* magazine, January, 1970, p. 42. (Campo-Giro pistol)

Gun Laws: Yesterday, Today and Tomorrow

Politics was once a dirty word among gun people. Lobbying was worse! For decades, the firearms industry and the shooting organizations alike shushed any mention of politics or lobbying, lest it draw fire from unnamed enemies. It was as if we were ashamed of our business, our sports, even of ourselves for being gun people.

There were reasons. Gunmakers wanted nothing so much as to forget the "Merchants of Death" labels stuck on them after World War One. Shooting groups wanted no attention drawn to their nonprofit tax exemptions. Millions of hunters, target shooters, gun owners generally, laughed at the threat of anti-gun legislation, smug in the belief that "It can't happen here! Not in America! We have the Second Amendment!"

So the courts took away our Second Amendment. (Now, we're shushed if we mention the Second Amendment. It's a dead issue, we're told; better forget it.) But the courts were mistaken. The word they tripped over was "militia," and the founding fathers defined the word in their debates. It meant "every citizen qualified to vote." It meant "the people." It did not mean any organized military organization, state or national, to be formed a century later. It was bred of the colonists' fear of the professional military systems of Europe, from which they had fled, and of their determination to establish here a means of national defense composed of citizens, armed and ready for a national need.

John F. Kennedy was well aware of the meaning, the intent, and the continuing importance of the Second Amendment. In a letter to my office in 1959, the then junior Senator from Massachusetts wrote:

> "By calling attention to 'a well regulated militia,' 'the security of the nation,' and the right of each citizen 'to keep and bear arms,' our founding fathers recognized the essentially civilian nature of our economy... The Second Amendment still remains an important declaration of our basic civilian-military relationships, in which every citizen must be ready to participate in the defense of his country. For that reason I believe the Second Amendment will always be important."

But it took the tragedies of Dallas and Memphis and Los Angeles, and the national hysterias that followed them, to shake our lethargy. So violent were the reactions to those assassinations that even the smug ones, even the timid ones who should have led us earlier but had shirked that leadership—even they were faced with the greater threat of extinction: extinction of the firearms industry and of the shooting sports. Belatedly, in sheer terror, even the smug and the fearful acknowledged that politics is, after all, by definition, only "the science of government," and that politics, even lobbying, was the only defense against the impending danger.

We reacted well. Not well enough, but better than our previous apathy portended. Thanks to a few staunch friends in Washington who kept their heads while all around them were losing theirs—and thanks especially to the determined groups of "little" people who refused to be shushed and went out and did the tedious, thankless tasks of grassroot politics—we weathered the worst of what our enemies intended. We took a licking in the enactment of the Gun Control Act of 1968; but in the national elections of that year we demonstrated at least a small part of the muscle that lies in our numbers. The defeats of Dodd, Tydings, Clark, and others were major triumphs, and there were other pro-gun victories at national and state, and local levels.

Those victories did not go unnoticed by other politicos. There has been a noticeable tendency in the Congress to heed ex-Senator Tydings' comment that only fools would ever again espouse the cause of anti-gun legislation, and the steady support of the Nixon administration has helped us lighten the GCA burden. But there is still a dangerously vocal, dangerously powerful hard core of anti-gun fanatics seeking to usurp the anti-gun springboard of free publicity which lifted Dodd to notoriety. Anti-gun-ism is not dead, will never die so long as a drooling media provides the publicity which is the life-blood of the movement—and so long as our cities need excuses for their crime problems. It is so easy, and so cheap, to say, "It's all because the crooks have guns!"

We know it's a lie, that gun laws have no effect on crime except actually to make crime safer for the criminal; but "It's a lie!" is not the answer. Shouting "It's a lie!"—and proving it—has not put Birch Bayh or Ted Kennedy or Stevenson or their cohorts out of office. Only one thing will do that: ballots. And only one thing will produce the ballots: work! Hard, door to door, thankless, persuasive, fact-spreading work at the political grass roots. Plus skillful, aggressive, make-no-secret-of-it lobbying in legislative halls, state and federal.

Given the work at the grassroots, and courageous leadership at the top, we could stud the future with accomplishments—defeat of the anti-gun fanatics, repeal of the GCA of '68, even re-interpretation by the courts of the Second Amendment. We have the political muscle to do it. Fifty million strong, united, who could stand against us?

Otherwise, the future of our industry and of our shooting sports is bleak. Apathy can never stand against fanaticism, and the threat is real. How will we meet it?

E. B. Mann

★SUPER★
SMOOTHBORES

Made in America

Now you can have that London-bespoke quality in a shotgun—or a rifle, for that matter—and at prices that'll surprise you! A great craftsman in Oregon, his skills and taste whetted to a fine edge, makes this seeming contradiction a reality.

by PEYTON AUTRY

EVERY AVID shotgunner has had a yen to own a highly personalized scattergun. Still, all too many of us have had to be satisfied with a yen or two, appeasing our expensive appetites with more mundane smoothbores. Now, though, there's more than a fond hope for the poor working stiff who yearns for that London-built double, one made every fraction of an inch just for him.

Typically, the budding fancier of fine shotguns is greatly taken by artistic engraving and fancy, figured wood. How does he get that way—and why? Let's take a close look.

First, he settles for a standard grade gun. Then, often without realizing it, he gradually works himself into the conviction that he should get one of the manufacturer's higher grade models, a gun with some nice engraving, a bit better wood and hand checkering. Later on comes the awakening, the realization that the ultimate gun is still much farther from his reach. He learns that other shotgun fanciers—for long years in some cases—have had guns built from the ground up to fit both their bodily framework and their artistic tastes as well. Such famed firms as Purdey, Boss, Holland & Holland, Rigby, Westley Richards and Francotte,

Merkel, Lebeau-Courally, Perazzi and Beretta on the Continent become names of enchantment. These people —and some others—in the past and now, will gladly build a completely personalized gun. For a price, and with delivery up to four years away. True, such made-to-measure guns are a far cry from any hand-me-down model, no matter how high the "grade." Such guns can't have the feel of a custom-fitted stock of ultra beautiful Circassian walnut or such niceties as the velvet smoothness of a gold-plated lock mechanism, specially cut stock hardware, special engraving designs, or a leather covered recoil pad.

The Browning superposed shown here was a high-priority project, made by McGuire especially for illustration with this article. All work—stocking, checkering and engraving—was done in McGuire's shop, including the London-style leather-covered stock pad mentioned in the story. McGuire also made another stock for this same Browning, equally beautiful, in pistol grip form. I very much regret we can't show this striking Browning in color, for the monochrome used here doesn't even begin to show the brilliant, flowing color of this Circassian wood—it's a riot of whirling golds, browns and rich blacks.

Considering the excellent quality of his work, McGuire's prices are moderate—$375 or so for boxlock stocks, $425 for sidelocks, $35 for his leather-covered pads.

You often hear it said that "they don't make 'em that way anymore." Unfortunately that's all too true, at least generally, even in Europe. They're not making them like they used to! However, it may surprise the "fine shotgun" nut to learn that truly top quality guns are available *today* in the United States!

It is no surprise that the U.S.A. is the birthplace of the custom built bolt action rifle. From the days of Sedgley, Hoffman, Owen, Niedner and Griffin & Howe to the Biesens, Goenses, Fischers, Brownells and Nelsons of today no finer sporters have been built anywhere else in the world. However, the truly custom-fitted, high grade double gun as made for the discerning shotgun shooter, has heretofore been conspicuously absent on these shores. Yes, a few such double guns have been built in the States but they have been done by knowledgeable customers who have coerced and cudgeled each artisan into doing each job separately. Unless the customer is an expert himself the end result is an expensive mal-coordinated hodge-podge, the truth of which is invariably revealed by the gun itself.

Bill McGuire Shotgun Specialist

Nevertheless, I know of one productive but little-known source of high grade personalized shotguns in this country. The gentleman's name is Bill McGuire of Seattle, Washington. For some years now McGuire has worked up fine custom shotguns, in his spare time, for a limited clientele of elite customers, such men as would be described by my old Oregon duck caller as "high falutin' shootin' gents."

Though McGuire is, then, well known to a relative handful of special customers and friends in the U.S., he's also recognized as a fellow craftsman and artist in the gunshops of London, having made many trips to Europe in connection with his custom gun work. He has tried out his guns on the red grouse of Scotland's moors as well as on the game birds of the Pacific Northwest.

Recently he resigned the post of research director for Eddie Bauer, the well-known Seattle outdoor outfitters, to form his own firm—Bill McGuire, Inc., Seattle. His new firm will take over manufacture of the Dem-Bart

line of hand checkering tools, but he'll also build fine custom-fitted, upgraded shotguns, his first love, and rifles as well. He has already made some fine rifles on Ruger's single shot actions.

His custom guns are built on a "you-order-it, we-make-it" basis. His shotguns are fitted to the customer in the finest Circassian walnuts, for he's developed a close association with the best sources of wood and other raw gun materials from all over the world. McGuire's long-time specialty is stock making and checkering, arts in which he excels. He is a master at glove-like inletting of sidelock guns. He has discovered several unusual, perhaps unique ways of speeding his work without any sacrifice of quality. Because of this he can produce excellent custom work at a price that is within reason. By contrast really good European work has risen tremendously during the last few years. McGuire's wood loft, happily, is well-stocked with exhibition grade blanks of luscious Circassian—and other fine woods—held in reserve for discerning customers.

The Browning over-under illus-

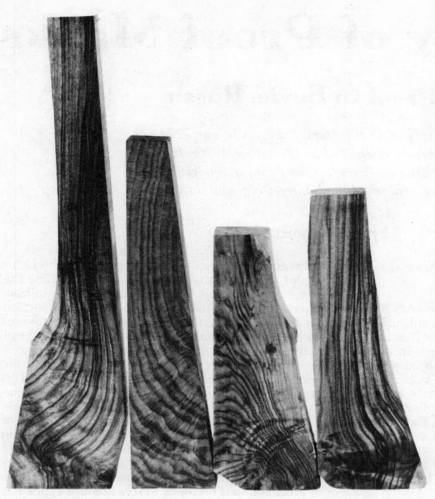

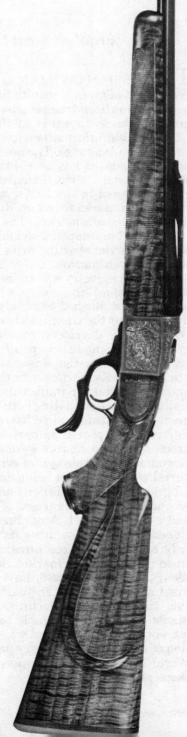

This Ruger single shot rifle was stocked with a superb piece of Claro walnut, then engraved and the action silver-greyed in McGuire's shop. The owner of this handsome rifle, modeled in classic fashion, is Dr. Dale Mitchell of Burien, Wash. ● Really good stock wood gets scarcer all the time, but McGuire obviously knows someone! From left—Circassian, Claro, two more Circassian.

trated here is a good example of a McGuire custom gun, the foundation a standard grade I Skeet gun, rebuilt by McGuire for a fastidious Skeet shooter to the latter's dimensions and desires. The action is gracefully rounded on the underside, which also helps to fend off finish wear of the edges. The safety-selector lever was removed (feasible on a tournament gun) resulting in a smooth-flowing tang and one presenting an attractive area for engraving. The action, tastefully engraved by a man on McGuire's staff, is greyed rather than blued, using a special process developed by Bill McGuire. McGuire contends that bluing the work of a first class engraver is like painting a Rolls Royce with a dimestore spray can. The leather-covered rubber recoil pads are hand-fitted, in a variety of colors, to match the wood used. The McGuire firm has a long list of optional extras which can be incorporated in a personalized gun.

All McGuire jobs may be had with the specialized features commonly associated with top quality European guns—hand-honed actions, gold plated action parts (any type of action can be specified), engraving, trunk cases, snap caps, special handmade fore-end irons and escutcheons.

McGuire's partner, George W. McVey, operates the Dem-Bart manufacturing division of the firm. He is also a master craftsman in handmade metal parts for McGuire custom guns.

●

Writers have been known to exaggerate a little, so I reached for the salt when Autry gave Bill McGuire such rave notices—not only in the article here but in letters and phone calls, where he was even more enthusiastic.

I'm no longer a skeptic—I saw and closely examined several guns by McGuire at the 1973 N.S.G.A. show, none of which was less than superb. McGuire's several skills are at the highest levels, and I envied the owners of the guns exhibited. Many London guns today, sad to say, aren't up to McGuire's work—or to their own former high standards.

Autry mentions "leather covered" recoil pads, a prosaic enough object normally. You'd have to see and handle McGuire's for real appreciation—they're honestly works of art!

The address for Bill McGuire, Inc., as well as for Dem-Bart, is 7749 15th Ave. N.W., Seattle, WA 98107. Descriptive brochures are now available from both.

J.T.A.

A History of Proof Marks

Gun Proof in Soviet Russia

This new "History of Proof Marks," begun in our 22nd edition, has been deeply researched by the author. With this issue we present our 7th installment, "Gun Proof in Soviet Russia," which we hope will be found interesting and instructive.

by Lee Kennett

Proof in Soviet Russia

THE RUSSIAN CIVILIAN arms industry has long been a sort of terra incognita for gun enthusiasts. In part this has been true because so few Russian civilian arms have appeared in the West; in addition, little reliable information has appeared, except in the Russian language. The dearth of information on proof procedures has been particularly noticeable. When Colonel Calvin Goddard compiled his monograph on proof in the 1930s, he was forced to show the various marks found on Russian military arms, for want of information. The data supplied here, while far from complete, should be of practical value now that Soviet sporting arms have been offered on the American market.

The arms industry was an important one in Russia as early as the 17th century, when several large centers were established to supply weapons for the armies of Peter the Great. Although the production of civilian arms developed rapidly, too, there was no system of compulsory proof during the Czarist regimes. The situation was unusual in that huge government plants, particularly those at Tula, Izhevsk, and Sestroretsk, manufactured both military and civilian arms, dominating both markets. The government plants also supplied barrels to private makers. Barrels were proved as part of the manufacturing process, but proofmarks were rarely applied. Baron Engelhardt was able to find evidence of two separate barrel proofs, the first being done, in 12 gauge, with 15 grams of black powder and a 30-gram ball; the second proof was composed of 13 grams of powder and a 30-gram ball. According to a Russian Encyclopedia of 1905, the arms factory at Tula was the only one which placed proofmarks on barrels destined for the civilian market. Several variant marks seem to have been used, having as a common element a smith's hammer (marks 1 and 2). At about this time the proof facilities of the government plants were made available to private gunmakers; moreover, the government was considering the adoption of a general compulsory proof system. The First World War and the Revolution of 1917 put an end to these plans.

Production of civilian arms resumed in the 1920s at the Tula and Izhevsk factories. By this time the arms industry had been completely nationalized, thus the government had a monopoly of production for both civilian and military arms. Since governmental controls could be exercised at every stage of manufacture, proof became but one of a series of tests for civilian guns. This is in part responsible for several unusual features of proof in the Soviet Union. While marks in other countries vary from time to time as changes are introduced, and thus provide a means of dating, marks on Soviet arms vary from one model to the next, and several with exactly the same meaning may be in use at the same time. While dating according to proofmarks is thus almost impossible, civilian arms rather consistently bear the year of proof stamped on them. Marks are also applied in a greater variety of places; in addition to barrel flats and water tables, they are also placed on the lumps or locking lugs, and on the upper surfaces of the barrels, usually near the breech.

Over the years a score of major shotgun models have been manufactured; the variation in marks is therefore considerable. The marks can be categorized according to their significance, but it should be borne in mind that no model will bear a mark of every category; thus the model MTS-6 shotgun, introduced in 1948, bore no proofmark, though it had been proved. The various categories follow:

Excess Pressure Proof

Testing was done for a number of years with both black and smokeless powders. The traditional series of black powder provisional, black powder definitive and smokeless powder definitive proofs was used in the case of some models. Certain models bore no proofmark on the arm itself, but proof data was supplied in an accompanying certificate. Provisional proofmarks are nos. 3 and 4; definitive proof nos. 5, 6, and 7; smokeless definitive marks are nos. 8 through 13.

Currently proof is standardized at Tula and Izhevsk, with only minor variations between the two plants. The following are the rules for proof of shotguns, the only type of arm for which detailed information is available:

Before being joined, barrels for doubles undergo provisional proof with smokeless powder, as follows:

Gauge	Proof Pressure	Proof Shot Charge
12	13,200psi	35 grams
16	13,900	30
20	14,700	25

Barrels intended for single barrel shotguns do not undergo this provisional proof; it is felt that the superior thickness of their walls makes this unnecessary.

All shotguns undergo definitive nitro proof as follows:

Gauge	Proof Pressure	Proof Shot Charge
12	11,800psi	35 grams
16	12,500	30
20	13,200	25
28	13,900	20
32	14,700	15

Accuracy and grouping proof: This type of test, virtually unknown in Western proof installations, is designed to verify accuracy and shot dispersion. For this purpose each barrel is fired at a circular target about a yard in diameter, at a distance of 40 yards. Not only must the gun put the shot where it is aimed, but there must also be even pellet dispersion and the pattern must conform to the degree of choke indicated on the gun. This test is designated by marks 14 and 15.

Maximum service pressure data: This is stamped on many guns as a guide to those who load their own cartridges. The pressure is given in metric atmospheres (marks 16-18).

Caliber and chamber designation: Either or both of these may be stamped (marks 19-25). Gauge may be indicated by the number "12," "16," etc., or by the chamber diameter in millimeters, or in case of mark no. 25, by both. Chamber length is given in millimeters (note that Russian and European practice generally is to mark off decimals by commas, rather than periods). The letter "K" in association with these marks stands for *kalibr* (caliber), or, as we say, gauge.

Choke designation: This may be indicated by giving bore diameters of choked and unchoked portions of the barrel (no. 26), or by use of symbols. In the case of marks 32 and 33, choke is indicated by "ds" numbers, these letters signifying *dulnoe suzhenie* or muzzle constriction. The numbers have the following meanings:

"ds" number	constriction in mm	U.S. equivalent
1	.25	Imp. cylinder
2	.50	Mod.
3	.75	Mod.-improved
4	1.00	Full
5	1.25	Extra full

Factory mark: Marks 34-40 are those used by the two main plants at Tula and Izhevsk. This is usually stamped, though in some cases the model stamp (MTS-6, etc.) may take its place.

OTK symbol: Each plant has what is known as an *otdel tekhnicheskovo kontrolya,* or technical control section. This is actually a quality testing division of the installation, charged with verifying the acceptable standards of workmanship, serviceability, etc. This is of great importance since the arms are not sold in a competitive market as we know it. The acceptance marks used by the OTK are nos. 41-45.

Steel type symbol: Such symbols are sometimes stamped on the arm itself, more often they appear in the data which accompanies the arm on the "passport," mentioned below. Marks 46-49 are examples of this type of mark.

Miscellaneous marks: Among these mark no. 50 indicates that the gun is intended for use with paper shells, rather than all-metal ones. Inspectors' or controllers' marks are frequently found; these are most commonly single letters enclosed within circles or triangles. All arms bear factory serial numbers, the digits often being preceded by a letter. Finally, most models are stamped with the year of manufacture; a few bear month and year (thus "VI-46" would mean production in June, 1946).

Accompanying each gun is a "passport," which is simply a descriptive folder. This gives complete details about the arm, information on the steel type and its physical properties, excess pressure proof, results of patterning tests, and even the type of wood from which the stock is made. The meaning of all marks stamped on the gun is given as well.

Current production is limited to a few tried and true models; the most recent export catalog lists one bolt action shotgun, one automatic, and seven doubles. There is a high degree of standardization. Only the 70mm chambering is currently used; doubles receive full choke in the left barrel and half choke in the right (different chokes may be had on special order).

In conclusion, Russian proof practices, though distinctive, seem thoroughly adequate. Proof pressures compare very favorably indeed with those used elsewhere. It seems logical to assume that such is also the case for centerfire hunting rifles now being developed for export.

Bibliography

There is a sizeable number of works on Soviet firearms; unfortunately none has been translated into English. For military arms to the end of the 19th century, there is an excellent work: M. M. Denisova, M. E. Portnov, and E. N. Denisov, *Russkoe Oruzhie* (The Russian Arm), Moscow, 1954. For civilian arms there are: M. N. Blium, *Sportivnoe Oruzhie* (The Sporting Arm), Moscow, 1954; and *Nastolnaya Kniga Okhotnika i Sportsmena* (Reference Book for the Hunter and Sportsman), Moscow, 1955. All have numerous illustrations and contain information about various marks.

The bulk of the information on proof itself was supplied through the kindness of Chief Engineer B. Robustov of the Tula Arms Factory and Engineer Nikolai Izmetinskii of the Mechanical Factory in Izhevsk.

Proof Marks of Soviet Russia

Schematic drawing of marks currently affixed to double barreled shotguns at Izhevsk.

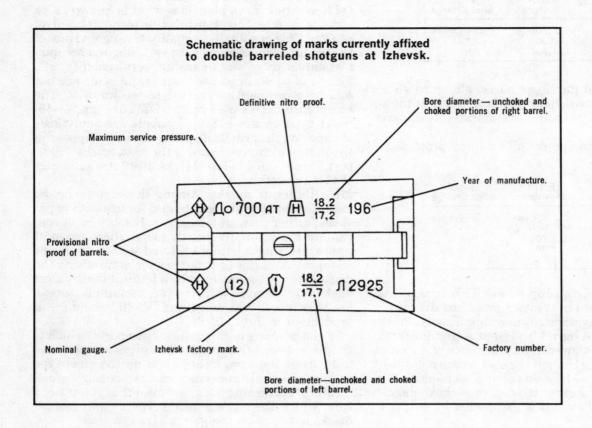

Definitive nitro proof.

Maximum service pressure.

Bore diameter — unchoked and choked portions of right barrel.

Year of manufacture.

Provisional nitro proof of barrels.

Nominal gauge.

Izhevsk factory mark.

Bore diameter—unchoked and choked portions of left barrel.

Factory number.

Schematic drawing of marks currently applied to double barreled shotguns at Tula.

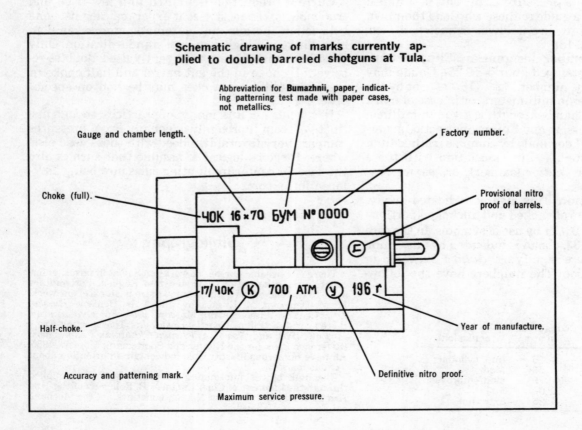

Abbreviation for **Bumazhnii**, paper, indicating patterning test made with paper cases, not metallics.

Gauge and chamber length.

Factory number.

Choke (full).

Provisional nitro proof of barrels.

Half-choke.

Year of manufacture.

Accuracy and patterning mark.

Definitive nitro proof.

Maximum service pressure.

Proofmarks affixed by the Tula Arms Factory before 1917.

1

2

Proofmarks at the Tula and Izhevsk Factories as of 1950.

Provisional proof marks.

3

4

Definitive proof marks.

Ⓤ

5

⬭У

6

(combined definitive proof and accuracy and grouping proof).

УК

7

Nitro definitive proof marks.

NITRO

8

НИТРО

9

Ⓗ

10

Ⓗ

11

$\dfrac{Б\ \overset{И}{\underset{Д}{}}\ П}{3,5\ г}$

12

ИСПЫТАНЫ БЕЗД. ПОРОХ.

13

Accuracy and grouping proof.

Ⓚ

14

Maximum service pressure marks.

700 АТМ.

15

До 700 ат

16

НЕ БОЛЕЕ 700 АТМ.

17

Caliber and chamber designations

⑫

18

16k

19

K16x70

20

12x70

21

70mm

22

$\dfrac{70}{20,7}$

23

$\dfrac{12X70,1}{20,65}$

24

Choke designations.

$\dfrac{16,9}{16,2}$

25

ЦИЛ
Cyl.

26

ЧОК
Full

27

⬥ 12/С
Full

28

П-ЧОК
Half

29

⬥ 12/%
Half

30

⬥ 12/4

31

$\dfrac{12К}{2ДС}$

32

Tula factory marks.

△T

33

34

△M

35

Izhevsk factory marks.

36

⬠☆

37

⬠ʎʎ

38

39

OTK symbols.

🛡K

40

Ⓚ

41

◇K

42

Ⓚ

43

⬭K

44

Steel-type symbols.

50РА

45

30ХН2МФА

46

50-А

47

ЗВХСА

48

(indicates gun designed to use paper cartridges).

БУМ

49

The Indian Enfield Carbine

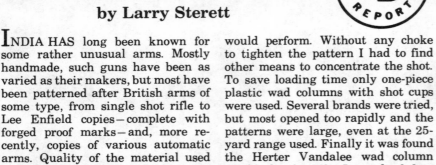

TESTFIRE GD REPORT

by Larry Sterett

INDIA HAS long been known for some rather unusual arms. Mostly handmade, such guns have been as varied as their makers, but most have been patterned after British arms of some type, from single shot rifle to Lee Enfield copies—complete with forged proof marks—and, more recently, copies of various automatic arms. Quality of the material used has been fair to good in the past, but now some standards have been set, and at least one enterprising firm has channeled the Indian effort into making black powder arms for the U.S. market. Two single shot smoothbores and a double barreled shotgun are currently available. One of the single shots—from the General Trading Co. of Clearfield, Utah—has recently been tested. Labeled the Enfield Carbine, and weighing 5¾ lbs., it has a 19½" barrel stamped .719" (bore diameter); the muzzle is a bit out of round, measuring from .720" to .734". It has been government proofed for 89 grains of black powder with 1¼ oz. of shot or ball. *It should not be used with smokeless powder of any type.*

The plastic-finished stock is said to be of teakwood, but that's questionable, and several knotty areas have been repaired. There are two iron bands used, with a sling swivel on the upper one and at the butt. The buttplate—held by two common wood screws—trigger guard and nosecap are brass. The front sight is an inverted V-block, the rear nothing more than a wide post with a small V-shaped notch—no adjustments of any kind. One of the handiest features is the swivel ramrod hinged below the barrel muzzle. Loading is simple and fast, once you establish a pattern or sequence, and you don't have to worry about leaving the ramrod lying somewhere. Being a smoothbore the Enfield can be used with shot as a brush gun on rabbits, or on deer when loaded with ball.

Next stop was the pattern board, to see how the cylinder bored barrel would perform. Without any choke to tighten the pattern I had to find other means to concentrate the shot. To save loading time only one-piece plastic wad columns with shot cups were used. Several brands were tried, but most opened too rapidly and the patterns were large, even at the 25-yard range used. Finally it was found the Herter Vandalee wad column would do the job. Instead of four slits, the Vandalee has only two, and they do not extend completely to the end of the cup. This means the cup does not peel back and release the shot charge as quickly.

Performance

At 25 yards, using 53.6 grains of Curtiss & Harvey's Fg black powder, a Vandalee wad column and one ounce of 5s, topped with a small wad of table paper as an over-shot wad, 5 shots averaged 100% in a 30-inch circle, with 75% inside the 20-inch ring. Switching to Herter's plastic "spinoff" overshot wads opened patterns to 63.4%, still not bad for a barrel without any choke. Some smaller shot sizes were also tried but the patterns were not as good or as consistent as with the 5s.

In many states shotguns and muzzleloading rifles may be used for hunting deer. Was the Enfield's accuracy with a solid ball good enough for whitetail, or similar size game?

A short search turned up some 69-cal. lead balls, which miked .680". The normal loading sequence for muzzle-loading arms consists of dropping a charge of powder, followed by ramming home a patched ball or lubed bullet. With the Enfield it seemed a better idea to load the lead ball into the plastic shotcup of a one-piece shotshell wad. Several wads were tried, but though they'd fit the bore when empty, adding the lead ball proved too much; it was impossible to ram the assembly home. Some walls were too thick, with others their ribs were in the way. Finally the Herter Chalice wad was tried. The shotcup has a rounded bottom which fits the lead ball perfectly, and the walls are thin enough to let the whole unit be pushed down the barrel without undue force.

Five of the lead balls averaged 466.3 grains each. A Mowrey "combination powder measurer and funnel" was set to throw 67.5 grains of C&H Fg powder. The standard military load for 69-cal muskets was 80 grains of FFg (C&H Fg is about the same grain size as du Pont FFg), and for 12-gauge shotguns it is about 82 grains with 1¼ oz. of shot. Thus all loads tried were well within the margin of safety and could be increased without any ill effects.

Firing was done at 50 yards from a kneeling position to determine if accuracy was good enough to make consistent hits on a deer size target—bench rests are fine for achieving maximum accuracy but they're seldom found afield when hunting, and the Enfield sights are crude and not adjustable. At 50 yards it was not hard to keep the 69-cal. balls on the target. The largest 3-shot group went just under 8 inches—remember this was from a kneeling position and with crude sights—and all shots were pretty much on the mark. There was some vertical stringing but almost no horizontal dispersion.

At 36⅝" the Enfield is a handy little black powder arm. It can be used with the 69-cal. Minie ball, too, if the ball is heavily lubed to hold it in the oversize bore, and even with regular home-cast 12-gauge slugs usually reserved for shotguns. Accuracy is satisfactory for short range shooting. If it had a pair of good sights it is probably capable of better accuracy, given proper load adjustment. Size 12 Remington percussion caps were a snug fit on the big nipple, but a standard nipple could be fitted.

If you want a rugged, big caliber, handy carbine-size black powder arm, then the Indian Enfield Carbine may be what you've been looking for. $75 may seem a bit steep but other black powder arms of lesser quality sell for more. It is fun to shoot, and it does produce a large cloud of smoke. •

Larry Sterett about to touch off the Indian Enfield carbine.

Shooter's Showcase

Ammo Boxes

Looking for paper boxes to hold your cartridges? This company has them — all sizes and shapes, from 22 Hornet to 45-90, also for nearly all handgun

and shotshell sizes. Prices run 20c-25c each. A full list is available — write to Shooters Supplies, 1251 Blair Ave., St. Paul, Minn. 55104.

Answering the Anti-Hunters

Sportsmen have an important and cogent answer to all the noisy nonsense currently coming out of the anti-hunting groups. That message is: *Hunters Pay for Conservation.* It's simple, to the point and absolutely true. Facts and figures prove it — the $108 million spent each year for hunting licenses goes to state game departments; $472 million has been collected for conservation since 1937 from the federal excise tax on sporting arms and ammunition; almost $8 million is spent each year on federal duck stamps.

To spread the word about the people who are really helping wildlife, the National Shooting Sports Foundation is offering a new *Hunters Pay for Conservation* kit. It contains a handsome, full-color 4″ brassard, with gold lettering, a matching automobile decal, and a pamphlet outlining the many contributions made by hunters to the welfare of wildlife.

Individual sportsmen can wear the Hunters Pay for Conservation emblem proudly. Clubs will want to sell the kits at a modest profit, give them to new members and award them as prizes to the winners of local shoots and matches.

With over $2.2 billion paid into the conservation coffers in less than 50 years, hunters are in a good position to argue for the future of their sport,

and it's high time the public knew about America's conservation financing. Putting on the patch and displaying the decal are steps in the right direction.

Individual kits are available at a cost of $2. Bulk packs of 24 kits are sold at a reduced price of $36. Orders can be placed by writing to John Chatellier, NSSF, 1075 Post Rd., Riverside, Conn. 06878.

Associated Industries

Old friend John R. (Jack) Hess, 8 years with the NRA as Public Relations Director, has joined A.I. in a similar job. Dwight F. Spear, head of the new A.I. firm, was formerly manager of membership promotion with the NRA. A.I. will specialize in firearm and outdoor products fields. The company is located at 1500 Massachusetts Ave., N.W., Washington, D.C. 20005.

Don Mitchell joins High Standard

Don Mitchell, formerly Marketing Director of Colt Firearms, is now chief executive at High Standard.

Mitchell, who started with Colt 7 years ago, created many programs there that were marked with success. He brought Colt into the black powder market with the Grant and Lee Commemorative revolvers, as well as directing their entire commemorative

program. Don also was responsible for the Combat Commanders, MK II revolvers, MK IV automatics, the New Frontier/Peacemaker, and the new Detective Special.

At home on the skeet and trap field, as well as on the business end of a fishing rod, Don is a real outdoorsman. He caught a record-class blue marlin in 1971 and is an avid big game hunter, using only a handgun in the field.

Omark-CCI

New for 1973 are CCI Maxi-Mag shotshells, intended for use solely in 22 WMR rifles or handguns. Each

cartridge contains ⅛-ounce of No. 11 shot, topped by a plastic capsule. Ten-inch patterns are obtained from a revolver at 15 feet, with excellent, uniform density. Packed 20 rounds to a flat plastic dispenser box of shirt-pocket size, the cost is $2.49.

Forest Service Cutback

Early in May (1973) DA Secretary E. L. Butz announced the closing of 5 regional U.S. Forest Service offices and the resultant loss of some 1000 jobs. Butz said "Early effort will be made to provide employment opportunities..." for them somewhere in the Forest Service.

We seriously doubt that even a small percentage of these people will be found jobs in the FS. More importantly, we also have grave doubts that "...these actions will enable the Forest Service to improve its efficiency and effectiveness in carrying out its resource management, research and state and private forestry programs." That is what Earl Butz said also, which amounts to getting more work done with fewer people and offices. This appears highly unlikely to us. J.T.A.

Sam Alvis-Wayne Leek

An old friend, Sam Alvis, is retiring at Remington, a man known to many of you through his answers to innumerable letters asking this, that and the other about Remington firearms, past or present. Samuel M. Alvis, Jr., who began working for Du Pont in 1928, went to Remington in 1941. For over 24 years Alvis was manager of the research division at Ilion, N.Y.

Taking on Sam's job is Wayne E. Leek, formerly manager of firearms research and design. Leek started his illustrious career with Remington in 1946 and, after serving in various capacities, became chief designer of firearms in 1961. Leek, liked and respected throughout the shooting world, headed design teams that produced the Nylon 66 rifles, the greatly successful Model 1100 auto shotgun and the brand new Model 3200 over-under 12 bore.

Hail and farewell to a couple of the great, good guys.

Hugger Hooks

Roman Products, long-time makers of the hooks that lock into pegboard (or other ⅛"-¼" boards, too), have added several new Hugger Hooks to an already extensive line, a line that includes plastic-covered styles that hold yet prevent injury to fine firearms.

The latest Hugger Hooks are called Mini-Brackets, designed to hold small parts jars, shelves, etc. Also new are J-Hooks, chiefly intended for the ceilings of rec vehicles with camper shells, but useful in many other places.

Roman Products will gladly send full information on styles and prices.

Plastic-covered Hugger Hooks hold firearms of all types safely, and they won't injure the finest guns.

Northern Instruments, Inc.

This company makes a wide range of rust- and corrosion-inhibiting products, some of which have high value for gun owners and outdoorsmen specifically. New for shotgun users is Stor-Safe Gun Protector, a simulated shotshell (12, 16, 20, and 410) which, placed in the chamber(s), protects barrel, action and magazine (if any) against rust and corrosion for two years. These can be carried afield and slipped into the gun after a day's shooting for full protection. Under $20.

Also new this year are Stor-Safe Vapor Strips and Sports Gear Protectors. Two Vapor Strips, placed in a tightly-closed container, protect the contents (up to 3 cubic feet) for two years. $1.49 for two units. Sports Gear Protectors work similarly but cover 5 cubic feet, and they're indicated for use in sleeping bags, tents in storage, gun cabinets, etc. $1.98 each. See your dealer or write to the firm at 4599 N. Chatsworth St., St. Paul, MN 55112, for more data on these and other products.

The Stor-Safe Gun Protector, made in 12, 16, 20 or 410, offers 2-year bore and action freedom from rust or corrosion.

Custer Battle Prints

Lisle Reedstrom is an artist whose work has appeared in the GUN DIGEST numerous times. He is also a General Custer buff. Combining his knowledge of the Little Big Horn fight and his skill with pen and brush, Reedstrom produced two prints on posters, each 29"x35", each depicting the salient figures who participated in that bloody battle.

One print shows the officers, the other portrays the Indians—three figures on each poster are in full color. Reedstrom has done a fine job, and these prints will be welcomed by enthusiasts of the period. The prints are available from Custer Battlefield, Attn: Mr. J. D. Young, Custer Battlefield National Monument, Crow Agency, MT 59022. Each print is $1, plus 50c postage, or $2.50 for both, postpaid.

Excise Revenues Increase

The 11% Federal excise tax on long guns and ammunition brought in over $35.7 million for conservation during fiscal 1972 compared to nearly $29.5 million for 1971. At the same time, excise revenues from handguns rose to $7.6 million, an increase over the 1971 figure of almost $400 thousand. That's $43 million for conservation-related purposes.

Targ-Dots

Want an instant, brilliant target? Targ-Dots are made of brightly fluorescent red paper, self-sticking, and come in 5 sizes—½", 1", 1½", 2" and 3"—and they're not expensive. The 3" diameter size costs $4 per 100, and the smaller sizes are less, of course. Just peel them off the roll supplied, and stick 'em onto most anything.

I've used Targ-Dots for years, and they're especially worthwhile when the day is dark—they really stand out.

Write to Peterson's Labels (Box 186, Redding Ridge, CT 06876) for details and data on these and other products—Ammo Box Labels, target pasters, new square Targ-Dots, etc.

Western Cutlery Co.

This old-line firm, makers of good factory knives since 1897, offers a 1973 complete line catalog that's yours for the asking. In it you'll find a great variety—pocket knives of many styles, sheath knives priced from $5.50 to $18.95, several Bowies (24 to $32) and knife axe combinations, with special sheaths.

Their best hunting knives are the Westmark brand, handcrafted from rust-resistant high-carbon steels, the handles laminated hardwoods. Each comes in a scabbard of triple-thick cowhide, moulded to the blade and heavily stitched. These are excellent knives; I've used the No. 702 Westmark for several years with full satisfaction. The Westmark illustrated here is the No. 701, an all-purpose type with 5½" blade.   J.T.A.

Coulter Flares

Hunters do get lost. These flares ignite at 500 feet above the shooter, produce a brilliant red glow 15 times brighter than a railroad flare, drop slowly and go out at 200 feet, falling to earth harmlessly. They're propelled from the hunter's rifle (or 12 gauge only shotgun), but calibers available are rather limited—30-06, 308, (300 Savage, 358, 30-30, 32 Spl., 303 Savage), 35 Remington, 300 H&H and 8x57 mm. A packet of any 3 is $2.95 list, and they're made by Marsh Coulter, Box 333, Tecumseh, MI 49286.

Well-Armed Britons

British authorities report that, between July and October of 1972, anti-hijacking measures at London airports resulted in the discovery of 19 firearms, 400 knives, axes and similar instruments, one package of rocket fuel and a camel whip. In a country where the tightest possible handgun controls have been in effect for 50 years, people still find ways to arm themselves for criminal purposes.

$53 Million to States

Distribution to the States of $53,145,000 in Federal aid was announced in January of this year by Secretary of the Interior. Over $12,100,000 is for sport fishing projects, $37,263,500 for wildlife and $3,781,500 for hunter safety programs.

Fish restoration funds come from a 10% excise tax on certain articles of fishing tackle. Distribution is made according to a formula based on the number of fishing license holders and the area of each State, including coastal and Great Lakes waters.

Wildlife restoration funds derive from the 11% excise tax on sporting arms and ammunition and the 10% excise tax on pistols and revolvers. The distribution for wildlife restoration is based on a formula which takes into account the number of hunting license holders and the area of each State. These funds may be used on approved State wildlife projects which include acquisition and development of land suitable for habitat, etc.

Hunter safety funds, based on the relative population of each State, may be used for hunter safety programs, including construction, operation, and maintenance of public outdoor target ranges. The States, however, may use these funds for wildlife restoration projects also.

Wilderness Survival

Every year sees a fair number of people lost in the wilderness. Some get home, some never do. Now, if you're a hunter intending to go into trackless areas, if you may find yourself, for any reason, heading into unknown country, there's a course in survival training you can take.

Write to Return Survival School, 1718 N. Normandie, Spokane, Wash. 99205 for the booklet on their 5-day courses.

John J. Schwarz

This owner-operator of Schwarz's Gun Shop—custom gunsmiths for 35 years—is also a maker of fine knives. The three shown are typical of Schwarz's work, but he's also prepared to copy any knife sent to him,

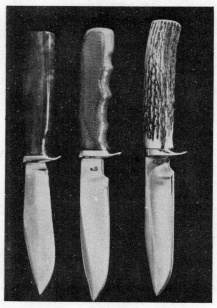

or a drawing thereof. The blade at left has a burl walnut handle, the middle knife one of natural Micarta, and the last one has handles of Sambar stag. The shop is at 41 Fifteenth St., Wellsburg, WV 26070.

Garcia Hunting Annual

Here's a big value for $1, and I hope you can find a copy—this 1973 issue was released last April. Full of good color photos, this 8½"x11" softcover book devotes 80 of its 130 pages to feature articles covering the gamut of hunting in the U.S. plus one on African safaris. The 48-page catalog section shows all Garcia firearms, plus camping gear, etc. Prices are not shown, but I'm sure a note to Garcia will fetch one.

Trajectoplots

These are small (about 3" x 5") card-like plottings of trajectories that may be carried handily in the shirt pocket, thus full data is instantly available on such load-performance factors as mid-range height, drop, etc. Most of us "know" these things to a degree, but often enough to a small degree. The Trajectoplot eliminates the guesswork. Available in 243, 6mm, 264, 270, 7mm Rem. Mag., 308, 30-06 and 300 Win. Mag., they're $1 each, any 6 for $5. Write to W. G. Dykes, P.E., 802 Santa Rosa Dr., Vicksburg, MS 39180.

Game Winner

One of my favorite hunting jackets, for mixed conditions, is Game Winner's reversible coat—green camouflage color one side, blaze orange on the other, both sides with good pocket space, and a snapped flap over the heavy-duty zipper. Included is a zip-attached hood. This jacket (their No. 12511) is lined with Dacron 88 for good warmth—with the hood up and drawstring closed, this coat handles a lot of cold weather. I've also got their reversible matching cap (No. 10099), which I find myself using when it turns a bit warmer.

Game Winner makes a very wide range of hunting clothing—jackets, vests and pants of various weights and colors, including some things for women. Write for their 1973 big full-color catalog. The address is 515 Candler Bldg., Atlanta, GA 30303

E.C. Prudhomme Master Gun Engraver

Jack Prudhomme—whom I've known for nearly 25 years, and who engraved several firearms for me during that time—had 56 handguns and shoulder arms on loan exhibit earlier this year at the R.W. Norton Art Gallery in Shreveport, La. All of the guns on view had been engraved by Prudhomme, many of them also inlaid with gold, platinum or silver.

This splendid tribute to Prudhomme's artistry ran from April 1 to May 13, the wide variety of arms handsomely displayed. A fully illustrated 32-page catalog of the exhibit (all but two of the 56 guns are illustrated, including some in color) is available from the Museum at $3 postpaid. Write to the R.W. Norton Art Gallery, 4700 Creswell Ave., Shreveport, La. 71106. This limited-issue catalog will probably become a collectors item.   J.T.A.

Profile Publications Ltd.

Profiles are paper bound booklets of some 24 pages or 10,000 words, including 40-50 illustrations—photos and diagrams plus color drawings—put together by a highly competent team of writers, editors and researchers. Technical and historical data are offered, objectively and factually treated. Mr. A. J. R. Cormack is the editor. All book production is done in England.

While *Profiles* cover warships, aircraft, cars, etc., what we'll comment on here are the small arms series, now totaling 17 titles, each $2.

So far covered are:
1. Webley and Scott—auto pistols
2. Browning—auto pistols
3. Luger—auto pistols
4. Thompson—SMGs
5. Colt—45 auto pistols
6. Walther—auto and flare pistols
7. Heckler & Koch—auto pistols
8. Erma—SMGs
9. Beretta—auto pistols
10. SIG—service rifles
11. Winchester—rifles mostly
12. Russia—SMGs
13. Bren guns
14. Enfield muzzleloaders
15. Astra—pistols and revolvers
16. Colt—percussion revolvers
17. Smith & Wesson—tip-up revolvers

These are excellent monographs, all of them, if necessarily brief in coverage. They should make fine introductions for the starting collector/gun buff, and they can be considered first class references.

Each of the 17 issues has, on the inside front cover, a 1934 Beretta auto pistol shown taken down, and a glossary keyed to the components. Why this page is used with such Profiles as Nos. 4, 8 or 10, et al, is unexplained.

The United States address for Profile Publications, Ltd., is Box 2368, Culver City, CA 90230.

Kwikfire Gun Sling

If you'd like to see how this new sling works, write Wayne Products Co., Box 247, Camp Hill, PA 17011, for a fully detailed brochure—I can only give you a hint in this space! Briefly, this 1-inch patented web sling lets the rifle or shotgun hang securely across your chest area, sort of port-arm fashion, leaving both hands free—which is a boon indeed in cold weather. Then, sighting game, the gun can be brought to the shoulder instantly, much faster than it could be from the usual slung-on-the-shoulder position. The new sling is $3.95, postpaid anywhere in the U.S.A.

One-Step Gun Care

What's that? TSI-300, a space-research derived chemical that cleans, lubricates, penetrates and prevents rust and corrosion. It is non-flammable, and it contains no petroleum-based components such as carbon tet, silicates, etc. TSI-300 lubricates efficiently and prevents rust because it displaces moisture—actual or potential, by creating a film on the surface of the metal. The original packaging—1¼-oz. plastic bottle at $1.49 or 4-oz. aerosol spray cans for $2.98—has been joined by a big spray can, the Professional Gunsmith's Package of 20 ounces, cost $6.98.

Our test supply of TSI-300 performed well, and as indicated. It makes a surprisingly good lube, I found—I tried it for case lubing in full-length sizing, and it worked as well as the many others I've used for years.

TSI (Glenside, PA 19038) has another product to interest handloaders particularly. This is TSI-400 Ammo Brass Cleaner, a product that's safe to use and non-etching. Just soak the cases for a moment, remove and rinse, then dry. All corrosion and oxidation, inside and out, has been removed, and the cleaner is indefinitely reusable! A 16-oz. plastic bottle sells for $2.98.

Shaw-Leibowitz

Until I saw their work a few years ago I hadn't believed that *etching* could be anything like as good as it really is. Pure ignorance, I guess. S-L work approaches fine hand engraving, and if you'd like to see numerous examples of their skill, ask for a new catalog, just received. It's full of well-photographed specimens—firearms, knives, medallions, et al—all done by hand, mind you, and therefore every piece is different, even if the same basic pattern is asked for.

Shaw-Leibowitz, Rt. 1, Box 421, New Cumberland, W. Va. 26047.

The Atlantic Flyway

A superbly done history of this great flyway, this is, too, an important book if its critical appraisal of the grave conditions threatening the Atlantic Flyway can be absorbed—it is fervently hoped—and acted upon. In a recent letter to me, the author said: "What happens to this great Flyway in the next couple of decades—whether it's preserved and even improved or whether it's buried under heaps of garbage, miles of factories, and endless housing developments—is pretty much up to people like your readers." I can't put it better.

Bob Elman wrote the text, the late Walter Osborne made the many great photographs in this 204-page book (including an extensive bibliography), and it was published by Winchester Press in 1973. $15.   J.T.A.

Knife Kits

Indian Ridge Traders (P.O. Box X-50, Ferndale MI 48220) is offering a complete line of do-it-yourself knives in kit form. The blades are shaped, polished and ready for final honing and are offered in a myriad of shapes and sizes to suit almost any need.

The Sheffield line of blades are made of high carbon cutlery steel, each heat treated to proper hardness for the particular uses of the pattern. All have an established edge grind. The tangs are drawn down in hardness so you can drill, saw, tap or thread them without trouble.

The "American Line" of blades features styles like the 4" Ripper, 5" Camp Knife, 5" Buffalo Skinner, and a line of kitchen blades for everything from paring work to slicing steaks and chops. The blades come in ancient patterns and designs chosen by those that work with knives eight hours every day. They are made of just plain old-fashioned high carbon steel that stains in use but sharpens so readily that it is still the steel choice among professionals.

You can order just the blade and fashion handles of your own material or order the blade, laminated hardwood pieces saturated with phenolic resin, rivets and epoxy cement and go to work from there.

Prices are surprisingly low—the 5" Buffalo Skinner blade sells for $2.00. Handles are $1.50, rivets $1.50 and the epoxy is $1.75. Write for their large, illustrated catalog for full facts and prices.   H.A.M.

Johnny Stewart Game Calls

Stewart's game and varmint calling instruments are too well known to need extensive review here. They're of consistently high quality, they're self-contained and battery-operated, with provision for 8-watt or 25-watt separate speakers; and that he offers a big variety of records. The record machines start at $69.95 and go to $149.95, this last including his 25-watt speaker and a microphone for public address usefulness.

The latest of Johnny's callers is the DeLuxe 600M, the only "cassette tape" machine on the market, I believe. Light and rugged (9 or 11¼ pounds, depending on the speaker selected, and cased in tough Cycolac), the 600M gets some 25 hours of operation from a set (12) of standard D-cells. I like the sound quality of this tape box very much, and it will handle all standard music or voice cassettes, not only his game-varmint calls. The cassettes are well protected against dust, too, via *two* dustproof covers— one for the tapes and the lid itself.

The Stewart cassettes sell for $7.95 each — and he's got them for all effects — playing time 30 minutes each side. The 600M with an 8-watt speaker is $169.95; add $20 if you want the 25-watt speaker. Write to J. S. at Box 7594, Waco, TX 76710 and you'll receive full details free.

Rusteprufe

This well-known powder solvent and rust preventive — in use now for 30 years — needs little introduction, but the company's Chamois Wiper Kit deserves more recognition. The Chamois (not fabric) is marketed in a tight, dust-free container which also holds a Rusteprufe-soaked felt disc. Wiping the gun — or other metal — leaves a thin film that inhibits rust indefinitely. Two ounces are 85c, pints and quarts $2.95 and $4.95.

Vibro Burgess

Vibro-Tools, Electric Pencils, Vibro-Markers — all are names for the several such tools made by Burgess Vibracrafters of Grayslake, Illinois.

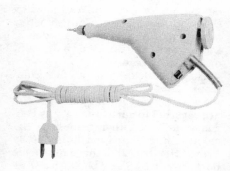

All are 110-volt powered, offer up to 7200 strokes on impact per minute for a multitude of uses — marking tools, leather, glass or anything you like; engraving the toughest metals, filing, the list is long indeed. A tungsten-carbide point is the means of doing these multi-chores, but Burgess offers a big variety of other points as well — 22 altogether.

The Vibro-Marker and Vibro-Graver have become increasingly popular for marking valuable objects in the home and in industry to decrease theft. "Operation Identification," now receiving national attention and wide approval by the media and numerous law-enforcement agencies, suggests the use of a marking tool. Burgess offers an "Operation Identification" package — the Vibro-Marker, two window warning stickers and 10 "Stop, Thief" labels for use on portable valuables, plus instructions on joining the national program. Price of the V-600-1 outfit is $9.95. Other Burgess vibro-tools run $7.95 to $23.95.

The 22 Rifle

That's the title of a new book that is highly recommended. If you have a youngster — boy or girl — that wants to shoot, or one just beginning the sport, this is their book. The author begins with a chapter on safety precepts and safe gun handling, quite rightly, and goes from there to cover the 22 rimfire rifle in all its many forms, its care, use, its sights, etc. There's even a chapter on 22 centerfire rifles.

The author is Dave Petzal, managing editor for *Field & Stream* and a long time shooter-hunter. 143 pages, plus an index, numerous illus., cloth-bound, $5.95.   J.T.A.

Public Servants Pack Pistols

The California Legislature recently passed a bill which will greatly increase the number of gun-toting peace officers in the Wild West. The measure, opposed by Golden State police spokesmen, allows various guards, messengers, inspectors and other public employees to go about armed. Oddly enough, the legislation was founded on a combination of urban lawlessness and anti-gun sentiment. State Senator Alfred Song told his colleagues the bill was particularly needed by Los Angeles City and County employees because the L.A. Sheriff refuses to approve handgun permits. Sen. Song said, "There have been murders, there have been shootings, there have been knifings, but no one — absolutely no one — can get a gun permit from the sheriff there."

W. C. Strutz

Custom gunsmith Strutz specializes in metal work — barreling, chambering, bolt alterations and all related work on bolt action rifles. He also supplies complete rifles (stocked by Bishop or Fajen), the actions most anything commercially available, and at this time he is offering extra-quality rifles on the Sako L461, L579 and 661 actions. These are barreled to the customer's choice in caliber and contour, then stocked in fancy grade woods. Strutz has a detailed brochure ready for the asking.

Golden Rods

These are low wattage (8 to 25, and 12" to 36" long) thermo-electric dryers designed to keep guns — or other objects — warm and dry, free from rust. The sealed electric elements, enclosed in a slim metal tube, are guaranteed for 5 years. At

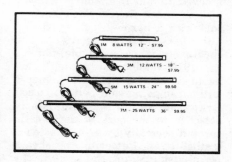

$7.95 to $9.95, each, and costing only pennies a day to operate, Golden Rods are good insurance and worry-free products. Write to Phinney-Hale Corp., Box 5286, Oxnard, CA 93030 or see your dealer.

Hunting Licenses Decline

Fishing licenses reached a record level last year, but hunting license sales in 1972 fell below the 1971 record.

In all, hunters and fishermen spent more than $214 million last year for licenses, tags, permits, and stamps, an increase of $6 million over 1971. Hunting license holders decreased by 675,084; the 1972 total was 15,298,243. Expenditures by hunters for licenses and permits, which exceeded $108 million in 1971, came to $107,310,803 last year.

Loc-Knife, Inc.

In general form the Loc-Knife is fairly normal—4 blade lengths are offered, 4½″ to 6″ in several configurations, mirror or satin finished, and with handles of brown or ivory Du Pont Zytel, skip-checkered and with

brass spacers at the hilt end. These knives are all full-tang type for great strength, the hilt knobs of dural and carrying a formed piece that lets the special Loc-Knife sheath be snap-fastened to the knife for safety and ready removal.

Each Loc-Knife is hammer forged from Swedish steel, and all have a grooved thumb rest and a cutaway for the index finger. Each knife is sold with a harness leather sheath, fiber lined to prevent corrosion. Two sheath styles are available, but it's the 1970 version that's highly unusual; it can be put on or removed without undoing your belt, and a soft Arkansas stone is permanently attached to the back of the sheath, covered normally by a snap-fastened leather strap. Removing the sheath permits sharpening the knife in the field, and the stone can't be lost.

Prices run about $26 to $40, and a full-color leaflet is yours for the asking on these U.S. patented products. Address the company at 11717 E. 23rd St., Independence, MO 64050

Knife Collectors Club

Behind this new organization is A. G. Russell, operator for some time of Morseth Knives, and a long-time source of the finest in Arkansas sharpening stones. Membership, at a one-time $4.50, is open to anyone who has bought one or more knives issued by the Club, and members only may buy the specially decorated grades of knives, and they're offered a discount on "collector grades."

The "Kentucky Rifle" knife is Commemorative No. 1. 11,867 of these were made in a $15 version, half of which are reported to have been sold by February, 1973. Another grade, the Excelsior, has engraved bolsters by Frank Hendrix and the main blade floral etched by Shaw-Leibowitz. Only 122 of these exist, their price $60.

In the Premier grade, all have 14K solid gold bolsters and an inlaid Kentucky rifle, also 14K, the engraving on these done by Lynton McKenzie. All three blades carry game/scroll etching by S-L. These are $350 for numbers 3 to 15 (five already sold), $400 for No. 2, and No. 1 sold at $500. Serial No. 0? A.G. is keeping that one for himself.

Write to the K.C.C. at 1705 Hiway 71 North, Springdale, Ark. 72764, for further details.

9422 Winchester Trigger Shoe

Williams Gun Sight Co. offers a wide, serrated trigger shoe for the new Winchester 9422. Closely machined for a snug fit, the shoe's extra width and natural contour provides a much better trigger feel, greater

comfort and control and, of course, more accurate shooting. Made from a rust-proof alloy and blued to match the attractive finish of the new 22 Winchester, the Guide Trigger Shoe sells for $2.95.

H&R

Harrington & Richardson, Inc., established in 1871, was bought in early 1973 by a small group of individuals headed by C. Edward (Ted) Rowe, Jr., president of H&R. Mr. Rowe then became chairman of the board as well. H&R operations will continue as usual and no personnel changes are anticipated.

H&R makes a complete line of sporting firearms and accessories. It is also exclusive U.S. distributor for Webley and Scott, Ltd., of Birmingham, England, makers of fine double barrel shotguns, and of Hardy Bros. (Alnwick, England), world-famous fly rods, reels and accessories.

Hoppes No. 9

Once upon a time that was about all that Frank Hoppe made and sold—and it's still, most likely, their

New Penguin "Sta-Put" trap.

leader in unit volume, if not in dollars. Today, though, following the merger or whatever between Hoppe and Penguin Industries a while back, they market more shooter-hunter products than I could describe if I covered this page and a couple more. The long list includes, to name only a few items, shooting sticks, bench rest bags, gun cases, glasses, traps, gun lamps (!), gun hangers, *ad inf*. O, yes, Hoppe's No. 9 and a host of cleaning and refinishing materials, too, including Reemay® patches for bore cleaning, a recent development by Du Pont made of spunbonded polyester fiber, said to give better scrubbing action, no lint, etc. Penguin address is Box 97, Parkesburg, PA 19350.

Remington Sportsman Library

Outdoor Tips is only one of a dozen or so titles on Remington's 1973-74 book list. In its 190 pages, this volume covers camping, rec vehicles, etc., plus a thousand and one valuable bits of information. Send $2.95 to Box 731, Bridgeport, Conn. 06601 and ask also for the complete list of RSL titles.

AMERICAN BULLETED CARTRIDGES

by KENNETH L. WATERS

A check list of current metallic cartridges, domestic and imported, plus a guide to performance and selection.

DEVELOPMENTS IN METALLIC CARTRIDGES

For a number of years past we have used this preface to American Bulleted Cartridges to inform readers of new developments in the field of metallic cartridges occurring during the previous twelve-month period. As readers of this section know well, the prevalence of product introductions and changes in the cartridge line-up have varied enormously, ranging from boom years when there was almost too much to cover, to periods of near-stagnation. In between, we've witnessed times of consolidation and—unfortunately—some retrogression in the form of un-announced deletions.

This writer, for one, does not believe that all of these mercurial ups-and-downs can be explained away because of shooters' demands. There have been too many innovations which failed of general acceptance, too many un-asked for and unwanted removals, and an insufficient response to requests for items clearly needed, readily discernible as practical and, in most instances, capable of economical development and production.

To their credit, Winchester-Western realized their error in dropping the great 220 Swift and reinstituted it in their line-up (as reported in last year's ABC section). Also several ammunition makers have recognized the existence of a wide-spread demand for light-bullet, high-velocity handgun cartridges, giving us some truly significant factory loads in this area. But all too frequently, opportunities to score successes have been either passed over or ignored.

1972-73 was just such a year, with little in the way of new items appearing. It was, in fact, more notable for those things which should have been brought out but never arrived. For this reason, it was decided to devote the current ABC section primarily to a discussion of what is truly needed in the factory ammo line-up, in the probably vain hope that someone in the industry will find themselves in agreement with us to the point of doing something about it.

I. New Loads Needed For Existing Calibers Rifles

Although the 220 Swift established its reputation for great velocity with a 48-gr. bullet, it would make a lot more sense if Winchester-Western were to load this fine cartridge with the ballistically better 55-gr. slug, more resistant to wind deflection and capable of retaining a higher percentage of its initial velocity and energy over long ranges. The superior 55-gr. PSP bullet is already being loaded in their 225 and 22-250 Super-X and Super-Speed cartridges, so no new manufacturing would be entailed.

Another good example of the practicality of my suggested process of using existing components to produce a more varied and useful factory cartridge line-up is to be seen in the little 25-20 round; both major ammunition makers have abandoned the 60-gr. hollow-point loading, thereby stripping away fully half of its potential as a combined varmint and small game cartridge, while retaining the un-needed and decidedly less accurate 86-gr. lead bullet. Since Winchester still makes a 25-caliber open-point expanding (OPE) bullet in 60-gr. weight for their 256 cartridge, I see no reason why this same slug couldn't be loaded in their 25-20, thereby restoring that round's usefulness for varmint shooting. I do it regularly with handloads for my 25-20s, finding it both more accurate and flatter shooting due to its very considerably higher velocity. This would surely prove a real boon to the owners of 25-20 rifles.

Peculiarly, Remington-Peters offer their 250-3000 Savage cartridge loaded with a well-designed 100-gr. PSP bullet while seemingly almost deliberately handicapping the fine 257 Roberts cartridge with a single loading comprising a velocity-shedding 117-gr. round-nose. At the same time, the newer 25-06 is being listed as available with an excellent selection of bullets including an 87-gr. hollow-point, a 100-gr. PSP and a 120-gr. PSP. Now the 257 Roberts was never intended to be a woods hunting cartridge in the first place, so I ask wouldn't it make sense to drop that old blunt-nosed, slow-moving 117-gr. loading, and offer the 257 loaded with the same three efficient bullets currently being put into the 25-06?

Also while they're at it, why not try that same 87-gr. hollow-point in the 250 Savage as a varmint loading? No new bullets required, just a re-mating of existing components to provide more effective and certainly more popular factory ammunition. Winchester already does this with the 250 Savage, besides offering 87- and 100-gr. loadings for the 257 Roberts. Remington has an opportunity here for some one-upmanship by increasing 257 Roberts velocities at the same time the improved bullets are added. Based upon their experience with the 6mm Remington it is obvious that a 100-gr. spitzer bullet could be given close to 3200 fps MV in the 257, and an 87-gr. around 3400 fps. Remington proved they could do it with the even older 25-06; why not do it to the 257?

The 6.5mm Remington Magnum is now factory loaded with PSP bullets of 100- and 120-gr. weights, while the 264 Winchester Magnum bullets run 100- and 140-grains. I submit that the 6.5 Remington would be a better big game cartridge if it were also to be made available with a 140-gr. bullet. By the same token, the 120-gr. would provide an excellent flat-shooting load for antelope in the 246 Magnum. Remington manufactures both bullets and they're of the same diameter, so again two new loadings to tickle shooters' appetites could be put together with utmost ease.

Originally the 280 Remington was offered in a 125-gr. loading, and a most useful one it was. I never heard anyone propose that it be dropped or even find any fault with it, yet dropped it was! Why? Certainly not because it entailed making a special bullet, for the identical 125-gr. PSP slug is currently loaded in the 7mm Remington Magnum by Remington-Peters. The fine 280 cartridge badly

needs the greater versatility which the 125-gr. loading provided, and it should definitely be reinstated.

The old 7×57 Mauser round, currently enjoying a rebirth of popularity, could also profit from this idea of multiple use of the same factory bullets loaded in different cases. Older shooters recall how the pre-war 139-gr. loading in 7mm Mauser improved long range performance, and the Federal Cartridge Company, as well as Dominion, still offer a factory round of this weight with a spitzer bullet rated at 2710 and 2800 fps MV respectively, versus only 2490 fps for the 175-gr. with its blunt round-nose. Remington would do well to consider the possibility of making up a 150-gr. loading for the 7mm Mauser using the bullets of that weight presently loaded in their 280 Remington case.

Winchester offers a 125-gr. PSP bullet for the 308 Winchester, but Remington omits this important step in their 308 offerings, despite the fact that they already have such a bullet for the 30-06. With the number of 308 users constantly on the increase, this would be a sure-fire addition to the R-P line.

There is a notable gap—or so it seems to me—in 30 caliber between the 180- and 220-gr. bullets, especially since all 220-grainers are of round-nose profile. For the always popular 30-06 and particularly for the 300 Magnums, to be used on large game at ranges which could be long, a 200-gr. spitzer loading might well be useful. Neither Winchester nor Remington offer such a factory load in '06, 300 H&H or 300 Winchester Magnum, yet Winchester has a 200-gr. Silvertip bullet which they load in the smaller 308 cartridge, an obvious deficiency that should be corrected.

By the same token, Winchester, Remington and Federal offer a single loading only in 8mm Mauser caliber. This is a mild deer loading, and while we all know that it's been kept purposely mild because of the old Commission rifles

and drillings in this caliber (many of which have the smaller .318″ bore size), there's no reason I can think of why a *heavier* bullet of some compromise diameter and construction couldn't be offered—say of 200 grains or thereabout. True, this one would require the production of a new bullet, but with all the tens-of-thousands of 8mm rifles in existence, which would thereby become better suited for taking large game, it seems logical to suppose that added sales of 8mm Mauser ammo would pay the freight.

Remember what we said about the 25-20? Well, another older but still widely used combination small game and varmint cartridge—the 32-20—has been accorded precisely the same treatment by the ammo makers. The varmint loading with 80-gr. hollow-point bullet was dropped, halving the 32-20's usefulness. We'd like to see the 80-gr. HP loading restored to the line-up of at least one manufacturer.

Finally we come to the big bores, they too having certain gaps which should be filled and, though fewer in numbers, they are none the less important. Unfortunately, in each instance a newly designed bullet (newly manufactured to *original* design in the first instance) will be required, but in four of the five cases I'll cite, bullets are already being offered for handloaders by component manufacturers, including Speer, Hornady and Herter, indicating there must be at least a fair-sized demand. So I'll propose the following additional factory cartridge loadings:

(1) A 250-gr. in 348 Winchester caliber (formerly made but unavailable today).

(2) A lighter bullet—235-gr. or thereabout—in 375 H&H Magnum caliber (also previously made).

(3) A heavier bullet for the 444 Marlin; that is, heavier in weight *and* construction for deeper penetration on really large game. 275 grains would be my suggestion as to weight.

(4) A lighter bullet in Express-type loading at higher velocity for the re-discovered 45-70, say either 350- or 300 grains.

(5) A 400-gr. bullet for the 458 Winchester Magnum, not so much to increase velocities, but rather as a means of reducing the very substantial recoil of that cartridge. This would also better adapt it for larger North American game, where the present 500-gr. loading is unnecessarily heavy.

New Loads Needed—Handguns

The past few years have witnessed considerable improvement in the line-up of factory loaded handgun cartridges, particularly in the area of lighter bullets at higher velocities, as noted in our introduction. Nowhere has this trend been more marked than in 38 Special and 357 Magnum calibers, but I submit that there are others needing adoption. Here are my nominations:

A 125-gr. (preferably) or a 110-gr. jacketed hollow-point (JHP)—or both—in 38 Special. (Remington already does this).

A 140-gr. JHP in 38 Special.

A 140-gr. JHP in 357 Magnum.

Note: Just as this was being written, word has come that Speer is offering *all* of these loadings in their new Lawman series of factory loaded cartridges, about which I'll have more to say further along.

Next, the autoloaders to consider. Most factory auto rounds are still based on full-jacketed bullets (except Super Vel and certain notable numbers in 9mm Luger and 45 ACP by other makers) despite the fact that custom bullets have established the practicality—at least in some instances—of loading these cartridges with soft nose or hollow-point bullets.

This writer is well aware of the need for *absolute* reliability in feeding auto pistol cartridges from magazine to chamber, and the difficulties experienced along this line with handloads containing some of the newer bullets. At the same time, I am convinced that, with such adequate design and testing as the large ammo makers would surely devote to such a project, all those problems could be overcome.

On this assumption, I'm going to recommend a 90-gr. JHP loading for the 380 Auto, a 115-gr. JHP in 38 Super Automatic, and a 200-gr. JHP in 45 ACP. We mustn't expect rifle-type expansion from such bullets, but against fluid-filled game tissues they're bound to show some improvement over the smooth unbroken nose surfaces of our present full-metal-jacketed pistol slugs.

Finally, after using Hornady's excellent 250-gr. jacketed hollow-points in handloads for the 45 Long Colt, I'm convinced that a factory loading with bullets of this type in the 45 would give it all the knock-down power most of us will ever need from a sidearm. With Ruger's new 45/45 Convertible Blackhawk added to Colt's enduring Single Action Army, more big bore sixgun shooters than ever would undoubtedly respond happily to the introduction of such a standard loading.

II. Proposed New Cartridges—Rifles

It's going to be doubly harder to convince ammunition makers of a need for totally new factory cartridges. As a realist, I'm unable to muster much more than hope that any of the proposals I'm about to suggest will ever be given a second look.

However, the way I figure it, soon or late new cartridges *will* be developed as the result of somebody's ideas, and its just possible that "somebody," whoever he is, might see some merit in one of the following:

(1) A 25-caliber *and* a 35-caliber—or if just one, then a 7mm—high velocity cartridge with a *rimmed* case. With the resurgence of single shot rifles we badly need a rimmed cartridge with modern ballistics. Conceivably 30-40 Krag or 303 British cases could be used as the foundation, with brass blown out to "Improved" sharp-shoulder form, but I'd prefer to see a longer case of perhaps 2½″ length. The 280 Remington, or the 25-06 Remington and 35 Whelen with rimmed cases would be just great.

(2) An entirely new short cartridge, again with an "Improved" rimmed case designed specifically for use in the Model 94 Winchester lever action. Contrary to what a lot of folks seem to think, the enormous popularity of the Model 94 carbine is *not* based on love for the 30-30 and 32 Special cartridges it currently chambers, but reflects instead the love of American deer hunters for this light, handy little carbine. Give it a new, more effective cartridge and its appeal would grow even greater, I believe. Once again, I'm going to suggest that the caliber of such a cartridge be 7mm.

(3) A modified version of the 458 Winchester for hunters of the largest North American game, preferably a 40-caliber on the 458 case necked down, or a 375 Short Magnum or the 338 Winchester case necked up. I'd expect such a round to find considerable favor in Alaska.

(4) Lastly, I'd personally like to see a large (non-belted) rimless cartridge developed duplicating the British 404 case dimensions. It wouldn't necessarily have to be in that caliber, but should definitely be designed with really large game in mind; that is to say it should be at least 338-caliber or larger, handling 275-gr. bullets or, better still, 300-gr. or heavier. Yes, I can hear a fellow gun-writer reminding his readers that at last count no Kodiak bears had been seen on Main Street, USA, but the indisputable fact remains that a large percentage of the 375s and 458s sold never get to Alaska or Africa. The obvious conclusion must be that more than a few shooters just happen to like owning and shooting the big bores. It's still a free country, isn't it?

Handguns

From where we sit there appear to be just two gaps which need filling in the factory line-up of handgun cartridges. Undoubtedly other pistol and sixgun shooters will have somewhat different ideas as to what is wanted, but I believe these would at least satisfy the major demands.

First and foremost, there *must* be a considerable market for a large-caliber, high-performance cartridge with rimless case for automatic pistols. Today, fanciers of the self-shuckers must choose between the fast-stepping but light-bullet 9mm or 38 Super Automatic, and the comparatively slow-moving 45 ACP. Something in between that would combine the best features of each is needed.

I don't believe the new 44 Auto-Mag fills this bill. Its unnecessarily great power requires too large and cumbersome a pistol to handle it, at least partially defeating our sought-after objective of a practical sidearm for holster wear afield, besides which I see no need to resort to using cut-off rifle cartridge cases in a pistol.

It would seem logical to simply develop a *rimless* version of the 41 S&W Magnum cartridge in that same caliber, intended specifically for use in a strengthened automatic pistol. Whether the big 1911 Colt could be successfully adapted to handle such a cartridge I'm not qualified to say. Maybe the over-all loaded cartridge length of the 41 would have to be reduced 0.30″ (to equal that of the 38 Super Auto) but, as far as strength is concerned, I believe that chamber pressures must run very nearly as high in the 38 Super as in the 41 Magnum.

Our primary sixgun cartridge need is at the opposite end of the caliber spectrum. Here we've got all the big bores necessary, but with the dubious exceptions of the 30 Carbine cartridge and the old 32-20, there aren't any medium caliber revolver rounds developing high velocity with light recoil. I'm thinking here of a round that would drive 100/110-gr. 30- or 32-caliber JHP bullets to perhaps 1600 fps at the muzzle, giving the field gunner adequate power and a flat trajectory for varmints without the accompanying recoil of a 357 Magnum.

The 30 Carbine cartridge would conceivably meet these requirements if produced in rimmed-case form so it could be used in the side-swing cylinders of double-action revolvers. The old 32-20 is out because of the many old revolvers chambered for it, but the factories should have no trouble in producing a rimmed 30 Magnum based on the straight-sided carbine case.

III. Resurrections

I realize it's not a usual thing for ammunition makers to bring back a cartridge once its been dropped from the line, but it's not entirely without precedent, either. It happened once with the 405 Winchester, and most recently with the 220 Swift, so it *isn't* impossible, and I believe I speak on behalf of a goodly number of riflemen and hunters in expressing the hope that it may happen again.

That famous pair of combination target and deer rounds—the 32-40 and 38-55—having been discontinued without prior warning, has left a void unfilled even by non-existent components, causing many a fine old, but still accurate and shootable rifle, to be shelved. They should be reinstated by at least one domestic company, even if only for a limited time, in order to give owners of such old rifles a chance to stock up on ammo for them.

The same request is made for at least a limited re-issue of the big 405 Winchester round, except that this one is still modern enough ballistically to fill the 40-caliber gap we referred to in Section II (3). With its 300-gr. soft point at 2260 fps MV, it would nicely take care of the present wide spacing between the 375 and 458 Magnums.

IV. New Developments

Bringing our readers up to date on what *has* happened, here are additional offerings announced by Federal Cartridge Company just too late to be included in last year's column. To their centerfire rifle line they've added the 44 Remington Magnum with 240-gr. *Hollow* S.P. bullet, claiming an M.V. of 1750 fps in 18½" barrels.

Federal's centerfire pistol cartridge list was expanded considerably by the addition of standard loadings with full metal cased bullets for the 25 Auto, 32 Auto, 380 Auto, 9mm Auto, and a fourth variety of 38 Special with 158-gr. lead semi-wadcutter bullet. So far, I've only tried the 380 rounds, but if they should all prove to equal previous Federal offerings, users can count on getting absolutely reliable and accurate ammunition.

Biggest news for 1973 (at the time of this writing) is Speer's new line of factory-loaded handgun cartridges for police use, identified as their "Lawman Series." These include two 9mm Luger rounds with 100-gr. JHP and 125-gr. JSP Speer bullets; *nine* 38 Specials offering bullet choices of 110-gr. JHP, 125-gr. JHP, 125-gr. JSP, 140-gr. JHP, 158-gr. SWC, 158-gr. R.N., 158-gr. JSP, 200-gr. R.N., and a Match load with 148-gr. HBWC (hollow-base wadcutter) bullets.

There are also five 357 Magnum loadings with 110-gr. JHP, 125-gr. JHP, 125-gr. JSP, 140-gr. JHP and 158-gr. JSP, plus shotshells loaded with #9 shot fitting both 38 Special and 357 Magnum revolvers, and a similar shotshell for the 44 Magnum. The very latest to appear are a pair of cartridges for the 44 Magnum with 200-gr. JHP and 240-gr. JSP Speers. All-in-all, a most comprehensive selection for law enforcement, defense, or hunting uses. Although I haven't had an opportunity to try them as this is written, considering the Speer bullets with which they are loaded, I fully expect them to prove effective as well as highly accurate.

Late News From Browning

In late January, 1973, Browning announced the following new loadings in centerfire cartridges:

25-06 — 87-gr. Spitzer S.P.
25-06 — 120-gr. Spitzer S.P.
30-06 — 180-gr. R.N.S.P.
32 S&W Long — 98-gr. Lead.
9mm Luger — 100-gr. JHP
357 — Magnum — 110-gr. Semi-Jacketed H.P.
44 Rem. Magnum — 240-gr. Semi-Jacketed H.P.
(for rifle or handgun)

Of course, none of these are new calibers or even new bullet weights or types, but they *are* new to the Browning factory cartridge line-up, and those shooters who found previous Browning ammo so satisfactory (as this tester did), will no doubt want to try these offerings, especially if acquiring one of the highly interesting new Browning Single Shot rifles.

Part 1. RIFLE CARTRIDGES
The Centerfires

17 REMINGTON For the shooter who already has everything he needs, but wishes to add a combination varmint cartridge and conversation piece to his battery, the 17 Remington offers a limited area of usefulness. Although it will kill varmints like lightning, it is neither as fast as the 220 Swift nor as hard hitting as a 22-250, and its extremely light bullets are more susceptible to the influence of wind over long ranges than are the high velocity 22s. In fact, I can't think of anything this caliber can do that can't be done as well or better by one or more of the 22s. The most that can be said for the 17 is that it is flat-shooting, has a low noise level and almost nonexistent recoil. Individual chronographers report that it doesn't quite reach 4000 fps at the muzzle of a 24" barrel. Above all, the 17 should never be used on any game animal!

22 HORNET One of the most useful smallbore cartridges, and the first standard 22 specifically for varmint hunting. Since its appearance in 1930 it has earned a reputation for fine accuracy, flat trajectory, and quick bullet expansion. Effective to 175 yards on foxes, woodchucks, and jack rabbits, excellent for wild turkeys, it should definitely not be used on deer.

218 BEE Introduced in 1938 for the lever action Model 65 Winchester, its use was extended to bolt actions where its greater powder capacity, higher velocity and flatter trajectory from a stronger case made it a better choice than the Hornet. Effective on the same game species as the Hornet. Not available in any rifle today.

22 REMINGTON JET See Part II — Handgun Cartridges.

220 SWIFT Highest velocity standard sporting rifle cartridge ever produced commercially in the U.S., its 48-gr. bullet leaving the muzzle at 4110 fps is virtually a bomb, unfit for use on large game animals. As a long range varmint cartridge it is one of the finest, needing only a longer, heavier bullet less sensitive to wind. In deference to popular demand, Winchester has resumed production of 220 Swift cartridges and components, but it remains to be seen whether rifles will ever again be offered in this caliber.

222 REMINGTON First of the post-WW II cartridges, the 222 has climbed rapidly to fame as a benchrest target and varmint round. Its better-designed bullets and finer accuracy have extended practical small varmint range to about 225 yards. This, together with its availability in numerous strong bolt action rifles, has made the older Bee and Zipper obsolete.

222 REMINGTON MAGNUM Big Brother to the standard 222, this later and longer cartridge combines increased power and velocity with the fine accuracy of its forerunner to give varmint shooters one of the best balanced, most practical 'chuck cartridges ever developed. 55- and 60-gr. spitzer bullets buck the wind better than the 50-gr. standard 222 bullet, and arrive at a 200-yard target with some 25% more energy to boot. Rifles for the 222 Magnum have been dropped because of its close similarity to the 223 Remington (or 5.56mm) in use by our military. Factory ammunition is still made by Remington in HP and PSP style, but not by Winchester.

222 SUPER RIMMED Developed in Australia, this rimmed version of our 222 Remington emigrated first to Canada and thence to the U.S. An ideal choice for chambering in single shot rifles, case dimensions (except for the rim), ballistics and loading data all duplicate those of the standard 222. Velocities may be somewhat higher however, in the longer barrels common to single shot rifles.

223 REMINGTON Adopted by the U.S. military forces as the 5.56mm with full metal jacketed 55-gr. bullets, its civilian name is 223 Remington, under which headstamp a soft point bullet is loaded. Identical ballistically to the 222 Magnum, the 223's case dimensions differ enough so that they should never be fired in a 222 Magnum chamber; they'll go in, but hazardous excess headspace will be present with a probability of case separations. Rifles for the 223 have a twist rate of 1-in-12″ rather than the 1-in-14″ of most 22 centerfires, this to insure bullet stability all the way out to 600-yards. Case capacity is about a grain less than the 222 Magnum and its neck is about 1/16″ shorter, making the 222 Magnum a better choice for handloaders. Future government surplus ammunition will probably be available for the 223, however.

225 WINCHESTER Intended as a successor to the 220 Swift (in Winchester rifles), this new high performance cartridge has done more than that; it has also superseded the discontinued 219 Zipper in its role as the most powerful rimmed 22 centerfire. Although officially classified as "semi-rimless," the 225 does have a rim, easily sufficient to permit its use in single shot rifles while still fitting the bolt heads and extractors (of 270, 30-06 dimensions) of modern standard rimless cartridge repeaters. Closely similar in design to the 219 Improved Zipper (but differing in certain vital dimensions), the 225 Winchester is loaded to higher pressures than the old standard 219 Zipper, developing 540 fps greater muzzle velocity for a trajectory that is almost twice as flat. Factory cartridges in this new caliber are loaded with outstanding uniformity and provide excellent accuracy.

22/250 REMINGTON A long time favorite wildcat with both varminters and benchrest shooters, the 22/250 was standardized by Remington in 1965 and shows signs of rapidly growing popularity. Generally considered to be better designed than the Swift, it will give nearly as high velocities with bullets of the same weight. Because it is slower, case and barrel life are longer. Case capacity to bore ratio in the 22/250 is most favorable, and its short over-all loaded cartridge length of 2.35″ makes it readily adaptable to short-action box magazine repeaters. Remington, Winchester, Federal, Norma and Browning all offer ammunition in this caliber.

243 WINCHESTER One of the new 6mm or 24 caliber compromises between 22 and 25 calibers, having in large measure the best features of both. A 100-gr. bullet with high sectional density at 3,070 fs for deer and antelope, and an 80-gr. at 3,500 for long range varmints, provide accuracy equal to the Swift and far better wind-bucking and killing power. Excellent for the one-gun hunter of game not larger than deer.

244 REMINGTON Remington's first 6mm or 24-cal. rifle, never very popular because of its 1-in-12″ rifling twist which kept bullet weight to 90 grains in spitzer form. Heavier bullets **can** be stabilized if made with a blunt round nose. Shooters wanted a dual-purpose rifle, however, one in which they could use 100-gr. spitzers for big game, so many picked the lesser-capacity 243. Despite the fact that neither shooters nor game could tell the difference between 90- and 100-gr. bullets, the 244 slipped and Remington ceased production of rifles in this caliber. Although officially removed from Remington's cartridge list for 1972 as a separate caliber, 6mm Remington cartridges with both 80-and 90-gr. bullets may be used interchangeably in 244 Remington rifles.

6mm REMINGTON Identical in case dimensions to the older 244

Remington, this newer cartridge is loaded with the 100-gr. bullet demanded by deer hunters. Remington lists MV as 3190 fps, and barrels have a rifling twist of 1-in-9″ to stabilize the longer bullet. Despite the fact that 75- and 90-gr. 244 cartridges can also be used in 6mm rifles, shooters wanted a varmint round bearing the 6mm headstamp. Hence, in 1965 Remington announced an additional load using their new 80-gr. Power-Lokt bullet, which has proven exceptionally accurate and flat shooting. The 6mm is therefore an even better dual purpose cartridge than the 243. Early in 1972, Remington announced the discontinuance of ammunition bearing the 244 Remington headstamp, and the addition of a new 90-gr. PSP bullet loading in 6mm Remington caliber.

25-20 WCF Prior to the coming of the Hornet and Bee, this 1893-born round was the top small-game/varmint cartridge. Today we have better pest loads, but there is still a useful place for the 25-20 among those who hunt for stew or seek the lordly wild turkey. W-W and R-P have dropped the 60-gr. open-point varmint loading—at 2250 fps such a good little 'chuck load — and henceforth will offer only a pair of 86-gr. loads at 1460 fps. It would have been better if they had dropped the old round with plain lead bullet instead of the more accurate and faster hollow point.

25-35 WINCHESTER Another cartridge from the 1890's, this one **can** be used for deer. Currently obtainable only as a 117-gr. soft point at 2,300 fs, the 25-35's chief claim to fame lies in its reputation as one of the most accurate cartridges ever developed for lever action rifles, and one of the lightest recoiling.

250 SAVAGE Popularly known as the "250-3000" because of its velocity with an 87-gr. bullet, this fine cartridge appeared in 1915 as one of our earliest really high speed loads. 100-gr. bullets are loaded to 2,820 fs. Quick killing power, flat trajectory, and light recoil have kept this cartridge popular for over 40 years. Use 100-gr. bullets for deer and 87's for varmints. In wind-swept areas, the 100 grain is preferred, even for varmints.

256 WINCHESTER MAGNUM See Part II—Handgun Cartridges.

257 ROBERTS Named for its famous originator, Major Ned Roberts, this was to have been an extra long range varmint cartridge, but with factory production came additional bullet weights, making it one of our more versatile rounds. Although no rifles of standard make are now being chambered for the 257, W-W still offers an 87-gr. load at 3200 fps for varmints, a 100-gr. Silvertip at 2900 fps for deer/antelope, and a 117-gr. Power-Point at 2650 fps for the woods hunter. Remington lists only a single loading—the least useful 117-gr. RN—but it can be efficiently reloaded with the newer 120-gr. spitzer bullets to equal or better 243/6mm performance.

25-06 REMINGTON Wisely, Remington decided to adopt and standardize this old wildcat based as much upon popular demand as upon its proven excellence ballistically. It is without doubt one of our very finest "all-round" cartridges for American game in the contiguous 48 states (that is, not including the great bears of Alaska). Ideally, it is not an elk or moose cartridge, but as a long range load for all medium game as well as varmints, it is superb with its 87-gr. HP at 3500 fps and 120-gr. PSP at 3120 fps. Sighted for 200 yards, either bullet drops only some 9″ at 400, and the heavier bullet has 1210 f.p. of energy left at that far-out range, or just slightly less than a 30-30 at only 100-yards. For all practical purposes, the 25-06 with 120-gr. bullet is the equal of the 6.5 Magnum, and treads close on the heels of the 270. In 1972 Remington wisely introduced a third loading for the 25-06, this new round containing a 100-gr. PSP bullet listed at 3300 fps MV from a 26″ barrel, providing a flatter trajectory at 500 yards than either the 87-gr. or 120-gr. loadings. This should be the best choice for deer hunting with the 25-06.
*As independently chronographed, actually about 3350. Ed.

6.5 REMINGTON MAGNUM One of a pair of short-short belted magnums developed by Remington for short-receiver bolt action rifles, powder capacity is very close to that of the 270, hence its ballistics are also much the same when using bullets of similar sectional density in equal length barrels. With its 100-gr. bullet at 3450 fps for varmints and 120-gr. game load at 3220 fps, it is even closer in performance to the 25-06, standing mid-way between the 6mm and the larger 7mm Remington Magnum. The only real advantage of the 6.5 over the 25-06 is in its ability to handle still heavier bullets, and for this purpose the 270 and 280 are even better.

264 WINCHESTER MAGNUM The third cartridge produced in Winchester's series of medium-short belted cases, the 264 offers magnum velocities and power from standard-length bolt actions. This is a cartridge with a specific purpose—the delivery of a controlled expansion bullet with flat trajectory and high residual energy at ultra long ranges. This it does. Accuracy with the 264 sometimes is less than it might be, chiefly because of a mismatching of bore-groove diameters and the bullets available. However, given the right combination, the 264 shoots very well. With the 264 or the 6.5 Magnum, select those bullets which will stand the high rotational forces of their quick-twist rifling.

270 WINCHESTER Superior to the 257 and 6mms for western use and for game larger than deer, the 270 has earned a good reputation among open country hunters. Its flat trajectory and high velocity with 130-gr. bullet at 3140 fps makes hitting easier over long, difficult-to-estimate ranges. Thus, as a mule deer, sheep and goat cartridge it is all anyone could ask for. For larger and heavier game of the caribou, elk and moose species, Winchester loads a 150-gr. Power-Point bullet to an increased muzzle velocity of 2900 fps, while Remington offers a 150-gr. round nose Core-Lokt at 2800 for woods hunting. The 100-gr. load is excellent for varmints, and is a good choice on antelope, too.

7mm REMINGTON MAGNUM Rifle cartridge of 1962, this short-case belted magnum mates the striking power of a 180-gr. 30-06 with the velocity and flat trajectory of a 130-gr. 270. The 175-gr. load has 21½% greater muzzle energy than the 180-gr. 30-06, and the 150-gr. is traveling 12% faster than the 130-gr. 270 bullet out at 300 yards. Various "wildcat" 7mm Magnum cartridges have evidenced their game killing ability in all corners of the globe, and now we have a factory standard cartridge capable of doing the same. In 1965, Remington added a 175-gr. factory loading having a pointed Core-Lokt bullet designed to retain high velocity over longer ranges. Starting out at the muzzle with the same 3070 fps as the round-nose bullet, remaining velocity of the new spitzer slug is 340 fs higher at 300 yards and 460 fs faster at 500 yards, even equaling the 150-gr. bullet by the time 300 yards is reached. In 1967, Remington added still another loading, this time a 125-gr. PSP at 3430 MV, thus making available a lightweight, high speed bullet with correspondingly flat trajectory for use on the smaller species of big game under long range conditions. This load should **not** be used in taking really large game, especially at short to medium ranges where velocity is still high.

280 REMINGTON One of our very best—if not the best—"all-round" cartridges, the 280 has been sadly overlooked, bucking, as it does, the popularity and head start of the closely similar 270, and over-shadowed by the newer 7mm Remington Magnum. Originally, its attraction lay in the splendid selection of factory loads available. Four bullet weights—100-, 125-, 150- and 165-gr. —gave the 280 a flexibility unequaled by the 270 unless the latter were handloaded, and with lower chamber pressures to boot. However, shooters have shown a preference for the 7mm Magnum, with the result that Remington has discontinued the 100- and 125-gr. 280 loads, and only their M742 autoloader is still being chambered for it—most regrettable.

284 WINCHESTER Unusual for American cartridges, this short-cased round has a body diameter larger than its rim, giving

it a powder capacity only about 1 grain less than the 280 Remington, even though ½-inch shorter, while retaining a "standard" size rim (common to such calibers as the 270, 280, 308 and 30-06), in order to permit use of the 284 cartridge with existing bolt face dimensions. Designed to give short action rifles (specifically the Winchester M88 lever action and M100 autoloader) ballistics equaling the longer 270 Winchester and 280 Remington cartridges, there is no reason why bolt action rifles shouldn't be chambered for it.

7mm MAUSER Originating as the Spanish military cartridge of 1893, the 7x57mm became popular the world over and today's factory loadings are better than ever. It will handle any game that the 270 will but, if used for antelope or other plains game at long range, either Federal's 139-gr. loading at 2710 fps, Dominion's 139-gr. at 2800 fps, or Norma's 150-gr. load at 2756 fps, should be selected. For varmints, Norma offers a loading with 110-gr. SP at 3067 fps MV. These modern high velocity versions have given the 7x57 new appeal. However, the standard U.S. cartridge with 175-gr. round-nose bullet of high sectional density is still the best choice for big game, especially when hunting in brush or woods.

30 CARBINE Commercial jacketed SP cartridges are loaded by W-W, R-P, Federal and Norma for use in the 30 M-1 Carbine and Ruger revolver. Winchester's 110-gr. is a hollow point; the other 3 are all RNSPs. All have a rated MV of 1970-1980 fps from an 18" barrel; at only 100-yards, velocity is down to 1540 fps with 575 f.p. energy. From this it should be obvious that the 30 Carbine is not an adequate deer load. If used on varmints, it may ricochet badly.

30-30 WCF & 32 WINCHESTER SPECIAL Old favorites of the deer hunter and rancher, these cartridges continue to be popular more because of the light, handy carbines which use them than because of any attribute of the cartridges themselves. For the indifferent marksman they are wounders, having neither great bullet weight nor high velocity. These are deer cartridges and should not be "stretched." They're neither flat shooting nor accurate enough for varmints, nor do they have the power to be good moose killers.

30 & 32 REMINGTON Rimless versions of the 30-30 and 32 Special for the Remington line of autoloaders and slide action rifles (Models 8, 81, 14 and 141), bullet weights and velocities are the same (except no 150-gr. bullets), and there is no difference in killing power. Depends solely on which rifle action the shooter chooses as to which cartridge he uses.

300 SAVAGE Developed by Savage to approximate early 30-06 ballistics in their Model 99 lever action, this cartridge had a phenomenal acceptance for a time. It has an extremely short case neck, making it difficult to reload, but with 150- and 180-gr. factory loads it is a quick killer on deer. The lighter bullet should be chosen where flat trajectory and rapid expansion counts, but for wooded country, or for bear, moose and caribou, use the 180-gr. bullet.

30-40 KRAG Generally called the "Krag," this old military cartridge looks good in "civies." Rifles are no longer made for it, but the Krag bolt actions and Winchester Model 95 lever actions just don't seem to wear out. 180- and 220-gr. bullet loadings are available, with the former as best choice for deer, or mountain hunting requiring the flattest possible trajectory, while the latter is a long brush-cutter slow to open up and offering deeper penetration on heavy game than the faster 30-06, assuming like bullets.

308 WINCHESTER Commercial version of the 7.62mm NATO cartridge, the 308 is a big stick in a small bundle. A stubby cartridge, resembling the 300 Savage with a longer neck but still half-an-inch shorter than the 30-06, this hot little number comes within 100 fs of equaling 30-06 velocities. When first brought out, only 150- and 180-gr. bullets were available in factory loads, but now there is a 110-gr. varmint load and a dandy 200-gr. for the heavier stuff. Because of its suitability for use in short actions especially, popularity of the 308 has been growing rapidly.

30-06 SPRINGFIELD American military cartridge since 1906, this has been the standard by which all other big game cartridges were compared. Many have called it our most versatile all-round cartridge, for there are many bullets available, from the 110-gr.

for varmints, through the flat-shooting 150-gr. to the 180-gr. "all-purpose," and finally up to a 220-gr. for big game and timber hunting. Except for Alaskan brown bear, buffalo, and rear-angling shots on elk, it is probably adequate for any North American game.

300 H&H MAGNUM Introduced in 1925 as the "Super-Thirty," this was the first factory cartridge giving a velocity in excess of 3000 fps with a 150-gr. bullet. Re-named "300 H&H Magnum" by Americans, it soon demonstrated its superiority as a big game cartridge and, starting in 1935, as a long range target load in the Wimbledon Cup Match at Camp Perry. By virtue of its larger belted case and heavier powder charge, the 300 H&H moves 180-gr. bullets 220 fps faster than the 30-06 with an additional quarter-ton of energy. This gives the shooter who is able to handle the increased recoil flatter trajectory with less wind deflection and more remaining knock-down power.

300 WINCHESTER MAGNUM Recognizing the average American hunter's predilection for 30-cal. rifles as the favorite all-round bore size, Winchester in 1963 introduced this modern 300 Magnum, thereby spelling the doom of the fine old 300 H&H after 38 years. MV of the new round runs 150 to 200 fps higher than the 300 H&H with equal bullet weights, delivering almost 24% greater remaining energy at 400 yards (180-gr. bullet), and 13% flatter trajectory at the same range. Ballistics also exceed by a considerable margin those of smaller bore magnums. The 300 Winchester Magnum with proper bullet weights is adequate for all our big game from deer and antelope to elk, caribou, moose and even the great bears, plus African game of similar weight.

303 BRITISH British service cartridge for over half a century, the 303 has long been popular in Canada, and now with thousands of surplus military rifles in the hands of U.S. shooters its use on this side of the border has increased enormously. Consequently, a wide variety of factory loads have been made available including the old standard 215-gr. round-nose from Remington, Norma and Dominion at 2180-2200 fps; a 180-gr. from Remington, Winchester, Federal, Dominion and Norma averaging 2540 fps (Dominion, 2610); 150-gr. Dominion and Norma at 2720 fps. and even a 130-gr. Norma load traveling 2790 fps. The 303 has thus become a quite effective multi-purpose cartridge for North American game.

303 SAVAGE Another light deer cartridge of the 30-30 class, but in this one some velocity was traded for more bullet weight, 180- and 190-gr. bullets being given 100 to 200 fs less speed. Although showing slightly less kinetic energy than a 30-30, the greater sectional density of these bullets results in deeper penetration for more actual killing power, especially on large game, although trajectory is not quite as flat.

32-20 WCF An almost obsolete little cartridge that refuses to die, it should have been named the 30-20 for it uses a 30-cal. bullet. Too light and under-powered for deer, and with the former 80-gr. high speed HP now gone, this old round with its 100-gr. bullet at 1290 fps is best used for turkeys and edible small game.

8mm MAUSER Underloaded by American ammunition makers because of the wide variations in quality and bore diameter of foreign rifles chambering it, this cartridge has ballistics about like the 30-40 Krag and is a good deer slayer. As loaded by Norma and imported into this country it is quite different, acquiring 30-06 powers. Caution here is to make sure of your rifle. Strength and accuracy vary widely with the individual rifle. Given a good one, this can be a fine big game cartridge using the stepped-up loadings. Do NOT mix with 30-06 rounds!

338 WINCHESTER MAGNUM Long awaited by many big game hunters, the 338 has shown itself to be a leading contender for the all-round rifle crown, killing large game such as brown bear and bison with the aplomb of a 375 H&H, or whitetail deer with less meat destruction than a quick-expanding 270 bullet. This is a modern, high-efficiency cartridge with flat trajectory slightly bettering the 30-06-180 gr. and 270-150 gr. loads, while delivering about 25% more striking energy at 200 and 300 yards than the

30-06. The great sectional density of the heavier bullets insures penetration and resistance to deflection by wind or brush, especially when the 275-grain Speer bullets are handloaded. Recoil is greater than with lesser cartridges, but not excessive for the shooter used to firing heavy 30-06 loads in light sporting rifles. The 338 will become increasingly popular with hunters who mix elk and moose with their regular deer menu.

348 WINCHESTER Lever action cartridge for really big game as well as deer, this is one of our most powerful rimmed cases. It appeared in 1936 for the Winchester Model 71—the only rifle ever commercially chambered for it—and originally offered considerable versatility with factory loads in 150-, 200- and 250-gr. bullet weights. Today, only a single loading with 200-gr. bullet is available, no rifles are made for it, and the cartridge is making a last stand in Alaska where its power, combined with a handy, smooth-working rifle keep it in use. The old 150-gr. load isn't missed much, but at least one ammo maker should produce the hard-hitting 250-gr. load.

35 REMINGTON With 200-gr. bullet, the 35 has been found to have considerably more anchoring power than the smaller 30's and 32's. Then too, it's good for getting through brush without deflection, and leaves a better blood trail. To 200 yards there's little difference in trajectory from the 30-30 and it has the advantage of being effective on larger game such as moose at moderate ranges, without excessive recoil. Highly recommended for Eastern deer and black bear, this praise does **not** include the pointed 150-gr. load. Stick to the 200-gr. for best results.

351 WINCHESTER SELF-LOADER Chambered only in the now-obsolete Winchester '07 autoloading rifle, the 351 hangs on because of its widespread use by police departments. For close wood ranges it can be used for deer and will kill with a proper hit.

358 WINCHESTER Larger caliber version of the 308 Winchester, the 358 drives 200-gr. bullets at 2530 fps, and 250-gr. at 2250. Each gives better than 2800 f.p. energy at the muzzle, and some 2200 f.p. at 100 yards. Trajectory of the 200-gr. matches that of the 180-gr. 300 Savage to 300 yards, hence it is not restricted to short ranges only. A splendid woods cartridge for moose, elk and deer, it has, unfortunately, been overlooked by many hunters.

350 REMINGTON MAGNUM First commercial cartridge to deserve the term Short Magnum, and one of the most practical big game rounds to appear in recent years, the 350 Magnum is especially notable for the restraint built into its design. Either standard length or short actions will accommodate its squat hull and deep-seated bullets, and its power is an almost perfect compromise, for American big game, between too much and not enough. This stems directly from its powder capacity, about 7% more than that of a 30-06 when both cases are filled to the base of their necks. 200-gr. bullets have a MV of 2710 fps, while 250-grainers reach 2410 fps, both from only a 20″ carbine barrel. The old 35 Remington is thus hopelessly outclassed and the 35 Whelen challenged by a cartridge that is still within the recoil limitations of once-a-year hunters. Deer hunters and those who are recoil-shy should use the 200-gr. load, which delivers noticeably less kick.

375 H&H MAGNUM World-wide big game cartridge and champion of the "mediums," the 375 H&H dates back to 1912 but can still boast no peer as an all-round load for big and dangerous game. It will dispatch the largest American game as well as most African species. If necessary, it will kill an elephant, and yet its big 270-gr. slug will travel over long ranges as flat as a 180-gr. 30-06 to kill mountain game without excessive meat destruction. There is also a 300-gr. bullet turning up over 2 tons of muzzle energy. Cartridges may be purchased in almost all of the big game regions of the world. Its one disadvantage is its quite heavy recoil.

38-40 WINCHESTER This "38" actually measures 40 caliber and should have been named "40-40." Many deer are still killed yearly by its 180-gr. bullet, loafing along at 1,330 fs, mostly because it punches a big enough hole to let out a lot of blood. It's obsolete and there are a lot of better cartridges, but for short ranges (under 100 yards), it will still do the trick.

44-40 WINCHESTER Big brother of the 38-40, this is the same type of short, low-velocity cartridge, varying only by being slightly larger in bullet diameter and weight (200 grains). Under 100 yards it will kill as well as a 30-30.

44 REMINGTON MAGNUM Originally developed as a super-powered revolver cartridge, the 44 Magnum gradually evolved into a carbine deer load. Remington and Norma load a 240-gr. Jacketed SP, and Winchester a hollow point of the same weight—all at some 1750 fps from 18½" barrels. Handy little rifles by Ruger, Winchester and Marlin, plus a bolt action from Remington, have helped popularize this round, but it should be restricted to woods ranges not exceeding 150 yards.

444 MARLIN In essence a "super" 44 Magnum since it uses the same 240-gr. .429" jacketed SP bullet but in a long, straight 2.22" case, the 444 Marlin provides 30% higher MV with 88% greater ME! At the muzzle its energy is greater even than that of the 30-06, at least on paper, but the blunt, relatively short bullet sheds velocity so fast that at only 100 yards it is down to the power level of the 7mm Mauser and 300 Savage. However, the 444 will be hitting as hard at 200 yards as the 35 Remington at 150, making it a fine deer and black bear cartridge to this range, while at 100 yards or less it is capable of handling just about any North American big game. Its biggest need is for a heavier constructed bullet that will not break up on the tough muscles and bone structure of such game or any intervening brush. Such bullets are already available to handloaders.

45-70 Still potent after 100 years, some of which was on the battlefield, but even more in the hunting fields, this old timer asks only to be used within ranges where its trajectory isn't too steep. Other than that, its user can count on a kill (if he does his part) whether the game be a small deer or a big moose. Excessive drop makes hitting tough beyond 150 yards, despite its ability to kill well-beyond that distance. Handloads with lighter (300-500-gr.) bullets will give somewhat higher velocities with less recoil, but extreme caution should be used with the old "Trapdoor" Springfields not to exceed pressure limitations.

458 WINCHESTER Second most powerful American cartridge, the 458 has already won its spurs in Africa; the special Model 70 rifle chambered for it is known as the "African" Model. It is well named, for the massive 500-gr. full-steel-jacketed and 510-gr. soft-points are an "over-dose" for practically all other game with the exceptions of Indian tiger, Asian gaur, and Alaskan brown bear. Heavy bullet weight and high speed for its caliber combine to make this more than just a good killing cartridge—it is a "stopping load," designed to break down the most ponderous and dangerous beasts, and this it will do. For an American going to Africa for elephant, buffalo and rhino it is top choice. The soft point should be used on even the largest soft-skinned game, for the solid bullet is a specialized number for elephants. Has greatest recoil of all American cartridges except the 460 Weatherby.

THE WEATHERBY CARTRIDGES

Weatherby Magnum cartridges have been factory produced for many years now, and are sold at sporting goods stores all over America and in many foreign countries. The brass cases are produced in Sweden, but all other components are American-made and assembled. They therefore qualify as American ammunition and merit inclusion in this analysis of cartridges on the U.S. market.

224 WEATHERBY VARMINTMASTER Smallest of the Weatherby's, the 224 also has the smallest capacity of any belted case. Despite its modest size, however, velocities over 3700 fps with 50-gr. bullets and 3600 fps with 55-gr. have been chronographed, making it a close competitor of the 22-250. It is thus an efficient case which, in combination with the added safety features of good base thickness and positive headspacing provided by the belt, rates as an impressive performer. For those varminters who

feel a need for more velocity than the 222 or 222 Magnum, but are willing to settle for less than the 220 Swift, the 224 Weatherby is an outstanding choice.

240 WEATHERBY MAGNUM Highest velocity of all factory-loaded 24 calibers, with the single exception of Holland & Holland's 244 Magnum, this medium capacity Weatherby features an entirely new belted case of reduced dimensions, capable of driving 70-gr. 6mm bullets to 3850 fps, 90-gr. to 3500, and 100-gr. to 3395 fps. It is thus some 200-300 fs faster than the 6mm Remington, and 300-400 fs ahead of the 243 Winchester. With loads giving sufficiently fine accuracy, this should prove to be an outstanding cartridge for open country deer and antelope shooting in combination with summer use as a long range varmint round.

257 WEATHERBY MAGNUM For varmint shooting at extremely long range or for the lighter species of big game in open country, where a premium is placed on flat trajectory and rapid bullet expansion, this cartridge is outstanding. Offering the flattest trajectory of any known 25-caliber cartridge, it utilizes the maximum loads of present-day powders that can be efficiently burned in this caliber to provide the highest striking energy for its bore size. In these combined respects, it is exceeded only by the 264 Winchester Magnum in cartridges under 270 caliber, and even there the difference is negligible.

270 WEATHERBY MAGNUM Next step up in the Weatherby line, the 270 WM is also a better choice for those who place more emphasis on big game hunting, but would still like to use the same rifle for off-season varminting. Bullets of 100, 130 and 150 grains are available with energies and trajectories close to Winchester's 264 Magnum with, however, a somewhat better bullet selection for greater flexibility. While 270 WM muzzle velocities are around 300 fps faster than the standard 270, at 300 yards the speed differential is little more than 100 fs with the lighter bullets but some 270 fs ahead in 150-gr. loadings.

7mm WEATHERBY MAGNUM This cartridge so closely parallels the 270 WM in almost all respects that little more need be said about it, except to note that there's a .007" bigger bullet and heavier bullet selection (to 175 grains) in the 7mm. In any event, there is little to choose between the 7mm WM and the newer 7mm Remington Magnum.

300 WEATHERBY MAGNUM Weatherby says this is his most popular and versatile caliber, and it's not hard to see why. With equal bullet weights, the 300 Weatherby develops from 285 to 355 fps more muzzle velocity than the 300 H&H Magnum for a noticeable increase in power. This cartridge is also liked for the nice balance it strikes between the large and small bores. For example, the 180-gr. 300 WM load offers some 500 fs velocity advantage over the 270-gr. 375 H&H Magnum with a consequent flattening of trajectory by 27%, and yet when loaded with a 150-gr. spitzer bullet it is both faster and flatter shooting than either the 270 or 7mm Weatherby Magnums. Despite some rather extreme claims for it the 300 Weatherby Magnum is doubtless one of the finest all-round big game cartridges.

340 WEATHERBY MAGNUM This is Weatherby's newest big game cartridge, produced to satisfy those hunters who want still more bullet weight than the 300's 220 grains, but at the same time wish to retain the 300's velocity and trajectory characteristics. This it does, giving a 250-gr. bullet only 55 fs less muzzle velocity than the 220-gr. 300 WM. Recoil is up, however, and the man who selects the 340 in preference to a 300 should be reasonably sure he needs its extra punch. For the great Alaskan bear it would appear to be a better choice, but for an all-round rifle involving mostly smaller game, the 300 would get the nod. The 340 WM uses the same bullets as the 338 Winchester Magnum, but boosts bullet speeds by 150 to 210 fps. An excellent moose, elk and bear cartridge.

378 WEATHERBY MAGNUM With this truly "magnum-size" cartridge we enter the field of specialized big game calibers. The latest Weatherby catalog states that it was "designed for the purpose of killing thick-skinned animals where extremely deep penetration is needed." With bullet weights of 270- and 300-gr. at velocities of 2900 to 3180 fps, it should be obvious that while striking power is unquestionably great, so is its recoil; entirely too much, in fact, for the average hunter not used to handling such heavy comeback. Experienced African and Arctic hunters, however, accustomed to the slam of the 375 H&H and larger rifles, report the 378 WM to be a most effective cartridge for the big stuff. With the adoption of the 378, Weatherby has discontinued production of the 375 WM, although ammunition for the older caliber is still being made. Despite its designation, the 378 uses the same bullets as the 375 Weatherby and the 375 H&H Magnum.

460 WEATHERBY MAGNUM Comments made on the 378 WM apply with even greater force to this largest and most powerful of all American cartridges. Using the same oversize belted case as the 378 Weatherby, its energy of 8000 fp with 500-gr. bullet is so great that it would normally be selected for only the very largest and dangerous game including elephant, rhino and buffalo. Some authorities feel that the 378 Weatherby would be adequate for such animals were it not for African game laws requiring rifles of 40 caliber or over for those species. Here again the name may be misleading, since the 460 WM uses the same size bullets as the 458 Winchester, only at a phenomenal increase of 570 fps muzzle velocity and nearly 3000 foot pounds of ME.

AMERICANIZED IMPORTED CARTRIDGES

We include here summaries on some of the popular and significant cartridges produced abroad for the U.S. market. Some were actually designed in this country, others of overseas origin were specifically intended for export to the States; since most of them are encountered with increasing frequency, it is reasonable to think of them as "American" by use if not by manufacture. Only those loaded with American-type "Boxer" primers are included.

6.5x54 MS An old but still liked cartridge for the Mannlicher-Schoenauer carbines, Norma offers five different versions with bullet weights of 77, 139 and 156 grains at muzzle speeds of 3117, 2580 and 2461 fps. A modest capacity round, the 6.5 MS built its reputation as a game cartridge **not** on velocity, but rather on the deep penetration of its long pencil-like round nose bullets. In its heaviest bullet weight, it has been well-liked in Maine as an effective black bear load.

6.5x55 SWEDISH Long the military cartridge of Sweden and Norway, the 6.5x55 has become quite common in the U.S., partly because of thousands of imported surplus military rifles and the fine Schultz & Larsen target rifles. With its light recoil, resistance to wind deflection and excellent accuracy, it has justified its Scandinavian reputation and is seen increasingly on our target ranges. Norma offers 6 different loadings with bullet weights of 77, 93, 139 and 156 grains at velocities somewhat above those of the smaller Mannlicher cartridge. The 139-gr. load is probably the most popular here.

7x61 S&H A modern high velocity big game round with Norma short belted case, the brain-child of Americans Phil Sharpe and Dick Hart, this shell is only 4mm longer than the old 7x57 Mauser case but velocity with 160-gr. boat-tails is 3100 fps at muzzle of a 26" barrel, according to the Norma table. In 1968, Norma improved the 7x61 case by changing its interior dimensions to provide thinner but stronger case walls, Known as the Super 7x61, exterior dimensions remain exactly the same as formerly, hence the new version will fit all rifles chambered for the older 7x61 S&H, but due to a slightly increased powder capacity, velocity is rated 50 fs higher; (3150 with 160-gr. bullet from 26" barrels).

30 U.S. CARBINE To satisfy the demand for 30 Carbine ammo,

Norma produces one with full metal jacket, the other in soft point, both 110 grain. This last, the one hunter-owners most sought, is at best little more than a small game cartridge, since velocity and energy are down to 1595 fs and 622 fp respectively at only 100 yards. Fast repeat shots should not be counted on to make up for inadequate power; this cartridge should not be selected for deer or other big game hunting.

7.5 SWISS Known officially at the 7.5x55mm Schmidt-Rubin, this cartridge is intended for the Swiss military rifles, Model 1911, of the same name, and is now being imported by Norma-Precision, loaded with a 180-gr. soft point boat-tail bullet at M.V. 2650 fps. Cases have a single central flash-hole for American primers and, as factory loaded in Sweden, are both non-corrosive and non-mercuric. This should make a fine deer load for owners of these military rifles, and cases can be readily reloaded with U.S. components.

308 NORMA MAGNUM A short magnum tailored to American big game fields. Its 180-gr. bullet steps out at a velocity 400 fs faster than the 180-gr. 30-06, is 180 fs ahead of the great 300 H&H, equals the new 300 Winchester Magnum and even approaches the much larger 300 Weatherby. Advantage of the Norma cartridge (true also of the 300 Win. Mag.) is that it has the same over-all length as a 30-06, hence will fit in '06 magazines any only requires re-chambering the barrel and opening up the bolt face, plus an extractor alteration, to convert an '06 to 308 Magnum. Pressures run pretty high in this case, so only rifles with strong actions should be converted to the new cartridge. Only factory load is with 180-gr. "Dual-Core" bullets, but the cases may be reloaded with American primers and any 30-cal. bullets from 110- to 220-gr. weight. It is thus a versatile as well as powerful high performance cartridge.

NORMA 7.62mm RUSSIAN Imported by Norma-Precision for American owners of Winchester Model 1895 and surplus military rifles in this caliber, the 7.62mm is furnished with the Tri-Clad soft point 180-gr. bullet developing 2625 fps muzzle velocity and more than 2750 fp energy. This is a rimmed bottle-necked case, ballistically almost identical to our 308, thus only slightly inferior to the 30-06. Formerly loaded in this country with either 145-gr. or 150-gr. bullets at 2820 fps, those ballistics may be reproduced in these new cases by handloaders desiring a lighter, faster bullet loading.

303 BRITISH HV Another modernized old cartridge is Norma's high velocity loadings of the 303 British. As loaded by Remington with a 215-gr. bullet and by Winchester with a 180-gr., pressure limitations of the Lee-Enfield action have held velocities to a sedate 2180-2540 fps, and owners of surplus 303's have wondered how they could obtain higher speeds. The safest way is to decrease bullet weight, and this is just what Norma has done. Two Norma factory loads include a 150-gr. bullet at 2720 fps and a 130-gr. at 2789, either of which will shoot flatter and open quicker on impact than the heavier bullets. If you use a 303 for open country hunting of deer or antelope, give these new loads a try.

7.65 ARGENTINE Originally known as the 7.65mm Belgian Mauser, this cartridge was once loaded in the U.S. and chambered in such popular rifles as the Remington 30-S and Winchester 54 and 70, but was discontinued about the time of WW 2 for lack of demand. Importation of surplus Argentine military Mausers has reversed the picture and there is once again a need for this surprisingly efficient round. Norma offers a single 150-gr. soft point with 2920 fs muzzle velocity and 2105 fs at **300** yards for a midrange trajectory height of only 5.8". Regardless of the fact that this cartridge was designed over 70 years ago, in its modern version it is still an excellent deer cartridge. Bullet (not cartridge) size is the same as a 303 British—.311"-.312".

8x57-JR and 8x57-JRS Rimmed versions of the famous 8x57 Mauser cartridge, the 8x57-JR is loaded by Norma with a 196-gr. .318" bullet, while the 8x57-JRS has the same weight but in .323" diameter. Post-war rifles generally have the larger bore size, while pre-war rifles usually (but not necessarily) have the .318" bore. In any event, the proof markings on the barrel should be carefully examined and only those cartridges with the proper size bullets used. Both of the 8x57 rimmed rounds are good deer and black bear cartridges.

358 NORMA MAGNUM First of the new line of Norma Magnums, this 35-caliber number was offered to the market in 1959 and since then has steadily gained favor among big game hunters here and abroad. In the Scandinavian countries, the 358 Norma has become a favorite of moose hunters, a use for which it is well-fitted almost anywhere. A 250-gr. bullet at 2790 fps from a 23″ barrel gives 4322 fp energy—some 1500 more than a 220-gr. 30-06—and energy close to the 4500 fp of a 375 Magnum. With a 200-gr. bullet, 3100 fps can be reached with permissible pressures, so that the 358 Norma may be thought of as a direct competitor of the 338 Winchester, both ballistically and as concerns adaptability to game species. It should fill the bill as a powerful "medium" bore for African hunting, and of course is a natural for Canadian and Alaskan large game.

RIMFIRE CARTRIDGES

5mm REMINGTON RIMFIRE MAGNUM Although originally announced in the fall of 1967, this 20-cal. bottle-necked high velocity rimfire was not offered on sale until 1970, for various problems arose in providing adequate breech support for case rims. These were finally overcome and this cartridge now ranks as our most powerful rimfire. It has a 38-gr. Power-Lokt HP bullet of .2045″ diameter with muzzle velocity of 2100 fps and 372 f.p. Remaining speeds are 1605 fps at 100 yards, and 1400 at 150, which is about its limit on varmints. You'll need a special cleaning rod for this one, as 22-cal. rods are too large.

22 SHORT The economical shooting gallery cartridge. Accurate to 50 yards, this old load is still a popular number. Three loadings—Standard, High Speed and Gallery—give it a usefulness second only to the indispensable 22 Long Rifle. It is **not** a game cartridge, however, and its use on live targets should be restricted to rats, snakes, starlings and the like, since even in the

high speed load its light bullet gives but half the energy of the Long Rifle.

22 LONG Only the High Speed loading of this little "betwixt and between" cartridge survives. Having neither the accuracy of the Short nor the power of the Long Rifle it is not recommended except for those few old repeating rifles chambered especially for it.

22 LONG RIFLE Finest and most versatile rimfire cartridge ever developed, it is today better than ever. Four loadings fit it for just about everything except big game hunting. This is everybody's cartridge, with the gilt-edged accuracy of the special Match loads for serious competition, the Standard rounds for economical practice, the High Speeds for small game hunting (with hollow-point bullets), and the Shot cartridges for pest destruction. The High Speed with plain bullet is not recommended for **any** of these uses. For hunting, better use the hollow-point for humane kills, and even try for a head shot. Pass up shots beyond 75 yards and be content with squirrels, rabbits and birds.

22 WINCHESTER AUTOMATIC Useful only to owners of the old Winchester Model 1903 autoloader, it is less powerful than the Long Rifle.

22 WRF (or REMINGTON SPECIAL) More powerful than any Long Rifle load and a far better hunting cartridge, it deserves to be more popular. Its flat-nose bullet, of slightly greater diameter and 5 grains more weight than a Long Rifle, is faster, and turns up a third more energy. For squirrel hunters it is hard to beat, and rifles for it should again be made.

22 WINCHESTER MAGNUM RIMFIRE Now in second place to the 5mm Remington Rimfire Magnum as far as velocity and energy are concerned, the 22 WMR remains an excellent choice for the rimfire rifleman who wants greater shock power than the 22 LR offers—and wants it in other than a Remington or Winchester rifle. Chambering for the 22 WMR is offered by numerous other rifle makers, and by a few handgun manufacturers as well.

Part II. HANDGUN CARTRIDGES
(Rimfire & Centerfire)

22 SHORT RF This little cartridge is currently experiencing a revival of popularity because of its adaptability to rapid-fire international-type shooting in the autoloading pistols made especially for it.

22 LONG RF See Rifle Cartridge Section.

22 LONG RIFLE RF Just as with rifles, this cartridge has done more than any other to popularize shooting and training with the handgun. In either revolver or "automatic" it is highly accurate and makes a fine companion for hunter and trapper. Ammo is easily carried, yet will kill small game better than some larger centerfires. Use high speeds for hunting and standards for target work.

22 REMINGTON JET First of the CF handgun cartridges to appear, this little bottleneck was introduced in March of 1961 when Smith & Wesson announced their Magnum M53 revolver. Besides the 22 Jet this gun handles (via cylinder inserts) 22 Shorts, Longs and Long Rifles. The factory-announced muzzle velocity of 2460 fps (obtained in closed-breech test barrels) has not been achieved in revolvers with their open gap between cylinder and barrel. However, the 1870 fps reached with 6″ barrels (2100 with 8⅜″) makes this a respectable handgun varmint cartridge in any man's language.

221 REMINGTON FIREBALL The second 22-cal. CF cartridge to be introduced by Remington, it established a precedent in 1963 by being chambered in the first American commercial bolt action pistol. 2650 fps has been reached with a 50-gr. bullet from its 10½″ barrel, equal to a factory 22 Hornet with 45-gr. bullet fired in a full-length rifle barrel.

256 WINCHESTER MAGNUM Winchester's entry in the high speed, flat trajectory handgun cartridge field had trouble getting off the ground after it was announced in April, 1961, but it has

finally developed as **both** a handgun and rifle cartridge. Early published factory velocities were **lower** than those actually attained, first tables saying 2000 fps for the 60-gr. SP bullet, whereas independent chronographs registered 2350 fps from the 8½″ barrel of a Ruger Hawkeye.

25 AUTO Smallest of production centerfires, this is strictly for use in defensive weapons—tiny automatics lacking both power and accuracy, firing 50-gr. metal case bullets with less energy than even the standard velocity 22 LR.

30 CARBINE In producing his Blackhawk revolver chambered for the 30 Carbine cartridge, Bill Ruger has made this round properly classifiable as a handgun load. For the considerable number of today's pistol shooters seeking a high speed, flat-shooting revolver cartridge without the heavy recoil of a 44 or 41 Magnum, but with more bullet weight and diameter than a 22 caliber, the 30 Carbine may provide the answer. Factory and GI loads produce velocities varying from 1400 to 1530 fps from our 7½″ barrel test revolver, giving them some 40% more muzzle energy than the 22 Jet. As a revolver load it will be liked particularly by owners of carbines in the same caliber as a companion piece.

30 LUGER A bottle-necked cartridge for automatic pistols firing a 93-gr. metal case bullet at 1,220 fs. Flat shooting with high paper energy, expansion is lacking due to bullet construction, severely limiting its game-killing or man-stopping capabilities. However, it far out-classes the 32 ACP.

32 AUTO Next step up in the caliber scale for automatics, this is a very popular cartridge here and abroad for pocket pistols. Many are used by foreign police where it is known as the 7.65mm, but again a small (71-gr.) round nose metal case bullet gives energy only in the high speed 22 Long Rifle class and no bullet expansion. Not recommended for hunting or defense use.

32 S&W & 32 S&W LONG These are the most popular of the 32's for revolvers, the shorter load used in innumerable old "bureau-drawer specials," the accurate Long in target and light police revolvers. The Long should always be chosen if the gun will handle it. A good small game cartridge but lacks power for police work.

32 COLT SHORT & LONG A pair of "obsolete" cartridges used in old-model Colt pocket revolvers, they are less accurate and less powerful than the 32 S&W Long, and will not chamber in modern 32-caliber revolvers.

32-20 WINCHESTER Best of all the 32s for revolvers, using 100-gr. bullets in both lead and soft point types with flat nose, this is the smallest caliber practical for serious police and defensive use. Trajectory is also flatter due to higher velocity, making this a good hunting cartridge for varmints and small game. Do NOT use the "High Velocity" rifle loads in revolvers.

38 AUTO and 38 SUPER AUTOMATIC The 38 Automatic cartridge is intended to be used in the original Colt 38 Automatic pistols, Models of 1900 and 1902. When the Colt Super 38 appeared about 1925, a new, more powerful loading was offered under the name of Super 38 for this stronger pistol. These Super 38 Automatic cartridges should not be fired in the early model Colt pistols in view of their system of slide attachment and the higher pressures of the Super cartridge. Even the regular 38 Automatic is closely comparable to the 9mm Luger in power, and the 38 Super will give the 357 Magnum a run for its money in barrels of equal length. If loaded with soft point bullets, both of these 38 Auto cartridges would make good game killing loads. Either cartridge will function properly in the Super automatic pistol.

380 AUTO Designed to give more power in a straight blowback automatic pistol than is provided by the 32 ACP cartridge, and yet keep down chamber pressure and recoil to stay within the limitations of small pocket pistols, it is the smallest auto pistol cartridge which can be recommended for defense. Super Vel's modern loading of an 80-gr. JHP bullet at 1026 fps considerably increases the effectiveness of this cartridge.

9mm LUGER Improved bullet designs and modern high speed loadings have greatly upped the stopping power and all-round utility of the well-known 9mm Parabellum or Luger. To the old 124-gr. metal cased loading at 1120 fps have been added a 115-gr. JHP at 1160 fps (Rem.), a 100-gr. Power Point at 1325 fps (Win.), and either a 110-gr. SP at 1325 or 90-gr. JHP at 1422 fps by Super Vel. Long a European military pistol cartridge, the 9mm has now become an International cartridge with wide spread civilian and growing police use as well.

38 S&W A favorite cartridge for pocket revolvers, with 146-gr bullet, and adopted by the British military during World War II, when it was known as the 38-200 (as it was loaded with a 200-gr. bullet). Nothing smaller is recommended for defensive use.

38 COLT SHORT & LONG The 38 Short was used in early Colt house defense guns and the Long was the cartridge which failed to stop fanatical Moros during the Philippine Insurrection. Either may be used in a 38 Special revolver, but both are outclassed by that cartridge for any purpose, hence seldom used.

38 SPECIAL As with the 9mm, this cartridge—once considered marginal for police, defensive and combat use—has become, with the introduction of new bullets and high speed loadings, a far more effective "stopper" than was formerly thought possible. Hollow point and expanding soft points ranging from 110-gr. and 125-gr. at 1370 fps, to 158-gr. bullets at 1150 fps (from 6" barrels) have given this old cartridge a new lease on life. In its milder loadings, it continues to be our most accurate centerfire target cartridge for handguns.

357 MAGNUM A high velocity revolver cartridge ideally suited to the needs of police officers and field shooters, it offers higher velocity, flatter trajectories, greater striking energy and deeper penetration than the 38 Special with same bullet weights and barrel length. With metal piercing bullets it will penetrate an

automobile body, and with expanding bullets is capable of killing game of considerable size if a proper hit is made. The newer jacketed soft point and hollow-point bullets are especially effective; these possess the added advantage of not leading barrels as did the original lead bullet loads. One of our three best long range revolver cartridges, a gun in this caliber has the extra attraction of chambering all 38 Special cartridges for target and practice shooting.

38-40 WINCHESTER See Part I—CF Rifle Cartridges.

41 MAGNUM Produced by Remington for Smith & Wesson revolvers in response to demands for a more potent police cartridge, this new 41 Magnum fills the gap between the 357 and 44 Magnums. Two loads are offered, one a 210-gr. SP at 1500 fps, the other a 210-gr. lead bullet at 1050 fps, both MV figures from 8⅜" bbls. In the more common 6" bbl., velocities run 1342 and 986. A potent and accurate cartridge in SP version, trajectory is practically as flat as the 44 Magnum is; it penetrates even deeper, though bullet energy is less. Recoil, only 75% of a 44 Magnum's, makes it a much more pleasant load to shoot. It may well find more use in the game fields than on the policeman's beat. Recoil and gun weight are both heavy for police use, and so far the lead bullet loads have shown only medoicre accuracy. Bullet diameter is .410" and will not interchange with the old 41 Long Colt.

44-40 WINCHESTER See Part I—CF Rifle Cartridges.

44 S&W SPECIAL Developed as a target cartridge from the earlier 44 S&W Russian, the 44 Special has never been loaded by the factories to its velocity potential. The 246-gr. lead bullets travel slowly (755 fs), which is of no matter on target ranges where their high accuracy is paramount. Only when properly handloaded is its true power capacity realized.

44 REMINGTON MAGNUM Quite in a class by itself, this extremely powerful revolver cartridge with standard factory loadings of 240-gr. lead or jacketed SP and HP bullets at 1470 fps (from 6½" barrels) ranks high in stopping power and recoil. Muzzle energy of 1150 f.p. is more than twice that of the hottest 38 Specials, but so is recoil, and gun weight too must be higher, making this a cartridge for specialized use by veteran handgunners. It most definitely cannot be recommended for beginning handgunners! Those shooters seeking a lighter load for target practice may use the mild old 44 S&W Special.

45 COLT Most famous of all American revolver cartridges and still one of the best, whether the target be criminal or beast. For close range work we would prefer its big 250-gr. bullet to the 357 Magnum. Now that new guns are again being made for the old 45, its historical background as well as its effective power should ensure a continued popularity and long life. Availability of new jacketed hollow-point bullets, such as Hornady's 250-gr. for reloaders, have increased the stopping power of this cartridge and eliminated bore leading with the heavier loads. Modern solid-head cases are much to be preferred for reloading.

45 AUTO Official U.S. Army sidearm cartridge since 1911 and spanning 4 wars, this largest American round for automatic pistols has thoroughly proven itself, both in combat and on the target range. Difficult to control until mastered, but inherently accurate in accurized pistols, its already wide popularity has been given assists in the form of special target loads with 185- and 210-gr. match bullets at very low velocity, plus some stepped up prescriptions, typical of which is Super Vel's 190-gr. JHP at 1060 fps. Probably more shooters than ever before are using this cartridge for a wide range of activities from police sidearm to hunting. On competitive target ranges it often supplants the 38 Special in the centerfire matches. It is a good all-round choice for big bore pistol shooters.

45 AUTO RIM Companion of the 45 ACP, this thick-rimmed cartridge was developed for use in revolvers chambered for the 45 Auto round, without the necessity of using half-moon clips. Its 230-gr. lead bullets at 810 fps MV (from 5½" barrel) makes it suitable for either police or field use. Shallow rifling in these revolvers requires that bullets be cast hard or jacketed.

CENTER RIFLE CARTRIDGES — BALLISTICS AND PRICES

Winchester-Western, Remington-Peters, Federal, Speer-DWM, Browning and Frontier

Most of these centerfire loads are available from Winchester-Western and Remington-Peters. Loads available from only one source are marked by a letter, thus: Winchester (a); Western (b); Remington (c); Peters (d); Speer-DWM (f). Those fewer cartridges also available from Federal are marked (e). Contrary to previous practice, W-W and R-P prices are not necessarily uniform. **All prices are approximate.**

Cartridge	Bullet Wt. Grs.	Bullet Type	Velocity (fps) Muzzle	Velocity 100 yds.	Velocity 200 yds.	Velocity 300 yds.	Energy (ft. lbs.) Muzzle	Energy 100 yds.	Energy 200 yds.	Energy 300 yds.	Mid-Range Trajectory 100 yds.	Mid-Range Trajectory 200 yds.	Mid-Range Trajectory 300 yds.	Price for 20*
17 Remington	25	HP, PL	4020	3290	2630	2060	900	600	380	230	Not Available			$ 5.10
218 Bee*	46	HP	2860	2160	1610	1200	835	475	265	145	0.7	3.8	11.5	11.35
22 Hornet*	45	SP	2690	2030	1510	1150	720	410	230	130	0.8	4.3	13.0	10.85
22 Hornet* (c, d)	45	HP	2690	2030	1510	1150	720	410	230	130	0.8	4.3	13.0	10.35
22 Hornet*	46	HP	2690	2030	1510	1150	740	420	235	135	0.8	4.3	13.0	10.35
222 Remington (e)	50	SP, MC, PL†	3200	2660	2170	1750	1140	785	520	340	0.5	2.5	7.0	4.35
222 Remington Magnum (c, d)	55	SP, PL†	3300	2800	2340	1930	1330	955	670	455	0.5	2.3	6.1	4.75
222 Remington Magnum (c, d)	55	HP, PL	3300	2830	2400	2010	1330	975	700	490	Not Available			5.10
223 Remington (c, d, e)	55	SP, PL†	3300	2800	2340	1930	1330	955	670	455	0.5	2.1	5.4	4.50
22-250 Remington	55	PSP	3810	3270	2770	2320	1770	1300	935	655	0.3	1.6	4.4	4.75
22-250 Remington (c, d, e)	55	HP, PL, SP	3810	3330	2890	2490	1770	1360	1020	760	Not Available			4.90
225 Winchester (a, b)	55	PSP	3650	3140	2680	2270	1630	1200	875	630	0.4	1.8	4.8	4.85
243 Winchester (a, e)	80	PSP, PL†	3500	3080	2720	2410	2180	1690	1320	1030	0.4	1.8	4.7	6.00
243 Winchester (c, d)	80	HP, PL	3450	3050	2675	2330	2115	1650	1270	965	Not Available			6.25
243 Winchester (a, c, e)	100	PP, CL, PSP	3070	2790	2540	2320	2090	1730	1430	1190	0.5	2.2	5.5	5.70
6mm Remington (c, d)	80	PSP, HP, PL†	3450	3130	2750	2400	2220	1740	1340	1018	0.4	1.8	4.7	6.40
6mm Remington (c, d)	100	PCL	3190	2920	2660	2420	2260	1890	1570	1300	0.5	2.1	5.1	6.00
244 Remington (d)	90	PSP	3200	2850	2530	2230	2050	1630	1280	995	0.5	2.1	5.5	5.70
25-06 Remington (c, d)	87	HP	3500	3070	2680	2310	2370	1820	1390	1030	Not Available			6.55
25-06 Remington (a, c, d)	120	PSP, CL	3120	2850	2600	2360	2590	2160	1800	1480	Not Available			6.55
25-20 Winchester*	86	L, Lu	1460	1180	1030	940	405	265	200	170	2.6	12.5	32.0	8.65
25-20 Winchester*	86	SP	1460	1180	1030	940	405	265	200	170	2.6	12.5	32.0	9.60
25-35 Winchester	117	SP, CL	2300	1910	1600	1340	1370	945	665	465	1.0	4.6	12.5	6.05
250 Savage (a, b)	87	PSP, SP	3030	2660	2330	2060	1770	1370	1050	820	0.6	2.5	6.4	5.65
250 Savage	100	ST, CL, PSP	2820	2460	2140	1870	1760	1340	1020	775	0.6	2.9	7.4	5.65
256 Winchester Magnum* (b)	60	OPE	2800	2070	1570	1220	1040	570	330	200	0.8	4.0	12.0	10.35
257 Roberts (a, b)	87	PSP	3200	2840	2500	2190	1980	1560	1210	925	0.5	2.2	5.7	6.20
257 Roberts (a, b)	100	ST, CL	2900	2540	2210	1920	1870	1430	1080	820	0.6	2.7	7.0	6.20
257 Roberts	117	PP, CL	2650	2280	1950	1690	1820	1350	985	740	0.7	3.4	8.8	6.20
6.5 Remington Magnum (c)	100	PSPCL	3450	3070	2690	2320	2640	2090	1610	1190	Not Available			8.15
6.5mm Remington Magnum (c)	120	PSPCL	3030	2750	2480	2230	2450	2010	1640	1330	0.5	2.3	5.7	8.15
264 Winchester Magnum	100	PSP, CL	3700	3260	2880	2550	3040	2360	1840	1440	0.4	1.6	4.2	8.15
264 Winchester Magnum	140	PP, CL	3200	2490	2700	2480	3180	2690	2270	1910	0.5	2.0	4.9	8.15
270 Winchester	100	PSP	3480	3070	2690	2340	2690	2090	1600	1215	0.4	1.8	4.8	6.55
270 Winchester (e)	130	PP, PSP	3140	2880	2630	2400	2850	2390	2000	1660	0.5	2.1	5.3	6.20
270 Winchester	130	ST, CL, BP, PP	3140	2850	2580	2320	2840	2340	1920	1550	0.5	2.1	5.3	6.55
270 Winchester (c, d)	150	CL	2800	2440	2140	1870	2610	1980	1520	1160	0.6	2.9	7.6	6.55
270 Winchester (a, b, e)	150	PP, SP	2900	2620	2380	2160	2800	2290	1890	1550	0.6	2.5	6.3	6.55
280 Remington (c, d)	150	PCL	2900	2670	2450	2220	2800	2370	2000	1640	0.6	2.5	6.1	6.55
280 Remington (c, d)	165	CL	2820	2510	2220	1970	2910	2310	1810	1420	0.6	2.8	7.2	6.25
284 Winchester (a, b)	125	PP	3200	2880	2590	2310	2840	2300	1860	1480	0.5	2.1	5.3	6.55
284 Winchester (a, b)	150	PP	2900	2630	2380	2160	2800	2300	1890	1550	0.6	2.5	6.3	6.55
7mm Mauser (a, e)	139	SP	2710	2440	2190	1960	2280	1850	1490	1190	0.7	3.0	7.8	6.55
7mm Mauser (a, e)	175	SP	2490	2170	1900	1680	2410	1830	1400	1100	0.8	3.7	9.5	6.55
7mm Remington Magnum	125	CL	3430	3080	2750	2450	3260	2630	2100	1660	0.6	1.8	4.7	8.15
7mm Remington Magnum (e)	150	PP, CL	3260	2970	2700	2450	3540	2940	2430	1990	0.4	2.0	4.9	7.95
7mm Remington Magnum (e)	175	PP	3070	2720	2400	2120	3660	2870	2240	1750	0.5	2.4	6.1	7.95
7mm Remington Magnum (c, d)	175	PCL	3070	2860	2660	2460	3660	3170	2740	2350	0.5	2.1	5.2	8.15
30 Carbine* (a, c, e)	110	HSP, SP	1980	1540	1230	1040	950	575	370	260	1.4	7.5	21.7	10.30
30-30 Winchester (c, d)	150	CL	2410	1960	1620	1360	1930	1280	875	616	0.9	4.5	12.5	5.15
30-30 Winchester (e)	150	HP	2410	2020	1700	1430	1930	1360	960	680	0.9	4.2	11.0	5.15
30-30 Winchester (a, b)	150	PP, ST, OPE	2410	2020	1700	1430	1930	1360	960	680	0.9	4.2	11.0	5.15
30-30 Winchester (e)	170	PP, HP, CL, ST, MC	2220	1890	1630	1410	1860	1350	1000	750	1.2	4.6	12.5	5.15
30 Remington	170	ST, CL	2120	1820	1560	1350	1700	1250	920	690	1.1	5.3	14.0	6.15
30-06 Springfield (a, b)	110	PSP	3370	2830	2350	1920	2770	1960	1350	900	0.5	2.2	6.0	6.55
30-06 Springfield	125	PSP	3200	2810	2480	2200	2840	2190	1710	1340	0.5	2.2	5.6	6.55
30-06 Springfield (c, d)	150	SP	2970	2710	2470	2240	2930	2440	2030	1670	0.5	2.4	6.0	6.55
30-06 Springfield (e)	150	PP	2970	2620	2300	2010	2930	2280	1760	1340	0.6	2.5	6.5	6.55
30-06 Springfield	150	ST, PCL, PSP	2970	2670	2400	2130	2930	2370	1920	1510	0.6	2.4	6.1	6.55
30-06 Springfield	180	PP, CL, PSP	2700	2330	2010	1740	2910	2170	1610	1210	0.7	3.1	8.3	6.55
30-06 Springfield (e)	180	ST, BP, PCL	2700	2470	2250	2040	2910	2440	2020	1660	0.7	2.9	7.0	6.55
30-06 Springfield (a)	180	MCBT, MAT	2700	2520	2350	2190	2910	2540	2200	1900	0.6	2.8	6.7	9.70
30-06 Springfield	220	PP, CL	2410	2120	1870	1670	2830	2190	1710	1360	0.8	3.9	9.8	6.40
30-06 Springfield (a, b)	220	ST	2410	2180	1980	1790	2830	2320	1910	1560	0.8	3.7	9.2	6.40
30-40 Krag	180	PP, CL	2470	2120	1830	1590	2440	1790	1340	1010	0.8	3.8	9.9	6.65
30-40 Krag	180	ST, PCL	2470	2250	2040	1850	2440	2020	1660	1370	0.8	3.5	8.5	6.65
30-40 Krag (a, b)	220	ST	2200	1990	1800	1630	2360	1930	1580	1300	1.0	4.4	11.0	6.65
300 Winchester Magnum (c, e)	150	PP, PCL, PSP	3400	3050	2730	2430	3850	3100	2480	1970	0.4	1.9	4.8	8.40
300 Winchester Magnum (c, e)	180	PP, PCL, PSP	3070	2850	2640	2440	3770	3250	2790	2380	0.5	2.1	5.3	8.40
300 Winchester Mag (a, b)	220	ST	2720	2490	2270	2060	3620	3030	2520	2070	0.6	2.9	6.9	9.35
300 H&H Magnum (a, b)	150	ST	3190	2870	2580	2300	3390	2740	2220	1760	0.5	2.1	5.2	9.35
300 H&H Magnum	180	ST, PCL	2920	2670	2440	2220	3400	2850	2380	1970	0.6	2.4	5.8	8.40
300 H&H Magnum (a, b)	220	ST, CL	2620	2370	2150	1940	3350	2740	2260	1840	0.7	3.1	7.7	9.35
300 Savage (e)	150	PP	2670	2350	2060	1800	2370	1840	1410	1080	0.7	3.2	8.0	6.20
300 Savage	150	ST, PCL	2670	2390	2130	1890	2370	1900	1510	1190	0.7	3.0	7.6	6.35
300 Savage (c, d)	150	CL	2670	2270	1930	1660	2370	1710	1240	916	0.7	3.3	9.3	6.35
300 Savage (e)	180	PP, CL	2370	2040	1760	1520	2240	1660	1240	920	0.9	4.1	10.5	6.35
300 Savage	180	ST, PCL	2370	2160	1960	1770	2240	1860	1530	1250	0.9	3.7	9.2	6.35
303 Savage (c, d)	180	CL	2140	1810	1550	1340	1830	1310	960	715	1.1	5.4	14.0	6.75
303 Savage (a, b)	190	ST	1980	1680	1440	1250	1650	1190	875	660	1.3	6.2	15.5	6.75
303 British (e)	180	PP, CL	2540	2300	2090	1900	2580	2120	1750	1440	0.7	3.3	8.2	6.60
303 British (c, d)	215	SP	2180	1900	1660	1460	2270	1720	1310	1020	1.1	4.9	12.5	6.60
308 Winchester (a, b)	110	PSP	3340	2810	2340	1920	2730	1930	1340	900	0.5	2.2	6.0	6.55
308 Winchester (a, b)	125	PSP	3100	2740	2430	2160	2670	2080	1640	1300	0.5	2.3	5.9	6.55
308 Winchester (e)	150	PP	2860	2520	2210	1930	2730	2120	1630	1240	0.6	2.7	7.0	6.55
308 Winchester	150	ST, PCL	2860	2570	2300	2050	2730	2200	1760	1400	0.6	2.6	6.5	6.55
308 Winchester (e)	180	PP, CL	2610	2250	1940	1680	2720	2020	1500	1130	0.7	3.4	8.9	6.55
308 Winchester	180	ST, PCL	2610	2390	2170	1970	2720	2280	1870	1540	0.8	3.1	7.4	6.55
308 Winchester (a, b)	200	ST	2450	2210	1980	1770	2670	2170	1750	1400	0.8	3.6	9.0	6.40
32 Winchester Special (c, d, e)	170	HP, CL	2280	1920	1630	1410	1960	1390	1000	750	1.0	4.8	12.5	5.30
32 Winchester Special	170	PP, ST	2280	1870	1560	1330	1960	1320	920	665	1.0	4.8	13.0	5.30
32 Remington (c, d)	170	CL	2120	1800	1540	1340	1700	1220	895	680	1.0	4.9	13.0	6.35
32 Remington (a, b)	170	ST	2120	1760	1460	1220	1700	1170	805	560	1.1	5.3	14.5	6.30
32-20 Winchester*	100	SP	1290	1060	940	840	370	250	195	155	3.3	15.5	38.0	9.20
32-20 Winchester*	100	SP, L, Lu	1290	1060	940	840	370	250	195	155	3.3	15.5	38.0	7.40

CENTERFIRE RIFLE CARTRIDGES — BALLISTICS AND PRICES (continued)

Cartridge	Wt. Grs.	Bullet Type	Velocity (fps) Muzzle	100 yds.	200 yds.	300 yds.	Energy (ft. lbs.) Muzzle	100 yds.	200 yds.	300 yds.	Mid-Range Trajectory 100 yds.	200 yds.	300 yds.	Price for 20*
8mm Mauser (a, c, e)	170	PP, CL	2570	2140	1790	1520	2490	1730	1210	870	0.8	3.9	10.5	$6.55
338 Winchester Magnum (a, b)	200	PP	3000	2690	2410	2170	4000	3210	2580	2090	0.5	2.4	6.0	8.80
338 Winchester Magnum (a, b)	250	ST	2700	2430	2180	1940	4050	3280	2640	2090	0.7	3.0	7.4	8.80
338 Winchester Magnum (a, b)	300	PP	2450	2160	1910	1690	4000	3110	2430	1900	0.8	3.7	9.5	8.80
348 Winchester (a)	200	ST	2530	2220	1940	1680	2840	2190	1765	1509	0.4	1.7	4.7	9.15
348 Winchester (c, d)	200	CL	2530	2140	1820	1570	2840	2030	1470	1090	0.8	3.8	10.0	9.15
35 Remington (c, d)	150	CL	2400	1960	1580	1280	1920	1280	835	545	0.9	4.6	13.0	5.95
35 Remington (e)	200	PP, ST, CL	2100	1710	1390	1160	1950	1300	860	605	1.2	6.0	16.5	5.95
350 Remington Magnum (c, d)	200	PCL	2710	2410	2130	1870	3260	2570	2000	1550	Not Available			8.15
350 Remington Magnum (c, d)	250	PCL	2410	2190	1980	1790	3220	2660	2180	1780	Not Available			8.15
351 Winchester Self-Loading*	180	SP	1850	1560	1310	1140	1370	975	685	520	1.5	7.8	21.5	13.00
358 Winchester (a, b)	200	ST	2530	2210	1910	1640	2840	2160	1610	1190	0.8	3.6	9.4	7.75
358 Winchester (a, b)	250	ST	2250	2010	1780	1570	2810	2230	1760	1370	1.0	4.4	11.0	7.75
375 H&H Magnum	270	PP, SP	2740	2460	2210	1990	4500	3620	2920	2370	0.7	2.9	7.1	10.45
375 H&H Magnum	300	ST	2550	2280	2040	1830	4330	3460	2770	2230	0.7	3.3	8.3	10.45
375 H&H Magnum	300	MC	2550	2180	1860	1590	4330	3160	2300	1680	0.7	3.6	9.3	10.20
38-40 Winchester*	180	SP	1330	1070	960	850	705	455	370	290	3.2	15.0	36.5	11.00
44 Magnum* (c, d)	240	SP	1750	1360	1110	980	1630	985	655	510	1.6	8.4		11.25
44 Magnum (b)	240	HSP	1750	1350	1090	950	1630	970	635	480	1.8	9.4	26.0	4.50
444 Marlin (c)	240	SP	2400	1845	1410	1125	3070	1815	1060	675	Not Available			6.65
44-40 Winchester*	200	SP	1310	1050	940	830	760	490	390	305	3.3	15.0	36.5	13.20
45-70 Government	405	SP	1320	1160	1050	990	1570	1210	990	880	2.9	13.0	32.5	8.10
458 Winchester Magnum	500	MC	2130	1910	1700	1520	5040	4050	3210	2570	1.1	4.8	12.0	19.40
458 Winchester Magnum	510	SP	2130	1840	1600	1400	5140	3830	2900	2220	1.1	5.1	13.5	12.80

*Price for 50 HP—Hollow Point SP—Soft Point PSP—Pointed Soft Point PP—Power Point L—Lead Lu—Lubaloy ST—Silvertip
HSP—Hollow Soft Point MC—Metal Case BT—Boat Tail MAT—Match BP—Bronze Point CL—Core Lokt PCL—Pointed Core Lokt
OPE—Open Point Expanding †PL—Power-Lokt (slightly higher price) (1) Not safe in handguns or Win. M73.

WEATHERBY MAGNUM CARTRIDGES — BALLISTICS AND PRICES

Cartridge	Wt. Grs.	Bullet Type	Velocity (fps) Muzzle	100 yds.	200 yds.	300 yds.	Energy (ft. lbs.) Muzzle	100 yds.	200 yds.	300 yds.	Mid-Range Trajectory 100 yds.	200 yds.	300 yds.	Price for 20
224 Weatherby Varmintmaster	50	PE	3750	3160	2625	2140	1562	1109	1670	1250	0.7	3.6	9.0	$5.95
224 Weatherby Varmintmaster	55	PE	3650	3150	2685	2270	1627	1212	881	629	0.4	1.7	4.5	5.95
240 Weatherby	70	PE	3850	3395	2975	2585	2304	1788	1376	1038	0.3	1.5	3.9	7.95
240 Weatherby	90	PE	3500	3135	2795	2475	2444	1960	1559	1222	0.4	1.8	4.5	7.95
240 Weatherby	100	PE	3395	3115	2850	2595	2554	2150	1804	1495	0.4	1.8	4.4	7.95
257 Weatherby	87	PE	3825	3290	2835	2450	2828	2087	1553	1160	0.3	1.6	4.4	8.95
257 Weatherby	100	PE	3555	3150	2815	2500	2802	2199	1760	1338	0.4	1.7	4.4	8.95
257 Weatherby	117	SPE	3300	2900	2550	2250	2824	2184	1689	1315	0.4	2.4	6.8	8.95
270 Weatherby	100	PE	3760	3625	2825	2435	3140	2363	1773	1317	0.4	1.6	4.3	8.95
270 Weatherby	130	PE	3375	3050	2750	2480	3283	2685	2183	1776	0.4	1.8	4.5	8.95
270 Weatherby	150	PE	3245	2955	2675	2430	3501	2909	2385	1967	0.5	2.0	5.0	8.95
7mm Weatherby	139	PE	3300	2995	2715	2465	3355	2770	2275	1877	0.4	1.9	4.9	8.95
7mm Weatherby	154	PE	3160	2885	2640	2415	3406	2874	2384	1994	0.5	2.0	5.0	8.95
300 Weatherby	150	PE	3545	3195	2890	2615	4179	3393	2783	2279	0.4	1.5	3.9	9.95
300 Weatherby	180	PE	3245	2960	2705	2475	4201	3501	2925	2448	0.4	1.9	5.2	9.95
300 Weatherby	220	SPE	2905	2610	2385	2150	4123	3329	2757	2257	0.6	2.5	6.7	9.95
340 Weatherby	200	PE	3210	2905	2615	2345	4566	3748	3038	2442	0.5	2.1	5.3	9.95
340 Weatherby	210	Nosler	3165	2910	2665	2435	4660	3948	3312	2766	0.5	2.1	5.0	9.95
340 Weatherby	250	SPE	2850	2580	2325	2090	4510	3695	3000	2425	0.6	2.7	6.7	9.95
375 Weatherby	270	SPE	3180	2850	2600	2315	6051	4871	4053	3210	0.5	2.0	5.2	10.95
378 Weatherby	300	SPE, FMJ	2925	2610	2380	2125	5700	4539	3774	3009	0.6	2.5	6.2	19.50
460 Weatherby	500	RN, FMJ	2700	2330	2005	1730	8095	6025	4465	3320	0.7	3.3	10.0	19.50

Trajectory is given from scope height. Velocities chronographed using 26″ bbls. Available with Nosler bullets; add $2.00 per box.
SPE—Semi-Pointed Expanding RN—Round Nose PE—Pointed Expanding FMJ—Full Metal Jacket

RIMFIRE CARTRIDGES — BALLISTICS AND PRICES

Remington-Peters, Winchester-Western, Federal & CCI

All loads available from all manufacturers except as indicated: R-P (a); W-W (b); Fed. (c); CCI (d). **All prices are approximate.**

CARTRIDGE	WT. GRS.	BULLET TYPE	VELOCITY FT. PER SEC. MUZZLE	100 YDS.	ENERGY FT. LBS. MUZZLE	100 YDS.	MID-RANGE TRAJECTORY 100 YDS.	HANDGUN BARREL LENGTH	BALLISTICS M.V. F.P.S.	M.E. F.P.	PRICE FOR 50
22 Short T22 (b)	29	C, L*	1045	810	70	42	5.6	6″	865	48	$ .93
22 Short Hi-Vel.	29	C, L	1125	920	81	54	4.3	6″	1035	69	.95
22 Short HP Hi-Vel. (a, b, c)	27	C, L	1155	920	80	51	4.2	—	—	—	1.03
22 Short (a, c)	29	D	1045	—	70	—	—	—	—	(per 500)	8.37
22 Short (a, c)	15	D	1710	—	97	—	—	—	—	(per 500)	8.37
22 Long Hi-Vel. (a, c)	29	C, L	1240	965	99	60	3.8	6″	1095	77	1.03
22 Long Rifle T22 (b)†-2	40	L*	1145	975	116	84	4.0	6″	950	80	1.08
22 Long Rifle (b)†-3	40	L*	1120	950	111	80	4.2	—	—	—	1.85
22 Long Rifle (b)†-3	40	L*						6¾″	1060	100	1.85
22 Long Rifle (d)†-4	40	C	1165	980	121	84	4.0	—	—	—	.99
22 Long Rifle Hi-Vel.	40	C, L	1285	1025	147	93	3.4	6″	1125	112	1.08
22 Long Rifle HP Hi-Vel. (b, d)	37	C, L	1315	1020	142	85	3.4	—	—	—	1.20
22 Long Rifle HP Hi-Vel. (a, c)	36	C	1365	1040	149	86	3.4	—	—	—	1.20
22 Long Rifle (a, b, c)	No.	12 Shot						—	—	—	2.24
22 WRF [Rem. Spl.] (a, b)	45	C, L	1450	1110	210	123		—	—	—	3.07
22 WRF Mag. (b)	40	JHP	2000	1390	355	170	1.6	6½″	1550	213	2.95
22 WRF Mag. (b)	40	MC	2000	1390	355	170	1.6	6½″	1550	213	2.95
22 Win. Auto Inside lub. (a)	45	C, L	1055	930	111	86		—	—	—	3.07
5mm Rem. RFM (a)	38	PLHP	2100	1605	372	217	Not Available				4.20

†—Target loads of these ballistics available in: (1) Rem. Match; (2) W-W Super Match Mark III; (3) Super Match Mark IV and Pistol Match; (4) CCI Mini-Group. C—Copper plated L—Lead (Wax Coated) L*—Lead, lubricated D—Disintegrating MC—Metal Case
HP—Hollow Point JHP—Jacket Hollow Point PLHP—Power-Lokt Hollow Point

NORMA C.F. RIFLE CARTRIDGES — BALLISTICS AND PRICES

Norma ammunition loaded to standard velocity and pressure is now available with Nosler bullets in the following loads: 270 Win., 130-, 150-gr.; Super 7x61 (S&H), 160-gr.; 308 Win., 180-gr.; 30-06, 150-, 180-gr., all at slightly higher prices. All ballistic figures are computed from a line of sight one inch above center of bore at muzzle. Write for their latest prices.

Cartridge	Bullet Wt. Grs.	Type	Velocity, feet per sec. V Muzzle	V 100 yds.	V 200 yds.	V 300 yds.	Energy, foot pounds E Muzzle	E 100 yds.	E 200 yds.	E 300 yds.	Max. height of trajectory, inches Tr. 100 yds.	Tr. 200 yds.	Tr. 300 yds.	Price for 20
220 Swift	50	SP	4111	3611	3133	2681	1877	1448	1090	799	.2	.9	3.0	$6.00
222 Remington	50	SP	3200	2660	2170	1750	1137	786	523	340	.0	2.0	6.2	4.50
223	55	SP	3300	2900	2520	2160	1330	1027	776	570	.4	2.4	6.8	5.10
22-250	50	SP	3800	3300	2810	2350	1600	1209	885	613	Not Available			5.10
	55	SP	3650	3200	2780	2400	1637	1251	944	704	Not Available			5.10
243 Winchester	80	SP	3500	3070	2660	2290	2041	1570	1179	873	.0	1.4	4.1	6.05
	100	SP	3070	2790	2540	2320	2093	1729	1433	1195	.1	1.8	5.0	6.05
6mm Remington	100	SP	3190	2920	2660	2420	2260	1890	1570	1300	.4	2.1	5.3	6.05
250 Savage	87	SP	3032	2685	2357	2054	1776	1393	1074	815	.0	1.9	5.8	5.80
	100	SP	2822	2514	2223	1956	1769	1404	1098	850	.1	2.2	6.6	5.80
6.5 Carcano	156	SP	2000	1810	1640	1485	1386	1135	932	764	Not Available			7.65
6.5 Japanese	139	SPBT	2428	2280	2130	1990	1820	1605	1401	1223	.3	2.8	7.7	7.65
	156	SP	2067	1871	1692	1529	1481	1213	992	810	.6	4.4	11.9	7.65
6.5 x 54 MS	139	SPBT	2580	2420	2270	2120	2056	1808	1591	1388	.2	2.4	6.5	7.65
	156	SP	2461	2240	2033	1840	2098	1738	1432	1173	.3	3.0	8.2	7.65
6.5 x 55	139	SPBT	2789	2630	2470	2320	2402	2136	1883	1662	.1	2.0	5.6	7.65
	156	SP	2493	2271	2062	1867	2153	1787	1473	1208	.3	2.9	7.9	7.65
270 Winchester	110	SP	3248	2966	2694	2435	2578	2150	1773	1448	.1	1.4	4.3	6.55
	130	SPBT	3140	2884	2639	2404	2847	2401	2011	1669	.0	1.6	4.7	6.55
	150	SPBT	2802	2616	2436	2262	2616	2280	1977	1705	.1	2.0	5.7	6.55
7.5 x 55 Schmidt Rubin (7.5 Swiss)	180	SP	2650	2450	2260	2060	2792	2350	1990	1665	Not Available			7.65
7 x 57	110	SP	3068	2792	2528	2277	2300	1904	1561	1267	.0	1.6	5.0	6.55
	150	SPBT	2756	2539	2331	2133	2530	2148	1810	1516	.1	2.2	6.2	6.55
	175	SP	2490	2170	1900	1680	2410	1830	1403	1097	.4	3.3	9.0	6.55
7mm Remington Magnum	150	SP	3260	2970	2700	2450	3540	2945	2435	1990	.4	2.0	4.9	8.25
	175	SP	3070	2720	2400	2120	3660	2870	2240	1590	.5	2.4	6.1	8.25
7 x 61 S & H (26 in.)	160	SPBT	3100	2927	2757	2595	3415	3045	2701	2393	.0	1.5	4.3	8.80
30 U.S. Carbine	110	SPRN	1970	1595	1300	1090	948	622	413	290	.8	6.4	19.0	4.15
308 Winchester	130	SPBT	2900	2590	2300	2030	2428	1937	1527	1190	.1	2.1	6.2	6.55
	150	SPBT	2860	2570	2300	2050	2725	2200	1762	1400	.1	2.0	5.9	6.55
	180	SPBT	2610	2400	2210	2020	2725	2303	1952	1631	.2	2.5	6.6	6.55
	180	SP	2610	2400	2210	2020	2725	2303	1952	1631	.7	3.4	8.9	7.50
7.62 Russian	180	PSPBT	2624	2415	2222	2030	2749	2326	1970	1644	.2	2.5	6.6	7.65
308 Norma Magnum	180	DC	3100	2881	2668	2464	3842	3318	2846	2427	.0	1.6	4.6	10.25
30-06	130	PSPBT	3281	2951	2636	2338	3108	2514	2006	1578	.1	1.5	4.6	6.55
	150	PS	2972	2680	2402	2141	2943	2393	1922	1527	.0	1.9	5.7	6.55
	180	PSPBT, SPDC	2700	2494	2296	2109	2914	2487	2107	1778	.1	2.3	6.4	6.55
	220	SPRN	2411	2197	1996	1809	2840	2358	1947	1599	.3	3.1	8.5	6.55
	220	FJBT	2410	2197	1996	1809	2840	2358	1947	1599	Not Available			6.55
	180	SPDC	2700	2494	2296	2109	2914	2487	2107	1778	Not Available			7.50
7.65 Argentine	150	SP	2920	2630	2355	2105	2841	2304	1848	1476	.1	2.0	5.8	7.65
303 British	130	SP	2789	2483	2195	1929	2246	1780	1391	1075	.1	2.3	6.7	6.65
	150	SP	2720	2440	2170	1930	2465	1983	1569	1241	.1	2.2	6.5	6.65
	180	SPBT	2540	2340	2147	1965	2579	2189	1843	1544	.2	2.7	7.3	6.65
7.7 Japanese	130	SP	2950	2635	2340	2065	2513	2004	1581	1231	.1	2.0	5.9	7.65
	180	SPBT	2493	2292	2101	1922	2484	2100	1765	1477	.3	2.8	7.7	7.65
8mm Mauser (.323 in.)	123	SP	2888	2515	2170	1857	2277	1728	1286	942	Not Available			6.60
	165	SP	2855	2563	2285	2028	2894	2405	1912	1506	Not Available			6.60
	196	SP	2526	2195	1894	1627	2778	2097	1562	1152	Not Available			6.60
358 Winchester	250	SP	2250	2010	1780	1570	2811	2243	1759	1369	Not Available			8.15
358 Norma Magnum	250	SP	2790	2493	2231	2001	4322	3451	2764	2223	.2	2.4	6.6	10.25
44 Magnum*	240	SPFP	1705				1526				Not Available			4.85
	236	HP	1705				1526							4.85

P—Pointed   SP—Soft Point   HP—Hollow Point   FP—Flat Point   RN—Round Nose   MC—Metal Case
DC—Dual Core   SPS—Soft Point Semi-Pointed   NA—Not announced   *Price for 50   BT—Boat Tail

CENTERFIRE HANDGUN CARTRIDGES — BALLISTICS AND PRICES

Winchester-Western, Remington-Peters, Norma, Federal, Browning & S&W/Fiocchi

Most loads are available from W-W and R-P. All available Norma loads are listed. Federal cartridges are marked with an asterisk. Other loads supplied by only one source are indicated by a letter, thus: Norma (a); R-P (b); W-W (c).

Cartridge	Bullet Gr.	Bullet Style	Muzzle Velocity	Muzzle Energy	Barrel Inches	Price Per 50
22 Jet (b)	40	SP	2100	390	8⅜	$10.05
221 Fireball (b)	50	SP	2650	780	10½	4.90
25 (6.35mm) Auto*	50	MC	810	73	2	5.85
256 Winchester Magnum (c)	60	HP	2350	735	8½	10.10
30 (7.65mm) Luger Auto	93	MC	1220	307	4½	9.30
32 S&W Blank (c)	No bullet		—	—	—	4.35
32 S&W Blank, BP (c)	No bullet		—	—	—	4.35
32 Short Colt	80	Lead	745	100	4	5.10
32 Long Colt, IL (b, c)	82	Lub.	755	104	4	5.30
32 Colt New Police	100	Lead	680	100	4	6.20
32 (7.65mm) Auto*	71	MC	960	145	4	6.70
32 (7.65mm) Auto Pistol (a)	77	MC	900	162	4	6.50
32 S&W	88	Lead	680	90	3	5.10
32 S&W Long	98	Lead	705	115	4	5.35
32-20 Winchester	100	Lead	1030	271	6	7.40
32-20 Winchester	100	SP	1030	271	6	9.20
357 Magnum (b)*	158	SP	1550	845	8⅜	8.80
357 Magnum	110	HP	1410	695	8⅜	8.80
357 Magnum	158	Lead	1410	696	8⅜	7.45
357 Magnum (a)	158	JHP	1450	735	8⅜	8.80
9mm Luger (a)	116	MC	1165	349	4	8.30
9mm Luger Auto*	124	MC	1120	345	4	8.30
38 S&W Blank	No bullet		—	—	—	4.50
38 Smith & Wesson	146	Lead	685	150	4	7.10
38 S&W (a)	146	Lead	730	172	4	6.15
38 Special Blank	No bullet		—	—	—	7.00
38 Special, IL (c)	150	Lub.	1060	375	6	6.60
38 Special, IL (c)	150	MP	1060	375	6	7.85
38 Special	158	Lead	855	256	6	7.00
38 Special	200	Lead	730	236	6	6.60
38 Special	158	MP	855	256	6	7.85
38 Special (b)	125	SJHP	Not available			7.85
38 Special (b)	158	SJHP	Not available			7.85
38 Special WC (b)	148	Lead	770	195	6	6.60
38 Special Match, IL (c)	148	Lead	770	195	6	6.60
38 Special Match, IL (b, c)	158	Lead	855	256	6	6.45
38 Special Hi-Speed*	158	Lead	1090	425	6	7.00
38 Special (a)	158	RN	900	320	6	6.45
38 Short Colt	125	Lead	730	150	6	5.75
38 Short Colt, Greased (c)	130	Lub.	730	155	6	5.60
38 Long Colt	150	Lead	730	175	6	6.35
38 Super Auto (b)	130	MC	1280	475	5	7.10
38 Auto, for Colt 38 Super (c)	130	MC	1280	475	5	7.10
38 Auto	130	MC	1040	312	4½	7.10
380 Auto*	95	MC	955	192	3¾	6.85
38-40 Winchester	180	SP	975	380	5	11.00
41 Remington Magnum (b)	210	Lead	1050	515	8¾	9.70
41 Remington Magnum (b)	210	SP	1500	1050	8¾	11.00
44 S&W Special	246	Lead	755	311	6½	8.60
44 Remington Magnum	240	SP	1470	1150	6½	11.25
44 Remington Magnum	240	Lead	1470	1150	6½	11.25
44-40 Winchester	200	SP	975	420	7½	13.20
45 Colt	250	Lead	860	410	5½	8.65
45 Colt, IL (c)	255	Lub., L	860	410	5½	8.65
45 Auto	230	MC	850	369	5	9.00
45 ACP (a)	230	JHP	850	370	5	9.45
45 Auto WC*	185	MC	775	245	5	9.45
45 Auto MC (a, b)	230	MC	850	369	5	9.45
45 Auto Match (c)	185	MC	775	247	5	9.50
45 Auto Match, IL (c)	210	Lead	710	235	5	9.45
45 Auto Match*	230	MC	850	370	5	9.50
45 Auto Rim (b)	230	Lead	810	335	5½	9.40

IL—Inside Lub. JSP—Jacketed Soft Point WC—Wad Cutter
RN—Round Nose HP—Hollow Point Lub—Lubricated
MC—Metal Case SP—Soft Point MP—Metal Point
LGC—Lead, Gas Check JHP—Jacketed Hollow Point

SUPER VEL HANDGUN CARTRIDGES — BALLISTICS AND PRICES

The cartridges listed below are perhaps the most powerful and destructive of these calibers commercially manufactured. Bullets listed can be had as components — other weights (not loaded by Super Vel) are also available.

Cartridge	Bullet Gs.	Bullet Style	Muzzle Velocity	Muzzle Energy	Barrel Inches	Price Per 50
380 ACP	88	JHP	1065	227	4	$8.45
9mm Luger	90	JHP	1485	441	4	9.45
9mm Luger	112	JSP	1330	439	4	9.45
9mm Luger	125	FMJ	995	274	4	9.45
9mm Luger	125	FMJ	1120	345	4	10.00
38 Special	110	JHP	1370	458	6	8.85
38 Special	110	JSP	1370	458	6	8.85
38 Special	125	JHP	1370	520	6	8.85
38 Special	158	SWC-lead	855	256	6	7.60
38 Special	158	RN-lead	855	256	6	7.60
38 Special	148	HBWC	775	196	6	7.60
357 Magnum	110	JHP	1690	697	6	9.70
357 Magnum	110	JSP	1690	697	6	9.70
357 Magnum	137	JSP	1620	796	6	9.70
357 Magnum	158	JHP	1300	593	6	9.70
357 Magnum	158	JSP	1300	593	6	9.70
45 Auto	190	JHP	1060	473	5	10.95
44 Magnum	180	JHP	2075	1591	8⅜	5.50
44 Magnum	180	JSP	2075	1591	8⅜	5.50

JHP—Jacketed Hollow Point SP—Jacketed Soft Point
HBWC—Hollow Base Wad Cutter †Price per 20

SHOTSHELL LOADS AND PRICES

Winchester-Western, Remington-Peters, Federal, Eley & S&W/Fiocchi

In certain loadings one manufacturer may offer fewer or more shot sizes than another, but in general all makers offer equivalent loadings. Sources are indicated by letters, thus: W-W (a); R-P (b); Fed. (c); Eley (d). Prices are approximate.

GAUGE	Length Shell Ins.	Powder Equiv. Drams	Shot Ozs.	Shot Size	PRICE FOR 25
MAGNUM LOADS					
10 (a[1], b)	3½	5	2	2	$10.65
12 (a, b, c)	3	4½	1⅞	BB, 2, 4	6.50
12 (a[1], b)	3	4¼	1⅝	2, 4, 6	6.50
12 (a)	3	Max	1⅜	2, 4, 6	6.10
12 (a[1], b, c, d)	2¾	4	1½	2, 4, 5, 6	5.95
16 (a, b, c, d)	2¾	3½	1¼	2, 4, 6	5.10
20 (a, b, c)	3	3¼	1¼	4, 6, 7½	5.30
20 (a[1])	3	Max	1 3/16	4	5.30
20 (a[1], b, c, d)	2¾	3	1⅛	2, 4, 6, 7½	4.05
LONG RANGE LOADS					
10 (a, b)	2⅞	4¾	1⅝	4	6.30
12 (a[1], b, c, d)	2¾	3¾	1¼	BB, 2, 4, 5, 6, 7½, 9	4.65
16 (a, b, c, d)	2¾	3¼	1⅛	4, 5, 6, 7½, 9	4.30
20 (a[1], b, c, d)	2¾	2¾	1	4, 5, 6, 7½, 9	4.05
28 (a, b)	2¾	2¼	¾	6, 7½, 9	4.05
28 (c)	2¾	2¼	⅞	4, 6, 7½, 9	4.05
FIELD LOADS					
12 (a, b, c)	2¾	3¼	1¼	7½, 8	4.00
12 (a, b, c, d)	2¾	3¼	1⅛	4, 5, 6, 7½, 8, 9	4.00
12 (a, b, c, d)	2¾	3	1	4, 5, 6, 8	3.70
16 (a, b, c, d)	2¾	2¾	1⅛	4, 5, 6, 7½, 8, 9	3.70
16 (a, b, c)	2¾	2½	1	6, 8	3.55
20 (a, b, c, d)	2¾	2½	1	4, 5, 6, 7½, 8, 9	3.60
20 (a, b, c)	2¾	2¼	⅞	6, 8	3.30
SCATTER LOADS					
12 (a, b)	2¾	3	1⅛	8	4.20
TARGET LOADS					
12 (a, b, c)	2¾	3	1⅛	7½, 8	3.90
12 (a, b, c)	2¾	2¾	1⅛	7½, 8	3.90
16 (a, b, c)	2¾	2½	1	9	3.70
20 (a, b, c)	2¾	2¼	⅞	9	3.30
28 (a, c)	2¾	2¼	¾	9	4.05
410 (a, b, c, d)	3	Max	¾	9	3.10
410 (a, b, c)	2½	Max	½	9	3.10
SKEET & TRAP					
12 (a, b, c, d)	2¾	3	1⅛	7½, 8, 9	3.90
12 (a, b, c, d)	2¾	2¾	1⅛	7½, 8, 9	3.90
16 (a, b, c, d)	2¾	2½	1	9	3.70
16 (c)	2¾	1⅛	1⅛	8, 9	3.70
20 (a, b, c)	2¾	2¼	⅞	9	3.30
BUCKSHOT					
12 (a, b, c)	3 Mag.	4½	—	00 Buck—12 pellets	7.05
12 (a, b, c)	3 Mag.	4½	—	4 Buck—41 pellets	8.15
12 (b)	2¾ Mag.	4	—	1 Buck—20 pellets	7.05
12 (a, b, c)	2¾ Mag.	4	—	00 Buck—12 pellets	7.05
12 (a, b, c)	2¾	3¾	—	00 Buck— 9 pellets	6.25
12 (a, b, c)	2¾	3¾	—	0 Buck—12 pellets	6.30
12 (a, b, c)	2¾	3¾	—	1 Buck—16 pellets	6.30
12 (a, b, c)	2¾	3¾	—	4 Buck—27 pellets	6.30
16 (a, b, c)	2¾	3	—	1 Buck—12 pellets	6.25
20 (a, b, c)	2¾	2¾	—	3 Buck—20 pellets	6.25
RIFLED SLUGS					
12 (a, b, c, d)	2¾	3¾	1	Slug	7.35
16 (a, b, c)	2¾	3	⅞	Slug	6.75
20 (a, b, c)	2¾	2¾	⅝	Slug	6.75
410 (a, b, c)	2½	Max	⅕	Slug	6.10

W-W 410, 28- and 10-ga. Magnum shells available in paper cases only, as are their scatter and target loads; their skeet and trap loads come in both plastic and paper.

RP shells are all of plastic with Power Piston wads except: 12 ga. scatter loads have Post Wad: all 10 ga., 410-3″ and rifled slug loads have standard wad columns.

Federal magnum, range, buckshot, slug and all 410 loads are made in plastic only. Field loads are available in both paper and plastic.

Eley shotshells are of plastic-coated paper.

1—These loads available from W-W with Lubaloy shot at higher price.

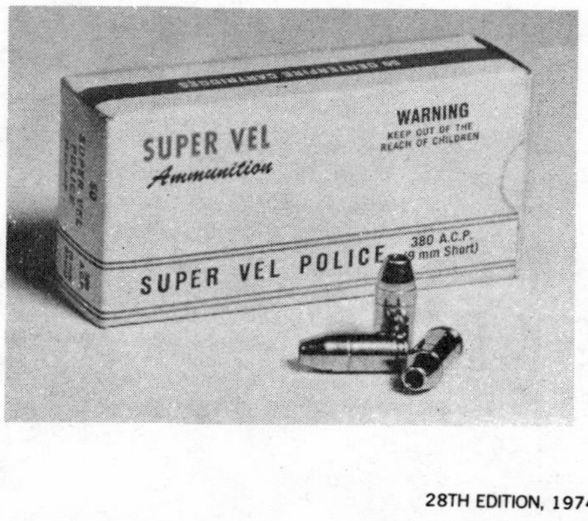

FEDERAL® AMMUNITION

FEDERAL CARTRIDGE CORPORATION 2700 FOSHAY TOWER MINNEAPOLIS, MINN. 55402

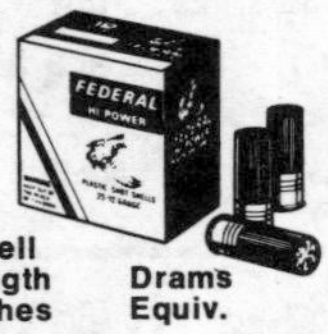

SHOT SHELL LOADS

Gauge	Shell Length Inches	Drams Equiv.	Shot Ozs.	Shot Sizes	Price Per Box
MAGNUM LOADS					
12	3	4	1⅞	BB,2,4	6.65
12	3	4	1⅝	2,4,6	6.15
12	2¾	3¾	1½	2,4,5,6	5.65
16	2¾	3¼	1¼	2,4,6	4.85
20	3	3	1¼	2,4,6,7½	5.00
20	2¾	2¾	1⅛	4,6,7½	4.45
HI-POWER® LOADS					
12	2¾	3¾	1¼	BB,2,4,5,6,7½,9	4.65
16	2¾	3¼	1⅛	4,5,6,7½,9	4.25
20	2¾	2¾	1	4,5,6,7½,9	4.05
28	2¾	2¼	⅞	6,7½,9	3.95
410	3	Max.	11⁄16	4,5,6,7½	3.60
410	2½	Max.	½	6,7½	3.10
FIELD AND GAME LOADS					
12	2¾	3¼	1¼	7½,8,9	3.95
12	2¾	3¼	1⅛	4,5,6,7½,8,9	3.80
12	2¾	3¼	1	6,8	3.15
16	2¾	2¾	1⅛	4,5,6,7½,8,9	3.50
16	2¾	2½	1	8	3.05
20	2¾	2½	1	4,5,6,7½8,9	3.40
20	2¾	2½	⅞	8	2.80
TARGET LOADS					
12[1]	2¾	2¾	1⅛	7½,8,8½,9	3.90
12[1]	2¾	3	1⅛	7½,8,8½,9	3.90
12	2¾	2¾	1⅛	7½,8,8½,9	3.55
12	2¾	3	1⅛	7½,8,8½,9	3.55
12[3]	2¾	3¼	1⅛	7½,8,9	4.00
16	2¾	2¾	1⅛	7½,8,9	3.70
20[2]	2¾	2½	⅞	8,9	3.25
28	2¾	2	¾	9	3.95
410	2½	Max.	½	9	3.00
BUCKSHOT & RIFLED SLUG LOADS					
12	3	Sup. Mag.	—	00 Buck, 15 Pellets	1.60
12	3	Sup. Mag.	—	No. 4 Buck, 41 Pellets	1.60
12	2¾	Mag.	—	00 Buck, 12 Pellets	1.38
12	2¾	Mag.	—	No. 1 Buck, 20 Pellets	1.38
12	2¾	Mag	—	No. 4 Buck, 34 Pellets	1.38
12	2¾	Max.	—	00 Buck, 9 Pellets	1.23
12	2¾	Max.	—	0 Buck, 12 Pellets	1.23
12	2¾	Max.	—	No. 1 Buck, 16 Pellets	1.23
12	2¾	Max.	—	No. 4 Buck, 27 Pellets	1.23
16	2¾	Max.	—	No. 1 Buck, 12 Pellets	1.23
20	2¾	Max.	—	No. 3 Buck, 20 Pellets	1.23
12	2¾	Max.	—	⅞ oz. Rifled Slug	1.45
16	2¾	Max.	—	4/5 oz. Rifled Slug	1.37
20	2¾	Max.	—	⅝ oz. Rifled Slug	1.33
410	2½	Max.	—	1/5 oz. Rifled Slug	1.25

All Plastic tubes except
[1]Paper [2]Offered in Plastic and Paper
[3]International Load.
Packaged 25 per box except Buckshot and slugs 5 per box.
Wad Columns: Triple-Plus in 12, 16, 20 Ga. Hi-Power and Fields.
Magnums, 28 Gauge, 410 use shot cup with conventional wads.
12 Gauge Target loads use plastic "Champion" air-chamber wad.
Buck and Rifled Slugs do not use shot cups.

CENTERFIRE PISTOL & RIFLE

Cartridge	Gr.	Bullet Style	Muzzle Velocity	Muzzle Energy	Barrel Length Inches	Price Per Box
PISTOL						
25 (6.35mm) Auto	50	MC	810	73	2	5.85
32 Auto	71	MC	905	128	4	6.65
357 Mag.,Ni.Pl.Cs.	158	JSP	1550	845	6	8.75
9 mm Luger Auto	123	MC	1120	345	4	8.30
380 Auto	95	MC	955	192	3¾	6.80
38 Special Match	148	WC	770	195	6	6.60
38 Special	158	Lead	855	256	6	6.30
38 Special	158	SWC	855	256	6	6.45
38 Special, Hi-Vel.	158	Lead	1090	415	6	7.00
45 Auto Match	230	MC	850	370	5	8.95
45 Auto Match	185	WC	775	247	5	9.40
RIFLE						
222 Remington	50	SP	3200	1140	26	4.10
*22250 Remington	55	SP	3810	1770	26	4.50
223 Remington	55	SP	3300	1330	26	4.50
*243 Winchester	80	SP	3500	2180	26	5.70
*243 Winchester	100	SP	3070	2090	26	5.70
*270 Winchester	130	HS	3140	2840	24	6.20
*270 Winchester	150	HS	2800	2610	24	6.20
*7 mm Mauser	175	HS	2490	2410	24	6.20
*7 mm Mauser	139	HS	2710	2280	24	6.20
*7 mm Rem. Mag.	150	HS	3260	3540	26	7.70
*7 mm Rem. Mag.	175	HS	3070	3660	26	7.70
30 Carbine	110	SP	1980	955	18	3.90
*3030 Winchester	150	HS	2410	1930	26	4.85
*3030 Winchester	170	HS	2220	1860	26	4.85
*3006 Springfield	150	HS	2970	2930	24	6.20
*3006 Springfield	180	HS	2700	2910	24	6.20
*3006 Springfield	125	SP	3200	2840	24	6.20
*300 Savage	150	HS	2670	2370	24	6.05
*300 Savage	180	HS	2370	2240	24	6.05
*300 Win. Mag.	150	HS	3400	3850	26	7.95
*300 Win. Mag.	180	HS	3070	3770	26	7.95
*303 British	180	HS	2540	2580	26	6.25
*308 Winchester	150	HS	2860	2730	24	6.20
*308 Winchester	180	HS	2610	2720	24	6.20
*8mm Mauser	170	HS	2570	2490	23½	6.20
*32 Win. Special	170	HS	2280	1960	26	5.00
*35 Remington	200	HS	2100	1950	22	5.65
44 Magnum	240	HP-SP	1750	1630	18½	4.40

Pistol Cartridges Packaged 50 per box
Rifle Cartridges Packaged 20 per box
MC-Metal Case JSP-Jacketed Soft Point WC-Wadcutter SWC-Semi-Wadcutter
SP-Soft Point HS-"Hi-Shok" Soft Point HP-Hollow Point
*Caliber with "Cartridge Carrier" pack.

RIMFIRE 22'S

Cartridge	Gr.	Bullet Style	Muzzle Velocity	Barrel Length	Price Per Box
HI-POWER®					
22 Short	29	Solid	1125	24	.90
22 Short	29	Hollow Point	1155	24	.98
22 Long	29	Solid	1240	24	.95
†22 Long Rifle	40	Solid	1285	24	1.03
†22 Long Rifle	38	Hollow Point	1315	24	1.15
22 Long Rifle	25	No. 12 Shot	—	24	2.10
CHAMPION STANDARD VELOCITY					
22 Short	29	Solid	1045	24	.90
†22 Long Rifle	40	Solid	1145	24	1.03

Packaged 50 per box. Items with † also available packaged 100 per plastic box.

BROWNING 22 AUTO CHALLENGER PISTOL
Caliber: 22 LR, 10-shot magazine.
Barrel: 4½" or 6¾".
Length: 8⅞" over-all (4½" bbl.). **Weight:** 35 oz. (4½" bbl.).
Stocks: Select walnut, hand checkered, wrap-around.
Features: Steel frame, manual stop-open latch (automatic after last shot); gold plated grooved trigger; trigger pull adjustment screw on rear face of frame.
Sights: ⅛" non-glare blade front; frame-mtd. rear, screw adj. for w. & e.
Price: Blue, either bbl. . . . . **$108.50**   Engraved and gold inlaid . . **$259.50**
Price: Renaissance Grade, engraved, chrome plated, 6¾" bbl. . . . **$294.50**

BROWNING 22 AUTO MEDALIST PISTOL
Caliber: 22 LR, 10-shot magazine.
Barrel: 6¾", med.-heavy vent. rib.
Length: 11⁵/₁₆" over-all. **Weight:** 46 oz. less weights.
Stocks: Full wrap-around thumbrest of select checkered walnut; matching fore-end. Left hand grips available.
Features: Dry-fire mechanism permits practice without mechanical harm. Fore-end holds variable weights. Trigger adj. for weight of pull and backlash.
Sights: ⅛" undercut removable blade front; rear frame-mtd., has micrometer clicks adj. for w. and e. Sight radius, 9½".
Price: Blued . . . . **$169.50**   Engraved and gold inlaid **$324.50**
Price: Renaissance Grade, chrome plated **$374.50**

BROWNING INTERNATIONAL MEDALIST PISTOL
Caliber: 22 LR, 10-shot magazine.
Barrel: 5.9", med.-heavy vent rib.
Length: 10¹⁵/₁₆" over-all. **Weight:** 42 oz.
Stocks: Select walnut, full wraparound with thumb rest, 1.8" max. width.
Features: The International Medalist pistol meets all International Shooting Union regulations. The regular Medalist qualifies under N.R.A. pistol regulations.
Sights: Identical to those of standard Medalist, sight radius is 8.6".
Price: Blued **$159.50**

COLT WOODSMAN MATCH TARGET AUTO PISTOL
Caliber: 22 LR, 10-shot magazine.
Barrel: 4" or 6".
Length: 9" (4" bbl.). **Weight:** 40 oz. (6" bbl.), 36 oz. (4" bbl.).
Stocks: Walnut with thumbrest; checkered.
Features: Wide trigger, automatic slide stop.
Sights: Ramp front with removable undercut blade; ⅛" standard, ¹/₁₀" on special order; Colt-Elliason adjustable rear.
Price: Colt Blue only **$119.95**

COLT WOODSMAN SPORT AND TARGET MODEL
Caliber: 22 LR, 10-shot magazine.
Barrel: 4" or 6".
Length: 9" (4" bbl.). **Weight:** 30 oz. (4" bbl.) 32 oz. (6" bbl.).
Stocks: Walnut with thumbrest; checkered.
Features: Wide trigger, automatic slide stop.
Sights: Ramp front with removable blade, adjustable rear.
Price: Colt Blue only **$99.95**

COLT TARGETSMAN
Same as Woodsman S&T model except: 6" bbl. only; fixed blade front sight, economy adj. rear; without auto. slide stop **$84.95**

COLT GOLD CUP NAT'L MATCH AUTO
Caliber: 45 ACP or Wad Cutter; 38 Spec. W.C. 7-shot magazine.
Barrel: 5", with new design bushing.
Length: 8½". **Weight:** 37 oz.
Stocks: Checkered walnut, gold plated medallion.
Features: Arched or flat housing; wide, grooved trigger with adj. stop; ribbed-top slide, hand fitted, with improved ejection port.
Sights: Patridge front, Colt-Elliason rear adj. for w. and e.
Price: Colt Royal Blue **$189.95**

COLT GOLD CUP NAT'L MATCH Mk IV SERIES 70 AUTO
Identical to the Gold Cup except fitted with a split-finger, collet-type barrel bushing and reverse-taper barrel to match for improved accuracy.
Price: **$199.95**

HI-STANDARD SUPERMATIC STANDARD CITATION

Caliber: 22 LR, 10-shot magazine.
Barrel: 5½" bull weight.
Length: 10" (5½" bbl.). **Weight:** 42 oz. (5½" bbl.).
Stocks: Checkered walnut with or w/o thumbrest, right or left.
Features: Adjustable trigger pull; over-travel trigger adjustment; double acting safety; rebounding firing pin.
Sights: Undercut ramp front; click adjustable square notch rear.
Price: 5½" bull barrel $130.00

HI-STANDARD S'MATIC CITATION MILITARY

Caliber: 22 LR, 10-shot magazine.
Barrel: 5½" bull, 7¼" fluted.
Length: 9¾" (5½" bbl.). **Weight:** 46 oz.
Stocks: Checkered walnut with or w/o thumbrest, right or left.
Features: Same as regular Citation plus military style grip, stippled front- and backstraps, positive magazine latch.
Sights: Undercut ramp front; frame mounted rear, click adj.
Price: Either bbl. length $130.00

HI-STANDARD VICTOR

Caliber: 22 LR, 10-shot magazine.
Barrel: 4½", 5½".
Length: 8¾" (4½" bbl.). **Weight:** 48 oz. (4½" bbl.), 52 oz. (5½" bbl.).
Stock: Checkered walnut.
Sights: Undercut ramp front, rib mounted click adj. rear.
Features: Vent. rib, interchangeable barrel, 2 - 2¼ lb. trigger pull, blue finish, back and front straps stippled.
Price: Either bbl. length $175.00

HI-STANDARD (*ISU) OLYMPIC AUTO PISTOL

Caliber: 22 Short, 10-shot magazine.
Barrel: 6¾" round tapered, with stabilizer.
Length: 11¼". **Weight:** 40 oz.
Stocks: Checkered walnut w or w/o thumbrest, right or left.
Features: Integral stabilizer with two removable weights. Trigger adj. for pull and over-travel; Citation grade finish.
Sights: Undercut ramp front; click adj., square notch rear.
Price: Blued $132.50
*Complies with all International Shooting Union regulations.
Olympic model with frame-mounted rear sight $145.00

HI-STANDARD SUPERMATIC TROPHY MILITARY

Caliber: 22 LR, 10-shot magazine.
Barrel: 5½" heavy, 7¼" fluted.
Length: 9¾ inches (5½" bbl.). **Weight:** 44½ oz.
Stocks: Checkered walnut with or w/o thumbrest, right or left.
Features: Grip duplicates feel of military 45; positive action mag. latch; front- and backstraps stippled. Trigger adj. for pull, over-travel.
Sights: Undercut ramp front; frame mounted rear, click adj.
Price: Either bbl. length $145.00

SMITH & WESSON 22 AUTO PISTOL Model 41
Caliber: 22 LR or 22 S, 10-shot clip.
Barrel: 5″ or 7⅜″, sight radius 9⁵/₁₆″ (7⅜″ bbl.).
Length: 12″, incl. detachable muzzle brake, (7⅜″ bbl. only).
Weight: 43½ oz. (7⅜″ bbl.).
Stocks: Checkered walnut with thumbrest, usable with either hand.
Features: ⅜″ wide, grooved trigger with adj. stop; wgts. available to make pistol up to 59 oz.
Sights: Front, ⅛″ Patridge undercut; micro click rear adj. for w. and e.
Price: S&W Bright Blue, satin matted bbl., either caliber **$145.00**

SMITH & WESSON 22 MATCH HEAVY BARREL M-41
Caliber: 22 LR, 10-shot clip.
Barrel: 5½″ heavy, without muzzle brake. Sight radius, 8″.
Length: 9″. **Weight:** 44½ oz.
Stocks: Checkered walnut with modified thumbrest, usable with either hand.
Features: ⅜″ wide, grooved trigger; adj. trigger stop.
Sights: ⅛″ Patridge on ramp base. S&W micro click rear, adj. for w. and e.
Price: S&W Bright Blue, satin matted top area **$145.00**

S & W 22 AUTO HEAVY BARREL EFS Model 41
Same as Model 41 Heavy Barrel but with extendible ⅛″ front sight. Without muzzle brake or weights. Blued **$160.50**

SMITH & WESSON CONVERSION KIT
Converts Models 41 and 46 from 22 Short to 22 LR and vice versa. Consists of barrel, slide, magazine, slide stop and recoil spring.
Price, parts only **$65.40**
Price, factory installed and tested **$74.85**
Price, 5½″ heavy bbl. only with sights for M41 or M46 .... **$37.40**

SMITH & WESSON 38 MASTER Model 52 AUTO
Caliber: 38 Special (for Mid-range W.C. with flush-seated bullet only). 5-shot magazine.
Barrel: 5″.
Length: 8⅝″. **Weight:** 41 oz. with empty magazine.
Features: Top sighting surfaces matte finished. Locked breech, moving barrel system; checked for 10-ring groups at 50 yards. Coin-adj. sight screws. Dry firing permissible if manual safety on.
Stocks: Checkered walnut.
Sights: ⅛″ Patridge front, S&W micro click rear adj. for w. and e.
Price: S&W Bright Blue **$225.00**

STERLING MODEL 283 TARGET
Caliber: 22 LR, 10-shot magazine.
Barrel: 4½″, 6″, and 8″.
Length: 9″ (4½″ bbl.). **Weight:** 36 oz. (4½″ bbl.).
Stocks: Checkered plastic.
Features: Adjustable trigger and balance weights; sear lock safety.
Sights: ⅛″ blade front; Click adj. square notch rear.
Price: Blued **$79.95**

RUGER Mark 1 TARGET MODEL AUTO PISTOL
Caliber: 22 LR only, 9-shot magazine.
Barrel: 6⅞″ or 5½″ bull barrel (6-groove, 14″ twist).
Length: 10⅞″ (6⅞″ bbl.). **Weight:** 42 oz. with 6⅞″ bbl.
Stocks: Checkered hard rubber.
Features: Rear sight mounted on receiver, does not move with slide; wide, grooved trigger.
Sights: ⅛″ blade front, micro click rear, adjustable for w. and e. Sight radius 9⅜″ (with 6⅞″ bbl.).
Price: Blued, either barrel length **$69.00**
Price: Checkered walnut panels with left thumbrest **$73.00**

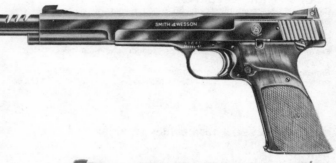

COLT DIAMONDBACK REVOLVER

Caliber: 22 S, L or LR, or 38 Special, 6 shot.
Barrel: 2½" or 4", with ventilated rib.
Length: 9" (4" bbl.). **Weight:** 25 oz. (2½" bbl.), 28½ oz. (4" bbl.).
Stocks: Checkered walnut, target type, square butt.
Features: Ventilated rib; grooved, crisp trigger; swing-out cylinder; wide hammer spur.
Sights: Ramp front, adj. notch rear.
Price: Colt Blue $139.95
Price: Nickel finish (38 Spl. only) $149.95

COLT PYTHON REVOLVER

Caliber: 357 Magnum (handles all 38 Spec.), 6 shot.
Barrel: 2½", 4" or 6", with ventilated rib.
Length: 9¼" (4" bbl.). **Weight:** 41 oz. (4" bbl.).
Stocks: Checkered walnut, target type, square butt.
Features: Ventilated rib; grooved, crisp trigger; swing-out cylinder; target hammer.
Sights: ⅛" ramp front, adj. notch rear.
Price: Colt Royal Blue ..... **$199.95** Nickeled **$224.95**

SMITH & WESSON 1953 Model 35, 22/32 TARGET

Caliber: 22 S, L or LR, 6 shot.
Barrel: 6 inches.
Length: 10½ inches. **Weight:** 25 oz.
Stocks: Checkered walnut, Magna.
Sights: Front, 1/10" Patridge, micro click rear, adjustable for w. and e.
Price: Blued $116.00

SMITH & WESSON 22 CENTER FIRE MAGNUM M-53

Caliber: Rem. 22 Jet and 22 S, L, LR with inserts. 6 shot.
Barrel: 4", 6" or 8⅜".
Length: 11¼" (6" bbl.). **Weight:** 40 oz.
Stocks: Checkered walnut, target.
Features: Grooved tangs and trigger, swing-out cylinder revolver.
Sights: ⅛" Baughman Quick Draw front, micro click rear, adjustable for w. and e.
Price: Blued $155.00
Price: Extra cylinder for 22 RF. (fitted) $37.40

SMITH & WESSON MASTERPIECE TARGET MODELS

Model: K-22 (M17).	K-22 (M48).
Caliber: 22 LR, 6 shot.	22 RF Magnum, 6 shot.
Barrel: 6", 8⅜".	4", 6" or 8⅜"
Length: 11⅛" (6" bbl.).	11⅛" (6" bbl.).
Weight: 38½ oz. (6" bbl.).	39 oz.(6" bbl.).
Model: K-32 (M16). (Illus.)	K-38 (M14).
Caliber: 32 S&W Long, 6 shot.	38 S&W Special, 6 shot.
Barrel: 6 inches.	6", 8⅜".
Length: 11⅛ inches.	11⅛ inches. (6" bbl.)
Weight: 38½ oz. (Loaded).	38½ oz. (6", loaded).

Features: All Masterpiece models have: checkered walnut, Magna stocks; grooved tang and trigger; ⅛" Patridge front sight, micro. adj. rear sights. Swing out cylinder revolver.
Price: Blued, all calibers $115.50

SMITH & WESSON COMBAT MASTERPIECE

Caliber: 38 Special (M15) or 22 LR (M18), 6 shot.
Barrel: 2" (M15) 4" (M18)
Length: 9⅛" (4" bbl.). **Weight:** Loaded, 22 36½ oz, 38 30 oz.
Stocks: Checkered walnut, Magna. Grooved tangs and trigger.
Sights: Front, ⅛" Baugham Quick Draw on ramp, micro click rear, adjustable for w. and e.
Price: Blued $115.50

U.S. HANDGUNS—TARGET REVOLVERS

SMITH & WESSON 1955 Model 25, 45 TARGET
Caliber: 45 ACP and 45 AR, 6 shot.
Barrel: 6½" (heavy target type).
Length: 11⅞ inches. **Weight:** 45 oz.
Stocks: Checkered walnut target.
Features: Tangs and trigger grooved; target trigger and hammer standard, checkered target hammer. Swing-out cylinder revolver.
Sights: ⅛" Patridge front, micro click rear, adjustable for w. and e.
Price: Blued **$155.00**

SMITH & WESSON ACCESSORIES
Target hammers with low, broad, deeply-checkered spur, and wide-swaged, grooved target trigger. For all frame sizes, **$5.00** (target hammers not available for small frames). Target stocks: for large-frame guns, **$10.65** to **$12.30**; for med/-frame guns, **$8.40-$10.65**; for small-frame guns, **$7.10**. These prices applicable only when specified on original order.
As separately-ordered parts: target hammers and triggers, **$7.65**; stocks, **$13.75-$15.60**.

U.S. HANDGUNS—SERVICE & SPORT

AMERICAN FIREARMS STAINLESS PISTOL
Caliber: 25 ACP, 8-shot.
Barrel: 2.1".
Length: 4.4". **Weight:** 15½ oz.
Stocks: Smooth walnut.
Sights: Fixed, open.
Price: Bright stainless steel finish **$79.95**
Price: Blued steel M & P model **$58.50**
Price: Deluxe Hi-Polish blued steel **$64.50**

AMERICAN FIREARMS DERRINGER
Caliber: 38 Special, 22 LR, 22 WRM, 2-shot.
Barrel: 3".
Length: 4¾". **Weight:** 15 oz.
Stocks: Checkered plastic, walnut optional ($3.00).
Sights: Fixed, open.
Features: Made entirely of stainless steel, spur trigger, positive hammer block safety.
Price: Hi-Polish **$67.50**
Price: Dura-Matt (police combat finish) **$76.50**

AMERICAN FIREARMS SAFEGUARD
Caliber: 380 ACP, 8-shot.
Barrel: 3½".
Length: 5½". **Weight:** 21 oz.
Stocks: Smooth walnut.
Sights: Fixed, open.
Features: Magazine safety, loaded chamber indicator. Made entirely from stainless steel.
Price: **$125.00**

AUTO MAG AUTO. PISTOL
Caliber: 44 Auto Mag or 357 Auto Mag, 7-shot.
Barrel: 6½".
Weight: 57 oz. (44), 54 oz. (357). **Length:** 11½" over-all.
Stocks: Checkered polyurethane.
Sights: Target-type ramp front, fully adj. rear.
Features: Short recoil, rotary bolt system. Made of stainless steel. Conversion unit available to change caliber using same frame. Comes in plastic carrying case with extra magazine, wrenches, lubricant and manual.
Price: 44 AMP or 357 AMP **$298.00**
Price: Conversion unit **$150.00**
Price: Engraved models from **$565.00**

BAUER 25 AUTOMATIC PISTOL
Caliber: 25 ACP, 6-shot.
Barrel: 2⅛".
Length: 4". **Weight:** 10 oz.
Stocks: Plastic pearl or checkered walnut.
Sights: Recessed, fixed.
Features: Stainless steel construction, positive manual safety, magazine safety. With padded zipper case.
Price: Satin stainless steel **$79.95**

BROWNING 22 AUTO NOMAD PISTOL

Caliber: 22 LR, 10-shot magazine.
Barrel: 4½" or 6¾".
Length: 8$^{15}/_{16}$" over-all (4½" bbl.). **Weight:** 34 oz. (4½ bbl.).
Stocks: Novadur plastic, checkered, wrap-around.
Features: Steel frame; thumb safety; bbls. interchangeable via lock screw on front of frame.
Sights: ⅛" non-glare blade front; frame-mtd. rear, screw adj. for w. & e.
Price: Blued, either bbl. $89.50

BROWNING 380

Caliber: 380 ACP.
Barrel: 4$^7/_{16}$".
Length: 7$^1/_{16}$". **Weight:** 23 oz.
Stock: Novadur plastic w/thumb rest.
Sights: Front, $^1/_{10}$" fixed blade. Rear, adjustable for w. & e.
Features: Fixed barrel, non-glare rear sight, magazine safety, loaded chamber indicator.
Price: Blue $89.50
Price: Renaissance Grade, engraved & chrome plated $249.50

BROWNING HI-POWER 9mm AUTOMATIC PISTOL

Caliber: 9mm Parabellum (Luger), 13-shot magazine.
Barrel: 4$^{21}/_{32}$ inches.
Length: 7¾" over-all. **Weight:** 32 oz.
Stocks: Walnut, hand checkered.
Features: External hammer with half-cock safety, thumb and magazine safeties. A blow on the hammer cannot discharge a cartridge; cannot be fired with magazine removed.
Sights: Fixed front; rear adj. for w.
Price: Blued $142.50
Price: 9mm Standard with rear sight adj. for w. and e. $156.50

BROWNING RENAISSANCE HI-POWER 9mm AUTO

Same as Browning Hi-Power 9mm Auto except: fully engraved, chrome plated, polyester pearl grips $349.50

BUDISCHOWSKY TP-70 AUTO PISTOL

Caliber: 25 ACP, 6-shot.
Barrel: 2.6".
Length: 4$^2/_3$". **Weight:** 12$^1/_3$ oz.
Stocks: Checkered walnut.
Sights: Fixed.
Features: Double action, exposed hammer, manual and magazine safeties. All stainless steel construction. Available in 22 LR—early 1974. Norarmco, manufacturer.
Price: $110.00

COLT PONY AUTOMATIC

Caliber: 380 ACP, 6-shot magazine.
Barrel: 3⅛".
Length: 5½" over-all.
Stocks: Checkered walnut.
Sights: Fixed blade front, drift-adj. rear.
Features: Blue finish, grooved trigger. Extra tang length gives protection from slide.
Price: $99.95

COLT COMMANDER AUTO PISTOL

Caliber: 45 ACP, 7 shot; 38 Super Auto, 9 shot; 9mm Luger, 9 shot.
Barrel: 4¼".
Length: 8". **Weight:** 26½ oz.
Stocks: Checkered Coltwood.
Features: Grooved trigger and hammer spur; arched housing; grip and thumb safeties.
Sights: Fixed, glare-proofed ramp front, square notch rear.
Price: Blued $134.95

COLT POCKET AUTOMATIC

Caliber: 25 ACP, 6-shot magazine.
Barrel: 2¼".
Length: 4⅜" over-all. **Weight:** 12 oz.
Stocks: Fully checkered walnut.
Sights: Fixed on full-length serrated rib.
Features: Thumb and magazine safeties; round top grooved visible hammer
Price: Colt blue $69.95

U.S. HANDGUNS—SERVICE & SPORT

COLT GOVT. SUPER 38 AUTO PISTOL
Caliber: 38 Super Auto, 9mm Luger 9 shot.
Barrel: 5".
Length: 8½". **Weight:** 39 oz.
Stocks: Checkered Coltwood. Grooved trigger.
Features: Grip and thumb safeties; grooved trigger and hammer; arched mainspring housing.
Sights: Fixed, glare-proofed ramp front, square notch rear.
Price: Blued .... $125.00   Nickeled $143.75

COLT MK IV/SERIES 70 45 GOV'T MODEL AUTO PISTOL
Identical to 38 Super and previous 45 Government Model except for addition of a split-finger, collet-type barrel bushing and reverse-taper barrel to match for improved accuracy.
Price: Blued .... $134.95   Nickeled $149.95

COLT CONVERSION UNIT
Permits the 45 and 38 Super Automatic pistols to use the economical 22 LR cartridge. No tools needed. Adjustable rear sight; 10-shot magazine. Designed to give recoil effect of the larger calibers. Not adaptable to Commander models. Blue finish $69.95

COLT HUNTSMAN AUTO PISTOL
Caliber: 22 LR, 10-shot magazine.
Barrel: 4", 6".
Length: 9" (4½" bbl.). **Weight:** 30 oz. (4" bbl.), 31½ oz. (6" bbl.).
Stocks: Checkered walnut. Wide trigger.
Sights: Fixed ramp front, square notch rear, non-adjustable.
Price: Colt Blue $74.95

COLT COMBAT COMMANDER
Same as Commander except steel frame, American walnut grips, weight 33 oz.
Price: Blue or satin nickel $134.95

COLT DERINGERS
Caliber: 22 Short, single-shot.
Barrel: 2½", side swing, blued.
Length: 4¹⁵/₁₆" overall. **Weight:** 7¾ oz.
Stocks: Brown plastic, smooth.
Features: Fixed open sights, stud trigger, auto. ejection, single action, presentation case
Price: Gold frame (cased pair) $59.95
Price: 14K Gold frame, pearlite grips (cased pair) $59.95

CLERKE TARGET AUTOMATIC
Caliber: 22 LR, 380 ACP (9-shots 22, 6-shots 380).
Barrel: 4¼".
Length: 8" over-all. **Weight:** 30 oz.
Stocks: Checkered plastic or simulated rosewood.
Sights: Blade front, fixed rear.
Features: Adj. trigger, target sights available at extra cost, grip safety, blue finish.
Price: 22 LR with standard sights $42.75
Price: 22 LR with target sights $50.00
Price: 380 ACP with standard sights $55.00
Price: 380 ACP with target sights $62.00

F.I.E. E27 TITAN PISTOL
Caliber: 25, 6-shot magazine
Barrel: 2⁷/₁₆".
Length: 4⅝" over-all. **Weight:** 12 oz.
Stocks: Checkered plastic.
Features: Visible hammer; fast simple takedown.
Sights: Fixed.
Price: Blued .... $35.95   Chromed: $39.95

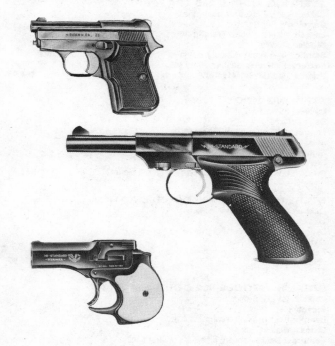

HI-STANDARD PLINKER AUTO PISTOL
Caliber: 22 LR, 9-shot magazine.
Barrel: 4½" or 6½".
Length: 9" (4½" bbl.). **Weight:** 32 oz. (4½" bbl.).
Stocks: Checkered plastic grips. Grooved thumb rest.
Features: Non slip trigger, interchangeable bbls., moulded target grips.
Sights: Fixed, ramp front, square notch rear.
Price: Blued $64.50

HI-STANDARD MODEL D-100 and DM-101 DERRINGER
Caliber: 22 S, L or LR: 22 Rimfire Magnum. 2 shot.
Barrel: 3½", over and under, rifled.
Length: 5" over-all. **Weight:** 11 oz.
Stocks: Smooth plastic.
Features: Hammerless, integral safety hammerblock, all steel unit is encased in a black, anodized alloy housing. Recessed chamber. Dual extraction. Top break, double action.
Sights: Fixed, open.
Price: Blued .... $51.50   Nickel $62.50
Price: 22 WMR, Blued .... $53.50   Nickel $64.50

U.S. HANDGUNS—SERVICE & SPORT

HI-STANDARD SHARPSHOOTER AUTO PISTOL
Caliber: 22 LR, 9-shot magazine.
Barrel: 5½".
Length: 9" over-all. **Weight:** 45 oz.
Stocks: Checkered laminated plastic.
Features: Wide, scored trigger; new hammer-sear design. Slide lock, push-button take down.
Sights: Fixed, ramp front, square notch rear adj. for w. & e.
Price: Blued **$99.50**

PLAINFIELD MODEL 71
Caliber: 22 LR (10-shot) and 25 ACP (8-shot).
Barrel: 1".
Length: 5⅛" over-all. **Weight:** 25 oz.
Stocks: Checkered walnut.
Sights: Fixed.
Features: Easily converts from 22 cal. to 25 cal. by changing bolt, bbl. and magazine. Stainless steel frame and slide.
Price: With conversion kit. . **$87.00** M71 in 22 cal. only **$66.00**
Price: M71 in 25 cal. only **$66.00**

LIBERTY RAVEN
Caliber: 25 ACP, 6-shot magazine.
Barrel: 2".
Length: 4¾". **Weight:** 15 oz.
Stocks: Plastic.
Sights: Fixed square notch.
Features: Available in either satin nickel or blue finish.
Price: **$39.95**

STERLING MODEL 286 TRAPPER
Caliber: 22 LR, 10-shot magazine.
Barrel: 4½" or 6".
Length: 9" (4½" bbl.). **Weight:** 36 oz. (4½" bbl.).
Stocks: Checkered plastic.
Sights: Fixed ramp (6" bbl.) or blade (4½" bbl.) front. Square notch rear.
Features: Interchangeable safety (4½" bbl.).
Price: Blued (M286) 4½" or 6" tapered **$64.95**

STERLING MODEL 300
Caliber: 25 ACP, 6-shot.
Barrel: 2½".
Length: 4½" over-all. **Weight:** 13 oz.
Stocks: Cycolac, black or white.
Sights: Fixed.
Features: All steel construction.
Price: Blued . . . . **$47.95** Satin nickel **$52.95**

STERLING MODEL 400 DOUBLE ACTION
Caliber: 380 ACP, 6-shot.
Barrel: 3¾".
Length: 6½" over-all. **Weight:** 24 oz.
Stocks: Cycolac, black.
Features: All steel construction. Double action.
Price: Blued . . . . **$79.95** Satin nickel **$84.50**

STERLING MODEL 402 DOUBLE ACTION
Caliber: 22 LR, 8-shot.
Barrel: 3¾".
Length: 6½" over-all. **Weight:** 24 oz.
Stocks: Black Cycolac.
Features: Double action, all steel construction.
Price: Blued . . . . **$79.95** Satin nickel **$84.50**

PLAINFIELD MODEL 72
Same as Model 71 except: has 3½" bbl. and aluminum slide.
Price: Model 72 & conversion kit **$95.95**
Price: 22 cal. only **$75.95**
Price: 25 cal. only **$75.95**

RUGER STANDARD MODEL AUTO PISTOL
Caliber: 22 LR, 9-shot magazine.
Barrel: 4¾" or 6".
Length: 8¾" (4¾" bbl.). **Weight:** 36 oz. (4¾" bbl.).
Stocks: Checkered hard rubber.
Sights: Fixed, wide blade front, square notch rear.
Price: Blued **$49.50**
Price: With checkered walnut grips **$53.50**

STERLING MODEL 302
Caliber: 22 LR, 6-shot.
Barrel: 2½".
Length: 4½" over-all. **Weight:** 13 oz.
Stocks: Cycolac, black or white.
Sights: Fixed.
Features: All steel construction.
Price: Blue or satin nickel **$59.95**

U.S. HANDGUNS—SERVICE & SPORT

SMITH & WESSON 9mm MODEL 39 AUTO PISTOL
Caliber: 9mm Luger, 8-shot clip.
Barrel: 4".
Length: 7⁷/₁₆". **Weight:** 26½ oz.; without magazine.
Stocks: Checkered walnut.
Features: Magazine disconnector, positive firing pin lock and hammer-release
    safety; alloy frame with lanyard loop; locked-breech, short-recoil double
    action; slide locks open on last shot.
Sights: ⅛" serrated ramp front, adjustable rear.
Price: Blued . . . . $125.00   Nickeled $135.00

SMITH & WESSON MODEL 59 DOUBLE ACTION
Caliber: 9mm Luger, 15-shot.
Barrel: 4".
Length: 7⁷/₁₆" over-all. **Weight:** 27½ oz., without clip.
Stocks: Checkered high impact moulded nylon.
Sights: ⅛" serrated ramp front, square notch rear adj. for w.
Features: Double action automatic. Furnished with two magazines. Blue finish.
Price: $150.00

STOEGER LUGER 22 AUTO PISTOL
Caliber: 22 LR, 12-shot (11 in magazine, 1 in chamber).
Barrel: 4½" or 5½".
Weight: 30 oz.
Stocks: Checkered wood, identical to P-08.
Features: Action remains open after last shot and as magazine is removed.
    Grip and balance identical to P-08.
Price: 4½" Barrel $78.95
Price: 5½" Barrel $78.95

U.S. HANDGUNS—REVOLVERS OVER $90

CHARTER ARMS BULLDOG
Caliber: 44 Special, 5-shot.
Barrel: 3".
Weight: 19 oz.
Stocks: Checkered American walnut, oil finished.
Sights: Patridge type 9/64" front, square notch rear.
Features: Wide trigger and hammer, chrome-moly steel frame, unbreakable
    firing pin, transfer bar ignition.
Price: $110.00

CHARTER ARMS "UNDERCOVER" REVOLVER
Caliber: 38 Special, 5 shot.
Barrel: 2" or 3.
Length: 6¼" (round butt). **Weight:** 16 oz.
Features: Wide trigger and hammer spur
Stocks: Smooth walnut, round or square butt available.
Sights: Fixed; matted ramp front, ⅛" wide blade.
Price: Polished Blue . . . . . . $87.00   Nickel $97.00
Price: With checkered, finger-rest bulldog grips (blue) $94.00

CHARTER ARMS PATHFINDER
    Same as Undercover but in 22 LR caliber, and has 3" bbl. Fitted with
    adjustable rear sight, ramp front. Weight 18½ oz.
Price: Blued $96.00
Price: With checkered, finger-rest bulldog grips $103.00

CHARTER ARMS UNDERCOVERETTE
    Like the Undercover, but a 6-shot 32 S&W Long revolver available with 2"
    barrel only, and weighing 16½ oz.
Price: Polished blue $88.00

COLT AGENT REVOLVER
Caliber: 38 Special, 6 shot.
Barrel: 2" (Twist, 1-16).
Length: 6¾" over-all. **Weight:** 14 oz.
Stocks: Checkered walnut, round butt. Grooved trigger.
Sights: Fixed, glare-proofed ramp front, square notch rear.
Price: Blued . . . . **$104.95**   With a hammer shroud installed . . **$109.95**

COLT COBRA REVOLVER
Caliber: 22 LR or 38 Special, 6 shot.
Barrel: 2", 3" (22 LR available in 3" only).
Length: 6¾" (2" bbl.). **Weight:** 15 oz. (2" bbl.).
Stocks: Checkered walnut, round butt. Grooved trigger.
Sights: Fixed, glare-proofed ramp front, square notch rear.
Price: Blued . . . . **$104.95** Nickeled **$119.95**
Price: Blued, 38 Spec. With hammer shroud installed **$109.95**

COLT DETECTIVE SPECIAL
Caliber: 38 Special, 6-shot.
Barrel: 2".
Length: 6⁹/₁₀" over-all. **Weight:** 23 oz.
Stocks: Full, checkered walnut, round butt.
Sights: Fixed, ramp front or blade, square notch rear.
Features: Glare-proofed sights, smooth trigger. Nickel finish, hammer shroud
    available as options. Two bbl. styles available—with or without shrouded
    ejector rod.
Price: $99.95

COLT OFFICIAL POLICE MK III REVOLVER
Caliber: 38 Special, 6 shot.
Barrel: 4" and 6".
Length: 9¼" (4" bbl.).
Weight: 36 oz. (38 cal., 6" bbl.).
Stocks: Checkered walnut, square butt.
Sights: Fixed, glare-proofed ramp front, square notch rear.
Price: Blued $119.95

COLT HAMMER SHROUD
Facilitates quick draw from holster or pocket. Hammer spur projects just
enough to allow for cocking for single action firing. Fits only Colt Detective
Special, Cobra and Agent revolvers. Factory installed on new guns, $5, or
as a kit for installation. Blued only $6.00
Factory installed on your gun (listed above). Blued only $7.50

COLT LAWMAN Mk III Revolver
Same as Official Police MK III but with 2" or 4" heavy barrel. Weight 36 oz.
38 Special only. Also as Metropolitan Mk III in 38 Spec. caliber.
Price: Blued . . . . **$119.95**   Nickeled **$124.95**

COLT POLICE POSITIVE REVOLVER
Caliber: 38 Special, 6 shot.
Barrel: 4".
Length: 8¾" over-all. **Weight:** 23 oz.
Stocks: Checkered walnut, round butt. Grooved trigger.
Sights: Fixed, glare-proofed ramp front, square notch rear.
Price: Blued $99.95

COLT TROOPER MK III REVOLVER
Caliber: 38 Special or 357 Magnum, 6-shot.
Barrel: 4" 6" (357 only).
Length: 9¼" (4" bbl.). **Weight:** 40 oz. (4" bbl.), 42 oz. (6" bbl.).
Stock: Checkered walnut, square butt. Grooved trigger.
Sights: Fixed ramp front with ⅛" blade, adj. notch rear.
Price: Blued $149.95. With wide spur hammer and target stocks . $142.00
Price: Nickeled $159.95

HI-STANDARD SENTINEL MKII, MKIII
Caliber: 357 or 38 Spec.
Barrel: 2½", 4", 6".
Weight: 38 oz. (4" bbl.). **Length:** 9" over-all (4" bbl.).
Stocks: Walnut, service type or combat.
Sights: Fixed on MKII. MKIII has fully adj. rear.
Features: Cylinder latch located in front of cylinder. Fast lock time. Blue finish
    only.
Price: MKII $92.95
Price: MKIII $124.95

RUGER SECURITY-SIX Model 117
Caliber: 357 Mag. (also fires 38 Spec.), 6-shot.
Barrel: 2¾", 4" or 6".
Weight: 35 oz. (4" bbl.) **Length:** 9¼" (4" bbl.) over-all.
Stocks: Hand checkered American walnut, semi-target style.
Sights: Patridge-type front on ramp, rear adj. for w. and e.
Features: Music wire coil springs throughout. Hardened steel construction. Integral ejector rod shroud and sighting rib. Can be disassembled using only a coin.
Price: $107.00

RUGER STAINLESS SECURITY-SIX Model 717
Caliber: 357 Mag. (also fires 38 Spec.), 6-shot.
Barrel: 2¾", 4" or 6".
Weight: 35 oz. (4 bbl.). **Length:** 9¼" (4" bbl.) over-all.
Stocks: Hand checkered American walnut.
Sights: Patridge-type front, fully adj. rear.
Features: All metal parts except sights made of stainless steel. Sights are black alloy for maximum visibility. Same mechanism and features found in regular Security-Six.
Price: $132.50

RUGER SPEED-SIX Models 207 and 208
Caliber: Model 207—357 Mag. (also fires 38 Spec.); Model 208—38 Spec. only, 6-shot.
Barrel: 2¾".
Weight: 31½ oz. **Length:** 7½" over-all.
Stocks: Round butt design, diamond pattern checkered American walnut.
Sights: Patridge-type front, square-notch rear.
Features: Same basic mechanism as Security-Six. Hammer without spur available on special order. All steel construction. Music wire coil springs used throughout.
Price: Model 207 (357 Mag.) $102.00
Price: Model 208 (38 Spec. only) $91.00

RUGER SECURITY-SIX Models 107 and 108
Caliber: 357 (Model 107), 38 Spec. (Model 108), 6-shot.
Barrel: 2¾" or 4".
Weight: 33½ oz (4" bbl.). **Length:** 9¼" (4 bbl.) over-all.
Stocks: Checkered American walnut, semi-target style.
Sights: Patridge-type front, square notch rear.
Features: Solid frame with barrel, rib and ejector rod housing combined in one unit. All steel construction. Field strips without tools.
Price: Model 107 (357) $102.00
Price: Model 108 (38) $91.00

SMITH & WESSON 38 M&P Heavy Barrel Model 10
Same as regular M&P except: 4" ribbed bbl. with ⅛" ramp front sight, square rear, square butt, wgt. 34 oz.
Price: Blued .... $96.00   Nickeled $106.00

SMITH & WESSON M&P Model 10 REVOLVER
Caliber: 38 Special, 6 shot.
Barrel: 2", 4", 5" or 6".
Length: 9¼" (4" bbl.). **Weight:** 30½ oz. (4" bbl.).
Stocks: Checkered walnut, Magna. Round or square butt.
Sights: Fixed, ⅛" ramp front, square notch rear.
Price: Blued .... $96.00   Nickeled $106.00

SMITH & WESSON 38 M&P AIRWEIGHT Model 12
Caliber: 38 Special, 6 shot.
Barrel: 2 or 4 inches.
Length: 6⅞" over-all. **Weight:** 18 oz. (2" bbl.)
Stocks: Checkered walnut, Magna. Round or square butt.
Sights: Fixed, ⅛" serrated ramp front, square notch rear.
Price: Blued .... $99.00   Nickeled $109.00

SMITH & WESSON TERRIOR MODEL 32
Caliber: 38 S&W, 5-shot.
Barrel: 2".
Length: 6½" over-all. **Weight:** 17 oz.
Stock: Checkered walnut.
Sights: Front, 1/10" serrated ramp, square notch rear.
Price: Blued .... $96.00   Nickeled $106.00

SMITH & WESSON KIT GUN AIRWEIGHT (Model 43, not illus.)
Same as M34 except 3½" barrel, square butt; weight 14¼ oz. 22LR.
Price: Blued .... $119.00   Nickeled $129.00

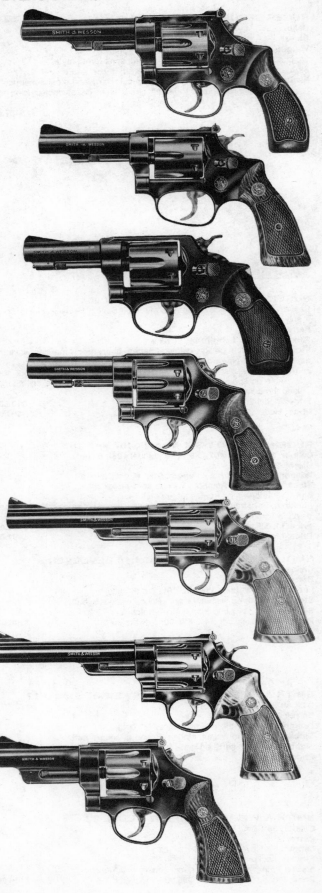

SMITH & WESSON 1953 Model 34, 22/32 KIT GUN
Caliber: 22 LR, 6 shot.
Barrel: 2″, 4″.
Length: 8″ (4″ bbl. and round butt). **Weight:** 22½ oz. (4″ bbl.).
Stocks: Checkered walnut, round or square butt.
Sights: Front, ¹/₁₀″ serrated ramp, micro. click rear, adjustable for w. & e.
Price: Blued . . . . $110.00   Nickeled $120.00

SMITH & WESSON Model 51 22/32 KIT GUN
Same as Model 34 except chambered for 22 WRF Magnum; 3½″ barrel; weight, 24 oz. Choice of round or square butt.
Price: Blued . . . . $119.00   Nickeled $129.00

SMITH & WESSON 32 HAND EJECTOR Model 30
Caliber: 32 S&W Long, 6 shot.
Barrel: 2″, 3″, 4″.
Length: 8 inches (4″ bbl.). **Weight:** 18 oz. (4″ bbl.).
Stocks: Checkered walnut, Magna.
Sights: Fixed, ¹/₁₀″ serrated ramp front, square notch rear.
Price: Blued . . . . $96.00   Nickeled $106.00

SMITH & WESSON 41 M&P Model 58 REVOLVER
Caliber: 41 Magnum, 6 shot.
Barrel: 4″.
Length: 9¼″ over-all. **Weight:** 41 oz.
Stocks: Checkered walnut, Magna.
Sights: Fixed, ⅛″ serrated ramp front, square notch rear.
Price: Blued . . . . $120.00   Nickeled $130.00

SMITH & WESSON 41 MAGNUM Model 57 REVOLVER
Caliber: 41 Magnum, 6 shot.
Barrel: 4″, 6″ or 8⅜″.
Length: 11⅜″ (6″ bbl.). **Weight:** 48 oz. (6″ bbl.).
Stocks: Oversize target type checkered Goncala Alves wood and target hammer. Tang and target trigger grooved.
Sights: ⅛″ red ramp front, micro. click rear, adj. for w. and e.
Price: S&W Bright Blue or Nickel $203.50

SMITH & WESSON 44 MAGNUM Model 29 REVOLVER
Caliber: 44 Magnum, 44 Special or 44 Russian, 6 shot.
Barrel: 4″, 6½″, 8⅜″.
Length: 11⅞″ (6½″ bbl.). **Weight:** 47 oz. (6½″ bbl.), 43 oz. (4″ bbl.).
Stocks: Oversize target type, checkered Goncala Alves. Tangs and target trigger grooved, checkered target hammer.
Sights: ⅛″ red ramp-front, micro. click rear, adjustable for w. and e.
Price: S&W Bright Blue or Nickel $203.50

SMITH & WESSON HIGHWAY PATROLMAN Model 28
Caliber: 357 Magnum and 38 Special, 6 shot.
Barrel: 4″, 6″.
Length: 11¼″ (6″ bbl.). **Weight:** 44 oz. (6″ bbl.).
Stocks: Checkered walnut, Magna. Grooved tangs and trigger.
Sights: Front, ⅛″ Baughman Quick Draw, on plain ramp. micro click rear, adjustable for w. and e.
Price: S&W Watin Blue, sandblasted frame edging and barrel top $123.00
Price: With target stocks $131.00

U.S. HANDGUNS—REVOLVERS OVER $90

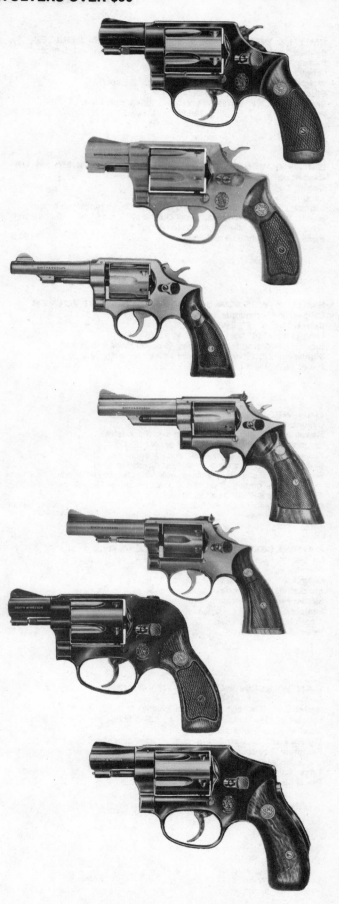

SMITH & WESSON 38 CHIEFS SPECIAL & AIRWEIGHT
Caliber: 38 Special, 5 shot.
Barrel: 2″, 3″.
Length: 6½″ (2″ bbl. and round butt).
Weight: 19 oz. (2″ bbl.) ; 14 oz. (AIRWEIGHT).
Stocks: Checkered walnut, Magna. Round or square butt.
Sights: Fixed, ¹/₁₀″ serrated ramp front, square notch rear.
Price: Blued std. M-36 .... **$96.00**   Standard weight Nickel ... **$106.00**
Price: Blued AIR'W M-37 .. **$99.00**   AIRWEIGHT Nickel **$109.00**

SMITH & WESSON 60 CHIEFS SPECIAL STAINLESS
   Same as Model 36 except: 2″ bbl. and round butt only.
Price: Stainless steel **$125.00**

SMITH & WESSON MODEL 64 STAINLESS M&P
Caliber: 38 Special, 6-shot.
Barrel: 4″.
Length: 9½″ over-all. **Weight:** 30½ oz.
Stocks: Checkered walnut, service style.
Sights: Fixed, ⅛″ serrated ramp front, square notch rear.
Features: Satin finished stainless steel, square butt.
Price: **$125.00**

**SMITH & WESSON MODEL 66 STAINLESS COMBAT
   MAGNUM**
Caliber: 357 Magnum and 38 Special, 6-shot.
Barrel: 4″.
Length: 9½″ over-all. **Weight:** 35 oz.
Stocks: Checkered Goncala Alves target.
Sights: Front, ⅛″ Baughman Quick Draw on plain ramp, micro click rear adj.
   for w. and e.
Features: Satin finish stainless steel, grooved trigger with adj. stop.
Price: **$170.00**

**SMITH & WESSON MODEL 67 K-38 STAINLESS COM-
   BAT MASTERPIECE**
Caliber: 38 special, 6-shot.
Barrel: 4″.
Length: 9⅛″ over-all. **Weight:** 34 oz. (loaded).
Stocks: Checkered walnut, service style.
Sights: Front, ⅛″ Baughman Quick Draw on ramp, micro click rear adj. for
   w. and e.
Features: Stainless steel. Square butt frame with grooved tangs, grooved
   trigger with adj. stop.
Price: **$145.00**

SMITH & WESSON BODYGUARD Model 38 REVOLVER
Caliber: 38 Special; 5 shot, double action revolver.
Barrel: 2″.
Length: 6⅜″. **Weight:** 14½ oz.
Features: Alloy frame; integral hammer shroud.
Stocks: Checkered walnut, Magna.
Sights: Fixed ¹/₁₀″ serrated ramp front, square notch rear.
Price: Blued .... **$97.00**   Nickeled **$109.00**

SMITH & WESSON BODYGUARD Model 49 REVOLVER
Same as Model 38 except steel construction. Weight 20½ oz.
Price: Blued .... **$97.00**   Nickeled **$107.00**

**SMITH & WESSON CENTENNIAL Model 40
& AIRWEIGHT Model 42 REVOLVERS**
Caliber: 38 Special, 5 shot.
Barrel: 2″.
Length: 6½″. **Weight:** 19 oz. (Standard weight), 13 oz. (AIRWEIGHT).
Stocks: Smooth walnut, Magna.
Sights: Fixed ¹/₁₀″ serrated ramp front, square notch rear.
Price: Blued, standard wgt. **$100.00**   Nickeled, standard wgt. **$110.00**
Price: Blued AIRWEIGHT . **$103.50**   Nickeled, AIRWEIGHT **$113.50**

SMITH & WESSON 32 & 38 REGULATION POLICE
Caliber: 32 S&W Long (M31), 6 shot. 38 S&W (M33) (Illus.), 5 shot.
Barrel: 2", 3", 4". (4" only in 38 S&W).
Length: 8½" (4" bbl.).
Weight: 18¾ oz. (4" bbl., in 32 cal.), 18 oz. (38 cal.).
Stocks: Checkered walnut, Magna.
Sights: Fixed, ¹/₁₀" serrated ramp front, square notch rear.
Price: Blued . . . . $96.00   Nickeled $106.00

SMITH & WESSON 357 COMBAT MAGNUM Model 19
Caliber: 357 Magnum and 38 Special, 6 shot.
Barrel: 2½", 4", 6".
Length: 9½" (4" bbl.). **Weight:** 35 oz.
Stocks: Checkered Goncala Alves, target. Grooved tangs and trigger.
Sights: Front, ⅛" Baughman Quick Draw on 2½" or 4" bbl., Patridge on 6"
  bbl., micro click rear adjustable for w. and e.
Price: S&W Bright Blue or Nickel $150.00

SMITH & WESSON 357 MAGNUM M-27 REVOLVER
Caliber: 357 Magnum and 38 Special, 6 shot.
Barrel: 3½", 5", 6", 8⅜".
Length: 11¼" (6" bbl.). **Weight:** 44 oz. (6" bbl.).
Stocks: Checkered walnut, Magna. Grooved tangs and trigger.
Sights: Any S&W target front, micro click rear, adjustable for w. and e.
Price: S&W Bright Blue or Nickel $175.00

DAN WESSON MODEL 11 REVOLVER
Caliber: 357 Magnum, 6-shot.
Barrel: 2½", 4" or 6" (optional and interchangeable).
Length: 9¼" (4" bbl.). **Weight:** 36 oz. (4" bbl.).
Stocks: Walnut, interchangeable and optional.
Sights: Front, ⅛" serrated ramp, rear dovetailed fixed.
Features: Wide spur (⅜") hammer, wide tang (⅜") trigger with adj. overtravel
  stop. Three grades of engraving available on all Dan Wesson revolvers
  priced from $175.00 to $550.00.
Price: Blue (satin) $91.00

DAN WESSON MODEL 12 REVOLVER
Caliber: 357 Magnum, 6-shot.
Barrel: 2½", 4" or 6" interchangeable.
Length: 9" (4" bbl.). **Weight:** 36 oz. (4" bbl.).
Stocks: Walnut, checkered, interchangeable.
Sights: Front, ⅛" serrated ramp, rear adj. for w. and e.
Features: Wide spur (⅜") hammer; wide tang; adj. trigger. Tools supplied for
  barrel. and grip changing.
Price: Blue (satin) $110.00

DAN WESSON MODEL 14 REVOLVER
Caliber: 357 Magnum, 6-shot.
Barrel: 2¼", 3¾" or 5¾" interchangeable.
Length: 9" (3¾" bbl.). **Weight:** 36 oz. (3¾" bbl.).
Stocks: Walnut, interchangeable.
Sights: Front, ⅛" serrated ramp, rear, dovetailed, fixed.
Features: Wide spur (⅜") hammer, wide tang (⅜") trigger with adj. overtravel
  stop, recessed barrel nut.
Price: Satin blue . . . . $89.95   Nickel $97.50
Price: Matte nickel $105.00

DAN WESSON MODEL 15 REVOLVER
Caliber: 357 Magnum, 6-shot. (38 Special optional).
Barrel: 2¼", 3¾" or 5¾" interchangeable.
Length: 9" (3¾" bbl.). **Weight:** 38 oz. (3¾" bbl.).
Stocks: Walnut, interchangeable and optional.
Sights: Front, ⅛" serrated ramp, rear, adj. for w. and e.
Features: Wide spur (⅜") hammer, wide tang (⅜") trigger with adj. overtravel
  stop, recessed barrel nut.
Price: Bright blue . . . . $118.50   Nickel $128.50
Price: Matte nickel $133.50

F.I.E. "38" Model F38 REVOLVER
Caliber: 38 Special.
Barrel: 2" or 4".
Length: 6¼" over-all (2" bbl.). **Weight:** 27 oz.
Features: Swing-out cylinder.
Stocks: Plastic Bulldog.
Sights: Fixed.
Price: Blued .... $50.95   4" bbl. $54.95

CLERKE FIRST REVOLVERS
Caliber: 22 S,L,LR, 32 S&W (6-shots 22, 5-shots 32).
Barrel: 2¼".
Length: 6¼" over-all. **Weight:** 17 oz.
Stocks: Checkered plastic, black, ivory or simulated rosewood.
Sights: Fixed.
Features: Swing-out cylinder, double action, square butt. Available in blue finish or nickel.
Price: 22 cal. $24.00
Price: 32 S&W $29.95

F.I.E. T18 TITAN REVOLVER
Caliber: 22 LR, 6-shot.
Barrel: 1¾".
Length: 5¾" over-all. **Weight:** 16 oz.
Features: Swing-out cylinder with quick release.
Stocks: Checkered plastic.
Sights: Fixed.
Price: Blued $20.95

GARCIA REGENT
Caliber: 22 LR, 8-shot.
Barrel: 3", 4" or 6" round (2½" or 4" in 32 S&W Long).
Weight: 28 oz. (3" bbl.).
Features: Swing-out cylinder, recessed for cartridge rims.
Stocks: Checkered composition.
Sights: Fixed; ramp front.
Price: Blued, 22 LR $40.00

H&R Model 940 Ultra "Side-Kick" REVOLVER
Caliber: 22 S, L or LR, 9 shot.
Barrel: 6" target weight with ventilated rib.
Weight: 33 oz.
Features: Swing-out, safety rim cylinder; safety lock and key.
Stocks: Checkered walnut with thumbrest.
Sights: Ramp front; rear adjustable for w. and e.
Price: H&R Crown-Luster Blue $62.95

H&R Model 939 Ultra "Side-Kick REVOLVER
Like the Model 940 but with a flat-sided barrel.
Price: H&R Crown-Luster Blue $64.95

HARRINGTON & RICHARDSON Model 732 Guardsman
Caliber: 32 S&W or 32 S&W Long, 6 shot.
Barrel: 2½" or 4" round barrel.
Weight: 23½ oz. (2½" bbl.), 26 oz. (4" bbl.).
Features: Swing-out cylinder with auto. extractor return. Pat. safety rim cylinder. Grooved trigger.
Stocks: Checkered, black Cycolac.
Sights: Blade front; adjustable rear on 4" model.
Price: Blued .... $49.95   Chromed (Model 733) 2½" bbl. only $54.95

HARRINGTON & RICHARDSON Model 926 REVOLVER
Caliber: 22 S, L, or LR, 9-shot, 38 S&W 5-shot.
Barrel: 4". **Weight:** 31 oz.
Features: Top-break, double or single action
Stocks: Checkered walnut.
Sights: Fixed front, read adj. for w.
Price: Blued $64.95

HARRINGTON & RICHARDSON Model 622 REVOLVER
Caliber: 22 S, L or LR, 6 shot.
Barrel: 2½", 4", round bbl.
Weight: 22 oz. (2½" bbl.).
Features: Solid steel, Bantamweight frame; snap-out safety rim cylinder; non-glare finish on frame; coil springs.
Stocks: Checkered black Cycolac.
Sights: Fixed, blade front, square notch rear.
Price: Blued, 2½", 4", bbl. $37.95

HARRINGTON & RICHARDSON Model 925 "Defender"
Caliber: 38 S&W 5 shot.
Barrel: 2½".
Length: 7½" over-all. **Weight:** 22 oz.
Features: Top-break double action, push pin extractor.
Stocks: Smooth walnut, birds-head style, one piece wrap-round.
Sights: Rear with windage adj.
Price: H&R Crown Luster Blue **$59.95**

HI-STANDARD SENTINEL
Caliber: 22 S, L, LR, 9-shot capacity.
Barrel: 2⅜", 4" or 6".
Length: 7¼". **Weight:** 15 oz. (2⅜" bbl.).
Stocks: Checkered plastic.
Sights: Blade front, square notch rear adj. for w.
Features: One-piece frame, wide, grooved trigger. Grips in brown or white.
Price: Blued **$59.95**
Price: Nickel **$64.95**

HIGH STANDARD LONG HORN CONVERTIBLE REVOLVER
Same as the Double-Nine convertible but with a 9½" bbl., fixed sights, blued only, Weight: 40 oz.
Price: . . . . **$99.50**   Magnum only **$94.50**

HARRINGTON & RICHARDSON SPORTSMAN Model 999 REVOLVER
Caliber: 22 S, L or LR, 9 shot.
Barrel: 6" top-break (16" twist), integral vent. rib.
Length: 10½". **Weight:** 30 oz.
Features: Wide hammer spur; rest for second finger.
Stocks: Checkered walnut, semi-thumbrest.
Sights: Front adjustable for elevation, rear for windage.
Price: Blued **$69.95**

HARRINGTON & RICHARDSON Model 929 "Side-Kick"
Caliber: 22 S, L or LR, 9 shot.
Barrel: 2½", 4" or 6".
Weight: 26 oz. (4" bbl.).
Features: Swing-out cylinder with auto. extractor return. Pat. safety rim cylinder. Grooved trigger. Round-grip frame.
Stocks: Checkered, black Cycolac.
Sights: Blade front; adjustable rear on 4" and 6" models.
Price: Blued, 2½", 4" or 6" bbl. **$49.95**
Price: Nickel (Model 930), 4" bbl. **54.95**

HARRINGTON & RICHARDSON M-949 FORTY-NINER
Caliber: 22 S, L or LR, 9 shot.
Barrel: 5½" round with ejector rod.
Weight: 31 oz.
Features: Contoured loading gate; wide hammer spur; single and double action. Western type ejector-housing.
Stocks: One-piece smooth walnut frontier style.
Sights: Round blade front, adj. rear.
Price: H&R Crown-Luster Blue **$47.95**
Price: Nickel (Model 1950) **$52.95**

HI-STANDARD KIT GUN
Caliber: 22 S, L, LR, 9-shots.
Barrel: 4".
Length: 9". **Weight:** 19 oz.
Stocks: Checkered walnut.
Sights: Ramp target type front, rear adj. for w. & e.
Features: Swing out cylinder, blue finish.
Price: **$69.95**

HIGH STANDARD DOUBLE-NINE CONVERTIBLE
Caliber: 22 S, L or LR, 9-shot (22 WRM with extra cylinder).
Barrel: 5½", dummy ejector rod fitted.
Length: 11" over-all. **Weight:** 32 oz.
Stocks: Smooth walnut, frontier style with medallion
Features: Western styling; rebounding hammer with auto safety block; spring-loaded ejection.
Sights: Fixed blade front, notched rear.
Price: Blued . . . . **$89.50**   Nickeled **$94.50**
   As above but in 22 WRM only (no extra cylinder for other rimfire cartridges)
Price: Blued . . . . **$84.50**   Nickeled **$89.50**
   Deluxe Double-Nine with adjustable Patridge type sights available in blue only.
Price: Convertible . . . . **$99.50**   Magnum only **$94.50**

HIGH STANDARD DURANGO REVOLVER

A variation of the High Standard Double-Nine with a brass finished trigger guard and backstrap. 4½" bbl., 10" over-all, weight 25 oz. 22 S, L or LR only. Walnut grips.
Price: Blued **$64.95**
As above but with 5½" bbl., weight 25 oz.
Price: Blued .... **$64.95**   Nickeled **$74.95**
Price: Blue with nickel back strap **$69.95**

IVER JOHNSON TARGET MODEL 57A REVOLVER

Caliber: 22 S or LR, 8 shot, double action.
Barrel: 4½", 6".
Length: 10¾" (6" bbl.). **Weight:** 30½ oz. (6" bbl.).
Features: Flash Control cylinder, adj. mainspring.
Stocks: Checkered thumbrest, Tenite.
Sights: Adjustable Patridge type.
Price: Blued **$49.15**

IVER JOHNSON CADET Model 55SA

Same as Model 55A except with 2½" barrel only, rounded tenite grips; weight 24 oz. Price, blued **$46.50**
Also available in 32 or 38 S&W caliber, 5 shot **$46.50**

IVER JOHNSON TARGET MODEL 55A REVOLVER

Same as Model 57A except without adjustable sights. Price **$46.50**

IVER JOHNSON MODEL 50A SIDEWINDER REVOLVER

Caliber: 22 S, L, LR, 8 shot.
Barrel: 6".
Length: 11¼". **Weight:** 31 oz.
Features: Wide spur hammer, half-cock safety, scored trigger, Flash Control cylinder, recessed shell head, push rod ejector.
Stocks: Plastic Stag Horn.
Sights: Fixed, blade front.
Price: Blued **$50.00**

IVER JOHNSON MODEL 67 VIKING REVOLVER

Caliber: 22 S, L, LR, 8-shot.
Barrel: 4½" or 6" chrome-lined heavy.
Length: 9½" (4½" bbl.). **Weight:** 34 oz. (6" bbl.).
Features: Cyl. front recessed for Flash Control, chambers also recessed for cartridge rims. Matted top, wide trigger. "Hammer-the-Hammer" action.
Stocks: Checkered, thumbrest plastic.
Sights: Adjustable Patridge type.
Price: Blued **$62.90**

IVER JOHNSON VIKING 67S SNUB REVOLVER

Sam as M67 Viking except has 2¾" barrel, smooth rounded stocks, 7" over-all, weight 25 oz. **$62.90**
Also available in 32 and 38 S&W calibers or Colt N.P., 5 shot ... **$62.90**

IVER JOHNSON TRAILSMAN 66 REVOLVER

Same as M67 Viking but with rebounding hammer. 6" bbl. only.
Price: **$59.15**

RMAC MINI REVOLVER

Caliber: 22 short, 5-shot.
Barrel: 1".
Length: 3¼" over-all.
Stocks: Polished walnut.
Features: Finished in hard chrome. Spur trigger.
Price: **$69.95**

U.S. HANDGUNS—SINGLE ACTION REVOLVERS

COLT SINGLE ACTION ARMY REVOLVER
Caliber: 357 Magnum or 45 Colt, 6 shot.
Barrel: 4¾", 5½" or 7½".
Length: 11½" (5½" bbl.). **Weight:** 37 oz. (5½" bbl.).
Stocks: Checkered hard rubber. (Walnut stocks **$5.00** extra).
Sights: Fixed. Grooved top strap, blade front.
Price: Blued and case hardened in color **$194.95**
Price: Nickel with walnut stocks **$229.95**
Price: Buntline Spec., cal. 45 only. 12 bbl., wood. stocks **$229.95**

COLT SINGLE ACTION ARMY—NEW FRONTIER
Same specifications as standard Single Action Army except: flat-top frame; high polished finish, blue and case colored; ramp front sight and target rear adj. for windage and elevation; smooth walnut stocks with silver medallion.
Price: **$229.95**

COLT NEW FRONTIER 22
Caliber: 22 LR, 22 Magnum.
Barrel: 4¾", 6" or 7½" (Buntline).
Length: 9⁵/₁₆", (10⁹/₁₆ in Mag., 12¾" for Buntline). **Weight:** 30 oz. (31 oz. in Mag., 28½ oz. for Buntline).
Stocks: Checkered black plastic.
Sights: Ramp front, adjustable rear.
Features: Blue finish, smooth trigger, knurled hammer spur.
Price: .... **$84.95**   (22 Magnum Dual Cyl., ... **$89.95**)
Buntline .... **$89.95**   (22 Magnum Dual Cyl., ... **$94.95**)

COLT PEACEMAKER 22
Caliber: 22 LR, 22 Magnum.
Barrel: 4¾", 6" or 7½" (Buntline).
Length: 9⁵/₁₆", (10⁹/₁₆ in Mag., 12¾" for Buntline). **Weight:** 30 oz. (31 oz. in Mag., 28½ oz. for Buntline).
Stock: Checkered black plastic (Buntline, checkered black rubber).
Sights: Fixed. Grooved top strap, blade front.
Features: Color case hardened frame, all steel construction, smooth trigger, knurled hammer spur.
Price: Blued .... **$74.95**   with Magnum cylinder **$79.95**
Buntline .... **$79.95**   with Magnum cylinder **$84.95**

F.I.E. E15 BUFFALO SCOUT REVOLVER
Caliber: 22 LR, 6-shot.
Barrel: 4¾.
Length: 10" over-all. **Weight:** 30 oz.
Stocks: Black plastic.
Features: Slide spring ejector.
Sights: Fixed.
Price: Blued, cylinder, ejector tube and handle chromed **$32.95**
Price: Model E15M with extra interchangeable 22 WMR Mag. cylinder, blue finish **$41.95**

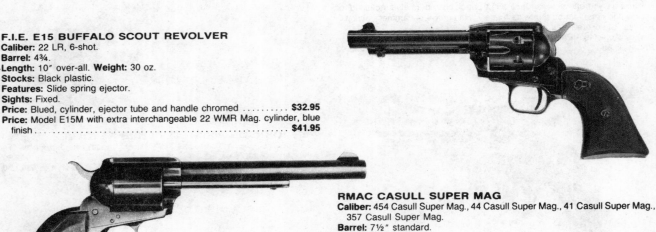

RMAC CASULL SUPER MAG
Caliber: 454 Casull Super Mag., 44 Casull Super Mag., 41 Casull Super Mag., 357 Casull Super Mag.
Barrel: 7½" standard.
Weight: 3 lbs.
Stocks: Highly polished one-piece.
Sights: Blade front, grooved top strap rear.
Features: Single action only, 4140 steel construction.
Price: 454, 44 and 41 .... **$295.00**   357 Casull Super Mag. ... **$275.00**

RUGER SUPER BEARCAT REVOLVER
Caliber: 22 S, L, or LR, 6 shot.
Barrel: 4" only.
Length: 8⅞" over-all. **Weight:** 22½ oz.
Stocks: American walnut with medallion.
Sights: Fixed; Patridge front, square notch rear.
Features: All steel construction, patented Ruger action, music wire coil springs throughout, non-fluted engraved cylinder.
Price: Blued **$54.00**

RUGER NEW MODEL SUPER BLACKHAWK
Caliber: 44 Magnum, 6-shot. Also fires 44 Spec.
Barrel: 7½" (6-groove, 20" twist).
Weight: 48 oz. **Length:** 13⅜" over-all.
Stocks: Genuine American walnut.
Sights: ⅛" ramp front, micro click rear adj. for w. and e.
Features: New Ruger interlocked mechanism, non-fluted cylinder, steel grip and cylinder frame, square back trigger guard, wide serrated trigger and wide spur hammer. Deep Ruger blue.
Price: **$135.00**

RUGER NEW MODEL BLACKHAWK REVOLVER
Caliber: 357 or 41 Mag., 6-shot.
Barrel: 4⅝" or 6½", either caliber.
Weight: 40 oz. (6½" bbl.). **Length:** 12¼" over-all (6½" bbl.).
Stocks: American walnut.
Sights: ⅛" ramp front, micro click rear adj. for w. and e.
Features: New Ruger interlocked mechanism, independent firing pin, hardened chrome-moly steel frame, music wire springs throughout.
Price: Blued **$109.00**

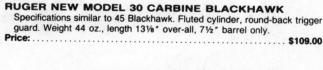

RUGER NEW MODEL SUPER SINGLE-SIX
Caliber: 22 S, L, LR, 6-shot. 22 WMR in extra cylinder.
Barrel: 4⅝", 5½", 6½" or 9½" (6-groove).
Weight: 32 oz. (6½" bbl.). **Length:** 11⅞" over-all (6½" bbl.).
Stocks: Smooth American walnut.
Sights: Improved patridge front on ramp, fully adj. rear protected by integral frame ribs.
Features: New Ruger "interlocked" mechanism, transfer bar ignition, gate-controlled loading, hardened chrome-moly steel frame, wide trigger, music wire springs throughout, independent firing pin.
Price: 4⅝", 5½", 6½" barrel **$87.50**
Price: 9½" barrel **$95.00**

RUGER NEW MODEL 30 CARBINE BLACKHAWK
Specifications similar to 45 Blackhawk. Fluted cylinder, round-back trigger guard. Weight 44 oz., length 13⅛" over-all, 7½" barrel only.
Price: **$109.00**

RUGER NEW MODEL 357/9MM BLACKHAWK
Same as the 357 Magnum except furnished with interchangeable cylinders for 9mm Parabellum and 357 Magnum cartridges **$119.00**
9mm cylinder, fitted to your 357 Blackhawk **$16.00**

RUGER NEW MODEL CONVERTIBLE BLACKHAWK
Caliber: 45 Colt or 45 Colt/45 ACP (extra cylinder).
Barrel: 4⅝" or 7½" (6-groove, 16" twist).
Weight: 40 oz. (7½" bbl.). **Length:** 13⅛" (7½" bbl.).
Stocks: Smooth American walnut.
Sights: ⅛" ramp front, micro click rear adj. for w. and e.
Features: Similar to Super Blackhawk, Ruger interlocked mechanism. Convertible furnished with interchangeable cylinder for 45 ACP.
Price: Blued, 45 Colt **$109.00**
Price: Convertible **$119.00**

U.S. HANDGUNS—SINGLE ACTION REVOLVERS

SMITH & WESSON K-38 SINGLE ACTION
Caliber: 38 Spec., 6-shot.
Barrel: 6″, 8⅜″.
Length: 11⅛″ over-all (6″ bbl.). **Weight:** 38½ oz. (6″ bbl.).
Stocks: Checkered walnut, service type.
Sights: ⅛″ Patridge front, micro click rear adj. for w. and e.
Features: Same as Model 14 except single action only.
Price: **$128.00**

U.S. HANDGUNS—MISCELLANEOUS

MBA GYROJET PISTOL
Caliber: 12 mm, 6-shot magazine.
Barrel: 8¼″.
Length: 9¾″ over-all. **Weight:** 16 oz.
Stocks: Walnut, smooth.
Sights: Fixed. Post front, square notch rear.
Features: Semi-automatic, fires rocket projectile instead of conventional cartridge.
Price: **$99.00**

MERRILL SPORTSMAN'S SINGLE SHOT
Caliber: 22 S, L, LR, 22WMR, 22WRF, 22 Rem. Jet, 22 Hornet, K-Hornet, 357, 38 Spl., 256 Win. Mag., 45 Colt/410 (3″).
Barrel: 9″ hinged type break-open. Semi-octagon.
Length: 10½″. **Weight:** 54 oz.
Stocks: Smooth walnut with thumb & heel rest.
Sights: Front 125″ blade, square notch rear adj. for w. & e.
Features: .355″ rib on top, grooved for scope mounts, auto. safety, cocking indicator, hammerless.
Price: **$150.00**
Price: Extra bbls. .... **$39.50**   Wrist rest attachment **$12.50**

REMINGTON MODEL XP-100 Bolt Action Pistol
Caliber: 221 Fireball, single shot.
Barrel: 10½ inches, ventilated rib.
Length: 16¾ inches. **Weight:** 60 oz.
Stocks: Brown nylon one-piece, checkered grip with white spacers.
Features: Fits left or right hand, is shaped to fit fingers and heel of hand. Grooved trigger. Rotating thumb safety, cavity in fore-end permits insertion of up to five 38 cal., 130-gr. metal jacketed bullets to adjust weight and balance. Included is a black vinyl, zippered case.
Sights: Fixed front, rear adj. for w. and e. Tapped for scope mount.
Price: Including case **$119.95**

THOMPSON-CENTER ARMS CONTENDER
Caliber: 17 Bumblebee, 17 Ackley-Bee, 17 Hornet, 17 K Hornet, 17 Mach IV, 22 S, L, LR, 22 WMR, 22 Rem. Jet, 22 Hornet, 22 K Hornet, 256 Win., 9mm Parabellum, 38 Super, 357/44 B & D, 38 Spl., 357 Mag., also 222 Rem., 30 M1, 45 ACP, 44 Mag. 5mm Rern., 45 Long Colt.
Barrel: 8¾″, 10″, tapered octagon. Single shot.
Length: 13¼″ (10″ bbl.). **Weight:** 43 oz. (10″ bbl.).
Stocks: Select checkered walnut grip and fore-end, with thumb rest. Right or left hand.
Sights: Under cut blade ramp front, rear adj. for w. & e.
Features: Break open action with auto-safety. Single action only. Interchangeable bbls., both caliber (rim & center fire), and length. Grooved for scope. Engraved frame.
Price: Blued (rimfire Cals.) **$135.00**
Price: Blued (centerfire Cals.) **$144.00**
Price: Extra bbls. (Rimfire) . **$36.00**   Extra bbls. (centerfire) **$45.00**
Price: 30 cal. Herrett bull bbl. with fore-end, less sights **$57.00**
Price: As above except with sights **$67.00**
Price: Bushnell Phantom scope base **$5.00**
Price: Fitted walnut case **$29.50**

UNIVERSAL ENFORCER AUTO CARBINE
Caliber: 30 M1 Carbine, 30-shot magazine.
Barrel: 10¼″ with 12-groove rifling.
Length: 17¾″. **Weight:** 4½ lbs.
Stocks: American walnut with handguard.
Features: Uses surplus 5- or 15-shot magazine. 4½-6 lb. trigger pull.
Sights: Gold bead ramp front. Peep rear adj. for w. and e. 14″ sight radius.
Price: Blue finish **$134.95**
Price: Nickel plated finish **$159.95**
Price: Gold plated finish **$184.95**

U.S. CENTERFIRE RIFLES—LEVER ACTION

BROWNING BLR LEVER ACTION RIFLE
Caliber: 243 or 308 Win. 4-shot detachable mag.
Barrel: 20″ round tapered.
Weight: 6 lbs. 15 oz. **Length:** 39¾″ over-all.
Stock: Checkered straight grip and fore-end, oil finished walnut (13¾″x1¾″x2⅜″).
Sights: Square notch adj. rear, gold bead on hooded ramp front.
Features: Wide, grooved trigger; half-cock hammer safety. Receiver tapped for scope mount. Recoil pad installed.
Price: **$179.50**

MARLIN 336T LEVER ACTION CARBINE
Same as the 336C except: straight stock; cal. 30-30 only. Brass saddle ring, squared finger lever. **$115.00**

MARLIN 336C LEVER ACTION CARBINE
Caliber: 30-30 or 35 Rem., 6-shot tubular magazine
Barrel: 20″ Micro-Groove
Weight: 7 lbs. **Length:** 38½″
Stock: Select American walnut, capped p.g. with white line spacers.
Sights: Wide-Scan ramp front, semi-buckhorn rear adj. for w. & e.
Features: Gold plated trigger, receiver tapped for scope mount, offset hammer spur, top of receiver sand blasted to prevent glare.
Price: **$115.00**

MARLIN 336 OCTAGON
Same as the 336T except: fully tapered 22″ octagon barrel, hard rubber buttplate, bead front sight. Weight about 7 lbs. Available in 30-30 Win. only.
.... **$135.00**

MARLIN 444 LEVER ACTION SPORTER
Caliber: 444 Marlin, 4-shot tubular magazine
Barrel: 22″ Micro-Groove
Weight: 7½ lbs. **Length:** 40½″
Stock: American walnut, capped p.g. with white line spacers, recoil pad.
Sights: Bead front, folding leaf rear adj. for w. & e.
Features: Gold plated trigger, receiver tapped for scope mount, offset hammer spur, leather sling with detachable swivels.
Price: **$145.00**

MARLIN GLENFIELD 30A LEVER ACTION CARBINE
Same as the Marlin 336C except: checkered walnut finished hardwood p.g. stock, 30-30 only 6-shot. **$105.00**

MARLIN 336A
Same action as the 336C with 24″ round barrel, ½-magazine tube with 5-shot capacity. Blued fore-end cap and sling swivels. Available in either 30-30 Win. or 35 Rem. **$119.95**

MARLIN 1894 OCTAGON LEVER ACTION CARBINE
Caliber: 44 Magnum, 10 shot tubular magazine
Barrel: 20″ Micro-Groove
Weight: 6 lbs. **Length:** 37½″
Stock: American walnut, straight grip and fore-end.
Sights: Bead ramp front, semi-buckhorn rear adj. for w. & e.
Features: Gold plated trigger, receiver tapped for scope mount, offset hammer spur, solid top receiver sand blasted to prevent glare.
Price: **$135.00**

MARLIN ZANE GREY CENTURY
Caliber: 30-30, 6-shot tubular magazine.
Barrel: 22″ fully tapered octagon.
Weight: 7 lbs. **Length:** 40½″.
Stock: American walnut, p.g.
Sights: Bead front, semi-buckhorn adj. for w. and e.
Features: Curved brass buttplate, brass fore-end cap, Zane Grey medallion, gold-plated trigger, offset hammer, receiver tapped for scope mount.
Price: **$150.00**

MARLIN 1895 LEVER ACTION RIFLE
Caliber: 45-70, 4-shot tubular magazine.
Barrel: 22″ round.
Weight: 7 lbs. **Length:** 40½″.
Stock: American walnut, straight p.g.
Sights: Bead front, semi-buckhorn rear adj. for w. and e.
Features: Solid receiver tapped for scope mounts or receiver sights, offset hammer spur.
Price: **$185.00**

MARLIN 1894 SPORTER
Same as 1894 Octagon except: 22″ round barrel, 6-shot capacity magazine tube. Over-all length 39½″. **$115.00**

MOSSBERG MODEL 472 LEVER ACTION

Caliber: 30-30, 6-shot magazine.
Barrel: 20".
Weight: 7½ lbs. **Length:** 38½" over-all.
Stock: Walnut, fluted comb, p.g., rubber buttplate, white line spacers at p.g. cap and butt.
Sights: Ramp front, rear adj. for e.
Features: Trigger moves with lever on opening, hammer-block safety. Solid top receiver with side ejection.
Price: **$99.95**

SAVAGE 99A LEVER ACTION RIFLE

Same as the 99E except: straight-grip walnut stock with schnabel fore-end, top tang safety. Folding leaf rear sight. Available in 250-3000 (250 Savage) 300 Savage, 243 or 308 Win. **$159.95**

SAVAGE 99E LEVER ACTION RIFLE

Caliber: 300 Savage, 243 or 308 Win., 5-shot rotary magazine.
Barrel: 20" Chrome-moly steel.
Weight: 7 lbs. **Length:** 39¾" over-all.
Stock: Walnut finished with checkered p.g. and fore-end (13½x1½x2½).
Sights: Ramp front with step adj. sporting rear. Tapped for scope mounts.
Features: Grooved trigger, slide safety locks trigger and lever.
Price: **$142.95**

SAVAGE 99F LIGHTWEIGHT CARBINE

Same as 99E except: 22" lightweight bbl. Mag. indicator on left side. Select walnut stock with checkered p.g. and fore-end, Wgt. 6½ lbs., 41¾" over-all. Cals. 300 Sav., 243 and 308 Win. **$154.95**

SAVAGE 99C LEVER ACTION CLIP RIFLE

Similar to M99F except: Detachable staggered clip magazine with push-button ejection. Wgt. about 6¾ lbs., 41¾" over-all with 22" bbl. Cals. 243, 284, 308 . . . . **$164.95**

SAVAGE 99DL CARBINE

Same as 99F except: High comb Monte Carlo stock; slim fore-end; sling swivels. Wgt. 6¾ lbs., 41¾" over-all. Cals: 243 and 308 Win. . . **$169.95**

WESTERN FIELD 72 LEVER ACTION CARBINE

Caliber: 30-30, 6-shot magazine.
Barrel: 20".
Weight: 7½ lbs. **Length:** 38½" over-all.
Stock: Walnut, fluted comb, p.g., rubber buttplate and p.g. cap with white spacers.
Sights: Ramp front, rear adj. for e.
Features: Trigger moves with lever on opening, hammer-block safety. Gold plated trigger. Solid top receiver with side ejection.
Price: Standard Model . . . . **$94.99**   With 2½x-7x scope and See Through mount **$124.00**

WESTERN FIELD COMMEMORATIVE 72

Same as Standard Model except: Select walnut stock and fore-end, hand checkered p.g. and fore-end. Gold plated trigger and bbl. band. Gold filled "deer" scenes on receiver sides, brass commemorative medallion imbedded in stock.
Price: **$140.00**

WINCHESTER 94 TEXAS RANGER COMMEMORATIVE

Caliber: 30-30, 7-shot.
Barrel: 20", round.
Length: 37¾" over-all. **Weight:** 7 lbs.
Stock: Semi-fancy walnut, square comb, curved metal buttplate.
Sights: Curved post front, semi-buckhorn rear.
Features: Patterned after Model 1894 rifle. Celebrates 150th anniversary of Texas Rangers. Limited edition of 5,000 rifles to be sold only in Texas. First 150 are special editions sold only through Texas Ranger Assn. Facsimile "Texas Ranger Star" imbedded in butt stock.
Price: Regular issue **$134.95**
Special edition models have hand checkered, full fancy stock, 16" bbl. with full buckhorn sights, special presentation case (star mounted on case)
$1,000.00

WINCHESTER 88 LEVER ACTION RIFLE
Caliber: 243 Win., (10″ twist), 308 Win., (12″ twist). 4-shot detachable mag.
Barrel: 22″ round bbl.
Weight: 7¼ lbs. **Length:** 42½″ over-all
Stock: One-piece basket-weave checkered p.g. stock (13¾″x1½″x2⅝″).
Sights: Bead front sight on ramp, with cover; folding leaf rear.
Features: Hammerless, rotating 3-lug bolt. Side ejection, cross-bolt safety.
Price: .... **$169.95**   Extra magazine **$5.75**

WINCHESTER 94 LEVER ACTION CARBINE
Caliber: 30-30, (12″ twist), 32 Special (16″ twist) 6-shot tubular mag.
Barrel: 20″
Weight: 6½ lbs. **Length:** 37¾″ over-all
Stock: Walnut straight grip stock and fore-end (13″x1¾″x2½″).
Sights: Bead front sight on ramp with removable cover; open rear. Tapped for receiver sights.
Features: Solid frame, top ejection, half-cock hammer safety.
Price: **$104.95**

WINCHESTER 94 ANTIQUE CARBINE
Same as M94 except: color case-hardened and scroll-engraved receiver, brass-plated loading gate and saddle ring. 30-30 only **$114.95**

WINCHESTER 64 LEVER ACTION RIFLE
Caliber: 30-30 only (12″ twist).
Barrel: 24″.
Weight: 6⅝ lbs. **Length:** 42″ over-all.
Stock: Walnut, semi-pistol grip stock and fore-end (13″x1¾″x2½″)
Sights: Hooded ramp and bead-post front, adj. semi-buckhorn rear.
Features: Contoured lever, half-magazine, top ejection, half-cock hammer safety, side scope mount accommodation, detachable sling swivels.
Price: **$124.95**

U.S. CENTERFIRE RIFLES—AUTOLOADING

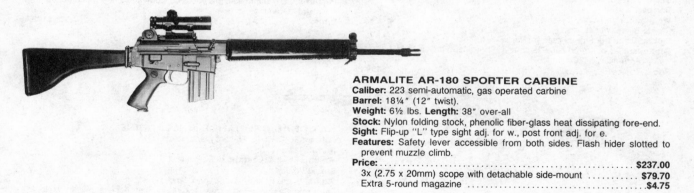

ARMALITE AR-180 SPORTER CARBINE
Caliber: 223 semi-automatic, gas operated carbine
Barrel: 18¼″ (12″ twist).
Weight: 6½ lbs. **Length:** 38″ over-all
Stock: Nylon folding stock, phenolic fiber-glass heat dissipating fore-end.
Sight: Flip-up "L" type sight adj. for w., post front adj. for e.
Features: Safety lever accessible from both sides. Flash hider slotted to prevent muzzle climb.
Price: **$237.00**
3x (2.75 x 20mm) scope with detachable side-mount **$79.70**
Extra 5-round magazine **$4.75**

BROWNING HIGH-POWER AUTO RIFLE
Caliber: 243, 270, 30-06, 308.
Barrel: 22″ round tapered.
Weight: 7⅜ lbs. **Length:** 43½″ over-all.
Stock: French walnut p.g. stock (13⅝″x2″x1⅝″) and fore-end, hand checkered.
Sights: Adj. folding-leaf rear, gold bead on hooded ramp front.
Features: Detachable 4-round magazine. Receiver tapped for scope mounts. Trigger pull 4 lbs.
Price: Grade I **$229.50**
Grade II. Same as Grade I except hand-rubbed selected French walnut stock, hand engraved receiver **$249.50**
Other Grades and prices to **$1,000.00**

BROWNING MAGNUM AUTO RIFLE
Same as the standard caliber model, except weighs 8½ lbs., 45¼″ over-all 24″ bbl., 3-round mag., Cals. 7mm Mag., 300 Win. Mag. and 338 Mag.
Grade I .... **$249.50**   Grade II **$269.50**
Other Grades and prices to **$1,000.00**

U.S. CENTERFIRE RIFLES—AUTOLOADING

COLT AR-15 SPORTER
Caliber: 223 Rem.
Barrel: 20".
Weight: 6¼ lbs. **Length:** 39" over-all.
Stock: Nylon. Phenolic fiber-glass ventilated fore-end.
Sights: Flip-up "L" type read adj. for w. & e., post front.
Features: 5-round detachable box magazine recoil pad, flash suppressor, sling swivels.
Price: **$234.95**

HARRINGTON & RICHARDSON 360 ULTRA AUTO
Caliber: 243, 308 Winchester. 3 round mag.
Barrel: 22" round, tapered.
Weight: 7½ lbs. **Length:** 43½" over-all.
Stock: One-piece American walnut Monte Carlo p.g. stock, roll-over cheek-piece.
Sights: Open adj. rear sight, gold bead ramp front.
Features: Sliding trigger guard safety. Manually operated bolt stop. Receiver tapped for scope mount.
Price: **$189.00**
Also available with full roll-over cheekpiece for left or right hand shooters as Model 361 . . . . **$199.95**

M-1 GARAND AUTO RIFLE
Caliber: 30-06, 8-shot clip.
Barrel: 24".
Length: 43½" over-all. **Weight:** 9½ lbs.
Stock: Birch, walnut finish.
Sights: Blade front, peep rear adj. for w. & e.
Features: Semi-automatic, gas operated, completely new manufacture. From National Ordnance.
Price: **$199.95**

M-1 TANKER GARAND
Caliber: 30-06, 8-shot clip.
Barrel: 17½".
Weight: 8½ lbs.
Stock: Birch, walnut finish.
Sights: Blade front, peep rear adj. for w. & e.
Features: Gas-operated semi-automatic. Shortened version of M-1 Garand rifle. From National Ordnance.
Price: **$199.95**

NATIONAL ORDNANCE M-1 CARBINE
Caliber: 30 Carbine, 15-shot magazine.
Barrel: 18".
Weight: 5½ lbs. **Length:** 35½" over-all.
Stock: Walnut.
Sights: Blade front, rear adj. for w. and e.
Features: Gas operated, cross lock safety, hammerless, military style.
Price: **$89.95**
With scope base mounted **$99.95**
With folding "paratrooper" stock and 30-shot magazine **$109.95**
With scope base mounted **$119.95**

PLAINFIELD MACHINE CO. CARBINE
Caliber: 30 U.S. Carbine or 223 (5.7mm)
Barrel: 18" six-groove.
Weight: 6 lbs. **Length:** 35½" over-all.
Stock: Glossy finished hard wood.
Sights: Click adj. open rear, gold bead ramp front.
Features: Gas operated semi-auto carbine. 15-shot detachable magazine.
Price: **$114.00**
Paratrooper. With telescoping wire stock, front vertical hand grip **$135.00**
Plainfielder. With walnut Monte Carlo sporting p.g. stock **$150.00**

U.S. CENTERFIRE RIFLES—AUTOLOADING

PJK M-68 CARBINE
Caliber: 9mm Luger, 30-shot magazine.
Barrel: 16³/₁₆".
Weight: 7 lbs. **Length:** 27".
Stock: Black plastic.
Sights: Blade front, aperature rear.
Features: Straight blowback operation, cross-bolt safety, removeable flash hider. Semi-automatic only.
Price: **$159.95**

REMINGTON 742 WOODMASTER AUTO RIFLE
Caliber: 243 Win., 6mm Rem., 280 Rem., 308 Win. and 30-06.
Barrel: 22" round tapered.
Weight: 7½ lbs. **Length:** 42" over-all
Stock: Walnut (13¼"x1⅝"x2¼") deluxe checkered p.g. and fore-end.
Sights: Gold bead front sight on ramp; step rear sight with windage adj.
Features: Positive cross-bolt safety. Receiver tapped for scope mount. 4-shot clip mag.
Price: **$179.95**
  Extra 4-shot clip magazine **$5.25**
  Sling strap and swivels (installed) **$9.10**
  Peerless (D) and Premier (F) grades . . . . **$595.00** and **$1295.00**
  Premier with gold inlays **$2000.00**
  Model 742 in foam lined case (30-06 & 308) **$199.94**

REMINGTON 742 CARBINE
  Same as M742 except: 18½" bbl., 38½" over-all, wgt. 6¾ lbs. Cals: 30-06, 308 Win. **$179.95**

REMINGTON 742 BDL WOODSMASTER
  Same as 742 except: "stepped" receiver, Monte Carlo with cheekpiece (right or left), whiteline spacers, basket-weave checkering on p.g. and fore-end, black fore-end tip, RKW finish (13⁵/₁₆"x1⅝"x1¹³/₁₆"x2½"). Cals. 30-06, 308 . . . . **$199.95**

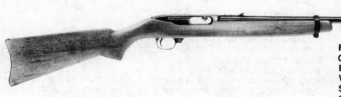

RUGER 44 AUTOLOADING CARBINE
Caliber: 44 Magnum, 4-shot tubular magazine.
Barrel: 18½" round tapered.
Weight: 5¾ lbs. **Length:** 36¾" over-all
Stock: One-piece walnut p.g. stock (13⅜"x1⅝"x2¼")
Sights: ¹/₁₆" front, folding leaf rear sights.
Features: Wide, curved trigger. Sliding cross-bolt safety. Receiver tapped for scope mount, unloading button.
Price: **$119.00**

RUGER 44 AUTOLOADING DELUXE CARBINE
Caliber: 44 Magnum, 4-shot tubular magazine.
Barrel: 18½" round tapered.
Weight: 5¾ lbs. **Length:** 36¾" over-all.
Stock: One piece American walnut with sling swivels.
Sights: Gold bead front, Ruger adj. peep rear.
Features: Automatic bolt hold-open after last shot, magazine unloading button. Drilled and tapped for scope mount.
Price: **$122.00**

RUGER MINI-14 223 CARBINE
Caliber: 223 Rem., 5-shot detachable box magazine.
Barrel: 18½".
Weight: 6½ lbs. **Length:** 37¼" over-all.
Stock: Walnut, steel reinforced.
Sights: Gold bead front, fully adj. rear.
Features: Fixed piston gas-operated, positive primary extraction. 20-shot magazine available only to police departments. **Factory accepting police orders only for balance of 1973.**
Price: **$200.00**

U.S. CENTERFIRE RIFLES—AUTOLOADING

UNIVERSAL 1000 AUTOLOADING CARBINE
Caliber: 30 M1, 5-shot magazine.
Barrel: 18″
Weight: 5½ lbs: **Length:** 35½″ over-all
Stock: Walnut stock inletted for "issue" sling and oiler;
Sights: Blade front aperture rear. With protective wings, adj.
Features: Gas operated, hammerless. Cross lock safety. Receiver tapped for scope mounts.
Price: **$112.50**

UNIVERSAL MODEL 1002 CARBINE
Same as Model 1000 except: Military type with metal handguard. Blue **$112.50**

UNIVERSAL MODEL 1005 CARBINE
Same as Model 1000 except: Select American walnut Monte Carlo stock, no sling swivels. Blue **$124.95**

WINCHESTER 100 AUTOLOADING RIFLE
Caliber: 243, (10″ twist), and 308 (12″ twist).
Barrel: 22″ round, tapered.
Weight: 7¼ lbs. **Length:** 42½″ over-all
Stock: One piece walnut p.g. stock (13¾″x1½″x2⅝″), semi-beavertail fore-end, basketweave checkered.
Sights: Bead front and folding-leaf rear sights.
Features: Detachable box magazine. Sling swivels installed.
Price: .... **$179.95** Extra magazine **$5.75**

U.S. CENTERFIRE RIFLES—SLIDE ACTION

REMINGTON 760 GAMEMASTER SLIDE ACTION
Caliber: 6mm Rem., 243, 270, 308 Win., 30-06.
Barrel: 22″ round tapered.
Weight: 7½ lbs. **Length:** 42″ over-all.
Stock: Checkered walnut p.g. and fore-end (13¼″x1⅝″x2⅛″) RKW finish.
Sights: Gold bead front sight on matted ramp, open step adj. sporting rear.
Features: Detachable 4-shot clip. Cross-bolt safety. Receiver tapped for scope mount.
Price: **$154.95**
  Sling strap and swivels (installed) **$9.10**
  Extra 4-shot clip **4.50**

REMINGTON 760 BDL GAMEMASTER
Same as 760 except: "stepped receiver," Monte Carlo stock with cheekpiece (right or left), whiteline spacer, basket-weave checkering on p.g. and fore-end, black fore-end tip, RKW finish. (13⁵/₁₆″x1⅝″x1¹³/₁₆″x2½″). Cals. 270, 30-06, 308 .... **$174.95**
Also in Peerless (D) and Premier (F) grades ..... **$595.00 and $1295.00**
(F), with gold inlay **$2000.00**

REMINGTON 760 GAMEMASTER CARBINE
Same as M760 except has 18½″ barrel. Wgt. 7¼ lbs., 38½″ over-all. Cals: 308 Win. and 30-60 .... **$154.95**

SAVAGE MODEL 170 SLIDE ACTION
Caliber: 30-30 only. 3-shot mag.
Barrel: 22″ round tapered.
Weight: 6¾ lbs. **Length:** 41½″ over-all.
Stock: Walnut (14″x1½″x2½″), with checkered p.g. Hard rubber buttplate.
Sights: Gold bead ramp front, folding-leaf rear.
Features: Hammerless, solid frame tapped for scope mount. Top tang safety.
Price: **$103.95**

AMERICAN FIREARMS STAINLESS RIFLE

Caliber: 22-250, 243, 6mm Rem., 6mm Win. Mag., 25-06, 257 Win. Mag., 264 Win. Mag., 6.5 Rem. Mag., 6.5x55, 270 Win., 270 Win. Mag., 284 Win., 7x57, 7mm Rem. Mag., 7.62x39, 308 Win., 30-06, 300 Win. Mag., 338 Win. Mag., 458 Mag.

Barrel: 16½", 18", 20", 22", 24", 26" or 28".

weight: 6½ to 11 lbs. **Length:** 44½" (24" bbl.)

Stock: Walnut, maple, laminated combinations. Handcheckered (13⅜"x1⅜"x2⅜" standard).

Sights: None furnished (drilled & tapped for scope mounts).

Features: Side safety, hinged floorplate, adjustable trigger. Made entirely of stainless steel. Blue or satin stainless steel.

Price: Grade I (Presentation)

$895.00   Grade II (Deluxe) $595.00

Grade III (Standard) ...... $395.00   Grade IV (Standard 338 & 458 Mag.) $550.00

BROWNING HIGH POWER RIFLE

Caliber: 222, 222 Mag., 22-250, 284, 243, 308, 270, 30-06, 7mm Rem. Mag., 300 Win. Mag., 308 Norma, 338 Win. Mag. 375 H&H, 458 Win. Mag.

Barrel: 22" standard, 24" Magnum.

Weight: 6⅛ to 8¼ lbs. **Length:** 43"

Stock: Checkered walnut p.g. with Monte Carlo (13⅝"x1⅝"x2⅜").

Sights: Hooded ramp front, removable adj. folding-leaf rear; except none on 458.

Features: 3-position side safety, hinged floorplate, receiver tapped for scope mount.

Price: Safari Grade .... $276.50 to $306.50

Medallion Grade .... $460.00 to $475.00

Olympian Grade .... $770.00 to $785.00

CHAMPLIN RIFLE

Caliber: All std. chamberings, including 458 Win. and 460 Wea. Many wildcats on request.

Barrel: Any length up to 26" for octagon. Choice of round, straight taper octagon, or octagon with integral quarter rib, front sight ramp and sling swivel stud.

Length: 45" over-all. **Weight:** About 8 lbs.

Stock: Hand inletted, shaped and finished. Checkered to customer specs. Select French, Circassin or claro walnut. Steel p.g. cap, trap buttplate or recoil pad.

Sights: Bead on ramp front, 3-leaf folding rear.

Features: Right or left hand Champlin action, tang safety or optional shroud safety, Canjar adj. trigger, hinged floorplate.

Price: From $890.00

COLT SAUER RIFLE

Caliber: 25-06, 270, 30-06, 7mm Rem. Mag., 300 Win. Mag.

Barrel: 24", round tapered.

Length: 43¾" over-all. **Weight:** 7½ lbs.

Stock: American walnut, cast-off M.C. design with cheekpiece. Fore-end tip and p.g. cap rosewood with white spacers. Hand checkering.

Sights: None furnished. Specially designed scope mounts for any popular make scope furnished.

Features: Unique barrel/receiver union, non-rotating bolt with cam-actuated locking lugs, tang-type safety locks sear. Detachable 3- and 4-shot magazines.

Price: Standard cals. ..... $394.95   Magnum cals. $399.95

COLT SAUER GRAND AFRICAN

Caliber: 458 Win. Mag.

Barrel: 26", round tapered.

Length: 44½" over-all. **Weight:** 10½ lbs.

Stock: Solid African bubinga wood, cast-off M.C. with cheekpiece, contrasting rosewood fore-end and p.g. caps with white spacers. Checkered fore-end and p.g.

Sights: Ivory bead hooded ramp front, adj. sliding rear.

Price: $425.00

84 PENNSY RIFLE

Caliber: All standard calibers from 17 Rem. to 460.
Barrel: 24".
Weight: 7¾ lbs. **Length:** 44½" over-all.
Stock: Walnut, contrasting p.g. cap and fore-end tip. Hand checkered.
Sights: None furnished.
Features: Sako action, Star Premium grade bbl., rubber recoil pad, sling studs, beaver tail fore-end, roll over cheek piece. "Ultra Modern" stock design.
Price: Standard grade .... **$340.00**   Grade 1 .... **$445.00**
Grade 2 .... **$715.00**   Grade 3 .... **$1425.00**
Grade 4 .... **$2970.00**

84 LOBO RIFLE

Same as Pennsy model except: Less radical stock design, slimmer fore-end and p.g. Weight is 7¼ lbs. Standard: **$330.00**; Grade 1: **$435.00**; Grade 2: **$685.00**; Grade 3: **$1415.00**; Grade 4: **$2960.00**.

84 CLASSIC RIFLE

Same as Lobo model except: Conventional stock design, weight is 7¼ lbs. Standard: **$320.00**; Grade 1: **$425.00**; Grade 2: **$675.00**; Grade 3: **$1405.00**; Grade 4: **$2950.00**.

HARRINGTON & RICHARDSON 300 BOLT ACTION

Caliber: 22-250, 243, 270, 308, 30-06 (5-shot), 7mm Rem. Mag., 300 Win. Mag. (3-shot)
Barrel: 22" round, tapered.
Weight: 7¾ lbs. **Length:** 42½" over-all.
Stock: American walnut, hand checkered p.g. and fore-end, Monte Carlo, roll-over cheekpiece.
Sights: Adjustable rear, gold bead ramp front.
Features: Hinged floorplate; sliding side safety; sling swivels, recoil pad. Receiver tapped for scope mount. Sako action.
Price: **$225.00**

HARRINGTON & RICHARDSON 301 ULTRA CARBINE

Similar to M300, except: Mannlicher style stock (no roll-over cheek-piece) metal fore-end tip. 18" bbl., 39" over all, wgt. 7¼ lbs., not available in 22-250. .... **$239.00**

HARRINGTON & RICHARDSON 317 ULTRA WILDCAT

Caliber: 17 Rem., 222, 223 or 17/223 (handload) 6-shot magazine.
Barrel: 20" round, tapered.
Weight: 5¼ lbs. **Length:** 38½" over-all.
Stock: Walnut, hand polished, hand checkered capped p.g. and fore-end, with Monte Carlo.
Sights: None. Receiver dovetailed for integral scope mounts.
Features: Sliding side safety, adj. trigger. included. Sliding side safety, adj. trigger.
Price: **$249.00**
Model 317P has better wood, basketweave checkering **$450.00**

HARRINGTON & RICHARDSON 370 ULTRA MEDALIST

Caliber: 22-250, 6mm Rem. and 243. 5-shot magazine.
Barrel: 24" heavy varmint-target weight.
Weight: 9½ lbs. **Length:** 44¾" over-all.
Stock: Oil finished walnut, full p.g. and roll-over comb; recoil pad installed.
Sights: None. Bbl. and receiver tapped for open sights and/or scope mounts.
Features: Sliding side safety, adj. trigger, sling swivels installed. Sako action.
Price: **$245.00**

ITHACA LSA-65 BOLT ACTION RIFLE

Same as the LSA-55 except in 25-06, 270 or 30-06 caliber (4-shot clip only).
Price: **$179.95**
Price: LSA-65 Deluxe **$219.95**
Price: 222 cal. **$219.95**

ITHACA LSA-55 DELUXE BOLT ACTION

Same as the std. except rollover cheekpiece, fore-end tip and pistol grip cap of rosewood with white spacers. Scope mount rings supplied. Sling swivels installed.
Price: 243, 308, 22-250 & 6mm **$199.95**
Price: 270 & 30-06 .... **$214.95**
Price: 222 cal. **$204.95**

ITHACA LSA-55 BOLT ACTION RIFLE

Caliber: 243, 308, 22-250, 6mm Rem. 270 and 30-06.
Barrel: 23" round tapered, full-floating.
Weight: About 6½ lbs. **Length:** 41½" over-all
Stock: Hand checkered walnut, Monte Carlo with built-in swell on p.g.
Sights: Removable rear adj. for w. & e. ramp front.
Features: Detachable 3-shot magazine, adj. trigger, top tang safety. Receiver tapped for scope mounts.
Price: 243, 308, 22-250 & 6mm **$164.95**
Price: 270 & 30-06 .... **$179.95**
Price: 222 Standard **$164.95**
Price: Deluxe Model **$204.95**

U.S. CENTERFIRE RIFLES — BOLT ACTION

MOSSBERG 810A BOLT ACTION RIFLE
Caliber: 30-06, 270, 4-shot magazine, 338, 3-shot.
Barrel: 22" AC-KRO-GRUV, straight taper.
Weight: 7½ to 8 lbs. **Length:** 42" over-all.
Stock: Walnut Monte Carlo with checkered fore-end and capped p.g. recoil pad and sling swivels installed.
Sights: Gold bead on ramp front, folding-leaf rear.
Features: Receiver tapped for metallic sight or scope mounts. Top tang safety. Detachable box magazine.
Price: **$133.35**
Price: With 4x scope as 810 ASM **$151.60**

MOSSBERG 810B BOLT ACTION RIFLE
Same as 810A except in 7mm Rem. Mag. only, length is 33" over-all **$147.60**
810 BSM with M 84 4x scope **$166.00**

MOSSBERG 810D BOLT ACTION RIFLE
Same as 810A except in 338 Win. Mag. **$147.60**
With 4x scope as 810 DSM **$166.00**

MOSSBERG 810C BOLT ACTION RIFLE
Same as 810A except in 270 Win. **$133.35**
With 4x scope as 810 CSM **$151.60**

MOSSBERG 800 V/T VARMINT TARGET RIFLE
Model 800 with heavy 24" bbl, target scope bases, no iron sights. Cals. 243 and 22-250 only. 44" overall, wgt. about 9½ lbs. **$125.75**

MOSSBERG 800SM SCOPED RIFLE
Same as M800 except has Mossberg M84 4x scope, but no iron sights. Wgt. 7½ lbs. **$136.95**

MOSSBERG 800 BOLT ACTION RIFLE
Caliber: 22-250, 243 and 308. 4-shot magazine.
Barrel: 22" AC-KRO-GRUV round tapered.
Weight: 6½ lbs. **Length:** 42" over-all.
Stock: Walnut, Monte Carlo, checkered p.g. and fore-end.
Sights: Gold bead ramp front, adj. folding-leaf rear.
Features: Top tang safety, hinged floorplate, 1" sling swivels installed. Receiver tapped for scope mounts.
Price: **$119.95**

MOSSBERG 800D DELUXE RIFLE
Super grade M800 with special finish and Monte Carlo rollover-comb stock with wgt. 6¾ lbs. **$156.00**

OMEGA III BOLT ACTION RIFLE
Caliber: 25-06, 270, 30-06, 7mm. Rem. Mag., 300 Win. Mag., 338 Win. Mag., 358 Norma Mag.
Barrel: 22" or 24".
Length: 42" over-all (24" bbl). **Weight:** 7¼ lbs.
Stock: Choice of three styles: Monte Carlo, Cassic or Thumbhole Varminter in either Claro walnut, English walnut or laminated.
Sights: None furnished.
Features: Right or left hand action, octagonal bolt, square locking system with enclosed bolt face gives 50 degree lift. Rotary magazine holds five standard or four belted cartridges, dual safety, fully adj. trigger, interchangeable stock and fore-end. Omega Arms Co.
Price: Left or right-hand version **$397.50**
Extra set of stocks **$97.50**

PEDERSEN 3000 BOLT ACTION RIFLE
Caliber: 270, 30-06, 7mm Rem. Mag., 338 Win. Mag., 3-shot magazine.
Barrel: 22" (270, 30-06), 24" (7mm Rem. Mag., 338 Win. Mag.).
Weight: 7 lbs. **Length:** 42" over-all.
Stocks: Walnut, roll-over cheekpiece, M.C., wrap-around checkering at p.g. and fore-end.
Sights: Drilled and tapped for scope mounts. Iron sight model available.
Features: Adjustable trigger, sling swivels, medium weight barrel, bull barrel on 338. Grades differ in extent of engraving and stock figure. Mossberg M800 action.
Price: Grade I **$650.00**
Price: Grade II **$450.00**
Price: Grade III **$375.00**

RANGER ARMS BOLT ACTION RIFLE
Caliber: All major calibers from 22-250 to 458 Win. Mag.
Barrel: Lengths up to 25½", & contour desired.
Length: Varies with bbl. lengths. **Weight:** Varies with options.
Stock: Rollover, cheekpiece, thumbhole, Mannlicher. Available in claro walnut, laminated walnut & maple, fiddleback & quilt maple, with hand checkering, rosewood p.g. & fore-end cap. Recoil pad installed.
Sights: None furnished. Drilled and tapped for scope mount.
Features: Push-button safety, adj. trigger. Available in left or right hand models at same price.
Price: .... **$375.00** & up.

REMINGTON 700 ADL BOLT ACTION RIFLE
Caliber: 222, 22-250, 6mm Rem., 243, 25-06, 270, 7mm Rem. Mag., 308 and 30-06.
Barrel: 22″ or 24″ round tapered.
Weight: 7 lbs. **Length:** 41½″ to 43½″
Stock: Walnut, RKW finished p.g. stock with impressed checkering, Monte Carlo (13⅜″x1⅝″x2⅜″).
Sights: Gold bead ramp front; removable, step-adj. rear with windage screw.
Features: Side safety, receiver tapped for scope mounts.
Price: (except 7mm Rem. Mag.) **$154.95**
7mm Rem. Mag. **$169.95**

REMINGTON 700 BDL BOLT ACTION RIFLE
Same as 700-ADL except: fleur-de-lis checkering; black fore-end tip and p.g. cap, white line spacers. Matted receiver top, quick release floorplate. Hooded ramp front sight. Q.D. swivels and 1″ sling **$174.95**
Available also in 6.5 Rem. Mag., 350 Rem. Mag., 7mm Rem. Mag., 264 and 300 Win. Mag., or 17 Rem. caliber. 44½″ over-all, weight 7½ lbs.**$189.95**
Peerless Grade .... **$595.00**   Premier Grade **$1295.00**

REMINGTON 700 SAFARI
Same as the 700 BDL except 375 H&H or 458 Win. Magnum calibers only. Hand checkered, oil finished stock with recoil pad installed. Delivery time is about five months. **$344.95**

REMINGTON 700 BDL VARMINT
Same as 700 BDL, except: 24″ heavy bbl., 43½″ over-all, wgt. 9 lbs. Cals. 222, 223, 22-250, 6mm Rem., 243 and 25-06. No sights. **$189.95**

REMINGTON 700BDL LEFT HAND
Same as 700 BDL except: mirror-image left-hand action, stock. 270, 30-06 **$179.95;** 7mm Rem. Mag. **$194.95**

REMINGTON 700 C CUSTOM RIFLE
Same as the 700 BDL except choice of 20″, 22″ or 24″ bbl. with or without sights. Jewelled bolt, with or without hinged floor plate. Select American walnut stock is hand checkered, rosewood fore-end & grip cap. Hand lapped barrel. 16 weeks for delivery after placing order **$345.00**
M700 C Custom Magnum **$357.00**
Optional extras: recoil pad **$12.00,** oil finish **$13.75,** left hand cheekpiece **$25.00.**

REMINGTON 788 BOLT ACTION RIFLE
Caliber: 222 (5-shot), 22-250, 6mm Rem., 243, and 308 (4-shot).
Barrel: 22″ round tapered (24″ in 222 and 22-250).
Weight: 7-7½ lbs. **Length:** 41⅝″ over-all.
Stock: Walnut finished hardwood with Monte Carlo and p.g. (13⅝″x1⅞″x2⅝″).
Sights: Blade ramp front, open rear adj. for w. & e.
Features: Detachable box magazine, thumb safety, receiver tapped for scope mounts.
Price: **$99.95**
Sling strap and swivels, installed **$5.40**
Model 788 with Universal Model UE 4x scope, mounts and rings in cals. 6mm Rem., 243 Win., 308 and 22-250 .... **$114.95**

REMINGTON 788 LEFT HAND BOLT ACTION
—Same as 788 except cals. 6mm & 308 only and left hand stock and action.
Price: **$104.95**

RUGER 77 BOLT ACTION RIFLE
Caliber: 22/250, 243, 6mm, 250-3000, 308 (5-shot), 6.5mm Mag., 284, 350 Mag. (3-shot).
Barrel: 22″ round tapered.
Weight: 6¾ lbs. **Length:** 42″ over-all.
Stock: Hand checkered American walnut (13¾″x1⅝″x2⅛″), p.g. cap, sling swivel studs and recoil pad.
Sights: Optional gold bead ramp front, folding leaf adj. rear, or scope rings.
Features: Integral scope mount bases, diagonal bedding system, hinged floorplate, adj. trigger, tang safety. Scope optional.
Price: With Ruger steel scope rings **$169.50**
Price: With rings and open sights **$183.50**

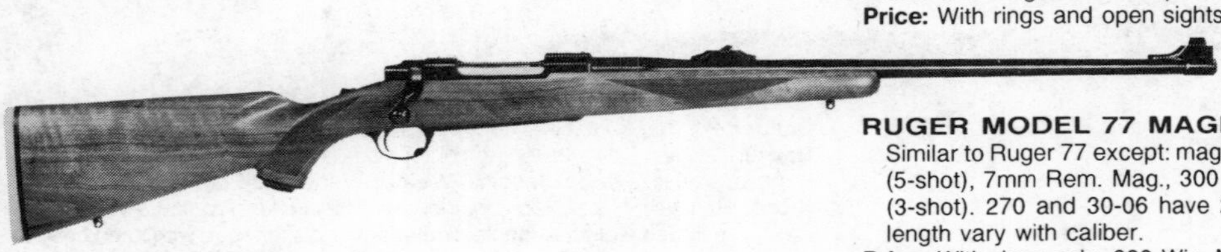

RUGER MODEL 77 MAGNUM RIFLE
Similar to Ruger 77 except: magnum-size action. Calibers 25-06, 270, 30-06 (5-shot), 7mm Rem. Mag., 300 Win. Mag., 338 Win. Mag., 458 Win. Mag. (3-shot). 270 and 30-06 have 22″ bbl., all others have 24″. Weight and length vary with caliber.
Price: With rings only, 300 Win. Mag. and 338 Win. Mag. **$179.50**
Price: With rings only, all cals. except 458 .... **$169.50**
Price: With rings and sights, 300 and 338 .... **$193.50**
Price: With rings and sights, 458 .... **$246.00**
Price: With rings and sights, other cals. **$183.50**

RUGER MODEL 77 MAGNUM ROUND TOP

Same as Model 77 except: round top receiver, drilled and tapped for standard scope mounts. Open sights are standard equipment. Calibers 25-06, 270, 30-06, 7mm Rem. Mag., 300 Win. Mag., 338 Win. Mag.

Price: All cals. except 300 and 338 .... **$169.50**
Price: 300 and 338 .... **$179.50**

RUGER MODEL 77 VARMINT

Caliber: 22-250, 243, 6mm, 25-06.
Barrel: 24″ heavy straight tapered.
Weight: Approx. 9 lbs. **Length:** Approx. 44″ over-all.
Stock: American walnut, similar in style to Magnum Rifle.
Sights: Barrel drilled and tapped for target scope blocks. Integral scope mount bases in receiver.
Features: Ruger diagonal bedding system, Ruger steel 1″ scope rings supplied. Fully adj. trigger. Barreled actions available in any of the standard calibers and barrel lengths.
Price: **$176.50**
Price: Barreled action only **$130.00**

SAVAGE 110E BOLT ACTION RIFLE

Caliber: 30-06, 4-shot. Also 7mm Rem. Mag., 3-shot.
Barrel: 20″ round tapered (7mm 24″ stainless).
Weight: 6¾ lbs. (7mm-7¾ lbs.) **Length:** 40½″ (20″ bbl.)
Stock: Walnut finished hardwood with Monte Carlo, checkered p.g. and fore-end, hard rubber buttplate.
Sights: Gold bead removable ramp front, step adj. rear.
Features: Top tang safety, receiver, tapped for peep or scope sights. Right or left hand models available.
Price: Right hand, std. cals.
$124.95   Left hand (110EL) std. cals.**$129.95**
Price: Right hand, magnum **$139.95**   Left hand magnum **$144.95**

SAVAGE 110 E/S SCOPEGUN

Standard Model 110E, caliber 30-06, factory fitted with 4x scope, rings and bases **$153.25**

SAVAGE 110C BOLT ACTION RIFLE

Same as the 110D except: Detachable box magazine. Cals. 243, 25-06, 270 and 30-06 (4-shot). Also in 7mm Rem. or 300 Win. Mag. (3-shot) at $15 extra.
Price Right hand std. cals. **$153.95**   Left hand (110 CL) std. cals.**$159.95**
Price: Right hand, magnum**$168.95**   Left hand, magnum **$171.95**

SAVAGE 110D BOLT ACTION RIFLE

Same as 110E except: 22″ bbl. (24″ on Mag.); walnut stock, cheekpiece; recoil pad on mag.; folding-leaf rear sight; weight 6¾-8 lbs. Cals. 243, 270 and 30-06. Also available in 7mm Rem. or 300 Win. Mag. at $15 extra.
Price: Right hand std. cals. **$153.95**   Left hand std. cals. **$159.95**
Price: Right hand, magnum**$168.95**   Left hand, magnum **$171.95**

SAVAGE 340 CLIP REPEATER

Caliber: 222 Rem. (4-shot) and 30-30 (3-shot).
Barrel: 24″ and 22″ respectively.
Weight: About 6½ lbs. **Length:** 40″-42″
Stock: Walnut, Monte Carlo, checkered p.g. and fore-end white line spacers.
Sights: Gold bead ramp front, folding-leaf rear.
Features: Detachable clip magazine, sliding thumb safety, receiver tapped for scope mounts.
Price: **$92.95**

SMITH & WESSON MODEL 125 RIFLE

Caliber: 30-06, 270, 5-shot.
Barrel: 24".
Length: 44¾" over-all. **Weight:** 7½ lbs.
Stock: Deluxe Grade features hand checkered European walnut, contrasting rosewood fore-end and p.g. cap with white spacers. Std. Grade omits fore-end and p.s. cap.
Sights: Hooded ramp front with gold bead, step rear adj. for w. & e.
Features: Drilled and tapped for scope mounts, positive thumb-type safety. Sights removable for scope mounting.
Price: Standard Grade ... **$169.95**   Deluxe Grade **$174.95**

SPRINGFIELD MODEL 1903-A3

Caliber: 30-06, 5-shot magazine.
Barrel: 24".
Length: 43¼" over-all. **Weight:** 8½ lbs.
Stock: Birch, walnut finish.
Sights: Military ramp front, peep rear adj. for w. & e.
Features: Bolt action. All parts, including receiver, are new manufacture. From National Ordnance.
Price: **$79.95**

WEATHERBY MARK V BOLT ACTION RIFLE

Caiber: All Weatherby Cals., 22-250 and 30-06.
Barrel: 24" or 26" round tapered.
Weight: 6½-10½ lbs. **Length:** 43¼"-46½"
Stock: Walnut, Monte Carlo with cheekpiece, high luster finish, checkered p.g. and fore-end, recoil pad.
Sights: Optional (extra).
Features: Cocking indicator, adj. trigger, hinged floorplate, thumb safety, quick detachable sling swivels.
Price: Cals. 224 and 22-250, std. bbl. **$319.50**
With 26" semi-target bbl. **$329.50**
Cals. 240, 257, 270, 7mm, 30-06 and 300 (24" bbl.) **$359.50**
With 26" No. 2 contour bbl. **$369.50**
Cal. 340 (26" bbl.) **$369.50**
Cal. 378 (26" bbl.) **455.00**
Cal. 460 (26" bbl.) **525.00**

WEATHERBY MARK V RIFLE Left Hand

Available in all Weatherby calibers except 224 and 22-250 (and 26" No. 2 contour 300WM). Complete left handed action; stock with cheekpiece on right side. Prices are $10 higher than right hand models except the 378 and 460WM are unchanged.

WEATHERBY VANGUARD BOLT ACTION RIFLE

Caliber: 25-06, 243, 270, 30-06 and 308 (5-shot), 7mm Rem. and 300 Win. Mag. (3-shot).
Barrel: 24" hammer forged.
Weight: 7⅞ lbs. **Length:** 44½" over-all.
Stock: American walnut, p.g. cap and fore-end tip, hand inletted and checkered, 13½" pull.
Sights: Optional, available at extra cost.
Features: Side safety, adj. trigger, hinged floorplate, receiver tapped for scope mounts.
Price: **$199.50**

WESTERN FIELD 780 BOLT ACTION RIFLE

Caliber: 243, 308, 5-shot mag.
Barrel: 22" round tapered.
Weight: 6½ lbs. **Length:** 43" over-all.
Stock: Walnut, Monte Carlo, checkered p.g. and fore-end.
Sights: Ramp, gold bead front; rear adj. for e.
Features: Recessed bolt head, top tang safety, hinged magazine floorplate, Receiver tapped for scope mount.
Price: **$113.99**

WESTERN FIELD 730 BOLT ACTION RIFLE

Caliber: 30-06 only.
Barrel: 22" round tapered.
Weight: 8 lbs. 8 oz.
Stock: Walnut with Monte Carlo comb, checkered p.g. and fore-end, recoil pad, sling swivels.
Sights: Bead ramp front, folding rear.
Features: Light weight sporter with removable magazine; top receiver safety.
Price: **$122.95**

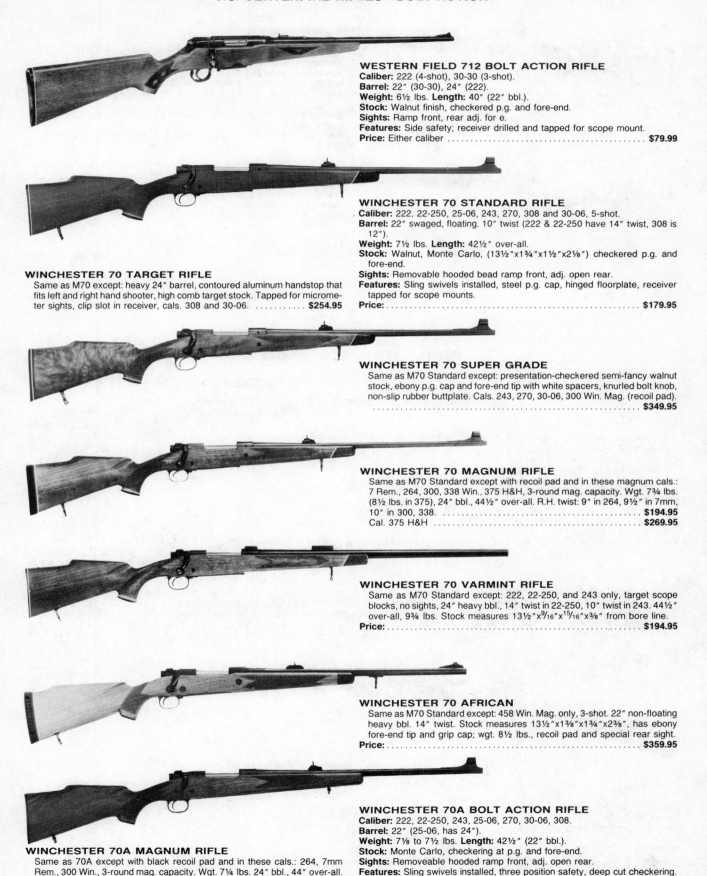

WESTERN FIELD 712 BOLT ACTION RIFLE
Caliber: 222 (4-shot), 30-30 (3-shot).
Barrel: 22" (30-30), 24" (222).
Weight: 6½ lbs. **Length:** 40" (22" bbl.).
Stock: Walnut finish, checkered p.g. and fore-end.
Sights: Ramp front, rear adj. for e.
Features: Side safety; receiver drilled and tapped for scope mount.
Price: Either caliber $79.99

WINCHESTER 70 STANDARD RIFLE
Caliber: 222, 22-250, 25-06, 243, 270, 308 and 30-06, 5-shot.
Barrel: 22" swaged, floating. 10" twist (222 & 22-250 have 14" twist, 308 is 12").
Weight: 7½ lbs. **Length:** 42½" over-all.
Stock: Walnut, Monte Carlo, (13½"x1¾"x1½"x2⅛") checkered p.g. and fore-end.
Sights: Removable hooded bead ramp front, adj. open rear.
Features: Sling swivels installed, steel p.g. cap, hinged floorplate, receiver tapped for scope mounts.
Price: $179.95

WINCHESTER 70 TARGET RIFLE
Same as M70 except: heavy 24" barrel, contoured aluminum handstop that fits left and right hand shooter, high comb target stock. Tapped for micrometer sights, clip slot in receiver, cals. 308 and 30-06. .... $254.95

WINCHESTER 70 SUPER GRADE
Same as M70 Standard except: presentation-checkered semi-fancy walnut stock, ebony p.g. cap and fore-end tip with white spacers, knurled bolt knob, non-slip rubber buttplate. Cals. 243, 270, 30-06, 300 Win. Mag. (recoil pad). $349.95

WINCHESTER 70 MAGNUM RIFLE
Same as M70 Standard except with recoil pad and in these magnum cals.: 7 Rem., 264, 300, 338 Win., 375 H&H, 3-round mag. capacity. Wgt. 7¾ lbs. (8½ lbs. in 375), 24" bbl., 44½" over-all. R.H. twist: 9" in 264, 9½" in 7mm, 10" in 300, 338. .... $194.95
Cal. 375 H&H $269.95

WINCHESTER 70 VARMINT RIFLE
Same as M70 Standard except: 222, 22-250, and 243 only, target scope blocks, no sights, 24" heavy bbl., 14" twist in 22-250, 10" twist in 243. 44½" over-all, 9¾ lbs. Stock measures 13½"x⁹⁄₁₆"x¹⁵⁄₁₆"x³⁄₈" from bore line.
Price: $194.95

WINCHESTER 70 AFRICAN
Same as M70 Standard except: 458 Win. Mag. only, 3-shot. 22" non-floating heavy bbl. 14" twist. Stock measures 13½"x1⅜"x1¾"x2⅜", has ebony fore-end tip and grip cap; wgt. 8½ lbs., recoil pad and special rear sight.
Price: $359.95

WINCHESTER 70A MAGNUM RIFLE
Same as 70A except with black recoil pad and in these cals.: 264, 7mm Rem., 300 Win., 3-round mag. capacity. Wgt. 7¼ lbs. 24" bbl., 44" over-all. R. H. twist: 9" in 264, 9½" in 7mm Rem. 10" in 300 Win. $169.95

WINCHESTER 70A BOLT ACTION RIFLE
Caliber: 222, 22-250, 243, 25-06, 270, 30-06, 308.
Barrel: 22" (25-06, has 24").
Weight: 7⅛ to 7½ lbs. **Length:** 42½" (22" bbl.).
Stock: Monte Carlo, checkering at p.g. and fore-end.
Sights: Removeable hooded ramp front, adj. open rear.
Features: Sling swivels installed, three position safety, deep cut checkering.
Price: $154.95

U.S. CENTERFIRE RIFLES—BOLT ACTION

WINCHESTER 670 BOLT ACTION RIFLE
Caliber: 243 and 30-06, 4-shot
Barrel: 22" full floating.
Length: 42½" over-all. **Weight:** 7 lbs. (30-06).
Stock: Monte Carlo stock (13½"x1¾"x1½"x2⅛"), checkered p.g. and fore-end.
Sights: Ramp front sight and adj. open rear (both easily detachable for scope-only use).
Features: Wide serrated trigger, two position safety, red cocking indicator.
Price: **$134.95**

WINSLOW BOLT ACTION RIFLE
Caliber: All standard cartridges (magnum add $10).
Barrel: 24" Douglas premium. (Magnums 26")
Weight: 7-7½ lbs. **Length:** 43" over-all.
Stock: Hand rubbed black walnut, choice of 3 styles
Sights: None. Metallics available at extra cost.
Features: Receiver tapped for scope mounts, QD swivels and recoil pad installed. 4-shot blind mag.
Price: Regal Grade **$390.00**
Regent, Regimental, Crown, Emperor and Imperial grades in ascending order of carving, engraving and inlaying, to **$3525.00**
Regal grade Varmint in 17/222 (std or Mag.) or 17/223.
Priced from **$430.00**
Left hand models at $60 extra.

U.S. CENTERFIRE RIFLES—SINGLE SHOT

BROWNING MODEL '78 SINGLE-SHOT RIFLE
Caliber: 30-06, 25-06, 6mm Rem. 22-250.
Barrel: 26", tapered octagon or medium round.
Length: 42" over-all. **Weight:** Oct. bbl. 7¾ lbs., round.
Stock: Select walnut, hand rubbed finish, hand checkered (13⅝"x1⅛"*x ¹⁹/₃₂"*). Rubber recoil pad. *Bore measurement.
Sights: None. Furnished with scope mount and rings.
Features: Closely resembles M1885 High Wall rifle. Falling block action with exposed hammer, auto. ejector. Adj. trigger (3½ to 4½ lbs.) Half-cock safety.
Price: **$229.50**

CLERKE DELUXE SINGLE-SHOT HI-WALL
Same as standard model except: Adj. trigger, features half-octagon barrel, presentation grade walnut checkered p.g. stock with cheekpiece. Plain trigger. Double set trigger avail. for $35.00 extra. Without slot cut in bbl. for rear sight **$240.00**

CLERKE SINGLE-SHOT HI-WALL RIFLE
Caliber: 222, 223, 22-250, 243, 6mm Rem., 250 Sav., 257 Rob., 25-06, 264 Win., 270, 7mm Rem. Mag., 30-30, 30-06, 300 Win., 375 H&H, 458 Win., 45-70.
Barrel: 26" medium weight.
Stock: Walnut p.g. stock and for-end, white line spacer with black buttplate.
Sights: None furnished. Drilled and tapped.
Features: Std. model: Exposed hammer, curved finger lever, Schnabel fore-end.
Price: **$190.00**

HARRINGTON & RICHARDSON OFFICERS MODEL 1873
Caliber: 45-70, single shot
Barrel: 26" round.
Weight: About 8 lbs. **Length:** 44" over-all.
Stock: Oil finished walnut, checkered at wrist and fore-end white metal tipped.
Sights: Blade front, vernier tang rear adj. for w. & e.
Features: Replica of the 1873 Springfield has engraved breech block, side lock and hammer. Each comes with commemorative plaque.
Price: **$260.00**

HARRINGTON & RICHARDSON CAVALRY MODEL CARBINE
Caliber: 45-70, single shot.
Barrel: 22".
Weight: 7 lbs. **Length:** 41".
Stock: American walnut with saddle ring and bridle.
Sights: Blade front, barrel mounted leaf rear adj. for e.
Features: Replica of the 1871 Springfield Carbine. Blue-black finish.
Price: **$150.00**
Deluxe version shown has engraved breech block, side lock & hammer $200.00
Springfield Armory Museum silver plated carbine **$1,000.00**

HARRINGTON & RICHARDSON L.B.H. COMMEMORA-TIVE CARBINE
Caliber: 45-70, single shot.
Barrel: 22".
Weight: 7 lbs., 4 oz. **Length:** 41".
Stock: American walnut with metal grip adapter.
Sights: Blade front, tang mounted aperature rear adj. for w. and e.
Features: Replica of the 1871 Springfield carbine. Engraved breech block, side lock and hammer. Action color case hardened. Each comes with book entitled "In the Valley of the Little Big Horn".
Price: **$200.00**

HARRINGTON AND RICHARDSON 158 TOPPER RIFLE
Caliber: 30-30
Barrel: 22" round tapered.
Weight: 5¼ lbs. **Length:** 37½"
Stock: Walnut finished stock and fore-end; recoil pad.
Sights: Lyman folding adj. rear and ramp front sights.
Features: Side lever break-open action with visible hammer. Easy takedown. Converts to 20 ga. Shotgun with accessory bbl. ($15 extra).
Price: **$44.95**

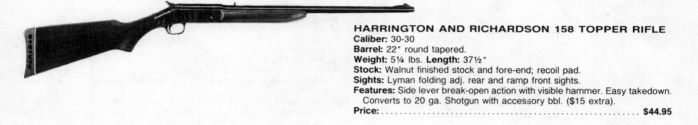

HYPER-SINGLE RIFLE
Caliber: All calibers, standard and wildcat.
Barrel: Choice of maker, weight, length (std. twist and contours).
Length: To customer specs. **Weight:** To customer specs.
Stock: To customer specs. AA fancy American black walnut is standard.
Sights: None furnished. Drilled and tapped for scope mounts.
Features: Falling block action. Striker rotates on bronze bearing and is powered by dual coil springs. Trigger adj. for weight, pull and travel. Tang safety. Octagon receiver on special order (same price).
Price: Complete Rifle . . . . **$590.00**   Barreled action **$315.00**
Price: Action only (blank extractor) **$230.00**
Price: Stainless steel barrel (extra) **$40.00**
Price: Fluted barrel (extra) **$60.00**

RUGER NUMBER ONE SINGLE SHOT
Caliber: 22-250, 243, 6mm Rem., 25-06, 270, 30-06, 7mm Rem. Mag., 300 Win., 45-70, 458 Win. Mag., 375 H&H Mag.
Barrel: 26" round tapered with quarter-rib.
Weight: 8 lbs. **Length:** 42" over-all.
Stock: Walnut, two-piece, checkered p.g. and fore-end (either semi-beavertail or Henry style).
Sights: None, 1" scope rings supplied for integral mounts.
Features: Under lever, hammerless falling block design has auto ejector, top tang safety.
Price: **$265.00**
Available also as Light Sporter, Medium Sporter, Special Varminter or Tropical Rifle **$265.00**

RUGER NO. 3 CARBINE SINGLE SHOT
Caliber: 22 Hornet, 30-40 Krag, 45-70.
Barrel: 22" round.
Weight: 6 lbs. **Length:** 38½".
Stock: American walnut, carbine-type.
Sights: Gold bead front, adj. folding leaf rear.
Features: Same action as No. 1 Rifle except different lever. Has auto ejector, top tang safety, adj. trigger.
Price: **$165.00**

ARMALITE AR-7 EXPLORER CARBINE
Caliber: 22 LR, 8-shot autoloading.
Barrel: 16″ alloy (steel-lined).
Weight: 2¾ lbs. **Length:** 34½″/16½″ stowed.
Stock: Moulded grey Cycloac, snap-on rubber butt pad.
Features: Take-down design stores bbl. and action in hollow stock. Light enough to float.
Price: **$59.95**

BROWNING AUTOLOADING RIFLE
Caliber: 22 LR,11-shot.
Barrel: 19¼ lbs.
Weight: 4¾ lbs. **Length:** 37″ over-all.
Stock: Checkered select walnut (13¾″x1¹³/₁₆″x2⅝″) with p.g. and semi-beavertail fore-end.
Sights: Gold bead front, folding leaf rear.
Features: Engraved receiver is grooved for tip-off scope mount; cross-bolt safety; tubular magazine in buttstock; easy take down for carrying or storage.
Price: Grade I .... **$114.50** Grade II ......**$179.50** Grade III **$319.50**
Also available in Grade I, 22 S (16-shot) **$114.50**

COLT COLTEER AUTOLOADING CARBINE
Caliber: 22LR, 15-shot tubular mag.
Barrel: 13⅜″ round.
Weight: 4¾ lbs. **Length:** 37″ over-all
Stock: Straight grip black walnut stock (13¾″x1⅝″x2¼″) beavertail fore-end.
Sights: Hooded gold bead front sight with notched rear adj. for w. and e.
Features: Full length magazine tube; Cross-bolt Safety. Receiver grooved for tip-off scope mount.
Price: **$64.95**

COLT COURIER AUTOLOADING RIFLE
Same as the Colteer except; p.g. stock with tapered fore-end (no fore-end bbl. band).
Price: **$65.00**

COLT STAGECOACH AUTOLOADING CARBINE
Similar to Colteer except: 16½″ bbl., 33¾″ over-all. Scroll engraved receiver, with saddle ring. 22 LR only.
Price: **$74.95**

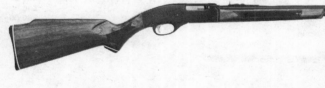

MARLIN 49DL AUTOLOADING RIFLE
Caliber: 22 LR, 18-shot tubular magazine
Barrel: 22″ Micro-Groove
Weight: 5½ lbs. **Length:** 40½″
Stock: American walnut, Monte Carlo capped p.g., checkered fore-end and p.g.,
Sights: Blade ramp front, step rear adj. for w. & e.
Features: Gold plated trigger, bolt hold-open for safety and cleaning, scroll-engraved receiver grooved for tip-off scope mounts.
Price: **$64.95**

MARLIN 99C AUTOLOADING RIFLE
Same as the Marlin 49DL except: one piece American walnut stock with checkered p.g. and fore-end.
Price: **$57.95**

MARLIN 99 M1 AUTOLOADING CARBINE
Caliber: 22 LR, 9-shot tubular magazine
Barrel: 18″ Micro-Groove
Weight: 4½ lbs. **Length:** 37″
Stock: Monte Carlo American walnut with p.g. and handguard. White buttplate spacer.
Sights: Blade on band type ramp front, removable flat-top mid-sight adj. for w. & e.
Features: Gold plated trigger, bolt hold-open, serrated receiver top is grooved for tip-off scope mount, sling swivels·attached.
Price: **$57.95**

MARLIN 989 M2 AUTOLOADING CARBINE
Same as the Marlin 99 M1 carbine except 7-shot detachable clip magazine.
Price: **$57.95**

MARLIN GLENFIELD 60 AUTOLOADER
Caliber: 22 LR, 18-shot tubular mag.
Barrel: 22″ round tapered.
Weight: About 5½ lbs. **Length:** 41″ Over-all.
Stock: Walnut finished Monte Carlo, checkered p.g. and fore-end.
Sights: Blade ramp front, step adj. rear.
Features: Chrome plated trigger, matted receiver is grooved for tip-off mounts.
Price: **$49.95**

MOSSBERG MODEL 353 RIFLE
Caliber: 22 LR, 7-shot clip.
Barrel: 18″ "AC-KRO-GRUV".
Weight: 5 lbs. **Length:** 38″ over-all.
Stock: Walnut, checkered at p.g. and fore-end. Black Tenite two-positions.
Sights: Open step adj. U-notch rear, bead front on ramp.
Features: Sling swivels and web strap on left of stock, extension fore-end folds down for steady firing from prone position. Receiver grooved for scope mounting.
Price: **$58.95**

REMINGTON MODEL 552BDL AUTO RIFLE
Same as Model 552A except: Du Pont RKW finished checkered fore-end and capped p.g. stock. Blade ramp front and fully adj. rear sights.
Price: **$84.95**

REMINGTON 552C AUTOLOADING CARBINE
Same as the Model 552A rifle except: 21″ bbl., weight 5½ lbs., 40″ over-all.
Price: **$74.95**

REMINGTON 552A AUTOLOADING RIFLE
Caliber: 22 S (20), L (17) or LR (15) tubular mag.
Barrel: 23″ round tapered.
Weight: about 5¾ lbs. **Length:** 42″ over-all.
Stock: Full-size, walnut with p.g.
Sights: Bead front, step adj. open rear.
Features: Positive cross-bolt safety, receiver grooved for tip-off mount.
Price: **$74.95**
Price: M552GS (22 Short only) **$86.95**

REMINGTON NYLON 66AB AUTO RIFLE
Same as the Model 66MB except: Apache Black Nylon stock, chrome plated receiver.
Price: **$64.95**

REMINGTON NYLON 66MB AUTO RIFLE
Caliber: 22 LR, 14-shot tubular mag.
Barrel: 19⅝″ round tapered.
Weight: 4 lbs. **Length:** 38½″ over-all.
Stock: Moulded Mohawk Brown Nylon, checkered p.g. and fore-end.
Sights: Blade ramp front, adj. open rear.
Features: Top tang safety, double extractors, receiver grooved for tip-off mounts.
Price: **$59.95**
Price: Model 66GS (22 Short only) **$69.95**

REMINGTON MOHAWK 10C AUTO RIFLE
Same as Nylon 66 rifle except: removable 10-shot 22 LR clip magazine.
Price: **$54.95**
Extra 5-shot clip . . . . **$2.75**   Extra 10-shot clip **$3.50**

RUGER 10/22 AUTOLOADING CARBINE
Caliber: 22 LR, 10-shot rotary mag.
Barrel: 18½″ round tapered.
Weight: 5 lbs. **Length:** 37″ over-all.
Stock: American walnut with p.g. and bbl. band.
Sights: Gold bead front, fully adj. folding leaf rear.
Features: Detachable rotary magazine fits flush into stock, cross-bolt safety, receiver tapped and grooved for scope blocks or tip-off mount.
Price: **$57.50**

RUGER 10/22 AUTO SPORTER
Same as 10/22 Carbine except: Hand checkered p.g. and fore-end with straight buttplate, no bbl., bands, sling swivels.
Price: **$74.50**

SAVAGE 88 AUTOLOADING RIFLE
Caliber: 22 LR, 15-shot tubular mag.
Barrel: 20″ round tapered.
Weight: About 6 lbs. **Length:** 40½″ over-all.
Stock: Walnut finish, checkered p.g. and semi-beavertail fore-end.
Sights: Blade front, Step adj. open rear.
Features: White line buttplate, top tang safety, receiver grooved for tip-off mount.
Price: **$49.95**

U.S. RIMFIRE—AUTOLOADING

WEATHERBY MARK XXII AUTO RIFLE, CLIP MODEL
Caliber: 22 LR only, 5- or 10-shot clip loaded
Barrel: 24″ round contoured.
Weight: 6 lbs. **Length:** 42¼″ over-all.
Stock: Walnut, Monte Carlo comb and cheekpiece, rosewood p.g. cap and fore-end tip. Skip-line checkering.
Sights: Gold bead ramp front, 3-leaf folding rear.
Features: Thumb operated side safety also acts as single shot selector. Receiver grooved for tip-off scope mount. Single pin release for quick take-down.
Price: $129.50
Extra 5-shot clip ....$3.95   Extra 10-shot clip $4.50

WEATHERBY MARK XXII TUBULAR MODEL
Same as Mark XXII Clip Model except: 15-shot tubular magazine.$129.50

WESTERN FIELD 868 AUTO RIFLE
Caliber: 22 LR, 15-shot tubular mag.
Barrel: 20″.
Weight: 6½ lbs. **Length:** 39½″ over-all.
Stock: Walnut finish p.g. and fore-end.
Sights: Ramp front, rear adj. for e.
Features: Sling swivels, plastic butt plate.
Price: $52.95

WESTERN FIELD 894 AUTO RIFLE
Caliber: 22 LR, 15-shot tubular mag.
Barrel: 20″ round.
Weight: 6¼ lbs. **Length:** 39″ over-all.
Stock: Walnut, checkered p.g. and fore-end, p.g. cap and butt plate with white line spacers.
Sights: Bead front on ramp, folding leaf rear.
Features: Top side safety, automatic bolt hold open after last shot.
Price: $63.95

WINCHESTER 290 AUTOLOADING RIFLE
Caliber: 22 L (17) or LR (15), tubular mag.
Barrel: 20½″ round tapered (16″ twist).
Weight: 5 lbs. **Length:** 39″ over-all.
Stock: 2-piece walnut finished hardwood. checkered p.g. and fore-end, (13⅝″x1¾″x2¾″).
Sights: Bead post front, step adj. rear.
Features: Cross-bolt safety, composition buttplate with white line spacer, receiver grooved for tip-off scope mount.
Price: $66.95

WINCHESTER 190 AUTO RIFLE
Same as M290 except: No checkering, pistol grip cap or buttplate spacer.
Price: $54.95

U.S. RIMFIRE—BOLT ACTION

BROWNING T-BOLT T-2 REPEATING RIFLE
Caliber: 22 LR, 5-shot clip.
Barrel: 24″ round, straight taper.
Length: 44¼″ over-all. **Weight:** 6 lbs.
Stock: Select walnut with checkered p.g. and fore-end.
Sights: Blade ramp front, aperture rear adj. for w. and e.
Features: 5-shot clip loading, straight-pull-back breech bolt, double extractors, side ejection. Left or right hand action.
Price: $97.50

HARRINGTON & RICHARDSON 865 PLAINSMAN RIFLE
Caliber: 22 S, L or LR. 5-shot clip mag.
Barrel: 22" round tapered.
Weight: 5 lbs. **Length:** 39" over-all.
Stock: Walnut finished hardwood with Monte Carlo and p.g.
Sights: Blade front, step adj. open rear.
Features: Cocking indicator, sliding side safety, receiver grooved for tip-off scope mounts.
Price: **$44.95**

MARLIN 780 BOLT ACTION RIFLE
Caliber: 22 S, L, or LR; 7-shot clip magazine.
Barrel: 22" Micro-Groove
Weight: 5½ lbs. **Length:** 41"
Stock: Monte Carlo American walnut with checkered p.g. White line spacer at buttplate.
Sights: Blade on band ramp front, open rear adj. for w. & e.
Features: Gold plated trigger receiver anti-glare serrated and grooved for tip-off scope mount.
Price: **$53.95**

MARLIN 781 BOLT ACTION RIFLE
Same as the Marlin 780 except: tubular magazine holds 25 Shorts, 19 Longs or 17 Long Rifle cartridges. Weight 6 lbs. **$55.95**

MARLIN 782 BOLT ACTION RIFLE
Same as the Marlin 780 except: 22 Rimfire Magnum cal. only, weight about 6 lbs. Sling and swivels attached. **$58.45**

MARLIN 783 BOLT ACTION RIFLE
Same as Marlin 782 except: Tubular magazine holds 13 rounds of 22 Rimfire Magnum ammunition. **$59.95**

MARLIN GLENFIELD 20 BOLT ACTION REPEATER
Similar to Marlin 780, except: Walnut finished checkered p.g. stock, without Monte Carlo, conventional rifling. **$43.95**

MOSSBERG MODEL 340B RIFLE
Caliber: 22 S, L, LR, 7-shot clip.
Barrel: 24" "AC-KRO-GRUV".
Weight: 6 lbs. **Length:** 43½" over-all.
Stock: Walnut finish with p.g., Monte Carlo and cheek piece, sling swivels.
Sights: Mossberg S331 receiver peep with ¼-minute adjustments for w. and e. S320 Mossberg hooded ramp front.
Features: Front sight offers choice of post or aperture elements. "Magic 3-Way" clip adjusts for Short, Long or Long Rifle cartridges. Receiver grooved for scope mount.
Price: **$55.40**

MOSSBERG MODEL 341 RIFLE
Caliber: 22 S, L, LR, 7-shot clip.
Barrel: 24" "AG-KRO-GRUV"
Weight: 6½ lbs. **Length:** 43½" over-all.
Stock: Walnut, checkered p.g. and fore-end, Monte Carlo and cheek piece. Buttplate with white line spacer.
Sights: Open, U-notch rear adj. for w. and e.
Features: Sliding side safety, 8 groove rifling, "Magic 3-way" clip adjusts to Short, Long or Long Rifle cartridges.
Price: **$51.90**

MOSSBERG MODEL 640K CHUCKSTER
Caliber: 22 WMR. 5-shot clip mag.
Barrel: 24" AC-KRO-GRUV.
Weight: 6 lbs. **Length:** 44¾" over-all.
Stock: Walnut, checkered p.g. and fore-end, Monte Carlo comb and cheek-piece.
Sights: Ramp front with bead, fully adj. leaf rear.
Features: Grooved trigger, sliding side safety, double extractors, receiver grooved for tip-off scope mounts and tapped for aperture rear sight.
Price: **$58.95**

MOSSBERG MODEL 321K
Caliber: 22 S, L, LR, single shot.
Barrel: 24".
Length: 43½" over-all. **Weight:** 6½ lbs.
Stock: Walnut finish, cheekpiece, checkered p.g. and fore-end.
Sights: Ramp front, adj. rear.
Features: Hammerless bolt action with drop-in loading platform and automatic safety, black buttplate. Model 321B has S330 peep sight with ¼-minute click adjustments.
Price: **$48.00**

U.S. RIMFIRE—BOLT ACTION

REMINGTON MODEL 541-S
Barrel: 24"
Weight: 5½ lbs. **Length:** 42⅝".
Stock: Walnut, checkered p.g. and fore end.
Sights: None. Drilled and tapped for scope mounts or receiver sights.
Features: Clip repeater. Thumb safety. Receiver and trigger guard scroll engraved.
Price: $134.95
Price: Extra 10-shot clip $3.50

REMINGTON MODEL 581 RIFLE
Caliber: 22 S, L or LR. 5-shot clip mag.
Barrel: 24" round.
Weight: 4¾ lbs. **Length:** 42⅜" over-all.
Stock: Walnut finished Monte Carlo with p.g.
Sights: Bead post front, screw adj. open rear.
Features: Sliding side safety, wide trigger, receiver grooved for tip-off scope mounts.
Price: $57.95
Price: Left hand action and stock $62.95

REMINGTON MODEL 582 RIFLE
Same as M581 except: tubular magazine under bbl. holds 20 S, 15 L or 14 LR cartridges. Wgt. 5½ lbs.
Price: $64.95

REMINGTON MODEL 591 RIFLE
Caliber: 5mm Remington RFM. 4-shot clip mag.
Barrel: 24" round.
Weight: 5 lbs. **Length:** 42⅜" over-all.
Stock: Walnut finished hardwood, Monte Carlo comb, black p.g. cap and buttplate.
Sights: Bead post front, screw adj. open rear.
Features: Sliding thumb safety, detachable sights, receiver grooved for tip-off scope mounts.
Price: $74.95

REMINGTON MODEL 592 RIFLE
Same as the M591 except: tubular magazine under bbl. holds ten 5mm Remington RFM cartridges.
Price: $79.95

SAVAGE/ANSCHUTZ 164 BOLT ACTION RIFLE
Caliber: 22 LR. 5-shot clip mag.
Barrel: 24" round tapered.
Weight: 6 lbs. **Length:** 40¾" over-all
Stock: Walnut, hand checkered p.g. and fore-end, Monte Carlo comb and cheekpiece, schnabel fore-end.
Sights: Hooded ramp gold bead front, folding-leaf rear.
Features: Fully adj. single stage trigger, sliding side safety, receiver grooved for tip-off mount.
Price: $119.95
Price: Model 164M in 22 WRM (4-shot) $129.95

SAVAGE/ANSCHUTZ MODEL 184 BOLT ACTION RIFLE
Caliber: 22 LR, 5-shot clip.
Barrel: 21½".
Weight: 4½ lbs. **Length:** 39½".
Stock: Walnut, Monte Carlo comb, hand checkered p.g. and fore-end, schnabel fore-end.
Sights: Hooded ramp gold bead front, folding-leaf rear.
Features: Side safety, crisp factory-set trigger, receiver grooved for scope mounting.
Price: $99.95

SAVAGE/ANSCHUTZ MODEL 54 SPORTER
Caliber: 22 LR. 5-shot clip mag.
Barrel: 23" round tapered.
Weight: 6¾ lbs. **Length:** 42" over-all.
Stock: French walnut, checkered p.g. and fore-end. Monte Carlo roll-over comb, schnabel fore-end tip.
Sights: Hooded ramp gold bead front, folding-leaf rear.
Features: Adj. single stage trigger, wing safety, receiver grooved for tip-off mount, tapped for scope blocks.
Price: $199.95
Price: Model 54M (22 WRM) $209.95

SAVAGE MODEL 65 RIFLE
Caliber: 22 S, L or LR. 5-shot clip mag.
Barrel: 20″ lightweight, free floating.
Weight: 5 lbs. **Length:** 39″ over-all.
Stock: Walnut, Monte Carlo comb. checkered p.g. and fore-end.
Sights: Gold bead ramp front, step adj. open rear.
Features: Sliding side safety, double extractors, receiver grooved for tip-off scope mount.
Price: $49.95
Price: Model 65M in 22 WMR (5-shot) $53.95

SAVAGE/STEVENS MODEL 34 RIFLE
Same as the Model 65 except: walnut finished hard wood stock, bead post front sight.
Price: $47.95
Price: Model 34M in 22 WMR (5-shot) $46.95

SAVAGE/STEVENS MODEL 46 RIFLE
Same as the Model 34 except: tubular magazine holds 22 S, 17 L or 15 LR cartridges. Available in 22 rimfire only (not magnum).
Price: $49.95

WINCHESTER 320 BOLT ACTION REPEATER
Caliber: 22 S, L, LR, 5-shot clip.
Barrel: 22″ round tapered.
Weight: 5⅝ lbs. **Length:** 39½″ over-all.
Stock: Walnut, Monte Carlo, checkered p.g. and fore-end. 13½″ pull.
Sights: Bead on ramp front, step adj. rear.
Features: Wide serrated trigger, positive safety, matted receiver is tapped for scope and micrometer sights. Sling swivels installed.
Price: $59.95
Extra 5-shot clip $3.15
Extra 10-shot clip $3.95

WESTERN FIELD 832 BOLT ACTION RIFLE
Caliber: 22 S, L, LR; 7-shot clip.
Barrel: 24″ round tapered.
Length: 43″ over-all. **Weight:** 6½ lbs.
Stock: Walnut p.g. and fore-end, checkered p.g.
Sights: Ramp front, rear adj. for e.
Features: Thumb operated safety, sling swivels.
Price: $46.95

U.S. RIMFIRE—LEVER ACTION

BROWNING BL-22 LEVER ACTION RIFLE
Caliber: 22 S(22), L(17) or LR(15). Tubular mag.
Barrel: 20″ round tapered.
Weight: 5 lbs. **Length:** 36¾″ over-all.
Stock: Walnut, 2-piece straight grip western style.
Sights: Bead post front, folding-leaf rear.
Features: Short throw lever, ½-cock safety, receiver grooved for tip-off scope mounts.
Price: Grade I $89.50
Price: Grade II, engraved receiver, checkered grip and fore-end .. $109.50

U.S. RIMFIRE—LEVER ACTION

ITHACA MODEL 72 SADDLEGUN
Caliber: 22 LR, 15-shot magazine tube.
Barrel: 18½".
Weight: 5 lbs.
Stock: American walnut.
Sights: Hooded front, step-adj. rear.
Features: Half-cock safety, steel receiver grooved for scope mounts.
Price: $79.95

MARLIN 39D LEVER ACTION CARBINE
Caliber: 22 S (21), L (16) or LR (15), tubular magazine.
Barrel: 20" Micro-Groove.
Weight: 5¾ lbs. **Length:** 36½"
Stock: American walnut with white line spacers at p.g. cap and buttplate.
Sights: Blade front, semi-buckhorn rear adj. for w. & e.
Features: Receiver tapped for aperture sights and scope mount (adapter base incl.), offset hammer spur.
Price: $99.95

MARLIN GOLDEN 39A LEVER ACTION RIFLE
Caliber: 22 S(26), L(21), LR(19), tubular magazine.
Barrel: 24" micro-groove.
Weight: 6¾ lbs. **Length:** 40".
Stock: American walnut with white line spacers at p.g. cap and buttplate.
Sights: Bead ramp front with detachable hood, rear semi-buckhorn adj. for w. and e.
Features: Take-down action, receiver tapped for scope mount (supplied), gold plated trigger, sling swivels, offset hammer spur. Scope $17.95 extra.
Price: $109.95

MARLIN 39A OCTAGON
Same as Golden 39A except: fully tapered 24" octagon barrel, blued trigger, hard rubber buttplate. $125.00

MARLIN GOLDEN 39M CARBINE
Caliber: 22 S(21), L(16), LR(15), tubular magazine.
Barrel: 20" micro-groove.
Weight: 6 lbs. **Length:** 36".
Stock: American walnut, straight grip, white line buttplate spacer.
Sights: Wide-Scan bead ramp front with hood, rear semi-buckhorn adj. for w. and e.
Features: Receiver tapped for scope mount or receiver sight, gold plated trigger, offset hammer spur, sling swivels, take-down action.
Price: $109.95

MARLIN 39M OCTAGON
Same as 39M except: fully tapered 20" octagon bbl., blued trigger, no buttplate spacer. $125.00

MARLIN 39 CENTURY LTD.
Same as Golden 39M Carbine except: 20" fully tapered octagon barrel, cartridge brass appointments, squared finger lever, brass medallion on receiver and stock.
Price: $125.00

WINCHESTER 150 LEVER ACTION CARBINE
Same as M250 except straight stock (no p.g.), no checkering or spacers. With barrel band and swivels.
Price: $62.95

WINCHESTER MODEL 250 LEVER ACTION RIFLE
Caliber: 22 S(21), L(17) or LR(15). Tubular mag.
Barrel: 20½" round (16" twist).
Weight: 5 lbs. **Length:** 39" over-all.
Stock: Two-piece walnut finished hardwood, checkered p.g. and fore-end (13⅝" x 1¾" x 2¾").
Sights: Bead post ramp front, step adj. open rear.
Features: Cross-bolt safety, composition buttplate with white line spacer, receiver grooved for tip-off scope mount.
Price: $69.95

WINCHESTER 9422M LEVER ACTION RIFLE
Same as the 9422 except chambered for 22 WMR cartridge, has 11-round mag. capacity $114.95

WINCHESTER 9422 LEVER ACTION RIFLE
Caliber: 22 S(21), L(17), LR(15). Tubular mag.
Barrel: 20½" (16" twist).
Length: 37⅛" over-all. **Weight:** 6½ lbs.
Stock: American walnut, 2-piece, straight grip (no p.g.).
Sights: Hooded ramp ront, adj. semi-byckhorn rear.
Features: Side ejection, receiver grooved for scope mounting, takedown action.
Price: $109.95

U.S. RIMFIRE—SLIDE ACTION

REMINGTON 572 FIELDMASTER PUMP RIFLE
Caliber: 22 S(20), L(17) or LR(14). Tubular mag.
Barrel: 24″ round tapered.
Weight: 5½ lbs. **Length:** 42″ over-all.
Stock: Genuine walnut with p.g. and grooved slide handle.
Sights: Bead post front, step adj. open rear.
Features: Cross-bolt safety, removing inner mag. tube converts rifle to single shot, receiver grooved for tip-off scope mount.
Price: $74.95

REMINGTON MODEL 572 BDL DELUXE
Same as the 572 except: p.g. cap, RKW finish, checkered grip and fore-end, ramp front and fully adj. rear sights.
Price: $84.95

REMINGTON MODEL 572 SB
Similar to the 572, but has smoothbore bbl. choked for 22 LR shot cartridges.
Sling and swivels installed. $7.50
Price: $84.95

WINCHESTER MODEL 270 PUMP RIFLE
Caliber: 22 S(21), L(17) or LR(15). Tubular mag.
Barrel: 20½″ round (16″ twist).
Weight: 5 lbs. **Length:** 39″ over-all.
Stock: Walnut finished hardwood, checkered p.g. and fore-end (13⅝″ x 1¾″ x 2¾″).
Sights: Square post ramp front, adj. open rear.
Features: Cross-bolt safety, composition buttplate with white line spacer, receiver grooved for tip-off scope mount.
Price: $72.95

U.S. RIMFIRE—SINGLE SHOT

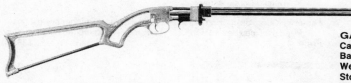

GARCIA BRONCO 22 RIFLE
Caliber: 22 S, L or LR. Single-shot.
Barrel: 16½″ round.
Weight: 3 lbs. **Length:** 32″ over-all.
Stock: Skeletonized crackle finished alloy casting.
Sights: Protected blade front, adj. rear.
Features: Cross-bolt safety, swing-out chamber, ultra lightweight for easy portability, instant takedown.
Price: $25.00

HARRINGTON & RICHARDSON MODEL 750 PIONEER
Caliber: 22 S, L or LR. Single-shot.
Barrel: 22″ round tapered.
Weight: 5 lbs. **Length:** 39″ over-all.
Stock: Walnut finished hardwood with Monte Carlo comb and p.g.
Sights: Blade front, step adj. open rear.
Features: Double extractors, feed platform, cocking indicator. sliding side safety, receiver grooved for tip-off scope mount, tapped for aperture sight.
Price: $33.95

ITHACA MODEL 49 DELUXE
Same as the M49 except: figured walnut stock, better finish, gold plated trigger and hammer, Sling and swivels installed.
Price: $44.95
Price: Presentation Model (engraved) $150.00

ITHACA MODEL 49 SADDLEGUN
Caliber: 22 S, L or LR. Single-shot.
Barrel: 18″ round.
Weight: About 5½ lbs. **Length:** 34½″ over-all
Stock: Two-piece walnut, checkered straight grip, fore-end has bbl. band.
Sights: Bead post front, step adj. open rear.
Features: Rebounding hammer safety, Martini-type lever action, rifle can be ordered with shorter (youth) stock at no extra cost.
Price: $34.95
Price: Chambered for 22 WRM only $44.95

U.S. RIMFIRE—SINGLE SHOT

MARLIN 101 SINGLE SHOT RIFLE
Caliber: 22 S, L or LR; Single shot.
Barrel: 22″ Micro-Groove
Weight: 4½ lbs. **Length:** 40″
Stock: Monte Carlo American walnut with p.g. and white line spacer at butt-plate.
Sights: Blade band ramp front, semi-buckhorn rear adj. for w. & e.
Features: Gold plated trigger, T-shaped cocking knob, non-jamming feed throat, receiver grooved for tip-off scope mount. Manual cocking action.
Price: **$37.95**

MARLIN GLENFIELD MODEL 10 RIFLE
Same as the Marlin 101 except: checkered walnut finished hardwood stock.
Price: **$31.95**

REMINGTON MODEL 580 SINGLE SHOT RIFLE
Caliber: 22 S, L or LR. Single-shot.
Barrel: 24″ round tapered.
Weight: 4¾ lbs. **Length:** 42⅜″ over-all.
Stock: Walnut finished hardwood, Monte Carlo comb and p.g., black composition buttplate.
Sights: Bead post front, screw-lock adj. rear.
Features: Single screw take-down, integral loading platform, sliding side safety, receiver grooved for tip-off mount, can be had with 1″ shorter (youth) stock.
Price: **$44.95**
Price: M580 SB (smooth bore) **$49.95**

SAVAGE STEVENS MODEL 73 SINGLE SHOT RIFLE
Caliber: 22 S, L or LR. Single-shot.
Barrel: 20″ round tapered.
Weight: 4¾ lbs. **Length:** 38½″ over-all.
Stock: Walnut finished hardwood.
Sights: Bead post front, step adj. open rear.
Features: Cocks on opening, automatic safety, key locks trigger against unauthorized use, may be had with 12½″ pull stock (youth model) at same cost.
Price: **$28.95**

SAVAGE STEVENS MODEL 72 CRACKSHOT
Caliber: 22 S, L, LR.
Barrel: 22″ octagonal.
Weight: 4½ lbs. **Length:** 37″.
Stock: Walnut, straight grip and fore-end.
Sights: Blade front, step adj. rear.
Features: Deluxe version of Model 74, color case hardened frame.
Price: **$59.50**

SAVAGE STEVENS LITTLE FAVORITE MODEL 74
Caliber: 22 S, L, LR.
Weight: 4½ lbs. **Length:** 37″.
Stock: Walnut finished straight grip.
Sights: Blade front, step adj. open rear.
Features: Black satin finish. Hammer must be manually cocked before each shot, black plastic buttplate.
Price: **$44.50**

WINCHESTER MODEL 310 RIFLE
Caliber: 22 S, L or LR. Single-shot.
Barrel: 22″ round tapered (16″ twist).
Weight: 5⅝ lbs. **Length:** 39½″ over-all.
Stock: Walnut, fluted Monte Carlo comb, checkered p.g. and fore-end (13½″ x 1⅝″ x 2⁷/₁₆″).
Sights: Bead post ramp front, step adj. open rear.
Features: Twin extractors, sliding side safety, wide serrated trigger, receiver grooved for tip-off scope mounts tapped for aperture rear sight.
Price: **$49.95**

ANSCHUTZ 1411 MATCH 54 RIFLE

Caliber: 22 LR. Single shot.
Barrel: 27½ round (¹⁵/₁₆" dia.)
Weight: 11 lbs. **Length:** 46" over-all.
Stock: French walnut, American prone style with Monte Carlo, cast-off cheekpiece, checkered p.g., beavertail fore-end with swivel rail and adj. swivel, adj. rubber buttplate.
Sights: None. Receiver grooved for Anshutz sights (extra). Scope blocks.
Features: Single stage adj. trigger, wing safety, short firing pin travel. Available from Savage Arms.
Price: **$245.00**
Price: Left hand stocked rifle, no sights **$265.00**

ANSCHUTZ 1413 SUPER MATCH RIFLE

Same as the model 1411 except: International type stock with adj. cheekpiece, adj. aluminum hook buttplate, weight 15½ lbs., 50" over-all. Available from Savage Arms.
Price: **$440.00**
Price: Left hand stocked rifle, no sights **$460.00**

ANSCHUTZ 1407 MATCH 54 RIFLE

Same as the model 1411 except: 26" bbl. (⅞" dia.), weight 10 lbs., 44½" over-all to conform to ISU requirements and also suitable for NRA matches. Available from Savage Arms.
Price: **$245.00**
Price: Left hand stocked rifle, no sights **$265.00**

SAVAGE/ANSCHUTZ 64 MATCH RIFLE

Caliber: 22 LR only. Single shot.
Barrel: 26" round (¹¹/₁₆" dia.)
Weight: 7¾ lbs. **Length:** 44" over-all.
Stock: Walnut finished hardwood, cheekpiece, checkered p.g., beavertail fore-end, adj. buttplate.
Sights: None (extra). Scope blocks.
Features: Sliding side safety, adj. single stage trigger, receiver grooved for Anschutz sights.
Price: .... **$104.95**   64L (Left hand) **$114.95**
As above but with Anschutz 6723 Match Sight Set.
Price: Model 64S (Right hand)
$134.95   64SL (Left hand) **$144.95**

MOSSBERG MODEL 144 TARGET RIFLE

Caliber: 22 LR only. 7-shot clip.
Barrel: 26" round (¹⁵/₁₆" dia.)
Weight: About 8 lbs. **Length:** 43" over-all.
Stock: Walnut with high thick comb, cheekpiece, p.g., beavertail fore-end, adj. handstop and sling swivels.
Sights: Lyman 17A hooded front with inserts, Mossberg S331 receiver peep with ¼-minute clicks.
Features: Wide grooved trigger adj. for wgt. of pull, thumb safety, receiver grooved for scope mounting.
Price: **$73.75**

U.S. TARGET RIFLES—CENTERFIRE AND RIMFIRE

REMINGTON INTERNATIONAL FREE RIFLE
Caliber: 22 LR, 222 Rem., 222 Rem. Mag., 223 Rem., 7.62 NATO (308 Win.), 30-06 only. Single shot.
Barrel: 27¼" heavy.
Weight: 15 lbs. **Length:** 47"
Stock: Semi-finished laminated walnut. Adj. hook buttplate, palm rest, and front sling swivel.
Sights: None. Scope blocks installed.
Features: Action is 40-XB type. 2 oz. trigger.
Price: Special order **$395.00**

REMINGTON 40-XB RANGEMASTER TARGET Centerfire
Caliber: 222 Rem., 222 Rem. Mag., 223 Rem., 22-250, 6mm x 47, 6mm Int., 6mm Rem., 243, 25-06, 6.5mm Rem. Mag., 7mm Rem. Mag., 30-338, 30-7mm Rem. Mag., 300 Win. Mag., 7.62 NATO (308 Win.), 30-06. Single shot.
Barrel: 27¼" round (Stand. dia.-¾", Hvy. dia.-⅞")
Weight: Std.—9¼ lbs., Hvy.—11¼ **Length:** 47"
Stock: American walnut with high comb and beavertail fore-end stop. Rubber non-slip buttplate.
Sights: None. Scope blocks installed.
Features: Adjustable trigger pull. Receiver drilled and tapped for sights.
Price: Standard ss., stainless steel **$269.95**
Price: Repeating model **$289.95**
Price: Extra for 2 oz. trigger **$40.00**

REMINGTON 40-XB RANGEMASTER TARGET RIMFIRE
Caliber: 22 LR only. Single shot.
Barrel: 28" standard or heavy.
Length: 47" over-all. **Weight:** 10¾ lbs. (std.), 12 lbs. (hvy.).
Stock: American walnut, p.g. guide rail with adj. swivel block and handstop, beavertail fore-end.
Sights: None. Receiver tapped for sights and scope blocks. (Redfield Olympic sight set optional at $35 extra.)
Features: Positive thumb safety, adj. trigger, loading platform, double extractors.
Price: **$199.95**

REMINGTON MODEL 40XB-BR
Caliber: 222 Rem., 222 Rem. Mag., 223, 6mm x 47, 7.62 NATO (308 Win.).
Barrel: 20" (light varmint class), 26" (heavy varmint class).
Length: 38" (20" bbl.), 44" (26" bbl.). **Weight:** Light varmint class, 7¼ lbs., Heavy varmint class, 12 lbs.
Stock: Select walnut.
Sights: None. Supplied with scope blocks.
Features: Unblued stainless steel barrel, trigger adj. from 1½ lbs. to 3½ lbs. Special 2 oz. trigger at extra cost. Scope and mounts extra.
Price: **$289.95**

REMINGTON 540X MATCH TARGET RIFLE
Caliber: 22 LR. Single shot.
Barrel: 26″ heavy.
Weight: 8 lbs. **Length:** 43½″ to 47″
Stock: Target style with Monte Carlo, cheekpiece and thumbrest groove. Adj. buttplate and full length guide rail.
Sights: Redfield #75 rear sight with ¼ min. clicks. #63 Globe front sight with 7 inserts. Optional.
Features: Adjustable trigger pull. Rear locking bolt with 6 lugs, double extractors.
Price: Without sights ..... **$104.95** With sights **$124.95**
For sling with front swivel block assembly installed add **$6.95.**

WINCHESTER 52D BOLT ACTION TARGET RIFLE
Caliber: 22 LR only. Single shot.
Barrel: 28″, standard or heavy weight.
Weight: 9¾ lbs. Std. 11 lbs. Hvy. **Length:** 46″
Stock: Marksman stock of choice walnut with full length accessory channel and adj. bedding device and non-slip butt pad.
Sights: None. Barrel tapped for front sight bases.
Features: Adjustable trigger.
Price: **$194.95**

WINCHESTER 70 INT'L ARMY MATCH RIFLE
Caliber: 308 (7.62mm NATO) 5-shot.
Barrel: 24″ heavy-contour.
Weight: 11 lbs. **Length:** 43¼″ over-all.
Stock: Oil finished walnut, (12″ x 1¼″ x 1¼″) meets ISU requirements.
Sights: None. Receiver tapped for M70 sights (available at extra cost).
Features: Fore-end rail takes most std. accessories, vertically adj. buttplate, externally adj. trigger, glass bedded action.
Price: Match .... **$399.95** Ultra Match **$344.95**

WINCHESTER 52 INTERNATIONAL MATCH RIFLE
Caliber: 22 LR. Single shot.
Barrel: 28″ heavy bbl.
Weight: 13½ lbs. **Length:** 44½″
Stock: Laminated International-style, aluminum fore-end assembly, adj. palm rest.
Sights: Receiver tapped for sights and scope bases; scope blocks are included.
Features: Non-drag trigger. Lead-lapped barrel with Winchester muzzle counterbore.
Price: **$389.00**
With Kenyon trigger **$425.00**
With ISU trigger **$425.00**

Browning Auto-5 Magnum 12

Same as Std. Auto-5 except: chambered for 3″ magnum shells (also handles 2¾″ magnum and 2¾″ HV loads). 28″ Mod., Full; 30″ and 32″ (Full) bbls. 14″x1⅝″x2½″ stock. Recoil pad. Wgt. 8¾ lbs.

Price: . . . . $248.50   With vent. rib. Wgt. 9 lbs. $266.50

Browning Auto-5 Light Skeet

Same as Light Standard except: 12 and 20 ga. only, 26″ or 28″ bbl. (Skeet). Wgt. 6¼-7¼ bls. $244.50
With vent. rib. Wgt. 6⅜-7½ lbs. $262.50

BROWNING AUTO-5 LIGHT 12, 20 and SWEET 16

Gauge: 12, 20, 16 (5-shot; 3-shot plug furnished). 2¾″ chamber.
Action: Recoil operated autoloader; takedown.
Barrel: 26″ (Skeet boring in 12 & 20 ga., Cyl., Imp. Cyl., Mod. in 16 & 20 ga.); 28″ (Skeet in 12 ga., Full in 16 ga., Mod., Full); 30″ (Full in 12 ga.).
Weight: 12 ga. 7¼ lbs., 16 ga. 6¾ lbs., 20 ga. 6⅜ lbs.
Stock: French walnut, hand checkered half-p.g. and fore-end. 14¼″ x 1⅝″ x 2½″.
Features: Receiver hand engraved with scroll designs and border. Double extractors, extra bbls. interchangeable without factory fitting; mag. cut-off; cross-bolt safety.
Price: $244.50
Price: Vent. rib $262.50

Browning Auto-5 Magnum 20

Same as Magnum 12 except barrels 28″ Full or Mod., or 26″ Full, Mod. or Imp. Cyl. 7 lbs. $248.50
With ventilated rib, 7½ lbs. $266.50

Browning Auto-5 Buck Special

Same as A-5 Light model except: 24″ bbl. choked for slugs, gold bead front sight on contoured ramp, rear sight adj. for w.&e. Wgt. (12 ga.) 7⅝ lbs.
Price: $262.50

BROWNING AUTO-5 Light 12, 16, 20, or 12 Buck Special

Same as Std. Buck Special except: with gold trigger and of less weight. Wgt. 12 ga., 7 lbs.; 16 ga., 6⅜ lbs.; 20 ga., 6 lbs. 2 oz.; 3″ Mag. 12, 8¼ lbs.
Price: $271.50
All Buck Specials are available with carrying sling, detachable swivels and swivel attachments for $9.00 extra.

Hi-Standard Supermatic Trap

Same features as Supermatic Skeet except: 30″ full choke barrel; stock (14⅜″x1½″x1⅞″); recoil pad. Wgt. 8 lbs. 12 ga. only.
Price: . . . . $194.95   With Monte Carlo stock . . . $209.95

HI-STANDARD SUPERMATIC DELUXE AUTOS

Gauge: 12 ga. (5-shot; 3-shot plug furnished). 20 ga. (3-shots only).
Action: Gas operated autoloader (12 ga. 2¾″, 20 ga. 3″ chambers).
Barrel: 12 gauge, 30″ (Full), 26″ (Imp. Cyl.), 12 and 20 gauge, 28″ (Mod. or Full). Plain Barrel.
Stock: 14″x1½″x2½″. Walnut, checkered p.g. and semi-beavertail fore-end. Recoil pad. 20 ga. guns have longer fore-end with sloped front.
Weight: 7½ lbs. (12 ga.) 47¾″ over-all (12, 28″).
Features: 12 ga. uses all 2¾″ shells, 20 ga. all 2¾″ or 3″ shells, including rifled slugs, manual adjustment, engraved receiver.
Price: Field, plain bbl., No rib $179.95
Price: Deluxe vent. rib, checkered stock, w/o adj. choke $199.95
Price: Checkered stock, vent.-rib, adj. choke $199.95
Price: Duck, 3″ Magnum, 12 ga., 30″ full, recoil pad, with vent. rib bbl.$199.95

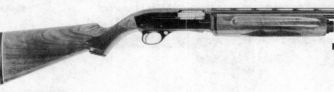

ITHACA MODEL XL 900

Gauge: 12 (2¾″), 20 (2¾″, 3″ chamber); 5 shot capacity.
Action: Gas-operated autoloader.
Barrel: 12 ga., Field Grade - 30″ (Full), 28″ (Full or Mod.), 26″ (Imp. Cyl.); 20 ga., 28″ (Full or Mod.,) 26″ (Imp. Cyl,), Trap - 30″ (Full or Imp. Mod.), Skeet - 26″ (Skeet).
Weight: 6¾ lbs. **Length:** 48″ overall.
Stock: 1½″x2½″x14″ (Field Grade). Walnut finish.
Sights: Ventilated rib with Raybar front sight on field grades; Bradley-type on target grades.
Features: Self-compensating gas system, reversible safety, action release button.
Price: Ventilated rib . . . . . . $194.95   Trap grade (12 ga. only) . . $224.95
Price: Skeet grade . . . . $224.95   Slug gun $194.95

Hi-Standard Supermatic Skeet

Same as Supermatic DeLuxe except: 26″ Skeet choke bbl.; all external parts high polished; internal parts super finished; better grade American walnut stock (no recoil pad) and fore-end with cabinet finish. weight about 7½ lbs. $204.95

ITHACA MODEL XL 300

Gauge: 12 (2¾″), 20 (2¾″ or 3″ chamber).
Action: Gas-operated autoloader.
Barrel: 12 ga. Field Grade - 30″ (Full), 28″ (Full or Mod.), 26″ (Imp. Cyl.). 20 ga. Field Grade - 28″ (Full or Mod.) 26″ (Imp. Cyl.). Trap Grade - 30″ (Full or Mod.); Skeet-26″ (Skeet).
Weight: 7½ lbs. **Length:** 48″ over-all.
Stock: 1½″x2½″x14″ (Field Grade). Walnut.
Sights: Raybar front sight on ventilated rib.
Features: Self-compensating gas system, reversible safety.
Price: Standard . . . . $179.95   Ventilated rib $194.95
Price: XL 300 recoil operated, standard grade $179.95
Price: XL 300 recoil operated with vent. rib $194.95

ITHACA MODEL 51 FEATHERLIGHT AUTOMATIC

Gauge: 12 ga. 2¾" chamber.
Action: Gas-operated, rotary bolt has three locking lugs. Takedown. Self-compensating for high or low base loads.
Barrel: Roto-Forged, 30" (Full), 28" (Full, Mod., or Skeet), 26" (Imp. Cyl. or Skeet). Extra barrels available. Raybar front sight. Vent. rib $25.00 extra.
Stock: 14"x1⅝"x2½". Hand checkered walnut, white spacers on p.g. and under recoil pad.
Weight: About 7½ lbs.
Features: Hand fitted, engraved receiver, 3 shot capacity, safety is reversible for left hand shooter.
Price: Standard **$189.95**

Ithaca Model 51 Featherlight Automatic Trap

Same gun as Model 51 with vent. rib, trap recoil pad, stock dimensions are 14¼"x1½"x1⅞".
Price: .... **$244.95**   With Monte Carlo stock ... **$254.95**

Ithaca Model 51 Featherlight Automatic Skeet

Same gun as Model 51 with vent. rib, skeet recoil pad, stock dimensions are 14"x1⅝"x2½".
Price: .... **$214.95**   Deluxe Skeet **$249.95**

ITHACA MODEL 51 MAGNUM

Same as Standard Model 51 except has 3" chambers.
Price: Magnum Standard **$209.95**
Price: Magnum vent. rib **$234.95**

Ithaca Model 51 Featherlight Deluxe Trap

Same gun as Model 51 Trap with fancy American walnut stock, 30" (Full or Imp. Cyl.) or 28" (Full or Imp. Mod.) barrel.
Price: .... **$269.95**   With Monte Carlo stock ... **$279.95**

Ithaca Model 51 Featherlight Deluxe Skeet

Same gun as Model 51 Skeet with fancy American walnut stock, 28" or 29" (Skeet) barrel.
Price: **$249.95**

Ithaca Model 51 20 Gauge

Gauge: 20 only, 2¾" or 3" chamber.
Action: Gas-operated rotary bolt.
Barrel: Standard Grade, 26" (Imp. Cyl.), 28" (Full, Mod.), Target Grade, 26" (Skeet).
Weight: 7½ to 8½ lbs.
Stock: 14"x1½"x2¼", American walnut.
Sights: Raybar front sight.
Features: Quick take-down, reversible safety, interchangeable barrels. Easily field stripped without tools.
Price: Standard model **$189.95**
Price: Standard model with vent. rib **$214.95**
Price: Standard magnum **$209.95**
Price: Vent. magnum **$234.95**
Price: Standard Skeet **$214.95**
Price: Deluxe Skeet **$249.95**

Ithaca Model 51 Deerslayer

Gauge: 12 or 20 ga., 2¾" chamber.
Action: Gas-operated, semi-automatic.
Barrel: 24", special bore.
Weight: 7½ lbs. (12 ga.), 7¼ lbs. (20 ga.).
Stocks: 14"x1½"x2¼", American walnut. Checkered p.g. and fore-end.
Sights: Raybar front, open rear adj. for w. and e.
Features: Sight base grooved for scope mounts. Easy takedown, reversible safety.
Price: **$209.95**

REMINGTON MODEL 1100 AUTO

Gauge: 12, 16, 20 (5-shot); 3-shot plug furnished.
Action: Gas-operated autoloader.
Barrel: 26" (Imp. Cyl.), 28" (Mod., Full), 30" Full in 12 ga. only.
Stock: 14"x1½"x2½" American Walnut, checkered p.g. and fore-end.
Weight: 12 ga. 7½ lbs., 16 ga. 7⅜ lbs., 20 ga. 7¼ lbs.; 48" over-all (28" bbl.).
Features: Quickly interchangeable barrels within gauge. Matted receiver top with scroll work on both sides of receiver. Crossbolt safety.
Price: .... **$189.95**   With vent. rib **$214.95**
Price: Left hand model with vent. rib **$219.95**

Remington 1100D Tournament Auto
Same as 1100 Standard except: vent. rib, better wood, more extensive engraving **$595.00**

Remington 1100 SA Skeet
Same as the 1100 except: 26″ bbl., special skeet boring, vent. rib, ivory bead front and metal bead middle sights. 14″x1½″x2½″ stock. 20 and 12 ga. Wgt. 7½ lbs.
Price: **$244.95**
Price: 1100 SB (better grade walnut) **$249.95**
  For Cutts Comp add **$25.00**
  Left hand model with vent. rib **$229.95**
  28 & 410 ga., 25″ bbl. **$234.95**

Remington 1100 Magnum
Same as 1100 except: chambered for 3″ magnum loads. Available in 12 ga. (30″) or 20 ga. (28″) Mod. or Full, 14″x1½″x2½″ stock with recoil pad, Wgt. 7¾ lbs. **$209.95**
Price: With vent. rib **$234.95**
Price: Left hand model with vent. rib **$239.95**

Remington 1100 Small Gauge
Same as 1100 except: 28 ga. 2¾″ (5-shot) or 410, 3″ (except Skeet, 2½″ 4-shot). 45½″ over-all. Available in 25″ bbl. (Full, Mod., or Imp. Cyl.) only.
Price: Plain bbl. .... **$199.95**   With vent. rib **$224.95**

Remington 1100 20 ga. Lightweight
Basically the same design as Model 1100, but with special weight-saving features that retain strength and dependability of the standard Model 1100.
Barrel: 28″ (Full, Mod.), 26″ (Imp. Cyl.).
Weight: 6½ lbs.
Price: .... **$199.95**   With vent. rib **$224.95**
Price: 20 ga. Lightweight magnum (28″ Full) **$219.95**
Price: With vent. rib **$244.95**

Remington 1100F Premier Auto
Same as 1100D except: select wood, better engraving **$1295.00**
With gold inlay **2000.00**

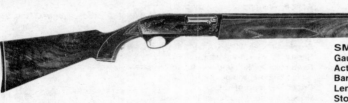

Remington 1100 Deer Gun
Same as 1100 except: 12 ga. only, 22″ bbl. (Imp. Cyl.), rifle sights adjustable for w. and e.; recoil pad with white spacer. Weight 7¼ lbs. **$209.95**

Remington 1100 TB Trap
Same as the 1100 except: better grade wood, recoil pad. 14⅜″x1⅜″x1¾″ stock. Wgt. 8¼ lbs. 12 ga. only. 30″ (Mod., Full) vent. rib bbl. Ivory bead front and white metal middle sight.
Price: .... **$259.95**   With Monte Carlo stock **$269.95**
Price: 1100TB Trap, left hand **$264.95**
Price: With Monte Carlo stock **$274.95**
Remington 1100 Extra bbls.: Plain **$49.95** (20, 28 & 410, **$52.95**). Vent. rib **$74.95** (20, 28 & 410, **$77.95**). Vent. rib Skeet **$79.95**. Vent. rib Trap **$79.95** Deer bbl. **$60.95**, Skeet, with cutts comp. **$104.95**. Available in the same gauges and chokes as shown on guns.

SMITH & WESSON MODEL 1000 AUTO
Gauge: 12 only, 2¾″ chamber, 4-shot.
Action: Gas-operated autoloader.
Barrel: 26″ (Skeet, Imp. Cyl.), 28″ (Imp. Mod., Mod., Full), 30″ (Full).
Length: 48″ over-all (28″ bbl.). **Weight:** 7½ lbs. (28″ bbl.).
Stock: 14″x1½″x2⅜″, American walnut.
Features: Interchangeable crossbolt safety, vent. rib with front and middle beads, engraved alloy receiver, pressure compensator and floating piston for light recoil.
Price: **$204.95**
Price: Extra barrels (as listed above) **$74.95**

UNIVERSAL AUTO WING SHOTGUN
Gauge: 12 only (5-shot; 3-shot plug furnished). 2¾″ chamber.
Action: Recoil operated autoloader; takedown; extra bbls. interchange without factory fitting; cross-bolt safety.
Barrels: 26″, 28″ or 30″ (Imp. Cyl., Mod., & Full). Vent. rib, Ivory bead front & middle sights.
Stock: 14¼″x1⅝″x2½″. Walnut checkered, full p.g. and grooved fore-end.
Weight: About 7 lbs.
Price: **$222.00**

WEATHERBY CENTURION AUTO
Gauge: 12 only, 2¾″ chamber.
Action: Gas operated autoloader with ''Floating Piston.''
Barrel: 26″ (Mod., Imp. Cyl, Skeet), 28″ (Full, Mod.), 30″ (Full), Vent. Rib.
Weight: About 7½ lbs. **Length:** 48¼″ (28″).
Stock: Walnut, hand checkered p.g. and fore-end, rubber recoil pad with white line spacer.
Features: Cross bolt safety, fluted bolt, gold plated trigger. Extra interchangeable bbls. **$79.95**
Price: Field or Skeet grade **$249.50**   Trap grade **$279.50**

U.S. SHOTGUNS—AUTOLOADING

Winchester 1400 Auto Skeet
Same as M1400 except: 12 and 20 ga. only, 26″ bbl., Skeet choke, wgt. 7½ lbs. Stock: 14″x1½″x2½″. Metal, middle, red front sights. Measures 46⅝″ over-all **$219.95**
Winchester 1400 Extra Barrels: Field, 12, 16, 20 ga. **$39.95**; with vent. rib **$59.95**; Deer Gun **$50.95**; Trap, Skeet **$67.95**

WINCHESTER 1400 AUTOMATIC MARK II
Gauge: 12, 16, and 20 (3-shot).
Action: Gas operated autoloader. Front-locking 4-lug rotating bolt locks in bbl. Alloy receiver. Push button action release.
Barrel: 26″ (Imp. Cyl.), 28″ (Mod., Full), 30″ (Full, 12 ga. only). Metal bead front sight.
Stock: 14″x1½″x2⅜″. American walnut, new-design checkered p.g. and fore-end; fluted comb, p.g. cap, recoil pad.
Weight: With 26″ bbl., 20 ga. 6½ lbs., 16, 12 ga. 6¾ lbs.; 46⅝″ over-all.
Features: Self-compensating valve adjusts for std. or magnum loads. Bbls. interchangeable without fitting. Crossbolt safety in front of trigger guard.
Price: .... **$149.95** With vent. rib **$169.95**

Winchester 1400 Auto Deer Gun
Same as M1400 except: 12 ga. only, 42⅝″ over-all with 22″ bbl. specially bored for rifled slugs. Ramp front sight, adj. open rear. Stock: 14″x1½″x2⅜″. Wgt. 6½ lbs. **$164.95**

Winchester 1400 Auto Trap
Same as M1400 except; 12 ga. only, 51″ over-all with 30″ full choke bbl. Stock: 14⅜″x1⅜″x1⅞″. Wgt., 8¼ lbs. Metal, middle, red front sights. **$219.95**. With Monte Carlo stock (14⅜″x1½″x2⅛″x1½″). With extended rib **$229.95**

U.S. SHOTGUNS—SLIDE ACTION

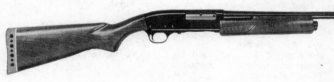

HARRINGTON & RICHARDSON 442 PUMP
Same as the 440 except: Full length vent. rib, checkered p.g. and fore-end.
Price: **$139.95**

HARRINGTON & RICHARDSON 440 PUMP
Gauge: 12, 20 (2¾″ and 3″ chamber), 16 (2¾″). 4-shot mag.
Action: Hammerless, side ejecting, slide action.
Barrel: 24″, 12 and 20 ga. (Imp. Cyl.); 26″, 12 and 20 ga. (Imp. Cyl. and Mod.); 28″, 12 ga. (Full and Mod.), 16 ga. (Mod. only), 20 ga. (Full and Mod.); 30″, 12 ga. (Full only).
Stock: Walnut p.g. stock and fore-end; recoil pad.
Weight: 6¼ lbs. 47″ over-all.
Price: **$112.00**

Hi-Standard Flite-King Skeet
Same as Flite-King DeLuxe except: Vent. rib, no recoil pad; 26″ Skeet choke bbl.; all external parts high polished; internal parts super finished; better grade American walnut stock (14″x1½″x2½″) and fore-end with cabinet finish. Wgt. 12 ga. 7½ lbs., 20, 6¼ lbs., 28 and 410 ga. 6¼ lbs. **$164.95**

Hi-Standard Flite-King Trap
Same features as Flite-King Skeet except: 30″ full choke; Monte Carlo stock with recoil pad. About 8¼ lbs. 12 ga. only **$174.95**

HI-STANDARD FLITE-KING DELUXE PUMP GUNS
Gauge: 12, 20, 28, and 410 (6 shots; 3-shot plug furnished).
Action: "Free-falling" slide action.
Barrel: 12 ga., 30″ (Full); 12, 20 ga., 28″ (Mod. or Full), 26″ (Imp. Cyl.); 410, 26″ (Full). 12 ga. barrels interchangeable.
Stock: 14″x1½″x2½″. Walnut, checkered p.g. and fore-end. Recoil pad except: 410 & Skeet guns.
Weight: 12 ga. 7¾ lbs., 20, 410 ga. 6½ lbs.
Features: Side ejection.
Price: Field **$129.95**
Price: 12 ga., with adj. choke, 27″ bbl **$134.95**
Price: De Luxe Rib, with vent. rib, w/o adj. choke **$149.95**
Price: 12 and 20 ga., as above with adj. choke **$154.95**
Price: Brush, 12 ga. only with 20″ cyl. bbl., grooved fore-end, adj. rifle sights. Stock (14¼″x1½″x1⅞″) 39¾″ over-all **$149.95**

Ithaca Model 37 Supreme
Same as Model 37 except: hand checkered beavertail fore-end and p.g. stock, Ithaca recoil pad and vent. rib **$259.95**
37 Supreme also with Skeet (14″x1½″x2½″) or Trap (14½″x1½″x1⅞″) stocks at no extra charge. Other options available at extra charge.

ITHACA MODEL 37 FEATHERLIGHT
Gauge: 12, 16, 20 (5-shot; 3-shot plug furnished).
Action: Slide; takedown; bottom ejection.
Barrel: 26″, 28″, 30″ in 12 ga. 26″ or 28″ in 16 or 20 ga. (Full, Mod. or Imp. Cyl.).
Stock: 14″x1⅝″x2⅝″. Checkered walnut capped p.g. stock and fore-end.
Weight: 12 ga. 6½ lbs., 16 ga. 6 lbs., 20 ga. 5¾ lbs.
Features: Ithaca Raybar front sight; decorated receiver; crossbolt safety; action release for removing shells.
Price: **$134.95**
Price: With vent. rib stock (14″x1½″x2½″) **$159.95**

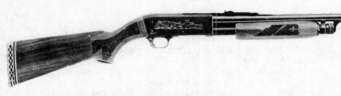

Ithaca Model 37 De Luxe Featherlight

Same as Model 37 except: checkered stock with p.g. cap; beavertail fore-end; recoil pad. Wgt. 12 ga. 6¾ lbs.

Price: . . . . $139.95   With vent. rib $164.95

Ithaca Model 37 Deerslayer

Same as Model 37 except: 26″ or 20″ bbl. designed for rifled slugs; sporting rear sight, Raybar front sight; rear sight ramp grooved for Redfield long eye relief scope mount. 12, 16, or 20 gauge. With checkered stock, beavertail fore-end and recoil pad.

Price: $149.95
Price: As above with special select walnut stock $169.95

MARLIN 120 MAGNUM PUMP GUN

Gauge: 12 ga. (2¾″ or 3″ chamber) 5-shot; 3-shot plug furnished.
Action: Hammerless, side ejecting, slide action.
Barrel: 26″ (Imp. Cyl.), 28″ (Mod.) or 30″ (Full), with vent. rib.
Stock: (14″x1½″x2⅜″). Checkered walnut, capped p.g., semi-beavertail checkered fore-end.
Length: 50½″ over-all (30″ bbl.). **Weight:** About 7¾ lbs.
Features: Interchangeable bbls., slide lock release; large button cross-bolt safety.
Price: $154.95

MARLIN 120 TRAP GUN

Same as 120 Magnum except: Monte Carlo stock and full fore-end with hand-cut checkering. Stock dimensions are 14¼″x1¼″x1¾″. Available with 30″ Full or Modified trap choke barrel with vent. rib. $229.95

MOSSBERG MODEL 500 PUMP GUN

Gauge: 12, 16 (2¾″), 20; 3″ (6-shot, 3-shot plug furnished).
Action: Slide, takedown; safety on top of receiver.
Barrel: 26″ (Imp. Cyl.) 28″ (Full or Mod.), 30″ (Full), 12 ga. only. Also 12 ga. 18½″ cylinder, for police only.
Stock: 14″x1½″x2½″. Walnut p.g., extension fore-end. Recoil pad. 13 oz. steel plug furnished for use with Magnum barrel.
Weight: 12 ga. 6¾ lbs., 45¼″ over-all (26″ bbl.).
Features: Easy interchangeability of barrels; side ejection; disconnecting trigger makes doubles impossible; straight-line feed.
Price: Standard barrel $106.95
Price: With C-Lect Choke, 3″ Mag., or 24″ Slugster bbls. $112.95
Price: Extra barrel, 2¾″ chamber $24.00
Price: Extra Magnum, C-Lect Choke or Slug, bbl. $31.65

Mossberg Model 500 Super Grade

Similar to the Model 500 except: vent. rib bbls. in 12 ga. (2¾″) or 20 ga. (3″); 26″ (Skeet), 28″ (Mod., Full), and 30″ Full (12 ga. only) 2¾″ or 3″ mag. Checkered p.g. and fore-end stock with fluted comb and recoil pad (14″x1½″x2½″).
Price: 12 or 20 ga. $124.00
Price: 12 ga. 3″ Magnum or C-Lect Choke 12 and 20 ga. $134.75

Mossberg Model 500E

Similar to Model 500 except: 410 bore only, 26″ bbl. (Full, Mod. or Imp. Cyl.); holds six 2¾″ or five 3″ shells. Walnut stock with smooth p.g. and grooved fore-end, fluted comb and recoil pad (14″x1¼″x2½″).
Weight: About 5¾ lbs., length over-all 46″.
Price: Standard barrels $106.95
Price: C-Lect Choke barrel $112.95
Price: Super Grade, 26″ Full, Mod., or Skeet bbl., vent. rib $124.00

Mossberg Model 500 APR Pigeon Grade

Similar to Model 500, but with vent. rib, rubber recoil pad, hand checkering, scroll engraving on action.
Price: $151.50
Price: 500 APTR trap gun 30″ full choke barrel, M.C. stock, 14½″x1½″x2″, additional barrels available. $157.95

REMINGTON 870 ALL AMERICAN

Gauge: 12 only.
Barrel: 30″ full choke.
Weight: 7 lbs.
Stock: Select walnut, fluted extension fore end, cut checkered.
Features: Receiver, trigger guard and breech fully engraved. Special "All American" shield fitted to left side of receiver. RK-W finished wood. Pistol grip cap has gold plate for initials. Supplied with luggage type, foam lined case.
Price: Standard or Monte Carlo stock $550.00

U.S. SHOTGUNS—SLIDE ACTION

Remington 870 Magnum
Same as the M870 except 3" chamber, 12 ga. 30" bbl. (Mod. or Full), 20 ga. 28" bbl. (Mod. or Full). Recoil pad installed. Wgt., 12 ga. 8 lbs., 20 ga. 7½ lbs.
Price: Plain bbl. .... **$154.95**   Vent. rib bbl. **$179.95**
Price: Left hand model, vent. rib. bbl. **$184.95**

Remington Model 870 Brushmaster Deluxe
Carbine version of the M870 with 20" bbl. (Imp. Cyl.) for rifled slugs. 40½" over-all, wgt. 6½ lbs. Recoil pad. Adj. rear, ramp front sights. 12 or 20 ga.
Deluxe **$154.95**

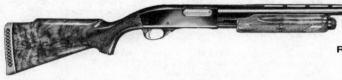

Remington 870D Tournament
Same as 870 except: better walnut, hand checkering, Engraved receiver & bbl. Vent.-rib. Stock dimensions to order **$595.00**

Remington 870F Premier
Same as M8700, except select walnut, better engraving **$1295.00**

Remington 870 Extra Barrels
Plain **$39.95**. Vent. rib **$64.95**. Vent. rib Skeet **$69.95**. Vent. rib Trap **$69.95**. 34" Trap **$74.95**. With rifle sights **$50.95**. Available in the same gauges and chokes as shown on guns.

REMINGTON 870 WINGMASTER PUMP GUN
Gauge: 12, 16, 20, (5-shot; 3-shot wood plug).
Action: Takedown, slide action.
Barrel: 12, 16, 20, ga. 26" (Imp. Cyl.); 28" (Mod. or Full); 12 ga. 30" (Full).
Stock: 14"x1⅝"x2½". Checkered walnut, p.g.; fluted extension fore-end; fitted rubber recoil pad.
Weight: 7 lbs., 12 ga. (7¾ lbs. with Vari-Weight plug); 6¾ lbs., 16 ga.; 6½ lbs., 20 ga. 48½" over-all (28" bbl.).
Features: Double action bars, crossbolt safety. Receiver machined from solid steel. Hand fitted action.
Price: Plain bbl. .... **$134.95**   Vent. rib **$159.95**
Price: Riot gun, 18" or 20" Riot bore, (12 ga. only) **$119.95**
Price: Riot gun, 20" Imp. Cyl., rifle sights **$129.95**
Price: Left hand, vent. rib., 12 and 20 ga. **$164.95**

Remington 870 SA Skeet
Same as the M870 except: 26" bbl. Skeet bored. Vent. rib with ivory front and white metal middle beads. 14"x1⅝"x2½" stock with rubber recoil pad, 12 or ga. only **$164.95**
Price: Add for Cutts comp. **$25.00**
Price: 28 and 410 ga., 25" bbl., no recoil pad **$174.95**

Remington 870 TB Trap
Same as the M870 except: 12 ga. only, 30" (Mod., Full) vent. rib. bbl., ivory front and white metal middle beads. Special sear, hammer and trigger assy. 14⅜"x1½"x1⅞" stock with recoil pad. Hand fitted action and parts. Wgt. 8 lbs. **$199.95**
Price: With Monte Carlo stock **$209.95**
Price: Add $5.00 for left hand model

Remington 870 Small Gauges
Exact copies of the large ga. Model 870, except that guns are offered in 20, 28 and 410 ga. 25" barrel (Full, Mod., Imp. Cyl.).
Plain barrel **$144.95**
D and F grade prices same as large ga. M870 prices.
Price: With vent. rib barrel **$169.95**
Price: Lightweight Magnum, 20 ga. plain bbl. (5¾ lbs.) **$164.95**
Price: Lightweight Magnum, 20 ga., vent. rib bbl. **$189.95**

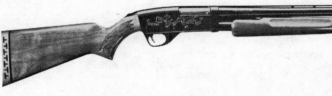

Savage Model 30-T
Same specifications as 12 ga., M30 except: 30" Full Choke bbl. with 3" chamber; Monte Carlo stock with trap dimensions (14⅝"x1½"x1½"x2¼"). Recoil pad. Over-all 50". 8 lbs. **$134.95**

Savage Model 30 Field Grade
Same as Model 30 except plain bbl. and receiver, hard rubber buttplate
Price: **$102.95**

SAVAGE MODEL 30-D PUMP GUN
Gauge: 12, 20, and 410, 5-shot (410, 4-shot) 3-shot plug furnished. All gauges chambered for 3" Magnum shells.
Action: Slide, hammerless, take-down; side ejection; top tang safety.
Barrel: Vent. rib. 12, 20 ga. 26" (Imp. Cyl.); 28" (Mod. or Full); 12 ga., 30" (Full); 410, 26" (Full).
Stock: 14"x1½"x2½". Walnut, checkered p.g., grooved extension fore-end, recoil pad.
Weight: 7 lbs. (410, 6¼ lbs.). Over-all 49½" (30" bbl.).
Features: Decorated lightweight receiver; plated trigger.
Price: **$124.95**

Savage Model 30 Slug Gun
Same as the Model 30 Field Grade but with 22" bbl., 12 or 20 ga. only, with rifle sights **$106.95**

SMITH & WESSON MODEL 916 EASTFIELD PUMP GUN
Gauge: 12, 20 (3"), 16 (2¾"), 6-shot (3-shot plug furnished).
Barrel: 20" (Cyl.), 26" (Imp. Cyl.), 28" (Mod., Full or adj. choke) 30" (Full), plain. Vent. rib 26", 28", 30".
Weight: 7¼ lbs. (28" plain bbl.).
Stock: 14"x2½"x1⅝", American walnut, fluted comb, finger-grooved fore-end.
Features: Vent. rib, vent. recoil pad, adj. choke available as options. Satin finish steel receiver with non-glare top.
Price: Plain bbl., no recoil pad **$98.25**
Price: Plain bbl. with adj. choke **$103.25**
Price: Plain bbl. with recoil pad **$100.75**
Price: Vent. rib and recoil pad (illus.) **$117.50**

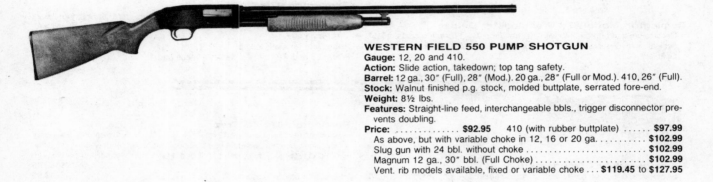

WEATHERBY PATRICIAN PUMP

Gauge: 12 only, 2¾" chamber.
Action: Short stroke slide action.
Barrel: 26" (Mod. Imp. Cyl, Skeet), 28" (Full, Mod.), 30" (Full) Vent. Rib.
Weight: About 7½ lbs. **Length:** 48⅛ (28" bbl.)
Stock: Walnut hand checkered p.g. and fore-end, white line spacers at p.g. cap and recoil pad.
Features: Short stroke action, hidden magazine cap, crossbolt safety. Extra interchangeable bbls. **$69.95**
Price: Field or Skeet grade **$189.50**   Trap grade **$219.50**

WESTERN FIELD 550 PUMP SHOTGUN

Gauge: 12, 20 and 410.
Action: Slide action, takedown; top tang safety.
Barrel: 12 ga., 30" (Full), 28" (Mod.). 20 ga., 28" (Full or Mod.). 410, 26" (Full).
Stock: Walnut finished p.g. stock, molded buttplate, serrated fore-end.
Weight: 8½ lbs.
Features: Straight-line feed, interchangeable bbls., trigger disconnector prevents doubling.
Price: .... **$92.95**   410 (with rubber buttplate) **$97.99**
As above, but with variable choke in 12, 16 or 20 ga. **$102.99**
Slug gun with 24 bbl. without choke **$102.99**
Magnum 12 ga., 30" bbl. (Full Choke) **$102.99**
Vent. rib models available, fixed or variable choke ... **$119.45** to **$127.95**

WINCHESTER 12 TRAP

Same as Model 12 except: 30" full choke vent. rib bbl. only. 49¾" overall.
14⅜"x1⅜"x1⅞" stock w/recoil pad **$375.00**
With Monte Carlo stock, 14⅜"x1½"x2⅛" **$385.00**

WINCHESTER 12 FIELD PUMP SHOTGUN

Gauge: 12 only, 6-shot (3-shot plug installed).
Barrel: 26" (Imp. Cyl.), 28" (Mod.), 30" (Full), 2¾" only.
Length: 45¾" (26" bbl.). **Weight:** 7¾ lbs.
Stock: 14"x1½"x2½". Semi-fancy walnut, checkered p.g. and fore-end.
Features: Ventilated rib, hand checkered, engine turned bolt.
Price: **$350.00**

WINCHESTER 12 SKEET

Same as Model 12 except available only with 26" Skeet bored bbl.
14"x1½"x2½" stock with recoil pad **$375.00**

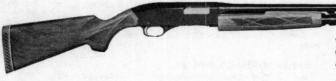

WINCHESTER 1200 FIELD PUMP GUN

Gauge: 12, 16 and 20 (5-shot; 3-shot plug installed).
Action: Slide; front locking 4-lug rotating bolt locks into bbl. Alloy receiver, cross-bolt safety in front of trigger guard. Take-down.
Barrel: 26" (Imp. Cyl.), 28" (Mod., Full) and 30" Full (12 ga. only). Metal bead front sight.
Stock: 14"x1⅜"x2⅜". American walnut with new-design checkered p.g. and fore-end; fluted comb, recoil pad. Steel p.g. cap.
Weight: 12 ga. 6½ lbs. with 26" bbl. 46⅝" over-all.
Price: .... **$123.95**   With vent. rib **$143.95**

Winchester 1200 Trap

Same as M1200 except: 12-ga. only, 30" Full choke vent. rib bbl., 51" over-all. 14⅜"x1⅜"x1⅞" stock with recoil pad, b. t. fore-end. Metal, middle, red front sights **$205.95**
With Monte Carlo stock, 14⅜"x1⁷⁄₁₆"x2⅛"x1½" **$215.95**

Winchester 1200 Deer Gun

Same as M1200 except: 12 ga. only, 22" bbl. bored for rifled slugs; rifle-type sights, rear adj. for e. only **$138.95**
Winchester 1200 Extra Barrels: Field and Riot w/o sights, 12, 16, 20 ga. **$39.45.** Field with vent. rib, 12, 16, 20 ga. **$59.45.** Riot with sights and Deer Gun, 12 ga. **$50.45.** Trap, 12 ga., Full choke 30" only .... **$64.95** Winchester 1200 with interchangeable choke tubes which are screwed into the barrel and tightened with supplied wrench. Available in 12, 16 and 20 ga. (28") Mod. tube. Price: Field **$123.95** Vent. rib **$143.95** Extra tubes in Full, Mod. or Imp. Cyl. **$4.95.** Wrench **$1.25.**

Winchester 1200 Field 3" Magnum

Same as 1200 except: 12 and 20 ga. only, 2¾" or 3" shells, 28" and 30" full choke bbls., 3 lbs. with 38" bbl., 48⅝" over-all.
Price: .... **$133.95**   With vent. rib **$153.95**

BROWNING B-SS
Gauge: 12 and 20 ga. (2¾" and 3" chambers).
Action: Top lever break-open action, top tang safety, single trigger.
Barrel: 26" (Mod. and Full or Imp. Cyl. and Mod.), 28" (Mod. and Full).
Weight: 6¾ lbs. (26" bbl.); 7 lbs. (28" bbl.).
Stock: 14¾"x1⅝"x2½". Walnut, hand checkered. Full p.g., full beavertail fore-end.
Features: Automatic safety, automatic ejectors. Hand engraved receiver, mechanical trigger.
Price: **$239.50**

ITHACA SKB 100 FIELD GRADE DOUBLE
Gauge: 12 (2¾" chambers) and 20 (3").
Action: Top lever, hammerless, boxlock, automatic safety, single selective trigger, non-automatic extractor.
Barrel: 12 ga. 26" (Imp. Cyl., Mod.). 28⅛ or 30" (Mod., Full). 20 ga. 28" (Mod., Full). 25" (Imp. Cyl., Mod.).
Stock: 14"x1½"x2⅝". Walnut, hand checkered p.g. and fore-end, p.g. cap, fluted comb.
Weight: 7 lbs. (12 ga.); 6 lbs. (20 ga.).
Features: Automatic safety. Chrome lined action and barrels, hand engraved receiver.
Price: **$214.95**

ITHACA SKB MODEL 150
Same as SKB 100 except: Beavertail fore-end and extensively etched scrollwork frame.
Price: **$239.95**

ITHACA SKB 200E DELUXE FIELD GRADE DOUBLE
Same as 100 Field Grade except: automatic selective ejectors, bead middle sight and scroll engraving on receiver, beavertail fore-end. White line spacers. Gold plated trigger and nameplate **$289.95**

Ithaca SKB 200E Skeet Grade
Same as 200E Deluxe Field Grade except: recoil pad, non-auto. safety. Bbls. 26" 12 ga. or 25" 20 ga. (Skeet, Skeet). Wgt. 7¼ and 6¼ lbs.
Price: **$289.95**

Ithaca-SKB Model 280 Quail Double
Gauge: 20 only, 3" chambers.
Barrel: 25" (I.C. & I.C.).
Weight: 6½ lbs.
Stock: 14"x1½"x2⅝", English style.
Features: Designed for quail and upland game shooting. Straight stock, wrap-around checkering, scroll game scene on frame, semi-beavertail fore-end. Auto. selective ejectors, single trigger.
Price: **$304.95**

Ithaca SKB 280 English Double
Like the 200 Field Grade except: hand-checkered straight grip stock with wrap-around checkering; semi-beavertail fore-end. Receiver hand engraved with quail and English scroll. Durable, simulated oil-finished walnut stock.
Price: **$304.95**

MARLIN L. C. SMITH FIELD DOUBLE
Gauge: 12 only (2¾" chambers).
Action: Sidelock, double trigger. Case hardened frame.
Barrel: 28" (Mod. & Full).
Stock: Select walnut with capped p.g. checkered, (14"x1½"x2½").
Weight: 6¾ lbs.
Features: Vent. rib, standard extractors, top auto. tang safety.
Price: **$325.00**

PEDERSEN 2500 GRADE III DOUBLE
Field gun version of Series 2000. No receiver engraving, standard stock dimensions. European walnut stock, hand checkered p.g. and beavertail fore-end.
Price: 12 or 20 ga. **$275.00**

PEDERSEN 2000 SERIES DOUBLE, GRADE I
Gauge: 12 or 20 ga.
Action: Boxlock.
Weight: To customer's specs. **Length:** To customer's specs.
Stock: Dimensions to customer's specs. Walnut, hand checkered p.g. and fore-end.
Features: Automatic selective ejectors, barrel selector/safety, gold filled engraving, automatic safety, single selective trigger. Gun is made entirely to customer specifications.
Price: Grade I **$970.00**

PEDERSEN 2000 SERIES DOUBLE, GRADE II
Same as Grade I except: standard stock dimensions (14"x2½"x1½"), different receiver engraving, less fancy wood.
Price: 12 or 20 ga. **$650.00**

U.S. SHOTGUNS—DOUBLE BARREL

SAVAGE FOX MODEL B-SE Double
Gauge: 12, 20, 410 (20, 2¾" and 3"; 410, 2½" and 3" shells).
Action: Hammerless, takedown; non-selective single trigger; auto. safety. Automatic ejectors.
Barrel: 12, 20 ga. 26" (Imp. Cyl., Mod.); 12 ga. (Mod., Full); 410, 26" (Full, Full). Vent. rib on all.
Stock: 14"x1½"x2½". Walnut, checkered p.g. and beavertail fore-end.
Weight: 12 ga. 7 lbs., 16 ga. 6¾ lbs., 20 ga. 6½ lbs., 410 ga. 6¼ lbs.
Features: Decorated, case-hardened frame; white bead front and middle sights.
Price: **$169.95**
Also available with double triggers, case hardened frame, without white line spacers and auto. ejectors as Model B **$144.95**

Savage Model 550 Double
Like the Fox B-SE except 12 or 20 ga. only, game scene and case hardened finish on receiver. White spacers at buttplate and capped p.g. . . **$174.95**

SAVAGE/FOX B 24" LIGHTWEIGHT
Gauge: 12, 20 2¾" & 3" chambers, 410, 2½" & 3" chambers.
Action: Hammerless, top lever, double triggers.
Barrel: 24", 12 & 20 ga. (Imp. Cyl. & Mod.), 26" (Imp. Cyl. & Mod.), 28" (Mod. & Full), 30" (Mod. & Full, 12 ga. only), 26", 410 ga. (Full & Full).
Weight: 7 to 8 lbs.
Stocks: 14"x1½"x2½", select walnut. Checkered p.g. and fore-end.
Features: Color case-hardened frame, beavertail fore-end, vent. rib.
Price: **$144.95**

SAVAGE-STEVENS MODEL 311 DOUBLE
Gauge: 12, 16, 20, 410 (12, 20 and 410, 3" chambers).
Action: Top lever, hammerless; double triggers, auto top tang safety.
Barrel: 12, 16, 20 ga. 36" (Imp. Cyl., Mod.); 12 ga. 28" (Mod., Full); 12 ga. 30" (Mod., Full); 410 ga. 26" (Full, Full).
Length: 45¾" over-all. **Weight:** 7-8 lbs. (30" bbl.).
Stock: 14"x1½"x2½". Walnut finish, p.g., fluted comb.
Features: Box type frame, case-hardened finish.
Price: **$112.95**

UNIVERSAL DOUBLE WING DOUBLE
Gauge: 12, 20 and 410, 3" chambers
Action: Top break, boxlock.
Barrel: 26" (Imp. Cyl., Mod.); 28" or 30" (Mod., Full; Imp., Mod.; Full & Full).
Stock: Walnut p.g. and fore-end, checkered.
Weight: About 7 lbs.
Features: Double triggers; Recoil pad. Beavertail style fore-end.
Price: **$182.50**
Price: 10 ga. 3½" chamber 32" Full and Full (M2030) **$199.95**

Winchester 21 Grand American
Same as Custom and Pigeon grades except: style "B" stock carving, with style "6" engraving, all figures gold inlaid; extra pair of bbls. with beavertail fore-end, engraved and carved to match rest of gun; full leather trunk case for all, with canvas cover **$4,950.00**

WINCHESTER 21 CUSTOM DOUBLE GUN
12, 16 or 20 ga. Almost any choke or bbl. length combination. Matted rib, 2¾" chambers, rounded frame, stock of AA-grade full fancy American walnut to customer's dimensions; straight or p.g., cheekpiece, Monte Carlo and/or offset; field. Skeet or trap fore-end.
Full fancy checkering, engine-turned receiver parts, gold plated trigger and gold oval name plate (optional) with three initials **$2,500.00**

Winchester 21 Pigeon grade
Same as Custom grade except: 3" chambers, available in 12 and 20 ga.; matted or vent. rib, leather covered pad (optional); style "A" stock carving and style "6" engraving (see Win. catalog); gold inlaid p.g. cap, gold name-plate or 3 gold initials in guard **$3,600.00**

U.S. SHOTGUNS—OVER-UNDER

BROWNING "LIEGE" O/U
Gauge: 12 only (2¾" or 3" mag.).
Action: Boxlock, top lever, single selective trigger.
Barrels: 26½", 2¾" (Full & Full, Mod. & Full. or Imp. Cyl. & Mod.); 28" 2¾" (Full & Full, Mod. & Full, Imp. Cyl. & Mod.); 28", 3" Mag. (Mod. & Full); 30", 3" Mag. (Full & Full or Mod. & Full).
Stock: 14¼"x1⅝"x2½". Select walnut, hand rubbed finish, hand checkered p.g. & fore-end.
Weight: 7¼ lbs. to 7¾ lbs.
Features: Mechanical trigger, manual safety with bbl. selector, 3-piece assembly, fore-end detaches for disassembly.
Price: **$429.50**

BROWNING SUPERPOSED LIGHTNING

Same as Super-Light except: 7-7¼ lbs. in 12 ga. 6-6¼ lbs. in 20 ga. Grade 1 **$590.00**, Pigeon **$880.00**, Diana **$1,170.00**, Midas **$1,640.00**.

Browning Superposed Magnum 12

Same as Browning Superposed Super-Light except 3″ chambers; 30″ (Full and Full or Full and Mod.) barrels, Stock, 14¼″x1⅝″x2½″ with factory fitted recoil pad. Weight 8 lbs. Grade 1, **$590.00**, Pigeon **$880.00**, Diana **$1,170.00**, Midas **$1,640.00**.

Browning Superposed Standard Skeet

Same as Superposed Standard except: 26½″ or 28″ bbls. (Skeet, Skeet). Wgt. 6½-7¾ lbs. 12 and 20 ga. Grade 1 **$585.00**; 28 and 410 ga, **$630.00**; Pigeon **$930.00**, Diana **$1,230.00**, Midas **$1,720.00**.

SUPERPOSED BROADWAY TRAP 12

Same as Browning Lightning Superposed except: ⅝″ wide vent. rib; stock, 14⅜″x1⁷/₁₆″x1⅝″. 30″ or 32″ (Imp. Mod, Full; Mod., Full; Full, Full). 8 lbs. with 32″ bbls. Grade 1 **$635.00**, Pigeon **$930.00**, Diana **$1,225.00**, Midas **$1,700.00**.

Browning Superposed Combinations

Standard and Lightning models are available with these factory fitted extra barrels: 12 and 20 ga., same gauge bbls.; 12 ga., 20 ga. bbls.; 20 ga., extra sets 28 and/or 410 gauge; 28 ga., extra 410 bbls. Extra barrels may be had in Lightning weights with Standard models and vice versa. Prices range from **$975.00** (12, 20 ga., one set extra bbls. same gauge) for the Grade 1 Standard to about **$2,850.00** for the Midas grade in various combinations, all as cased sets.

BROWNING SUPERPOSED SUPER-LIGHT

Gauge: 12, & 20 2¾″ chamber.
Action: Boxlock, top lever, single selective trigger. Bbl. selector combined with manual tang safety.
Barrels: 26½″ (Mod. & Full, or Imp. Cyl. & Mod.)
Stock: Straight grip (14¼″ x 1⅝″ x 2½″) hand checkered (fore-end and grip) select walnut.
Weight: 6⅜ lbs., average.
Features: Slender, tapered solid rib. Hand rubbed finish, engraved receiver.
Price: Grade 1 .... **$630.00**
   Pigeon **$940.00**
   Diana **$1,250.00**
   Midas **$1,760.00**

Browning Superposed Lightning Trap 12

Same as Browning Lightning Superposed except: semi-beavertail fore-end and ivory sights; stock, 14⅜″x1⁷/₁₆″x1⅝″. 7¾ lbs. 30″ (Full & Full, Full & Imp. Mod. or Full and Mod.) Grade 1 **$600.00** Pigeon **$890.00**, Diana **$1,180.00**, Midas **$1,650.00**.

Browning Superposed Lightning Skeet

Same as Standard Skeet except: 12 and 20 ga. only. Wgt. 6½-7¾ lbs. Grade 1 **$600.00**, Pigeon **$890.00**, Diana **$1,180.00**, Midas **$1,650.00**.

BROWNING SUPERPOSED ALL-GAUGE SKEET SET

Consists of four matched sets of barrels in 12, 20, 28 and 410 ga. Available in either 26½″ or 28″ length. Each bbl. set has a ¼″ wide vent. rib with two ivory sight beads. Grade 1 receiver is hand engraved and stock and fore-end are checkered. Weight 7 lbs., 10 oz. (26½″ bbls.), 7 lbs., 12 oz. (28″ bbls.). Grade 1 **$1,950.00**, Pigeon **$2,500.00**, Diana **$2,850.00**, Midas **$3,550.00**.

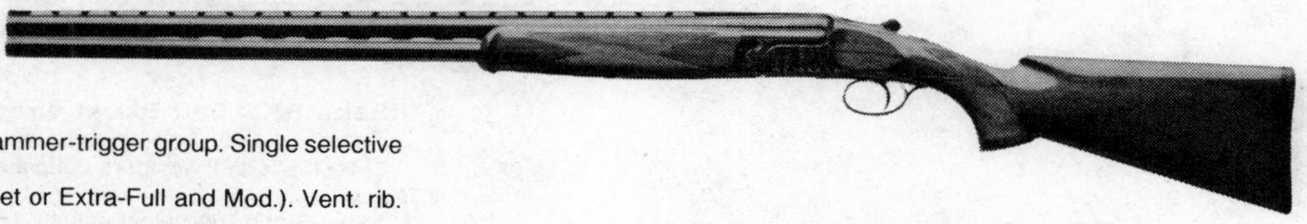

ITHACA MIRAGE O/U

Gauge: 12 only (2¾″ chambers).
Action: Boxlock type, interchangeable hammer-trigger group. Single selective trigger, specify choice of firing order.
Barrel: 28″, 30″, or 32″ (Skeet and Skeet or Extra-Full and Mod.). Vent. rib.
Weight: 8¼ lbs. **Length:** 44″ over-all.
Stock: Walnut, hand checkered with schnabel fore-end, 1½″x2⅜″x14″. Rubber recoil pad.
Price: Trap model **$1,395.00**
Price: Skeet model **$1,395.00**

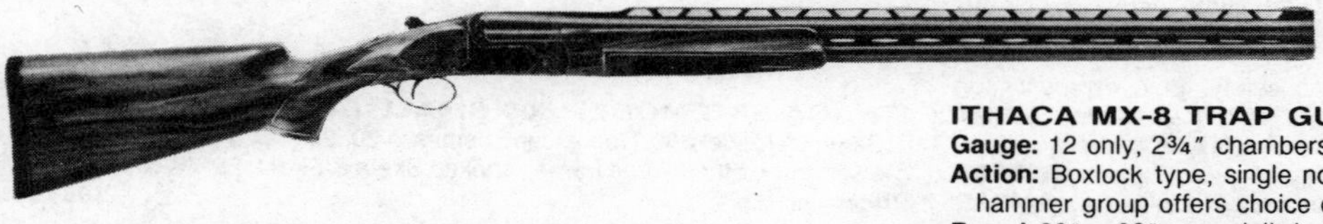

ITHACA COMPETITION I TRAP O/U

Gauge: 12 only, 2¾″ chambers.
Action: Boxlock type, interchangeable hammer-trigger group. Single non-selective trigger, specify choice of firing order.
Barrel: 30″ or 32″, upper Full; lower, Imp.-Mod., vent rib has concave surface with deep cuts.
Stock: Interchangeable, 6 standard (1³/₁₆″ to 1½″ at comb x1⅜″ to 1⅞″ at heel) and 3 Monte Carlo (1⅜″ to 1⁹/₁₆″x1⅜″ to 1⁹/₁₆″) of walnut; all have 14½″ pull. Fore-end has slight taper and finger groove for firm grip.
Weight: About 7¾ lbs.
Features: Extra trigger-hammer groups are available to change firing sequence and/or trigger pull. Custom stocks also available.
Price: **$895.00**
   Extra trigger-hammer group **75.00**
   Extra stock **85.00**

ITHACA MX-8 TRAP GUN

Gauge: 12 only, 2¾″ chambers.
Action: Boxlock type, single non-selective trigger; interchangeable trigger-hammer group offers choice of firing order.
Barrel: 30″ or 32″, especially bored for international clay target shooting. High concave vent rib has 5″ ramp.
Stock: Custom, finely checkered (oiled or lacquer finish) European walnut, interchangeable with other models, 9 available including Monte Carlo.
Weight: About 8 lbs.
Features: Ventilated middle rib has additional vent ports for maximum heat dissipation, better balance and smoother swing.
Price: **$1,395.00**
   Extra trigger-hammer group **75.00**
   Extra stock **85.00**

ITHACA MX-8 COMBINATION

Same as MX-8 Trap Gun except comes with interchangeable single barrel (32″ or 34″).
Price: **$1,895.00**

ITHACA COMPETITION I SKEET O/U

Gauge: 12 only, 2¾" chambers.
Action: Boxlock type, interchangeable hammer-trigger group. Single non-selective trigger.
Barrel: 26¾" (Skeet & Skeet). Vent rib has concave surface with deep cuts.
Stock: 14½"x1½"x2⅜", interchangeable walnut, custom stocks available.
Weight: About 7¾ lbs.
Features: Extra trigger-hammer groups to change firing order and/or weight of pull. Leather faced recoil pad has bevelled heel that will not catch. Extra stocks interchange for different style and dimension.
Price: $975.00
Extra trigger-hammer group 75.00

ITHACA LIGHT GAME MODEL

Gauge: 12 only (2¾" chambers).
Action: Boxlock type interchangeable hammer-trigger group. Offers choice of firing order. Single non-selective trigger.
Barrel: 27⅝" (Mod. and Full, Imp. Cyl. and Full, Imp. Cyl. and Mod.) Vent. rib.
Weight: 6¾ lbs. **Length:** 44½ overall.
Stock: French walnut. Hand checkered p.g., fore-end and butt, schnabel fore-end, 1½"x2⅜"x14".
Features: Hand engraved, case hardened frame.
Price: $895.00

ITHACA SKB 600 TRAP GRADE O/U

Same as 500 Field Grade except 30" bbl. (Imp. Mod., Full, or Full, Full), fine scroll engraved receiver; bead middle sight; Monte Carlo stock (14½"x1½"x1½"x2"), p.g. white line spacer and recoil pad.
Price: $379.95
Field Grade 600, on recoil pad or Monte Carlo $369.95
Trap Grade 700, features select walnut oil finished stock and band engraved receiver $449.95

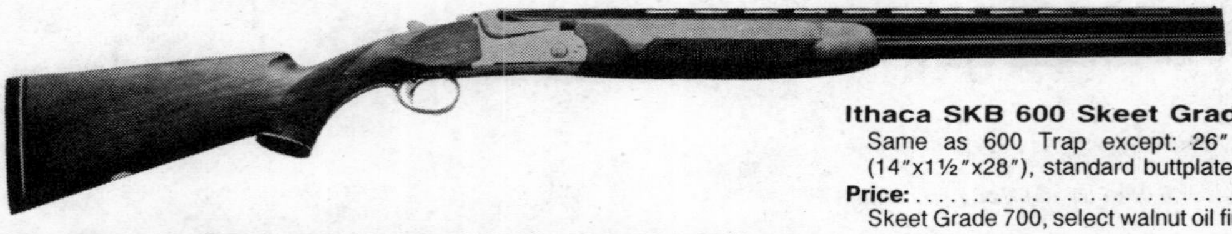

ITHACA SKB 500 FIELD GRADE O-U

Gauge: 12 (2¾" or 3" chambers), 20 (3").
Action: Top lever, hammerless, boxlock; gold-plated single selective trigger; automatic ejectors, non-auto safety.
Barrel: 26" vent. rib (Imp. Cyl., Mod.); 28" (Imp. Cyl., Mod. or Mod., Full); 30" (Mod., Full); 12 ga., 2¾" chambers. 26" (Imp. Cyl., Mod.); 28" (Mod., Full); 20 ga., 3" chambers.
Stock: 14"x1½"x2⅝". Walnut, checkered p.g. and fore-end, p.g. cap, fluted comb.
Weight: 7½ lbs. (12); 6½ lbs. (20).
Features: Border scroll engraved receiver. Chrome lined bbls. and action. Raybar front sight.
Price: $304.95
Price: Magnum model $314.95

ITHACA-SKB TRAP DOUBLES MODEL 600, 700 O/U

Gauge: 12, 2¾".
Barrel: 30" or 32", special bore.
Weight: 8 lbs.
Stocks: 14"x1½"x1⅞", American walnut, hand fitted, hand checkered, curved trap pad. Available with M.C. stock.
Sights: Bradley-type.
Features: Double locking lugs, non-automatic safety. Built expressly for shooting doubles and Continental/International style trap. Model 700 has select wood, extra-wide rib, more detailed scroll work on frame.
Price: Model 600 .... $384.95
Price: Model 700 (deluxe version of 600) $449.95

Ithaca SKB 600 Skeet Grade O/U

Same as 600 Trap except: 26" or 28" bbls. (Skeet, Skeet), stock (14"x1½"x28"), standard buttplate and whiteline spacer. Weight 7½ lbs.
Price: $379.95
Skeet Grade 700, select walnut oil finished stock and band engraved receiver $449.00

ITHACA-SKB MODEL 600 SMALL BORE SKEET

Same as Model 600 Trap except: comes in 20, 28 (2¾") and 410 (2½") as a set (three barrels, one frame), choked Skeet & Skeet, 28". Weight 7¼ lbs.
Price: $389.95

ITHACA TURKEYGUN

Caliber: 12 ga./.222.
Barrel: 24½" (Full).
Weight: 7½ lbs.
Stock: 14"x1⅝"x1⅞"x2¼", walnut.
Sights: Ramp front, folding leaf rear.
Features: Detachable choke tubes (Full choke supplied, Mod., Imp. Cyl. available), rifle barrel, sling swivels, grooved for scope mounts. Imported by Ithaca.
Price: $239.95

U.S. SHOTGUNS—OVER-UNDER

Ithaca-SKB Model 680 English O/U
Gauge: 12 or 20 ga.
Action: Boxlock.
Barrel: 26″ or 28″ (Full & Mod., Mod. & I.C.).
Weight: 7 lbs.
Stock: 14″x1½″x2⅝″, straight grip, walnut, wrap-around checkering.
Features: Auto. selective ejectors, Bradley-type sights on target grades. Single selective trigger, chrome lined barrels with black chrome exteriors.
Price: $379.95

ITHACA-SKB MODEL 880 CROWN GRADE O/U
Gauge: 12 or 20.
Action: Boxlock with sideplates.
Barrel: Trap 30″ or 32″ (Full & Imp. Mod.), Skeet 26″ (Skeet & Skeet), 20 ga. Skeet 28″ (Skeet & Skeet).
Weight: 7 lbs. (Skeet), 8 lbs. (Trap).
Stock: 14½″x2″x1½″x1½″ Trap with M.C., 14″x2½″x1½″ Skeet. Full fancy French walnut.
Sights: Bradley-type.
Features: Hand-honed action, extensive engraving and checkering. Gold-inlaid "crown" on bottom of frame.
Price: $999.95

PEDERSEN 1000 SERIES CUSTOM O/U
Gauge: 12 or 20 ga.
Action: Boxlock.
Barrel: To customer specs.
Weight: To customer specs. **Length:** To customer specs.
Stock: Dimensions to customer specs. American walnut, hand checkered p.g. and fore-end, rubber recoil pad.
Features: Vent. rib, single selective trigger, automatic ejectors, gold filled, hand engraved receiver, gun made entirely to customer specifications.
Price: 12 or 20 ga. $970.00
Price: Trap or Skeet models $970.00

Pedersen 1000 Series O/U, Grade II
Same as Grade I except: standard stock dimensions (14″x2½″x1½″x2″), less fancy wood, different receiver engraving.
Price: 12 or 20 ga. $650.00
Price: Trap model (with trap dimensions) $675.00
Price: Skeet model $660.00

PEDERSEN 1000 SERIES O/U, GRADE III
Same as Grade I except: standard stock dimensions (14″x2½″x1½″x2″), no receiver engraving. Gold plated trigger and fore-end release.
Price: 12 or 20 ga. $500.00
Price: Trap model $525.00
Price: Skeet model $510.00

PEDERSEN 1500 O/U
Gauge: 12 only.
Action: Boxlock.
Barrel: 26″ to 32″.
Weight: 7 to 7½ lbs. **Length:** 44″ over-all (26″ bbl.).
Stock: 14″x2½″x1½″x2″. European walnut, hand checkered p.g. and fore-end, rubber recoil pad.
Features: Field gun version of Series 1000. Automatic selective ejectors, vent. rib, choice of sights on target guns, Field model has Raybar type.
Price: 12 ga., Field $400.00
Price: Trap (has M.C. stock and pad) $420.00
Price: Skeet (skeet chokes) $410.00

REMINGTON 3200 O/U
Gauge: 12, 2¾″ chambers.
Action: Top lever, break open. Single selective trigger.
Barrel: 26″ (Imp. Cyl. & Mod., Skeet & Skeet), 28″ (Mod. & Full, Skeet & Skeet), 30″ (Mod. & Full, Full & Full, Imp. Mod. & Full). Vent. rib.
Weight: 7¾ lbs. (26″ bbl.).
Stock: 14″x1½″x2⅛″, American walnut. Checkered p.g. and fore-end. Modified beavertail fore-end on field model, full on trap and Skeet.
Features: Super-fast lock time, separated barrels, engraved receiver, unbreakable firing pins, combination barrel selector/safety, wide trigger, shield-covered breech.
Price: Field (illus.) .... $450.00   Skeet $470.00
Price: Trap .... $490.00   Special Trap $540.00
Price: "One of 1,000" Trap $1,050.00

SAVAGE MODEL 24-D O/U
Caliber: Top bbl. 22 S, L, LR or 22 Mag.; bottom bbl. 20 or 410 gauge.
Action: Two-way top lever opening, low rebounding visible hammer, single trigger, barrel selector spur on hammer, separate extractors, color case-hardened frame.
Barrel: 24″, separated barrels.
Weight: 6¾ lbs. **Length:** 40″.
Stock: Walnut, checkered p.g. and fore-end (14″x1½″x2½″).
Sights: Ramp front, rear open adj. for e.
Features: Receiver grooved for scope mounting.
Price: $82.95

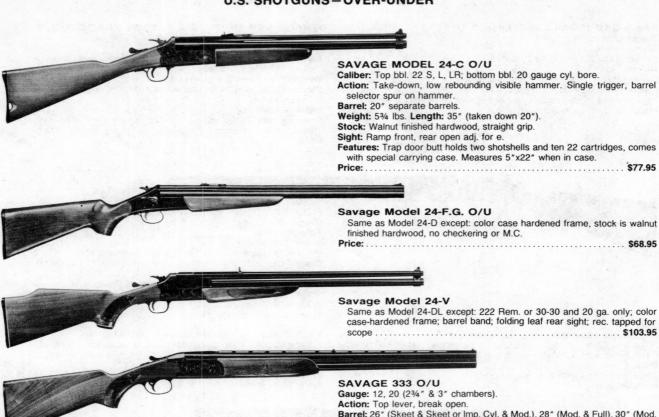

SAVAGE MODEL 24-C O/U
Caliber: Top bbl. 22 S, L, LR; bottom bbl. 20 gauge cyl. bore.
Action: Take-down, low rebounding visible hammer. Single trigger, barrel selector spur on hammer.
Barrel: 20″ separate barrels.
Weight: 5¾ lbs. **Length:** 35″ (taken down 20″).
Stock: Walnut finished hardwood, straight grip.
Sight: Ramp front, rear open adj. for e.
Features: Trap door butt holds two shotshells and ten 22 cartridges, comes with special carrying case. Measures 5″x22″ when in case.
Price: **$77.95**

Savage Model 24-F.G. O/U
Same as Model 24-D except: color case hardened frame, stock is walnut finished hardwood, no checkering or M.C.
Price: **$68.95**

Savage Model 24-V
Same as Model 24-DL except: 222 Rem. or 30-30 and 20 ga. only; color case-hardened frame; barrel band; folding leaf rear sight; rec. tapped for scope **$103.95**

SAVAGE 333 O/U
Gauge: 12, 20 (2¾″ & 3″ chambers).
Action: Top lever, break open.
Barrel: 26″ (Skeet & Skeet or Imp. Cyl. & Mod.), 28″ (Mod. & Full), 30″ (Mod. & Full, 12 ga. only).
Weight: 6¼ to 7¼ lbs.
Stock: 14″x1½″x2½″, French walnut. Fleur-de-lis checkering.
Features: Single selective trigger, auto. safety, ejectors, cocking indicators. Engraved steel receiver.
Price: **$237.50**

Savage Model 330 O/U Set
Identical to the Model 330 but with two sets of barrels, one in 12 ga. the other in 20 (Mod. & Full). Same fore-end fits both sets of bbls. Comes with padded case with pocket for extra bbl.
Price: Factory fitted **$310.00**
Price: Extra 20 ga. bbl. only (must be fitted at the factory) **$110.00**

SAVAGE 333-T
Same specifications as Model 330 except has trap specifications and features: 30″ bbl. choked Imp. Mod. and Full, manually operated top tang safety (disconnects trigger from sears), stock measures 14½″x1½″x1½″ at Monte Carlo, 2½″ heel. Over-all length 47″, taken down 30″, weight 7¾ lbs. Has extra-wide ventilated rib, extractors, recoil pad.
Price: **$288.50**

SAVAGE MODEL 330 O/U
Gauge: 12, 2¾″ chambers, 20 ga. 3″ chambers.
Action: Top lever, break open. Selective single trigger, auto top tang safety locks trigger, coil springs.
Barrel: 26″ (Mod. & Imp. Cyl.), 28″ or 30″ (Mod. & Full).
Stock: 14″x1½″x2½″). Walnut, checkered p.g. and fore-end, hard rubber plate.
Weight: About 7 lbs., 46½″ (30″ bbl.) over-all.
Features: Monoblock locking rails are engaged by locking shield that snaps forward as gun is closed. This shield overlaps the breech for added strength.
Price: **$217.50**

UNIVERSAL OVER WING O/U SHOTGUN
Gauge: 12, 20. 3″ chamber.
Action: Top lever, hammerless, box lock, double triggers.
Barrel: 26″ vent. rib (Imp. Cyl., & Mod.); 28″ or 30″ (Mod. & Full). Front & middle sights.
Stock: 14″x1½″x2⅝″. Walnut, checkered p.g. and fore-end. Recoil Pad.
Weight: 7½ lbs. (12); 6½ lbs. (20).
Price: **$269.95**
With single-trigger, engraved receiver and fancier stock **$288.00**

WEATHERBY REGENCY O/U SHOTGUN
Gauge: 12 ga. (2¾″ chambers), 20 ga. (3″ chambers).
Action: Boxlock (simulated side-lock) top lever break-open. Selective auto ejectors, single selective trigger (selector inside trigger guard).
Barrel: 28″ with vent rib and bead front sight, Full & Mod., Mod. & Imp. Cyl. or Skeet & Skeet.
Stock: American walnut, checkered p.g. and fore-end (14¼″x1½″x2½″).
Weight: 12 ga. 7⅜ lbs., 20 ga. 6⅞ lbs.
Features: Mechanically operated trigger. Top tang safety, Greener cross-bolt, fully engraved receiver, recoil pad installed.
Price: 12 or 20 ga. Field and Skeet **$599.00**
Price: 12 ga. Trap Model **$649.50**

U.S. SHOTGUNS—OVER-UNDER

Winchester 101 Trap Gun
Same as the 101 Field gun except: Metal front and middle bead sights. 30″ (Full & Full) bbl. only. 14⅜″x1⅜″x1⅞″ stock with 1¼″ pitch down and recoil pad. 12 ga. only **$395.00**
With Monte Carlo stock (14⅜″x1⅜″x1⅜″x1⅞″), 30″ or 32″, Full and Full or Imp. Mod. and Full **$405.00**

Winchester 101 Combination Skeet Set
Same as 101 20 ga. Skeet except: Includes Skeet bbls. in 410 & 28 ga. Vent. ribs match 20 ga. frame. With fitted trunk case **$915.00**

Winchester 101 Skeet
Same as M-101 except: 12 ga., 26″ bbls., 20, 26½″, 28 & 410, 28″. Bored Skeet and Skeet only, 12 or 20 ga. **$395.00**
M101 in 28 or 410 .... **$420.00**

WINCHESTER 101 OVER/UNDER Field Gun
Gauge: 12 and 28, 2¾″; 20 and 410, 3″.
Action: Top lever, break open. Manual safety combined with bbl. selector at top of receiver tang.
Barrel: Vent. rib 26″ 12, 26½″, 20 and 410 (Imp. Cyl., Mod.), 28″ (Mod & Full), 30″ 12 only (Mod. & Full). Metal bead front sight. Chrome plated chambers and bores.
Stock: 14″x1½″x2½″. Checkered walnut p.g. and fore-end; fluted comb.
Weight: 12 ga. 7¾ lbs. Others 6¼ lbs. **Length:** 44¾″ over-all (28″ bbls.).
Features: Single selective trigger, auto ejectors. Hand engraved receiver.
Price: 12 or 20 ga. **$360.00**
Price: 28 or 410 ga. **$385.00**

Winchester 101 Magnum Field Gun
Same as 101 Field Gun except: chambers 3″ Magnum shells; 12 & 20 ga. 30″ (Full & Full or Mod. & Full); hand-engraved receiver, select French walnut stock with fluted comb, hand-checkered pistol grip and beavertail fore-end with recoil pad **$370.00**

U.S. SHOTGUNS—SINGLE BARREL

BROWNING BT-99 SINGLE BARREL TRAP
Gauge: 2¾″ 12 gauge only.
Action: Top lever break-open hammerless, engraved.
Barrel: 32″ or 34″ (Mod., Imp. Mod. or Full) with ¹¹/₃₂″ wide, high post floating vent rib.
Stock: French walnut, hand checkered full p.g. and beavertail fore-end, factory fitted recoil pad (14⅜″x1⁷/₁₆″x1⅝″).
Weight: 8 lbs. (32″ bbl.), 8⅛ lbs. (34″ bbl.).
Features: Automatic ejector, gold plated trigger has about 3½ lb. pull, no safety.
Price: **$349.50**

CLERKE FALLING BLOCK SHOTGUN
Gauge: 12, 20, 410 (2¾″ or 3″ magnums).
Weight: 6¼ lbs. (12 ga.). **Length:** 42″ to 52″ (12 ga.).
Stock: Walnut finish stock and fore-end. Full pistol grip.
Features: Exposed rebounding hammer, falling block side lever action, color case hardened frame. Vent. rib, trap grade stock and rubber recoil pad available as options.
Price: **$49.95**

GARCIA BRONCO 410 SHOTGUN
Lightweight single shot (3″ chamber), featuring swing-out chamber, skeletonized 1-pc. receiver and p.g. stock, push-button safety, 3½ lbs., instant take-down.
Price: **$33.00**

H & R HARRICH NO. 1
Gauge: 12 gauge only. (2¾″).
Barrel: 32″ or 34″
Weight: 8½ lbs.
Stock: Select walnut, checkered p.g. and beavertail fore-end 14¾″x1¼″x1¼″x2″.
Features: Anson & Deeley type locking system with Kersten top locks and double under-locking lugs. Full length high line vent. rib. Hand engraved side locks.
Price: **$1500.00**

H & R TOPPER JR. MODEL 490
Like M158 except ideally proportioned stock for the smaller shooter. Can be cheaply changed to full size. 20 ga. (Mod.) or 410 (Full) 26″ bbl. Weight 5 lbs., 40½″ over-all **$42.50**

H & R TOPPER MODELS 158 and 198
Gauge: 12, 20 and 410. (2¾″ or 3″ chamber), 16 (2¾″ only).
Action: Takedown. Side lever opening. External hammer, auto ejection. Case hardened frame.
Barrel: 12 ga., 28″, 30″, 32″, 36″; 20 and 410 ga., 28″. (Full choke). 12, 16, 20 ga. available 28″ (Mod.).
Stock: Walnut finished hardwood; p.g., recoil pad. (14″x1¾″x2½″).
Weight: 5 to 6½ lbs., according to gauge and bbl. length.
Features: Self-adj. bbl. lock; coil springs throughout; auto. rebound hammer.
Price: M158 .... **$39.95**
Model 198, Topper Deluxe Chrome frame, ebony finished stock. 20 ga. and 410, 28″ bbl. **$44.95**

H & R TOPPER BUCK MODEL 162
Same as M158 except 12 ga. 24″ cyl. bored bbl., adj. Lyman peep rear sight, blade front, 5½ lbs.; over-all 40″. Cross bolt safety: push-button action release, ... **$46.95**

Ithaca Model 66 Supersingle Youth
Same as the 66 Standard except: 20 (26″ Bbl., Mod.) and 410 ga. (26″ Bbl., Full) shorter stock with recoil pad **$49.95**
With vent. rib, 20 ga. only **$59.95**

ITHACA MODEL 66 SUPERSINGLE
Gauge: 12, 20, 410 (3″ chamber).
Action: Non-takedown; under lever opening.
Barrel: 12, 20 ga. 28″ (Mod., Full); 12 ga., 30″ (Full), 410, 26″ (Full).
Stock: Straight grip walnut-finish stock and fore-end.
Weight: About 7 lbs.
Features: Rebounding hammer independent of the lever.
Price: **$44.95**
With vent. rib, 20 ga. only **$57.95**

U.S. SHOTGUNS—SINGLE BARREL

Ithaca Model 66 RS Supersingle Buckbuster
Same as the Model 66 Standard except: 12 and 20 ga. only, 22″ bbl. with rifle sights, designed to shoot slugs **$54.95**
Heavy bbl. (12 ga. only) **$54.95**

Ithaca 5E Grade Single Barrel Trap
Same as 4E except: Vent. rib bbl., better wood, more extensive engraving, and gold inlaid figures. Custom made: **$2,500.00**

Ithaca $4500 Grade Ejector
Same as 5E except: Special wood, better engraving, figures inlaid in green and yellow gold and platinum, gold plated trigger. **$4,500.00**

ITHACA 4E GRADE SINGLE BARREL TRAP GUN
Gauge: 12 only.
Action: Top lever break open hammerless, dual locking lugs.
Barrel: 30″ or 32″, rampless rib.
Stock: (14½″x1½″x1⅛″). Select walnut, checkered p.g. and beavertail fore-end, p.g. cap, recoil pad, Monte Carlo comb, cheekpiece, Cast-on, cast-off or extreme deviation from standard stock dimensions $100 extra. Reasonable deviation allowed without extra charge.
Features: Frame, top lever and trigger guard engraved. Gold name plate in stock.
Price: Custom made: **$1,750.00**

ITHACA PERAZZI SINGLE BARREL
Gauge: 12 (2¾″ chamber)
Action: Top lever, break open, top tang safety.
Barrel: 32″ or 34″; custom choking; ventilated rib.
Stock: Custom fitted European walnut in lacquered or oil finish.
Weight: About 8½ lbs.
Features: Hand-engraved receiver; interchangeable stocks available with some fitting.
Price: **$895.00**

Stevens M94-Y Youth's Gun
Same as Model 940 except: 26″ bbl., 20 ga. Mod. or 410 Full, 12½″ stock with recoil pad. Wgt. about 5½ lbs. 40½″ over-all. **$44.95**

SAVAGE-STEVENS MODEL 94-C Single Barrel Gun
Gauge: 12, 16, 20, 410 (12, 20 and 410, 3″ chambers).
Action: Top lever break open; hammer; auto. ejector.
Barrel: 12 ga. 28″, 30″, 32″, 36″; 16, 20 ga. 28″; 410 ga. 26″. Full choke only.
Stock: 14″x1½″x2½″. Walnut finish, checkered p.g. and fore-end.
Weight: About 6 lbs. Over-all 42″ (26″ bbl.).
Features: Color case-hardened frame, low rebounding hammer.
Price: 26″ to 32″ bbls. .... **$43.50**   36″ bbl. **$44.95**

IVER JOHNSON CHAMPION
Gauge: 12, 20 or 410 (3″ chamber).
Barrel: 12 gauge, 28″ or 30″; 20 gauge, 28″; 410, 26″; full choke.
Stock: Walnut finish, trap style fore-end.
Features: Takedown action, automatic ejection.
Price: Either gauge **$53.75**

ITHACA-SKB CENTURY SINGLE BARREL TRAP
Gauge: 12 only, 2¾″.
Barrel: 32″ or 34″ (Full).
Weight: 8 lbs.
Stock: 14½″x1½″x1⅞″ (Trap). French walnut, hand checkered, curved pad, full beavertail fore-end. M.C. stock available.
Sights: Bradley-type front, middle bead.
Features: Scroll-engraved silver-finish frame, chrome lined barrel, semi-wide vent. rib, auto. ejector.
Price: M.C. or straight stock **$419.95**

WESTERN FIELD 100 Single Barrel Gun
Gauge: 12, 16, 20, 410 (410, 3″ chamber).
Action: Hammerless; thumb slide break open.
Barrel: 12 ga., 30″; 16, 20 ga., 28″; 410 ga., 26″. All Full choke.
Stock: Walnut finished, p.g., recoil pad.
Weight: 6¼ to 7 lbs.
Features: Automatic safety, auto ejector.
Price: **$48.99**
Also available as Youth's Model. 26″ barrel, 20 or 410 gauge. Wgt. 6 lbs., 41″ over-all **$49.99**

WINCHESTER 37A SINGLE SHOT
Gauge: 12, 20, 410 (3″ chamber), 16, 28 (2¾″ chamber).
Action: Top lever break-open, exposed hammer.
Barrel: 26″, 410 ga. (Full). 28″, 20 & 28 ga. (Full). 30″, 16 ga. (Full). 30″, 32″ 36″, 12 ga. (Full).
Length: 42¼″ over-all (26″ bbl.). **Weight:** 5½ to 6¼ lbs.
Stock: 14″x1⅜″x2⅜″, walnut finish.
Sights: Metal bead front.
Features: Checkered p.g. and fore-end bottom, gold plated trigger, engraved receiver, concave hammer spur. Grip cap and buttplate have white spacers. Auto. ejector. Top lever opens right or left.
Price: Standard Model, 12 ga. **$47.95**
Price: 16, 20, 28 410 ga. **$46.95**

WINCHESTER 37A YOUTH MODEL
Same as std. 37A except: shorter 26″ bbl., youth-size stock (12½″ pull), 40¾″ over-all length. Rubber recoil pad. Available only in 20 ga. (Imp. Mod.) or 410 (Full). **$47.95**

MARLIN GOOSE GUN BOLT ACTION
Gauge: 12 only, 2-shot (3″ mag. or 2¾″).
Action: Bolt action, thumb safety, detachable clip.
Barrel: 36″, Full choke.
Stock: Walnut, p.g., recoil pad, leather strap & swivels.
Weight: 7¼ lbs., 57″ over-all.
Features: Double extractors, tapped for receiver sights. Swivels and leather carrying strap. Gold-plated trigger.
Price: **$68.95**

MARLIN 55S SLUG GUN
Same as Goose Gun except: 24″ barrel, iron sights (rear adj.), drilled and tapped for scope mounting. Comes with carrying strap and swivels. Weight is 7 lbs., over-all length 45″. **$73.95**

Marlin-Glenfield Model 50 Bolt Action
Same as the Marlin Goose Gun Except: 12 and 20 ga., 3″. No sling or swivels. Walnut-finished hardwood stock. Bbls. 12 ga. 28″, 20 ga. 26″ (Full). Wgt. 7 lbs., 49″ over-all (28″ bbl.)
Price: **$52.95**

MOSSBERG MODEL 183K BOLT ACTION
Gauge: 410, 3-shot (3″ chamber).
Action: Bolt; top-loading mag.; thumb safety.
Barrel: 25″ with C-Lect-Choke.
Stock: Walnut finish, p.g., Monte Carlo comb., rubber recoil pad w/spacer.
Weight: 6¾ lbs. **Length:** 43½″ over-all.
Features: Moulded trigger guard with finger grooves, gold bead front sight.
Price: **$52.35**
Price: As 183T without choke **$48.65**

MOSSBERG MODEL 395K BOLT ACTION
Gauge: 12, 3-shot (3″ chamber).
Action: Bolt; takedown; detachable clip.
Barrel: 28″ with C-Lect-Choke.
Stock: Walnut finish, p.g. Monte Carlo comb; recoil pad.
Weight: 6¾ lbs. 47½″ over-all.
Features: Streamlined action; top safety; grooved rear sight.
Price: **$63.00**
Also available in 20 ga. 3″ chamber 28″ bbl. 6¼ lbs., as M385K, **$58.35,** and in 16 ga. 28″ bbl., 6¾ lbs., as M390K **$61.45**

Mossberg Model 395S Bolt Action
Same as Model 395K except 24″ barrel with adjustable folding leaf rear sight and ramp front, for use with slugs. Sling supplied **$63.60**

SAVAGE-STEVENS 58 BOLT ACTION SHOTGUN
Gauge: 12, 20 2¾″ chambers. 20 ga. also in 3″. (2-shot detachable clip).
Action: Self-cocking bolt; double extractors; thumb safety.
Barrel: 25″, Full choke.
Stock: Walnut finish, checkered fore-end and p.g., recoil pad.
Weight: 7-7½ lbs. Over-all 46″ (43½″ in 410)
Features: Crisp trigger pull.
Price: **$59.95**
Also available in 410 ga., 3″ chamber, 3-shot detachable clip, 5½ lbs. 43½″ over-all (24″ bbl.) **$49.95**

Savage-Stevens 59 Bolt Action
Same as Model 58 410 ga. except: tubular mag. holding five 3″ or six 2½″ shells; 3-shot plug furnished; no recoil pad. Wgt. 6 lbs. 24″ bbl., 44½″ over-all **$61.95**

WESTERN FIELD 150 BOLT ACTION SHOTGUN
Gauge: 410 (3″ chamber).
Action: Self cocking, bolt action. Thumb safety. 3-shot magazine.
Barrel: 24″, full choke.
Weight: 5½ lbs. **Length:** 44½″ over-all.
Stock: Hardwood, Monte Carlo design.
Features: Top loading.
Price: **$46.95**

WESTERN FIELD 172 BOLT ACTION SHOTGUN
Gauge: 12 (3″ chamber).
Action: Self-cocking bolt. Thumb safety, double locking lugs, detachable clip.
Barrel: 28″ adj. choke, shoots rifled slugs.
Stock: Walnut, Monte Carlo design, p.g., recoil pad.
Features: Quick removable bolt with double extractors, grooved rear sight.
Price: **$58.95**
M175 Similar to above except 20 ga., **$54.95.** Without recoil pad and adj. choke **$52.95**

WESTERN FIELD 170 SLUG GUN
Gauge: 12 only, 2-shot clip.
Action: Self-cocking bolt action. Thumb safety, double locking lugs, detachable clip. Take-down action.
Barrel: 24″.
Weight: 6¾ lbs. **Length:** 43¼″ over-all.
Stock: Walnut finish p.g. stock.
Features: Rifle sights, rubber recoil pad; leather sling, sling swivels.
Price: **$60.89**

ASTRA CONSTABLE AUTO PISTOL

Caliber: 22 LR, 10-shot; 32 ACP, 8-shot; and 380 ACP, 7-shot.
Barrel: 3½".
Weight: 26 oz.
Stocks: Moulded plastic.
Sights: Adj. rear.
Features: Double action, quick no-tool takedown, non-glare rib on slide. Imported from Spain by Garcia.
Price: $100.00

BERETTA MODEL 70T AUTO PISTOL

Caliber: 32 ACP, 9-shot magazine.
Barrel: 6".
Weight: 19 oz. **Length:** 9½".
Stocks: Checkered plastic wrap-around.
Sights: Fixed front, adj. rear.
Features: External hammer, target-length bbl., slide stays open after last shot. Imported from Italy by Garcia.
Price: $98.00

BERETTA MODEL 101 AUTO PISTOL

Same as Model 70T except 22 LR, 10-round magazine. Imported from Italy by Garcia.
Price: $98.00

BERETTA MODEL 76 AUTO PISTOL

Caliber: 22 LR, 10-shot magazine.
Barrel: 6".
Weight: 35 oz. **Length:** 9½".
Stocks: Checkered plastic wrap-around.
Sights: Interchangeable blade front, adj. rear.
Features: Competition-type, non-glare ribbed heavy bbl., external hammer. Imported from Italy by Garcia.
Price: $140.00

BERETTA MODEL 70S AUTO PISTOL

Caliber: 380 ACP, 7-shot magazine.
Barrel: 3⅝".
Weight: 23¼ oz. **Length:** 6¼".
Stocks: Checkered plastic wrap-around.
Sights: Fixed front and rear.
Features: External hammer. Imported from Italy by Garcia.
Price: $120.00

BERETTA MODEL 90 AUTO PISTOL

Caliber: 32 ACP, 8-shot magazine.
Barrel: 3⅝".
Weight: 19½ oz. **Length:** 6¾".
Stocks: Moulded plastic wrap-around.
Sights: Fixed.
Features: Double action, chamber loaded indicator, sighting rib on slide, external hammer, stainless steel bbl. Imported from Italy by Garcia.
Price: $175.00

BERETTA MODEL 951 AUTO PISTOL
Caliber: 9mm Para., 8-shot magazine.
Barrel: 4½".
Weight: 31 oz. **Length:** 8".
Stocks: Moulded plastic.
Sights: Fixed.
Features: Crossbolt safety, external hammer, slide stays open after last shot. Imported from Italy by Garcia.
Price: **$200.00**

BERNARDELLI MATCH 22 AUTO PISTOL
Caliber: 22 LR, 10-shot magazine.
Barrel: 5¾".
Weight: 36 oz. **Length:** 9".
Stocks: Hand checkered walnut with thumbrest.
Sights: Post front, adj. rear.
Features: Manual and magazine safeties, external hammer, fitted case. Imported from Italy by Gold Rush.
Price: **$119.00**

BERNARDELLI MODEL 60 AUTO PISTOL
Caliber: 22 LR, 10-shot; 32 ACP, 8-shot; and 380, 7-shot.
Barrel: 3½".
Weight: 26 oz. **Length:** 6⅓".
Stocks: Checkered plastic.
Sights: Post front, click adj. rear.
Features: Manual and magazine safeties. Optional thumb rest grips, $10.00. Imported from Italy by Gold Rush, Kleingunther's, Liberty, Sloan's.
Price: **$84.50**

ERMA KGP 68 AUTO PISTOL
Caliber: 32 ACP, 6-shot; 380 ACP, 5-shot.
Barrel: 3½".
Weight: 22½ oz. **Length:** 6¾".
Stocks: Checkered walnut.
Sights: Fixed rear, adj. blade front.
Features: Sidelock manual safety. Imported from Germany by R. G. Industries.
Price: **$83.95**

ERMA KGP 69 AUTO PISTOL
Caliber: 22 LR, 8-shot magazine.
Barrel: 4".
Weight: 29 oz. **Length:** 7⁵⁄₁₆".
Stocks: Checkered walnut.
Sights: Fixed rear, adj. front.
Features: Stays open after last shot. Imported from Germany by R. G. Industries.
Price: **$81.95**

HAMMERLI STANDARD, MODELS 208 & 211
Caliber: 22 LR.
Barrel: 5.9", 6-groove.
Weight: 37.6 oz. (45 oz. with extra heavy barrel weight). **Length:** 10".
Stocks: Walnut. Adj. palm rest (208), 211 has thumbrest grip.
Sights: Match sights, fully adj. for w. and e. (click adj.). Interchangeable front and rear blades.
Features: Semi-automatic, recoil operated. 8-shot clip. Slide stop. Fully adj. trigger (2 lbs. and 3 lbs.). Extra barrel weight available. H. Grieder, importer.
Price: Model 208, approx. **$320.00**   Model 211 approx. **$305.00**

HAMMERLI MODEL 230 RAPID FIRE PISTOL
Caliber: 22 S.
Barrel: 6.3", 6-groove.
Weight: 43.8 oz. **Length:** 11.6".
Stocks: Walnut. Standard grip w/o thumbrest (230-1), 230-2 has adj. grip.
Sights: Match type sights. Sight radius 9.9". Micro rear, click adj. Interchangeable front sight blade.
Features: Semi-automatic. Recoil-operated, 6-shot clip. Gas escape in front of chamber to eliminate muzzle jump. Fully adj. trigger with three different lengths available. Designed for International 25 meter Silhouette Program. H. Grieder, importer.
Price: Model 230-1 .... **$345.00**
Price: Model 230-2 .... **$360.00**

HECKLER & KOCH HK-4 AUTO PISTOL
Caliber: 380 ACP, 8 shots.
Barrel: 3½".
Weight: 24 oz. **Length:** 6".
Stock: Checkered black plastic.
Sights: Front, fixed, rear adj. for w.
Features: Double action, 22 LR conversion kit available. Imported from Germany by Harrington & Richardson.
Price: .... **$110.00**   Conversion Kit for 22 LR ... **$37.50**

HECKLER & KOCH P9S AUTO PISTOL
Caliber: 9mm Para., 9-shot magazine.
Barrel: 4".
Weight: 33½ oz. **Length:** 5.4".
Stocks: Checkered plastic.
Sights: Fixed
Features: Double action, quick takedown, hammer cocking lever, loaded and cocked indicators. Special target model and 7.65mm Para. bbls. available. Imported from Germany by Gold Rush.
Price: **$179.00**

LLAMA MODELS VIII, IXA AUTO PISTOLS
Caliber: Super 38 (M. VIII), 45 ACP (M. IXA).
Barrel: 5".
Weight: 30 oz. **Length:** 8½".
Stocks: Checkered walnut.
Sights: Fixed.
Features: Grip and manual safeties, ventilated rib. Engraved, chrome engraved or gold damascened finish available. Imported from Spain by Stoeger Arms.
Price: **$115.95**

LLAMA MODELS XV, XA, IIIA AUTO PISTOLS
Caliber: 22 LR, 32 ACP and 380.
Barrel: 3¹¹/₁₆".
Weight: 23 oz. **Length:** 6½".
Stocks: Checkered plastic, thumb rest.
Sights: Fixed front, adj. notch rear.
Features: Ventilated rib, manual and grip safeties. Model XV is 22 LR, Model XA is 32 ACP, and Model IIIA is 380. Models XA and IIIA have loaded indicator; IIIA is locked breech. Imported from Spain by Stoeger Arms.
Price: **$83.95**

LLAMA XI AUTO PISTOL
Caliber: 9mm Para.
Barrel: 5".
Weight: 38 oz. **Length:** 8½".
Stocks: Moulded plastic.
Sights: Fixed front, adj. rear.
Features: Also available with engraved, chrome engraved or gold damascened finish. Imported from Spain by Stoeger Arms.
Price: **$108.95**

MAB PA15 AUTO PISTOL
Caliber: 9mm Para., 15-shot magazine.
Barrel: 4½".
Weight: 38 oz. **Length:** 8".
Stocks: Checkered plastic.
Sights: Fixed front and rear.
Features: External hammer, manual safety. 15-round magazine. Target model available on special order. Imported from France by Gold Rush.
Price: **$125.00**

MAUSER HSc AUTO PISTOL
Caliber: 32 ACP, 380 ACP, 7-shot.
Barrel: 3⅜".
Weight: 23 oz. **Length:** 6.05".
Stocks: Checkered walnut.
Sights: Fixed.
Features: Double action, manual and magazine safeties. Imported from Germany by Interarms.
Price: . . . . **$120.00**   Nickel plated **$135.00**

MAUSER PARABELLUM AUTO PISTOL
Caliber: 7.65mm, 9mm Para., 8-shot.
Barrel: 6", 4" (9mm only).
Weight: 32 oz. **Length:** 8⅔" (4" bbl.).
Stocks: Checkered walnut.
Sights: Fixed.
Features: Manual and grip safeties, American eagle over chamber. Imported from Germany by Interarms.
Price: **$219.00**

MKE MODEL TPK AUTO PISTOL
Caliber: 32 ACP, 8-shot; 380, 7-shot.
Barrel: 4".
Weight: 23 oz. **Length:** 6½".
Stocks: Checkered black plastic.
Sights: Fixed front, adj. notch rear.
Features: Double action with exposed hammer; safety blocks firing pin and drops hammer. Chamber loaded indicator pin. Imported from Turkey by Firearms Center.
Price: **$89.95**

SIG 210 AUTO PISTOL
Caliber: 22 LR, 7.65mm or 9mm Para., 8-shot.
Barrel: 4¾".
Weight: 34 oz. **Length:** 8½".
Stocks: Grooved walnut or checkered plastic.
Sights: Blade front, fixed notch rear.
Features: Thumb safety, external hammer. Available with various finishes including custom engraving. Conversion unit to convert CF pistol to 22 LR $100.00. Imported from Switzerland by Gold Rush.
Prices: . . . . from **$250.00.**

STAR MODELS A, B AND P AUTO PISTOLS
Caliber: 38 Super (Model A), 9-shot; 9mm Para. (Model B), 9-shot; and 45 ACP (Model P), 7-shot.
Barrel: 5".
Weight: 37½ oz. **Length:** 8½".
Stocks: Checkered walnut.
Sights: Fixed.
Features: Magazine and manual safeties, wide-spur hammer. Imported from Spain by Garcia.
Price: Models A, P and SM**$110.00**   Model B **$125.00**

STAR STARLIGHT AUTO PISTOL
Caliber: 9mm Para., 8-shot magazine.
Barrel: 4¼".
Weight: 25 oz.
Stocks: Checkered plastic.
Sights: Fixed.
Features: Magazine and manual safeties, external hammer. Imported from Spain by Garcia.
Price: **$110.00**

IMPORTED HANDGUNS—AUTOLOADERS

STAR SUPER SM
Caliber: 380 ACP, 10-shot.
Barrel: 4".
Weight: 22 oz. **Length:** 6⅝" over-all.
Stocks: Plastic, checkered.
Sights: Blade front, adj. rear.
Features: Loaded chamber indicator, thumb safety. Imported from Spain by Garcia.
Price: Approx. $115.00

STAR FRS AUTO PISTOL
Caliber: 22 LR, 10-shot magazine.
Barrel: 6".
Weight: 30 oz.
Stocks: Checkered plastic.
Sights: Fixed front, adj. rear.
Features: External hammer, manual safety. Available in blue or chrome (Model FRS-C). Alloy frame. Imported from Spain by Garcia.
Price: Blue $75.00
Price: Chrome $85.00

STAR MODEL FM AUTO PISTOL
Caliber: 22 LR, 10-shot magazine
Barrel: 4¼".
Weight: 30 oz.
Stocks: Checkered plastic.
Sights: Fixed front, adj. rear.
Features: External hammer, manual safety. Imported from Spain by Garcia.
Price: $75.00

WALTHER P-38 AUTO PISTOL
Caliber: 22 LR, 7.65mm or 9mm Para., 8-shot.
Barrel: 4¹⁵/₁₆".
Weight: 28 oz. **Length:** 8½".
Stock: Checkered plastic.
Sights: Fixed.
Features: Double action, safety blocks firing pin and drops hammer, chamber loaded indicator. Matte finish standard, polished blue, engraving and/or plating available. Imported from Germany by Interarms.
Price: (9mm) $139.00
Price: (22 LR, 7.65mm) $160.00
Price: 9mm polished blue finish $185.00
Price: Engraved models start at $425.00

WALTHER PP AUTO PISTOL
Caliber: 22 LR, 32 ACP, 8-shot; 380 ACP, 7-shot.
Barrel: 3.86".
Weight: 23½ oz. **Length:** 6⁵/₁₆".
Stocks: Checkered plastic.
Sights: Fixed, white markings.
Features: Double action, manual safety blocks firing pin and drops hammer, chamber loaded indicator on 32 and 380, finger rest extra magazine provided. Imported from Germany by Interarms.
Price: (22 LR) $155.00
Price: (32 and 380) $149.00
Price: Engraved models start at $315.00

WALTHER PPKS AUTO PISTOL
Same as PP except bbl. 3.27", length 5⁷/₁₆" o.a.
Price: $155.00
Price: Engraved models start at $315.00

WALTER GSP MATCH PISTOL
Caliber: 22 LR, 32 S&W wadcutter (GSP-C), 5-shot.
Barrel: 5¾".
Weight: 41 oz. **Length:** 11⅞".
Stock: Walnut, special hand-fitting design.
Sights: Fixed front, rear adj. for w. & e.
Features: Available with either 2.2 lb. (1000 gm) or 3 lb. (1360 gm) trigger. Spare mag., bbl. weight, tools supplied. Imported from Germany by Interarms.
Price: $275.00
Price: 22 cal. conversion unit for GSP-C $150.00

WALTHER OSP RAPID-FIRE PISTOL
Similar to Model GSP except 22 short only, stock has adj. free-style thumb rest.
Price: $250.00

IMPORTED HANDGUNS—REVOLVERS

ARMINIUS REVOLVERS
Caliber: 38 Special, 32 S&W Long (6-shot); 22 Magnum, 22 LR (8-shot).
Barrel: 4" (38 Spec., 32 S&W, 22 LR); 6" (38 Spec., 22 LR); 9½" (22 Mag. only).
Weight: 35 oz. (6" bbl.). **Length:** 11" (6" bbl. 38).
Stocks: Checkered plastic.
Sights: Ramp front, fixed rear on standard models, w. & e. adj. on target models.
Features: Ventilated rib, solid frame, swing-out cylinder. Interchangeable 22 Mag. cylinder available with 22 cal versions. Imported from West Germany by Firearms Import & Export.
Price: . . . . $52.95 to $74.95

ASTRA 357 MAGNUM REVOLVER
Caliber: 357 Magnum, 6-shot.
Barrel: 3", 4", 6".
Weight: 40 oz. (6" bbl.). **Length:** 11¼" (6" bbl.).
Stocks: Checkered walnut.
Sights: Fixed front, rear adj. for w. and e.
Features: Swing-out cylinder with countersunk chambers, floating firing pin. Imported from Spain by Garcia
Price: $110.00

BISON SINGLE ACTION REVOLVER
Caliber: 22 LR.
Barrel: 4¾".
Weight: 20 oz.
Stocks: Imitation stag.
Sights: Fixed front, adj. rear.
Features: 22 WRM cylinder also available ($5.95 additional). Imported from Germany by Jana.
Price: $26.00

APACHE REVOLVERS
Caliber: 22 LR, 8 shot; 32 S&W, 7 shot; 38 Special, 6 shot.
Barrel: 4", 3" (available in 38 Special only).
Stocks: Checkered plastic.
Sights: Fixed front, rear adj. for w. & e.
Features: Ventilated rib on bbl. Imported from Germany by Jana.
Price: $50.00

CATTLEMAN TRAILBLAZER
Caliber: 22 S, L, LR, 22 Mag.
Barrel: 5½" or 6½".
Weight: 2½ lbs.
Stocks: Smooth walnut.
Sights: Ramp front, rear adj. for w. and e.
Features: Comes with interchangeable magnum cylinder. Single action. Case-hardened frame, brass back strap and trigger guard. Imported by L.A. Distributors.
Price: $86.95

CATTLEMAN BUNTLINE BUCKHORN MAGNUM
Caliber: 357, 38 Spec., 44 Mag., 45 LC, 6-shot.
Barrel: 18".
Weight: 3½ lbs.
Stocks: Smooth walnut.
Sights: Ramp front, rear adj. for w. and e.
Features: Single action. Blued barrel, case-hardened frame, brass trigger guard and back strap. Comes with detachable shoulder stock. Imported by L.A. Distributors.
Price: 357, 45 LC . . . . $210.00   44 Mag. $220.00

CATTLEMAN BUCKHORN MAGNUM
Caliber: 357, 38 Spec., 44 Mag., 45 LC.
Barrel: 6½", 7½" (44 Mag.), 5¾" or 7½" (357, 38, 45).
Weight: 2¾ lbs.
Stocks: Smooth walnut.
Sights: Ramp front, rear adj. for w. and e.
Features: Single action. Blued barrel, case-hardened frame, brass back strap and trigger guard. Imported by L.A. Distributors.
Price: 357, 45 LC $109.95
Price: 44 Mag. $125.95

CATTLEMAN MAGNUM
Caliber: 357, 44 Mag., 45 LC, 6-shot.
Barrel: 4¾", 5½" or 7½". 44 Mag. avail. with 6", 6¼" or 7½".
Weight: 2½ lbs.
Stocks: Smooth walnut.
Sights: Fixed.
Features: Case-hardened frame, single action, blued barrel, brass backstrap and trigger guard. Imported by L.A. Distributors.
Price: 357, 45 LC . . . . $99.95   44 Mag. $115.95

DAKOTA SINGLE ACTION REVOLVER
Caliber: 22 S, L, LR, 22 Mag., 357 Mag., 44-40, 45 Colt.
Barrel: 4⅝″, 5½″, 7½″.
Weight: 40 oz. (357 w/5½″ bbl.). **Length:** 10¼″ (4⅝″ bbl.) over-all.
Stocks: One-piece walnut.
Sights: Blade front, notch rear.
Features: Blued barrel and cylinder, case hardened frame, brass trigger guard and back strap. Imported by Intercontinental Arms.
Price: .... $99.75   Engraved model $175.00

SUPER DAKOTA REVOLVER
Caliber: 41 Mag., 44 Mag.
Barrel: 5½″, 7½″.
Weight: 44 oz. **Length:** 11½″ (5½ bbl.) over-all.
Stock: Walnut, one-piece.
Sights: Ramp front with matted and ribbed blade, integral ramp rear open notch adj. for w. & e.
Features: Flat-top single action. Brass trigger guard and back strap, rest blued. Imported by Intercontinental Arms.
Price: $117.50

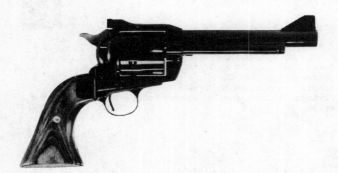

HAWES CHIEF MARSHAL REVOLVER
Caliber: 357 Magnum, 44 Magnum, 45 Long Colt; 6-shot.
Barrel: 6″.
Weight: 48 oz. **Length:** 11¾″.
Stocks: Extra large smooth rosewood.
Sights: Ramp target front, rear adj. for w. & e.
Features: Single action. Extra heavy frame. Imported from West Germany by Hawes.
Price: $119.95

HAWES WESTERN MARSHAL REVOLVERS
Caliber: 357 Magnum, 44 Magnum, 45 Long Colt, 22 Magnum, 22 LR, 6-shot.
Barrel: 6″ (357 Mag., 44 Mag., 45) and 5½″ (22 Mag., 22 LR).
Weight: 44 oz. (big bore), 40 oz. (small bore). **Length:** 11¾″ and 11¼″.
Stocks: Rosewood (big bore), moulded stag (small bore).
Sight: Blade front.
Features: Single action. Interchangeable cylinders available for all caliber guns: 357 Mag. with 9mm, 44 Mag. with 44/40, 45 LC with 45 ACP, 22 LR with 22 Mag. Imported from West Germany by Hawes.
Price: 357 Mag., 44 Mag., 45 LC **$99.95**
Price: Above calibers with interchangeable cylinder **$119.95**
Price: 22 Mag., 22 LR **$64.95**
Price: 22 LR with 22 Mag. cylinder **$76.95**

HAWES VIRGINIA CITY REVOLVER
Same as Western Marshal except with solid brass back strap and trigger guard.
Price: ....**$74.95** to **$114.95**

HAWES TEXAS MARSHAL REVOLVER
Similar to Western Marshal except full nickel finish and black or white Pearlite grips.
Price: ....**$79.95** to **$114.95**

LIBERTY MUSTANG
Caliber: 22 LR, 22 Mag. or combination, 8-shot.
Barrel: 5″.
Weight: 34 oz. **Length:** 10¼″ over-all.
Stocks: Smooth rosewood.
Sights: Blade front, adj. rear.
Features: Single action, slide ejector rod. Imported by Liberty.
Price: With one cylinder **$36.95**
Price: With two cylinders **$44.95**

LIBERTY KODIAK REVOLVER
Caliber: 22 LR, 22 MWR (8-shot), 32 S&W, 38 Spec. (6-shot).
Barrel: 24″, 4″.
Weight: 27 oz. (2″ bbl.). **Length:** 6¾″ (2″ bbl.).
Stocks: Smooth wood.
Sights: Fixed.
Features: Swing-out cylinder. Blue finish (22 and 32 cals.), blue or chrome (38 cal.). Imported by Liberty.
Price: 22 cal. **$39.95**
Price: 32 cal. **$44.95**
Price: 38 cal. **$49.95**

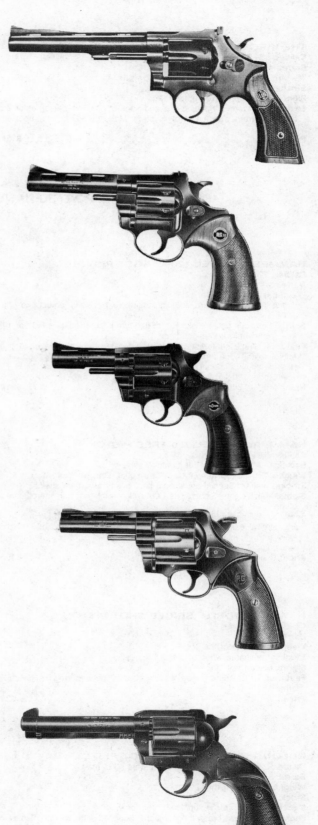

LLAMA "MARTIAL" REVOLVERS
Caliber: 22 LR, 22 RFM, 38 Special.
Barrel: 6″, 4″ (except 22 LR).
Weight: 22 LR 24 oz., 38 Special 31 oz. **Length:** 9¼″ (4″ bbl.).
Stocks: Checkered walnut.
Sights: Fixed blade front, rear adj. for w. & e.
Features: Ventilated rib, wide spur hammer. Chrome plating, engraved finishes available. Imported from Spain by Stoeger Arms.
Price: **$87.95**

RG30 REVOLVER
Caliber: 22 LR and 32, 6-shot.
Barrel: 4″.
Weight: 30 oz. **Length:** 9″.
Stocks: Checkered plastic.
Sights: Fixed front, rear adj. for w.
Features: Swing-out cylinder, choice of blue or nickel ($8.00 additional) finish. Imported from Germany by R. G. Industries.
Price: (22) . . . . **$37.95**   (32) **$39.95**

RG 38S REVOLVER
Caliber: 38 Special, 6-shot.
Barrel: 3″ and 4″.
Weight: 3″, 31 oz.; 4″, 34 oz. **Length:** 3″, 8½″; 4″, 9¼″.
Stocks: Checkered plastic.
Sights: Fixed front, rear adj. for w.
Features: Swing out cylinder with spring ejector, choice of blue or nickel finish. Imported from Germany by R. G. Industries.
Price: Blue **$47.95**
Price: Nickel **$54.95**

RG 57 REVOLVER
Caliber: 357 Magnum.
Barrel: 4″.
Weight: 44 oz. **Length:** 9½″.
Stocks: Checkered plastic.
Sights: Fixed rear.
Features: Swing out cylinder, spring ejector, steel frame. Imported from Germany by R. G. Industries.
Price: **$74.95**

RG63 WESTERN STYLE REVOLVER
Caliber: 22 LR & 22 Mag., 8-shot; 32 S&W & 38 Spec., 6-shot.
Barrel: 5″.
Weight: 34-36 ozs. **Length:** 10¼″.
Stocks: Checkered plastic.
Sights: Fixed.
Features: Slide ejector rod, choice of blue or nickel. Model 63M is combo set with both 22 LR and 22 Mag. cylinders. Imported from Germany by R. G. Industries.
Price: Blue . . . .(22) **$31.95**; (22M, 38) **$39.95**; (Model 63M) **$48.95**
Price: Nickel . . . .(22) **$46.95**; (22M, 38) **$48.95**; (Model 63M) **$58.95**

RG 66 SUPER SINGLE ACTION REVOLVER
Caliber: 22 LR, 22 Mag., 6-shot.
Barrel: 4¾″.
Weight: 32 oz. **Length:** 10″.
Stocks: Checkered plastic.
Sights: Fixed front, rear adj.
Features: Slide ejector rod, choice of blue or nickel finish. Model 66M is combo set with both 22 LR and 22 mag. cylinders. Imported from Germany by R. G. Industries.
Price: Blue . . . .$29.95; (Model 66M) **$34.95**
Price: Nickel . . . .$34.95; (Model 66M) **$42.95**
Price: Blue (6″) . . . .$34.95; Magnum **$39.95**
Price: Blue (9″) . . . .$34.95; Magnum **$39.95**

RG 121 SINGLE ACTION REVOLVER
Caliber: 357 Mag., 6-shot.
Barrel: 5½″
Weight: 44½ oz. **Length:** 11¼″.
Stocks: Simulated stag.
Sights: Fixed.
Features: Slide ejector rod, steel frame. Imported from Germany by R. G. Industries.
Price: **$82.95**

THE VIRGINIAN SINGLE ACTION REVOLVER

Caliber: 357 Mag., 45 Colt, 6-shot.
Barrel: 4⅝", 5½", 7½".
Weight: 2½ lbs. (357 w/5½" bbl.). **Length:** 11" over-all (5½" bbl.).
Stocks: One-piece walnut.
Sights: Blade front, fixed notch rear.
Features: Chromed trigger guard and back strap, blue barrel, color case-hardened frame, unique safety system. Made by Hammerli. Imported by Interarms.
Price: $159.00

IMPORTED HANDGUNS—SINGLE SHOT

HAMMERLI MODEL 120 TARGET PISTOL

Caliber: 22 LR.
Barrel: 10", 6-groove.
Weight: 44.1 oz. **Length:** 14.8".
Stocks: Walnut. Standard grip with thumb rest (120-1), adjustable grip on 120-2.
Sights: Fully adj. micro click rear (match type), sight radius is 9.9" or 14.6". Interchangeable front sight blade.
Features: Single shot with new action operated by lateral lever. Bolt fully encloses cartridge rim. Target trigger adj. from 3.5 oz. to 35.3 oz. Trigger position adj. H. Grieder, importer.
Price: Model 120-1 . . . . $205.00
Price: Model 120-2 . . . . $218.00

HAMMERLI MODEL 150 FREE PISTOL

Caliber: 22 LR.
Barrel: 11.4", 6-groove. Free floating.
Weight: 42.4 oz. Up to 49.4 oz. with weights. **Length:** 15.4".
Stocks: Walnut. Special anatomical design with adj. palm shelf.
Sights: Match sights. Sight radius 14.6". Micro-click rear with interchangeable blade.
Features: Single shot Martini-type action operated by a lateral lever. Straight line hammerless ignition is vibration-free with an ignition time of 0.0016 sec. New set-trigger design fully adj. Low barrel and sight line. Extra weights available. H. Grieder, importer.
Price: Approx. $400.00

HAWES FAVORITE SINGLE SHOT PISTOL

Caliber: 22 S, L, LR.
Barrel: 8".
Weight: 20 oz. **Length:** 12".
Stocks: Laminated wood or plastic.
Sights: Fixed front, adj. rear.
Features: Tilt up action, blued bbl., chromed frame. Imported by Hawes Firearms.
Price: $39.95

ROLLING BLOCK SINGLE SHOT PISTOL

Caliber: 22 LR, 22 WRM, 5mm Rem. Mag., 357 mag.
Barrel: 8".
Weight: 2 lbs. **Length:** 12".
Stock: Walnut.
Sights: Front adj. for w., buckhorn adj. for e.
Features: Polished brass trigger guard. Supplied with wooden display box. Imported by Navy Arms.
Price: $125.00

IMPORTED CENTERFIRE RIFLES—AUTOLOADING & LEVER ACTION

BERETTA BM-69 AUTO RIFLE
Caliber: 7.62mm NATO (308).
Barrel: 17".
Weight: 8½ lbs. **Length:** 38½".
Stock: Walnut.
Sights: Post front, adj. peep rear.
Features: Folding bipod available, $21.00. Mag. cap 20 rounds. Imported from Italy by Gold Rush.
Price: **$249.00**

BERETTA M-59 ASSAULT RIFLE
Caliber: 308 (7.62mm NATO), 20 round box mag.
Barrel: 21" with compensator.
Weight: 8½ lbs.
Stock: Walnut.
Sights: Blade front, rear adj. for w. & e.
Features: Gas-operated, semi-auto., Garand-type receiver, detachable box magazine, compensator/flash hider. From Federal Ordnance.
Price: **$225.00**

CETME SPORT AUTO RIFLE
Caliber: 308, 5-shot.
Barrel: 17¾".
Weight: 10½ lbs. **Length:** 40".
Stock: Walnut with walnut fore-end.
Sights: Blade front, flip up aperture rear, scope blocks.
Features: Scope rings, bipod, 20-shot mag. avail. Imported from Spain by Mars Equipment.
Price: **$209.95**

SAKO MODEL 73 LEVER ACTION RIFLE
Caliber: 243, 308.
Barrel: 23".
Weight: 6¾ lbs. **Length:** 42½".
Stock: Hand-checkered European walnut, Monte Carlo, one-piece.
Sights: Hooded front, dovetail blocks rear for tip-off scope mount or iron sights.
Features: Hammerless, short-throw lever, solid top, side ejection, 3-shot detachable mag. Imported from Finland by Garcia.
Price: **$260.00**

NAVY ARMS "1873" MODEL RIFLE
Caliber: 357 Mag., 44-40.
Barrel: 24" (rifle, octagon); 20" (carbine, round).
Weight: 9 lbs. (rifle); 7½ lbs. (carbine).
Stock: Walnut.
Sights: Blade front, step adj. rear.
Features: Available in blue or case-hardened finish. Sliding dust cover, lever latch. Imported by Navy Arms.
Price: Rifle **$200.00**
Price: Carbine **$175.00**

CLASSIC 1873 LEVER ACTION RIFLE
Caliber: 357 Magnum, 44-40.
Barrel: 20".
Weight: 7 lbs. **Length:** 39".
Stock: Walnut, straight grip, carbine buttplate.
Sights: Fixed front, adj. rear.
Features: Exact copy of 1873 Winchester, with full length tubular mag., center hammer, top ejection. Imported from Italy by Gold Rush, Jana.
Price: . . . . **$175.00** to **$200.00**
Price: Carbine model with round bbl., bbl. band. Navy only **$175.00**

VALMET M-62/S RIFLE
Caliber: 7.62x39mm, 15- and 30-shot detachable box magazines.
Barrel: 16⅝".
Weight: 8¾ lbs. **Length:** 36⅝" over-all.
Stock: Fixed metal tube. Walnut optional.
Sights: Hooded post front adj. for w., tangent peep rear adj. for e.
Features: Finnish semi-automatic version of the AK-47. Basic Kalashnikov design (gas piston operating a rotating bolt assy.). Imported by Interarms.
Price: Metal stock version **$258.00**
Price: Wood stock version **$266.00**

The product prices mentioned in these catalog pages were correct at presstime, but may be higher when you read this.

BSA MONARCH BOLT ACTION RIFLE
Caliber: 22-250, 222 Rem., 243 Win., 270 Win., 308 Win., 30-06, 7mm Rem. Mag., 300 Win. Mag.
Barrel: 22".
Weight: 7 lbs.
Stock: Hand checkered European walnut, Monte Carlo, white line spacers on p.g. cap, fore-end tip and recoil pad.
Sights: Hooded ramp front, flip up rear.
Features: Adj. trigger, hinged mag. floor plate, silent sliding safety locks bolt and trigger. Imported from England by Galef.
Price: **$174.95**

CHURCHILL "ONE OF ONE THOUSAND"
Caliber: 270, 308, 30-06, 7mm Rem. Mag., 300 Win. Mag., 375 H&H, 458 Win.
Barrel: 24" (average).
Weight: 8 lbs. (30-06). **Length:** 44" (24" bbl.).
Stock: Select European walnut.
Sights: Hooded gold bead ramp front, 3-leaf folding rear.
Features: Commercial Mauser action, adj. trigger, hinged floorplate swivel-mounted rubber recoil pad with cartridge trap, p.g. cap recess holds extra front sight, bbl. mounted sling swivel. Lifetime guarantee. Only 1,000 rifles being produced. Fitted leather case available. By Churchill (Gunmakers) Ltd., imported by Interarms.
Price: . . . . **$1,000.00**   Fitted case **$249.00**

DSCHULLNIGG BOLT ACTION RIFLE
Caliber: All standard calibers.
Barrel: 24 or 26".
Weight: 7 lbs.
Stock: Select Austrian walnut with choice of finish, checkering, carving and inlay.
Sights: Fixed iron sights or choice of European scopes and mounts.
Features: Available in Grade IV (engraved) or Custom Grade (to buyer's specifications). Imported from Austria by Firearms Center.
Price: . . . . from **$650.00**

DUMOULIN BOLT ACTION RIFLE
Caliber: All commercial calibers.
Barrel: 25".
Weight: 7 lbs. **Length:** 43".
Stock: French walnut with rosewood p.g. cap and fore-end tip, standard or skip line checkering, recoil pad.
Sights: Optional, available at extra cost.
Features: Made to customer requirements using Sako or FN action, with or without engraving (3 grades available). Imported from Belgium by Firearms Center.
Price: . . . . from **$315.00**

FN MAUSER BOLT ACTION RIFLE
Caliber: 243, 7x57mm, 270, 308, 30-06, 264 Mag., 7mm Mag., 300 Win. Mag.
Barrel: 24".
Weight: 8½ lbs.
Stock: Hand-checkered European walnut, Monte Carlo.
Sights: Hooded front, adj. peep rear.
Features: Adj. grooved trigger, hinged floorplate, sliding safety. Also available as actions or barrelled actions. Imported from Belgium by Garcia.
Price: Standard calibers **$430.00**
Price: Magnums **$445.00**

CARL GUSTAV GRADE II
Caliber: 22-250, 243 win., 6mm Rem., 250 Savage, 257 Rob., 25-06, 6.5x55, 270, 7x57, 280 Rem., 30-06, 308, 358, 35 Whelen Imp., 5-shot (3-shot magnum).
Barrel: 23½".
Weight: 7⅛ lbs. **Length:** 44" over-all.
Stock: European walnut, hand checkered.
Sights: Hooded ramp front, folding leaf rear.
Fatures: Externally adj. trigger, silent safety, 80° bolt lift, enclosed bolt face, hinged floor plate. Also available in left hand version. Imported from Sweden by FFV Sports.
Price: **$259.95**
Price: **$274.95**

The product prices mentioned in these catalog pages were correct at presstime, but may be higher when you read this.

IMPORTED CENTERFIRE RIFLES—BOLT ACTION

CARL GUSTAV GRADE II MAGNUM

Same as Grade II except: has rubber recoil pad. Available in 264 Win., 7mm Rem., 300 Win., 308 Norma, 338 Win., 358 Norma, 458 Win. Also available in left-hand version.

Price: **$269.95**
Price: Left-hand **$284.95**

CARL GUSTAV GRADE III MAGNUM

Same as Grade III except: has recoil pad and internal modifications to handle magnum calibers. Also available in left-hand version.

Price: **$319.95**
Price: Left-hand **$334.95**

CARL GUSTAV GRADE III

Caliber: 22-250, 243 Win., 6mm Rem., 250 Sav., 257 Rob., 25-06, 6.5x55, 270, 7x57, 280 Rem., 30-06, 308, 358, 35 Whelen Imp., 5-shot (3-shot magnum).
Barrel: 23½".
Weight: 7⅛ lbs. **Length:** 44" over-all.
Stock: French walnut, hand checkered.
Sights: None furnished.
Features: Engraved floor plate, detachable swivels, jeweled bolt. Also available in left-hand version. Imported from Sweden by FFV.

Price: **$309.95**
Price: Left-hand **$324.95**

CARL GUSTAV "SWEDE"

Can be had in standard or deluxe versions utilizing the Grade II or Grade III barreled actions. Choice of either Monte Carlo design or sloping comb with schnabel fore-end.

Price: Standard **$229.95**
Price: Deluxe **$264.95**

CARL GUSTAV GRADE V

Caliber: Available in any caliber listed for all other Carl Gustav rifles.
Barrel: 24".
Weight: 7⅛ lbs. **Length:** 44" over-all.
Stock: French walnut.
Sights: None furnished. Drilled and tapped for scope mounting.
Features: Scroll-type engraving on receiver, trigger guard and floorplate. Owners initials inlaid in gold on bolt sleeve. Special order only. Imported from Sweden by FFV.

Price: Standard cals. **$544.95**
Price: Magnum cals. **$559.95**
Price: Left-hand **$559.95**
Price: Left-hand magnum **$569.95**

CARL GUSTAV V-T

Caliber: 222 Rem., 22-250, 243 Win., 6.5x55, 17 Rem., 223, 6mm Rem., 25-06.
Barrel: 27". Bbl. diameter .850".
Weight: 9½ lbs. **Length:** 47½" over-all.
Stock: European walnut.
Sights: None furnished. Drilled and tapped for scope mounts.
Features: Wundhammer p.g., full-floating barrel, externally adj. trigger, large bolt handle. Imported from Sweden by FFV.

Price: **$309.95**

CARL GUSTAV CG-T

Caliber: 6.5x55, 308, 30-06, single shot.
Barrel: 26".
Weight: 11½ lbs. **Length:** 46" over-all.
Stock: American walnut, straight comb, full p.g., palm swell.
Sights: None furnished. Drilled and tapped for scope mounts.
Features: 5-shot magazine and clip slot. Stainless steel barrel optional at extra cost. Imported from Sweden by FFV.

Price: **$349.50**

HERTER'S MARK J9 RIFLE

Caliber: 22-250, 25-06, 243, 6mm, 270, 308, 30-06, 264, 7mm mag., 300 Win. Mag.
Barrel: 23½".
Weight: 8 lbs. **Length:** 42½".
Stock: Black walnut, rollover cheek piece, ebonite p.g. cap and butt plate.
Sights: Ramp front, rear adj. for w. and e.
Features: Also available w/o sights, with Mannlicher or beavertail style stocks. Three grades (Hunter's, Supreme, Presentation) differ stock finish, style. Also available as actions or barreled actions. Imported from Yugoslavia by Herter's.

Price: Hunter's Grade **$93.80**
Price: Supreme Grade **$104.70**
Price: Presentation Grade **$118.70**

HERTER'S MARK U9 RIFLE

Caliber: 222, 222 mag., 223, 22-250, 25-06, 243, 6mm, 284, 308, 270, 30-06, 264, 7mm mag., 300 Win.
Barrel: 23½".
Weight: 6¼ lbs. **Length:** 42½".
Stock: American walnut, Monte Carlo, p.g.
Sights: Ramp front, rear adj. for w. and e.
Features: Also available less sights, with Mannlicher style stock, Douglas barrels (338 and 458 mag. plus above cals.). Three grades (Hunter's, Supreme, Presentation) differ in stock finish, style. Also available as actions or bbld. actions, bench rest, target or varmint versions. Imported from England by Herter's.

Price: Hunter's Grade **$120.90**
Price: Supreme Grade **$129.70**
Price: Presentation Grade **$144.70**

KLEINGUENTHER K-14 INSTA-FIRE RIFLE
Caliber: 243, 25-06, 270, 7mm Rem. Mag., 30-06, 300 Win. Mag., 308 Win., 308 Norma, 375 H&H, 458 Win.
Barrel: 24", 26".
Weight: 7⅛ lbs. **Length:** 43½" over-all.
Stock: Walnut, Monte Carlo, hand checkered, cheekpiece, rosewood fore-end tip, rosewood p.g. cap with diamond inlay.
Sights: None furnished. Drilled and tapped for scope mounts.
Features: Ultra fast lock/ignition time. Rubber recoil pad, hidden clip, external trigger adj., recessed bolt face, 60° bolt lift. Imported from Germany by Kleinguenther's.
Price: Std. cals. .... **$248.43**   **Mag. cals.** **$259.42**

MARK X RIFLE
Caliber: 22-250; 243, 270 & 308 Win.; 30-06; 25-06; 7 mm Rem. Mag; 300 Win. Mag.
Barrel: 24".
Weight: 7½ lbs. **Length:** 44".
Stock: Hand checkered walnut, Monte Carlo, white line spacers on p.g. cap, buttplate and fore-end tip.
Sights: Ramp front with removeable hood, folding-leaf rear adj. for w. and e.
Features: Sliding safety, quick detachable sling swivels, hinged floorplate. Adj. trigger available ($10.00 additional). Also available as actions or bbld. actions. Imported from Europe by Interarms.
Price: .... **$179.00**   **With adj. trigger** **$189.00**

MAUSER MODEL 3000 BARRELED ACTIONS
Available in both right or left hand models in 243 Win., 270 Win., 7mm Rem. Mag. and 375 H&H Mag. Drilled and tapped for Redfield, Weaver, Conetrol, B&L Leupold and Holden Iron Sighter bases. Prices start at **$184.95**

MAUSER MODEL 660 RIFLE
Caliber: 25-06, 243 Win., 25-06, 270 Win., 308, 30-06, 7x57, 7mm Rem. Mag.
Barrel: 24".
Weight: 7¾ lbs. **Length:** 41".
Stock: Hand checkered walnut, Monte Carlo, with white line p.g. cap, fore-end and recoil pad spacers, detachable swivels.
Sights: Drilled and tapped for scope mounts.
Features: Quickly interchanged bbls., new short action, adj. single stage trigger, push-button safety. Double set trigger, iron sights, engraving and hand carving all available at extra cost. Imported from German by Mauser-Bauer.
Price: **$418.95**
Price: Fitted case **$79.95**

MAUSER VARMINTER 10
Caliber: 22-250.
Barrel: 24", heavy barrel.
Weight: 7 lbs. **Length:** 43" over-all.
Stock: Walnut, M.C., checkered p.g. and fore-end.
Sights: Drilled and tapped for scope mounts.
Features: Heavy barrel version of the Model 3000 sporter. Externally adj. trigger for pull and travel, hammer-forged barrel, available as right-hand action only. Redfield scope blocks available (optional). Imported from Germany by Mauser-Bauer.
Price: **$271.95**

MAUSER MODEL 660 SAFARI RIFLE
Same as Model 660 except cals. 458 Win. Mag., 375 H&H Mag., 7mm Rem. Mag., 338 Win. Mag., 28" bbl., 9 lbs. Fixed front and express rear sights.
Price: **$507.95**
Price: Interchangeable barrels **$169.95**

MAUSER MODEL 3000 RIFLE
Caliber: 243 Win., 270 Win., 308, 30-06, 375 H&H Mag., 7mm Rem. Mag.
Barrel: 22" (standard), 26" (Magnum).
Weight: 7¼ lbs. **Length:** 43".
Stock: Hand checkered walnut, Monte Carlo, white line spacer for p.g. and fore-end caps, vent. recoil pad.
Sights: Drilled and tapped for scope mounts.
Features: 5-round capacity standard cals., 3-round magnums. Sliding safety, fully adj. trigger. Open sights, left hand action available at extra cost. Imported from Germany by Mauser-Bauer.

MAUSER CONVERSION UNITS
Interchangeable barrel assemblies for 25-06, 243, 270, 308, 20-06, 7x57, 7mm Rem. Mag. **$144.95**
Conversion Kit. Includes new bolt face and barrel to convert standard 660 to 7mm Rem. Mag. **$80.95**

Price: Standard calibers .. **$254.95**   **Magnums** **$259.95**
Price: Left hand .... **$294.95**   **Left hand** **$322.95**

IMPORTED CENTERFIRE RIFLES—BOLT ACTION

MUSGRAVE VALIANT NR6
Caliber: 243, 270, 30-06, 308, 7mm Rem. Mag., 5-shot magazine.
Barrel: 24" medium weight.
Weight: 7¾ lbs. **Length:** 46" over-all.
Stock: Select walnut with straight comb, vent. recoil pad, swivel studs, skip-line checkering.
Sights: Hooded ramp front, fixed leaf rear. Action drilled and tapped for scope mounts.
Features: Improved Mauser action, hinged floorplate, wing-type safety, three forward locking lugs, hammer forged barrel. Imported from South Africa by J. J. Sherban.
Price: With open sights $179.95

MUSGRAVE PREMIER NR5
Caliber: 243 Win., 270 Win., 30-06, 308, 7mm Rem. Mag., 5-shot mag.
Barrel: 25½", medium weight.
Weight: 8¼ lbs. **Length:** 48" over-all.
Stock: Select walnut with M.C., recoil pad. Hand finished, hand checkered, swivel studs, fore-end and p.g. cap of contrasting wood.
Sights: None furnished. Drilled and tapped for scope mounts.
Features: Improved Mauser action, hinged floorplate, wing-type safety, three forward locking lugs. Machine tested for accuracy. Imported from South Africa by J. J. Sherban.
Price: $244.95

PARKER-HALE SUPER 1200 BOLT ACTION RIFLE
Caliber: 22-250, 243 Win., 6mm Rem., 25-06, 270 Win., 30-06, 308 Win., 7mm Rem. Mag., 300 Win. Mag.
Barrel: 24".
Weight: 7¼ lbs. **Length:** 45".
Stock: 13.5" x 1.8" x 2.3". Hand checkered walnut, rosewood p.g. and fore-end caps, fitted rubber recoil pad with white line spacers.
Sights: Bead front, folding adj. rear. Receiver tapped for scope mounts.
Features: 3-way side safety, single-stage adj. trigger, hinged mag. floorplate. Model 1200P has scroll engraved action, trigger guard and mag. floorplate, detachable swivels, no sights; not avail. in 22-250. Varmint Model (1200V) has glass-bedded action, free-floating bbl., avail. in 22-250, 6mm Rem., 25-06, 243 Win., without sights. Imported from England by Jana.
Price: .... $174.95 ($189.95, mag. cals.)
Price: 1200P .... $219.95 1200V $184.95

SAKO MODEL 72 BOLT ACTION RIFLE
Caliber: 222, 223, 22-250, 243, 308, 25-06, 270, 30-06, 7mm Mag., 300 Mag., 338 Mag., 375 H & H Mag.
Barrel: 23" (222, 223, 22-250, 243 and 308), 24" (other cals.).
Weight: 6½ lbs. (23" bbl.), 7 lbs. (others).
Stock: Hand-checkered European walnut.
Sights: Hooded front, adj. rear.
Features: Adj. trigger, hinged floorplate. 222 and 223 have short action, 22-250, 243 and 308 medium action, others are long action. Imported from Finland by Garcia.
Price: Standard calibers $185.00
Price: Magnums $195.00

The product prices mentioned in these catalog pages were correct at presstime, but may be higher when you read this.

STEYR-MANNLICHER MODELS SL, L BOLT RIFLES
Caliber: 222 Rem., 222 Rem. Mag., 223 Rem. (Model SL): 22-250, 6mm Rem., 243 Win., 308 Win. (Model L).
Barrel: 20" (carbine), 23⅝ (rifle).
Weight: 6 lbs. 6 oz. **Length:** 39" (carbine,) 42½" (rifle).
Stock: Checkered walnut.
Sights: Hooded post front, adj. rear.
Features: Choice of single or double-set trigger. 5-round detachable rotary magazine. Also available in heavy-barreled Varmint Models, without sights, cals. 222, 223 and 22-250 only. Imported from Austria by Stoeger Arms.
Price: (Model SL) .. $264.00 (rifle); $282.00 (carbine)
Price: (Model L) ... $284.00 (rifle); $302.00 (carbine)

IMPORTED CENTERFIRE RIFLES—BOLT ACTION

TRADEWINDS HUSKY MODEL 5000 BOLT RIFLE
Caliber: 270, 30-06, 308, 243, 22-250.
Barrel: 23¾".
Weight: 6 lbs. 11 oz.
Stock: Hand checkered European walnut, Monte Carlo, white line spacers on p.g. cap, fore-end tip and butt plate.
Sights: Fixed hooded front, adj. rear.
Features: Removeable mag., fully recessed bolt head, adj. trigger. Imported by Tradewinds.
Price: **$184.50**

STEYR-MANNLICHER MODEL M, S BOLT RIFLES
Caliber: 7 x 57mm, 270, 30-06 (Model M); 7mm Rem., 257 Weatherby, 264, 300 H&H, 338, 375 H&H and 458 Magnum (Model S).
Barrel: 20" (carbine), 24" (rifle); Model S (rifle only) 25½".
Weight: 7 lbs. **Length:** 39" (carbine), 43" (rifle); Model S (rifle only) 45".
Stock: European walnut, hand checkered.
Sights: Hooded post front, open rear.
Features: Choice of single or double-set trigger. 5-round detachable rotary magazine (4-round in magnum Model S). Model S available in single trigger rifle only. Imported from Austria by Stoeger Arms.
Price: (Model M) ....**$328.00** (rifle); **$346.00** (carbine)
Price: (Model S) ....**$364.00** (rifle only)

WALTHER SSV BOLT ACTION RIFLE
Same as KKJ except bbl. 25½", heavier Monte Carlo stock, weight 6½ lbs., no sights (scope rails provided). Also available in 222 Rem.
Price: 22 Hornet **$225.00**
Price: With double set trigger **$244.00**

TYROL CUSTOM CRAFTED RIFLE
Caliber: 243, 25-06, 308, 30-06, 7mm, 300 Win.
Barrel: 24".
Weight: 7 lbs. **Length:** 42½" over-all.
Stock: Hand checkered walnut, rosewood fore-end and p.g. cap, rubber recoil pad and detachable swivels.
Sights: Hooded ramp front, 100 and 200 yd. rear. Drilled and tapped for scope mounting.
Features: Shotgun-type tang safety, adj., trigger. Imported from Austria by Firearms Center, Inc.
Price: **$220.95**

WALTHER KKJ BOLT ACTION RIFLE
Caliber: 22 Hornet, 5 shot.
Barrel: 22½".
Weight: 5½ lbs. **Length:** 41½".
Stock: Hand checkered walnut, p.g., cheek piece.
Sights: Hooded ramp front, adj. rear; dove tailed for slide-on scope mounts.
Features: Double set triggers available. Imported from Germany by Interarms.
Price: .... **$225.00** With double set trigger ... **$244.00**

IMPORTED CENTERFIRE RIFLES—REPLICAS

MARTINI TARGET RIFLES
Caliber: 45-70 or 444.
Barrel: 18", 26" or 30".
Weight: 9 lbs. **Length:** 35½" over-all (18" bbl.).
Stock: Walnut.
Sights: Blade front, U-notch middle, fully adj. vernier tang peep.
Features: Action color case hardened. Half-round half-octagon barrel, p.g. stock, schnabel fore-end, long cocking lever. Imported by Navy Arms.
Price: **$175.00**

NAVY ARMS ROLLING BLOCK RIFLE
Caliber: 45-70, 444 Marlin.
Barrels: 26½".
Stock: Walnut finished.
Sights: Fixed front, adj. rear.
Features: Reproduction of classic rolling block action. Available in Buffalo Rifle (octagonal bbl.) and Creedmore (half round, half octagonal bbl.) models. Imported by Navy Arms.
Price: **$150.00**

NAVY ARMS MODEL 1875 REVOLVING RIFLE
Caliber: 38 Special, 44-40.
Barrel: 20".
Weight: 5 lbs. **Length:** 38".
Stock: Walnut, brass butt plate.
Sights: Front blade adj. for w., buckhorn rear adj. for e.
Features: Action resembles Remington Model 1875 revolver. Polished brass trigger guard. Imported by Navy Arms.
Price: **$125.00**

STAR ROLLING BLOCK CARBINE
Caliber: 30-30, 357 Mag., 44 Mag.
Barrel: 20".
Weight: 6 lbs. **Length:** 35" over-all.
Stock: Walnut, straight grip.
Sights: Square bead ramp front, folding leaf rear.
Features: Color case-hardened receiver, crescent buttplate. Forged steel receiver. Imported by Garcia.
Price: Approx. **$90.00**

IMPORTED RIMFIRE RIFLES—LEVER ACTION

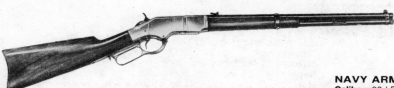

ERMA EG71 LEVER ACTION RIFLE
Caliber: 22 LR, 15-shot.
Barrel: 18½".
Weight: 5 lbs., 5 ozs. **Length:** 35⅞".
Stock: Walnut.
Sights: Fixed front, adj. rear, receiver grooved for scope mts.
Features: Looks and operates like traditional 30-30. Imported from Germany by R. G. Industries.
Price: $82.95

NAVY ARMS MODEL 66 LEVER ACTION RIFLE
Caliber: 22 LR, 38 Special, 44-40.
Barrel: 19".
Weight: 7 lbs. **Length:** 39½".
Stock: Walnut.
Sights: Fixed front, folding rear.
Features: Replica of Winchester Model 1866 "Yellowboy." Available with three grades of engraving, selected stock and fore-end at additional cost. 22 LR also available with 16" bbl. (Trapper's Model). Imported by Navy Arms.
Price: $120.00

IMPORTED RIMFIRE RIFLES—AUTOLOADING

AP-15 AUTO RIFLE
Caliber: 22 LR, 15- or 20-shot magazine.
Barrel: 20" including flash reducer.
Weight: 6¾ lbs. **Length:** 38½" over-all.
Stock: Black plastic.
Sights: Ramp front, adj. peep rear.
Features: Pivotal take-down, easy disassembly. AR-15 look-alike. Sling and sling swivels included. Imported by Intercontinental Arms.
Price: $125.00

ERMA EM1 22 AUTOLOADING CARBINE
Caliber: 22 LR, 10-shot.
Barrel: 17¾".
Weight: 5¾ lbs. **Length:** 35⅜".
Stock: Walnut, semi p.g.
Sights: Fixed front, rear adj. for w. & e., grooved for scope mts. Looks and operates like U.S. M1 carbine. 15-shot mag. also available. Imported from Germany by R.G. Industries.
Price: $83.95

FRANCHI CENTENNIAL AUTO RIFLE
Caliber: 22 LR. (11-shot).
Barrel: 21".
Weight: 5 lbs. 2 oz. **Length:** 39⅛".
Stock: Epoxy-finished walnut.
Sights: Gold bead front, adj. rear.
Features: Quick takedown, cross-bolt safety, receiver grooved for tip-off scope mounts. Available in standard and deluxe (engraved action) grades. Imported from Italy by Stoeger Arms.
Price: $165.95

TRADEWINDS MODEL 260 AUTO RIFLE
Caliber: 22 LR, 5-shot (10-shot mag. avail.).
Barrel: 22½".
Weight: 5¾ lbs. **Length:** 41½".
Stock: Walnut, with hand checkered p.g. and fore-end.
Sights: Ramp front with hood, 3-leaf folding rear, receiver grooved for scope mt.
Features: Double extractors, sliding safety. Imported by Tradewinds.
Price: $99.95

CARL GUSTAV CG-22T
Caliber: 22 LR.
Barrel: 19.7″. Muzzle diameter .825″.
Weight: 9½ lbs. **Length:** 46″ over-all.
Stock: Length of pull 13.8″. Walnut, target-type. Rubber recoil pad.
Sights: None supplied, drilled and tapped for scope mounts.
Features: Lock time of 1.8 millisec. Firing pin fall of .09″, 65 degree bolt lift. Trigger pull adj. from 1.1 to 1.7 lbs.
Price: **$259.50**

KLEINGUNTHER K-10 BOLT ACTION RIFLE
Caliber: 22 LR, single shot.
Barrel: 21¼″.
Weight: 4.2 lbs. **Length:** 38¼″.
Stock: Beechwood, walnut stained.
Sights: Hooded front, Mauser type tangent rear.
Features: Mauser type thumb safety locks firing pin. Imported from Europe by Kleingunther
Price: **$39.00**

KLEINGUNTHER K-12 BOLT ACTION RIFLE
Caliber: 22 LR, 5-shot or 10-shot.
Barrel: 21¼″.
Weight: 5.7 lbs. **Length:** 40″.
Stock: Hand checkered walnut, p.g., rosewood fore-end tip.
Sights: Hooded front, 2 leaf folding rear. Receiver grooved for scope mts.
Features: Adj. trigger, thumb lever safety. Imported from Europe by Kleingunther
Price: **$86.00**

KLEINGUNTHER K-13 BOLT ACTION RIFLE
Same as K-12 except chambered for 22 WMR, weight 5.9 lbs.
Price: **$128.00**

ROSSI GALLERY PUMP RIFLE
Caliber: 22 S, L or LR (Standard), 22 RFM (Magnum).
Barrel: 22½″.
Weight: 5¼ lbs.
Stock: Walnut, straight grip, grooved fore-end.
Sights: Fixed front, adj. rear.
Features: Capacity 20 Short, 16 Long or 14 Long Rifle. Quick takedown. Imported from Brazil by Garcia.
Price: Standard **$80.00**
Price: Magnum **$90.00**

TRADEWINDS MODEL 311 BOLT ACTION RIFLE
Caliber: 22 LR, 5-shot (10-shot mag. avail.).
Barrel: 22½″.
Weight: 6 lbs. **Length:** 41¼″.
Stock: Walnut, Monte Carlo with hand checkered p.g. and fore-end.
Sights: Ramp front with hood, folding leaf rear, receiver grooved for scope mt.
Features: Sliding safety locks trigger and bolt handle. Imported by Tradewinds.
Price: **$99.95**

WALTHER KKJ RIMFIRE RIFLE
Caliber: 22 LR, 5 or 8 shot; 22 WRM, 5 shot.
Barrel: 22½″.
Weight: 5½ lbs. **Length:** 41½″.
Stock: Hand checkered walnut, p.g., cheek piece.
Sights: Hooded ramp front, adj. rear; dove tailed for slide-on scope mounts.
Features: Double set triggers available. Imported from Germany by Interarms.
Price: 22 LR **$199.00**
Price: 22 WRM **$225.00**
Price: 22 LR with double set trigger **$218.00**
Price: 22 WRM with double set trigger **$244.00**

WALTHER SSV RIMFIRE RIFLE
Same as KKJ except bbl. 25½″, heavier Monte Carlo stock, weight 6¾ lbs. no sights (scope rails provided), 22LR (single shot) only.
Price: **$215.00**
Price: With double set trigger **$233.00**

IMPORTED TARGET RIFLES

MUSGRAVE RSA NR1 TARGET RIFLE
Caliber: 308 (7.62mm). Single shot.
Barrel: 26″, heavy.
Weight: 10 lbs. **Length:** 48½″ over-all.
Stock: Select walnut. Target type p.g., beavertail fore-end with handguard. Solid rubber recoil pad.
Sights: Musgrave tunnel front; takes Auschutz-type inserts. Aperture rear with ½ minute clicks for w. and e.
Features: Closed top bolt action for strength. Three forward locking lugs, claw-type extractor, gas deflection ports. Sling swivel beneath action and on front band. Fully adj. trigger. Wing-type safety. Imported from South Africa by J. J. Sherban Co.
Price: With sights **$299.95**

PARKER-HALE 1200 TX TARGET RIFLE
Caliber: 7.62mm NATO (308), 30-06.
Barrel: 26″.
Weight: 10½ lbs. **Length:** 46¾″.
Stock: 13³⁄₁₆″ x 1¹¹⁄₁₆″ x 1¹⁵⁄₁₆″. Oil finish, full beavertail, p.g., vent. rubber butt pad.
Sights: Micro adj. ¼″ click rear, interchangeable element tubular front.
Features: Full floating bbl., epoxy bedded action, fully adj. trigger, selected bbl. Imported from England by Jana.
Price: **$219.95**

WALTHER U.I.T. MATCH RIFLE
Caliber: 22 LR.
Barrel: 25½″.
Weight: 10 lbs., 3 oz. **Length:** 44¾″.
Stock: Walnut, adj. for length and drop; fore-end guide rail for sling or palm rest.
Sights: Interchangeable post or aperture front, micro adj. rear.
Features: Conforms to both NRA and U.I.T. requirements. Fully adj. trigger. Left hand stock available on special order. Imported from Germany by Interarms.
Price: **$255.00**

WALTHER RUNNING BOAR MATCH RIFLE
Caliber: 22 LR.
Barrel: 23.6″.
Weight: 8 lbs. 5 oz. **Length:** 42″ over-all.
Stock: Walnut thumb-hole type. Fore-end and p.g. stippled.
Sights: Globe front, micro adj. rear.
Features: Especially designed for running boar competition. Receiver grooved to accept dovetail scope mounts. Adjustable cheekpiece and butt plate. 1.1 lb. trigger pull. Imported by Interarms.
Price: **$245.00**

WALTHER "PRONE 400" MATCH RIFLE
Especially designed for prone shooting with split stock to allow cheekpiece adjustment. Caliber 22 LR with scope blocks.
Price: **$285.00**

WALTHER KKM MATCH RIFLE
Caliber: 22 LR.
Barrel: 28″.
Weight: 15½ lbs. **Length:** 46″.
Stock: Walnut, with fully adj. hook butt plate, hand shelf and selection of ball-type offset yoke palm rest.
Sights: Olympic front with post and aperture inserts, micrometer rear click adj. for w. & e.
Features: Fully adj. match trigger. Imported from Germany by Interarms.
Price: **$395.00**

FERLACH O/U TURKEY RIFLE/SHOTGUN
Gauge: 12, 16, 20, and 22 Hornet, 222 Rem., 243, 257, 6.5x55, 270, 7x57, 30-06.
Action: Anson & Deeley boxlock.
Barrel: 22" or 24".
Weight: 6½ lbs.
Stock: Circassian walnut, hand checkered at p.g. and split fore-end, horn p.g. cap and buttplate.
Features: Double triggers, auto safety, engraved action. With or without cheekpiece, recoil pad. Imported from Austria by Flaig's.
Price: **$950.00**

KRIEGHOFF "TECK" DOUBLE RIFLE
Caliber: All standard rimless and rimmed American and metric calibers, including 375 H & H and 458 Win. Mag.
Action: Kersten double cross bolt, double under-lug locking system.
Barrel: 25", separated, free-floating.
Weight: From 8 lbs. **Length:** 41" over-all.
Stock: 14¼"x1¼"x2¼", European walnut.
Sights: Sourdough front, express rear.
Features: Imported by Unordco.
Price: Std. cals. **$1,450.00**
Price: Belted magnum cals. **$1,650.00**
Price: Model Ulm (sidelocks) **$2,150.00**
Price: Model Ulm (engraved, hand-detachable sidelocks) **$2,550.00**
Price: Interchangeable o/u shotgun barrel **$400.00**
Price: Interchangeable o/u rifle barrel **$550.00**

KRIEGHOFF TRUMPF DRILLING
Caliber: 12 and 12 ga. (2¾") and 30-06, 20 and 20 (3") and 243 Win.
Action: Sidelock or boxlock.
Barrel: 25", solid rib.
Weight: 7½ lbs. **Length:** 41" over-all.
Stock: 14¼"x1¼"x2¼", European walnut.
Sights: Sourdough front, express rear.
Features: Shot barrel locks cock on opening, rifle barrel cocked and rear sight raises by action of tang mounted slide. Split extractors. American scope can be mounted at factory with claw mounts. Imported by Unordco.
Price: Boxlock action with optional engraving coverage and special stock features **$1,350.00**
Price: Sidelock version (Neptun) **$2,275.00**
Price: Deluxe Neptun (engraved) with hand-detachable locks **$2,800.00**

DSCHULLNIGG DOUBLE RIFLES
Caliber: All standard calibers.
Barrel: 24 or 26".
Stock: Circassian walnut, hand checkered.
Sights: Open.
Features: Double rifles, over and under rifles and drillings available on custom order basis. Imported from Austria by Firearms Center.
Price: . . . . Individually quoted to customer specifications.

KRIEGHOFF RIFLE-SHOTGUN COMBO
Caliber Gauge: Top-12, 16, 20 (2¾"), 20 ga. 3"; lower-all popular U.S. and metric cartridges, rimless and rimmed.
Action: Boxlock.
Barrel: 25", solid rib.
Weight: 6¼ lbs. **Length:** 41" over-all.
Stock: 14¼"x1¼"x2¼", European walnut.
Sights: Sourdough front, express rear.
Features: Interchangeable rifle barrels in 22 Hornet, 222 Rem., 222 Rem. Mag. priced at $175.00. Scope optional. Imported by Unordco.
Price: 12 ga./30-06 or 222 Rem. **$1,275.00**
Price: Sidelock Ulm model **$1,900.00**
Price: Ulm Primus (deluxe) **$2,375.00**
Price: 12 ga. double barrels (only) with ejectors **$400.00**

> **The product prices mentioned in these catalog pages were correct at presstime, but may be higher when you read this.**

BERETTA AL AUTO SHOTGUNS
Gauge: 12 or 20 (4-shot, 3-shot plug furnished). 2¾″ chambers.
Action: Gas-operated autoloader.
Barrel: 12 ga., 30 or 28″ (Full), 28″ (Mod.), 26″ (Imp. Cyl.); 20 ga., 28″ (Full or Mod.), 26″ (Imp. Cyl.); 12 ga. Trap, 30″ (Full); 12 or 20 ga. Skeet, 26″ (Skeet).
Weight: 12 ga. 7 lbs., 20 ga. 6½ lbs., Trap 7½ lbs.
Stock: Hand checkered European walnut, p.g. Monte Carlo on trap models.
Features: AL-2 has hand-engraved receiver and ventilated rib; AL-1 has satin-finished receiver and plain bbl. AL-1 not available in 12 ga. 28″ (Full), Trap or Skeet. Crossbolt safety. Imported from Italy by Garcia.
Price: AL-2 . . . . **$195.00**
Price: AL-2 Trap or Skeet **$245.00**
Price: AL-2 Magnum **$235.00**

CHARLES DALY AUTO SHOTGUN
Gauge: 12 (2¾″ chamber).
Action: Recoil-operated semi-auto.
Barrel: 26″ (I.C.), 28″ (Mod. or Full), 30″ (Full), vent. rib.
Stock: Hand-checkered walnut, p.g.
Features: Button safety, 5-shot capacity (3-shot plug furnished). Imported by Charles Daly.
Price: . . . . **$240.00**　　Extra barrels **$74.50**

FRANCHI SLUG GUN
Same as Standard automatic except 22″ cylinder bored bbl., adj. rear sight, sling swivels.
Price: **$259.95**

FRANCHI STANDARD AUTO SHOTGUN
Gauge: 12 or 20.
Action: Recoil-operated automatic.
Barrel: 24″ (Cyl.); 26″ (Imp. Cyl. or Mod.); 28″ (Mod. or Full); 30″, 12 ga. (Full).
Weight: 12 ga. 6¼ lbs., 20 ga. 5 lbs. 2 oz.
Stock: Epoxy-finished walnut.
Features: Chrome-lined bbl., easy takedown, 3-round plug provided. Available with plain round or ventilated rib barrel. Imported from Italy by Stoeger Arms.
Price: Plain bbl. 12 or 20 ga. **$219.95**
Price: Vent. rib 12 or 20 ga.[$259.95

FRANCHI MAGNUM AUTO SHOTGUN
Gauge: 12 or 20, 3-inch shells.
Action: Recoil-operated automatic.
Barrel: 32″, 12 ga.; 28″, 20 ga., both Full.
Weight: 12 ga. 8¼ lbs., 20 ga. 6 lbs.
Stock: Epoxy-finished walnut with recoil pad.
Features: Chrome-lined bbl., easy takedown. Available with ventilated rib barrel. Imported from Italy by Stoeger Arms.
Price: . . . . **$279.95** (20 ga.); **$289.95** (12 ga.)

TRADEWINDS H-170 AUTO SHOTGUN
Gauge: 12 only, 2¾″ chambers.
Action: Recoil-operated automatic.
Barrel: 26″, 28″ (Mod.) and 28″ (Full), chrome lined.
Weight: 7 lbs.
Stock: Select European walnut stock, p.g. and fore-end hand checkered.
Features: Light alloy receiver, 5-shot tubular magazine, ventilated rib. Imported by Tradewinds.
Price: **$179.95**

IMPORTED SHOTGUNS—DOUBLE BARREL

ATLAS MODEL 208 DOUBLE BARREL SHOTGUN
Gauge: 12, 20, 28 and 410 (3″ chambers).
Action: Anson & Deeley-type, engraved.
Barrel: 26″ (I.C. & Mod.), 26″, 28″ (Mod. & Full).
Weight: 6-7 lbs.
Stock: Walnut with checkered semi p.g. and beavertail fore-end.
Features: Chromed bores, double trigger. Imported from Italy by Atlas Arms.
Price: **$250.00**

ATLAS 145 DOUBLE BARREL SHOTGUN
Similar to M208 except: vent. rib, choice of p.g. or straight stock, full hand engraving, entire gun of nickel-chrome steel. 12 & 20 ga., 2¾″ chambers only. Available with 2 sets of bbls., 26″ (Skeet 1 & 2), 28″ (Mod. & Full), on special order. Imported from Italy by Atlas Arms.
Price: **$350.00**

ATLAS 500 MAGNUM DOUBLE BARREL SHOTGUN
Gauge: 10 (3½″ chambers); 12, 20 (3″ chambers).
Action: Anson & Deeley box lock, Purdey type locks.
Barrel: 32″ (Full & Full), 28″ (Mod. & Full).
Weight: 8 lbs.
Stock: Hand checkered walnut, semi p.g., beavertail fore-end, recoil pad.
Features: Vent. rib, double triggers. Imported from Italy by Atlas Arms.
Price: **$270.00**

ATLAS MODEL 520 HAMMER DOUBLE SHOTGUN
Gauge: 12 (3″ chambers).
Action: Greener Crossbolt.
Barrel: 18½″ (Cyl. & Cyl.).
Weight: 6 lbs.
Stock: Hand checkered walnut, p.g., push button release fore-end.
Features: External hammers, engraved action. Imported from Italy by Atlas Arms.
Price: **$119.95**

AYA MODELS 56 & 53E DOUBLE BARREL SHOTGUNS
Gauge: 12, 20 (2¾″ chambers standard, 3″ on request).
Action: Heavy Competition sidelock frame, triple bolting.
Barrel Up to 30″ (length and choke customer specified).
Stock: Made to customer specifications.
Features: Auto safety and ejectors, loading indicators, matted rib, gas escape valves, folding front trigger, engraved frame. Made to customer requirements, 10-12 month delivery. Model 53-E same except has hand detachable locks, concave rib. Imported from Spain by JBL Arms.
Price: 56 . . . . **$795.00**
Price: 53E **$685.00**

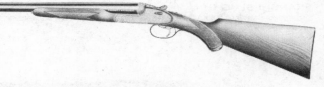

AYA NO. 1 DOUBLE BARREL SHOTGUN
Same as 56 except lightweight frame, concave rib, double bolting, 2¾″ chambers only.
No. 2 similar to No. 1 except without loading indicators or folding front trigger.
Price: No. 1 . . . . **$795.00**
Price: No. 2 . . . . **$569.00**

AYA XXV/SL DOUBLE BARREL SHOTGUN
Same as 56 except 12 ga., 2¾″ chamber only, narrow top rib, 25″ bbl.
Price: **$654.00**

AYA 117 DOUBLE BARREL SHOTGUN
Similar to 53-E except without loading indicators; has folding front trigger.
Price: **$388.00**

BERETTA GR DOUBLE BARREL SHOTGUN
Gauge: 12 (2¾″ chambers), 20 (3″ chambers).
Action: Improved Greener action.
Barrel: 12 ga. 30″ or 28″ (Mod., Full), 26″ (Imp. Cyl., Mod.) 20 ga. 28″ (Mod., Full), 26″ (Imp. Cyl., Mod.)
Weight: 12 ga. 7 lbs., 20 ga. 6½ lbs., 12 ga. Mag. 8 lbs.
Stock: 14″ x 1½″ x 2½″ hand checkered European walnut stock and semi-beavertail fore-end.
Features: Ventilated rib. Model GR-2 has double triggers; GR-3 has single selective trigger; GR-4 has single selective trigger, auto ejectors, engraved action and select wood. Imported from Italy by Garcia.
Price: . . . . **$300.00**(GR-2) to **$465.00**(GR-4)

IMPORTED SHOTGUNS—DOUBLE BARREL

BERETTA SO DOUBLE BARREL SHOTGUNS
Gauge: 12 (2¾″ chambers).
Action: Heavy underlug locking. Single selective or double triggers, gold plated on SO-7.
Barrel: 28″ (Mod. and Full), 26″ (I.C. and Mod.); 30″ bbl. and different choke combos available.
Weight: 7 to 7¼ lbs.
Stock: Select European walnut, 14⅛″ x 1½″ x 2½″ or custom fitted, p.g. or straight grip.
Features: Made to order to customer's specifications. SO-7 has more ornamentation. Auto safety on Field models, manual on Skeet and Trap. Imported from Italy by Garcia.
Price: SO-6 .... $2,875.00
Price: SO-7 .... $4,000.00

BERNARDELLI GAME COCK DOUBLE SHOTGUN
Gauge: 12 or 20.
Action: Hammerless boxlock, auto safety, double triggers.
Barrel: 25″ (Imp. Cyl. & Mod.), 28″ (Mod. & Full).
Weight: 12 ga. 6 lbs., 20 ga. 5½ lbs.
Stock: 14″ x 1½″ x 2½″ hand-checkered walnut.
Features: Available in Standard, Deluxe (light scroll engraving, auto ejectors) or Premier (engraving, auto ejectors, non-selective single trigger). Imported from Italy by Stoeger Arms.
Price: .... $325.00 (Standard); $435.00 (Deluxe); $525.00 (Premier)

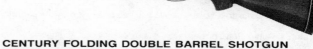

BRESCIA DOUBLE BARREL SHOTGUN
Gauge: 12, 20 (2¾″ chambers).
Action: Anson & Deeley.
Barrel: 28″ (Full & Mod. or I.C. & Mod.), chrome lined.
Weight: 6½ lbs.
Stock: Hand checkered walnut, p.g. or straight, recoil pad.
Features: Double triggers, engraved action. Imported from Italy by Klein-gunther.
Price: $216.20

CENTURY FOLDING DOUBLE BARREL SHOTGUN
Gauge: 410 (3″ chambers).
Action: Hammer, side lever to open action.
Barrel: 27¾″ (Full & Full).
Weight: 4¾ lbs.
Stock: Hand checkered walnut, semi p.g.
Features: Depressing button on frame allows gun to be folded for carrying or storage. Imported from Spain by Century Arms.
Price: $34.50

CHARLES DALY P-O-S DOUBLE BARREL SHOTGUN
Gauge: 10, 12, 20 or 410 (3″ chambers except 10, 3½″; 28, 2¾″).
Action: Hammerless, double triggers.
Barrel: 32″ 10, 30″ 12 (Full & Full); 30″ 12, 28″ 12 or 20, 26″ 28 or 410 (Mod. & Full); 26″ 12 or 20 (I.C. & Mod.).
Stock: Checkered walnut, p.g. cap and buttplate with white line spacers.
Features: Imported from Spain by Charles Daly.
Price: $150.00

DARNE SLIDING BREECH DOUBLE
Gauge: 12, 16, 20 or 28.
Action: Sliding breech.
Barrel: 25½″ to 27½″, choice of choking.
Weight: 5½ to 6½ lbs.
Stock: European walnut, hand checkered p.g., and fore-end. English style or semi-p.g.
Features: Double triggers, selective ejectors, plume or raised rib, case-hardened or engraved receiver. Available in 8 grades, stock or custom made. Imported from France by Firearms Center, Inc.
Price: From $355.00

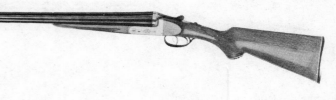

DAVIDSON MODEL 63B DOUBLE BARREL SHOTGUN
Gauge: 12, 20, 28 (2¾″ chambers); 410 (3″ chambers).
Action: Anson & Deeley with crossbolt (no crossbolt on 28 and 410).
Barrel: 30″ 12 (Mod. & Full); 26″ (I.C. & Mod.) and 28″ (Mod. & Full) all except 410; 410, 25″ (Full & Full) only.
Weight: 12 ga., 7 lbs.; 16, 20, 28 ga., 6½ lbs.; 410 ga., 5 lbs. 11 oz.
Stock: Hand finished checkered European walnut, white line spacers on p.g. cap and butt plate.
Features: Auto safety, manual extractors, gold-plated double triggers, engraved nickel-plated frame. Imported from Europe by Davidson.
Price: $129.95

IMPORTED SHOTGUNS—DOUBLE BARREL

F.I.E. DOUBLE BARREL SHOTGUN
Gauge: 12, 20, 410.
Action: Boxlock.
Barrel: 30″ 12 only (Full & Full); 28″ all exc. 410 (Mod.& Full); 26″ all exc. 410 (I.C.& Mod.); 26″ 410 (Mod.& Full or Full & Full).
Stock: Hand checkered walnut, beavertail fore-end, white line spacers on p.g. cap and butt plate.
Features: Raised matted rib, double triggers, engraved case hardened receiver. Imported by Firearms Import & Export.
Price: $99.95

DIXIE HAMMER DOUBLE BARREL SHOTGUN
Gauge: 12, 28 ga. regular.
Action: Front and back action.
Barrel: 28″ to 32″ barrels.
Stock: Straight, semi-pistol or full pistol-grip halfstocks, some with checkered grip and fore-end, some smooth.
Weight: Varies.
Features: Proofed for heaviest smokeless powder loads. Case-hardened frames with modest engraving. Imported from Belgium by Dixie Gun Works.
Price: .... $125.00 to $140.00

DAVIDSON 63B MAGNUM DOUBLE SHOTGUN
Gauge: 10 (3½″ chambers), 12 and 20 (3″ chambers) magnum.
Barrel: 32″ 10 (Full & Fyll), 30″ 12 (Mod. & Full), 28″ 12, 20 (Mod. & Full).
Weight: 10 ga., 10 lbs. 10 oz.; 12 ga., 7½ lbs.; 20 ga. 6¾ lbs.
Stock: Hand finished checkered European walnut, beavertail fore-end, white line spacers on p.g. cap and recoil pad.
Features: Auto safety, manual extractors, gold-plated double triggers (front hinged), engraved nickel-plated action. Imported from Europe by Davidson.
Price: 12, 20 ga $139.95
Price: 10 ga $179.95

FALCON GOOSE DOUBLE BARREL SHOTGUN
Gauge: 10 (3½-inch chambers).
Action: Anson & Deeley with Holland type extractors, double triggers.
Barrel: 32″ (Full and Full).
Weight: 11 lbs.
Stock: Hand checkered walnut, plastic p.g. cap and rubber recoil pad with white spacers.
Features: Auto safety, rubber recoil pad, engraved action. Imported from Spain by American Import.
Price: $199.00

LOYOLA MAGNUM DOUBLE BARREL SHOTGUN
Gauge: 10 (3½ chambers); 12, 20 and 410 (all 3″ chambers).
Action: Hammerless, double trigger, auto. safety.
Barrel: 12, 20 ga. 26″ (Imp. Cyl., Mod.), 28″ (Full, Mod.); 10, 12 ga. 30″ (Full, Mod.); 10 ga. 32″, 12 ga. 30″ and 410 ga. 26″ (Full, Full).
Stock: Checkered walnut, p.g., fitted rubber recoil pad.
Features: Available with solid or vent. rib. ($20.00 additional). Imported from Spain by Jana.
Price: .... $110.00 (12, 20, 410 ga.), $130.00 (10 ga.)

MAUSER MODEL 580 DOUBLE BARREL SHOTGUN
Gauge: 12, 20 (3″ chambers).
Action: Holland & Holland type side lock.
Barrel: 28″ (Full & I.M. or I.C. & Mod.).
Weight: 7 lbs.
Stock: Hand checkered French walnut.
Features: Auto selective ejectors, choice of double or single ($50.00 additional) trigger. English scroll engraved. Imported from Germany by Mauser Bauer.
Price: Single trigger $1,129.95
Price: Double trigger $1,079.95

MERCURY MAGNUM DOUBLE BARREL SHOTGUN
Gauge: 10 (3½″), 12 or 20 (3″) magnums.
Action: Triple-lock Anson & Deeley type.
Barrel: 28″ (Full & Mod.), 12 and 20 ga.; 32″ (Full & Full), 10 ga.
Weight: 7¼ lbs. (12 ga.); 6½ lbs. (20 ga.); 10⅛ lbs. (10 ga.). **Length:** 45″ (28″ bbls.).
Stock: 14″ x 1⅝″ x 2¼″ walnut, checkered p.g. stock and beavertail fore-end, recoil pad.
Features: Double triggers, front hinged, auto safety, extractors; safety gas ports, engraved frame. Imported from Spain by Tradewinds.
Price: .... $149.95 (12, 20 ga.)
Price: .... $179.95 (10 ga.)

IMPORTED SHOTGUNS—DOUBLE BARREL

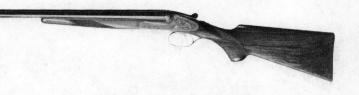

GEBRUDER MERKEL 475 SIDE BY SIDE
Gauge: 12, 16, 20, 3″ chambers on request.
Action: Sidelock with double hook bolting and Greener breech.
Barrel: To customer's specs., choice of chokes.
Weight: 6¼ to 6¾ lbs.
Stock: To customer's specs. Walnut with p.g. or English style.
Features: Double, single or single selective trigger. Cocking indicators. English arabesque engraving. Imported by Champlin Firearms.
Price: With single trigger **$743.00**

PREMIER AMBASSADOR DOUBLE BARREL SHOTGUN
Gauge: 12, 16 (2¾″); 20, 410 (3″).
Action: Triple Greener crossbolt, Purdey avail. on 410; side locks.
Barrels: 22″ exc. 410; 26″ all (Mod. & Full).
Weight: 7¼ lbs. (12) to 6¼ lbs. (410). **Length:** 44½″.
Stock: 14″ x 1⅝″ x 2½″ checkered walnut, p.g., beavertail fore-end.
Features: Cocking indicators, double triggers, auto safety. Imported from Europe by Premier.
Price: **$187.00**

PREMIER CONTINENTAL DOUBLE HAMMER SHOTGUN
Same as Ambassador except outside hammers, not avail. in 410.
Price: **$170.00**

PREMIER REGENT DOUBLE BARREL SHOTGUN
Gauge: 12, 16, 28 (2¾″ chambers); 20, 410 (3″ chambers).
Action: Triple Greener crossbolt; Purdey optional on 28, 410.
Barrels: 26″ (I.C. & Mod.) exc. 28 and 410 only (Mod. & Full); 28″ (Mod. & Full); 30″ 12 only (Mod. & Full).
Weight: 7¼ lbs. (12) to 6⅛ lbs. (410). **Length:** 42½″ (26″ bbls.).
Stock: 14″ x 1⅝″ x 2½″ checkered walnut, p.g. and fore-end.
Features: Matted tapered rib, double triggers, auto safety. Extra bbl. sets avail. Imported from Europe by Premier.
Price: **$137.95**

PREMIER BRUSH KING DOUBLE BARREL SHOTGUN
Same as Regent except 12 and 20 ga. only, 22″ bbls. (I.C. & Mod.), weight 6¼ lbs. (12), 5¾ lbs. (20).
Price: **$148.00**

PREMIER MAGNUM DOUBLE BARREL SHOTGUN
Similar to Regent except 10 ga. (3½″ chambers) 32″ or 12 ga. (3″ chambers) 30″, both Full & Full. Recoil pad, beavertail fore-end.
Price: 12 ga. **$155.00**
Price 10 ga. **$169.00**

ROSSI OVERLAND DOUBLE BARREL SHOTGUN
Gauge: 12, 20 and 410 (3-in. chambers).
Action: Sidelock with external hammers; Greener crossbolt.
Barrel: 12 ga., 20″ (Imp. Cyl., Mod.) 28″ (Mod., Full); 20 ga., 20″ or 26″ (Mod., Full); 410 ga., 26″ (Full, Full).
Weight: 6 lbs. (410 ga., 26″ bbls.) to 7 lbs. (12 ga., 28″ bbls).
Stock: Walnut p.g. with beavertail fore-end.
Features: Solid raised matted rib. Imported from Brazil by Garcia.
Price: **$105.00**

The product prices mentioned in these catalog pages were correct at presstime, but may be higher when you read this.

IMPORTED SHOTGUNS—DOUBLE BARREL

ROSSI HAMMERLESS
Gauge: 12, 20, 410, 3″ chambers.
Action: Greener crossbolt, top lever, break-open.
Barrel: 12 and 20 ga. 26″ (Imp. Cyl. & Mod.), 12 ga. 28″ (Mod. & Full), 410 26″ (Full & Full).
Weight: 6 to 7¾ lbs.
Stock: Brazilian hardwood, walnut finish.
Features: Double triggers, raised matted rib with bead front, beavertail fore-end, extractors. Imported from Brazil by Garcia.
Price: **$115.00**

STAR GAUGE DOUBLE BARREL SHOTGUN
Gauge: 12 (2¾″ chambers), 20 (3″ chambers).
Action: Anson & Deeley with double under-locks.
Barrel: 26″ (I.C. & Mod.), 28″ (Full & Mod.); 26″ (Full & Mod.) 20 ga. only; ventilated rib.
Weight: 7¼ lbs. (12), 6¾ lbs. (20)
Stock: Hand checkered walnut, p.g. and semi-beavertail fore-end, fitted recoil pad.
Features: Available with double (Standard) or single triggers (Deluxe). Deluxe has auto ejectors. Imported from Spain by Interarms.
Price: ....**$149.00** (Standard); **$179.00** (Deluxe).

UGARTECHEA DOUBLE BARREL SHOTGUN
Gauge: 12 (Model 1302), 20 (Model 1303), 28 (Model 1304), 410 (Model 1305). All 3-inch chambers except 28 ga.
Action: Anson & Deeley, gold plated double triggers.
Barrel: 30″ (Mod. and Full) 12 ga., 28″ (Mod. and Full) 12 and 20 ga., 26″ (Imp. Cyl. and Mod.) 12 and 20 ga., (Mod. and Full) 28 ga., (Full and Full) 410 ga.
Stock: Hand checkered walnut, ebonite p.g. cap and butt plate with white spacers, beavertail fore-end.
Features: Scroll engraving. Imported from Spain by American Import.
Price: **$155.00**

A & F ZANOTTI DOUBLE BARREL SHOTGUN
Gauge: 12, 20, 28.
Action: Boxlock.
Barrel: 28″ 12 only (Mod.& Full), 26″ (I.C.& Mod.).
Stock: 12 ga. has semi-p.g. walnut stock and beavertail fore-end; 20 and 28 ga. have straight grip and slim fore-end.
Features: Single non-selective trigger, ejectors, gold stock inlay for initials. Custom made. Imported from Italy by Abercrombie & Fitch.
Price: 12 or 20 ga. ....**$675.00** 28 ga. **$750.00**

ZABALA DOUBLE BARREL SHOTGUN
Gauge: 10 (3½″); 12, 20, 410 (3″); 16, 20 (2¾″).
Action: Modified Anson & Deeley boxlock.
Barrels: 32″ 10, 12 only (Full & Full); 30″ 12 only (Mod.& Full); 28″ all exc. 410 (Mod.& Full); 26″ 12, 20, 28 (I.C.&Mod.); 26″ 410 only (Mod.& Full); 22″ 12 only (I.C.& I.C.).
Weight: 10½ lbs.(10), 7¾ lbs.(12) to 6 lbs.(410).
Stock: Hand checkered European walnut, p.g., beavertail fore-end, rubber recoil pad. Dimensions vary with gauge.
Features: Auto safety, plain extractors. Imported from Spain by Galef.
Price: 10 ga. .... **$175.95**   12 - 410 .... **$142.95**

IMPORTED SHOTGUNS—OVER-UNDER

ATLAS MODEL 800 O/U SHOTGUN
Gauge: 12, 20 (3″ chambers).
Action: Merkel-type.
Barrel: 26″ or 28″, standard chokes, vent. rib.
Weight: 7 lbs.
Stock: 14¼″x1½″x2½″ p.g., hand checkered.
Features: Highly engraved, non-ejector, non-selective single trigger. Detachable sideplates. Imported from Italy by Atlas Arms.
Price: **$295.00**

ATLAS GRAND PRIX O/U SHOTGUN
Gauge: 12, 20.
Action: Merkel-type, sidelocks.
Barrel: 26″ or 28″ vent. rib barrels, choice of chokes.
Weight: 7¼ lbs.
Stock: Straight or p.g. to order.
Features: Fully engraved, automatic ejectors, single selective trigger. Available on special order only. Imported from Italy by Atlas Arms.
Price: .... **$1,000.00 up.**

IMPORTED SHOTGUNS—OVER-UNDER

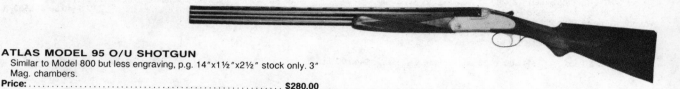

ATLAS MODEL 65 O/U SHOTGUN
Gauge: 28, 410 (3" chambers).
Action: Merkel-type.
Barrel: 26", 28" (I.C.& Mod., Mod.&Full, Skeet & Skeet).
Weight: 5½ lbs.
Stock: Hand checkered walnut.
Features: Extractors, single or double triggers. Imported from Italy by Atlas Arms.
Price: **$248.00**

ATLAS MODEL 95 O/U SHOTGUN
Similar to Model 800 but less engraving, p.g. 14"x1½"x2½" stock only. 3" Mag. chambers.
Price: **$280.00**

BERETTA BL O/U SHOTGUNS
Gauge: 12, 28 (2¾" chambers); 12 mag., 20 (3" chambers).
Action: Hammerless with gold-plated single-selective trigger. BL-6 has Beretta boxlock action.
Barrel: 12 ga., 30" or 28" (Mod., Full), 26" (Imp. Cyl., Mod.); 20 ga., 28" (Mod., Full), 26" (Mod., Full); 28 ga., 28" (Mod., Full), 26" (Imp. Cyl Mod.); 12 ga. Trap, 30" (Imp. Mod., Full); 12 or 20 ga. Skeet, 26" (Skeet, Skeet).
Weight: 7¼ lbs. (12 ga.), 6 lbs (20 and 28 ga.), 7½ lbs (Trap and 12 ga. Mag.).
Stock: 14⅛"x1½"x2½" (Standard), 14⅜"x1⅜"x1¾" (Trap), hand-checkered European walnut, p.g.
Features: Hand-engraved receivers, ventilated rib. BL-4 has more engraving and checkering than BL-3, is available with two sets of barrels. BL-6 has additional hand-engraved sideplates, specially selected wood. Imported from Italy by Garcia.
Price: .... From **$360.00** (BL-3) to **$700.00** (BL-6 Trap or Skeet)

CONDOR TRAP O/U SHOTGUN
Same as Field Grade except wide rib, Monte Carlo stock, 12 ga. only, 28" (Full & Mod.); 30" or 32" (I.M.& Full, Full & Full), weight 7 lbs.7oz.
Price: **$397.40**

BERETTA SO SERIES O/U SHOTGUNS
Gauge: 12 (2¾" chambers).
Action: Sidelock, with modified Greener crossbolt, hand-detachable on SO-4 and 5. Single selective or double triggers, gold plated on SO-5 only.
Barrel: 28" (Mod. and Full), 26" (I.C. and Mod.). 30" and different choke combos available.
Weight: 7 to 7¼ lbs.
Stock: Select European walnut, 14⅛"x1½"x2½" or custom fitted, p.g. or straight grip.
Features: Made to order to customer's specifications. Ornamentation varies with grade, SO-2 through SO-5. Auto safety on Field models, manual on Skeet and Trap. Imported from Italy by Garcia.
Price: SO-2, SO-5; depends on grade and engraving **$1,500.00** to **$4,000.00**

CONDOR O/U SHOTGUN
Gauge: 12, 20 (2¾" or 3" chambers).
Action: Purdey type double lock.
Barrel: 26" (I.C. & Mod., Skeet & Skeet); 28" (Full & Mod., I.M.& Mod.); 30" (Full & Full, Full & Mod.) 12 mag. only.
Weight: 6½ lbs. (26"20) to 7 lbs.3oz. (30"12).
Stock: 14"x1½"x2½" handcheckered walnut, p.g. and fore-end, recoil pad.
Features: Single selective trigger, auto ejectors, manual tang safety, vent. rib. Skeet Grade has extra wide rib. Imported from Italy by Kleingunther.
Price: Field grade **$367.00**
Price: Skeet **$387.83**

CHARLES DALY FIELD GRADE O/U SHOTGUNS

Gauge: 12, 28 (2¾″ chambers); 12 mag., 20, 410 (3″ chambers).
Action: Boxlock, single selective inertia trigger, auto safety (exc. Skeet).
Barrel: 30″ 12 (Skeet&Sheet), 12 Mag. (Full&Full); 28″ 12, 20 (Mod.&Full); 26″ 12, 20, 28, 410 (Skeet&Skeet, I.C.& Mod.); 28, 410 (Mod.&Full).
Weight: 12 ga., 7 lbs.; others, about 6¼ lbs.
Stock: 14″x1½″x2½″ walnut, p.g. 12 Mag. has recoil pad.
Features: Ventilated rib, selective auto ejectors. Imported from Japan by Charles Daly.
Price: 12 and 20 ga. ..... **$415.00**   28 and 410 ga. **$440.00**

CHARLES DALY SUPERIOR GRADE O/U SHOTGUN

Gauge: 12, 20, 28, 410 (2¾″ chambers except 20 and 410 ga. Field models, 3″)
Action: Boxlock, single selective inertia trigger.
Barrel: Same as Field Grade plus 28″ 12, 20, 410 (Skeet & Skeet).
Weight: 12 ga., 7¼ lbs.; others, 6 lbs. 10 oz.
Stock: 14″x1½″x2½″ checkered walnut, p.g., beavertail fore-end.
Features: Ventilated rib. "Selexor" permits shooter to select auto ejection or merely extraction. Imported from Japan by Charles Daly.
Price: .... **$440.00** to **$550.00**

CHARLES DALY VENTURE GRADE O/U SHOTGUNS

Gauge: 12 (2¾″ chambers), 20 (3″ chambers).
Action: Box lock, single selective inertia trigger.
Barrel: 26″ (I.C. and Mod.), 28″ (Mod. and Full).
Weight: 12 ga., 7 lbs.; 20 ga., 6 lbs. 5 oz.
Stock: 14″x1½″x2½″ checkered walnut, p.g.
Features: Ventilated rib, manual safety, auto ejectors. Imported from Japan by Charles Daly.
Price: **$370.00**

FALCON SUPER 8 O/U

Gauge: 410 ga., 3″ chambers.
Barrel: 26″ (Mod. & Full).
Weight: 5¾ lbs.
Stock: Walnut finish, hand checkered.
Features: Single non-selective trigger, chrome bores, hard plastic buttplate. Imported by American Import.
Price: **$149.00**

FRANCHI FALCONET O/U SHOTGUN

Gauge: 12, 16, 20, 28 and 410.
Action: Hammerless with overhead-sear trigger and auto. safety.
Barrel: 24″, 12 or 20 ga. (Cyl. & Imp. Cyl.); 26″, all except 410 (Imp. Cyl. & Mod.), 410 (Mod. & Full); 28″, all (Mod. & Full); 30″, 12 ga. (Mod. & Full); 26″, all except 16 ga. (Skeet 1-Skeet 2); 30″ 12 ga. Trap (Mod. & Full).
Weight: 6 lbs. (approx.) except Skeet 7½ lbs. and Trap 8¼ lbs.
Stock: Epoxy finished walnut.
Features: Chrome-lined barrels, selective single trigger, auto ejectors. Available with "Buckskin" or "Ebony" (Blue) colored Frames. Skeet and Trap models have 10mm rib, middle sight, non-auto safety. Imported from Italy by Stoeger Arms.
Price: (Ebony) .... **$379.95** (12, 16, 20 ga.); **$399.95** (28, 410 ga.).
Price: (Buckskin) .... **$354.75** (12, 16, 20 ga.); **$378.75** (28, 410 ga.).
Price: (Skeet) .... **$659.95** (12, 20 ga.); **$715.95** (28, 410 ga.)
Price: (Trap) .... **$659.95** (12, 20 ga.).

KRIEGHOFF MODEL 32 O/U SHOTGUN

Gauge: 12, 20, 28 & 410.
Action: Boxlock.
Barrel: 28″, 30″, 32″, 34″.
Stock: Hand checkered walnut, p.g., beavertail fore-end.
Features: Three-way safety (manual, auto or inoperative). Selective single trigger, ejectors and ventilated rib. Other barrel lengths, chokes to order. Available with fancier walnut and relief engraving and silver and gold inlays. Extra barrels available. Imported from Germany by Krieghoff Gun Co.
Price: .... **$895.00** to **$6,945.00**

IMPORTED SHOTGUNS—OVER-UNDER

KRIEGHOFF "TECK" O/U SHOTGUN
Gauge: 12, 16, 20 (2¾"), 20 (3").
Action: Boxlock.
Barrel: 28½" (Full & Mod.), vent. rib.
Weight: 7 lbs. **Length:** 44" over-all.
Stock: 14¼"x1¼"x2¼", European walnut.
Features: Kersten double crossbolt system. Interchangeable barrels. Imported from Germany by Unordco.
Price: With ejectors $1,200.00
Price: Interchangeable double rifle barrels up to 7mm Rem. Mag. **$825.00**
Price: Interchangeable double rifle barrels as above, with ejectors **$875.00**
Price: Double rifle barrels, 7mm, 375, 458 Win. Mag. $1,000.00
Price: As above with ejectors.
Price: Interchangeable shotgun-rifle barrel combination $550.00
Price: Model Ulm with sidelocks $1,800.00
Price: Model Ulm with hand-detachable engraved sidelocks $2,350.00

LAURONA MODEL 71-G O/U SHOTGUN
Gauge: 12 (3" chambers).
Action: Hammerless, gold-plated double selectable triggers, auto. safety.
Barrel: 26" (Imp. Cyl. & Mod.); 28" (Full & Mod.); 30" (Full & Full), 30" (Full & Mod.), vent. rib.
Stock: Hand-checkered walnut, p.g., vent. rubber recoil pad.
Feature: Chromed bores, vent. rib. Imported from Spain by Jana.
Price: $230.00

LAURONA MODEL 71-G-EX O/U SHOTGUN
Same as Model 67-G except supplied with both 12 and 20 ga. bbls., 28" (Full & Mod.).
Price: $360.00

LAMES O/U SHOTGUN
Gauge: 12 (2¾").
Action: Boxlock.
Barrels: 32", 30" (Full & Full or Imp.Mod.& Full), 28" (I.C.& Mod. or Mod.& Full), 26" (I.C.& Mod.).
Stock: Hand checkered walnut, semi p.g.
Features: Gold-plated single selective trigger, auto safety, vent. rib. Imported by LA Distributors.
Price: $329.95

LAMES O/U TRAP SHOTGUN
Gauge: 12 (2¾").
Action: Boxlock.
Barrels: 30" or 32" (Full & Full or Mod.& Full).
Stock: Hand checkered walnut, Monte Carlo, p.g., beavertail fore-end, recoil pad.
Features: Single selective trigger, manual safety, double vent. rib. Fitted 20 ga. bbl. set available. Imported by LA Distributors.
Price: $399.95

MAUSER 620 O/U SHOTGUN
Gauge: 12 (2¾" chambers).
Action: Greener crossbolt.
Barrel: 30" (Full & I.Mod.), 28" (Mod.& Full, I.C.& Mod. or Skeet & Skeet).
Weight: 7½ lbs. **Length:** 45" (28" bbls.).
Stock: Hand checkered walnut, p.g., beavertail fore-end, recoil pad.
Features: Single non-selective adj. trigger, vent. rib, auto ejectors. Selective or double triggers, engraving available at extra cost. Imported from Germany by Mauser Bauer.
Price: $895.00

MAUSER MODEL 610 PHANTOM O/U
Gauge: 12 ga., 2¾" chambers.
Barrel: 26", 28" (Skeet), 30", 32" (trap).
Weight: 8 lbs.
Stock: 14½"x1½"x2", European walnut.
Features: Double vented barrels, raised rib, rubber recoil pad, color case-hardened action, checkered p.g. and fore-end. Imported by Mauser-Bauer.
Price: Trap or Skeet $799.95
Price: Skeet set with Purbaugh tubes in 12, 20, 28, 410. 26" or 28" lengths, choked Skeet & Skeet $1,299.00

IMPORTED SHOTGUNS—OVER-UNDER

GEBRUDER MERKEL 201E O/U
Gauge: 12, 16, 20, 3″ chambers on request.
Action: Kersten double crossbolt.
Barrel: To customer's specs with choice of chokes.
Weight: 7½ lbs.
Stock: To customer's specs. Walnut with p.g. or English style.
Features: Double, single or single selective trigger, cocking indicators. Fine hunting scene engraving. Imported by Champlin Firearms.
Price: With single selective trigger $1,037.00

GEBRUDER MERKEL 200E O/U
Similar to 201E except: English arabesque engraving and color case-hardening.
Price: With single non-selective trigger $646.00

GEBRUDER MERKEL MODEL 203E O/U
Gauge: 12, 16, 20, 3″ chambers on request.
Action: Merkel H&H hand-detachable side locks with double sears. Double crossbolt breech.
Barrel: To customer's specs, choice of chokes.
Weight: 7½ lbs.
Stock: Deluxe walnut with p.g. or English style. To customer's specs.
Features: Double, single or single selective trigger. Cocking indicators. Choice of arabesque or fine hunting scene engraving. Imported by Champlin Firearms.
Price: With single selective trigger $1,675.00

GEBRUDER MERKEL MODEL 303E O/U
Similar to Model 203E except: double hook-bolting in conjunction with double crossbolt breech. Finer quality.
Price: $2,500.00

MIIDA MODEL 612 O/U
Gauge: 12 only.
Action: Boxlock-type.
Barrels: 28″ (Full & Mod.), 26″ (Mod. & Imp. Cyl.). Vent. rib.
Weight: 6¾ lbs. **Length:** 42¾″ (26″ bbl.).
Stock: French walnut (14″x1½″x2½″), hand checkered. Black buttplate & p.g. cap.
Features: Automatic selective ejectors, single selective trigger, tang safety. Chrome-plated bores. Blued bbls., trigger guard and locking lever, silver, engraved receiver. Imported from Japan by Marubeni America Corp.
Price: Field Grade $395.00

MIIDA MODEL 2100 SKEET
Same as Model 612 except: 27″ bbl. bored Skeet & Skeet, 50% engraving coverage, weighs 7¾ lbs., length is 43¾″. White line spacers at buttplate and p.g. cap.
Price: $445.00

MIIDA MODEL 2300 TRAP & SKEET
Same as Model 2200 except: 70% engraving coverage, fancy French walnut, semi-beavertail fore-end. Imported by Marubeni.
Price: Trap model . . . . $550.00   Skeet model $525.00

MIIDA MODEL GRANDEE TRAP & SKEET
Gauge: 12 only.
Action: Boxlock type.
Barrel: 29″ (Full & Full), 26″ (Skeet & Skeet).
Weight: 7¾ lbs. **Length:** 42¾″ over-all (Skeet).
Stock: 14⅜″x1⅜″x2⅛″x1⅜″ (Trap), 14″x1½″x2½″ (Skeet). Super fancy French walnut. Deep fluted comb. Trap model has Pachmayr pad. Semi-beavertail fore-end. Fine checkering.
Features: Ivory p.g. cap, outer surfaces of breech block, ejectors, and locking levers engine-turned, wide vent. rib. Frame, bbl. (breech end), trigger guard, locking lever fully hand engraved with gold inlays. Imported by Marubeni.
Price: Skeet or Trap $1,195.00

MIIDA MODEL 2200 TRAP & SKEET
Same as Model 612 except: white line spacers at buttplate and p.g. cap, bbls. 29¾″ (Full & Imp. Mod.) or 27″ (Skeet & Skeet), wide rib, 60% engraving coverage, gold plated trigger, Skeet or Trap stock dimensions. Trap model has Pachmayr pad.
Price: Trap . . . . $510.00   Skeet $485.00

ZOLI GRAY EAGLE O/U SHOTGUN
Gauge: 12 (Model 300) or 20 (Model 302), 3-inch chambers.
Action: Hammerless, with auto safety and top lever release.
Barrel: 28" (Mod. and Full), 26" (Imp. Cyl. and Mod.).
Weight: 6 lbs. 13 oz. (12); 6¼ lbs. (20).
Stock: Hand checkered selected walnut, p.g., ebonite butt plate with white spacer.
Features: Ventilated rib, chrome plated bore. Imported from Italy by American Import.
Price: **$275.00**
Also available with single non-selective trigger, 12 ga. (M304), 20 ga. (M306) **$299.00**

PARKER BROS. FIELD MODEL O/U
Gauge: 12 only, 3" chambers.
Action: 26" (Imp. Cyl. & Mod.), 28" (Mod. & Full), 30" (Mod. & Full or Full & Full).
Weight: 8½ lbs.
Stock: Walnut, checkered p.g. and fore-end, rubber recoil pad.
Features: Vent. rib with front bead, engraved receiver, auto. ejectors, single selective trigger. Imported from Italy by Jana.
Price: **$275.00**

PARKER BROS. SKEET MODEL
Same as Field Model except: semi-beavertail fore-end with wrap-around checkering, stock with Skeet dimensions, double vent. ribs, 2¾" chambers, 26" (Skeet & Skeet).
Price: **$335.00**

PARKER BROS. DOUBLE VENT. RIB MODEL
Same as Field Model except: has conventional top vent. rib plus ventilated separation between barrels. Imported from Italy by Jana.
Price: **$320.00**

PARKER BROS. CALIFORNIA TRAP
Same as Standard Trap except: double vent. ribs, M.C. stock, luminous front and center sights.
Price: **$620.00**

PARKER BROS. STD. TRAP "MONTE CARLO"
Same as Field Model except: M.C. type stock, checkered semi-beavertail fore-end, wide vent. rib, front and center bead sights. 2¾" chambers. 30" (Full & Full or Imp. Mod. & Full), 32" (Imp. Mod. & Full.
Price: .... **$360.00**   With standard stock design **$340.00**

A & F PERAZZI O/U SHOTGUN
Gauge: 12.
Action: Boxlock.
Barrel: 29" (Trap); 28" (Pigeon); 26" (Skeet).
Weight: 7 - 7½ lbs.
Stock: Hand checkered walnut, p.g., beavertail fore-end.
Features: Interchangeable stocks for Trap or Field, and interchangeable double or single trigger assemblies. Ventilated rib, bright-finished action. Imported from Italy by Abercrombie & Fitch.
Price: Trap, Pigeon .... **$875.00** Skeet **$950.00**

ZOLI SILVER SNIPE O/U SHOTGUN
Gauge: 12, 20 (3" chambers).
Action: Purdey type double boxlock, crossbolt.
Barrels: 26" (I.C.& Mod.), 28" (Mod.&Full), 30", 12 only (Mod.& Full); 26" Skeet (Skeet & Skeet), 30" Trap (Full & Full).
Weight: 6½ lbs. (12 ga.).
Stock: Hand checkered European walnut, p.g. and fore-end.
Features: Auto safety (exc. Trap and Skeet), vent rib, single trigger, chrome bores. Imported from Italy by Galef.
Price: Field .... **$251.45** Skeet and Trap **$302.65**

ZOLI GOLDEN SNIPE O/U SHOTGUN
Same as Silver Snipe except selective auto ejectors.
Price: Field .... **$296.95** Skeet & Trap **$353.85**

IMPORTED SHOTGUNS—SINGLE BARREL

ATLAS SINGLE BARREL TRAP GUN
Gauge: 12 only.
Action: Boxlock.
Barrel: 30" or 32" (Extra Full), vent. rib, chromed bore.
Weight: 8 lbs.
Stock: 14½"x1⅜"x1⅞"x2¼" checkered walnut Monte Carlo, beavertail fore-end. Recoil pad.
Features: Engraved action, auto. ejector. Avail. with custom engraving, gold trigger and gold lettering (Deluxe). Imported from Italy by Atlas Arms.
Price: Std. .... **$420.00** Deluxe **$460.00**

The product prices mentioned in these catalog pages were correct at presstime, but may be higher when you read this.

BERETTA MARK II SINGLE BARREL TRAP SHOTGUN
Gauge: 12 only; (2¾" chamber).
Action: BL type, full width hinge, top snap tip down.
Barrel: 32" or 34", (Full), matted high tapered vent. rib.
Weight: 8¼ lbs.
Stock: 14⅜" x 1⅜" x 1¾". Hand checkered European walnut, p.g.; rubber recoil pad, beavertail fore-end, Monte Carlo.
Features: Hand engraved receiver. Imported from Italy by Garcia.
Price: **$425.00**

BERETTA TR-2 TRAP SHOTGUN
Gauge: 12 only (2¾" chamber).
Action: Hammerless, under-bbl. release.
Barrel: 32", Full, matted vent. rib.
Weight: 8¼ lbs.
Stock: 14⅜"x1⅜"x1⅝" hand checkered European walnut Monte Carlo stock, p.g., trap-style recoil pad. Beavertail fore-end.
Features: Hand engraved receiver, matted ventilated rib, crossbolt safety. Imported from Italy by Garcia.
Price: **$190.00**

DAINO SINGLE BARREL SHOTGUN
Gauge: 12, 20, 410.
Action: Folding, underlever.
Barrel: 27½", Full or Mod.
Weight: 5½ lbs. **Length:** 44½".
Stock: Hand checkered walnut, semi p.g.
Features: Folds to 27½", choice of plain or vent rib ($5.25 additional) barrel, engraved action. Imported by Kleingunther
Price: **$68.50**

DICKSON BOLT ACTION SHOTGUN
Gauge: 410.
Action: Bolt, sliding thumb safety.
Barrel: 25" (Full).
Weight: 5 lbs. 5 oz.
Stock: Oiled walnut, p.g., black plastic buttplate.
Features: 3-round capacity. Imported from Europe by American Import.
Price: **$41.95**

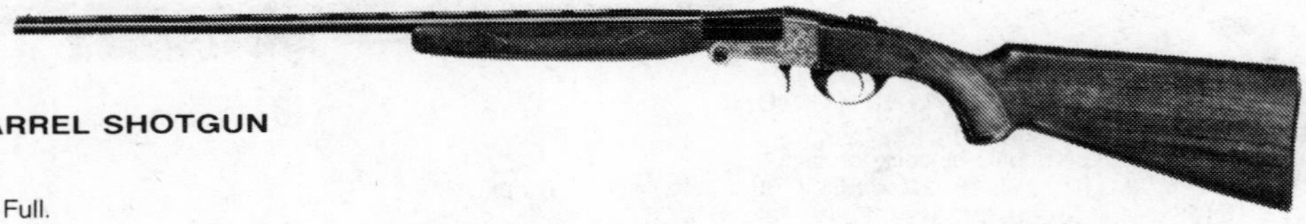

GALEF COMPANION SINGLE BARREL SHOTGUN
Gauge: 12, 20, 410 (3"); 16, 28 (2¾").
Action: Folding boxlock.
Barrel: 28" exc. 12 (30") and 410 (26"), all Full.
Weight: 5½ lbs. (12) to 4½ lbs. (410).
Stock: 14"x1½"x2⅝" hand checkered walnut, p.g.
Features: Non-auto safety, folds. Vent. rib $5.00 additional. Imported from Italy by Galef.
Price: Plain bbl. .... **$51.95**   Vent. rib **$56.95**

MONTE CARLO SINGLE BARREL SHOTGUN
Gauge: 12 (2¾" chamber).
Action: Monte Carlo, bottom release.
Barrel: 32" (Trap).
Weight: 8¼ lbs.
Stock: 14½"x1⅛"x1⅝" hand checkered walnut, p.g., beavertail fore-end, recoil pad.
Features: Auto ejector, slide safety, gold plated trigger. Imported from Italy by Galef.
Price: **$149.95**

MAUSER MODEL 496 SINGLE BARREL SHOTGUN
Gauge: 12 (2¾" chamber).
Action: Greener-type cross bolt, 4 locking lugs.
Barrel: 32" (Mod.), 34" (Full).
Weight: 8 lbs. **Length:** 49".
Stock: Walnut Monte Carlo, p.g., beavertail fore-end.
Features: Front and middle sights, no manual safety, chrome lined bbl., auto ejector. Imported from German by Mauser Bauer.
Price: .... **$564.00**   Competition model **$699.95**

KRIEGHOFF SINGLE BARREL TRAP SHOTGUN
Gauge: 12.
Action: Boxlock, short hammer fall.
Barrel: 32" or 34" (Full).
Weight: About 8½ lbs.
Stock: Monte Carlo with checkered p.g. and grooved beavertail fore-end.
Features: Thumb safety, vent. rib. Extra bbls. available $445.00. Available with various grades of decoration, wood. Imported from Germany by Krieghoff Gun Co.
Price: Standard .... **$945.00**   San Remo **$1,695.00**
Monte Carlo Grade ..... **$3,795.00**   Crown **$4,195.00**
Super Crown Grade **$4,495.00**

KRIEGHOFF VANDALIA TRAP MODEL
Gauge: 12 only.
Action: Boxlock.
Barrel: 30", 32", 34". Available as either single or over/under.
Stock: Hand checkered walnut, p.g., beavertail fore-end.
Weight: About 9 lbs.
Features: Three-way safety (manual, auto or inoperative). Selective single trigger, ejectors, full length vent. rib. Other bbl. lengths, chokes to order. Available with fancier walnut and relief engraving and silver and gold inlays. Extra bbls. available. Imported from Germany by Krieghoff Gun Co.
Price: 30" .. **$1,245.00 to $5,445.00**   32" and 34" **$1,295.00 to $5,495.00**

BLACK POWDER GUNS

The following pages catalog the black powder arms currently available to U.S. shooters. These range from quite precise replicas of historically significant arms to totally new designs created expressly to give the black powder shooter the benefits of modern technology.

Most of the replicas are imported, and many are available from more than one source. Thus examples of a given model such as the 1860 Army revolver or Zouave rifle purchased from different importers may vary in price, finish and fitting. Most of them bear proof marks, indicating that they have been test fired in the proof house of their country of origin.

A list of the importers and the retail price range are included with the description for each model. Many local dealers handle more than one importer's products, giving the prospective buyer an opportunity to make his own judgment in selecting a black powder gun. Most importers have catalogs available free or at

nominal cost, and some are well worth having for the useful information on black powder shooting they provide in addition to their detailed descriptions and specifications of the guns.

A number of special accessories are also available for the black powder shooter. These include replica powder flasks, bullet moulds, cappers and tools, as well as more modern devices to facilitate black powder cleaning and maintenance. Ornate presentation cases and even detachable shoulder stocks are also available for some black powder pistols from their importers. Again, dealers or the importers will have catalogs.

The black powder guns are arranged in four sections: Single Shot Pistols, Revolvers, Muskets & Rifles, and Shotguns. The guns within each section are arranged by date of the original, with the oldest first. Thus the 1836 Texas Patterson replica leads off the revolver section, and flintlocks precede percussion arms in the other sections.

BLACK POWDER SINGLE SHOT PISTOLS—FLINT & PERCUSSION

ZANOTTI FLINTLOCK PISTOL
Extremely ornate replica of an early Italian flintlock dueling pistol complete with case, bullet mould and powder flask. Carved walnut stock, deep relief engraved metal. Imported by Navy, Hawes.
Price: . . . . **$100.00** to **$125.00**

TOWER FLINTLOCK PISTOL
Caliber: 45.
Barrel: 8¼".
Weight: 40 oz. **Length:** 14" over-all.
Stock: Walnut.
Sights: Fixed.
Features: Engraved lock, brass furniture. Specifications, including caliber, weight and length may vary with importers. Available as flint or percussion. Imported by The Armoury, F.I.E., Hawes, C.V.A., Sloan's, Centennial.
Price: . . . . **$23.00** to **$42.95.**

HARPER'S FERRY 1806 PERCUSSION PISTOL
Caliber: 54.
Barrel: 10".
Weight: 40 oz. **Length:** 16" over-all.
Stock: Walnut.
Sights: Fixed.
Features: Case hardened lock, brass mounted browned bbl. Replica of the first U.S. Gov't.-made flintlock pistol. Imported by Navy Arms, Sloan's.
Price: . . . . **$50.00** to **$95.00**

KENTUCKY FLINTLOCK PISTOL
Caliber: 44.
Barrel: 10⅛".
Weight: 32 oz. **Length:** 15½" over-all.
Stock: Walnut.
Sights: Fixed.
Features: Case hardened lock, blued bbl.; available also as brass bbl. flint Model 1821 ($95.00, Navy). Imported by Navy, Replica, The Armoury, Century, Centennial, F.I.E., Sloan's, Jana.
Price: . . . . **$40.95** to **$85.00**

KENTUCKY PERCUSSION PISTOL
Similar to above but percussion lock. Imported by Centennial, The Armory, Navy, F.I.E., Hawes, Jana, Replica.
Price: . . . . **$26.95** to **$85.00**

BLACK POWDER SINGLE SHOT PISTOLS—FLINT & PERCUSSION

KENTUCKY BELT PERCUSSION PISTOL
Caliber: 45.
Barrel: 7", rifled.
Weight: 29 oz. **Length:** 12" over-all.
Stock: Walnut.
Sights: Fixed.
Features: Engraved lock, brass furniture, steel ramrod. Available as flint or percussion. Imported by The Armoury, C.V.A., Hawes.
Price: ....$22.95 to $31.95.

HOPKINS & ALLEN M-L BOOT PISTOL
Caliber: 36 or 45, single shot percussion.
Barrel: 6 inch octagonal, regular or gain twist.
Length: 13 inches. **Weight:** 34 oz.
Stocks: Smooth walnut, birdshead style.
Sights: Fixed blade front, adj. rear.
Features: Underhammer lockwork, match trigger. From High Standard.
Price: $39.95

ENGLISH BELT PISTOL
Caliber: 44 (.451" bore).
Barrel: 7", octagonal, rifled.
Length: 12" over-all.
Stock: Walnut.
Features: Case-hardened lock, brass furniture, fixed sights. Available in either flint or percussion. Imported by CVA.
Price: ....$29.95 to $34.95
Also available in kit form, either flint or percussion. Stock 90% inletted.
Price: ....$19.95 to $25.95

SINGLE SHOT PERCUSSION TARGET PISTOL
Caliber: 44.
Barrel: 9" octagonal.
Weight: 42 oz.
Stocks: Walnut.
Sights: Bead front, rear adj. for w. and e.
Features: Engraved scenes on frame sides; brass backstrap and trigger guard; case hardened frame and hammer. Imported by Replica, Navy.
Price: ....$64.95 to $70.00

HARPER'S FERRY MODEL 1855 PERCUSSION PISTOL
Caliber: 58.
Barrel: 11¾", rifled.
Weight: 56 oz. **Length:** 18" over-all.
Stock: Walnut.
Sights: Fixed.
Features: Case hardened lock and hammer; brass furniture; blued bbl. Shoulder stock available, priced at $35.00. Imported by Navy Arms.
Price: $90.00

KENTUCKIAN PISTOL
Caliber: 44.
Barrel: 9½".
Weight: 40 oz. **Length:** 15" over-all.
Stock: Select walnut.
Sights: Dovetailed brass blade front, open notch rear.
Features: Brass trigger guard, side plate, barrel cap. Case hardened action with engraved lockplate. Imported by Intercontinental Arms.
Price: Flint or Percussion $59.95
Price: Cased set (includes fitted case, flask, mould, wrench and tool)$99.50

DRAGOON REPLICA PERCUSSION PISTOL
Caliber: 58.
Barrel: 11¾".
Weight: 5½ lbs. **Length:** 29" over-all (with stock).
Stock: Walnut finish.
Sights: Dual folding leaf rear, post front.
Features: Comes complete with detachable extension stock. Sling swivels, brass fittings. Imported by American Import.
Price: $125.00

BLACK POWDER SINGLE SHOT PISTOLS—FLINT & PERCUSSION

RENEGADE PISTOL
Caliber: 44 or 36.
Barrel: 8¼".
Weight: Approx. 31 oz. **Length:** 13¼" over-all.
Stock: Walnut.
Sights: Bead front.
Features: Double barrel, double trigger percussion pistol with rifled barrels. Engraved side plates and hammers. Engraved brass trigger guard and butt cap. Steel ramrod with brass tip. Imported by Intercontinental Arms.
Price: Pistol only **$49.95**
Price: Cased set (includes fitted case, pistol, powder flask, bullet mould, wrench, and tool) **$89.50**

RIPOLL BOOT PISTOL
Caliber: 45.
Barrel: 4", rifled.
Length: 8¼" over-all.
Stock: Walnut.
Features: Miquelet lock, cold-forged barrel, proof tested. Imported by CVA.
Price: **$64.95**

THOMPSON/CENTER PATRIOT PERCUSSION PISTOL
Caliber: 45.
Barrel: 9¼".
Weight: 36 oz. **Length:** 16" over-all.
Stock: Walnut.
Sights: Patridge-type. Rear adj. for w. and e.
Features: Hook breech system; ebony ramrod; double set triggers; coil mainspring. From Thompson/Center Arms.
Price: **$112.00**
With accessory pack (Ohaus bullet mould, TC patches, adj. powder measure, short starter, black powder solvent, extra nipple and nipple wrench.
Price: **$132.50**

PHILADELPHIA DERRINGER PERCUSSION PISTOL
Caliber: 41.
Barrel: 3⅛".
Weight: 14 oz. **Length:** 7" over-all.
Stock: Walnut, checkered grip.
Sights: Fixed.
Features: Engraved wedge holder and bbl. Also available in flintlock version (Armoury, $29.95). Imported by C.V.A., Century, The Armoury, Hawes.
Price: . . . .**$18.37 to $24.95.**

MOWREY KENTUCKY PISTOL
Caliber: 45 or 50.
Barrel: 8".
Weight: 3½ lbs. **Length:** 15" over-all.
Stock: Walnut.
Sights: Bead front.
Features: Percussion only. Brass stock furniture. Also available in kit form.
Price: Complete . . . . **$109.50**   Kit **$88.95**

TINGLE BLACK POWDER M1960 PISTOL
Caliber: 40, single shot, percussion.
Barrel: 8", 9", 10", or 12" octagon.
Length: 11¾ inches. **Weight:** 33 oz. (8" bbl.).
Stocks: Walnut, one piece.
Features: 6-groove bbl., easily removable for cleaning; 1-in-30 twist.
Sights: Fixed blade front, w. adj. rear.
Price: **$64.95**
Price: With detachable shoulder stock, ...**$19.50** extra.

RIPOLL BELT PISTOL
Caliber: 61.
Barrel: 8¾" rifled.
Length: 15".
Stock: Walnut.
Features: Miquelet lock, cold-forged barrel, proof tested. Imported by CVA.
Price: **$69.95**

BLACK POWDER REVOLVERS

TEXAS PATERSON 1836 PERCUSSION REVOLVER
Caliber: 36, 5-shot.
Barrel: 6", 7½", 9", 12".
Weight: 24 oz. **Length:** 10" (6" bbl.).
Stocks: Walnut.
Sights: Fixed.
Features: Indian scene engraved on cylinder; folding trigger; all blue finish. Imported by Replica, Navy.
Price: . . . .**$100.00 to $104.50**

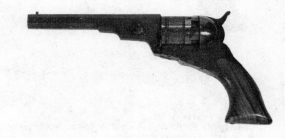

> **The product prices mentioned in these catalog pages were correct at presstime, but may be higher when you read this.**

BLACK POWDER REVOLVERS

WALKER 1847 PERCUSSION REVOLVER
Caliber: 44, 6-shot.
Barrel: 9″.
Weight: 72 oz. **Length:** 15½″ over-all.
Stocks: Walnut.
Sights: Fixed.
Features: Case hardened frame, loading lever and hammer; iron back strap; brass trigger guard; engraved cylinder. Imported by Replica, Navy, Jana.
Price:..$100.00 to $115.00

SECOND MODEL DRAGOON 1848 REVOLVER
Caliber: 44, 6-shot.
Barrel: 7½″.
Weight: 64 oz. **Length:** 14″ over-all.
Stocks: One piece walnut.
Sights: Fixed.
Features: Case hardened frame, loading lever and hammer; engraved cylinder scene; safety notches on hammer, safety pin in cylinder. Imported by Replica, Navy. First and Third Models also available from Navy priced from $100.00.
Price:..................................... $90.00 to $110.00

BABY DRAGOON 1848 PERCUSSION REVOLVER
Caliber: 31, 5-shot.
Barrel: 4″, 5″, 6″.
Weight: 24 oz. (6″ bbl.). **Length:** 10½″ (6″ bbl.).
Stocks: Walnut.
Sights: Fixed.
Features: Case hardened frame; safety notches on hammer and safety pin in cylinder; engraved cylinder scene; octagonal bbl. Imported by Replica, Navy Arms, F.I.E., Jana.
Price:.. $38.15 to $76.25

1849 WELLS FARGO PERCUSSION REVOLVER
Caliber: 31, 5-shot.
Barrel: 3″, 4″, 5″, 6″.
Weight: 22 oz.
Stocks: Walnut.
Sights: Fixed.
Features: No loading lever; square-back trigger guard; case hardened frame and hammer; engraved cylinder; brass trigger guard and back-strap. Imported by Replica, Navy, Jana. Bbl. lengths may vary with importer.
Price:.. $60.00 to $75.00

1851 NAVY-SHERIFF
Same as 1851 Sheriff model except: 4″ barrel, fluted cylinder, belt ring in butt. Imported by American Import.
Price:.. $50.00

1851 SHERIFF'S MODEL POLICE REVOLVER
Caliber: 36.
Barrel: 5″.
Weight: 38 oz. **Length:** 10½″ over-all.
Stocks: Walnut.
Sights: Fixed.
Features: Richly blued steel frame, fluted cylinder and lanyard ring. Also available with 7½″ bbl. (wgt. 43 oz., 12½″ o.a.), same price. Imported by Centennial Arms, American Import.
Price:.. $40.95

POCKET MODEL 1849 PERCUSSION REVOLVER
Caliber: 31, 5-shot.
Barrel: 4″, 6″.
Weight: 26 oz.
Stocks: Walnut finish.
Sights: Fixed.
Features: Round trigger guard; Colt stagecoach hold-up scene on cylinder. Imported by Navy Arms.
Price:.. $75.00

BLACK POWDER REVOLVERS

COLT 1851 NAVY PERCUSSION REVOLVER

Caliber: 36, 5-shot.
Barrel: 7½".
Weight: 40 oz. **Length:** 13⅛" over-all.
Stocks: Black walnut.
Sights: Bead-type front, hammer notch rear.
Features: Color case hardened frame; barrel and cylinder blued. Silver plated trigger guard and backstrap. Naval scene engraving on cylinder. From Colt's.
Price: **$149.95**

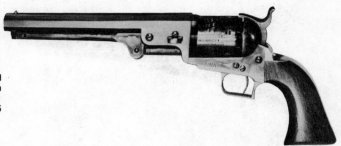

ARMY 1851 PERCUSSION REVOLVER

Caliber: 44, 6-shot.
Barrel: 7½".
Weight: 45 oz. **Length:** 13" over-all.
Stocks: Walnut finish.
Sights: Fixed.
Features: 44 caliber version of the 1851 Navy. Imported by Valor, The Armoury, Jana.
Price: .... **$33.50** to **$65.00**

1851 SHERIFF MODEL PERCUSSION REVOLVER

Caliber: 36, 6-shot.
Barrel: 5".
Weight: 40 oz. **Length:** 10½" over-all.
Stocks: Walnut.
Sights: Fixed.
Features: Brass back strap and trigger guard; engraved navy scene; case hardened frame, hammer, loading lever. Available with brass frame from some importers at slightly lower prices. Imported by Centennial, The Armoury, Navy, Hawes.
Price: Steel frame .... **$41.95** to **$90.00**
Price: Brass frame .... **$34.95** to **$49.95**

NAVY MODEL 1851 PERCUSSION REVOLVER

Caliber: 36 or 44 6-shot.
Barrel: 7½".
Weight: 42 oz. **Length:** 13" over-all.
Stocks: Walnut finish.
Sights: Fixed.
Features: Brass backstrap and trigger guard; engraved cylinder with navy battle scene; case hardened frame, hammer, loading lever. Imported by Centennial, The Armoury, Navy, Hawes, Valor, Century, F.I.E., American Import, Jana.
Price: Brass frame .... **$31.50** to **$49.95**
Price: Steel frame .... **$40.95** to **$90.00**

NEW MODEL 1858 ARMY PERCUSSION REVOLVER

Caliber: 36 or 44, 6-shot.
Barrel: 8".
Weight: 40 oz. **Length:** 13½" over-all.
Stocks: Walnut.
Sights: Fixed.
Features: Replica of Remington Model 1858. Also available from some importers as Army Model Belt Revolver in 36 cal., shortened and lightened version of the 44. Target Model (Centennial, Navy Arms) has fully adj. target rear sight, target front, 36 or 44 ($74.95—$125.00). Imported by Navy, Century, F.I.E., Hawes, C.V.A., Valor, American Import, Jana, The Armoury, Centennial.
Price: .... **$49.95** to **$95.00**

1860 ARMY PERCUSSION REVOLVER

Caliber: 44, 6-shot.
Barrel: 8".
Weight: 40 oz. **Length:** 13⅝" over-all.
Stocks: Walnut.
Sights: Fixed.
Features: Engraved navy scene on cylinder; brass trigger guard; case hardened frame, loading lever and hammer. Some importers supply pistol cut for detachable shoulder stock, have accessory stock available. Imported by Navy, Centennial, The Armoury, Hawes, Jana, Replica.
Price: .... **$44.95** to **$89.95**
1861 Navy: Same as Army except 36 cal., 7½" bbl., wt. 41 oz., cut for stock; round cylinder (fluted avail.), from Replica **$89.95**

GRISWOLD & GRIER PERCUSSION REVOLVER

Caliber: 36, 44, 6-shot.
Barrel: 7½".
Weight: 44 oz. (36 cal.). **Length:** 13" over-all.
Stocks: Walnut.
Sights: Fixed.
Features: Replica of famous Confederate pistol. Brass frame, backstrap and trigger guard; case hardened loading lever; rebated cylinder (44 cal. only). Imported by Navy Arms.
Price: **$50.00**

1862 POLICE MODEL PERCUSSION REVOLVER

Caliber: 36, 5-shot.
Barrel: 4½", 5½", 6½".
Weight: 26 oz. **Length:** 12" (6½" bbl.).
Stocks: Walnut.
Sights: Fixed.
Features: Half-fluted and rebated cylinder; case hardened frame, loading lever and hammer; brass trigger guard and back strap. Imported by Replica.
Price: **$89.95**

BLACK POWDER REVOLVERS

RUGER 44 OLD ARMY PERCUSSION REVOLVER
Caliber: 44, 6-shot. Use .457" dia. lead bullets.
Barrel: 7½" (6-groove, 16" twist).
Weight: 46 oz. **Length:** 13½" over-all.
Stock: Smooth walnut.
Sights: Ramp front, rear adj. for w. and e.
Features: Stainless steel standard size nipples, chrome-moly steel cylinder and frame, same lockwork as in Super Blackhawk. Made in USA. From Sturm, Ruger & Co.
Price: Blued **$115.00**

LYMAN 44 NEW MODEL ARMY REVOLVER
Caliber: 44, 6-shot.
Barrel: 7¾".
Weight: 42 oz. **Length:** 13½" over-all.
Stock: Walnut.
Sights: Fixed.
Features: Replica of 1858 Remington. Brass trigger guard. Solid frame with top strap. Heavy duty nipples. From Lyman Gunsight Corp.
Price: **$96.95**

LYMAN 36 NEW MODEL NAVY PERCUSSION REVOLV-ER
Caliber: 36, 6-shot.
Barrel: 6½".
Weight: 42 oz. **Length:** 12⅜" over-all.
Stock: Walnut.
Sights: Fixed.
Features: Replica of 1860 Remington. Brass trigger guard. Solid frame with top strap. Heavy duty nipples. From Lyman Gunsight Corp.
Price: **$94.95**

BLACK POWDER MUSKETS & RIFLES

FLINTLOCK BLUNDERBUSS
Caliber: 70.
Barrel: 15½".
Weight: 6¼ lbs. **Length:** 30".
Stock: Walnut finish, hand rubbed.
Sights: None.
Features: Brass barrel and fittings, steel lock from Navy; others have steel bbl., brass fittings. Imported by Navy Arms, The Armory, Dixie.
Price: . . . . **$37.95** to **$100.00**

BROWN BESS FLINTLOCK MUSKET
Caliber: 70.
Barrel: 42".
Weight: 10½ lbs. **Length:** 59" over-all.
Stock: Walnut.
Sights: Fixed.
Features: Replica of Revolutionary War period model. Replica bayonet ($12.00) available. Carbine version (30½" bbl., 7¾ lbs.) also available. Can be purchased as kit ($165.00). Imported by Navy Arms.
Price: **$275.00**

KENTUCKY FLINTLOCK RIFLE
Caliber: 44.
Barrel: 35".
Weight: 7 lbs. **Length:** 50" over-all.
Stock: Walnut stained, brass fittings.
Sights: Fixed.
Features: Available in Carbine model also, 28" bbl. Some variations in detail, finish. Kits also available from some importers. Imported by Navy Arms, Centennial, The Armory, Intercontinental, Century, Dixie and Challanger.
Price: . . . . **$72.50** to **$145.00**

BLACK POWDER MUSKETS & RIFLES

KENTUCKY PERCUSSION RIFLE
Similar to above except percussion lock. Finish and features vary with importer. Imported by Jana, Centennial, Navy Arms, Firearms Import & Export, The Armory, Century, Challanger, Dixie, Connecticut Valley, Valor and Replica.
Price: . . . . **$65.00** to **$229.95**

HOPKINS AND ALLEN MINUTEMAN RIFLE
Caliber: 36, 45, single-shot.
Barrel: 39″.
Weight: 9½ lbs. **Length:** 55″ over-all.
Stock: Maple.
Sights: Fixed.
Features: Brass furniture, patch box. Available in either flint or percussion. From High Standard.
Price: Either caliber, either ignition system **$179.95**

PENNSYLVANIA LONG RIFLE
Caliber: 36 or 45
Barrel: 39″ octagonal.
Weight: 10½ lbs. **Length:** 55″ over-all.
Stock: Full-length tiger striped maple, traditional Pennsylvania form.
Sights: Brass blade front, open notch rear.
Features: Solid brass engraved furniture (crescent buttplate, patch box, fore-end cap, etc.) From High Standard.
Price: Flint or percussion form **$179.95**

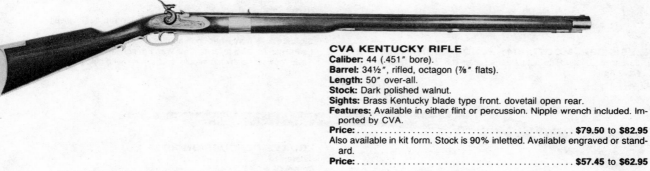

CVA KENTUCKY RIFLE
Caliber: 44 (.451″ bore).
Barrel: 34½″, rifled, octagon (⅞″ flats).
Length: 50″ over-all.
Stock: Dark polished walnut.
Sights: Brass Kentucky blade type front. dovetail open rear.
Features: Available in either flint or percussion. Nipple wrench included. Imported by CVA.
Price: . . . . **$79.50** to **$82.95**
Also available in kit form. Stock is 90% inletted. Available engraved or standard.
Price: . . . . **$57.45** to **$62.95**

KENTUCKIAN RIFLE & CARBINE
Caliber: 44.
Barrel: 35″ (Rifle), 27½″ (Carbine).
Weight: 7 lbs. (Rifle), 5½ lbs. (Carbine). **Length:** 51″ (Rifle) over-all, carbine 43″.
Stock: Walnut stain.
Sights: Brass blade front, steel V-Ramp rear.
Features: Octagon bbl., case-hardened and engraved lock plate. Brass furniture. Imported by Intercontinental Arms.
Price: Rifle (illus.) or carbine, flint or percussion **$135.00**

BERDAN PERCUSSION RIFLE
Caliber: 45.
Barrel: 25″.
Weight: 8 lbs.
Stock: Walnut, brass fittings.
Sights: Fixed front, rear adj. for e.
Features: Double set trigger. Replica of Wesson rifle. Imported by Replica Arms.
Price: **$99.95**

REVOLVING PERCUSSION CARBINE
Caliber: 44, 6-shot.
Barrel: 18″, 20″.
Weight: 5 lbs. **Length:** 38″ over-all.
Stock: Walnut, brass butt plate.
Sights: Blade front adj. for w., buckhorn rear adj. for e.
Features: Action based on 1858 Remington revolver. Brass trigger guard. Imported by Navy Arms.
Price: **$130.00**

BLACK POWDER MUSKETS & RIFLES

ENFIELD PATTERN 1858 NAVAL RIFLE
Caliber: .577".
Barrel: 33".
Weight: 8½ lbs. **Length:** 48½" over-all.
Stock: European walnut.
Sights: Blade front, step adj. rear.
Features: Two-band Enfield percussion rifle with heavy barrel. 5-groove progressive depth rifling, solid brass furniture. All parts made exactly to original patterns. Imported from England by Jana.
Price: **$199.95**

ENFIELD MODEL 1861 PERCUSSION CARBINE
Caliber: 577.
Barrel: 24".
Weight: 7½ lbs. **Length:** 40¼" over-all.
Stock: Walnut.
Sights: Fixed front, adj. rear.
Features: Percussion muzzle loader, made to original 1861 English patterns. Imported from England by Jana.
Price: **$199.95**

MISSISSIPPI MODEL 1841 PERCUSSION RIFLE
Similar to Zouave Rifle but patterned after U.S. Model 1841. Imported by Navy Arms.
Price: **$125.00**

H & R SPRINGFIELD STALKER
Caliber: 45 or 58.
Barrel: 28" round.
Weight: 8 lbs. (45 cal.), 7½ lbs. (58 cal.). **length:** 43" over-all.
Stock: American walnut.
Sights: Blade front, rear open adj. for w. and e.
Features: Action similar to Civil War Springfield. Supplied with solid brass ramrod with hardwood handle, spare nipple and nipple wrench. Blue-black finish.
Price: **$150.00**

CVA ZOUAVE RIFLE KIT
Caliber: 58.
Barrel: 33¼", rifled.
Weight: About 9½ lbs. **Length:** 49" over-all.
Stock: Walnut.
Sights: Fixed front, rear adj. for e.
Features: Cold forged rifled bbl., authentic lock, solid brass hardware. Imported by CVA.
Price: **$89.95**

ZOUAVE PERCUSSION RIFLE
Caliber: 58.
Barrel: 32½".
Weight: 9½ lbs. **Length:** 48½" over-all.
Stock: Walnut finish, brass patch box and butt plate.
Sights: Fixed front, rear adj. for e.
Features: Also available from Navy Arms as carbine, with 22" bbl. Extra 20 ga. shotgun bbl. $45.00. Imported by Navy Arms, Centennial, The Armory, Gold Rush, Lyman.
Price: .... **$88.95 to $145.00**

DICKSON BUFFALO HUNTER RIFLE/SHOTGUN
Similar to standard Buffalo Hunter except: over-all length 42", no checkering, 26" bbl. Comes with extra 20ga. shotgun barrel. Imported by American Import.
Price: **$199.00**

BUFFALO HUNTER PERCUSSION RIFLE
Caliber: 58.
Barrel: 25½".
Weight: 8 lbs. **Length:** 41½" over-all.
Stock: Walnut finished, hand checkered, brass furniture.
Sights: Fixed.
Features: Designed for primitive weapons hunting. 20 ga. shotgun bbl. also available ($45.00). Imported by Navy Arms.
Price: **$125.00**

HAWKEN HURRICANE
Caliber: 45 or 50.
Barrel: 28", octagon.
Weight: 6 lbs. **Length:** 44¾" over-all.
Stock: American walnut.
Sights: Blade front, open fixed rear.
Features: American made. Curved buttplate, brass stock furniture. From Navy Arms.
Price: **$175.00**
Price: Hawken Hunter (58 cal.) **$175.00**

BLACK POWDER MUSKETS & RIFLES

MOWREY HAWK
Caliber: 45, 50 54 or 58.
Barrel: 32″.
Weight: 9½ lbs. **Length:** 49″ over-all.
Stock: Walnut, sporter-type with cheek-piece, walnut fore-end.
Sights: Open, fully adj. for w. and e.
Features: Hawkins-type buttplate and action housing of brass. Adj. trigger. Also available in kit form.
Price: Complete .... $174.50   Kit $118.47

MOWREY HAWKINS FULLSTOCK
Caliber: 45, 50, 54, 58.
Barrel: 27½″.
Weight: 8¼ lbs. **Length:** 45″ over-all.
Stock: Select maple. Hand rubbed oil finish, brass furniture.
Sights: Blade front, step adj. rear.
Features: Hawkins replica, fullstock design. Double set triggers. Also available in kit form.
Price: Percussion .... $285.00   Flint $295.00

MOWREY HAWKINS HALFSTOCK REPLICA
Caliber: 45, 50, 54 or 58.
Barrel: 27½″.
Weight: 11 lbs. **Length:** 50″ over-all.
Stock: Select maple with brass furniture. Hand rubbed oil finish.
Sights: Open, fully adj. for w. & e.
Features: Available in flint or percussion. Double set trigger. Built in limited quantities.
Price: Percussion .... $250.00   Kit $159.50
Price: Flint .... $260.00   Kit $165.00

MOWREY ALLEN & THURBER SPECIAL
Caliber: 45, 50, 54 or 58.
Barrel: 32″ octagonal.
Weight: 10 lbs. **Length:** 48″ over-all.
Stock: Walnut with curved brass buttplate, walnut fore-end.
Sights: Open, fully adj.
Features: Same design as A&T Replica except has walnut fore-end. Polished brass furniture. Also available in kit form.
Price: Complete .... $164.50   Kit $115.27

MOWREY "TEXAS CARBINE"
Caliber: 58, takes .575″ mini-ball or round ball.
Barrel: 24″ octagon, 4-groove.
Weight: 8 lbs. **Length:** 39″ over-all.
Stock: Dark maple (walnut optional).
Sights: Adjustable front and rear.
Features: "1 of 100" inscribed on first 100, "1 of 1000" on remaining 1000. Saddle ring with leather thong and Texas seal imbedded in stock. Distributed by Trail Guns Armory.
Price: $179.50

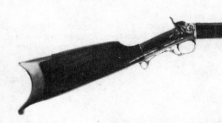

MOWREY ALLEN & THURBER REPLICA
Caliber: 45, 50, 54 or 58.
Barrel: 32″, 8-groove rifling, octagon.
Weight: 10¼ lbs. **Length:** 48″ over-all.
Stock: Walnut with curved brass butt plate.
Sights: Open, adj. for w. & e.
Features: Polished brass furniture, brass fore-end, ramrod. Also available in kit form.
Price: Complete .... $159.50   Kit $108.67

THOMPSON/CENTER HAWKEN RIFLE
Caliber: 45 or 50.
Barrel: 28″ octagon, hooked breech.
Stock: American walnut.
Sights: Blade front, rear adj. for w. & e.
Features: Solid brass furniture, double set triggers, button rifled barrel, coil-type main spring. From Thompson/Center Arms.
Price: Percussion Model .. $175.00   Flintlock Model $190.00

THOMPSON/CENTER SENECA RIFLE
Caliber: 36, 45.
Barrel: 28″.
Weight: 6½ lbs.
Stock: American walnut.
Sights: Post front semi-globe, open square notch rear fully adj. for w. and e.
Features: Coil spring lock, octagon bbl. measures $^{13}/_{16}$″ across flats, brass stock furniture.
Price: Rifle $175.00
Price: Rifle with accessory kit (includes Ohaus mould, patches, powder measure, short starter, Bucheimer's Black Powder Solvent) $195.50

BLACK POWDER MUSKETS & RIFLES

NAVY 1861 SPRINGFIELD RIFLE
Caliber: 58.
Barrel: 40", rifled.
Weight: 8½ lbs. **Length:** 54¾" over-all.
Stock: American walnut.
Sights: Blade front, open step adj. rear.
Features: Full-size three-band musket reproduction. Imported by Navy Arms.
Price: **$175.00**

LYMAN PLAINS RIFLE
Caliber: 45.
Barrel: 28".
Weight: 8¾ lbs. **Length:** 45" over-all.
Stock: European walnut.
Sights: Blade front, fully adj. rear.
Features: Double set trigger, hooked breech system, brass stock furniture, patch box. Imported from Italy by Lyman.
Price: Rifle only **$175.00**
Price: Rifle and kit (includes single cavity round ball mould, handles, nipple wrench, ball starter, Hodgdon's "Spit Patch", patches, Lyman manual **$193.50**

RICHLAND YORKSHIRE RIFLE
Caliber: 45.
Barrel: 36", rifled, ⅞ octagon.
Weight: 7½ lbs. **Length:** 51¾" over-all.
Stock: Select maple.
Sights: Blade front, open U-notch rear.
Features: Adj. double set triggers. Brass front and rear sights, trigger guard, patch box, buttplate and fore-end. Case hardened lock plate.
Price: **$129.50**

H & R HUNTSMAN PERCUSSION RIFLE
Caliber: 45, 58, 12 gauge, single shot.
Barrel: 28".
Weight: 6¼ lbs. (12 ga.), 7¼ lbs. (58 cal.), 8 lbs. (45 cal.). **Length:** 43".
Stock: Walnut finished hardwood.
Sights: Open, rear adj. for w. and e., blade front.
Features: Action similar to Model 158 Topper. Enclosed nipple (#11 size). Supplied with rifle are brass ramrod with wood handle, spare nipple and nipple wrench. Blue-black finish with color case hardened frame. From Harrington & Richardson.
Price: **$59.95**

MORSE/NAVY RIFLE
Caliber: 45, 50 or 58.
Barrel: 26".
Weight: 6 lbs. (45 cal.). **Length:** 41½" over-all.
Stock: American walnut, full p.g.
Sights: Blade front, open fixed rear.
Features: Brass action, trigger guard, ramrod pipes. From Navy Arms.
Price: **$80.00**
Price: 45 or 50 caliber, straight stock **$80.00**

ESOPUS TB-1 O/U PERCUSSION RIFLE
Caliber: 45, 2-shot.
Barrels: 28".
Weight: 8½ lbs. **Length:** 44½" over-all.
Stock: Black walnut stock and fore-end, brass fittings.
Sights: Brass blade front, open rear.
Features: Percussion turn-barrel design with one lock, trigger and hammer. From Esopus Gun Works.
Price: **$139.95**

BLACK POWDER MUSKETS & RIFLES

CHALLENGER GOLDEN EAGLE PERCUSSION RIFLE
Caliber: 36, 45 or 58.
Barrel: 32" octagonal (also 20" carbine 45-cal.)
Weight: 9 lbs. **Length:** 49" over-all.
Stock: Oil finished walnut, half-stock fore-end.
Sights: Brass blade front, both notch open and aperture rear sights.
Features: Under hammer design, solid brass furniture, (buttplate, engraved patch box, fore-end tip, etc.)
Price: **$109.95**

ROCKY MOUNTAIN ARMS BREECH LOADING PER-CUSSION RIFLE
Caliber: 22, 36, 44, single-shot.
Barrel: 20", 22½", 28".
Weight: 3 lbs., 5¼ lbs., 6½ lbs. **Length:** 35¼", 39½", 46".
Stock: Walnut or Ash.
Sights: Blade front, open rear adj. for e.
Features: Percussion. Breech-turret loading action, half-cock safety. From Rocky Mountain Arms.
Price: 22 cal. with wood stock **$49.50**
Price: With polyurethane stock **$37.50**
Price: 36 or 44 cals. **$99.50**

HOPKINS AND ALLEN OFFHAND DELUXE RIFLE
Same as Deer Stalker except: 36 or 45 cal., weight 8½ lbs.
Price: Either caliber **$87.95**

HOPKINS AND ALLEN HERITAGE MODEL
Same as Deer Stalker except: 36 or 45 cal.; weight 8½ lbs.; hooded front sight with ring aperture, "Kentucky" open notched rear and H&A aperture target tang rear sights; brass crescent-shaped buttplate, cap box and trigger guard extension.
Price: Either caliber **$99.50**

HOPKINS AND ALLEN DEER STALKER RIFLE
Caliber: 58 (.575").
Barrel: 32".
Weight: About 9½ lbs. **Length:** 49" over-all.
Stock: Walnut stock and fore-end.
Sights: Hooded front, open notch rear.
Features: Under-hammer action. Blue finish. From High Standard.
Price: **$87.95**

HOPKINS AND ALLEN DELUXE BUGGY RIFLE
Same as Deer Stalker Model except: 20" bbl.; 36 or 45 cal.; weight about 6½ lbs; over-all length 37"; fully adj. notch rear sight.
Price: Either caliber **$84.95**

HOPKINS AND ALLEN 45 TARGET RIFLE
Same as Deer Stalker except: 45 cal., weight about 9½ lbs., long-range 3-aperture tang rear sight, no fore-end or ram rod ferrules. Barrel flats measure 1⅛" **$84.95**

HOPKINS AND ALLEN TURNBARREL O/U RIFLE
Caliber: 45, 2-shot.
Barrels: 28".
Weight: About 8½ lbs. **Length:** 43" over-all.
Stock: Walnut.
Sights: Blade front, open notch fixed rear.
Features: Rotating barrels shoot to same point. Crescent buttplate. From High Standard.
Price: **$139.95**

TINGLE M1962 MUZZLE LOADING RIFLE
Caliber: 36 or 44
Barrel: 32" octagon, hook breech, 52" twist.
Weight: 10 lbs. **Length:** 48" over-all.
Stock: One-piece walnut with concave cheekpiece.
Sights: Blade front, step adj. V-notch rear.
Features: Solid brass furniture, double-set trigger with adj. pull, percussion lock.
Price: **$139.95**

BUGGY RIFLE CASED SET
Caliber: 45.
Barrel: 16".
Stock: Detachable butt stock with brass furniture.
Sights: Tube sight with interchangeable apertures. Not a telescope.
Features: Cased set contains false muzzle, concentric bullet starter, ramrod, cleaning equipment, bullet mould and swage, powder flask and measure, funnel, nipple wrench, oil bottle, bullet and patch block. Rifle has brass frame and p.g. cap, blued octagon bbl. Imported by Intercontinental Arms.
Price: Cased set complete **$500.00**

The product prices mentioned in these catalog pages were correct at presstime, but may be higher when you read this.

BLACK POWDER SHOTGUNS

MOWREY 12 GAUGE SHOTGUN
Gauge: 12 ga. only.
Barrel: 32", half octagon, half round.
Weight: 7½ lbs. **Length:** 48" over-all.
Stock: Maple, oil finish, brass furniture.
Sights: Bead front.
Features: Available in percussion only. Uses standard 12 ga. wadding. Also available in kit form.
Price: Complete .... $149.50   Kit $102.07

DOUBLE BARREL PERCUSSION SHOTGUN
Gauge: 12.
Barrel: 30" (I.C.& Mod.).
Weight: 6¼ lbs. **Length:** 45" over-all.
Stock: Hand checkered walnut, 14" pull.
Features: Double triggers, light hand engraving. Details vary with importer. Imported by Navy Arms, The Armory, Century, Dixie, and Replica.
Price: .... $125.00 to $134.95

FRONTIER PERCUSSION SHOTGUN
Gauge: 12 ga.
Barrels: 30". (Mod. & Imp. Cyl.). Patent breech with threaded breech plugs.
Length: 46½" over-all.
Stock: Walnut. Length of pull 14".
Features: Patent breech for easy cleaning & disassembly. Front bead sight. Engraving on hardware. Brass patch box. Imported by CVA.
Price: $99.95

SINGLE BARREL FLINTLOCK SHOTGUN
Gauge: 28.
Barrel: 28".
Weight: 4½ lbs. **Length:** 43" over-all.
Stock: Walnut finish, choice of half or full stock. Imported by The Armory.
Price: $37.95

TINGLE PERCUSSION SINGLE BARREL SHOTGUN
Gauge: 12 only.
Barrel: 30" straight bored, no choke.
Weight: 5 lbs.
Stock: Lacquered walnut.
Features: Mule ear side hammer lock, iron trigger guard, rubber recoil pad.
Price: Blued $99.75

MORSE/NAVY SINGLE BARREL SHOTGUN
Gauge: 12 ga.
Barrel: 26".
Weight: 5 lbs. **Length:** 41½" over-all.
Stock: American walnut, full p.g.
Sights: Front bead.
Features: Brass receiver, black buttplate. From Navy Arms.
Price: $80.00

SINGLE BARREL PERCUSSION SHOTGUN
Gauge: 12, 20, 28.
Barrel: 28".
Weight: 4½ lbs. **Length:** 43" over-all.
Stock: Walnut finish, choice of half or full stock.
Features: Finish and features vary with importer. Imported by Navy Arms, The Armory, Century, Dixie.
Price: .... $32.95 to $65.00

PELLET GUNS—HANDGUNS

Guns in this section are powered by: A) disposable CO_2 cylinders, B) hand-pumped compressed air released by trigger action, C) air compressed by a spring-powered piston released by trigger action. Calibers are generally 177 (BB or pellet) and 22 (ball or pellet); a few guns are made in 20 or 25 caliber. Pellet guns are usually rifled, those made for BB's only are smoothbore.

AMPELL CO_2 PISTOL KIT
Caliber: BB, 177 or 22. (BB only has 80-shot mag., others single shot.)
Barrel: 8½", rifled.
Length: 11¾". **Weight:** 36 oz.
Sights: Sq. notch rear adj. for w. and e., blade front.
Power: Standard CO_2 cylinder.
Features: Up to 365 f.p.s. M.V.; 2-lb. trigger pull. Kit includes pistol, 250 pellets, Ampow'r CO_2. BB kit includes pistol, 1200 BB's and Ampow'r CO_2.
Price: **$26.50**

BENJAMIN 422 SEMI-AUTOMATIC PISTOL
Caliber: 22, 10-shot.
Barrel: 5⁹/₁₆", rifled bronze liner.
Length: 9" **Weight:** 2 lbs.
Power: Standard CO_2 cylinder. Muzzle velocity about 400 fps.
Features: Trigger and hammer safeties, checkered plastic thumbrest grips, adj. rear sight, blade front.
Price: Blued **$28.20**

BENJAMIN SUPER S. S. TARGET PISTOL SERIES 130
Caliber: BB, 22 and 177; single shot.
Barrel: 8 inches; BB smoothbore; 22 and 177, rifled.
Length: 11". **Weight:** 2 lbs.
Power: Hand pumped.
Features: Bolt action; fingertip safety; adj. power.
Price: M130, BB **$37.90**
Price: M132, 22 .... **$37.90** M137, 177 .... **$37.90**

CROSMAN MODEL "1300" MEDALIST II
Caliber: 22, single shot.
Barrel: 8", button rifled.
Length: 11¾". **Weight:** 37 oz.
Power: Hand pumped.
Features: Moulded plastic grip, hand size pump forearm. Cross bolt safety, self-cocking.
Price: **$31.95**

CROSMAN 454 BB PISTOL
Caliber: BB, 16-shot.
Length: 11" over-all. **Weight:** 30 oz.
Stocks: Contoured with thumb-rest.
Sights: Patridge-type front, fully adj. rear.
Power: Crosman CO_2 Powerlet
Features: Gives about 80 shots per Powerlet, slide-action safety, steel barrel, die-cast receiver.
Price: **$24.00**

CROSMAN PEACEMAKER "44"
Caliber: 22, 6 shot.
Barrel: 4¾", button rifled.
Length: 10⅜". **Weight:** 34 oz.
Power: Crosman CO_2 Powerlet
Features: Revolving cylinder, walnut finished grips. Simulated gold hammer and trigger, positive valve design. Single-action.
Price: **$27.50**

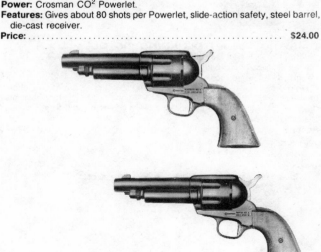

CROSMAN FRONTIER "36"
Caliber: BB, 18-shot.
Barrel: 4¾", smoothbore.
Length: 10⅜". **Weight:** 34 oz.
Power: Crosman CO_2 Powerlet
Features: Single-action, steel barrel, revolving cylinder. Walnut finish grips.
Price: **$27.50**

PELLET GUNS—HANDGUNS

CROSMAN MARK I TARGET PISTOL
Caliber: 22, single shot.
Barrel: 7¼", button rifled.
Length: 11". **Weight:** 42 oz.
Power: Crosman Powerlet CO_2 cylinder.
Features: New system provides same shot-to-shot velocity, adj. from 300- to 400 fps. Checkered thumbrest grips, right or left. Patridge front sight, rear adj. for w. & e. Adj. trigger.
Price: 22 or 177 .... **$29.95**

CROSMAN MARK II TARGET PISTOL
Same as Mark I except 177 cal. **$29.95**

CROSMAN 38 TARGET REVOLVER M9
Caliber: 22, 6-shot.
Barrel: 6", rifled.
Length: 11 inches. **Weight:** 43 oz.
Power: CO_2 Powerlet cylinder.
Features: Double action, revolving cylinder. Adj. rear sight.
Price: **$37.95**

CROSMAN 38 COMBAT REVOLVER
Same as 38 Target except 3½" bbl., 38 oz. **$37.95**

DAISY 179 SIX GUN
Caliber: BB, 12-shot.
Barrel: Steel lined, smoothbore.
Length: 11½". **Weight:** NA
Power: Spring.
Features: Forced feed from under-barrel magazine. Single action, molded wood grained grips.
Price: **$10.50**

DAISY 5679 TEXAS RANGER COMMEMORATIVE PISTOLS
Caliber: BB, 12-shot.
Barrel: Steel. Inscribed with "1823-The Texas Rangers-1973".
Length: 11½" over-all. **Weight:** 2½ lbs.
Stock: Wood grained, moulded grips, mounted with Texas Ranger commemorative seal miniature and on the reverse a miniature of the Ranger badge.
Features: Matched set. "Spittin' image" of the Western Peacemaker. Exclusive case-hardened plating on receiver. Comes with 48-page history of the Texas Rangers.
Price: Per pair **$27.50**

DAISY 177 BB PISTOL
Caliber: BB, 150-shot.
Barrel: Formed steel, smoothbore.
Length: 11¼". **Weight:** NA.
Power: Spring.
Features: Gravity feed, adjustable rear sight, moulded plastic thumbrest grips.
Price: **$10.50**

DAISY CO_2 200 AUTOLOADING PISTOL
Caliber: BB, 175-shot semi-auto.
Barrel: 7½", steel-lined, smoothbore.
Length: 11⅞", sight radius 9". **Weight:** 24 oz.
Power: Daisy CO_2 cylinders, 8½ grams (100 shots) or 12 grams (160 shots).
Features: 175-shot magazine; constant full power valve system eliminates gas leakage; checkered thumbrest stocks; undercut ramp front sight and adjustable rear.
Price: **$28.00**

DAISY/FWB 65 TARGET PISTOL
Caliber: 177, single shot.
Barrel: 7½", rifled, fixed to receiver.
Length: 15½". **Weight:** 42 oz.
Power: Spring, cocked by left-side lever.
Features: Recoiless operation, may be set to give recoil; Micro. rear sight, 14" radius. Adj. trigger; normal 17.6 oz. pull can be raised to 48 oz. for training. Checkered, thumbrest target grips. Air Rifle Hdqtrs. or Daisy, importer.
Price: **$230.00**

FEINWERKBAU F-65 AIR PISTOL
Caliber: 177.
Barrel: 7½″.
Length: 14¾″ over-all. **Weight:** 42 oz.
Power: Spring, sidelever cocking.
Stock: Walnut, stippled thumb-rest.
Sights: Front, interchangeable post element system, open rear, click adj. for w. & e. and for sighting notch width.
Features: 2-stage trigger, 4 adjustments. Programs instantly for recoil or recoiless operation. Permanently lubricated. Special switch converts trigger from 17.6 oz. pull to 42 oz. let-off. Imported by Air Rifle Hdq.
Price: **$178.50**

FEINWERKBAU MODEL 65 INTERNATIONAL MATCH PISTOL
Same as FWB 65 pistol except: new adj. wood grips to meet international regulations, optional 3 oz. barrel sleeve weight. Available from A.R.H., Beeman's.
Price: .... To be announced.

HAMMERLI MODEL 454 "MASTER" CO_2 TARGET
Caliber: .177 waisted pellets.
Barrel: 6.7″, 12-groove.
Length: 16″. **Weight:** 38 oz.
Stocks: Plastic with thumbrest and checkering.
Sights: Ramp front, micro rear, click adj.
Features: Single shot, manual loading. Residual gas vented automatically. 4-way adj. trigger. Imported by HY-SCORE, H. Grieder.
Price: Approx. **$69.00**

HAMMERLI MODEL 452 "SINGLE" CO_2 TARGET PISTOL
Caliber: .177 waisted pellets.
Barrel: 4.5″, 12-groove.
Length: 12″. **Weight:** 35.3 oz.
Stocks: Plastic with thumb rest and checkering.
Sights: Ramp front, micro-click rear. Adj. sight radius from 11.5″ to 13.5″ V-notch or square notch.
Features: Single shot, easy manual loading, 4-way adj. trigger. Imported by HY-SCORE, H. Grieder.
Price: Approx. **$54.00**

HEALTHWAYS SHARPSHOOTER
Caliber: BB, 50-shot.
Barrel: 6¼″.
Weight: 28 oz.
Power: Spring (barrel cocking).
Features: Easy cocking action. Loading pocket speeds and simplifies loading. Spring mechanism housed in grip.
Price: **$14.00**

HEALTHWAYS ML 175 CO_2 AUTOMATIC PISTOL
Caliber: BB, 100-shot repeater.
Barrel: 5¾″, smooth.
Length: 9½″. **Weight:** 28 oz.
Power: Standard CO_2 cylinder.
Features: 3 position power switch. Auto. ammunition feed. Positive safety.
Price: **$21.00**

HY-SCORE 816 M TARGET PISTOL
Caliber: 177, single shot.
Barrel: 7″ precision rifled.
Length: 16″. **Weight:** 50 oz.
Power: Spring, bbl. cocking.
Features: Recoil-less firing, adj. trigger. Hooded front sight with 3 apertures, click adj. rear with 4 apertures. Plastic thumbrest target grips.
Price: In plastic case **$49.95**

HY-SCORE 814 JUNIOR PISTOL
Caliber: 177 darts, BBs, single shot.
Barrel: Smoothbore.
Length: About 10″. **Weight:** NA.
Power: Spring, compressed by screwing in breech plug.
Features: Checkered wooden grips.
Price: Blued $5.95

HY-SCORE 815 TARGET PISTOL
Same as Hy-Score M816 except: without recoil-less system; is slightly shorter and lighter; has fixed aperture front sight. In plastic case. Also in 22 cal. **$29.95**

PELLET GUNS—HANDGUNS

MARKSMAN REPEATER PISTOL
Caliber: 177, 20-shot repeater.
Barrel: 2½", smoothbore.
Length: 8¼". **Weight:** 24 oz.
Power: Spring.
Features: Thumb safety. Uses BBs, darts or pellets. Repeats with BBs only.
Price: Black finish **$11.95**
    Also available in either antique gold or silver finish with moulded plastic
    display box **$15.95**

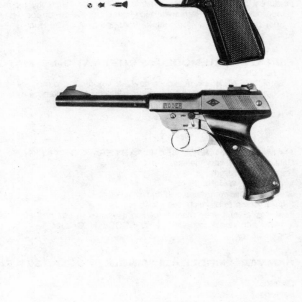

ROGER CO² BB PISTOL
Caliber: BB, 100-shot.
Barrel: 6", smooth.
Length: 10½" over-all.
Power: Standard CO_2 cartridge.
Features: Semi-automatic. Checkered plastic thumbrest target grips. Precise
Imports, importer.
Price: **$21.95**

TEX 086 AIR PISTOL
Caliber: 177, single-shot.
Barrel: 7¼".
Length: 13½" over-all. **Weight:** 2¾ lbs.
Power: Spring, barrel cocking.
Features: Plastic checkered thumbrest target grips. Precise Imports.
Price: **$30.00**

SMITH & WESSON MODELS 78G & 79G
Caliber: 22 cal. pellet (78G), 177 cal. pellet (79G), single-shot.
Barrel: 8½", rifled steel.
Weight: 42 oz.
Power: 12.5 gram CO_2 cartridge.
Stocks: Simulated walnut, checkered. Thumb rest. Left or right hand.
Sights: Patridge front, fully adj. rear with micro. click windage adjustment.
Features: Pull-bolt action, crossbolt safety, double sear trigger with adj. en-
gagement. High-low power adjustment. Gun blue finish.
Price: **$35.00**

WALTHER MODEL LP-3
Caliber: 177, single shot.
Barrel: 9½", rifled.
Length: 13³/₁₆". **Weight:** 45½ oz.
Power: Spring-air, lever cocking.
Features: Recoil-less operation, cocking in grip frame. Micro-click rear sight,
adj. for w. & e., 4-way adj. trigger. Plastic thumbrest grips; wood grip at extra
cost. Interarms, Air Rifle HQ, Beeman's.
Price: **$109.00**

WALTHER MODEL LP-3 MATCH PISTOL
    Same specifications as LP-3 except for grips and weight. Has adjustable
walnut grips to meet international shooting regulations. Available from Beeman's, Interarms.
Price: . . . . To be announced.

WALTHER MODEL 53 PISTOL

Caliber: 177, single shot.
Barrel: 9⅜", rifled.
Length: 12¼" over-all. **Weight:** 42 oz.
Power: Spring.
Features: Micrometer rear sight. Interchangeable rear sight blades. Adj. trigger. Target grips. Bbl. weight available at extra cost. Interarms, Alexandria, Va.
Price: **$59.00**

WEBLEY AIR PISTOLS

Model:	Junior	Premier
Caliber:	177	177 or 22
Barrel:	6⅛"	6½"
Weight:	24 oz.	37 oz.
Power:	Spring, barrel cocking	Same
Sights:	Adj. for elev.	Adj. for w.&e.
Trigger:	Fixed	Adj.
Price:	**$44.50**	**$49.95**

Features: Single stroke cocking, heavy steel construction, blued. From Harrington & Richardson, A.R.H., Beeman's.

WEIHRAUCH HW-70 AIR PISTOL

Caliber: 177, single shot.
Barrel: 6¼", rifled.
Length: 12¾" over-all. **Weight:** 38 oz.
Sights: Hooded post front, square notch rear adj. for w. and e.
Power: Spring, barrel cocking.
Features: Adj. trigger. 24-lb. cocking effort, 365 f.p.s. M.V.; automatic safety. Air Rifle HQ, importer.
Price: **$44.50**

WINCHESTER 363 TARGET PISTOL

Caliber: 177, single shot.
Barrel: 7" rifled.
Length: 16". **Weight:** 3 lbs.
Power: Spring, barrel cocking.
Features: Recoil-less firing, adj. double pull type trigger, hooded front sight with 3 apertures, click adj. rear sight. Plastic thumbrest target grips. M.V. 378 fps.
Price: **$63.95**

WINCHESTER 353 TARGET PISTOL

Caliber: 177 or 22, single shot.
Barrel: 7" rifled.
Length: 16". **Weight:** 2 lbs. 11 oz.
Power: Spring, barrel cocking.
Features: Plastic thumbrest target grips. Adj. double pull trigger, Micro rear sight, detachable bead front with hood. M.V. 378 fps.
Price: **$41.95**

WISCHO CUSTOM MATCH PISTOL

Caliber: 177, single shot.
Barrel: 7" rifled.
Length: 15¾" over-all. **Weight:** 44 oz.
Sights: Bead front, rear adj. for w. and e.
Power: Spring, barrel cocking.
Features: Cocking effort of 17 lbs.; M.V. 472 f.p.s.; adj. trigger. Air Rifle HQ, importer.
Price: **$59.95**

> **The product prices mentioned in these catalog pages were correct at presstime, but may be higher when you read this.**

PELLET GUNS—LONG GUNS

AMPELL BB MAGNUM RIFLE
Caliber: BB, 48-shot magazine.
Length: 38" over-all. **Weight:** 4¼ lbs.
Sights: Blade front, rear square notch adj. for w. and e.
Power: Pump cocking spring.
Features: Hardwood stock, cross-bolt safety, 4-5 lb. trigger pull.
Price: **$26.50**

ANSCHUTZ 250 TARGET RIFLE
Caliber: 177, single shot.
Barrel: 18½", rifled, one piece with receiver.
Length: 45". **Weight:** 11 lbs. with sights.
Power: Spring, side-lever cocking, 17 lb. pull.
Features: Recoil-less operation. Two-stage adj. trigger. Checkered walnut
   p.g. stock with Monte Carlo comb & cheekpiece; adj. buttplate; accessory
   rail. Air Rifle Hdqtrs., Beeman's.
Price: Without sights **$179.50**
   With #6723 match sight set **$204.50**

ANSCHUTZ 335 RIFLE
Caliber: 177, single-shot.
Barrel: 18½", 12-groove, rifled.
Length: 43" over-all. **Weight:** 7 lbs.
Power: Spring, barrel-cocking.
Stock: Checkered M.C. Stock with cheekpiece and white line spacer butt-
   plate.
Sights: Tunnel front with blade, open rear adj. for w. & e.
Features: Special safety latch to prevent barrel backlash when breech is
   open. Available from Beeman's, A.R.H.
Price: With open sight **$59.95**
Price: With #6706 match aperture sight **$84.95**

BSA METEOR SUPER
Caliber: 177 or 22, single-shot.
Barrel: 18½", rifled.
Length: 42". **Weight:** 6 lbs.
Power: Spring, bbl. cocking.
Features: Beechwood Monte Carlo stock, recoil pad. Adjustable single-stage
   trigger. Bead front, adjustable rear sight. Positive relocation of barrel for
   same zero shot to shot. Galef, importer.
Price: **$41.95**

BENJAMIN 3030 CO² REPEATER
Caliber: BB only.
Barrel: 25½", smoothbore, takedown.
Length: 36". **Weight:** 4 lbs.
Power: Standard CO² cylinder.
Features: Bolt action. 30-shot repeater with permanent-magnet, shot-holder
   ammo feed.
Price: **$26.15**

BENJAMIN SERIES 3100 SUPER REPEATER RIFLES
Caliber: BB, 100-shot; 22, 85-shot.
Barrel: 23", rifled or smoothbore.
Length: 35". **Weight:** 6¼ lbs.
Power: Hand pumped.
Features: Bolt action. Piggy back full view magazine. Bar V adj. rear sight.
   Walnut p.g. stock with monte carlo.
Price: M3100, BB .... **$45.00** M3120, 22 rifled **$45.00**

BENJAMIN SERIES 340 AIR RIFLE
Caliber: 22 and 177 pellets or BB; single shot.
Barrel: 23", rifled and smoothbore.
Length: 35". **Weight:** 6 lbs.
Power: Hand pumped.
Features: Bolt action, walnut Monte Carlo stock and pump handle. Ramp-type
   front sight, adj. leaf type rear. Push-pull safety.
Price: M340, BB **$43.95**
Price: M342, 22 .... **$43.95** M347, 177 .... **$43.95**

SCOPES & MOUNTS

Hunting, Target and Varmint Scopes—Continued

Maker and Model	Magn.	Field at 100 Yds. (feet)	Relative Brightness	Eye Relief (in.)	Length (in.)	Tube Diam. (in.)	W&E Adjustments	Weight (ozs.)	Other Data	Price
Redfield										
Westerner 4x	4	24½	27	3½	9½	.75	Int.	6	Constantly centered reticles; scratchproof TufCoat finish; W. & E. dials adjustable to zero; weatherproof sealed. Reticle same size at all powers. Add $10 for Accu-Range, $10 for dot (not avail. in Sportster). 12X has separate parallax adj. knob, ¼ clicks.	29.95
Frontier 4x	4	28½	46	3½	11⅜	1	Int.	9¾		53.50
Widefield 2¾	2¾	55½	49	3	10½	1	Int.	8		64.95
Widefield 4	4	37½	46	3	11½	1	Int.	10		74.95
Widefield 6	6	25	44	3	13½	1	Int.	11½		84.95
12X	12	10	13.7	3-3¾	14⅞	1	Int.	13.5		119.95
Frontier 2-7x	2-7	42-14	216-22	3½	11¼	1	Int.	12		77.25
Widefield	1¾-5	70-27	100-16	3-3¾	10¾	1	Int.	11½	Mounts solidly. Fine CH, Med. CH, ¼" dot.	95.95
Widefield	2-7	49-19	121-25	3½	11¾	1	Int.	13		105.95
Widefield	3-9	39-15	144-20	3½	12½	1	Int.	14		115.95
Variable	4-12	27½-9	100-22	3-3¾	13⅞	1	Int.	14		129.95
Variable	6-18	16-5½	44.5	3½	14	1	Int.	18		139.95
3200 Target	12, 16, 20, 24,	6½, 5¼, 4, 3¾	9, 6, 3¼, 2¼	2½	23¼	1	Int.	21		169.95
Sanders										
Bisley 2½x20	2½	42	64	3	10¾	1	Int.	8¼	Alum. alloy tubes, ¼" adj., coated lenses. Two other scopes are also offered: a 3-9x at $56.50, and a 6x45 at $42. Rubber lens covers (clear plastic) are $2.50. Choice of reticles in CH, PCH, 3-post.	32.50
Bisley 4x33	4	28	64	3	12	1	Int.	9		36.50
Bisley 6x40	6	19	45	3	12½	1	Int.	9½		38.50
Bisley 8x40	8	18	25	3¼	12½	1	Int.	9½		40.50
Bisley 10x40	10	12½	16	2½	12½	1	Int.	10¼		42.50
Bisley 5-13x40	5-13	29-10	64-9	3	14	1	Int.	14		58.50
Sears										
No. 53801	4	30		2	11½	.75	Int.	6	First three scopes for 22's only, complete with rings for grooved receivers. Crosshair or post and crosshair reticle. Big game scopes come with mount rings. Bases available to fit almost all H.P. rifles. Fixed crosshair reticle remains in center regardless of adjustment. No 53824 for Sears M54.	12.75
No. 53802	4	28		2	11½	.75	Int.	8		8.75
No. 53803	3-6	20-16					Int.	6½		13.50
No. 53824	3	37		3-6	10⅜	1	Int.	8½		34.50
No. 53821	4	30		3¼	11¼	1	Int.	12		39.50
No. 43901	1				8	1	Int.	8½		39.50
Southern Precision										
562	2½	40	144	3½	12	1	Int.	9¼	Centered reticles, CH or post. All elements sealed.	26.50
564	4	30	64	3½	12	1	Int.	9¼		26.50
566	6	21	28	3¼	12	1	Int.	9¼		26.95
Stoeger										
4x	4	30	64	3	12	1	Int.	9	CH only. ½" clicks. Obj. tube diam. 1½" in fixed powers, 1⅞" in variable.	24.95
6x	6	20	28	3	12¾	1	Int.	9		29.95
8x	8	16	25	3	12	1	Int.	13		35.95
3x-9x	3-9	38-11	170-20	3	11½	1	Int.	12¾		46.95
Swift										
Stag	4	28½	64	3	11.7	1	Int.	8.5	Dot, tapered post & CH or Rangefinder reticles available on all but Zoom & Game, $2.50 extra. Rangefinder optional on Zoom & Game. All have self-centering reticles.	28.00
Aerolite	4	28½	64	3	11¾	1	Int.	9½		23.00
Aerolite	2½-8	32-13	164-16	3	13¼	1	Int.	11¼		40.00
Yukon	2½-8	32½-13	164-16	3	13¼	1	Int.	11.3		45.00
Tasco										
Zoom Utility	3-7	28-12	130-24	2¼	12	⅞	Int.	9½	Lens covers furnished. Constantly centered reticles. Write the importer, Tasco, for data on complete line.	19.95
Pistol Scope	1¾	23	216	19	8⅝	⅞	Int.	7½		29.95
Sniper	2-5	58-19	100-16	3¼	11¼	1	Int.	10		49.95
Super Marksman	3-9	35-14	266-29	3.2	12⅜	1	Int.	12½		69.95
Omni-View	3-9	43-16	114-13	3	12½	1	Int.	12¼		99.95
Thompson/Center										
Puma	1½	16	—	11-20	7¾	.87	Int.	5	Handgun scope, with mount for Contender, S&W or Ruger.	39.50
Tops										
4X	4	28½	64	3	11½	1	Int.	9½	Hard-coated lenses, nitrogen filled, shock-proof tested. Write Ed Paul, importer, for data on complete line.	23.95
8X	8	14½	16	3	13	1	Int.	10		29.95
3X-9X	3-9	33-15	175-19	3	12¾	1	Int.	14		39.95

Williams "Wide Guide" scope is offered in 4x only and has a 35 foot field of view. Ocular piece remains round. Comes with crosshair, T.N.T. or guide reticule.

SCOPES & MOUNTS

Hunting, Target and Varmint Scopes—Continued

Maker and Model	Magn.	Field at 100 Yds. (feet)	Relative Bright-ness	Eye Relief (in.)	Length (in.)	Tube Diam. (in.)	W&E Adjust-ments	Weight (ozs.)	Other Data	Price
United										
Golden Hawk	4	30	64		11⅞	—	Int.	9½	Anodized tubes, nitrogen filled. Write United for data on complete line.	44.50
Golden Grizzly	6	18½	44		11⅞	1	Int.	11		55.00
Golden Falcon	4-9	29½-14	100-20		13½	1	Int.	12¼		89.50
Golden Plainsman	3-12	33-12½	169-11		13½	1	Int.	12¾		110.00
Unertl										
Falcon	2¾	40	75.5	4	11	1	Int.(1′)	10	Black dural tube in hunting models. (2 oz. more with steel tube.)	57.50
Hawk	4	34	64	4	11¾	1	Int.(1′)	10.5		62.50
Condor	6	17	40	3-4	13½	1	Int.(1′)	12		78.50
◆1″ Target	6,8,10	16-10	17.6-6.25	2	21½	.75	Ext.	21	Dural ¼ MOA click mounts. Hard coated lenses. Non-rotating objective lens focusing.	78.00
◆1¼″ Target	8,10,12,14	12-6	15.2-5	2	25	.75	Ext.	25		104.00
◆1½″ Target	8,10,12,14 16,18,20,24	11.5-3.2		2¼	25½	.75	Ext.	31		121.00
◆2″ Target	8,10,12,14 16,18,24 30,36		22.6-2.5	2¼	26¼	1	Ext.	44		168.00
◆Varmint, 1¼″	6,8,10,12	14.1-7	28.7-1	2½	19½	.875	Ext.	26	¼ MOA dehorned mounts. With target mounts.	106.00 110.00
◆Ultra Varmint, 2″	8,10 12,15	12.6-7	39.7-11	2½	24	1	Ext.	34	With dehorned mount. With calibrated head.	133.00 152.00
◆Small Game	4,6	25-17	19.4-8.4	2¼	18	.75	Ext.	16	Same as 1″ Target but without objective lens focusing.	57.00
◆Vulture	8 10	11.2 10.9	29 18½	3-4	15⅝ 16⅛	1	E or I	15½	Price with internal adj. Price with ¼ MOA click mounts.	94.50 112.50
◆Programer 200	8,10,12,14 16,18,20,24 30,36	11.3-4	39-1.9		26½	1	Ext.	45	With new Posa mounts.	222.00
◆BV-20	20	8	4.4	4.4	17⅞	1	Ext.	21¼	Range focus unit near rear of tube. Price is with Posa mounts. Magnum clamp. With standard mounts and clamp ring, $148.00.	158.00
Universal										
Deluxe UC	2½	32	172	3½	12	1	Int.	9¼	Aluminum alloy tubes, centered reticles, coated lenses. Similar Standard series available at lower cost.	27.95
Deluxe UE	4	29	64	3½	12	1	Int.	9		27.95
Deluxe UG	6	17½	28	3¼	12	1	Int.	9		31.50
Deluxe UL	3-9	34-12	177-18	3	12¾	1	Int.	15¼		49.50
Weatherby										
Mark XXII	4	25	50	2½-3½	11¾	⅞	Int.	9¼	Focuses in top turret.	29.50
Imperial	2¾	47½	90	3¼-5	10½	1	Int.	9¼	¼ MOA adj. for e., 1 MOA for w. in all models. Reticles: CH, post and CH, Lee Dot or Open Dot ($12.50 extra).	89.50
Imperial 4x	4	33	81	3¼-4½	11⅛	1	Int.	10¼		99.50
Imperial 6x	6	21½	62	3¼-4½	12½	1	Int.	12⅜		109.50
Imperial Variable	2-7	48-17¾	324-27	4.3-3.1	11$\frac{3}{16}$	1	Int.	12		119.50
Imperial Variable	2¾-10	37-14.6	296-22	4½-3½	12½	1	Int.	14⅛		129.50
Weaver										
K1.5	1½	56		3-5	9¾	1	Int.	7		29.95
K2.5	2½	43		3-6	10⅜	1	Int.	8½		39.95
K3	3	37		3-6	10⅜	1	Int.	8½		44.95
K4	4	31		3-5½	11¼	1	Int.	9½		54.95
K6	6	20		3-5	13⅝	1	Int.	11		59.95
K8	8	15		3-5	15⅜	1	Int.	12¼	Crosswires, post, rangefinder or Dual X reticle optional on all K and V scopes (except no RF in K1½, post in K8, 10, 12, or RF in V22). Dot $7.50 extra in K and V models only. Objective lens on K8, K10, K12, V9, V12 and V9-W focuses for range.	64.95
K10	10	12		3-5	15½	1	Int.	12½		69.95
K12	12	10		3-5	15¾	1	Int.	12½		79.95
K3-W	3	55	—	3¾	10¾	1	Int.	12½		59.95
K4-W	4	37½	—	3¾	12	1	Int.	13¼		69.95
K6-W	6	25	—	3¾	13¾	1	Int.	14¼		74.95
V4.5-W	1½-4½	70-26	—	4	10¾	1	Int.	14		74.95
V7-W	2½-7	53-20	—	3¾	12½	1	Int.	16		84.95
V9-W	3-9	41-16	—	3¾	13¾	1	Int.	19¾		94.95
V4.5	1½-4½	54-21		3-5	10	1	Int.	8½		59.95
V7	2½-7	40-15		3-5	11⅝	1	Int.	10½		69.95
V9	3-9	33-12		3-5	13	1	Int.	13		79.95
V12	4-12	24-9		4	13		Int.	13		89.95
V22	3-6	30-16		2	12½	.875	Int.	4½	$1 extra for Dual X reticle.	15.95
D4	4	28	—	2	11⅝	.875	Int.	4	D model prices include N or Tip-Off mount.	10.95
D6	6	18	—	2	12	.875	Int.	4		12.95
Qwik-Point	1	—	—	6	—	—	Int.	8	For rifles and shotguns. Projects red dot aiming point.	39.95
Williams										
Guide Line	4	29½	64	3¾	11¾	1	Int.	9½	Coated lenses, mitrogen filled tubes, ½ MOA adj. CH, dot, TNT or Guide reticle. Dot covers 3 MOA at 4x in all models.	75.00
Guide Line	1½-4½	78-26	196-22	4⅓-3¼	9½	1	Int.	7¾		105.00
Guide Line	2-6	60-20	169-18	3¼	10¼	1	Int.	10		105.00
Guide Line	3-9	39-13	161-18	3¾-3¼	12	1	Int.	14½		115.00
Twilight	2½	32	64	3¾	11¼	1	Int.	8½	$5 more for TNT reticle.	32.50
Twilight	4	29	64	3½	11¾	1	Int.	9½		36.50
Twilight	2-6	45-17	256-28	3	11½	1	Int.	11½		54.00
Twilight	3-9	36-13	161-18	3	12¾	1	Int.	13½		62.00
Wide Guide	4	35	64	3¼	12¼	1	Int.	14	CH, TNT or Guide reticle.	75.00

◆Signifies target and/or varmint scope.

Hunting scopes in general are furnished with a choice of reticle—cross hairs, post with crosshairs, tapered or blunt post, or dot crosshairs, etc.

The great majority of target and varmint scopes have medium or fine crosshairs but post or dot reticles may be ordered.

W—Windage E—Elevation MOA—Minute of angle or 1″ (approx.) at 100 yards, etc.

SCOPES & MOUNTS
TELESCOPE MOUNTS

Maker, Model, Type	Adjust.	Scopes	Suitable for	Price
Bausch & Lomb				
Custom One Piece (T)	Yes	B&L, other 1" scopes.	Most popular rifles.	$34.90-$39.90
Custom Two Piece (T)	Yes			29.90
Trophy (T)	No	1". With split rings	Rings for Weaver bases—$11.95	21.90
Browning				
One Piece (T)	W only	1" split rings	Browning FN rifles.	25.00
One Piece (T)	No	¾" split rings	Browning 22 semi-auto.	5.00
One Piece Barrel Mount Base	No	Groove mount	22 rifles with grooved receiver	6.00
Two Piece	No	¾" ring mount.	For Browning T-bolt 22.	9.50
B-Square Co.				
Mono-Mount	No	Leupold M8-2x (mounts ahead of action)	M94 Win.	11.50
			M1 Carbine.	9.50
Buehler				
One Piece (T)	W only	¾" or 1" solid rings; ⅞", 1" or 26mm split rings. 4" or 5" spacing.	All popular models.	Solid rings—21.75 Split rings—26.75
One Piece "Micro-Dial" Universal	Yes	Same. 4" ring spacing only.	Most popular models.	Solid—28.25 Split—33.25
Two Piece (T)	W only	Same. Rings for 26.5—27 mm adjust to size by shims.	Rem. 700, 721, 722, 725; Win. 70, 52; FN; Rem. 37; Mathieu; Schultz & Larsen; Husq.	Solid—21.75 Split—26.75
One Piece Pistol Base	W only	Uses any Buehler rings.	S&W K. Colt, Ruger, Thompson	Bases only—11.25
One Piece (T)	W only	Same.	Rem. 600 rifle and XP100 pistol.	Base only—11.25
Burris			Most popular rifles.	Rings—15.95
Supreme One Piece (T)	W only	1" split rings, 3 heights		1 piece base— 9.95
Trophy Two Piece (T)	W only	1" split rings, 3 heights		2 piece base— 8.95
Bushnell			Most popular rifles.	Rings— 6.95
Detachable (T)	No	1" only, 2 heights.		Bases, each— 1.40
				1 pc. bridge base— 1.40
Pivot (T)	No	1" only.	Most popular rifles.	Rings— 7.95
				Bases, each— 1.60
				1 pc. bridge base— 1.40
All Purpose	No	Phantom	V-block bottoms lock to chrom-moly studs seated into two 6-48 holes.	6.50
Rigid	No	Phantom	Heavy loads in Colt, S&W, Ruger revolvers, Rem. XP100, Ruger Hawkeye.	5.00
94 Win.	No	Phantom	M94 Win., end of bbl. clamp or center dovetail.	6.50
Collins				
Bulittco (T)	E only	1" split rings	Rimfire rifles with grooved receivers.	4.98
Conetrol				
One Piece (T)	W only	1" solid or split rings.	Sako dovetail bases (14.95);	Huntur $20.95
Two Piece (T)	W only	Same.	for S&K bases on M1 Carb., SMLE 4 & 5, $9.90.	Gunnur $25.85 Custum $32.85
Griffin & Howe				
Standard Double Lever (S)	No	All standard models.	All popular models. (Garand $37.50; Win. 94 $30.00).	30.00
E. C. Kerkner Echo (S)	No	All standard models.	All popular models. Solid or split rings.	14.50—19.75
Holden				
Ironsighter (T)	No	1" split rings.	Many popular rifles. Rings have oval holes to permit use of iron sights. For 22 rimfire groover receivers, ¾, ⅞ or 1 inch tubes, $6.95. For long eye relief scopes on M94, $19.95.	14.95

International Guns Inc. handles the complete line of Parker-Hale (British) Roll-Over and other scope mounts.

Maker, Model, Type	Adjust.	Scopes	Suitable for	Price
Jaeger				
QD, with windage (S)	W only	1", 26mm; 3 heights.	All popular models.	38.00
QD Railscope Mount	W only		For scopes with dovetail rib.	38.00
Jaguar				
QD Dovetail (T)	No	1", 26mm and 26½mm rings.	For BSA Monarch rifle (Galef, importer).	16.95
Kesselring				
Standard QD (T)	W only	¾", ⅞", 1", 26mm—30 mm split or solid rings.	All popular rifles, one or two piece bases.	12.50-20.00
See-Em-Under (T)	W only	Same.	Rem. 760, 740, 788, Win. 100, 88, Marlin 336	16.50
QD Dovetail (T)	W only	1", 26mm.	Steyr 22, Sako, BSA, Brno, Krico	16.50
Kwik-Site (T)	No	1" split rings	Wider-View, $15.75. Mounts scope high to permit iron sight use.	14.75
			Offset base for 94 Win.	19.95

Burris one- and two-piece mounts (right) and rings (below, left). Rings have special coating inside to prevent slippage of scope under recoil.

SCOPES & MOUNTS

Maker, Model, Type	Adjust.	Scopes	Suitable for	Price
Leupold				
STD (T)	W only	1″ only, 3 heights. Interchange with Redfield Jr. and Sr. components.	Most popular rifles.	Rings—15.95 Base— 9.95
M3 (T)	Yes	1″ only.	Rem. 700, 740, Win. 70, 88, 100, Wby. Mark V, FN, others. Bases reversible to give wide latitude in mounting.	33.50
Lyman All-American				
Tru-lock (T)	No	¾″, ⅞″, 1″, 26mm, split rings.	All popular post-war rifles, plus Savage 99, 98 Mauser. One or two piece bases.	11.00
Marble				
Game Getter (T)	No	1″ only.	Many popular rifles. Has see-through base to permit use of iron sights.	14.95
Marlin				
One Piece QD (T)	No	1″ split rings.	Most popular models. Glenfield model. 5.00.	6.95
Numrich				
Side mount	No	1″ split rings.	M-1 carbine.	6.95
Pachmayr				
Lo-Swing (S)	Yes	¾″, ⅞″, 1″, 26mm solid or split loops.	All popular rifles. Scope swings aside for instant use of iron sights.	20.00
Lo-Swing (T)	Yes	¾″, ⅞″, 1″, 26mm split rings.	Adjustable base. Win. 70, 88; Rem. 721, 722, 725, 740, 760; Mar. 336; Sav. 99.	25.00
Precise Imports				
M-21 (rings only)	No	1″ tube; not over 32mm obj.	Fit Weaver bases.	3.95
M-22 (rings only)	No	1″ tube; 40mm obj. scopes.		3.95
Realist				
V lock QD (T)	No	1″ split rings.	Most popular rifles.	13.00
Redfield				
JR-SR (T)	W only	¾″, 1″, 26mm.	Low, med. & high, split rings. Reversible extension front rings for 1″. 2-piece bases for Mannlicher-Schoenauer and Sako. JR-SR comes with integral folding peep sight.	25.90-43.90
Swing-Over (T) base only	No	1″. (Not for variables.)	Standard height split rings. Also for shotguns.	14.95
Ring (T)	No	¾″ and 1″.	Split rings for grooved 22's.	7.95—9.95
Frontier (T) bases	No	Takes ¾″ or 1″ rings.	See-thru bases $4.95; shotgun model $4.95. Rings $9.95.	1.95
S&K				
Insta-Mount (T) base only	No	Takes Conetrol, Weaver, Herter or United rings.	M1903, A3, M1 Carbine, Lee Enfield #3, #4 #5, P14, M1917, M98 Mauser, FN Auto, AR-15. For M1 Garand, steel rings.	7.50-30.00 41.50
Conventional rings and bases	No	1″ split rings.	Most popular rifles. For "see through underneath" risers, add $4.	19.00
Sako				
QD Dovetail (T)	W only	1″ or 26mm split rings.	Sako, or any rifle using Sako action. 3 heights and extension rings available. Garcia, importer.	18.95—20.65
Savage				
Detachable (T)	No	1″ split rings.	Most modern rifles. One or two piece bases.	9.75-10.25
No. 40 (S)	No	1″	For Savage 340.	3.00
Tasco				
700(T) and 800(S) series	No	1″ split rings, regular or high.	Many popular rifles. Swing mount, 9.95.	4.50—10.45
M722	No	Split rings.	For 22s with grooved receivers.	3.00
Unertl				
Posa (T)	Yes	¾″, ⅞″, 1″ scopes	Unertl target or varmint scope.	26.00-30.00
¼ Click (T)	Yes	¾″, 1″ target scopes	Any with regular dovetail scope bases.	27.00-28.00
Dehorned Varmint (T)	Yes	¾″, ⅞″, 1″ scopes	Add $3 for Posa.	23.00-25.00
Weaver				
Detachable Mount (T & S)	No	¾″, ⅞″, 1″, 26mm.	Nearly all modern rifles. Extension rings, 1″ $11.00	9.95
Type N (S)	No	¾″ scopes only.	Same. High or low style mounts.	2.00
Pivot Mount (T)	No	¾″, 1″, 26mm.	Most modern big bore rifles.	12.50
Tip-Off (T)	No	⅞″.	22s with grooved receivers.	3.00
Tip-Off (T)	No	1″, two-piece	Same. Adapter for Lee Enfield—$1.75	8.00
Williams				
Offset (S)	No	¾″, ⅞″, 1″, 26mm solid, split or exxtension rings.	Most rifles (with over-bore rings, $18.00). Br. S.M.L.E. (round rec.) $2.50 extra.	15.35
QC (T)	No	Same.	Same. Add $4.70 for micro. windage ring.	17.85
QC (S)	No	Same.	Most rifles.	15.35
Sight-Thru	No	1″, ⅞″ sleeves $1	Many modern rifles.	15.00

(S)—Side Mount   (T)—Top Mount   22mm = .866″   25.4mm = 1″   26mm = 1.024″   26.5mm = 1.045″   30mm = 1.181″

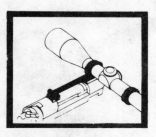

SCOPE REMOVED EASILY

Leupold's new "STD" mount is available for most rifles with a selection of three ring heights.

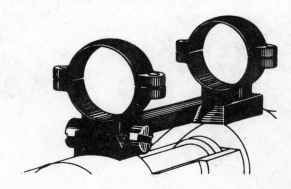

SPOTTING SCOPES

BAUSCH & LOMB BALSCOPE Sr.—60mm objective, 20X. Field at 100 yds. 11.1 ft. Relative brightness, 9. Wgt., 48 oz. Length closed, 16⁷/₁₆". Rapid prismatic focusing..**$139.95**
    Also 15X, 30X, and 60X eyepieces, each....................**29.95**
    Triple eyepiece turret (without eyepiece)..................**19.95**
    Combination auto window/camera tripod adaptor............**24.95**
    Carrying case..**24.95**
    Tele-Master camera adapter..............................**34.95**
BAUSCH & LOMB BALSCOPE ZOOM—15X to 60X variable power. 60mm objective. Field at 1000 yards. 150 ft. (15X) to 37½ feet (60X). Relative brightness 16 (15X) to 1 (60X). Wgt., 48 oz., 16¹¹/₁₆" overall. Integral tripod lug. Straight eyepiece..................................**169.95**
    With 45° eyepiece......................................**179.95**
BAUSCH & LOMB BALSCOPE 20—40mm objective. 20X. Field at 100 yds., 7.5 ft. 15⅜" over-all, Wgt., 22 oz..................................**$29.95**

BAUSCH & LOMB BALSCOPE 10—30mm objective. 10X. Field at 100 yds. 7.5 ft. 10¼" over-all, weight, 9 oz..................................**$11.95**
BUSHNELL SPACEMASTER—60mm objective, 25X. Field at 100 yds., 10.5 ft. Relative brightness, 5.76. Wgt., 39 oz. Length closed, 15¼". Prism focusing, sliding sunshade..**$110.50**
    15X, 20X, 25X, 40X and 60X eyepieces, each..............**$25.00**
    20X wide angle eyepiece................................**$30.00**
BUSHNELL SPACEMASTER 45°—Same as above except: Wgt., 43 oz., length closed 16¼". Eyepiece at 45°...............................**$114.50**
BUSHNELL SPACEMASTER II—20X-45X zoom. 60mm objective. Field at 100 yards 12-7.2 ft. Relative brightness 9-1.7. Wgt. 36 oz., length 11⅝" **$124.50**
BUSHNELL SENTRY II—20X. 50mm objective. Field at 100 yards 12 ft. Relative brightness 6.25...**$64.50**
    Also 32X and 48X eyepieces, each......................**$22.50**
BUSHNELL ZOOM SPOTTER—40mm objective. 9X-30X var. power **$33.50**
HUTSON CHROMATAR 60—63.4mm objective. 22.5X eyepiece at 45D. Wgt. 24 oz. 8" over-all. 10½" foot field at 100 yards............**$119.00**
    15X or 45X eyepieces, each............................**22.00**
HY-SCORE MODEL 460—60mm objective. 15X, 20X, 25X, 40X and 60X eyepieces included. Field at 100 yds. 15.8 to 3.2 ft. Length closed 11". Wgt., 35 oz. With tripod and case..................................**$182.00**
PRECISE IMPORTS, T-15—60mm objective, 15X to 30X zoom scope. About 15" long, weighs approximately 6 lbs. with adj. tripod...........**$49.95**
PRECISE IMPORTS, T-19—60mm objective, interchangeable eyepieces of 15X, 20X, 30X, 40X, 60X. Sliding sunshade. Weighs about 6 lbs. with adj. tripod...**$69.95**

REDFIELD FIFTEEN-SIXTY—15X-60X zoom. 60mm objective. Field at 100 yards 15.6-3.7 ft. Relative brightness 16-1. Wgt. 48 oz., length 16¾" **$149.50**
    Tripod stand..**27.50**
    Bipod stand..**$29.95**
    Carrying case...**29.95**
SOUTHERN PRECISION MODEL 549—60mm objective and 5 eyepieces from 15X to 60X; extensible sunshade and folding tripod. Closed, 14¾", Wgt., 4¼ lbs..**$79.50**
SOUTHERN PRECISION ZOOM MODEL 547—60mm objective, 25X to 50X; ext. sunshade folding tripod. Closed, 18", wgt. 4½ lbs. with tripod (included)..**$96.00**

SOUTHERN PRECISION MODEL 546—50mm objective, 25X. Folding tripod, leather case included. Closed, 13", wgt. 3 lbs..................**$41.00**
SWIFT TELEMASTER M841—60mm objective. 15X to 60X variable power. Field at 1000 yards 160 feet (15X) to 40 feet (60X). Wgt. 3.4 lbs. 17.6" over-all...**$210.00**
    Tripod for above......................................**$46.50**
    Photo adapter...**$12.95**
    Case for above..**$32.95**
SWIFT MODEL 821—60mm objective. 15X, 20X, 30X, 40X and 60X eyepieces included. Field at 100 yds., 158 to 32 ft. 18" tripod with friction clutch adj. handle. Length 13½" (without sunshade). 6 lbs.....**$154.50**
TASCO ZOOM—60mm objective. 20X to 60X variable power. Field at 1000 yards 158 feet (16X) to 40 feet (50X). Wgt. 4½ lbs. 18" overall.**$119.95**
TASCO 28T ANGLEVIEW—60mm objective. 25X, resolves to 2 sec. at 100 yds. Rapid focus knob. Table top tripod with adj. elevation leg. Camera tripod adapter, extending sun shade. Wgt., 6 lbs., length 16½". Complete with lens covers..**$159.95**
TASCO 8T SPOTTING 60—60mm objective, 4 par-focal, variable power eye-lenses 15X, 30X, 40X and 60X. Resolves 2.8 sec. at 100 yds. Wgt., 4 lbs., length 16½"..**$119.95**
UNERTL RIGHT ANGLE—63.5mm objective. 24X. Field at 100 yds., 7 ft. Relative brightness, 6.96. Eye relief, ½". Wgt., 41 oz. Length closed, 19". Push-pull and screw-focus eyepiece. 16X and 32X eyepieces $18 each. Price..**$127.00**

UNERTL STRAIGHT PRISMATIC—Same as Unertl Right Angle except: straight eyepiece and Wgt. of 40 oz..................................**$106.00**
UNERTL 20X STRAIGHT PRISMATIC—54mm objective. 20X. Field at 100 yds., 8.5 ft. Relative brightness, 6.1. Eye relief, ½". Wgt., 36 oz. Length closed, 13½". Complete with lens covers.........................**$86.00**
UNERTL TEAM SCOPE—100mm objective. 15X, 24X. 32X eyepieces. Field at 100 yds. 13 to 7.5 ft. Relative brightness, 39.06 to 9.79. Eye relief, 2" to 1½". Weight, 13 lbs. 29⅞" overall. Metal tripod, yoke and wood carrying case furnished (total weight, 80 lbs.)..........................**$450.00**
WEATHERBY—60mm objective, 20X-45X zoom................**$112.00**
    Tripod for above......................................**17.50**

SCOPE ATTACHMENTS

DAVIS TARGETEER—Objective lens/tube units that attach to front of low power scopes, increase magnification to 8X. 1¼" lens, $25, 1½" lens**$29.50**
HERMANN DUST CAPS—Connected leather straps, hand made, natural color. For all popular scopes.....................................**$4.00**
LEE TACKHOLE DOTS—Various size dots for all scopes. Priced from**$7.50** to **$17.50**
LYMAN HAZE FILTER—For morning and late afternoon hunting. Filters out blue and violet rays allowing only the best part of the spectrum to transmit through your telescope lenses. For all reflescopes..........**$2.75**
PGS SCOPE SHIELDS—Flexible rubber, usable at front and rear, protect scopes from snow or rain. Made for all scopes....................**$3.95**
PREMIER RETICLES—Various size dots for all scopes, also special reticles to order. Price—**$7.00** to **$18.50. PREMIER WEATHER CAPS**— transparent, high light transmission. For all popular scopes. Price **$3.50** Special sizes...**$5.00**
W. P. SIEBERT—Converts Lyman, Leupold and Weaver K model varmint scopes to 15X-24X....................................**$25.00-$30.00**
STORM KING LENS CAPS—A hinged glass-and-rubber protector set (2), made in various sizes for all scopes. May be unhinged or sighted through. Anderson Gun Shop. Per pair.......................................**$3.45**
SUPREME LENS COVERS—Hinged protectors for most scope models, front and rear lenses shielded. Butler Creek Corp. Per pair, postpaid.**$7.50**

SPOTTING SCOPE STANDS

DAVIDSON MARK 245—Bipod adjustable for elevation, 9½"-14½". Side mount with two straps. Black crinkle finish. Length folded 16½". Price **$23.95**
FREELAND ALL ANGLE—Tripod adjustable for elevation. Left or right side mount with worm drive clamp. Folding legs. Clamps available for any scope tube size. Black, gray, or green crinkle finish. Price.......**$22.75**
    Also 12" 18", 24" extensions available...................**$3.00-5.00**
FREELAND OLYMPIC—Bipod adjustable for elevation. All angle mount with padded worm drive clamp. Folding legs. Clamps available for any scope tube size. Black, grey, or green crinkle finish. Price......**$24.75**
    Also 12", 18", 24" extensions available..................**$3.00-5.00**
    Zoom head for tripod or bipod..........................**$11.00**
FREELAND REGAL BIPOD—Choice of saddle or zoom head. All adjustment knobs are oversize for easy adjusting. Large "ball" carrying knob. Gray or green finish...**$26.75**
    Above with stability weight..............................**34.25**
    Extensions 12"-24"....................................**$3.00-5.00**

A selection of books—old, new and forthcoming—for everyone in the arms field, with a brief description by . . . RAY RILING

ballistics and handloading

Ballistics in the Seventeenth Century, by A. R. Hall. 1st J. & J. Harper ed. 1969 [from the Cambridge University Press ed. of 1952]. 186 pp., illus., with tables and diagrams. $13.50.
A profound work for advanced scholars, this is a study in the relations of science and war, with reference principally to England.

The Bullet's Flight, from Powder to Target, by F. W. Mann. Ray Riling Arms Books Co., Phila., PA, 1965. A reprint of the very scarce original work of 1909. Introduction by Homer S. Powley, 384 pp. illus. $12.50.
One of the best known and scholarly-developed works on basic ballistics.

Cartridges, by Cyril Waterworth. Farleigh Press Lindfield, N.S.W. 2070, Australia, N.D. 80 pp., illus. $1.50.
Rifle, handgun and collectors cartridges are shown and briefly described, but no prices are given.

Cartridges of the World, by Frank C. Barnes, John T. Amber ed., Digest Books, Inc., Northfield, IL, 1972. 8½"x11", 378 pp. Profusely illus. Paperbound. $6.95.
The third edition of a comprehensive reference for hunters, collectors, handloaders and ballisticians. Covering over 1000 cartridges, loads, components, etc., from all over the world.

Centerfire American Rifle Cartridges, 1892-1963, by Ray Bearse, A. S. Barnes & Co., S. Brunswick, NJ, 1966. 198 pp., illus. $6.98
Identification manual covering caliber, introduction date, origin, case type, etc. Self-indexed and cross-referenced. Headstamps and line drawings are included.

Centerfire Pistol and Revolver Cartridges, by H. P. White, B. D. Munhall and Ray Bearse. A. S. Barnes, NY, 1967, 85 pp. plus 170 pp., illus. $10.00.
A new and revised edition covering the original Volume I, Centerfire Metric Pistol and Revolver Cartridges and Volume II, Centerfire American and British Pistol and Revolver Cartridges, by White and Munnall, formerly known as Cartridge Identification.

Complete Guide to Handloading, by Phil Sharpe. Funk & Wagnalls, NYC, 1953 (3rd ed., 2nd rev.) 734 pp., profusely illustrated, numerous line and halftone charts, tables, lists, etc., $10.00.
The bible of handloaders ever since its first appearance in 1937, but badly dated now.

Handbook for Shooters and Reloaders, by P. O. Ackley, Salt Lake City, UT, 1970. *Vol. I,* 567 pp., illus. $9.00. *Vol. II,* a new printing with specific new material. 495 pp., illus. $9.00. Both volumes. $17.50.

Handloader's Digest, ed. by John T. Amber. Digest Books, Inc., Northfield, IL, 1972. 320 pp., very well illus., stiff paper covers. $5.95.
This 6th edition contains the latest data on ballistics, maximum loads, new tools, equipment, reduced loads, etc., plus a fully illus. catalog section, current prices and specifications.

Home Guide to Cartridge Conversions, by Geo. C. Nonte, Jr., Stackpole Books, Harrisburg, PA, 1967. 404 pp., illus. $8.95.
A new, revised and enlarged ed. of instructions, charts and tables for making ammunition no longer available, or which has become too expensive on the commercial market.

Hornady Handbook of Cartridge Reloading. Hornady Mfg. Co., Grand Island, Nebr., 1967. 360 pp., illus. $3.50.
Handloader's reference, with much detail on projectiles, ballistics, etc., on many popular U.S. and imported firearms. An excellent work with particularly needed ballistic detail.

Interior Ballistics, How a Gun Converts Chemical Energy to Projectile Motion, by E. D. Lowry. Doubleday and Co., NY, 1968. 168 pp., including index and bibliography., illus. with 4 halftones and 17 line drawings. $4.50.
An introduction to the history of small arms and weapons relative to the science of internal ballistics, especially for the layman and student.

Lee Reloading Handbook, by R. Lee, Lee Custom Engineering, Hartford, WI. 98 pp., illus. Paper, 98¢.
Manual on reloading ammunition of various types.

Lyman Cast Bullet Handbook. Lyman Gunsight Corp., Middlefield, CT, 1973. 260 pp., illus. Paper covers. $4.95.
A long-awaited and fine reference for handloaders.

Lyman Handbook No. 45. Lyman Gunsight Corp., Middlefield, CT, 1967. $3.50.
Latest edition of a favorite reference for ammunition handloaders, whether novice or veteran.

Make Muzzle Loader Accessories, by R. H. McCrory, R. H. McCory, Publ., 1971, 46 pp. Paper $2.25.
A revised 2nd ed. covering over 20 items from powderhorns to useful tools. Well illus.

Manual of Pistol and Revolver Cartridges, Vol. I, by H. A. Erlmeier and J. H. Brandt. C. D. Associates, Wiesbaden, Germany, 1967. 268 pp., illus. $21.50.
Both English and German text on centerfire and metric calibers.

Modern Handloading, by Maj. Geo. C. Nonte. Winchester Press, NY, 1972. 416 pp., illus. $10.00.
Covers all aspects of metallic and shotshell ammunition loading, plus more loads than any book in print; state and Federal laws, reloading tools, glossary.

The NRA Handloader's Guide. Ashley Halsey, Jr., ed. Nat'l Rifle Assn., Washington, DC, 1969, 312 pp., illus., paperbound. $5.00.
Revised edition of a reloading handbook, based on material published in *The American Rifleman.*

Pocket Manual for Shooters and Reloaders, by P. O. Ackley. publ. by author, Salt Lake City, UT, 1964. 176 pp., illus., spiral bound. $3.50.
Good coverage on standard and wildcat cartridges and related firearms in popular calibers.

Principles and Practice of Loading Ammunition, by Lt. Col. Earl Naramore. Stackpole Books, Harrisburg, PA, 1954. 915 text pages, 240 illustrations. $14.95.
Actually two volumes in one. The first part (565 pp.) deals with ballistics and the principles of cartridge making—and the chemistry, metallurgy, and physics involved. The second part (350 pp.) is a thorough discussion of the mechanics of loading cartridges. 1967 printing.

Professional Loading of Rifle, Pistol and Shotgun Cartridges . . ., by G. L. Herter, Waseca, MN, 1970, 830 pp., illus. $7.50
Detailed technical loading information on small arms ammunition, with related articles on firearms and their use. A "condensed" paper-cover version of the above, 430 pp., illus. $4.50.

Rifle/Pistol Cartridge Reloading Manual, rev. ed. 1972. Pacific Tool Co., Grand Island, NB, 1972. 336 pp., illus. Paper covers. $3.50.
Up-to-date loading data for a multitude of caliber-cartridge combinations, including wildcats.

Shooter's Bible Black Powder Guide, by George Nonte, Shooter's Bible, Inc., S. Hackensack, NJ, 1969. 214 pp., well illus. $3.95.
Information on black powder weapons, ammunition, shooting, etc.

Reloading Simplified, 5th ed., by Cyril Waterworth. Farleigh Pres, Lindfield, N.S.W. 2070 Australia, 1970. 120 pp., illus. Paper, $1.50.
Australia's only handloading manual—and an excellent one—it covers rifles, handguns and shotgun loading, plus how-to-do-it chapters.

Shooter's Bible Reloader's Guide, 2nd ed., by R. A. Steindler. Shooter's Bible, Inc., S. Hackensack, NJ, 1968, 220 pp., fully illus. $3.95.
Comprehensive coverage of technology and methods of handloading all types of small arms ammunition. This is a useful work.

Shotshell Handbook, by Lyman Handbook Staff. Lyman Gunsight Corp., Middlefield, CT, 1969. 160 pp., illus., stiff paper spiral-binding. $3.00.
The first book devoted exclusively to shotshell reloading. Considers: gauge, shell length, brand, case, loads, buckshot, etc., plus excellent reference section. Some color illus.

Shotshell Reloading Manual, rev. ed., 1972. Pacific Tool Co., Grand Island, NB, 1972. 96 pp., illus. Paper covers. $3.50.
Complete data for more than 300 modern shotshell loads, with detailed sequential drawings.

Sierra Bullets Reloading Manual, by Robert Hayden. Sierra Bullets, Santa Fe Springs, CA, 1971. 350 pp., illus. In loose-leaf binder. $4.85.
Reference manual on cartridge reloading, including ballistics and ammunition data on rifles and pistols.

Small Arms Ammunition Identification Guide. Normount Tech. Pub., Forest Grove, OR, 1971. 151 pp., illus. Paper, $3.00.
A reprint of the guide originally published as FSTC-CW-07-02-66, revised.

Small Arms Ammunition Identification Guide, An Army Intelligence Document, Paladin Press, Boulder, CO, 1972. 254 pp., illus. Paper, $5.00.
An exact reprint of FSTC-CW-7068, 1969 updated. An identification guide for most countries.

Speer Manual for Reloading Ammunition No. 8. Speer, Inc., Lewiston, ID, 1970. 382 pp., illus. $3.95.
A popular manual on handloading, with authoritative articles on loading, ballistics, and related subjects. Decorated paper wrappers.

Why Not Load Your Own? by Col. T. Whelen. A. S. Barnes, New York, 1957, 4th ed., rev. 237 pp., illus, $5.95.
A basic reference on handloading, describing each step, materials and equipment. Loads for popular cartridges are given.

The Winchester-Western Ammunition Handbook. Thomas Nelson & Sons, NYC, 1964. 185 pp., illus. $2.95.
Called the world's handiest handbook on ammunition for all types of shotguns, rifles and handguns. Full of facts, photographs, ballistics and statistics.

COLLECTORS

About Cannon in 1862, by Robert F. Hudson, American Archives Publ. Co., Topsfield, MA, 1971. 44 pp., illus. Paper, $4.00.
Reprint of an 18th century monograph on artillery pieces, with historical notes.

Accoutrement Plates, North and South, 1861-1865, by Wm. G. Gavin. Geo. Shumway, York, PA, 1963. 236 pp., 220 illus. $12.00
The 1st detailed study of Civil War belt buckles and cartridge box insignia. Dimensions, materials, details of manufacture, relative and dollar values given.

The Age of Firearms, by Robert Held. Digest Books, Inc., Northfield, IL, 1970. New, fully rev. and corrected ed., paper covers. 192 pp., fully illus. $4.95.
A popular review of firearms since 1475 with accent on their effects on social conditions, and the craft of making functional/artistic arms.

Air Guns, by Eldon G. Wolff. Milwaukee Public Museum, Milwaukee, WI, 1958. 198 pp., illus. Paper, $6.00.
A scholarly and comprehensive treatise, excellent for student and collectors' use, of air gun history. Every form of arm is described, and a list of 350 makers is included.

Air Guns and Air Pistols, by L. Wesley. A. S. Barnes Co., NY, 1964. 210 pp., illus. $5.00.
Latest, enlarged ed. of a standard work.

American Axes, by H. J. Kauffman. Stephen Greene Press, Brattleboro, VT, 1972. 151 pp., illus. $12.50.
A history of American axes and their makers.

The American Bayonet, 1776-1964, by A. N. Hardin, Jr. Geo. Shumway, York, PA, 1964. 252 pp., profusely illus. $20.00.
First comprehensive book on U.S. bayonets of all services, a standard reference for collectors. All bayonets made for long arms and described in full detail, with outstanding photographs, and historical development of principal types. Full references and bibliography.

American, British & Continental Pepperbox Firearms, by Jack Dunlap. H. J. Dunlap, Los Altos, CA, 1964. 279 pp., 665 illus. $15.00.
Comprehensive history of production pepperpots from early 18th cent. through the cartridge pepperbox. Variations are covered, with much data of value to the collector.

American Engraved Powder Horns, by Stephen V. Grancsay. Originally published by The Metropolitan Museum of Art, at NYC, 1945. The 1st reprint publ. by Ray Riling Arms Books Co., Phila., PA, 1965. 96 pp. plus 47 full-page plates. $15.00.
A study based on the J. H. Grenville Gilbert collection of historic, rare and beautiful powder horns. A scholarly work by an eminent authority. Long out of print and offered now in a limited edition of 1000 copies.

American and European Swords in the Historical Collections of the U.S. National Museum, by T. T. Belote. Benchmark Pub. Co., Glendale, NY, 1970. 163 pp., illus. $7.50
A reprint of Smithsonian Institution Bulletin 163, first published in 1932.

American Knives, the First History and Collectors' Guide, by Harold L. Peterson. Scribner's, N.Y.C., 1958. 178 pp., well illus. $6.95.
A timely book to whet the appetite of the ever-growing group of knife collectors.

The American Percussion Revolver, by F. M. Sellers and Sam E. Smith. Museum Restoration Service, Ottawa, Canada, 1970. 200 pp., illus. $15.00.
All inclusive from 1826 to 1870. Over 200 illus., with profuse coverage on lesser-known arms.

American Polearms, 1526-1865, by R. H. Brown. N. Flayderman Co., New Milford, Conn., 1967. 198 pp., 150 plates. $14.50.
Concise history of pikes, spears, and similar weapons used in American military forces through the Civil War.

American Socket Bayonets, 1717-1873, by D. B. Webster, Jr. Museum Rest. Service, Ottawa, Can. 1964. 48 pp., 60 illus. paperbound. $1.50.
Concise account of major types, with nomenclature, characteristics, and dimensions. Line drawings.

The American Sword 1775-1945, by H. L. Peterson. Ray Riling Arms Books Co., Phila., PA, 1973. 286 pp. plus 60 pp. of illus. $16.50.
1973 reprint of a survey of swords worn by U.S. uniformed forces, plus the rare "American Silver Mounted Swords." (1700-1815).

Ancient Armour and Weapons in Europe, by John Hewitt. Akademische Druck- u. Verlagsanstalt, Graz, Austria, 1967. 3 vols., 1151 total pp., illus. $50.00.
Reprint of a renowned British work first published 1855-1860; covers armor, weapons, military history and tactics through the 17th century.

Antique Arms Annual, ed. by R. L. Wilson, S. P. Stevens, Texas Gun Coll. Assn., Waco, Texas. 1971. 262 pp., profusely illus. $15.00.
A magnificent work showing hundreds of fine color photographs of rare firearms. Decorated paper covers.

Antique European and American Firearms in the Hermitage Museum, by L. Tarassuk. Arco Pub. Co., NY, 1972. 224 pp., 130 pp. of illus., 54 pp. in full color. $20.00.
Selected from the museum's 2500 firearms dating from the 15th to 19th centuries, including the magnificently decorated Colt rifle and pistols presented by Samuel Colt to Tzars Nicholas 1st and Alexander II.

Antique Firearms, by Frederick Wilkinson. Guinness Signatures, London. 1st ed., 1969. 256 pp., Well illus. $15.00.
Sixteen monographs on important aspects of firearms development from the 14th century to the era of the modern repeating rifle. Shows museum-quality arms, many in full color.

Antique Pistols, by S. G. Alexander, illus. by Ronald Paton. Arco Publ. Co., New York, 1963. 56 pp., 12 color plates. $15.00.
The large 8-color plates show 14 examples of the pistol-maker's art in England and U.S.A., 1690-1900. Commentary on each by a knowledgeable English collector.

Antique Weapons, A-Z, by Douglas J. Fryer. G. Bell & Sons, London, 1969. 114 pp. illus. $7.50.
A concise survey of collectors' arms, including firearms, edged weapons, polearms, etc., of European and Oriental design, classified by types.

Antique Weapons for Pleasure and Investment, by R. Akehurst. Arco Pub. Co., N.Y., 1969. 174 pp., illus. $5.95.
Reprint of an English book covering an extensive variety of arms, including Japanese and Hindu edged weapons and firearms.

L'Aristocratie Du Pistolet (Handgun Aristocracy), by Raymond Caranta & Pierre Cantegrit. Balland, Paris, France, 1971. 357 pp., illus. $25.00.
Covers the most glamorous handguns made during the industrial period, 1847 to date, with references to the men who designed or used them. French text.

Les Armes Americaines 1870-1871 de las Defense Nationale, by P. Lorain and J. Boudriot. Librarie Pierre Petitot, Paris, France, 1970. French text, 96 pp., illus. $12.50.
Covers all U.S. weapons bought by the French government a century ago.

Armes a Feu Francaises Modeles Reglementaires, by J. Boudriot. Paris, 1961-1968. 4 series of booklets; 1st and 2nd series, 5 booklets; 3rd and 4th, 6 booklets. Each series, $6.75, $9.75, $10.75, $11.75, resp.
Detailed survey of all models of French military small arms, 1717-1861, with text in French and fine scale drawings. Each series covers a different period of development; the last covers percussion arms.

Armes Blanches Militaires Francaises, by Christian Aries. P. Petitot, Paris, 1968. Unpaginated, paperbound, 11 volumes. $9.50 per vol., $95.00 complete.
Pictorial survey of French military swords, in French text and line drawings in exact detail. The classifications in the various volumes are the author's own and do not follow any specific sequence. The work must be used as a complete set for maximum benefit.

Le Armi da Fuoco Portatili Italiane, dalle Origini al Risorgimento, by Gen. Agostino Gaibi. Bramante Editrice, Milan, Italy, 1962. 527 pp., 320 illus. (69 in color), in slip case. $65.00.
A magnificently produced volume covering Italian hand firearms from their beginning into the 18th cent. Italian text. Superb illus. of historic weapons, engraving, marks, related equipment. A companion book to *Armi e Armature Italiane.*

Armi e Armature Italiane, Fino al XVIII Secolo, by Aldo Mario Aroldi. Bramante Editrice, Milan, Italy, 1961. 544 pp., profusely illus. (Much in color). In slip case, $65.00.
A luxurious work on the golden age of Italian arms and makers through the 18th cent., emphasizing body and horse armor, edged weapons, crossbows, early firearms. Italian text. Beautiful and scholarly work for the advanced collector.

Armi e Armature Orientali, by Gianni Vianello, Bramante Editrice, Milano, Italy, 1966. 423 pp. Magnificently illustrated, mainly in full-color tip-ins. $56.00 with slip case. Ed. ltd. to 1600 copies.
A new addition to a notable series of fine books in the arms and armor field. The introduction is 68 pp., 105 pp. of commentary on the 250 pp. of illus.

Arming the Troops, by Paul C. Boehret, Publ. by the author at Chalfont, Pa., 1967. 39 pp., illus. $7.50. The same in paper wrappers $5.00.
A catalog of arms makers of the early years of U.S. history, from 1775 to 1815.

The Armourer and his Craft, by Charles ffoulkes. Frederick Ungar Publ. Co., N.Y., 1967. 199 pp., illus. $18.50.
Standard British reference on body armor, 11th-16th cent.; covering notable makers, construction, decoration, and use. 1st ed. 1912, now reprinted.

Armourers Marks, by D. S. H. Gyngell. Thorsons, Ltd., England, 1959. 131 pp., illus. $10.00.
Some of the marks of armourers, swordsmiths and gunsmiths of almost every foreign country.

Arms Archives, by H. B. Lockhoven, International Small Arms Publ., Cologne, W. Germany, 1969. Unpaginated but coded. Illus. English and German text, loose-leaf format. Available in 4 series; "A" Handguns, "B" Automatic Weapons, "C" Longarms, "D" Antique Arms. Each series in 4 installments at $10 per installment. Binders for each series $5.50.
A major breakthrough in arms literature. Scaled photographs of guns and their cartridges, fully described. Only 1st installment now available in series "D".

Arms and Armor, by Vesey Norman. Putnam's N.Y.C., 1964. 128 pp., 129 illus. $5.95.
Authoritative, compact coverage of European armor and weapons prior to the age of firearms. Excellent illus., many in color.

Arms & Armor from the Atelier of Ernst Schmidt, Munich, by E. Andrew Mowbray, compiler. Mowbray Co., Providence, R.I., 1967. 168 pp., well illus. $11.95.
Principally a compilation of plates from the extremely rare Schmidt catalog displaying the famous replicas of medieval armor and weapons made in his shop from about 1870 to 1930. Limited edition.

Arms and Armor in Colonial America, 1526-1783, by H. L. Peterson. Crown, New York, reprint ed., 1964. 350 pp., illus. $3.95.
Well-organized account of arms and equipment used in America's colonization and exploration, through the Revolutionary period.

Arms and Armour, by Frederick Wilkinson, A. & C. Black Ltd., London. Reprint of 1969, 63 pp., well illus. $2.95.
A concise work for young readers describing edged weapons, polearms, armor, etc., mainly of European origin.

Arms and Armour Digest, edited by Robert Held. Digest Books, Inc., Northfield, IL, 1973. 320 pp., illus. Paper covers. $7.95.
Written by the world's greatest gun authorities, this book is of incomparable scope and historical integrity.

Arms and Armour, 9th to 17th Century, by Paul Martin, C. E. Tuttle Co., Rutland, Vt., 1968. 298 pp., well illus. $15.00.
Beautiful illustrations and authoritative text on armor and accessories from the time of Charlemagne to the firearms era.

Arms and Armour of the Western World, by B. Thomas, O. Gamber & H. Schedelmann, McGraw Hill, N.Y.C., 1964. 252 pp., illus. (much in color), $27.50.
Museum quality weapons and armor shown and described in a magnificent book, which gives the association of specimen arms with the men and events of history. Superb photographs in color. Pub. 1963 in German as "Die Schonsten Waffen . . ." price $25.00.

Arms Collection of Colonel Colt, by R. L. Wilson. Herb Glass, Bullville, N.Y., 1964. 132 pp., 73 illus. Lim. deluxe ed., $16.50; trade ed., $6.50.
Samuel Colt's personal collection is well-described and photographed, plus new technical data on Colt's arms and life. 51 Colt guns and other revolving U.S. and European arms are included.

Arms and Equipment of the Civil War, by Jack Coggins, Doubleday & Co., Inc, NY, 1962. 160 pp., $5.95.
Tools of war of the blue and the grey. Infantry, cavalry, artillery, and navy: guide to equipment, clothing, organization, and weapons. Over 500 illus.

Arms Making In the Connecticut Valley, by F. J. Deyrup. George Shumway Publ., York, Pa., 1970. Reprint of the noted work originally publ. in 1948 by Smith College. 290 pp., line maps, $10.00.
A scholarly regional study of the economic development of the small arms industry 1798-1870. With statistical appendices, notes, bibliography.

Arms of the World—1911, ed. by Joseph J. Schroeder, Jr., Digest Books, Inc., Northfield, IL, 1972, 420 pp., profusely illus. $5.95.
Reprint of the Adolph Frank ALFA 21 catalog of 1911 in 4 languages—English, German, French, Spanish.

Artillery and Ammunition of the Civil War, by Warren Ripley. Van Nostrand Reinhold Co., New York, N.Y., 1st ed., 1970. 384 pp., well illus. with 662 black and white photos and line drawings. $22.50.
A fine survey covering both Union and Confederate cannon and projectiles, as well as those imported.

Artillery of the United States Land Service. Vol. I, Field Artillery 1848-1865, comp. by D. E. Lutz, Antique Ordnance Artificers, Jackson, MI, 1970. 64 pp. Paper, $5.00.
First of series containing drawings of artillery used during the Civil War. Limited ed., each copy numbered.

Artillery Through the Ages, by A. Manucy, Normount Armament Co., Forest Grove, OR, 1971. 92 pp., illus. Paper, $2.50
A short history of cannon, emphasizing types used in America.

Arts of the Japanese Swords, by B. W. Robinson. Chas. E. Tuttle Co., Rutland, Vt., 1961. 110 pp. of descriptive text with illus., plus 100 full page plates, some in full color. $15.00.
An authoritative work, divided into 2 parts—the first on blades, tracing their history to the present day; the second on mounts and fittings. It includes forging processes; accounts of the important schools of swordsmiths; techniques employed, plus a useful appendix on care and cleaning.

Badges & Emblems of the British Forces 1940, Arms and Armour Press, London, 1968. 64 pp. Paper, $3.00.
Reprint of a comprehensive guide to badges and emblems worn by all British forces in 1940, including Welfare, Aux. Services, Nursing Units, etc. Over 350 illus.

Ballard Rifles in the H. J. Nunnemacher Coll., by Eldon G. Wolff. Milwaukee Public Museum, Milwaukee, Wisc., 2nd ed. 1961. Paper, 77 p. plus 4 pp. of charts and 27 plates. $2.50.
A thoroughly authoritative work on all phases of the famous rifles, their parts, patent and manufacturing history.

The Bannerman Catalogue 1903, Francis Bannerman Sons, New York, N.Y. Reprint released in 1960. 116 pp., well illus., $3.50.
A reprint in facsimile of this dealer's catalog of military goods of all descriptions, including weapons and equipment.

The Bannerman Catalog 1965, Francis Bannerman Sons, Blue Point, N.Y. The 100th anniversary ed., 1966. 264 pp., well illus. $5.00.
Latest dealer catalog of nostalgic interest on military and collector's items of all sorts.

Basic Documents on U.S. Marital Arms, commentary by Col. B. R. Lewis, reissue by Ray Riling, Phila., Pa., 1956 and 1960.
Rifle Musket Model 1855. The first issue rifle of musket caliber, a muzzle loader equipped with the Maynard Primer, 32 pp. $2.50.
Rifle Musket Model 1863. The Typical Union muzzle-loader of the Civil War, 26 pp. $1.75.
Breech-Loading Rifle Musket Model 1866. The first of our 50 caliber breechloading rifles, 12 pp. $1.75.
Remington Navy Rifle Model 1870. A commercial type breech-loader made at Springfield, 16 pp. $1.75.
Lee Straight Pull Navy Rifle Model 1895. A magazine cartridge arm of 6mm caliber. 23 pp. $3.00.
Breech-Loading Rifle Musket Model 1868. The first 50-70 designed as such. 20 pp. $1.75.
Peabody Breech-Loading Arms (five models)—27 pp. $2.75.
Ward-Burton Rifle Musket 1871—16 pp. $2.50.
Springfield Rifle, Carbine & Army Revolvers (cal. 45) model 1873 including Colt and Smith & Wesson hand arms. 52 pp. $3.00.
U.S. Magazine Rifle and Carbine (cal. 30) Model 1892 (the Krag Rifle) 36 pp. $2.50.

Bayonets Illustrated, by Bert Walsh, Bashall Eaves, Ireland, 1970. 49 pp., illus. $5.00.
162 detailed line drawings of bayonets from many countries and periods.

Bayonets, an Illustrated History and Reference Guide, by F. J. Stephens. Arms and Armour Press, London, 1968. 76 pp., stiff paper wrappers, 134 photographs. $5.00.
A general historical survey of all categories of the weapon, from the U.S. and many other countries.

Bellifortis [The War Hero], by Conrad Kyeser. Verlag des Vereins Deutscher Ingenieure, Dusseldorf, W. Germany. 1967. Two large facsimile volumes, 391 pp., combining Latin and German text. Superbly illus.
For the advanced collector, this is a reproduction of the oldest [A.D. 1405] German manuscript on weapons and warfare. Limited to 1,000 copies, bound in white half-vellum and boxed. $120.00.

Bilderatlas zum Grundriss der Waffenlehre, by K. T. VonSauer. Pawlas, Nurnberg, Germany, 1968. Paper folder containing 28 pp. text and 26 plates. $7.50.
Facsimile of an 1869 set of plates depicting military rifles of Germany, with explanatory pamphlet in German text.

Blades and Barrels, by H. Gordon Frost. Walloon Press, El Paso, TX, 1972. 298 pp., illus. $16.95.
The first full-scale study about man's attempts to combine an edged weapon with a firearm.

Blunderbusses, by D. R. Baxter. Stackpole Books, Harrisburg, Pa., 1970. 80 pp., 60 illus. $4.95.
Traces blunderbuss development from the 16th century, covering basic designs, firing systems, the double blunderbuss and revolving pepperbox design.

The Book of Colt Firearms, by R. Q. Sutherland and R. L. Wilson, Privately printed, Kansas City, Mo., 1971. 604 pp. 9x12", profusely illus. $50.00.
This exhaustive large work, highly informative and scholarly, contains 40 color plates showing 420 Colt firearms, plus 1258 black and white photographs.

The Book of the Continental Soldier, by Harold L. Peterson. Stackpole Books, Harrisburg, Pa, 1968. 287 pp., of large format profusely illus. with halftone, line, and including art work by H. Charles McBarron, Jr., Clyde A. Risley and Peter Copeland, $12.95.
A thorough and commendable work in every pertinent aspect. Covers in satisfying detail every facet of the soldier's existence.

Bowie Knives, by R. Abels. Pub. by the author, NYC, 1960. 48 pp. profusely illus. Paper covers. $2.00.
A booklet showing knives, tomahawks, related trade cards and advertisements.

Bowie Knives From the Collections of Robert Abels and the Ohio Historical Society, by Wm. G. Keener and D. A. Hutslar. The Ohio Historical Society, 1962. 124 pp., profusely illus. Paper covers. $4.50.
Limited ed. of an original Museum Catalog of a special exhibit by the Ohio Historical Society.

Brass Spikes & Horsehair Plumes: A Study of U.S. Army Dress Helmets, 1872-1903, by Gordon Chappell, Arizona Pioneers Hist. Soc., Tucson, Ariz. 1966. 50 pp., illus. Paper covers. $2.00.
Historical monograph on military headgear of the period.

The Breech-Loader in the Service, 1816-1917, by Claud E. Fuller, N. Flayderman, New Milford, Conn., 1965. 381 pp., illus. $14.50.
Revised ed. of a 1933 historical reference on U.S. standard and experimental military shoulder arms. Much patent data, drawings, and photographs of the arms.
A voluminous work that covers handloading—and other things—in great detail. Replete with data for all cartridge forms.

British and American Flintlocks, by Fred. Wilkinson. Country Life Books, London, 1971. 64 pp., illus. $2.95.
Historical and technical aspects of flintlock firearms, in military and civilian use.

British and American Infantry Weapons of World War II, by A. J. Barker. 1st ed., 1969, Arco Publishing Co., New York, N.Y. 76 pp., illus., $3.50.
A British officer's survey that includes numerous specialized weapons, all are illustrated and described.

British Cut and Thrust Weapons, by John Wilkinson-Latham. Charles E. Tuttle Co., VT, 1971. 112 pp., illus. $7.50.
Well-illustrated study tracing the development of edged weapons and their adoption by the British armed forces. Describes in detail swords of cavalry and mounted troops, infantry, general officers, yeomanry, militia, the navy and air force.

British Military Bayonets from 1700 to 1945, by R. J. W. Latham. Arco Publ. Co., N.Y.C., 1969. 94 pp., ilus. $8.50.
History and identification catalog of British bayonets, with fine illustrations, marks, dimensions, and equipment of various British army units.

British Military Firearms 1650-1850, by H. L. Blackmore. Arco Publ. Co. Inc., New York, 1962. 296 pp. and 83 plates of photographs, line drawings, appendices and index. $10.00.
This excellent work admirably and authoritatively covers the subject in every detail. Highly recommended.

British Military Longarms 1715-1815, by D. W. Bailey, Stackpole Books, Harrisburg, PA, 1971. 80 pp., $4.95.
The Regulation service longarms of the British Army and Navy during a century of conflict in Europe, America and India, are fully described and illus.

British Military Longarms 1815-1865, by D. W. Bailey. Stackpole Books, Harrisburg, PA, 1972. 79 pp., illus. $4.95.
Concise account, covering muskets, carbines, rifles and their markings.

British Military Swords, From 1800 to the Present Day, by J. W. Latham, Crown Publishers, NY, 1967, 91 pp., illus. $3.95.
Survey of British swords used by various branches of the Army, with data on their manufacture, specifications, and procurement.

British Pistols and Guns, 1640-1940, by Ian Glendenning. Arco Publ. Co., NY, 1967. 194 pp., photos and drawings. $7.50.
Historical review of British firearms, with much data and illustration of furniture and decoration of fine weapons.

British Smooth-Bore Artillery, by Maj.-Gen. B. P. Hughes. Stackpole Books, Harrisburg, PA, 1969. 144 pp., illus. $14.95.
On the muzzle-loading artillery of the 18th and 19th centuries, covering dimensions, ammunition, and application.

The British Soldier's Firearm, 1850-1864, by C. H. Roads. Herbert Jenkins, London, 1964. 332 pp., illus. $14.50.
Detailed account of development of British military arms at the acme of the muzzle-loading period. All models in use are covered, as well as ammunition.

Buttons of the British Army 1855-1970, by Howard Ripley, Arms & Armour Press, London, 1971. 64 pp. $5.00.
Guide for collectors with over 650 buttons illus.

The Canadian Bayonet, by R. B. Manarey, Century Press, Alberta, Can. 1970. 51 pp. $5.00.
Illustrated history of the Canadian bayonet.

The Canadian Gunsmiths 1608-1900, by S. James Gooding. Museum Restoration Service, Canada, 1962. 322 pp., illus. $17.50.
Comprehensive survey of the gunmakers of Canada and the products of their skill, from early settlement to the age of the breech-loader.

Cartridge Headstamp Guide, by H. P. White and B. D. Munhall. H. P. White Laboratory, Bel Air, MD, 1963. 263 pp., illus. $10.00.
An important reference on headstamping of small arms ammo, by manufacturers in many countries. Clear illus. of 1936 headstamps of every type.

Cartridges for Collectors, by Fred A. Datig. Borden Publishing Co., Alhambra, Calif, Vol. I (Centerfire), 1958; Vol. II (Rimfire and Misc.) Types, 1963; Vol. III (Additional Rimfire, Centerfire, and Plastic,) 1967. Each of the three volumes 176 pp., well illus. and each priced at $7.50.
Vol. III supplements the first two books and presents 300 additional specimens. All illus. are shown in full-scale line drawings.

Cavalry Equipment 1874, 4 reprint of *U.S. Ordnance Memoranda No. 18* by Francis Bannerman Sons, Blue Point, NY, 1969. 119 pp., 12 plates. $6.50.
An officers' report on details of equipment issued to U.S. cavalry units.

Civil War Carbines, by A. F. Lustyik. World Wide Gun Report, Inc., Aledo, ILL, 1962. 63 pp., illus. paper covers, $2.00.
Accurate, interesting summary of most carbines of the Civil War period, in booklet form, with numerous good illus.

Civil War Collector's Encyclopedia, by Francis A. Lord, Stackpole books, Harrisburg, PA, 1963, 384 pp., 350 illus. $17.95.
A reference work on Civil War relics, for museums, students, writers, and collectors of Union and Confederate items. Identifies arms, uniforms, accoutrements, ordnance material, currency, postage, etc. Many patent drawings. Lists of manufacturers and vendors, North and South, are given.

Civil War Guns, by Wm. B. Edwards, Stackpole Books, Harrisburg, PA, 1962. 464 pp., over 400 illus. $5.95.
Comprehensive survey of Civil War arms, identification data, procurement procedures, and historical data. Important information on replicas, imitations, and fakes.

Classic Bowie Knives, by Robert Abels. R. Abels, Inc., NY, 1967. 97 pp., illus. with numerous fine examples of the subject. $7.50.
A nostalgic story of the famous blades, with trade advertisements on them, and photos of users.

The Collecting of Guns, ed. by Jas. E. Serven. Stackpole Books, Harrisburg, PA, 1964. 272 pp., illus. $24.50.
A new and massive compendium of gun lore for serious collectors by recognized experts. Separate chapters cover major categories and aspects of collecting. Over 600 firearms illus. Handsomely designed, deluxe binding in slip case. Reprint of 1966, $5.95.

Collector's Guide to American Cartridge Handguns, by Dewitt E. Sell. Stackpole Books, Harrisburg, PA, 1963, 234 pp., illus. $3.98.
Catalogs the important U.S. makers in its field, with histories of the firms and their production models. Photos, descriptions and features of many older and current handguns are included.

Collector's Guide to Luger Values 1972-73 Edition, by Michael Reese. Pelican Pub. Co., Gretna, LA, 1972. 10 pp., paper covers. $1.00.
Collector's guide to top prices.

A Collector's Pictorial Book of Bayonets, by F. J. Stephens, Stackpole Books, Harrisburg, PA, 1971. 127 pp., illus. $5.95.
Instant identification of bayonet types, plus their history and use.

Colt Firearms from 1836, by James E. Serven. New 7th ed. Foundation Press, La Habra, CA, 1973. 398 pp., illus. $19.95.
Excellent survey of the Colt company and its products. Updated with new SAA production chart and commemorative list.
Colt Tips, by E. Dixon Larson. Pioneer Press, Union City, TN, 1972. 140 pp., illus. Paper covers. $3.95.
Comprehensive, discriminating facts about Colt models from 1836 to 1898.
Colt's Variations of the Old Model Pocket Pistol, 1848 to 1872, by P. L. Shumaker. Borden Publishing Co., Alhambra, CA 1966, a reprint of the 1957 edition. 150 pp., illus. $6.00.
A useful tool for the Colt specialist and a welcome return of a popular source of information that had been long out-of-print.
The Complete Book of Gun Collecting, by Charles E. Chapel. Coward-McCann, Inc., N.Y.C., 1960. 222 pp., illus. $5.95.
Answers hundreds of questions for the beginner, and is a reference for the advanced collector and student of firearms. It covers hand cannon of the 14th century to arms of the present day.
Confederate Arms, by Wm. A. Albaugh III, and E. N. Simmons. Stackpole Books, Harrisburg, PA, 1957. 278 pp., illus. $3.95.
Contains much heretofore unpublished information on the arms and associated material of the Confederacy.
Confederate Handguns, by Wm. A. Albaugh III. Hugh Benet Jr., and Edw. N. Simmons. Geo. Shumway, York, PA, 1963. 272 pp., 125 illus. $5.95.
Every known true Confederate pistol and revolver is described and illus., with the story of its maker and procurement by the C.S.A. Much new information includes listing of C. W. makers and dealers, information on replicas and fakes. Indispensable to the collector and student of these arms and their period.
Cut and Thrust Weapons, by E. Wagner, Spring Books, Longdon, 1967. 491 pp., line drawings. $17.50.
English translation of a survey of European edged weapons, their traditions, manufacture, and use.
Deanes' Manual of the History and Science of Fire-arms, by J. Deane. Standard Publications, Huntington, WV, 1946 facsimile reprint of the rare English original of 1858. 291 pp., three folding plates. $6.00.
A history of firearms, plus design and manufacture of military and sporting arms.
Decoy Collector's Guide 1963-1964-1965, ed. by H. D. Sorenson, Burlington, IA, 1971. Irregular pagination, illus., $15.00.
This volume includes all of the 12 booklets originally published as quarterlies.
Decoy Collector's Guide 1966-67 Annual, ed. by H. D. Sorenson, Burlington, IA, 1966. 125 pp., illus. $5.00.
Well-illustrated articles on American decoys.
Decoy Collector's Guide, 1968, ed. by H. D. Sorenson, 1967, Burlington, IA 128 pp, 75 photos. Spiral bound. $5.00.
History, decoy patents, carving, collecting, etc.
Digest of Patents Relating to Breech-Loading and Magazine Small Arms (1836-1873), by V. D. Stockbridge, WA, 1874. Reprinted 1963 by E. N. Flayderman, Greenwich, Conn. 180 pp., 880 illus. $12.50.
An exhaustive compendium of patent documents on firearms, indexed and classified by breech mechanism types, valuable reference for students and collectors.
Early Firearms of Great Britain and Ireland from the Collection of Clay P. Bedford. The Metropolitan Museum of Art, NY, 1971. 187 pp., illus. $17.50.
Authoritative account of an exceptional body of historic firearms, and a detailed survey of three centuries of gunmaking.
Early Indian Trade Guns—1625 to 1775, by T. M. Hamilton. Museum of the Great Plains, Lawton, Okla. 1969. 34 pp., well illus., paper covers. $2.50.
Detailed descriptions of subject arms, compiled from early records and from the study of remnants found in Indian county.
Early Japanese Sword Guards, by Masayuki Sasano. Japan Pub. Trading Co., San Francisco, CA, 1972. 256 pp., illus. $12.50.
220 of the finest open-work sword guards, dating from early periods and representing most of the major schools.
Early Loading Tools and Bullet Molds, by R. H. Chamberlain. The Farm Tribune, Porterville, GA, 1971. 75 pp., illus. Paper covers, $3.00.
An excellent aid to collectors.
Early Percussion Firearms, by Lewis Winant, Wm. Morrow & Co., Inc., N.Y.C., 1959. 292 pp., illus. $2.98.
A history of early percussion firearms ignition—from Forsyth to Winchester 44-40, from flintlocks of the 18th century to centerfires. Over 230 illus. of firearms, parts, patents, and cartridges—from some of the finest collections here and abroad.
Edged Weapons, by Fred. Wilkinson. Guinness Signatures, London, 1970, 256 pp., plus 14-page index. Excellently illus., many in full color. $12.95.
Scholarly treatment of all kinds of blades—from flint to steel, rapiers, smallswords, knives, daggers, hunting weapons, polearms, etc., plus construction and decoration.
The Encyclopedia of Military History, by R. Ernest and Trevor N. Dupuy. Harper & Row, New York, NY, 1970. 1st ed., 1406 pp., well illus., in line and halftone. $20.00.
This massive single volume covers the subject from 3500 B.C. to the present time. A complete reference guide to the world's military history; narration of war and combat, tactics, strategy and weaponry. Over 250 maps, illus. of weapons, fortifications, etc.
English, Irish and Scottish Firearms, by A. Merwyn Carey. Arco Publishing Co., Inc., NY, 1967. A reprint. 121 pp., illus. in line and halftone. $6.50.
Out-of-print since 1954, this work covers the subject from the middle of the 16th century to the end of the 19th.
English Pistols & Revolvers, by J. N. George. Arco Publ. Co., Inc., N.Y.C., 1962, 256 pp., 28 plates, $6.50.
The 2nd reprinting of a notable work first publ. in 1938. Treats of the historical development and design of English hand firearms from the 17th cent. to the present. A much better book than the former reprint, particularly as to clarity of the tipped-in plates.
English Sporting Guns and Accessories, by Macdonald Hastings. Ward Lock & Co., London. 1st ed., 1969. 96 pp., well illus. $4.00.
A delightful monograph on shotguns and accessory equipment for hunting from 1800 to the advent of the breech loader, including historic arms and ammunition.
European & American Arms, by Claude Blair, Batsford, London, and Crown Publ., N.Y.C., 1962, 192 pp., 9"x12". Profusely and magnificently illus. $6.95.
A complete visual encyclopedia on all sorts of arms of Europe and America with over 600 photographs of pieces from nearly all the major collections of Western Europe, America, and Russia, from about 1100 to 1850. A splendid text describes historical and technical developments.
European Armour in the Tower of London, by A. R. Dufty. H. M. Stationery Office, London, England, 1968. 17 pp. text, 164 plates, $12.60.
Pictorial record of almost 400 pieces of armor, helmets, and accoutements in the famous Tower of London collection.
European Arms & Armour, by Chas. H. Ashdown, Brussel & Brussel, NY, 1967. A reprint, 384 pp., illus. with 42 plates and 450 drawings. $5.95.
Historical survey of body armor up to the era of gunpowder, with some coverage on weapons and early firearms,
European Hand Firearms of the 16th, 17th, and 18th Centuries, by H. J. Jackson and C. E. Whitlaw. Bramhall house, New York, NY. A reprint of the noted original. 108 pp., fine photographic plates. $5.95.
A work for scholars and collectors, including a list of arms makers. Not without error.
The Evolution of the Colt, by R. L. Wilson, R. Q. Sutherland, Kansas City, MO, 1967. 54 pp., illus. $3.00.
Pictures the fine Colt arms of the publisher from percussion to cartridge. Includes a Colt bibliography.
Famous Guns from the Smithsonian Collection, by H. W. Bowman. Arco. Publ. Co., Inc., NY, 1967. 112 pp., illus. $3.50.
The finest of the "Famous Guns" series.
Famous Guns from the Winchester Collection, by H. W. Bowman. Arco Publ. Co., NYC, 1958 and later. 144 pp., illus. $3.50.
The gems of the hand and shoulder arms in the great collection at New Haven, CT.
Feuerwaffen von 1300 bis 1967, by Hans-Bert Lockhoven. International Small Arms Publ., Cologne, W. Germany, 1969. 96 pp., illus. $6.95.
Review of the principal developments in military smallarms from early times, German text.
'51 Colt Navies, by N. L. Swayze. Gun Hill Publ. Co., Yazoo City, MS, 1967. 243 pp., well illus. $15.00.
The first major effort devoting its entire space to the 1851 Colt Navy revolver. There are 198 photos of models, sub-models, variations, parts, markings, documentary material, etc. Fully indexed.
Firearms Curiosa, by Lewis Winant, Ray Riling, Philadelphia, PA, 2nd and deluxe reissue 1961, 281 pp., well illus. $5.00.
Reissue publ. by Bonanza Books, N.Y.C., 1965. $2.98.
An important work for those with an interest in odd, distinctive and unusual forms and firing.
The Firearms Dictionary, by R. A. Steindler. Stackpole Books, Harrisburg, PA, 1970. 256 pp., nearly 200 illus. $7.95.
A super single-source reference to more than 1800 English and Foreign gun-related words, phrases and nomenclature, etc. Highly useful to all armsmen—collectors, shooters, hunters, etc.
Firearms in England in the Fourteenth Century, by T. F. Tout. Geo. Shumway, York, PA, 1958. 58 pp., illus., Paper covers. $4.00.
Reprint of a 1911 monograph on the history and manufacture of early British firearms, by a distinguished historian.
Flintlock Guns and Rifles, by F. Wilkinson, Stackpole Books, Harrisburg, PA, 1971. 80 pp., $4.95.
Illus. reference guide for 1650-1850 period showing makers, mechanisms and users.
The Flintlock, Its Origin and Development, by Torsten Lenk; J. T. Hayward, Editor, Holland Press, London, 1964. 192 pp., 134 illus. $6.95.
First English-text version of the 1939 Swedish work termed "the most important book on the subject." Original illus. are reproduced, and a new index and bibliography complete this valuable book.
Flintlock Pistols, by F. Wilkinson. Stackpole Books, Harrisburg, PA, 1968. 75 pp., illus. $4.95.
Illustrated reference guide by a British authority, covering 17th-19th century flintlock pistols.
Forsyth & Co.—Patent Gunmakers, by W. Keith Neal and D. H. L. Back. G. Bell & Sons, London, 1st ed., 1969, 280 pp., well illus. $12.95.
An excellent study of the invention and development of the percussion system by the Rev. Alexander Forsyth in the early 19th century. All Forsyth types are covered, plus a diary of events from 1768 to 1852.
.45-70 Rifles, by J. Behn, Rutgers Book Center, Highland Park, NJ, 1972. New ed., 150 pp., illus. $5.95.
Covers the official U.S. Army small arms cartridge and the weapons for its use.
The French Army in America, by E. P. Hamilton. Museum Restoration Service, Ottawa, 1967. 108 pp., illus. $3.00.
Concise historical coverage, illus. with contemporary documents and manual-of-arms plates. Text in English and French. Paper wrappers.
French Pistols and Sporting Guns, by A. N. Kennard. Transatlantic Arts, Inc., Levittown, NY, 1972. 63 pp., illus. $2.95. Traces the technical evolution of French pistols and sporting guns from matchlock to breechloader.
French Military Weapons, 1717-1938, by James E. Hicks. N. Flayderman & Co., New Milford, CT, 1964. 281 pp., profusely illus. $9.50.
A valuable reference work, first publ. 1938 as *Notes on French Ordnance*, this rev. ed. covers hand, shoulder, and edged weapons, ammunition and artillery, with history of various systems.
The Fuller Collection of American Firearms, by H. L. Peterson. Eastern National Park & Monument Assn., 1967. 63 pp., illus. $2.50.
Illustrated catalog of principal military shoulder arms in the collection. Decorated paper wrappers.
Gamle Danske Militaervaben, by Th. Moller. Host & Sons, Denmark, 1st reprinting, 1968. 64 pp., well illus. in line. Heavy paper covers. $4.00.
Old Danish military weapons, with Danish and English text, covering Weapons from 1971 to 1832, plus accoutrements.
The Gatling Gun, by Paul Wahl & D. R. Toppel. Arco Publ., N.Y.C., 1971. 168 pp., illus. $5.95.
History of the famed rapid-fire weapon used by many of the world's armies and navies from 1861.
German Mauser Rifle—Model of 1898, by J. E. Coombes and J. L. Aney. A reprint in paper covers by Francis Bannerman Sons, New York, NY, of their 1921 publication. 20 pp., well illus. $1.50.
Data on the subject weapon and its W. W. I development. Bayonets and ammunition are also described and illus.
German Pistols and Holsters 1934 to 1945, by R. D. Whittington III. Brownlee Books, College Station, Tex., 1969. 1st ed., limited to 2000 numbered copies, 223 pp., well illus., in halftone. $15.00.
A manual for collectors on subject items issued to the military, police and NSDAP. Covers all models of various designs, including those of foreign manufacture.
German Submachine Guns and Assault Rifles. WE, Inc., Old Greenwich, CT, 1967. 161 pp. $5.95.
Aberdeen Proving Ground reports on over 50 models of World War II German rapid-fire weapons are reprinted.
Die Geschichtliche Entwicklung Der Handfeuerwaffen, by M. Thierbach, Akademische Druck, Graz, Austria, 1965. Vol. 1, 590 pp., German text: Vol. II, 36 Plates. $37.00.
The famous German work on history and development of firearms, accessories and ammunition, first published in 1886 in Dresden.
A Glossary of the Construction, Decoration and Use of Arms and Armor in all Countries and in all Times, by Geo. C. Stone, Jack Brussel, NY, 2nd reprint, 1966, 694 pp., illus. $9.95.
The outstanding work on its subject, authoritative and accurate in detail. The major portion is on oriental arms.
The Great Guns, by H. L. Peterson and Robt. Elman. Grosset & Dunlap, NY, 1972. $14.95.
Basic and general history with 70 full color illustrations and 140 photos of some of the finest guns from American collections. A well written text.
Great Weapons of World War I, by Com. G. Dooly, Walker & Co., NY, 1969, 340 pp., illus. $14.50.
Describes all the important weapons and system developments used during WWI.

A Guide to Oriental Daggers and Swords, by Michael C. German. M. C. German, London, Eng., 1967. 59 pp., illus. Paper covers. $3.95.
Excellent, inexpensive guide for identifying and classifying hundreds of different Oriental daggers.

The Gun and its Development, by W. W. Greener. Bonanza Books, NY, 1967. A reprint. 804 pp., profusely illus. $5.95.
A facsimile of the famous 9th edition of 1910. Covers history and development of arms in general with emphasis on shotguns.

Gun Collector's Digest, edited by Jos. J. Schroeder, Jr. Digest Books, Inc., Northfield, IL, 1973. 320 pp., illus. Paper covers. $6.95.
Articles on guns as an investment; rating gun condition; display and security; gun collecting and the law; building a collector's library, etc. A special section on values.

The Gun Collector's Handbook of Values, by C. E. Chapel. Coward, McCann & Geoghegan, Inc NY, 1972. 398 pp., illus. $12.50.
10th rev. ed. of the best-known price reference for collectors, with values for 1973-74.

The Gun Digest Book of Knives, edited by Jack Lewis. Digest Books, Inc. Northfield, IL, 1973. 288 pp., illus. Paper covers. $5.95.
Authoritative, in-depth study. How to collect, buy and care for knives. Illus. catalog section gives current prices for blades from custom cutlers and knife factories.

Gunmakers of Indiana, by A. W. Lindert. Publ. by the author, Homewood, IL, 1968, 3rd ed. 284 pp., illus. Large format. $15.00.
An extensive and historical treatment, illus. with old photographs and drawings.

Guns and Gun Collecting, by De Witt Bailey; et al. Octopus Books, London, Eng., 1972. 128 pp., illus. $5.95.
A new look at the world of firearms, including not only the historical aspects but hunting and sporting guns and 19th and 20th century weapons of war. Nearly 180 photos, 78 in full color.

Guns of the Old West, by C. E. Chapel. Coward-McCann Inc., N.Y.C., 1961. 306 pp., illus. $6.95.
A definitive book on American arms that opened the frontier and won the West. Shows arms, rare pictures, advertisements, and pertinent associated material.

Guns Through the Ages, by Geoffrey Boothroyd. Sterling Publ. Co., N.Y.C., 1962, 192 pp., illus. $1.69.
A detailed illustrated history of small arms from the invention of gunpowder to today. Covers ignition methods, proof marks, fakes, ammo, etc. Bibliography.

Haandskydevaabens Bedommelse, by Johan F. Stockel. Udgivet Af Tojuhusmuseet, Copenhagen, Denmark, 2nd limited reprint, 1966. Vol. I, 397 pp., plus 6 plates, Vol. II, 1080 pp. illus. Both $35.00.
Printed in Danish but considered by scholars to be the finest and most complete source for the "marks" and "touches" of gunmakers. Both are well illus.

Hall System Military Firearms and Conversions in the Museum Collection. Veteran Association of the First Corps of Cadets Museum, Boston, MA, 1973. 20 pp., illus. Paper covers. $1.00
Illustrates and describes various models, including several Confederate conversions.

Hall's Breechloaders, by R. T. Huntington, Geo. Shumway, Publ. 1972. 369 pp., illus. $15.00. Paper, $12.00.
Definitive treatise on John H. Hall and his inspectors. Shows all known models of the Hall rifle, appurtenances and pistol.

Handbuch Der Waffenkunde, by Wendelin Boeheim. Akademische D. U. V., Graz, Austria, 1966, 694 pp., illus. $14.00.
One of the famous works of 1890—long out-of-print. Now in a new printing, German text. Historical weapons and armor from the Middle Ages through the 18th century.

Handfeuerwaffen, by J. Lugs, Deutscher Militarverlag, Berlin, 1956. 2 Vol., 315 pp., illus. German text, $40.00.
Noted reference on small arms and their development in many nations. All types of weapons are listed described, and illustrated, with data on manufacturers.

Die Handfeuerwaffen, by Rudolf Schmidt, Vienna, Austria, 1968, Vol. I, text 225 pp., Vol. II, 76 plates. $20.00.
Reprint of an important 1875 German reference work on military small arms, much prized by knowledgeable collectors. The fine color plates in Vol. II show detailed and exploded views of many longarms and handguns.

Handfeuerwaffen System Vetterli, by Hugo Schneider; et al. Stocker-Schmid, A. G. Dietikon-Zurich, Switzerland, 1972. 143 pp., illus. $26.00.
Describes and illustrates the many models of Vetterli rifles and carbines, the bayonets and ammunition used with them. Many large clear illustrations. German text.

Heavy Artillery Projectiles of the Civil War 1861-1865, by S. C. Kerksis & T. S. Dickey. Phoenix Press, Kennesaw, GA, 1972. 277 pp., illus. $19.50. Privately pub., limited ed.
Covers use of the projectiles used by both combatants.

Hints to Riflemen, by H. W. S. Cleveland. Distributor, Robert Halter, New Hope, PA, 286 pp., illustrated. $10.00.
A reprint of the original 1864 edition, to which *Practical Directions for the use of the Rifle* has been added.

History and Collecting Case Pocket Knives, by D. P. Ferguson. D. P. Ferguson, Fairborn, OH, 1970. 24 pp., illus., paper, $1.00.
Handbook on knives made by W. R. Case & Sons Cutlery Co.

A History of Body Armor, by H. L. Peterson, Charles Scribner's Sons, NY, 1968. 64 pp., illus. $4.95.
From the fur and leather armor of primitive man to the nylon body armor and steel helmet of today.

A History of the Colt Revolver, by C. T. Haven and F. A. Belden. Bonanza Books, NY, 1967. A reprint. 711 pages large format, profusely illus. in line and halftone. $8.95.
A great and massive work, including details on other Colt arms from 1836 to 1940. A must for every Colt collector.

A History of Firearms, by W. Y. Carman. Routledge & Kegan Paul Ltd., London, England, 1955. 207 pp., illus. $4.50.
A concise coverage, from earliest times to 1914, with emphasis on artillery.

A History of Firearms, by H. L. Peterson. Chas. Scribner's Sons, N.Y.C., 1961. 57 pp., profusely illus. $4.95.
From the origin of firearms through each ignition form and improvement to the M-14. Drawings by Daniel D. Feaser.

A History of Shooting, by Jaroslav Lugs, Spring Books, Feltham, England. 1st printing, 1968. 227 pp., well illus., with contemporary drawings and photographs. $4.98.
Historical survey dealing mainly with marksmanship, duelling and exhibition shooting in Europe and America.

A History of Spanish Firearms, by James D. Lavin. Arco Co., NY, 1965. 304 pp., illus. $9.95.
This history, beginning with the recorded appearance of gunpowder in Spain, traces the development of hand firearms through their golden age —the eighteenth century—to the death in 1825 of Isidro Soler. Copious reproductions of short and long arms, list of gun makers and their "marks" a glossary, bibliography and index are included.

A History of Weaponry, by Courtlandt Canby, Hawthorne Books, Inc., NY, 1963, 112 pp., illus. $2.98.
From the caveman's club to the M-14 rifle, from Greek fire to the ICBM.

The History of Winchester Firearms 1866-1966, ed. by T. E. Hall and P. Kuhlhoff, Winchester-Western Press, New Haven, CT, 1966. 159 pp., illus. $10.00.
Called the collector's item of the century, this 3rd ed. of Geo. R. Watrous' work rises to new glory in its scope and illustrations, beautifully produced, with a slip case showing old hunting scenes by A. B. Frost and Frederic Remington. Limited ed.

Home Service Helmet 1878-1914 With Regimental Plates, The Collectors Series, London, n.d., 32 pp., illus. Paper, $4.00.
Taken from the Wilkinson-Latham collection.

Hopkins & Allen Gun Guide and Catalog (ca. 1913). Wagle Publ., Lake Wales, FA, 1972. 32 pp., illus. Paper covers. $3.75.
Facsimile of the original catalog. Shows the firms rifles, shotguns and pistols, and includes prices. Full color cover painting by Dan Smith.

The Identification and Analysis of Luger Proof Marks, by Robt. B. Marvin. R. B. Marvin, Jasper, FA, 1972. 88 pp., illus. Paper covers. $7.50.
Shows Luger pistol markings and their use in identifying the type of pistol. Complete cross index. **Identifying Old U.S. Muskets, Rifles & Carbines,** by Col. A. Gluckman. Stackpole Books, Harrisburg, PA, 1973. 487 pp., illus. $2.98. Collector's guide to U.S. long arms, first publ. 1959. Numerous models of each type are described and shown, with histories of their makers.

Illustrated British Firearms Patents 1714-1853, comp. and ed. by Stephen V. Grancsay and Merrill Lindsay. Winchester Press. NY, 1969. Unpaginated. $15.00.
Facsimile of patent documents with a bibliography. Limited, numbered ed. of 1000, bound in ¾ leather and marbled boards.

Insignia, Decorations and Badges of the Third Reich and Occupied Countries, by R. Kahl, Military Collectors Service, Kedichem, Holland, 1970. 135 pp., $9.95.
Handbook of regalia with descriptive text and over 800 line illus.

An introduction to British Artillery in North America, by S. J. Gooding. Museum Rest. Serv., Ottawa, 1965. 54 pp., illus., Paperbound. $2.00.
Concise account of such equipment used in America 1750-1850.

Italian Fascist Daggers, by Fred. J. Stephens. Militaria Pub. Ltd., London, England, 1972. 25 pp., illus., some in color. Paper covers. $5.
First publ. devoted to collecting the daggers of Fascist Italy.

Japanese Armour, by L. J. Anderson. Stackpole Books, Harrisburg, PA, 1968. 84 pp., illus. $4.95.
British reference on museum quality armor made by the Myochin and Saotome families between the 15th and 20th centuries.

Japanese Military Handguns and Holsters 1893-1945, by John C. Van Lund. J. C. Van Lund, Donelson, TN, 1972. 467 pp., illus. $15.
A help in identifying Japanese handguns and holsters. Gives variations, serial ranges, and production totals. Limited ed. Signed by the author.

Japanese Polearms, by R. M. Knutsen. Holland Press, London, 1963. 271 pp., well-illus. Line drawings and photos. $18.00.
Each category of Japanese spear is described and illus. in this hist. treatment, including schools of spear and sword fencing. Lists leading makers and glossary.

Japanese Sword Blades, by Alfred Dobree, George Shumway, York, PA, 1967. 39 pp., illus., in paper wrapers. $4.50.
A two-part monograph, reprinted from a notable work.

Japanese Sword Fittings: The Naunton Collection, by Henri L. Joly. W. M. Hawley, Hollywood, CA, 1973. 434 pp., illus. $50.
Reprint of the finest work ever done in English on the subject. 88 plates show 1300 fittings full size.

Kentucky Knife-Traders Manual, compiled by R. B. Ritchie. R. B. Ritchie, Hindman, KY, 1971. 66 pp., illus. Paper covers. $5.75.
Lists some 2000 pocket knives and their values by brands, pattern and condition, plus a listing of about 400 collectible razors.

The Kentucky Rifle, by J. G. W. Dillin. Geo. Shumway, York, PA, 1967. 5th ed. 202 pp., illus. $20.00
A respected work on the long rifles developed in colonial days and carried by pioneers and soldiers. Much information of value to collectors and historians. Limited ed.

The Kentucky Rifle: A True American Heritage in Picture, compiled by Philip Cowan, et al. The Kentucky Rifle Assn. Wash., D.C., 1967. 110 pp., illus. $15.
Presents an outstanding group of Kentucky Rifles, most of them never before pictured.

The Kentucky Rifle, by Merrill Lindsay. Arma Press, NY/The Historical Society of York County, York, PA, 1972. 100 pp., 81 large colored illustrations. $15.
Presents in precise detail and exact color 77 of the finest Kentucky rifles ever assembled in one place. Also describes the conditions which led to the development of this uniquely American arm.

Kentucky Rifle Patchboxes & Barrel Marks, by Roy F. Chandler, Valley View Offset, Duncannon, PA, 1971. 400 pp., $20.00.
Reference work illustrating hundreds of patchboxes, together with the mark or signature of the maker.

Robert Klaas Sword and Dagger Catalog, Robt. Klaas, Solingen-Ohligs, W. Germany 1938. 32 pp., illus. Paper, $5.00.
Reprint of the original 1938 catalog. A rare reference work. 16 pp. of swords and daggers with original prices.

The Leather Jacket Soldier, by O. B. Faulk. Socio-Technical Pub., Pasadena, CA, 1971, 80 pp., illus. $10.00.
History of such Spanish military equipment of the late 18th century as lances, horse accoutrements, guns, uniforms, etc.

Longrifles of North Carolina, by John Bivins, Jr. Geo. Shumway, York, PA, 1968, 200 pp., profusely illus. $24.00.
Historical survey of North Carolina gunmakers and their production during the 18th and 19th centuries. Over 400 gunsmiths are included. Fine photographs.

Longrifles of Note, by Geo. Shumway, Geo. Shumway, York, PA, 1967. 90 pp., illus. Paper covers, $3.95.
A review of 35 fine American long rifles, with detailed illustrations showing their art work, plus descriptive material.

The Luger Pistol, by Fred A. Datig. Privately published, Los Angeles, CA, 1962. 328 pp. well-illus. $8.50.
Larger, revised ed. of the story behind the most famous pistol of all time.

Manhattan Firearms, by Waldo E. Nutter, Stackpole Books, Harrisburg, PA, 1958. 250 pp., illus., in halftone. $7.95.
Complete history of the Manhattan Firearms Mfg. Co., and its products. Excellent specialized reference.

Manual of Rifling and Rifle Sights, by Lt.-Col. Viscount Bury, M.P., Ray Riling Arms Books Co., Phila., PA, 1971. 47 pp., Paper, $5.00.
Reprint of 1864 London edition done for the British National Rifle Ass'n. 141 illus., plus 3 folding plates.

The Manufacture of Armour and Helmets in 16th Century Japan, by Sakakibara Kozan. Holland Press, London, 1963. 156 pp., 32 pp. of illus. $20.00.

Important reference on styles and steps of making Japanese armor, first publ. Tokyo, 1800. Eng. trans., revised by H. R. Robinson of Tower of London Armouries.

Mauser-Gewehre & Mauser-Patente, by R. H. Korn. Akademische Druck Graz, Austria, 1971. 440 pp. German text, most completely illustrated with copious line drawings, charts, many of them folding plates. $30.00.

Fine reprint of the extremely-rare original. Truly a must for every Mauser buff, it has never been surpassed.

Metal Uniform Insignia of the US Army in the Southwest, 1846-1902, by S. B. Brinckerhoff, Arizona Pioneers Hist. Soc., Tucson, Ariz., 1972, 28 pp., illus. Paper covers. $2.50.

Monograph on buttons, badges, buckles, and other uniform insignia.

Metallic Cartridges, T. J. Treadwell, compiler. The Armoury, NYC, 1959. Unpaginated. 68 plates. Paper, $2.95. Cloth, $5.95.

A reduced-size reproduction of U.S. Ordnance Memoranda No. 14, originally publ. in 1873, on regulation and experimental cartridges manufactured and tested at Frankford Arsenal, Philadelphia, Pa.

Militaria, by Frederick Wilkinson. Hawthorn Books, New York, NY, 1969. 1st U.S. ed. 256 pp., well illus. in halftone. $5.95.

Introduction to military items of interest to collectors, including prints, medals, uniforms, military miniatures, weapons, badges etc.

Military Arms of Canada, by Upper Canada Hist. Arms Soc. Museum Restoration Serv., West Hill, Ont., 1963. 43 pp., illus. $1.50.

Booklet cont. 6 authoritative articles on the principal models of Canadian mil. small arms. Gives characteristics of each, makers, quantities produced.

Military Edged Weapons of the World, 1880-1965, by H. A. Mauerer, College Pt., NY, 1967. 151 pp., illus. $4.50.

Various swords, blades, etc., in a private collection are dimensioned, described, and photographed. A guide for collectors. Paper wrappers.

Military Headgear in the Southwest, 1846-1890, by S. B. Brinckerhoff, Arizona Pioneers Hist. Soc., Tucson, Ariz., 1963. 16 pp., illus. Paper covers. $1.50.

Historical monograph, reprinted from the journal *Arizoniana.* With bibliography.

Military Sharps Rifles and Carbines, by R. E. Hopkins. Hopkins, Campbell, Calif., 1967. 141 pp., illus. $11.50.

A guide to the principal types, with photographs, patent data, technical details, etc.

Miniature Arms, by Merrill Lindsay. Winchester Press, New York, NY, 1970. 111 pp., illus. $5.95.

A concise study of small-scale replicas of firearms and other weapons of collector interest. Fine color photographs.

Monographie der K. K. Osterr.-Ung: Blanken und Handfeuer-Waffen, by Anton Dolleczek. Akademische Druck, Graz, Austria, 1970. 197 pp., illus. $10.00.

Facsimile reprint of a standard 1896 German work on military weapons. In German text, illus. with line drawings and color plate of regimental colors.

Montgomery Ward & Co. 1894-1895, reproduction of a 600-page catalog, ed. by Jos. J. Schroeder, Jr., Digest Books, Inc., Northfield, IL, 1970. profusely illus. $4.95.

A nostalgic look at the past, and for the gun enthusiast a look at models and prices prevailing in the late 19th century.

The NRA Collector's Series, Digest Books, Inc., Northfield, IL, 1971, 84 pp. paper covers $2.95.

Reprint of the three predecessors of *American Rifleman* magazine and the first edition of *American Rifleman.*

The NRA Gun Collectors Guide, by staff members of NRA. National Rifle Assn., Washington, D.C., 1972. 256 pp., well illus. $4.50.

A wealth of information on collecting and collectors arms, with 64 major and 41 short articles, selected from the last 18 years of in "The American Rifleman."

Louis Napoleon on Artillery: The Development of Artillery from the 14th to the 17th Century, by W. Y. Carman, Arms and Armour Press, Middlesex, England, 1967. 24 pp., illus. Paper covers. $2.75.

A reprinting of rare original material—10 finely engraved plates, with 70 drawings, on the development of artillery, plus brief text.

Native American Bows, by T. M. Hamilton. George Shumway, York, PA, 1972. 148 pp., illus. $12.

Summary of the history and development of bows native to America, from early times to the present.

The New Highland Military Discipline, by Geo. Grant. Museum Restoration Service, Ottawa, 1967. 32 pp., illus. $1.50.

Reprint of a Scottish drill manual, regimental history, with illus. contemporary and modern. Paper wrappers.

The 9-pdr. Muzzle Loading Rifle, by J. D. Chown. Museum Restoration Service, Ottawa, 1967. 32 pp., illus. $1.50.

Reprint of an early Canadian artillery manual, with historical notes. Paper wrappers.

Simeon North: First Official Pistol Maker of the United States, by S. North and R. North, Rutgers Book Center, Highland Park, NJ, 1972. 207 pp., illus. $7.95.

Exact reprint of the original. Includes chapters on New England pioneer manufacturers and on various arms.

The Northwest Gun, by Chas. E. Hanson Jr. Nebraska State Historical Society, Lincoln, NB, 1970. 85 pp., illus. Paper covers. $4.50.

The corner-stone of collecting Indian trade guns.

Notes on U.S. Ordnance, vol. II, 1776-1941, by James E. Hicks. Modern Books & Crafts, Greens Farms, Conn., 1971. 252 pp., illus. $8.00.

Updated version of a standard work on development of military weapons used by U.S. forces, from handguns to coast artillery and aerial bombs. This is not to be confused with Hicks 1940 United States Ordnance, referring mainly to Ordnance correspondence as Vol. II.

One Hundred Great Guns, by Merrill Lindsay. Walker & Co., NY, 1967. 379 pp., fine color illus. $9.95.

Deluxe illus. history of firearms, covering all principal types of small arms and their makers. Bibliography.

A super-deluxe edition is available at $75.00.

Ordnance Memoranda No.22. The Fabrication of Small Arms for the U.S. Service, by Lt. Col. James G. Benton. Benchmark Pub. Co., Glendale, NY, 1970. 229 pp., 35 plates. $9.50.

Reprint of an 1878 War Dept. pub. on U.S. production of military firearms and edged weapons.

Oriental Armour, by W. R. Robinson. Reprint by Outlet Book Co., New York, NY, 1970. 256 pp., well illus. $4.95.

Traces the subject material from earliest times until it was finally discarded.

The Original Mauser Magazine Sporting Rifles. Shooter's Bible, S. Hackensack, NJ, 56 pp., illus., paperbound. $1.00.

Facsimile reprint of a Mauser firearms brochure, with English text.

An Outline of the History and Development of Hand Firearms, from the Earliest Period to About the End of the Fifteenth Century, by R. C. Clephan [Original ed., 1906]. A reprint in 1946 by Standard Publications, Inc., Huntington, W.Va. 60 pp., illus. $4.00.

A worthy facsimile of a very scarce, concise and scholarly work.

The Peacemaker and Its Rivals, by John E. Parsons. Morrow, NYC, 1950. 140 pp., illustrated. Appendix, bibliography, and index. $7.50.

Detailed history and development of the Single Action Army Colt, with an over-all study of the six-shooter's significance in American history.

The Pennsylvania-Kentucky Rifle, by Henry J. Kauffman. Bonanza Books, NY, 1968. A reprint. 374 pp., illus. $4.95.

A classic work first publ. in 1960 on early long rifles. Makers descriptions, and manufacturing methods are covered.

Percussion Guns & Rifles, by D. W. Bailey. Stackpole Books, Harrisburg, PA, 1972. 79 pp., illus. $5.95.

A guide to the muzzle-loading percussion guns and rifles of the 19th century.

Percussion Revolvers of the United States, by R. Thalheimer. Von Hoffman Press, St. Louis, 1970. 224 pp., illus, $7.95.

Reference work on U.S. and Confederate percussion revolvers, plus a history of firearms from the hand-cannon to percussion revolvers.

Photographic Supplement of Confederate Swords, by Wm. A. Albaugh III. Wm. A. Bond, Vernon, TX, 1963. 205 pp., 300 photos. $6.95.

Over 200 specimens of C. W. Edged weapons are shown, with data on their owners and makers. Useful for collectors and students.

The Powder Flask Book, by Ray Riling. Bonanza Books, NY 1968. A reprint. 520 pp., large format, profusely illus. First re-issue of the 1953 original ed. $9.95. A limited number of the originals are available for inscription and autograph at $35.00.

Covers the literature on flasks, their makers, and users—hunters, shooters and the military—as well as showing the arms, cased or not, short and long. A relative price listing for collector advantage is included.

Price List of the U.S. Cartridge Company's Ammunition, A 1969 reprint of the 1891 original, publ. by J. C. Tillinghast, Marlow, N.H. 29 pp., illus., paper covers. $2.50.

Displays many of the now hard-to-find cartridges.

A Primer of World Bayonets. G. Hughes, London, 1969. Unpaginated, illus. Paper, $5.00.

A comprehensive (2 vol.) manual on the bayonet.

Quellen zur Geschichte de Feuerwaffen, by A. Essenwein [ed./compiler] Akademische Druck, Graz, Austria, 1969. One volume of text [German] plus another of fascinating plates. 178 pp., text and 197 plates. $50.00.

A fine facsimile of a rare and most interesting German source book on the "History of Firearms," taken from original drawings of 1390-1700. A treasury for the serious scholar and/or artillery buff.

The Rampant Colt, by R. L. Wilson. Thomas Haas, Spencer, Ind., 1969. 107 pp., well illus. $10.00.

Study of Samuel Colt's coat-of-arms and the rampant colt figure used on Colt firearms and in advertising.

Rapiers, by Eric Valentine. Stackpole Books, Harrisburg, Pa., 1968. 76 pp., 58 photos., 3 drawings. $4.95.

A desirable monograph, first on its subject, to be publ. in English. Covers methods of authentication, renovation, cleaning and preservation.

Red Coat and Brown Bess, by Anthony D. Darling. Museum Restoration Service, Ottawa, Ontario, Can., 1970. Paper covers, 63 pp., very well illus., in line and halftone. $3.00.

An unusually excellent treatise on the British Army in 1774-1775. Includes detailed text and illus. of various models of the "Brown Bess," plus "Records of the Battles, Sieges and Skirmishes of the American Revolution."

Regulation Military Swords, by J. Wilkinson-Latham, Star Products, London, 1970. 32 pp., illus. Paper, $4.00.

Survey of military swords of U.S., England, France and Germany.

Remington Arms in American History, by A. Hatch, Rinehart & Co., NY, 1956. 359 pp., illus. $6.50.

Collector's guide with appendix of all Remington arms, ballistics tables, etc.

Remington Catalog [Price List] of 1885, a reprint in facsimile, by The Wyoming Armory, Inc., Cheyenne, Wyo., 1969. 48 pp., well illus., paper covers. $2.50.

All rifles, handguns, cane gun, sights, cartridges, shotguns, accessories etc. A priced catalog.

The Remington Historical Treasury of American Guns, by Harold L. Peterson. Thomas Nelson & Sons, N.Y.C., 1966. 199 pp., illus. $2.95.

A historical saga woven into first-rate Americana through the facts and details of the Remington firm and their products.

The Revolver, Its Description, Management, and Use, by P. E. Dove. Arms and Armour Press, London, 1968. 57 pp., 6 engravings, stiff paper wrappers. $3.75.

A facsimile reprint of a rare classic, dealing principally with the Adams revolver compared to the qualities of the Colt.

Revolving Arms, by A. W. F. Taylerson, Walker and Co., New York, 1967. 123 pp., illus. $8.50.

A detailed history of mechanically-rotated cylinder firearms in Europe and the U.S. Primarily on handguns, but other types of revolving guns are included.

Rifled Infantry Arms, by J. Schon; trans. by Capt. J. Gorgas, USA. Dresden, 1855; facsimile reprint by W. E. Meuse, Schuylersville, NY, 1965. 54 pp., illus. $2.50.

Reprint of classic essay on European military small arms of the mid-19th century. Paper covers.

The Rifled Musket, by Claud E. Fuller. Stackpole Books, Harrisburg, Pa., 1958. 302 pp., illus. $4.95.

The authoritative work of the late Claud E. Fuller and basically an account of the muskets whose model dates fell within the Civil War years—1861, 1863 and 1864. Part Two treats of the contract muskets. Some reproduced material, notably Bartlett & Gallatin's "Digest of Cartridges," is almost wholly illegible, as is much of an 1860 Ordnance Dept. report.

Romance of Knife Collecting, by Dewey P. Ferguson, Dewey P. Ferguson, Fairborn, OH, 1970. 100 pp., illus. Paper covers, spiral binding. $5.00.

From stone to steel knives, care, patterns, counterfeiting, history of knife companies, etc.

Price Guide to above title, by D. P. Ferguson, same place, 1972. 60 pp., illus. Paper covers. $4.00.

G. Roth Aktiengesellschaft. Horn Co., Burlington, Vt., 1968. 28 pp., illus., paperbound. $2.50.

Reprint of a German cartridge catalog of 1913, with drawings and dimensions.

Royal Sporting Guns at Windsor, by H. L. Blackmore. H. M. Stationery Office, London, England, 1968. 60 pp. text, 52 plates. $9.54.

Catalog of the most decorative and interesting guns in the Royal Armoury collection at Windsor Castle.

Russian Military Swords, 1801-1917, by E. Mollo. Historical Research Unit, London, Eng., 1969. 56 pp., illus. $7.50.

First book in English to examine and classify the various swords used by the Russian Army from Alexander I to the Revolution. 42 photos, 27 line drawings, 10 in color.

Russian Pistols in the 17th Century, by L. Tarassuk. Geo. Shumway, York, Pa., 1968. 35 pp. plus plates. $4.00.

Monograph on museum quality Russian handguns of the 17th century. Fine, detailed photographs.

Samuel Colt's New Model Pocket Pistols, by S. G. Keogh. Priv. publ., 1964. 31 pp., 20 illus., paperbound. $3.00.

"The story of the 1855 Root model revolver," with detailed classification data and descriptions. Well-illus.

The Samurai Swords, by J. M. Yumoto. Tuttle Co., Rutland, Vt., 1958. 191 pp., illus. $4.50.

Detailed information on evaluation of specimens, including origin and development of the Japanese blade.

Savage Automatic Pistols, by James R. Carr. Publ. by the author, St. Charles, Ill., 1967. A reprint. 129 pp., illus. with numerous photos. $6.50.

Collector's guide to Savage pistols, models 1907-1922, with features, production data, and pictures of each. A reprint of the circa 1912 Savage promotional and instructive booklet titled *It Banishes Fear* is recommended to accompany the above. Paper wrappers, 32 pp. $1.50.

Schuyler, Hartley & Graham Catalog. publ. by Norm Flayderman, Greenwich, Conn., 1961. 176 pp., illus. $9.50.

A reprint of a rare 1864 catalog of firearms, military goods, uniforms, etc. An extensive source of information for Civil War collectors.

Scottish Swords and Dirks, by John Wallace. Stackpole Books, Harrisburg, Pa., 1970. 80 pp., illus. $4.95.

An illustrated reference guide to Scottish edged weapons.

Scottish Swords from the Battlefield at Culloden, by Lord Archibald Campbell, Mowbray Co., Providence, RI, 1971. 63 pp., illus. $5.00.

Modern reprint of an exceedingly rare 1894 limited private ed.

Sears, Roebuck & Co. Catalogue No. 117, J. J. Schroeder, ed. A reprint of the 1908 work. Digest Books, Inc., Northfield, Ill., 1969, profusely illus., paper covers. $3.95.

This reprint of a famous catalog brings to all arms collectors a treasured replica of the collectibles and prices of yesteryear.

The Sharps Rifle, by W. O. Smith. Morrow, NYC, 1943, reprinted 1965. 138 pp., illus. $10.00.

Study of America's first successful breech-loader patented 1848, with information on its history, development, and operation.

Shooter's Bible Gun Trader's Guide, by Paul Wahl. Stoeger Arms Corp., So. Hackensack, NJ, 1973. 254 pp., 6th rev. ed. Paper covers. $4.95.

Fully illus. guide to identification of modern firearms, plus current market values.

Shosankenshu, by H. L. Joly. Holland Press, London, 1963. Unpaginated. $12.50.

List of Japanese artists' names and kakihan found on sword furniture by the late European authority. Completed in 1919, previously unpubl., this is a facsimile of Joly's MS. and line drawings. Lists nearly 3,000 names.

Shotgun Shells: Identification, Manufacturers and Checklist for Collectors, by F. H. Steward. B. and P. Associates, St. Louis, Mo., 1969. 101 pp., illus., paper covers. $4.95.

Historical data for the collector.

Single-Shot Rifles, by James J. Grant. Wm. Morrow & Co., NYC, 4th printing 1964. 385 pp., illus. $8.50.

A detailed study of these rifles by a noted collector.

Small Arms, by Frederick Wilkinson, Hawthorne Books, Inc., New York, 1966. 256 pp., illus. $4.95.

A history of small firearms, techniques of the gunsmith, equipment used by combatants, sportsmen and hunters.

Small Arms and Ammunition in the United States Service, 1776-1865, by B. R. Lewis. Smithsonian Inst., Washington, D.C., 1968. 338 pp. plus 52 plates. $12.50.

2nd printing of a distinguished work for historians and collectors. A limited number of deluxe, signed and numbered copies (1st reprinting 1960) are available in full leather and gilt top at $25.

Small Arms of the Sea Services, by Robt. H. Rankin. N. Flayderman & Co., New Milford, CT, 1972. 227 pp., illus. $14.50.

Encyclopedic reference to small arms of the U.S. Navy, Marines and Coast Guard. Covers edged weapons, handguns, long arms and others, from the beginnings.

Smith and Wesson 1857-1945, by Robert J. Neal and Roy J. Jenks. A. S. Barnes and Co., Inc., NYC, 1966. 500 pp., illus. with over 300 photos and 90 radiographs. $25.00.

A long-needed book, especially for knowledgeable enthusiasts and collectors. Covers an investigation of the series of handguns produced by the Smith and Wesson Company.

The Soldier's Manual, by J. H. Nesmith. (First publ. in Philadelphia in 1824.) Geo. Shumway, York, Pa., 1963. 108 pp., frontis, and 11 color plates. $4.95.

Facsimile reproduction of an important early American militia drill manual, covering exercises with musket, pistol, sword, and artillery. The color plates depict accurately the picturesque uniforms and accoutrements of elite militia corps of Phila. and vicinity. Intro. by Anne S. K. Brown traces the origin of the text matter and the early engravers.

Southern Derringers of the Mississippi Valley, by Turner Kirkland. Pioneer Press, Tenn., 1971. 80 pp., illus., paper covers. $2.00.

A guide for the collector, and a much-needed study.

Spanish Military Weapons in Colonial America, 1700-1821, by S. B. Brinckerhoff & P. A. Chamberlain. Stackpole Books, Harrisburg, PA, 1972. 160 pp., illus. $14.95.

Spanish arms and armaments described and illustrated in 274 photographic plates. Includes firearms, accoutrements, swords, polearms and cannon.

Sporting Guns, by Richard Akehurst. G. P. Putnam's Sons, New York, NY, 1968. 120 pp., excellently illus. and with 24 pp. in full color. $5.95.

One of the noted Pleasures and Treasures series. A nostalgic tracing of the history of shooting, and of the guns and rifles used by the sportsman.

Springfield Armory, Pointless Sacrifice, by C. L. Dvarecka. Prolitho Pub., Ludlow, Mass., 1968. 177 pp., illus. Paper covers. $1.00.

Story of the armory's closing; contains names, particulars and the quantities made of Springfield arms.

Springfield Muzzle-Loading Shoulder Arms, by C. E. Fuller, F. Bannerman Sons, NYC, reprinted 1968. 176 pp., illus. $12.50.

Long-awaited reprint of an important 1930 reference work on weapons produced at Springfield Armory, 1795-1865, including ordnance reports, tables, etc., on flintlock and percussion models.

Stahlhelm; Evolution of the German Steel Helmet, by F. R. Tubbs, F. R. Tubbs, 1971. 104 pp., illus. Paper, $5.50.

Helmets used by the German Army from 1916 to date. Shields, frontal plates, liners, detailed drawings, camouflage, etc.

Stevens Pistols and Pocket Rifles, by K. L. Cope, Museum Restoration Service, Ottawa, Can., 1971. 104 pp. $8.50.

All are shown, identified, detailed, variations, listings of dates, etc.

The Story of Allen and Wheelock Firearms, by H. H. Thomas. C. J. Krehbiel, Cincinnati, 1965, 125 pp., illus. $6.50.

Brief history of the Allen & Wheelock guns produced in mid-19th century, and their maker. Well illus. with descriptions of specimens.

The Story of Pope's Barrels, by Ray M. Smith. Stackpole Books, Harrisburg, PA, 1964., 211 pp., illus. $10.00.

Detailed account of the achievements and life of Harry M. Pope, master rifle bbl. maker.

Superimposed Load Firearms 1360-1860, by D. R. Baxter. Privately printed for the author in Hong Kong, 1966. $22.00. Foreword by Keith Neal. Ltd. ed., 500 copies only.

Excellently illustrated with photographs, diagrams, figures and patent drawings. Covers over-under arms of all countries, and a list of gunmakers and inventors is included.

Sword, Lance and Bayonet, by Charles ffoulkes and E. C. Hopkinson. Arco Publishing Co., NY, 1967. 145 pp., well illus. in line and halftone. $7.50.

A facsimile reprint of the first attempt at a consecutive account of the arms, both general and official use, since the discarding of armor.

The Sword and Same, by H. L. Joly and I. Hogitaro, Holland Press Ltd., London, 1971. 241 pp. plates and line drawings. $18.00.

New printing of Arai Hakuseki, "The Sword Book in Honcho Gunkiko" and "The Book of Same Ko Hi Sei Gi of Inaba Tsurio."

Swords & Blades of the American Revolution, by Geo. C. Neumann. Stackpole Books, Harrisburg, PA, 1973. 288 pp. well illus. $24.95.

An encyclopedia of 1,600 bladed weapons—swords, bayonets, spontoons, halberds, pikes, knives, daggers, and axes—used by both sides, on land and sea, in America's struggle for independence.

Swords for Sea Service, by Commander W. E. May, R. N. & P. G. W. Annis, H.M. S.O., London, 1970. 398 pp. in 2 volumes, $30.00.

Study based on the swords, dirks and cutlasses in the National Maritime Museum in Greenwich, plus many other outside weapons, and information on the British sword trade, industry, makers and retailers. 140 black and white plates, 3 color plates and many other illus.

The 36 Calibers of the Colt Single Action Army, by David M. Brown. Publ. by the author at Albuquerque, NM, new reprint 1971. 222 pp., well-illus. $15.00.

Edited by Bev Mann of *Guns Magazine.* This is an unusual approach to the many details of the Colt S.A. Army revolver. Halftone and line drawings of the same models make this of especial interest.

Thoughts on the Kentucky Rifle in its Golden Age, by Joe Kindig, Jr. George Shumway, York, PA, 1970. A facsimile reprint of the 1960 original. 561 pp., replete with fine arms and data on many makers. $14.50.

Covers mainly the arms and their makers in the Lancaster area of Pennsylvania. An authoritative work.

Toxophilus, by Roger Ascham. S. R. Pub. Ltd., Yorkshire, Eng., 1968. 230 pp., illus. $7.00.

A facsimile reprint of the 1788 ed. still regarded as the classic text on archery.

Treasury of the Gun, by H. L. Peterson, Crown Publishing Co.'s reprint, NYC, 1965. 252 pp. profusely illus., some in color. $7.95.

A beautiful production, presenting a new high in authoritative text. Virtually every significant type of firearm of the past 650 years is shown.

A Treatise on Ancient Armour and Weapons, by F. Grose, Benchmark Publ., Glendale, NY, 1970. Irreg. pagination, illus. $12.50.

Reprint of a 1786 monograph from the collection in the Tower of London and other sites.

Underhammer Guns, by H. C. Logan. Stackpole Books, Harrisburg, PA, 1964. 250 pp. illus. $4.98.

A full account of an unusual form of firearm dating back to flintlock days. Both American and foreign specimens are included.

Uniforms and Badges of the Third Reich, by Rudolph Kahl, Military Collectors Service, Kedichem, Holland, 1970.

Volume I; NSDAP. 76 pp., 260 illus. $6.95.
Volume II: SA, NSKK, and SS. 120 pp., 523 illus. $8.95.
Volume III: HJ, NSFK, and RAD. 100 pp., 452 illus. $7.95.

Uniforms of the American, British, French, and German Armies in the War of the American Revolution, 1775-1783, by Lt. Charles M. Lefferts, We Inc., Old Greenwich, CT, 1970. 292 pp., illus. $8.00.

Reprint of the original 1926 ed. and the only book on its subject today.

U.S. Army Headgear to 1854, Vol. I, by E. M. Howell and D. E. Kloster. Smithsonian Institution, Wash., D.C., 1969. 75 pp., illus. $3.75.

U.S. National Museum Bulletin 269. Illustrates and describes specimens of 1776 to 1854.

U.S. Cartridge Co. Collection of Firearms, We, Inc., Old Greenwich, CT., 1970. 142 pp., illus. $6.00.

Describes each arm in detail as to manufacture, action, period of use, function, markings, patents, makers, etc.

U.S. Firearms: The First Century, 1776-1875, by D. F. Butler. Winchester Press, NY, 1971. 320 pp., illus. $15.00.

A rich mine of carefully researched information and data on American firearms of this period. Illustrated with photos, schematics and historical documents.

U.S. Martial and Collectors Arms, by D. Verlag. Military Arms Research Service, San Jose, CA, 1971. 83 pp. Paper covers. $2.50.

Complete listing of U.S. arms inspectors: names, initials used, types of guns inspected circa 1790s through 1964. Detailed tabulations of guns bought by U.S.; quantities; serial number ranges; contractors.

U.S. Martial and Semi-Martial Single-Shot Pistols, by C. E. Chapel, Coward-McCann Inc., NYC, 1962. 352 pp., over 150 illus. $7.50.

Describes in detail all single shot martial pistols used by the US armed forces and by military units of the states. A definitive guide.

U.S. Military Firearms, 1776-1956, by Maj. Jas. E. Hicks. J. E. Hicks & Son. La Canada, Calif., 216 pp., incl. 88 pages of fine plates. $12.50.

Covering 180 years of America's hand and shoulder weapons. The most authoritative book on this subject. Packed with official data.

U.S. Military Small Arms 1816-1865, by R. M. Reilly. The Eagle Press, Inc., Baton Rouge, La., 1970. 275 pp., illus. $22.50.

Describes and superbly illustrates every known type of primary and secondary martial firearm of the period 1816-1865. Limited, numbered ed.

U.S. Ordnance Manual 1862, compiled by T. T. S. Laidley, Bvt. Major, Capt. of Ordnance. Ordnance Park Corp., Lyons, CO, 1970. 559 pp., illus., 33 plates. A limited numbered ed. $15.40.

Facsimile of the 3rd ed. of the 1862 *Ordnance Manual for the Use of the Officers of the United States Army.*

U.S. Sword Bayonets, 1847-1865, by R. V. Davis, Jr. Priv. prt., Pittsburgh, PA, 1963. 36 pp., 17 pl., paper. $4.00

Histories, production data, and good photos of U.S. military sword bayonets of Civil War era.

U.S. Weapons Development 1920-25. An abridged reprint from official sources, this Section 1 covering rifles, pistols and some miscellaneous items. Design Publ., Inc. Hyattsville, Md. [circa 1968]. 57 pp., illus., paper covers. $5.00.

Dependable material for the collector and shooter.

A Universal Military Dictionary, by Captain George Smith. The rare original book was published at London in 1779. This facsimile reprint was released in 1969 by Museum Restoration Service, Ottawa, Ontario, Can. 336 pp., 16 fold-out plates. $27.50.

A most useful reference for mean of arms interest. Offered only in a numbered, limited issue of 700 copies.

Waffen: Beitrag zur Historischen Waffenkunde, by J. H. Hefner-Alteneck. Akademische Druck, Graz, Austria, 1969. 58 pp., German text plus 100 plates. $30.00.
A descriptive text complements the fine illustrations depicting armor and weapons used in Europe from the middle ages through the 17th century.

Weapons, by E. Tunis. World Publishing Co., NYC, 1954. 153 pp., a large book, well-illus. $6.95.
A pictorial history of arms with complementing narrative. Coverage: from the first tied stone thrown by pre-historic man to super bombs.

Weapons of the British Soldier, by Col. H. C. B. Rogers. Seeley Service & Co., London, 1960. 259 pp., illus. in line and halftone plus full color frontis. $8.75.
The story of weapons used by the British soldier throughout the ages and the many developments in personal arms during the course of history.

The Webley Story, by Wm. C. Dowell, Skyrac Press, Leeds, Eng. 337 pp., profusely illus. $21.00.
Detailed study of Webley pistols and revolvers, covering over 250 specimens. This important reference also gives detailed listing of English small arms cartridge patents through 1880.

The Whitney Firearms, by Claud Fuller. Standard Publications, Huntington, W. Va., 1946. 334 pp., many plates and drawings. $12.50.
An authoritative history of all Whitney arms and their maker. Highly recommended. An exclusive with Ray Riling Arms Book Co.

Winchester—The Gun That Won the West, by H. F. Williamson. Combat Forces Press, Washington, D.C., 1952. Later eds. by Barnes, NY 494 pp., profusely illus. $5.95.
A scholarly and essential economic history of an honored arms company, but the early and modern arms introduced will satisfy all but the exacting collector.

The Winchester Book, by Geo. Madis. Art & Reference House, Lancaster, Texas, 1971. 542 pp., illus. $20.00.
First release of 1,000 autographed deluxe copies at this special price. After these are sold only a standard ed. will be available, the price the same. $20.00.

The World of Guns, by Richard Akehurst. Crown Publ., NY, 1972. 127 pp., illus. $3.95.
Many full color plates tell the story of guns from the first simple handguns: guns in warfare, sporting guns, rifles, the American West, duelling pistols, etc.

GENERAL

A.B.C. of Snap Shooting, by Horace Fletcher, Americana Archives Publ. Co., Topsfield, MA., 1971. 48 pp., illus. Paper, $3.00.
Authentic reproduction of a rare 1881 original.

African Antelope, paintings by Peter Skirka, intro. and text by Wendell Swank. Winchester Press, NY, 1972. 144 pp., slipcased. $27.50.
Superbly illus. study, with full-color paintings of all 34 principal African antelope. The text describes the range, life cycle and characteristics of each animal.

Age of Great Guns, by Frank E. Comparato. Stackpole Books, Harrisburg, Pa. 1965, 386 pp. illus. $11.95.
Of cannon kings and cannoneers who forged the fire-power of artillery. A highly acclaimed work of importance to artillery enthusiasts.

Air Gun Batteries, by E. G. Wolff. Public Museum, Milwaukee, Wisc., 1964. 28 pp., illus., paperbound. 75¢.
Study of discharge mechanisms on reservoir air guns.

Air Organizations of the Third Reich, Volume I, R. J. Bender, compiler. R. J. Bender, Mountain View, CA, 192 pp., illus., some in color. $9.95.
Concise survey of the World War II Luftwaffe organizations. Shows uniforms, weapons, identification marks and badges.

The Album of Gunfighters, by J. Marvin Hunter and Noah H. Rose, Warren Hunter, Helotes, Texas, 1965. 4th printing. 236 pp., wonderfully illus., with spectacular oldtime photos. $17.50.
For the serious gunfighter fan there is nothing to equal this factual record of the men-behind-the-star and the human targets that they faced.

To All Sportsmen; and Particularly to Farmers and Gamekeepers, by Col. Geo. Hanger, Richmond Publ. Co., Richmond, England, 1971. 226 pp. $9.50.
Reprint of an 1814 work on hunting, guns, horses, veterinary techniques, etc.

The American B.B. Gun, by A. T. Dunathan, A. S. Barnes, S. Brunswick, NJ, 1971. 154 pp., illus. $10.00.
Identification reference and a price guide for B.B. guns, plus a brief history and advertising plates.

American Bird Decoys, by W. J. Mackey Jr. Bonanza Books, NY, 1972. 256 pp., illus. $3.95.
The history and fine points of decoys for all gamebird species, with much data for collectors and hunters.

American Game Birds of Field and Forest, by F. C. Edminster, Book Sales, NY, 1972 490 pp. 99 plates. $6.95.
18 species; their origin, history, range, food, diseases, etc.

American Handmade Knives of Today, by B. R. Hughes. Pioneer Press, Union City, TN, 1972. 56 pp., illus. Paper covers. $2.95.
A primer for those developing an interest in handmade blades. Knowledgeable.

American Indian Tomahawks, by H. L. Peterson, Museum of the American Indian Heye Foundation, 1971. 142 pp., $10.00.
Brief description of various types and their makers. 314 illustrations, and many line drawings.

Americans and their Guns, compiled by Jas. B. Trefethen, ed. by Jas. E. Serven, Stackpole Books, Harrisburg, Pa., 1967. 320 pp., illus. $9.95.
The National Rifle Association of America story through nearly a century of service to the nation. More than a history—a chronical of help to novice and expert in the safe and proper use of firearms for defense and recreation, as well as a guide for the collector of arms.

America's Camping Book, by Paul Cardwell, Jr. C. Scribner's Sons, New York, NY 1st ed., 1969. 591 pp., well illus., in line and halftone. $10.00.
A fine illustrated guide to camping and woodcraft, with data on equipment, techniques, emergencies and nature study.

Ammunition General, TM 9-1900 to 11A-1-20, Dept. of the Army, Paladin Press, Boulder, CO, 1971. 320 pp., Paper, $6.00.
Reprint of army manual covering propellants, low and high explosives, chemical agents, rockets, etc. 215 illus., 19 color plates.

Animals in Africa, by Peter and Philippa Scott. Clarkson N. Potter, NY, 1963. Profusely, magnificently illus. Unpaginated. Large format. $7.95.
The enchanting story, in words and pictures, of a journey by the authors through the National Parks of Kenya to Murchison Falls Park in Uganda. Over 180 pictures in black-and-white, 20 in full color.

Archery: Its Theory and Practice, by H. A. Ford. Geo. Shumway, York, PA, 1971. 128 pp., illus. $6.00.
Reprint of the scarce 1856 ed.

Archery, by C. J. Longman and H. Walrond. Frederick Ungar Co., NY, 1967. 534 pp., illus. in line and halftone. $5.95.
Reproduction of a standard, important British reference work, first publ. in 1894, on the history, uses and techniques of archery.

Arco Gun Book, ed. by Larry Koller. Arco Publ. Co. Inc., NYC, 1962 397 pp., illus. $7.50.
A concise encyclopedia for arms collectors, shooters and hunters.

Armour, by Viscount Dillon. Geo. Shumway, York, PA, 1968. 78 pp., illus., paperbound. $4.00.
Facsimile of British monographs titled *An Elizabethan Armourer's Album* and *Armour Notes.*

Armoured Fighting Vehicles, by Malcolm McGregor, Walker & Co., New York, 1967. 56 pp., illus. $15.00.
Describes 12 tanks and armored cars, representative of those used in the two World Wars. The illustrations in full-color are true scale drawn from actual models.

Armoured Forces, by R. M. Ogorkiewicz. Arco Pub. Co., NY, 1970. 475 pp., illus. $7.95.
A history of the armored forces and their vehicles.

Arms of the World: The 1911 Alfa Catalogue. Edited by Joseph J. Schroeder, Jr. Digest Books, Northfield, IL., 701 pp., Paper, $5.95.
Reprint in 4 languages of thousands of guns, cartridges, swords, helmets, tools, etc. Profusely illus., and priced the 1911 way.

The Art of Archerie, by Gervase Markham. A reprint of the 1634 original, publ. in London. Geo. Shumway, York, PA, 1968. 172 pp. $12.00.
This classic treatise, written to keep alive the art of archery in warfare, treats with the making of longbows and their use. A scholarly introduction to the new issue by S. V. Grancsay adds an enlightening historical perception.

Art for Conservation; The Federal Duck Stamps, by Jene C. Gilmore, with introd. by Robt. Hines, Barre Publ., Barre, MA, 1971. 94 pp., illus. $14.95.
Contains all the duck stamp illustrations from 1934 to 1972 with pertinent biographical, historical and philatelic data.

The Art and Science of Taking to the Woods, by C. B. Colby and B. Angier, Stackpole Books, Harrisburg, Pa. 1970, 288 pp. illus. $7.95. Also in paper covers. $3.95.
Illustrated camper's manual covering all types of outdoor living and transportation, for novice and expert alike.

The Art of Shooting, by C. E. Chapel. Barnes, NYC, 1960. 424 pp., illus. $3.95.
A comprehensive, simplified guide to every aspect of pistol, revolver, and rifle shooting. A history of rifle development is included.

The Art of Survival, by C. Troebst. Doubleday & Co., Garden City, NY. 1965. 312 pp. illus. $5.95.
Narratives of devices of survival in difficult terrain or circumstances and evaluation of rescue and life-saving procedures.

The Art of the Decoy: American Bird Carvings, by Adele Earnest. Clarkson N. Potter, Inc., NYC, 1966. $4.95.
The origin of a lost art explained, plus some data on the most famous carvers. Over 106 black-and-white photos, 35 line drawings and an 8-page insert in full color.

The Artillerist's Manual, by Lieut, John Gibbon, Benchmark Pub. Co., Glendale, NY, 1970. 568 pp., illus. $16.50.
Reprint of an 1860 textbook on U.S. artillery, covering guns, ammunition, transportation, many other facets.

Asian Fighting Arts, by D. F. Draeger and R. W. Smith. Kodansha International Ltd., Tokyo, Japan. 2nd printing, 1969. 207 pp., well illus., in line and halftone. $12.50.
A work of monumental research, interesting to all involved in the science of fighting techniques. Covers eleven Asian skills, ranging from Chinese T'ai-chi and Burmese Bando to Japanese Jujitsu and the lethal Pentjak-silak of Indonesia.

The Atlantic Flyway, by Robt. Elman and Walter Osborne. Winchester Press, NY, 1972. 288 pp., illus. $15.
Fascinating word and picture study of one of the world's great migratory corridors. Past history, present problems and future prospects of wildfowling in this area. Over 250 magnificent color and black-and-white photos.

Author and Subject Index to the American Rifleman Magazine 1961-1970, by W. R. Burrell, Galesburg, MI, 1971. 64 pp. $6.50.
Alphabetical listing by author, title and subject.

Bannerman Military Goods Catalog, 1907. Benchmark Publ. Co., NY, 260 pp., illus. Paper, $3.95.
Exact reprint of original catalog with thousands of items listed.

Bayonet Fighting, by the Dept. of the Army, Normount Armament Co., Forest Grove, OR, 1972. 76 pp., illus. Paper, $1.50.
Reprint of FM 23-25. Its principles, purpose, use, positions, training, etc.

Baron von Steuben and his Regulations, by Joseph R. Riling, Ray Riling Arms Books Co., Philadelphia, Penna., 1966. 207 pp., illus. $12.50.
A documented book on this great American Major General and the creation by him of the first official "Regulations." Includes the complete facsimile of these regulations.

Basic Nazi Swords & Daggers, by Peter Stahl. Die Wehrmacht Military Publ., Stanford, CA, 1972. 30 pp., illus. Paper covers. $2.
Pictures and identifies Nazi swords and daggers.

Battle Ships of World War I, by Anthony Preston. Stackpole Books, Harrisburg, PA, 1972. 259 pp. $19.95.
Illus. encyclopedia of the battlewagons of all nations, 1914-1918.

Being Your Own Wilderness Doctor, by Dr. E. Russel Kodet and Bradford Angier. Stackpole Books, Harrisburg, Pa., 1968. 127 pp., illus. In line drawings. $3.95.
Called the "outdoorsman's emergency manual" It offers security of knowing what to do best—in case of the worst.

A Bibliography of Military Books up to 1642, by Maurice J. D. Cockle. A new reprint of the Holland Press, London, 1965. 320 pp., illus. $15.00.
Describes the important military books from the invention of gunpowder to subject date. A standard reference.

Birds in Our Lives, ed. by A. Stefferud and A. L. Nelson. Gov't. Prtg. Office, Washington, D.C. 20402, 1966, 576 pp., 80 drawings, 372 photos. $9.00.
61 authors have contributed to this great book, the illus. by Bob Hines. A successful effort to bring any and all readers an appreciation of—and an interest in—the part birds play in their lives.

Black Powder Gun Digest, edited by T. Bridges. Digest Books, Inc., Northfield, IL, 1972. 288 pp., illus. Paper covers. $5.95.
Comprehensive, authoritative book on black powder rifles, handguns, scatterguns and accessories. With a where-to-buy it directory.

Black Powder Guide, by Geo. Nonte, Jr. Shooter's Bible Publ., S. Hackensack, NJ, 1969. 214 pp., fully illus., $3.95.
A complete guide to muzzle-loading firearms of all types, their loading, repair and maintenance.

Black Powder Snapshots, by Herb Sherlock. Standard Publications. Huntington, W. VA, 50 pp., illus. $10.00.
Deluxe large volume containing 23 major Sherlock drawings and 95 punchy, marginal sketches.

The Book of the American West, ed. by Jay Monaghan. Julian Messner, New York, 1963. 608 pp., 200 illus. (many in color). $9.95.
A special chapter on frontier firearms is a feature of this massive work. 10 experts on Western hist. in as many fields of study contributed to the book. Illus. includ. works by the best contemporary artists.

The Book of the American Woodcock, by Wm. G. Sheldon, Ph.D. University of Mass. Press, Amherst, 1967. 227 pp., bibliography, appendices and index. $8.50.

Bow & Arrow Archer's Digest, ed. by Jack Lewis. Digest Books, Inc., Northfield, Ill., 1971. 320 pp., profusely illus. $5.95.
Comprehensive treatment of the art and science of archery.

The Boy's Book of Backyard Camping, by A. A. Macfarlan. Stackpole Books, Harrisburg, Pa. 1st ed. 1968. 160 pp., illus. in line. $4.50.
"How to use at-home space for the development of camping skills." Chapters on tents, equipment, cooking—all for out-of-doors enjoyment.

Boys in the Revolution, by Jack Coggins, Stackpole Books, Harrisburg, Pa., 1967. 96 pp., illus. $4.50.
Young Americans tell their part in the war for independence—what they did, what they wore, the gear they carried, the weapons they used, the ships they sailed on, the campaigns in which they fought.

British and American Tanks of WW II, by P. Chamberlain and C. Ellis. Arco Pub. Co., New York., 1969 222 pp., illus. $9.95.
Complete, illus. history of American, British and Commonwealth tanks, 1939-1945. Photos, and precise specifications of each.

The British Code of Duel, Richmond Publ. Co., Richmond, England, 1971. 144 pp. Reprint of the 1824 ed. Reference on the laws of honour and the character of gentlemen. Together with **The Art of Duelling,** same publ., 1971. 70 pp. Reprint of the 1836 London ed. Both books $9.00.
Information useful to young Continental tourists.

The Cabinet of Natural History and American Rural Sports. Imprint Society, Barre Publ., Barre, MA, 1973. Unpaginated. $40.
Edited facsimile version of the extremely scarce sporting magazine published in America, 1830-31. Illus. with 56 lithographs, 12 in color, the remainder in one tint. The originals were the first colored sporting plates actually done in America.

Camper's Digest, by Cecil Coffey. Digest Books, Inc., Northfield, Ill. 60093 320 pp., paper covers, over 500 illus. $4.95.
Everything needed to be known about camping. Trails, tools, clothes, cooking, hundreds of camp grounds listed, and more.

The Camping Manual, compiled by Fred Sturges, Stackpole Books, Harrisburg, PA, 1967. 160 pp., illus. $3.95.
An excellent refresher on the fundamentals, with a digest of the newest methods and latest advice for those who want to enjoy camping more.

Carbine Handbook, by Paul Wahl. Arco Publ. Co., N.Y.C., 1964. 80 pp., illus. $6.00. Paperbound, $3.95.
A manual and guide to the U.S. Carbine, cal. .30, M1, with data on its history, operation, repair, ammunition, and shooting.

The Chi-Com Series, by Granville Rideout, Yankee Publ. Co., Ashburnham, MA, 1971. 246 pp., illus. $12.95
New definitive reference work on Chinese Communist weapons in Southeast Asia. Limited and numbered ed.

Classic African Animals: The Big Five, text by Anthony Dyer, painting by Bob Kuhn. Winchester Press, NY, 1973. 128 pp., illus. $10.00.
The famed "Big Five" of Africa—lion, leopard, rhino, buffalo and elephant. A story of the animals themselves, magnificently illus. with 6 pages of color plus black-and-white drawings from Kuhn's African sketchbook. A deluxe limited, signed ed. $100.

The Classic Decoy Series, Ed Zern, text; M. C. Weiller, illustrator. Winchester Press, New York, NY 1969. A beautiful work picturing 24 American duck decoys in full color, printed on special paper and loose for framing. Decorated covers in slip case. Anecdotal text on each species shown. $100.00.
This deluxe collectors' work is offered in a strictly limited issue of 1000 copies, each signed by the artist and numbered.

The Code of Honor; or Rules for the Government of Principals and Seconds in Duelling, by John Lyde Wilson, Ray Riling Arms Books Co., Phila., PA, 1971. 48 pp. Paper, $5.00.
Reprint of the rare 1858 edition.

Colt Commemorative Firearms, by R. L. Wilson. Chas. Kidwell, Wichita, KS, 1969. 108 pp., $10.00.
A chronological listing and a precise description of all Colt commemoratives from 1961 through 1969.

The Complete Book of the Air Gun, by G. C. Nonte Jr. Stackpole Books, Harrisburg, PA, 1970. 288 pp., illus. $7.95.
From Plinking to Olympic competition, from BB guns to deluxe rifles, pistols, the air shotgun.

The Complete Book of Game Conservation, by Chas. Coles, Barrie & Jenkins, London, 1971. 394 pp., $18.50.
Definitive work on the subject. 181 illustrations including color reproductions of rare prints and original paintings.

Complete Book of Rifles and Shotguns, by Jack O'Connor, Harper & Bros., N.Y.C., 1961, 477 pp., illus. $6.95.
A splendid two-part book of encyclopedic coverage on every detail of rifle and shotgun.

Complete Book of Shooting, by Jack O'Connor et al. Outdoor Life—Harper & Row, N.Y.C., 1965. 385 pp., illus. $5.95.
Fundamentals of shooting with rifle, shotgun, and handgun in the hunting field and on target ranges.

The Complete Book of Trick and Fancy Shooting, by Ernie Lind, Winchester Press, NY, 1972. 159 pp., illus. $5.95.
Step-by-step instructions for acquiring the whole range of shooting skills with rifle, pistol and shotgun; includes practical hints on developing your own shooting act.

The Complete Cannoneer, compiled by M. C. Switlik. Antique Ordnance Artificers, Jackson, MI, 1971. 106 pp., illus., paper covers. $4.50.
A must for the modern cannoneer. Compiled in two sections. Part first contains "School of the Piece" as orginally published in Artillery Drill by George S. Patton, in 1861. Part second contains current observations on the safe use of cannon.

Coping with Camp Cooking, by M. W. Stephens and G. S. Wells. Stackpole Books, Harrisburg, PA 1966. 94 pp., illus., decorated boards. $2.95.
Hints and recipes selected from the editors' writings appearing in *Camping Guide Magazine.*

The Crossbow, by Sir Ralph Payne-Gallwey, Holland Press Ltd., London, 1971. 375 pp., illus. $21.00.
New printing of the only work devoted to the crossbow and such related weapons as the siege engine, balistas, catapults, Turkish bows and the Chinese repeating crossbow.

Crusade for Wildlife, by J. B. Trefethen. Stackpole Books, Harrisburg, PA, 1961. 377 pp., illus. $7.50.
History of the Boone and Crockett Club and its efforts to preserve wildlife in America, with accounts of the plight of threatened species.

Current American War Medals and Decorations, 1963-69, by E. E. Kerrigan. Medallic Publishing Co., Noroton Heights, CT 1st ed. 1969. Paper covers, 23 pp., illus. $3.00.
This supplement updates the author's *American War Medals and Decorations,* listing recently created awards and recipients.

Daggers, Bayonets & Fighting Knives of Hitler's Germany, by John R. Angolia. James Bender Pub. Co., Mountain View, CA. 1st ed. 1971. 334 pp., profusely illus. $14.95.
An exceptionally fine, useful compilation for collector, historian and student.

The Daggers and Edged Weapons of Hitler's Germany, by Maj. J. P. Atwood, Publ. privately for the author in Berlin, Germany, 1965. 240 pp. illus. New edition, 1967. $15.00.
Lavishly illus. with many plates in full color, this is an outstanding production, easily the best information (for the collector) on the subject.

Daggers and Fighting Knives of the Western World: From the Stone Age Unitl 1900, by Harold L. Peterson, Walker and Co., New York, 1967. 256 pp., illus. $2.98.
The only full-scale historical and analytical work on this subject, from flint knives of the stone age to British and American naval dirks.

Decoys and Decoy Carvers of Illinois, by P. W. Parmalee and F. D. Loomis. Northern Illinois University Press, DeKalb, IL. 1st ed., 1969, 506 pp., illus. $17.50.
A comprehensive and handsome survey, replete with photographs—many in color. The work of the makers is analyzed, with comments on Illinois duck shooting over the past century.

Deer of the World, by G. Kenneth Whitehead. The Viking Press, NY, 1972. 194 pp., illus. $14.95.
Important reference. Covers all 40 species of deer and many sub-species. Describes appearances, habits, status and distribution.

Description of U.S. Military Rifle Sights, by Edw. A. Tolosky, E. A. Tolosky, Publ., 1971. 117 pp. Paper, $8.50.
Covers period from 1861 to 1940. New and excellent work for collectors and fans of the U.S. Military. Definitive text, full-size line drawings.

The Details of the Rocket System, by Col. Wm. Congreve. Museum Restoration Service, Ottawa, Canada, 1970. 85 pp., illus. $10.00.
Reprint of the 1814 1st ed. with details, photos and plates of rockets and their launchers. Edition limited and numbered.

The Diary of Colonel Peter Hawker, by Col. P. Hawker, Richmond Publ. Co., Richmond, England. 1971. 759 pp., illus. $16.95.
Reprint of the 1893 ed. covers shooting in every way and how to outwit your opponent!

Die Handwaffen, by Werner Eckardt and Otto Morawietz. H. G. Schulz, Hamburg, 1957. 265 pp., 15 plates, 175 illus. $10.00.
An important work (in German) on German Service arms from their beginnings through World War II. A symposium on the subject—ancient, obsolete, semi-modern and modern.

The Double-Armed Man, by Wm. Neade, Geo. Shumway, Publ., York, PA, 1971. 51 pp., 7 woodcuts. $8.00.
Facsimile ed. of a little book published in London in 1625. Describes use of the longbow in combination with the pike. Limited to 400 numbered copies.

Eat the Weeds, by B. C. Harris. Barre Publ., Barre, MA, 1968. 223 pp., illus., paper covers $3.95.
Practical directions for collecting and drying herbs, for using edible plants and fruits as food and for medical purposes or as substitutes for cultivated vegetables.

Elephant, by Commander D. E. Blunt. A reprint by Neville Spearman, Ltd., London, 1971. 260 pp., illus. $10.00.
A hunter's account of the ways of the elephant in Africa and elsewhere—on hunting and conservation practices.

Encyclopedia of Continental Army Units; Battalions, Regiments and Independent Corps, by Fred A. Berg, Stackpole Books, Harrisburg, PA, 1972. 160 pp. $6.95.
The official and unofficial designations, organizational history, commanding officers and ethnic composition for every unit of the Continental Army for which these facts are known.

Encyclopedia of British, Provincial, and German Army Units 1775-1783, by P. R. Katcher. Stackpole Books, Harrisburg, PA, 1973. 160 pp., illus. $6.95.
Definitive study of America's opposing forces, meant for historians, buffs, and students; covers units, placement, commanders, arms, etc.

Encyclopedia of Firearms, ed. by H. L. Peterson. E. P. Dutton, N.Y.C., 1964. 367 pp., 100 pp. of illus. incl. color. $14.95.
Fine reference work on firearms, with articles by 45 top authorities covering classes of guns, manufacturers, ammunition, nomenclature, and related topics.

Encyclopedia of Modern Firearms, Vol. 1, compiled and publ. by Bob Brownell, Montezuma, IA, 1959. 1057 pp. plus index, illus. $22.50. Dist. by Bob Brownell, Montezuma, IA 50171.
Massive accumulation of basic information of nearly all modern arms pertaining to "parts and assembly." Replete with arms photographs, exploded drawings, manufacturers' lists of parts, etc.

The English Bowman, by T. Roberts. George Shumway, York, PA, 1973. 347 pp. $6.
Facsimile of the original work of 1801, with a new intro. by E. G. Heath. The art and practice of archery, the techniques of shooting and the elements of toxophily are examined, with comments on an earlier and similar work by Roger Ascham, called *Toxophilus.*

The Exercise of Arms, by Jacob de Gehyn, McGraw-Hill Book Co., NY, 1971. 250 pp. plus separate commentary by J. B. Kist, Dutch historian. $45.00.
Exact facsimile of original 1807 ed. now in Dutch archives, and based on concepts of troop organization and training developed by Prince Johann II. 117 copper engravings.
Special deluxe-bound ed. in full hard covers, limited to ten (10) copies. $1,000.00.

The Experts Book of the Shooting Sports, ed. by D. E. Petzal. Simon and Schuster, NY, 1972. 320 pp., illus. $9.95.
America's foremost shooting and hunting experts disclose the secrets of their specialties.

Explosives and Bomb Disposal Guide, by Robt. R. Lenz. Chas. C. Thomas, Springfield, IL, 1971. 303 pp., illus. $14.00.
Course of instruction on handling clandestine and sabotage devices; now being taught to all military bomb disposal technicians.

Explosives and Demolitions, U.S. Field Manual 5-25, Normount Armament Co., Forest Grove, OR. 215 pp., illus., paperbound. $4.00.
A reprint of the Army FM dated 14 May 1959.

Explosives and Homemade Bombs, by Jos. Stoffel. Chas. C. Thomas, Springfield, IL, 1972. 304 pp., illus. $14.00.
Elementary text on design and manufacture of explosive devices, for use as a text in training bomb disposal personnel.

Falconry, by Gilbert Blaine, Neville Spearman, London, 1970. 253 pp., illus. $7.50.

Reprint of a 1936 classic on training, handling, types, furniture, etc., of hawks, plus a glossary and list.

Die Faustfeuerwaffen von 1850 dis zur Gegenwart, by Eugene Heer, Akademische D.-u. V., Graz, Austria, 1972. 234 pp. of German texts, 215 pp. of illus. $30.00.

First volume in a series which will cover the history of Swiss firearms from 1800. The handguns issued between 1850 and 1950 are described and illustrated in considerable detail.

Feasting Free on Wild Edibles, by Bradford Angier. Stackpole Books, Harrisburg, PA, 1972. 285 pp., illus. $4.95.

More than 500 ways to banquet on nature's bounty. A one-vol. issue combining Angier's *Free for the Eating* and *More Free for the Eating Wild Foods.*

Fell's Guide to Guns and How to Use Them, by B. G. Wels. Frederick Fell, New York, NY 1969. 173 pp., illus. in line and halftone. $4.95.

Aspects of the safe use of firearms for sportsmen, hunters and collectors.

Fighting Vehicles, by C. Ellis & P. Chamberlain. Hamlyn Publ., London, Eng., 1972. 96 pp. $3.95.

Illus. story of the tank, going back centuries. Covers mobile fortresses through Patton and W.W. II tanks to today's varied types.

Firearms, by Walter Buehr. Crowell Co., N.Y.C., 1967. 186 pp., illus. $5.95.

From gunpowder to guided missile, an illustrated history of firearms for military and sporting uses.

Firearms Dictionary, by R. A. "Bob" Steindler. Stackpole Books, Harrisburg, PA, 288 pp., illus. $7.95.

Firearm Silencers, by D. B. McLean. Normount Armament Co., Forest Grove, OR, 1968. 123 pp., illus., paperbound. $4.00.

The history, design, and development of silencers for U.S. military firearms.

Firearms, Traps & Tools of the Mountain Men, by Carl P. Russell. A. A. Knopf, NY, 1967. 448 pp., illus. in line drawings. $15.00.

Detailed survey of fur traders' equipment in the early days of the west.

The Fireside Book of Guns, by Larry Koller. Simon & Schuster, N.Y.C., 1959. 284 pp., illus. in artistic photography and full-color plates. $12.95.

On all counts the most beautiful and colorful production of any arms book of our time, this work adequately tells the story of firearms in America—from the first explorers to today's sportsmen.

Four Studies on the History of Arms, by Arne Hoff, et al. Tjhusmuseet, Copenhagen, 1964. 145 pp., illus., paperbound. $6.75.

A Danish museum publication containing in English text scholarly monographs on arms topics of historic interest.

Frederic Remington and the Spanish-American War, by Douglas Allen, Crown Publ., Inc., NY, 1971. 178 pp., $4.95. Deluxe numbered and signed ed. limited to 150 copies, slip-cased. $50.

Copiously illus. with reproductions of the artist's drawings, paintings and bronzes.

Free for the Eating, by Bradford Angier, Stackpole Books, Harrisburg, PA, 1966. 191 pp., illus. $4.95.

Discusses and illustrates 100 wild plants and 300 ways to use them.

More Free for the Eating, Wild Foods, by Bradford Angier, Stackpole Books, Harrisburg, PA, 1969. 192 pp., illus. $4.95.

A sequel to *Free for the Eating*, being a nature-study cookbook with an additional 200 ways to prepare common wild plants.

The A. B. Frost Book, by Henry M. Reed. Charles E. Tuttle Co., Rutland, VT, 1967. 149 pp., of large format with over 70 plates, 44 in color, and many line drawings. $20.00.

A collection of the sketches, drawings and paintings by a famous outdoor artist (1851-1928). Includes his noted sporting and shooting masterpieces.

Fundamentals of Small Arms, U.S. TM9-2205. Normount Armament Co., Forest Grove, OR. 236 pp., illus., paperbound. $3.50.

Reprint of the U.S. Army technical manual dated 7 May 1952.

Game Animals, by Leonard Lee Rue III. Harper & Row, NY, 1968. 655 pp., incl. appendix and index. Illus. with maps and photos. $6.50.

A concise guide to and field book of North American species.

Game and Bird Calling, by A. C. Becker, Jr., A. S. Barnes and Co., NY, 1972. 147 pp., illus. $7.95.

Discusses various types of calls and techniques used by hunters—tyros and professionals.

Game Bird Carving, by Bruce Burk. Winchester Press, NY, 1972. 256 pp. $12.50.

The first step-by-step book on bird carving techniques. Over 700 photographs and line drawings by the author.

Game and Fish Cookbook, by H. and J. Barnett. Grossman Publ., New York, NY 1968, 162 pp., illus. $7.95.

Special culinary attention to fish and game, with interesting and different touches.

Game in the Kitchen, by B. Flood and W. C. Roux (eds.). Barre Publ., Barre, MA 1st ed., 1968, 234 pp., illus. $7.50.

A fish and game cookbook, with menus and information on preservation, cooking and serving.

Gas, Air and Spring Guns of the World, by W. H. B. Smith. Stackpole Books, Harrisburg, PA, 1957. 279 pp., well illus. $4.98.

A detailed, well-documented history of the air and gas gun industry throughout the world. It includes ancient and modern arms, and it devotes a chapter to accurate velocity tests of modern arms.

German Army Uniforms and Insignia 1933-1945, by B. L. Davis. World Publ. Co., NY, 1972. 224 pp. $12.

Every aspect of the uniforms, insignias, and accoutrements of the Third Reich Army are covered in detail. Many illus. in full color.

German Infantry Weapons, ed. by D. B. McLean. Normount Armament Co., Forest Grove, OR, 1966. 191 pp., illus., paperbound. $3.00.

World War II German weapons described and illustrated, from military intelligence research.

German Infantry Weapons of World War II, by A. J. Barker. Arco Publ. Co., New York, NY 1969, 76 pp., illus. $3.50.

Historical and statistical data on all types of the subject weapons, ammunition, etc.

German Machineguns, by D. D. Musgrave & S. H. Oliver, Mor Associates, WA, DC, 1971. 472 pp., $17.50.

Covers aircraft and ground types, including rare and little-known weapons, plus information on ammunition, accessories, and mounts. Over 500 illus..

German Secret Weapons of World War II, by I. V. Hogg. Arco Pub. Co., NY, 1970. 80 pp., illus. $3.50.

Compact, comprehensive account of Germany's secret weapons, eccentric and brilliant. Includes plans and technical details.

German Tanks of World War II, by F. M. von Senger und Etterlin. Stackpole Books, Harrisburg, PA, 1969. 176 pp., nearly 300 photos and drawings. Large format. $11.95.

A fully illustrated and definitive history of German armoured fighting vehicles, 1926-1945. Written in English.

German Weapons-Uniforms-Insignia 1841-1918, by Maj. J. E. Hicks. J. E. Hicks & Son, La Canada, CA, 1958. 158 pp., illus. $6.00.

Originally published in 1937 as *Notes on German Ordnance 1841-1918,* this new edition offers the collector a wealth of information gathered from many authentic sources.

The Golden Guide to Guns, by Larry Koller. Golden Press, N.Y.C., 1966. 160 pp., illus., paperbound, pocket-size. $1.00.

Introduction to rifles, shotguns, and handguns for all uses. Profusely illus., much in color.

Gourmet Cooking for Free, by Bradford Angier. Stackpole Books. Harrisburg, PA 1970. 190 pp. illus. $4.95.

Cookery of large and small game, seafood and wild plants.

The Grey Goose Wing, by E. G. Heath. Osprey Publ., Reading, Berkshire, Eng., 1971. 343 pp. plus index. $25.

A history of archery. Profusely illus. with paintings, photographs, prints, posters, etc., many in full color.

Great American Guns and Frontier Fighters, by Will Bryant, Grosset & Dunlap, NY, 1961. 160 pp., illus. $3.95.

Popular account of firearms in U.S. history and of the events in which they played a part.

The Great American Shooting Prints, selections and text by Robt. Elman. A. A. Knopf, NY, 1972. Large format. 72 full color plates. $25.

The hunting life in America as portrayed in paintings and lithographs from the 1820s to the present.

The Great Art of Artillery, by Casimir Simienowicz, with a new foreword by Brig. O. F. G. Hogg. S. R. Publi., Ltd., London, Eng., 1971. $12.50.

Facsimile of the original 1729 ed. Red-hot shot, chain shot and other incendiary "globes" are described in detail, and rockets are covered most extensively. Basically a work on fireworks—military and civil.

Great Weapons of World War II, by J. Kirk and R. Young. Bonanza Books, NY, 1968. 348 pp., profusely illus. The latest reprint. $4.95.

Covers, in text and picture, great and powerful weapons, planes, tanks as well as small arms, miscellaneous arms and naval attack vessels.

Grundriss der Waffenlehre, ed. by J. Schott, Akademische D. U. V., Graz, Austria, 1971. 395 pp. of German text, plus a 24 pp. Atlas. $22.50

Facsimile reprint of the 1876 ed. written by Edw. Zernin and publ. in Darmstadt and Leipzig.

Guide to the Soviet Navy, by Siegfried Breyer, U.S. Naval Institute, Annapolis, MD, 1971. 353 pp. $10.00.

Compact, comprehensive, up-to-date view of organization, construction, weapons, equipment, forces, bases and ports. Over 100 photos, plans, tables and maps, specifications and profiles.

Guide to United States Machine Guns, by K. F. Schreier, Jr., Normount Armament Co., Forest Grove, OR, 1971. 178 pp., illus. Paper, $4.00.

All machine guns procured by the U.S. Armed Forces and some of an experimental nature.

Gun Carriages: An Aide Memoire to the Military Sciences, 1846, by R. J. Nelson. Museum Restoration Service, Ottawa, Canada, 1972. 64 pp. Paper covers.

Originally prepared in 1846 as a manual for the officers of the British Army. Illus. with detailed scaled drawings, plus tables of dimensions and weights.

Gun Digest, 28th ed., edited by John T. Amber. Digest Books, Inc., Northfield, IL, 1973. 480 pp., illus. Paper covers. $7.95.

Known as the world's greatest gun book because of its factual, informative data for shooters, hunters, collectors, reloaders and other enthusiasts.

Gun Digest Treasury, ed. by J. T. Amber, 4th ed., 1972. Digest Books, Inc. Northfield, IL. 352 pp. illus. Paper, $5.95.

The best from 25 years   selected from the annual editions.

The Gun, 1834, by Wm. Greener, with intro. by D. B. McLean. Normount Technical Publ., Forest Grove, OR, 1971. 240 pp., illus. Paper, $4.95.

Reprint of the 1835 British ed. on various small firearms.

Gundogs, Their Care and Training, by M. Brander. A. & C. Black, London, Eng., 1969. 97 pp., illus. $4.95.

A British manual on hunting dogs.

Gun Fun with Safety, by G. E. Damon. Standard Publications, Huntington, W. VA, 1947. 206 pp., well illus. $6.00.

A long out-of-print work that is still much sought. A fine general coverage of arms and ammunition, old and new, with chapters on shooting, targets, etc., with safety always upper-most.

The Gun that Made the Twenties Roar, by W. J. Helmer, Macmillan Co., NY 1969. 286 pp. illus. $7.95.

Historical account of John T. Thompson and his invention, the Thompson submachine gun. Includes virtually a complete manual in detail.

Gun Talk, edited by Dave Moreton. Winchester Press, NY, 1973. 256 pp., illus. $7.95.

A treasury of original writing by the top gun writers and editors in America. Practical advice about every aspect of the shooting sports.

The Gunfighter, Man or Myth? by Joseph G. Rosa, Oklahoma Press, Norman, OK, 1969. 229 pp., illus., (including weapons). $5.95.

A well-documented work on gunfights and gunfighters of the West and elsewhere. Great treat for all gunfighter buffs.

The Gunfighters, by Dale T. Schoenberger, The Caxton Printers, Ltd., Caldwell, ID, 1971. 207 pp., illus. $12.95.

Startling expose of our foremost Western folk heroes.

The Gun-Founders of England, by Charles ffoulkes, Geo. Shumway, York, PA, 1969. 133 pp., illus. $10.00.

Detailed study of cannon, casting. Describes preparation of moulds, castings, mfg. of powder and shot, etc.

The Gunner's Bible, by Bill Riviere. Doubleday, N.Y.C., 1965. 192 pp., illus. Paperbound. $1.95.

General Guide to modern sporting firearms and their accessories, for all shooters.

Gunology, by P. M. Doane. Winchester-Western, N.Y.C., 1968. 64 pp., illus., paperbound. $2.95.

A comprehensive course for professional sporting arms salesmen. Of great help to the arms man are the hundreds of questions on arms and hunting.

Guns, by Dudley Pope. Delacorte Press, N.Y.C., 1965. 256 pp., illus. $9.98.

Concise history of firearms, stressing early museum-quality weapons. Includes small arms as well as artillery, naval, and airborne types. Fine photographs, many in color.

Guns, by F. Wilkinson, Grosset & Dunlap, NY, 1971. 168 pp., $3.95.

From the discovery of gunpowder to the complex weapons of today. Over 100 photos in color.

Guns & Ammo 1973 Annual, Guns & Ammo magazine, Petersen Publ. Co., Los Angeles, CA, 1973. 378 pp. illus. Paper covers. $3.95.

Annual catalog of sporting firearms and accessories, with numerous articles for gun enthusiasts.

Guns Annual for 1973, edited by Jerome Rakusan, Publishers Development Corp., Skokie, IL, 1972. 134 pp., well illus., decorated paper wrappers. $2.00.

An annual publication describing and illustrating firearms available in current markets, plus articles by experts in the field of collecting, shooting, ammunition, etc.

Guns Illustrated 1974, 6th ed., edited by Jos. J. Schroeder, Jr. Digest Books, Inc., Northfield, IL, 1973. 288 pp., illus. Paper covers. $4.95.

The all-new 1974 ed. combines a variety of information on shooting, collecting and handloading.

Guns; An Illustrated History of Artillery, ed. by Jos. Jobe, New York Graphic Society, Greenwich, CT, 1971. 216 pp., illus. $30.00.

Traces the history and technology of artillery from its beginnings in the 14th century to its 20th century demise in the face of aerial bombs and guided missiles.

Guns and Rifles of the World, by Howard L. Blackmore, The Viking Press, NY, 1965. 290 pp. 1042 halftone and line illustrations. $9.98.

One of the finest books to come out of England. Covers firearms from the handgun to air, steam, and electric guns.

Guns and Shooting, by Maj. Sir Gerald Burrard. Barnes & Co., N.Y.C., 1962. 147 pp. $1.95.

Expanded from the author's earlier *In the Gunroom*, this contains 153 often-asked questions on shotguns and rifles, with authoritative answers covering guns, ammunition, ballistics, etc.

Guns and Shooting, a Bibliography, by R. Riling. Greenberg, N.Y.C., 1951. 434 pp., illus. $20.00.

A selected listing, with pertinent comments and anecdote, of books and printed material on arms and ammunition from 1420 to 1950.

The Guns of Harpers Ferry, by S. E. Brown Jr. Virginia Book Co., Berryville, VA, 1968. 157 pp., illus. $12.50.

Catalog of all known firearms produced at the U.S. armory at Harpers Ferry, 1798-1861, with descriptions, illustrations and a history of the operations there.

Guns of the Wild West, by Elsie Hanauer. A. S. Barnes & Co., NY, 1973. 112 pp. $12.

History and development of the gun, the early frontiersmen who needed firearms to survive, and the early outlaws who used guns as part of their trade. Nearly 100 pages of full-color illus.

The Hall Carbine Affair; An Essay in Historiography, by R. Gordon Wasson, Privately Printed, Danbury, CT, 1971. 250 pp., illus. Deluxe slip-cased ed. of 250 copies. $75.00.

Based on the original work (limited to 100 copies) of 1941 and a 1948 revised ed. of only 750 copies. This issue, enlarged and re-researched, relates to sales and purchases of Hall carbines in the Civil War, in which J. Pierpont Morgan was involved.

Handbook on German Military Forces, a reprint of *TM-E30-451*, originating with U.S. Military Intelligence. Publ. by the Military Press, Gaithersburg, Md. 1970. 550 pp., copious illus., many in color. $14.95.

A rare restricted handbook [many destroyed] covering military systems, doctrines, SS Policy, home defense, etc.

Handbook on German Military Forces, by Founder's Ltd., Des Moines, IA. Paper, 372 pp., illus. $7.50.

Reprint of a restricted Military Intelligence Division handbook TM-E-30-451.

Handbook for Hythe, by H. Busk, Richmond Pub. Co., Richmond, England, 1971. 194 pp., illus. $8.50.

Reprint of the 1860 ed. explaining laws of projectiles with an introduction to the system of musketry.

Handbook of Self-Defense for Law Enforcement Officers, by John Martone. Arco Publ. Co., New York, NY, 1968. 1st ed., 4th printing, 111 pp., $3.50.

A clearly-illustrated manual on offensive and defensive techniques recommended for the use of policemen.

Hardtack and Coffee, or The Unwritten Story of Civil War Army Life, by John D. Billings, Benchmark Publ. Corp., Glendale, NY, 1970. 408 pp., illus. $9.50.

Reprint of original 1887 ed., with data on army life in tents, huts, enlisting, foraging, punishment, etc.

Hatcher's Notebook, by Maj. Gen. J. S. Hatcher. Stackpole Books, Harrisburg, Pa., 1952. 2nd ed. with four new chapters, 1957. 629 pp., illus. $11.95.

A dependable source of information for gunsmiths, ballisticians, historians, hunters, and collectors.

Hibbard, Spencer, Bartlett & Co. Catalog. American Reprints, St. Louis, MO, 1969. 92 pp., illus. Paper, $5.00.

Reprint of 1884 catalog on guns, rifles, revolvers, ammo, powder flasks, etc. Descriptions and contemporary prices.

History of the British Army, by P. Young and J. P. Lawford. G. P. Putnam's Sons, NY, 1970. 304 pp., profusely illus., much in color. $15.00.

Traces history of the British Army from the early 17th century to the present.

A History of the Dress of the British Soldier, by Lt. Col. John Luard, Frederick Muller Ltd., London, 1971. 171 pp., illus. 50 plates. $15.00.

Reprint of the 1852 ed., limited to 400 numbered copies.

A History of Knives, by Harold L. Peterson. Charles Scripner's Sons, N.Y.C., 1966. 64 pp., illus. $5.00.

The fine drawings of Daniel D. Feaser combine with the author's commendable text to produce an important work. From the earliest knives of prehistoric man through the evolution of the metal knife.

A History of War and Weapons, 449 to 1660, by A. V. B. Norman and D. Pottinger. Thomas Y. Crowell Co., NY, 1966. 224 pp., well illus. with sketches. $6.95.

An excellent work for the scholar on the evolution of war and weapons in England. Many sketches of arms and weapons of all sorts add importance.

The History of Weapons of the American Revolution, by Geo. C. Neumann. Harper & Row, NY, 1967, 373 pp., fully illus. $15.00.

Collector's reference covering long arms, handguns, edged and pole weapons used in the Revolutionary War.

The Hitler Albums, Vol. I, by Roger J. Bender, R. J. Bender Publ. Co., Mountain View, CA, 1970. 144 pp., $10.95.

Complete photographic study of Mussolini's state visit to Germany in September, 1937. 175 photos and illus.

Home Book of Taxidermy and Tanning, by G. J. Grantz, Stackpole Books, Harrisburg, PA, 1969. 160 pp., illus. $7.95.

Amateur's primer on mounting fish, birds, animals, and trophies.

Home in Your Pack, by Bradford Angier, Stackpole Books, Harrisburg, PA, 1965. 192 pp., illus. $4.50.

An outdoorsman's handbook on equipment, woodcraft, and camping techniques.

Horse Equipments and Cavalry Accoutrements 1891. A reprint of U.S. Ordnance Memoranda No. 29 by Francis Bannerman Sons, Blue Point, NY, 1969, 23 pp., plus 20 plates. $3.50.

U.S. army cavalry equipment described and illustrated in line.

How to Build Your Home in the Woods, by Bradford Angier, Stackpole Books, Harrisburg, PA, 1967, 310 pp., illus. $7.00.

Detailed instructions on building cabins, shelters, etc., with natural materials. How to obtain food from nature, and how to live in the wilderness in comfort.

How to Defend Yourself, your Family, and your Home, by Geo. Hunter. David McKay, N.Y.C., 1967, 307 pp., illus. $6.95.

The only book available for the public at large that advocates their ownership of firearms—including handguns. Covers laws of self-defense, setting up home protection, and much else.

How to Live in the Woods on Pennies a Day, by Bradford Angier, Stackpole Books, Harrisburg, PA, 1971. 192 pp., illus. $6.95.

New reprint on modern-day wilderness living in America, plus cooking and recipes.

The Identification and Registration of Firearms, by Vaclav "Jack" Krcma, C. C. Thomas, Springfield, IL, 1971. 173 pp., illus. $17.50.

Analysis of problems and improved techniques of recording firearms data accurately.

Indian and Oriental Armour, by Lord Egerton of Tatton. Stackpole Books, Harrisburg, PA, 1968. 178 pp., well illus., some in color. $14.95.

New edition of a rare work which has been a key reference for students of the subject, plus a creditable source on Oriental history.

Infantry Equipment 1875. A reprint of U.S. Ordnance Memoranda No. 19 by Francis Bannerman Sons, Blue Point, NY, 1969. 62 pp., plus 9 plates. $6.50.

A report covering materials, supplies, etc., to outfit troops in field and garrison.

Instinct Shooting, by Mike Jennings. Dodd, Mead & Co., N.Y.C., 1959. 157 pp., 20 line drawings, illus. $3.95.

All about Lucky McDaniel and his surprisingly successful discovery of a new aerial shooting technique, one which will let almost anyone, novices preferred, hit flying targets with only minutes of instruction.

Instructions to Young Sportsmen: Guns and Shooting, by Col. P. Hawker, Richmond Publ. Co., Richmond, England, 1971. 507 pp., illus. $13.95.

Reprint of the 1833 British work on guns, shooting and killing game.

Introduction to Muzzle Loading, by R. O. Ackerman. Publ. by the author, Albuquerque, NM, 1966. 20 pp., illus. with author's sketches. $1.50.

This booklet, in paper wrappers, will be Book No. 1 of a projected series. Contains a glossary of muzzle loading terms, and is aimed at the novice.

An Introduction to Tool Marks, Firearms and the Striagraph, by J. E. Davis. Chas. C. Thomas, Springfield, IL, 1st ed., 1958. 282 pp. $8.50.

Textbook on micro-contour analysis in criminalistics, with emphasis upon the striagraph in analysis of evidence.

Ironmaker To The Confederacy, by C. B. Dew. Yale Univ. Press, New Haven, 1966. 345 pp., illus. $10.00.

History of Joseph R. Anderson's Tredegar Iron works in Richmond, VA, which produced weapons and military equipment essential to the Confederacy's armed forces.

Jane's Weapons Systems: 1970-71, by R. T. Pretty and D. H. R. Archer, Editors. Jane's Yearbooks, London, 1970. 606 pp. illus. $55.00.

Catalog of military hardware of the major nations.

Japanese Infantry Weapons, ed. by D. B. McLean. Normount Armament Co., Forest Grove, OR, 1966. 241 pp., well illus., paperbound. $3.50.

Survey of World War II Japanese weapons, based on military intelligence research.

The Japanese Sword and Its Fittings, by members of the Japanese Sword Society of New York. Cooper Union Museum, N.Y.C., 1966. Paper covers. 26 pp. of text plus many illus. $3.50.

The authoritative text in the form of a catalog describing the illus. of items in the possession of members of the society.

John Groth's World of Sport, by J. Groth. Winchester Press. NY, 1970. 160 pp., illus. $6.95.

Exotic and exciting sports recorded by a man whose vital drawings convey the essence of the action. 40 color paintings.

Johnson Rifles and Light Machine Guns, ed. by D. B. McLean. Normount Armament Co., Forest Grove, OR, 1968. 55 pp., illus., paperbound. $2.00.

Manual on the only recoil-operated auto-loading rifle issued to U.S. forces.

Knife Throwing as a Modern Sport, by H. K. McEvoy and C. V. Gruzanski. Charles C. Thomas, Springfield, IL, 1965. 57 pp., illus. $5.50.

For first time, a concise, easy-to-read and complete story on this modern sport.

Knife Throwing: A Practical Guide, by H. K. McEvoy. C. E. Tuttle Co., VT, 1973. 112 pp., illus. Paper covers. $2.95.

For the amateur sportsman and experienced thrower as well. Building targets, buying information, etc. How to use knives and tomahawks in hunting game.

A Knight and His Armour, 95 pp. $3.25.
A Knight and His Castle, 108 pp. $3.25.
A Knight and His Horse, 96 pp. $3.25.
A Knight and His Weapons, 95 pp. $3.25.

A series planned for young readers, by R. E. Oakeshott. Lutterworth Press, London, 1966. All illus. Of interest to adults as well.

Knights in Armor, by S. Glubok, Harper & Row, NY, 1969. 48 pp., illus. $5.50.

Story of European body armor told for young readers.

Kuhlhoff on Guns, by Pete Kuhlhoff, Winchester Press, NY, 1970. 180 pp., illus. $5.95.

A selection of firearms articles by the late Gun Editor of *Argosy* Magazine.

Lewis Automatic Machine Gun, publ. originally by Savage Arms Co., Utica, NY. A reprint by L. A. Funk, Puyallup, WA, 1969. 47 pp., illus., paper covers. $1.50.

This facsimile covers the Model 1916 gun, explaining all features of operation, action, nomenclature, stripping and assembly.

The Long African Day, by Norman Myers. The Macmillan Co., Riverside, NJ, 1973. 400 pp. $25.

300 magnificent photos and a perceptive text explore East Africa, an area whose wildlife and countryside may be the most beautiful, fascinating, and varied in the world.

The Machine Gun, Vol., II, Part VII, by Lt. Col. G. M. Chinn. Paladin Press, Boulder, Col., n.d. 215 pp., illus. $15.00.

Reprint of a 1952 Navy publication of Soviet WW II rapid fire weapons.

Machine Guns and Gunnery for Machine Guns. Normount Armament Co., Forest Grove, OR, 1968. 218 pp., illus. Paper, $3.00.

Complete manual on 30- and 50-caliber machine guns and 45-caliber sub-machine guns.

Marksmanship: Secrets of High Scoring from a World Champ, by Gary L. Anderson. Simon & Schuster, NY, 1972. 79 pp. $4.95.

Illus. step-by-step guide to target shooting. Covers equipment, ammunition, breath control, arm position, etc.

Marlin Catalog of 1897. A reprint in facsimile by the Wyoming Armory, Inc., Cheyenne, WY, 1969. 192 pp. Well illus., paper covers, $3.50.

All models are covered, cartridges, sights, engraving, accessories, reloading tools, etc.

Marlin Catalog, 1905, Wyoming Armory, Inc., Cheyenne, WY, 1971. 128 pp. Paper, $4.00.

Reprint. Rifles, shotguns, pistols, tools, cartridge information, factory engraving and carving illustrated and described.

Mexican Military Arms, The Cartridge Period, by James B. Hughes, Jr. Deep River Armory, Inc., Houston, TX, 1967. 135 pp., photos and line drawings. $4.50.

An interesting and useful work, in imprinted wrappers, covering the period from 1866 to 1967.

Military Modelling, by Donald Featherstone, A. S. Barnes and Co., NY, 1971. 159 pp., illus. $6.95.

Describes the art of moulding and casting, soldering, glueing, painting and construction of small figures.

Military Small Arms of the 20th Century, by Ian V. Hogg & John S. Weeks. Digest Books, Inc., Northfield, IL, 1973. 256 pp. Paper covers. $7.95.

Weapons from the world over are meticulously examined in this comprehensive encyclopedia of those military small arms issued since 1900. Over 500 illus.

Military Uniforms, 1686-1918, by Rene North. Grosset & Dunlap, NY, 1970. 159 pp., illus. $3.95.

Concise survey of European and U.S. military dress and its history during the principal wars. Profusely illus., with some colored drawings.

Military Uniforms of the World in Color, by Preben Kannik, translated by W. Y. Carman. MacMillan Co., N.Y., NY, 1968. 278 pp. incl. index, 512 illus. figures in full color. $4.95.

An excellent handbook for the collector and student. The descriptive text gives good details of equipment.

The Minute Men, by J. R. Galvin. Hawthorn Books, N.Y.C., 1967. 286 pp. $6.95.

History of the colonial militia to the beginning of the Revolutionary War, including data on the battles of Lexington and Concord.

Modern ABC's of Bow and Arrow, by G. H. Gillelan. Stackpole Books, Harrisburg, PA, 1967. 160 pp., illus. $4.95.

Survey of techniques for beginners and experts in target archery as well as bowhunting.

Modern ABC's of Guns, by R. A. Steindler. Stackpole Books, Harrisburg, PA, 1965. 191 pp., illus. $4.95.

Concise lexicon of today's sporting firearms, their components, ammunition, accessory equipment and use.

NRA Firearms & Ammunition Fact Book. National Rifle Assn., Wash., D.C., 1970. 352 pp., illus. Paper covers. $2.

Articles, questions and answers, definitions, charts and tables. A wealth of accurate, sound information on everything connected with shooting.

NRA Question and Answer Handbook. National Rifle Assn., Wash., D.C., 1973. 48 pp., illus. Paper covers. $2.50.

A reprint of 150 basic questions most often asked of *The American Rifleman's* arms and shooting specialists, and the answers to them.

Navies of the World, by Hans Busk, Richmond Publ. Co., Richmond, England, 1971. 456 pp., illus. $13.50.

Reprint of the London 1859 ed.

New England Militia Uniforms and Accoutrements, by J. O. Curtis and Wm. H. Guthman. Old Sturbridge Inc., Sturbridge, MA, 1971. 102 pp. Paper covers. $4.

An identification guide which illustrates uniforms, epaulettes, helmets, helmet plates, belt buckles and cartridge pouches.

New Principles of Gunnery, by Benjamin Robins. Richmond Publ. Co., London, 1972. 190 pp. $10.95.

Facsimile of the rare 1742 ed. For anyone, including libraries, interested in gunnery, military history and technology.

The New Way of the Wilderness, By Calvin Rutstrum. Macmillan Co., New York, NY 1st ed., 1966 [4th printing]. 276 pp., illus. in line. $4.95.

An outdoorsman's manual on traveling and living in the open, with chapters on transportation, equipment, food, hunting and fishing for food.

L. D. Nimschke, Firearms Engraver, by R. L. Wilson. John J. Malloy, publisher, Teaneck, NJ, 1965. Quarto, 107 pp., profusely illus. $17.50.

Showing a wide variety of designs, initials and monograms and ever-so-many portions of collectors' arms. A thoroughly interesting work for the collector and an inspiration to the engraver.

No Second Place Winner, by Wm. H. Jordan, publ. by the author, Shreveport, LA (Box 4072), 1962. 114 pp., illus. $6.00.

Guns and gear of the peace officer, ably discussed by a U.S. Border Patrolman for over 30 years, and a first-class shooter with handgun, rifle, etc.

The Order of the Death's Head, by Heinz Hohne, Coward-McCann, Inc., NY, 1970. 690 pp., illus. $12.50.

The Story of Hitler's S.S., the most horrifying organization ever invented by the Germans. Based on Himmler's personal staff files, the Nuremberg trials and the Reich Security Office.

The Other Mr. Churchill, by Macdonald Hastings. Dodd Mead, N.Y.C., 1965. 336 pp., illus. $1.98.

Important biography of a great London gunmaker and forensic ballistics expert, who contributed much to the color and excellence of British firearms tradition.

Outdoor Tips, by L. W. Johnson, Robt. Elman & Jerry Gibbs. Benjamin Co., NY, 1972. 190 pp., illus. Paper covers. $2.95.

Authoritative chapters on American hunting, fishing, camping, other outdoor activities.

Pageant of the Gun, by Harold L. Peterson. Doubleday & Co., Inc., Garden City, NY, 1967. 352 pp., profusely illus. $3.95.

A storehouse of stories on firearms, their romance and lore, their development and use through 10 centuries. A most satisfying history of firearms chronologically presented.

Paradise Below Zero, by Calvin Rutstrum. Macmillan Co., New York, NY 1st ed., 1968. 244 pp., illus. in line and halftone. $5.95.

On the rewards and methods of camping and travel in Eskimo country, including check lists of provisions, tools, equipment, clothing and ways of getting about.

The Pictorial Field-Book of the Revolution, 1775-1783; or "Illustrations by Pen and Pencil of the History, Biography, Scenery, Relics and Traditions of the War for Independence," by Benson J. Lossing. Benchmark Publ. Corp. Glendale, NY, 1970. 1555 pp. in 2 Vol. $36.50.

Reprint of the original 1855 ed. Over 1100 engravings and index.

The Pictorial Field-Book of the War of 1812; or "Illustrations by Pen and Pencil of the History, Biography, Scenery, Relics and Traditions of the Last War for American Independence," by Benson J. Lossing. Benchmark Publ. Corp., Glendale, NY, 1970. 1084 pp., $24.50.

Reprint of the 1869 ed. Several hundred engravings.

Pictorial History of Tanks of the World 1915-45, by P. Chamberlain & C. Ellis. Stackpole Books, Harrisburg, PA, 1972. 256 pp., illus. $19.95.

All tanks produced for military service are pictured, including many rarely seen experimental models and prototypes.

Pictorial History of the Machine Gun, by F. W. A. Hobart. Drake Publ., Inc., NY, 1972. 256 pp. $9.95.

Text is enhanced by over 240 photos and diagrams and a table of machine-gun data giving essential details on a large number of guns—some of which never got beyond the prototype stage.

Picture Book of the Continental Soldier, by C. K. Wilbur. Stackpole Books, Harrisburg, PA, 1969. 96 pp., well illus. $4.95.

A wealth of detailed material in text and fine drawings, depicting Revolutionary War weapons, accouterments, field equipment, and the routine of the solder's life. Included are artillery, edged weapons, muskets, rifles, powder horns, etc.

Picture Book of the Revolution's Privateers, by C. Keith Wilbur. Stackpole Books, Harrisburg, PA, 1973. 96 pp. $4.95.

Hundreds of drawn illus., plus explanatory text, show the privateersmen, their ships, gear, weapons, tactics, etc.

Pocket Guide to Archery, by H. T. Sigler. Stackpole Co., Harrisburg, PA, 1960. 96 pp., illus. $2.95.

Useful introduction to the subject, covering equipment, shooting techniques, and bow hunting of small game and deer.

Practical Wildlife Management, by Geo. V. Burger. Winchester Press, NY, 1973. 224 pp., illus. $8.95. Anyone interested in wildlife will find this an invaluable reference as well as entertaining, informative reading.

Presenting America's Aristocracy of Fine Cutlery, Grawolf Trading Co., Milwaukee, WI, 1971. Vol. 2 of a limited, numbered ed. Paper, $3.50.

Unpaginated with hundreds of illus. and explanations.

Reading the Woods, by Vinson Brown. Stackpole Books, Harrisburg, PA, 1969. 160 pp., illus. $5.95.

Clues to the past, present and future development of wooded areas by observation of signs of change, decay, influences of water and wildlife, and the impact of man's presence.

The Records and Badges of Every Regiment and Corps in the British Army, by H. M. Chichester and Geo. Burges-Short. Fred. Muller, Ltd., London, 1970. A reprint of the 2nd ed. of 1900. 240 illus., in the text and 24 color plates $27.50.

A magnificent facsimile with gilt top giving the history, uniforms, colors and insignia in satisfying detail of much-wanted data on subject.

Records of the Scottish Volunteer Force 1859-1908, by Lt. Gen. Sir James Moncrieff Grierson. Frederick Muller, Ltd., London, 1972. 372 pp. $29.50.

Limited reprint of the rare classic on the history and uniforms of the Scottish Volunteers before the re-organization of 1908. 47 full-color plates show 239 different uniforms.

The Redbook of Used Gun Values, rev. 1973 ed., publishers Dev. Corp., Skokie, IL, 1972. 130 pp., illus., paper covers. $2.50.

Today's values for commercial firearms, listed by manufacturers with a bonus listing of antique gun values.

Remington Arms Revised Price-List, 1902. Arthur McKee, Northport, NY, n.d. 64 pp. Paper covers. $3.50.

Reprint, fully illustrated.

Remington Firearms, 1906 Catalog, Arthur McKee, Northport, NY, n.d., 48 pp., illus. Paper covers. $3.50.

Reprint. Guns, parts, ammo., prices, etc.

Riot Control—Materiel and Techniques, by Rex Applegate. Stackpole Books, Harrisburg, PA 1969. 320 pp., illus. $9.95.

Originally released as *Kill or Get Killed,* later as *Crowd and Riot Control.* Designed for law officer training, plus deployment of personnel, chemicals and special equipment for best results.

Round Shot and Rammers, by H. L. Peterson. Stackpole Books, Harrisburg, PA, 1969. 128 pp., illus. $9.95.

Artillery in America Through the Civil War years, with much detail on manufacture, history, accessory equipment, and use of all types of cannon. Fine line drawings show the guns, their equipment, and the men who used them.

Russian Infantry Weapons of World War II, by A. J. Barker and John Walter, Arco Publ. Co., NY, 1971. 80 pp., $3.50.

History and development of World War II infantry weapons used by the Red Army. Each weapon is fully described and illus.

Sam Colt: Genius, by Robt. F. Hudson, American Archieves Publ. Co., Topsfield, MA, 1971. 160 pp., illus. Plastic spiral bound. $6.50.

Historical review of Colt's inventions, including facsimiles of patent papers and other Colt information.

Sam Colt and His Gun, by Gertrude H. Winders. John Day Co., NY, ca. 1959. 159 pp., illus. $4.50.

Concise biography of the "inventor" of the revolver.

Scloppetaria, by Capt. H. Beaufroy, Richmond Publ. Co., Richmond, England, 1971. 251 pp. $11.00.

Reprint of the 1808 edition written under the pseudonym "A Corporal of Rilfemen". Covers rifles and rifle shooting, the first such work in English.

The Search for the Well-Dressed Soldier 1865-1890, by Gordon Chappell. Arizona Hist. Society, Tucson, AR, 1972. 51 pp., illus. Paper covers. $2.50.

Developments and innovations in U.S. Army uniforms on the western frontier.

Second World War Combat Weapons, by Hoffschmidt & Tantum. WE, Inc., Old Greenwich, CT, 1968. 212 pp., illus. $7.95.

German weapons, vehicles, and projectiles illustrated and described. First of a 7-vol. series.

Secret Fighting Arts of the World, by J. F. Gilbey. Tuttle, Rutland, VT 1963. 150 pp., illus. $4.15.

20 chapters on advanced techniques of unarmed combat, described in anecdotal form.

Secret Weapons of the Third Reich, by L. E. Simon, We, Inc., Old Greenwich, CT, 1971. 248 pp., illus. $8.95.

Review of German World War II military research and its products.

Shooter's Bible, No. 64, John Olson, ed. Shooter's Bible, S. Hackensack, NJ, 1973. 576 pp., illus. $4.95.

An annually-published guide to firearms, ammunition, and accessories.

Shooter's Bible Game Cook Book, by Geraldine Steindler. Follett Publ. Co., Chicago IL 1965. 224 pp., illus., cloth, $6.95; paper, $4.95.

Full information on preparing game for the table, including recipes and methods of field-dressing.

The Shooter's Guide: or Complete Sportsman's Companion, by B. Thomas, Richmond Publ. Co., Richmond, England, 1971. 264 pp., illus. $9.00.

Reprint of an 1816 British handbook on hunting small game, game laws, dogs, guns and ammunition.

Shooting, by M. Turner and St. Tucker, Cogswell & Harrison, London, 1970. 176 pp., illus. $2.95.

Instruction manual for novices and the young in sports.

Shooting Muzzle Loading Hand Guns, by Charles T. Haven. Guns Inc., MA, 1947. 132 pp., illus. $6.50.

A good summary of shooting methods, both contemporary and modern. Duelling with M.L. handguns is also covered.

The Shorebirds of North America, by Peter Matthiesen, ed. by Gordon Stout, with species accounts by R. S. Palmer. Viking Press, N.Y.C., 1967, 288 pp., 32 6-color plates, 10″x14″, $22.50. De Luxe ltd. ed., extra bound, $50.00.

A magnificent book, probably the outstanding work on the shorebirds of the northern western world. 32 chapters cover 59 species. The illustrations are superb.

Silencers. Paladin Press, Boulder, CO, 1971 205 pp., illus. $9.95.

Reprint of Frankford Arsenal Report R-1896. The functional and physical details on foreign and domestic silencers, including patent drawings, engineering data, manufacture, etc.

Silencers, Snipers & Assassins, by J. David Truby, Paladin Press, Boulder, CO, 1972. 209 pp., illus. $15.95.

Traces development of silencers from their invention by Hiram Maxim in 1908 to American snipers' use during the Korean conflict.

Six-guns and Saddle Leather, by Ramon F. Adams. University of Oklahoma Press, Norman, OK, 1969, 801 pp., $19.95.

A bibliography of books and pamphlets on western outlaws and gunmen. A brand new revised and enlarged edition.

Sketch Book 76: The American Soldier 1775-1781, by R. Klinger and R. A. Wilder, Arlington VA, 1967. 53 pp., illus. Paper covers. $2.50.
Sketches, notes, and patterns compiled from a study of clothing and equipment used by the American foot soldier in the Revolutionary War.

Skills for Taming the Wilds, by Bradford Angier, Stackpole Books, Harrisburg, PA, 1967. 320 pp., illus. $6.95.
A handbook of woodcraft wisdom, by a foremost authority, showing how to obtain maximum comfort from nature.

Small Arms Identification and Operation Guide—Eurasian Communist Countries, by Harold E. Johnson, Inco., 1972. 218 pp., illus. Paper covers. $4.00.
Reprint of 1970 U.S. Army manual FSTC-CW-07-03-70.

Small Arms Lexicon and Concise Encyclopedia, by Chester Mueller and John Olson. Stoeger Arms, So. Hackensack, NJ, 1968. 312 pp., 500 illus. $14.95.
Definitions, explanations, and references on antiques, optics, ballistics, etc., from A to Z. Over 3,000 entries plus appendix.

Small Arms of the World, by W. H. B. Smith and J. E. Smith. 9th ed., 1969. Stackpole Books, Harrisburg, PA. 786 pp., profusely illus. $17.95.
A most popular firearms classic for easy reference. Covers the small arms of 42 countries, clearly showing operational principles. A timeless volume of proven worth.

The Sportsman's Eye, by James Gregg, Winchester Press, NY, 1971. 210 pp., illus. $6.95.
How to make better use of your eyes in the outdoors.

Stoeger's Catalog & Handbook: New York World's Fair 1939 Jubilee Issue, Stoeger Arms, NY, 1970. 512 pp., illus. Paper, $4.95.
Reprint describing pre-W.W.II sporting arms.

Stoeger Mail Order and Gun Parts Catalog, 2nd ed. Stoeger Arms, So. Hackensack, NJ, 1972. 416 pp., illus. Paper covers. $3.95.
Lists over 1000 parts for handguns, rifles and shotguns, domestic and foreign. Includes gunsmith tools and accessories.

Stories of the Old Duck Hunters and Other Drivel, by Gordon MacQuarrie and compiled by Zack Taylor. Stackpole Books, Harrisburg, PA, 1967. 223 pp., illus. $5.95.
An off-beat relaxing and enjoyable group of 19 best-remembered outdoor stories, previously publ. in magazines.

The Story of the Guns, by Emerson Tennent. Richmond Publ. Co., Surrey, Eng., 1972. 364 pp. $11.50.
Reprint of the original 1864 London ed. Part I—The Rifled Musket, Part 2—Rifled Ordnance, Part 3—The Iron Navy.

Submachine Guns Caliber .45, M3 and M3A1, U.S. FM23-41 and TM 9-1217. Normount Armament Co., Forest Grove, OR, 1967. 141 pp., illus., paperbound. $3.00.
Reprint of two U.S. Army manuals on submachine guns.

The Survival Handbook, by W. K. Merrill. Winchester Press, NY, 1972. 320 pp., illus. $5.95.
How to stay out of trouble in all kinds of terrain and weather. Detailed advice on shelter, food and first aid for those caught unexpectedly in disaster situations.

Swords & Daggers, by Frederick Wilkinson. Hawthorn Books, NY, 1968. 256 pp., well illus. $5.95.
Good general survey of edged weapons and polearms of collector interest, with 150 pp. of illustrations and descriptions of arms from Europe, Africa and the Orient.

Swords of Hitler's Third Reich, by Major J. R. Angolia, F. J. Stephens, Essex, England, 1969. Over 100 pp., well illus. $8.95.
A comprehensive work on the swords of the German Army, Navy, Air Force, SS, Police, Fire Dept., and many other government departments—plus belts, hangers, and accouterments—all described and illus.

Tank Data 3, by H. E. Johnson. We Inc., Old Greenwich, CT, 1972. 208 pp., illus. $10.
Proving Ground Series. A collection of photos and data on tanks of all nations.

Tanks; An Illustrated History of Fighting Vehicles, by Armin Halle & Carlo Demand, New York Graphic Society, Greenwich, CT, 1971. 175 pp., illus. $24.95.
Comprehensively traces the development and technology of one of man's most complex and ingenious weapons.

Tanks and Other AFV's of the Blitzkrieg Era, 1939-1941, by B. T. White. The Macmillan Co., Riverside, NJ, 1973. 180 pp. $4.95.
Comprehensive, carefully illus. encyclopedia of the most important armored fighting vehicles developed by the principal countries at war.

Teaching Kids to Shoot, by Henry M. Stebbins. Stackpole Books, Harrisburg, PA 1966. 96 pp. illus. $2.95.
Designed for parents and leaders who want to develop safety conscious firearms-users.

Tear Gas Munitions. by T. F. Swearengen, Charles C. Thomas, Springfield, IL, 1966. 569 pp., illus. $34.50.
An analysis of commercial (riot) gas guns, tear gas projectiles, grenades, small arms ammunition, and related tear gas devices.

Technical Dictionary for Weapon Enthusiasts, Shooters and Hunters, by Gustav Sybertz. Publ. by J. Neumann-Neudamm, 3508 Melsungen, W. Germany, 1969, 164 pp., semi-soft covers. $7.50.
A German-English and English-German dictionary for the sportsman. An excellent handy work.

Tenting on the Plains, by Elizabeth Bacon Custer, Univ. of Oklahoma Press, Norman, OK, 1971. 706 pp. in 3 volumes, plus a 30-page intro. by Jane R. Stewart. Slip-cased. $8.85.
Deals with period after the Civil War when General Custer was stationed in Texas and Kansas.

The Thompson Gun, publ. by Numrich Arms, West Hurley, NY, 1967, 27 pp., illus., paper covers. $1.95.
A facsimile reprint, excellently done, of a 1923 catalog of Thompson sub-machine guns.

Thompson-Submachine Guns, compiled from original manuals by the publ. Normount Armament Co., Forest Grove, OR, 1968. Over 230 pp., well illus., many exploded views. Paper wrappers. $4.00.
Five reprints in one book: Basic Field Manual, Cal. 45, M1928AI (U.S. Army); Cal. 45, Model 1928, (for British); Cal., 45 (U.S. Ordnance); Model M1, Cal., 45 (U.S. Ordnance) and Ultra Modern Automatic Arms (Auto-Ordnance Corp.).

The Tournament, its periods and phases, by R. C. Clephan. Frederick Ungar Co., NY, 1967. A reprint. 195 pp., illus. with contemporary pictures plus half-tones of armor and weapons used by contestants, $9.95.
A rare and eagerly-sought work, long out-of-print. A scholarly, historical and descriptive account of jousting.

Training Your Own Bird Dog, by Henry P. Davis, G. P. Putnam's Sons, New York, NY. New rev. ed., 1969, 168 pp., plus 10 pp. of field trial records. Illus. with photographs. $5.95.
The reappearance of a popular and practical book for the beginner starting his first bird dog—by an internationally recognized authority.

A Treatise on Ancient Armour and Weapons, by Francis Grose. Benchmark Pub. Co., Glendale, NY, 1970. Irregular pagination. $12.50.
Reprint of a 1786 British monograph showing numerous items from the Tower of London and other sites.

Treatise on Military Small Arms and Ammunition 1888, compiled by Col. J. Bond, R. A. Arms and Armour Press, London, Eng., 1971. 142 pp., illus. $10.
Facsimile of the original compiled in 1888 at the School of Musketry, Hythe, and accepted by the British Army as a definitive textbook.

Triggernometry, by Eugene Cunningham. Caxton Printers Lt., Caldwell, ID, 1970. 441 pp., illus. $7.95. A classic study of famous outlaws and lawmen of the West—their stature as human beings, their exploits and skills in handling firearms. A reprint.

The True Book About Firearms, by R. H. Walton, Frederick Muller, Ltd., London, 1965. 143 pp., illus. $4.00.
How modern weapons work, are used and their effect on history.

Unconventional Warfare Devices and Techniques, a reprint of Army TM 31-200-1 234 pp., illus., paper covers. $10.00.
Published primarily for U.S. Army Special Forces. Deals with destructive techniques and their applications to targets in guerrilla warfare.

Uniforms, Organization and History of the Waffen SS, by R. J. Bender and H. P. Taylor. R. J. Bender, Mountain View, CA, 1969-1973. Various pagination. $9.95 each volume.
A projected 4-vol. set, of which 3 books are now ready. Detailed and intriguing study of Hitler's elite supermen.

United States Military Medals & Ribbons, by Philip K. Robles, Charles E. Tuttle Co., Rutland, VT, 1971. 187 pp., $12.50.
A definitive work; 139 plates in full color.

Use and Maintenance of the Browning "Hi-Power" Pistol, (No. 2 MK 1 and Commercial Models), by D. B. McLean. Normount Armament Co., Forest Grove, OR, 1966. 48 pp., illus., paperbound. $1.50.
Covers the use, maintenance, and repair of various Browning 9mm parabellum pistols.

Warriors and Weapons of Early Times, by Niels M. Saxtorph. The Macmillan Co., Riverside, NJ, 1973. 244 pp. $4.95.
128 pages of superb color illus. of uniforms and military accoutrements from 300 B.C. to 1700, from all over the Old World.

Warriors' Weapons, by Walter Buehr. Crowell Co., NYC, 1963. 186 pp., illus. $5.95.
Illustrated history of pre-gunpower arms, from stone ax to crossbow and catapult.

Weapons of the American Revolution, and Accoutrements, by Warren Moore. Funk & Wagnalls, NY, 1967. 225 pp., fine illus. $10.00.
Revolutionary era shoulder arms, pistols, edged weapons, and equipment are described and shown in fine drawings and photographs, some in color.

Weapons and Fighting Arts of the Indonesian Archipelago, by Donn F. Draeger. Chas. E. Tuttle Co., VT, 1972. 254 pp., illus. $12.50.
The varied combative forms of the islands, from empty-hand techniques to the use of spears, knives, the kris, etc.

The Weapons Merchants, by Bernt Engelmann, Crown Publ., inc., Inc., NY, 1968. 224 pp., illus. $4.95.
A true account of illegal traffic in death-dealing arms by individuals and governments.

Weapons and Tactics, Hastings to Berlin, by Jac Weller, St. Martin's Press, New York, 1966. 238 pp., illus. $6.00.
Primarily on the infantry weapons of today, with basic data on those of the past.

Weapons of War, by P. E. Cleator. Crowell Co., NYC, 1968. 224 pp., illus. $6.95.
A British survey of warfare from earliest times, as influenced by the weapons available for combat.

A. A. White Engravers, Inc. A catalog, unpaginated, n.d. Paper covers. $2.00.
Current prices and illus. for the engraving of arms.

Whitewings: The White-winged Dove, ed. by C. Cottam & J. B. Trefethen. D. Van Nostrand Co., Princeton, NJ, 1968. 348 pp. $7.50.
Compendium of research publications on an important game bird of Texas and Arizona, the Southwest, including Mexico. Excellent photographs.

Wild Game Cookbook, by L. E. Johnson. Benjamin Co., NYC, 1968. 160 pp. $2.95.
Recipes, sauces, and cooking hints for preparation of all types of game birds and animals.

Wild Sanctuaries . . ., by Robert Murphy. E. P. Dutton & Co., Inc., New York, NY, 1968, 288 pp., over 250 photographs in color and monochrome, plus 32 maps, including those of the flyways. $12.95.
Concerns America's national wildlife refuges. An all-encompassing treatise on its subject with fascinating pertinent text.

The Wild Turkey, its History and Domestication, by A. W. Schorger, Univ. of Oklahoma Press, Norman, Okla., 1966. 625 pp., illus. $15.00.
Detailed coverage of habitats, characteristics, breeding, and feeding of the American wild turkey. Bibliography.

Wilderness Cookery, by Bradford Angier. Stackpole Books, Harrisburg, PA, 1969. 256 pp., illus. $4.95.
An excellent work, one that will be of big interest to hunters, fishermen, campers, et al.

Wilderness Gear You Can Make Yourself, by Bradford Angier. Stackpole Books, Harrisburg, PA, 1973. 192 pp., illus. $6.95.
Detailed, illus. guide to let you make your own outdoor necessities.

The Wilderness Route Finder, by C. Rutstrum, Macmillan Co., NY, 1970. 214 pp. $4.95.
Complete guide to finding your way in the wilderness.

Wildwood Wisdom, by Ellsworth Jaeger. The Macmillan Company, New York, NY, 1964. 491 pp. well-illus. by author. $6.95.
An authoritative work, through many editions; about all there is to know about every detail for the outdoorsman.

Williams 1972-73 Blue Book of Gun Dealing, Williams Gun Sight Co., Davison, MI, 1972. 92 pp., illus. Paper covers. $2.95.
A guide to modern gun values based on past experience by this famous concern.

The World of the Moose, by Joe Van Wormer. J. B. Lippincott Co., Phila., PA, 1972. 160 pp., illus. $5.95.
A record of the life style of these animals in their wild and remote habitats.

The World of the Ruffed Grouse, by Leonard Lee Rue, III. J. B. Lippincott, Phila., PA, 1973. 160 pp., illus. $5.95.
A year-round survey of the ruffed grouse and its environment, habitat, enemies, and relation to man.

The World of the White-Tailed Deer, by L. L. Rue III. J. B. Lippincott Co., Phila., 1967. A reprint. 137 pp., fine photos. $5.95.
An eminent naturalist-writer's account of the year-round activities of the white-tailed deer.

The World of the Wild Turkey, by J. C. Lewis. J. B. Lippincott Co., Phila., PA, 1973. 158 pp., illus. $5.95.
The author takes the reader into the wilderness world of the turkey's 6 surviving subspecies.

The World's Assault Rifles (and Automatic Carbines), by D. D. Musgrave and T. B. Nelson. T. B. N. Enterprises, Alexandria, VA, 1967. 546 pp., profusely illus. $19.50.
High velocity small-bore combat rifles are shown and described in much detail, arranged by type and nationality. A companion volume to *The World's Submachine Guns*, by Nelson and Lockhoven.

The World's Submachine Guns (and Machine Pistols), by T. B. Nelson and H. B. Lockhoven. T. B. N. Enterprises, Alexandria, VA, 1962. 739 pp., profusely illus. $15.50.
The 2nd printing (1964) of the first work with descriptive data on all significant SMGs to date, arranged by national origin. A glossary in 22 languages is included. It is a companion volume to the *The World's Assault Rifles* by Musgrave and Nelson.
You and Your Retriever, by R. W. Coykendall, Jr. Doubleday & Co., Garden City, NY, 1963. 155 pp., illus. $4.95.
A text on early, intermediate and advanced training of retrievers, with full information for handlers.
The Young Sportsman's Guide to Camping, by J. L. Holden. Thomas Nelson & Sons, Camden, NJ, 1962. 96 pp., illus. $2.75.
A concise and dependable guide to basic techniques of camping in comfort and safety.
The Young Sportsman's Guide to Dogs, by J. R. Falk. Thomas Nelson & Sons, Camden, NJ, 1964. 96 pp., illus. $2.75.
A creditable and concise work on the history and characteristics of 29 breeds of dogs, both working and nonsporting types.
The Young Sportsman's Guide to Target Shooting, by Gene Seraphine. Thomas Nelson & Sons, Camden, NJ, 1964. 94 pp., illus. $2.95.
A basic introduction to marksmanship, including selection of firearms, sights, equipment, ammunition and range behavior.

Gunsmithing

Antique Firearms: Their Care, Repair and Restoration, by Ronald Lister. Crown Publ., New York, 1964. 220 pp., 66 plates, 24 fig. $2.98.
A workshop manual for collectors and gunsmiths, giving correct procedures for every step in preserving firearms.
Artistry in Arms. The R. W. Norton Gallery, Shreveport, LA., 1970. 42 pp., illus. Paper, $2.50.
The art of gunsmithing and engraving.
Building the Kentucky Rifle, by J. R. Johnston. Golden Age Arms Co., Worthington, OH, 1972. 44 pp., illus. Paper covers. $5.
How to go about it, with text and drawings.
Checkering and Carving of Gun Stocks, by Monte Kennedy. Stackpole Books, Harrisburg, PA, 1962. 175 pp., illus. $10.00.
Rev., enlarged clothbound ed. of a much sought-after, dependable work.
Complete Guide to Gunsmithing, by C. E. Chapel. Barnes & Co., NYC, 1962. 479 pp., illus. $6.95.
2nd rev. edition, known earlier as *Gun Care and Repair,* of a comprehensive book on all details of gunsmithing for the hobbyist and professional.
The Complete Rehabilitation of the Flintlock Rifle and Other Works, by T. B. Tryon. Limbo Library, Taos, NM, 1972. 112 pp., illus. Paper covers. $6.95.
A series of articles which first appeared in various issues of the *American Rifleman* in the 1930s.
Firearms Blueing and Browning, by R. H. Angier. Stackpole Books, Harrisburg, PA, 151 pp., illus. $5.00.
A useful, concise text on chemical coloring methods for the gunsmith and mechanic.
Gun Engraving Review, by E. C. Prudhomme. G.E.R. Publ. Co., Shreveport, LA, 1965. 150 pp., profusely illus. (some in color.) $21.95. Deluxe limited ed., signed and notarized. $40.
Excellent examples of the gun engraver's art to serve as a guide to novice or expert. Selection of tools, techniques and pertinent comments by practicing gunsmiths the world over.
Gunsmith Kinks, by F. R. [Bob] Brownell. F. Brownell & Son., Montezuma, I. 1st ed., 1969. 496 pp., well illus. $9.95.
A widely useful accumulation of shop kinks, short cuts, techniques and pertinent comments by practicing gunsmiths from all over the world.
The Gunsmith's Manual, by J. Stelle and W. Harrison, Rutgers Book Center, Highland Park, NJ, 1972. 376 pp., illus. $9.95.
Exact reprint of the original. For the American gunsmith in all branches of the trade.
Gunsmithing, by Roy F. Dunlap. Stackpole Books, Harrisburg, PA, 714 pp., illus. $10.00.
Comprehensive work on conventional techniques, incl. recent advances in the field. Valuable to rifle owners, shooters, and practicing gunsmiths.
Gunsmithing Simplified, by H. E. Macfarland. Washington, DC, 1950, A. S. Barnes, NYC, 1959. 303 pp., illus. $6.95.
A thorough dependable concise work with many helpful short-cuts.
Gunstock Finishing and Care, by A. D. Newell. Stackpole Books, Harrisburg, PA. A new printing, 1966. 473 pp. illus. $9.50.
Amateur's and professional's handbook on the selection, use and application of protective and decorative coatings on gun stocks.
Hobby Gunsmithing, by Ralph Walker, Digest Books, Inc., Northfield, IL, 1972, 320 pp., illus. Paper, $5.95.
Kitchen table gunsmithing for the budding hobbyist.
Home Gun Care & Repair, by P. O. Ackley. Stackpole Books, Harrisburg, PA, 1969. 191 pp., illus. $5.95.
Basic reference for safe tinkering, fixing, and converting rifles, shotguns, handguns.
Home Gunsmithing Digest, by Tommy Bish. Digest Books, Inc., Northfield, IL, 1970, 320 pp., very well illus. within stiff decorated paper covers. $4.95.
An unusually beneficial assist for gun owners doing their own repairs, maintenance, etc. 45 chapters on tools, techniques and theories.
HOW . . . by L. Cowher, W. Hunley, and L. Johnston. NMLR Assn., IN, 1961. 107 pp., illus. Paper covers. $2.95.
This 1961 rev. ed., enlarged by 3 chapters and additional illustrations, covers the building of a muzzle-loading rifle, target pistol, and powder horn, and tells how to make gunflints.
How to Convert Military Rifles, by Harvey Williams, *et al.* Digest Books, Inc., Northfield, IL, 1970. 88 pp., very well illus., stiff paper covers. $1.95.
The 6th and latest ed. of a popular work formerly distributed by the author's company. Gives step-by-step instructions to convert a military rifle to a good looking and easy to handle sporter.
Introduction to Modern Gunsmithing, by H. E. MacFarland. Stackpole Books, Harrisburg, PA, 1965. 320 pp., illus. $6.95.
Up-to-date reference for all gunsmiths on care, repair, and modification of firearms, sights, and related topics.
Lock, Stock and Barrel, by R. H. McCrory. Publ. by author at Bellmore, NY, 1966. Paper covers, 122 pp., illus. $4.00.
A handy and useful work for the collector or the professional with many helpful procedures shown and described on antique gun repair.
Master French Gunsmith's Designs of the 17th-18th Centuries, compiled by S. V. Grancsay. Winchester Press, New York, NY, 1970. A brand new work of 208 pp., beautifully illus. in facsimile. Numbered, limited issue of 1000 copies. $24.95.
Magnificient ornamentation of weapons taken from a superb collection of design books, gathered by a world authority. An inspiration and a must for the gunsmith-engraver.
The Modern Gunsmith, by James V. Howe. Funk & Wagnalls. NYC, 1970 reprint ed. (2 vols.). 910 pp., illus. $25.00.
Guide for amateur and professional gunsmiths on firearms design, construction, repair, etc.
The Modern Kentucky Rifle, How to Build Your Own, by R. H. McCrory. McCrory, Wantagh, NY, 1961. 68 pp., illus., paper bound. $3.50.
A workshop manual on how to fabricate a flintlock rifle. Also some information on pistols and percussion locks.
The NRA Firearms Assembly Guidebook to Shoulder Arms. National Rifle Assn., Wash., D.C., 1973. 203 pp. Paper covers. $4.
Text and illus. explaining the takedown of 96 rifles and shotguns, domestic and foreign.
The NRA Firearms Assembly Guidebook to Handguns. National Rifle Assn., Wash., D.C., 1973, 206 pp. Paper covers. $4.
Illus. articles on the takedown of 101 pistol and revolver models.
The NRA Gunsmithing Guide, National Rifle Association, Wash., DC, 1971. 336 pp., illus. Paper. $5.50.
Information of the past 15 years from the "American Rifleman," ranging from 03A3 Springfields to Model 92 Winchesters.
Professional Gunsmithing, by W. J. Howe, Stackpole Books, Harrisburg, PA, 1968 reprinting. 526 pp., illus. $10.00.
Textbook on repair and alteration of firearms, with detailed notes on equipment and commercial gunshop operation.
Recreating the Kentucky Rifle, by Wm. Buchele. Geo. Shumway, York, PA, 1970. 189 pp., illus. $10.00.
How to build a Kentucky rifle, illustrated with line drawings and separate full-scale drawings. In paper covers. $6.50.
Restocking a Rifle, by Alvin Linden. Stackpole Books, Harrisburg, PA, 1969. 138 combined pp., of text. Well illus. Large format. $9.95.
A re-issue in one volume of the 3 earlier Linden instruction guides on: Stock Inletting; Shaping; Finishing of the Springfield, Enfield and Winchester M70 rifles.
Rifle Making in the Great Smoky Mountains, comp. by Gene Fries. Buffalo Bull Press, Cedar Rapids, IA, 1972. 40 pp., illus. Paper covers. $2.50.
Reprint of National Park Service Popular Study Series No. 13 by Dr. Arthur Kendall, publ. in 1941. Describes making the rifle, tools and operations involved, plus other short articles of interest to the muzzleloader.

handguns

Automatic Firearm Pistols, by Elmer Swanson, Wesmore Book Co., Weehawken, NJ. 1st (and only) ed. 1955, 210 pp., well illus. $15.00.
A veritable catalog exclusively on automatic handguns for collectors, with many line drawings and descriptions, plus then-market market values of each.
Automatic Pistols, by H. B. C. Pollard, WE Inc., Old Greenwich, CT, 1966. 110 pp., illus. $5.95.
A facsimile reprint of the scarce 1920 original. Covers historical development of military and other automatics, shooting, care, etc.
Book of Pistols & Revolvers, by W. H. B. Smith. Stackpole Books, Harrisburg, PA, 1968. 758 pp., profusely illus. $6.00.
Rev. and enlarged, this encyclopedic reference, first publ. in 1946, continues to be the best on its subject.
Browning Hi-Power Pistols. Normount Armament Co., Forest Grove, OR, 1968. 48 pp., illus., paperbound. $1.50.
A handbook on all models of Browning Hi-Power Pistols, covering their use, maintenance and repair.
Colt Commemorative Firearms, by R. L. Wilson. Charles Kidwell, Wichita, Kans., 1969, Unpaginated, well illus. paper covers $5.95. In hard deluxe covers, limited issue of 1000 copies, each numbered. $10.00.
Description and fine color photographs of commemorative handguns issued by the Colt company, 1961-1969, all replicas of famous earlier models.
Combat Shooting for Police, by Paul B. Weston. Charles C. Thomas, Springfield, IL, 1967. A reprint. 194 pp., illus. $10.00.
First publ. in 1960 this popular self-teaching manual gives basic concepts of defensive fire in every position.
The Encyclopedia of the Third Reich, Book 1, by R. B. Marvin. Universal Research, Inc., Fort Lauderdale, Fla., 1969, from offset typewritten copy. 37 pp., very clear and sharp illustrations, paper covers. $4.00
This volume considers only handguns, but is a concise collector's guide to the main types of W.W. II German pistols and revolvers.
Die Faustfeuerwaffen von 1850 bis zur Gegenwart, by Eugen Heer. Graz, Austria, 1971. 457 pp., illus. $30.
Historical treatment of pistols and revolvers for military use in the last half of the 19th century. German text.
Georgian Pistols; The Art and Craft of the Flintlock Pistol, 1715-1840, by Norman Dixon, Geo. Shumway, York, PA, 1971. 184 pp., illus. $14.00.
The art of the Georgian gunmaker, describing the evolution of the holster pistol and the duelling pistol, with the parallel changes in style of the turn-off pistol.
German Pistols and Revolvers 1871-1945, by Ian V. Hogg, Stackpole Books, Harrisburg, PA, 1971. 160 pp. $12.95.
Over 160 photos and drawings showing each weapon, plus exploded views of parts, including markings, firms, patents, mfg. codes, etc.
The Handbook of Handgunning, by Paul B. Weston. Crown Publ., NYC, 1968. 138 pp., illus. with photos. $4.95.
FFNew concepts in pistol and revolver shooting," by a noted firearms instructor and writer.
Handbuch der Faustfeuerwaffen, by Gerhard Bock and W. Weigel. J. Neumann-Neudamm, Melsungen, Germany, 1968. 4th and latest ed., 724 pp., including index. Profusely illus. $21.00.
A truly encyclopedic work in German text on every aspect of handguns. Highly recommended for those who read German.

The Handgun, by Geoffrey Boothroyd. Crown Publishers, Inc., New York, NY, 1970. 564 pp., profusely illus., plus copious index. $19.95.

A massive and impressive work, excellently covering the subject from matchlocks to present-day automatics. Many anecdotes, much comment and pertinent data, including ammunition, etc.

Handguns Americana, by De Witt Sell. Borden Publ. Co., Alhambra, CA, 1972. 160 pp., illus. $8.50.

The pageantry of American enterprise in providing handguns suitable for both civilian needs and military purposes.

Home Gunsmithing the Colt Single Action Revolvers, by Loren W. Smith, Ray Riling Arms Books Co., Phila., PA, 1971. 119 pp., illus. $7.95.

Detailed, information on the operation and servicing of this famous and historic handgun.

Japanese Hand Guns, by F. E. Leithe, Borden Publ. Co., Alhambra, CA, 1968. Unpaginated, well illus. $8.50.

Identification guide, covering models produced since the late 19th century. Brief text material gives history, descriptions, and markings.

Law Enforcement Handgun Digest, by Dean Grennell and Mason Williams. Digest Books, Inc., Northfield, IL, 1972. 320 pp., illus. Paper covers. $5.95.

Written especially for law enforcement officers and handgun-enthusiasts. From selection of weapon to grips, ammo, training, etc.

The Luger Pistol (Pistole Parabellum), by F. A. Datig. Borden Publ. Co., Alhambra, CA, 1962. 328 pp., well illus. $8.50.

An enlarged, rev. ed. of an important reference on the arm, its history and development from 1893 to 1945.

Lugers at Random, by Charles Kenyon, Jr. Handgun Press, Chicago, IL. 1st ed., 1970. 416 pp., profusely illus. $15.00.

An impressive large side-opening book carrying throughout alternate facing-pages of descriptive text and clear photographs. A new boon to the Luger collector and/or shooter.

Lugers Unlimited, by F. G. Tilton, World-Wide Gun Reports, Inc., Aledo, IL, 1965. 49 pp., illus. Paper covers $2.00.

An excellent monograph about one of the most controversial pistols since the invention of hand firearms.

Mauser Pocket Pistols 1910-1946, by Roy G. Pender, Collectors Press, Houston, TX, 1971. 307 pp., $14.50.

Comprehensive work covering over 100 variations, including factory boxes and manuals. Over 300 photos. Limited, numbered ed.

The Mauser Self-Loading Pistol, by Belford & Dunlap. Borden Publ. Co., Alhambra, CA. Over 200 pp., 300 illus., large format. $12.50.

The long-awaited book on the "Broom Handles," covering their inception in 1894 to the end of production. Complete and in detail: pocket pistols, Chinese and Spanish copies, etc.

Mauser, Walther & Mannlicher Firearms, by W.H.B. Smith, with a intro. by John T. Amber. Stackpole Books, Harrisburg, PA, 1971. 673 pp., illus. $14.95.

W.H.B. Smith's three classics, now in one convenient volume.

The Military Four, by Claude V. Holland. C. V. Holland, Bonita Springs, FL, 1972. 64 pp., illus. Paper covers. $2.98.

Technical data, photographs and history of the Luger, Colt, P-38 and Mauser broomhandle pistols.

Military Pistols and Revolvers, by I. V. Hogg. Arco Pub. Co., NY, 1970. 80 pp., illus. $3.50.

The handguns of the two World Wars shown in halftone illus., with brief historical and descriptive text.

The Modern Handgun, by Robert Hertzberg. Arco Publ. Co., New York, NY, 1965. 112 pp., well illus. $3.50.

Pistols and revolvers of all types are traced from their beginnings. Data on modern marksmanship included.

Modern Pistol Shooting, by P. C. Freeman. Faber & Faber, London, England, 1968, 176 pp., illus. $5.00.

How to develop accuracy with the pistol. Fine points in technique are covered, with information on competitive target shooting.

The Official U.S. Army Pistol Marksmanship Guide, first authorized repro. of original U.S. Army work. J&A Publ., NY, 1972. 144 pp., illus. Paper covers. $4.95.

Every detail from sight alignment to International Pistol programs—technical and fundamental for championship shooting in easy-to-read illus. form.

The "Parbellum" Automatic Pistol, the English version of the official DWM handbook on Luger pistols. Normount Armament Co., Forest Grove, OR, 1968. 42 pp., illus. Paper wrappers. $1.25.

A user's handbook, a reference work for collectors. A reprint of the original detailed instructions on use, disassembly and maintenance. Includes three folding plates.

Pistol and Revolver Guide, by George Nonte. Stoeger Arms Corp., So. Hackensack, NJ, 1967. 192 pp., well illus. Paper wrappers. $3.95.

A history of the handgun, its selection, use and care, with a glossary and trade directory.

The Pistol Shooter's Treasury, by Gil Hebard; et al. Gil Hebard Guns, Knoxville, IL, 1972. 128 pp., illus. Paper covers. $2.95.

Articles by noted handgun experts on all phases of selecting and shooting handguns.

Pistolen Atlas, by Karl R. Pawlas, Nuremberg, Germany, 1970. Arranged alphabetically by maker and model in loose-leaf binding. Each vol. $10.00.

Carefully planned and researched for the "automatic arms buff," shooter and collector, depicts hundreds of auto. pistols of all nations and of all calibers with excellent illus. and descriptive text in English, French, German and Spanish. 13 volumes projected, of which vols. 1, 2, 3, 5, 6, 7 and 8 are now ready.

Pistols, A Modern Encyclopedia, by Stebbins, Shay & Hammond. Stackpole Co., Harrisburg, PA, 1961. 380 pp., illus. $4.98.

Comprehensive coverage of handguns for every purpose, with material on selection, ammunition, and marksmanship.

Pistols of the World, by Claude Blair, Viking Press, NYC, 1968. 206 pp., plus plates, $9.98.

Authoritative review of handguns since the 16th century, with chapters on major types, manufacture, and decoration. Fine photographic illustrations.

Pistols, Revolvers, and Ammunition, by M. H. Josserand and J. Stevenson, Crown Publ. Co., NY, 1972. 341 pp., illus. $7.50.

Basic information classifying the pistol, revolver, ammunition, ballistics and rules of safety.

Report of Board on Tests of Revolvers and Automatic Pistols. From The *Annual Report* of the Chief of Ordnance, 1907. Reprinted by J. C. Tillinghast, Marlow, NH, 1969. 34 pp., 7 plates, paper covers. $3.00.

A comparison of handguns, including Luger, Savage, Colt, Webley-Fosbery and other makes.

The Revolver, 1818-1865, by Taylerson, Andrews, & Frith. Crown Publ. NYC, 1968. 360 pp., illus. $7.50.

Noted British work on early revolving arms and the principal makers, giving production data and serial numbers on many models.

The Revolver, 1865-1888, by A. W. F. Taylerson. Crown Publ., NYC, 1966. 292 pp., illus. $3.49.

Detailed study of 19th-century British and U.S. revolvers, by types and makers, based on study of patent records.

The Revolver 1889-1914, by A. W. F. Taylerson. Crown Pub. NY, 1971. 324 pp., illus. $7.50.

The concluding volume of this definitive work deals with Continental arms, American rimfire and centerfire, British centerfire, and obsolescent arms in use.

Saga of the Colt Six-Shooter, and the famous men who used it, by G. E. Virgines. Frederick Fell Co., New York, NY, 1969. 220 pp., well illus. $7.95.

History of the Colt Single action army revolver since 1873, with much information of interest to collectors and shooters.

Sixguns by Keith, by Elmer Keith. Stackpole Co., Harrisburg, PA, 1968 (reprint of 1961 edition). 335 pp., illus. $4.95.

Long a popular reference on handguns, this work covers all aspects, whether for the shooter, collector or other enthusiasts.

Smith and Wesson Catalog of 1901, a reprint facsimile by The Wyoming Armory, Inc., Cheyenne, WY, 1969. 72 pp., well illus., paper covers. $2.25.

All models, engraving, parts and break-down lists, etc.

The Story of Colt's Revolver, by Wm. B. Edwards, Castle Books, NY, 1971. 470 pp. $9.98.

Biography of Samuel Colt and his invention. Hundreds of photos, diagrams, patents and appendix of original advertisements.

System Mauser, a Pictorial History of the Model 1896 Self-Loading Pistol, by J. W. Breathed, Jr., and J. J. Schroeder, Jr. Handgun Press, Chicago, IL, 1967. 273 pp., well illus. 1st limited ed. hardbound. $12.50.

10 Shots Quick, by Daniel K. Stern. Globe Printing Co., San Jose, CA, 1967. 153 pp., photos. $8.50.

History of Savage-made automatic pistols, models of 1903-1917, with descriptive data for shooters and collectors.

U.S. Pistols and Revolvers Vol. 1, D. B. McLean, compiler. Normount Armament Co., Forest Grove, OR, 1968. 2nd printing, 198 pp., well illus., paper covers. $3.50.

A useful and reliable work from authoritative sources on M1911/M1911A1 Colt Pistols; M1917 S & W revolvers; M1917 and Detective Special Colt revolvers. Excellent for their use, maintenance and repair.

United States Single Shot Martial Pistols, by C. W. Sawyer, WE, Inc., Old Greenwich, CT, 1971. 101 pp., illus. $5.00.

History of pistols used by the U.S. Armed Services 1776-1871.

U.S. Test Trials 1900 Luger, by Michael Reese II. Coventry Publ. Co., Gretna, LA, 1970. illus. $7.00.

For the Luger Pistol collector.

The Webley-Fosbery Automatic Revolver. A reprint of the original undated booklet pupl. by the British makers. Deep River Armory, Houston, TX, 1968. 16 pp., illus., paper. $3.00.

An instruction manual, parts list and sales brochure on this scarce military handgun.

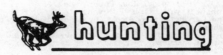

hunting

African Hunting, by Wm. C. Baldwin. Abercrombie & Fitch Library, NY, 1967. 451 pp., illus. $12.95.

Limited printing of a much-desired book giving vivid accounts of big game hunting exploits in Africa. First publ. in 1863.

After Wild Sheep in the Altai and Mongolia, by Prince Demidoff. Abercrombie & Fitch Library, NY, 1966. 324 pp., with photographs and drawings. $10.00.

Limited printing of a famous British work of 1900, on hunting big game in Asia. Long out-of-print.

American Partridge & Pheasant Shooting, by Frank Schley. Abercrombie & Fitch Library, NYC, 1968. 238 pp., illus. $7.95.

Facsimile of an American sporting classic work, including detailed engravings of game birds.

The American Sportsman, by Elisha J. Lewis. Abercrombie & Fitch Library, NY, 1967, 510 pp., illus. $10.95.

Limited issue of a scarce classic American work on the hunting field, first publ. in 1851.

Art of Small Game Hunting, by Francis Sell. Stackpole Books, Harrisburg, PA, 1973. 192 pp., illus. $2.95.

An invaluable primer and skill sharpener for any hunter.

Art of Successful Deer Hunting, by F. E. Sell, Stackpole Books, Harrisburg, PA, 1971. 192 pp., paper, $2.95.

Illus. re-issue of "The Deer Hunter's Guide." Western hunting lore for rifle and bow-hunter.

The Art of Wing Shooting, by W. B. Leffingwell. Abercromble & Fitch Library, NYC, 1968. 190 pp., illus. $7.95.

An outstanding treatise on shotgun marksmanship, first publ. 1894, with explicit drawings on techniques of leading the target.

Asian Jungle, African Bush, by Charles Askins. Stackpole Books, Harrisburg, PA, 1959. 258 pp., illus. $5.95.

A where-to-go and how-to-do guide for game-rich Indo-China. The African section deals with game, the use of various arms and ammo on specific species.

The Australian Hunter, by Col. Allison with Ian Coombes. Cassell Australia Ltd., No. Melbourne, Australia, 1970. 212 pp., 58 photos, and 60 distribution maps and drawings. $11.50.

A comprehensive guide to game, equipment, hunting and photography.

Bell of Africa, by W. D. M. Bell, with foreword and introduction by Wally Taber and Col. T. Whelen. N. Spearman and Holland Press, London, 1960. 236 pp., illus. $5.75.

On elephants and the hunter extracted from Bell's own papers, it includes an appendix on rifles and rifle shooting.

The Best of Nash Buckingham, by Nash Buckingham, selected, edited and annotated by George Bird Evans. Winchester Press, NY, 1973. 320 pp. $10.

Thirty pieces that represent the very cream of Nash's output on his whole range of outdoor interests—upland shooting, duck hunting, even fishing.

Big Game Hunting in the West, by Mike Cramond. Mitchell Press, Vancouver, B.C., Can., 1965. 164 pp., illus. $5.95.

Accounts of hunting many species of big game and predators are given plus a section on rifles, equipment, and useful tips for the field.

Big Game Hunting Around the World, by B. Klineburger and V. Hurst, Exposition Press, NY, 1969. 376 pp., illus. $15.00.

From hunting tigers in India to polar bears in the Arctic.

Big Game Hunting in New Zealand, by Gary Joll. Whitcombe & Tombs, Christchurch, NZ, 1971. 214 pp., illus. $6.50.
An experienced hunter's advice on various species of New Zealand game, guns, equipment, and other aspects of hunting.
Big Game Shooting in Africa, ed. by Major H. C. Maydon. Seeley, Service & Co., London, n.d., 445 pp. illus. $8.50.
Vol. 14 of the Lonsdale Library, with chapters by various British writers on African big game and on hunting in various sections of Africa.
Bird Hunting Know-How, by D. M. Duffey. Van Nostrand, Princeton, NJ, 1968. 192 pp., illus. $5.95.
Game-getting techniques and sound advice on all aspects of upland bird hunting, plus data on guns and loads.
The Bobwhite Quail, its Life and Management, by Walter Rosene. Rutgers University Press, New Brunswick, NJ. 1st ed., 1969. 418 pp., photographs, maps and color plates. $20.00.
An exhaustive study of an important species which has diminished under the impact of changing agricultural and forestry practices.
The Book of Saint Albans, by Dame Juliana Berners, Abercrombie & Fitch, NY, 1966. Illus. $18.00.
Reprint of the rare 1810 Haselwood ed. on hawking, hunting, fishing etc. The first English sporting book.
Bow & Arrow Archer's Digest, by J. Lewis, Digest Books, Northfield, IL, 1971. 320 pp., illus. Paper, $5.95.
The encyclopedia for all archers, from picking a bow to varmint calling.
Bowhunting for Deer, by H. R. Wambold. Stackpole Books, Harrisburg, PA, 1964. 160 pp., illus. $5.95.
Useful tips on deer, their habits, anatomy, and how-when-where of hunting, plus selection and use of tackle.
A Boy and His Gun, by Edward C. Janes. A. S. Barnes & Co., New York, NY. 207 pp., illus., $5.00.
Introduction to rifles, shooting and hunting techniques for young shooters with practical hints on game shooting with rifle or shotgun.
Buckshot and Hounds, by C. J. Milling. A. S. Barnes, NY, 1967. 132 pp., illus. $4.95.
Deer-driving methods and traditions of the South and West, with present-day adaptations described.
Calling All Game, by Bert Popowski. Stackpole Books, Harrisburg, PA, 1952, 306 pp. Illus. $7.50.
Practical methods of attracting game, from quail to moose, using artificial decoys and calls.
Charles Morgan on Retrievers, ed. by Ann Fowler and D. L. Walters. Abercrombie & Fitch, NYC, 1968, 168 pp., illus. $12.50.
Based on years of success in schooling hunting dogs, this work gives full details of an expert's proven methods to guide experienced trainers.
Complete Book of Bow and Arrow, by G. H. Gillelan, Stackpole Books, Harrisburg, PA, 1971. 320 pp., illus. $9.95.
Encyclopedic reference on archery, gear, rules, skill, etc.
Complete Book of Hunting, by Clyde Ormond. Harper & Bros., NYC, 1962. 467 pp., well-illus. $6.95.
Part I is on game animals, Part II is on birds. Guns and ammunition, game, habitats, clothing, equipment, etc. hunters' tips are discussed.
The Complete Deer Hunt, by Joe DeFalco. Madison Publ. Co., New York, NY, 1970. 133 pp., well illus., in line and halftone. Stiff paper covers. $3.95.
A concise work covering field dressing, skinning, equipment and arms, methods of hunting, etc.
Complete Guide to Hunting Across North America, by Byron Dalrymple. Outdoor Life, Harper & Row, NY, 1970. 848 pp., illus. with photos and 50 maps. $10.00.
A large reference work on hunting conditions, locating game, clothing, techniques, transportation, equipment for every region, etc.
Crow Shooting, by Bert Popowski. A. S. Barnes and Co., NYC, 1946. (4th printing 1957). 216 pp., illus. $5.00.
Practical and entertaining, telling how to locate roosts, build blinds and employ cover; the use of various decoys for shooting with rifle or shotgun.
Crow Shooting Secrets, by Dick Mermon. Winchester Press, New York, 1970. 149 pp., illus. $5.95.
An expert shares his secrets and touches all the bases.
Danger, by B. East, E. P. Dutton, NY, 1970. 323 pp., illus. $5.95.
The dangers in hunting and the weird things that can happen.
Decoying Waterfowl, by A. C. Becker Jr. A. S. Barnes and Co., NY, 1973. 256 pp., illus. $12.
An in-depth study of decoy shape, paint finishes, and formations on the water, etc. Over 100 photos and drawings.
The Deer Hunter's Bible, by Geo. Laycock. Doubleday, Garden City, NY, 1963. 154 pp., illus. paperbound. $1.95.
Handy summary of deer hunting lore, by an expert. Guns, loads, bowhunting, care of vension, field techniques are covered.
The Deer of North America, edit. by W. P. Taylor. Stackpole Books. Harrisburg, PA, 1956. 668 pp., illus. incl. full-color plates. $12.50.
Leading authorities in all parts of the deer range have contributed their intimate studies of the animal.
Ducks of the Mississippi Flyway, ed. by John McKane. North Star Press, St. Cloud, MN, 1969. 54 pp., illus. $4.95.
A duck hunter's reference. Full color paintings of some 30 species, plus descriptive text.
Elephant, by D. E. Blunt, Neville Spearman, London, 1971. 260 pp., illus. $10.00.
Reprint of a rare book, a hunter's account of the ways of an elephant.
The End of the Game, by P. H. Beard. Viking Press, NYC, 1965. 256 pp., fine illus. $12.95.
Account of recent changes in African game country and decline of the game population.
Game Animals in New Zealand, by Gordon Roberts. A. H. & A. W. Reed, Sydney, Australia, 1968. 112 pp., illus. $6.25.
Pictures of wild, live animals in their natural and often remote habitats.
Game Bird Hunting in the West, by Mike Cramond. Mitchell Press, Vancouver, B.C., Can., 1967. 246 pp., illus. $5.95.
Identification and hunting methods for each species of waterfowl and upland game birds, plus a section on shotgun types, equipment, and related subjects for the hunter.
Good Hunting, by Jas L. Clark, Univ. of Oklahoma Press, Norman, Okla., 1966. 242 pp., illus. $7.95.
Fifty years of collecting and preparing habitat groups for the American Museum.
A Good Keen Man, by Barry Crump. A. H. & A. W. Reed, Sydney, Australia, 1969. 192 pp., illus. $4.50.
A popular tale of deer hunting in the New Zealand back-country.
The Great Arc of the Wild Sheep, by J. L. Clark, Univ. of Oklahoma Press, Norman, Okla., 1964. 247 pp., illus. $8.95.
Every classified variety of wild sheep is discussed, as found in North America, Asia & Europe. Numerous hunting stories by experts are included.
Great Game Animals of the World, by Russell B. Aitken. Winchester Press, NY, 1969. 192 pp. profusely ills. in monochrome and color. $22.50.
Accounts of man's pursuit of big game in all parts of the world, told in many fine pictures.
Green Hills of Africa, by Ernest Hemingway. Charles Scribner's Sons, NY, 1963. 285 pp., illus. $6.95.
A famous narrative of African big-game hunting, first published in 1935.
The Grizzly Bear, edited by B. D. and E. Haynes, Univ. of Oklahoma Press, Norman, Okla., 1966. 386 pp., illus. $7.95.
Collected stories about various encounters with the grizzly by mountain men, settlers, naturalists, scouts and others.
Grizzly Country, by Andy Russell. A. A. Knopf, NYC, 1968, 302 pp., illus. $7.95.
Many-sided view of the grizzly bear and his world, by a noted guide, hunter and naturalist.
Grouse Feathers, by Burton L. Spiller. Crown Publ., NY, 1972. 207 pp., illus. $7.50.
Facsimile of the original Derrydale Press issue of 1935. How to hunt the ruffed grouse, with stories of the author's experiences with dogs and guns from boyhood. Illus. by Lynn Bogue Hunt.
Grouse and Grouse Hunting, by Frank Woolner. Crown Pub., Co., NY, 1970. 192 pp., illus. $7.50.
The history, habits, habitat and methods of hunting one of America's great game birds.
Guide to Safaris, by Burk H. Steizner. Charles Scribner's Sons, New York, NY, 1970. 178 pp., illus. $6.95.
Discussions of the different African regions, types of safari, minimal costs, etc. Highly informative for the would-be safari-goers seeking basic information.
Gun Dog, by Richard A. Wolters, E. P. Dutton, New York, NY, 1969. 1st ed., 11th Printing. 150 pp., well illus. $5.95.
A popular manual for upland bird shooters who want to train their dogs to perfection in minimum time.
Highland Stage of Otago, by D. Bruce Banwell. A. H. & A. W. Reed, Sydney, Australia, 1968. 169 pp., illus. $7.75.
The romantic history of Otago's red deer. Trophy statistics, fully checked for accuracy, are given. An invaluable reference work.
How to Hunt American Game, by R. B. Vale. Stackpole Books, Harrisburg, PA. 5th printing, 1954. 199 pp., illus. $4.00.
Wildlife habits, conservation and the encouragement of hunting. Including the author's experiences in hunting game throughout America.
How to Hunt Small American Game, by L. A. Anderson. Funk and Wagnalls, New York, NY, 1969. 167 pp., well illus. $5.95.
A new basic guide for the small game hunter, similar to the author's 1959 *How to Hunt Deer and Small Game.* Written for beginner and expert, covers game, guns, equipment and game habits.
How to Hunt Whitetail Deer, L. A. Anderson. Funk & Wagnalls, NYC, 1968. 116 pp., illus. $5.95.
Useful reference for deer hunters, both novice and experienced, giving basic information and valuable pointers.
Hunt the Far Mountain, by Keith Severinsen. A. H. & A. W. Reed, Wellington, N.Z., 1970. 182 pp., illus. $7.
An introduction to every hunting trophy New Zealand offers.
Hunter's Digest, edited by Erwin A. Bauer. Digest Books, Inc., Northfield, IL, 1973. 320 pp., illus. Paper covers. $6.95.
The best ways, times and places to hunt the most popular species of large and small game animals in North America.
A Hunter's Fireside Book, by Gene Hill Winchester Press, NY, 1972. 192 pp., illus. $7.95
An outdoor book that will appeal to every person who spends time in the field—or who wishes he could.
The Hunter's World, by C. F. Waterman. Random House, NY, 1970. 250 pp., illus. $15.00.
A book for those who welcome an expert's guidance, one who understands the terrain, feed, cover, etc., of the game they hunt. Profusely illus. in color.
Hunting Dog Know-How, by D. M. Duffey, Van Nostrand, Princeton, NJ, 1965. 177 pp., illus. $5.95.
Covers selection, breeds, and training of hunting dogs, problems in hunting and field trials.
Hunting Hounds: How to Choose, Train and Handle America's Trail and Tree Hounds, by David Michael Duffey. Winchester Press, NY, 1972. 192 pp., illus. $5.95.
Origin, development, selection, care and usage of every breed and strain, with entertaining anecdotes and practical training tips.
Hunting Our Biggest Game, by Clyde Ormond. Stackpole Books, Harrisburg, PA, 1956. 197 pp., illus. $8.95.
Practical advice for hunters on moose, elk, bear, wild sheep, trophy data, field methods, etc.
Hunting Our Medium Size Game, by Clyde Ormond. Stackpole Books, Harrisburg, PA, 1958. 219 pp., illus. $5.00.
Covers deer, whitetails and mules; black bear; antelope; coyotes; bobcats and cougar. Included are sections on equipment, use of rifles, and care of venison.
Hunting Pronghorn Antelope, by Bert Popowski. Stackpole Books, Harrisburg, PA, 1959. 227 pp., illus. $6.50.
Hunting the Ruffed Grouse, by Nick Sisley. Copyright, Nick Sisley, 1970. 136 pp., illus. $3.50.
A must for hunting this great game bird. The author, a grouse expert, is vice president of the Ruffed Grouse Society of America.
Hunting with Bow and Arrow, by George Laycock and Erwin Bauer. Arco Publ. Co., Inc., NYC, 1966. $3.50.
A practical guide to archery as a present-day sport. Mentions equipment needed and how to select it. Illus. instructions on how to shoot with ease and accuracy.
Hunting Upland Birds, by Chas. F. Waterman. Winchester Press, NY, 1972. 320 pp., illus. $8.95.
Excellent treatment of game habits and habitat, hunting methods, and management techniques for each of the 18 major North American gamebird species.
Hunting Weapons, by Howard L. Blackmore. Walker & Co., NY, 1971. 401 pp., illus. $17.50.
Covers sporting arms from the Middle Ages to the present, by a prominent British expert on historical weapons.
Hunting in Westland, by Lew Sutherland. A. H. & A. W. Reed, Sydney, Australia, 1970. 95 pp., illus. Paper covers. $3.75.
Intended to assist parties of experienced hunters in planning an expedition.
The Imperial Collection of Audubon Animals, original text by John James Audubon and Rev. John Bachman, illus. by John James and John Woodhouse Audubon. A magnificent quarto reproduction of the rare original by Hammond, Inc., Maplewood, NJ, 1967. 307 pp., 150 animals pictured in full color. $6.95.
Each illus. accompanied by engaging text, as in the 1st ed. of 1848, including accounts of Audubon's exploring trips. A most useful work for hunters who want to know their game.
Inside Safari Hunting, by D. Holman. G. P. Putnam's Sons, NY, 1970. 296 pp., illus. $6.95.
The work of the white hunter in Africa, based on the experiences of a second-generation professional.

Key to North American Waterfowl, by S. R. Wylie and S. S. Furlong. Livingston Publ. Co., Wynwood, PA, 1972. 32 pp., color illus. Plastic covers. $3.95.

Designed to help the hunter identify all species of ducks, geese and swans in winter plumage. Illustrated with color plates. Printed on waterproof, greaseproof, washable plastic.

Krider's Sporting Anecdotes, edited by Milnor H. Klapp. Abercrombie & Fitch Library, NY, 1966. 292 pp., illus. $8.00.

Limited issue of the much-wanted work on Philadelphia's renowned gunsmith, John Krider, publ. first in 1853. A rich fund of knowledge on upland shooting, dogs and match shooting, etc.

Living Off the Country, by B. Angier. Stackpole Books, Harrisburg, PA, 1959. 241 pp., illus. $5.00.

In a simple and entertaining manner the author explains how to live off nature when emergency arises and how to stay alive in the woods.

Meditations on Hunting, by Jose Ortega y Gasset. Chas. Scribner's Sons, NY, 1972. 152 pp., illus. $9.95.

First publ. in Lisbon 1942. Translated by Howard B. Wescott. Provocative insights into anthropology and ecology by the great Spanish thinker.

Modern ABC's of Bird Hunting, by Dave Harbour, Stackpole Books, Harrisburg, PA, 1966. 192 pp., illus. $4.95.

From city's edge to wilderness this gives the occasional hunter the quickest way on how to increase his bag. Covers all game birds of the U.S. and Canada.

Modern Hunting with Indian Secrets, by Allan A. Macfarlan. Stackpole Books, Harrisburg, PA, 1971. 222 pp., $6.50.

How to acquire the new-old skills of the Redman, how to apply them to modern hunting.

More Grouse Feathers, by Burton L. Spiller. Crown Publ., NY, 1972. 238 pp., illus. $7.50.

Facsimile of the original Derrydale Press issue of 1938. Guns and dogs, the habits and shooting of grouse, woodcook, ducks, etc. Illus. by Lynn Bogue Hunt.

NRA Hunting Annual, 1973. National Rifle Assn., Washington, D.C., 1973. 160 pp., illus. Paper covers. $1.75.

A directory of North American hunting, with features on guides, knives, calls and calling.

The New Hunter's Encyclopedia, edited by Leonard Miracle and James B. Trefethen, plus specialized articles by over 60 outstanding contributors. Stackpole Books, Harrisburg, PA, 1972. 1054 pp., with 2047 photos, diagrams, drawings and full-color plates. $24.95.

A massive work covering every detail of every sort of hunting in the U.S., Canada and Mexico.

Nine Centuries of Hunting Weapons, by L. G. Boccia, Editrice Edam, Firenze, Italy, 1967. 181 pp., illus. with many fine photos of superb museum quality in full color. $15.00.

In Italian text, a historical survey of hunting weapons of Italian origin and their makers.

North American Big Game 1971 Edition, ed. by Robt. C. Alberts, Boone and Crockett Club, Pittsburgh, PA, 1971. 403 pp., illus. $15.00.

Tabulations of outstanding trophies compiled by the B & C Club.

The North American Waterfowler, by Paul S. Bernsen. Superior Publ. Co., Seattle, WA, 1972. 206 pp. $14.95.

The complete inside and outside story of duck and goose shooting. Big and colorful, illus. by Les Kouba. Contains an 8-minute 45 RPM duck calling record in back.

On Your Own in the Wilderness, by Col. T. Whelen and B. Angier. Stackpole Books, Harrisburg, PA, 1958. 324 pp., illus. $5.00.

Two eminent authorities give complete, accurate, and useful data on all phases of camping and travel in primitive areas.

Pack and Rifle, by Philip Holden. A. H. & A. W. Reed, Sydney, Australia, 1971. 194 pp., illus. $7.75.

The hunting days of a New Zealand Forest Service professional shooter. Hunts after red deer, sika, rusa, and sambar.

Paw Prints; How to Identify Rare and Common Mammals by Their Tracks. O. C. Lempfert, NY, 1972. 71 pp., illus. with actual size prints. $7.50.

An authoritive manual for hunters and outdoorsmen.

Pocket Guide to Animal Tracks, by L. M. Henderson, Stackpole Books, Harrisburg, PA, 1968. 57 pp., profusely illus., and bound in paper boards. $2.95.

Delightful text plus Henderson's most accurate line drawings show many signatures—paw and hoof prints, habits and characteristics, of 44 North American small and big game.

The Practical Hunter's Dog Book, by John R. Falk, Winchester Press, NY, 1971. 314 pp., illus. $8.95.

Helps to choose, train and enjoy your gun dog.

Prehistoric Animals and Their Hunters, by I. W. Cornwall. F. A. Praeger, NY, 1968. 214 pp., illus. $7.50.

Describes animal species and hunting methods used in this period, plus uses made of the kills.

The Puma, Mysterious American Cat, by S. P. Young and E. A. Goldman, Dover Publ., NY, 1964, 358 pp., illus. Paper covers $3.00.

A two-part work: the first on the history, economic status and control: the second on classifications of the races of the puma.

Ranch Life and the Hunting Trail, by Theodore Roosevelt, 1894. A fine reprint by the Winchester Press, New York, NY, 1969, with introduction by Kermit Roosevelt. 168 pp., and includes the Frederic Remington illustrations from the original and those added from the 1908 edition. $6.98.

The far west of the 1880's of hunting and bags, of men and manners.

The Red Stags of the Rakaia, by D. Bruce Banwell. A. H. & A. W. Reed, Sydney, Australia, 1972. 165 pp., illus. $7.75.

An invaluable standard reference, and a lively, readable saga of a herd whose trophies have become world-famous.

The Rifle and Hound in Ceylon, by Samuel White Baker. Abercrombie & Fitch Library, NY, 1967. 422 pp., well illus. $12.95.

Limited printing of a classic description of elephant-hunting, deer-coursing and elk-hunting in the East. First published in the 1850s.

Rowland Ward's Records of Big Game, 14th ed., comp. by G. A. Best, Rowland Ward Pub., Ltd., 1971. 438 pp., illus. $45.00.

New edition of the authoritive record of big game kills in Africa, by species.

Safari, by Elmer Keith. Safari Publ., La Jolla, CA, 1968. 166 pp., illus. $7.95.

Guide to big game hunting in Africa, with anecdote and expert advice on hunting many species of game. Information on guns, ammunition, equipment, and planning the safari is included. Fine photographs.

Safari by Jet, through Africa and Asia, by Sister Maria del Rey, Charles Scribner's Sons, New York, NY, 1962. 308 pp., profusely illus., with photos, and line. $5.95.

Off-beat reading about an African-Asian grand tour, with tales of the land and the people of Tanganyika, Ceylon, the Philippines, Hong Kong, Taiwan, et al.

Selected American Game Birds, by David Hagerbaumer and Sam Lehman, The Caxton Printers, Ltd., Caldwell, ID, 1972. The entire text of this book is executed in decorated calligraphy. $30.00.

Twenty-six of David Hagerbaumer's exquisite original watercolors, representing 29 bird species. A must for every book collector and art lover.

The Sharp Shooter, by Matt & Bruce Grant. A. H. & A. W. Reed, Sydney, Australia, 1972. 270 pp., illus. $8.50.

How to get the best out of rifles and ammunition. Covers hunting rifles, sights, stalking, ballistics, etc.

Shooting, A Complete Guide for Beginners, by John Marchington. Faber & Faber, London, Eng., 1972. 158 pp., illus. $9.75.

Guide to all aspects of shooting in the British manner, for all types of game.

Shooting for the Skipper, by Jack McNair. A. H. & A. W. Reed, Sydney, Australia, 1971. 153 pp., illus. $8. Memories of a veteran New Zealand deer hunter.

Shooting Pictures, by A. B. Frost, with 24 pp. of text by Chas. D. Lanier. Winchester Press, NY, 1972. 12 color plates. Enclosed in a board portfolio. Ed. limited to 750 numbered copies. $50.

Frost's twelve superb 12″ by 16″ pictures have often been called the finest sporting prints published in the U.S. A facsimile of the 1895-6 edition printed on fine paper with superb color fidelity.

Shots at Mule Deer, by Rollo S. Robinson. Winchester Press, NY, 1972. 256 pp., illus. $8.95.

Describes the mule deer itself, its life cycle and its ways. There is a complete run-down of all appropriate deer rifles and cartridges, plus advice on their selection and proper field use.

Shots at Whitetails, by Larry Koller. A. A. Knopf, NY, 1970. 359 pp., illus. $7.95.

A new reprint, with all information on guns, loads, scopes, etc., brought up to date.

Small Game Hunting, by Clyde Ormond. Outdoor Life Books, NY, 1969. 126 pp., illus. $4.50.

Field-tested advice for increasing your take of chucks, squirrels, rabbits, crows, hawks, etc. Good information on guns, loads, field tips, etc.

A Sporting Chance . . . , by D. P. Mannix. E. P. Dutton & Co., NY, 1967. 248 pp., illus. with 50 photos. $1.98.

Unusual methods of hunting the exotic species from hounds to falcons. Inspiring reading for those desiring to get away from the commonplace.

Sporting Guns, by Richard Akehurst. G. P. Putnam's Sons, NYC, 1968. 120 pp., illus. $5.95.

History of shooting and of the guns and rifles developed to meet the hunter's needs, with anecdotes of the hunting field.

The Sportsman's Companion, by Lee Wulff. Harper & Row, N.Y.C., 1968. 413 pp., illus. $11.95.

Compendium of writings by various experts on hunting and fishing for American game. A useful reference for the outdoorsman.

Sportman's Guide to Game Animals, by Leonard Lee Rue III. Harper & Row [Outdoor Life Books], New York, NY, 1st ed., 2nd printing, 1969. 635 pp., illus. with photographs and maps. $6.50.

Exhaustive and capable coverage of the behavior and habits of all North American game animals.

Squirrels and Squirrel Hunting, by Bob Gooch. Tidewater Publ., Cambridge, MD, 1973. 148 pp., illus. $6.

A complete book for the squirrel hunter, beginner or old hand. Details methods of hunting, squirrel habitat, management, proper clothing, care of the kill, cleaning and cooking.

The Standard Book of Hunting and Shooting, R. B. Stringfellow, ed. 1st ed., in 1950 by the Greystone Press, New York, NY, 564 pp., very well illus. $10.00.

An excellent anthology on hunting in America, giving meaningful information on all major species and on all types of guns, sights, ammunition, etc. An abridgement of the larger *Hunters Encyclopedia.*

Three Years' Hunting & Trapping America and the Great Northwest, by J. Turner-Turner Abercrombie & Fitch Library, N.Y.C., 1967. 182 pp., illus. $10.95.

Reprint of an 1888 account of a determined quest for valuable furs in one of the world's least hospitable regions.

Topflight; A Speed Index to Waterfowl, by J. A. Ruthven & Wm. Zimmerman, Moebius Prtg. Co., Milwaukee, WI, 1968. 112 pp. $5.95.

Rapid reference for specie identification. Marginal color band of book directs reader to proper section. 263 full color illustrations of body and feather configurations.

Tracks of an Intruder, by Gordon Young. Winchester Press, NY, 1970. 191 pp., illus. $5.95.

Fascinating, first hand account of how an American naturalist gained recognition as a master hunter from the Montagnard Lahu tribesmen of Southeast Asia.

Travel & Adventure in Southeast Africa, by F. C. Selous. A & F Press, N.Y.C., 1967. 522 pp., illus. $11.95.

New edition of a famous African hunting book, first published in 1893.

A Treasury of African Hunting, ed. by Peter Barrett. Winchester Press, NY, 1970. 251 pp., illus. $6.95.

Outstanding accounts by noted writers and experts on African hunting, covering big game and small in many sections of the continent.

The Treasury of Hunting, by Larry Koller, Odyssey Press, N.Y.C., 1965. 251 pp., illus. $7.95.

Concise accounts of all types of hunting in the U.S. Excellent illustrations, many color photographs taken in various hunting fields.

Trophy Hunter in Asia, by E. T. Gates, Winchester Press, NY, 1971. 272 pp., illus. $12.50.

Hunting the rarest of game animals.

The Truth About Hunting in Today's Africa and how to go on a safari for $690.00, by G. L. Herter, Herter's, Inc., Waseca, Minn., 1970. 314 pp., well illus. $3.95.

Tells how to arrange safari costs, plus new data on weights, rifles and bullets derived from actual field tests.

Two Dogs and a Rifle, by Ken Cuthbertson. A. H. & A. W. Reed, Sydney, Australia, 1968. 180 pp., illus. $7.75.

Forty years' accumulation of knowledge on the habits of wild pigs, and on the dogs and rifles with which to hunt them.

The Unnatural Enemy, by Vance Bourjaily. The Dial Press, 1963. 182 pp., illus. $2.49.

Beautifully written episodes of bird-hunting.

The Upland Game Hunter's Bible, by Dan Holland. Doubleday, N.Y.C., 1961. 192 pp., illus. paper covers. $1.95.

Hunter's manual on the principal species of American upland game birds and how to hunt them.

The Upland Shooting Life, by George Bird Evans. A. A. Knopf, NY, 1971. 301 pp., illus. $10.

A basic shooting book by a writer-hunter. His experience in the fields, the pines, the birches, the alder swamps and the bushy borders in pursuit of upland game.

The Varmint and Crow Hunter's Bible, by Bert Popowski. Doubleday & Co., N.Y.C., 1962. 185 pp., 150 illus. Paper covers. $1.95.

Hunting and trapping techniques described by a well-known authority. Chapters on woodchucks, crows, foxes, snakes, guns, etc.

Water Dog, by R. A. Wolters, E. P. Dutton & Co., NY, 1964. 179 pp., illus. $5.95.

Rapid training manual for working retrievers.

Waterfowl in the Marshes, by A. C. Becker Jr. A. S. Barnes and Co., New York, NY, 1969. 155 pp., photographs. $7.50.
A highly informative and practical guide to waterfowl hunting in America.
Whitetail, by George Mattis. World Publ. Co., New York, NY, 1969. 273 pp., including index. Illus. $6.95.
Fundamentals and fine points of compelling interest for the deer hunter.
Wild Fowl Decoys, by Joel Barber. Dover Publ., N.Y.C., 1954. 156 pp., 134 illus., paperbound. $4.00.
A fine work on making, painting, care and use of decoys in hunting, recently reprinted. Full data on design and construction.
Wildfowling, by James Andrews, et al. Seeley, Service & Co., London, n.d. 352 pp., illus. $7.50.
Articles by British sportsmen on shooting wildfowl, guns, punting, and conditions in various areas. Vol. 29 of the Lonsdale Library.
Winchester Hunter's Handbook 1972-73, comp. by Dr. Edw. Kozicky, John Madson and David Petzal. Winchester Press, NY, 1972. 191 pp., illus. Paper covers. $1.95.
Articles by America's finest outdoor writers. Full of facts, figures, and practical information.

RIFLES

The Accurate Rifle, by Warren Page. Winchester Press, NY, 1973. 256 pp., illus. $8.95.
A masterly discussion. A must for the competitive shooter hoping to win, and highly useful to the practical hunter.
The Big-Game Rifle, by Jack O'Connor, Alfred A. Knopf, N.Y.C., 1951. 371 pp., plus XI pp. Well illus. $10.00.
Discusses construction, purpose and use for all types of big game as well as ammo., sights, accessories, etc.
Bolt Action Rifles, by Frank de Haas, ed. by John T. Amber, Editor of GCUND DCIGESTD. Digest Books, Inc., Northfield, IL, 1971. 320 pp., illus. Paper, $6.95.
The definitive work, covering every major design since the Mauser of 1871.
The Book of Rifles, by W. H. B. Smith. Stackpole Books, Harrisburg, PA, 1963 (3rd ed.). 656 pp., profusely illus. $6.00.
An encyclopedic reference work on shoulder arms, recently up-dated. Includes rifles of all types, arranged by country of origin.
The Boy's Book of Rifles, by C. E. Chapel. Coward-McCann, N.Y.C., 1948, rev. ed., 1960. 274 pp., illus. $3.95.
For all young men of Boy Scout age at every phase of small-caliber marksmanship and safe gun handling. It tells how to qualify for NRA medals and Scout Merit Badges for Marksmanship.
Boy's Single-Shot Rifles, by Jas. J. Grant, William Morrow & Co., Inc., NY, 1967. 608 pp., illus. $10.00.
A wealth of important new material on an ever-popular subject, authoritatively presented. By the author of *Single Shot Rifles* and *More Single Shot Rifles.*
Browning Automatic Rifles, Normount Armament Co., Forest Grove, OR, 81 pp., illus. Paper, $2.00.
Reprint of Ordnance Manual TM 9-1211, on all types of caliber 30's.
Carbines Cal. .30 M1, M1A1, M2 and M3, by D. B. McLean. Normount Armament Co., Forest Grove, OR, 1964. 221 pp., well illus., paperbound. $3.00.
U.S. field manual reprints on these weapons, edited and reorganized.
Description and Instructions for the Management of the Gallery-Practice Rifle Caliber .22—Model of 1903. Inco., 1972. 12 pp., 1 plate. Paper, $1.00.
Reprint of 1907 War Dept. pamphlet No. 1925.
Description of Telescopic Musket Sights, Inco, 1972. 10 pp., 4 plates. Paper, $1.00.
Reprint of 1917 War Dept. pamphlet No. 1957, first publ. in 1908.
Fifteen Years in the Hawken Lode, by John D. Baird, The Buckskin Press, Chaska, MI, 1971. 120 pp., illus. $10.00.
Complements "The Hawken Rifle" by the same author. Collection of thoughts and observations over many years on the famed Hawkens.
The First Winchester, by John E. Parsons. Winchester Press, New York, NY, 1969. 207 pp., well illus., $8.95.
This new printing of *The Story of the 1866 Repeating Rifle* [1st publ. 1955]] is revised, and additional illustrations included.
Garand Rifles M1, M1C, M1D, by Donald B. McLean. Normount Armament Co., Forest Grove, OR, 1968. Over 160 pp., 175 illus., paper wrappers. $3.00.
Covers all facets of the arm: battlefield use, disassembly and maintenance, all details to complete lock-stock-and-barrel repair, plus variations, grenades, ammo., and accessories; plus a section on 7.62mm NATO conventions.
Hawken Rifles; The Mountain Man's Choice, by John D. Baird, The Buckskin Press, Chaska, MI, 1971. 95 pp., illus. $10.00.
History and collector's reference on Hawken rifles, developed and used in the West in the fur trade.
How to Select and Use Your Big Game Rifle, by Henry M. Stebbins, Combat Forces Press, Washington, 1952. 237 pp., illus. $6.50.
Concise valuable data on rifles, old and new—slide action, lever, semi automatic, and single shot models are covered.
The Hunting Rifle, by Jack O'Connor. Winchester Press, NY, 1970. 352 pp., illus. $8.95.
An analysis, with wit and wisdom, of contemporary rifles, cartridges, accessories and hunting techniques.
Johnson Semi-Automatic Rifle, Rotary Feed Model, 1941 Instruction Manual, by the Johnson Arms Co. Design Publ., Hyattsville, Md., 1969. 72 pp. illus., paper covers. $4.00.
A reprint of the original instruction manual.
The Lee-Enfield Rifle, by E. G. B. Reynolds. Arco Publ. Co., NY, 1968. 224 pp., drawings and photos. $9.50.
New U.S. edition of a standard reference on models and modifications of the famous British military rifle.
Major Ned H. Roberts and the Schuetzen Rifle, by Gerald O. Kelver, G: O. Kelver, Publ., Mentone, IN, 1972. 99 pp., illus. $4.00.
Selected writings on old single shot rifles, sights, loads, etc.
Maynard Catalog of 1880, a reprint in facsimile by the Wyoming Armory, Inc., Cheyenne, WY, 1969. 32 pp., illus., paper covers. $2.25.
All models, sights, cartridges, targets etc.
Modern Breech-Loaders, Sporting and Military, by W. W. Greener, with intro. by D. B. McLean. Normount Tech. Publ., Forest Grove, OR, 1971. 256 pp., illus. Paper covers. $3.50.
Reprint of the 1870 ed. Covers rifles, carbines, and the "new" breech-loading pistols.
Same title, this is a reprint of the 1871 ed. Lujac Publ., Pueblo, CO, 1972. 275 pp., illus. $4.95.
Reprint of original 1870 ed. Covers rifles, carbines, and the "new" breech-loading pistols.
Pictorial History of the Rifle, By G. W. P. Swenson. Ian Allan Ltd., Shepperton, Surrey, England, 1971. 184 pp., illus. $9.50.
Essentially a picture book, with over 200 rifle illustrations. The text furnishes a concise history of the rifle and its development.
Position Rifle Shooting, by Bill Pullum and F. T. Hanenkrat. Winchester Press, NY, 1973. 256 pp., illus. $10.00.
The single most complete statement of rifle shooting principles and techniques, and the means of learning, teaching and using them, ever to appear in print.
The Rifle: and How to Use it, by H. Busk, Richmond Publ. Co., Richmond, England, 1971. 225 pp., illus. $9.00.
Reprint of the 1859 ed. Covers mid-19th century military rifles.
The Rifle Book, by Jack O'Connor. Random House (Knopf), N.Y.C., 1948. 3rd ed., 1964. 338 pp., illus. $10.00.
A definitive work, out-of-print until recently, which covers actions, design, ammunition, sights and accessories.
Rifles, a Modern Encyclopedia, by H. M. Stebbins. Book Sales, New York, NY, 1970. A reprint of the original of 1958. 376 pp., well illus. $4.98.
A comprehensive work covering subject for target and game. A limited number of original, deluxe and numbered full-leather bound copies at $25.00.
Rifles AR15, M16, and M16A1, 5.56 mm, by D. B. McLean. Normount Armament Co., Forest Grove, OR, 1968. Unpaginated, illus., paper covers. $3.50.
Descriptions, specifications and operation of subject models are set forth in text and picture.
Schuetzen Rifles, History and Loading, by Gerald O. Kelver, Gerald O. Kelver, Publisher, Brighton, CO, 1972. Illus. $4.00.
Reference work on these rifles, their bullets, loading, telescopic sights, accuracy, etc. A limited, numbered ed.
Sharps Firearms, *v. 3, Pt. 3, Model 1874 Rifles,* by Frank M. Sellers and Dewitt Bailey II. Frank M. Sellers, Denver, Colo., 1969. 20 pp., illus., paper covers. $7.50.
A separately printed section of a continuing comprehensive collector's reference. This current work shows and describes the known M1874 variations.
Shooter's Bible Gunsight Guide, by George Nonte. Shooter's Bible, Inc., So. Hackensack, NJ, 1968. 224 pp., illus. $3.95.
Catalog data, descriptions and comment, plus articles on all types of modern gun sights.
Shooting the Percussion Rifle, by R. O. Ackerman. Publ. by the author, Albuquerque, N.M., 1966. 19 pp., illus. in line by the author. Paper wrappers, $1.50.
This well prepared work is Book No. 2 of a projected series. This one gives basic information on the use of the muzzle-loading rifle.
Single Shot Rifles and Actions, by Frank de Haas. Ed. by J. T. Amber. Published by Digest Books, Inc., Northfield, IL, 1969. 342 pp., illus. paper bound. $7.95.
A definitive book on over 60 single shot actions and rifles, their use, repair, remodelling, etc.
Sir Charles Ross and His Rifle, by Robt. Phillips and J. J. Knap, Museum Restoration Service, Ottawa, Canada., 1969. 32 pp., illus. Paper covers. $2.00.
The story of the man who invented the "Ross Model 1897 Magazine Sporting Rifle," the 1900 under the name of Bennett, and many others.
Small Bore Target Shooting, by H. G. B. Fuller. Herbert Jenkins, London, 1964. 264 pp., well illus. $8.50.
Authoritative English work, covering rifle types, buying hints, ammunition, accessories, and range technique.
Sniper Rifles of Two World Wars, by W. H. Tantum IV. Museum Restoration Service, Ottawa, Can., 1967. 32 pp., illus. $1.50.
Monograph on high-accuracy rifles used by troops in world wars I and II and in Korea. Paper wrappers.
Springfield Rifles, M1903, M1903A1, M1903A4, compiled by the publ. Normount Armament Co., Forest Grove, OR, 1968. Over 115 pp., illus., paper wrappers. $2.50.
Routine disassembly and maintenance to complete ordnance inspection and repair; bore sighting, trigger adjustment, accessories, etc.
The '03 Springfields, by Clark S. Campbell, Ray Riling Arms Books Co., Phila, PA, 1971. 320 pp., illus. $16.50.
New, completely revised, enlarged and updated ed. based on the 1957 issue.
Target Rifle Shooting, by E. G. B. Reynolds & Robin Fulton. Barrie & Jenkins, London, Eng., 1972. 200 pp., illus. $9.50.
For the novice and intermediate shooter who wants to learn the basics needed to become a rifle marksman.
Twenty-Two Caliber Varmint Rifles, by C. S. Landis. Stackpole Books, Harrisburg, PA, 1947. 521 pp., profusely illustrated. $7.50.
A vast amount of data on the many Wildcat 22's, including numerous scale drawings of cartridges and chambers.
The .22 Rifle, by Dave Petzal. Winchester Press, NY, 1972. 244 pp., illus. $5.95.
All about the mechanics of the .22 rifle. How to choose the right one, how to choose a place to shoot, what makes a good shot, the basics of small-game hunting.
United States Rifle, Cal. .30, Model of 1917, a reprint of an official government booklet by Normount Publ. Co., Forest Grove, OR, 1969. 80 pp., line illus., paper covers. $2.00.
A training manual issued by the War Department in 1918. A much-wanted and useful booklet.
United States Rifle 7.62 mm, M14 and M14E2, a reprint of an official government booklet by Normount Armament Co., Forest Grove, OR, 1968. 50 pp., illus., paper covers. $2.00.
U.S. Army Field Manual 23-8, first published in 1965.
Westley Richards Modern Sporting Rifles and Cartridges. A reprint of an original undated catalog of the British makers. Safari Outfitters, Richfield, Conn., 1968. 60 pp. illus., paper. $4.95.
Facsimile of issue, covers big game rifles and ammunition.
Winchester '73 & '76, the First Repeating Center-Fire Rifles, by D. F. Butler. Winchester Press, New York, NY, 1st ed., 1970. 95 pp., well and tastefully illus. in line, halftones and photos. Color frontispiece. $7.95.
A complete history of the subject arms and their then-new ammunition, plus details of their use on America's western frontiers.

shotguns

American Partridge and Pheasant Shooting, Frank Schley. Abercrombie & Fitch Library, NY, 1967. 222 pp., illus. with detailed engravings of game birds. $7.95.
Limited printing of the rare sporting classic of 1877, considered for years the most important book available on the use of the scattergun.
The American Shotgun, by David F. Butler. Winchester Press, NY, 1973. 256 pp. $15.
Authoritive and profusely illus. Traces the entire evolution of the American shotgun and modern American shotshells.
The Art of Wing Shooting, by Wm. B. Leffingwell. Abercrombie & Fitch Library, NY, 1967. 192 pp., illus. $7.95.
Limited issue of a practical treatise on the use of the shotgun, first publ. in 1894. Contains a wealth of period anecdotes.
Automatic and Repeating Shotguns, by R. Arnold. Barnes & Co., N.Y.C., 1960. 173 pp., illus. $2.95.
Their history and development, with expert professional advice on choosing a gun for clay target shooting, game shooting, etc.
Book of Shotgun Sports, by Sports Illustrated eds. J. B. Lippincott Co., Phila, PA, 1967. 88 pp., illus., $3.50.
Introduction to target shooting, game shooting, and gunmanship.
Clay Pigeon Marksmanship, by Percy Stanbury and G. L. Carlisle. Herbert Jenkins, London, 1964. 216 pp., illus. $6.00.
Handbook on learning the skills, with data on guns & equipment and competition shooting at all types of clay targets; by two eminent British writers.
Field, Skeet and Trapshooting, by C. E. Chapel. Revised ed. Barnes & Co., NYC, 1962. 291 pp., illus. $6.95.
A useful work on shotgun shooting, including gun types, ammo, accessories, marksmanship, etc.
The Fowler in Ireland. by Sir Ralph Payne-Gallwey, Richmond Publ. Co., Richmond, England, 1971. 503 pp., illus. $13.95.
Reprint of the 1882 work on wildfowling and wildlife in Ireland.
The Game Shot's Vade Mecum, by Michael Brander, A. & C. Black, London, 1st ed., 1965. 242 pp., illus. $6.00.
A British guide on the use of the shotgun in the hunting field, covers selection, marksmanship, game behavior and hunt management.
The Golden Age of Shotgunning, by Bob Hinman, Winchester Press, NY, 1971. 175 pp., illus. $8.95.
The story of American shotgun and wingshooting from 1870 to 1900.
Gough Thomas's Gun Book, by G. T. Garwood. A. & C. Black, London, England, 1969. 160 pp., illus. $8.95.
Excerpts of articles on the shotgun published in *Shooting Times,* by a noted British authority. Wide-ranging survey of every aspect on the shotgun, its use, behavior, care, and lore.
Gough Thomas's Second Gun Book, by G. T. Garwood, A. & C. Black, London, 1971. 227 pp., illus. $8.95.
More—and excellent—shotgun lore for the sportsman.
High Pheasants, by Sir Ralph Payne-Gallwey, Richmond Publ. Co., Richmond, England, 1970. 79 pp. $6.60.
The first and last word on its subject.
How to Shoot Straight, by Macdonald Hastings. A. S. Barnes and Co., New York, NY, 1970. 133 pp., illus., index ed. $5.95.
A companion volume to the author's *Churchill on Game Shooting,* and designed as a standard work on the modern game gun—a "teach-yourself" book.
New England Grouse Shooting, by W. H. Foster, Chas. Scribner's, NY, 193 pp., illus. $12.50.
Many interesting and helpful points on how to hunt grouse.
The New Wildfowler in the 1970's by N. M. Sedgwick, et al. Barrie & Jenkins, London, Eng., 1970. 375 pp., illus. $11.50.
A compendium of articles on wildfowling, hunting practices and conservation. An updated reprint.
Parker, America's Finest Shotgun, by P. H. Johnson. Outlet Book Co., Inc., NY, 1968. 260 pp., illus. $2.95.
An account of a great sporting arm—from post Civil War until 1947, when it was sold to Remington. Values, models, etc.
Parker Brother Gun Catalog, 1869. B. Palmer, Tyler, TX, 1972. 14 pp., illus. Paper covers. $4.
Facsimile of Charles Parker's first issued catalog on "Parker Breech-Loading Shot Guns."
Pigeon Shooting, by Richard Arnold. Faber & Faber, London, Eng., 1966. 162 pp., illus. $5.00.
A practical, specialized work on pigeon shooting in flight, over decoys, how to make hideouts, decoys, etc.
Rough Shooting, by G. A. Gratten & R. Willett. Faber & Faber, London, Eng., 1968. 242 pp., illus. $6.75.
The art of shooting, dogs and their training, games, rearing and their diseases, proof marks, etc.
Score Better at Skeet, by Fred Missildine, with Nick Karas. Winchester Press, NY, 1972. 160 pp., illus. $5.95. In paper covers, $2.95.
The long-awaited companion volume to *Score Better at Trap.*
Score Better at Trap, by Fred Missildine. Winchester Press, NY, 1971. 192 pp., illus. $5.95.
Step-by-step instructions, fully illustrated, on mastering the game by one of the world's leading coaches. In paper covers, $2.95.
Shooting For Beginners, by E. N. Barclay. Percival Marshal & Co., London, 1963. 74 pp., illus. $1.75.
Concise introduction to British techniques and customs in shotgunning for game birds.
Shooting Preserve Management (The Nilo System), by E. L. Kozicky and John Madson, Winchester Press, New York, NY, 1969. 312 pp., photos., line drawings and diagrams. $10.00.
The new look in 13 chapters, a full account of American field shooting at Nilo Farms, the show-case of the shooting-preserve concept.
The Shotgun, by T. D. S. & J. A. Purdey. A. & C. Black, London, Eng., 1969. 144 pp., illus. with Photos and diagrams. $3.95.
Reprinted 4th ed. of a well-known British work by two members of the notable gunsmith family. Covers the gun and its use in the field, at traps, and for skeet.
The Shotgun Book, by Jack O'Connor. Alfred A. Knopf, NY, 1965. 332 pp., plus index, illus. with line and photos. $10.00.
The definitive, authoritative book with up-to-date chapters on wild-fowling, upland gunning, trap and Skeet shooting. It includes practical advice on shotgun makes, models and functions, as well as data on actions.
Shotgun and Shooter, by G. Carlisle and P. Stanbury, Barrie & Jenkins, London, 1970. 217 pp., illus. $6.95.
On guns, wildfowling, dog training, decoys, safety, etc.
Shotgun Marksmanship, by P. Stanbury & G. L. Carlisle. A. S. Barnes & Co., NY, 1969. 224 pp., illus. $6.95.
A new and revised edition for beginners, veterans, skeet shooters, hunters, etc. Valuable tips on improving marksmanship, etc.
The Shotgun Stock, by Robt. Arthur. A. S. Barnes & Co., NY, 1971. 175 pp., illus. $12.00.
The first and only book about the shotgun stock. Its design, construction, and embellishment. A much-needed work.
The Shotgunner's Bible, by George Laycock. Doubleday & Co., Garden City, NY, 1969. 173 pp., illus., paper covers. $1.95.
Coverage of shotguns, ammunition, marksmanship, hunting of various types of game, care and safety, etc.
Shotguns & Cartridges, by Gough Thomas. A. & C. Black, London, Eng., 1970. 136 pp., illus. $5.00.
An excellent work on the choice and use of guns and loads, by the gun editor of *The Shooting Times* (England).
Shotguns by Keith, by E. Keith. Stackpole Books, Harrisburg, PA, 1967. 307 pp., illus. A new edition, $2.98.
Guns and their accessories from history to ornamentation, their ammunition, and the practical use of American, English and European arms.
Skeet Shooting with D. Lee Braun, Robt. Campbell, ed. Grosset & Dunlap, NY, 1967. 160 pp., illus. Paper covers $1.95.
Thorough instructions on the fine points of Skeet shooting.
Successful Shotgun Shooting, by A. A. Montague. Winchester Press, NY, 1970. 160 pp., illus. $5.95.
The work of a superb shot and a great teacher; even the experts can read with profit.
Sure-Hit Shotgun Ways, by F. E. Sell, Stackpole Books, Harrisburg, PA, 1967. 160 pp., illus. $5.95.
An expert with the scatter gun uncomplicates its effective use in every field, gives quick-skill methods for the sportsman.
Trapshooting with D. Lee Braun and the Remington Pros., ed. by R. Campbell. Remington Arms Co., Bridgeport, CT, 1969. 157 pp., well illus., $5.95. Also in paper covers. $2.95.
America's masters of the scattergun give the secrets of professional marksmanship.
Wing & Shot, by R. G. Wehle, Country Press, Scottsville, NY, 1967. 190 pp., illus. $8.50.
Step-by-step account on how to train a fine shooting dog.

Lightner Reprints

The following titles come from the Lightner Library Coll., Cocoa Beach, Fla. All have paper covers, all were publ. in 1973.
Browning Arms Co. Catalog, 1935. 188 pp., illus. $4.
Facsimile reprint showing first superposed models and grades.
Charles Daly (Prussian) Catalog, ca. 1930. 24 pp., illus. $4.
Facsimile catalog showing Regent and Diamond grades, over-unders, 3-barrel trap models.
A.H. Fox Gun Co. Catalog, 1923. 40 pp., illus. $4.
Facsimile of the 1923 catalog. All models and grades including single barrel trap models, and information on the Fox-Kautsky single trigger.
A.H. Fox Gun Catalog, 1934. 23 pp., illus. $4.
Facsimile showing all models, parts, prices, of Fox guns made by Savage Arms Corp., Utica, NY.
Ithaca Gun Co. Catalog, 1915. 25 pp., illus. $4.
Facsimile reprint of a large format catalog. Shows hammerless models.
Ithaca Gun Co. Catalog 51-F, 1930. 22 pp., illus. $4.
Facsimile of a large format catalog. Shows new lock models, gives prices.
Lefever Arms Catalog, 1892. 32 pp., illus. $4.
Facsimile of a very rare catalog.
The Parker Gun Catalog, 1934. 15 pp., illus. $3.
Facsimile of the last catalog issued by the original Parker Bros. Company.
The Parker Gun Catalog, 1937. 34 pp., illus. $5.
Facsimile of the 1937 catalog, publ. by the Parker Gun Works, Remington Arms Co., Inc. Their largest, most beautiful and last regular catalog issued. The only one displaying all Parker trap and Skeet models.
The Parker Gun Dealer's Illustrated Price Catalog, 1940. 8 pp., illus. $2.
Last wholesale and retail price catalog issued by Parker Gun Works, Remington Arms Co. Shows all models and accessories.
Remington Arms Co. Catalog, 1910. 62 pp., illus. $4.
Facsimile showing all double barreled models, including special 750 grade, autos, rifles, parts.
L.C. Smith (Hunter Arms Co.) Catalog, 1907. 34 pp., $5.
Facsimile of a large, beautifully illus. catalog. Shows early hammerless models, parts and prices.
L.C. Smith (Hunter Arms Co.) Catalog, 1928. 28 pp., illus. $4.
Facsimile reprint showing all models—trap, Skeet, eagle, etc.
L.C. Smith (Hunter Arms Co.) Catalog, 1918. 24 pp., illus. $4.
Facsimile reprint showing all hammerless models and prices.
L.C. Smith (Hunter Arms Co.) Catalog, 1939. 24 pp., illus. $4.50.
Facsimile of the Golden Anniversary Issue. Separate anniversary brochure included.
L.C. Smith (Hunter Arms Co.) Catalog, 1945. 24 pp., illus. $4.
Facsimile of the last L.C.S. catalog. Shows most modern models.

IMPORTANT NOTICE TO BOOK BUYERS

Books listed above may be bought from Ray Riling Arms Books Co., 6844 Gorsten St., Phila., PA, 19119. Ray Riling, the proprietor, is the researcher and compiler of "The Arms Library" and a seller of gun books for the past 30 years.
The Riling stock includes the books classic and modern, many hard-to-find items, and many not obtainable elsewhere. The above pages list a portion of the current stock. They offer prompt, complete service, with delayed shipments occurring only on out-of-print or out-of-stock books.
NOTICE FOR ALL CUSTOMERS: Remittance in U.S. funds must accompany all orders. For U.S. add 15¢ postage per book on all orders under $20.00 plus 25¢ for insurance. Orders over $20.00 add 40¢ for insurance.
All foreign countries add 60¢ per book for postage and handling, plus 95¢ per 10-lb. Package or under for safe delivery by registered mail.
Payments in excess of order or for "Backorders" are credited or fully refunded at request. Books "As-Ordered" are not returnable except by permission and a handling charge on these of $1.00 per book is deducted from refund or credit. Only Pennsylvania customers must include current sales tax.
Full variety of arms books are also available from N. Flayderman & Co., Inc., Squash Hollow. RFD 2, New Milford, CT 06776 and Rutgers Book Center, 127 Raritan Ave., Highland Park, NJ 08904.

ARMS ASSOCIATIONS IN AMERICA AND ABROAD

UNITED STATES

ALABAMA

Alabama Gun Collectors Assn.
Thomas M. Stewart, P.O. Box 20021, Birmingham, Ala. 35216
North Alabama Gun Coll. Assn.
P.O. Box 564, Huntsville, Ala. 35804

ARIZONA

Arizona Gun Collectors Assn. Inc.
Miles S. Vaughn, 1129 S. 6th Ave., Tucson, Ariz. 85701
International Cartridge Coll. Assn., Inc.
A. D. Amesbury, 4065 Montecito Ave., Tucson, Ariz. 85711

ARKANSAS

Ft. Smith Dealers & Coll. Assn.
Tony Smith, 1407 57 Terrace, Ft. Smith, Ark. 72901

CALIFORNIA

Calif. Hunters & Gun Owners Assoc.
V. H. Wacker, 2309 Cipriani Blvd., Belmont, Cal. 94002
Greater Calif. Arms & Collectors Assn.
Donald L. Bullock, 8291 Carburton St., Long Beach, Cal. 90808
Los Angeles Gun & Ctg. Collectors Assn.
F. H. Ruffra, 20810 Amie Ave., Torrance, CA 90503
Northern California Historical Arms Coll. Assn.
Julia Lundwall, 25 Mizpah St., San Francisco Ca. 94131
San Bernardino Valley Arms Collectors, Inc.
F. Schaperkotter, 2697 Acacia Ave., San Bernardino, Cal. 92405
Santa Barbara Antique Arms Coll. Assn., Inc.
P.O. Box 6291, Santa Barbara, CA. 93111
Southern California Arms Collectors Assn.
Frank E. Barnyak, 4204 Elmer Ave., No. Hollywood, Cal. 91602
U. S. International Trap and Skeet Assn.
Box 1437, Huntington Beach, CA. 92647

COLORADO

Arapahoe Gun Collectors
Bill Rutherford, 2968 S. Broadway, Englewood, Colo. 80110
Colorado Gun Collectors Assn.
Arnie Dowd, 5970 Estes Ct., Arvada, Colo. 80002
Pikes Peak Gun Collectors Guild
Charles Cell, 406 E. Uintah St., Colorado Springs, Colo. 80903

CONNECTICUT

Antique Arms Coll. Assn. of Conn.
T. N. Reiley, 17 Philip Rd., Manchester, Conn. 06040
National Shooting Sports Fdtn., Inc.
Warren Page, President, 1075 Post Rd., Riverside, Conn. 06878
Stratford Gun Collectors Assn., Inc.
P.O. Box 52, Stratford, Conn. 06497
Ye Conn. Gun Guild, Inc.
Rob. L. Harris, P.O. Box 67, Cornwall Bridge, Conn. 06754

DELAWARE

Delaware Antique Arms Collectors
C. Landis, 2408 Duncan Rd., Wilmington, Del. 19808

DISTRICT OF COLUMBIA

American Military Inst.
Box 568, Washington, D.C. 20044
American Ordnance Assn.
819 Union Trust Bldg., Washington, D.C. 20005
National Rifle Assn.
1600 Rhode Island Ave., Washington, D.C. 20036

FLORIDA

American Police Pistol & Rifle Assn.
1100 N.E. 125th St., No. Miami, Fl. 33161 (law enforcement members and gun enthusiasts).

Florida Gun Collectors Assn.
Bob Marvin, P.O. Box 470, Jasper, Fla. 32052
National Police Officers Assn. of America
Natl. Police Hall of Fame Bldg., Venice, Fla. 33595
Tampa Bay Gun Collectors Assn.
Col. Emmet M. Jeffreys, 401 49th St., N., St. Petersburg, Fla. 33710

GEORGIA

Georgia Arms Collectors
Aubrey C. Oliveras, P.O. Box 450, Atlanta, Ga. 30301

ILLINOIS

Central Illinois Gun Collectors Assn., Inc.
Donald E. Bryan, R.R. #2, Jacksonville, Ill. 62650
Fort Dearborn Frontiersmen
Al Normath, 8845 Pleasant Ave., Hickory Hills, IL 60457
Fox Valley Arms Fellowship, Inc.
P.O. Box 301, Palatine, Ill. 60618
Illinois State Rifle Assn.
2800 N. Milwaukee Ave., Chicago, Ill. 60618
Illinois Gun Collectors Assn.
P. E. Pitts, P.O. Box 1524, Chicago, Ill. 60690
Little Fort Gun Collectors Assn.
Ernie Robinson, P.O. Box 194, Gurney, Ill. 60031
Mississippi Valley Gun & Cartridge Coll. Assn.
Mel Sims, Box 426, New Windsor, Ill. 61465
Sauk Trail Gun Collectors
L. D. Carlock, Rte. 1, Box 169, Prophetstown, Ill. 61277
Wabash Valley Gun Collectors Assn., Inc.
Mrs. Betty Baer, 1002 Lincoln Pk. Ave., Danville, Ill. 61832

INDIANA

American Single Shot Rifle Assn.
Dennis Hrusosky, 411 David Ave., Joliet, Ill. 60433
Central Indiana Gun Coll. Assn.
Paul E. Daugherty, 421 E. Washington St., Hartford City, Ind. 47348
Crawfordsville Gun Club, Inc.
Rob. J. K. Edmonds, R.R. 2, Crawfordsville, Ind. 47933
Midwest Gun Traders Inc.
c/o Glen Wittenberger, 4609 Oliver St., Ft. Wayne, IN 46806
National Muzzle Loading Rifle Assn.
Box 67, Friendship, Ind. 47021
Northern Indiana Gun Collectors Assn.
Joe Katona, 16150 Ireland Rd., Mishawaka, Ind. 46544
Southern Indiana Gun Collectors Assn., Inc.
Harold M. McClary, 509 N. 3rd St., Boonville, Ind. 47601
Tippecanoe Gun and Cartridge Collectors Club
Leonard Ledman, RR 12, Box 212, Lafayette, Ind.

IOWA

Cedar Valley Gun Coll.
R. L. Harris, 1602 Wenig Rd., N.E., Cedar Rapids, Iowa 52402
Central States Gun Collectors Assn.
Chas. J. Versluis, 701 Broadway, Watterloo, IA 50703
Eastern Iowa Gun and Cartridge Collectors Assn.
F. Fitzpatrick, 305 N. Eliza St., Maquoketa, IA. 52060
Quad City Arms Coll. Assn.
A. Squire, 1845 W. 3rd St., Davenport, IA. 52802

KANSAS

Chisholm Trail Antique Gun Coll. Assn.
P.O. Box 13093, Wichita, Kans. 67213
Four State Collectors Assn.
M. G. Wilkinson, 915 E. 10th, Pittsburgh, Kan. 66762
Kansas Cartridge Coll. Assn.
Bob Linder, Box 84, Plainville, Kans. 67663
Missouri Valley Arms Collectors Assn.
Chas. F. Samuel, Jr., Box 8204, Shawnee Mission, Kans. 66208
Solomon Valley Gun Collectors
Frank Wheeler, Box 230, Osborne, Kan. 67473

KENTUCKY

John Hunt Morgan Gun Coll. Inc.
P.O. Box 525, Paris, Ky. 40361
Kentuckiana Arms Coll. Assn.
Charles R. Phelps, Box 1776, Louisville, Ky. 40201
Kentucky Gun Collectors Assn., Inc.
J. A. Smith, Box 64, Owensboro, Ky. 42301

LOUISIANA

Ark-La-Tex Gun Collectors Assn.
Ray Franks, 1521 Earl St., Shreveport, La. 71108
Bayou Gun Club
Dave Dugas, c/o Le Petit Soldier Shop, 528 Rue Royale, New Orleans, La. 70130
Pelican Arms Collectors
B. Thompson, 9142 Cefalu Dr., Baton Rouge, La. 70811

MARYLAND

Cumberland Valley Arms Collectors Assn.
Mrs. S. Naylor, Rte. #2, Hagerstown, Md. 21740
Penn-Mar-Va Antique Arms Soc.
T. Wibberley, 54 E. Lincoln Ave., Hagerstown, Md. 21740

MASSACHUSETTS

Bay Colony Weapons Collectors Inc.
Ronald B. Santurjian, 47 Homer Rd., Belmont, Mass. 02178
Massachusetts Arms Collectors
John J. Callan, Jr., 15 Montague St., Worcester, Mass. 01603
U. S. Revolver Assn.
Stanley A. Sprague, 59 Alvin St., Springfield, Mass. 01104

MICHIGAN

Michigan Antique Arms Coll., Inc.
W. H. Heid, 8914 Borgman Ave., Huntington Woods, Mich. 48070
Michigan Rifle & Pistol Assn.
Betty Swarthout, 8384 Perrin, Westland, Mich. 48185
Royal Oak Historical Arms Collectors, Inc.
Nancy Stein, 25487 Hereford, Huntington Woods, Mich. 48070

MINNESOTA

Minnesota Weapons Coll. Assn., Inc.
Ken Molenaar, Box 662, Hopkins, MN 55343
Twin Ports Weapons Collectors
Jack Puglisi, 6504 Lexington St., Duluth, MN. 55807

MISSISSIPPI

Dixie Arms Collectors
Ruth Creecy, 1509 W. 7th, Hattiesburg, Miss. 39401
Mississippi Gun Collectors Assn.
Mrs. J. E. Swinney, Box 1332, Hattiesburg, Miss. 39401

MISSOURI

Edwardsville, Ill. Gun Collectors
A. W. Stephensmeier, 317 N. Grand Bl., St. Louis, Mo. 62178
Meramec Valley Gun Collectors
L. W. Olson, Star Route, St. Clair, Mo.
Mineral Belt Gun Coll. Assn.
G. W. Gunter, 1110 E. Cleveland Ave., Monett, Mo. 65708

MONTANA

Montana Arms Collectors Assn.
Chris Sorensen, 175 6th Ave., W.N. Kalispell, Mont. 59901
North American Sportsmen's Assn.
Box 1943—2501 4th Ave. N., Billings, Mont. 59103

NEBRASKA

Nebraska Gun & Cartridge Collectors
E. M. Zalud, 710 West 6th St., North Platte, Neb. 69101
Pine Ridge Gun Coll.
Loren Pickering, 509 Elm St., Crawford, Neb. 69339

NEW MEXICO

New Mexico Gun Collectors Assn.
P.O. Box 14145, Albuquerque, NM. 87111

NEW HAMPSHIRE

Maple Tree Gun Coll. Assn.
E. P. Hector, Meriden Rd., Lebanon, N.H. 03766
New Hampshire Arms Collectors Inc.
James Tillinghast, Box 5, Marlow, N.H. 03456

NEW JERSEY

Experimental Ballistics Associates
Ed Yard, 110 Kensington, Trenton, N.J. 08618
Jersey Shore Antique Arms Collectors
Bob Holloway, 1755 McGallard Ave., Trenton, N.J. 08610
New Jersey Arms Collectors Club, Inc.
Joseph Rixon, 122 Bender Ave., Roselle Park, N.J. 07204

NEW YORK

Armor & Arms Club
J. K. Watson, 51 W. 51st St., New York, N.Y. 10019
Fort Lee Arms Collectors
W. E. Sammis, R.D. 776 Brookridge Dr., Valley Cottage, N.Y. 10989
Hudson-Mohawk Arms Collectors Assn., Inc.
Bennie S. Pisarz, 108 W. Main St., Frankfort, N.Y. 13340
International Benchrest Shooters
Donalee Sterl, R.D. 1, Robinson Rd., Mowhawk, N.Y. 13407
Iroquois Arms Collectors Assn.
Dennis Freeman, 12144 McNeeley Rd., Akron, N.Y. 14001
Long Island Antique Gun Coll. Assn.
Frank Davison, 8 Johnson Pl., Baldwin, N.Y. 11510
Mid-State Arms Coll. & Shooters Club
Bennie S. Pisarz, 108 W. Main St., Frankfort, N.Y. 13340
New York State Arms Collectors Assn., Inc.
Marvin Salls, R. D. 1,Ilion, N.Y. 13357
Sporting Arms and Ammunition Manufacturers' Inst.
420 Lexington Ave., N.Y., N.Y. 10017
Westchester Arms Collectors Club, Inc.
F. E. Falkenbury, Jr., Secy., 75 Hillcrest Rd., Hartsdale, N.Y. 10530

NORTH CAROLINA

Carolina Gun Collectors Assn.
N. C. Bill Harvey, P.O. Box 464, Wilson, N.C. 27893

OHIO

Amateur Trap Shooting Assn.
P.O. Box 246, Vandalia, O. 45377
American Society of Arms Collectors, Inc.
Rob. F. Rubendunst, 6550 Baywood Ln., Cincinnati, O. 45224
Barberton Gun Collectors Assn.
R. N. Watters, 1108 Bevan St., Barberton, O. 44203
Central Ohio Gun and Indian Relic Coll. Assn.
Coyt Stookey, 134 E. Ohio Ave., Washington C.H., O. 43160
Lakeshore Gun Collectors
R. N. Watters, 1108 Bevan St., Barberton, Ohio 44203
Maumee Valley Gun Collectors Assn.
J. Jennings, 3450 Gallatin Rd., Toledo, O. 43606
National Bench Rest Shooters Assn., Inc.
Bernice McMullen, 607 W. Line St., Minerva, O. 44657
Ohio Gun Collectors, Assn., Inc.
Mrs. C. D. Rickey, 130 S. Main St., Prospect, O. 43342
The Stark Gun Collectors, Inc.
Russ McNary, 147 Miles Ave., N.W., Canton, O. 44708
Tri-State Gun Collectors
Doyt S. Gamble, 1115 N. Main St., Lima, OH 45801

OKLAHOMA

Indian Territory Gun Collectors Assn.
P.O. Box 4491, Tulsa, Okla. 74104

OREGON

Jefferson State Arms Collectors
Art Chipman, 2251 Ross Lane, Medford, Ore. 97501
National Reloading Mfrs. Assn., Inc.
1220 Morrison St., S.W., Portland, OR 97205

Oregon Cartridge Coll. Assn. Inc.
Dick Hamilton, P.O. Box 152, Junction City, OR 97448
Oregon Arms Coll. Assn., Inc.
Ted Dowd, 2375 S.W. 76th, Portland, OR 97225
Willamette Valley Arms Coll. Assn.
M. Brooks, 2110 W. 20th, Eugene, Ore. 97405

PENNSYLVANIA

Boone & Crockett Club
C/O Carnegie Museum, 4400 Forbes Ave., Pittsburgh, Pa. 15213
Central Penn Antique Arms Assn.
Geo. Smithgall, 549 W. Lemon St., Lancaster, Pa. 17603
Forks of the Delaware Weapons Assn., Inc.
John F. Scheid, 348 Bushkill St., Easton, Pa. 18042
Lancaster Muzzle Loading Rifle Assn.
James H. Frederick, Jr., R.D. 1, Box 447, Columbia, Pa. 17512
Northern Tier Antique Gun Collectors
Cliff Breidinger, Trout Run, Pa. 17771
Pennsylvania Antique Gun Collectors Assn.
Ray Petry, 801 N. Jackson, Media, PA 19063
Pennsylvania Gun Collectors Assn.
Arch Waugh, 37 Woodside Dr., Washington, PA 15301
Presque Isle Gun Collectors Assn.
James Welch, 156 E. 37th St., Erie, Pa. 16506
Somerset Rifle & Pistol Club
J. Richard Ross, 2 Stein Bldg., Somerset, Pa. 15501
Two Lick Valley Gun Collectors
Carl Steel II, 158 N. 14th St., Indiana, PA 15701

SOUTH CAROLINA

Belton Gun Club Inc.
J. K. Phillips, P.O. Box 605, Belton S.C. 29627
South Carolina Arms Coll. Assn.
J. W. McNelley, 3215 Lincoln St., Columbia, S.C. 29201

TENNESSEE

Memphis Antique Weapons Assn.
F. Dauser, 3429 Jenkins, Memphis, Tenn. 38118
Smoky Mountain Gun Collectors Assn.
P.O. Box 22, Oak Ridge, Tenn. 37830
Tennessee Gun Collectors Assn., Inc.
M. H. Parks, 3556 Pleasant Valley Rd., Nashville, Tenn. 37204

TEXAS

Alamo Arms Collectors
Bill Brookshire, 410 Rector, San Antonio, Tex. 78216
Houston Gun Collectors Assn.
P.O. Box 53435, Houston, TX 77052
National Skeet Shooting Assn.
James M. Leer, Jr., 212 Linwood Bldg., 2608 Inwood Rd., Dallas, Tex. 75235
Paso Del Norte Gun Collectors Inc.
Ken Hockett, 1216 Mescalero, El Paso, Tex. 79925
Permian Basin Rifle & Pistol Club, Inc.
E. L. Good, Box 459, Midland, Tex. 79701
Sabine Gun Collectors Club
Mrs. Irene Vivier, 1042 Iowa, Beaumont, Tex. 77705
Texas Gun Collectors Assn.
Mrs. Taska Clark, 3119 Produce Row, Houston, TX. 77023
Waco Gun Collectors
C. V. Pruitt, 4021 N. 26th, Waco, Tex. 76708

UTAH

Utah Gun Collectors Assn.
S. Gerald Keogh, 875 20th St., Ogden, Utah 84401

VIRGINIA

North-South Skirmish Assn.
John L. Rawls, P.O. Box 114, McLean, Va. 22101
Shenandoah Valley Gun Coll. Assn.
Daniel E. Blye, P.O. Box 926, Winchester, Va. 22601

Virginia Arms Collectors & Assn.
W. H. Bacon, 4601 Sylvan Rd., Richmond, Va. 23225

WASHINGTON

Washington Arms Collectors, Inc.
Don Zwicker, 446 Pelly Ave., Renton, WA 98055

WISCONSIN

Chippewa Valley Weapons Collectors
J. M. Sullivan, 504 Ferry St., Eau Claire, Wis. 54701
Great Lakes Arms Coll. Assn., Inc.
E. Warnke, 2249A N. 61 St., Wauwatosa, Wis. 53213
Wisconsin Gun Collectors Assn., Inc.
Rob. Zellmer, W180N8996 Leona Lane, Menomonee Falls, WI. 53051

WYOMING

Wyoming Gun Collectors
Bob Funk, 224 N. 2W., Riverton, Wyo. 82501

AUSTRALIA

Nat'l. Sporting Shooters' Assn. of Australia
G. O. Nelis, P.O. Box 90, Stafford, Brisbane, Qld., Australia 4053

CANADA

ALBERTA

Canadian Historical Arms Society
P.O. Box 901, Edmonton, Alb., Canada T5J 2L8

ONTARIO

Niagara Arms Collectors
Box 948, Beamsville, Ont. Canada
Ontario Arms Collectors Assn.
P. Peddle, 174 Ellerslie Ave., Willowdale, Ont., Canada
Oshawa Antique Gun Coll. Inc.
Gordon J. Dignem, 613 Rosmere St., Oshawa, Ont., Canada

QUEBEC

Lower Canada Arms Collectors Assn.
Secretary, P.O. Box 1162, St. B. Montreal 101, Quebec, Can.

EUROPE

ENGLAND

Arms and Armour Society of London
F. Wilkinson, 40 Great James St., Holborn, London, N. 3HB W.C.1.
Muzzle Loaders' Assn. of Great Britain
Membership Records, 12 Frances Rd., Baginton, Coventry, England
National Rifle Assn. (British)
Bisley Camp, Brookwood, Woking, Surrey, England

FRANCE

Les Arquebusiers de France,
Mme, Marckmann, 70 Rue des Chantiers, 78-Versailles, France

NEW ZEALAND

New Zealand Deerstalkers Assn.
J. M. Murphy, P.O. Box 263, Wellington, New Zealand

SOUTH AFRICA

Historical Firearms Soc. of South Africa
"Minden" 11 Buchan Rd., Newlands, Cape Town, South Africa

PERIODICAL PUBLICATIONS

ALASKA Magazine
Alaska Northwest Pub. Co., Box 4-EEE, Anchorage, Alaska 99503. $8.00 yr. Hunting and fishing articles.

American Field†
222 W. Adams St., Chicago, Ill. 60606. $9.00 yr. Field dogs and trials, occasional gun and hunting articles.

The American Rifleman (M)
National Rifle Assn., 1600 Rhode Island Ave., N.W., Wash., D.C. 20036. $7.50 yr. Firearms articles of all kinds.

The American West*
American West Publ. Co., 599 College Ave., Palo Alto, Ca. 94306. $9.00 yr.

Argosy
Popular Publ., Inc., 420 Lexington Ave., New York, N.Y. 10017. $7.00 yr.

Army (M)
Assn of the U.S. Army, 1529 18th Ave. N.W., Wash., D.C. 20036. $10.00 yr. Occasional articles on small arms

Australian Shooters' Journal
P.O. Box 12, Elizabeth, South Australia 5112. $5.50 yr. locally; $7.50 yr. overseas. Hunting and shooting articles.

Canadian Journal of Arms Collecting (Q)
Museums Restoration Service P.O. Box 2037, Sta. D, Ottawa, Ont., Canada. $4.00 yr.

Deutsches Waffen Journal
Journal-Verlag Schwend GmbH, Postfach 340, D7170 Schwabisch Hall, Germany. $11.50 yr. Antique and modern arms, their history, technical aspects, etc. German text.

Ducks Unlimited, Inc. (M)
P.O. Box 66300, Chicago, Ill. 60666.

Enforcement Journal (Q)
Natl. Police Officers Assn., Natl. Police Academy Bldg., 1890 S. Tamiami Trail, Venice, Fla. 33595. $6.00 yr.

The Field†
The Harmsworth Press Ltd., 8 Stratton St., London W.I., England. $29.50 yr. Hunting and shooting articles.

Field & Stream
Holt, Rinehart and Winston, Inc., 383 Madison Ave., New York, N.Y. 10017. $5.00 yr. Articles on firearms plus hunting and fishing.

Fur-Fish-Game
A. R. Harding Pub. Co., 2878 E. Main St., Columbus, Ohio 43209. $4.00 yr. "Gun Rack" column by M. H. Decker.

The Gun Report
World Wide Gun Report, Inc., Box 111, Aledo, Ill. 61231. $7.00 yr. For the gun collector.

Gunsport & Gun Collector
The Clark Bldg., Suite 2100, Pittsburgh, PA 15222. Md. 20637. $5.00 yr.

Gun Week‡
Amos Press, Inc., P.O. Box 150, Sidney, Ohio 45365. $5.00 yr. U.S. and possessions; $6.00 yr. Canada; $7.00 yr. foreign. Tabloid paper on guns, hunting, shooting.

Gun World
Gallant Publishing Co., 3424 Camino Capistrano, Capistrano Beach, CA 92624. $7.50 yr. For the hunting, reloading and shooting enthusiast.

Guns & Ammo
Petersen Pub. Co., 8490 Sunset Blvd., Los Angeles, Calif. 90069. $7.50 yr. Guns, shooting, and technical articles.

Guns
Guns Magazine, 8150 N. Central Park Ave., Skokie, Ill. 60076. $7.50 yr. Articles for gun collectors, hunters and shooters.

Guns Review
Ravenhill Pub. Co. Ltd., Standard House, Bonhill St., London E.C. 2, England. $10.20 yr. For collectors and shooters.

The Handgunner (M)
U.S. Revolver Assn., 59 Alvin St., Springfield, Mass. 01104. $5.00 yr. General handgun and competition articles.

The Handloader Magazine*
Dave Wolfe Pub. Co., Box 3030, Prescott, Ariz. 86301 $5.00 yr.

Hobbies
Lightner Pub. Co., 1006 S. Michigan Ave., Chicago, Ill. 60605. $6.00 yr.; Canada $7.00; foreign $7.50. Collectors departments.

International Shooting Sport*
Union Internationale de Tir, 62 Wiesbaden-Klarenthal, Klarenthalerstr., Germany. $7.20 yr., p.p. For the International target shooter.

The Journal of the Arms & Armour Society (M)
F. Wilkinson (Secy.), 40 Great James St., Holborn, London WC1, England. $4.00 yr. Articles for the collector.

Law and Order
Law and Order Magazine, 37 W. 38th St., New York, N.Y. 10018. $7.00 yr. Articles on weapons for law enforcement.

The Luger Journal
Robt. B. Marvin, Publ., P.O. Box 326, Jasper, FL 32052. $6.00 yr.

Muzzle Blasts (M)
National Muzzle Loading Rifle Assn. P.O. Box 67, Friendship, Ind. 47021. $8.00 yr. For the black powder shooter.

National Rifle Assn. Journal (British)
Natl. Rifle Assn. (BR.), Bisley Camp, Brookwood, Woking, Surrey, England.

National Wildlife*
Natl. Wildlife Fed. Inc., 1412 16th St. N.W., Washington, D.C. $6.00 yr. World/Assoc. membership *includes Intl. Wildlife;* 12 issues $11.00.

New Zealand Wildlife (Q)
New Zealand Deerstalkers Assoc. Inc., P.O. Box 263, Wellington, N.Z. $2.00 U.S. and Canada, elsewhere on application. Hunting and shooting articles.

Ordnance* (M)
American Ordnance Assn., 819 Union Trust Bldg., Wash., D.C. 20005. $8.00 yr. Occasional articles on small arms and related subjects.

Outdoor Life
Popular Science Pub. Co., 355 Lexington Ave., New York, N.Y. 10017. $6.00 yr. Arms column by Jim Carmichel.

Outdoor World*
Country Beautiful Corp., 24198 W. Bluemound Rd., Waukesha, Wis. 53186. $7.95 yr. Conservation and wildlife articles.

Police Times (M)
1100 N.E. 125th St., No. Miami, Fla. 33161.

Popular Mechanics
Hearst Corp., 224 W. 57th St., New York, N.Y. 10019. $5.97 yr., $7.97 Canada, $9.97 foreign. Hunting and shooting articles.

Precision Shooting
Precision Shooting, Inc., Box 6, Athens, PA 18810. $5.00 yr. Journal of the International Benchrest Shooters.

The Rifle Magazine*
Dave Wolfe Publishing Co., Box 3030, Presott, Ariz. 86301. $5.00 yr. Journal of the NBRSA.

The Rifleman (Q)
National Smallbore Rifle Assoc., 113 Southwark St., London, S. E. 1, Englnd. $7.00 (5 yrs.). Data on British Matches and International Matches, and technical shooting articles.

Rod and Gun in Canada
Rod and Gun Pub. Corp., 1219 Hotel deVille, Montreal 129, P.Q. Canada. $3.00 yr., $5.00 2 yrs., out of Canada, postage $1.00 p. yr. extra. Regular gun and shooting articles.

Saga
Gambi Public., 333 Johnson Ave., Brooklyn, N.Y. 11026. $6.00 yr. U.S., $6.50 Canada.

The Shooting Industry
Publisher's Dev. Corp., 8150 N. Central Pk., Skokie, Ill. 60076. $7.00 yr.

The Shooting Times & Country Magazine (England) †
Cordwallis Estate, Clivemont Rd., Maidenhead, Berksh., England. $20 yr. Game shooting, wild fowling and firearms articles.

Shooting Times
PJS Publications, News Plaza, Peoria, Ill., 61601 $5.85 yr. Guns, shooting, reloading; articles on every gun activity.

The Shotgun News‡
Snell Publishing Co., Box 1147, Hastings, NB 68901. $5.00 yr. Sample copy 75¢. Gun ads of all kinds.

The Skeet Shooting Review
National Skeet Shooting Assn., 212 Linwood Bldg., 2608 Inwood Rd., Dallas. Tex. 75235. $9.00 yr. (Assn. membership of $10.00 includes mag.) Scores, averages, skeet articles.

Sporting Goods Business
Gralla Publications, 1501 Broadway, New York, NY 10036, Trade journal.

The Sporting Goods Dealer
1212 No. Lindbergh Blvd., St. Louis, Mo. 63166. $4.00 yr. The sporting goods trade journal.

Sports Afield
The Hearst Corp., 250 W. 55th St., New York, N.Y. 10019. $5.00 yr. Pete Brown on firearms plus hunting and fishing articles.

Sports Illustrated†
Time, Inc., 541 N. Fairbanks Court, Chicago, Ill. 60611. $12.00 yr. U.S. Poss. and Canada; $16.00 yr. all other countries. Articles on the current sporting scene.

Trap & Field
110 Waterway Blvd., Indianapolis, Ind. 46202. $8.00 yr. Official publ. Amateur Trapshooting Assn. Scores, averages, trapshooting articles.

True
Fawcett Publ., Inc., Fawcett Bldg., Greenwich, Conn. 06830. $7.00 yr. U.S. Poss., and Canada; $10.00 yr. all other countries.

Wildlife Review (Q)
Dep't of Rec. and Conservation Parliament Bldgs., Victoria, B.C., Canada $1.00 yr.

---

* Published bi-monthly
† Published weekly
‡ Published twice per month.

M Membership requirements; write for details.
Q Published Quarterly.
All others are published monthly.

Shooting Publications

Write directly to the sources noted for titles listed and ask for their latest catalog. Do not order from the GUN DIGEST.

A Joint Resolution—A 4-page statement by the National Police Officers Assn. and the National Shooting Sports Foundation, outlining the role of firearms in U.S. history and voicing their stand against ill-planned restrictive gun laws. Free.[1]

Basic Pistol Marksmanship—Textbook for basic pistol courses. 25¢[2]

Basic Rifle Marksmanship—Textbook for basic rifle courses. 25¢ ea.[2]

The Elk—125-page report on the hunting and management of this game animal, more properly called *wapiti*. Extensive biblio. $1.00.[4]

Free Films—Brochure listing outdoor movies available to sportsmen's clubs. Free.[1]

The Gun Law Problem—Information about firearms legislation. Free.[2]

How to be a Crack Shot—A 14-page booklet detailing everything necessary to becoming an outstanding shot. Free.[3]

Fundamentals of Claybird Shooting—A 39-page booklet explaining the basics of Skeet and trap in non-technical terms. Many diagrams. 25¢ ea.[4]

Hunter Safety Instructor's Guide—How to conduct an NRA Hunter Safety Course. 25¢ ea.[2]

Hunting and Shooting Sportsmanship—A 4-page brochure defining the "true sportsman" and giving information on the outdoor field. Free.[1]

Junior Rifle Handbook—Information about the NRA junior program with short instruction course. (25 copies issued to each new affiliated junior club without charge.) 25¢ ea.[2]

NRA Hunter Safety Handbook—Textbook for students. 10¢ ea.[2]

National Shooting Preserve Directory—Up-to-date listing of small game preserves in the U.S. and Canada. Free.[1]

Game, Gunners and Biology—A thumbnail history of American wildlife conservation. 50¢ ea.[4]

Shooting's Fun for Everyone—The why, when, where, and how of riflery for boys and girls. 20 pp. 5¢ ea.[1]

Trap or Skeet Fundamentals—Handbooks explaining fundamentals of these two sports, complete with explicit diagrams to start beginners off right. Free.[3]

25 Foot Shooting Program—Complete information on a short range shooting program with CO_2 and pneumatic rifles and pistols. 35¢[2]

What Every Parent Should Know When a Boy or Girl Wants a Gun—Straightforward answers to the 15 questions most frequently asked by parents. 8 pp. 5¢ ea.[1]

The Cottontail Rabbit—56-page rundown on America's most popular hunting target. Where to find him, how to hunt him, how to help him. Bibliography included. $1.00 ea.[4]

For the Young Hunter—A 32-page booklet giving fundamental information on the sport. Single copies free, 15¢ each in bulk.[4]

Gray and Fox Squirrels—112-page paperbound illustrated book giving full rundown on the squirrel families named. Extensive bibliography. $1.00 ea.[4]

How to Have More Pheasant Hunting—A 16-page booklet on low cost hunting, including data on in-season stocking and how to start a small preserve. 25¢.[1]

The Mallard—80-page semi-technical report on this popular duck. Life cycle, laws and management, hunting—even politics as they affect this bird—are covered. Bibliography. $1.00 ea.[4]

NRA Booklets—Ranging from 12 to 36 pages, these are articles on specific arms or arms types. Titles available are: Sighting In; The 45 Automatic; The M1 Rifle; Telescopic Sights; Metallic Sights; Duck Hunting; U.S. Cal. 30 Carbine; Remodeling the 03A3; Remodeling the 303 Lee-Enfield; Remodeling the U.S. 1917 Rifle; M1903 Springfield Rifle; Military Rifles and Civil War Small Arms, 50¢ ea. Gun Cabinets, Racks, Cases & Pistol Boxes, 75¢. Deer Hunting, $1.00.[2]

Under the heading of "Range Plans" are 15 booklets priced from 10¢ to $1.00. All are described in an order form pamphlet available from the NRA.

NRA Digest of the Federal Gun Control Act of 1968—A 12-page booklet clearly explaining the new law and its provisions. Free to NRA members.[2]

NRA Federal Firearms Laws—A 28-page booklet digesting the several U.S. gun laws affecting the citizen today. Free to NRA members.[2]

NRA Firearms & Ammunition Fact Book—352-page book of questions and answers, ballistic charts and tables, descriptions of firearms and ammunition. NRA, Washington, D.C., 1964. $2.00 ea. ($1.75 to NRA members).

NRA Firearms Assembly Handbook, Volumes I and II—Articles describing the assembly and disassembly of various arms. Vol. I, 160 pp., covers 77 guns, Vol. II, 176 pp., 87 guns. Illustrated with exploded-view and supplementary drawings. NRA, Washington, D.C., 1960 and 1964. $3.50 ea. (2.50 to NRA members).

NRA Firearms Handling Handbook—21 major articles on the proper useage of most types of small arms available to civilians. Illus. NRA, Washington, D.C., 1962, 80 pp. $2.75 ($1.75 to NRA members).

NRA Gun Collectors Handbook—20 feature articles on all phases of gun collecting, plus a listing of all important museums. NRA, Washington, D.C., 1959. 48 pp., illus. $2.50 ($1.50 to NRA members).

NRA Handloader's Guide—Enlarged & Revised. A successor to the *NRA Illustrated Reloading Handbook*, this excellent new work covers all aspects of metallic-case and shotshell reloading. Washington, D. C., 1969, fully illus. $5.00 (NRA members, $4.00).

NRA Hunters Handbook—51 major pieces, 18 shorter ones. NRA, Washington, D.C., 1960. 72 pp., illus. $3.00 ($2.00 to NRA members).

NRA Illustrated International Shooting Handbook—18 major articles detailing shooting under ISU rules, training methods, etc. NRA, Washington, D.C., 1964. $2.50 ea. ($1.50 to NRA members).

NRA Illustrated Shotgun Handbook—50 articles covering every phase of smoothbore shooting, including exploded views of many shotguns. NRA, Washington, D.C. 1964. 128 pp. $3.00 ea. ($2.00 to NRA members).

NRA Questions and Answers Handbook—150 queries and replies on guns and shooting. NRA, Washington, D.C., 1959. 46 pp. with index, illus. $2.50 ($1.50 to NRA members).

NRA Shooters Guide—40 articles of high interest to shooters of all kinds. Over 340 illus. NRA, Washington, D.C., 1959. 72 pp., $3.00 ($2.00 to NRA members).

NRA Shooting Handbook—83 major articles plus 35 shorts on every phase of shooting. NRA, Washington, D.C., 1961. 224 pp., illus. $4.50 ($3.50 to NRA members).

Principles of Game Management—A 25-page booklet surveying in popular manner such subjects as hunting regulations, predator control, game refuges and habitat restoration. Single copies free, 15¢ each in bulk.[4]

The Ring-Necked Pheasant—Popular distillation of much of the technical literature on the "ringneck." 104-page paperbound book, appropriately illustrated. Bibliography included. $1.00 ea.[4]

Ruffed Grouse, by John Madson—108-page booklet on the life history, management and hunting of *Bonasa umbellus* in its numerous variations. Extensive biblio. $1.00.[4]

Start A Gun Club—All of the basic information needed to establish a club with clay bird shooting facilities. 24 pp. 50¢[1]

Where To Shoot Muzzle Loaders In The U.S.A.—Publ. for black powder burners, and lists more than 100 muzzle loading clubs. 10¢.[1]

The White-Tailed Deer—History, management, hunting—a complete survey in this 108-page paperbound book. Full bibliography. $1.00 ea.[4]

You and Your Lawmaker—A 22-page citizenship manual for sportsmen, showing how they can support or combat legislation affecting shooting and outdoor sports. 10¢ ea.[1]

[2]National Rifle Association of America, 1600 Rhode Island Ave., Washington, D. C. 20036

[3]Remington Arms Company, Dept. C—Bridgeport, Conn. 06602

[4]Olin Mathieson Conservation Dept., East Alton, Ill. 62024

[1]National Shooting Sports Foundation, Inc. 1075 Post Road, Riverside, Conn. 06878

Publishers: Please send review copies to John T. Amber, 20604 Collins Rd., Marengo, Ill. 60152

Directory of the Arms Trade

Zip Code Abbreviations

Alaska	AK	Kentucky	KY	North Dakota	ND
Alabama	AL	Louisiana	LA	Ohio	OH
Arizona	AZ	Maine	ME	Oklahoma	OK
Arkansas	AR	Maryland	MD	Oregon	OR
California	CA	Massachusetts	MA	Pennsylvania	PA
Canal Zone	CZ	Michigan	MI	Puerto Rico	PR
Colorado	CO	Minnesota	MN	Rhode Island	RI
Connecticut	CT	Mississippi	MS	South Carolina	SC
Delaware	DE	Missouri	MO	South Dakota	SD
District of Columbia	DC	Montana	MT	Tennessee	TN
Florida	FL	Nebraska	NB	Texas	TX
Georgia	GA	Nevada	NV	Utah	UT
Guam	GU	New Hampshire	NH	Vermont	VT
Hawaii	HI	New Jersey	NJ	Virginia	VA
Idaho	ID	New Mexico	NM	Virgin Islands	VI
Illinois	IL	New York	NY	Washington	WA
Indiana	IN	North Carolina	NC	West Virginia	WV
Iowa	IA			Wisconsin	WI
Kansas	KS			Wyoming	WY

AMMUNITION (Commercial)

Alcan Shells, (See: Smith & Wesson Ammunition Co.)
Cascade Cartridge Inc., (See Omark)
DWM (see RWS)
Dynamit Nobel of America, Inc., 105 Stonehurst Ct., Northvale, NJ 07647 (DWM, RWS)
Federal Cartridge Co., 2700 Foshay Tower, Minneapolis, Minn. 55402
Frontier Cartridge Co., Inc., Box 1848, Grand Island, Neb. 68801
Omark-CCI, Inc., Box 856, Lewiston, Ida. 83501
RWS (see Dynamit Nobel)
Remington Arms Co., Bridgeport, Conn. 06602
Service Armament, 689 Bergen Blvd., Ridgefield, N.J. 07657
Smith & Wesson Ammunition Co., 3640 Seminary Rd., Alton, IL 62002
Super-Vel Cartridge Co., Box 40, Shelbyville, Ind. 46176
Weatherby's, 2781 E. Firestone Blvd., South Gate, Calif. 90280
Winchester-Western, East Alton, Ill. 62024

AMMUNITION (Custom)

Ed Agramonte, Inc., 41 Riverdale Ave., Yonkers, NY 10701
Ammodyne, Box 1589, Los Angeles, Calif. 90053
Bill Ballard, P.O. Box 656, Billings, Mont. 59103
Caldwell's Loading Serv., 1314 Monroe Dr., N.E., Atlanta, Ga. 30306
Russell Campbell, 219 Leisure Dr., San Antonio, Tex. 78201
Collectors Shotshell Arsenal, 365 S. Moore, Lakewood, CO 80226
Cumberland Arms, 1222 Oak Dr., Manchester, Tenn. 37355
Custom Ammo & Gunsmithing, 2325 E. 15th St., Farmington, NM 87401
J. Dewey Gun Co., Clinton Corners, N.Y. 12514
E. W. Ellis Sport Shop, RFD 1, Box 139, Corinth, N.Y. 12822
Ellwood Epps (Orillia) Ltd., Hwy. 11 North, Orillia, Ont., Canada
David J. Gaida, 1109 S. Millwood, Wichita, KS 67203
R. H. Keeler, 1304 S. Oak, Port Angeles, Wash. 98362
KTW Inc., 710 Cooper-Foster Pk. Rd., Lorain, O. 44053 (bullets)
Dean Lincoln, P.O. Box 1886, Farmington, NM 87401
Pat B. McMillan, 1828 E. Campo Bello Dr., Phoenix, Ariz. 85022
Mansfield Gunshop, Box 83, New Boston, N.H. 03070
Man-Tol Shells, Box 134, Bunnell, Fla. 32010
Numrich Arms Corp., 203 Broadway, W. Hurley, N.Y. 12491
Robert Pomeroy, Morrison Ave., East Corinth, ME 04427 (custom shells)
A. F. Sailer, 707 W. 3d St., Owen, WI 54460
Sanders Cust. Gun Serv., 2358 Tyler Lane, Louisville, Ky. 40205
Shooter's Service & Dewey, Inc., Clinton Corners, N.Y. 12514
Geo. Spence, Box 333, Steele, MO 63877 (box-primed cartridges)
3-D Co., Inc., 6020 Colfax, Lincoln, NB 68507
James C. Tillinghast, Box 568, Marlow, N.H. 03456
Whitney Cartridge Co., P.O. Box 608, Cortez, CO 81321 (shotshells)
H. Winter Cast Bullets, 422 Circle Dr., Clarksville, TN 37040

AMMUNITION (Foreign)

Abercrombie & Fitch, Madison at 45th St., New York, N.Y. 10017
Canadian Ind. Ltd. (C.I.L.), Box 10, Montreal, Que., Canada
C-I-L Ammunition Inc., P.O. Box 831, Plattsburgh, N.Y. 12901
Colonial Ammunition Co., Box 8511, Auckland, New Zealand
DWM, Speer Prods. Inc., Box 896, Lewiston, Ida. 83501

Dynamit Nobel of America, Inc., 105 Stonehurst Court, Northvale, NJ 07647 (RWS)
Gevelot of Canada, Box 1593, Saskatoon, Sask., Canada
Hy-Score Arms Co., 200 Tillary, Brooklyn, N.Y. 11201
Paul Jaeger Inc., 211 Leedom St., Jenkintown, Pa. 19046
S. E. Laszlo, 200 Tillary, Brooklyn, N.Y. 11201
L.E.S., 3642 Dempster, Skokie, IL 60076 (Hirtenberg)
NORMA-Precision, South Lansing, N.Y. 14882
Oregon Ammo Service, Box 19341, Portland, Ore. 97219
RWS (Rheinische-Westfalische Sprengstoff) see: Stoeger
Stoeger Arms Corp., 55 Ruta Ct., So. Hackensack, N.J. 07606 (RWS)
James C. Tillinghast, Box 568, Marlow, N.H. 03456

AMMUNITION COMPONENTS—BULLETS, POWDER, PRIMERS

Accuracy Bullet Co., 2443 41st St., San Francisco, Calif. 94116 (Perfecast bullets)
Alcan, (see: Smith & Wesson Ammunition Co.)
Ammo-O-Mart, P.O. Box 66, Hawkesbury, Ont., Canada (Curry bullets)
Austin Power Co. (see Red Diamond Dist. Co.)
Bahler Die Shop, Box 386, Florence, Ore. 97439 (17 cal. bull.)
Lee Baker, 10314 Langmuir Ave., Sunland, CA 91040 (17 cal. bull.)
Joe J. Balickie, 6108 Deerwood Pl., Raleigh, NC 27607
Ballistic Research Industries, see: S & W-Fiocchi (12 ga. Sabot bullets)
Bitterroot Bullet Co., Box 412, Lewiston, Ida. 83501
The Bullet Boys, Box 367, Jaffrey, NH 03452 (cast bullets)
Centrix, 2116 N. 10th Ave., Tucson, Ariz. 85705
Kenneth E. Clark, 18738 Highway 99, Madera, CA 93637 (Bullets)
Colorado Custom Bullets, Rt. 1, Box 507-B, Montrose, Colo. 81401
Curry Bullets Canada, P.O. Box 66, Hawkesbury, Ont., Canada
Division Lead, 7742 W. 61 Pl., Summit, Ill. 60502
DuPont, Explosives Dept., Wilmington, Del. 19898
Elk Mountain Shooters Supply, Star Route, Box 1157, Pasco, WA 99301 (Alaskan bullets)
Farmer Bros. Mfg. Co., 1102 Washington St., Eldora, IA 50627 (Lage shotshell wads)
Forty Five Ranch Enterprises, 119 S. Main, Miami, Okla. 74354
Godfrey Reloading Supply, R.R. 1, Box 688, Brighton, Ill. 62012 (cast bullets)
Lynn Godfrey, see: Elk Mtn. Shooters Supply
G. J. Godwin, 455 Fox Lane, Orange Park, Fla. 32073 (cast bullets)
Green Bay Bullets, 233 No. Ashland, Green Bay, Wis. 54303 (lead)
Frank A. Hemsted, Box 281, Sunland, Calif. 91040
Hercules Powder Co., 910 Market St., Wilmington, Del. 19899
Herter's Inc., Waseca, Minn. 56093
Hi-Precision Co., 109 Third Ave., N.E., Orange City, Ia. 51041
B. E. Hodgdon, Inc., 7710 W. 50th Hwy., Shawnee Mission, Kans. 66202
Hornady Mfg. Co., Box 1848, Grand Island, Neb. 68801
N. E. House Co., Middletown Rd., E. Hampton, Conn. 06424 (zinc bases only)
David Ingram, Box 4263, Long Beach, CA 90804 (17/20 cal. bullets)
Jurras Munition Corp., Box 140, Shelbyville, Ind. 46176
Kush Plastics, P.O. Box 366, Palatine, IL 60067 (shotshell wads)
L. L. F. Die Shop, 1281 Highway 99 North, Eugene, Ore. 97402
LAGE wads, see Farmer Bros.
Lee's Precision Bullets, 10314 Langmuir Ave., Sunland, CA 91040 (17 cal.)
Ljutic Ind., Inc., Box 2117, Yakima, WA 98902 (Mono-wads)
Lomont Precision Bullets, 4425 Fairfield, Ft. Wayne, IN 46807

Lyman Gun Sight Products, Middlefield, Conn. 06455
Markell, Inc., 4115 Judah St., San Francisco, Calif. 94112
Meyer Bros. Mfgrs., Wabasha, Minn. 55981 (shotgun slugs)
Michael's Antiques, Box 233, Copiague, L.I., NY 11726 (Balle Blondeau)
Miller Trading Co., 20 S. Front St., Wilmington, N.C. 28401
G. E. Murphy, 2443-41 Ave., San Francisco, CA 94116 (Acc. Perfecast bullets)
Norma-Precision, So. Lansing, N.Y. 14882
Northridge Bullet Co., P.O. Box 1208, Vista, Ca. 92083
Nosler Bullets, P.O. Box 688, Beaverton, OR 97005
Oregon Ammo Service, Box 19341, Portland, Ore. 97219
Pattern Perfect, P.O. Box 366, Palatine, IL 60067 (shotshell wads)
Robert Pomeroy, Morrison Ave., East Corinth, ME 04427
Red Diamond Distributing Co., 1304 Snowdon Dr., Knoxville, TN 37912 (black powder)
Remington-Peters, Bridgeport, Conn. 06602
Sanderson's, 724 W. Edgewater, Portage, Wis. 53901 (cork wad)
Sierra Bullets Inc., 421 No. Altadena Dr., Pasadena, Ca. 91107
Sisk Bullet Co., Box 874, Iowa Park, TX 76367
Smith & Wesson Ammunition Co., 3640 Seminary Rd., Alton, IL 62002
Speedy Bullets, Box 1262, Lincoln, Neb. 68501
Speer Products Inc., Box 896, Lewiston, Ida. 83501
C. H. Stocking, Rte. 3, Hutchinson, Minn. 55350 (17 cal. bullet jackets)
Super-Vel Cartr. Corp., 129 E. Franklin St., Shelbyville, Ind. 46176
Taylor Bullets, P.O. Box 21254, San Antonio, Tex. 78221
James C. Tillinghast, Box 568, Marlow, N.H. 03456
Vitt & Boos, Sugarloaf Dr., Wilton, Conn. 06897
Winchester-Western, New Haven, Conn. 06504
F. Wood, Box 386, Florence, Ore. 97439 (17 cal.)
Xelex Ltd., Hawksbury, Ont., Canada (powder, Curry bullets)
Zero Bullet Co., P.O. Box 1012, Cullman, AL 35055

ANTIQUE ARMS DEALERS

Robert Abels, P.O. Box 428, Hopewell Junction, NY 12533 (Catalog $1.00)
Ed Agramonte, Inc., 41 Riverdale Ave., Yonkers, NY 10701
F. Bannerman Sons, Inc., Box 126, L.I., Blue Point, NY 11715
Wm. Boggs, 1243 Grandview Ave., Columbus, Ohio 43212
Ellwood Epps (Orillia) Ltd., Hwy. 11 North, Orillia, Ont., Canada
Farris Muzzle Guns, 1610 Gallia St., Portsmouth, Ohio 45662
A. A. Fidd, Diamond Pt. Rd., Diamond Pt., N.Y. 12824
N. Flayderman & Co., Squash Hollow, New Milford, Conn. 06776
Fulmer's Antique Firearms, Rte. #3, Detroit Lakes, MN 56501
Herb Glass, Bullville, N.Y. 10915
Goergen's Gun Shop, 707 8th St. S.E., Austin, MN 55912
Gold Rush Guns, P.O. Box 33, Afton, VA 22921
Goodman's for Guns, 1101 Olive St., St. Louis, Mo. 63101
Griffin's Guns & Antiques, R.R. 4, Peterboro, Ont., Canada K9J 6X5
The Gun Shop, 6497 Pearl Rd., Cleveland, O. 44130
Hansen & Company, 244 Old Post Rd., Southport, CT 06490
Heritage Firearms Co., 27 Danbury Rd., Rte. 7, Wilton, Conn 06897
Holbrook Arms Museum, 12953 Biscayne Blvd., N. Miami, Fla. 33161
Ed Howe, 2 Main, Coopers Mills, Me. 04341
Jackson Arms, 6209 Hillcrest Ave., Dallas, Tex. 75205
Jerry's Gun Shop, 9220 Ogden Ave., Brookfield, Ill. 60513
Kenfix Co., 3500 E. Hillsborough Ave., Tampa, FL 33610
Lever Arms Serv. Ltd., 771 Dunsmuir St., Vancouver 1, B.C., Canada
Wm. M. Locke, 3607 Ault Pk. Rd., Cincinnati, O. 45208
John J. Malloy, Briar Ridge Rd., Danbury, Conn. 06810
Charles W. Moore, R.D. 2, Schenevus, N.Y. 12155
Museum of Historical Arms, 1038 Alton Rd., Miami Beach, Fla. 33139
National Gun Traders, Inc., 225 S.W. 22nd Ave., Miami, Fla. 33135
New Orleans Arms Co., Inc., 240 Chartres St., New Orleans, La. 70130
Old West Gun Room, 3509 Carlson Blvd., El Cerrito, Cal. 94530 (write for list)
Pioneer Guns, 5228 Montgomery, Cincinnati (Norwood), OH 45212
Powell & Clements Sporting Arms, 210 E. 6th St., Cincinnati, O. 45202
Glode M. Requa, Box 35, Monsey, N.Y. 10952
Martin B. Retting Inc., 11029 Washington, Culver City, Calif. 90230
Ridge Guncraft, Inc., 234 N. Tulane Ave., Oak Ridge, Tenn. 37830
S.G. Intl., P.O. Box 702, Hermosa Beach, CA. 90254
Safari Outfitters Ltd., 71 Ethan Allen Highway, Ridgefield, CT 06877
San Francisco Gun Exch., 124 Second St., San Francisco, Calif. 94105
Santa Ana Gunroom, P.O. Box 1777, Santa Ana, Calif. 92702
Ward & Van Valkenburg, 402-30th Ave. No., Fargo, N. Dak. 58102
M. C. Wiest, 234 N. Tulane Ave., Oak Ridge, Tenn. 37830
Yale's Gun Shop, R.D. 1, Box 133, Bel Air, MD 21014
Yeck Antique Firearms, 579 Tecumseh, Dundee, Mich. 48131

BOOKS (ARMS), Publishers and Dealers

CB Press, Box 4087, Bartonville, IL 61607
Digest Books, Inc., 540 Frontage Rd., Northfield, IL 60093
Norm Flayderman, RFD 2, Squash Hollow, New Milford, CT 06776
Handgun Press, 5832 S. Green, Chicago, IL 60621
Johnson's Book Service, 9 Hill Place, Stoney Creek, Ont., Canada
Normount Technical Publications, P.O. Drawer N-2, Wickesburg, AZ 85358
Personal Firearms Record Book, Box 201, Park Ridge, IL 60068
Ray Riling Arms Books Co., 6844 Gorsten St., Philadelphia, PA 19119
Rutgers, Mark Aziz, 127 Raritan Ave., Highland Park, NJ 08904

BULLET & CASE LUBRICANTS

Alpha-Molykote, Dow Corning Corp., 45 Commerce Dr., Trumbull, Ct. 06601
Birchwood-Casey Co., Inc., 7900 Fuller Rd., Eden Prairie, Minn. 55343 (Anderol)
Bullet Pouch, Box 4285, Long Beach, Calif. 90804 (Mirror-Lube)

Chopie Mfg. Inc., 531 Copeland, La Crosse, Wis. 54601 (Black-Solve)
Cooper-Woodward, Box 972, Riverside, Cal. 92502 (Perfect Lube)
Green Bay Bullets, 233 N. Ashland, Green Bay, Wis. 54303 (EZE-Size case lube)
Herter's, Inc., Waseca, Minn. 56903 (Perfect Lubricant)
IPCO (Industrial Products Co.), Box 14, Bedford, MA 01730
Javelina Products, Box 337, San Bernardino, Cal. 92402 (Alox beeswax)
Jet-Aer Corp., 100 Sixth Ave., Paterson, N.J. 07524
Lenz Prod. Co., Box 1226, Sta. C, Canton, O. 44708 (Clenzoil)
Lyman Gun Sight Products, Middlefield, Conn. 06455 (Size-Ezy)
Micro Shooter's Supply, Box 213, Las Cruces, N. Mex. 88001 (Micro-Lube)
Mirror Lube, American Spl. Lubricants, Box 4275, Long Beach, CA 90804
Nutec, Box 1187, Wilmington, Del. 19899 (Dry-Lube)
Pacific Tool Co., P.O. Drawer 2048, Ordnance Plant Rd., Grand Island, NB 68801
Phelps Rel. Inc., Box 4004, E. Orange, N.J. 07019
RCBS, Inc., Box 1919, Oroville, Calif. 95965
SAECO Rel. Inc., 726 Hopmeadow St., Simsbury, Conn. 06070
Scientific Lubricants Co., 3753 Lawrence Ave., Chicago, Ill. 60625
Shooters Accessory Supply (SAS), Box 250, N. Bend, Ore. 97459
Sports Distr. Co., Rte. 1, Rapid City, S.D. 57701 (Reloader No. 7)
Testing Systems, Inc., 2832 Mt. Carmel, Glenside, PA 19038

BULLET SWAGE DIES AND TOOLS

Bahler Die Shop, Box 386/412 Hemlock St., Florence, OR 97439
Belmont Products, Rte. #1, Friendsville, TN 37737
C-H Tool & Die Corp., P.O. Box L, Owen, WI 54460
Clymer Mfg. Co., 14241 W. 11 Mile Rd., Oak Park, MI 48237
Lester Coats, 416 Simpson St., North Bend, OR 97459 (lead wire cutter)
Hemp Dies, Frank A. Hemsted, P.O. Box 281, Sunland, CA 91040
Herter's Inc., Waseca, MN 56093
Hollywood, Whitney Sales Inc., P.O. Box 875, Reseda, CA 91335
Independent Machine & Gun Shop, 1416 N. Hayes, Pocatello, ID 83201 (TNT)
L.L.F. Die Shop, 1281 Highway 99 North, Eugene, OR 97402
Rorschach Precision Products, P.O. Box 1613, Irving, TX 75060
SAS Dies, P.O. Box 250, North Bend, OR 97459
Robert B. Simonson, Rte. 2, 2129 Vanderbilt Rd., Kalamazoo, MI 49002
TNT (see Ind. Mach. & Gun Shop)

CARTRIDGES FOR COLLECTORS

Antique Arsenal, 365 So. Moore St., Lakewood, Colo. 80226
J. A. Belton, 52 Sauve Rd., Mercier, Chateauguay Cty, Quebec, Canada
Peter Bigler, 291 Crestwood Dr., Milltown, N.J. 08850 (ctlg. $1.50)
Geo. Blakeslee, 3135 W. 28th St., Denver, CO 80211
Cameron's, 16690 W. 11th Ave., Golden, Colo. 80401
Carter Gun Works, 2211 Jefferson Pk. Ave., Charlottesville, Va. 22903
Gerry Coleman, 163 Arkell St., Hamilton, Ont., Canada
Chas. E. Duffy, Williams Lane, West Hurley, N.Y. 12419
Tom M. Dunn, 1342 So. Poplar, Casper, Wyo. 82601
Ellwood Epps (Orillia) Ltd., Hwy. 11 North, Orillia, Ont., Canada
Ed Howe, 2 Main St., Coopers Mills, Me. 04341
Walt Ireson, 47 Chedoke Ave., Hamilton 12, Ont., Canada
Jackson Arms, 6209 Hillcrest Ave., Dallas, Tex. 75205
George Kass, 30 Ivy Circle, West Haven, CT 06516
Oregon Ammo Service, Box 19341, Portland, Ore. 97219 (catlg. $2.00)
Powder Horn, 3135 W. 28th, Denver, CO 80211
Martin B. Retting, Inc., 11029 Washington, Culver City, Calif. 90230
San Francisco Gun Exchange, 124 Second St., San Francisco, CA 94105
Perry Spangler, 519 So. Lynch, Flint, Mich. 48503 (list 50¢)
Ernest Tichy, 365 S. Moore, Lakewood, Colo. 80226
James C. Tillinghast, Box 568, Marlow, N.H. 03456 (list 50c)

CASES, CABINETS AND RACKS—GUN

Alco Carrying Cases Inc., 601 W. 26th St., New York, N.Y. 10001
Artistic Wood Specialties, 923-29 W. Chicago Ave., Chicago, Ill. 60622
Morton Booth Co., Box 123, Joplin, Mo. 64801
Boyt Co., Div. of Welsh Sportg. Gds., Box 1108, Iowa Falls, Ia. 50126
Brewster Corp., Old Lyme, Conn. 06371
Browning, Rt. 4, Box 624-B, Arnold, MO 63010
Cap-Lex Gun Cases, Capitol Plastics of Ohio, Inc., 333 Van Camp Rd., Bowling Green, OH 43402
Castle Westchester Prods. Co., Inc., 498 Nepperhan Ave., Yonkers, N.Y. 10701
Challanger Mfg. Co., 118 Pearl St., Mt. Vernon, NY 10550
Cincinnati Ind. Inc., (Cindus), Cincinnati (Lockland), O. 45215
Coladonato Bros., Box 156, Hazleton, Pa. 18201
Do-All Mfg. Co., 3206 Plant Dr., Boise, ID 83703
E & C Enterprises, P.O. Box 823, So. Pasadena, CA 91030 (gun socks)
East-Tenn Mills, Inc., Box 1030, Johnson City, TN 37601 (gun socks)
Ellwood Epps (Orillia) Ltd., Hwy. 11 North, Orillia, Ont., Canada
Farber Bros., Inc., 821 Linden Ave., Memphis, Tenn. 38101 (truck pouch)
Ferrell Co., Rte. 3, Gallatin, Tenn. 37066 (Redi-Rack)
Flambeau Plastics Corp., 801 Lynn, Baraboo, Wis. 53913
Gun-Ho Case Mfg. Co., 110 East 10th St., St. Paul, Minn. 55101
Gun Racks, Inc., P.O. Box 22675, Houston, Tex. 77027
B. E. Hodgdon, Inc., 7710 W. 50 Hiway, Shawnee-Mission, Kans. 66202
Ithaca Gun Co., Terrace Hill, Ithaca, N.Y. 14850
J-K Imports, Box 403, Novato, Cal. 94947 (leg 'o mutton case)
Jumbo Sports Prods., P.O. Box 280-Airport Rd., Frederick, MD 21701
Kolpin Bros. Co., Inc., Box 231, Berlin, Wis. 54923
Marble Arms Corp., 420 Industrial Park, Gladstone, Mich. 49837
W. A. Miller Co., Inc. (Wamco), Mingo Loop, Oguossoc, ME 04964 (wooden handgun cases)
National Sports Div., 19 E. McWilliams St., Fond du Lac, Wis. 54935

Nortex Co., 2821 Main St., Dallas, Tex. 75226 (automobile gun rack)
North Star Devices, Inc., P.O. Box 2095, North St., Paul, MN 55109 (Gun-Slinger portable rack)
Paul-Reed, Inc., P.O. Box 227, Charlevoix, Mich. 49720
Penguin Industries, Inc., Box 97, Parkesburg, Pa. 19365
Precise Imp. Corp., 3 Chestnut, Suffern, N.Y. 10901
Protecto Plastics, Inc., 201 Alpha Rd., Wind Gap, Pa. 18091 (carrying cases)
Richland Arms Co., 321 W. Adrian, Blissfield, Mich. 49228
Saf-T-Case, Box 10592, Dallas, Tex. 75207
San Angelo Die Castings, Box 984, San Angelo, Tex. 76901
Buddy Schoellkopf, 4100 Platinum Way, Dallas, Tex. 75237
Sile Distr., 7 Centre Market Pl., New York, N.Y. 10013 (leg o'mutton case)
Stearn Mfg. Co., Div. & 30th St., St. Cloud, Minn. 56301
Tread Corp., P.O. Box 5497, Roanoke, VA 24012 (security gun chest)
Western Holder Co., Box 33, Menomonee Falls, Wis. 53051
Woodstream Corp., Box 327, Lititz, Pa. 17543
Yield House, Inc., RFD, No. Conway, N.H. 03860

CHOKE DEVICES & RECOIL ABSORBERS

Arms Ingenuity Co., Box 1, Weatogue, Conn. 06089 (Jet-Away)
Contra-Jet, 7920 49th Ave. So., Seattle, Wash. 98118
Dahl's Gun Shop, Rt. 2, Billings, Mont. 59101
Diverter Arms, Inc., 6520 Rampart St., Houston, TX 77036 (shotgun diverter)
Edwards Recoil Reducer, 269 Herbert St., Alton, Ill. 62002
Emsco Chokes, 101 Second Ave., S.E., Waseca, Minn. 56093
Herter's Inc., Waseca, Minn. 56093. (Vari-Choke)
Lyman Gun Sight Products, Middlefield, Conn. 06455 (Cutts Comp.)
Mag-Na-Port Arms, Inc., 34341 Groesbeck, Fraser, MI 48026 (muzzle-brake system)
Pendleton Dekickers, 1210 S. W. Hailey Ave., Pendleton, Ore. 97801
Poly-Choke Co., Inc., Box 296, Hartford, Conn. 06101
St. Louis Precision Products, 902 Michigan Ave., St. Louis, Mich. 48880 (Gun-Tamer)

CHRONOGRAPHS AND PRESSURE TOOLS

Avtron, 10409 Meech Ave., Cleveland, Ohio, 44105
B-Square Co., Box 11281, Ft. Worth, Tex. 76110
Chronograph Specialists, P.O. Box 5005, Santa Ana, Calif. 92704
Display Electronics, Box 1044, Littleton, CO 80120
Diverter Arms, Inc., 6520 Rampart St., Houston, TX 77036 (press. tool)
Herter's, Waseca, Minn. 56093
Micro-Sight Co., 242 Harbor Blvd., Belmont, Calif. 94002 (Techsonic)
Oehler Research, P.O. Box 9135, Austin, Tex. 78756
Sundtek Co., P.O. Box 744, Springfield, Ore. 97477
Telepacific Electronics Co., Inc., 3335 W. Orange Ave., Anaheim, CA 92804
M. York, 19381 Keymar Way, Gaithersburg, MD 20760 (press. tool)

CLEANING & REFINISHING SUPPLIES

ADSCO, Box 191, Ft. Kent, Me. 04743 (stock finish)
Allied Products Co., 734 N. Leavitt, Chicago, Ill. 60612 (Cor-O-Dex)
Armite Labs., 1845 Randolph St., Los Angeles, CA 90001 (pen oiler)
Armoloy, 206 E. Daggett St., Ft. Worth, TX 76104
Backus Co., 411 W. Water St., Smethport, Pa. 16749 (field gun-cleaner)
Ber Big Enterprises, P.O. Box 291, Huntington, CA 90255 (gunsoap)
Birchwood-Casey Chem. Co., 7900 Fuller Rd., Eden Prairie, Minn. 55343 (Anderol, etc.)
Bisonite Co., Inc., 2250 Military Rd., Tonwanda, NY 14150
Jim Brobst, 299 Poplar St., Hamburg, Pa. 19526 (J-B Compound)
Geo. Brothers, Great Barrington, Mass. 01230 (G-B Linspeed Oil)
Browning Arms, Rt. 4, Box 624-B, Arnold, Mo. 63010
J. M. Bucheimer Co., Airport Rd., Frederick, MD 21701
Bullet Pouch, Box 4285, Long Beach, Cal. 90804 (Mirror Lube)
Burnishine Prod. Co., 8140 N. Ridgeway, Skokie, Ill. 60076 (Stock Glaze)
C & R Distr. Corp., 449 E. 21st So., Salt Lake City, Utah 84115
Cherry Corners Mfg. Co., 11136 Congress Rd., Lodi, Ohio 44254 (buffing compound)
Chopie Mfg. Inc., 531 Copeland, La Crosse, Wis. 54601 (Black-Solve)
Clenzoil Co., Box 1226, Sta. C, Canton, O. 44708
Craftsman Wood Serv. Co., 2729 S. Mary, Chicago, Ill. 60608 (ctlg. 50¢)
Dex-Kleen, Box 509, Des Moines, Ia. 50302 (gun wipers)
J. Dewey Gun Co., Clinton Corners, N.Y. 12514
Dri-Slide, Inc., Industrial Park, Fremont, Mich. 49412
Forty-Five Ranch Enterpr., 119 S. Main St., Miami, Okla. 74354
Garcia Sptg. Arms Corp., 329 Alfred Ave., Teaneck, N.J. 07666
Gun-All Products, Box 244, Dowagiac, Mich. 49047
Percy Harms Corp., 7349 N. Hamlin, Skokie, Ill. 60076
Frank C. Hoppe Div., P.O. Box 97, Parkesburg, Pa. 19365
Hunting World, 247 E. 50th St., N.Y. 10022 (P-H Safari Kit)
J & G Rifle Ranch, Turner, MT 59542
Jet-Aer Corp., 100 Sixth Ave., Paterson, N.J. 07524 (blues & oils)
K.W. Kleinendorst, 48 Taylortown Rd., Montville, N.J. 07045 (rifle clg. rods)
Knox Laboratories, 2335 S. Michigan Ave., Chicago, Ill. 60616
LPS Res. Labs. Inc., 2050 Cotner Ave., Los Angeles, Calif. 90025
Carl Lampert Co., 2639 So. 31st St., Milwaukee, Wis. 53215 (gun bags)
LEM Gun Spec., Box 31, College Park, Ga. 30337 (Lewis Lead Remover)
Liquid Wrench, Box 10628, Charlotte, N.C. 28201 (pen. oil)
Lynx Line Gun Prods. Div., Protective Coatings, Inc., 20626 Fenkell Ave., Detroit, MI 48223
Marble Arms Co., 420 Industrial Pk., Gladstone, Mich. 49837
Micro Sight Co., 242 Harbor Blvd., Belmont, Ca. 94002 (bedding)
Mill Run Prod., 1360 W. 9th, Cleveland, O. 44113 (Brite-Bore Kits)
Mint Luster Cleaners, 1102 N. Division, Appleton, Wis. 54911

Mirror-Lube Div., Amer. Spec. Lubricants, Box 4275, Long Beach, CA 90804
Mistic Metal Mover, Inc., R.R. 2, P.O. Box 336, Princeton, Ill. 61356
Mitchell Chemical Co., Wampus Lane, Milford, CT 06460 (Gun Guard)
New Method Mfg. Co., Box 175, Bradford, Pa. 16701 (gun blue)
Northern Instruments, Inc., 4643 No. Chatsworth St., St. Paul, MN 55112 (Stor-Safe rust preventer)
Numrich Arms Co., West Hurley, N.Y. 12491 (44-40 gun blue)
Nutec, Box 1187, Wilmington, Del. 19899 (Dry-Lube)
Outers Laboratories, Box 37, Onalaska, Wis. 54650 (Gunslick kits)
Radiator Spec. Co., 1400 Independence Blvd., Charlotte, N.C. 28201 (liquid wrench)
Realist Inc., N. 93 W. 16288 Megal Dr., Menomonee Falls, Wis. 53051
Reardon Prod., 323 N. Main St., Roanoke, Ill. 61561 (Dry-Lube)
Reese Arms Co., R.R. 1, Colona, IL 61241 (Dry-film lube)
Rice Dry Film Gun Coatings, 1521-43rd St., West Palm Beach, FL 33407
Riel & Fuller, 423 Woodrow Ave., Dunkirk, N.Y. 14048 (anti-rust oil)
Rig Products Co., Box 279, Oregon, Ill. 61061 (Rig Grease)
Rocket Chemical Co., Inc., 5390 Napa St., San Diego, Calif. 92110 (WD-40)
Rusteprufe Labs., 605 Wolcott St., Sparta, Wis. 54656
Saunders Sptg. Gds., 338 Somerset, No. Plainfield, NJ 07060 (Sav-Bore)
Service Armament, 689 Bergen Blvd., Ridgefield, N. J. 07657 (Parker-Hale)
Sheldon's Inc., Box 508, Antigo, Wis. 54409 (shotgun brushes)
Shooter's Serv. & Dewey (SS&D), Clinton Corners, N.Y. 12514
Silicote Corp., Box 359, Oshkosh, Wis. 54901 (Silicone cloths)
Silver Dollar Guns, P.O. Box 489, Franklin NH 03235 (Silicone oil)
A. D. Soucy, Box 191, Ft. Kent, Me. 04743 (ADSCO stock finish)
Southeastern Coatings, Ind., (SECOA), Bldg. 132, P.B.I. Airport, W. Palm Beach, Fla. 33406 (Teflon Coatings)
Sportsmen's Labs., Inc., Box 732, Anoka, Minn. 55303 (Gun Life lube)
Surcon, Inc., P.O. Box 277, Zieglerville, Pa. 19492
Taylor & Robbins, Box 164, Rixford, Pa. 16745 (Throat Saver)
Testing Systems, Inc., 2832 Mt. Carmel, Glenside, PA 19038 (gun lube)
Texas Platers Supply Co., 2458 W. Five Mile Parkway, Dallas, TX 75233 (plating kit)
C. S. Van Gorden, 120 Tenth Ave., Eau Claire, Wis. 54701 (Instant Blue)
WD-40 Co., 5390 Napa St., San Diego, Ca 92110
W&W Mfg. Co., Box 365, Belton, Mo. 64012 (shotgun cleaner)
West Coast Secoa, Inc., Rt. 5, Box 138, Lakeland, FL 33801 (Teflon coatings)
Williams Gun Sight, 7389 Lapeer Rd., Davison, Mich. 48423 (finish kit)
Winslow Arms Co., P.O. Box 578, Osprey, Fla. 33595 (refinishing kit)
Wisconsin Platers Supply Co., see: Texas Platers Supply Co.
Woodstream Corp., P.O. Box 327, Lititz, Pa. 17543 (Mask)

DECOYS

Carry-Lite, Inc., 3000 W. Clarke, Milwaukee, WI 53245
Deeks, Inc., P.O. Box 2309, Salt Lake City, UT 84114
G & H Decoy Mfg. Co., P.O. Box 937, Henryetta, OK 74437
Tex Wirtz Ent., Inc., 1925 Hubbard St., Chicago, IL 60622
Woodstream Corp., P.O. Box 327, Lititz, PA 17543

ENGRAVERS, ENGRAVING, TOOLS

Austrian Gunworks Reg'd., P.O. Box 136, Eastman, Que., Canada
E. Averill, Rt. 1, 60 Chestnut St., Cooperstown, N.Y. 13326
Joseph Bayer, Sunset Ave., Sunset Hill, RD 1, Princeton, N.J. 08540
Sid Bell, Box 188, Tully, N.Y. 13159
John T. Bickett, 401 Westmark Ave., Colorado Springs, CO 80906
Weldon Bledsoe, 6812 Park Place Dr., Fort Worth. Tex. 76118
Henry D. Bonham, Box 656 (Main St.), Brownville, Me. 04414
Ray Bossi, 3574 University Ave., San Diego, CA 92104
Max E. Bruehl, 781 No. 9th Ave., Canton, Il. 61520
Burgess Vibrocrafters (BVI), Rt. 83, Grayslake, Ill. 60030
Chizar Engr. Serv., 690—12th Ave., San Francisco, Cal. 94118
Joe Condon, 1008 Pyramid, Las Vegas, Nev. 89106
Carl E. Courts, 2421 E. Anaheim St., Long Beach, Cal. 90804
Creative Carvings Inc., R.D. 2, Tully, N.Y. 13159
Bill Dyer, P.O. Box 75255, Oklahoma City, Okla. 73107
Ken Eyster, Heritage Gunsmiths Inc., 6441 Bishop Rd., Centerburg, O. 43011
Ken Flood, 63 Homestead, Stratford, Conn. 06497
Jos. Fugger, c/o Griffin & Howe, 589-8th Ave., N.Y., N.Y. 10017
Donald Glaser, 1520 West St., Emporia, Kans. 66801
Howard V. Grant, P.O. Box 396, Lac Du Flambeau, WI 54538
Griffin & Howe, 589-8th Ave., N.Y., N.Y. 10017
F. R. Gurney, Engraving Methods Ltd., #205 Birks Building, Edmonton, Alberta, Can.
Bryson J. Gwinnell, 2895 Seneca St., Buffalo, NY 14224
Neil Hartliep, Box 733, Fairmont, Minn. 56031
Frank E. Hendricks, Rt. 2, Box 189J, San Antonio, Tex. 78228
Heide Hiptmayer, P.O. Box 136, Eastman, Que., Canada
Bob Izenstark, 101 Wolpers Rd., Park Forest, IL 60466
Paul Jaeger, 211 Leedom, Jenkintown, Pa. 19046
Robert C. Kain, R.F.D. Rte. #30, Newfane, Vermont 05345
T. J. Kaye, 4745 Dellwood, Beaumont, TX 77706
Lance Kelly, P.O. Box 1072, Pompana Beach, Fla. 33061
Kleinguenther's, P.O. Box 1261, Seguin, TX 78155
John Kudlas, 622 14th St. S.E., Rochester, MN 55901
Lynton S.M. McKenzie, 240 Chartres St., New Orleans, La. 70130 (booklet $3.00)
Wm. H. Mains, 2895 Seneca St., Buffalo, N.Y. 14224
Rudy Marek, Rt. 1, Box 1A, Banks, Ore. 97106
Franz Marktl, c/o Davis Gun Shop, 7211 Lee Hwy., Falls Church, VA 22046

S. A. Miller, Central P.O. Box 619, Naha, Okinawa, Japan
Frank Mittermeier, 3577 E. Tremont Ave., New York, N.Y. 10465
New Orleans Jewelers Supply, 206 Chartres St., New Orleans, LA 70130
Albin Obiltschnig, Ferlach, Austria
Pachmayr Gun Works, Inc., 1220 S. Grand Ave., Los Angeles, Calif. 90015
Hans Pfeiffer, 286 Illinois St., Elmhurst, IL 60126
E. C. Prudhomme, 302 Ward Bldg., Shreveport, La. 71101
John R. Rohner, Sunshine Canyon, Boulder, Colo. 80302
Robert P. Runge, 94 Grove St., Ilion, N.Y. 13357
Shaw-Leibowitz, Rt. 1, Box 421, New Cumberland, W.Va. 26047 (etchers)
Russell J. Smith, 231 Springdale Rd., Westfield, Mass. 01085
Robt. Swartley, 2800 Pine St., Napa, Calif. 94559
Ray Viramontez, 5258 Robinwood, Dayton, O. 45431
Floyd E. Warren, Rt. 3, Box 87, Cortland, O. 44410
John E. Warren, P.O. Box 72, Eastham, Mass. 02642
A. A. White Engr., Inc., P.O. Box 68, Manchester, Conn. 06040

GAME CALLS

Black Duck, 1737 Davis, Whiting, Ind. 46394
Burnham Bros., Box 100-C, Marble Falls, Tex. 78654
Electronic Game Calls, Inc., 210 W. Grand, Wisconsin Rapids, Wis. 54494
Faulk's, 616 18th St., Lake Charles, La. 70601
Lohman Mfg. Co., 320 E. Spring, Neosho, Mo. 64850
M. L. Lynch, 306 Edgewood Blvd., Birmingham, Ala. 35209
Mallardtone, 2901 16th St., Moline, Ill. 61265
Edward J. Mehok, 1737 Davis Ave., Whiting, IN 46394
Phil. S. Olt Co., Box 550, Pekin, Ill. 61554
Penn's Woods Products, Inc., 19 W. Pittsburgh St., Delmont, Pa. 15626
Sport-Lore, Inc., 1757 Cherry St., Denver, Colo. 80220
Johnny Stewart Wildlife Calls, Box 7954, Waco, Tex. 76710
Thomas Game Calls, P.O. Box 336, Winnsboro, TX 75494
Weems Wild Calls, Box 7261, Ft. Worth, Tex. 76111
Wightman Electronics, Box 989, Easton, Md. 21601
Wildlife Prod. Inc., Prof. Bldg., 513 East Perkins Ave., Sandusky, Ohio 44870 (Lectro Hunter)
Tex Wirtz Ent., Inc., 1925 W. Hubbard St., Chicago, Ill. 60622

GUNS (Foreign)

Abercrombie & Fitch, Madison at 45th, New York, N.Y. 10017
Alaskan Rifles, Box 30, Juneau, Alaska 99801
American Import Co., 1167 Mission St., San Francisco, Calif. 94103
Armi Fabbri, Casella 206, Brescia, Italy 25100
Armi Famars, Via Cinelli 33, Gardone V.T. (Brescia), Italy 25036
Armoury Inc., Rte. 25, New Preston, Ct. 06777
Atlas Arms, Inc., 7952 Waukegan Rd., Niles, Ill. 60648
Benet Arms Co., Box 33, Afton, Va. 22920
Blumenfeld Co., 80 W. Virginia Ave., Memphis, Tenn. 38100
Browning, Rt. 4, Box 624-B, Arnold, Mo. 63010
Centennial Arms Corp., 3318 W. Devon, Chicago, (Lincolnwood) Ill. 60645
Century Arms Co., 3-5 Federal St., St. Albans, Vt. 05478
Champlin Firearms, Inc., Box 3191, Enid, OK 73701 (Gebruder Merkel)
Connecticut Valley Arms Co., Candlewood Hill Rd., Higganum, CT 06441 (CVA)
Continental Arms Corp., 697 Fifth Ave., New York, N.Y. 10022
W. H. Craig, Box 927, Selma, Ala. 36701
Crusader Arms Co., Box 2801, 800 S. 4th St., Louisville, Ky. 40202
Daiwa, 14011 Normandie Ave., Gardena, CA 90247
Charles Daly, Inc., 90 Chambers St., New York, N.Y. 10007
Davidson Firearms Co., 2703 High Pt. Rd., Greensboro, N.C. 27403 (shotguns)
Davis Gun Shop, 7213 Lee Highway, Falls Church, VA 22046 (Fanzoj, Ferlach; Spanish guns)
Dixie Gun Works, Inc., Hwy 51, South, Union City, Tenn. 38261 ("Kentucky" rifles)
Euroarms, Via Solferino 13/A, 25100 Brescia, Italy
FFV Sports Inc., P.O. Box 195, Billings, NY 12510 (Husqvarna)
J. Fanzoj, P.O. Box 25, Ferlach, Austria 9170
R. C. Fessler & Co., 1634 Colorado Blvd., Los Angeles, Calif. 90041
Firearms Center Inc. (FCI), 113 Spokane, Victoria, TX 77901
Firearms Imp. & Exp. Co., 2470 N.W. 21st St., Miami, Fla. 33142
Firearms International Corp., 515 Kerby Hill Rd., Washington, DC 20022
Flaig's Lodge, Millvale, Pa. 15209
Florida Firearms Corp., P.O. Box 237, Hialeah, FL 33010
Freeland's Scope Stands, Inc., 3737 14th Ave., Rock Island, Ill. 61201
J. L. Galef & Son, Inc., 85 Chambers, New York, N.Y. 10007
Garcia Sptg. Arms Corp., 329 Alfred Ave., Teaneck, N.J. 07666
Gevarm (see Blumenfeld Co.)
Gevelot of Can. Ltd., Box 1593, Saskatoon, Sask., Canada
Gold Rush Guns, Box 33, Afton, Va. 22921 (SIG)
H. F. Grieder, Box 487, Knoxville, Ill. 61448 (Hammerli)
Harrington & Richardson Arms Co., 320 Park Ave., Worcester, Mass. 01610 (HK pistol)
Hawes Firearms Co., 8224 Sunset Blvd., Los Angeles, Calif. 90046
Healthways, Box 45055, Los Angeles, Calif. 90061
A. D. Heller, Inc., Box 268, Grand Ave., Baldwin, NY 11510
Herter's, Waseca, Minn. 56093
Husqvarna, see FFV Sports Inc.
Interarmco, see: Interarms (Walther)
Interarms Ltd., 10 Prince St., Alexandria, Va. 22313 (Mauser)
Intercontinental Arms, 2222 Barry Ave., Los Angeles, Calif. 90064
International Firearms Co., Ltd., Montreal 1, Que., Canada
Ithaca Gun Co., Terrace Hill, Ithaca, N.Y. 14850 (Perazzi)
Italguns, Via Leonardo da Vinci 36, 20090 Zingoni Di Trezzano, Milano, Italy
JBL Arms Co., 4315 Warren St., Davenport, IA 52806
J-K Imports, Box 403, Novato, Cal. 94947 (Italian)
Paul Jaeger Inc., 211 Leedom St., Jenkintown, Pa. 19046

Jana Intl. Co., Box 1107, Denver, Colo. 80201 (Parker-Hale)
J. J. Jenkins, 462 Stanford Pl., Santa Barbara, CA 93105
Guy T. Jones Import Co., 905 Gervais St., Columbia, S. Car. 29201
Kassnar Imports, P.O. Box 3895, Harrisburg, PA 17105
Kleinguenther's, P.O. Box 1261, Seguin, TX 78155
Knight & Knight, 5930 S.W. 48 St., Miami, FL 33155 (made-to-order only)
Krieghoff Gun Co., P.O. Box 48-1367, Miami, FL 33148
L. A. Distributors, 4 Centre Market Pl., New York, N.Y. 10013
Jos. G. Landmann, 2308 Preetz/Holstein, W. Germany (JGL)
S. E. Laszlo, 200 Tillary St., Brooklyn, N.Y. 11201
Lever Arms Serv. Ltd., 771 Dunsmuir, Vancouver 1, B.C., Canada
Liberty Arms Organization, Box 306, Montrose, Calif. 91020
McKeown's Guns, R.R. 1, Pekin, Ill. 61554
McQueen Sales Co. Ltd., 1760 W. 3rd Ave., Vancouver 9, B.C., Canada
Marietta Replica Arms Co., 706½ Montgomery St., Marietta, OH 45750
Marketing Unlimited, Inc., 1 Ranch Rite Rd., Yakima, WN 98901
Marubeni America Corp., 200 Park Ave., New York, NY 10017
Mars Equipment Corp., 3318 W. Devon, Chicago, Ill. 60645
Mauser-Bauer Inc., 34577 Commerce Rd., Fraser, MI 48026
Miida, see: Marubeni
Musgrave Firearms, J. J. Sherban & Co., 2655 Harrison Ave. S.W., Canton, OH 44706
Navy Arms Co., 689 Bergen Blvd., Ridgefield, N.J. 07657
Omnipol, Washingtonova 11, Praha 1, Czechoslovakia
Harry Owen, P.O. Box 774, Sunnyvale, Ca. 94088.
Pachmayr Gun Works, 1220 S. Grand Ave., Los Angeles, Calif. 90015 (Fabbri)
Pacific Intl. Import Co., 2416 - 16th St., Sacramento, CA 91605
Palmetto State, Inc., P.O. Box 4008, Columbia, SC 29204
Parker-Hale, Whittall St., Birmingham 4, England
Ed Paul Sptg. Goods, 172 Flatbush Ave., Brooklyn, N.Y. 11217 (Premier)
Precise Imp. Corp. (PIC), 3 Chestnut, Suffern, N.Y. 10901
Premier Shotguns, 172 Flatbush Ave., Brooklyn N.Y. 11217
J.L. Quick & Son Co., 1301 Laurence St., Birmingham, AL 35210
RG Industries, Inc., 2485 N.W. 20th St., Miami, FL 33142 (Erma)
Richland Arms Co., 321 W. Adrian St., Blissfield, Mich. 49228
Sanderson's, 724 W. Edgewater, Portage, Wis. 53901
Savage Arms Corp., Westfield, Mass. 01085 (Anschutz)
Security Arms Co., 1815 No. Ft. Myer Dr., Arlington, VA 22209 (Heckler & Koch)
Service Armament, 689 Bergen Blvd., Ridgefield, N.J. 07657 (Greener Harpoon Gun)
Sherwood Dist., Inc., 9470 Santa Monica Blvd., Beverly Hills, Ca. 90210
Simmons Spec., Inc., 700 Rogers Rd., Olathe, Kans. 66061
Skinner's Gun Shop (see Alaskan Rifles)
Sloan's Sprtg. Goods, Inc., 88 Chambers St., New York, N.Y. 10001
Solingen Cutlery, Box 306, Montrose, Calif. 91020
Spesco Corp., 3540 Browns Mill Rd. S.E., Atlanta, Ga. 30315
Sportex Intl. Ltd., 10389 W. Olympic Blvd, W. Los Angeles, CA 90064
Stoeger Arms Co., 55 Ruta Ct., S. Hackensack, N.J. 07606
Tradewinds, Inc., P.O. Box 1191, Tacoma, Wash. 98401
Twin City Sptg. Grds., 217 Ehrman Ave., Cincinnati, OH 45220
Universal Firearms Corp., 3746 E. 10th Ct., Hialeah, Fla. 33013
Universal Ordnance Co., P.O. Box 15723, Nashville, TN 37215 (Krieghoff combination guns)
Valor Imp. Corp., 5555 N.W. 36th Ave., Miami, FL 33142
Voere (see Marketing Unlimited)
Waffen-Frankonia, Box 380, 87 Wurzburg, W. Germany
Weatherby's, 2781 Firestone Blvd., So. Gate, Calif. 90280 (Sauer)
Dan Wesson Arms, 293 So. Main, Monson, Mass. 01057
Zavodi Crvena Zastava, 29 Novembra St., No. 12, Belgrade, Yugosl.

GUNS & GUN PARTS, REPLICA AND ANTIQUE

Antique Gun Parts, Inc., 569 So. Braddock Ave., Pittsburgh, Pa. 15221 (ML)
Armoury Inc., Rte. 25, New Preston, Conn. 06777
Artistic Arms, Inc., Box 23, Hoagland, IN 46745 (Sharps-Borchardt replica)
Bannerman, F., Box 126, Blue Point, Long Island, N.Y. 11715
Shelley Braverman, Athens, N.Y. 12015 (obsolete parts)
Carter Gun Works, 2211 Jefferson Pk. Ave., Charlottesville, Va. 22903
Cornwall Bridge Gun Shop, P.O. Box 67, Cornwall Bridge, CT 06754 (parts)
R. MacDonald Champlin, Box 74, Wentworth, N.H. 03282 (replicas)
David E. Cumberland, 3509 Carlson Blvd., El Cerrito, CA 94530 (Replica Gatling guns)
Darr's Rifle Shop, 2309 Black Rd., Joliet, Ill. 60435 (S.S. items)
Dixie Gun Works, Inc., Hwy 51, South, Union City, Tenn. 38261
Federal Ordnance Inc., 9643 Alpaca St., So. El Monte, CA 91733
Kindig's Log Cabin Sport Shop, R.D. 1, P.O. Box 275, Lodi, Ohio 44254
Lever Arms Service Ltd., 771 Dunsmuir, Vancouver, B.C., Canada
Edw. E. Lucas, 32 Garfield Ave., Old Bridge, N.J. 08857 (45-70)
Lyman Gun Sight Products, Middlefield, CT 06455
R. M. Marek, Rt. 1, Box 1-A, Banks Ore. 97106 (cannons)
Numrich Arms Co., West Hurley, N.Y. 12491
Replica Models, Inc., 610 Franklin St., Alexandria, VA 22314
Riflemen's Hdqs., Rt. 3, RD 550-E, Kendallville, IN 46755
S&S Firearms, 88-21 Aubrey Ave., Glendale, N.Y. 11227
C. H. Stoppler, 1426 Walton Ave., New York, NY 10452 (miniature guns)
Rob. Thompson, 1031-5th Ave., N., Clinton, Ia. 52732 (Win. only)
C. H. Weisz, Box 311, Arlington, Va. 22210
W. H. Wescombe, P.O. Box 488, Glencoe, CA 95232 (Rem. R.B. parts)

GUN PARTS, U. S. AND FOREIGN

American Firearms Mfg. Co., Inc., 1200 Warfield, San Antonio, Tex. 78216 (clips)
Badger Shooter's Supply, Owen, Wisc. 54460
Shelley Braverman, Athens, N.Y. 12015
Philip R. Crouthamel, 817 E. Baltimore, E. Lansdowne, Pa. 19050
Charles E. Duffy, Williams Lane, West Hurley, N.Y. 12491
Federal Ordnance Inc., 9634 Alpaca St., So. El Monte, CA 91733

Greeley Arms Co., Inc., 223 Little Falls Rd., Fairfield, N.J. 07006
Hunter's Haven, Zero Prince St., Alexandria, Va. 22314
International Sportsmen's Supply Co., Inc., Arapaho-Central Park, Suite 311, Richardson, TX 75080 (bbld. actions)
M. C. Matthews, Box 33095, Decatur, GA 30031 (ctlg. $1)
Numrich Arms Co., West Hurley, N.Y. 12491
Pacific Intl. Import Co., 2416-16th St., Sacramento, CA 95818
Reed & Co., Shokan, N.Y. 12481
Martin B. Retting, Inc., 11029 Washington, Culver City, Cal. 90230
Ruvel & Co., 3037 N. Clark, Chicago, IL 60614
Sarco, Inc., 192 Central, Stirling, N.J. 07980
R. A. Saunders, 3253 Hillcrest Dr., San Antonio, Tex. 78201 (clips)
Sherwood Distr. Inc., 7435 Greenbush Ave., No. Hollywood, CA 91605
Simms, 2801 J St., Sacramento, CA 95816
Clifford L. Smires, R.D., Columbus, N.J. 08022 (Mauser rifles)
Sporting Arms, Inc., 9643 Alpaca St., So. El Monte, CA 91733 (M-1 carb. access.)
N. F. Strebe, 4926 Marlboro Pike, S.E., Washington, D.C. 20027
Triple-K Mfg. Co., 568-6th Ave., San Diego, CA 92101

GUNS (Pellet)

Air Rifle Hq., 247 Court St., Grantsville, W. Va. 26147
AmPell Playtime Prods., Inc., 24 E. Main St., Honeoye, NY 14471
Beeman's Precision Airguns, P.O. Box 542, San Anselmo, CA 94960
Benjamin Air Rifle Co., 1525 So. 8th St., Louis, Mo. 63104
Continental Arms Corp., 697 5th Ave., New York, N.Y. 10022
Crosman Arms Co., Inc., Fairport, N.Y. 14450
Daisy Mfg. Co., Rogers, Ark. 72756 (also Feinwerkbau)
Fanta Air Rifles, Box 8122, La Crescenta, Calif, 91214
J. L. Galef & Son, Inc., 85 Chambers St., New York, N.Y. 10007 (B.S.A.)
H. F. Grieder, Box 487, Knoxville, IL 61448 (Hammerli)
Harrington & Richardson Arms Co., 320 Park Ave., Worcester, Mass. 01610 (Webley)
Healthways, Box 45055, Los Angeles, Calif. 90061
Gil Hebard Guns, Box 1, Knoxville, Ill. 61448
Hy-Score Arms Co., 200 Tillary St., Brooklyn, N.Y. 11201
Interarms, 10 Prince, Alexandria, Va. 22313 (Walther)
Kerrco, Inc., Box 368, Hastings, Nebr. 68901
Marksman Products, P.O. Box 2983, Torrance, CA 90509
Precise Imports Corp. (PIC), 3 Chestnut, Suffern, N.Y. 10901
Sears, Roebuck & Co., 825 S. St. Louis, Chicago, Ill. 60607
Service Armament, 689 Bergen Blvd., Ridgefield, N.J. 07657 (Webley, Jaguar)
Sheridan Products, Inc., 3205 Sheridan, Racine, Wis. 53403
Smith & Wesson, Inc., 7710 No. 30th St., Tampa, FL 33610
Solingen Cutlery, Box 306, Montrose, Calif. 91020
Stoeger Arms Corp., 55 Ruta Ct., S. Hackensack, N.J. 07606 (Peerless)
Stuart Distr. Co., 6 Riverside Dr., Baltimore, Md. 21221
Dan Wesson Arms, 293 S. Main, Monson, Mass. 01057

GUNS, SURPLUS PARTS AND AMMUNITION

Century Arms, Inc., 3-5 Federal St., St. Albans, Vt. 05478
W. H. Craig, Box 927, Selma, Ala. 36701
Cummings Intl. Inc., 41 Riverside Ave., Yonkers, N.Y. 10701
Eastern Firearms Co., 790 S. Arroyo Pkwy., Pasadena, Calif. 91105
Hunter's Lodge, 200 S. Union, Alexandria, Va. 22313
Lever Arms Serv. Ltd., 771 Dunsmuir St., Vancouver 1, B.C., Canada
Mars Equipment Corp., 3318 W. Devon, Chicago, Ill. 60645
National Gun Traders, 225 S.W. 22nd, Miami, Fla. 33135
Pacific Intl. Imp. Co., 2416-16th St., Sacramento, CA 95818
Plainfield Ordnance Co., Box 447, Dunellen, N.J. 08812
Potomac Arms Corp., Box 35, Alexandria, Va. 22313
Ruvel & Co., 3037 N. Clark St., Chicago, Ill. 60614
Service Armament Co., 689 Bergen Blvd., Ridgefield, N.J. 07657
Sherwood Distrib. Inc., 9470 Santa Monica Blvd., Beverly Hills, CA 90210
Z. M. Military Corp., 31 Legion Dr., Bergenfield, NJ 07621

GUNS, U.S.-made

Agawam Arms Co., 916 Suffield St., Agawam, Mass. 01001
American Firearms Mfg. Co., Inc., 1200 Warfield, San Antonio, Tex. 78216
ArmaLite, 118 E. 16th St., Costa Mesa, Calif. 92627
Artistic Arms, Inc., Box 23, Hoagland, IN 46745 (Sharps-Borchardt)
Bauer Firearms, 34750 Klein Ave., Fraser, MI 48026
Caraville Arms, P.O. Box 377, Thousand Oaks, CA 91360
Challanger Mfg. Corp., 118 Pearl St., Mt. Vernon, NY 10550 (Hopkins & Allen)
Champlin Firearms, Inc., Box 3191, Enid, Okla. 73701
Charter Arms Corp., 265 Asylum, Bridgeport, Conn. 06610
Clerke Products, 2219 Main St., Santa Monica, Ca. 90405
Colt's, 150 Huyshope Ave., Hartford, Conn. 06102
Commando Arms, Inc., Box 10214, Knoxville, Tenn. 37919
Cumberland Arms, 1222 Oak Dr., Manchester, Tenn 37355
Day Arms Corp., 7515 Stagecoach Ln., San Antonio, Tex. 78227
84 Gun Co., Inc., P.O. Box 54, Eighty Four, PA 15330
Esopus Gun Works, Port Ewen, NY 12466 (muzzle loaders)
Falling Block Works, P.O. Box 22, Troy, MI 48084
Firearms Imp. & Exp. Co., 2470 N.W. 21st St., Miami, FL 33142 (FIE)
Firearms Intl. Corp., (see: Garcia)
Golden Age Arms Co., 657 High St., Worthington, O. 43085
Gyrojet (see Intercontinental Arms)
Harrington & Richardson, Park Ave., Worcester, Mass. 01610
A. D. Heller, Inc., Box 268, Grand Ave., Baldwin, NY 11510
High Standard Mfg. Co., 1817 Dixwell Ave., Hamden, Conn. 06514

Hopkins & Allen, see: High Standard
Indian Arms Corp., 13503 Joseph Campar, Detroit, MI 48212
Intercontinental Arms, Inc., 2222 Barry Ave., Los Angeles, Ca. 90064
International Sportsmen's Supply Co., Inc., Arapaho-Central Park, Suite 311, Richardson, TX 75080 (Santa Barbara bbld. actions)
Ithaca Gun Co., Ithaca, N.Y. 14850
Iver Johnson Arms & Cycle Works, Fitchburg, Mass. 01420
Jackson Hole Arms Corp., Box T, Jackson, Wyo. 83001
J & R carbine: see: PJK Inc.)
Ljutic Ind., Inc., P.O. Box 2117, Yakima, WA 98902 (Mono-Gun)
MBAssociates, (see Intercontinental Arms)
Marlin Firearms Co., 100 Kenna Dr., New Haven, Conn. 06473
Merrill Co. Inc., Box 187, Rockwell City, IA 50579
O. F. Mossberg & Sons, Inc., 7 Grasso St., No. Haven, Conn. 06473
W. L. Mowrey Gun Works, Inc., Box 711, Olney, TX 73674
Natl. Ordance Inc., 9643 Alpaca, S. El Monte, CA 91733
Navy Arms Co., 689 Bergen Blvd., Ridgefield, N.J. 07657
Norarmco, 41471 Irwin, Mt. Clemens, MI 48043 (D.A. 25 auto)
North Star Arms, R.2, Box 74A, Ortonville, MN 56278 (The Plainsman)
Numrich Arms Corp., W. Hurley, N.Y. 12491
Omega Arms Inc., 218 Austin St., Denton, TX 76201
PJK, Inc., 1527 Royal Oak Dr., Bradbury, Ca 91010 (J&R Carbine)
Pedersen Custom Guns, Div. of O. F. Mossberg & Sons, Inc., 7 Grasso Ave., North Haven, CT 06473
Plainfield Machine Co., Inc., Box 447, Dunellen, N.J. 08812
Plainfield Ordnance Co., P.O. Box 251, Middlesex, NJ 08846
Potomac Arms Corp., P.O. Box 35, Alexandria, Va. 22313 (ML replicas)
R G Industries, 2485 N.W. 20th SE., Miami, FL 33142
Ranger Arms Co., Box 704, Gainesville, Tex. 76240 (Texan Mag.)
Remington Arms Co., Bridgeport, Conn. 06602
Riedl Rifles, P.O. Box 308, San Juan Capistrano, CA 92675 (S.S.)
Rocky Mountain Arms Corp., Box 224, Salt Lake City, UT 84110
Savage Arms Corp., Westfield, Mass. 01085
Sears, Roebuck & Co., 825 S. St. Louis, Chicago, Ill. 60607
Seventrees Ltd., 315 W. 39th St., New York, N.Y. 10018
Smith & Wesson, Inc., 2100 Roosevelt Ave., Springfield, MA 01101
Sporting Arms, Inc., 9643 Alpaca St., So. El Monte, CA 91733 (M-1 carbine)
Sterling Arms Corp., 2207 Elmwood Ave., Buffalo, N.Y. 14216
Sturm, Ruger & Co., Southport, Conn. 06490
T.D.E. Corp., 11609 Vanowen St., No. Hollywood, CA 91605 (Auto-Mag)
Thompson-Center Arms, Box 2405, Rochester, N.H. 03867 (Contender pistol)
Tingle, 1125 Smithland Pike, Shelbyville, Ind. 46176 (muzzleloader)
Trail Guns Armory, 2115 Lexington, Houston, TX 77006 (muzzleloaders)
Universal Firearms Corp., 3746 E. 10th Ct., Hialeah, Fla. 33013
Ward's, 619 W. Chicago, Chicago, Ill. 60607 (Western Field brand)
Weatherby's, 2781 E. Firestone Blvd., South Gate, Calif. 90280
Dan Wesson Arms, 293 So. Main St., Monson, Mass. 01057
Winchester Repeating Arms Co., New Haven, Conn. 06504
Winslow Arms Co., P.O. Box 578, Osprey, Fla. 33595

GUNSMITHS, CUSTOM

Abe-Van Horn, 5124 Huntington Dr., Los Angeles, CA 90032
P. O. Ackley, 2235 Arbor Lane, Salt Lake City, UT 84117
Ed Agramonte, 41 Riverdale Ave., Yonkers, NY 10701
Ahlman Cust. Gun Shop, R.R. 1, Box 20, Morristown, Minn. 55052
R. E. Anderson, 706 S. 23rd St., Laramie, Wyo. 82070
Andrews' Ammunition, 7114 So. Albion, Littleton, Colo. 80120
R. J. Anton, 1016 Riehl St., Waterloo, Ia. 50703
Arms Divs., M. R. Co., 5920 Smith Ave., Baltimore, MD 21209
Atkinson Gun Co., P.O. Box 512, Prescott, AZ 86301
Bacon Creek Gun Shop, Cumberland Falls Rd., Corbin, Ky. 40701
Bain and Davis Sptg. Gds., 599 W. Las Tunas Dr., San Gabriel, Calif. 41776
Joe J. Balickie, 6108 Deerwood Pl., Raleigh, N.C. 27607
Wm. G. Bankard, 4211 Thorncliff Rd., Baltimore, MD 21236 (Kentuckys)
Barta's, Rte. 1, Box 129-A, Cato, Wis. 54206
Bayer's Gun Shop, 213 S. 2nd, Walla Walla, Wash. 99362
Bennett Gun Works, 561 Delaware Ave., Delmar, N.Y. 12054
Irvin L. Benson, Saganaga Lake, Pine Island Camp, Ontario, Canada
Gordon Bess, 708 River St., Canon City, Colo. 81212
Bruce Betts Gunsmith Co., 26 Rolla Gardens Dr., Rolla, Mo. 65401
John Bivins, Jr., 446 So. Main St., Winston-Salem, N.C. 27101
Edwin T. Blackburn, Jr., 474 E. McKinley, Sunnyvale, CA 94086 (precision metal work)
Boone Mountain Trading Post, Averyville Rd., St. Marys, Pa. 15857
T. H. Boughton, 410 Stone Rd., Rochester, N.Y. 14616
Kay H. Bowles, Pinedale, Wyo. 82941
Breckheimers, Parish, NY 13131
L. H. Brown, Rte. 2, Airport Rd., Kalispell, Mont. 59901
Lenard M. Brownell, Box 25, Wyarno, WY 82845
George Bunch, 7735 Garrison Rd., Hyattsville, Md. 20784
Tom Burgess, Rte. 3, Kalispell, MT 59901 (metalsmithing only)
Leo Bustani, P.O. Box 8125, W. Palm Beach, Fla. 33407
Gus Butterowe, 2520 W. Mockingbird Lane, Dallas, Tex. 75235
Cameron's Guns, 16690 W. 11th Ave., Golden, Colo. 80401
Carpenter's Gun Works, Gunshop Rd., Box C, Plattekill, N.Y. 12568
Carter Gun Works, 2211 Jefferson Pk. Ave., Charlotteville, Va. 22903
Cassell Gun Shop, 403 West Lane, Worland, Wyo. 82401
Ray Chalmers, 18 White Clay Dr., Newark, Del. 19711
N. C. Christakos, 2832 N. Austin, Chicago, IL 60634
Kenneth E. Clark, 18738 Highway 99, Madera, Calif. 93637
Cloward's Gun Shop, 4023 Aurora Ave., Seattle, WA 98102
Crest Carving Co., 14849 Dillow St., Westminster, Ca. 92683
Philip R. Crouthamel, 817 E. Baltimore, E. Lansdowne, Pa. 19050
Custom Rifle Shop, 4550 E. Colfax Ave., Denver, Colo. 80220

Jim Cuthbert, 715 S. 5th St., Coos Bay, Ore. 97420
DS Antique Arms Co., P.O. Box 35109. Houston, TX 77035 (Hawken copies)
Dahl's Gunshop, Rt. 2, Billings, Mont. 59101
Dave's Gun Shop, 3994 Potters Rd. West, Ionia, Mich. 48846
Davis Gun Shop, 7213 Lee Highway, Falls Church, VA 22046
Dee Davis, 5658 So. Mayfield, Chicago, Ill. 60638
Jack Dever, Box 577, Jackson, Wyo. 83001 (S. S. Work)
J. Dewey Gun Co., Clinton Corners, N.Y. 12514
Joe E. Dillen, 1206 Juanita S.W., Massillon, Ohio 44646
Dominic DiStefano, 4303 Friar Lane, Colorado Springs, CO 80907
Drumbore Gun Shop, 119 Center St., Lehigton, PA 18235
Charles Duffy, Williams Lane, W. Hurley, N.Y. 12491
Gerald D. Eisenhauer, Rte. #3, Twin Falls, Ida. 83301
Bill English, 4411 S. W. 100th, Seattle, Wash. 98146
Ken Eyster, Heritage Gunsmiths Inc., 6441 Bishop Rd., Centerburg, O. 43011
N. B. Fashingbauer, Box 366, Lac Du Flambeau, Wis. 54538
Ted Fellowes, Beaver Lodge, 9245-16th Ave., S.W., Seattle, Wa. 98106 (muzzle loaders)
The Fergusons, 27 W. Chestnut St., Farmingdale, NY 11735
H. J. and L. A. Finn, 12565 Gratiot Ave., Detroit, MI 48205
Loxley Firth Firearms, 8563 Oswego Rd., R. D. 4, Baldwinsville, N.Y. 13027
Marshall F. Fish, Westport, N.Y. 12993
Jerry Fisher, 1244—4th Ave. West, Kalispell, Mont. 59901
Flagler Gun Clinic, Box 8125, West Palm Beach, Fla. 33407 (Win. 92 & 94 Conv.)
Frazier's Custom Guns, Box 3, Tyler, WA 99035
Freeland's Scope Stands, 3737—14th Ave., Rock Island, Ill. 61201
Fred's Gun Shop, Box 725, Juneau, Alaska 99801
Frederick Gun Shop, 10 Elson Drive, Riverside, R.I. 02915
Frontier Arms, Inc., 420 E. Riding Club Rd., Cheyenne, Wyo. 82001
Fuller Gunshop, Cooper Landing, Alas. 99572
Geo. M. Fullmer, 2499 Mavis St., Oakland, Cal. 94501 (metal work)
Georgia Gun & Smith, 5170 Thistle Rd., Smyrna, GA 30080
Gibbs Rifle Products, Viola, Ida. 83872
Ed Gillman, Upper High Crest Dr., R.F.D. #1, Butler, N.J. 07405
Dale Goens, Box 224, Cedar Crest, NM 87008
A. R. Goode, R.D. 1, Box 84, Thurmont, MD 21788
Griffin & Howe, 589-8th Ave., New York, N.Y. 10017
Dale M. Guise, Rt. 2, Box 239, Gardners, Pa. 17324 (Rem. left-hand conversions)
H & R Custom Gun Serv., 68 Passaic Dr., Hewitt, N.J. 07421
Paul Haberly, 2364 N. Neva, Chicago, IL 60635
Chas. E. Hammans, Box 788, Stuttgart, AR 72160
Harkrader's Cust. Gun Shop, 111 No. Franklin St., Christiansburg, Va. 24073
Elden Harsh, Rt. 4, London, O. 43140
Rob't W. Hart & Son, 401 Montgomery St., Nescopeck, Pa. 18635 (actions, stocks)
Hal Hartley, Box 147, Blairs Fork Rd., Lenoir, N.C. 28654
Hubert J. Hecht, 55 Rose Mead Circle, Sacramento, CA 95831
Edw. O. Hefti, 300 Fairview, College Sta., Tex. 77840
Iver Henriksen, 1211 So. 2nd, Missoula, Mont. 59801
Wm. Hobaugh, Box 657, Philipsburg, Mont. 59858
Richard Hodgson, 9081 Tahoe Lane, Boulder, Colo. 80301
Hoenig-Rodman, 853 So. Curtis Rd., Boise, ID 83705
Hollis Gun Shop, 917 Rex St., Carlsbad, N.M. 88220
Huckleberry Gun Shop, 10440 Kingsbury Rd., Delton, Mich. 49046 (rust blueing)
Hurt's Specialty Gunsmithing, Box 1033, Muskogee, Okla. 74401
Hyper-Single Precision SS Rifles, 520 E. Beaver, Jenks, OK 74037
Independent Machine & Gun Shop, 1416 N. Hayes, Pocatello, Ida. 83201
Jackson's, Box 416, Selman City, TX 75689
Paul Jaeger, 211 Leedom, Jenkintown, Pa. 19046
J. J. Jenkins, 462 Stanford Pl., Santa Barbara, CA 93105
Jerry's Gun Shop, 9220 Ogden Ave., Brookfield, Ill. 60513
Jerry's Gun Shop, 1527 N. Graceland Ave., Appleton, Wis. 54911
Johnson Automatics Assoc., Inc., Box 306, Hope Valley, R.I. 02832
Johnson's Gun Shop, 1316 N. Blackstone, Fresno, Calif. 93703
Kennedy Gun Shop, Rt. 6, Clarksville, Tenn. 37040
Monte Kennedy, R. D. 2-B, Kalispell, Mont. 59901
Kennon's Custom Rifles, 5408 Biffle, Stone Mtn., Ga. 30083
Kerr Sport Shop, Inc., 9584 Wilshire Blvd., Beverly Hills, Calif. 90212
Kess Arms Co., 12515 W. Lisbon Rd., Brookfield, Wis. 53005
Kesselring Gun Shop, 400 Pacific Hiway 99 No., Burlington, Wash. 98233
Knights Gun Store, Inc., 103 So. Jennings, Ft. Worth, Tex. 76104
Ward Koozer, Box 18, Walterville, Ore. 97489
R. Krieger & Sons, 34923 Gratiot, Mt. Clemens, Mich. 48043
Lacy's Gun Service, 1518A West Blvd., Charlotte, N.C. 28208
Sam Lair, 520 E. Beaver, Jenks, OK 74037
R. H. Lampert, 520 Hugo St. N.E., Fridley, MN 55432 (metalsmithing only)
LanDav Custom Guns, 7213 Lee Highway, Falls Church, VA 22046
Harry Lawson Co., 3328 N. Richey Blvd., Tucson, Ariz. 85716
John G. Lawson, 1802 E. Columbia, Tacoma, Wa. 98404
Gene Lechner, 636 Jane N.E., Albuquerque, NM 87123
LeDel, Inc., Main and Commerce Sts., Cheswold, Del. 19936
Art LeFeuvre, 1003 Hazel Ave., Deerfield, Ill. 60015
LeFever Arms Co., R.D. 1, Lee Center, N.Y. 13363
Max J. Lindauer, R.R. 1, Box 114, Washington, Mo. 63090
Robt. L. Lindsay, 9416 Emory Grove Rd., Gaithersburg, Md. 20760 (services only)
Ljutic Ind., Box 2117, Yakima, WA 98902 (Mono-Wads)
Llanerch Gun Shop, 2800 Township Line, Upper Darby, Pa. 19083
McCormick's Gun Bluing Service, 4936 E. Rosecrans Ave., Compton, Calif. 90221
Harry McGowen, Momence, IL 60954
Bill McGuire, Inc., 7749 15th Ave., N.W., Seattle, WA 98117
Pat B. McMillan, 1828 E. Campo Bello Dr., Phoenix, Ariz. 85022

R. J. Maberry, 511 So. K, Midland, Tex. 79701
Harold E. MacFarland, Star Route, Box 84, Cottonwood, Ariz. 86326
E. H. Martin, 937 S. Sheridan Blvd., Denver, CO 80226
Maryland Gun Exchange, Rte. 5, Frederick, Md. 21701
Mashburn Arms Co., 1020 N.W. 6th St., Oklahoma City, OK 73102
Mathews & Son, 10224 S. Paramount Blvd., Downey, Calif. 90241
Maurer Arms, 2366 Frederick Dr., Cuyahoga Falls, Ohio 44221 (muzzleloaders)
Middaugh's Nodak, 318 2nd St., Bismarck, N.D. 58501
C.D. Miller Guns, St. Onge, SD 57779
Earl Milliron, 1249 N.E. 166th Ave., Portland, Ore. 97230
Mills (D.H.) Custom Stocks, 401 N. Ellsworth, San Mateo, Calif. 94401
Mitchell's Gun Repair, Rt. 1, Perryville, Ark. 72126
Natl. Gun Traders, Inc., 225 S.W. 22nd Ave., Miami, Fla. 33135
Clayton N. Nelson, 1725 Thompson Ave., Enid, Okla. 73701
Newman Gunshop, 119 Miller Rd., Agency, Ia. 52530
Nu-Line Guns, Inc., 3727 Jennings Rd., St. Louis, Mo. 63121
Oak Lawn Gun Shop, Inc., 9618 Southwest Hwy., Oak Lawn, Ill. 60453
O'Brien Rifle Co., 324 Tropicana No. 128, Las Vegas, Nev. 89109
Pachmayr Gun Works, 1220 S. Grand Ave., Los Angeles, Calif. 90015
Harry Pagett Gun Shop, 125 Water St., Milford, Ohio 45150
Charles J. Parkinson, 116 Wharncliffe Rd. So., London, Ont., Canada N6J2K3
Pendleton Gunshop, 1210 S. W. Haley Ave., Pendleton, Ore. 97801
C. R. Pedersen & Son, Ludington, Mich. 49431
Al Petersen, Box 8, Riverhurst, Sask., Canada S0H3P0
A. W. Peterson Gun Shop, 1693 Old 44 No., Mt. Dora, Fla. 32757 (ML rifles, also)
Gene Phipps, 10 Wood's Gap Rd., Floyd, Va. 24091
Purcell's Gunshop, 915 Main St., Boise, Idaho 83702
Ready Eddie's Gun Shop, 501 Van Spanje Ave., Michigan City, IN 46360
Marion Reed Gun Shop, 1522 Colorado, Bartlesville, Okla. 74003
Ridge Guncraft, Inc., 234 N. Tulane, Oak Ridge, Tenn. 37830
Riedl Rifles, P.O. Box 308, San Juan Capistrano, CA 92675 (S.S.)
Rifle Shop, Box 657, Philipsburg, Mont. 59858
Riflemen's Hdqs., Rte. 3, RD 550-E, Kendallville, IN 46755
Carl Roth, P.O. Box 2593, Cheyenne, WY 82001
Royal Arms, Inc., 10064 Bert Acosta, Santee, Calif. 92071
Murray F. Ruffino, Rt. 2, Milford, ME 04461
Rush's Old Colonial Forge, 106 Wiltshire Rd., Baltimore, MD 21221 (Ky.-Pa. rifles)
Sam's Gun Shop, 25 Squam Rd., Rockport, Mass. 01966
Sanders Custom Gun Serv., 2358 Tyler Lane, Louisville, Ky. 40205
Sandy's Custom Gunshop, Rockport, Ill. 62370
Saratoga Arms Co., R.D. 3, Box 387, Pottstown, Pa. 19464
Roy V. Schaefer, 965 W. Hilliard Lane, Eugene, Ore. 97402
George Schielke, Washington Crossing, Titusville, N.J. 08560
N.H. Schiffman Cust. Gun Serv., 963 Malibu, Pocatello, ID 83201
Schuetzen Gun Works, 1226 Prairie Rd., Colorado Springs, Colo. 80909
Schumaker's Gun Shop, 208 W. 5th Ave., Colville, Wash 99114
Schwab Gun Shop, 1103 E. Bigelow, Findlay, O. 45840
Schwartz Custom Guns, 9621 Coleman Rd., Haslett, Mich. 48840
Schwarz's Gun Shop, 41-15th St., Wellsburg, W. Va. 26070
Jim Scott, Hiway 2-East, Leon, IA 50144
Scotty's Gun Shop, Second and Rancier, Killeen, TX 76541
Joseph M. Sellner, 1010 Stelton Rd., Piscataway, N.J. 08854
Shaw's, 1655 S. Euclid Ave., Anaheim, Calif. 92802
George H. Sheldon, P.O. Box 489, Franklin, NH 03235 (45 autos only)
Shilen Rifles, Inc., 205 Metropark Blvd., Ennis, TX 75119
Harold H. Shockley, Box 355, Hanna City, Ill. 65126 (hot bluing & plating)
Shooters Service & Dewey Inc., Clinton Corner, N.Y. 12514
Walter Shultz, R.D. 3, Pottstown, Pa. 19464
The Sight Shop, 1802 E. Columbia Ave., Tacoma, Wa. 98404
Silver Dollar Guns, P.O. Box 489, Franklin, NH 03235
Simmons Gun Spec., 700 Rogers Rd., Olathe, Kans. 66061
Simms Hardward Co., 2801 J St., Sacramento, Calif. 95816
Skinner's Gun Shop, Box 30, Juneau, Alaska 98801
Markus Skosples, 1119-35th St., Rock Island, Ill. 61201
Jerome F. Slezak, 1290 Marlowe, Lakewood (Cleveland), OH 44107
Small Arms Eng., P.O. Box 306, Des Plaines, IL 60018 (restorations)
John Smith, 912 Lincoln, Carpentersville, Ill. 60110
K. E. Smith, 8766 Los Choches Rd., Lakeside, Calif. 92040
Smitty's Gunshop, 308 S. Washington, Lake City, Minn. 55041
Snapp's Gunshop, 6911 E. Washington Rd., Clare, Mich. 48617
R. Southgate, Rt. 2, Franklin, Tenn. 37064 (new Kentucky rifles)
Sportsman's Den, 1010 Stelton Rd., Piscataway, N.J. 08854
Sportsmens Equip. Co., 915 W. Washington, San Diego, Calif. 92103
Jess L. Stark, 12051 Stroud, Houston, TX 77072
Ikey Starks, 1058 Grand Ave., So. San Francisco, Calif. 94080
Keith Stegall, Box 696, Gunnison, Colo. 81230
W. C. Strutz, 3230 Sunnyside Ave., Brookfield, IL 60513
Suter's House of Guns, 332 N. Tejon, Colorado Springs, Colo. 80902
Swanson Custom Firearms, 1051 Broadway. Denver, Colo. 80203 .
A. D. Swenson's, P.O. Box 884, Lawndale, CA 90260
T-P Shop, 212 E. Houghton, West Branch, Mich. 48661
Talmage Ent., 1309 W. 12th St., Long Beach, Calif. 90813
Taylor & Robbins, Box 164, Rixford, Pa. 16745
Daniel Titus, 119 Morlyn Ave., Bryn Mawr, PA 19010
Tom's Gunshop, 600 Albert Pike, Hot Springs, Ark. 71901
Dave Trevallion, 3442 S. Post Rd., Indianapolis, IN 46239
Trinko's Gun Serv., 1406 E. Main, Watertown, Wis. 53094
Herb. G. Troester's Accurizing Serv., Cayuga, ND 58013
C. Hunt Turner, 618 S. Grove, Webster Groves, Mo. 63119 (shotguns only)
Upper Missouri Trading Co., Inc., Box 181, Crofton, NB 68730
Roy Vail, R. 1, Box 8, Warwick, N.Y. 10990
J. W. Van Patten, Box 145, Foster Hill, Milford, Pa. 18337
Herman Waldron, Box 475, Pomeroy, WN 99437 (metalsmithing)
Walker Arms Co., R. 2, Box 38, Selma, Ala. 36701
Harold Waller, 1288 Camillo Way, El Cajon, CA 99347
R. A. Wardrop, Box 245, Mechanicsburg, Pa. 17055

Weatherby's, 2781 Firestone Blvd., South Gate, Calif. 90280
Wells Sport Store, 110 N. Summit St., Prescott, Ariz. 86301
R. A. Wells, 3452 N. 1st, Racine, Wis. 53402
Robert G. West, 6626 S. Lincoln, Littleton, Colo. 80120
Western Stocks & Guns, 2206 E. 11th, Bremerton, Wash. 98310
M. C. Wiest, 234 N. Tulane Ave., Oak Ridge, Tenn. 37830
W. C. Wilber, 400 Lucerne Dr., Spartanburg, SC 29302
Williams Gun Sight Co., 7389 Lapeer Rd., Davison, Mich. 48423
Lou Williamson, 129 Stonegate Ct., Bedford, TX 76021
Wilson Gun Store Inc., R.D. 1, Rte. 225, Dauphin, Pa. 17018
Robert M. Winter, Box 484, Menno, SD 57045
Lester Womack, Box 17210, Tucson, AZ 85710
W. H. Womack, 2124 Meriwether Rd., Shreveport, La. 71108
York County Gun Works, RR 4, Tottenham, Ont., Canada (muzzleloaders)
Russ Zeeryp, 1601 Foard Dr., Lynn Ross Manor, Morristown, TN 37814
R. E. Zellmer, W180 N8996 Leona Ln., Menomonee Falls, WI 53051

GUNSMITHS, HANDGUN

Alamo Heat Treating, Box 55345, Houston, Tex. 77055
Allen Assoc., 7448 Limekiln Pike, Philadelphia, Pa. 19138 (speed-cock lever for 45 ACP)
Bain and Davis Sptg. Gds., 559 W. Las Tunas Dr., San Gabriel, Cal. 91776
Bar-Sto Precision Machine, 633 So. Victory Blvd., Burbank, CA 91502 (S.S. bbls. f. 45 Acp)
Behlert & Freed, Inc., 33 Herning Ave., Cranford. N.J. 07016 (short actions)
R. M. Champlin, P.O. Box 74, Wentworth, N.H. 03282
F. Bob Chow, Gun Shop, 3185 Mission, San Francisco, Calif. 94110
J.E. Clark, Rte. 2, Box 22A, Keithville, LA 71047
Custom Gunshop, 33 Herning Ave., Cranford, N.J. 07016
Day Arms Corp., 7515 Stagecoach Lane, San Antonio, Tex. 78227
Alton S. Dinan, Jr., P.O. Box 6674, Canaan, Conn. 06018
Dominic DiStefano, 4303 Friar Lane, Colorado Springs, CO 80907 (accurizing)
Dan Dwyer, 915 W. Washington, San Diego, Calif. 92103
Giles' 45 Shop, Rt. 1, Box 47, Odessa, Fla. 33556
H. H. Harris, 1237 So. State, Chicago, Ill. 60605
Gil Hebard Guns, Box 1, Knoxville, Ill. 61448
Rudy Marent, 9711 Tiltree, Houston, Tex. 77034 (Hammerli)
Maryland Gun Exchange, Inc., Rte. 40 W., RD 5, Frederick, Md. 21701
Match Arms Co., 831 Mary St., Springdale, Pa. 15144
Pachmayr Gun Works, 1220 S. Grand Ave., Los Angeles, Calif. 90015
R. L. Shockey Guns, Inc., 1614 S. Choctaw, E. Reno, Okla. 73036
Silver Dollar Guns, 7 Balsam St., Keene, N.H. 03431 (45 auto only)
Sportsmens Equipmt. Co., 915 W. Washington, San Diego, Calif. 92103
A. D. Swenson's, P.O. Box 884, Lawndale, CA 90260
Dave Woodruff, 116 Stahl Ave., Wilmington Manor, New Castle, DE 19720

GUNSMITH SCHOOLS

Colorado School of Trades, 1545 Hoyt, Lakewood, CO 80215
Lassen Community College, Highway 139, Susanville, Calif. 96130
Oregon Technical Institute, Klamath Falls, Ore. 97601
Penn. Gunsmith School, 812 Ohio River Blvd., Avalon, Pittsburgh, Pa. 15202
Trinidad State Junior College, Trinidad, Colo. 81082

GUNSMITH SUPPLIES, TOOLS, SERVICES

Alamo Heat Treating Co., Box 55345, Houston, Tex. 77055
Albright Prod. Co., P.O. Box 1027, Winnemucca, NV 89445 (trap buttplates)
Alley Supply Co., Carson Valley Industrial Park, Gardnerville, NV 89410
American Edelstaal, Inc., 1 Atwood Ave., Tenafly, NJ 07670
American Firearms Mfg. Co., Inc., 1200 Warfield, San Antonio, Tex. 78216 (45 Conversion Kit)
Anderson & Co., 1203 Broadway, Yakima, Wash. 98902 (tang safe)
Armite Labs., 1845 Randolph St., Los Angeles, Cal. 90001 (pen oiler)
Atlas Arms Inc., 2952 Waukegan Rd., Niles, Ill. 60648
B-Square Co., Box 11281, Ft. Worth, Tex. 76110
Jim Baiar, Rt. 1-B, Box 352, Columbia Falls, Mont. 59912 (hex screws)
Bonanza Sports Mfg. Co., 412 Western Ave., Faribault, Minn. 55021
Brookstone Co., 13 Brookstone Bldg., Peterborough, NH 03458
Brown & Sharpe Mfg. Co., Precision Pk., No. Kingston, R.I. 02852
Bob Brownell's, Main & Third, Montezuma, Ia. 50171
W. E. Brownell, 1852 Alessandro Trail, Vista, Calif. 92083 (checkering tools)
Maynard P. Buehler, Inc., 17 Orinda Hwy., Orinda, Calif. 94563 (Rocol lube)
Burgess Vibrocrafters, Inc. (BVI), Rte. 83, Grayslake, Ill. 60030
M. H. Canjar, 500 E. 45th, Denver, Colo. 80216 (triggers, etc.)
Centerline Prod., Box 14074, Denver, Colo. 80214
Chapman Mfg. Co., Rte. 17, Durham, CT 06422
Chicago Wheel & Mfg. Co., 1101 W. Monroe St., Chicago, Ill. 60607 (Handee grinders)
Christy Gun Works, 875-57th St., Sacramento, Calif. 95819
Clymer Mfg. Co., 14241 W. 11 Mile Rd., Oak Park, Mich. 48237 (reamers)
Colbert Industries, 10107 Adella, South Gate, Calif. 90280 (Panavise)
A. Constantine & Son, Inc., 2050 Eastchester Rd., Bronx, N.Y. 10461 (wood)
Cougar & Hunter, 6398 W. Pierson Rd., Flushing, Mich. 48433 (scope jigs)
Dayton-Traister Co., P.O. Box 593, Oak Harbor, Wa. 98277 (triggers)
Dem-Bart Hand Tool Co., 7749 15th Ave. N.W., Seattle, WA 98107 (checkering tools)
Ditto Industries, 527 N. Alexandria, Los Angeles, Cal. 90004 (clamp tool)

Dixie Diamond Tool Co., Inc., 6875 S.W. 81st St., Miami, Fla. 33143 (marking pencils)
Dremel Mfg. Co., P.O. Box 518, Racine, Wis. 53401 (grinders)
Chas. E. Duffy, Williams Lane, West Hurley, N.Y. 12491
E-Z Tool Co., P.O. Box 3186, 25 N.W. 44th Ave., Des Moines, Ia. 50313 (lathe taper attachment)
Edmund Scientific Co., 101 E. Glouster Pike, Barrington, N.J. 08007
F. K. Elliott, Box 785, Ramona, Calif. 92065 (reamers)
Foredom Elec. Co., Rt. 6, Bethel, Conn. 06801 (power drills)
Forster Appelt Mfg. Co., Inc., 82 E. Lanark Ave., Lanark, Ill. 61046
Keith Francis, Box 343, Talent, Ore. 97540 (reamers)
Frantz Tools, 913 Barbara Ave., Placentia, Cal. 92670
G. R. S. Corp., Box 1157, Boulder, Colo. 80302 (Gravermeister)
Gager Gage and Tool Co., 27509 Industrial Blvd., Hayward, CA 94545 (speedlock triggers f. Rem. 1100 & 870 pumps)
Gilmore Pattern Works, 1164 N. Utica, Tulsa, Okla. 74110
Gold Lode, Inc., P.O. Box 31, Addison, Ill. 60101 (gold inlay kit)
Grace Metal Prod., Box 67, Elk Rapids, Mich. 49629 (screw drivers, drifts)
Gopher Shooter's Supply, Box 246, Faribault, Minn. 55021 (screwdrivers, etc.)
Gunline Tools Inc., 719 No. East St., Anaheim, CA 92805
H. & M. 24062 Orchard Lake Rd., Farmington, Mich. 48024 (reamers)
Half Moon Rifle Shop, Rt. 1B, Box 352, Columbia Falls, MT 59912 (hex screws)
Hartford Reamer Co., Box 134, Lathrup Village, Mich. 48075
O. Iber Co., 626 W. Randolph, Chicago, Ill. 60606
Paul Jaeger, Inc., 211 Leedom St., Jenkintown, PA. 19046
Kasenite Co., Inc., 3 King St., Mahwah, N.J. 07430 (surface hrdng. comp.)
LanDav Custom Guns, 7213 Lee Highway, Falls Church, VA 22046
John G. Lawson, 1802 E. Columbia Ave., Tacoma, WA 98404
Lea Mfg. Co., 237 E. Aurora St., Waterbury, Conn. 06720
Lock's Phila. Gun Exch., 6700 Rowland Ave., Philadelphia, Pa. 19149
Marker Machine Co., Box 426, Charleston, Ill. 61920
Michaels of Oregon Co., P.O. Box 13010, Portland, Ore. 97213
Viggo Miller, P.O. Box 4181, Omaha, Neb. 68104 (trigger attachment)
Miller Single Trigger Mfg. Co., Box 69, Millersburg, Pa. 17061
Frank Mittermeier, 3577 E. Tremont, N.Y., N.Y. 10465
Moderntools Corp, Box 407, Dept. GD, Woodside, N.Y. 11377
N&J Sales, Lime Kiln Rd., Northford, Conn. 06472 (screwdrivers)
Karl A. Neise, Inc., 5602 Roosevelt Ave., Woodside, N.Y. 11377
P & S Sales, P.O. Box 45095, Tulsa, OK 74145
Palmgren, 8383 South Chicago Ave., Chicago, Ill. 60167 (vises, etc.)
C. R. Pedersen & Son, Ludington, Mich. 49431
Ponderay Lab., 210 W. Prasch, Yakima, Wash. 98902 (epoxy glass bedding)
Redford Reamer Co., Box 6604, Redford Hts. Sta, Detroit, MI 48240
Richland Arms Co., 321 W. Adrian St., Blissfield, Mich. 49228
Riley's Supply Co., 121 No. Main St., Avilla, Ind. 46710 (Niedner buttplates, caps)
Rob. A. Saunders, (see Amer. Firearms Mfg.)
Ruhr-American Corp., So. Hwy #5, Glenwood, Minn. 56334
A. G. Russell, 1705 Hiway 71N, Springdale, AR 72764 (Arkansas oilstones)
Schaffner Mfg. Co., Emsworth, Pittsburgh, Pa. 15202 (polishing kits)
Schuetzen Gun Works, 1226 Prarie Rd., Colo. Springs, Colo. 80909
Shaw's, 1655 S. Euclid Ave., Anaheim, Calif. 92802
A. D. Soucy Co., Box 191, Fort Kent, Me. 04743 (ADSCO stock finish)
L. S. Starrett Co., Athol, Mass. 01331
Technological Devices, Inc., P.O. Box 3491, Stamford, Conn. 06905 (Accu-Orb circle cutters)
Texas Platers Supply Co., 2458 W. Five Mile Parkway, Dallas, TX 75233 (plating kit)
Timney Mfg. Co., 5624 Imperial Hwy., So. Gate, Calif. 90280 (triggers)
Stan de Treville, Box 33021, San Diego, Calif. 92103 (checkering patterns)
Twin City Steel Treating Co., Inc., 1114 S. 3rd, Minneapolis, Minn. 55415 (heat treating)
R. G. Walters Co., 3235 Hancock, San Diego, Ca. 92110
Ward Mfg. Co., 500 Ford Blvd., Hamilton, O. 45011
Will-Burt Co., P.O. Box 160, Orrville, O. 44667 (vises)
Williams Gun Sight Co., 7389 Lapeer Rd., Davison, Mich. 48423
Wilson Arms Co., Box 364, Stony Creek, Branford, Conn. 06405
Wilton Tool Corp., 9525 W. Irving Pk. Rd., Schiller Park, Ill. 60176 (vises)
Wisconsin Platers Supply Co., see: Texas Platers
W. C. Wolff Co., Box 232, Ardmore, PA 19003 (springs)
Woodcraft Supply Corp., 313 Montvale, Woburn, MA 01801

HANDGUN ACCESSORIES

A & R Sales Co., 99163¾ Rush St., So. El Monte, CA 91733
Barami Corp, 6250 E. 7 Mile Rd, Detroit, Mich. 48234 (Hip-Grip)
Bar-Sto Precision Machine, 633 S. Victory Blvd., Burbank, CA 91502
B. L. Broadway, Rte. 1, Box 381, Alpine, CA 92001 (machine rest)
C'Arco, P.O. Box 2043, San Bernardino, CA 92406 (Ransom Rest)
Case Master, 4675 E. 10 Ave., Miami, Fla. 33013
Central Specialties Co., 6030 Northwest Hwy., Chicago, Ill. 60631
John Dangelzer, 3056 Frontier Pl., N.E., Albuquerque, N.M. 87106 (flasks)
Bill Dyer, 503 Midwest Bldg., Oklahoma City, Okla. 73102 (grip caps)
R. S. Frielich, 396 Broome St., New York, N.Y. 10013 (cases)
Hunt Eng., 121—17th St., Yucaipa, Calif. 92399 (Multi-Loader)
Jeffersontown Speclty. Co., Inc., 9815 Taylorsville Rd., Jeffersontown, KY 40299 (pin pads)
R. G. Jensen, 16153½ Parthenia, Sepulveda, Calif. 91343 (auxiliary chambers)
Lee Prec. Mfg., 21 E. Wisconsin, Hartford, WI 53027 (pistol rest holders)
Los Gatos Grip & Specialty Co., P.O. Box 1850, Los Gatos, CA 95030 (custom-made)
Marcon, 1720 Marina Ct., Suite D, San Mateo, CA 94403 (Mellmark pistol safe)
Matich Loader, Box 958, So. Pasadena, Calif. 91030 (Quick Load)

J. McArthur, 1961 Overlook Ave., Youngstown, O. 44509 (sling)
W. A. Miller Co., Inc., Mingo Loop, Oguossoc, ME 04964 (cases)
No-Sho Mfg. Co., 10727 Glenfield Ct., Houston, TX 77035
Pachmayr, 1220 S. Grand, Los Angeles, Calif. 90015 (cases)
Platt Luggage, Inc., 2301 S. Prairie, Chicago, Ill. 60616 (cases)
Jules Reiver, 4104 Market St., Wilmington, Del. 19899 (cases)
Roger A. Smith, 19320 Heber St., Glendora, Ca. 91740 (Wrist-Loc)
Sportsmen's Equipment Co., 415 W. Washington, San Diego, Calif. 92103
M. Tyler, 1326 W. Britton, Oklahoma City, Okla. 73114 (grip adaptor)

HANDGUN GRIPS

Beckelhymer's, Hidalgo & San Bernardo, Laredo, Tex. 78040
Belmont Prods., Rte. #1, Friendsville, TN 37737
Cloyce's Gun Stocks, Box 1133, Twin Falls, Ida. 83301
Crest Carving Co., 8091 Bolsa Ave., Midway City, CA 92655
Custom Combat Grips, 148 Shepherd Ave., Brooklyn, N.Y. 11208
Fitz, Box 49797, Los Angeles, Calif. 90049
Herret's, Box 741, Twin Falls, Ida. 83301
Hogue Custom Grips, Box 1001, Cambria, CA 93428
Mershon Co., Inc., 1230 S. Grand Ave., Los Angeles, Calif. 90015
Mustang Pistol Grips, P.O. Box 214, Temecula, CA 92390
Safety Grip Corp., Box 456, Riverside St., Miami, Fla. 33135
Sanderson Custom Pistol Stocks, 17695 Fenton, Detroit, Mich. 48219
Jay Scott, 81 Sherman Place, Garfield, N.J. 07026
Sile Dist., 7 Centre Market Pl., New York, N.Y. 10013
Sports Inc., P.O. Box 683, Park Ridge, IL 60068 (Franzite)
John W. Womack, 3006 Bibb St., Shreveport, La 71108

HEARING PROTECTORS

American Optical Corp., Mechanic St., Southbridge, Mass. 01550 (ear valve)
Bausch & Lomb, 635 St. Paul St., Rochester, N.Y. 14602
David Clark Co., 360 Franklin St., Worcester, Mass. 01604
Curtis Safety Prod. Co., Box 61, Webster Sq. Sta., Worcester, Mass. 01603 (ear valve)
Hodgdon, 7710 W. 50 Hiway, Shawnee Mission, Kans. 66202
Sigma Eng. Co., 11320 Burbank Blvd., No. Hollywood, Ca. 91601 (Lee-Sonic ear valve)
Safety Direct, P.O. Box 8907, Reno, NV 89507 (Silencio)
Sellstrom Mfg. Co., Sellstrom Industrial Park, Palatine, IL 60067
Smith & Wesson, 2100 Roosevelt Ave., Springfield, MA 01101
Vector Scientific, P.O. Box D, Ft. Lauderdale, FL 33315
Willson Prods Div., P.O. Box 622, Reading, Pa. 19603 (Ray-O-Vac)

HOLSTERS & LEATHER GOODS

American Sales & Mfg. Co., P.O. Box 677, Laredo, Tex. 78040
Andy Anderson, 6100 Vineland Ave., No. Hollywood, CA 91606 (Gunfighter Custom Holsters)
Berns-Martin, 1307 Spring St. N.W., Atlanta, GA 30309
Bianchi Holster Co., 100 Calle Cortez, Temecula, CA 92390
Edward H. Bohlin, 931 N. Highland Ave., Hollywood, Calif. 90038
Boyt Co., Div. of Welch Sptg., Box 1108, Iowa Falls, Ia. 51026
Brauer Bros. Mfg. Co., 817 N. 17th, St. Louis, Mo. 63106
Browning, Rt. 4, Box 624-B, Arnold, MO 63010
J. M. Bucheimer Co., Airport Rd., Frederick, Md. 21701
Cathey Enterprises, P.O. Box 3545, Chula Vista, CA 92011
Clements Custom Leathercraft, 538 E. 18th Ave., Denver, CO 80203
Cole's Acku-Rite, Box 25, Kennedy, N.Y. 14747
Colt's, 150 Huyshope Ave., Hartford, Conn. 06102
Custom Leathercraft, 538 E. 18th Ave., Denver, CO 80203
Daisy Mfg. Co., Rogers, Ark. 72756
Eugene DeMayo & Sons, Inc., 2795 Third Ave., Bronx, N.Y. 10455
Ellwood Epps (Orillia) Ltd., Hwy. 11 North, Orillia, Ont., Canada
Filmat Enterpr., Inc., 200 Market St., East Paterson, N.J. 07407
Flintrop Arms Co., 4034 W. National Ave., Milwaukee, Wis. 53215
Goerg Ent., 3009 S. Laurel, Port Angeles, Wash. 98362
Gunfighter (See Anderson)
Hoyt Holster Co., P.O. Box 1783, Costa Mesa, Cal. 92626
Hudson Holsters, P.O. Box 132, Chula Vista, CA 92012
Don Hume, Box 351, Miami, Okla. 74354
The Hunter Co., 1215 12th St., Denver, Colo. 80204
Jet Sports Corp., 4 Centre Market Pl., New York, N.Y. 10013
Jumbo Sports Prods., P.O. Box 280, Airport Rd., Frederick, MD 21701
George Lawrence Co., 306 S. W. First Ave., Portland, Ore. 97221
Leathercrafters, 710 S. Washington, Alexandria, VA 22314
MMGR Corp., 5710 12th Ave., Brooklyn, N.Y. 11219
S. D. Myres Saddle Co., Box 9776, El Paso, Tex. 79988
Alfonso Pineda, 4850 Lankershim Blvd., No. Hollywood, CA 91062 (custom holstermaker)
Pony Express Sport Shop, 17460 Ventura Blvd., Encino, Calif. 91316
Red Head Brand Co., 4100 Platinum Way, Dallas, Tex. 75237
Rickenbacker's, P.O. Box 532, State Ave., Holly Hill, SC 29059
R. E. Roseberry, 810 W. 38th, Anderson, Ind. 46014
Safariland Leather Products, 1941 Walker Ave., Monrovia, Calif. 91016
Safety Speed Holster, Inc., 910 So. Vail, Montebello, Calif. 90640
Saguaro Holsters, 1508 Del Carlo Circle, Seagoville, TX 75159 (custom)
Buddy Schoellkopf Products, Inc., 4100 Platinum Way, Dallas, Tex. 75237
Seventrees, 315 W. 39 St., New York, N.Y. 10018
Sile Distr., 7 Centre Market Pl., New York, N.Y. 10013
Smith & Wesson Leather Co., 2100 Roosevelt, Springfield, Mass. 01101
Swiss-Craft Co., Inc., 33 Arctic St., Worcester, MA 01604
Tandy Leather Co., 1001 Foch, Fort Worth, Texas 76107
Tayra Corp., 1529-19th St. N.W., Canton, O. 44709

Triple-K Mfg. Co., 568 Sixth Ave., San Diego, CA 92101
Whitco, Box 1712, Brownsville, Tex. 78520 (Hide-A-Way)
Woodland Sport and Gift Shop, Box 107, Mayfield, N.Y. 12117

HUNTING AND CAMP GEAR, CLOTHING, ETC.

Abercrombie & Fitch, 45th & Madison Ave., N.Y., N.Y. 10017
Action Sports, Box 1264, Wausau, WI 54401 (rain gear)
Eddie Bauer, 1737 Airport Way So., Seattle, Wash. 98134
L. L. Bean, Freeport, Me. 04032
Bear Archery Co., R.R. 1, Grayling, Mich. 49738 (Himalayan backpack)
Bernzomatic Corp., 740 Driving Pk. Ave., Rochester, N.Y. 14613 (stoves & lanterns)
Big Beam, Teledyne Co., 290 E. Prairie St., Crystal Lake, Ill. 60014 (lamp)
Thos. Black & Sons, 930 Ford St., Ogdensburg, N.Y. 13669 (ctlg. 25¢)
Bill Boatman & Co., So. Maple St., Bainbridge, OH 45612
Browning, Rte. 1, Morgan, Utah 84050
Camouflage Mfg. Co., P.O. Box 5437, Pine Bluff, AR 71601
Camp and Trail Outfitters, 21 Park Place, N.Y., N.Y. 10007
Camp Trails, P.O. Box 14500, Phoenix, Ariz. 85031 (packs only)
Camp Ways, 415 Molino St., Los Angeles, CA 90013
Challanger Mfg. Co., Box 550, Jamaica, N.Y. 11431 (glow safe)
Coleman Co., Inc., 250 N. St. Francis, Wichita, Kans. 67201
Colorado Outdoor Sports Co., 5450 N. Valley Hwy., Denver, Colo. 80216
Converse Rubber Co., 2000 Mannheim Rd., Melrose Park, IL 60160
Corcoran, Inc., 2 Canton Street, Stoughton, Mass, 02072
Dana Safety Heater, J. L. Galef & Son, Inc., 85 Chamber St., N.Y. N.Y. 10007
DEER-ME Prod. Co., Box 345, Anoka, Minn. 55303 (tree steps)
Dunham's Footwear, RFD 3, Brattleboro, Vt. 05301 (boots)
Edmont-Wilson, 1300 Walnut St., Coshocton, O. 43812 (gloves)
Fabrico Mfg. Corp., 1300 W. Exchange, Chicago, Ill. 60609
Farber Bros., Inc., 821 Linden Ave., Memphis, TN 38101 (Westex Truck Pouch)
Filmat Enterpr., Inc., 200 Market St., East Paterson, N.J. 07407 (field dressing kit)
Freeman Ind., Inc., 100 Marblehead Rd., Tuckahoe, N.Y. 10707 (Trak-Kit)
Game-Winner, Inc., 515 Candler Bldg., Atlanta, GA 30336 (camouflage suits)
Gander Mountain, Inc., Box 248, Wilmot, Wis. 53192
Gerry Mountain Sports, Inc. (see Colorado Sports)
Gokey, 94 E. 4th St., St. Paul, Minn. 55101
Greenford Products, Inc., 64 Old Orchard, Skokie, Ill. 60076 (heaters & ranges)
Gun Club Sportswear, Box 477, Des Moines, Ia. 50302
Gun-Ho Case Mfg. Co., 110 E. 10th St., St. Paul, Minn. 55101
Hawthorn Co., Div. of Kellwood Co., New Haven, Mo. 63068 (tents)
Herter's Inc., Waseca, Minn. 56093
Himalayan Back Packs, P.O. Box 5668, Pine Bluff, AR 71601
Bob Hinman, 1217 W. Glen, Peoria, Ill. 61614
Holubar Mountaineering, Box 7, Boulder, Colo. 80302
Hunting World, 247 E. 50th St., New York, N.Y. 10022
Kelty Pack, Inc., Box 3645, Glendale, Calif. 91201
Peter Limmer & Sons, Box 66, Intervale, N.H. 03845 (boots)
H. O. McBurnette, Jr., Rte. 4, Box 337, Piedmont, AL 36272 (camouflage suits)
Marble Arms Corp., 420 Industrial Park, Gladstone, Mich. 49837
Moor & Mountain, 14 Main St., Concord Center, Mass. 01742
National Sports Div., 19 E. McWilliams St., Fond du Lac, Wis. 54935
Nimrod & Wayfarer Trailers, 500 Ford Blvd., Hamilton, O. 45011
Charles F. Orvis Co., Manchester, Vt. 05254 (fishing gear)
Palco Prods., 15 Hope Ave., Worcester, Mass. 01603
Paulin Infra-Red Prod. Co., 30520 Lakeland Blvd., Willowick, OH 44094
Primus-Sievert, 354 Sackett Pt. Rd., No. Haven, CT 06473 (stoves)
Raemco, Box 882, Somerville, N.J. 08876 (stoves)
Ranger Mfg. Co., Inc., P.O. Box 3676, Augusta, GA 30904
Red Head Brand Co., 4100 Platinum Way, Dallas Tex. 75237
Red Wing Shoe Co., Rte. 2, Red Wing, Minn. 55066
Refrigiwear, Inc., 71 Inip Dr., Inwood, L.I., N.Y. 11696
Reliance Ltd., 1830 Dublin Ave., Winnipeg 21, Man., Can. (tent peg)
W. R. Russell Moccasin Co., 285 S.W. Franklin, Berlin, WI 54923
Buddy Schoellkopf, Inc., 4100 Platinum Way, Dallas, Tex. 75237
Servus Rubber Co., 1136 2nd St., Rock Island, Ill. 61201 (footwear)
Sportsgear, Inc., 4909 Fremont Ave. So., Minneapolis, Minn. 55409 (pack sack & port. chair)
Sportsmen Prod. Inc., Box 1082, Boulder, Colo. 80302 (snowshoes)
Stearns Mfg. Co., Division & 30th St., St. Cloud, Minn. 56301
Sterno Inc., 105 Hudson St., Jersey City, N.J. 07302 (camp stoves)
Teledyne Co., Big Beam, 290 E. Prairie St., Crystal Lake, IL 60014
10-X Mfg. Co., 6185 Arapahoe, Boulder, CO 80303
Thermos Div., KST Co., Norwich, Conn. 06361 (Pop Tent)
Therm'x Corp., Inc., 1280 Columbus, San Francisco, Calif. 94133
Norm Thompson, 1805 N.W. Thurman St., Portland, Ore. 97209
Trailwise-The Ski Hut, 1615 University Ave., Berkeley, Calif. 94703
Travel Industries, Box 108, Oswego, Kan. 67356 (Dreamer pickup fleet)
Ute Mountain Corp., Box 3602, Englewood, Colo. 80110 (Metal Match)
Utica Duxbak Corp., 815 Noyes St., Utica, N.Y. 13502
Visa-Therm Prod., Inc., P.O. Box 486, Bridgeport, Conn. 06601 (Astro/Electr. vest)
Waffen-Frankonia, Box 380, 87 Wurzburg, W. Germany
Ward Mfg. Co., 500 Ford Blvd., Hamilton, O. 45015 (trailers)
Weinbrenner Shoe Corp., Polk St., Merrill, WI 54452
Wenzel Co., 1280 Research Blvd., St. Louis, MO 63132
Wilson Certified Foods, Inc., Box 7345, Omaha, Neb. 68107
Wisconsin Shoe Co., 1039 So. Second, Milwaukee, Wis. 53204
Woods Bag & Canvas Co., Ltd., 16 Lake St., Ogdensburg, N.Y. 13669
Woodstream Corp., Box 327, Lititz, Pa. 17543 (Hunter Seat)
Woolrich Woolen Mills, Woolrich, Pa. 17779
Yankee Mechanics, Lacey Place, Southport, CT 06490 (hand winches)
Zeus Portable Generator Co., 500 Mildred, Primos, Ohio 19018

KNIVES, AXES AND HATCHETS—HUNTING

John Applebaugh, Box 68, Blackwell, Okla. 74631 (custom-knives)
Baker Forged Knives, P.O. Box 514, Hinsdale, IL 60521 (custom-made, folder $1)
L. L. Bean, Freeport, Maine 04032
Bear Archery Co., R.R. 1, Grayling, MI 49738
Lee Biggs, 3816 Via La Silva, Palo Verde, CA 92266 (custom-knives)
Ralph Bone Knife Co., 806 Avenue J, Lubbock, Tex. 79401
H. Gardner Bourne, 1252 Hope Ave., Columbus, O. 43212 (custom-knives)
L. E. "Red" Brown, 301 E. Neece St., Long Beach, CA 90805 (custom-knives)
Buck Knives, Inc., P.O. Box 1267, El Cajon, CA 92022
Busch Custom Knives, 940 Orion, Metairie, LA 70005
Pete Callan, 17 Sherline Ave., New Orleans, LA 70124 (custom-knives)
Camillus Cutlery Co., Camillus, NY 13031
W. R. Case Knives, 20 Russell Blvd., Bradford, Pa. 16701
Challanger Mfg. Co., 118 Pearl St., Mt. Vernon, NY 10550
Collins Brothers Div., 593 Westminster Dr., N.E., Atlanta, GA 30324 (belt-buckle knife)
Cooper Knives, P.O. Box 1423, Burbank, CA 91505 (custom, ctlg. 50¢)
Custom Cutlery, 907 Greenwood Pl., Dalton, GA 30720
Custom Knifemaker's Supply, P.O. Box 11448, Dallas, TX 75223
Dan-D Custom Knives, Box 4479, Yuma, AZ 85364
Davis Custom Knives, North 1405 Ash, Spokane, WA 99201
Philip Day, Rte. 1, Box 465T, Bay Minetter, AL 36507 (custom-knives)
J. R. Dennard, 907 Greenwood Pl., Dalton, GA 30720 (custom-knives)
Chas. E. Dickey, 803 N.E. A St., Bentonville, AR 72712 (custom-knives)
T. M. Dowell, 139 St. Helen's Pl., Bend, OR 97701 (TMD custom-knives, ctlg. $1)
Draper Blade, Inc., 519 E. State Rd., American Fork, UT 84003 (custom knives, ctlg. 50¢)
John Ek, 1547 NW 119th St., No. Miami, FL 33167
Eze-Lap Diamond Prods., Box 2229, Westminster, CA 92683 (knife sharpeners)
Fischer Custom Knives, Rt. 1, Box 170-M, Victoria, TX 77901
H. H. Frank, #1 Mountain Meadows, Whitefish, MT 59937 (custom-knives)
James Furlow, 2499 Brookdale Dr. N.E., Atlanta, GA 30345 (custom-knives)
Garcia Sptg. Arms Corp., 329 Alfred Ave., Teaneck, NJ 07666
Gerber Legendary Blades, 14200 S.W. 72nd St., Portland, OR 99223
Gutman Cutlery Co., Inc., 3956 Broadway, New York, NY 10032
Gyrfalcon Inc., Kutz Bldg., 1104 Fernwood Ave., Camp Hill, PA 17011 (Skachet)
H & B Forge Co., Rte. 2, Greenwich, OH 44837 (tomahawks)
Hale Handmade Knives, Box 5988, Texarkana, TX 75501
Virgil W. Hartley, 1602 S. Hunter Rd., Indianapolis, IN 46239 (Bamsen knives)
C. M. (Pete) Heath, 119 Grant St., Winnecone, WI 54986 (custom-knives)
J. A. Henckels Twinworks, 1 Westchester Plaza, Elmsford, NY 10523
G. H. Herron, 920 Murrah Ave., Aiken, SC 29801 (custom-knives)
Gil Hibben, Box 773, Springdale, AR 72764 (custom-knives)
Chubby Hueske, 4808 Tamarisk Dr., Bellaire, TX 77401 (custom-knives)
Bill Imel (see Ramrod Knife & Gun Shop)
Indian Ridge Traders, P.O. Box X-50, Ferndale, MI 48220
Jet-Aer Corp., 100 Sixth Ave., Paterson, NJ 07524 (G96 knives)
LaDow (Doc) Johnston, 2322 W. Country Club Parkway, Toledo, OH 43614 (custom-knives)
KA-BAR Cutlery, Inc., 5777 Grant Ave., Cleveland, OH 44105
Jon W. Kirk, 800 N. Olive, Fayetteville, AR 72701 (custom-knives)
W. Kneubuhler, P.O. Box 327, Pioneer, OH 43554 (custom-knives)
Kustom Made Knives, 418 Jolee, Richardson, TX 75080
Lile Handmade Knives, Rte. 1, Box 56, Russellville, AR 72801
LocKnife, Inc., 11717 E. 23rd St., Independence, MO 64050
R. W. Loveless, P.O. Box 7836, Arlington Sta., Riverside, CA 92503 (custom-knives, ctlg. $1)
Bob Ludwig, 1028 Pecos Ave., Port Arthur, TX 77640 (custom-knives)
MAC Intl. Corp., 4848 W. Main, Skokie, IL 60076
Marble Arms Corp., 420 Industrial Park, Gladstone, MI 49837
Joe S. Martin, Box 6652, Lubbock, TX 79413 (custom-knives)
John T. Mims, 620 S. 28th Ave., Apt. 327, Hattiesburg, MS 39401 (custom-knives)
Mitchell Knives, 511 Ave. B, So. Houston, TX 77587 (custom)
W. F. Moran, Jr., Rt. 5, Frederick, MD 21701 (custom-knives, ctlg. 50¢)
Morseth Sports Equip. Co., 1705 Hiway 71N, Springdale, AR 72764 (custom-knives)
Normark Corp., 1710 E. 78th St., Minneapolis, MN 55423
Ogg Custom Knives, Rt. 1, Box 230, Paris, AR 72855
Olsen Knife Co., Inc., 7 Joy St., Howard City, MI 49329
Ramrod Knife & Gun Shop, Route 5, State Road 3 North, Newcastle, IN 47362 (custom-knives)
Randall-Made Knives, Box 1988, Orlando, FL 32802 (ctlg. 25¢)
Razor Edge, Box 203, Butler, WI 53007 (knife sharpener)
F. J. Richtig, Clarkson, NB 68629 (custom-knives)
Rigid Knives, P.O. Box 460, Santee, CA 92071 (custom-made)
Ruana Knife Works, Box 574, Bonner, MT 59823 (ctlg. 50¢)
Sanders, 2358 Tyler Lane, Louisville, KY 40205 (Bahco)
Jack D. Schmier, 16787 Mulberry Ct., Fountain Valley, CA 92708 (custom-knives)
Bob Schrimsher, Custom Knifemaker's Supply, P.O. Box 11448, Dallas, TX 75223
John J. Schwarz, 41 Fifteenth St., Wellsburg, WV 26070 (custom-knives)
N. H. Schiffman Custom Knives, 963 Malibu, Pocatello, ID 83201
Sewell Custom Knives, 1307 Spring St. N.W., Atlanta, GA 30309
C. R. Sigman, Star Rte., Box 3, Red House, WV 25168
Skachet, (see: Gyrfalcon Inc.)
Smith & Wesson, 2100 Roosevelt Ave., Springfield, MA 01101
John T. Smith, 6048 Cedar Crest Dr., So. Haven, MS 38671 (custom-knives)
W. J. Sonneville, 1050 Chalet Dr. W., Mobile, AL 36608 (custom-knives)

Bernard Sparks, Box 32, Dingle, ID 83233 (custom-knives)
Stone Knives, 703 Floyd Rd., Richardson, TX 75080
Thompson/Center, P.O. Box 2405, Rochester, NH 03867
Track Knives, 1313 2nd St., Whitefish, MT 59937
Tru-Balance Knife Co., 2115 Tremont Blvd., Grand Rapids, MI 49504
True-Temper, 1623 Euclid, Cleveland, OH 44100
Unique Inventions, Inc., 3727 W. Alabama St., Houston, TX 77027 (throwing knife)
W-K Knives, P.O. Box 327, Pioneer, OH 43554
Western Cutlery Co., 5311 Western Ave., Boulder, CO 80302
Ronnie Wilson, P.O. Box 2012, Weirton, WV 26062 (custom-knives)
Don Zaccagaino, P.O. Box Zack, Pahokee, FL 33476 (custom-knives)

LABELS, BOXES, CARTRIDGE HOLDERS

Milton Brynin, Box 162, Fleetwood Station, Mount Vernon, NY 10552 (cartridge box labels)
E-Z Loader, Del Rey Products, P.O. Box 91561, Los Angeles, CA 90009
Jasco, J. A. Somers Co., P.O. Box 49751, Los Angeles, CA 90049 (cartridge box labels)
Llanerch Gun Shop, 2800 Township Line, Upper Darby, PA 19083 (cartridge box labels)
C. W. Paddock, Shooters Supplies, 1251 Blair Ave., St. Paul, MN 55104 (cartridge boxes)
Peterson Label Co., P.O. Box 186Z, Redding Ridge, CT 06876 (cartridge box labels; Targ-Dots)
Ramco, P.O. Box 741, Loveland, CO 80537 (ammo organizer)
N. H. Schiffman, 963 Malibu, Pocatello, ID 83201 (cartridge carrier)

LOAD TESTING & CHRONOGRAPHING

Carter Gun Works, 2211 Jefferson Pk. Ave., Charlottesville, Va. 22903
Custom Ballistics' Lab., 3354 Cumberland Dr., San Angelo, Tex. 76901
Horton Ballistics, North Waterford, Me. 04267
Hutton Rifle Ranch, Box 898, Topanga, CA 90290
Jurras Co., Box 163, Shelbyville, Ind. 46176
Kennon's, 5408 Biffle, Stone Mountain, Ga. 30083
Plum City Ballistics Range, Box 29C, Plum City, Wis. 54761
Shooters Service & Dewey, Inc., Clinton Corners, N.Y. 12514 (daily fee range also)
Gene West, 137 Baylor, Pueblo, Colo. 81005
H. P. White Lab., Box 331, Bel Air, Md. 21014

MISCELLANEOUS

Accurizing Service, Herbert G. Troester, Cayuaga, ND 58013
Adhesive Flannel, Forest City Prod., 722 Bolivar, Cleveland, OH 44115
Archery, Bear Co., R.R. 1, Grayling, Mich. 49738
Arms Research, American Arms Co., 1641 Maplecrest Dr., Bloomington, Ind. 47401
Arms Restoration, J. J. Jenkins, 462 Stanford Pl., Santa Barbara, CA 93105
Barrel Band Swivels, Phil Judd, 83 E. Park St., Butte, Mont. 59701
Barrel Bedding Device, W. H. Womack, 2124 Meriwether Rd., Shreveport, La. 71108
Bedding Kit, Bisonite Co., 2250 Military Rd., Tonawanda, NY 14150
Bedding Kit, Fenwal, Inc., Resin Systems Div., 400 Main St., Ashland, Mass. 01721
Binocular/Camera Harness, Jack Worsfold Assoc., Box 25, Forest Hill, Md. 21050
Bootdryers, Baekgaard Ltd., 1855 Janke Dr., Northbrook, Ill. 60062
Breech Plug Wrench, Swaine Machine, 195 O'Connell, Providence, R.I. 02905
Cannons, South Bend Replicas Inc., 61650 Oak Rd., So. Bend, IN 46614 (ctlg. $1)
Case Gauge, Plum City Ballistics Range, Box 29C, Plum City, Wis. 54761
Chrome Brl. Lining, Marker Mach. Co., Box 426, Charleston, Ill. 61920
Color Hardening, Alamo Heat Treating Co., Box 55345, Houston, Tex. 77055
Crow Caller, Wightman Elec. Inc., Box 989, Easton, Md. 21601
Custom Bluing, J. A. Wingert, 124 W. 2nd St., Waynesboro, Pa. 17268
Distress Flares, Marsh Coulter Co., P.O. Box 333, Tecumseh, MI 49286
Dog House, Canine Pal Sales, 421 E. 39th Ave., Gary, Ind. 46409 (portable)
Dryer, Thermo-Electric, Golden-Rod, (Phinney-Hale, Inc., Box 5286, Oxnard, CA 93030
E-Z Loader, Del Rey Prod., P.O. Box 91561, Los Angeles, CA 90009
Ear-Valv, Sigma Eng. Co., 11320 Burbank Blvd., N. Hollywood, Cal. 91601 (Lee-Sonic)
Emergency Food, Chuck Wagon, Micro Dr., Woburn, Mass. 01801
Fill N'File, Apsco Packaging Co., 9325 W. Bryon St., Schiller Park, IL 60176
Flares, Colt Industries, Huyshope Ave., Hartford, Conn. 06102
Flares, Intercontinental Arms, 2222 Barry Ave., Los Angeles, Ca. 90064 (MBA)
Flares, Smith & Wesson Chemical Co., 2399 Forman Rd., Rock Creek, OH 44084
Flat Springs, Alamo Heat Treating Co., Box 55345, Houston, Tex. 77055
Game Hoist, Flanders Mfg. Co., Box 33363, Houston, Tex. 77033
Game Hoist, PIC, 3 Chestnut, Suffern, N.Y. 10901
Game Scent, Buck Stop, Inc., 3015 Grow Rd., Stanton, Mi 4888
Game Scent, Pete Rickard, R.D. 1, Carlisle Rd., Box 1002, Cobleskill, N.Y. 12043 (Indian Buck lure)
Gas Pistol, Penguin Ind., Inc., Box 97, Parkesburg, Pa. 19365
Golden-Rod, Phinney-Hale, Inc., P.O. Box 5286, Oxnard, CA 93030 (Thermo-Electric Dryers)
Gun Bedding Kit, Resin Systems Div., Fenwal, Inc., 400 Main St., Ashland, Mass. 01721
Gun Jewelry, Sid Bell, Originals, Box 188, Tully, N.Y. 13159
Gun Jewelry, Al Popper, 614 Turnpike St., Stoughton, Mass. 02072
Gun Lock, E & C Enterprises, P.O. Box 823, So. Pasadena, CA. 91030

Gun Lock Chain, Lundy Corp., 1123-24 Davenport Bk. Bldg., Davenport, Ia. 52801
Gun Sling, Kwikfire, Wayne Prods. Co., P.O. Box 247, Camp Hill, PA 17011
Hollow Pointer, Goerg Ent., 3009 S. Laurel St., Port Angeles, Wash. 98362
Hugger Hooks, Roman Products, Box 891, Golden, Colo. 80401
Hunting Bag, Dan Barr, Rte. 1, Thornville, OH 43076
Insect Repellent, Armor, Div. of Buck Stop, Inc., 3015 Grow Rd., Stanton, Mich. 48888
Insert Barrels, (22 RF) H. Owen, P.O. Box 774, Sunnyvale, Calif. 94088
Lightnin-Loader, Hunter Mfg. Co., Box 2882, Van Nuys, Cal. 91404
Locks, Gun, Bor-Lok Prods., 105 5th St., Arbuckle, CA 95912
Magazine Clip (Colyer), Great Northern Trading Post, 13001 Hwy. 65 N.E., Rte. 4, Anoka, Minn. 55303
Magazine Clips, Amer. Firearms Mfg. Co., Inc., 1200 Warfield, San Antonio, Tex. 78216
Locks, Gun, Master Lock Co., 2600 N. 32nd St., Milwaukee, WI 53245
Military Museum, Lt. Col. E.H. Hoffman, 768 So. Main St., Woodstock, Va. 22664
Miniature Guns, C. H. Stoppler, 1426 Walton Ave., N.Y., N.Y. 10452
Monte Carlo Pad, Frank A. Hoppe Div., P.O. Box 97, Parkesburg, Pa. 19365
Muzzle-Top, Allen Assoc., 7502 Limekiln, Philadelphia, PA 19150 (plastic gun muzzle cap)
Pell Remover, A. Edw. Terpening, 838 W. Darlington Rd., Tarpon Springs, Fla. 33589
Powder Storage Magazine, C & M Gunworks, 4201 36th Ave., Moline, IL 61265
Pressure Testg. Machine, M. York, 19381 Keymar Way, Gaithersburg, MD 20760
Ransom Handgun Rests, C'Arco, P.O. Box 2043, San Bernardino, CA 92406
Retriev-R-Trainer, Scientific Prods. Corp., 426 Swann Ave., Alexandria, VA 22301
Rifle Slings, Bianchi, 212 W. Foothill Blvd., Monrovia, Cal. 91016
Rifle Sling, Ready Sling Co., P.O. Box 536, Delano, CA 93215
RIG, NRA Scoring Plug, Rig Prod. Co., Box 279, Oregon, Ill. 60161
Rubber Cheekpiece, W. H. Lodewick, 2816 N. E. Halsey, Portland, Ore. 97232
Safeties, Williams Gun Sight Co., 7389 Lapeer Rd., Davison, Mich. 48423
Salute Cannons, Naval Co., Rt. 611, Doylestown, Pa. 18901
Sav-Bore, Saunders Sptg. Gds., 338 Somerset St., N. Plainfield, NJ 07060
Scrimshaw Engraving, C. Milton Barringer, 217-2nd Isle N., Port Richey, FL 33568
Scrimshaw Engraving, A. Douglas Jacobs, Box 1236, Cutchogue, NY 11935
Sharpening Stones, Russell's Arkansas Oilstones, 1705 Hiway 71N., Springdale, AR 72764
Shell Shrinker Mfg. Co., Box 6143, Lubbock, Tex. 79413
Shok-Baton Co., 440 W. Nixon St., Savage, MN 55378
Shooting Bench/Porto, Universal Standard Prods. Inc., 926 N. Memorial Dr., Racine, WI 53404
Shooting Coats, 10-X Mfg. Co., 6185 Arapahoe, Boulder, CO 80303
Shooting Ranges, Shooting Equip. Inc., 10 S. LaSalle, Chicago, IL 60603
Shotgun Sight, bi-ocular, Trius Prod., Box 25, Cleves, O. 45002
Silver Grip Caps, Bill Dyer, P.O. Box 75255, Oklahoma City, Okla. 73107
Snap Caps, Filmat, 200 Market, East Paterson, N.J. 07407
Snap Caps, G & S Engineering Co., Box 590, Clinton, MI 49236 (Practicaps)
Snowshoes, Sportsmen Prod. Inc., Box 1082, Boulder, Colo. 80302
Springfield Safety Pin, B-Square Co., P.O. Box 11281, Ft. Worth, Tex. 76110
Springs, W. Wolff Co., Box 232, Ardmore, Pa. 19003
Stock-Lo-Kater, Bill Matthews Co., 5004 Encinita Ave., Temple City, Ca. 91780
Supersound, Edmund Scientific Co., 101 E. Gloucester Pike, Barrington, NJ 08007 (safety device)
Swivels, Michaels, P.O. Box 13010, Portland, Ore. 97213
Swivels, Sile Dist., 7 Centre Market Pl., New York, N.Y. 10013
Swivels, Williams Gun Sight Co., 7389 Lapeer Rd., Davison, Mich. 48423
Trophies, L. G. Balfour Co., Attleboro, Mass. 02703
Trophies, Blackinton & Co., 140 Commonwealth, Attleboro Falls, Mass. 12763
Trophies, F. H. Noble & Co., 559 W. 59th St., Chicago, Ill. 60621
Universal 3-shot Shotgun Plug, LanDav Custom Guns, 7213 Lee Highway, Falls Church, VA 22046
Worldhunting Info., Jack Atcheson, 2309 Hancock Ave., Butte, Mont. 59701
World Hunting Info., Denver Jonas Bros., 1037 Broadway, Denver, CO 80203

MUZZLE LOADING BARRELS OR EQUIPMENT

Luther Adkins, Box 281, Shelbyville, Ind. 47176 (breech plugs)
Anderson & Co., 1203 Broadway, Yakima, WA 98902
Armoury, Inc., Rte. 25, New Preston, Conn. 06777
Barney's Cannons, Inc., 61650 Oak Rd., South Bend, IN 46614 (ctlg. $1)
Dan Barr, Rte. 1, Thornville, OH 43076 (hunting bag)
Henry S. Beverage, New Gloucester, Me. 04260 (brass bullet mould)
John Bivins, Jr., 446 So. Main, Winston-Salem, N.C. 27101
Jesse F. Booher, 2751 Ridge Ave., Dayton, Ohio 45414
G. S. Bunch, 7735 Garrison, Hyattsville, Md. 20784 (flask repair)
Pat Burke, 3339 Farnsworth Rd., Lapeer, Mich. 48446 (capper)
Caution Tool Co., Scout Rd., Southbury, CT 06488
Challanger Mfg. Co., 118 Pearl St., Mt. Vernon, NY 10550
Cherry Corners Mfg. Co., 11136 Congress Rd., Lodi, Ohio 44254
Chopie Mfg. Inc., 531 Copeland Ave., LaCrosse, WI 54601 (nipple wrenches)
Cornwall Bridge Gun Shop, P.O. Box 67, Cornwall Bridge, CT 06745
Earl T. Cureton, Rte. 6, 7017 Pine Grove Rd., Knoxville, Tenn. 37914 (powder horns)

John N. Dangelzer, 3056 Frontier Pl. N.E., Albuquerque, N. Mex. 87106 (powder flasks)
Ted Fellowes, Beaver Lodge, 9245 16th Ave. S.W., Seattle, Wash. 98106
Firearms Imp. & Exp. Corp., 2470 N.W. 21st St., Miami, Fla. 33142
Golden Age Arms Co., 657 High St., Worthington, Ohio 43085 (ctlg. $1)
Golden Strip Enterprises, Box 457, Simpsonville, SC 29681 (powder horns)
A. R. Goode, R.D. 1, Box 84, Thurmont, MD 21788
Green River Forge, 4326 120th Ave. S.E., Bellevue, WA 98006 (Forge-Fire flints)
Virgil W. Hartley, 1602 S. Hunter Rd., Indianapolis, IN 46239 (ML pouch)
International M. L. Parts Co., 19453 Forrer, Detroit, MI 48235
JJJJ Ranch, Wm. Large, Rte. 1, Ironton, Ohio 45638
K & W Cap and Ball Dispenser, Rte. 2, 5073 Townsley Rd., Cedarville, OH 45314
Kindig's Log Cabin Sport Shop, R.D. 1, Box 275, Lodi, OH 44254
Art LeFeuvre, 1003 Hazel Ave., Deerfield, Ill. 60015 (antique gun restoring)
Les' Gun Shop (Les Bauska), Box 511, Kalispell, Mont. 59901
Lever Arms Serv. Ltd., 771 Dunsmuir, Vancouver 1, B.C., Canada
J. Lewis Arms Mfg., 3931 Montgomery Rd., Cincinnati, Ohio 45212 (pistol)
McKeown's Guns, R.R. 1, Pekin, IL 61554 (E-Z load rev. stand)
Maryland Gun Exchange Inc., Rt. 40 West, RD 5, Frederick, MD 21701
Maywood Forge, Foley, MN 56329 (cannons)
Jos. W. Mellott, 334 Rockhill Rd., Pittsburgh, Pa. 15243 (barrel blanks)
W. L. Mowrey Gun Works, Inc., Box 711, Olney, Tex. 73674
Muzzle Loaders Supply Co., Rte. 25, New Preston, CT 06777
Numrich Corp., W. Hurley, N.Y. 12491 (powder flasks)
R. Paris & Son, R.D. 5, Box 61, Gettysburg, Pa. 17325 (barrels)
Penna. Rifle Works, 319 E. Main St., Ligonier, Pa. 15658 (ML guns, parts)
Rush's Old Colonial Forge, 106 Wiltshire Rd., Baltimore, MD 21221
H. M. Schoeller, 569 So. Braddock Ave., Pittsburgh, Pa. 15221
Shilo Ind., Inc., 173 Washington Pl., Hasbrouck Heights, NJ 07604 (4-cavity mould)
C. E. Siler, 181 Sandhill School, Asheville, N.C., 28806 (flint locks)
Upper Missouri Trading Co., Inc., Box 181, Crofton, NB 68730
Thos. F. White, 5801 Westchester Ct., Worthington, O. 43085 (powder horn)
Lou Williamson, 129 Stonegate Ct., Bedford, TX 76021
R. E. Zellmer, W180 N8996 Leona Ln., Menomonee Falls, WI 53051 (Kentucky Fullstocks)

REBORING AND RERIFLING

P.O. Ackley, 2235 Arbor Lane, Salt Lake City, UT 84117
Atkinson Gun Co., P.O. Box 512, Prescott, AZ 86301
Bain & Davis Sptg. Gds., 559 W. Las Tunas Dr., San Gabriel, Calif. 91776
Carpenter's Gun Works, Gunshop Rd., Box C, Plattekill, N.Y. 12568
Fuller Gun Shop, Cooper Landing, Alaska 99572
Ward Koozer, Box 18, Walterville, Ore. 97489
Les' Gun Shop, Box 511, Kalispell, Mont. 59901
Morgan's Cust. Reboring, 707 Union Ave., Grants Pass, OR 97526
Nu-Line Guns, 3727 Jennings Rd., St. Louis, Mo. 63121
Al Petersen, Box 8, Riverhurst, Saskatchewan, Canada S0H3P0
Schuetzen Gun Works, 1226 Prairie Rd., Colorado Springs, Colo. 80909
Sharon Rifle Barrel Co., P.O. Box 106, Kalispell, Mont. 59901
Siegrist Gun Shop, R.R. #1, Whittemore, MI 48770
Small Arms Eng., P.O. Box 306, Des Plaines, IL 60018
Snapp's Gunshop, 6911 E. Washington Rd., Clare, Mich. 48617
R. Southgate, Rt. 2, Franklin, Tenn. 37064 (Muzzleloaders)
J. W. Van Patten, Box 145, Foster Hill, Milford, Pa. 18337
Robt. G. West, 6626 So. Lincoln, Littleton, Colo. 80120

RESTS—BENCH, PORTABLE, ETC.

Bausch & Lomb, 635 St. Paul St., Rochester, NY 14602 (rifle rest)
Gene Beecher Prods., 2155 Demington Dr., Cleveland Hgts., OH 44106
Jim Brobst, 299 Poplar St., Hamburg, PA 19526 (bench rest pedestal)
C'Arco, P.O. Box 2043, San Bernardino, CA 92401 (Ransom handgun rest)
Central Specialties Co., 630 Northwest Hwy., Chicago, IL 60631 (portable gun rest)
Cole's Acku-Rite Prod., Box 25, Kennedy, N.Y. 14747
F & H Machining, 4645 Cambio Ct., Fremont, CA 94536
The Fergusons, 27 W. Chestnut St., Farmingdale, N.Y. 11735 (rifle rests)
Frontier Arms, Inc., 420 E. Riding Club Rd., Cheyenne, Wyo. 82001
The Gun Case, 11035 Maplefield, El Monte, Cal. 91733
Harris Engr., Inc., Box 305, Fraser, Mich. 48026 (bipods)
Rob. W. Hart & Son, 401 Montgomery St., Nescopeck, Pa. 18635
North Star Devices, Inc., P.O. Box 2095, North St. Paul, MN 55109 (Gun Slinger)
Porto/Shooting bench, Universal Std. Prods., 926 N. Memorial, Racine, WI 53404
Rec. Prods., Res., Inc., 158 Franklin Ave., Ridgewood, N.J. 07450 (Butts Pipod)
Suter's, 332 Tejon, Colorado Springs, CO 80902
Basil Tuller, 29 Germania, Galeton, PA 16922 (Protecktor sandbags)
Walden Leisure Prods., 1040 Matley Lane, Bldg. 4, Reno, NV 89502 (bench rest accessory case; portable bench)
W. H. Womack, 2124 Meriwether Rd., Shreveport, La. 71108

RELOADING TOOLS AND ACCESSORIES

Acme Ind. Inc., Box 101, Kaukauna, WI 54130 (loader & wingtraps)
Alcan, (See: Smith & Wesson Arms Co.)
Alpha-Molykote, Dow Corning Corp., 45 Commerce, Trumbull, Ct. 06601
Anchor Alloys, Inc., 966 Meeker Ave., Brooklyn, N.Y. 11222 (chilled shot)
Anchor Plastics, Inc., P.O. Box 300, Logansport, IN 46947
Anderson Mfg. Co., Royal, Ia. 51357 (Shotshell Trimmers)
Aurands, 229 E. 3rd St., Lewistown, Pa. 17044

B-Square Eng. Co., Box 11281, Ft. Worth, Tex. 76110
Bahler Die Shop, Box 386, Florence, Ore. 97439
Bair Machine Co., Box 4407, Lincoln, Neb. 68504
Bill Ballard, P.O. Box 656, Billings, Mont. 59103
Belding & Mull, P.O. Box 428, Philipsburg, Pa. 16866
Belmont Prods., Rte. 1, Friendsville, TN 37737 (lead cutter)
H. S. Beverage, New Gloucester, Me. 04260 (brass bullet mould)
Blackhawk SAA East, K2274 POB, Loves Park, Ill. 61111
Blackhawk SAA West, Box 285, Hiawatha, KS 66434
Bonanza Sports, Inc., 412 Western Ave., Faribault, Minn. 55021
Gene Bowlin, 3602 Hill Ave., Snyder, Tex. 79549 (arbor press)
Brown Precision Co., 5869 Indian Ave., San Jose, Calif. 95123 (Little Wiggler)
A. V. Bryant, 72 Whiting Rd., East Hartford, CT 06118 (Nutmeg Universal Press)
C-H Tool & Die Corp., Box L, Owen, Wis. 54460
Camdex, Inc., 18619 W. Seven Mile Rd., Detroit, Mich. 48219
Carbide Die & Mfg. Co., Box 226, Covina, Calif. 91706
Carter Gun Works, 2211 Jefferson Pk. Ave., Charlottesville, Va. 22903
Cascade Cartridge, Inc., (See Omark)
Clymer Mfg. Co., 14241 W. 11 Mile Rd., Oak Park, MI 48237 (½-jack. swaging dies)
Lester Coats, 416 Simpson St., No. Bend, Ore. 97459 (core cutter)
Cole's Acku-Rite Prod., P.O. Box 25, Kennedy, N.Y. 14747 (die racks)
Containter Development Corp., 424 Montgomery St., Watertown, Wis. 53094
Continental Kite & Key Co., Box 40, Broomall, PA 19008 (primer pocket cleaner)
Cooper-Woodward, Box 972, Riverside, Calif. 92502 (Perfect Lube)
J. Dewey Gun Co., Clinton Corners, N.Y. 12514 (bullet spinner)
Diverter Arms, Inc., 6520 Rampart St., Houston, TX 77036 (bullet puller)
Division Lead Co., 7742 W. 61st Pl., Summit, Ill. 60502
Eagle Products Co., 1520 Adelia Ave., So. El Monte, Cal. 91733
W. H. English, 4411 S. W. 100th, Seattle, Wash. 98146 (Paktool)
Farmer Bros. Mfg. Co., 1102 Washington St., Eldora, IA 50627 (Lage wads)
The Fergusons, 27 W. Chestnut St., Farmingdale, N.Y. 11735
Fitz, Box 49797, Los Angeles, Calif. 90049 (Fitz Flipper)
Flambeau Plastics, 801 Lynn, Baraboo, Wis. 53913
Forster-Appelt Mfg. Co., Inc., 82 E. Lanark Ave., Lanark, Ill. 61046
Gene's Gun Shop, 3602 Hill Ave., Snyder, Tex. 79549 (arbor press)
John R. Gillette, 4514 W. 123d Place, Alsip, IL 60658
Goerg Enterprises, 3009 S. Laurel, Port Angeles, WA 98362 (hollow pointer)
Gopher Shooter's Supply, Box 246, Faribault, Minn. 55021
Griffin Shooter's Supplies, 7801-A9 Hillmont, Houston, TX 77040 (Electric operator for MEC tools)
The Gun Clinic, 81 Kale St., Mahtomedi, Minn. 55115
Hart Products, 401 Montgomery St., Nescopeck, Pa. 18635
Ed Hart, U.S. Rte. 15, Cohocton, NY 14826 (Meyer shotgun slugs)
Frank A. Hemsted, Box 281, Sunland, Cal. 91040 (swage dies)
Hensley & Gibbs, Box 10, Murphy, Ore. 97533
E. C. Herkner Co., Box 5007, Boise, Ida. 83702
Herter's Inc., RR1, Waseca, Minn. 56093
B. E. Hodgdon, Inc., 7710 W. 50 Hiway, Shawnee Mission, Kans. 66202
Hollywood Reloading, see: Whitney Sales, Inc.
Hulme Firearm Serv., Box 83, Millbrae, Calif. 94030 (Star case feeder)
Hunter Bradlee Co., 2800 Routh St., Dallas, TX 75201 (powder measure)
Independent Mach. & Gun Shop, 1416 N. Hayes, Pocatello, Ida. 83201
JASCO, Box 49751, Los Angeles, Calif. 90049
J & G Rifle Ranch, Turner, Mont. 59542 (case tumblers)
Javelina Products, Box 337, San Bernardino, Cal. 92402 (Alox beeswax)
Kexplore, Box 22084, Houston, Tex. 77027
Kuharsky Bros., 2425 W. 12th, Erie, Pa. 16500 (primer pocket cleaner)
Kush Plastics, P.O. Box 366, Palatine, IL 60067 (shotshell wads)
Lachmiller Eng. Co., 11273 Goss St., Sun Valley, CA 91352
Lage universal shotshell wad, see: Farmer Bros.
LanDav, 7213 Lee Highway, Falls Church, VA 22046 (X-15 bullet puller)
Lee Engineering, 21 E. Wisconsin St., Hartford, Wis. 53027
Leon's Reloading Service, 3945 No. 11 St., Lincoln, Neb. 68521
L. L. F. Die Shop, 1281 Highway 99 N., Eugene, Ore. 97402
Ljutic Industries, 918 N. 5th Ave., Yakima, Wash. 98902
Lock's Phila. Gun Exch., 6700 Rowland, Philadelphia, Pa. 19149
J. T. Loos, P.O. Box 41, Pomfret, CT. 06258 (primer pocket cleaner)
Lyman Gun Sight Products, Middlefield, Conn. 06455
McKillen & Heyer, Box 627, Willoughby, O. 44094 (case gauge)
Paul McLean, 2670 Lakeshore Blvd., W., Toronto 14, Ont., Canada (Universal Cartridge Holder)
Pat B. McMillan, 1828 E. Campo Bello Dr., Phoenix, Ariz. 85022
MTM Molded Prod., 5680 Webster St., Dayton, OH 45414
Magma Eng. Co., P.O. Box 881, Chandler, AZ 85224
Mayville Eng. Co., 715 South St., Mayville, Wis. 53050 (shotshell loader)
Merit Gun Sight Co., P.O. Box 995, Sequim, Wash. 98382
Minnesota Shooters Supply, 1915 E. 22nd St., Minneapolis, Minn. 55404
Murdock Lead Co., Box 5298, Dallas, Tex. 75222
National Lead Co., Box 831, Perth Amboy, N.J. 08861
Normington Co., Box 156, Rathdrum, Ida. 83858 (powder baffles)
Ohaus Scale Corp., 29 Hanover Rd., Florham Park, N.J. 07932
Omark-CCI, Inc., Box 856, Lewiston, Ida. 83501
Pacific Tool Co., P.O. Drawer 2048, Ordnance Plant Rd., Grand Island, NB 68801
C. W. Paddock Shooters Supplies, 1251 Blair Ave., St. Paul, MN 55101 (cartridge boxes)
Pak-Tool Co., 4411 S.W. 100th, Seattle, WA 98146
Pattern Perfect, P.O. Box 366, Palatine, IL 60067 (shotshell wads)
Perfection Die Co., 1614 S. Choctaw, El Reno, Okla. 73036
Personal Firearms Record Book, Box 201, Park Ridge, Ill. 60068
Ferris Pindell, R.R. 3, Box 205, Connersville, IN 47331 (bullet spinner)
Plum City Ballistics Range, Box 29C, Plum City, Wis. 54761
Ponsness-Warren, Inc., P.O. Box 861, Eugene, OR 97401

Potter Eng. Co., 1410 Santa Ana Dr., Dunedin, FL 33528 (electric pots only)
Marian Powley, 19 Sugarplum Rd., Levittown, Pa. 10956
Quinetics Corp., 3740 Colony Dr., San Antonio, Tx. 78230 (kinetic bullet puller)
RCBS, Inc., Box 1919, Oroville, Calif. 95965
Redco, Box 15523, Salt Lake City, Utah 84115
Redding-Hunter, Inc., 114 Starr Rd., Cortland, N.Y. 13045
Remco, 1404 Whitesboro St., Utica, N.Y. 13502 (shot caps)
Rifle Ranch, Rte. 1, Prescott, Ariz. 86301
Rochester Lead Works, Rochester, N.Y. 14608 (leadwire)
Rorschach Precision Prods., P.O. Box 1613, Irving, Tex. 75060
Rotex Mfg. Co. (see Texan)
Ruhr-American Corp., So. East Hwy. 55, Glenwood, Minn. 56334
SAECO Rel. Inc., P.O. Box 778, Carpinteria, Calif. 93013
Savage Arms Co., Westfield, Mass. 01085
Scientific Lubricants Co., 3753 Lawrence Ave., Chicago, Ill. 60625
Shilo IV, Inc., 173 Washington Pl., Hasbrouck Heights, NJ 07604 (4-cavity bullet mould)
Shoffstalls Mfg. Co., 740 Ellis Place, E. Aurora N.Y. 14052
Shooters Accessory Supply, Box 250, N. Bend, Ore. 97459 (SAS)
Shooters Serv. & Dewey, Inc., Clinton Corners, N.Y. 12514 (SS&D) (bullet spinner)
Sil's Gun Prod., 490 Sylvan Dr., Washington, Pa. 15301 (K-spinner)
Jerry Simmons, 713 Middlebury St., Goshen, Ind. 46526 (Pope de- & recapper)
Rob. B. Simonson, Rte. 7, 2129 Vanderbilt Rd., Kalamazoo, Mich. 49002
Smith & Wesson Ammunition Co., Inc., 3640 Seminary Rd., Alton, IL 62002
J. A. Somers Co., P.O. Box 49751, Los Angeles, CA 90049 (Jasco)
Star Machine Works, 418 10th Ave., San Diego, Calif. 92101
Sullivan Arms Corp., see: Anchor Plastics
Texan Reloaders, Inc., P.O. Box 5355, Dallas, Tex. 75222
VAMCO, Box 67, Vestal, N.Y. 13850
W. S. Vickerman, 505 W. 3rd Ave., Ellensburg, Wash. 98926
Walker Mfg. Inc., 8296 So. Channel, Harsen's Island, MI 48028 (Berdan decapper)
Weatherby, Inc., 2781 Firestone Blvd., South Gate, Calif. 90280
Webster Scale Mfg. Co., Box 188, Sebring, Fla. 33870
Whitney Cartridge Co., P.O. Box 608, Cortez, CO 81321 (shotshells)
Whitney Sales, Inc., P.O. 875, Reseda, CA 91335 (Hollywood)
L. E. Wilson, Inc., Box 324, Cashmere, Wash. 98815
Xelex, Ltd., Hawksbury, Ont., Canada (powder)
Zenith Ent., RFD, Nordland, WA 98358
A. Zimmerman, 127 Highland Trail, Denville, N.J. 07834 (case trimmer)

RIFLE BARREL MAKERS

P.O. Ackley, 2235 Arbor Lane, Salt Lake City, UT 84117
Apex Rifle Co., 7628 San Fernando, Sun Valley, Calif. 91352
Atkinson Gun Co., P.O. Box 512, Prescott, AZ 86301
Christy Gun Works, 875 57th St., Sacramento, Calif. 95819
Clerke Prods., 2219 Main St., Santa Monica, Calif. 90405
Cuthbert Gun Shop, 715 So. 5th, Coos Bay, Ore. 97420
Darr's Rifle Shop, 2309 Black Rd., Joliet, IL 60435
J. Dewey Gun Co., Clinton Corners, N.Y. 12514
Douglas Barrels, Inc., 5504 Big Tyler Rd., Charleston, W. Va. 25312
Douglas Jackalope Gun & Sport Shop, Inc., 1205 E. Richards St., Douglas, WY 82633
Federal Firearms Co., Inc., Box 145, Oakdale, Pa. 15071 (Star bbls., actions)
A. R. Goode, R.D. 1, Box 84, Thurmont, MD 21788
Hart Rifle Barrels, Inc., RD 2, Lafayette, N.Y. 13084
Wm. H. Hobaugh, Box 657, Philipsburg, Mont. 59858
Intern'l Casting Co., 19453 Forrer, Detroit, Mich. 48235
Johnson Automatics, Box 306, Hope Valley, R.I. 02832
Gene Lechner, 636 Jane N.E., Albuquerque, NM 87123
Les' Gun Shop, Box 511, Kalispell, Mont. 59901
McGowen Rifle Barrels, Rte. 3, St. Anne, Ill. 60964
D. M. Manley, 295 Main St., Brookville, PA 15825
Nu-Line Guns, Inc., 3727 Jennings Rd., St. Louis, Mo. 63121
Numrich Arms, W. Hurley, N.Y. 12491
R. Paris & Son, R.D. 5, Box 61, Gettysburg, Pa. 17325
Rheinmetall (see John Weir)
SS & D, Inc., Clinton Corners, N.Y. 12514 (cold-formed bbls.)
Sanders Cust. Gun Serv., 2358 Tyler Lane, Louisville, Ky. 40205
Scotty's Gun Shop, Second & Rancier, Killeen, TX 76541
Sharon Rifle Barrel Co., P.O. Box 106, Kalispell, Mont. 59901
Ed Shilen Rifles, Inc., 205 Metropark Blvd., Ennis, TX 75119
W. C. Strutz, 3230 Sunnyside Ave., Brookfield, IL 60513
Titus Barrel & Gun Co., Box 151, Heber City, Ut. 84032
John E. Weir, 3304 Norton Ave., Independence, Mo. 64052
Wilson Arms, Box 364, Stony Creek, Branford, Conn. 06405

SCOPES, MOUNTS, ACCESSORIES, OPTICAL EQUIPMENT

Alley Supply Co., Carson Valley Industrial Park, Gardnerville, NV 89410 (Scope collimator)
American Import Co., 1167 Mission, San Francisco, Calif. 94103
Anderson & Co., 1203 Broadway, Yakima, Wash. 98902 (lens cap)
Avery Corp., P.O. Box 99, Electra, TX 76360 (Mini-Light)
Ball-One Buck Scope Lens Cover, Box 426, Midway City, CA 92655
Bausch & Lomb Inc., 635 St. Paul St., Rochester, N.Y. 14602
Bennett, 561 Delaware, Delmar, N.Y. 12054 (mounting wrench)
Bridge Mount Co., Box 3344, Lubbock, Tex. 79410 (one-piece target mts.)
Browning Arms, Rt. 4, Box 624-B, Arnold, Mo. 63010

Maynard P. Buehler, Inc., 17 Orinda Highway, Orinda, Calif. 94563
Burris Co., 351 E. 8th St., Greeley, CO 80631
D. P. Bushnell & Co., Inc., 2828 E. Foothill Blvd., Pasadena, Calif. 91107
Butler Creek Corp., Box GG, Jackson Hole, WY 83001 (lens caps)
Kenneth Clark, 18738 Highway 99, Madera, Calif. 93637
Clear View Sports Shields, P.O. Box 255, Wethersfield, CT 06107 (shooting/testing glasses)
Colt's, Hartford, Conn. 06102
Compass Instr. & Optical Co., Inc., 104 E 25th St., New York, N.Y. 10010
Conetrol, Hwy 123 South, Seguin, Tex. 78155
Continental Arms Corp., 697-5th Ave., New York, N.Y. 10022 (Nickel)
Davis Optical Co., P.O. Box 6, Winchester, Ind. 47934
Del-Sports, Main St., Margaretville, N.Y. 12455 (Kahles)
Diana Imports, Main St., Margaretville, N.Y. 12455 (Habicht)
M. B. Dinsmore, Box 21, Wyomissing, PA 19610 (shooting glasses)
Duo Mount see: Firearms Service
Eder Instrument Co., 5115 N. Ravenswood, Chicago, IL 60640 (borescope)
Firearms Service, 2 Lewelling Blvd., San Lorenzo, CA 94580
Flaig's, Babcock Blvd., Millvale, Pa. 15209
Freeland's Scope Stands, Inc. 3734 14th, Rock Island, Ill. 61201
Griffin & Howe, Inc., 589-8th Ave., New York, N.Y. 10017
E. C. Herkner Co., Box 5007, Boise, Idaho 83702
Herter's Inc., Waseca, Minn. 56093
J. B. Holden Co., Box H-1495, Plymouth, Mich. 48170
The Hutson Corp., P.O. 1127, Arlington, Tex. 76010
Hy-Score Arms Corp., 200 Tillary St., Brooklyn, N.Y. 11201
Paul Jaeger, 211 Leedom St., Jenkintown, Pa. 19046 (Nickel)
Jana Intl. Co., Box 1107, Denver, Colo. 80201
Jason Empire, 1211 Walnut, Kansas City, Mo. 64106
Kesselring Gun Shop, 400 Pacific Hiway 99 No, Burlington, Wash. 98283
Kuharsky Bros., 2425 W. 12th St., Erie, Pa. 16500
Kwik-Site, 27367 Michigan, Inkster, Mich. 48141 (rings)
LanDav, 7213 Lee Highway, Falls Church, VA 22046 (steel leverlock side mt.)
T. K. Lee, Box 2123, Birmingham, Ala. 35201 (reticles)
E. Leitz, Inc., Rockleigh, N.J. 07647
Leupold & Stevens Inc., P.O. Box 688, Beaverton, Ore. 97005
Jake Levin and Son, Inc., 1211 Walnut, Kansas City, Mo. 64106
W. H. Lodewick, 2816 N.E. Halsey, Portland, OR 97232 (scope safeties)
Lyman Gun Sight Products, Middlefield, Conn. 06455
Marble Arms Co., 420 Industrial Park, Gladstone, MI 49837
Marlin Firearms Co., 100 Kenna Dr., New Haven, Conn. 06473
Mitchell's Shooting Glasses, Box 539, Waynesville, MO 65583
O. F. Mossberg & Sons, Inc., 7 Grasso Ave., North Haven, Conn. 06473
Normark Corp., 1710 E. 78th St., Minneapolis, Minn. 55423 (Singlepoint)
Numrich Arms, West Hurley, N.Y. 12491
Nydar Div., Swain Nelson Co., Box 45, Glenview, Ill. 60025 (shotgun sight)
PGS, Peters' Inc., 622 Gratiot Ave., Saginaw, Mich. 48602 (scope shields)
Pachmayr Gun Works, 1220 S. Grand Ave., Los Angeles, Calif. 90015
Pacific Tool Co., P.O. Drawer 2048, Ordnance Plant Rd., Grand Island, NB 68801
Ed Paul's Sptg. Goods, Inc., 172 Flatbush Ave., Brooklyn, N.Y. 11217 (Tops)
Pickering Co., 2110 Walnut, Unionville, Mo. 63565
Precise Imports Corp., 3 Chestnut, Suffern, N.Y. 10901 (PIC)
Ranging Inc., P.O. Box 9106, Rochester, N.Y. 14625
Ray-O-Vac, Willson Prod. Div., P.O. Box 622, Reading, PA 19603 (shooting glasses)
Realist, Inc., N. 93 W. 16288, Megal Dr., Menomonee Falls, Wis. 53051
Redfield Gun Sight Co., 5800 E. Jewell Ave., Denver, Colo. 80222
Rifleman's Bore Sighter Co., P.O. Box 1701, Saginaw, MI 48605
S & K Mfg. Co., Box 247, Pittsfield, Pa. 16340 (Insta-mount)
Sanders Cust. Gun Serv., 2358 Tyler Lane, Louisville, Ky. 40205 (MSW)
Savage Arms, Westfield, Mass. 01085
Sears, Roebuck & Co., 825 S. St. Louis, Chicago, Ill. 60607
W. H. Siebert, 22443 S.E. 56th Pl., Issaquah, Wn. 98027
Singlepoint (see Normark)
Southern Precision Inst. Co., 3419 E. Commerce St., San Antonio, TX 78219
Spacetron Inc., Box 84, Broadview, IL 60155 (bore lamp)
Stoeger Arms Co., 55 Ruta Ct., S. Hackensack, N.J. 07606
Swift Instruments, Inc., 952 Dorchester Ave., Boston, Mass. 02125
Tasco, 1075 N.W. 71st, Miami, Fla. 33138
Thompson-Center Arms, P.O. Box 2405, Rochester, N.H. 03867 (handgun scope)
Tradewinds, Inc., Box 1191, Tacoma, Wash. 98401
John Unertl Optical Co., 3551-5 East St., Pittsburgh, Pa. 15214
United Binocular Co., 9043 S. Western Ave., Chicago, Ill. 60620
Universal Firearms Corp., 3746 E. 10th Ct., Hialeah, Fla. 33013
Vissing (see: Butler Creek Corp.)
H. P. Wasson, Box 15, Vacation Village, FL 33071 (eyeglass apertures)
Weatherby's, 2781 Firestone, South Gate, Calif. 90280
W. R. Weaver Co., 7125 Industrial Ave., El Paso, Tex. 79915
Wein Prods. Inc., 115 W. 25th St., Los Angeles, CA 90007 (Cronoscope)
Williams Gun Sight Co., 7389 Lapeer Rd., Davison, Mich. 48423
Willrich Precision Instrument Co., 37-13 Broadway, Rte. 4, Fair Lawn, NJ 07410 (borescope)
Carl Zeiss Inc., 444 Fifth Ave., New York, N.Y. 10018 (Hensoldt)

SIGHTS, METALLIC

B-Square Eng. Co., Box 11281, Ft. Worth, Tex. 76110
Bo-Mar Tool & Mfg. Co., Box 168, Carthage, Tex. 75633
Maynard P. Buehler, Inc., 17 Orinda Highway, Orinda, Calif. 94563
Christy Gun Works, 875 57th St., Sacramento, Calif. 95819
Cornwall Bridge Gun Shop, P.O. Box 67, Cornwall Bridge, CT 06754 (vernier)
E-Z Mount, Ruelle Bros., P.O. Box 114, Ferndale, MT 48220

Firearms Dev. Lab., Box 3, Lincoln, CA 95648
Freeland's Scope Stands, Inc., 3734-14th Ave., Rock Island, Ill. 61201
P. W. Gray Co., Fairgrounds Rd., Nantucket, Mass. 02554 (shotgun)
Paul T. Haberly, 2364 N. Neva, Chicago, IL 60635
Paul Jaeger, Inc., 211 Leedom St., Jenkintown, PA 19046
Lyman Gun Sight Products, Middlefield, Conn. 06455
Marble Arms Corp., 420 Industrial Park, Gladstone, Mich. 49837
Merit Gunsight Co., P.O. Box 995, Sequim, Wash. 98382
Micro Sight Co., 242 Harbor Blvd., Belmont, Calif. 94002
Miniature Machine Co., 212 E. Spruce, Deming, N.M. 88030
Oxford Corp., 100 Benbro Dr., Buffalo, N.Y. 14225 (Illum. Sight)
C. R. Pedersen & Son, Ludington, Mich. 49431
Poly Choke Co., Inc., P.O. Box 296, Hartford, CT 06101
Redfield Gun Sight Co., 5800 E. Jewell St., Denver, Colo. 80222
Ruelle Bros. Co., P.O. Box 114, Ferndale, MI 48220
Schwarz's Gun Shop, 41 - 15th St., Wellsburg, W. Va. 26070
Simmons Gun Specialties, Inc., 700 Rodgers Rd., Olathe, Kans. 66061
Slug Site Co., 3835 University, Des Moines, Ia. 50311
Tradewinds, Inc., Box 1191, Tacoma, WA 98401
Williams Gun Sight Co., 7389 Lapeer Rd., Davison, Mich. 48423
W. H. Womack, 2124 Meriwether Rd., Shreveport. La. 71108

STOCKS (Commercial and Custom)

Abe-Van Horn, 5124 Huntington Dr., Los Angeles, CA 90032
Adams Custom Gun Stocks, 13461 Quito Rd., Saratoga, CA 95070
Ahlman's Inc., R.R. 1, Box 20, Morristown, MN 55052
R. E. Anderson, 706 So. 23rd St., Laramie, Wyo. 82070
Dale P. Andrews, 7114 So. Albion, Littleton, Colo. 80120
R. J. Anton, 1016 Riehl St., Waterloo, Ia. 50703
Austrian Gunworks Reg'd., P.O. Box 136, Eastman, Que., Canada
Jim Baiar, Rt. 1-B, Box 352, Columbia Falls, Mont. 59912
Joe J. Balickie, Custom Stocks, 6108 Deerwood Pl., Raleigh, N.C. 27607
Bartas, Rte. 1, Box 129-A, Cato, Wis. 54206
John Bianchi, 212 W. Foothill Blvd., Monrovia, Calif. 91016 (U. S. carbines)
Al Biesen, West 2039 Sinto Ave., Spokane, Wash. 99201
E. C. Bishop & Son Inc., Box 7, Warsaw, Mo. 65355
Nate Bishop, Box 334, Minturn, CO 81645
Kay H. Bowles, Pinedale, Wyo. 82941
Brown Precision Co., 5869 Indian Ave., San Jose, CA 95123
Lenard M. Brownell, Box 25, Wyarno, WY 82845
Cadmus Ind. Sporting Arms, Inc., 6311 Yucca St., Hollywood, Calif. 90028 (U. S. carbines)
Calico Hardwoods, Inc., 1648 Airport Blvd., Windsor, Calif. 95492 (blanks)
Dick Campbell, 1445 So. Meade, Denver, Colo. 80219
Cloward's Gun Shop, 4023 Aurora Ave., Seattle, WA 98102
Mike Conner, Box 208, Tijeras, N.M. 87059
Crane Creek Gun Stock Co., 25 Shephard Terr., Madison, WI 53705
Crest Carving Co., 8091 Bolsa Ave., Midway City, CA 92655
Charles De Veto, 1087 Irene Rd., Lyndhurst, O. 44124
Custom Gunstocks, 1445 So. Meade, Denver, Colo. 80219
Reinhart Fajen, Box 338, Warsaw, Mo. 65355
N. B. Fashingbauer, Box 366, Lac Du Flambeau, Wis. 54538
Ted Fellowes, Beaver Lodge, 9245 16th Ave. S. W., Seattle, Wash. 98106
Clyde E. Fischer, Rt. 1, Box 170-M, Victoria, Tex. 77901
Jerry Fisher, 1244-4th Ave. W., Kalispell, MT 59901
Flaig's Lodge, Millvale, Pa. 15209
Horace M. Frantz, Box 128, Farmingdale, N.J. 07727
Freeland's Scope Stands, Inc., 3734 14th Ave., Rock Island, Ill. 61201
Aaron T. Gates, 3229 Felton St., San Diego, Calif. 92104
Dale Goens, Box 224, Cedar Crest, N.M. 87008
Gould's Myrtlewood, 1692 N. Dogwood, Coquille, Ore. 97423 (gun blanks)
Rolf R. Gruning, 315 Busby Dr., San Antonio, Tex. 78209
Gunstocks-Rarewoods, Haleiwa, Hawaii 97612 (blanks)
Gunwoods (N.Z.) Ltd., Box 18505, New Brighton, Christchurch, New Zealand (blanks)
Half Moon Rifle Shop, Rte. 1B, Box 352, Columbia Falls, MT 59912
Hank's Stock Shop, 1078 Alice Ave., Ukiah, Calif. 95482
Harper's Custom Stocks, 928 Lombrano St., San Antonio, Tex. 78207
Harris Gun Stocks, Inc., 12 Lake St., Richfield Springs, N.Y. 13439
Elden Harsh, Rt. 4, London, O. 43140
Hal Hartley, Box 147, Blairsfork Rd., Lenoir, N.C. 28654
Hayes Gunstock Service Co., 914 E. Turner St., Clearwater, Fla. 33516
Hubert J. Hecht, 55 Rose Mead Circle, Sacramento, CA 95831
Edward O. Hefti, 300 Fairview, College Sta., Tex. 77840
Herter's Inc., Waseca, Minn. 56093
Klaus Hiptmayer, P.O. Box 136, Eastman, Que., Canada
Richard Hodgson, 9081 Tahoe Lane, Boulder, CO 80301
Hollis Gun Shop, 917 Rex St., Carlsbad, N.M. 88220
Jack's Walnut Woods, 10333 San Fernando Rd., Pacoima, CA 91331 (English and Claro blanks)
Jackson's, Box 416, Selman City, Tex. 75689 (blanks)
Paul Jaeger, 211 Leedom St., Jenkintown, Pa. 19046
I. D. Johnson, Rt. 1, Strawberry Point, Ia. 52076 (blanks)
Johnson's Gun Shop, 1316 N. Blackstone, Fresno, CA 93703
Monte Kennedy, R.D. 2B, Kalispell Mont., 59901
Leer's Gun Barn, Rt. 3, Sycamore Hills, Elwood, Ind. 46036
LeFever Arms Co., Inc., R.D. 1, Lee Center, N.Y. 13363
Bill McGuire, Inc., 7749 - 15th Ave. N.W., Seattle, WA 98117
Maryland Gun Exchange, Rte. 5, Frederick, Md. 21701
Maurer Arms, 2366 Frederick Dr., Cuyahoga Falls, O. 44221
Leonard Mews, R.2, Box 242, Hortonville, W. 54944
Robt. U. Milhoan & Son, Rt. 3, Elizabeth, W. Va. 26143
C. D. Miller Guns, St. Onge, S.D. 57779
Mills (D.H.) Custom Stocks, 401 N. Ellsworth Ave., San Mateo, Calif. 94401
Nelsen's Gun Shop, 501 S. Wilson, Olympia, Wash. 98501
Oakley and Merkley, Box 2446, Sacramento, Calif. 95801 (blanks)

Ernest O. Paulsen, Chinook, Mont. 59523 (blanks)
Peterson Mach. Carving, Box 1065, Sun Valley, Calif. 91352
Andrew Redmond, Inc., No. Anson, Me. 04958 (birchwood blanks)
Richards Micro-Fit Stocks, P.O. Box 1066, Sun Valley, CA. 91352 (thumb-hole)
Roberts Wood Prod., 1400 Melody Rd., Marysville, Calif. 95901
Carl Roth, Jr., P.O. Box 2593, Cheyenne, Wy. 82001
Royal Arms, Inc., 10064 Bert Acosta Ct., Santee, Calif. 92071
Sanders Cust. Gun Serv., 2358 Tyler Lane, Louisville, Ky. 40205 (blanks)
Saratoga Arms Co., R.D. 3, Box 387, Pottstown, Pa. 19464
Roy Schaefer, 965 W. Hilliard Lane, Eugene, Ore. 97402 (blanks)
Shaw's, 1655 S. Euclid Ave., Anaheim, Calif. 92802
Sile Dist., 7 Centre Market Pl., New York, N.Y. 10013
Ed Sowers, 8331 DeCelis Pl., Sepulveda, Calif. 91343
Sportsmen's Equip. Co., 915 W. Washington, San Diego, Calif. 92103 (carbine conversions)
Keith Stegall, Box 696, Gunnison, Colo. 81230
Stinehour Rifles, Box 84, Cragsmoor, N.Y. 12420
Swanson Cust. Firearms, 1051 Broadway, Denver, Colo. 80203
Talmage Enterpr., 1309 W. 12 St., Long Beach, CA 90813
D. W. Thomas, Box 184, Vineland, N.J. 08360
Trevallion Gunstocks, 3442 S. Post Rd., Indianapolis, IN 46239
Brent L. Umberger, R.R. 4, Cambridge, OH 43725
Roy Vail, Rt. 1, Box 8, Warwick, N.Y. 10990
Harold Waller, 1288 Camillo Way, El Cajon, CA 92021
Weatherby's, 2781 Firestone, South Gate, Calif. 90280
Western Stocks & Guns, Inc., 2206 E 11th, Bremerton, Wash. 98311
Joe White, Box 8505, New Brighton, Christchurch, N.Z. (blanks)
Lou Williamson, 129 Stonegate Ct., Bedford, TX 76021
Robert M. Winter, Box 484, Menno, S.D. 57045
Fred Wranic, 6919 Santa Fe, Huntington Park, Calif. 90255 (mesquite)
Paul Wright, 4504 W. Washington Blvd., Los Angeles, Calif. 90016

TAXIDERMY

D. Anderson, 140 E. 13800 South, Draper, UT 84020
Jack Atcheson, 2309 Hancock Ave., Butte, MT 59701
Clearfield Taxidermy, 603 Hanna St., Clearfield, PA 16830
Jonas Bros., Inc., 1037 Broadway, Denver, CO 80203 (catlg. $2)
Knopp Bros., N. 6715 Division St., Spokane, WA 99208
Mac's Taxidermy, 1316 West Ave., Waukesha, WI 53186

TARGETS, BULLET & CLAYBIRD TRAPS

Black Products Co., 13513 Calumet Ave., Chicago, Ill. 60627
Caswell Target Carriers, Box 344, Anoka, Minn. 55303
Cole's Acku-Rite Prod., Box 25, Kennedy, N.Y. 14747 (Site Rite targets)
Detroit Bullet Trap Co., 2233 N. Palmer Dr., Schaumburg, Ill. 60172
Electro Ballistic Lab., P.O. Box 5876, Stanford, CA 94305 (Electronic Trap Boy)
Ellwood Epps (Orillia) Ltd., Hwy. 11 North, Orillia, Ont., Canada (hand traps)
Gopher Shooter's Supply, Box 246, Faribault, Minn. 55021 (Lok-A-Leg target holders)

Millard F. Lerch, Box 163, 10842 Front St., Mokena, Ill. 60448 (bullet target)
National Target Co., 4960 Wyaconda Rd., Rockville, Md. 20853
Outers Laboratories, Inc., Onalaska, Wis. 54650 (claybird traps)
Peterson Label Co., P.O. Box 186Z, Redding Ridge, CT 06876 (paste-ons)
Professional Tape Co., 355 E. Burlington Rd., Riverside, Ill. 60546 (Time Labels)
Ranger Arms Co., Box 704, Gainesville, Tex. 76240 (paper targets)
Recreation Prods. Res. Inc., 158 Franklin Ave., Ridgwood, N.J. 07450 (Butts bullet trap)
Remington Arms Co., Bridgeport, Conn. 06602 (claybird traps)
Scientific Prod. Corp., 426 Swann Ave., Alexandria, VA 22301 (Targetter)
Sheridan Products, Inc., 3205 Sheridan, Racine, Wis. 53403 (traps)
Shooting Equip. Inc., 2001 N. Parkside Ave., Chicago, Ill. 60639 (electric range)
Sterling-Fleischman Inc., 176 Penna Ave., Malvern, Pa. 19355
Time Products Co. (See Prof. Tape Co.)
Trius Prod., Box 25, Cleves, O. 45002 (claybird, can thrower)
Winchester-Western, New Haven, Conn. 06504 (claybird traps)
Wisler Western Target Co., 1685 Industrial Way, Sparks, Nev. 89431 (NRA targets)

TRAP & SKEET SHOOTERS EQUIP.

Creed Enterprises, P.O. Box 3029, Arcadia, CA 91006 (ammo pouch)
Filmat Ent., Inc., 200 Market St., East Paterson, NJ 07407 (shotshell pouches)
The I and I Co., 709 12th St., Altoona, PA 16601 (multiple shell catcher)
Old Mill Trap & Skeet, 300 Mill Ridge Rd., Secaucus, NJ 07094 (Seymour shotshell catcher)
Outers Laboratories, Inc., P.O. Box 37, Onalaska, WI 54650 (trap, claybird)
Remington Arms Co., Bridgeport, CT 06602 (trap, claybird)
Safe-T-Shell, Inc., 4361 Woodhall Rd., Columbus, OH 43221 (shotgun)
Trius Products, Box 25, Cleves, OH 45002 (can thrower; trap, claybird)
Daniel Titus, 119 Morlyn Ave., Bryn Mawr, PA 19010 (hull bag)
Winchester-Western New Haven, CT 06504 (trap, claybird)

TRIGGERS, RELATED EQUIP.

M. H. Canjar Co., 500 E. 45th Ave., Denver, CO 80216 (triggers)
Flaig's, Babcock Blvd. & Thompson Run Rd., Millvale, PA 15209 (trigger shoe)
Gager Gage & Tool Co., 27509 Industrial Blvd., Hayward, CA 94545 (speedlock triggers f. Rem. 1100 and 870 shotguns)
Michaels of Oregon Co., P.O. Box 13010, Portland, OR 97213 (trigger guards)
Ohaus Corp., 29 Hanover Rd., Florham Park, NJ 07932 (trigger pull gauge)
Pachmayr Gun Works, 1220 S. Grand Ave., Los Angeles, CA 90015 (trigger shoe)
Pacific Tool Co., P.O. Drawer 2048, Ordnance Plant Rd., Grand Island, NB 68801 (trigger shoe)
Schwab Gun Shop, 1103 E. Bigelow, Findlay, OH 45840 (trigger release)
Melvin Tyler, 1326 W. Britton Ave., Oklahoma City, OK 73114 (trigger shoe)
L. H. Waltersdorf, 29 Freier Rd., Quakertown, PA 18951 (release trigger)
Williams Gun Sight Co., 7389 Lapeer Rd., Davison, MI 48423 (trigger shoe)

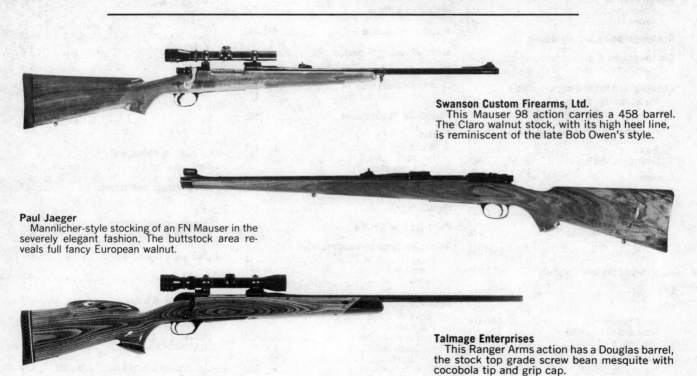

Swanson Custom Firearms, Ltd.
This Mauser 98 action carries a 458 barrel. The Claro walnut stock, with its high heel line, is reminiscent of the late Bob Owen's style.

Paul Jaeger
Mannlicher-style stocking of an FN Mauser in the severely elegant fashion. The buttstock area reveals full fancy European walnut.

Talmage Enterprises
This Ranger Arms action has a Douglas barrel, the stock top grade screw bean mesquite with cocobola tip and grip cap.

INDEX

to the departmental and display page
of the **GUN DIGEST**—*28th Edit*